ENVIRONMENTAL LAW HANDBOOK

by PATTON, BOGGS & BLOW

ENVIRONMENTAL LAW HANDBOOK

by PATTON, BOGGS & BLOW

TIMOTHY A. VANDERVER, JR.
Editor-in-Chief

J. Gordon Arbuckle
Mary Beth Bosco
Elliott P. Laws
John C. Martin
Marshall Lee Miller
W. Caffey Norman, III
Russell V. Randle
Peter D. Robertson
Duane A. Siler
Paul A. J. Wilson

The Bureau of National Affairs, Inc., Washington, D.C.

Library of Congress Cataloging-in-Publication Data

Environmental law handbook / by Patton, Boggs & Blow; Timothy A. Vanderver, Jr., editor-in-chief ... [et al.].
p. cm.
Includes index.
ISBN 0-87179-811-5
1. Environmental law--United States. I. Vanderver, Timothy A. II. Patton, Boggs & Blow.
KF3775.E474 1994
344.73'046--dc20
[347.30446] 93-47638
CIP

Published by BNA Books
1250 23rd St. NW, Washington, DC 20037
International Standard Book Number: 0-87179-811-5
Printed in the United States of America

Preface

Before 1970, the existence of a subject called environmental law legitimately could be questioned. Most law schools had no such course offering. Practitioners dealt with many of the elements that since have been brought under the rubric of environmental law, but these topics were thought of as belonging to other legal specialties, such as common law litigation.

Growing public concern for the environment has changed that dramatically and emphatically. Since the National Environmental Policy Act of 1969, the Clean Air Amendments of 1970, and the Federal Water Pollution Control Act of 1972, the floodgates have opened, loosing a torrent of environmental legislation and an even greater flood of environmental regulations. Extensive regulatory activities, enforcement actions, and litigation have followed.

In these circumstances and in view of the growing importance of environmental law, there is a widely recognized need for a comprehensive and understandable, yet manageable, handbook for the environmental professional, the legal practitioner, and the student.

The *Environmental Law Handbook by Patton, Boggs & Blow* is intended to fill this need for a guide to federal environmental law. Written by members of Patton, Boggs & Blow's nationally known environmental practice group, this book presents and analyzes the entire scope of federal environmental law and related topics that impact on it. Different chapters also examine regulatory activities and, where relevant, enforcement actions and litigation. Perhaps the most useful aspect of the book, however, is the practical insight the authors provide on the various topics. The book's focus is on what is important, and we have tried to avoid detailed expositions of topics of little significance.

Thus, the *Environmental Law Handbook by Patton, Boggs & Blow* is intended to be a comprehensive, understandable, and manageable guide to federal environmental law. We hope that it satisfies this difficult objective.

Eleven authors are listed on the frontispiece as contributing to this work. A number of other people have made significant contributions to preparing this book, and they are recognized at the beginning of various chapters. Others whose assistance is deeply appreciated include Jennifer Parker Lake and Michele Wilt for their patience, word processing and administrative skills in completing the work. We also thank Jim Fattibene of BNA, who achieved a miracle by his courteous and patient encouragement of the authors: this book finally got published. Finally, we thank our editors at BNA for their untiring efforts in turning draft chapters into a highly polished book.

About the Authors

Timothy A. Vanderver, Jr., a partner in the Washington, D.C. law firm of Patton, Boggs & Blow, is an acknowledged expert in environmental law. He has given many seminars on a variety of environmental subjects. Vanderver has represented clients in a variety of Clean Air Act matters, including the 1990 legislation, and has wide experience in representing and counseling clients concerning Superfund and RCRA. He previously practiced environmental law in the Solicitor's Office at the U.S. Department of the Interior and the U.S. Department of Housing and Urban Development, where he developed a knowledge of NEPA and other early environmental legislation. He is a co-author of the *Environmental Law Handbook* (Government Institutes, 1991), *Emergency Planning and Community Right-to-Know Handbook,* and *Clean Air Law and Regulation.* He is a co-author of the recent article in the *Toxics Law Rep.* on the 1986 Superfund Amendments. He was a Rhodes scholar, earning his law degrees from Oxford University and Harvard Law School.

J. Gordon Arbuckle is a partner with Patton, Boggs & Blow who has practiced environmental and natural resources law for over 20 years. Among his major endeavors are a number of big projects that have required careful attention to environmental impacts. These include the Louisiana Offshore Oil Port, the Alaska natural gas pipeline, and the first deep seabed mining license. He was active in connection with specific issues arising under other environmental legislation, including AHERA, RCRA, the Clean Water Act, CERCLA, and the Oil Pollution Act of 1990. He participated on the negotiated rulemaking panel that developed the EPA asbestos in school regulations. Mr. Arbuckle has represented clients in administrative and judicial proceedings arising under the CAA, RCRA, the Clean Water Act, TSCA, OCSLA, CZMA, the Endangered Species Act, and other environmental laws. He has also been extensively involved in Superfund litigation. He is an author of the *Environmental Law Handbook* (Government Institutes, 1991), the *Clean Water Act Handbook,* and the *Environmental Managers Handbook,* texts widely read by environmental practitioners. He has authored numerous other articles concerning criminal liability under environmental statutes and other developing compliance incentives.

Mary Beth Bosco is a partner with the law firm of Patton, Boggs & Blow where she specializes in environmental law and litigation. Her experience includes representing clients before EPA in connection with the underground storage tank and used oil regulations, as well as Superfund litigation. She is a contributing author to *Regulation of the Gas Industry* (Mathew Bender, 1989) and the *Environmental Law Handbook* (Government Institutes, 1991). Ms. Bosco is a 1978 graduate of Yale University and a 1983 graduate of George Washington University Law School with honors.

Elliott P. Laws, a former partner at the Washington, D.C. law firm of Patton, Boggs & Blow where he specialized in environmental law, legislation, and litigation, is now Assistant Administrator of the Environmental Protection Agency for the Office of Solid Waste and Emergency Response. Before joining Patton, Boggs & Blow he was a trial attorney in the Environmental Defense Section of the Department of Justice's Land (now Environment) and Natural Resources Division. Prior to that, he was an enforcement attorney with EPA's Water Enforcement Division. He has experience under a wide variety of environmental statutes, including CERCLA, the Clean Water Act, the Clean Air Act and RCRA. Mr. Laws currently serves as Co-Chair of the Environment Committee of the Bar Association of the District of Columbia and has co-authored several books and articles on environmental issues. He is a graduate of Georgetown University Law Center.

John C. Martin, a partner at the law firm of Patton, Boggs & Blow, specializes in natural resources and environmental law. He worked as a trial attorney in the Environmental Enforcement Section at the Department of Justice from 1982 through 1985. There, he litigated cases on behalf of the EPA, and was the recipient of a Special Achievement Award for his efforts. Mr. Martin successfully litigated many penalty cases under the Clean Air Act and the Clean Water Act. A frequent lecturer on various environmental topics, Mr. Martin is also the co-author of three other books and several articles on various aspects of environmental law. He is a graduate of Georgetown University Law Center.

Marshall Miller, a partner in the Washington, D.C. office of the Baker & Hostetler law firm, has over two decades of environmental experience. He was formerly the acting Administrator of the U.S. Occupational Safety and Health Administration (OSHA). His experience includes service as the Special Assistant to the first Administrator of the U.S. Environmental Protection Agency (EPA), Chief EPA Judicial Officer, and Associate Deputy Attorney General in the U.S. Department of Justice.

W. Caffey Norman III is a partner with Patton, Boggs & Blow in Washington, D.C. He has extensive experience representing trade associations and other clients in connection with the regulation of chemicals by the Environmental Protection Agency, the Occupational Safety and Health Administration, the Consumer Product Safety Commission, and various state regulatory agencies. He has been particularly active in the subject areas of toxic substances, stratospheric ozone depletion, and global warming. His practice also includes appellate litigation in the U.S. Court of Appeals and legislative work. Mr. Norman is a graduate of the University of Virginia Law School and he served as law clerk to Judge Walter P. Gewin of the U.S. Court of Appeals for the Fifth Circuit.

Russell V. Randle is a partner in the Washington office of Patton, Boggs & Blow, where he has represented direct and indirect industrial dischargers, municipalities, and oil transportation companies in connection with Clean Water and Oil Pollution Act compliance, done legislative work concerning coal slurry pipelines, recycling standards, and clean air permits, and practiced under most federal environmental statutes, including considerable CERCLA litigation and negotiation. In addition to his representation of private industry and municipalities, Mr. Randle has represented environmental groups in designating a sole source aquifer under the Safe Drinking Water Act and other efforts, and provided environmental education assistance to the Episcopal Diocese of Virginia as well as extensive training for a number of federal military and Energy Department installations. Mr. Randle received his legal training at Yale Law School, where he was an editor of the Law Journal, followed by a clerkship for U.S. District Judge John H. Pratt. His environmental experience also includes work at the National Commission on Water Quality, EPA, and Capitol Hill. Mr. Randle has published frequently in the environmental area, as well as on legal problems involved in export controls.

Peter Robertson is an attorney with Patton, Boggs & Blow specializing in environmental and legislative law. He has experience lobbying and litigating on the Clean Air Act, CERCLA, the Clean Water Act, the Safe Drinking Water Act, and other environmental statutes. He is a frequent lecturer on environmental legislation and is one of the co-authors of *The Clean Water Handbook.* Mr. Robertson earned a B.A. degree from the University of Oklahoma. After pursuing graduate studies at the University of Virginia, he worked on Capitol Hill for seven years, first on the personal staff of Congressman James R. Jones and later as a professional staff member of the Committee on the Budget of the House of Representatives. He took his J.D. degree at Georgetown University Law Center.

Duane A. Siler, a partner in Patton, Boggs & Blow, specializes in environmental law, including counseling and litigation on behalf of corporate and trade association clients and review of environmental aspects of acquisitions and financings. Mr. Siler has served as trial counsel in environmental cases arising under CERCLA, RCRA, and the common law. He is a graduate of Boalt Hall School of Law, University of California at Berkeley.

Paul A. J. Wilson is a partner in the Washington D.C. office of Patton, Boggs & Blow specializing in matters arising out of the regulation of hazardous substances under CERCLA, RCRA, EPCRA, TSCA, and the OSH Act. He spent over five years with the Environmental Protection Agency and twice received the EPA Bronze Medal for Commendable Service. Mr. Wilson graduated from the University of Virginia School of Law where he was the executive editor of the Virginia Journal of Natural Resources Law. He is the author of six other books and articles on environmental matters.

Summary Table of Contents

Detailed Table of Contents

1

Environmental Law: What It Is and How It Works

By J. Gordon Arbuckle

Environmental law is more than just a collection of laws on environmental subjects. It is a discipline that cannot be mastered by rote learning of various specific requirements of individual laws and regulations. It requires understanding.

To understand the environmental law system we must know some specifics. More important, however, we must understand the unifying principles and the ways the parts work together to achieve environmental objectives.

I. What Is Environmental Law?

The best definition of environmental law that we have been able to formulate is:

> The environmental law system is an organized way of using *all* of the laws in our legal system to minimize, prevent, punish, or remedy the consequences of actions that damage or threaten the environment.

The thing that makes a law or regulation a part of the environmental law system is not its label or original function but the purpose for which it is used. It would be a mistake to assume that a compilation of the federal "environmental statutes" enacted since about 1970 to regulate the various activities that pollute or might pollute the environment would include all of the environmental law or even most of it. The criminal code and the Administrative Procedure Act also function as important "environmental" laws.

The environmental law system includes all aspects of the U.S. legal system—the Constitution, statutes, regulations, rules of evidence, rules of procedure, judicial interpretations, the common law, and, indeed, the criminal law—to the extent that they are being used to protect the environment. Environmental law is not a compilation of certain laws. It is instead a focus or *method* for using *all* of the laws for environmental purposes.

II. How Does It Work?

Most legal systems develop characteristic sets of duties and compliance requirements adapted to the subject matter and circumstances being regulated. The environmental law system is no exception to this rule. There are eight generic compliance obligations—the "Eight Commandments"—that are used, in some combination, by virtually all environmental laws.

These eight compliance obligations or commandments are *notification* requirements, *discharge* limits, *process* controls, *product* controls, *activity* controls, *transportation* standards, *response* requirements, and *compensation* requirements.

1. INFORMATION, REPORTING, AND NOTIFICATION REQUIREMENTS.

ADVISE APPROPRIATE AUTHORITIES, EMPLOYEES, AND OFTEN THE PUBLIC OF INTENDED OR ACTUAL RELEASES OF POLLUTANTS, VIOLATIONS OF DISCHARGE LIMITS OR OTHER PROHIBITIONS, AND OF THE COMMENCEMENT OF ACTIVITIES, SUCH AS RESOURCE EXTRACTION OR CONSTRUCTION, THAT MAY HAVE SIGNIFICANT ENVIRONMENTAL IMPACTS.

Like our tax laws, the environmental laws obligate the regulated community to provide the regulators with the information required to regulate and the information needed to protect those put at risk. These duties to notify, the cornerstone of virtually all of the environmental statutes, take various forms: requirements to file permit applications before commencing an activity or discharge; periodic monitoring and compliance reporting; noncompliance reporting; spill, release, and other event-oriented reporting; product labeling; risk and exposure notifications; duties to warn; annual inventory reporting; and so on.

Since these notifications, monitoring, and self-reporting requirements are so critical to operation of the environmental law system, they are broadly interpreted and vigorously enforced. The questions of "Is notice required?" and "How should it be given and kept current?" are central to operation of the system and among the most important to be faced in environmental law practice and compliance efforts.

2. DISCHARGE LIMITS.

PREVENT OR ACCEPTABLY MINIMIZE THE RELEASE OF POLLUTANTS INTO THE ENVIRONMENT.

These controls, variously referred to as "emission limits," "effluent limitations," "exposure limits," "design, construction and operating standards," "closure requirements," or "discharge prohibitions," are imposed at the point where pollutants are discharged, disposed of, or released to the environment. They are probably the oldest and probably still the most prevalent type of pollution control requirement. The level of effectiveness or "standard of performance" required to be achieved by these point-of-discharge controls is generally set by reference to the limits of technological practicability or possibility, health effects levels, environmental effects levels, or a combination of these factors.

3. POLLUTION PREVENTION OR PROCESS CONTROLS.

REDUCE THE QUANTITIES, PREVENT THE RELEASE, AND MINIMIZE THE HAZARDOUS CHARACTERISTICS OF WASTES THAT ARE GENERATED.

Sometimes it is more practical to require protective actions in the plant or process before waste is generated than it is to directly control the discharge of pollutants. The simplest example of this type of control approach is that used with unanticipated spills. Since these discharges are unanticipated, it is usually impractical to treat them. Instead, it is preferable to prevent them by requiring the adoption of spill prevention and containment programs and by requiring maintenance of tank integrity and leak detection systems. Similarly, if it is impractical to treat plant site runoff, management practices should be mandated to keep the runoff from becoming contaminated and to minimize its volume. More sophisticated process-oriented controls, such as substitution of solvents and other materials used and aggressive reduction in the use of water and other waste-generating consumables, are becoming increasingly popular ways of attaining environmental objectives and are sometimes mandated. For example, those companies that create hazardous waste must certify to implementation of a waste minimization program before shipping wastes for disposal.

4. PRODUCT CONTROLS.

ENSURE THAT PRODUCTS ARE DESIGNED, FORMULATED, PACKAGED, OR USED SO THAT THEY DO NOT PRESENT UNREASONABLE RISKS TO HUMAN HEALTH OR THE ENVIRONMENT WHEN EITHER USED OR DISPOSED OF.

Environmental effects of the use or disposal of a product can be as severe as effects of the process by which the product is manufactured. This is clearly true, for example, in the case of the automobile, where it has long been recognized that tailpipe emissions and fuel efficiency are appropriate subjects for environmental regulation. Other products, such as asbestos building materials, have been perceived to be so inherently hazardous as to require a ban on new product sales and regulation of the product in place. Regulation of polychlorinated biphenyls (PCBs) under the Toxic Substances Control Act is another example of stringent product control regulation extending to a phasing out of nearly all existing product uses. Product controls are the primary regulatory mechanism for pesticide products under the Federal Insecticide, Fungicide and Rodenticide Act. The states are becoming increasingly active in the development of product and packaging standards focused on minimization of solid waste generation and disposal problems, and it is expected that federal law will follow that lead.

5. ACTIVITY CONTROLS.

PROTECT RESOURCES, SPECIES, AND ECOLOGICAL AMENITIES.

In some instances, an activity, regardless of the stringency with which we control its processes, waste streams, and products, cannot take place at a particular location or time, exploit a particular resource, or otherwise be conducted without impacts that are arguably unacceptable.

The regulatory approaches that seek to protect resources, species, or environmental amenities through control or curtailment of activities have usually focused on the protection of especially significant areas: wetlands under the Clean Water Act section 404 permit program; beaches and coastal margins under the Coastal Zone Management Act; fragile species, such as the northern spotted owl and the Arizona red squirrel under the Endangered Species Act; or irreplaceable amenities, such as ancient forests, that environmentalists are seeking to preserve under the National Environmental Policy Act, the Endangered Species Act, and other laws.

These arguments about threatened species, fragile ecosystems, and priceless amenities do not find ready compromises, are often not solvable by the expenditure of money or application of technology, and almost always involve scientific issues, both real and spurious, on the margins of available knowledge. Procedures to handle these issues are developed in the heat of battle, and these matters are therefore often hard to resolve without resorting to courts and Congress. This kind of focus on direct regulation of activities, rather than their consequences, will become more common as the focus of environmental law continues to shift from local issues, like toxic hot spots, to ''problems of the planet,'' like global warming, species diversity, and desertification, that can be dealt with, some argue, only by major and wide-scale changes in the way people live and organize their institutions. This form of regulation will likely continue to occupy a place on the cutting edge of the environmental law system's development.

6. TRANSPORTATION STANDARDS.

ACCEPTABLY MINIMIZE THE RISKS INHERENT IN TRANSPORTATION OF HAZARDOUS WASTES OR MATERIALS, OIL, OR OTHER POTENTIALLY HARMFUL SUBSTANCES.

Laws and regulations intended to protect the environment from spills and other incidents occurring during transportation are an important part of the environmental law system. These laws include the Hazardous Materials Transportation Act, the Oil Pollution Act of 1990, the tank vessel statutes and implementing Coast Guard regulations, the international agreements and treaties overlaying the above, sections 311 and 312 of the Clean Water Act, the Resource Conservation and Recovery Act manifest requirements, and the other complex parts of the system of laws and regulations applicable to transportation.

These laws require, in essence, that covered substances be identified; packed properly in proper containers; labeled; loaded onto a placarded, properly designed, built, and maintained truck, tanker, pipeline, or other transportation mode; and delivered to an appropriate site. Adequate financial responsibility must be maintained and demonstrated and careful records must be kept of everything picked up and everything delivered to its ultimate destination. In some instances, the ability to respond to a spill must be maintained. If there is a spill, an appropriate notification must be given.

7. RESPONSE REQUIREMENTS.

CLEAN UP POLLUTANTS THAT HAVE BEEN RELEASED, PREVENT THE THREAT OF RELEASE, OR PAY THE COSTS OF THAT CLEANUP OR PREVENTION.

After a release or threatened release is discovered, through notification or otherwise, the response and remediation provisions of laws like section 311 of the Clean Water Act, sections 104, 106, and 107 of the Comprehensive Environmental Response, Compensation and Liability Act (the "Superfund" law governing cleanup of abandoned hazardous waste dump sites), and the closure provisions of the Resource Conservation and Recovery Act, require "responsible parties" to clean up the problem or authorize the government or private parties to clean up the problem and recover the cleanup costs from the responsible parties. The requirements that responsible parties bear the cost of remedying problems alleged to result from their wastes are among the most complicated and controversial in the environmental law system. Critical questions include: Who is responsible for the release or threatened release? What is the technical fix or remedy? and How will the costs of the remedy be shared among the responsible parties?

8. COMPENSATION REQUIREMENTS.

MAKE RESPONSIBLE PARTIES PAY PRIVATE PARTIES, OR GROUPS, FOR DAMAGES DONE TO THEIR HEALTH OR ENVIRONMENT OR ALLOW REPRESENTATIVES OF THE PUBLIC INTEREST IN NATURAL RESOURCES AND THE ENVIRONMENT TO RECOVER FOR INJURIES DONE TO THOSE PUBLIC ASSETS.

If all other regulatory approaches are unsuccessful in preventing or remedying damage to health or the environment, one should examine the possibility of making the responsible party pay for that damage. The Superfund and the Oil Pollution Act of 1990, for example, have provisions creating a public right of action for damage to natural resources. Those laws may also create private rights of action for damages caused by spills. Another effective set of mechanisms for enforcing obligations to compensate for damage, including that to the environment, is embodied in the common law that has been developed by courts and judges through the resolution of cases and controversies that have arisen in the last 700 or so years. These compensation cases involve larger dollar amounts, probably more complex scientific issues, and perhaps more public attention than any other category of environmental law cases.

III. Laws That Spell Out the Commandments

There are at least eight categories of laws that define the Eight Commandments.

A. The Federal Environmental Statutes

The later chapters of this book describe the regulatory programs in place under the major federal environmental statutes. The major ones are listed below as a preview of what is coming and as an introduction to the acronyms.

- Clean Air Act (CAA)
- Clean Water Act (CWA)

- Occupational Safety and Health Act (OSH Act)
- Safe Drinking Water Act (SDWA)
- Resource Conservation and Recovery Act (RCRA) and the Underground Storage Tank (UST) program
- Hazardous Materials Transportation Act (HMTA)
- Comprehensive Environmental Response, Compensation and Liability Act (CERCLA or Superfund)
- Emergency Planning and Community Right-to-Know Act (EPCRA)
- Toxic Substances Control Act (TSCA)

This system of federal laws has evolved over time to meet perceived needs for environmental protection and provides a fairly logical and nearly complete umbrella of coverage for most activities and events affecting or threatening the environment. Arising out of controversy and developed in debate, these statutes are clearly the most comprehensive and complicated system of such laws that the world has yet devised. Surprisingly, the overall system also makes a certain amount of sense and the overall structure seems reasonably adapted to achieve the objectives for which it was created.

The following sketch of these laws' general dynamics should prove helpful in putting together ''the big picture'' of the environmental law system.

1. The Media-Focused Statutes—CAA, CWA, SDWA, and the OSH Act

The first four entries on the list of federal laws focus on the major environmental media—air, water, groundwater, and the indoor environment of the workplace—and seek to protect them through a combination of the regulatory methods that have just been discussed.

The CAA seeks to protect the ambient outdoor atmosphere through a combination of notification, permitting, waste treatment, and pollution prevention requirements.

The CWA focuses on surface water and seeks to protect it by a combination of notification, permitting, treatment, and pollution prevention similar to that in place under the CAA.

The SDWA, though it has some elements of product regulation in that it regulates the quality of drinking water provided by community water systems, is the primary federal law protecting underground aquifers or groundwater. It uses permit and notification mechanisms to regulate the disposal of wastes by underground injection (discharge into a hole deeper than it is wide) and provides more comprehensive protective regimes for certain critical underground water resources designated as ''sole source aquifers.'' Because comprehensive regulation under SDWA is limited in its applicability to sole source aquifers and the generally applicable underground injection control program does not cover all activities potentially affecting groundwater, the federal program to protect the groundwater medium is unfinished and incomplete. A comprehensive federal groundwater protection act has been on the congressional agenda for several years and sooner or later will be enacted.

The OSH Act, administered by the Department of Labor, has not been traditionally thought of as an environmental statute, but, particularly in its health focus, has become so intertwined with the traditional environmental statutes that it must be treated as an environmental law. The OSH Act protects the indoor environment of the workplace with a comprehensive system of notification (hazcomm) requirements, requires prevention and response planning for events (hazwoprs), and establishes exposure limits for noise and hazardous chemicals in the workplace.

These four media-focused statutes provide a fairly comprehensive shield against damage to the protected media resulting from acts of the regulated community. There are, however, chinks in the armor and those chinks are filled by the laws remaining to be discussed.

2. *Statutes Regulating Waste Activities—RCRA, HMTA*

Perhaps because of the incompleteness of the regulatory scheme protecting groundwater, the need was perceived for an additional layer of protection for all environmental media by specifically focusing on certain activities related to waste and particularly hazardous waste. In response to this perceived need, Congress enacted RCRA to regulate the operation, maintenance, and closure of landfills. RCRA also provides a detailed system of permitting, treatment, notification (manifesting), and operational requirements applicable to the treatment, storage, or disposal of hazardous wastes and works together with HMTA to ensure that those wastes are safely transported to appropriate disposal sites. Consistent with its role as an activity-focused backstop to the media-protective statutes, RCRA does not cover activities specifically permitted and regulated under those other regimes.

3. *Statutes Regulating Releases*

Although the media-specific statutes all have permitting, notification, and response provisions applicable to releases to the media they protect, gaps were perceived, particularly in respect to coverage of releases occurring prior to the date of enactment of those statutes. To fill those gaps Congress enacted Superfund, or CERCLA. CERCLA provides a comprehensive reporting, clean-up, and compensation regime for all releases of harmful quantities of hazardous substances or pollutants that are not permitted under the other statutes discussed above.

4. *Statutes Notifying the Public and Planning for Emergencies*

Although there are notification and pollution prevention provisions in all of the laws discussed above, events like the Bhopal, India, and Institute, West Virginia, releases convinced Congress of the need for more information that is more accessible both to ordinary citizens at the local level and to state and local officials responsible for emergency planning and preparedness. The response to this need, properly referred to as the Emergency Planning and Community Right-to-Know Act, will eventually become the informational underpinning of the environmental law system; even now it is the primary source of information on the progress being made in implementing that system.

5. *The NEPA Context*

The National Environmental Policy Act (NEPA), though it is asserted to be procedural only, should also be considered a major environmental statute since it is so important in establishing the overall context of federal actions within which the more substantive laws operate.

These environmental statutes, enacted by the U.S. Congress since the beginning of the new environmental consciousness in the late 1960s and early 1970s, along with a few others like the Endangered Species Act and the Coastal Zone Management Act, define most of the substantive compliance obligations or regulatory requirements of the environmental law system.

The major federal environmental statutes do not, however, operate in a vacuum. There are other important categories of environmental laws that supplement, complement, or go beyond the programs that the federal environmental statutes establish, including federal agency regulations and guidance, state laws and regulations, tax and business laws, and local ordinances and land use plans.

B. The Federal Agency Regulations and Guidance Documents

Although the federal environmental statutes themselves are pushing hard at 2,000 pages of text, Congress leaves the "details" of statutory implementation for federal agencies to establish in rules and regulations adopted in administrative proceedings under the Administrative Procedure Act. These rules and regulations are supposed to answer the day-to-day questions that must be dealt with before a statute's precise requirements can be ascertained. There are three points to remember about these rules and regulations:

- It takes at least 10 and maybe 100 pages of regulations to clarify and implement one page of statute. The regulations are more complex than the statutes.
- Regulations take longer to develop and adopt than statutes. The regulations are never completed on time and when they are done, it is usually time to change them, producing continuing uncertainty.
- Regulations are supposed to be based on science but are usually written by lawyers based on comments submitted in a public comment procedure.

Considering these factors, environmental regulations have proved workable, but they still leave much to be desired.

Partly because of the difficulty of working out detailed technical instructions in public proceedings that are, at least to some extent, adversarial, the various agencies have developed their own mechanisms for working out the details. These are called "guidance documents," "technical support documents," or sometimes just "guidance." Generally, guidance is even longer and more complicated than regulations. However, it does not go through the public comment process and, therefore, gets done more quickly. Guidance, like regulations, seems to be in a constant state of flux—drafts are finalized, agency opinions are updated, and policies changed with each new administration. Also, since guidance is often written by technical people, technical people often can understand it. Lawyers often cannot. While guidance is not supposed to have any legal status or to be binding on the issuing agency, sometimes, in practical effect, the guidance determines the case. More arcane subject matter, like water quality based toxics control, is particularly susceptible to handling by guidance, and some subjects apparently cannot be dealt with in any other manner. Concerning certain subjects, guidance begets guidance, in bewildering profusion/abundance.

To summarize, federal regulations and guidance documents are extremely important aspects of the environmental law system. They are probably the most complex aspect of the system and are one of the points at which scientific and technical issues are handled most directly. Because of their technical content, federal regulations and guidance are heavily used in state programs and are often the only available authoritative resolution of a technical issue, even at the state level. Understanding the applicable regulations and guidance is often the key to answering environmental compliance questions. Participation in the process that determines what the regulations will require is a critical, but often difficult and unsatisfying, part of the environmental management function.

C. State Statutes and Regulations Implementing the Federal Statutes

Many of the federal statutes, like CAA, CWA, and RCRA, establish "federal-state regulatory programs" in which the states are given the opportunity to enact and enforce laws, meeting federal minimum criteria, to achieve the regulatory objectives that the U.S. Congress has established. In most instances where the states have had the opportunity to take over regulatory programs in their jurisdictions, they have done so.

Thus, under CAA, CWA, and RCRA, states are generally the primary permitting and enforcement authorities, subject to federal intervention only if the states do not enforce effectively or rigorously enough or if the states ask for help. The states are almost never precluded from enforcing criteria more stringent than those required by the federal laws and are given considerable leeway to follow enforcement interpretations that may not be fully consistent with those applied at the federal level. The laws and interpretations used to apply and enforce the federal laws may vary considerably from state to state and these variations may not be carefully noticed or even published. Where a state is the implementing authority, careful and continuing consultation with the state regulatory officials is necessary.

D. State Laws Independent of the Federal Requirements

Except in extremely rare circumstances, states are not preempted or precluded from adopting their own environmental laws that go beyond or regulate subject matter not covered by environmental laws at the federal level. The trend is for states, particularly certain states like California and New Jersey, to take initiatives to provide their citizens and their environments with protections or information beyond that generally available under the federal statutes. Examples of laws generated by this trend include:

- *Toxic Waste Minimization Laws.* A recent one in Massachusetts imposes mandatory waste reduction objectives on companies that use or generate toxic or hazardous wastes.
- *Environmental Full Disclosure Laws.* California Proposition 65 requires extraordinary efforts to make the public aware of health risks associated with products or environments to which they are exposed.
- *Investigate and Cleanup Before Property Transfer Laws.* New Jersey requires extensive investigation and cleanup of contaminated sites before they are sold or transferred.
- *State Land Application and Groundwater Protection Laws.* Although the federal government has not yet adopted comprehensive groundwater protection legislation, many, if not most of the states, have detailed permit programs.

The list goes on, including state citizens' action laws, laws compelling response at hazardous substance sites not on the federal Superfund list, facility siting laws, laws governing the operation of publicly owned treatment works and landfills, and asbestos abatement laws. The bottom line is that independent state laws in many states may be a more important factor in dictating the focus of compliance programs than the laws that exist at the federal level. Attention is clearly warranted.

E. Tax Laws and Economic Incentives

There is an increasing tendency at both the state and federal levels towards using the tax laws to create incentives in favor of environmentally benign products and activities and disincentives against products and activities considered to be environmentally detrimental. Gas guzzler taxes, recycling tax credits, taxes on use of virgin materials, taxes on hazardous waste generation, and excise taxes on various products are among the approaches that have been adopted or seriously discussed. These approaches and other economic incentive-oriented strategies will be more vigorously promoted over the next few years.

F. Business Regulatory Laws

The Federal Trade Commission and a number of state attorneys general have recently announced initiatives to use their ordinary business regulatory authorities to police environmental claims made for products, and the Securities and Exchange Commission has for some time required full disclosure of environmental liabilities in statements and reports falling under its jurisdiction. Other business regulatory laws, like the requirement to register in order to do business, are likely to be mobilized for environmental purposes.

It seems likely that the innovative abilities of both state and federal officials will continue to be applied toward effective use of all the laws in their arsenal in an effort to enforce increasingly stringent standards of protection for health, safety, and the environment. The limits on this kind of creativity are yet to be seen and are unlikely to be reached in the immediate future. The federal and the state governments, however, are not the end of the story.

G. Local and Municipal Laws

While local governmental entities probably have not been as pervasively involved in environmental regulation as their counterparts at the state and federal levels, the localities do have great power to control the location and operation of facilities within their jurisdictions and are often able to effectively use this authority. Active community involvement and participation in consideration of local ordinances is, for a number of businesses, essential to continued ability to operate profitably. While it is difficult to generalize, issues that warrant particularly careful attention include the operation of the local waterworks and waste treatment plants, local recycling initiatives and associated product initiatives, zoning and noise control ordinances, nuisance laws, air emission requirements, landfill restrictions or closures, local emergency planning, and initiatives relating to waste site cleanup. The impact of this kind of local action can be as immediate and severe as that of any taken at the state or federal level. From the perspective of an environmental law compliance program, local does not mean trivial. It means immediate, important, largely unreviewable, and deserving of considerable attention. Effective practitioners and compliers will become familiar with such local requirements and become proactive members of the local community.

H. Judicial Decisions and the Common Law

The last kind of environmental law discussed here is not written out in statutes or ordinances, but it is derived from common law cases—decisions by the courts. In the English and American legal systems, a body of law has been established case by case and controversy by controversy, in judicial decisions resolving issues in accordance with the "custom of the people." Each decision is a precedent and this judge-made, or at least judge-declared, customary law plays a major role in filling gaps not occupied by the statutes. Traditional common law remedies and notions of liability are increasingly being used to force compliance with environmental duties and obtain compensation for environmental harm.

Common law theories that have supported successful actions in environmental contexts include the following:

Negligence	Defective Product
Nuisance	Failure to Warn
Trespass	Inherently Dangerous Activities
Riparian Rights	Other Strict Liability Theories
Constructive Eviction	Assault and/or Battery

A kind of hybrid common law/statutory approach is involved in cases where plaintiffs are injured by conduct that violates the environmental statutes.

This conduct is often "negligence per se" and the injured can often collect damages without proving negligence but simply by showing a causal link between the violation of environmental duty and the damage suffered.

Private litigation under the common law and common law augmented by statutes will continue to be an important factor in determining the substance of the environmental law system.

IV. Laws That Enforce the Commandments—Permits, Prohibitions, and Penalties

Although the environmental law's mechanisms for enforcing its mandates are essentially the same as those available in other legal disciplines, there is a distinctive aspect to the enforcement package. This is the way in which the available mechanisms are used together to effectively compel fulfillment of the environmental compliance obligations.

A. Permits

Perhaps the most distinctive aspect of the environmental law enforcement package is its extensive and effective use of permitting mechanisms. Particularly with laws as complex and technical as most of the environmental statutes, it is critical that there be an effective mechanism for bridging from generalities like "effluents shall be treated in compliance with best available technology" to specifics like "permittee is authorized to discharge from outfall 001 x pounds per day of pollutant y, subject to the condition that the discharge be monitored in accordance with specified protocols and that periodic reports be provided."

The permit fulfills this need by, in effect, establishing the "law" for a particular discharge or activity. The requirement to obtain a permit and operate in compliance with it is an individualized and highly effective way of ensuring that regulators are notified of releases or activities of which they need to be aware. It is also an effective way of ensuring and demonstrating that persons required to comply are on notice of their obligations. The role of permits in bridging between the substantive requirements of the environmental laws—notification, discharge controls, and so forth—and the other enforcement mechanisms discussed below and in section C, is an important part of the system as we know it.

Permitting requirements, however, are by no means the only weapon in environmental law's enforcement arsenal.

B. Enforcement Provisions of the Federal and State Environmental Statutes

Each of the major federal environmental statutes provides an array of enforcement tools to compel compliance with its mandates. Generally, these include:

- *Civil penalties* ranging from $10,000 to $50,000 per violation or day of violation;

- *Administrative orders* to respond or abate, typically stipulated penalties to enhance likelihood of compliance, enforceable by civil and criminal sanctions;
- *Civil actions for relief* including prohibition or mandatory injunction enforced by judicial decree;
- *Citizens civil actions* to compel compliance with or collect damages for violation of the statute; and
- *Criminal sanctions* against organizations and responsible individuals for misrepresentation or knowing or negligent violation of the statutes.

There is no doubt that the federal environmental statutes and the regulations under them present a formidable set of reasons for businesses and other organizations to institute programs for aggressive compliance with the environmental laws. They are supported and complemented by similar enforcement provisions in the state environmental statutes as well as in local laws and ordinances.

C. General Purpose Heavy Duty Criminal Laws

The last major category of ''environmental laws that enforce'' are laws from the criminal code, originally enacted to punish more traditional crimes, that have been adopted and adapted to the prosecution of crimes that are essentially environmental. The criminal code provisions that have proven particularly useful in this connection include:

- The prohibition against false statements to the federal government—18 U.S.C. §1001;
- The mail fraud statutes—18 U.S.C. §§1341, 1343; and
- The conspiracy laws—18 U.S.C. §371.

Even more traditional criminal laws, such as the murder statutes, have been used, at least at the state level, to successfully prosecute environmental offenses. These nonenvironmental laws have become almost as important as the environmental statutes in defining the liability of violators.

The environmental law enforcement package, then, is a carefully structured combination of methods—environmental and general purpose, traditional and newly conceived—that work together to bring negative consequences to those who fail to fulfill their environmental compliance obligations. This interaction has been extremely effective and will become even more formidable as the environmental law system matures.

V. Procedural Laws, Administrative Procedures, Codes, and Rules of Evidence

As with most areas of law, the business of environmental law is to find the facts and decide what to do about them. While the substantive laws outlined above will greatly affect the way this business is conducted, the required procedures—the process by which business is done—will be equally if not more influential in determining the outcomes of cases. In cases where there is significant scientific opinion on all sides of an issue, like causation, the critical questions can be who has the burden of proof and what must be done to carry it. In a case where an administrative agency has made a decision or promulgated a rule, the issue is not whether the rule or decision is good or bad, but whether it was within the agency's authority, consistent with required procedures, and otherwise in accordance with law. The critical questions of environmental practice—the cutting edge issues of science, risk assessment, application of technology, and analytical methods—are often resolved, not through the scientific and engineering disciplines, but through the *process* used to determine the facts and decide the issue.

A. Administrative Law and Procedure

Administrative law may not be a favorite course in law school and it is probably not an area in which the average practitioner has much experience. It is probable, however, that administrative law issues are at the heart of somewhere between 80 percent and 97 percent of all disputes concerning the federal environmental laws and regulations. Following is a brief outline of the most important aspects of administrative practice:

- Administrative agencies have no inherent or residual authority but can act only pursuant to authority delegated to them in the statutes enacted by Congress. If an agency acts beyond the scope of its delegated authority, its action is illegal.
- Agencies' opinions in interpreting their own regulations, and the statutes they administer, will, particularly if consistently held over a substantial period of time, be given deference by the courts.
- Agencies must act in accordance with the procedures specified in their enabling legislation, or if none are so specified, in accordance with the Administrative Procedure Act. The required procedures normally entail publication in the *Federal Register,* opportunity for public comment, sometimes a public hearing, response to public comment, and final publication.
- Agencies must act in accordance with their own rules and regulations and failure to follow those rules results in invalid actions.
- Agencies must maintain a docket or record in support of their action and there must be evidence in that record to support the agency action. The record must be open for public examination throughout the period when public comments are being received.
- Agency actions may not be "arbitrary and capricious," which means that there must be at least some evidence in the record to support the agency decision. When a statute specifically so requires, agencies must support their decisions with "substantial evidence." Although the difference between "some evidence" and "substantial evidence" is somewhat obscure, agencies hate substantial evidence requirements.
- Agency decisions may be appealed to the courts either under specific judicial review provisions in the enabling statutes or the general provision in the Administrative Procedure Act. Aggrieved parties cannot go

to court, however, unless they have standing, the issue is "ripe," administrative remedies have been exhausted, and a final agency decision has been issued.
- On appeal, administrative agency actions are generally upheld in the absence of some glaring procedural defect or a clearly inadequate record. These circumstances occur frequently, however, and successful appeals, while not the rule, are far from a rarity.

B. Determining Facts in Courts, Judicial Codes, Rules of Evidence, and Apportioning Liability

Most environmental cases do not get to court. Of the few that do, many involve the issue of causation, while most of the rest involve the question of who is responsible and what it takes to prove it. Some of these questions turn on evidentiary determinations, others on questions of responsibility, liability sharing, and contribution. What follows is a quick discussion of some of the major concepts.

1. Burden of Proof and Presumptions

Where, as is often the case, the scientific facts of a controversy are being hotly debated in the scientific community or the facts are otherwise unclear, the outcome of the case may turn on the question of who has the "burden of proof" and the obligation of going forward with the evidence.

In our legal system, plaintiffs in civil cases normally have the burden of proving their cases. They must do so by a preponderance of the evidence. However, as noted above, attorneys and courts have developed special liability concepts, like strict liability, to shift the burden to defendants in some circumstances. Since the party with the burden will often lose the case, the question is one of the most contentious issues in civil litigation in the environmental context.

In criminal cases, the prosecutor has the burden of proving guilt beyond a reasonable doubt and defendants are presumed innocent until proven guilty, though that presumption is not always reflected in public opinion.

Finally, where the issue involves an effort to set aside an agency regulation or other action, there is a presumption of validity and the contesting party has the obligation of proving conclusively that the action is arbitrary and capricious, unsupported by the evidence, or otherwise not in accordance with law.

2. Joint and Several Liability and Contribution

Although it is not strictly an evidentiary matter, the concept of joint and several liability in clean-up and toxic tort cases has developed in response to the extreme difficulty of making the factual determinations required in order to apportion liability among, say, numerous contributors to a hazardous waste landfill. The theory is that the public or the injured party should not bear the risk and cost of sorting out these complex situations but, instead, should rest the burden on those who caused the problems. Thus, what the law does is make each of the responsible parties responsible for *all* of the damage or clean-up costs and leave it to each to make the other responsible parties come up with a ''contribution'' for their share.

These issues of contribution and liability sharing were among the most hotly contested issues of the 1980s and the dispute will continue into the 1990s and perhaps beyond. The public may eventually ''win'' this dispute by making sure that clean-up costs are initially paid by parties who had at least some share in the responsibility for causing those costs. As usual, however, the public will pay for this victory (with transaction costs added for good measure) in the cost of goods and services it buys. There clearly is a need for improved procedures to determine and assess responsibility for environmental harms.

VI. Conclusion

The need for a working understanding of the environmental law system is probably more crucial now than it ever has been. Our actions and inactions, what we know, and, perhaps most important, what we ought to know, can have dramatic effects on the financial well-being of organizations as well as the financial and personal futures of the individuals who work for them. Knowledge of and strict adherence to the mandates of the environmental laws are not luxuries only for the largest companies and organizations. Executives, managers, and line employees, in companies and organizations of all sizes, need this knowledge and need to know how to use it. We hope this book will help.

2

Environmental Protection and the Common Law

By Timothy A. Vanderver, Jr. and John C. Martin
with John A. Gillan

I. Introduction

The foundation upon which our modern legal system is built is known as the common law. Originating in medieval England, the common law has been passed down through generations in the form of precedent—previous decisions of the courts. The common law is not a fixed body of rules, but rather a set of general principles arising out of the gradual accumulation of judicial decisions on the myriad of cases that come before courts. Although change in the common law occurs gradually, these principles are continually being adapted to meet new legal problems. Thus, most decisions can be traced back to earlier rulings. These common threads are the glue that binds the common law together.

Redressing wrongs of an environmental nature has a long history in the common law. Therefore, as public awareness of environmental issues increased in the 1960s, environmentalists and others first turned to the common law in their search for legal solutions to environmental dilemmas.[1] A number of common law doctrines address the burdens pollution problems place upon individuals.[2] Nuisance law protects against interference with the use and enjoyment of land,[3] while trespass provides protection from unpermitted physical intrusions.[4] If an intrusion results in direct physical or property damage, the injured party might sue in negligence. If certain types of hazardous activities are at issue, a cause of action in strict liability might arise.[5]

These legal theories were well developed, albeit at times contradictory and confusing, by the time the public and the courts developed their modern sensitivity to environmental issues. Not long after turning to the common law, however, environmentalists and their supporters came to believe that it was inadequate as a means of addressing environmental issues.[6] Pollution control under the common law was reactive rather than proactive. The common law

---

[1] Daniel P. Selmi & Kenneth A. Manaster, State Environmental Law 2–2 (1991).
[2] *Id.*
[3] Restatement (Second) of Torts §821 (1979).
[4] *Id.* §158.
[5] Selmi & Manaster, *supra* note 1, at 2–3.
[6] Krier, Environmental Litigation and the Burden of Proof in Law and the Environment (1970).

generally required that there be a private plaintiff with both sufficient injury and resources to warrant a legal action; sufficient relief under the common law could prove difficult to obtain.[7] With these realizations, in the late 1960s the emphasis in environmental protection turned to legislation specifically designed to address environmental concerns.

Over the past 20 years a wide variety of statutes have been enacted at both the state and federal level to address everything from air pollution to hazardous waste management. These statutes have, for the most part, imposed detailed control standards that dischargers must meet. These statutes have also created administrative agencies with expertise in the regulated area and the power to enforce relevant standards. Given this massive effort, many commentators believed that the demise of environmental common law was imminent.[8] Their predictions, however, have proven to be premature.

Far from being a clean break from the common law, regulatory statutes have incorporated both common law concepts and vices into their fabric. Courts and plaintiffs have used the common law to supplement, interpret, and even bypass environmental statutes. Thus, it has been held that the mere existence of an environmental statute will not necessarily preempt claims under common law theories,[9] and that the common law may be used to fill in the gaps in statutory language.[10] Finally, and perhaps most important, the common law is often used by private parties who have suffered environmental injury to recover damages in those instances where the relevant environmental statutes do not provide for such recovery.[11]

Taken together, the foregoing indicates that the common law is alive and well in the environmental arena. It provides a refuge for those plaintiffs who are ignored by statutory law and a means by which courts may interpret voids left in statutes by their drafters. It is, however, generally underutilized and poorly understood by both practitioners and the courts.

This chapter will discuss various theories of recovery under the common law. As part of this examination, we will trace the evolution of these theories from pre-seventeenth century England to the present. By gaining a more complete understanding of the various theories of liability, the reader can learn of the impact—both real and potential—of the common law on environmental issues.

II. Historical Development of the Environmental Common Law

A. Pre-Industrial Revolution

The earliest efforts by common law courts to deal with environmental issues focused on protection of property rights. In order to best understand this

---

[7] SELMI & MANASTER, *supra* note 1, at 2–3, n.5.

[8] SELMI & MANASTER, *supra* note 1, at 2–4.

[9] State, Dep't of Envtl. Protection v. Ventron, 94 N.J. 473, 468 A.2d 150, 163 (1983); Wilsonville v. SCA Servs. 86 Ill. 2d 1, 426 N.E.2d 824, 837 (1981).

[10] United States v. Alcan Aluminum Corp., 964 F.2d 252, 268 (3d Cir. 1992); United States v. Chem-Dyne Corp., 572 F. Supp. 802, 808 (S.D. Ohio 1983); O'Neil v. Picillo, 883 F.2d 176, 178 (1st Cir. 1989).

[11] In fact, most environmental statutes are designed to provide recompense for injury to the public rather than to the individual. The most notable exceptions to this rule are the cost recovery provisions of the Comprehensive Environmental Response, Compensation and Liability Act (CERCLA), 42 U.S.C. §9601 *et seq.*

approach, one must recognize that prior to the Industrial Revolution land was still the principal method by which wealth could be amassed, transferred, and passed on through inheritance. It was at once both means of exchange and method of livelihood, providing to its owners innumerable benefits that "ran with the land." Thus it was said that:

> [B]y the laws of England every invasion of private property, be it ever so minute, is a trespass. No man can set his foot upon my ground without my licence, but he is liable to an action, though the damage be nothing.[12]

Generally, the right to recover for environmental damage in preindustrial England was tied to the plaintiff's rights as a landowner.[13] The first tort developed by the medieval courts to address environmental concerns was *trespass quare clausum fregit* or trespass to land.[14] Technically this tort governed those instances where there was an actual "breach of the close" or physical invasion of the plaintiff's property. As time passed, however, courts came to recognize that trespass-like invasions, which fell short of actual physical entry but nevertheless interfered with the plaintiff's rights in his land, should be actionable.

In response to this recognition, the tort of nuisance was developed.[15] Thus, nuisance came to govern "such unlawful conduct as annoyance or disturbance in the enjoyment of property rather than forcible physical injury."[16] However, even though trespass and nuisance were clearly distinct actions, in practice the line between the two was sufficiently blurred so as to engender substantial confusion.[17] We will not examine this distinction further but will proceed from the premise that trespass and nuisance were the causes of action available to a landowner injured by pollution from his neighbor in the preindustrial era.

The standard of liability attaching to actions in trespass and nuisance in preindustrial England was, in general, one of strict liability.[18] Application of this standard was not, however, absolute; several commentators have identified cases as early as 1569[19] that allowed for mitigation based upon individual circumstances. Nevertheless, the strict liability standard, which was handed down from medieval times, continued in force in trespass and nuisance actions

---

[12] Entick v. Carrington, 19 S.T. at 1066 (Lord Camden, C.J. 1765).

[13] Larry D. Silver, *The Law of Environmental Risk and Some Recent Applications*, 10 HARV. ENVTL. L. REV. 61 (1986).

[14] J.H. BAKER, AN INTRODUCTION TO ENGLISH LEGAL HISTORY 71 (3d ed. 1990); F. KEMPIN, HISTORICAL INTRODUCTION TO ANGLO-AMERICAN LAW IN A NUTSHELL 165–67 (2d ed. 1973). *See also* 7 F. HOLDSWORTH, HOLDSWORTH'S HISTORY OF ENGLISH LAW 57–74 (2d ed. 1937).

[15] It is not clear whether nuisance was an outgrowth of trespass or a separate development. *See* 7 HOLDSWORTH, *supra* note 14, at 57–74; BAKER, *supra* note 14, at 478.

[16] BAKER, *supra* note 14, at 478.

[17] For example, courts held men absolutely liable in trespass for cattle that broke out of their property and entered the lands of another. 8 HOLDSWORTH, *supra* note 14, at 465–66. However, an action in nuisance lay for the flooding of plaintiff's land occasioned by defendant's negligent maintenance of a seawall. BAKER, *supra* note 14, at 481, citing, Bernardeston v. Heighlynge, 32 SS 309, 103 SS 457 (1342–1344). In each instance there was a physical invasion of the plaintiff's close by something originating on the defendant's property, yet different theories were applied. Thus, the distinction between these two causes is unclear.

[18] W. PROSSER, THE LAW OF TORTS §§13, 86 (4th ed. 1971); P. Keeton, *Trespass, Nuisance & Strict Liability*, 59 COLUM. L. REV. 457 (1959); 8 HOLDSWORTH, *supra* note 14, at 465–67.

[19] BAKER, *supra* note 14, at 486–88.

well into the nineteenth century.[20] In practice this meant that generally even the smallest invasion was actionable without regard to fault.[21]

By and large, the majority of cases of the preindustrial period dealing with environmental contamination appear to have been styled in nuisance rather than trespass. Early nuisance actions were maintained for smelly privies,[22] smoke and vibrations,[23] and disturbances and pollution of watercourses.[24] However, not until the seventeenth century was a hard and fast rule for addressing these cases developed in *Aldred v. Benton.*[25] That case involved a complaint regarding a neighbor's pigsty that was alleged to be constructed so near the plaintiff's property that "a fetid and unwholesome stink" flowed into his house and rendered it uninhabitable without risk of infection. The court applied the principle *sic utero tuo alienum non laedes* (use your own property so as not to injure your neighbor's) to enjoin the operation as a nuisance that lay, not for interfering with plaintiff's comfort, but for infecting the air.[26] This principle remained the lodestar of nuisance law well into the nineteenth century. Thus, in *Tenant v. Goldwin,*[27] the court applied the principle to allow an action where the defendant's privy wall collapsed and filth flowed into the plaintiff's cellar contaminating his coal and beer supplies. The court further observed that the result would be the same if a large dung heap collapsed onto the plaintiff's land.[28]

Despite the fact that the standard in nuisance actions was strict liability, common law courts did not permit unrestricted claims for nuisance. Instead, the use of the doctrine of *sic utero tuo* was restricted to protection of matters of necessity. Activities on neighboring property would not be enjoined for aesthetic reasons or other trifling inconveniences.[29] Thus in *Jeffrey's Case,*[30] the court refused to enjoin the operation of a school where the plaintiff complained that the "jabbering of the boys" disturbed the quiet of his study.

In addition to enjoining present nuisances, common law courts also, at least theoretically, found that threats of future harm could be enjoined. In *Ripon v. Hobart,*[31] the court found that such threats could be actionable depending on a balancing of the probability and the magnitude of the potential harm. Despite this theoretical possibility, it appears that preindustrial common law courts typically refused to enjoin potential nuisances prior to their construction.[32] Moreover, the present fear of future harm was deemed to be nonactionable under nuisance theory in this period.[33]

---

[20] T.F. PLUCKNETT, A CONCISE HISTORY OF THE COMMON LAW 408–09 (2d ed. 1936).

[21] *Id.*

[22] Luter v. Ware, London Assize, at 88, pl.364 (1341).

[23] Yonge v. Chadenesfeld, London Assize, at 160, pl.617 (1378) (smoke and vibrations from armorer's forge).

[24] Lowth v. Abbott of Lesnes, 103 SS 348 (1317) (diverting and polluting water).

[25] B. & M. 599 (1610), 77 Eng. Rep. 816 (1611).

[26] *Id. See also* BAKER, *supra* note 14, at 487.

[27] 2 Lyd. Ram. 1089, 6 Mod. Rep. 311 (1704).

[28] *Id. See also* BAKER, *supra* note 14, at 491.

[29] Silver, *supra* note 13, at 7.

[30] B. & M. 592 (c.1560).

[31] 40 Eng. Rep. 65 (1834).

[32] Ramsay v. Riddle, 20 F. Cas. 212 (C.C.D.C. 1807).

[33] *In Anonymous,* 26 Eng. Rep. 1230 (Ch. 1752).

Although many of the early efforts of common law courts appear to have concerned nuisance claims, trespass claims for environmental harm were not unknown. In *Wiseman v. Denham,*[34] both trespass and nuisance claims lay for the failure of the defendant to remove noxious substances from the plaintiff's property when he was under a duty to do so. In that case, the plaintiff had set out milk and butter as tithes and the defendant, the local rector, had failed to collect them until they had become moldy. Similarly, in *Hales Case,*[35] a defendant who had a "horrible sickness" and who would not leave the plaintiff's house was found liable for both trespass and nuisance. The remaining on the land was a trespass and the infection of the air was a nuisance.[36]

Taken together, the foregoing indicates that by the beginning of the Industrial Revolution there was a well-developed body of cases upon which a party suffering environmental injury could rely. Moreover, under both trespass and nuisance theories, the plaintiff could, in most cases, count upon the application of a strict liability standard being applied to the defendant's conduct. Thus, whether his complaint was for foul smells emanating from his neighbor's property or actual invasion of his land by noxious substances, the plaintiff/landowner could proceed knowing that the law was predisposed to favor his case. However, as society began to undergo fundamental change because of its burgeoning industrialization, so too did the courts begin to reexamine that predisposition to the landowner's interests that had been handed down from medieval times.

B. Industrial Revolution

Between 1700 and 1910 England and America underwent a radical transformation from predominantly agrarian to largely industrial nations. This massive shift reduced, to a certain extent, the traditional value of land, and brought with it a host of complex new problems, both social and environmental. The response of the common law to these changes was gradual. Nonetheless, although many traditional concepts continued to be applied, over the course of the nineteenth century the case-by-case evaluation of liability that had made some inroads into the strict liability standard during the 1500s[37] gradually came to replace that standard in both trespass and nuisance actions.[38]

For the first half of the nineteenth century, the main feature of the common law's approach to environmental problems was continued application of old doctrines. Of particular import in this regard was continued emphasis on the denial of injunctive relief for prospective nuisances. The lengths to which the courts went during the Industrial Revolution to avoid enjoining potential nuisances is illustrated by the case of *Attorney General v. Mayor, Alderman & Corporation of Kingston-on-Thames.*[39] In that case the town proposed to construct a drainage system that would discharge the untreated sewage from the

[34] Palm. 341, Ley 69 (1623).
[35] B. & M. 592, 593 (1569).
[36] *See* BAKER, *supra* note 14, at 487.
[37] *Id.* at 486–89.
[38] PLUCKNETT, *supra* note 20, at 408–13.
[39] 6 New. Rep. 248, 13 WR 888 (Wood, V.C. 1865).

entire town of Kingston into the Thames, thereby increasing the amount of sewage discharged by the town to 10 times the preconstruction level. Despite testimony indicating that this discharge would foul waters downstream making them unfit for fishing and bathing and the possibility of pollution of the town's own upstream water supply, Vice Chancellor Wood found that there was no evidence of immediate and irreparable harm. His opinion stated:

> Something which might happen in a hundred years time would not justify the interposition of the court; inasmuch as by that time a variety of chemical contrivances might be found to prevent the evil, and a variety of contrivances might be discovered by which the very thing that was now being done might be done without the evil effect anticipated.[40]

A similar result obtained in *Salvin v. North Brancepeth Coal Co.*,[41] where plaintiff sought an injunction claiming that smoke and vapors from coal ovens constituted a nuisance to his land. Although the court conceded that the emissions might have done some slight damage to the plaintiff's lands, it would not enjoin the operation of the ovens because there was no injury that could be discerned by a layman.[42] The court's antipathy to relief from future environmental harm was plainly stated by Mr. Justice James when he wrote:

> So if it were made out that every minute a millionth of a grain of poison were absorbed by a tree, or a millionth of a grain of dust deposited on a tree, that would not afford a ground for interfering, although after a lapse of a million minutes the grains of dust or the grains of poison could be easily detected.[43]

The most extreme example of this philosophy is embodied in the decision of *Fletcher v. Bealy.*[44] In that case the owner of a paper mill complained that the dumping of sulfuric vat waste by the defendant on the upstream banks of the river running adjacent to his mill was a nuisance in that his mill needed almost pure water to operate. Despite the fact that both plaintiff and defendant agreed that as a result of the dumping, chemicals from these piles would begin to seep into the river in a year or two and continue to seep for upwards of 50 years, the court found no nuisance arguing that it was possible that science would find a remedy for the problem before it got to such a point as to destroy plaintiff's business.[45]

Although the common law continued to employ old doctrines during the nineteenth century, it was not static. The most significant change in the common law's treatment of environmental harm during the Industrial Revolution was the gradual weakening of the doctrine of *sic utero tuo* and the abandonment of the strict liability standard, first in regard to injunctive relief and later in connection with damages claims. The origins of this change are found in the case of *St. Helen's Smelting.*[46] There, the House of Lords used the doctrine of *sic utero tuo* to uphold a lower court decision enjoining the operation of a copper smelter.

[40] 6 New. Rep. at 253.
[41] 9 L.R.-Ch. 705 (1874).
[42] 9 L.R.-Ch. at 708 n.1.
[43] *Id.* at 709.
[44] 28 Ch.D. 688 (1885).
[45] *Id.* at 695.
[46] 11 Eng. Rep. 1483 (H.L. 1865).

The plaintiff in that case alleged that the smelter spewed "noxious vapours" onto his land, damaging his trees and shrubs and disturbing the occupants. Though finding in favor of the plaintiff, Lord Cranworth quoted in dicta an unreported case where although it was proved that smoke interfered to a certain degree with the plaintiff's use of his land, no action lay. The unreported case provided that:

> You must look at it not with a view to the question whether, abstractedly, that quantity of smoke was a nuisance, but whether it was a nuisance to a person living in the town of Shields.[47]

Misconstruing this dicta in *St. Helens* as establishing a balancing approach that overrode the previous doctrine of *sic utero tuo,* the common law courts gradually[48] adopted as a general rule a utilitarian doctrine that considered the value and reasonableness of the defendant's enterprise in relation to the locality, overriding the once absolute guarantees made to the passive property owner.[49] This shift effectively "devalued" the sanctity of the plaintiff's property right by inquiring into the reasonableness of both the defendant's activities and the plaintiff's expectations. Moreover, based on an examination of the nuisance actions brought against entrepreneurs in nineteenth century America, it appears that courts came to view the rights of the entrepreneur as weighing more heavily in this balancing test than the rights of the individual plaintiff.[50] This devaluation or shift clearly reflects the broader societal change in which the landowner was being supplanted by the entrepreneur as society's prime economic mover.

The adoption of a balancing standard in the environmental area was first seen in the treatment of claims for injunctive relief in nuisance actions. Though the approach by the courts to such requests reflected their long-standing antipathy to injunctive relief for potential nuisances, the balancing approach gradually became the new basis for the denials. Thus, in *Auburn & Cato Plank Road Co. v. Douglass,*[51] the court stated: "While . . . *sic utero tuo,* etc. may be a very good moral precept, it is utterly useless as a legal maxim. . . ."[52]

In contrast to their approach to injunctive relief, common law courts, particularly in the United States, continued to uniformly apply the traditional strict liability rule to damages cases in nuisance for the first half of the nineteenth century.[53] Thus in *Scott v. Bay,*[54] the court found that the precautions taken by defendant, while they might have been proper and appropriate, were no bar to liability where defendant's quarrying operation had damaged plaintiff's land. As the century began to move to a close, however, U.S. courts began to adopt the balancing test in damages cases that had up to that point been used

---

[47] 11 Eng. Rep. at 1487.

[48] Not until 1856 did an American court expressly adopted a balancing test for a nuisance injunction. Grey v. Ohio & Pa. R.R., 1 Grant Cas. 412 (Pa. 1856). The use of balancing for nuisance damages cases did not come into vogue until much later in the century.

[49] *See* Hole v. Barlow, 140 Eng. Rep. 1113, 1118 (C.P. 1858); Silver, *supra* note 13, at 9. *See generally* P. Kurtz, *Nineteenth Century Anti-Entrepreneurial Nuisance Injunctions—Avoiding the Chancellor,* 17 WM. & MARY L. REV. 621 (1976).

[50] *See generally* Kurtz, *supra* note 49.

[51] 9 N.Y. 444 (1854).

[52] *Id.* at 445. *See also* Kurtz, *supra* note 49, at 644–46.

[53] Kurtz, *supra* note 49, at 644.

[54] 3 Md. 431 (1853).

only in the injunctive setting.[55] In *McCarty v. Natural Carbonic Gas Co.,*[56] the court described the law of substantive nuisance as "a law of degree [that] usually turns on the question of fact whether the use is reasonable under the circumstances."[57]

The move to balancing and the bias in favor of the entrepreneur, evidenced by the foregoing cases, had two notable exceptions. First, during the Industrial Revolution courts for the first time explicitly allowed a cause of action in nuisance for fear of future harm, in particular fear of infection.[58] Moreover, courts held that such fear did not even have to be founded in scientific fact to be actionable. Thus, in the case of *Everett v. Paschall,*[59] the Supreme Court of Washington enjoined the operation of a sanitorium for the treatment of tuberculosis based on the plaintiff's fear of infection, even though the lower court found that due to the distance from the property, the plaintiff's fear was scientifically unfounded.[60]

The second exception to the bias in favor of the entrepreneur was the continued use of a strict liability standard for "non-natural" uses of a defendant's land. In the landmark case of *Rylands v. Fletcher,*[61] plaintiff sought recovery where defendants, mill owners in a mining region, constructed a reservoir on their property. Unbeknownst to them, the land below the reservoir was crisscrossed with the passages and filled shafts of an abandoned mine. The waters of the reservoir "escaped" into the abandoned mine and from there flooded the working mine of the plaintiff.[62] As explained by Prosser,

> No trespass could be found, since the flooding was not direct or immediate; nor any nuisance, as the term was then understood, since there was nothing offensive to the senses and the damage was not continuing or recurring.[63]

The failure of the "traditional" remedies to provide redress in this instance did not prevent the Court of Exchequer Chamber from finding the mill owner strictly liable. The court stated:

> We think that the true rule of law is that the person who for his own purposes brings on his land and collects and keeps there anything likely to do mischief if it escapes, must do so at his peril, and if he does not do so, is prima facie answerable for all damage which is the natural consequence of its escape.[64]

The House of Lords, while affirming liability on appeal, used a narrower construction of the rule. Discussing the rule set out by the Court of Exchequer Chamber, the opinion of Lord Cairns provides:

---

[55] Kurtz, *supra* note 49, at 663.

[56] 189 N.Y. 40, 81 N.E. 549 (1907).

[57] *Id.*, 81 N.E. at 549. *See also* Eller v. Koehler, 68 Ohio St. 51, 67 N.E. 89 (1903).

[58] PROSSER, *supra* note 18, §87, n.80.

[59] 61 Wash. 47, 111 P. 879 (1910).

[60] *Id.* It should be noted that although this decision was not consistent with the general approach of the preindustrial common law, it was not the first time that fear of infection was taken into account in a nuisance decision. *See* Hale's Case, B. & M. 592, 593 (1569).

[61] Fletcher v. Rylands, 3 H. & C. 774, 159 Eng. Rep. 737 (1865), *rev'd*, L.R.1 Ex. 265 (1866), *aff'd. sub nom.* Rylands v. Fletcher, L.R.3 H.L. 330 (1868).

[62] *Id.*

[63] PROSSER, *supra* note 18, §78, at 505.

[64] Fletcher v. Rylands, L.R. 1 Ex. at 279–80.

> The general rule as stated above seems on principle just. The person whose grass or corn is eaten down by the escaping cattle of his neighbor, or whose mine is flooded by the water from his neighbor's reservoir, or whose cellar is invaded by the filth of his neighbor's privy, or whose habitation is made unhealthy by the fumes and vapours of his neighbor's alkali works, is damnified without any fault of his own; and it seems but reasonable and just that the neighbor, who has brought something on his property which was not naturally there, harmless to others so long as it is confined to his own property, but which he knows to be mischievous if it gets on his neighbor's, should be obliged to make good the damage which ensues if he does not succeed in confining it to his own property.[65]

Although the House of Lords failed to define nonnatural uses, later commentators have concluded that the standard enunciated in *Rylands* required examination of the suitability of the activity in the particular locale. Thus, not all reservoirs are unnatural uses, only those located in areas where the property owner should know that local conditions make the likelihood of damage great.[66] Although it is often described as new law, the rule enunciated in *Rylands* has its roots in the traditional rule of strict liability for trespassing cattle.[67] Moreover, as Holdsworth points out, the common law had long recognized the principle that the doing of obviously dangerous acts should impose a stricter standard of liability.[68]

Based upon the foregoing, it is clear that at the close of the Industrial Revolution the common law had made some significant modifications in the way in which it had approached environmental problems since the Middle Ages. The abandonment of the *sic utero tuo* doctrine ushered in an age when courts would balance all the facts and circumstances in each case when deciding whether trespass or nuisance would lay. As they did for civil liability in general, courts abandoned strict liability standards in favor of fault and negligence theories. At the same time, they continued to apply their traditional strict scrutiny to requests for injunctive relief. This state of affairs continued in effect for most of the first half of the century. In the flush of post-World War II prosperity, however, a green revolution would occur that would force a reexamination of these principles.

III. The Modern Era

With the notable exception of the fear of harm cases, common law concepts as developed in the nineteenth century have changed very little in this century.[69] However, the way in which courts have applied those concepts has changed significantly in the last 30 years. While during the nineteenth century and the first part of the twentieth, courts were predisposed to favor the entrepre-

---

[65] Rylands v. Fletcher, L.R.3 H.L. at 339–40.

[66] *See* Selmi & Manaster, *supra* note 1, at 4–7; State, Dep't of Envtl. Protection v. Ventron, 94 N.J. 473, 489–90, 468 A.2d 150 (1983).

[67] Prosser, *supra* note 18, §78, at 505.

[68] 8 Holdsworth, *supra* note 14, at 468–71.

[69] Silver, *supra* note 13, at 14. According to Silver, the courts of the twentieth century severely reduced the ability of plaintiffs to recover for fear of environmental harm. *Id.*

neur at the expense of the environment,[70] courts in the post-1970 period exhibited a willingness to use the common law to protect the environment and innocent injuried parties.[71] However, despite the willingness of the courts to use common law theories in favor of the environment, the results have not always been satisfactory in the eyes of the environmental community. Principally, environmentalists have discovered that the reactive nature of the common law does not foster the pollution prevention that they sought.

Recognition of the limitations of the common law in protecting the environment has led to the passage of a series of comprehensive statutes designed to regulate those activities perceived to have the greatest impact on the environment. By and large, these statutes seek to implement and enforce various permitting and regulatory schemes by which the government (on behalf of the public) regulates the introduction of pollutants into the environment. Thus limits are set, standards are imposed, penalties assessed, and cleanups required that are intended to prevent environmental harm and protect the rights of the public as a whole in the natural world.

Despite the comprehensive nature of these statutes, however, significant environmental interests are not protected under their ambit, namely the interest of the private individual. With the notable exception of the Comprehensive Environmental Response, Compensation, and Liability Act's (CERCLA or Superfund) cost recovery provisions, federal environmental statutes have ignored the interest of the individual who has incurred environmental harm. It is in this statutory void that the common law continues to flourish. This section will examine each of the most prevalent common law causes of action available in the environmental area today.

A. Nuisance

The modern formulation of the tort of nuisance harkens back to that of the Industrial Revolution. Thus the *Restatement (Second) of Torts* provides that a private nuisance is an invasion of another's interest in the private use and enjoyment of land.[72] The invasion will be actionable only if (1) the conduct giving rise to the invasion is tortious and (2) an interest associated with the use and enjoyment of plaintiff's land has been invaded.[73]

A public nuisance, on the other hand, is an interference with a right of the public at large, which is not limited to the use and enjoyment of land.[74] As in the

[70] *See* Rose v. Socony-Vacuum Corp., 54 R.I. 411, 173 A. 627 (1934) (contamination of aquifer originating at defendant's oil refinery not actionable because caused by percolating waters whose courses not known); Turner v. Big Lake Oil Co., 128 Tex. 155, 96 S.W.2d 221 (1936) (escape of salt water from detention pond on defendant's property that contaminated plaintiff's fresh water supply found not actionable for similar reasons).

[71] *See* Reserve Mining Co. v. EPA, 514 F.2d 492 (8th Cir. 1975); *Ventron,* 94 N.J. 473, 489–90.

[72] RESTATEMENT, *supra* note 3, §§821D, 822; Copart v. Consolidated Edison Co., 41 N.Y.2d 564, 362 N.E.2d 968, 971 (1977). This should be distinguished from invasions of and harm to the property itself.

[73] RESTATEMENT, *supra* note 3, §821 cmt. a. *See also* Wright v. Masonite Corp., 368 F.2d 661, 663–65 (4th Cir. 1966), *cert. denied,* 386 U.S. 934 (1967) (plaintiff brought a nuisance action for damages for the loss of goods resulting from the discharge of gas from defendant's neighboring plant; court held that the nonnegligent and unintentional discharge of gases by the defendant created no private nuisance nor a cause of action therefor).

[74] RESTATEMENT, *supra* note 3, §821B.

case of private nuisance, the plaintiff must prove both tortious conduct and an actionable invasion resulting therefrom.[75] Only where the plaintiff can prove some special injury may he or she recover under this theory.[76] However, in environmental cases the showing of special injury is often easily made.[77] Thus in *Anderson v. W.R. Grace & Co.,*[78] plaintiffs claimed that defendant's contamination of groundwater constituted a public nuisance. The court found that the special injury requirement was satisfied by plaintiffs' allegation that they had suffered a variety of illnesses due to exposure to the water. The public interest was in uncontaminated groundwater, the special injury arose by the effect the contaminated water had on the particular plaintiffs.[79]

A claim for nuisance can be made for an invasion caused by conduct that is both intentional and unreasonable. An invasion will be considered intentional if the defendant (1) acts for the purpose of causing the invasion or (2) knows that the invasion results or is substantially certain to result from the conduct.[80] A prime example of such substantial certainty is *Hughes v. Emerald Mines Corp.*[81] In that case plaintiffs alleged that defendant's acts were intentional where it injected grout into the ground that sealed off water from plaintiffs' nearby wells. The court found that reasonable persons could deduce that defendant knew that its grouting process would seal off water, that the grout had traveled and sealed off wells in the past, and that in this instance the danger of this recurring was substantial. Thus the invasion was unreasonable.[82]

An invasion will not be actionable in nuisance unless it is substantial, i.e., if it offends normal persons in that particular locality.[83] As a general rule, the unsightliness of a thing, without more, does not render it a nuisance.[84] This does not mean that nuisance will be restricted to physical or tangible impact. Use and enjoyment of property encompasses all the pleasures and comforts people derive from the use and occupancy of their lands.[85]

Codifying the balancing tests that arose in the nineteenth century, the *Restatement* provides that an invasion will be found to be unreasonable if either (1) the gravity of the harm outweighs the utility of the actor's conduct or (2) the harm caused is serious and the financial burden of compensating for this and similar harm to others would make the continuation of the harm not feasible.[86] The gravity of the harm will be determined by weighing five factors: (1) the extent of the harm, (2) the character of the harm, (3) the social value of the use invaded, (4) the suitability of the invaded use to the location, and (5) the burden

---

[75] *Id.* §821B cmt. c.

[76] SELMI & MANASTER, *supra* note 1, at 3–2; Philadelphia Elec. Co. v. Hercules, Inc., 762 F.2d 303 (3d Cir. 1985), *cert. denied,* 106 S. Ct. 384 (1985).

[77] SELMI & MANASTER, *supra* note 1, at 3–3.

[78] 628 F. Supp. 1219, 1233 (D. Mass. 1986).

[79] *See* RESTATEMENT, *supra* note 3, §821C cmt. d.

[80] *Id.* at §825; Hughes v. Emerald Mines Corp., 450 A.2d 1, 4–5 (Pa. Super. 1982).

[81] 450 A.2d 1 (Pa. Super. 1982).

[82] *Id. See also* Padilla v. Lawrence, 685 P.2d 964, 968 (N.M. 1984); Morgan v. Quailbrook Condominium Co., 704 P.2d 573, 577 (Utah 1985).

[83] Page County Appliance Center, Inc. v. Honeywell, Inc., 347 N.W.2d 171, 175 (Iowa 1984); Burgess v. Omahawaks Radio Control Org., 219 Neb. 100, 362 N.W.2d 27 (1985).

[84] Coty v. Ramsey Assocs., Inc., 546 A.2d 196, 201 (Vt. 1988).

[85] Exxon Corp. v. Yarema, 516 A.2d 990, 1002 (Md. App. 1986); RESTATEMENT, *supra* note 3, at §821D.

[86] RESTATEMENT, *supra* note 3, at §826.

on the person harmed to avoid the harm.[87] The utility of the harmful conduct will be determined through an examination of (1) the social value attached to the primary purpose of the conduct, (2) the suitability of the conduct to the location in question, and (3) the impracticality of preventing or avoiding the invasion.[88] Finally, a harm will be considered per se unreasonable if it could have been avoided with minimal cost to the actor.[89]

Putting all of these principles into practice, modern courts have been willing to uphold claims of nuisance for all manner of environmental problems. For example, in *Ozark Poultry Products, Inc. v. Garmon,*[90] the plaintiffs claimed that the odors from a rendering plant caused them to lose sleep at night and to feel nauseous. The court found the odors emanating from the plant to be a nuisance and ordered the defendants to close the plant unless the conditions causing the nuisance were corrected. In *O'Neil v. Carolina Freight Carriers Corp.,*[91] plaintiffs claimed that the noise from defendant's trucking terminal kept them awake at night and disturbed them enough at other times during the day to interfere with their enjoyment of their home. The court found that the noise was a nuisance and both issued an injunction and awarded damages to plaintiffs. In *Burgess v. M.V. Tamano,*[92] plaintiff clam diggers and fishermen were able to maintain a public nuisance action for damages to coastal waters resulting from defendant's oil spill. The court found that there was a public right in the use and enjoyment of the coastal waters and the marine life contained therein, and that the fishermen and clam diggers had a special injury from the interference with their exercise of that public right to fish and harvest clams.

Despite the fact that the common law continues to permit recovery under nuisance theories, its coverage is not unlimited. First, as noted above, the common law has not, since the nineteenth century, allowed claims for trifling inconveniences. Thus a defendant may claim that the harm alleged is not substantial and therefore not actionable.[93] Second, a defendant may argue that plaintiff's suit is barred by the statute of limitations. Such a defense will only be applicable in those cases where the nuisance is not continuing.[94] Third, a defendant may be able to convince the court that under the applicable balancing test the utility of the activity at issue outweighs the harm that has been caused.[95] This defense may have limited applicability where the plaintiff's use is a residential one as there is some preference for residential uses in the balancing process employed by modern courts.[96] Fourth, a defendant may argue that it has complied with all laws and the terms of all applicable permits. The success of this defense is unclear as many courts have been reluctant to consider such

[87] *Id.* at §827. *See* Great Atl. & Pac. Tea Co. v. LaSalle Nat'l Bank, 395 N.E.2d 1193 (Ill. 1979); Crest Chevrolet-Oldsmobile-Cadillac, Inc. v. Willemsen, 384 N.E.2d 692, 696 (Wis. 1986).

[88] RESTATEMENT, *supra* note 3, at §828.

[89] *Id.* at §830.

[90] 472 S.W.2d 714 (Ark. 1971).

[91] 244 A.2d 372 (Conn. 1988).

[92] 370 F. Supp. 247, 250–251 (D. Me. 1973).

[93] *See Coty,* 546 A.2d at 201.

[94] SELMI & MANASTER, *supra* note 1, at 3–30 through 3–33.

[95] *Id.* at 3–16 through 3–17.

[96] *Id.*

compliance as a bar to recovery.[97] In such cases, however, courts have placed a heavier burden on plaintiffs to prove that the defendant's conduct was unreasonable by taking the defendant's compliance into account in the balancing test.[98] Finally, a defendant may argue that the plaintiff is a successor in title to him and thus is not entitled to recovery.[99]

The value of both public and private nuisance claims lies in the fact that a plaintiff may use them to obtain relief for injuries to that bundle of intangible rights accompanying the property interest that make up "use and enjoyment." Economic damages, like those claimed in *Burgess,* and damages relating to physical discomfort and noise, like those claimed in *O'Neil* and *Ozark Poultry,* would not have been recoverable under any federal statute. Moreover, unlike federal statutes, nuisance theory provides for damages beyond those that can be obtained under current environmental laws.

B. Trespass

Second only to nuisance, trespass also has its roots in pre-twentieth century jurisprudence. The *Restatement* provides that one who either intentionally or negligently or recklessly (1) enters or causes a third party or thing to enter the plaintiff's land, (2) remains on the plaintiff's land, or (3) fails to remove from the plaintiff's land a thing that he was under a duty to remove, will be liable in trespass for any harm thereby caused to any legal interest of the plaintiff.[100]

Although this formulation seems to provide a bright line test, in practice the distinction between trespass and nuisance has often blurred. This is particularly apparent in cases where there is a physical invasion but the offending object (particle, etc.) is not visible to the naked eye. In such cases some courts have styled the action as nuisance[101] while others view it as trespass.[102] Some courts have even used the two doctrines interchangeably, thus adding to the confusion.[103] Plaintiffs are therefore wise to allege both trespass and nuisance when dealing with issues of environmental damage as not all cases are easily classified. For the purposes of this section, however, we will use the definition of trespass enunciated in *Borland v. Sanders Lead Co.,*[104] as only the actual physical invasion of the property itself and damage resulting therefrom.

As indicated by the *Restatement's* definition, courts have retained the nineteenth century requirement that a showing of either intent or fault is a prerequisite to a trespass. To show the requisite intent on the part of the defendant, the plaintiff does not need to prove that the defendant acted for the purpose of causing the invasion. Intent may be established if the defendant knows that there is a substantial certainty that its actions will result in the

---

[97] *Padilla,* 685 P.2d at 968.

[98] SELMI & MANASTER, *supra* note 1, at 3–26; Rose v. Chaikin, 453 A.2d 1378 (N.J. 1982).

[99] Philadelphia Elec. Co. v. Hercules, Inc., 762 F.2d 303 (3d Cir. 1985).

[100] RESTATEMENT, *supra* note 3, at §§158, 165.

[101] *Padilla,* 685 P.2d at 968 (court would only allow nuisance and not trespass claim where the plaintiff's expert could not measure the dust deposited on plaintiff's land).

[102] Hall v. DeWeld Mica Corp., 93 S.E.2d 56 (1956) (cloud of dust sufficient to support claim for trespass).

[103] Stacy v. Vepco, 7 E.R. Cases 1443 (E.D. Va. 1975).

[104] 369 So.2d 523, 2 A.L.R.4th 1042, 1051 (Ala. 1979).

invasion.[105] Absent intent, a showing of negligence will also suffice to establish fault on the part of the defendant.[106]

In addition to fault or intent, the plaintiff must also show that the harm suffered is substantial. The degree of substantiality will depend, as in nuisance, on the facts of the case and the outlook of the court that is examining those facts. Thus in *Martin v. Reynolds,*[107] the court found that the discharge of fluoride compounds in the form of gases and particulates could constitute a trespass. In contrast, the court in *Padilla*[108] found that the dust that landed on the plaintiff's property but that could not be measured by plaintiff's expert did not amount to a trespass. It is likely that a court will take a harder look at indirect invasions than at direct ones.[109]

One of the most important issues in a suit for trespass is whether in the course of committing the alleged trespass the defendant violated any statute or ordinance. In *Springer v. Schlitz Brewing Co.,*[110] plaintiffs alleged that Schlitz violated their riparian rights by overloading the local publicly owned treatment works (POTW), causing several fish kills in the river running adjacent to their property. The court instructed the jury that if it found Schlitz had violated the local sewage ordinance, that would be negligence per se and if that negligence were the cause of the damages claimed, Schlitz would be liable.

Trespass may be seen to have more limited utility than nuisance in the environmental context as it is limited in application to invasions of the plaintiff's property, whereas nuisance goes to rights attached to property other than those owned by the plaintiff. Nevertheless, trespass, like nuisance, provides its best service when the private litigant seeks to recover damages other than those directly associated with cleaning up the property, such as economic loss or damage. Such damages are not recoverable under federal statutes. Moreover, because of the confusion over the trespass/nuisance distinction, a trespass claim may be all that is needed in some jurisdictions to recover damages for interference with the plaintiff's use and enjoyment of its property. Thus in *French v. Ralph E. Moore, Inc.,*[111] plaintiffs sued defendant, the owner of a service station, for damages caused by gasoline contamination of their property. In finding for the plaintiffs, the court stated that where there was a trespass to land, damages for discomfort and annoyance of the occupant, in addition to damage to the land itself, were recoverable and long recognized. No federal statute currently provides for such damages.

C. Abnormally Dangerous/Ultrahazardous Activities

The third common law doctrine of the nineteenth century still in use in the environmental area is the doctrine of abnormally dangerous/ultrahazardous

[105] SELMI & MANASTER, *supra* note 1, at 4–4; RESTATEMENT, *supra* note 3, at §158 cmt. (i); Dial v. City of O'Fallon, 411 N.E.2d 217, 221 (Ill. 1980).

[106] RESTATEMENT, *supra* note 3, at §165.

[107] 342 P.2d 790, 794 (Or. 1969).

[108] Padilla v. Lawrence, 685 P.2d 964, 968 (N.M. 1984).

[109] *Borland,* 369 So.2d 523, 2 A.L.R.4th 1042, 1051 (Ala. 1979).

[110] 510 F.2d 468 (4th Cir. 1975).

[111] 203 Mont. 327, 661 P.2d 844, 847 (1983).

activities. The doctrine of strict liability for unnatural uses of land enunciated in *Rylands v. Fletcher* has been codified in two different forms over the years in the *Restatement.* The first *Restatement* provided that defendants would be strictly liable for the damages caused by ultrahazardous activities in which they engaged.[112] These activities were defined as activities that necessarily involve a serious risk of harm that cannot be eliminated and that are not a matter of common usage.[113] It would appear that this definition is more constricted than that of the House of Lords in *Rylands* by limiting its applicability to activities with serious risks of harm.[114]

The second *Restatement* significantly modified the language of the first *Restatement,* dispensing with the requirement of a risk of serious harm. This formulation, which appears to be more faithful to *Rylands,* provides:

> One who carries on an abnormally dangerous activity is subject to liability for harm to the person, land or chattels of another resulting from the activity, although he has exercised the utmost care to prevent the harm.[115]

The *Restatement* goes on to provide that an activity may be found abnormally dangerous based upon an evaluation of six factors: (1) the existence of a high degree of risk of some harm to the person, land, or chattels of another; (2) the likelihood that the harm that results will be great; (3) the inability to eliminate the risk by the exercise of reasonable care; (4) the extent to which the activity is not a matter of common usage; (5) the inappropriateness of the activity to the location; and (6) the extent to which the value to the community is outweighed by its dangerous attributes.[116] This balancing test is highly dependent upon the evidence presented by both sides regarding the character of the activity at issue. Moreover, as with all such balancing tests, it is a highly subjective endeavour, the results of which will depend upon the outlook of the particular court involved.

Despite the fact that it would appear that the second *Restatement* was intended to replace the first, courts continue to use both formulations somewhat indiscriminately.[117] Moreover, some courts have applied the tests interchangeably thus adding to the confusion. In *Cities Service Co. v. State,*[118] the court discussed both the first and second *Restatements* before finding defendants' conduct to be a nonnatural use of the land, subjecting defendants to strict liability.

Application of the abnormally dangerous/ultrahazardous activity doctrine in the environmental context has been fairly widespread in recent years. In the definitive case in this regard, *State, Department of Environmental Protection v. Ventron,*[119] the state sued both present and former owners of a site where mercury processing operations had resulted in mercury contamination of both

---

[112] RESTATEMENT, *supra* note 3, at §520.
[113] *Id.*
[114] SELMI & MANASTER, *supra* note 1, at 4–7.
[115] RESTATEMENT, *supra* note 3, at §519.
[116] *Id.* at §520.
[117] SELMI & MANASTER, *supra* note 1, at 4–7 through 4–8.
[118] 312 So.2d 799 (Fla. App. 1979).
[119] 94 N.J. 473, 468 A.2d 150, 163 (1983).

the site itself and the tidal creek running through it. Citing the *Restatement* factors, the court examined the facts and found that:

> mercury and other toxic wastes are "abnormally dangerous" and . . . the disposal of them, past or present, is an abnormally dangerous activity. We recognize that one engaged in disposing of toxic waste may be performing an activity that is of some use to society. Nevertheless, "the unavoidable risk of harm that is inherent in it requires that it be carried on at his peril, rather than at the expense of the innocent person who suffers harm as a result of it."[120]

Numerous other cases have adopted this approach in the environmental context. Thus it has been held that storage of toxic wastes in underground tanks, chemical contamination from oil wells, leaking gasoline tanks, and radioactive emissions all give rise to strict liability.[121]

Despite the large number of cases imposing liability under this theory of abnormally dangerous activities, not all courts have been willing to adopt it outright. Even the New Jersey court, which so strongly embraced the concept, recently rejected a claim that the storage of gasoline in underground tanks is an ultrahazardous activity.[122]

In addition to proving that an activity is not ultrahazardous in the facts and circumstances of a given case, the defendant may also avoid liability by arguing that its activity was not in fact a cause of the harm complained of. In *State Department of Environmental Protection v. Exxon Corp.,*[123] the court held that ownership of the land, without active participation in the injury, was not sufficient to impose liability. Another defense that may be raised in response to a strict liability claim is assumption of the risk.[124] In *Allied Corp. v. Frola,*[125] the U.S. district court in New Jersey ruled that assumption of the risk could be a defense if the defendant could show that the plaintiff/landlord assumed the risk of contamination of his property from the activities of his tenant. In a similar vein, a defendant may also raise the defense of contributory negligence.[126] A defendant may not claim, however, that the intervening acts of a third party should prevent the application of strict liability.[127]

One of the most significant advantages of a claim under this theory is that an activity that is otherwise lawful may nonetheless be considered abnormally dangerous/ultrahazardous depending upon the circumstances of the case. Thus, storage of gasoline, which is not unlawful, gave rise to liability in *Exxon Corp. v. Yarema*[128] due to the specific circumstances of that case. Moreover, unlike the strict liability associated with CERCLA, liability under this theory is not limited to any statutorily defined set of costs, but rather encompasses traditional tort damages.

---

[120] 94 N.J. at 493.

[121] New York v. Shore Realty, 759 F.2d 1032 (2d Cir. 1985); Branch v. Western Petroleum, Inc., 657 P.2d 267 (Utah 1982); Exxon Corp. v. Yarema, 516 A.2d 990 (Md. App. 1986); Bennett v. Mallinckrodt, Inc., 698 S.W.2d 854 (Mo. Ct. App. 1985).

[122] McKay v. Cities Serv. Oil & Gas Co., No. A 1594-91T-1 (N.J. Super. Ct. 1990).

[123] 376 A.2d 1339 (N.J. 1977).

[124] RESTATEMENT, *supra* note 3, at §523.

[125] 730 F. Supp. 630 (D.N.J. 1990).

[126] Prospect Indus. Corp. v. Singer, 569 A.2d 908, 909–11 (N.J. Super. 1989).

[127] RESTATEMENT, *supra* note 3, at §522.

[128] 516 A.2d 990 (Md. App. 1986).

D. Toxic Torts

An outgrowth of the more traditional theories of recovery, the field of toxic torts has grown significantly in recent years. Toxic torts involve a wide variety of factual situations, many of which were known to the common law before the label "toxic tort" was invented. Others involve products or situations that common law judges never even dreamed of.[129] Toxic tort actions can be based either in traditional common law theories of liability (i.e., negligence, nuisance, and so on) or in newly developed areas (i.e., product liability, market share liability, and so on).

Although a comprehensive list of the characteristics common to all toxic torts is not possible, the main characteristics of such actions include the following: (1) the injuries involved allegedly arose from exposure to a toxic substance, (2) the nature of the exposure is such that a large number of people have suffered a comparable injury, (3) the full consequences of the exposure may not be immediately apparent, (4) the connection between the exposure and the injuries suffered is open to reasonable dispute, (5) the identity of the particular party responsible for the agent allegedly causing injury is open to question, (6) the evidence used to establish causation is on the frontiers of medical science, and (7) the injuries suffered are so serious or the claimant's situation so sympathetic that traditional legal defenses such as assumption of risk are looked on extremely critically by the courts.[130]

Perhaps the most significant challenges that plaintiffs face in toxic tort cases center around causation. Some of the most significant decisions in this area have dealt with the degree of certainty and the type of evidence that will be required to establish liability.[131] Among the other defenses that have proved important in these cases are the state of the art defense, traditional tort defenses of assumption of risk and contributory negligence, and the inadequacy of the plaintiff's expert testimony.[132]

Toxic tort actions, like the common law theories on which they are based, fill a gap in federal statutory law. In particular, federal statutory law governs manufacturing, processing, storage, disposal, cleanup, and even exposure levels of most of the products (pesticides, chemicals, asbestos, and so on) on which toxic torts have been based. However, it does not go the final step, assessing liability for those personal injuries that may occur despite the existence of such controls. Only in the toxic tort action may such personal injury damages be recovered.

E. Negligence

Although neligence as a separate tort theory of recovery traces back to the early 1800s, it is only within the last 100 years that it has come into its own as a tort.[133] The traditional formula for the elements necessary to a cause of action in

[129] M. Dore, Law of Toxic Torts 2–1 (9th ed. 1992).
[130] *Id.* at 2–1, 2–2.
[131] *See* Dore, *supra* note 129, part F.
[132] *See generally* Dore, *supra* note 129.
[133] Prosser, *supra* note 18, at 160.

negligence is as follows: (1) a duty or obligation requiring the defendant to conform to a certain standard of conduct for the protection of others against unreasonable risks, (2) a failure on the defendant's part to conform to that standard, (3) the defendant's failure being the proximate cause of the injuries alleged, and (4) actual loss or damage.[134]

Negligence claims will most often be seen in the environmental context as the basis for either nuisance or trespass actions. However, negligence has also been used as an independent basis of liability for environmental wrongs by modern courts. Thus, courts have examined negligence claims for asbestosis,[135] cancer from coke oven emissions,[136] and violations of environmental statutes to name just a few instances.[137]

IV. Developing Trends

The foregoing focused on the traditional remedies that have been used in the modern environmental context. But the common law continues to develop, and this section examines trends that are likely to have an increasing impact in the environmental area in coming years as the common law expands to fill existing gaps in the federal statutory universe.

A. Product Liability Theories

"The liability of manufacturers, distributors and resellers of products has undergone substantial changes in recent decades."[138] Traditionally, product liability could only be imposed upon a showing of fault. Beginning in the 1960s, however, most states adopted a strict liability standard under which all parties in the distribution chain were strictly liable for damage caused by defects in their products.[139] Product liability theories have been advanced against the distributors of pharmaceutical products,[140] pesticides,[141] and industrial materials.[142]

The vast majority of environmental product liability cases have involved claims for personal injury. The use of these theories for property damage claims remains largely unexplored as the majority of such cases have proceeded under statutory or other common law theories. However, there is no reason to believe that property damage could not be equally compensable under this theory. In particular, although CERCLA's liability scheme proceeds a good distance along the chain of title by including generators in the definition of responsible party, it does not impose liability on the manufacturer of the "raw materials" with which the customer "makes" hazardous waste. Application of product liability theory in such instances would allow the potential plaintiff to cast a much wider

---

[134] *Id.* at 164–65.

[135] Locke v. Johns-Manville Corp., 275 S.E.2d 900 (Va. 1981).

[136] Anthony v. Koppers Co., 425 A.2d 428 (Pa. Super. 1980).

[137] Springer v. Schlitz Brewing Co., 510 F.2d 468 (4th Cir. 1975).

[138] DORE, *supra* note 129, at 3–2.

[139] *Id.*

[140] Sindell v. Abbott Laboratories, 607 P.2d 924 (Cal. 1980), *cert. denied,* 449 U.S. 912 (1980) (DES); *In re* A.H. Robins Co. Dalkon Shield I.U.D. Prod. Liab. Litig., 406 F. Supp. 540 (J.P.M.L. 1975) (Dalkon Shield).

[141] Arnett v. Dow Chem. Co., No. 12-954 (Cal. Super. Ct. 1983).

[142] Bloomington v. Westinghouse Elec. Corp., 30 ER Cases 1801 (7th Cir. 1989) (PCBs).

net. Although the harm is of a less sympathetic type than in personal injury cases, the development of this theory in regard to property damage does bear watching.

B. Market Share Liability

A second development that may have wider application in the environmental arena is the use of market share liability theory. In *Sindell v. Abbott Laboratories,*[143] the plaintiff sued certain manufacturers of DES, an antinausea drug given to pregnant women, alleging that her mother's use of the drug was the cause of personal injuries she had suffered. Although she had been able to prove all other elements of her case, the plaintiff did not know which manufacturer had made the particular drug taken by her mother. Rather than deny her claim, the court adopted a market share theory of liability that provides that once the plaintiff joins a substantial portion of those manufacturers who marketed the product in a particular area and establishes all other elements of a prima facie case, the burden of proof shifts to the defendants to prove that they are not the cause of the injury. In *Sindell,* defendants could do this only by proving that they did not manufacture the drug taken by plaintiff's mother. Barring such proof, they were each held liable for a percentage of the damages awarded based upon their share of the market.[144]

While a permutation of this theory has been used by defendants at Superfund sites to apportion liability based on volumetric share, it has not enjoyed wider applicability in the environmental area. Its most likely potential applicability is where damage is caused by a recognized substance, whose manufacture can be traced to a limited number of entities. Such a theory might even gain some support in the regulated community in that it offers a way in which strict joint and several liability under CERCLA may be avoided.

C. Medical Surveillance Claims

A third area of toxic tort law that may have broader applicability in the environmental arena concerns claims for costs of medical monitoring where there is a known risk of harm. In *Ayers v. Jackson Township,*[145] the New Jersey Supreme Court held that parties who could establish significant exposure to toxic substances can recover the cost of required medical surveillance. In so finding, the court stated that

> the cost of medical surveillance is a compensable item of damages where the proofs demonstrate . . . that such surveillance to monitor the effect of exposure to toxic chemicals is reasonable and necessary.[146]

Claims for future medical monitoring costs should be distinguished from claims for future risk of harm. Claims for medical monitoring have been far more successful because experts can testify that exposure to toxic substances creates a

---

[143] 607 P.2d 924 (Cal. 1980).

[144] *Id.*

[145] 106 N.J. 557, 525 A.2d 287 (1987).

[146] 525 A.2d at 312. *See also* Tyminski v. United States, 481 F.2d 257 (3d Cir. 1973); Askey v. Occidental Chem. Corp., 477 N.Y.S.2d 242, 247 (4th Dept. 1984).

need for ongoing medical examinations for exposed individuals. This contrasts to the inability of experts to say that a specific individual will contract a disease or suffer ill-effects from current exposure at some time in the future.[147]

D. Joint and Several Liability

During the 1960s, Dean Prosser argued that tort law should move to a standard of strict joint and several liability. His theme was readily adopted by the government in the environmental area, particularly in the context of Superfund, and has been accepted by many courts.[148] However, recent decisions indicate that imposition of joint and several liability will not be automatic, but will depend upon a case-by-case analysis of the nature of the injury and its causes. In *United States v. Alcan Aluminum Corp.*,[149] the U.S. Court of Appeals rejected EPA's contention that joint and several liability must always be applied in the Superfund context. The court held instead that Alcan must be allowed to prove to what extent, if any, the materials it sent to the site caused EPA to incur response costs recoverable under the statute. In so holding, the court undertook a comprehensive examination of the *Restatement of Torts* in order to determine whether joint and several liability should be applied, thus using common law to fill the interstices of CERCLA. It concluded that where a harm is indivisible, common law principles allow for imposition of joint and several liability.[150] However, where the harm is capable of division or there is a reasonable basis for apportioning liability, each party should only be liable as to that portion of the harm for which it was responsible.[151] Although other courts have indicated that joint and several liability might not apply in all instances,[152] the *Alcan* case was the first in which the harm was held to be divisible.

While the *Alcan* line of cases does not represent a wholesale rejection of joint and several liability in the environmental context, it does signal a willingness to look at the call for joint and several liability in an unbiased fashion. As scientific knowledge regarding the cleanup of pollution and the way in which pollutants act on the environment develops, we may see more cases in which joint and several liability is rejected in favor of apportionment. Although this may disappoint environmentalists and EPA, it may eliminate some of the gravely distorted results that have marked some cases, particularly in the CERCLA context.

V. Conclusions

Despite numerous predictions to the contrary, the common law is alive and well in the environmental area. Although it will probably never be as effective

[147] DORE, *supra* note 129, at 7–13.

[148] *See, e.g.*, United States v. R.W. Meyer, 889 F.2d 1497 (6th Cir. 1989).

[149] 964 F.2d 252, 268 (3d Cir. 1992).

[150] *Alcan*, 964 F.2d at 267–68; RESTATEMENT, *supra* note 3, at §875.

[151] *Alcan*, 964 F.2d at 267–68, citing RESTATEMENT, *supra* note 3, at §§433A and 881.

[152] United States v. Chem-Dyne Corp., 572 F. Supp. 802, 808 (S.D. Ohio 1983); O'Neil v. Picillo, 883 F.2d 176, 178 (1st Cir. 1989); United States v. Monsanto Co., 858 F.2d 160, 171 (4th Cir. 1988), *cert. denied*, 490 U.S. 1106 (1989).

as environmental statutes in regulating and controlling the discharge of pollutants, it may be said to be a far more effective tool where the rights of individuals have been affected. Despite this advantage, both practitioners and courts have been remiss in their attempts to understand and use the common law.

An understanding of the long history of common law approaches to environmental problems is critical to a full utilization of common law theories in the modern context. While modern courts apply permutations of traditional common law rules that were shaped by the Industrial Revolution, in the last 30 years they have applied these principles in defense of the environment rather than of industry. Thus the common law has, in some respects, returned to its roots in the preindustrial age, recognizing that the way in which individuals use their land can have serious adverse consequences on the lives and property of their neighbors. In light of this return to a more environmentally protective stance, old precedents may take on new life. Thus, even if the modern common law does not address a particular situation, an older precedent may.

The common law's current course is unclear. Numerous new theories have been developed, particularly in the field of toxic torts, which have cast a wider and wider net, harkening back to the days of the preindustrial era. At the same time, however, some courts have come to reexamine the issues of liability that have been at the forefront of the debate for the last 30 years. In so doing, they have begun to consider whether the shifting of all the risk from one party to another is the best answer to environmental problems. Regardless of which path the common law takes, its journey is one that no one concerned with environmental issues can afford to miss.

3

Clean Air Act

By Russell V. Randle
with Anne B. Walton

I. Introduction

The Clean Air Act of 1970 (CAA) federalized air pollution regulation to a large degree, imposed emission standards on new industrial plants based on technological and economic feasibility, and on existing plants through a complex air quality control program administered by the states under federal supervision. It also imposed stringent federal emission limits on new cars.

Congress overhauled the Act in 1977 by (1) imposing substantial new requirements in areas that the Environmental Protection Agency (EPA) determines have not attained National Ambient Air Quality Standards (NAAQSs) in a timely way, (2) requiring Prevention of Significant Deterioration (PSD) to protect areas where air quality is better than national standards and industrial growth threatens degradation of the air quality, and (3) extending the time for automotive compliance.

Between 1977 and 1990, numerous efforts were made to amend the Act, some to relax or delay its standards, others to impose controls to reduce acid rain, tighten automotive emission controls, and better address emissions of hazardous air pollutants. For the most part, these efforts failed, blocked by interest group politics, Administration unease with further government regulation, and environmentalists' defense of existing law. During this period, air quality improved somewhat on a nationwide basis, despite substantial economic growth and large increases in motor vehicles and the miles they traveled. Few people appreciated that without the Clean Air Act program, air quality in the United States might have resembled that of Eastern Europe and the Soviet Union, if American trends of the 1940s through the early 1970s had continued.

By 1989, it was evident to almost all parties in the debate that extensive changes had to be made in the CAA, partially because the last deadlines for compliance had passed, putting nonattainment areas in danger of having most industrial growth stopped. The resulting legislation, based in part on a Bush Administration proposal and in part on congressional initiatives, finally became law in November 1990, after running a marathon legislative gauntlet.

The 1990 Amendments were comprehensive, over 700 pages long. The major changes were to entirely rewrite the nonattainment provisions, to adopt a technology-based program to regulate toxic or hazardous air pollutants, to tighten automotive emission controls, to add an elaborate permit program, a phase-out program for chlorofluorocarbons (CFCs) and other ozone-depleting substances, and an acid rain control program that initially focused on about 110 large coal- and oil-fired power plants. Moreover, Congress armed EPA with expanded authority to enforce the Act. These changes will dramatically change the way and cost of doing business in the United States; estimated additional compliance costs are $25 billion each year.

Despite Congress's ambitious mandate under the Amendments, EPA failed to meet numerous statutory deadlines for its implementation, in part because the statutory schedules were unrealistic in light of EPA's inadequate resources, and in part because of regulatory gridlock in the latter half of the Bush Administration. This gridlock resulted from efforts by conservative elements that sought to limit the economic effects of the Clean Air Act and other federal environmental statutes. Over 50 regulations were delayed well beyond their statutory deadlines.[1]

The change in administrations may reduce some of the delays resulting from ideological warfare within the Executive Branch. Court mandates are also pushing EPA to issue many long-delayed rules, a number of which were signed on January 19, 1993, the last full day of the Bush Administration. Nonetheless, the change in administrations does nothing to increase EPA's resources, and the Clinton Administration's emphasis on deficit reduction suggests EPA will not have the personnel or funding to meet the statutory deadlines on a regular basis.

This chapter sets forth the implementation schedule, notes where EPA has failed to meet deadlines, and where possible, provides EPA's anticipated schedule for implementing the Act. But the reader should note that regulatory delay is a perennial Clean Air Act problem, and that will probably never entirely change.

Each of the CAA's six major titles focuses on resolving a different air pollution control problem:

Title I generally addresses stationary sources. Under its authority EPA sets National Ambient Air Quality Standards (NAAQSs) to use in regulating most existing stationary sources and determining compliance by different areas of the country. This title also requires EPA to set technology-based emission standards for new or modified stationary sources under the New Source Performance Standards (NSPSs), Prevention of Significant Deterioration (PSD), and nonattainment provisions.

---

[1] Two public interest groups have attempted to force EPA to comply with statutory deadlines through court proceedings. Sierra Club v. EPA, No. 92-1749 (D.D.C. Nov. 20, 1992) (addressing the sulfur dioxide (SO_2) allowance trading program, nitrogen oxide (NO_2) emissions for utility boilers, air toxics emissions controls for new and existing municipal waste incinerators, lists of major and area sources of hazardous air pollutants, and vehicle evaporative emissions controls); NRDC v. EPA, No. 92-2196 (D.D.C. Sept. 25, 1992) (addressing national emissions standards for hazardous organics to reduce toxic air pollution). The Sierra Club had threatened a second lawsuit to compel EPA to issue 23 additional overdue rules.

Recently, EPA entered into an agreement to settle a case brought privately by Congressman Waxman, Chairman of the Health and Environment Subcommittee of the House Energy and Commerce Committee. In an unusual initiative, Congressman Waxman sued EPA for the Agency's failure to meet Congress's statutory deadlines for CAA implementation. Waxman v. EPA, No. 92-1320 (D.C. Cir. Nov. 20, 1992). Under the settlement, EPA agreed to a strict schedule for promulgating numerous overdue regulations.

Title II addresses mobile sources. It regulates both vehicles and the fuels they use.

Title III provides for certain administrative and enforcement measures as well as economic impact analyses for implementation of the statute.

Title IV establishes a program to control acid rain by placing a cap on sulfur dioxide emissions and measures to reduce nitrogen dioxide emissions which are precursors to acid rain.

Title V establishes a federal permit program for stationary sources that states are required to implement.

Title VI establishes a program to control stratospheric ozone depletion by freezing production and consumption levels of ozone depleting substances (ODS), and eventually phasing them out altogether. Title VI additionally contains monitoring, reporting, labeling, recycling, and disposal requirements for ODSs.

II. Title I

Title I grants EPA authority to establish National Ambient Air Quality Standards (NAAQSs) that are designed to limit permissible levels of air pollutants in outdoor air. Primary NAAQSs are supposed to protect human health while secondary NAAQSs are supposed to address public welfare protection.

The CAA makes a distinction in Title I between sources of air pollutants located in areas that have air quality that is better than national standards require and sources located in areas that have air quality that is worse than national standards. New or modified sources located in areas in which ambient air complies with or is better than NAAQSs require are subject to the Prevention of Significant Deterioration (PSD) program, which was added to the CAA by the 1977 Amendments, and before that by judicial decision and EPA regulation. By the same token, stationary sources located in areas where ambient air quality is dirtier than NAAQSs allow are subject to elaborate nonattainment area provisions, a program added by EPA ruling in 1976, then by the 1977 Amendments, and extensively revised and expanded as part of the 1990 Amendments. Put simply, in addition to or as part of emission limits based on air quality standards, existing sources must use Reasonably Available Control Technology (RACT) and new or modified sources must use control technology set on the basis of Lowest Available Emission Rate (LAER).

The process for establishing and administering State Implementation Plans (SIPs) to control stationary source emissions is also contained in Title I. Through SIPs, existing sources must reduce emissions in order for the state to comply with NAAQSs. New or modified sources are subject to federally promulgated New Source Performance Standards (NSPSs). Title I additionally includes a program to establish National Emissions Standards for Hazardous Air Pollutants (NESHAPs) and imposes technology-based standards on new and existing sources that emit those air pollutants.

A. National Ambient Air Quality Standards

Section 108 of the CAA requires EPA to produce and periodically to revise a list of pollutants emitted from stationary or mobile sources that have an adverse effect on the public health or welfare.[2] From this list EPA establishes ambient air quality standards.[3] EPA is required to produce a report for each pollutant that contains a compilation of all available scientific studies concerning the pollutant's health effects at various concentrations in the ambient air. EPA must publish these "criteria" documents that "accurately reflect the latest scientific knowledge"[4] prior to establishing air quality standards.

1. Primary and Secondary NAAQSs

Congress directed EPA to set primary and secondary national ambient air quality standards or NAAQSs for criteria pollutants under sections 108 and 109.[5] EPA set these basic standards in 1971 for six pollutants: sulfur dioxide, nitrogen dioxide, particulate matter, photochemical oxidants, carbon monoxide, and hydrocarbons. Despite much controversy, and some revision, many of these standards continue today, and only lead has been added to this list.

Once established, the NAAQSs serve as a ceiling for permissible concentrations of the criteria pollutant that cannot be exceeded anywhere in the United States. The primary NAAQSs are based on the criteria document discussed above and are directed toward protection of public health.[6] Secondary NAAQSs are directed at public welfare protection from "any known or anticipated adverse effects" that a pollutant causes by its presence in the ambient air.[7] Although it would appear that the public welfare protection standard should be stricter than the public health protection standard, secondary NAAQSs are typically set at the same level as primary standards.[8] Despite challenges, EPA's primary standards and subsequent revisions have not been overturned.[9]

---

[2] §108, 42 U.S.C. §7408. EPA is required to establish criteria when the Administrator determines that the pollutant can "cause or contribute to air pollution which may reasonably be anticipated to endanger public health or welfare." *Id.* §108(a)(1)(A).

[3] In NRDC v. Train, 411 F. Supp. 864 (S.D.N.Y.), *aff'd,* 545 F.2d 320 (2d Cir. 1976), the court required EPA to list lead as a pollutant once the Agency determined that it endangered public health or welfare. The decision reduced EPA's flexibility in listing decisions.

[4] Lead Indus. Ass'n v. EPA, 647 F.2d 1130, 1136–37 (D.C. Cir. 1980), *cert. denied,* 449 U.S. 1042 (1981).

[5] 42 U.S.C. §§7409 and 7408.

[6] §7409(b)(1).

[7] §109(b)(2), 42 U.S.C. §7409(b)(2). The public welfare standard extends to wildlife, water, vegetation, man-made materials, property damage, and more generally effects on "economic values and on personal comfort and well-being." §302(h), 42 U.S.C. §7602(h).

[8] EPA has only issued primary standards for carbon monoxide (CO). The SO_2 secondary standards are more stringent than the primary standards.

[9] The primary and secondary standards for particulate matter smaller than 10 microns in size (PM10) and lead were upheld respectively in NRDC v. EPA, 902 F.2d 962, 980 (D.C. Cir. 1990); Lead Indus. Ass'n v. EPA, 647 F.2d 1130, 1180–81 (D.C. Cir. 1980), *cert. denied,* 449 U.S. 1042 (1981). These cases, however, were decided on jurisdictional and procedural grounds, and did not specifically address EPA's basis for setting the standards. The secondary standard for SO_2 was remanded in 1973 and revised by EPA, Kennecott Copper Corp. v. EPA, 462 F.2d 846 (D.C. Cir. 1972).

In establishing NAAQSs, EPA must base standards only on health protection considerations that exclude technical feasibility or cost factors.[10] This reflects Congress's goal of ''technology-forcing'' through the legislation. The policy requires regulated entities to invent and install necessary control technology or cease operations altogether. Consequently, NAAQSs affect where new sources can be located and the extent of control imposed on existing sources. Although the NAAQSs are not directly enforceable against sources, EPA and the states have enforcement authority over emissions limitations and controls that the NAAQSs help to establish.

2. *Criteria Pollutants*

Currently there are NAAQSs set for six criteria pollutants: sulfur dioxide (SO_2), particulate matter smaller than 10 microns in size (PM10), carbon monoxide (CO), ozone (O_3), nitrogen dioxide (NO_2), and lead (Pb).[11] Pursuant to court order, EPA added the lead standard in 1978.[12] In 1979, the ozone rule was relaxed by 50 percent after extensive debates concerning the sufficiency of data about its health effects.[13] In 1987, EPA changed the particulate standard from total suspended particulates (TSP) to particulate matter smaller than 10 microns in size (PM10).[14] Emission limits based on the earlier TSP standards remain effective until new emission limitations are formulated. Although the need for controls on fine particulate had been evident since the mid-1970s, the decade of debate and development work surrounding the PM10 limitation demonstrates the complexity and high stakes, in health and financial terms, at issue when NAAQSs are set.

The CAA requires EPA to review NAAQSs for criteria pollutants every five years to determine whether they are adequate to protect public health,[15] a mandate EPA has proven slow to carry out. Thus far, EPA has not changed the SO_2, O_3, or NO_2 standards despite scientific arguments that revisions may be needed and despite litigation by environmental groups to compel the Agency to make adjustments.[16] Moreover, EPA has not altered the averaging times that are

---

[10] American Petroleum Inst. v. Costle, 665 F.2d 1176 (D.C. Cir.), *cert. denied,* 455 U.S. 1034 (1981); Lead Indus. Ass'n v. EPA, 647 F.2d 1130 (D.C. Cir. 1980), *cert. denied,* 449 U.S. 1042 (1981); NRDC v. EPA, 902 F.2d 962 (D.C. Cir. 1990).

[11] 40 C.F.R. pts. 50.4, 50.6, 50.8, 50.9, 50.11, 50.12.

EPA has issued proposed regulations on ambient air quality surveillance for monitoring ozone, nitrogen oxide (NO_2), and volatile organic compounds (VOCs). The regulations would require states to establish monitoring stations as part of their SIPs to provide a database for air pollution control agencies to evaluate, track, and refine control strategies for attaining the NAAQSs for ozone. 57 Fed. Reg. 7687 (1992).

[12] NRDC v. Train, 411 F. Supp. 864 (S.D.N.Y.), *aff'd,* 545 F.2d 320 (2d Cir. 1976).

[13] EPA completed its review of the ozone NAAQS in March 1993. *See* 58 Fed. Reg. 25,080 (1993).

In 1971, EPA promulgated a NAAQS for hydrocarbons (HC) to help control the formation of photochemical oxidants or smog, now referred to as ozone. Hydrocarbons are not necessarily independently harmful, but they are believed to be a precursor to the formation of ozone and related photochemical oxidants. Ozone precursors, usually referred to as volatile organic compounds (VOCs), are strictly controlled under many state implementation plans (SIPs).

[14] In NRDC v. EPA, 902 F.2d 962 (D.C. Cir. 1990), the court upheld the PM10 standard.

[15] §109(d), 42 U.S.C. §7409(d).

[16] Environmental Defense Fund v. EPA, 27 E.R. Cases 2008 (S.D.N.Y. 1988) (finding that SO_2 standard revisions were not required); NRDC v. EPA, 27 E.R. Cases 1572 (D.C. Cir. 1988) (upholding change in averaging times on procedural grounds). EPA announced publication of a document assessing SO_2 acute health effects on asthmatics and a review of NAAQSs for sulfur oxides in August 1993. 58 Fed. Reg. 44,379 (1993).

critical to monitoring compliance and setting standards. For example, standards using shorter averaging times for the same numerical limits are more stringent than standards with a longer averaging time and the same numerical limit. The longer averaging time for NAAQSs allows weather variations to be cancelled out, just as emission limits with long averaging times allow process variability extremes to be diminished. The NAAQSs are a major factor in the subtitle D nonattainment provisions because numerical concentrations of criteria pollutants in excess of the NAAQSs trigger additional compliance obligations through state implementation plans.

B. State Implementation Plans

Once EPA establishes NAAQSs, section 110 of the CAA requires states to develop, and after an opportunity for public comment, submit to EPA state implementation plans or SIPs that provide for implementation, attainment, maintenance, and enforcement of those standards. The first set of these SIPs was developed in 1971 and 1972, and many major SIP revisions have occurred since as a result of court decisions, failure to meet attainment obligations, and legislative changes.

Through SIPs, states develop emission limitations that are imposed to control emissions from specific stationary sources. Once EPA approves a SIP, it is federally enforceable as well as enforceable by the state and through citizens suits pursuant to sections 110(d), 113, and 304.[17]

Under the 1990 Amendments, EPA has one year to accept or reject the SIP in whole or in part.[18] EPA may approve the SIP, disapprove the SIP, partially approve the SIP, or conditionally approve the SIP with a time limit for making necessary revisions. If it disapproves or partially approves the SIP, it must call for revisions to address substantial inadequacies in the state's measures to attain and maintain national standards. If these deficiencies are not timely remedied, EPA must promulgate a Federal Implementation Plan (FIP) to correct them.

Sections 110 and 179 require EPA to impose such FIPs within two years after a state fails to adopt or submits an inadequate SIP.[19] After 18 months of

---

The American Lung Association recently sued EPA claiming that the absence of a short-term (e.g., 5-minute) standard from the current SO_2 standards threatens asthma sufferers. American Lung Ass'n v. EPA, No. 92-5316 (E.D.N.Y. Nov. 12, 1992). The American Lung Association filed a similar suit in 1991 to compel EPA to review the ozone standard. American Lung Ass'n v. EPA, 22 E.R. Cases 1608 (E.D.N.Y. 1991). As part of the settlement of that case, EPA agreed to review the ozone standard, but ultimately concluded that the current standard was adequate.

[17] 42 U.S.C. §§7410(d), 7413, 7604; 40 C.F.R. pt. 52.

[18] 42 U.S.C. §7410(k).

[19] Federal revisions to correct SIP deficiencies have been promulgated on only a few occasions. EPA issued revisions to VOC Reasonably Available Control Technology rules in the Illinois SIP for ozone. Even in this instance, EPA only issued revisions after the state of Wisconsin filed a complaint against the Administrator for approving the Illinois SIP. *See* 55 Fed. Reg. 26,814 (1990). Similarly, in response to an order by the Ninth Circuit in Delaney v. EPA, 898 F.2d 687, 695 (9th Cir. 1990), EPA promulgated a FIP for the CO nonattainment areas of Phoenix and Tucson, Arizona. *See also* 56 Fed. Reg. 5458 (1991).

EPA has resisted promulgating a FIP for two California areas. Recently, the Ninth Circuit refused EPA's and the Justice Department's request for a review of the court's order requiring EPA to issue a FIP for Los Angeles, Sacramento, and Ventura, California. Coalition for Clean Air v. EPA, 971 F.2d 219 (9th Cir. 1992), *cert. denied,* 113 S. Ct. 1361 (1993). The U.S. District Court for the Eastern District of California ordered EPA to promulgate a FIP for improving air quality in Sacramento. Environmental Council of Sacramento v. EPA, CIVS-87-0420 (9th Cir. Nov. 13, 1992), *cert. denied,* 113 S. Ct. 1256 (1993).

such failure, a state is subject to mandatory sanctions, including the loss of federal highway money or imposition of tighter emission standards for new or modified sources, if it fails to submit an adequate SIP.[20] After two years, both sanctions are imposed. EPA has discretionary authority to impose both such sanctions prior to that time;[21] the importance of the mandatory sanctions is that if EPA fails to impose them, environmentalists may act through the courts to do so.

The 1990 Amendments require elaborate SIP modifications and set detailed schedules for establishing, reviewing, and approving these changes. The schedules depend primarily on the nonattainment provisions discussed below, with specific revisions due at different dates. EPA must determine whether the submissions are complete within 60 days of submission, and act to approve the SIP, in whole or in part, within one year of a determination that submissions are complete.[22]

1. SIP Content

With the 1990 Amendments, section 110(a)(2)(A)-(M) requires an acceptable SIP to contain provisions for

- Emission limitations, control measures, and compliance schedules;
- Monitoring devices and analysis of ambient air quality;
- Enforcement of emission limits, monitoring requirements, and a permit program for major or new stationary sources;
- Prevention of interstate pollution that interferes with other states' attainment of air quality standards and PSD requirements;
- Adequate state legal authority, funds, and personnel to oversee and enforce the program;
- An operations and maintenance (O&M) program with periodic emission and compliance reporting by sources;
- Authority and contingency plans to act in emergency circumstances;
- Compliance with the nonattainment provisions of the Act;
- Compliance with the PSD provisions of the Act;
- Demonstrations as to performance of the SIP's effect on air quality;
- A permit program and fee schedule for major stationary sources;
- Local government consultation and participation.

Despite this imposing list of SIP requirements, states have flexibility in determining how they will satisfy section 110 criteria and implement the SIP.[23]

---

[20] EPA has proposed criteria for exercising discretionary sanctions pursuant to requirements for consultation with political subdivisions under §7410(m). Under the proposal, EPA will determine whether a political subdivision of a state is primarily responsible for deficiencies in state air quality plans in order to avoid imposition of statewide sanctions. Before EPA applies sanctions to political subdivisions, rather than the state, the subdivision must (1) have legal authority to perform the required activity; (2) have traditionally performed or been delegated the authority to perform the required activity; (3) have agreed to perform the required activity or will accept responsibility to perform it; (4) have received funding or the authority to get funding from the state to perform the activity; and (4) have failed to perform the required activity. *See* 57 Fed. Reg. 44,534 (1992).

[21] §§110(m), 179(b), 42 U.S.C. §§7410(m), 7509(b).

[22] *See* 40 C.F.R. pt. 51 (providing SIP minimum requirements).

[23] EPA has issued guidance for SIPs developed between 1990 and 1996. The guidance is designed to assist states in their programs to reduce ozone and CO pollution. *See* 57 Fed. Reg. 13,498 (1992). It also provides guidance for new source review, permitting provisions, and sanctions.

As long as the state demonstrates that its air pollution control measures comply with section 110 and are sufficient to achieve and maintain NAAQSs, EPA should approve the SIP.[24]

2. *Compliance With NAAQSs*

Under the 1970 Act, states were required to meet primary NAAQSs ''as expeditiously as practicable,'' but not later than three years after the SIP, with only one possible two-year extension.[25] Under the 1977 Amendments, two five-year extensions lasting until 1987 were possible, and that deadline was legislatively extended until August 1988.

The 1990 Amendments further extended attainment dates for nonattainment areas. For carbon monoxide and ozone, the nonattainment provisions of subtitle D now base compliance on the pollutant involved and the amount by which a nonattainment area exceeds numerical standards. In contrast, secondary NAAQSs must be attained within a ''reasonable time,'' but there is no specification in the CAA as to a time limit.[26]

Numerous states failed to meet NAAQSs attainment dates specified in the 1970 Act. They were unable to meet NAAQSs for one or more criteria pollutants in air quality control regions (AQCRs) located within the state. In 1977, Congress revised the nonattainment provisions and required each state to designate which AQCRs exceeded NAAQSs. For areas designated ''nonattainment,'' SIPs were to impose a moratorium on construction and modification of major stationary sources. Nonattainment areas under the 1977 Amendments were reduced in size by making such designations on a county-by-county basis rather than by AQCRs. The 1990 Amendments extend nonattainment designations to consolidated or standard metropolitan statistical areas (CMSA or SMSA), a Census Bureau designation—rather than by county boundary. These definitional changes increase the geographic area where new and modified sources will face more stringent standards, and in which vehicles will be subject to special inspection and maintenance obligations.

3. *Early SIP Provision Challenges*

Implementation of clean air requirements through the SIP process sparked numerous challenges by industry and environmental groups. EPA maintained that its role in approving a SIP only involved a determination that the SIP provided adequate controls to meet NAAQSs. States were entitled to shut down sources as one means of meeting NAAQSs. Industry argued that EPA was required to consider technological and economic factors during its SIP review. The Supreme Court upheld EPA's position in *Union Electric v. EPA.*[27] The Court noted that in adopting a ''technology-forcing'' approach in the statute, Congress was prepared to compel polluters to invent, install, and use control technologies or cease operations. Thus, industry could initiate challenges con-

[24] NRDC v. Train, 421 U.S. 60 (1975); Union Elec. v. EPA, 427 U.S. 246 (1976).

[25] §110(e), 42 U.S.C. §7410(e).

[26] EPA by regulation indicated that, where controls were reasonably available, a ''reasonable time'' for achievement of the secondary standards for sulfur oxides and particulates would be three years, unless the state could show that good cause exists for choosing a later date. 40 C.F.R. §51.13(b)(1) and (2). When setting attainment dates for secondary NAAQSs, states may consider economic and technological factors.

[27] 427 U.S. 246 (1976).

cerning technological and economic feasibility at the state level through administrative and judicial channels, but EPA was not required to undertake its own review of such issues.[28] While some have criticized the technology-forcing approach as unreasonable, others have credited the policy with the development of "scrubber" technology which the utility industry currently uses to control SO_2 emissions.[29]

4. *The "Bubble" Policy*

EPA has adopted a policy for intrasource emissions trading commonly referred to as the "bubble" policy.[30] After much litigation, the courts upheld EPA's decision to allow such trading among emission points at a single plant.[31] Each emission point within a facility is not required to independently meet emissions requirements. Thus, one source can be used to offset emissions increases at another emission point within the facility if total emissions within the bubble are not increased. Only total emissions from the bubble encompassing the facility are considered. EPA and the states allow this averaging through the elastic language defining what a "source" is.

5. *Dispersion Techniques and Intermittent Control Systems*

When Congress passed the 1970 Act, many states were unwilling to impose emission limitations requiring continuous emissions reductions (CERs) on sources to attain NAAQSs. A vast disparity developed nationwide in the stringency of SIPs. Measures employed by sources in some states were not truly emission reduction programs. Rather, sources such as coal-fired electric utilities attempted to rely on pollution dispersion techniques through use of tall stacks and/or revised operations during adverse weather. Tall stacks could disperse pollutants over a wider area, thereby reducing concentrations at ground level. Another control measure that did not employ CER involved intermittent controls. Sources such as smelters would curtail or increase emissions according to meteorological conditions to control total emissions levels.

Environmentalists did not believe that these measures were reliable as a permanent means to control emissions. EPA took several conflicting positions. The utility and smelter industries, among others, advocated use of dispersion techniques and intermittent controls to meet emissions requirements. Courts generally agreed with the environmentalist's position that tall stacks and intermittent control systems could not be used to attain NAAQSs unless all available continuous emissions controls were first applied.[32] In 1977, Congress codified this interpretation in section 123, but in section 119 carved out an exception

---

[28] The Court did not decide what consideration EPA must give to technological or economic feasibility when the Agency itself promulgates SIP measures.

[29] Note, *Forcing Technology: The Clean Air Act Experience,* 88 YALE L.J. 1713, 1722–30 (1979).

[30] *See* 51 Fed. Reg. 43,814 (1986) for EPA guidance on the "bubble policy."

[31] *See* Chevron, U.S.A. v. EPA, 467 U.S. 837 (1984) (bubble allowed in nonattainment areas); Alabama Power v. Castle, 636 F.2d 323 (D.C. Cir. 1979) (bubble allowed in PSD program).

[32] NRDC v. Train, 489 F.2d 390 (5th Cir. 1974), *reversed in part on other grounds,* 421 U.S. 60 (1975); Big Rivers Elec. Coop. v. Train, 523 F.2d 16, 20–22 (6th Cir. 1975), *cert. denied,* 425 U.S. 934 (1976); Kennecott Copper Corp. v. Train, 526 F.2d 1149 (9th Cir. 1975), *cert. denied,* 425 U.S. 935 (1976); Kennecott Copper Corp. v. Costle, 572 F.2d 1349 (9th Cir. 1978).

until 1987 for nonferrous smelters.[33] EPA's regulations implementing section 123 have largely been upheld by the appeals courts.[34] Under these regulations, SIP emission limitations must be calculated based on a stack height that does not exceed 65 meters or two and a half times building height, whichever is greater. If the stack heights are higher than 65 meters, stack heights must be based on "good engineering practice" which the regulations specify as two and one-half times the height of the facility.[35]

6. *SIP Revisions and Variances*

Prior to the 1990 Amendments, EPA allowed states to approve variances for sources through SIP revisions as long as the revisions did not interfere with NAAQSs attainment. The procedural requirements for a SIP revision were far easier to satisfy than the requirements for a variance under section 110(f). Under that provision, formal hearings were required if the variance threatened to interfere with timely attainment of NAAQSs. EPA's position was vigorously challenged by environmentalists, but ultimately the Supreme Court approved the agency's approach to reviewing SIP revisions.[36] EPA's leisurely pace in reviewing such revisions lead some courts to bar EPA enforcement actions where EPA rejected a SIP revision several years after a state approved it. The Supreme Court ultimately held that EPA could maintain such enforcement actions, but that its dilatory conduct would mitigate any penalties.[37]

With the adoption of the 1990 Amendments and the permit program, source-specific SIP revisions should become increasingly rare, as such issues will be handled through the permit process.

C. New Source Performance Standards

Under section 111 of the Act, new source performance standards (NSPSs) are nationwide emission limits applicable to new facilities and to existing sources that undergo major modifications. Section 111(b)(1)(A) requires EPA

[33] 42 U.S.C. §7419. Under §119, copper, lead, or zinc smelters could defer compliance with SIP SO_2 emissions limits if there was no reasonably available control technology (RACT) to attain those limits. The factors for a RACT determination included cost of compliance, energy considerations, and impacts on health and the environment not associated with air quality. §119(b). Although smelter sources could use dispersion techniques or intermittent controls, §119 extension authority has now expired.

[34] NRDC v. EPA, 838 F.2d 1224 (D.C. Cir. 1988); Sierra Club v. EPA, 719 F.2d 436 (D.C. Cir. 1983). Although most substantive aspects of the regulations were upheld, the court struck down EPA's policy of "grandfathering" many plants from §123's requirements, a decision that could require many power plants to recalculate, and, consequently, to tighten emission limitations. Many of the affected power plants will now have to cut back emissions under the Title IV acid rain control program.

[35] Under some circumstances sources are permitted to use a greater height after a complex air quality modeling demonstration. 40 C.F.R. pt. 51.164.

The Title IV acid rain program will have an impact on debates over stack heights. It has been argued that stack heights over 200 feet enhance long-range SO_2 and NO_2 transport thereby increasing acid rain formation. It has been suggested that lower stack heights would reduce acid rain, but §123 is not consistent with that strategy. *See* B. Ackerman & W. Hassler, *Beyond the New Deal: Coal and the Clean Air Act,* 89 YALE L.J. 1466, 1531, 1534 (1980); R. Randle & L. Smith, *Comment on Beyond the New Deal,* 90 YALE L.J. 1398, 1410 (1981) (critiquing this strategy).

[36] The Natural Resources Defense Council challenged this approach, claiming that under §110(f), EPA must review each variance to a SIP. The courts of appeals divided several ways over the issue. The Supreme Court finally reviewed the dispute and affirmed EPA's position. Train v. NRDC, 421 U.S. 60 (1975).

[37] General Motors v. United States, 496 U.S. 530 (1990).

to identify those sources that "contribute significantly to air pollution which may reasonably be anticipated to endanger public health or welfare."[38] EPA then must set emission standards applicable to new sources of the types identified, as well as to modifications of existing sources of that type. The standards must reflect the "degree of emission reduction achievable" through the best technology EPA determines has been "adequately demonstrated," considering costs and "nonair quality health and environmental impacts and energy requirements."[39]

States must develop a program which assures that the NSPSs' technology-based emission limitations for new or modified sources are enforced.[40] The NSPSs requirements reflect Congress's view that new plants have the greatest flexibility to incorporate the latest, most effective pollution control technology. Moreover, NSPSs require equivalent controls for similar new sources in the same industry, thereby preventing some states from adopting more lenient air pollution requirements as a way of attracting or retaining industry.

1. Major Stationary Sources

EPA is required to list all major stationary source categories for which NSPSs had not been established and then set NSPSs for those categories. As of December 1992, EPA has promulgated NSPSs for 71 source categories.[41] Where the agency has identified major sources, but not set NSPSs, rulemaking for those additional source categories must be completed by 1996.[42] The 1990 Amendments also require EPA to review NSPSs on an eight-year schedule and to revise them if appropriate. Detailed review is mandatory if EPA determines that emission limitations and percentage reductions better than those required by the NSPSs are now achieved in practice.[43]

With the development of the subtitle C and D programs to prevent significant deterioration of air quality and for nonattainment areas, the role of NSPSs has changed substantially. They now provide minimum emission standards, based on the capabilities and expense of control technology. They do not, by their terms, mandate use of a specified technology, but instead mandate performance, leaving to the source the choice of the best means to achieve the limitations.

EPA or the states are free to impose more stringent limits to reflect air quality needs and subsequent technological advances. Thus, it should be expected that the longer it has been since the NSPSs for a particular industry have been revised, the more the NSPSs will differ from Best Available Control

[38] 42 U.S.C. §7411(b)(1)(A).

[39] Because EPA is authorized to consider costs and nonenvironmental concerns in developing NSPSs, the agency may determine that prohibitively expensive equipment is not the "best system" even if it provides a significantly higher degree of emissions control. Because this is a performance standard requiring achievement of a limit, rather than an equipment standard, EPA must allow alternative methods of continuous emission reduction if they are equally effective. Although EPA may specify equipment and work practice standards under §111(h) where it is impractical to set numerical emission limits, the Agency must revise the NSPSs to numerical limits if it becomes feasible to do so. EPA, however, can engage in technology-forcing strategies by determining that certain equipment has been "adequately demonstrated" even though it is not widely used in the regulated community.

[40] §111(c), 42 U.S.C. §7411(c).

[41] 40 C.F.R. §60.

[42] §111(f), 42 U.S.C. §7411(f).

[43] 42 U.S.C. §7411(b)(1)(B).

Technology (BACT) requirements for sources in areas subject to PSD, and from Lowest Achievable Emissions Rate (LAER) requirements for sources located in nonattainment areas. As technology improves, the disparity between NSPSs on the one hand and BACT and LAER on the other should increase until the NSPSs are revised on a national basis.

2. *NSPSs for Fossil-Fuel-Burning Facilities*

The most controversial aspect of section 111 under the 1977 Amendments was the requirement that EPA set NSPSs for fossil-fuel-burning sources that would achieve both a percentage reduction and an emission limitation.[44] Thc 1990 Amendments repealed this aspect of section III and may allow low sulfur coal to be used as a compliance strategy. This repeal resulted from the adoption of the acid rain provisions in Title IV, which in their first stage impose stringent and widespread limitations on sulfur dioxide emissions from about 110 large coal- and oil-fired power plants, and upon almost 800 sources under the second stage.

The NSPSs and new source review requirements under the PSD program sparked another controversy among EPA, environmentalists, and utilities. The language of section 111(a)(4) defines "modification" very broadly to mean physical changes or changes in operating methods that increase emissions or cause emissions of air pollutants not previously emitted.[45] The statutory language contains no de minimis level to accommodate changes, so that fuel switching, repairs, and similar events—including possible installation of new control equipment—might subject a source to NSPSs. One utility, Wisconsin Electric Power Company, challenged EPA's imposition of NSPSs and PSD requirements on its plans to install new equipment which would have extended the life expectancy of the plant. That challenge failed, as the court held that such changes did constitute "modifications" triggering the NSPSs if they increased emissions.[46] As the changes increased the plant's operating capacity, emissions would increase. The court also held, however, that EPA could not base its calculation of emissions increase on the assumption the plant would operate around the clock when it had never operated that way in the past.

In response to utility industry concerns, in mid-1992 EPA announced that utility pollution control projects are exempt from new source review requirements, unless the agency determines that the projects are not environmentally beneficial.[47] EPA plans to exclude physical and operational changes from

[44]This provision effectively required flue gas desulfurization (scrubbers) or other technology to be installed in almost all cases, and forbade compliance simply by the use of untreated low sulfur fuels as had been allowed under the 1971 version of the NSPSs. The requirement was intended to discourage sources from switching to low-sulfur western coals from high-sulfur eastern and midwestern coals and made use of the high-sulfur coal desirable. (This preference for local coal has been reinforced by high coal freight rates.) The Court of Appeals for the District of Columbia Circuit has twice upheld EPA's NSPSs for coal-fired power plants: the 1971 version was upheld in Portland Cement Ass'n v. Ruckelshaus, 486 F.2d 375 (D.C. Cir. 1973), *cert. denied,* 417 U.S. 921 (1974), and the 1979 version was upheld in Sierra Club v. Costle, 657 F.2d 298 (D.C. Cir. 1981), a book-length opinion.

[45]42 U.S.C. §7411(a)(4).

[46]Wisconsin Elec. Power Co. v. EPA, 893 F.2d 901 (7th Cir. 1990).

[47]The proposed exemption was reported at 56 Fed. Reg. 27,630 (1991). Modified existing facilities would still be subject to strict review standards. §111(a)(1), 42 U.S.C. §7411(a)(1). Revised regulations to assure that emissions do not increase from the affected plants are due in May 1994.

NSPSs and new source review, unless they increase emissions.[48] The policy remains controversial.

3. Effective Date of an NSPS

Unlike most EPA rules, which take effect upon promulgation, NSPSs take effect when EPA proposes them, which in practice can be a year or more before final promulgation. Construction of new facilities or modification of existing facilities that occur after the proposal date are subject to the NSPS. Thus, the timing of construction projects could affect whether they are subject to the NSPS.

The regulatory definition of when construction "commences" does not set a bright-line standard. Rather, construction commences when the owner "has undertaken a continuous program of construction or modification or . . . has entered into a contractual obligation to undertake and complete, within a reasonable time, a continuous program of construction or modification."[49] The contractual commitments involved must require the owner to incur significant financial loss in the event the construction work is canceled, e.g., if a boiler fabrication project were stopped when work was half done.[50] In the PSD program, section 169(2)(A) narrows this definition, but the language still leaves room for debate.[51] In practice, owners and operators contemplating construction of new or modified sources should obtain the views of EPA and the state agencies on the applicable standards very early in the process, lest regulators apply a very different, and far more costly rule.

4. NSPSs Special Source Categories

Section 111(d) requires states to regulate emissions from existing sources in any source category for which EPA sets an NSPS for new and modified sources. This obscure requirement applies only to pollutants that are not defined as criteria pollutant governed by NAAQSs or as hazardous air pollutants under section 112.[52] It is intended to assure that pollutants controlled from new source categories only by an NSPS are also subject to some federally supervised regulation by states.

Sulfuric acid mist and fluorides have been subject to regulation under this provision affecting the phosphate fertilizer, aluminum, sulfuric acid, and kraft

---

[48] Some argue that this exemption will allow older, dilapidated facilities that upgrade operations to avoid new source review when they should be phased out completely.

[49] 40 C.F.R. pt. 60.2(i)(1992). Despite indications that a revised definition was warranted, EPA has not adopted a new definition for the commencement of construction. 44 Fed. Reg. 31,596 (1979); 44 Fed. Reg. 55,173 (1979).

[50] *See* Potomac Elec. Power Co. v. EPA, 650 F.2d 509 (4th Cir.), *cert. denied,* 455 U.S. 1016 (1981) (interpretation of when construction "commences" in light of boiler contract dates).

[51] 42 U.S.C. §7479(2)(A) provides: "The term 'commenced' as applied to construction of a major emitting facility means that the owner or operator has obtained all necessary preconstruction approvals, air permits required by Federal, State, or local air pollution emissions and air quality laws or regulations and either has (i) begun, or caused to begin, a continuous program of physical on-site construction of the facility or (ii) entered into binding agreements or contractual obligations, which cannot be canceled or modified without substantial loss to the owner or operator, to undertake a program of construction of the facility to be completed within a reasonable time."

See Montana Power Co. v. EPA, 429 F. Supp. 683 (D. Mont. 1977), *rev'd,* 608 F.2d 334 (9th Cir. 1979) (addressing the "commenced construction" definition).

[52] 42 U.S.C. §7412.

pulp industries. EPA must approve each state's standards or establish its own substitute standards. Most states which have existing sources that emit those pollutants have developed standards for them based on EPA's control technology guidelines.

5. *NSPSs for Municipal Solid Waste Incinerators*

The 1990 Amendments added section 129 to address municipal and industrial solid waste emissions from incineration. Few environmental subjects are more controversial at the local level and increasingly at the national level than municipal waste incineration.[53] Section 129 combines section 111 NSPSs requirements and section 112 toxic air pollutant requirements. Section 129(d) includes a mandatory training requirement for municipal solid waste incinerator operators. EPA was to develop this program by November 1992. It will be unlawful to operate incinerators without certified operators after November 15, 1993. Permits last up to 12 years, but permit conditions must be reviewed every five years.[54]

EPA was required to promulgate standards for new and existing solid waste incineration units, including municipal solid waste (MSW) units, burning 250 or more tons of waste per day pursuant to sections 111, 111(d), and 129, by November 1991.[55] EPA is behind schedule, and has failed to meet court ordered deadlines that required it to propose standards for such sources by June 1993 and final standards by December 1993. Standards for smaller MSW and medical waste incinerators were due in November 1992. Commercial and industrial waste incinerator standards are due in November 1994.[56]

The new standards are required to address total and fine particulate matter, sulfur dioxide, hydrogen chloride, nitrogen oxides, carbon monoxide, lead, cadmium, mercury, dioxins, and dibenzofurans.[57] Many of these toxic metal emissions result from batteries in the municipal waste stream. Emission standards for new units must be at least as stringent as that achieved by the best similarly controlled unit. Emission standards for existing units must be at least as stringent as the best performing 12 percent of existing units.[58] These two standards for new and existing sources are very close to the definition of Lowest Achievable Emission Rate (LAER) under the nonattainment provisions and the

---

[53] The Clinton Administration is not expected to favor incineration as a means of waste disposal. Vice-President Gore had advocated a ban on construction of new incinerators.

[54] §129(e), 42 U.S.C. §7429(e).

[55] §129(a)(1)(A)-(D), 42 U.S.C. §7429(a)(1)(A)-(D). EPA expects to issue final NSPSs for both large and small municipal incinerators by November 1993. Pursuant to a settlement agreement with Congressman Waxman, EPA was to issue a schedule for promulgation of remaining standards required under §129 by December 31, 1993.

[56] The current EPA timetable anticipates final NSPSs for medical waste incinerators by February 1995.

[57] §129(a)(4), 42 U.S.C. §7429(a)(4). The language imposing emission standards borrows from both §§111 and 112:

> [Emission standards] shall reflect the maximum degree of reduction of emissions of [listed] air pollutants . . . taking into consideration the cost of achieving such emission reduction, and any non-air quality health and environmental impacts and energy requirements, determine[d to be] achievable for new or existing units in each category.

§129(a)(2), 42 U.S.C. §7429(a)(2).

[58] If there are less than 30 existing units, emissions standards from the best five will apply. §129(a)(2), 42 U.S.C. §7429(a)(2).

definition of Maximum Available Control Technology (MACT) under section 112. Section 129(a)(3) appears to allow EPA to impose recycling requirements by authorizing the agency to adopt ''methods and technologies for removal or destruction of pollutants before, during or after combustion.''[59] The 1990 Amendments also impose requirements for locating new incinerators in order to reduce health and environmental risks. These siting standards may overlap with PSD requirements covering units that incinerate more than 50 tons per day.[60]

D. Prevention of Significant Deterioration

The PSD program applies to new or modified facilities located in areas where the air is cleaner than NAAQSs require. The objective is to protect air quality that is cleaner than national standards by preventing degradation down to the national minimum health standards set by NAAQSs. The PSD provisions—subtitle C of Title I—contain elaborate air quality requirements referred to as the increment program in addition to those established for NAAQSs compliance as well as technology-based requirements known as Best Available Control Technology (BACT).

EPA initially resisted imposing regulations to prevent degradation of air quality, claiming that the agency had no authority to do so under the 1970 CAA. In 1972, the Sierra Club successfully brought suit to compel EPA to address PSD. The Sierra Club cited section 101(b), which stated that the purpose of the 1970 Act was to ''protect and enhance'' the nation's air resources. The trial court held, based on the legislative history, that EPA both had the authority and the obligation to implement PSD regulations.[61] EPA promulgated regulations in 1975 to implement the PSD program, regulations upheld by the court of appeals,[62] and used in a modified form as the basis for Congress's adoption in 1977 of a detailed statutory PSD program in subtitle C of Title I. The 1990 Amendments made very few changes in this program.

The statutory PSD program and the implementing regulations are exceedingly intricate. They have two major components that new or modified sources larger than a certain size must satisfy. First, there is an air quality component. It is implemented through the three-class zoning system that defines in precise numerical terms (increments) the permissible amount of air quality degradation the source may cause. That determination is made on the basis of air quality modeling.

Second, there is a technological component that requires new sources to use BACT, a technological determination which is to be made on a case-by-case basis. The resulting limit under BACT requirements must be at least as stringent as the level that would be required by applicable new source performance standards.

---

[59] 42 U.S.C. §7429(a)(3).

[60] Section 169(1) is modified to reduce the threshold for PSD review to municipal incinerators capable of charging more than 50 tons per day. 42 U.S.C. §7479(1).

[61] Sierra Club v. Ruckelshaus, 344 F. Supp. 253 (D.D.C. 1972), *aff'd mem.*, 4 ER Cases 1815 (D.C. Cir), *aff'd without opinion by an equally divided court,* 412 U.S. 541 (1973).

[62] Sierra Club v. EPA, 540 F.2d 1114 (D.C. Cir. 1976), *cert. denied,* 430 U.S. 959 (1977).

EPA promulgated elaborate rules in 1978 to implement the statutory program, rules which were largely upheld in 1979. EPA promulgated revised regulations in 1980, and challenges to them have largely been resolved by settlements involving small revisions to the rules. The Agency is scheduled to propose further revisions by June 1994.

1. PSD Class Designation

The 1977 Amendments used EPA's three-class zoning system, but significantly tightened applicable increments—numerically defined amounts of air quality degradation. Section 162 defines all national parks and national wilderness areas above 6,000 acres in size as Class I areas that cannot be redesignated.[63] Those areas have increments of permissible deterioration set quite low, so that location of a large source of emissions nearby would probably be infeasible.[64]

Section 162(b) designates the rest of the United States as Class II, for which the increments are larger than Class I. The Class II increments are designed to permit moderate well-controlled growth which will not lead to significant deterioration.[65]

The Class III designation has the most expansive increments, and allows additional pollution up to the secondary NAAQSs.[66] Class III areas are designed to allow states to promote industrial development by relaxing applicable increments. Rigorous procedures are included for states or Indian tribes that redesignate areas to different Classes. To date, however, no state or Indian tribe has chosen to redesignate any area as Class III.[67] Several efforts have been made to change a Class II designation to Class I.

2. PSD Increments

The statute defined numerical increments for two pollutants—total suspended particulates (TSP) and SO_2—and gave EPA authority to promulgate increments for other pollutants. Under the statute and subsequent regulations, EPA designated three types of areas, each with assigned permissible increments of SO_2, TSP, and, more recently, NO_2 pollution.[68] The 1990 Amendments gave EPA the authority to substitute PM10 increments for the prior TSP increments.[69] An air quality "increment" is a numerically defined amount of air quality degradation, which corresponds to a fraction of the applicable NAAQS.

---

[63] The 1990 Amendments changed §§162(a) and 164(a) to provide that Class I area boundary alterations, e.g., national parks, subsequent to the 1977 Amendments are to be reflected in the boundaries of these areas for PSD purposes. 42 U.S.C. §§7472(a), 7474(a).

[64] §§162, 164, 42 U.S.C. §§7472, 7474 (1988). *See also* 56 Fed. Reg. 50,513 (1991).

[65] 56 Fed. Reg. 14,861 (1991).

[66] 56 Fed. Reg. 14,861 (1991).

[67] Certain federal lands cannot be redesignated as Class III areas. §164(a), 42 U.S.C. §7474(a).

[68] EPA was required by court order to add annual NO_2 increments. 53 Fed. Reg. 40,656 (1988). As a result of a subsequent court order, EPA must also consider adding short-term NO_2 increments. This step is unusual because there is no short-term NAAQS for NO_2. Environmental Defense Fund v. EPA, 898 F.2d 183 (D.C. Cir. 1990).

Section 166(a) required EPA by August 1979 to adopt increments or other measures for hydrocarbons, carbon monoxide, ozone, and possibly lead. 42 U.S.C. §7476(a).

[69] With the 1990 Amendments, EPA is now authorized by §166(f), 42 U.S.C. §7476(f), to substitute PM10 increments for the prior statutory TSP increments in §§163(b) and 165(d).

Section 163 defines the increments for particulate matter and SO_2 in micrograms per cubic meter for various time frames. The increment is measured from a baseline concentration which is determined as part of the process of reviewing the first PSD permit application for an area.[70]

3. "Major Emitting Facilities" and BACT

Any new or modified "major emitting facility"[71] must obtain a preconstruction permit that requires it to use BACT and to show that its emissions using BACT will not violate increment requirements. BACT is defined as the

> maximum degree of [emission] reduction . . . which the permitting authority, on a case-by-case basis, taking into account energy, environmental, and economic impacts and other costs, determines is achievable for such facility.[72]

BACT limitations must be at least as stringent as applicable NSPSs or NESHAPs. Because NSPSs revisions occur on a slow schedule, the BACT provision gives EPA or the state the ability to tighten emission control requirements by incorporating more recent control technology developments. Some NSPSs requirements have not been revised since the early 1970s. Consequently, technology-forcing through BACT requirements typically results in more stringent emission controls than NSPSs alone would require.

Under EPA's 1987 BACT guidance, available technologies are listed according to the degree of emission reductions expected. The guidance required industry to apply best technology unless it could show that the technology would be economically or technologically infeasible. EPA recently proposed revisions to that guidance which presently allows states to press for more stringent controls through EPA's so-called "top-down" policy. Under the top-down policy, EPA proposes the best control technology for a new or modified source, eliminating distinctions between BACT and Lowest Achievable Emissions Rate (LAER) under the nonattainment provisions. The proposed change would allow industries to make the initial determinations of what constitutes

---

[70] §169(4), 42 U.S.C. §7479(4). Baseline concentration refers to "the ambient concentration levels which exist at the time of the first application for a permit . . . based on air quality data available in the Environmental Protection Agency and on such monitoring data as the permit applicant is required to submit."

An applicant's installation may not exceed the amount of increment left in the area in which it is located at the time the PSD application is submitted. There is no assurance, however, that any applicant will be allowed by the permitting authority to consume the entire amount of the remaining increment.

[71] Major emitting facilities are defined by the Act in two ways: first, as one of 28 designated sources which "emit, or have the potential to emit, one hundred tons per year or more of any air pollutant . . . [or] second, as any [other] source with the potential to emit two hundred fifty tons per year or more of any air pollutant." §169(1), 42 U.S.C. §7479(1).

The major sources at the 100 TPY level include the following stationary sources: fossil-fuel-fired steam electric plants with more than 250 million Btu per hour heat input, coal cleaning plants (thermal dryers), kraft pulp mills, Portland Cement plants, primary zinc smelters, iron and steel mill plants, primary aluminum ore reduction plants, primary copper smelters, municipal incinerators capable of charging more than 50 tons of refuse per day, hydroflouric, sulfuric, and nitric acid plants, petroleum refineries, lime plants, phosphate rock processing plants, coke oven batteries, sulfur recovery plants, carbon black plants (furnace process), primary lead smelters, fuel conversion plants, sintering plants, secondary metal production facilities, chemical process plants, fossil-fuel boilers with more than 250 Btu per hour heat input, petroleum storage and transfer facilities with a capacity exceeding 300,000 barrels, taconite ore processing facilities, glass fiber processing plants, charcoal production facilities. 42 U.S.C. §7479(1).

[72] §169(3), 42 U.S.C. §7479(3).

BACT. Application of the "top-down BACT" approach has been controversial and the subject of recent litigation.[73]

4. PSD Permit Program

EPA administers a preconstruction permit system under the PSD program.[74] This permit system predates and is in addition to the permit program under Title V. A source must undergo new source review if it falls in one of 28 specifically designated industrial categories and has the "potential to emit" more than 100 tons per year of any pollutant regulated by the CAA, not just SO_2 or particulates.[75] (The amount is 250 tons for sources outside the 28 specific categories.) "Potential to emit" refers to the maximum design capacity of the source after application of pollution controls.[76] A modification of an existing major stationary source must undergo review if it creates a "significant net increase," as defined by EPA regulation, in emissions of a pollutant regulated under the CAA. The amounts differ depending on the toxicity of the pollutant.

In determining the "source" to which the regulations apply, EPA examines the largest grouping of pollutant-emitting activities located on contiguous or adjacent properties that are under the control of the same person and within the same Standard Industrial Classification (SIC) code major group.[77] The definition of source is important because new source review applies only to a net increase in emissions from the source. If emissions can be reduced at other locations within the source to levels below 100 tons, new source review may be avoided.

A new source seeking a PSD permit must demonstrate not only that it will use BACT and not violate any NAAQSs, but also that its emissions will not result in air quality degradation greater than the amount of increment available.[78] This demonstration is costly and lengthy because, among other things, the applicant must present one year of continuous air quality monitoring data.[79] The CAA requires public hearings to be held on permit applications. In addition to the quantitative analysis required to determine the amount of increment consumed, the applicant must also submit information about (1) the air quality

[73] The American Paper Institute sued EPA in 1989, arguing that the "top-down BACT" guidance represents a departure from PSD regulations and should be subject to a formal rulemaking proceeding. American Paper Inst. v. EPA, No. 89-2030 (D.D.C. July 18, 1989). API claims that companies are unable to prove that less costly technology is appropriate and thus must install costly equipment unnecessarily. Two related suits are also pending in the court of appeals. American Petroleum Inst. v. EPA, No. 89-1428 (D.C. Cir. July 10, 1989); American Petroleum Inst. v. EPA, No. 90-1363 (D.C. Cir. July 13, 1990).

[74] The PSD permit program is established in 40 C.F.R. §52.21.

[75] Source categories are listed at 40 C.F.R. §52.21(b)(1)(i)(a).

[76] EPA is revising this definition as a result of the decision in Wisconsin Elec. Power Co. v. EPA, 893 F.2d 901 (7th Cir. 1990).

[77] 40 C.F.R. §52.21(b)(6).

[78] There are numerous exemptions to the PSD program. According to the statute, nonprofit health or educational institutions exempted by a state cannot be classified as a major emitting facility. In addition, fugitive emissions cannot be considered when determining whether a potential source qualifies as "major" except for specific source categories. 45 Fed. Reg. 52,680 (1980). If the area is designated nonattainment for a pollutant, a new source emitting that pollutant is subject to nonattainment provisions rather than preconstruction review.

[79] §166(e), 42 U.S.C. §7476(e). Quality assurance requirements for PSD air monitoring are provided at 40 C.F.R. §58, App. B (1992).

effects projected for the area as a result of growth associated with the facility, (2) effects on vegetation, and (3) effects on visibility.

5. *Visibility Protection Under the PSD Program*

Although the PSD and secondary NAAQSs theoretically should eliminate visibility protection concerns, the 1977 Amendments required initiation of a program for "the prevention of any future, and the remedying of any existing, impairment of visibility in Class I areas."[80] There are two aspects of visibility impairment that are usually a concern under this statutory program: "plume blight" which ordinarily refers to impacts from a particular plant's emission plume and "regional haze" which usually refers to more widespread visibility reduction from SO_2 (or NO_2) emissions by multiple sources. This provision requires best available retrofit technology (BART) to be determined for existing facilities affecting Class I areas.[81] EPA is authorized to exempt a facility from this requirement if the Agency determines that the source is not likely to emit pollutants, by itself or in combination with other sources, that will significantly impair visibility.[82] EPA issued regulations that are designed to preserve the public's ability to view national landmarks.[83] A list of these views, referred to in the regulations as "integral vistas," however, has never been published. Efforts are underway using statutory authorities existing prior to 1990 to require substantial emission reductions on power plants whose emissions degrade visibility in the Grand Canyon area.

The 1990 Amendments added section 169B which required the establishment of a Visibility Transport Commission that will address impairment of visibility in the Grand Canyon area.[84] This section authorizes establishment of similar commissions to oversee protection and improvement of visibility in Class I areas.

E. Nonattainment Provisions

The 1977 Amendments imposed substantial new requirements for areas that had not attained NAAQSs. New and modified existing major sources in those areas were subject to special technology-based and air-quality-based requirements in addition to NSPSs. The technology-based portions of these requirements for new sources are referred to as Lowest Achievable Emission Rate (LAER). The air quality portion of the program required such new or modified sources to obtain "offsets" for emissions: a reduction of an equivalent or greater quantity of emissions of that pollutant from an existing source equal or greater than the emissions the new source would emit using LAER. Offset requirements for emissions are imposed through a permit system.

Existing stationary sources in nonattainment areas are also required to use Reasonably Available Control Technology (RACT). RACT refers to control

[80] §169A(a), 42 U.S.C. §7491(a).
[81] §169A(b)(2)(A), 42 U.S.C. §7491(b)(2)(A).
[82] §169A(c)(1), 42 U.S.C. §7491(c)(1).
[83] 40 C.F.R. §51.301(n).
[84] §169B(c)(2), (f), 42 U.S.C. §7492(c)(2), (f).

equipment that is both reasonably available and economically feasible to achieve the lowest emission limit applicable to an existing source in a nonattainment area. The 1990 Amendments strengthened the RACT requirements and the offset obligations and made the amount of emissions requiring the application of LAER and RACT in many nonattainment areas lower than that imposed by the 1977 Amendments.

The 1990 Amendments made other major changes to the nonattainment area provisions, but retained aspects of the prior offset policy, LAER, and sanctions against states that fail to comply with attainment goals. Attainment deadlines vary according to the criteria pollutant involved. For ozone, carbon monoxide, and particulate matter, the deadlines vary according to the severity of the nonattainment.

In adopting staggered deadlines, Congress recognized that areas face varying degrees of difficulty in meeting NAAQSs. For example, the deadline for ozone attainment in the Los Angeles area extends until the year 2010, the longest extension under the Amendments. In exchange for receiving longer deadlines, those areas face increasingly severe requirements on their stationary and mobile sources as well as obligations to make reasonable further progress.

1. LAER and Offsets

The 1970 CAA required SIPs to include a program for preconstruction review of new or modified stationary sources to ensure that such sources would not interfere with attainment or maintenance of NAAQSs.[85] It was clear that any new or modified facility emitting a pollutant for which NAAQSs were violated would interfere with attainment. Consequently, EPA issued its ''offset ruling'' in late 1976, to allow growth under certain conditions.

New sources were required to secure a reduction in emissions, or ''offset,'' from existing sources, whether or not the applicant owned the source. The reductions were required to provide an offset greater than a one-for-one exchange in the total emissions from the new or modified facility. The offset policy required new sources to install BACT and to certify that other sources of air pollution in the same state under common ownership also met applicable requirements.

The 1977 Amendments retained the offset policy until SIP revisions substituted for it a preconstruction review program.[86] The nonattainment area provisions required all new or modified sources with the potential[87] to emit 100 tons or more per year of the pollutant to obtain a permit. A source was ''modified'' if its emissions increased by a certain percentage. EPA eventually defined ''source'' under the nonattainment area provisions the same way it does under the PSD provision, to include the entire plant, not just separate equipment within the plant.[88]

Depending on the type of nonattainment area in which a source is located (marginal, moderate, serious, severe, or extreme), the definition of ''source''

[85] §110(a)(2)(D), 42 U.S.C. §7410(a)(2)(D).

[86] §172, 42 U.S.C. §7502.

[87] The ''potential'' to emit refers to design capacity after application of emission controls.

[88] The Supreme Court upheld EPA's definition of source in Chevron, U.S.A. v. NRDC, 467 U.S. 837 (1984).

varies. Consequently, the worse the nonattainment problem, the lower the tonnage threshold at which a source is to be considered major for the purposes of LAER requirements and offsets. In "extreme" nonattainment areas, the threshold is 10 tons, as opposed to the prior threshold of 100 tons.

For purposes of new source review, any new major or modified existing source is subject to procedural review designed to determine its compatibility with NAAQSs attainment. These sources must demonstrate LAER, the strictest possible limits on emissions from new or existing sources in nonattainment areas. Furthermore, unless other sources owned or operated by the applicant in the state meet all applicable emission limits or at least meet all compliance schedule steps, the operator cannot obtain a permit for a new source. Finally, the new or modified source must provide offsets to its emissions.

Offset requirements will force new and modified sources to reduce emissions from existing sources by more than a one-to-one ratio with new emissions. The worse the nonattainment area, the greater the offset required.[89] Ratios range from 1.1 to 1 in "marginal" nonattainment areas to 1.5 to 1 in "extreme" nonattainment areas. Moreover, emission reductions required by the Clean Air Act and its implementing regulations—such as RACT requirements—cannot be used for offset purposes. Offsets must only be granted for measures by existing sources that go beyond compliance requirements—usually RACT.[90] Under some circumstances offsets obtained from within the same source or group of commonly controlled sources are permitted, though in serious, severe, and extreme nonattainment areas such offsets within a source are more difficult. It may also be possible for sources to use offsets from upwind nonattainment areas.[91]

2. *Classification of Nonattainment Areas*

The 1990 Amendments require EPA and the states to review the attainment status of all areas of the country and to decide how each nonattainment area should be classified for regulatory purposes. Under section 107 of the 1970 CAA, EPA was required to divide the country into air quality control regions (AQCRs) in order to treat interstate and intrastate areas with common meteorological, industrial, and socioeconomic factors as one unit.[92] EPA designated 275 AQCRs,[93] but the 1977 Amendments diminished the role of AQCRs by requiring states to identify and EPA to classify areas of the country that met or failed to meet NAAQSs and those for which there was insufficient information. Now, under the 1990 Amendments, nonattainment area designations are ordinarily to be made on the basis of county boundaries as opposed to AQCRs.[94]

---

[89] Additionally, the 1990 Amendments revised §176(b), 42 U.S.C. §7506(b), to forbid the practice of offsetting new emissions against a "growth allowance" provided under a SIP for areas that are in nonattainment status and have SIPs that are no longer approved. This change may raise questions about so-called "banked" emission credits, whereby a source shuts down emissions in one year and reserves the right to emit or sell such emission rights in later years.

[90] §173(c)(2), 42 U.S.C. §7503(c)(2).

[91] §172(c)(1), 42 U.S.C. §7502(c)(1).

[92] 42 U.S.C. §7407.

[93] 40 C.F.R. §81.

[94] As a consequence of diminished role of AQCRs, the impact of sanctions was somewhat reduced because smaller area boundaries are implicated under nonattainment designations.

3. *Reclassification of Nonattainment Areas*

Section 107 sets forth the detailed process for review and reclassification of an area's attainment status. It also imposes conditions on a state in order to move an area from nonattainment to attainment status. These conditions are intended to keep areas which may not stay in attainment from moving into that status without assurances that acceptable air quality will be maintained. The current nonattainment designations remain in force until EPA changes them.[95]

EPA cannot change a nonattainment designation to the unclassifiable[96] category under the 1990 Amendments.[97] Instead, in order to change the classification of a nonattainment area to attainment, EPA must determine that (1) the air quality in the area meets NAAQSs, (2) the state has a fully approved SIP, (3) the improvements in air quality result from permanent and enforceable emission reductions, and (4) an air quality maintenance plan is in place under section 175A.[98] A maintenance plan must assure attainment for 10 years. Until the reclassification is approved by EPA, the area retains its nonattainment status.

4. *Schedule for Classification*

States were required to submit designations for ozone and carbon monoxide attainment and nonattainment status of areas within their boundaries by March 1991.[99] After making appropriate changes to state submissions, EPA was required to promulgate a list of nonattaiment areas by July 15, 1991. Appendix A provides the current list of ozone, carbon monoxide, and particulate matter (PM10) nonattainment areas as of the time of this writing. The boundaries of ozone and carbon monoxide nonattainment areas are extended to include the entire standard (or consolidated) metropolitan statistical area (SMSA or CMSA) affected, if the nonattainment problem is classified as "serious," "severe," or "extreme," the three most stringent nonattaiment area designations.

5. *Particulate Matter Classification*

For particulate matter, where the NAAQSs changed in 1987 from one addressing total suspended particulates (TSP) to particulate matter smaller than 10 microns in size (PM10), the nonattainment provisions use a different approach.[100] At the time EPA promulgated the PM10 standard in 1987, it split air quality control regions into different Group areas, depending on the severity of the PM10 problem. Under the 1990 Amendments, areas EPA classified as having a high likelihood of violating the PM10 standard (Group I areas) are now classified as nonattainment for the PM10 standard as well as areas for which violations had been measured before 1989. All other areas are initially classified as attainment for PM10.

---

[95] §107(d)(1)(C), 42 U.S.C. §7407(d)(1)(C).

[96] Under prior versions of the Act, EPA had sometimes used the unclassifiable designation where data were incomplete or where they suggested a borderline case.

[97] §107(d)(3)(F), 42 U.S.C. §7407(d)(3)(F).

[98] §107(d)(3)(E), 42 U.S.C. §7407(d)(3)(E).

[99] §107(d)(4)(A), 42 U.S.C. §7407(d)(4)(A).

[100] §107(d)(4)(B), 42 U.S.C. §7407(d)(4)(B).

6. *Deadlines for Compliance with NAAQSs*

Area designations and redesignations are not subject to judicial review until final action is taken by EPA on SIP revisions.[101] In general, nonattainment areas have five years from designation in which to comply, which EPA can extend up to five more years.[102] EPA may further extend this time twice, each time for a year where there is an approved SIP, and the exceedances have been minimal. These general requirements are largely superseded, however, by the pollutant-specific time frames that the 1990 Amendments now include. The general requirements will be important if additional NAAQSs are promulgated, or existing ones are revised.

7. *Requirements for Specific Nonattainment Area Pollutants*

The 1990 Amendments set forth nonattainment requirements based in part upon the pollutant involved, and in part upon the degree by which that pollutant exceeds the NAAQSs. These requirements become more stringent the more serious the nonattainment problem. Usually, each more stringent level includes the measures required of the step below it, and adds additional requirements for the area in exchange for more time for the area to comply.

For each of the nonattainment steps, the definition of sources changes and the threshold decreases as the nonattainment problem becomes more severe. As the severity of the nonattainment increases, offset ratios become more stringent and additional restrictions on offsets are imposed. If automobiles contribute to the nonattainment problem, as in the case of ozone and carbon monoxide, inspection and maintenance (I&M) requirements become more stringent, and special requirements are imposed for the use of clean fuels and the reduction of vehicle traffic.[103]

a. Requirements for Ozone Nonattainment. Ozone is a problem resulting in large part from emissions of volatile organic compounds (VOCs) from cars and trucks, from industrial operations such as painting, coating, and degreasing, from some natural sources, and from handling petroleum. Ozone is also thought to result in part from nitrogen oxide (NO_2) emissions, although the relationship is not well understood. Consequently, the ozone nonattainment provisions focus both on stationary sources and on vehicle requirements.

The 1990 Amendments added the most detailed nonattainment requirements affecting any criteria pollutant for ozone. At the time of enactment, about 100 areas were classified as nonattainment for ground level ozone—formerly referred to as "photochemical oxidants."[104] As a result of changes made in the Amendments, the geographic area of many ozone nonattainment areas spread beyond county boundaries to include the entire standard or consolidated metropolitan statistical area (SMSA or CSMA). Increased area boundaries affect a larger number of stationary sources since reasonably available control technol-

---

[101] §172(a)(1)(C), 42 U.S.C. §7502(a)(1)(C).

[102] §172(a)(2), 42 U.S.C. §7502(a)(2).

[103] Section 108(f), as amended in 1990, lists a variety of transportation control measures that will be required in the worst nonattainment areas for ozone and carbon monoxide. 42 U.S.C. §7408(f).

[104] Subpart 2, subtitle D, §§181–185B; 42 U.S.C. §§7511–7511(b).

ogy (RACT) is required, as well as subjecting more vehicles to inspection and maintenance (I&M) requirements.

(1) Ozone design values. Section 181(a) classifies ozone nonattainment areas based on the "design value" ozone levels. The ozone design value is derived from monitoring data and represents a site's fourth highest daily maximum exceedance during a three-year period.[105] The highest site design value among all sites in a given area sets the design value for an area. These levels and the appropriate classifications are:

Areas Class	*Design Value*	*Attainment Deadline*
Marginal	0.121 to 0.138 ppm	November 1993
Moderate	0.138 to 0.160 ppm	November 1996
Serious	0.160 to 0.180 ppm	November 1999
Severe (I)	0.180 to 0.189 ppm	November 2005
Severe (II)[106]	0.190 to 0.280 ppm	November 2007
Extreme	0.280 ppm and above	November 2010

At the time of initial classification under the 1990 Amendments, and for 90 days thereafter, EPA had the discretion to vary the design value by plus or minus 5 percent.[107] This revision in design value is to be based on the number of exceedances, the amount of transport of ozone from other areas, and the mix of sources and pollutants in that area. EPA's designations for ozone nonattainment are provided in Appendix A.[108]

(2) SIP revisions for marginal nonattainment areas. Marginal nonattainment areas are those that were closest to meeting NAAQSs at the time of enactment of the 1990 Amendments. They had three years from enactment to attain standards. States with marginal nonattainment areas in their boundaries must submit SIP revisions with the following components:

- An inventory of emissions that identifies actual emissions of VOCs or NO_2. This inventory must be updated every three years until EPA redesignates the area as an attainment area.[109]
- Provisions to require Reasonably Available Control Technology (RACT) on all major sources that emit more than 100 tons VOCs or NO_2 per year for which EPA issued control technology guidelines (CTGs) as of November 1990.[110] Under this provision EPA's guidance documents are adopted as rules and made applicable to existing sources of VOC

[105] Industry critics believe this calculation does not take into consideration fluctuations in pollution levels.

[106] Severe areas with a 1988 designs value between 0.190 and 0.280 have 17 years in lieu of the 15 years for Severe I areas to achieve attainment standards. §181(a)(2), 42 U.S.C. §7511(a)(2).

[107] §181(a)(4), 42 U.S.C. §7511(a)(4). Section 185A provides that for areas without violations from January 1987 to December 1989, the applicability of the Subpart 2 ozone nonattainment provisions is suspended for a year in order to determine if the so-called "transitional" area comes into compliance.

[108] Nonattainment area designation were published on October 26, 1991, by the EPA Policy Development Section, Ozone/Carbon Monoxide Programs Branch, Air Quality Management Division, Office of Air Quality Planning and Standards, Research Triangle Park, NC.

[109] §182(a)(1)(3), 42 U.S.C. §7511a(a)(1)(3). The inventory provision is significant because states have different methods for collecting data on sources. States occasionally use permits for the inventory, but they typically reflect maximum, rather than actual, operating conditions.

[110] §182(a)(2)(A), 42 U.S.C. §7511a(a)(2)(A).

emissions. SIP revisions are due six months after EPA classifies nonattainment areas.

- States must continue vehicle inspection and maintenance (I&M) programs.[111] States must update the I&M programs in accordance with EPA's most recent guidance and submit SIP revisions upgrading I&M programs by November 1992.
- States must upgrade the permit program for major and modified sources of VOCs to be consistent with EPA guidance. SIP revisions for these programs are due by November 1992.[112]

Also, offset requirements are imposed on marginal areas. The offset ratio for marginal nonattainment areas must be at least 1.1 to 1.0 for VOCs. This requires existing sources to reduce emissions in the area by 11 tons for every 10 tons that emissions in the area increase from new sources.[113] These offsets must be arranged for by the new sources which is often done by purchasing these reductions from the existing sources. SIPs must require sources to submit annual emissions reports of VOCs and NO_2 with the first statement due in November 1993.[114] Offset arrangements that exchange reductions in maximum permitted emissions for real emission increases will be far more difficult to make once the inventory requirement takes effect.

(3) Moderate nonattainment area SIP revisions. There are about 35 moderate nonattainment areas. States must implement the same measures in moderate nonattainment areas as in marginal nonattainment areas. In addition, they must submit SIP revisions with the following requirements:

- The baseline emissions inventory must be cut 15 percent by November 1996.[115] Both VOC and NO_2 emissions reductions are required. The reductions must be achieved in annual increments.[116] Some reductions resulting from requirements imposed before November 1990—such as restrictions on fuel vapor pressures—cannot be applied towards the 15 percent requirement.
- RACT must be required for all existing major sources of VOC emissions, as well as sources for which EPA has issued CTGs (or those for which the 1990 Amendments require EPA to issue CTGs).[117] SIP revisions were due in November 1992, and VOC source compliance is required by May 1995.

---

[111] §182(a)(2)(B), 42 U.S.C. §7511a(a)(2)(B).

[112] §182(a)(2)(C), 42 U.S.C. §7511a(a)(2)(C).

[113] §182(a)(3), (4), 42 U.S.C. §7511a(a)(3), (4).

[114] §182(a)(3)(B), 42 U.S.C. §7511a(a)(3)(B). The state may waive this requirement for sources emitting less than 25 tons per year of these pollutants. Nitrogen oxides are included because they too can be a precursor of ozone, although the chemical transformation is extremely complicated.

[115] EPA may allow less than a 15% reduction if the state imposes new source review measures equivalent to those for extreme nonattainment areas; imposes RACT on all sources that emit five tons or more VOCs annually; adopts all technologically feasible measures in its SIP and otherwise requires SIP measures achieved in practice by similar sources in serious nonattainment areas. §182(b)(1)(A)(ii), 42 U.S.C. §7511a(b)(1)(A)(ii).

[116] §182(b)(1)(A), 42 U.S.C. §7511a(b)(1)(A). EPA has the discretion not to require the NO_2 reductions where such reductions will not contribute to attainment. The definition of "reasonable further progress," one of the general statutory requirements for nonattainment areas under §171(1), was changed to "annual incremental reductions in emissions of the relevant air pollutant."

[117] §182(b)(2), 42 U.S.C. §7511a(b)(2). Basic I&M programs, if not already required, were to be developed by November 1990. §182(b)(4), 42 U.S.C. §7511a(b)(4).

- States must adopt a vehicle I&M program equal to I&M programs that nonattainment areas adopted pursuant to the 1977 Amendments.
- Owners or operators of gasoline dispensing systems selling more than 10,000 gallons a month must install Phase II vapor recovery devices.[118]
- The offset ratio for new VOC emissions is increased to 1.15 to 1.0.

(4) SIP revisions for serious areas. States must revise SIPs for serious areas in order to take the same steps as those required for moderate nonattainment areas. In addition, these revised SIPs must require the following:

- Enhanced monitoring of VOCs, NO_2, and ozone.[119]
- Demonstrations of "reasonable further progress" in SIP revisions due by November 1994.[120] In total, a 24 percent cut in emissions from those shown in the baseline emissions inventory is required.[121] Thus, in addition to the 15 percent reduction required of moderate nonattainment areas by 1996, another 9 percent in reductions (3 percent annually) must also be achieved by 1999.
- I&M programs that include annual testing, registration denials for cars that cannot pass tests, diagnostic systems inspections, and no waivers for repairs unless they exceed costs of $450 (except for defective parts under warranty).[122] States must have programs operating by November 1992.
- Clean fuel vehicle programs must be operating by April 1994.[123] These provisions must be implemented in model year 1998. Requirements cover vehicle fleets and require fleet operators to use alternative fuels such as methanol and ethanol.
- Transportation control measures if vehicle miles traveled (VMT) in 1996 exceed levels used in SIPs for purposes of demonstrating ozone NAAQS attainment.[124] These measures must be reviewed every three years to determine whether VMTs have increased beyond those projected. If so, transportation control measures must be imposed.
- Strict contingency measures that are effective automatically if the area fails to meet applicable milestones or deadlines.[125]

New source review requirements are stricter with a 1.2 to 1.0 offset ratio.[126] The threshold emissions for regulated sources are reduced from those emitting 100 tons to those emitting 50 tons or more VOCs or NO_2 annually.[127] Revised SIPs

---

[118] §182(b)(3), 42 U.S.C. §7511a(b)(3).

[119] §182(c)(1), 42 U.S.C. §7511a(c)(1). The EPA guidance specifying enhanced monitoring requirements was due in April 1992. Pursuant to a settlement agreement with Congressman Waxman, EPA will promulgate rules for enhanced monitoring of pollutants by April 30, 1993.

[120] §182(c)(2), 42 U.S.C. §7511a(c)(2).

[121] These reductions need not be made for NO_2 if EPA determines that such reductions will not move the area towards attainment. Additionally, EPA is to issue guidance under which NO_2 control may be substituted for VOC controls in some circumstances.

[122] §182(c)(3), 42 U.S.C. §7511a(c)(3).

[123] §182(c)(4), 42 U.S.C. §7511a(c)(4).

[124] §182(c)(5), 42 U.S.C. §7511a(c)(5).

[125] §182(c)(9), 42 U.S.C. §7511a(c)(9).

[126] §182(c)(10), 42 U.S.C. §7511a(c)(10).

[127] §182(c), 42 U.S.C. §7511a(c). The requirements for stationary sources in serious, severe, and extreme ozone nonattainment areas apply to sources of VOCs and NO_2, but EPA has far more discretion to waive or adjust the NO_2 requirements. §182(f), 42 U.S.C. §7511a(f).

must impose restrictions on sources that average emission increases and decreases to remain below threshold requirements.[128]

(5) Severe nonattainment area SIP revisions. Severe areas are divided into the categories Severe I and Severe II. Severe I areas are those with a design value of 0.180 to 0.189 ppm of ozone. These areas have 15 years to achieve standards. Severe II areas are those with a design value of 0.190 to 0.280 ppm of ozone. These areas have 17 years to achieve standards.[129] Measures taken for severe nonattainment areas include those steps taken by serious nonattainment areas as well as the following:

- States must adopt enforceable transportation control measures to offset emissions from increases in vehicle use by November 1992.[130]
- States must adopt additional transportation control measures that require employers with more than 100 employees to increase average passenger occupancy in commuting trips by 25 percent to reduce VMT.[131]
- States must impose monetary penalties of $5,000 per ton exceedance on some major VOC sources if the area fails to meet deadlines.

The offset ratio for severe areas is increased to 1.3 to 1.0.[132] The threshold emissions for major stationary sources subject to regulation is decreased to 25 tons per year.

(6) Extreme nonattainment areas. Los Angeles is the only ozone nonattainment area classified as ''extreme.'' It must take the same steps as those imposed on severe nonattainment areas as well as:

- Require boilers that emit over 25 tons of NO_2 annually to use low polluting fuels such as natural gas, methanol, or ethanol, or require use of advanced control technologies such as catalytic controls by November 1998.
- Certain types of vehicles may be subject to restrictions during peak traffic hours in addition to those control measures in effect for severe nonattainment areas.
- The threshold emissions for regulation of major stationary sources is reduced to 10 tons per year.
- The offset ratio for new source emissions is increased to 1.5 to 1.0.[133]

(7) Compliance deadline extensions. If a nonattainment area fails to meet the deadline by one exceedance in the prior year, and if the state has met its commitments under the SIP for that nonattainment area, then EPA may grant a one-year extension in the attainment date.[134] If a nonattainment area fails to meet the deadline by more than six months and does not qualify for the one-year extension, then the area is moved either to the next highest classification, or, if

---

[128] §182(c)(6)-(8), 42 U.S.C. §7511a(c)(6)-(8).

[129] §181(a)(2), 42 U.S.C. §7511(a)(2).

[130] §182(d)(1)(A), 42 U.S.C. §7511(d)(1)(A).

[131] §182(d)(1)(B), 42 U.S.C. §7511a(d)(1)(B).

[132] §182(d)(2), 42 U.S.C. §7511a(d)(2).

[133] §182(e)(1), 42 U.S.C. §7511(e)(1).

[134] §181(a)(5), 42 U.S.C. §7511(a)(5). That one-year extension may be extended by one additional year if the same conditions, i.e., one exceedance, are met.

monitoring data are worse than the values addressed by the next level, to an even higher level.[135]

(8) Consequences for failure to meet NAAQSs. Where serious, severe, or extreme ozone nonattainment areas do not achieve milestones or deadlines, section 182(g) requires the state to choose one of three consequences: (1) reclassification of the area into a higher category subject to more stringent requirements; (2) imposition of contingency provisions of the SIP; or (3) imposition of an economic incentive program that includes emission fees, marketable permits, and fees to reduce VMT and use of ozone-forming products.[136]

Most important, section 185 economic penalties are applicable to areas that fail to meet attainment deadlines.[137] Among other things, a major VOC source must pay a penalty of $5,000 per ton of VOCs emitted for every ton over 80 percent of the baseline amount. This $5,000 penalty will be adjusted for inflation, beginning in 1990. States must submit SIP revisions, including these economic measures by December 2000.

(9) Ozone transport problems. Many nonattainment areas in the Northeast face compliance problems because of ozone transport across their boundaries. Congress exempted areas from certain penalty provisions if states demonstrate that nonattainment results from ozone transport. An ozone transport region was created in the Northeast that imposes enhanced I&M programs, CTG on all VOC sources, and refueling controls on nonattainment areas in this region pursuant to section 184.[138] An Interstate Transport Commission was created to review and recommend control measures for the ozone transport region. Once the Commission issues recommendations, EPA has nine months to take action and possibly require additional SIP revisions to control ozone transport problems.

(10) Ozone control standards. In addition to section 182 ozone nonattainment area provisions, EPA is required to revise existing CTGs and issue new ones for stationary sources of VOCs.[139] Furthermore, EPA in conjunction with the Coast Guard was required to set standards for tanker VOC emissions by November 1992,[140] though EPA missed that deadline.

More significant, under section 183(e) EPA must develop a regulatory program to reduce releases of ozone-forming substances that result from use of many commercial and consumer products. EPA must study the problems associated with the use of certain consumer and commercial products resulting in VOC emissions and report to Congress by November 1993. In its regulation of these products, EPA must consider

- Benefits, uses, and consumer demand;
- Products' health and safety functions;

[135] §181(b)(2), 42 U.S.C. §7511(b)(2). For severe areas, there are special restrictions which apply, but they are not moved to the extreme category.

[136] §182(g), 42 U.S.C. §7511a(g).

[137] §185, 42 U.S.C. §7511d. An EPA guidance covering economic incentive plans must be adopted by the state before alternatives under §184 are applicable.

[138] 42 U.S.C. §7511c.

[139] §183(a)-(c), 42 U.S.C. §7511b(a)-(c).

[140] §183(f), 42 U.S.C. §7511b(f). Similarly, the 1990 Amendments added §328, 42 U.S.C. §7627, which requires EPA to set nonattainment standards for VOC emissions from outer continential shelf activities with Atlantic and Pacific shorelines, taking back authority from the Secretary of Interior.

- Products' contribution to ozone formation;
- Cost-effectiveness of controls; and
- Available alternatives for the product, as well as the costs, health, and environmental impacts of the substitutes.

(11) Products contributing to VOC emissions. The 1990 Amendments require EPA to list categories of products that cause more than 80 percent of such evaporative VOC emissions. By November 1993, the Agency must issue an eight-year timeline for promulgating regulations governing those products. Furthermore, EPA must issue rules for products that require application of best available controls (BAC). BAC refers to the degree of emission reduction that EPA determines can be achieved on the basis of technological and economic feasibility, health, environmental, and energy impacts. The reduction in emissions must reflect "application of the most effective equipment, measures, processes, methods, systems, or techniques, including chemical reformulation, product or feedstock substitution, repackaging, directions for use, consumption, storage, or disposal."[141] Rules for VOC emitting products are applicable to manufacturers, processors, wholesalers, and importers. The rules do not apply to retailers or consumers, though they will certainly affect the availability of many important products now in use and their effectiveness.

Use of BAC gives EPA discretion in regulating VOC-emitting products. Furthermore, section 183(e)(3) allows EPA to prohibit or control the manufacture or sale of any consumer or commercial product which results in VOC emissions. To implement the program, EPA is authorized to use registration, labeling, self-monitoring and reporting, prohibitions, limitations, and economic incentives. Restrictions on the size, shape, and labeling requirements are not encouraged under section 183(e)(8) except where EPA determines these controls are useful to meet NAAQSs.[142]

b. Carbon Monoxide Nonattainment Provisions. Although many carbon monoxide (CO) nonattainment areas overlap with ozone nonattainment areas, CO nonattainment problems are particularly difficult in cold weather and in high altitude areas, while ozone nonattainment—photochemical smog—is more of a summertime, hot weather condition. The CO nonattainment provisions largely address motor vehicles, the primary source of CO. Section 186(a) classifies CO nonattainment areas according to the following design values:

Area Class	*Design Value*	*Attainment Deadline*
Moderate	9.1 to 16.4 ppm	December 1995
Serious	16.5 ppm and above	December 2000

EPA had discretion to adjust the design value by 5 percent within 90 days of initial area classification.

(1) Moderate nonattainment area SIP revisions. There are several SIP revisions required for moderate CO nonattainment areas, some of which are quite demanding:

[141] §183(e)(1), 42 U.S.C. §7511b(e)(1).
[142] §183(e)(8), 42 U.S.C. §7511(e)(8).

- States must supply a comprehensive, current, and accurate inventory of CO emissions by November 1992.[143]
- States must project VMT and other traffic congestion or car use measures for areas with a design value of 12.7 ppm or above.
- SIPs must include specific transportation control measures that will be effective after any year in which the VMT projection proves too low or the area fails to meet the attainment deadline.
- States must have an operational enhanced I&M program by November 1992 for areas with a design value above 12.7 ppm.

(2) Serious nonattainment area SIP revisions. In addition to meeting the requirements for moderate CO nonattainment areas, serious areas must require the following:

- States must impose transportation control measures to reduce VMT by November 1992.
- The SIP must require an increase in the oxygen content of gasoline sold in the area during the high CO emissions season, generally the winter months.[144]
- SIP revisions must be made for major stationary sources that have threshold CO emissions of 50 tons per year.[145]

(3) Compliance deadline extensions. A state can obtain two one-year extensions of the deadline if it has met all its other SIP obligations and exceedances are insignificant. If a moderate CO nonattainment area does not meet the 1995 deadline or qualify for an extension, it must be reclassified as a serious nonattainment area.

(4) Consequences of failure to meet NAAQSs. Serious CO nonattainment areas must meet reductions deadlines beginning in 1995, or economic sanctions will be imposed. In addition, the transportation controls for severe ozone nonattainment areas will be imposed on serious CO nonattainment areas. If a serious CO nonattainment area misses the attainment deadline of December 2000, a SIP revision is required to mandate CO reductions of 5 percent a year.[146]

c. *Particulate Matter (PM10) Nonattainment Provisions.* Congress legislated separate particulate matter (PM10) nonattainment area requirements but did not set specific numerical criteria in terms of a design value, because EPA did not set the NAAQSs until 1987, and there was uncertainty about the proper classification of some areas. Under the statute, all PM10 nonattainment areas are initially classified as moderate. These areas generally must meet a compliance date of December 1994.[147] The compliance date may be extended for two one-year periods, but only if the state has met its SIP obligations and the exceedances are insignificant.[148]

---

[143] §187(a), 42 U.S.C. §7512a(a).

[144] §187(b), 42 U.S.C. §7512a(b). These oxygenated fuel requirements have already been put into force in some areas, resulting in driver complaints about reduced mileage.

[145] §187(g), 42 U.S.C. §7512a(g).

[146] *Id.*

[147] §188(a)-(c), 42 U.S.C. §7513(a)-(c).

[148] §188(d), 42 U.S.C. §7513(d).

(1) Classification of serious PM10 nonattainment areas. The 1990 Amendments required EPA to determine which areas to classify as serious PM10 nonattainment areas by December 1991.[149] Serious PM10 nonattainment areas must comply with NAAQSs "as expeditiously as practicable" and no later than December 2001.[150] One five-year extension may be allowed for serious areas that cannot meet the 2001 deadline if the state has met its SIP obligations and imposes the most stringent PM10 measures in practice in any state.[151] Moreover, EPA may grant waivers if the nonattainment problem results from natural sources or foreign countries.[152]

(2) Moderate nonattainment area SIP revisions. Moderate PM10 nonattainment areas were to submit SIP revisions by June 1992, which required the following:

- Permits must be prepared for new and modified sources of particulate matter and precursors of PM10.[153]
- Reasonably Available Control Measures (RACM) must be implemented by December 10, 1993. Attainment must be demonstrated or states must demonstrate that it is impracticable to achieve attainment by that date.

(3) Serious nonattainment area SIP revisions. Serious PM10 nonattainment areas must take the same steps as moderate nonattainment areas except that SIP revisions must require:

- Application of Best Available Control Measures (BACM) in the place of RACM.[154] BACM must be applied no later than four years after the date that an area is classified as serious. EPA was to issue RACM and BACM guidance by April 1992[155] to address, among other things, urban fugitive dust, residential wood combustion, and agricultural and forestry burning practices.

d. Sulfur Dioxide, Nitrogen Oxide, and Lead Nonattainment Area Provisions. There are only a few pollutant-specific requirements imposed on SO_2, NO_2, and lead nonattainment areas.[156] EPA expects to designate SO_2 nonattainment areas by February 1993.[157] SIP revisions for these pollutant nonattainment areas must demonstrate that the area will be in compliance promptly, with November 1995 as the compliance deadline. For nonattainment areas classified after the 1990 Amendments, compliance is required five years after that classifi-

---

[149] §188(b)(1), 42 U.S.C. §7513(b)(1). Pursuant to a settlement agreement arising from a case brought by Congressman Waxman to compel EPA to issue overdue regulations, EPA agreed to reclassify moderate PM10 nonattainment areas to serious if those areas cannot meet the NAAQSs by December 31, 1994. *See* 57 Fed. Reg. 43,486 (1992) (providing EPA's proposed redesignation of PM10 nonattainment areas).

[150] §188(c), 42 U.S.C. §7513(c).

[151] §188(e), 42 U.S.C. §7513(e).

[152] §188(f), 42 U.S.C. §7513(f). Mexican border areas suffer severe air quality problems from industrial and automotive sources in Mexico. Section 815 creates a special program with Mexico and §179B, 42 U.S.C. §7509a, is directed at air quality problems involving foreign countries.

[153] §189(a), 42 U.S.C. §7513a(a).

[154] §189(b), 42 U.S.C. §7513a(b).

[155] §190, 42 U.S.C. §7513b.

[156] §§191–192, 42 U.S.C. §§7514–7514a.

[157] EPA proposed its redesignations for SO_2 nonattainment areas in September 1992. 57 Fed. Reg. 43,846 (1992).

cation. If a SIP covering a SO_2 nonattainment area is not fully approved, a construction moratorium must be imposed on new or modified sources of SO_2. This moratorium will stay in effect until the SIP adds permit requirements for new and modified SO_2 sources pursuant to section 172(c)(5) or sections 191 and 192.

e. Sanctions for Nonattainment Areas. Section 179, which was added by the 1990 Amendments, provides for sanctions on states that fail to submit an acceptable SIP or to comply with attainment deadlines.[158] States have 18 months to correct SIPs that EPA rejects in whole or in part. If an inadequate SIP is not corrected, EPA must withhold federal highway funds[159] or increase the offset ratio to two-to-one or higher.[160] EPA must prepare a Federal Implementation Plan (FIP) if the state does not correct SIP problems within two years of a nonattainment designation or a notice of disapproval.[161]

III. Air Toxics

When Congress adopted the 1990 Amendments, it completely rewrote the prior air toxics provision found in old section 112. Though still entitled National Emission Standards for Hazardous Air Pollutants (NESHAPs), the NESHAPs abbreviation is one of the few aspects of this program that Congress did not change.

Under old section 112, Congress sought to regulate emissions of pollutants that "may reasonably be anticipated to result in an increase in mortality, or an increase in serious irreversible, or incapacitating reversible illness." These pollutants are distinct from the criteria pollutants defined under sections 108 and 109 of the Act. Though the statutory mandate in the old NESHAPs was broad, between 1970 and 1990, EPA regulated few hazardous air pollutants—eight in all—and not necessarily from all the major sources which emitted them.[162]

EPA was hamstrung by an unworkable statutory mandate, which required it to protect public health "with an ample margin of safety," a charge that logically resulted in zero emission limitations if one accepts, as EPA often does, the scientific argument that there is no safe threshold of exposure to a substance which is carcinogenic. EPA sought to administer the statute as one requiring the application of best available control technology to sources of such emissions, but the courts rejected this approach, finally directing EPA to set standards based on risk levels higher than zero risk of cancer.[163]

Congress rejected this cumbersome approach in favor of one that resembled the Clean Water Act's regulation of toxic or priority pollutants, including the use of statutorily defined lists of pollutants and of industries emitting these

---

[158] §179, 42 U.S.C. §7509.

[159] §179(b)(1), 42 U.S.C. §7509(b)(1). Funds cannot be withheld for projects whose goals promote safety or air quality improvement.

[160] §179(b)(2), 42 U.S.C. §7509(b)(2).

[161] §110, 42 U.S.C. §7410.

[162] EPA regulated emissions of arsenic, asbestos, beryllium, mercury, radionuclides, benzene, and vinyl chloride under the old provision.

[163] NRDC v. EPA, 824 F.2d 1146 (D.C. Cir. 1987) (en banc).

pollutants, together with a mandate to impose technology-based controls on a strict schedule. Under section 112, these technology-based controls are to correspond to Maximum Available Control Technology (MACT).

Technology-based controls were only the first step in the regulation of NESHAPs under the 1990 Amendments, however. Similar to the Clean Water Act's approach, under which EPA and the states were to tighten toxic discharge standards based on water quality considerations where technology-based controls failed to result in compliance with toxic water quality standards, the new NESHAPs program requires EPA, after it has set MACT, to go back and to assure that emission standards protect public health from residual risks greater than one in one million.

The revised provisions define with some precision what sources and pollutants are subject to the regulations, set a detailed schedule for implementation through technology-based and residual risk-based standards, coordinate the NESHAPs program with the permit program under Title V, address specific problems facing certain named industries, and establish a program to prevent, reduce, and respond to accidental releases of specified hazardous air pollutants as well as extremely hazardous substances (EHSs) as defined under section 304 of the Emergency Planning and Community Right-to-Know Act (EPCRA).

The program is ambitious, and has already proven expensive and highly controversial. There is every reason to expect that it will remain so.

A. What Are Hazardous Air Pollutants?

A major defect in the old NESHAPs program was the slow process by which pollutants were listed: the legislative history shows that Congress had expected about 25 substances to be listed by the early 1970s, but only eight had been by 1990. Congress resolved this problem by enacting a list of 189 hazardous air pollutants (HAPs), of which 167 were specific chemicals, complete with Chemical Abstract Service (CAS) number, and of which the remaining 22 were classes of substances, e.g., nickel and compounds, defined either chemically (e.g., polycyclic organic matter), or by their source (e.g., coke oven emissions), or by physical characteristics (e.g., fine mineral fibers).[164] The list is reprinted as an appendix to this chapter.

The substances Congress listed included many already defined as toxic chemicals under EPCRA section 313, as well as a number identified by the Agency for Toxic Substances and Disease Registry (ATSDR) and state or local air pollution agencies.[165]

There are elaborate processes for the addition or deletion of chemicals from the list, including the filing of petitions to add or delete specific compounds.[166] Experience with similar provisions defining "toxic chemicals"

[164] §112(b)(1), 42 U.S.C. §7412(b)(1). Unless otherwise specified, the listing of a chemical without a CAS number and its compounds includes any unique chemical compound that contains the named chemical as part of that compound. Fine mineral fibers and polycyclic organic matter are specifically defined in the statute.

[165] SENATE COMMITTEE ON ENVIRONMENT AND PUBLIC WORKS REPORT ON S.1630, S. REP. NO. 228, 101st Cong., 1st Sess. 160 (1989).

[166] The 1990 Amendments permit any person as of May 1991 to petition the agency to add or delete a substance from the list. Petitions must provide adequate data demonstrating the substances' health or

under section 313 of EPCRA suggests that there will be ongoing adjustments to the NESHAPs list as a result of such petitions.

Congress also acted to coordinate regulation of these listed pollutants with rules under other provisions of the Act. Thus, a substance is not to be defined as both a criteria pollutant under section 108 and a HAP under section 112.[167] Certain volatile organic compounds (VOCs), however, may be regulated both as precursors of ground level ozone—photochemical smog—pursuant to nonattainment provisions, SIPs, and so forth, and as HAPs. Substances regulated under NESHAPs provisions are not to be regulated from the same source pursuant to the PSD provisions. Similarly, substances regulated under Title VI, related to protection of upper atmospheric ozone, are not to be regulated under this section 112 *solely* because of such adverse environmental effects.

One regulatory consequence of this statutory listing of HAPs is to change release reporting and cleanup obligations under the Comprehensive Environmental Response, Compensation and Liability Act (CERCLA) section 103. Under CERCLA section 101(14), listing of a substance as a HAP under section 112 of the Clean Air Act automatically makes the substance a ''hazardous substance'' under CERCLA, requiring those persons releasing more than the reportable quantity of that substance in a 24-hour period to report that release immediately to the National Response Center. Additionally, as explained more fully in the CERCLA chapter, the presence of such substances at a Superfund site could give rise to a liability for a party that previously had none.

B. Who Is Regulated?

EPA is directed to list major and area source categories of pollution, rather than attempt to control individual substances.[168] A major source is defined as a facility that emits 10 tons of any single air toxic annually or 25 tons of any combination of air toxics annually.[169] An area source is any *stationary* source of HAPs that is not a major source.[170] A local dry cleaning facility emitting less than 10 tons of a single HAP per year, for example, would be categorized as an area source. EPA failed to meet the November 1991 statutory deadline for designating major and area source categories and subcategories that emit HAPs. In July 1992, EPA published an initial list of 174 source categories, but

environmental effects. Within 18 months of submission, EPA must deny in writing petitions that are inadequately supported by data. The Agency has authority, however, to obtain necessary data to make its own determination. EPA must add a substance if the petition is adequately supported or EPA independently concludes that emissions, ambient concentration, bio accumulation, or deposition of the substance causes or is reasonably anticipated to cause adverse human health or environmental effects. §112(b)(2) and (b)(3)(C), 42 U.S.C. §7412(b)(2) and (b)(3)(C).

[167] The arguable exception is elemental lead, which §112(b)(7) makes clear is to be regulated under the criteria pollutant provision; lead compounds remain to be regulated as HAPs under §112(b)(1).

[168] §112(c)(1), 42 U.S.C. §7412(c)(1).

[169] The definition applies to any stationary source or group of stationary sources located within a contiguous area and under common control. §112(a)(1), 42 U.S.C. §7412(a)(1). Congress attempted in this definition to prevent facilities from separating operations at one site into separate emissions points to escape regulation under more stringent requirements for major sources.

[170] §112(a)(2), 42 U.S.C. §7412(a)(2). Mobile sources were excluded from area source categories, despite attempts during 1990 to regulate them under §112.

acknowledged that the list is likely to be revised as new emissions standards are established.[171]

EPA must revise the list of categories and subcategories at least every eight years if public comment or other evidence indicates that a revision is necessary.[172] The source category list can be revised by: (1) delisting petitions, (2) redefinition of major source emissions for a category, or (3) the agency's determination that a source addressed by an existing NESHAP needs more stringent regulation. The list must, to the extent possible, be consistent with NSPS and PSD provisions.[173] EPA's decisions to list pollutants or source categories and subcategories are subject to judicial review.[174]

C. Technological Emissions Standards

Once EPA completes the source category and subcategory list, it must identify and impose technology-based controls for each HAP source.[175] Different technology controls can be imposed for separate classes, types, or sizes of sources. EPA is required to consider cost, non–air quality health and environmental impacts, and energy factors in its formulation of MACT standards.[176] Possible MACT requirements include those that

- Reduce or eliminate emissions of pollutants through process changes, modifications, or substitution of materials;
- Address enclosed processes or systems to control emissions;
- Collect, capture, or treat pollutants released from various emissions points;
- Include design, equipment, work practice, or operating standards; or
- Include a combination of the preceding measures.[177]

MACT standards will be imposed on new and existing major sources.[178] Application of MACT to new sources requires standards to be as stringent as the

---

[171] 57 Fed. Reg. 31,578 (1992). The July 1992 list contains 166 major sources and 8 area sources. EPA's preliminary list contained approximately 750 categories grouped into 17 industry groups. The July 1992 list concentrated that list largely in the area of production and use of synthetic organic chemicals. Among the listed industry categories are: fuel combustion, nonferrous metals processing, mineral products processing, petroleum and natural gas production and refining liquids distribution, surface coating processes, waste treatment and disposal, agricultural chemical production, fibers production processes, food and agriculture processes, pharmaceutical production processes, polymers and resins production, production of inorganic chemicals, miscellaneous processes, and area source categories. Excluded from the list are electric utility steam generating units and solid waste incinerators.

[172] §112(c)(1), 42 U.S.C. §7412(c)(1).

[173] §112(c)(1), 42 U.S.C. §7412(c)(1).

[174] §307, 42 U.S.C. §7607 (1990).

[175] §112(d), 42 U.S.C. §7412(d).

[176] §112(d)(2), 42 U.S.C. §7412(d)(2).

[177] *Id.*

[178] §112(d)(3), 42 U.S.C. §7412(d)(3).

In addition to EPA's selection of MACT or residual risk standards, §112(h)(1) allows EPA to promulgate standards for design, equipment, work practice, and operational standards "when it is not feasible to prescribe or enforce an emissions standard." 42 U.S.C. §7412(h)(1). Such standards are applicable when HAPs cannot be captured through devices or the devices do not comport with federal, state, or local law. After an owner or operator submits a petition and there is opportunity for notice and comment, EPA may authorize those standards which it determines are consistent with the technology-based or residual risk standards. §112(h)(4), 42 U.S.C. §7412(h)(4).

emission controls achieved in practice by the best controled similar source.[179] This is similar to the statutory definition of LAER under the nonattainment provisions.

Less stringent MACT standards are applicable to existing or modified sources. Existing sources still must employ controls that are at least as stringent as those used by the best performing 12 percent of existing sources.[180] These percentage standards are applicable to categories or subcategories with 30 or more sources. For categories or subcategories with less than 30 sources, the standard is based on an average of the five top performing sources.[181] Even though technology-based standards for new and existing major sources differ, once EPA adopts a state's permit program under Title V, no major source can be constructed, reconstructed, or modified unless the state or EPA determines the source will achieve the MACT standard for existing sources.[182]

EPA must develop and submit to Congress a national plan to control HAP emissions from area sources in urban areas that is to be implemented by November 1999.[183] EPA must at a minimum name 30 HAPs emitted by area sources that are the most hazardous to public health in urban areas. Source categories that collectively emit 90 percent or more of each listed HAP will be subject to technology-based standards.[184] EPA will implement a national strategy to reduce incidence of cancer attributable to area source emissions by 75 percent pursuant to its authority under the CAA, other federal statutes, and state law.[185]

In addition to listing major source categories, EPA is required to list each category or subcategory of area sources. EPA then must either establish a MACT standard under section 112(d)(3) for the area source category considering factors applied in establishing major source standards, or require area sources to achieve emissions levels based on generally available control technology (GACT).[186] GACT refers to "methods, practices and techniques which are commercially available and appropriate for application by sources in the category."[187] GACT makes allowances for a plant's technical ability to operate and maintain emissions controls systems and considers the systems' economic impacts. Area sources regulated under section 112(d)(5) are not subject to the residual risk standards discussed below.

1. Schedule for Compliance

Existing sources must be in compliance no later than three years after the effective date of the standards with the possibility of a one-year extension for

---

[179] §112(d)(3), 42 U.S.C. §7412(d)(3).

[180] §112(d)(3)(A), 42 U.S.C. §7412(d)(3)(A).

[181] §112(d)(3)(B), 42 U.S.C. §7412(d)(3)(B).

[182] §112(g)(2)(A), 42 U.S.C. §7412(g)(2)(A).

[183] §112(k)(3), 42 U.S.C. §7412(k)(3).

[184] §112(d), 42 U.S.C. §7412(d).

[185] §112(k)(3)(1), 42 U.S.C. §7412(k)(3)(1). Other federal statutes include the Resource Recovery and Conservation Act (RCRA), the Toxic Substances Control Act (TSCA), and the Federal Insecticide, Fungicide, and Rodenticide Act (FIFRA). §112(k)(3)(C), 42 U.S.C. §7412(k)(3)(C).

[186] §112(d), 42 U.S.C. §7412(d).

[187] §112(d)(5), 42 U.S.C. §7412(d)(5).

installation of controls.[188] New stationary sources will be subject to NESHAPs through operating and preconstruction permits.[189] EPA must issue a compliance date for each category or subcategory of sources.[190] Upon the effective date of any standard, new major sources, existing major sources, or reconstructed sources must comply with those standards.[191] When construction of a new source commences after a standard is proposed, but before it is finalized, the source has three years after promulgation to comply.[192] Sources that install BACT or LAER technology under PSD or nonattainment provisions are allowed five years following such installation to achieve technological or residual risk standards under NESHAPs.[193]

Modified sources usually must comply with MACT requirements for existing sources.[194] The statute allows exceptions where an increase in one pollutant is offset by a decrease in emissions of another pollutant. Any physical change in a source or method that results in more than a de minimis increase in emissions will not be considered a modification subject to MACT where the increase is offset by equal or greater reductions in emissions of a pollutant considered more hazardous. EPA was required to rank relative hazards of HAPs in a guidance that was due in May 1992, but missed that deadline.[195]

In addition, the statute authorizes compliance date extensions to sources that voluntarily reduce emissions before scheduled compliance dates.[196] Participants in the program can receive a six-year extension to achieve compliance with MACT standards if their source emissions are reduced 90 percent (95 percent for particulates) by January 1994. In order to participate, emissions reductions must be made before a NESHAPs' proposed date.[197] Where NESHAPs have been proposed, participants can make an enforceable commitment to reduce emissions before January 1994.[198] This commitment will become part of a company's operating permit. States have until November 1993 to submit operating permit programs for EPA's approval.

2. *Residual Risk Standards*

Once EPA adopts technology-based controls, the second stage of air toxics regulation requires the development of risk-based standards.[199] This second phase of emissions controls reflects Congress's concern that, even with application of technology-based standards, certain HAP emissions will continue to endanger public health and the environment. To address this concern, EPA is to

---

[188] §112(i)(3)(B), 42 U.S.C. §7412(i)(3)(B).

[189] §112(i)(1), 42 U.S.C. §7412(i)(1).

[190] §112(i)(2), 42 U.S.C. §7412(i)(2). When construction or reconstruction begins following proposal of technological standards, but before proposal of a residual risk standard, the source has 10 years from the commencement of construction or reconstruction to meet the residual risk standard. §112(i)(7), 42 U.S.C. §7412(i)(7).

[191] §112(i), 42 U.S.C. §7412(i).

[192] §112(i)(2), 42 U.S.C. §4212(i)(2). The promulgated standard must be stricter than the proposed standard and the source must be in compliance during the three-year period.

[193] §112(i)(6), 42 U.S.C. §7412(i)(6).

[194] §112(g)(2)(A), 42 U.S.C. §7412(g)(2)(A).

[195] §112(g)(1)(B), 42 U.S.C. §7412(g)(1)(B).

[196] §112(i)(5), 42 U.S.C. §7412(i)(5). EPA issued a rule covering voluntary early reductions of air toxics in October 1992. 57 Fed. Reg. 61,970 (1992). The extension is not applicable to residual risk standards.

[197] §112(i)(5)(A), 42 U.S.C. §7412(i)(5)(A).

[198] §112(i)(5)(B), 42 U.S.C. §7412(i)(5)(B).

[199] §112(f), 42 U.S.C. §7412(f).

promulgate residual risk standards in those instances where technological controls have not reduced risk from carcinogenic substances to less than one in one million for the individual most exposed to the emissions from a source in the category or subcategory.[200] EPA is to consult with the Surgeon General, undertake an investigation, and report to Congress regarding residual risk by November 1996.[201] In addition, the National Academy of Sciences is required to evaluate the validity of HAP carcinogenic risk assessment methodology and to recommend improvements in risk assessment techniques by April 1993.[202] Following the National Academy study, EPA must issue guidelines for carcinogenic risk assessment that implement the Academy's recommendations or explain why the Agency has not adopted them. EPA has to develop the residual risk standards through the same two-step process set forth for development of NESHAPs under the pre-1990 statute after *NRDC v. EPA*.[203]

EPA must issue residual risk standards within eight years after promulgating technology-based standards.[204] Once EPA proposes regulations for a particular source, any new source in that category must meet the residual risk standards when it commences operations. Existing sources must comply within 90 days of the effective date of residual risk standards.[205]

3. *Schedules for MACT and Emissions Standards*

Section 112(e) imposes on EPA a strict schedule for promulgating MACT standards.[206] EPA was required to list MACT standards for the first 40 source categories and to set a schedule for issuing emissions standards by November

[200] §112(f)(2)(A), 42 U.S.C. §7412(f)(2)(A).

[201] The report to Congress will cover (1) the methods for determining the remaining risk; (2) the level of public health risk remaining; (3) the methods and costs to reduce residual risks; (4) the actual health effects of those living close to sources, reservations about risk assessment determinations and other health studies; and (5) recommendations to address residual risk through legislation. §112(f)(1), 42 U.S.C. §7412(f)(1).

[202] §112(o), 42 U.S.C. §7412(o).

[203] 824 F.2d 1146 (D.C. Cir. 1987) (en banc).

Under §112 of the 1970 CAA, EPA was required to list each HAP that the Agency intended to regulate and issue proposed emissions standards within six months. EPA was directed to set levels providing "an ample margin of safety to protect the public health." EPA resisted complying with this directive, because for certain air toxics thought to cause cancer, EPA believed that no safe level of emissions could be set. A ban on emissions, however, would close down numerous industrial activities. Consequently, in 1976, EPA proceeded to set levels for HAPs and regulated sources through application of Best Available Control Technology (BACT). In this approach, the Agency balanced health effects against costs and technological feasibility when it set HAP standards.

The U.S. Court of Appeals for the District of Columbia Circuit reviewed EPA's method for establishing NESHAPs in a dispute involving the vinyl chloride standard in 1987. In NRDC v. EPA, the court ruled that §112 did not require HAP emissions reductions to an absolute no-risk factor. 824 F.2d 1146 (D.C. Cir. 1987) (en banc). NRDC's assertion that §112 required a ban on pollutants that create a potential risk was rejected. *Id.* at 1152–54. The court, however, determined that EPA's application of BACT was improper. *Id.* at 1147–48. In *NRDC*, the court established a two-step process for setting NESHAPs. In the first step, EPA must determine a safe level for emissions to evaluate whether certain HAP sources create significant risks to public health. EPA cannot consider costs and feasibility at this stage. *Id.* at 1164. Second, EPA must calculate what further HAP emissions reductions are necessary to provide an ample margin of safety. In this second step, the Agency is permitted to consider limitations on risk assessment and scientific data and to set the standards even lower than levels considered to be safe. According to the court, safe emissions levels do not require risk free or zero emissions. *Id.*

[204] §112(f)(2)(A), 42 U.S.C. §7412(f)(2)(A). Residual risk standards are immediately effective upon promulgation. §112(f)(3), 42 U.S.C. §7412(f)(3).

[205] §112(f)(4), 42 U.S.C. §7412(f)(4). EPA is authorized to grant a two-year waiver if the existing source installs controls to protect the public from imminent danger.

[206] 42 U.S.C. §7412(e).

1992.[207] EPA additionally must issue emissions standards for 25 percent of listed categories and subcategories by November 1994, another 25 percent by November 1997, and all remaining standards by November 2000.[208] When promulgating emissions standards, EPA must consider known or anticipated adverse public health effects of HAPs, and the quantity and location of HAP emissions in each category or subcategory according to the pollutants emitted, or processes or technologies used.[209]

D. Hazardous Organic NESHAPs

Although EPA has failed to meet the statutory deadlines for issuing NESHAPs pursuant to section 112(e), the Agency recently proposed revised standards for synthetic organic chemicals under its hazardous organic NESHAPs—commonly referred to as the "HON" rule.[210] The HON rule covers 149 chemicals from 370 synthetic organic chemical manufacturers (SOCMI) in 40 states. Under the HON rule, companies can either apply control technologies to various emission points or use emission averaging (bubbling) to meet the standards.

Emission averaging is measured over a one-year period.[211] Under the proposed rule, emissions from process vents must be reduced 98 percent or 20 parts per billion by using combustion. Air emissions of these chemicals from wastewater streams must be reduced 95 to 98 percent or be controlled by target concentration. Storage tank emissions must be reduced by 95 percent through tank modifications or use of control devices such as vapor recovery. With the exception of equipment leaks, sources can obtain credits by overcontrolling

---

[207] §112(e)(1)(A), 42 U.S.C. §7412(e)(1)(A). A proposed schedule for regulating source categories of HAPs was published at 57 Fed. Reg. 44,147 (1992).

A proposed NESHAP for coke oven emissions from coke oven charging, door leaks, and topside leads on coal charged batteries was expected in November 1992. In the 1990 Amendments, Congress provided for separate emissions control standards for coke oven batteries because of concern over foreign competition with the domestic steel industry and the general economic climate. §112(d)(8)(A), 42 U.S.C. §7412(d)(8)(A). In order to avoid shutting down plants that could not achieve residual risk standards, Congress established three sets of emissions controls and exempted plants that comply with those standards from residual risk standards until 2020. EPA was required to issue the first set of emissions controls by December 31, 1992. Plants must comply with control standards by December 31, 1995.

[208] §112(e)(B)-(E), 42 U.S.C. §7412(e)(B)-(E).

EPA was authorized, but not required, to study HAP emissions from publicly owned treatment works (POTW). §112(n)(5), 42 U.S.C. §7412(n)(5). EPA has discretion to determine technology and control measures that may be applied to POTWs, including pretreatment of discharges and substitution or limitation on products used in their operations.

EPA is required to study public health risks associated with HAP emissions from electric utility steam generating units and report findings to Congress by November 1993. §112(n)(1), 42 U.S.C. §7412(n)(1). If the study indicates that controls are warranted, EPA has discretion to regulate HAP emissions from utilities. EPA is further directed to study and report to Congress by November 1994 on mercury emissions from utilities, municipal incinerators, and other sources. §112(n)(1)(B), 42 U.S.C. §7412(n)(1)(B). Special HAP provisions that require EPA to study and report to Congress on risks associated with hydrogen sulfide and hydrofluoric acid emissions are also included. §112(n)(5), (6), 42 U.S.C. §7412(n)(5), (6).

[209] §112(e)(2), 42 U.S.C. §7412(e)(2). Under §307, each standard is subject to judicial review. 42 U.S.C. §7607.

[210] 57 Fed. Reg. 62,608 (1992).

[211] Emission averaging particularly benefits batch processors who frequently change their operations. Emission averaging under the proposed rule is permitted only among same source categories. In addition, there are substantial recordkeeping, reporting, and monitoring requirements under the proposed rule.

certain emission points beyond the 95 to 98 percent levels. Credits can be used to offset insufficient control over other source emission points.

EPA may control new sources even more strictly under the HON rule. For example, emissions controls would be required for existing vents if their cost does not exceed $1,800 per ton. New sources must control emissions up to a cost of $9,900 per ton under the proposed rule. The equipment leak provisions of the proposed HON rule apply to sources in seven types of non-SOCMI processes. These include: styrene and butadiene rubber production, polybutadiene production, chlorine production, pesticide production, chlorinated hydrocarbon use, pharmaceutical production, and miscellaneous butadiene use.

E. MACT Hammer

Under section 112(j) of the 1990 Amendments, Congress included a "MACT hammer" provision applicable to sources through the Title V permit program. The hammer provisions take effect when EPA fails to establish standards for categories or subcategories of major sources in a timely manner.[212] Major sources must apply for a permit 18 months after EPA fails to meet a deadline to establish standards for a category or subcategory. The state permitting authority must issue a permit that contains emission limitations determined on a case-by-case basis that is at least as strict as the standard that would apply if EPA had issued an emission standard.[213] If EPA issues a standard after the permit is issued, the source must comply with the new standard when its permit is renewed.

F. How Are Accidental Releases Minimized and Controlled?

Though most of section 112 regulates ongoing and predictable releases of the list of 189 substances defined as HAPs, Congress recognized that not all dangerous releases of materials to the air are intentional. Consequently, Congress added section 112(r) in 1990 in order to prevent, detect, and control accidental releases to the air.

Section 112(r) duplicates, to a significant degree, the emergency planning requirements of EPCRA. Nonetheless, this subsection may have some of the earliest and most widespread effects of section 112 by imposing highly specific release prevention and accident response requirements. The statutory requirements are not limited by industry source category like the emission control requirements. Nor is there a phased implementation period for development, issuance, and compliance with section 112(r) requirements. Instead, section 112(r) applies to all persons who meet the threshold test which is to be set by EPA. (The requirements will also include federal facilities, which are excluded from coverage under EPCRA.) Moreover, the rules have a countrywide compliance deadline of 1996. Thus, potentially many thousands of installations will be affected well before EPA establishes MACT standards for many industry categories.

---

[212] §112(j), 42 U.S.C. §7412(j).

[213] §112(j)(5), 42 U.S.C. §7412(j)(5).

Section 112(r)(1) imposes a general duty, modeled on the general duty clause of the Occupational Safety and Health Act (OSH Act) to maintain a safe workplace, to prevent accidental releases of EHSs and regulated substances, and to minimize the effects of such accidental releases.[214] Only the government can enforce this general duty requirement; the statute makes clear that this is not to be the basis for citizen suits under section 304 or for private tort actions. This general duty is reinforced by the criminalization of "negligent endangerment" and "knowing endangerment." These violations consist of (1) the negligent or knowing release into the ambient air of any hazardous air pollutant listed under section 112 or any EHS *not* listed under section 112; and (2) the negligent or knowing placement of another person in imminent danger of death or serious bodily injury.[215]

1. Regulated Substances

In adding section 112(r), Congress focused on a group of substances that overlap somewhat with, but do not entirely correspond to the list of 189 hazardous air pollutants in section 112(a). Section 112(r) focuses on the 366 Extremely Hazardous Substances (EHSs) as defined by EPA under section 304 of EPCRA, as well as on an overlapping list of 100 "regulated substances" which EPA is to define. EPA's definition of such regulated substances must include 16 substances specified in section 112(r)(3). These 16 range from common chemicals such as ammonia and chlorine to methyl isocyanate, which was involved in the Bhophal disaster in 1984.

EPA must include in its list of regulated substances those that it believes pose the greatest risks when accidental releases occur. Other factors EPA must consider in listing regulated substances are the severity of adverse effects, the likelihood of accidental releases, and the potential magnitude of human exposure.[216] EPA may establish threshold quantities of substances which presumably will focus on the riskiest sources.[217] Section 108 criteria pollutants, and substances regulated under Title VI ozone protection provisions, are excluded from section 112(r)(3) regulations. The list may be revised on petition and must be revised by EPA every five years.

The key regulatory component in the accident prevention program is found in section 112(r)(7). This provision gives EPA extensive authority to issue "release prevention, detection, and correction requirements, including monitoring, reporting, training, vapor recovery, secondary containment, and other design, equipment, work practice and operational requirements."[218] EPA is required to promulgate "reasonable regulations and appropriate guidance" to prevent, detect, and require responses to releases of regulated substances by November 1993. The regulations must cover training, maintenance, monitoring, storage, and handling of these substances.

Owners and operators of affected sources have until November 1996 to comply with these rules. Owners and operators of sources that have more than a

[214] §112(r)(1), 42 U.S.C. §7412(r)(1).
[215] §113(c)(4), (5), 42 U.S.C. §7413(c)(4), (5).
[216] §112(r)(4), 42 U.S.C. §7412(r)(4).
[217] §112(r)(5), 42 U.S.C. §7412(r)(5).
[218] §112(r)(7)(A), 42 U.S.C. §7412(r)(7)(A).

threshold quantity of a regulated substance must prepare a risk management plan to prevent, detect, and respond to accidental releases. There are elaborate requirements for risk management plans that resemble the spill prevention control and countermeasure (SPCC) plan requirements that sources storing oil must meet pursuant to section 311(j)(5) of the Clean Water Act.

The risk management plan must include

- A hazard assessment of the effects of the worst case accidental release, including estimates of potential quantities of regulated substances released, downwind exposures, and previous release history of the source;
- A prevention program including safety precautions and maintenance, monitoring, and employee training measures to be used at the source; and
- A response program stating the specific actions to be taken in response to an accidental release, including measures to protect health and the environment, contact with state and local agencies, and employee training.[219]

Owners and operators must submit plans to EPA by November 1996. The same plans must also be submitted to the appropriate state and local agencies (probably the State Emergency Response Commission and Local Emergency Planning Committee), as well as the new Chemical Safety and Hazard Investigation Board discussed below. EPA is required to develop an auditing program to review the plans and require appropriate revisions. Both EPA and the source submitting the plans must make the plans available to the public.

To the extent possible, EPA's regulations under section 112(r)(7) are to be consistent with standards established by the American Society of Mechanical Engineers, the American National Standards Institute, and the American Society of Testing Materials. EPA is also to coordinate with the Occupational Safety and Health Administration and with the Nuclear Regulatory Commission in order to avoid duplicating those agencies' existing requirements. The release prevention requirements should distinguish between types and classes of facilities, devices, or systems and evaluate factors such as the size, location, process, process controls, amount of substance handled, concentration of substances, and the stationary source's current response capabilities.[220]

For enforcement purposes, these regulations are to be treated as if they were standards under section 112(d) and any violation of the regulations after their effective date will be a violation of section 1129(d). Section 112(r)(9) grants EPA additional emergency order authority to act where there is an imminent and substantial endangerment to health or the environment because of an actual or threatened accidental release. EPA was required to issue guidance by April 1991 that harmonizes its new emergency order authority with its authority under CERCLA, the Clean Water Act, the Resource Conservation and Recovery Act, the Safe Drinking Water Act, and other provisions of the Clean Air Act.

---

[219] §112(r)(7)(B)(ii), 42 U.S.C. §7412(r)(7)(B)(ii).

[220] *Id.*

2. *Chemical Safety and Hazard Investigation Board*

The 1990 Amendments created the Chemical Safety and Hazard Investigation Board (CSHIB),[221] which somewhat resembles the National Transportation Safety Board. It is an independent agency that investigates the cause of accidental releases of regulated substances that result in death, serious injury, or substantial property damage, and makes recommendations for means to prevent as well as to report such releases.[222]

CSHIB is required to issue periodic reports to Congress, federal, state, and local agencies, as well as to assist in developing accidental release prevention and response regulations.[223] CSHIB was supposed to make recommendations to EPA by April 1992 that address measures to minimize risks of EHS releases.[224] Within six months, EPA must initiate rulemaking to implement or to explain its departures from the CSHIB recommendations.[225]

CSHIB also was required to make recommendations to EPA and the Department of Labor in November 1992 for risk management plan regulations, accident prevention rules, and mitigation measures for releases that are applicable to sources handling more than a threshold quantity of a regulated substance.[226] EPA and the Department of Labor must act on the recommendations within six months. Despite these deadlines, the Board has not yet been appointed.

G. State Air Toxics Programs

States are authorized under section 112(l) of the 1990 Amendments to develop and submit programs to enforce EPA emissions standards as well as requirements to prevent and minimize consequences of accidental releases of EHSs.[227] EPA was required to issue guidelines by November 1991 to assist development and implementation of state and local air toxics programs.[228] Pursuant to court order, EPA agreed to propose guidelines for the overdue state air toxics program by April 30, 1993, and to finalize the guidelines by November 1993.[229] EPA must accept or reject a state program within six months of its submission.[230] EPA can withdraw approval if it determines that a state improp-

---

[221] §112(r)(6), 42 U.S.C. §7412(r)(6).

[222] *Id.* The President is authorized to appoint five technically qualified professionals to the CSHIB. §112(r)(6)(B), 42 U.S.C. §7412(r)(6)(B). The CSHIB has extensive authority to collect information as well as to hold hearings, subpoena witnesses, and inspect facilities and their files. §112(r)(6)(L), 42 U.S.C. §7412(r)(6)(L). Evidence gathered during CSHIB investigations, however, cannot provide the basis for a private action seeking damages resulting from accidental releases. §112(r)(6)(G), 42 U.S.C. §7412(r)(6)(G).

[223] §112(r)(6)(C)(ii), 42 U.S.C. §7412(r)(6)(C)(ii).

[224] §112(r)(6)(H), 42 U.S.C. §7412(r)(6)(H).

[225] §112(r)(6)(I), 42 U.S.C. §7412(r)(6)(I).

[226] §112(r)(6)(K), 42 U.S.C. §7412(r)(6)(K).

[227] 42 U.S.C. §7412(l).

[228] §112(l)(2), 42 U.S.C. §7412(l)(2).

[229] The Administrator signed the proposed guidelines on April 30 and they were published in May. 58 Fed. Reg. 29,296 (1993). EPA expects to meet its court ordered deadline of November 15 for finalizing the regulatory guidance.

[230] §112(l)(5), 42 U.S.C. §7412(l)(5). The program must (1) assure compliance with new §112 standards and requirements by all facilities in the state, (2) have sufficient authority and resources to ensure compliance,

erly implements its program.[231] Grants and assistance from the National Air Toxics Information Clearinghouse (NATIC)[232] are available to help states with their air toxics programs.

IV. Title IV—Acid Rain

The burning of fossil fuels, particularly coal and oil, releases sulfur dioxide (SO_2) and nitrogen oxide (NO_2) into the atmosphere. Although the process by which SO_2 and NO_2 emissions create acidic precipitation is not fully understood, once in the atmosphere, SO_2 and NO_2 undergo a series of chemical reactions. During this process, SO_2 and NO_2 are transformed into sulfate and nitrate particles, sulfuric and nitric acid, or other compounds that fall to the earth as snow, rain, fog, or even dry acidic particles. These acidic compounds, commonly referred to as ''acid rain,'' are believed to harm ecosystems by changing the PH levels in lakes and streams as well as soils. In addition, significant damage to crops, soil fertility, man-made structures, and paint and masonry has been attributed to acid rain.

Most SO_2 and NO_2 emissions have been attributed to coal-fired power plants located in the East and Midwest. Because these areas are more densely populated, utilities burn more coal to accommodate the energy needs of consumers. In addition, the sulfur content of the extensive coal reserves mined locally in these regions is much higher than coal mined in the Northern Great Plains. Problems associated with acid rain, however, are not limited to those local areas where coal is burned because the prevailing winds in the United States usually transport SO_2 and NO_2 toward the eastern and northeastern states and southeastern Canada. These pollutant transport problems were exacerbated by the widespread installation of very tall smokestacks by many utilities—stacks as high as 1,000 feet in some cases.

Before the 1990 Amendments, the Clean Air Act was not well-suited to address acid rain. Until the Amendments, the Act was focused primarily upon preventing excessive ground level concentrations of pollutants. Acid rain, however, is better understood as a ''mass-balance'' problem: specifically emitting nearly 20 million tons of SO_2 emissions annually east of the Mississippi cannot help but have widespread and detrimental effects regardless of ambient ground level concentrations at any particular time. The 1990 Amendments recognize that the total amount of these emissions is a major part of the problem, and seek to systematically reduce the overall amount of such emissions.

After nearly 15 years of debate over reducing emissions that contribute to acid rain, Congress enacted Title IV in 1990. To meet Title IV objectives, a maximum annual SO_2 emissions cap was created to reduce the nation's annual

---

(3) provide a schedule to implement the program promptly, and (4) be consistent with the EPA guidance or other objectives of §112. §112(l)(5)(A)-(D), 42 U.S.C. §7412(l)(5)(A)-(D).

[231] §112(l)(6), 42 U.S.C. §7412(l)(6).

[232] §112(l)(4), 42 U.S.C. §7412(l)(4) (grants) and §112(l)(3), 42 U.S.C. §7412(l)(3) (NATIC). NATIC collects technical information on potentially toxic air pollutants, health and ecological risk assessment, risk analysis, ambient monitoring and modeling, and control technology.

SO_2 emissions by more than 50 percent from 1980 levels.[233] The acid rain program requires electric utility SO_2 sources to obtain allowances for each ton of SO_2 that they emit annually. By the year 2000, utilities nationwide will not be permitted to exceed an 8.9 million ton cap on total SO_2 emissions.

Affected sources are provided with unprecedented flexibility in their plans to comply with Title IV emissions limitations. Rather than relying solely upon traditional regulatory approaches to reduce SO_2 emissions, such as imposing plant-by-plant emission limitations requiring the use of scrubber technology or of low sulfur fuels, Title IV allows affected sources to buy, sell, or bank their allowances. The allowance system is designed to permit utilities to choose the most cost-effective means to reduce their emissions, as long as the overall total meets the national target. This flexibility should result in substantially lower compliance costs.

A. Sulfur Dioxide Allowance Program

Pursuant to sections 402 and 403, EPA will issue annual SO_2 allowances to affected sources, primarily fossil-fuel-fired electric generating units. These allowances are issued without cost to the source. Each allowance authorizes the source to emit one ton of SO_2 in the year that the allowance is issued, or if not used in the year issued, in a later year.[234] Owners and operators of affected units, upon application and approval from EPA, may reassign an allowance granted from one unit to another under their control.[235] Sources must hold sufficient allowances at the close of the year to cover their total SO_2 emissions or face the penalties described below.

When the allowance program is fully operational, after the year 2000, the total number of allowances available for allocation will represent about a 50 percent reduction in utility SO_2 emissions. Thus, a utility that plans to generate the same amount of SO_2 as it did during 1985 through 1987, must either obtain additional allowances or reduce its emissions. The allowance system recognizes that it will be more economically feasible for some sources to reduce SO_2 emissions than others. Consequently, those sources that are able to reduce emissions below their allocated allowances can sell their surplus allowances to sources that cannot meet emissions limits as cheaply.

1. Phase I Sulfur Dioxide Requirements

The 1990 Amendments established two phases for implementation of the allowance program. Phase I begins in 1995 and continues through 1999. The first phase addresses the 111 large fossil-fuel-fired electricity generating plants in 21 states with emissions levels exceeding 2.5 pounds of SO_2 per million

---

[233] §403(a)(1), 42 U.S.C. §7651b(a)(1).

As noted in the discussion of §112(n)(1), EPA also is required to conduct a risk assessment study of hazards associated with HAP emissions from electric utility steam generating units. 42 U.S.C. §7412(n)(1). Depending on the outcome of that study, EPA may adopt regulations to control utilities' HAP emissions.

[234] §§402(3), 403(b), 42 U.S.C. §§7651a(3), 7651b(b). EPA issued final rules for the allowance system in January 1993. 58 Fed. Reg. 3590 (1993).

[235] §403(a)(1), 42 U.S.C. §7651b(a)(1).

British Thermal Units (Btu) heat input.[236] This emission limit is not technologically difficult to meet; indeed, in 1971 the first NSPS for coal-fired power plants was 1.2 pounds of SO_2 per million Btu heat input. For oil-fired plants the standard was 0.8 pounds of SO_2 per million Btu heat input. Emission rates in Title IV are expressed in pounds per million Btu heat input (lbs./mmBtu), the standard measure used in setting power plant emission limits such as NSPSs. Allowance allocations for these plants are determined by their baseline fuel consumption during the years 1985 through 1987 and a maximum allowable emissions ratc fixed by the statute.[237]

In addition to the allowance program, Title IV provides several incentives for utilities to install emission control technology during Phase I.[238] EPA may authorize a two-year extension from the Phse I emissions limitations as long as the owner or operator of the source holds allowances to emit the unit's total annual emissions for each of the two years of the extension.[239] An extension application must demonstrate that the affected unit will be modified to use a qualifying Phase I emissions reduction technology or that the owner or operator will transfer its Phase I emissions reduction obligation to a unit employing a qualifying Phase I technology.[240]

Thus, units that agree to install scrubbers by 1997 to comply with Phase I regulations are given a two-year extension until 1997 to reduce emissions.[241] Sources that use scrubbers in Phase I receive a bonus allowance for each ton of emissions reduction achieved below the 1.2 lbs. SO_2/mmBtu emission level.[242] An additional 300,000 incentive allowances are available to utilities that use energy conservation measures or renewable energy to achieve SO_2 emission reductions.[243] EPA's final rules for the acid rain allowance program did not include provisions for affected sources that want to opt in to the Phase I SO_2 allowance program. EPA is expected to develop separate regulations for these sources.[244]

---

[236] §404, 42 U.S.C. §7651c. A list of the 111 power plants is set forth in §404.

[237] §403(a)(1), 42 U.S.C. §7651b(a)(1). The records for baseline fuel consumption have been routinely kept by the Federal Energy Regulatory Commission (FERC).

[238] Units that agree to install scrubbers by 1997 to comply with Phase I regulations are entitled to a two-year extension until then. §404(d)(1), 42 U.S.C. §7651c(d)(1). Units that use scrubbers in Phase I receive one bonus allowance for every ton of emission reduction they achieve below the 1.2 lbs./mmBtu emission level. §404(d)(6), 42 U.S.C. §7651c(d)(6). Units that use scrubbers to reduce emissions in 1995 and 1996 can bank allowances they earn and use them in the future.

[239] §404(d)(1), 42 U.S.C. §7651c(d)(1).

[240] *Id.* A "qualifying phase I technology" is defined as a technological system of continuous emission reduction that achieves a 90% reduction in emissions of SO_2 from the emissions that would have resulted from the use of fuels that were not subject to treatment prior to combustion. §402(19), 42 U.S.C. §7651a(19).

This is almost equivalent to the repealed percentage reduction requirements under the new source performance standard set for coal-fired power plants in the 1979 NSPSs. *See* Sierra Club v. Costle, 657 F.2d 298 (D.C. Cir. 1981) (detailed review of this standard).

[241] §404(d)(1), 42 U.S.C. §7651c(d)(1).

[242] §404(d)(6), 42 U.S.C. §7651c(d)(6).

[243] §404(f), 42 U.S.C. §7651c(f).

[244] Industrial sources may elect to participate in the allowance program even though units at the source are not covered by sections 7651b(c), 7651c, or 7651d. §404, 42 U.S.C. §7651(i). Among the affected sources, apart from utilities, that may benefit from participation in the allowance program are: fossil-fuel-fired boilers to power industrial operations, nonferrous smelters, primary aluminum reduction plants, on-shore natural gas processing plants, petroleum refineries, kraft and sulfite pulp mills, and sulfuric acid manufacturing plants.

2. *Phase II Sulfur Dioxide Requirements*

Beginning in the year 2000, fossil-fuel-fired units with an output capacity of greater than 75 megawatts will be regulated under Phase II of the allowance program.[245] Phase II reduces the average allowable emissions rate from the Phase I level of 2.5 lbs./mmBtu to 1.2 lbs./mmBtu.[246] Annual allowances are to be allocated on the basis of sources' fuel consumption rates, emissions rates, and baseline fuel consumption during 1985 through 1987.[247]

EPA is authorized to establish a "reserve" pool and "bonus" Phase II allowances.[248] States with 1985 statewide annual emissions from sources within their boundaries below 0.8 lbs./mmBtu, so-called "clean" states, may elect to receive 125,000 extra Phase II allowances that are to be distributed on the basis of each utility's relative share of all Phase II allowances for the first 10 years of Phase II. The reserve is calculated for the entire state rather than from other bonus allowances available under the Act.[249]

Pursuant to section 405, EPA is authorized to allocate extra Phase II allowances for units in high growth states beginning in the year 2000.[250] This refers to states whose population increased more than 25 percent between 1980 and 1988.[251] Title IV of the CAA limits these allowances to 530,000 per year.[252] There are several incentives and bonus allowances authorized for midwestern and eastern states with units that have been dependent on high sulfur coal.[253]

Units whose construction had not begun by November 1990 are not eligible for the allowance allocations.[254] New units' annual SO_2 emissions cannot exceed the allowances that they obtain through purchases in the allowance market or by transferring them from units owned and operated by the same corporate entity.

3. *Allowance Auction System*

The most novel feature of the Title IV program is the ability of affected sources to freely transfer emission allowances. EPA expects that a market will develop for buying and selling allowances. As of the spring of 1993, a successful auction of emission allowances had taken place at the Chicago Board of Trade (CBT), a hopeful sign for the future viability of the market. The flexibility of the market approach, assuming that it is fully used by utilities, should reduce overall compliance costs. To administer the allowance system, EPA will pro-

---

[245] §405(b), 42 U.S.C. §7651d(b).

[246] §405(b)(1), 42 U.S.C. §7651d(b)(1). This 1.2 lbs./SO_2 mmBtu level corresponds to the 1971 NSPS for coal-fired power plants.

[247] In July 1992, EPA made available its National Allowance Data Base and technical support documents, which will be used for allocation of allowances to affected units during Phase II. 57 Fed. Reg. 30,034 (1992).

[248] EPA proposed allocation of basic allowances, bonus allowances, and miscellaneous allowances in July 1992. 57 Fed. Reg. 29,940 (1992).

[249] §406, 42 U.S.C. §7651e.

[250] 42 U.S.C. §7651d(i).

[251] 42 U.S.C. §7651d(i). Under this provision of the statute, population growth is determined according to a Commerce Department publication, *State Population and Household Estimates, With Age, Sex & Components of Change: 1981–1988.*

[252] §405(a)(2), 42 U.S.C. §7651d(a)(2).

[253] §405(a)(2), 42 U.S.C. §7651d(a)(2). The units will receive a pro rata share of bonus allowances based on a percentage of total Phase I allocations that units receive statewide. 57 Fed. Reg. 29,940, 29,955 (1992).

[254] §405(j), 42 U.S.C. §7651d(j).

vide each unit's account with a specified number of allowances based on the formulas discussed above. In order to track allowances, EPA will assign a unique identification number to each allowance.[255]

At the end of each year, EPA will deduct from the unit's account the sum of its SO_2 emissions during that year based on continuous emissions monitoring system (CEMS) data. If a unit's account is running low, the designated representative for the unit may purchase additional allowances to maintain an adequate balance. Any unused allowances at the end of the year carry over to the following year.[256] Units must pay $2,000 per ton for emissions in excess of their allowance balance, and their allowances for the following year will be reduced by the amount that they exceeded the authorized emissions in the previous year.[257]

The owner and operator of a unit, its designated representatives, and any other person holding allowances are authorized to buy and sell allowances in the market. EPA will transfer allowances upon receipt of transfer certifications signed by both parties. Transfers are effective only after they are registered by EPA.[258] Utilities cannot consume expected future allowances, but they can freely transfer them before they are issued. Thus, a utility in 1995 could buy or sell allowances it is not scheduled to receive until 2000. There are no geographic restrictions on buying or selling allowances.

To promote the trading market, section 416 requires EPA to sell a small number of allowances each year at auction and some at a fixed price on a first-come, first-served basis.[259] To supply the allowances sold by EPA without exceeding the emissions cap, the agency withholds 2.8 percent of each unit's annual allowance allocation.[260] The auctions will be conducted with sealed bids resulting in the sale of allowances to the highest bidder.[261] Allowance holders may offer additional allowances for sale in EPA auctions.[262] Income from the direct sales and auction will be distributed to utilities from which these allowances were withheld on the basis of each utility's relative contribution to the total sale.

4. *Chicago Board of Trade*

EPA has delegated authority to the Chicago Board of Trade (CBT) to conduct the sale and auction of SO_2 allowances for three years beginning in March 1993. The CBT will handle the 2.8 percent of reserve allowances that EPA withholds from utilities to stimulate the allowance trading market pursuant to section 416.[263] CBT will collect bids and payments, conduct the auction, publish the results, and administer direct sales of allowances. EPA will disburse

[255] 58 Fed. Reg. 3590, 3692 (1993) (to be codified at 40 C.F.R. §73.34).

[256] §403(b), 42 U.S.C. §7651b(b).

[257] *Id.*

[258] *Id.*

[259] §416, 42 U.S.C. §7651o.

[260] §416(b), 42 U.S.C. §7651o(b).

[261] §416(d)(2), 42 U.S.C. §7651o(d)(2).

[262] §416(d)(4), 42 U.S.C. §7651o(d)(4).

[263] 42 U.S.C. §7651o(b). At the end of the year, any allowances offered for sale, but not sold will be returned without charge on a pro rata basis to owners and operators of affected units from whom the allowances were originally withheld. §416(d)(3)(B), 42 U.S.C. §7651o(d)(3)(B).

payments and allowances following auctions and direct sales. The results of the auction will be published in the *Federal Register.*

Participants in the allowance program are not charged for CBT's sales services, but CBT expects to profit from futures trading. For a small fee, CBT will lock in future allowance prices for utilities. The CBT anticipates that the auction process will guide price determinations for the developing futures market. With somewhat stable prices, it is hoped that utilities will be better able to budget for allowance purchases and sales. Because Title IV authorizes anyone to trade in the allowance market, including speculators, environmental groups, and equipment makers,[264] the CBT program should make it easier for investors to access the allowance market.

It is not clear whether utilities will rely on short term buying and selling of allowances to meet emissions limits. General uncertainty about the market and allowance prices have made utilities hesitant to participate in the program. High growth areas such as Florida, however, may use the market to offset their increased energy production. The market also may serve as a safety net for utilities that are caught short in their allowance balance near the year's end.

B. Nitrogen Oxide Emission Reduction Program

Although scientists believe utility NO_2 emissions play a significant role in acid precipitation, that role is less well understood than the role of SO_2. The atmospheric chemistry is quite complex, as NO_2 is also thought to play an important, but nonlinear, role in the formation of photochemical smog, or ozone. Not only is the atmospheric chemistry of nitrogen oxide imperfectly understood, but its formation in combustion is also far more complex than is the formation of SO_2. Sulfur dioxide is formed when fuel containing sulfur is burned, just as some nitrogen oxides are formed when fuel containing some nitrogen is burned. Even if fuel contains no nitrogen, however, combustion can form nitrogen oxides because air is about 79 percent nitrogen, and the heat of combustion forms nitrogen oxide compounds. This reaction depends on the heat of combustion, on the configuration of the combustion chamber, and numerous other factors. Thus, control measures for nitrogen oxides must vary according to the type of utility boiler involved, the fuel burned, and many related factors not required to determine sulfur dioxide emission control techniques and emission limitations.

Under the 1990 Amendments, NO_2 emissions are to be capped at two million tons below 1980 emissions levels.[265] This level actually represents little, if any, reduction from NO_2 emissions in the late 1980s. As part of the SO_2 allowance program, EPA is required to study the feasibility of interpollutant

[264] Some speculate that equipment producers such as scrubber manufacturers will buy allowances and offer them as assurances to customers who buy their equipment. If, for example, the equipment fails to achieve the emissions reductions promised, the manufacturer would provide allowances that the buyer needs to comply with emissions limits. Equipment manufacturers could also offer the allowances as incentive for customers to buy their equipment. The allowance would provide an interim means for sources to meet emissions limitations while the new equipment is installed.

[265] §401(b), 42 U.S.C. §7651a(b).

trading that would allow a unit to offset NO_2 increases with SO_2 reductions and the converse.[266]

EPA was directed to establish annual allowable NO_2 limitations and revised performance standards for a number of boilers effective January 1, 1995.[267] EPA failed to meet its statutory deadline of May 1992 for issuing these regulations, but pursuant to court order the Agency agreed to promulgate rules for NO_2 emissions limits and averaging by October 1993.[268] NO_2 emissions from tangentially fired boilers must be limited to 0.45 lbs./mmBtu. In addition, the maximum emissions limit for dry bottom wall-fired boilers, except for those using cell burner technology, cannot exceed 0.5 lbs./mmBtu.[269] If EPA determines that there is no low NO_2 burner technology available,[270] the Agency is authorized to set higher emissions limits for affected boiler units.[271]

Application of low NO_2 burner technology to tangentially fired and dry bottom wall-fired boilers has been controversial. Emission rates cannot exceed limits set in the statute except where EPA determines that mandated levels cannot be achieved using low NO_2 burner technology. Those subject to regulations contend that EPA must base NO_2 emission rates for these types of boilers on the use of low NO_2 burners. Under section 407(b)(2), EPA may impose more stringent standards for tangentially fired and dry bottom wall-fired boilers by 1997, if the Agency determines that more effective low NO_2 burner technology is available.[272] The regulated community contends that this provision requires EPA to set initial limits based on low NO_2 burner technology. Environmentalists, however, claim that under section 407(b)(1), EPA has discretion to impose NO_2 emission limits stricter than these maximum levels authorized under the statute.[273] Consequently, they argue that EPA can consider additional control technologies in setting these limits. The debate is likely to continue once EPA adopts rules for NO_2 emissions limitations.

By January 1997, EPA must issue regulations for average annual NO_2 emission limits for wet bottom wall-fired boilers, cyclones, units applying cell burner technology, and other types of utility boilers.[274] These rates must reflect achievable reductions using the best system of continuous emission reduction that can be retrofitted to existing units. In setting these limits, EPA must consider available technology, energy and environmental impacts, and costs,

---

[266] §403(c), 42 U.S.C. §7651b(c).

[267] §404(b)-(c), 42 U.S.C. §7651f(b)-(c).

[268] EPA's proposed NO_2 emissions limits were issued in November 1992. 57 Fed. Reg. 55,632 (1992). The proposed limit does not go beyond the statutory limit, despite urgings from some state regulators and environmentalists.

[269] 57 Fed. Reg. 55,632 (1992).

[270] The definition of low NO_2 burner technology has sparked controversy. Environmentalists and some state authorities contend that several technologies, such as catalytic reduction and separated overfire air technology, fall into this definition. Industry officials assert that low NO_2 burner technology would not include requirements to use overfire air or catalytic reduction in combination with low NO_2 burners. During its development of NO_2 regulations, EPA has indicated that overfire air controls would be required unless the system was technically infeasible.

[271] §407(b)(1), 42 U.S.C. §7651f(b)(1).

[272] 42 U.S.C. §7651f(b)(2).

[273] 42 U.S.C. §7651f(b)(1).

[274] §407(b)(2), 42 U.S.C. §7651f(b)(2).

which must be comparable to costs of NO_2 controls available for dry bottom wall-fired boilers.[275] The NO_2 emissions limits are effective January 2000.[276]

Both the Title I nonattainment provisions and the acid rain program are applicable to utility sources of NO_2 emissions. Owners and operators of affected utilities assert that NO_2 emission reductions achieved under nonattainment provisions should be included in calculating NO_2 emission averages under Title IV.[277] Environmentalists, on the other hand, argue that Title I and Title IV impose requirements that are independent of one another. They contend that emission reductions required pursuant to nonattainment provisions should not be used to satisfy acid rain requirements. They are concerned that if such offsets were allowed, utilities would simply shift operations from urban nonattainment areas to rural areas to average their overall emissions.

Under some circumstances, utilities can request alternative limits for individual units upon a demonstration that they cannot meet applicable emission standards using appropriate technology.[278] The owner or operator seeking alternative limits must (1) show that control equipment designed to meet the emission rate was properly installed, (2) show that the equipment was operated continuously for 15 months and monitoring data demonstrate the affected unit cannot achieve the emission rate, and (3) specify what emission limit is feasible for the unit to achieve on an average annual basis.[279] A 15-month extension from the compliance deadline may be available to tangentially fired or dry bottom wall-fired units, if the owner or operator demonstrates that necessary technology is not available in sufficient supply for installation and operation at its units by January 1995.[280]

In addition, owners and operators of multiple affected units may petition the agency to average emissions of those units.[281] The average, however, must be less than the Btu weighted average annual emission rate that the same units would have achieved if each had been operated in accordance with the applicable emission rate.[282] Thus, overcontrol of some units can be used to offset exceedances by others.

C. Permits and Compliance Plans

In order to implement and enforce the allowance system, each affected source must obtain a permit that specifies all applicable acid rain requirements for the source and each affected unit within that source.[283] The permit must include (1) a designated representative for each affected source and each affected unit at a source, (2) continuous emission monitoring requirements, (3) SO_2 allowance requirements, (4) NO_2 emission limitations, (5) excess emission and offset requirements, (6) recordkeeping and reporting requirements, and (7)

---

[275] *Id.*

[276] §407(a), 42 U.S.C. §7651(a).

[277] EPA supplemented its general preamble on implementation of Title I regarding RACT for NO_2 emissions in November 1992. 57 Fed. Reg. 55,620 (1992).

[278] §407(d), 42 U.S.C. §7651f(d).

[279] §407(d)(2), 42 U.S.C. §7651f(d)(2).

[280] §407(a), (d), 42 U.S.C. §7651(a), (d).

[281] §407(e), 42 U.S.C. §7651f(e).

[282] §407(e), 42 U.S.C. §7651f(e).

[283] 58 Fed. Reg. 3590, 3677 (1993) (to be codified at 40 C.F.R. §72.70).

liability provisions.[284] Phase I sources were required to file permit applications by February 15, 1993.[285] EPA has six months to accept or reject a permit application.[286] Once issued, permits have a fixed term of five years effective January 1995.[287] Sources covered only by Phase II must submit permit applications by January 1996 for SO_2 emissions limits and January 1998 for NO_2 emissions limits.[288] New units must submit permit applications by January 1998 or two years before the unit commences commercial operations.[289] States will incorporate the acid rain permits into Title V operating permits by the year 2000.[290] If the state does not have an approved Title V operating program, EPA will issue Phase II permits to affected sources.[291]

1. *Permit Content*

Each permit must specify a designated representative who will be accountable to EPA and the state on acid rain matters. This person must file a certificate of representation stating that the owners are fully bound and liable for the actions of the designated representative.[292] Designated representatives must submit signed and verified reports certifying compliance with applicable requirements.[293]

Each unit at a source is subject to SO_2 and NO_2 limitations and, consequently, each unit must comply with separate planning requirements.[294] Owners and operators of affected sources have flexibility, however, in the compliance plan they adopt. A conditionally approved option will be ineffective, unless the source amends its permit and activates the option.[295]

Compliance planning options that cover multiple units at a single source and units at different sources include the following:

1. *Phase I substitution plans.* A Phase I unit emitting SO_2 at levels that exceed its annual allowances may reduce emissions at one or more of the utility's Phase II units.[296]
2. *Phase I extension plans.* Units that install equipment that reduces SO_2 by 90 percent, such as scrubbers, or units that transfer their emissions reduction requirements to another unit or units that install such equipment are eligible for a two-year extension of the January 1995 Phase I deadline.[297]

---

[284] 58 Fed. Reg. 3590, 3661–62 (1993) (to be codified at 40 C.F.R. §72.9).

[285] 58 Fed. Reg. 3590, 3665 (1993) (to be codified at 40 C.F.R. §72.30).

[286] 58 Fed. Reg. 3590, 3675 (1993) (to be codified at 40 C.F.R. §72.60).

[287] 58 Fed. Reg. 3590, 3677 (1993) (to be codified at 40 C.F.R. §72.69).

[288] 58 Fed. Reg. 3590, 3679 (1993) (to be codified at 40 C.F.R. §72.73).

[289] 58 Fed. Reg. 3590, 3665 (1993) (to be codified at 40 C.F.R. §72.30(b)(3)(ii)).

[290] 58 Fed. Reg. 3590, 3679 (1993) (to be codified at 40 C.F.R. §72.73(b)(ii)).

[291] 58 Fed. Reg. 3590, 3679 (1993) (to be codified at 40 C.F.R. §72.74).

[292] 58 Fed. Reg. 3590, 3663 (1993) (to be codified at 40 C.F.R. §72.20).

[293] 58 Fed. Reg. 3590, 3681 (1993) (to be codified at 40 C.F.R. §72.90).

[294] 58 Fed. Reg. 3590, 3661–62 (1993) (to be codified at 40 C.F.R. §72.9(c), (d)).

[295] 58 Fed. Reg. 3590, 3667 (1993) (to be codified at 40 C.F.R. §72.40).

[296] 58 Fed. Reg. 3590, 3668 (1993) (to be codified at 40 C.F.R. §72.41). Emissions reductions at the Phase II unit must be as great as the emissions reductions at the Phase I unit would have been without relying on a substitute plan.

[297] 58 Fed. Reg. 3590, 3669 (1993) (to be codified at 40 C.F.R. §72.42). Equipment must be installed no later than December 31, 1996.

3. *Phase I reduced utilization.* A utility that reduces utilization at a higher emitting unit can increase utilization of a lower emitting unit.[298]
4. *Phase II repowering extensions.* A unit that repowers with a qualifying clean coal technology (any technology applied at precombustion, combustion, or post-combustion stage which will achieve significant SO_2 and NO_2 emissions and which is not in widespread use as of November 1990) is eligible for up to a four-year extension to meet Phase II requirements.[299]

2. *Permit Revisions*

EPA must provide notice and an opportunity for public comment before issuing permits. Like the Title V permit procedures, Title IV provides for permit revisions through modifications and administrative amendments.[300] Permit modifications require an application for a permit and opportunity for public comment before the change is made. Changes requiring handling as modifications include relaxation of emission offset requirements, incorporation of a final NO_2 emission limitation, and determinations concerning failed repowering projects.[301]

Administrative permit amendments are not subject to advance public comment. Administrative permit amendments include changes that require more frequent monitoring, ownership changes, changes in the designated representative, activation or termination of a compliance plan option authorized under the initial permit, changes in substitution or reduced utilization plans, changes in date of commencement of qualifying phase I technology, and changes in NO_2 alternative emissions limitations.[302] Properly recorded allowance transactions automatically amend the permit to reflect the new number of allowances held by the affected source.[303]

EPA has adopted a procedure for fast-track modification of acid rain permit provisions. Under this procedure the designated representative provides notice to EPA and the state.[304] Public notice also must be given to any other interested party through a generally circulated publication. The public has 30 days to make comments after which the permitting authority has another 30 days to approve the modification in whole or in part.[305]

D. Repowered Sources

An extension until the year 2004 is available to units subject to Phase II SO_2 requirements that certify they will be repowered by a qualifying clean coal technology. A unit is "repowered" if the existing coal-fired boiler is replaced with one of the following technologies: magnetohydrodynamics (MHD), inte-

---

[298] 58 Fed. Reg. 3590, 3671 (1993) (to be codified at 40 C.F.R. §72.43).
[299] 58 Fed. Reg. 3590, 3673 (1993) (to be codified at 40 C.F.R. §72.44).
[300] 58 Fed. Reg. 3590, 3680 (1993) (to be codified at 40 C.F.R. §72.80).
[301] 58 Fed. Reg. 3590, 3680 (1993) (to be codified at 40 C.F.R. §72.81).
[302] 58 Fed. Reg. 3590, 3680–81 (1993) (to be codified at 40 C.F.R. §72.83).
[303] 58 Fed. Reg. 3590, 3680 (1993) (to be codified at 40 C.F.R. §72.84).
[304] 58 Fed. Reg. 3590, 3680 (1993) (to be codified at §72.82(a)).
[305] 58 Fed. Reg. 3590, 3680 (1993) (to be codified at 40 C.F.R. §72.82).

grated gasification cells, atmospheric or pressurized fluidized bed combustion (FBC), integrated gasification combined cycle, or direct and indirect coal-fired turbines.[306] To qualify for the extension, the unit's owner or operator must submit a binding contract for the majority of the equipment necessary to repower the unit.[307] The Department of Energy and EPA may determine that an alternative technology qualifies as repowering if it is capable of controlling multiple combustion emissions simultaneously with improved boiler or generation efficiency, along with significantly greater waste reduction relative to performance of technology in common use as of November 1990.[308]

Technology applied at precombustion, combustion, and post-combustion stages at a new or existing facility that will achieve significant reductions in the air emissions of SO_2 or NO_2 that was not in common use in November 1990 constitutes "clean coal technology."[309] The 1990 Amendments provide incentives to develop and install clean coal technology including partial federal funding for temporary or permanent clean coal demonstration projects and an exemption from NSPS requirements under section 111.[310]

E. Monitoring, Reporting, and Recordkeeping

Without accurate monitoring and data reporting, EPA will have no way to ensure that goals for reducing SO_2 and NO_2 emissions are achieved. Furthermore, in order for the allowance trading program to function, it is essential that EPA maintain complete and accurate data about sources. Otherwise, the allowance trading system will be unstable. Consequently, section 412 requires owners and operators of affected sources to install continuous emissions monitoring systems (CEMSs) to monitor SO_2, NO_2, opacity, and volumetric flow for each regulated unit.[311]

Title IV also provides for alternative monitoring systems that have the proven ability to provide information with the same precision, reliability, accessibility, and timeliness as CEMSs as well as recordkeeping and reporting requirements for both CEMSs and alternative monitoring systems.[312] Final CEMSs regulations were issued in January 1993.[313] (The CEMSs regulations additionally require sources to monitor for CO_2.)[314]

EPA's implementing regulations require each CEMS and its component monitors to be performance tested and certified before they become operational.[315] Furthermore, operators of affected units must ensure the quality of emission data for SO_2, NO_2, opacity, and volumetric flow.[316] Each operator of an affected unit must develop and implement a written quality control plan for

---

306 §402(12), 42 U.S.C. §7651a(12).
307 §409(a), 42 U.S.C. §7651h(a).
308 §402(12), 42 U.S.C. §7651a(12).
309 §413(a), 42 U.S.C. §7651n(a).
310 §413, 42 U.S.C. §7651n.
311 42 U.S.C. §7651k(a).
312 §412(a), 42 U.S.C. §7651k(a); 58 Fed. Reg. 3590, 3717 (1993) (to be codified at 40 C.F.R. §74.40).
313 58 Fed. Reg. 3590, 3701 (1993) (to be codified at 40 C.F.R. §75).
314 58 Fed. Reg. 3590, 3706 (1993) (to be codified at 40 C.F.R. §75.13).
315 58 Fed. Reg. 3590, 3709–10 (1993) (to be codified at 40 C.F.R. §75.20).
316 §412(a), 42 U.S.C. §7651k(a); 58 Fed. Reg. 3590, 3712 (1993) (to be codified at 40 C.F.R. §75.21).

the CEMS and its components. Assessments of the CEMSs' performance must be made on a daily, quarterly, semiannual, and annual basis.[317]

CEMSs must be operational in all Phase I units by November 15, 1993.[318] CEMSs must be operational in all Phase II units by January 1, 1995.[319] Pursuant to section 412(d), EPA issued regulations for calculating emissions from affected units during periods when emission data are unavailable, presumably during periods of a CEMS failure.[320]

Each unit must install a data collection and handling system to gather and produce a continuous readout of the data required pursuant to section 412.[321] Thus, data from the separate monitoring systems are combined to report total emissions.[322] EPA is also required to issue CEMSs regulations for NO_2.[323] Although each unit must monitor CO_2 emissions, a CEMS is not required for CO_2 monitoring.[324]

Operators need not install separate CEMSs for units that use a common stack so long as flue gases from an affected unit cannot bypass the CEMS.[325] In the latter case, a separate CEMS must be installed on the bypass flue or duct.[326] If an owner or operator installs a CEMS on a common stack to measure the combined SO_2 emissions of affected and nonaffected units, the emissions from the nonaffected units can be calculated by installing a separate CEMS on ducts leading to the common stack and subtracting them from total common stack emissions. The owner may choose to designate the nonaffected unit as an opt-in unit and comply with reporting requirements for multiple affected units.[327] The owner or operator may also petition the Agency to approve a substitute apportionment method.[328]

The CAA requires EPA to issue regulations for calculating emissions during periods that a CEMS is inoperable.[329] This calculation is crucial to the allowance trading system and to assess possible penalties for operations beyond emissions allowances. EPA has generally adopted a measure that calculates the period of time for which data are missing as a percentage of an annual monitor using data from the previous year.[330] With respect to SO_2 emissions, these data can be cross-checked to some degree with information the Federal Energy Regulatory Commission (FERC) routinely collects about the sulfur and Btu content of fuels burned in fossil-fuel-fired utility boilers.

---

[317] 58 Fed. Reg. 3590, 3726 (1993) (to be codified at 40 C.F.R. §75.64 and App. B).

[318] §412(b), 42 U.S.C. §7651k(b).

[319] §412(c), 42 U.S.C. §7651k(c).

[320] 42 U.S.C. §7651k(d).

[321] 58 Fed. Reg. 3590, 3704 (1993) (to be codified at 40 C.F.R. §75.10).

[322] 58 Fed. Reg. 3590, 3705 (1993) (to be codified at 40 C.F.R. §75.11).

[323] 58 Fed. Reg. 3590, 3705 (1993) (to be codified at 40 C.F.R. §75.12).

[324] 58 Fed. Reg. 3590, 3706 (1993) (to be codified at 40 C.F.R. §75.13).

[325] §412(a), 42 U.S.C. §7651k(a).

[326] 58 Fed. Reg. 3590, 3708 (1993) (to be codified at 40 C.F.R. §75.16).

[327] 58 Fed. Reg. 3590, 3708 (1993) (to be codified at 40 C.F.R. §75.16(a)(2)(A)).

[328] 58 Fed. Reg. 3590, 3708 (1993) (to be codified at 40 C.F.R. §75.16(a)(2)(C)).

[329] §412(d), 42 U.S.C. §7651k(d).

[330] 58 Fed. Reg. 3590, 3713 (1993) (to be codified at 40 C.F.R. §75.30). If the annual monitor availability is equal to or greater than 95%, the substitute emission value will depend on the length of the missing data period. *Id.* at 3714–15 (to be codified at 40 C.F.R. §75.33(b)). If the missing data period is less than 24 hours, the substitute emission value for each missing hour will be the average of the emissions recorded for the hour before and the hour after the missing data period. *Id.* If the data period is more than 24 hours, the substitute emission value will be equal to 90th percentile of the emissions recorded over the previous 30 days, or the average of the emissions recorded for the hour before and the hour after missing data, whichever is higher. *Id.*

F. Enforcement

There are strict penalties for failure to comply with the acid rain provisions, starting with a mandatory penalty of $2,000 (to be adjusted for inflation) for each ton of excess SO_2 or NO_2 emissions emitted by an affected source annually.[331] This penalty is independent of any other civil or criminal penalty for which the unit's owners or operators may be liable.[332] The designated representative must calculate and pay penalties owed, plus interest, from January 1. EPA will assess interest on delayed payments and impose joint and several liability on multiple owners, operators, and designated representatives of violating units. In addition to monetary penalties, EPA is required to deduct one ton of allowances for each ton of SO_2 excess emissions during the following year.[333] Operators of units with excess emissions must present to EPA and the state a plan to achieve offsets of SO_2 emissions. The offset plan is incorporated into the unit's operating permit.[334]

V. Title V—Permits

The 1990 Amendments established a nationwide permit program for stationary sources under Title V.[335] In many respects, this program resembles the National Pollutant Discharge Elimination System (NPDES) permit program administered by EPA and the states under section 402 of the Clean Water Act.[336] That resemblance is intentional, but the air permit program is by no means a carbon copy of the NPDES permit program.

Under current law, EPA is to approve and oversee the air permit program while the states are responsible for its implementation. This program will become the primary means of regulating stationary sources, which, before the 1990 Amendments, were primarily regulated by SIP programs that specified emission limitations calculated to comply with federal NAAQSs.

While many states prior to the 1990 Amendments adopted permit programs and required construction or operating permits for some sources, the decision to issue permits was made largely at the state level. The new federal program requires all states to implement a permit program that covers the following sources:

- Major stationary sources that emit or have the potential to emit more than 100 tons per year of any air pollutant, taking into account federally enforceable physical or operational limitations on emissions;[337]

---

[331] §412(a), (c), 42 U.S.C. §7651j(a), (c).

[332] §412(e), 42 U.S.C. §7651j(e).

[333] §412(b), 42 U.S.C. §7651j(b).

[334] *Id.*

[335] The §112 air toxics and Title IV acid rain provisions include additional permit requirements for sources affected by those titles.

[336] 33 U.S.C. §1342.

[337] §502(a) and §302(j), 42 U.S.C. §7661a(a) and §7602(j). For 26 categories of sources, EPA regulations require fugitive emissions to be taken into account in making this calculation. 40 C.F.R. §70.2. A source's "potential to emit" was originally viewed by EPA as a source's potential emissions from continual operations during a one-year period. This definition has proved contentious for many, especially batch processors who frequently change operations, and those processors who operate seasonally. The definition was challenged and partially rejected in Wisconsin Elec. Power Co. v. EPA, 893 F.2d 901 (7th Cir. 1990).

- Major sources as defined under section 112 hazardous air pollutant (HAP) provisions with the potential to emit 10 tons of any single HAP, 25 tons per year of any combination of HAP, or any lesser quantity of HAP specified by EPA through rulemaking;
- Area sources subject to HAP standards under section 112;
- Sources subject to section 111 new source performance standards (NSPS);[338]
- New or modified sources subject to prevention of significant deterioration (PSD) requirements (including any source that has the potential to emit more than 250 tons per year of SO_2, NO_2, or PM10 and for 28 source categories that emit 100 tons or more per year);[339]
- New or modified sources located in nonattainment areas, and those existing major sources in nonattainment areas affected by lower threshold emissions requirements;[340]
- Sources regulated under Title IV acid rain provisions, including the 111 coal- or oil-fired electric power plants and sources that participate in the emissions trading program; and
- Any other stationary source category that the Administrator designates.

The new operating permits provide a mechanism for SIP implementation and achievement of NAAQSs. Even sources that already hold a state permit must obtain an operating permit under Title V. With the exception of major sources, EPA has authority to exempt source categories from permit requirements if the Agency determines that they are unnecessarily burdensome, infeasible, or impracticable.[341] States still could require sources exempted by EPA to obtain an operating permit.

A. State Permit Program Requirements

EPA was required to adopt final regulations establishing minimum elements of state permit programs by November 15, 1991.[342] Under Title V, state permit programs must include

- Monitoring, recordkeeping, and reporting requirements for permitted facilities;[343]
- Adequate personnel and funding to administer the program;[344]

---

[338] EPA has promulgated NSPSs for approximately 70 source categories and imposed emissions controls, monitoring, reporting, and recordkeeping requirements on designated sources. 40 C.F.R. §60.

[339] Section 167 provisions govern source PSD permits, but Title V subjects those sources to annual fees. 42 U.S.C. §7476.

[340] The threshold for major stationary sources is lower in some nonattainment areas than under §302(j). 42 U.S.C. §7602(j). The definition of a major source changes in serious, severe, and extreme ozone nonattainment areas to a source that emits or has potential to emit 50, 25, and 10 tons per year respectively. For serious carbon monoxide nonattainment areas, the definition of a major source is one that emits or has potential to emit 50 tons per year. For serious particulate nonattainment areas, the definition of a major source is one that emits or has potential to emit 70 tons per year. §§182(c)-(e), 187(b), 189(b), 42 U.S.C. §§7511a(c)-(e), 7512a(b), 7513a(b).

[341] §502(a), 42 U.S.C. §7661a(a).

[342] EPA promulgated its final operating permits rule in July 1992. 57 Fed. Reg. 32,250 (1992).

[343] §502(b)(2), 42 U.S.C. §7661a(b)(2). Unlike the Title IV acid rain program, continuous monitoring of sources, although preferable, is not required under the permit program.

[344] §502(b)(4), 42 U.S.C. §7661a(b)(4).

- Adequate legal authority to issue, terminate, modify, or revoke permits during a fixed period of up to five years;[345]
- Enforcement mechanisms including civil penalties of up to $10,000 per day per violation and appropriate criminal penalties;[346]
- Procedures for prompt processing of applications;[347]
- Provisions for periodic permit revisions to reflect regulatory requirements promulgated after the permit is issued;[348]
- Allowances for minor changes upon seven days' notice to the permitting authority as long as the modifications are not subject to PSD, nonattainment, NSPS, or otherwise cause the facility to exceed the permit's emissions limits;[349]
- Provisions for a permit "shield" so that compliance with the permit is deemed compliance with Title V requirements;[350]
- Provisions for public notice and opportunity to comment on and obtain judicial review of permit applications;[351]
- Provisions for public access to permit applications, compliance plans, monitoring, and compliance reports;[352]
- Provisions for citizen suits against permit authorities who fail to act on permit applications within the time required under section 503;[353] and
- Requirements for owners and operators of all sources subject to permit requirements to pay annual fees to cover all reasonable costs associated with the development and administration of the permit program.[354]

B. State Permit Program Submissions and Approval

Each state is required to develop and submit to EPA by November 15, 1993, a permit program that incorporates the statutory and regulatory requirements set forth above. Although EPA's Title V implementing regulations were nine months overdue, states are not relieved of their obligation to meet the statutory deadline. Under section 502(d) provisions, EPA has one year to accept or reject state programs, and there must be notice and opportunity for public comment before EPA can act on the program.[355] If EPA disapproves the program, in whole or part, the Agency must notify the state, which then has six months to revise and resubmit the program. Once approved, the state permit program is effective immediately.[356] During the transition period, EPA will stop issuing permits for sources covered under the state program, but continue to

---

[345] §502(b)(5)(A), (D), 42 U.S.C. §7661a(b)(5)(A), (D).

[346] §502(b)(5)(E), 42 U.S.C. §7661a(b)(5)(E). Section 503(b) enforcement provisions require permittees to certify at least annually that the covered source is in compliance with applicable requirements and report deviations from permit requirements to appropriate authorities. 42 U.S.C. §7661b(b).

[347] §502(b)(6), 42 U.S.C. §7661a(b)(6).

[348] §502(b)(9), 42 U.S.C. §7661a(b)(9).

[349] §502(b)(10), 42 U.S.C. §7661a(b)(10). *See* 40 C.F.R. §70.4(b)(12).

[350] §504(f), 42 U.S.C. §7661c(f).

[351] §502(b)(7), 42 U.S.C. §7661a(b)(7).

[352] §503(e), 42 U.S.C. §7661b(e).

[353] §502(b)(7), 42 U.S.C. §7661a(b)(7).

[354] §502(b)(3), 42 U.S.C. §7661a(b)(3).

[355] §502(d), 42 U.S.C. §7661a(d).

[356] §502(h), 42 U.S.C. §7661a(h).

administer and enforce permits it has already issued or those that are under administrative or judicial review.[357]

1. Interim and Partial Approval

If a state program substantially meets the requirements for approval, EPA may grant interim approval pursuant to section 502(g).[358] Interim approval is conditional and cannot exceed a two-year period. EPA must specify revisions needed for full approval.[359] In order to obtain interim approval, the state program must at least assure compliance with the Title IV acid rain provisions, section 112 major and area source HAP requirements, and Title I NAAQS, PSD, and NSPS requirements.[360] Furthermore, the program must ensure the state's ability to enforce its provisions and MACT standards for hazardous air pollutants on a case-by-case basis for new, reconstructed, or modified sources where EPA has not yet specified MACT standards.[361]

EPA is also authorized to approve a partial permitting program applicable to all sources within a limited geographic area.[362] If EPA disapproves the partial program, the state has six months to revise and resubmit the program. Otherwise EPA will administer the permit program.

2. General Permits and Flexibility for Certain Sources

States are authorized after public notice and comment, to issue general permits for similar types of sources pursuant to section 504(d).[363] Under general permits, the terms and conditions for operation of a class of sources are specified. Individual sources must demonstrate that they satisfy the criteria for coverage. Use of general permits will reduce the permitting authority's administrative tasks, but their use does not promise any particular benefits to sources covered by them.

Permitting authorities retain flexibility to permit multiple or unique sources. For example, under section 502(c), one permit could be issued for multiple sources at the same facility.[364] This allows a large manufacturing facility to take advantage of "bubbling"—offsetting emissions from different pieces of equipment within a source—in order to comply with emissions requirements. Temporary sources such as mobile incinerators may be covered by a single permit pursuant to section 504(e).[365]

3. Sanctions for Noncompliance

States must continue to revise their permit programs until they are fully approved. If a state fails to submit an approvable permit program[366] or EPA

---

[357] §502(e), 42 U.S.C. §7661a(e).
[358] 42 U.S.C. §7661a(g).
[359] §502(g), 42 U.S.C. §7661a(g).
[360] §502(f), 42 U.S.C. §7661a(f).
[361] 56 Fed. Reg. 21,722 (1991).
[362] 40 C.F.R. §70.4(c).
[363] 42 U.S.C. §7661c(d).
[364] 42 U.S.C. §7661a(c).
[365] 42 U.S.C. §7661c(e).
[366] §502(d)(2)(A), 42 U.S.C. §7661a(d)(2)(A).

determines that the state is not administering or enforcing the program during an 18-month period after EPA gives the state notice of the deficiency, EPA may impose sanctions.[367] EPA must impose sanctions if the state fails to resubmit programs rejected by the Agency or fails to administer or enforce the program following the 18-month notice period.[368] Penalties for noncompliance include loss of federal highway funds and a 2 to 1 offset ratio for new or modified sources that are to be located in nonattainment areas.

C. Permit Fee System

Congress attempted to address the financial burden associated with imposition of the permit program through a fee system.[369] Owners or operators of the nearly 34,000 sources that will require a permit will have to pay yearly fees to cover all reasonable costs associated with the development and administration of the program. Generally, for each regulated pollutant, a state must collect from each permitted source at least $25 per ton, up to 4,000 tons per pollutant annually.[370] Regulated pollutants include VOCs, section 112 HAPs, section 111 NSPS pollutants, and pollutants for which a NAAQS (other than carbon monoxide) have been set. EPA may collect reasonable fees from covered sources if the agency determines that a state is not adequately administering or enforcing an approved fee program.[371]

D. Permit Applications

An individual source's permit application is due within one year of the date that EPA fully approves the state's program. Deadlines imposed on sources under the Title IV acid rain provisions, however, preempt Title V deadlines.[372] Although Title V does not specify the information that applicants must provide, EPA's operating permit regulations (finalized in July 1992) list basic data requirements.[373] The application must include at least:

- A description of the plant's processes and products;[374]
- Citation and description of applicable state and federal air pollution requirements;[375]

---

367 §502(i)(1), 42 U.S.C. §7661a(i)(1).

368 §§502(d)(2)(B) and 502(i)(2), 42 U.S.C. §§7661a(d)(2)(B) and 7661a(i)(2).

369 §502(b)(3), 42 U.S.C. §7661a(b)(3).

370 §502(b)(3)(B), 42 U.S.C. §7661a(b)(3)(B). The fee is adjusted on September 1 of each year to reflect changes in the U.S. Consumer Price Index. The most recent (1992) inflation adjustment raised the fee to more than $28 per ton.

371 §502(b)(3)(C)(i), 42 U.S.C. §7661a(b)(3)(C)(i). The state may charge a lower fee if the state demonstrates that it can adequately cover its administrative costs. 57 Fed. Reg. 32,291 (1992). This demonstration may be quite burdensome for the state under EPA's regulations. Nonetheless, at least one state is attempting to do so.

372 §502(b)(3)(B), 42 U.S.C. §7661a(b)(3)(B). The 111 affected utility plants must submit applications for Phase I SO_2 permits by February 15, 1993. These plants and other sources subject to Phase II requirements must submit applications for Phase II permits by January 1996. §408(c)(2), 42 U.S.C. §7651g(c)(2); §408(d), 42 U.S.C. §7651h(d).

373 57 Fed. Reg. 32,302 (1992).

374 40 C.F.R. §70.5(c)(2).

375 40 C.F.R. §70.6(a)(ii).

- If applicable, prohibitions of SO_2 emissions that exceed allowances held under Title IV acid rain provisions and emission trading provisions;[376]
- Enforceable emission limitations and standards;[377]
- If applicable, terms and conditions for trading emission increases and decreases in the facility;[378]
- Terms and conditions for alternative operating scenarios;[379]
- A compliance plan, along with a schedule of compliance and a schedule for progress reports to be issued no less frequently than every six months;[380]
- Requirements to certify compliance;[381]
- Inspection and entry requirements for permitting authorities;[382]
- Emissions related data such as types of regulated pollutants emitted, rate of emissions in tons per year, raw materials and fuels used, air pollution control equipment, and applicable limits on source operations or work practice standards;[383] and
- A statement that the permit may be modified, revoked, reissued, or reopened.[384]

A "responsible official" must sign each permit application and certify the truth, accuracy, and completeness of the information submitted.[385]

Upon receipt of a permit application, the state permitting authority must take final action within 18 months.[386] The permitting authority must establish a phased schedule for processing applications within the first year after a state's permit program goes into effect.[387] Under the schedule, action must be taken on at least one-third of the applications during each of the first three years of the program. If a source provides a complete permit application by the applicable deadline—one year from the effective date of a state's program—the source will be deemed to be in compliance with the requirement of obtaining a permit.[388] In effect, this provision allows a source to operate before obtaining its permit so that it is not penalized by the length of the approval process. Thus, it is important for owners and operators required to obtain a permit to prepare a complete and timely application, and to provide additional information required

---

[376] 40 C.F.R. §70.6(a)(1), (8).

[377] 40 C.F.R. §70.6(a)(1).

[378] 40 C.F.R. §70.6(a)(8).

[379] 40 C.F.R. §70.5(c)(7).

[380] §503(b), 42 U.S.C. §7661b(b). The plan must disclose whether the applicant is in compliance with each applicable requirement. This may subject the source to public scrutiny for acknowledging violations. 40 C.F.R. §70.5(c)(8). Adoption of a compliance plan, however, does not relieve a source from enforcement action or penalties for existing or preexisting violation of applicable requirements.

[381] 40 C.F.R. §70.5(c)(9).

[382] 40 C.F.R. §70.6(c)(2).

[383] 40 C.F.R. §70.5(c)(3).

[384] Permits may be reopened if (1) additional requirements for major sources with an existing permit term of three or more years are imposed under the Act, (2) the acid rain program adds requirements, (3) material mistakes are discovered in the original permit, or (4) the state or EPA determines that the permit must be revised to assure compliance. 40 C.F.R. §70.7(f).

[385] A responsible official is an officer of a corporation or a manager of manufacturing, production, or operating facilities employing more than 250 persons or having gross annual sales or expenditures exceeding $25 million, to whom authority to sign such documents has been delegated in accordance with corporate procedures. A general partner of a partnership is considered the responsible official. 40 C.F.R. §70.2.

[386] §503(c), 42 U.S.C. §7661b(c).

[387] §503(c), 42 U.S.C. §7661b(c).

[388] §503(d), 42 U.S.C. §7661b(d). *See* 57 Fed. Reg. 32,307 (1992).

by the permitting authority, in order to avoid the penalties for operating without a permit.

E. Permit Shield

The permit shield provisions under section 504(f) provide owners and operators with greater certainty about compliance with legal requirements. Under this provision, if a source complies with its permit requirements, it is considered to be in compliance with all other provisions of the CAA. The shield applies if the permit includes certain requirements or the permitting authority determines that those requirements are not applicable.[389] Sources raising the permit shield need not comply with new regulatory requirements not addressed in the permit until the permit is reopened to incorporate such changes.

In order to create the shield, the permit shield provisions must be expressly provided for in the permit and must specify requirements that apply to the source.[390] EPA interpreted the permit shield provisions in the final rules narrowly to apply only to those legal requirements in effect when the permit is issued. For example, the permit would not shield sources from MACT standards and future emissions limits later set by EPA pursuant to section 112. The shield does not exempt sources from legal or regulatory requirements that are enacted subsequent to the issuance of a permit. Furthermore, owners and operators of sources cannot rely on the shield to avoid liability for operational changes not provided for in the permit.

F. Operational Flexibility and Alternative Operating Scenarios

EPA has maintained that changes in industrial practices and procedures that do not violate the terms of a permit can be implemented without having to secure a new permit or modify the existing one. Thus, emissions or practices not prohibited by a permit are allowed if they are otherwise lawful under federal or state law. Under section 502(b)(10), permits must allow for changes on seven days' notice to the permitting authority provided that the changes do not result in emissions that exceed levels authorized under the permit.[391] The notice provisions have been controversial, and at least one public interest group has filed a lawsuit to challenge the rule, asserting that all operational changes should be subject to public notice and comment.[392]

Sources can incorporate alternative operating scenarios by describing products or processes associated with anticipated alternative operations. The permitting authority can add alternative operating scenarios upon assurance that the source can meet all applicable requirements when operating under each scenario.[393] The regulations do not state that sources must give notice to the permitting authority before making changes pursuant to alternative operating

---

[389] §504(f), 42 U.S.C. §7661c(f).

[390] 57 Fed. Reg. 32,306 (1992).

[391] 42 U.S.C. §7661a(b)(10); 57 Fed. Reg. 32,301 (1992).

[392] NRDC v. EPA, No. 92-1353 (D.C. Cir. 1992).

[393] The source owner need only record operational changes at the plant. It is not necessary to notify the permitting authority or EPA.

scenarios provided for in the permit.[394] (Alternative operating scenarios may also be protected by the permit shield.)

G. Off-Permit Changes

States are authorized to allow operational changes that the permit does not cover or prohibit.[395] These off-permit changes must (1) meet applicable permit requirements, (2) comply with existing permit terms and conditions, (3) not constitute Title I modifications, and (4) comply with Title IV acid rain provisions and other federal standards. Both EPA and state permitting authorities must receive written notice of off-permit changes.[396]

H. Permit Modifications and Administrative Amendments

Permitting authorities must review significant permit modifications in accordance with procedures for issuing new operating permits.[397] There are, however, several categories of permit changes, and it is not always clear which changes require permit modification. Those changes that can be made without permit modification are considered administrative amendments. They cover changes that (1) require more frequent monitoring, (2) reflect changes in ownership, or (3) correct simple typographical errors.[398] No public notice is required for administrative amendments and the permitting authority must take action within 60 days of receiving a request.[399]

1. Minor Modifications

A permit modification is one that cannot be made by administrative amendment. The most controversial of these are minor permit modifications—those that do not (1) violate applicable requirements, (2) cause significant changes to monitoring, reporting, or recordkeeping requirements, or (3) change an emissions limitation, permit term, or condition. EPA must be notified of minor permit modifications and the Agency has 45 days to review it.[400] A series of minor modifications can be grouped together for review if they do not exceed specified emissions thresholds.[401] No public comment period is provided for minor modifications. Upon receiving a completed application for minor modifications, the permitting authority must take action within 90 days or 15 days following EPA's review period, whichever is later. The permit shield does not apply to minor modifications.

---

[394] 57 Fed. Reg. 32,269 (1992).
[395] 57 Fed. Reg. 32,269 (1992).
[396] 57 Fed. Reg. 32,269 (1992). Source owners must keep records of off-permit changes.
[397] 40 C.F.R. §70.7(d)(3).
[398] 40 C.F.R. §70.7(d).
[399] 40 C.F.R. §70.7(d).
[400] 40 C.F.R. §70.7(e)(2)(iv).
[401] 57 Fed. Reg. 32,308 (1992). Specified thresholds are: (1) 10% of allowable emissions, (2) 20% of applicable major source defintion, or (3) 5 tons per year.

2. *Major Modifications*

Major permit modifications are usually designated by the permitting authority. They cover changes in (1) monitoring, (2) permit terms and conditions, and (3) reporting or recordkeeping requirements.[402] Significant permit changes are subject to EPA and public review using the same procedures specified for initial permit issuance and renewal.

I. Permit Renewal

Operating permits cannot exceed a fixed term of five years except for municipal solid waste incinerators governed by section 129, which can be for 12 years. Most renewal applications will have to be submitted 18 months before the existing permit expires so that the permitting authority will have 18 months to process them.[403] A source may continue to operate following the expiration of its permit provided that the renewal application is timely and complete. The same shield provisions apply to sources waiting for application renewals as sources waiting for an initial permit. EPA may allow a grace period before it assesses penalties against sources that fail to submit timely or complete renewal applications. Nevertheless, the shield provisions should be incentive enough for owners and operators of permitted sources to comply promptly or face fines and injunctions that could close their plants until a proper renewal application is submitted.[404]

J. Small Business Assistance

Section 507 includes provisions to assist small businesses with operating permit compliance.[405] To quality for assistance, a source must (1) be owned or operated by a person employing no more than 100 employees, (2) not be a major source, (3) emit no more than 50 tons per year of a regulated pollutant or 75 tons per year of any combination of regulated pollutants.[406] Pursuant to section 507, states were required to submit a program by November 1992 to which mechanisms to develop and distribute data about compliance technologies and measures for small business sources. The plan must establish a compliance advisory panel to monitor small businesses' implementation of the program. Furthermore, the program must offer assistance with obtaining permits, pollution prevention, accidental release detection and prevention requirements, and compliance audits.

K. Role of EPA, Other States, and the Public

As an integral part of an approved state permit program, section 505 provides EPA, other states, and the public with an opportunity to participate in

[402] 57 Fed. Reg. 32,309 (1992).
[403] 57 Fed. Reg. 32,307 (1992).
[404] *Id.*
[405] 42 U.S.C. §7661f.
[406] §507(a), 42 U.S.C. §7661f(a).

the permitting process.[407] With the exception of certain confidential business information,[408] the public is provided access to all permit applications, compliance plans, emissions or compliance monitoring reports, certification, and final permits pursuant to section 503(e).[409] The state cannot act on a permit without providing notice and opportunity for public comment.

The state must send copies of all permit applications to EPA and notify adjacent states, states within 50 miles of the source, and states that could be affected by the source.[410] Those states are authorized to comment and make recommendations on the proposed permit's terms and conditions. If the recommendations are not accepted, a written explanation must be provided to the interested state.

EPA can reject any part of the permit that fails to comply with CAA requirements or SIP provisions. Written objections are due from EPA within 45 days of its receiving notice of a proposed permit or receipt of another state's objections. The permitting state has 90 days to issue a permit that incorporates EPA's revisions.[411] If the state does not act on EPA's objections, EPA must deny the permit or issue the revised permit itself.[412]

If EPA does not object to a proposed permit within the 45-day review period, private parties have 60 days to raise objections in a petition to the Agency. The petition must be reasonably specific and based on concerns raised during the public comment period, unless the basis for objection arose after the public proceedings. EPA has 60 days to accept or reject a petition. In the meantime, the source can operate under the permit. Once EPA notifies the state that it has granted a petition, the state must change the permit or EPA can terminate, modify, or reissue a revised permit.[413] Pursuant to section 307, petitioners may seek judicial review of the Agency's decision to deny their petitions.[414]

The public will have access to monitoring and compliance reports for all permits issued. If these reports demonstrate noncompliance, they can provide the basis for citizen suits. Just as the NPDES permit program is enforced in significant part by citizen enforcement actions under the Clean Water Act, Congress intended to encourage similar actions to enforce CAA requirements, and has ensured that data needed to bring such actions are easily available.

VI. Title VI—Stratospheric Ozone Protection

The stratospheric ozone layer, located about 20 miles above the earth's surface, screens harmful ultraviolet radiation that can lead to skin cancer,

[407] 57 Fed. Reg. 32,309 (1992). Notice of a permit application must be provided in a newspaper of general circulation in the area where the source is located or in a state publication generally used for public notice purposes. *Id.*

[408] Section 114(c) may exempt certain business information from disclosure requirements. 42 U.S.C. §7414(c).

[409] 42 U.S.C. §7661b(e).

[410] §505(a), 42 U.S.C. §7661d(a).

[411] §505(b)(1)-(3), 42 U.S.C. §7661d(b)(1)-(3).

[412] §505(c), 42 U.S.C. §7661d(c).

[413] §505(b)(2), 42 U.S.C. §7661d(b)(2).

[414] *Id.* EPA may waive the review and objection process for minor sources categories. §505(d), 42 U.S.C. §7661d(d).

cataracts, crop damage, and injury to marine life. Research conducted over the past 20 years suggests that the release into the environment of certain industrially produced halocarbons, such as chlorofluorocarbons (CFCs), carbon tetrachloride, and methyl chloroform, contribute to depletion of the stratospheric ozone layer. These ozone depleting substances (ODSs) are stable in the atmospheric layer closest to the earth's surface, but when they migrate to the stratosphere they break down, releasing chlorine and bromine to react with ozone. It is believed that chlorine and bromine react with ozone and sunlight to form new compounds, thereby depleting or "scavenging" ozone in the stratosphere in quantities far out of proportion to the quantity of CFCs which reach that altitude.

The 1990 Amendments added Title VI in order to phase out production and importation of ODSs over a 40-year period as well as to impose restrictions on their production and use during that period. The phase-out of CFCs and methyl chloroform is much faster than for other ODSs. Provisions are included in Title VI to regulate ODSs and products that contain or are made with them.

A. Early Regulation of ODSs

In response to scientific studies released in 1975 which first connected the use of CFCs to the depletion of the stratospheric ozone layer, Congress added subtitle B to Title I in the 1977 CAA Amendments. Under subtitle B, EPA was directed to study substances, practices, processes, and activities that could adversely affect the ozone layer. The Agency was required to establish regulations to control ODSs, and the government was directed to enter into international agreements that would protect the stratosphere consistent with those regulations. In 1978, EPA prohibited the use of CFCs as aerosol propellants pursuant to its authority under section 6 of the Toxic Substances Control Act.[415] That same year, the Food and Drug Administration banned use of CFCs in food, drug, and cosmetic products.[416]

B. The Montreal Protocol

Negotiations for an international agreement to control ODSs commenced in 1982. In 1987, the United States along with most industrial nations signed the Montreal Protocol on Substances that Deplete the Ozone Layer.[417] The Protocol, in part, provided for (1) a phased reduction of CFCs to 50 percent of 1986 levels, (2) a halon production freeze at 1986 levels, (3) 10 additional years for developing countries to comply with reductions, and (4) trade restrictions against nonsignatory nations. EPA adopted implementing regulations in 1988 pursuant to its authority under then section 157.[418]

Shortly after the Montreal Protocol was signed, new evidence suggested that ozone depletion was much more serious than originally reported. Efforts were made to achieve greater reductions of ODSs on a tighter schedule. In 1990

---

[415] 15 U.S.C. §2605.
[416] 43 Fed. Reg. 11,316 (1978).
[417] 26 I.L.M. 1541 (1987), *reprinted in* 52 Fed. Reg. 47,515 (1987).
[418] 40 C.F.R. §82.

and 1992, the Montreal Protocol was amended to hasten the CFC and halon phaseout schedule. In addition, methyl chloroform, carbon tetrachloride, and methyl bromide were added to the production phase-out.[419] Title VI of the 1990 Amendments is largely designed to implement the terms and conditions of the Montreal Protocol. In the event of conflict between terms of the Protocol and the CAA, the more stringent term or condition controls.[420]

C. Listing of Class I and II Substances

Under the 1990 Amendments, EPA was directed to publish preliminary lists of substances for two separate classes of ODSs and assign numerical values reflecting the substances' potential to deplete ozone.[421] Class I substances are those believed to be most damaging to the ozone layer along with all isomers of those substances, with the exception of one methyl chloroform isomer, 1,1,2-trichloroethane. Class II includes chemicals considered less harmful to the ozone layer, such as hydrochlorofluorocarbons (HCFCs) and their isomers.[422] EPA must add substances that the Agency subsequently determines to have a specified ozone depleting potential.[423] In addition, private parties are authorized to petition EPA to list a substance.[424] EPA has one year to grant or deny listing petitions. Class I substances cannot be removed from the list and only a class II substance that is added to the list of class I substances can be removed from the list of class II substances.[425]

D. Monitoring and Reporting Requirements

The 1990 Amendments require each person who produces, imports, or exports a class I or II substance to file annual reports quantifying the amount of those substances produced, imported, or exported.[426] EPA, in turn, must monitor the production, use, and consumption of controlled substances. At least every three years EPA must report to Congress about both national and international production, use, and consumption.[427] Consumption is a term of art that

[419] The phase-out schedules exclude essential uses of ODSs—those necessary for health, safety, or critical to functioning society. Amendments to the Protocol in 1992 call for a complete phase-out of CFC, carbon tetrachloride, and methyl chloroform production by January 1996. Halons were given a phase-out date of 1994. Consumption of hydrochlorofluorocarbons (HCFCs) are frozen as of 1996 with a full phase-out by 2030. Methyl bromide was listed as an ODS and Montreal Protocol signatories agreed to freeze production and consumption of methyl bromide at 1991 levels beginning in 1995. Parties also agreed to a full phase-out of hydrobromofluorocarbons by the year 1996.

[420] §614, 42 U.S.C. §7671m.

[421] §602(a)-(e), 42 U.S.C. §7671a(a)-(e). EPA published numerical values at 56 Fed. Reg. 2420 (1991).

[422] §602(a)-(b), 42 U.S.C. §7671a(a)-(b).

[423] §602(c), 42 U.S.C. §7671a(c). A substance with an ozone depleting potential greater than 0.2 should be listed by the agency. §602(a), 42 U.S.C. §7671a(a).

[424] §602(c)(3), 42 U.S.C. §7671a(c)(3).

[425] §602(c)(4), 42 U.S.C. §7671a(c)(4).

[426] §603(b), 42 U.S.C. §7671b(b).

[427] §603(d)(1), 42 U.S.C. §7671b(d)(1). EPA must also report to Congress on the environmental and economic effects of stratospheric ozone depletion at least every six years. *Id.* In addition, the National Aeronautics and Space Administration and the National Oceanic and Atmospheric Administration must monitor and report to Congress on concentrations of chlorine and bromine in the troposphere and on levels of ozone depletion. §603(d)(2), 42 U.S.C. §7671b(d)(2).

refers to production plus imports less exports. By 2015, EPA must inform Congress about any technological development problems that will delay introduction of alternatives to class II substances needed to meet the phase-out schedule.[428]

E. Phase-Out of Class I Substances

Under the 1990 Amendments, reductions in production of class I substances under section 604 were specified according to percentages listed in the table below.[429] The table refers to the maximum allowable production as a percentage of the quantity of the substance produced in the baseline year. For most class I substances the baseline year is 1986. The baseline year for carbon tetrachloride, methyl chloroform, and certain CFCs is 1989. Production and consumption of class I substances must cease by January 2000, with the exception of methyl chloroform which cannot be produced or consumed after January 2002.[430]

Date	*Carbon Tetrachloride*	*Methyl Chloroform*	*Other Class I Substances*
1991	100%	100%	85%
1992	90%	100%	80%
1993	80%	90%	75%
1994	70%	85%	65%
1995	15%	70%	50%
1996	15%	50%	40%
1997	15%	50%	15%
1998	15%	50%	15%
1999	15%	50%	15%
2000		20%	
2001		20%	

This phase-out schedule will be revised pursuant to 1992 amendments to the Montreal Protocol. EPA proposed a revised phase-out schedule in March 1993;[431] the final version is expected in late 1993 with an effective date of January 1994.[432]

---

[428] §603(e), 42 U.S.C. §7671b(e).

[429] §604(a), 42 U.S.C. §7671c(a).

[430] §604(b), 42 U.S.C. §7671c(b).

[431] The proposed accelerated phase-out schedule is published at 58 Fed. Reg. 15,014, 15,022 (1993). The following table provides the proposed schedule for the percentage of baseline production and consumption allowed, subject to exceptions for essential uses:

Date	CFCs	Halons	Carbon Tetrachloride	Methyl Chloroform
1994	25%	0	50%	50%
1995	15%	0	15%	30%
1996	0	0	0	0

[432] 58 Fed. Reg. 15,014 (1993).

1. Exceptions

EPA may allow, after specific recommendations, notice, and comment, the limited production of certain ODSs where there are no safe or effective substitutes. Consequently, EPA may authorize production of methyl chloroform in limited quantities until January 2005 for use in essential applications.[433] After consultation with the Food and Drug Administration, EPA may allow the production of class I substances solely for use in medical devices.[434] After consultation with the Federal Aviation Administration, EPA may allow production of a limited quantity of halons solely for use to ensure aviation safety.[435] Until January 2010 (2012 for methyl chloroform), EPA may authorize production of class I substances for export solely to satisfy basic economic needs in developing countries which are parties to the Montreal Protocol.[436] Finally, until December 1999, EPA may authorize production of halons solely for fire suppression and explosion prevention.[437]

In addition to the exceptions listed above, the President may authorize production and use of CFC-114 and halons upon a finding that there are no satisfactory substitutes available and their production and use is essential to protect national security interests.[438] Exemptions pursuant to the President's order may not exceed one year, but the exemption is renewable.

F. Phase-Out of Class II Substances

Beginning January 2015, no person can introduce any class II substance into interstate commerce unless the substance has been (1) used, recovered, and recycled, (2) entirely consumed in the production of other chemicals (except for trace quantities), or (3) used as a refrigerant in appliances manufactured before January 1, 2020.[439] Furthermore, no person may produce class II substances in annual quantities that exceed production levels during a baseline year that is to be determined by EPA.[440] Production of any class II substance is prohibited as of January 1, 2030.[441] EPA must restrict consumption of class II substances according to the same production phase-out schedule for class II substances.[442]

1. Exceptions

The 1990 Amendments carve out exceptions to the class II substance phase-out that resemble certain class I exceptions under section 604.[443] EPA

---

433 §604(d)(1), 42 U.S.C. §7671c(d)(1).

434 §604(d)(2), 42 U.S.C. §7671c(d)(2).

435 §604(d)(3)(A), 42 U.S.C. §7671c(d)(3)(A). Provisions are included for the FAA to consult with EPA regarding safe and effective substitutes for methyl chloroform used in testing for metal fatigue and corrosion of airplane engines and parts after January 2005. §604(d)(3)(B), 42 U.S.C. §7671c(d)(3)(B).

436 §604(e), 42 U.S.C. §7671c(e). A cap is placed on this exception under §604(e)(2). 42 U.S.C. §7671c(e)(2).

437 §604(g)(1), 42 U.S.C. §7671c(g)(1).

438 §604(f), 42 U.S.C. §7671c(f).

439 §605(a), 42 U.S.C. §7671d(a).

440 §605(b)(1), 42 U.S.C. §7671d(b)(1).

441 §605(b)(2), 42 U.S.C. §7671d(b)(2).

442 §605(c), 42 U.S.C. §7671d(c).

443 §605(d), 42 U.S.C. §7671d(d).

may authorize production and use of limited quantities of class II substances solely for use in medical devices.[444] In addition, EPA may allow limited quantities of class II substances to be produced solely for export to satisfy basic economic needs of developing countries which are signatories to the Montreal Protocol.[445] Until January 2015, additional production of class II substances authorized pursuant to this exception cannot exceed 110 percent of baseline year production. Authorized additional production levels will decrease after the year 2030 and EPA may not authorize this exception after January 2040.[446]

G. Accelerated Phase-Out Schedule

EPA is required to issue regulations that accelerate the phase-out schedule of class I and class II substances if scientific evidence demonstrates that such action is necessary to protect human health and the environment.[447] In addition, an accelerated schedule is required if technological progress makes acceleration practicable due to the availability of substitutes for listed substances. After notice and opportunity for public comment, EPA must issue regulations to implement modifications in the terms and conditions of the Montreal Protocol terms and conditions.[448] The Agency recently proposed regulations to implement amendments to the Montreal Protocol adopted in 1992.[449] Section 606 also authorizes any person to petition EPA to accelerate the reduction schedule.[450]

H. Exchange Authority

EPA must provide for trading of class I and class II production allowances between regulated entities.[451] Exchanges will be permitted on the basis of the ozone depletion potential of the chemical being traded.[452] Allowances for class I or class II substances can only be exchanged for allowances of substances in the same group of the same class. Thus, CFCs of similar ozone depletion potential can be traded, but CFCs cannot be traded for halons, carbon tetrachloride, or methyl chloroform. Allowance traders are subject to enforceable and quantifiable reductions in annual productions.[453] Those reductions must ''result in greater total reductions in the production in each year of class I and class II substances than would occur in that year in the absence of such transactions.''[454] In addition, EPA must issue rules providing for the exchange of consumption allowances.[455]

---

[444] §605(d)(1), 42 U.S.C. §7671d(d)(1).

[445] §605(d)(2)(A), 42 U.S.C. §7671d(d)(2)(A).

[446] §605(d)(2)(B), 42 U.S.C. §7671d(d)(2)(B).

[447] §606, 42 U.S.C. §7671e.

[448] §606(a)(2)-(3), 42 U.S.C. §7671e(a)(2)-(3).

[449] 58 Fed. Reg. 15,014 (1993).

[450] §606(b), 42 U.S.C. §7671e(b).

[451] §607(a), 42 U.S.C. §7671f(a).

[452] §607(b), 42 U.S.C. §7671f(b).

[453] §607(c), 42 U.S.C. §7671f(c).

[454] §607(a), 42 U.S.C. §7671f(a).

[455] §607(d), 42 U.S.C. §7671f(d). Final regulations were published in July 1992. 57 Fed. Reg. 33,754 (1992).

I. Recycling and Emission Reduction Program

Section 608 requires EPA to adopt regulations for safe use and disposal of controlled substances. While the other sections of Title VI only address production and consumption of listed substances, section 608 has an impact on manufacturers that make products containing listed substances or use them to manufacture other commodities such as electronics. EPA failed to meet its statutory deadline for promulgating regulations that govern the use and disposal of class I and class II substances used in appliances and industrial process refrigeration.[456] Once promulgated, the regulations must prohibit anyone who services, repairs, or disposes of appliances from knowingly releasing or disposing listed substances.[457]

EPA must require listed substances present in bulk in appliances, machines, or other goods to be removed for recovery and recycling prior to delivery or disposal of those affected products.[458] Furthermore, manufacture and sale of appliances, machines, or other goods containing listed substances in bulk are prohibited unless the commodities are equipped to recapture listed substances during servicing or disposal.[459] Disposal of items containing listed substances must be conducted so as to minimize the release of the substances into the environment.

For those class I and class II substances not previously addressed pursuant to section 608(a)(1), EPA must promulgate regulations establishing standards and requirements for their use and disposal by November 15, 1994.[460] EPA must require (1) reductions in the use and emission of substances to the lowest achievable level, (2) maximization of recycling, and possibly (3) use of alternative substances.[461]

EPA was required to promulgate regulations for motor vehicle air conditioner servicing by November 1991.[462] As of January 1992, servicers of motor vehicle air conditioners must use refrigerant recycling equipment certified by EPA.[463] In addition, those using the equipment must be trained and certified in the use of the approved equipment.

J. Nonessential Products

EPA was required to promulgate regulations that prohibit the sale of nonessential products that release class I substances into the environment at any time during their manufacture, use, storage, or disposal effective November 15,

---

456 §608(a)(1), 42 U.S.C. §7671g(a)(1).

457 §608(c)(1), 42 U.S.C. §7671(c)(1). Small releases of listed substances that occur during good faith efforts to capture, recycle, or dispose of class I and class II substances are exempt from this provision.

458 §608(b), 42 U.S.C. §7671g(b).

459 §608(b)(2), 42 U.S.C. §7671g(b)(2).

460 §608(a)(2), 42 U.S.C. §7671g(a)(2).

461 §608(a)(2), 42 U.S.C. §7671g(a)(2).

462 §609(a), 42 U.S.C. §7671h(a). Regulations were proposed in September 1991 with supplemental provisions in April 1992. 56 Fed. Reg. 43,842 (1991); 57 Fed. Reg. 14,764 (1992). EPA issued the final rule in July 1992. 57 Fed. Reg. 31,242 (1992); *see also* 58 Fed. Reg. 28,660 (1993).

463 §609h(c), 42 U.S.C. §7671h(c).

1992.[464] The following products are specifically identified under section 610: (1) CFC-propelled plastic party streamers and noise horns, (2) cleaning fluids for noncommercial electronic and photographic equipment, and (3) other consumer products that EPA determines to be nonessential.[465]

In addition, as of January 1994, no person can sell or distribute any aerosol product or pressurized container that contains a class II substance or any plastic foam product that contains or is manufactured with a class II substance.[466] An exception is carved out for foam insulation or products used for vehicle safety where no substitute substance meets safety standards. Certain aerosol or pressurized dispensers, such as fire fighting equipment, are exempted from this prohibition if EPA determines that they are essential for worker safety.[467]

K. Labeling

By May 15, 1993, warning labels must be conspicuously displayed on all containers and certain products containing[468] class I and class II substances. The warning must state that the substance identified on the label harms the public health and environment by destroying ozone in the upper atmosphere.[469] Products manufactured with[470] class I substances also must be so labeled by May 15, 1993. Labels for those products will not be required if EPA determines that there are no alternative products or manufacturing processes that (1) do not rely on use of the class I substance, (2) reduce the overall risk to human health and the environment, and (3) are currently or potentially available.[471] After January 2015, all products manufactured with a class I substance must display a warning label.

Products containing or manufactured with a class II substance must display a warning label if the Agency determines that there are alternative products and manufacturing processes that (1) do not rely on the use of the class II substance,

---

[464] §610(c), 42 U.S.C. §7671i(c). EPA proposed regulations in January 1992 which were made final in January 1993. *See* 57 Fed. Reg. 1992 (1992); 58 Fed. Reg. 4768 (1993).

[465] In making its determination about the essential nature of products, EPA is directed to consider "the purpose of intended use of the product, the technological availability of substitutes for such products and for such class I substance, safety, health, and other relevant factors." §610(b)(3), 42 U.S.C. §7671i(b)(3).

[466] §610(d), 42 U.S.C. §7671i(d).

[467] §610(d)(2), 42 U.S.C. §7671i(d)(2).

[468] In its implementing regulations, EPA did not adopt a de minimis exclusion for products containing trace quantities of a controlled substance. The Agency, however, concluded that a label would not be required for products in which trace quantities of a controlled substance remain as a residue or impurity due to a chemical reaction, and where the controlled substance serves no useful purpose in or for the product itself. 40 C.F.R. §82.106(b)(1).

[469] §611(b), 42 U.S.C. §7671j(b). EPA published proposed implementing regulations in May 1992 and final regulations in February 1993. *See* 57 Fed. Reg. 19,166 (1992); 58 Fed. Reg. 8135 (1993).

[470] EPA's implementing regulations define the phrase "manufactured with" to mean that the manufacturer of the product itself used a controlled substance directly in the product's manufacturing. Component parts included with the final product that are manufactured using controlled substances presumably would not constitute "manufacturing with" ODSs. Nor is a product deemed to be manufactured with ODSs if (1) the product has had no physical contact with the controlled substance, (2) the manufacturing equipment has had only intermittent contact with an ODS, or (3) the ODS has been transformed (used and consumed), except for trace quantities. 58 Fed. Reg. 8135, 8165 (1993); 40 C.F.R. §82.106(b).

[471] §611(d)(2), 42 U.S.C. §7671j(d)(2). In its implementing regulations, EPA excluded all products manufactured using methyl chloroform or CFC-113 by persons who certify a 95% reduction over the 1990 usage of that substance during the previous year. 58 Fed. Reg. 8135, 8165 (1993); 40 C.F.R. §82.106(b)(2).

(2) reduce the risk to human health and the environment, and (3) are currently or potentially available.[472] All products containing or manufactured with a class II substance must display a warning label after January 2015.[473] Products intended for export outside of the United States are exempt from labeling because they are not "introduced into interstate commerce."[474]

Any person may petition the Agency to impose the labeling requirements on products that contain a class II substance or any listed substance not otherwise subject to labeling requirements.[475] EPA has six months to grant the petition and another six months to adopt a rule imposing labeling requirements. EPA must provide a written explanation for petition denials. Compliance with labeling requirements does not create a defense to product liability claims, or allow for a reduction in damages in federal or state civil and criminal actions other than a suit brought for failure to comply with labeling requirements.[476]

L. Safe Alternatives

Section 612 emphasizes a policy to maximize and expedite replacement of class I and class II substances with substances less harmful to public health and the environment. EPA was required to promulgate rules by November 1992 to prohibit substitution of listed substances with alternatives that EPA determines to cause adverse effects to human health or the environment.[477] EPA, however, must identify an available alternative before prohibiting substitutes to listed substances. Thus, EPA must produce a list of safe alternatives and those substitutes the Agency deems unsafe for particular uses. Any person is authorized to petition EPA to add or delete a substance from either the list of safe alternatives or the list of prohibited substitute substances.[478]

EPA is required to promote research to identify safe alternatives to class I and class II substances as well as alternatives to manufacturing processes that use them.[479] In this program, EPA is directed to use federal research facilities and recommend programs to aid users of listed substances in developing alternatives. The program must include recommendations for a federal procurement policy that promotes prompt transition by the federal government to the use of safe alternatives. Initiatives such as commercial technology transfers and provisions for a public clearinghouse to collect and provide information concerning alternative chemicals and manufacturing processes must also be included in the program.[480] Furthermore, any person producing an alternative to

---

[472] §611(c)(1), (d)(1), 42 U.S.C. §7671j(c)(1), (d)(1).

[473] §611(c)(2), (e)(5), 42 U.S.C. §7671j(c)(2), (e)(5).

[474] 40 C.F.R. §82.106(b)(3).

[475] §611(e), 42 U.S.C. §7671j(e).

[476] §611(f), 42 U.S.C. §7671j(f).

[477] EPA issued proposed rules in January 1992 and May 1993. 57 Fed. Reg. 1984 (1992) and 58 Fed. Reg. 28,094 (1993). The final rule is expected in February 1994.

[478] EPA has three months to grant or deny the petition and must explain in writing its decision to deny a petition. If the petition is granted, the Agency has six months to publish the revised list. §612(d), 42 U.S.C. §7671k(d).

[479] §612(a), 42 U.S.C. §7671k(a).

[480] §612(b), 42 U.S.C. §7671k(b).

a class I substance must provide EPA with health and safety studies conducted in evaluating the substitute substance.[481]

VII. Title II—Mobile Sources

The CAA contains a program for motor vehicle emission controls and fuels that works in conjunction with the state and local emission reductions programs for stationary sources discussed above. Vehicle emissions are primarily regulated through tailpipe standards that specify permissible levels of emissions from cars, light duty trucks, and heavy duty trucks. Different standards apply depending on the vehicle age and mileage. In addition, presale certification, inspection and maintenance, on-board diagnostics systems, reporting requirements, and manufacturers' warranties are included in Title II to ensure that the emission standards are met. Mobile source provisions in the 1990 Amendments require further reductions in emissions from conventional vehicles and fuels, and tighten the standards for compliance and related maintenance requirements. Motor vehicles also may be subject to air toxics requirements because the 1990 Amendments require EPA to study and develop regulations to control HAP emissions from vehicles and fuels.

The 1990 Amendments added new requirements for motor vehicle fuels. To implement the Title I nonattainment programs, EPA was required to issue regulations for reformulated fuels to be used in the worst ozone nonattainment areas. Moreover, motor vehicles in certain CO nonattainment areas will be required to use oxygenated gasoline. The 1990 Amendments further required EPA to develop clean fuel standards for a pilot program to be implemented in California. Vehicle fleets as well as urban buses are covered in the pilot program.

A. Early Vehicle Emission Controls

The 1965 Motor Vehicle Air Pollution Control Act[482] created the first federal program to control emissions from new motor vehicles. Public health, technological feasibility, and economic costs were the basis of these early emission standards.

The most radical feature of the 1970 CAA was its prescribed emission standards for passenger cars, expressed in terms of grams per mile. These prescribed standards represented a 90 percent reduction from 1970 hydrocarbon (HC) and carbon monoxide (CO) levels by 1975, and nitrogen oxides (NO_2) by 1976.[483] The 1970 CAA authorized EPA to suspend the effective date of those standards for one year, which was done in 1973.[484] Congress extended it one year further in 1974.

---

[481] §612(e), 42 U.S.C. §7671k(e). The Toxic Substances Control Act may impose similar, but additional requirements to provide EPA copies of such studies.

[482] Pub. L. No. 89-272, 79 Stat. 992.

[483] Pub. L. No. 91-604, 84 Stat. 1676, §6(a); 42 U.S.C. §7521(a)(1), (2).

[484] EPA issued standards in July 1972. 36 Fed. Reg. 12,658 (1972). EPA initially denied manufacturers' applications to suspend the effective date of the standards. The Agency's decision was successfully challenged despite the technology-forcing nature of the statute. International Harvester v. Ruckelshaus, 478 F.2d 615 (D.C. Cir. 1973). The extensions for standards were issued in 1973. 38 Fed. Reg. 10,317 (1973).

Because the automobile industry had not fully met these requirements by 1977, Congress further extended the effective date of HC and CO emissions standards until 1980, and until 1981 for NO_2.[485] Moreover, the NO_2 standard was relaxed to 1 gpm (gram per mile) for major light duty vehicle (LDV) manufacturers and 2.0 gpm for low volume manufacturers.[486] The 1977 Amendments also prescribed standards for heavy duty vehicles (HDV).[487] The same 90 percent reduction of HC and CO was required of HDVs and LDVs by model year 1983 as well as a requirement for 75 percent reduction in NO_2 by model year 1985.[488] EPA badly missed the deadlines for these standards—by more than four years in some cases.

The 1977 Amendments added nonconformance penalties for manufacturers who do not comply with the emissions standards on new motor vehicles, but remain below an upper limit determined by EPA. Section 206(g) permitted manufacturers to pay a penalty equal to the cost of compliance as determined by EPA.[489]

Until the 1990 Amendments, only California was allowed to set automotive emission standards more stringent than federal requirements; all other states had to enforce federal standards if they imposed any. The 1990 Amendments allowed states to adopt either the federal standard or the more stringent California standard. In 1990, Congress also added extensive programs for clean fuel vehicles and clean fuel components together with the revised tailpipe emissions standards and attainment schedules.

B. Tailpipe Standards

EPA has broad authority to set tailpipe standards for new motor vehicles under section 202(a).[490] The 1990 Amendments set short term (Tier I) and longer term (Tier II) standards for cars and LDVs which effectively require at least another 50 percent reduction in automotive emissions by model year 1996.

[485] Pub. L. No. 95-95, 91 Stat. 685, §201; 42 U.S.C. §7521(b)(1)(A)(Supp. 1984–1990).

[486] 42 U.S.C. §7521(b)(1)(B)(Supp. 1984–1990). LDVs are passenger cars that hold 12 passengers or less. 40 C.F.R. pt. 86.082.2 (1990).

LDVs no longer include trucks with a gross weight below 6,000 lbs. following International Harvester v. Ruckelshaus, 478 F.2d 615 (D.C. Cir. 1973). The 1977 Amendments additionally authorized manufacturers developing innovative emissions control technology to comply with a NO_2 standard of 1.5 gpm. 42 U.S.C. §7521(B)(4)(Supp. 1984–1990). EPA was authorized to grant extensions for compliance with CO standards up to two years, but this provision was repealed by the 1990 Amendments. 42 U.S.C. §7521(B)(5)(A), (B).

New tailpipe emissions rules are expected to further reduce NO_2 as well as HC and CO. 56 Fed. Reg. 25,724 (1991).

[487] §202(b)(3)(C), 42 U.S.C. §7521(b)(3)(C). HDVs are those trucks, buses, or other vehicles designed for use on public roads that have a gross weight exceeding 6,000 lbs.

Although the 1977 Amendments suspended EPA's discretionary regulation of HDVs, EPA retained authority to impose standards consistent with best available technology if the statutory standards were infeasible.

[488] The ''model year'' affected by CAA standards refers to the manufacturer's production period which included January 1 even if the production commences during the year prior to the effective date. §202(a)(3)(A)(ii), 42 U.S.C. §7521(a)(3)(A)(ii)(Supp. 1984–1990). EPA did not promulgate standards for 1985 model year HDVs until early 1985. The standards for NO_2 and PM were designed to become more rigid for model years 1991 and 1994. EPA's regulations were upheld against interest group challenges. NRDC v. EPA, 805 F.2d 410 (D.C. Cir. 1986).

[489] 42 U.S.C. §7525(g)(Supp. 1984–1990). EPA proposed nonconformance penalties that manufacturers of heavy duty engines and vehicles that do not meet standards can pay to receive a certificate of nonconformity. 57 Fed. Reg. 22,675 (1992).

[490] 42 U.S.C. §7521(a).

The requirements are phased in over three model years, ending in model year 1996. The standards are phased in for vehicles with a gross vehicle weight rating (GVWR) up to 6,000 pounds, effective for model year 1994,[491] and for vehicles with a GVWR greater than 6,000 pounds, effective for model year 1995.[492] Before new cars and light duty trucks (LDTs) can be sold to the public, manufacturers must meet certification standards.[493] For the first two years that they are subject to short term (Tier I) standards, intermediate in-use requirements apply. To facilitate the transition to compliance with the emissions standards, these standards are phased in over a period of three years by making them applicable to an increasing percentage of a manufacturer's total sales volume. Thus, pursuant to section 202, 40 percent of model year 1994 vehicles, 80 percent of model year 1995 vehicles, and 100 percent of vehicles manufactured after model year 1995 must comply with emissions standards.[494] EPA is required to consider technological feasibility and cost effectiveness of more stringent tailpipe standards and review the current standards for useful life of a car or LDT.[495]

1. *Refueling and Evaporative Emission Controls*

The 1990 Amendments required EPA to consult with the Department of Transportation (DOT) and develop standards to control motor vehicle refueling evaporative emissions by use of vehicle-based (on-board) controls pursuant to

---

[491] §202(g), 42 U.S.C. §7521(g).

Emissions Standards* for LDVs and LDTs
GVWR up to 6,000 lbs.

	Column A (5 Yrs/50,000 mi)				Column B (10 Yrs/100,000 mi)			
	NMHC**	CO	NO_2	PM (diesel)	NMHC	CO	NO_2	PM (diesel)
LDT (0–3,750 lbs. LVW) and light duty vehicles	0.25	3.4	0.4	0.08	0.31	4.2	0.6	0.10
LDTs (3,750–5,750 lbs. LVW)	0.32	4.4	0.7	0.08	0.40	5.5	0.97	0.10

*Standards are expressed in grams per mile.
**Nonmethane Hydrocarbons

[492] §202(h), 42 U.S.C. §7521(h).

Emissions Standards* for LDT
GVWR above 6,000 lbs.

LDT Test Weight	Column A (5 Yrs/50,000 mi)			Column B (11 Yrs/120,000 mi)			
	NMHC	CO	NO_2	NMHC	CO	NO_2	PM
3,751–5,750 lbs.	0.32	4.4	0.7	0.46	6.4	0.98	0.10
Above 5,750 lbs.	0.39	5.0	1.1	0.56	7.3	1.53	0.12

*Standards are expressed in grams per mile.

[493] EPA proposed test procedures for certification of natural gas fueled and liquified petroleum gas fueled LDVs, LDTs, HDVs, engines, and motorcycles in November 1992 to be effective model year 1994. 57 Fed. Reg. 52,912 (1992). The regulations also include fuel economy test procedures for model year 1993 vehicles.

[494] §202(g), 42 U.S.C. §7521(g).

[495] §202(i), 42 U.S.C. §7521(i). Section 203 extends the useful life of LDVs and engines. The term "useful life" refers to the period of time for which vehicles must comply with applicable standards. It is significant because it sets the durability standards for certifying a vehicle model and the duration that a specified class of vehicles is subject to recall for its failure to conform to emission standards. Thus, useful life provides a mechanism for enforcing motor vehicle emissions standards and controls.

section 202(a)(6). DOT aruged that installation of on-board controls increases the risk of explosions when vehicles collide. Consequently, EPA declined to promulgate regulations[496] but lost a court challenge,[497] and is now drafting such standards. Section 202(k) of the 1990 Amendments requires EPA to issue regulations to control evaporative emissions that occur while the vehicle is in operation or while the vehicle is at rest two or more days during hot weather conditions when emissions are increased.[498] The 1990 Amendments required EPA to commence rulemaking for section 202(k) by November 1991, something it failed to do.

2. *Mobile Source Related Air Toxics*

The 1990 Amendments require EPA to study hazardous air pollutants from motor vehicles and motor fuels pursuant to section 202.[499] The study must examine the feasibility and necessity of controlling these toxic pollutants as well as the means for controlling such emissions. EPA's April 1992 deadline for issuing the report has passed, but pursuant to court order, EPA finalized the study in April 1993.[500] The study must address emissions of the most toxic pollutants emitted by cars, including at a minimum, benzene and formaldehyde.[501] Following the study, EPA must promulgate regulations for vehicles, fuels, or both by April 1995, which reflect "the greatest degree of emission reduction achievable . . . [as well as] costs of the technology, and noise, energy and safety factors, and lead time."[502] The debates over these standards are likely to focus initially on the need for controls, and whether those controls should be imposed on motor fuels or motor vehicles, and upon what particular toxic pollutants.

3. *On-Board Diagnostic Systems*

On-board diagnostics (OBD) systems identify emission-related system malfunctions or deterioration during the vehicle's useful life. An OBD alerts a vehicle operator to maintain and repair the system and also stores diagnostic fault codes that can be retrieved by a mechanic in order to help in the repair of emission control systems. All passenger cars and light duty trucks are subject to OBD requirements pursuant to section 202(m).[503] In addition, EPA may require manufacturers of heavy duty vehicles to install OBD systems. States must

---

[496] 57 Fed. Reg. 13,046 (1992); 57 Fed. Reg. 13,220 (1992).

[497] NRDC v. EPA, No. 92-1137 (D.C. Cir. Apr. 2, 1992). The NRDC has continued to challenge EPA's position on on-board evaporative emissions controls asserting that because the CAA is a technology-forcing statute, a safe system must be devised even if one is not currently available. EPA maintains that Stage II controls installed at service stations will provide adequate controls without any associated safety concerns. On January 22, 1993, the court of appeals ruled that EPA is required by the CAA to issue standards that required passenger cars and LDTs to be equipped with vapor recovery systems. 23 Env't Rep. 2575 (Jan. 28, 1993).

[498] 42 U.S.C. §7521(k). Regulations for emissions lost while vehicles are at rest on hot surfaces are provided at 40 C.F.R. pt. 86.090-8(b). In October 1992, EPA issued a draft final rule requiring state inspection and maintenance programs to include two evaporative emissions tests to check the system for leaks and proper purging of reclaimed fuel.

[499] 42 U.S.C. §7521(l).

[500] 58 Fed. Reg. 27,283 (1993).

[501] §202(a), 42 U.S.C. §7521(a).

[502] §202(l)(2), 42 U.S.C. §7521(l)(2).

[503] 42 U.S.C. §7521(m).

establish programs to inspect OBD systems as part of their routine inspection and maintenance programs. The regulations are required to take effect in model year 1994. Pursuant to court order, EPA agreed to promulgate overdue regulations by January 1993, requiring manufacturers to install OBD systems.[504]

4. *Cold Temperature CO Emissions Standards*

The 1990 Amendments require EPA to establish an emissions standard of 10.0 gpm for model year 1994 cars or LDTs below 3,750 pounds and 12.5 gpm for LDTs above 3,750 pounds operated at 20 degrees Fahrenheit. With this provision, Congress recognized that automotive engines usually run ''dirtier'' under very cold weather conditions, especially with respect to carbon monoxide (CO).[505] The cold temperature CO standards are phased in over a three-year period requiring compliance by 40 percent of the manufacturer's sales volume in 1994, 80 percent in 1995, and 100 percent thereafter.[506] Section 202(j)(2) requires EPA to determine by June 1997 whether additional cold weather CO emission reductions are necessary for model year 2001 and later LDVs and LDTs operated at 20 degrees Fahrenheit. Furthermore, if by June 1997, the CO design value of six or more nonattainment areas is 9.5 ppm or above, EPA must establish phase II cold temperature CO standards of 3.4 gpm for passenger cars and 4.4 gpm for LDTs below 6,000 pounds with a comparable level for HDVs above 6,000 pounds beginning with model year 2002.[507]

C. Urban Bus Standards

Section 219 of the 1990 Amendments set performance standards to regulate emissions from urban buses beginning with model year 1994. These standards must be based on the best technology that can be reasonably anticipated to be available when regulations are imposed and must consider costs, safety, energy, and lead time. The particulate emissions from HDVs must be reduced by 50 percent.[508] EPA must conduct annual tests beginning with model year 1994 urban buses to determine whether they are meeting the standards when in

---

[504] Proposed regulations were published in September of 1991. 56 Fed. Reg. 48,272 (1991). Final regulations were issued on February 19, 1993. 58 Fed. Reg. 9468 (1993).

[505] EPA issued the overdue final regulations in July 1992. 57 Fed. Reg. 31,888 (1992). Currently CO emissions are measured at temperatures between 68 and 86 degrees Fahrenheit. More than half the nonattainment area violations for CO, however, occur at temperatures below 45 degrees. The regulations apply for the useful life of 50,000 miles. The motor vehicle industry is not permitted to average the 10 gpm standard over the entire fleet. Consequently, each vehicle must meet the limit.

[506] §202(j)(1), 42 U.S.C. §7521(j)(1).

[507] §202(j)(2)(B)(i), 42 U.S.C. §7521(j)(2)(B)(i). Certain nonattainment areas are excluded from EPA's determination where CO problems result primarily from stationary sources. §202(j)(2)(B)(ii), 42 U.S.C. §7521(j)(2)(B)(ii).

[508] EPA proposed regulations that would delay particulate standards for model year 1993 buses. 56 Fed. Reg. 24,242 (1991). In 1993, buses must comply with the standards limiting particulate emissions to .1g/BHP Hr (grams per brake horse power hour).

EPA issued revised regulations in July 1992, applicable to urban buses built in or before 1993, whose engines are rebuilt or retrofitted after January 1995. The program is applicable to areas where more than 80% of buses are in use in areas with a population of 750,000 and above. 57 Fed. Reg. 33,141 (1992). EPA provides one option for averaging particulate emissions in those urban bus fleets or a second option for allowing bus operators to install equipment that would meet an alternative standard if engine repairs would otherwise exceed a specified cost.

full use during their useful life. If the annual study reveals that a percentage of the buses tested does not meet the standards, EPA must promulgate low-pollution fuel requirements for urban buses, which will be phased in over a period of three years. New urban buses must operate exclusively on low polluting fuels.[509] EPA was required to issue regulations for urban bus emission standards and control technology by May 1992. EPA has not met those deadlines, but pursuant to court order, agreed to issue enforcement procedures by the end of May 1993 and urban bus emission standards and standards for emissions from rebuilt bus engines by February 1995.

D. Motor Vehicle and Engine Compliance Testing Certification, and Information Collection

EPA must require manufacturers to provide data so that the agency can determine whether vehicles will meet emission standards throughout their useful life pursuant to section 206(a).[510] Manufacturers must test vehicles in accordance with EPA regulations[511] in order to obtain a certificate of conformity before that model can be sold to the public. If manufacturers sell vehicles without a certificate, they are subject to civil penalties of up to $25,000 per vehicle under section 205.[512]

EPA was required by November 1991 to devise a new certification test procedure that evaluates whether model year 1994 passenger cars, LDVs, and LDTs could pass state emissions inspections. The test procedures are required to evaluate emission levels anticipated under actual driving conditions and conditions encountered during inspection and maintenance procedures.[513] EPA was required to review and modify certification test procedures as needed by June 1992. EPA failed to complete its review, but has agreed to take final action to revise or maintain current testing procedures by December 1994 pursuant to court order.[514]

Manufacturers must maintain records and submit reports on the results of testing to the Agency so that EPA can verify compliance with the Act.[515] EPA has expanded authority under the 1990 Amendments to inspect manufacturers' facilities and records.

---

[509] §219(c)(2), 42 U.S.C. §7554(c)(2). Low polluting fuels include propane, natural gas, and fuels that use ethanol and methanol.

[510] 42 U.S.C. §7525(a).

[511] 40 C.F.R. Subchapter C.

[512] 42 U.S.C. §7524.

[513] §206(h), 42 U.S.C. §7525(h).

For HDVs, EPA has authorized emission averaging under §206. This allows a manufacturer to certify one vehicle type even though its emissions exceed regulatory standards if the same manufacturer certifies that another vehicle it produces has lower emissions, as long as the average of the two, based on number of such vehicles sold, does not exceed the standard. EPA's position on emissions averaging was challenged and upheld by the courts in NRDC v. EPA, 805 F.2d 410, 425 (D.C. Cir. 1986).

EPA has also allowed banking of emissions credits by manufacturers that allow them to average emissions over a period of years as well as trading credits between manufacturers. 55 Fed. Reg. 30,584 (1990). EPA is also authorized to test cars under production for their compliance with emission standards even though the manufacturer has completed certification procedures. §206(b)(1), 42 U.S.C. §7525(b)(1).

[514] In addition, §215 requires manufacturers to ensure emission performance standards at high altitudes. 42 U.S.C. §7549.

[515] §211, 42 U.S.C. §7542.

E. Emission Control Warranties

Since the 1970 Act, automotive manufacturers have had to warrant that vehicles or engines are designed, built, and equipped to conform to emission standards at the time of their sale and for their useful life pursuant to section 207(a).[516] Manufacturers must further guarantee that the vehicle or engine is free from defects in material or workmanship that could lead to noncompliance during the vehicle's or engine's useful life. Thus, the warranty applies to latent defects as well as defects existing at the time of manufacture. Moreover, section 207(b) requires manufacturers to warrant that the vehicle will operate in compliance with emission standards if properly used and maintained during its useful life.

The 1990 Amendments extend the warranty duration for 1995 and later model year major emission control components used in passenger cars, LDTs, and engines. The prior warranty period was five years or 50,000 miles. The warranty period beginning with model year 1995 is eight years or 80,000 miles, whichever occurs first for major emissions components that include catalytic converters, electric emissions control units, and OBD systems.[517] Other emission control components are subject to a warranty period if they were not in general use on vehicles and engines before 1990 and have an installation cost that exceeds $200. The warranty for all other components is two years or 24,000 miles, whichever occurs first. EPA has authority to compel manufacturers to recall and repair vehicles upon the agency's determination that a substantial number of any class of vehicles or engines does not conform to the regulations when in actual use during their useful life. Manufacturers contesting an EPA recall order are entitled to a public hearing before an administrative law judge.[518]

F. State Standards

The CAA provisions for motor vehicle emissions standards preempt state standards, with the exception of certain ones adopted by the state of California. California had imposed its own emission standards before the federal program was legislated and many of the federal standards are modeled on the California program.[519] Under section 209, EPA may grant a waiver to California if EPA determines that California's program is at least as stringent as the federal program and is not otherwise excessive or arbitrary and capricious.[520] Thus far, EPA has approved California's waiver requests since the 1970 Act. In addition, section 177 was amended in 1990 to authorize states with approved SIPs

---

516 42 U.S.C. §7541(a).

517 §207(c), 42 U.S.C. §7541(c).

518 Under the regulations, recalls are typically initiated voluntarily at the request of manufacturers. *See* 40 C.F.R. §85.1901.

519 California first issued motor vehicle emissions regulations in 1959. 1959 Cal. Stat. ch. 200, §1 (repealed 1967). The California Air Resources Board (CARB) has promulgated comprehensive regulations which have been incorporated in the California Health and Safety Code. CAL. HEALTH & SAFETY CODE §43101.

520 The waiver requirements for the California standards are addressed in Motor & Equip. Mfrs. Ass'n v. EPA, 627 F.2d 1095 (D.C. Cir. 1979).

to adopt California's standards that EPA has authorized through waivers if they adopt them two years before a specified model year's effective date.[521] So far, New York,[522] Massachusetts, and Texas have adopted the California standards.[523]

G. Nonroad Engines and Vehicles

By November 1991, EPA was required to complete a study of the public health and welfare effects of nonroad engines and vehicle emissions pursuant to section 213.[524] If the study reveals that nonroad engines and vehicles (excluding locomotive engines) contribute to ozone or CO in nonattainment areas, EPA will have to develop regulations to control their emissions. The regulations must require the greatest degree of emission reductions possible while taking into consideration technological feasibility, cost, noise, energy, safety, and lead time. The implementation schedule for these standards is not provided in the Act.

A separate provision in section 213 is included for locomotives and locomotive engines.[525] EPA is required to issue regulations to control emissions from these sources by November 1995 with an effective date as early as possible taking into account lead time and development of control technology. The locomotive emission standards must require best available technology, taking into account cost, energy, and safety and noise considerations.

H. Aircraft Emission Standards

The 1970 CAA required EPA to study and investigate emissions of air pollutants from aircraft to determine how their emissions affected air quality control regions (AQCRs) and the technological feasibility of controlling their emissions.[526] The CAA requires EPA, after consultation with DOT, to issue rules to control such emissions from many types of aircraft engines, rules that reflected costs of compliance and the development of requisite technology.[527] These emission standards must be coordinated with noise standards applicable to aircraft and aircraft engines.

---

[521] 42 U.S.C. §7507.

[522] Two auto industry groups have challenged New York State's adoption of the California standards. Motor Vehicle Mfrs. Ass'n v. NYSDEC, No. 92-CV-869 (N.D.N.Y. July 9, 1992). Plaintiffs claim that New York's adoption of California vehicle standards which are designed to operate on California fuels requires complete redesign of the New York vehicles. They argue this has the effect of creating a third type of car, a burden that the CAA did not intend to impose on manufacturers. The legal challenge to New York's adoption of the California standards is currently on appeal to the Second Circuit following the district court's determination that there was insufficient evidence from the automobile manufacturers and the state regarding the effect of standard fuels on emission control systems.

[523] The following states are considering adopting the California program: Connecticut, Illinois, Maine, Maryland, New Hampshire, New Jersey, Pennsylvania, Rhode Island, Vermont, Virginia, and Washington.

[524] 42 U.S.C. §7547.

[525] §213(a)(5), 42 U.S.C. §7547(a)(5).

[526] §231, 42 U.S.C. §7571.

[527] Aircraft emission standards are codified at 40 C.F.R. pt. 87. Regulations could be disapproved by the President if DOT determined that they threaten aircraft safety.

I. Regulation of Fuels

EPA has had authority to control or prohibit mobile source fuels and fuel additives since passage of the 1970 CAA.[528] Manufacturers must notify EPA of any fuel additive and make reports about them available to the public, unless the manufacturer demonstrates the need for confidentiality.[529] Fuels and fuel additives cannot be marketed unless they are first registered with EPA.[530] Section 211 makes it unlawful for any manufacturer to introduce into commerce any fuel or fuel additive that is not substantially similar to a fuel or additive used to certify model year 1975 or later vehicles.[531] This prohibition is not absolute, however, because a manufacturer can apply and receive a waiver if it demonstrates that the fuel or fuel additive will not cause or contribute to increases in emissions.[532] EPA holds applicants for waivers to a high standard.[533]

The Agency must first determine that emissions from regulated fuels and fuel additives cause or contribute to air pollution that may "reasonably be anticipated to endanger the public health or welfare"[534] or will impair to a "significant degree the performance of any emission control device or system likely to be in general use."[535] In making this determination, EPA is required to consider all available scientific and economic data, including a cost benefit analysis comparing emission control devices in use with and without imposition of section 211 controls.[536] EPA has exercised section 211 authority to regulate lead and phosphorus content in gasoline, sulphur content in diesel fuel, and gasoline volatility. These regulations, though quite controversial at the time they were first adopted, are now recognized as a major cause of air quality improvement.

1. Lead Content Regulations

EPA first issued lead content regulations in 1973 in anticipation of auto manufacturers' need to meet 1975 emissions standards though the use of catalytic converters. The catalysts are "poisoned"—ruined—by lead after a

---

[528] §211(a), 42 U.S.C. §7545(a). Regulations are found at 40 C.F.R. pts. 79 and 80.

[529] §208, 42 U.S.C. §7542; 40 C.F.R. §80.26.

[530] §211(a), 42 U.S.C. §7545(a).

[531] §211(f)(1)(B), 42 U.S.C. §7545(f)(1)(B). The "substantially similar" language of this provision has been controversial. An interpretive rule for "substantially similar" under §211(f) is found at 46 Fed. Reg. 38,583 (1981) and amended at 56 Fed. Reg. 5352 (1991). EPA also proposed an interpretive rule with regard to diesel fuel and fuel additives to clarify the meaning of "substantially similar" at 56 Fed. Reg. 24,362 (1991).

[532] §211(f), 42 U.S.C. §7545(f).

[533] EPA's decision to grant a waiver is based on long term durability testing or adequate alternative means for evaluating effects of alternative fuels or fuel additives. It is not necessary for EPA to determine that a fuel or fuel additive will not cause or contribute to "any" emission increase. Motor Vehicle Mfr's Ass'n v. EPA, 768 F.2d 385, 390–93 (D.C. Cir. 1985). The D.C. Circuit has held that once a waiver is granted, EPA can only revoke it through its §211(c) regulatory authority. American Methyl Corp. v. EPA, 749 F.2d 826, 835 (D.C. Cir. 1984). In Motor Vehicle Mfrs. Ass'n v. EPA, the D.C. Circuit also held that although EPA cannot revoke a §211(f) waiver, the courts can reverse an arbitrary and capricious decision by EPA to grant a waiver. 768 F.2d 385, 393–402 (D.C. Cir. 1985).

[534] §211(c)(1)(A), 42 U.S.C. §7545(c)(1)(A). EPA has proposed procedures to test the health effects of over 6,000 on-road fuel additives. The regulations also specify performance test standards for fuel additives. 57 Fed. Reg. 3168 (1992).

[535] §211(c)(1)(B), 42 U.S.C. §7545(c)(1)(B).

[536] §211(c), 42 U.S.C. §7545(c).

vehicle uses one or two tanks of leaded fuel. These regulations were based on EPA's authority under section 211 to prevent impairment of emissions control devices.[537] These early lead content regulations did not prohibit leaded gasoline, but required cars with a catalytic converter to be labeled as such and fitted with inlets with which only specially designed gasoline pump nozzles would be compatible.[538] This regulation required retailers to make one grade of unleaded gasoline available at larger stations throughout the country.[539]

EPA also issued lead content regulations in 1973 based on its authority to protect health and welfare under section 211.[540] These regulations sought to reduce use of leaded gasoline through the gradual phasing down of lead content by 1979. In 1982 and 1985, EPA revised the lead content regulations and tightened phase-down requirements.[541] With the 1990 Amendments, Congress imposed a complete ban on the sale of leaded gasoline for on-road motor vehicles after December 1995[542] and imposed a ban on new engines that require leaded gasoline effective in 1992.[543]

2. *Lead Substitute Gasoline Additives*

The 1990 Amendments require EPA to develop a test procedure for evaluating lead substitute gasoline additives under section 211(j)(2).[544] Independent testing of the proposed substitutes must be arranged by EPA and the results published in the *Federal Register*. EPA is authorized to impose a user fee to recover costs of testing gasoline additives proposed as lead substitutes.

3. *Phosphorus Content Regulations*

Use of phosphorus, like the use of lead, poisons catalytic converters. Phosphorus was used primarily as a detergent in gasoline. In 1973, EPA issued regulations that set maximum limits on phosphorus content in gasoline.[545]

4. *Sulfur Content Regulations*

Although EPA considered regulating sulfur content in gasoline because its presence affects the efficiency of catalytic converters, no standard has been set.[546] These sulfur emissions were an issue in the 1974 congressional action to

---

[537] §211(c)(1)(B), 42 U.S.C. §7545(c)(1)(B). Lead poisons catalytic converters that are designed to reduce HC and CO emissions.

[538] 38 Fed. Reg. 1254 (1973).

[539] The 1973 unleaded gasoline regulations were upheld in Amoco Oil Co. v. EPA, 501 F.2d 722 (D.C. Cir. 1974). The court, however, rejected provisions in the regulations for vicarious liability which would have held refiners, those at the top of the distribution chain, strictly and vicariously liable for any violation of the regulations during distribution. EPA's revised vicarious liability provisions were successfully challenged in Amoco Oil v. EPA, 543 F.2d 270 (D.C. Cir. 1976) (finding that EPA could not impose general vicarious liability for violations without a "closely integrated relationship" between those in the distribution chain).

[540] §211(c)(1)(A), 42 U.S.C. §7545(c)(1)(A).

[541] 44 Fed. Reg. 49,322 (1979); 50 Fed. Reg. 9386 (1985). A banking feature was later added to the regulations along with additions for transferable credits to give the gasoline industry greater flexibility with compliance. 50 Fed. Reg. 13,118 (1985).

[542] §211(n), 42 U.S.C. §7545(n).

[543] §218, 42 U.S.C. §7553.

[544] 42 U.S.C. §7545(j)(2).

[545] 38 Fed. Reg. 1254 (1973).

[546] *Id.*

extend the automotive compliance date. EPA has issued regulations requiring an 80 percent reduction of sulfur in diesel fuel effective October 1993.[547] Combustion of diesel fuel, as opposed to gasoline, results in releases of particulate matter containing larger concentrations of sulfur.

5. *Gasoline Volatility*

EPA issued regulations to address gasoline volatility—usually measured as Reid Vapor Pressure (RVP)—in 1989 and 1990.[548] These regulations are designed to reduce VOC emissions resulting from the evaporation of gasoline. The rules do so by requiring reductions in fuel volatility, usually in warm weather months. The RVP regulations vary for different seasons and regions of the country because ambient temperatures affect motor vehicle fuel performance. EPA was required by April 1991 to promulgate regulations imposing stricter RVP standards on nonattainment areas, effective in the summer of 1992. During the high ozone season (the summer months) gasoline cannot be sold with a RVP in excess of 9 psi (pounds per square inch), pursuant to section 211(h).[549] Some SIPs impose more stringent requirements, some as low as 7.8 psi RVP. Fuel blends that contain gasoline and 10 percent ethanol are permitted an RVP of 10 psi.[550] These regulations became an issue in the 1992 presidential election, because of political pressure from corn and grain interests producing ethanol.

6. *Reformulated Gasoline*

Reformulated gasoline refers to gasoline that is certified by EPA under section 211(k).[551] The general requirements for reformulated gasoline include limits on NO_2 emissions, a minimum oxygen content, a maximum benzene content, and no heavy metals. EPA was required to issue regulations for reformulated fuels used in certain nonattainment areas by November 1991. EPA is under a court order to supplement proposed regulations or issue final regulations for reformulated fuels by March 1993.[552] These regulations must require the greatest reduction in ozone forming VOCs and toxic air pollutants available through reformulated gasoline.[553] In defining performance standards for reformulated fuels, the 1990 Amendments identify the following air toxics:

---

[547] 55 Fed. Reg. 34,120 (1990). Final rules for sulfur content of highway diesel fuel were promulgated at 57 Fed. Reg. 19,535 (1992).

[548] 54 Fed. Reg. 11,868 (1989), 55 Fed. Reg. 23,658 (1990).

[549] 42 U.S.C. §7545(h). Proposed revisions to existing regulations restricting the volatility of gasoline sold in summer time months were released in May 1991. 56 Fed. Reg. 24,242 (1991).

[550] §211(h)(4), 42 U.S.C. §7545(h)(4).

[551] 42 U.S.C. §7545(k).

[552] EPA proposed standards and an enforcement scheme for reformulated gasoline and emission models for gasoline certification and enforcement. 56 Fed. Reg. 31,176 (1991), 57 Fed. Reg. 13,416 (1992), and 58 Fed. Reg. 11,722 (1993). The final rule was signed on December 15, 1993.

[553] Use of ethanol in reformulated fuels has been controversial. The Bush Administration had authorized reformulated fuels using ethanol 1 psi RVP higher than the psi RVP specified for other reformulated fuels. The Bush Administration was under increasing pressure from midwestern farmers who produce corn for ethanol production to make reformulated fuels using ethanol more competitive. EPA has maintained, however, that use of ethanol could increase evaporative emissions as well as emissions of NO_2 and VOCs which are precursors to ozone. Rulemaking on ethanol use in reformulated fuel is likely to continue.

benzene, 1,3 butadiene, polycyclic organic matter (POM), acetaldehyde, and formaldehyde.[554]

To satisfy VOC or air toxic performance standards, producers of reformulated gasoline must demonstrate that beginning in 1995, aggregate emissions of pollutants from use of reformulated fuels are at least 15 percent less than model year 1990 motor vehicle emissions.[555] Beginning in the year 2000, emissions must be reduced 25 percent, with a limited exception for feasibility problems.[556] In order to evaluate reformulated fuels compliance with section 211(k) provisions, EPA must establish certification procedures.

Effective January 1995, section 211(k) prohibits sale or dispensing of conventional gasoline to consumers in nine major nonattainment areas or any ozone nonattainment areas later designated as severe.[557] Also, northeast ozone transport area states—from Virginia to Maine—may request that EPA extend reformulated requirements to other areas within their boundaries that experience ozone nonattainment problems.

7. *Reformulated Gasoline Credit Program*

Those subject to reformulated gasoline requirements can participate in a credit program for fuels that exceed minimum oxygen content requirements and are below maximum aromatic HC and benzene content. These credits are marketable, but only within the nonattainment area in which the gasoline is sold. Earned credits may be used to offset the sale of gasoline with lower oxygen content and higher aromatic HC or benzene content than is required for reformulated gasoline. Credits cannot be transferred, however, where average oxygen, HC, and benzene would exceed required levels specified for reformulated fuels. EPA has not specified the averaging period used in the credit program, and it is not clear whether EPA will allow the banking of credits. Averaging and banking rules, once issued, will be important for enforcement purposes, as has been the case with lead phase-down requirements.

J. California Pilot Test Program

The 1990 Amendments included provisions for a California pilot test program to develop and observe an alternative clean fuel and clean vehicle program applicable only to LDVs and LDTs. Under the California pilot test program, 150,000 LDVs and LDTs must be manufactured and introduced into the stream of commerce effective model years 1996 through 1998.[558] By 1999, and thereafter, 300,000 clean fuel vehicles must be produced and distributed annually. Section 249 authorizes transferable credits to manufacturers that sell more than the required allocation of clean fuel vehicles.[559] Moreover, manufacturers are entitled to receive credits for selling clean fuel vehicles that meet

[554] §211(k)(10)(C), 42 U.S.C. §7545(k)(10)(C).
[555] §211(k)(10)(A), 42 U.S.C. §7545(k)(10)(A).
[556] §211(k)(3)(B)(i)(ii), 42 U.S.C. §7545(k)(3)(B)(i)(ii).
[557] §211(k)(5)(A), 42 U.S.C. §7545(k)(5)(A).
[558] §249(c)(1), 42 U.S.C. §7589(c)(1).
[559] §249(d)(1)(A), 42 U.S.C. §7589(d)(1)(A).

more rigorous clean fuel standards than otherwise are required.[560] EPA was required to establish regulations to implement the California pilot test program by November 1992.[561] EPA must report to Congress on the status of the program by June 1994 and the effectiveness of the program by June 1998.[562]

Other states are authorized to opt-in to the California pilot program.[563] The pilot program can be adopted for their serious, severe, and extreme ozone nonattainment areas.[564] To promote the voluntary opt-in program, states are authorized to collect a 1 percent registration fee from new motor vehicles that are not clean fuel vehicles and use these funds to provide financial incentives to clean fuel vehicle dealers and purchasers.[565] Additional incentives include exemptions from high occupancy requirements and parking place preferences.[566] State adoption of the California pilot test program through SIP revisions, however, cannot mandate production and sale of clean fuel vehicles or clean alternative fuels. This reflects Congress's intent to avoid imposition requirements that have the effect of necessitating the creation of a third type of low emissions vehicle. The general prohibition on mandated production and sale of clean fuel vehicles and clean fuel alternatives (with the exception of the California pilot test program) is repeated in section 250.[567]

K. Clean Fuel Vehicles

With the 1990 Amendments, Congress included provisions for unconventional fuels, the use of which can allow vehicles to meet very stringent emission limitations. Unlike reformulated or oxygenated gasoline, these fuel requirements cannot generally, at least not without dramatic modification, function in conventional vehicles. Thus, both a fleet program and a pilot test program developed by California are included to further the clean fuel vehicle provisions. EPA was required to issue clean fuel vehicle standards for LDVs, LDTs, flexible dual fuel vehicles (those capable of operating on more than one fuel), and HDTs by November 1992. The standards must be set for LDVs and LDTs below a certain weight in two phases: Phase I commences with model year 1996, and Phase II commences with model year 2001.[568] Standards for heavier LDTs and HDTs must be met in 1998. Nonmethane organic gas emissions

---

[560] §249(d)(1)(B), 42 U.S.C. §7589(d)(1)(B). The California SIP must be revised to provide a clean fuel plan that ensures alternative clean fuels will be available at an adequate number of locations throughout the state. §249(c)(2)(A), 42 U.S.C. §7589(c)(2)(A). California is authorized to adopt a clean fuel program that has more stringent requirements than the federal clean fuel program if necessary to promote health, welfare, safety, vehicle maintenance, or performance. §249(c)(2)(C), 42 U.S.C. §7589(c)(2)(C). The 1990 Amendments also require EPA to establish a federal implementation plan by November 1994 if California does not implement an adequate clean fuel program. §249(c)(2)(F), 42 U.S.C. §7589(c)(2)(F).

[561] §249(c), 42 U.S.C. §7589(c).

[562] §249(e), 42 U.S.C. §7589(e).

[563] §249(f), 42 U.S.C. §7589(f).

[564] States with ozone nonattainment areas designated as serious to extreme are already under an obligation to revise SIPs to include measures to ensure effectiveness of their clean fuel programs. §182(c)(4)(A). *See* 57 Fed. Reg. 13,498 (1992).

[565] §249(f)(3), 42 U.S.C. §7589(f)(3).

[566] §249(f)(3)(B), (C), 42 U.S.C. §7589(f)(3)(B), (C).

[567] §250(b), 42 U.S.C. §7590(b).

[568] §243(a)-(d), 42 U.S.C. §7583(a)-(d).

(NMOG) standards for flexible or duel fueled vehicles must be met beginning in model year 1996.

California may implement its own clean fuel vehicle standards if its standards are in the aggregate at least as protective of public health as the federal standards.[569] California has received a preemptive waiver from federal clean fuel vehicle standards thereby allowing its standards to be more stringent.[570] The California standards are only applicable to ozone nonattainment areas covered by the California pilot test program[571] and specified CO and ozone nonattainment areas covered by the fleet program.[572]

L. Centrally Fueled Fleets

States must revise SIPs for serious, severe, and extreme CO nonattainment areas with populations that exceed 250,000 (1980 census) to impose requirements concerning fleet use. In these areas, owners and operators of motor vehicle fleets must purchase a specified percentage of ''clean-fuel'' vehicles for use in those nonattainment areas.[573] These section 246 provisions apply to fleets of 10 or more vehicles that are owned and operated by a single person and capable of being centrally fueled.[574] The provisions cover federal[575] and state agency fleets and some local and privately owned fleets, but several fleet classes are exempted from the definition of covered fleets.[576] The fleet provisions recognize that fleet vehicles generally travel more miles than nonfleet vehicles and that their operators have greater control over their refueling.

States with serious or severe ozone or CO nonattainment areas must submit to EPA by June 1994 revised SIPs that include fleet provisions.[577] States can obtain a waiver from these requirements if EPA approves states' additional measures to achieve long term reductions in emissions of ozone-forming air pollutants.[578] States that do not obtain a waiver from fleet provisions must consider factors such as cost, safety, equipment, and resale value after consultation with fleet operators, vehicle manufacturers, fuel suppliers, and other interested parties.[579] Final SIPs must incorporate a phase-in schedule requiring a 50 percent reduction in emissions from heavy duty trucks commencing in model year 1998.[580] For LDTs and LDVs, model year 2001 standards specified

---

[569] §243(e)-(f), 42 U.S.C. §7583(e)-(f).

[570] California expects manufacturers to begin producing low emission vehicles in 1997.

[571] §249, 42 U.S.C. §7589.

[572] §246, 42 U.S.C. §7586. In June 1992, EPA issued a waiver of federal standards authorizing California to enforce its standards and test procedures for compressed natural gas and liquefied petroleum gas. 57 Fed. Reg. 24,788 (1992).

[573] §246(a), 42 U.S.C. §7586(a).

[574] §241(5), 42 U.S.C. §7581(5).

[575] Although federal agency fleet provisions are included in the Act, the Secretary of Defense can exempt certain heavyduty or combat vehicles because of national security considerations. §248(a) and (e), 42 U.S.C. §7588(a) and (e).

[576] §241(5), 42 U.S.C. §7581(5). Motor vehicles leased or rented to the public, those held for sale by dealers, those used as law enforcement or emergency vehicles, and nonroad vehicles are exempted from the clean fleet provisions.

[577] §246(a)(1)(3), 42 U.S.C. §7586(a)(1)(3).

[578] §182(c)(4)(B), 42 U.S.C. §7502(c)(4)(B).

[579] §246(a)(4), 42 U.S.C. §7586(a)(4).

[580] §246(b), 42 U.S.C. §7586(b).

in section 243 must be met by 30 percent of the fleet vehicles in model year 1998, 50 percent in model year 1999, and 70 percent in model year 2000.[581] SIPs must include provisions for clean fuel availability at locations where fleets are centrally refueled.[582]

VIII. Enforcement and Judicial Review

The 1990 Amendments greatly expanded EPA's enforcement authority and provided the government and citizens with additional means to enforce the Act, implementing regulations, and emission limits contained in permits. The adoption of the air permit program will ensure that citizen suits play a much greater role in enforcement of emission limits. Further, changes to section 113 of the CAA largely track the Clean Water Act (CWA) and Resource Conservation and Recovery Act (RCRA) enforcement provisions and reflect congressional efforts to harmonize criminal, civil, and administrative penalty provisions. There remain some important differences between the enforcement provisions of the CAA and of these environmental laws, however.

The CAA criminal enforcement provisions now include criminal fines and imprisonment for negligent endangerment, for knowing offenses, and for knowing endangerment. The endangerment offenses focus on hazardous air pollutants under section 112(a) and extremely hazardous substances under section 302 of EPCRA. Knowing failures to pay required fees are felonies as are tampering with monitors and falsification of data. Congress, EPA, and the Department of Justice (DOJ) consider such offenses threats to the whole environmental protection program because that program rests so heavily on self-reporting.

Section 114 monitoring and compliance provisions, and the permit provisions' periodic reporting requirements, have further enhanced citizens' ability to enforce the CAA and the rules and permits issued under it by providing easier access to compliance data. Further public participation in the federal enforcement program is encouraged by the "bounty" provisions of the 1990 Amendments, which authorizes EPA to award persons, besides government employees, up to $10,000 for information that leads to criminal convictions or assessment of certain judicial and administrative penalties.[583] This provision parallels similar language in CERCLA, the CWA, and RCRA, among other environmental statutes.

A. Criminal Enforcement Authority

Congress rewrote the stationary source enforcement provision (section 113) in the 1990 Amendments in order to ensure compliance with the many new and revised provisions and in order to make it more consistent with the CWA's and RCRA's criminal and civil enforcement provisions. The latter is an impor-

[581] §246(b) and (c), 42 U.S.C. §7586(b) and (c).
[582] §246(e), 42 U.S.C. §7586(e).
[583] §113(f), 42 U.S.C. §7413(f).

tant consideration when the authorities are focusing on multimedia enforcement. The types of criminal offenses under new section 113(c) include knowing offenses, negligent endangerment, knowing endangerment, tampering with monitors, falsification, failure to comply with reporting requirements, and failure to pay required fees.[584]

1. Knowing Offenses

In contrast to the pre-1990 Act, which limited criminal offenses to knowing violations of a relatively short list of provisions, e.g., NESHAPs and NSPSs, the 1990 version of the Act expanded the criminal penalties of section 113 to cover virtually every major stationary source provision. (The automotive and fuel requirements of Title II have separate criminal, civil, and administrative enforcement provisions.) For the following stationary source requirements, prosecutors must demonstrate that the violator ''knowingly'' committed violations of (1) federally enforceable SIP provisions, (2) administrative orders, (3) NSPSs, (4) NESHAPs, (5) solid waste combustion provisions, (6) preconstruction requirements under PSD provisions, (7) section 303 emergency orders, (8) Title IV acid rain provisions, (9) Title V operating permit provisions and permits issued under them, (10) Title VI ozone protection provisions, and (11) nonpayment of fees required by the CAA (except those under Title II). A more detailed explanation of the standards applied to convict offenders for ''knowing'' violations is provided in Chapter 16, Enforcement and Defense Strategies.

For those who operate in highly regulated areas, such as those subject to the CAA provisions, courts typically interpret the knowledge requirement to include knowledge that owners and operators ''should have known'' based on the pervasive statutory and regulatory scheme governing their operations. There are, however, several aspects of knowing violations specific to the Clean Air Act which are important to note, and which may limit to some degree the expansive interpretations given by the courts in RCRA and CWA criminal cases.

In criminal prosecutions under the CWA and RCRA, courts have allowed charges to be pressed against relatively low-ranking individuals.[585] In the 1990 Amendments, however, Congress, under pressure from unions, added a definition of ''operator'' which appears to protect employees from criminal charges resulting from carrying out their ''normal activities'' when ''acting under orders from the employer.''[586] These employees can be held liable only for ''knowing and willful'' violations, not simply ''knowing'' offenses or for ''negligent endangerment.''[587] Though the terms ''knowing'' and ''willful'' are used almost interchangeably in statutory drafting,[588] Congress apparently

[584] 42 U.S.C. §7413(c). Criminal penalty provisions for knowing offenses under the old version of §113 simply provided for a maximum fine of $25,000 and one year maximum jail sentences. Criminal prosecutions under the old version of the Act mainly focused on hazardous air pollutant violations, such as improper conduct of asbestos abatement programs, tampering with monitors, and falsification of data.

[585] See Chapter 16, Enforcement and Defense Strategies.

[586] §113(h), 42 U.S.C. §7413(h).

[587] *Id.*

[588] BLACK'S LAW DICTIONARY 784, 1434 (5th ed. 1979).

intended to impose a higher ''knowledge'' standard—perhaps actual knowledge—for prosecuting individual employees than for prosecuting an organization, a ''corporate officer,'' or ''any person who is senior management personnel.''[589] Individuals who are ''corporate officers'' or ''senior management personnel'' apparently *can* be prosecuted for negligent endangerment according to a negligence standard or for knowing offenses according to a ''knowing'' standard that has been interpreted as ''know or should have known'' under other environmental criminal provisions. Though the term ''senior management personnel'' is not separately defined, the term specifically excludes ''any person who is a stationary engineer or technician responsible for the operation, maintenance, repair, or monitoring of equipment and facilities and who often has supervisory and training duties but who is not senior management personnel or a corporate officer.''[590] Thus, the definition will exclude not only hourly employees, but many and, perhaps, most salaried employees as well. Though the express protection of this provision does not extend to senior management personnel and corporate officers, the effect may be to make prosecutions against them more difficult to bring, as it will be harder to threaten prosecution against lower ranking personnel and then trade immunity from prosecution for favorable testimony against their supervisors.

A second limitation on the prosecution of ''knowing'' offenses comes not from the 1990 Amendments, but the Conference Report explaining them. Environmental audits are a useful tool for organizations that seek to find and correct problems before they reach the level where enforcement action is warranted.[591] The audits are, however, potentially strong evidence of actual knowledge of violations on the part of organizations and senior management personnel, and have been used in some past federal criminal prosecutions in the environmental area. The House-Senate conferees stated that such reports should not ordinarily be used in criminal prosecutions.[592] The language was not written into the statute, but is simply an aid to interpretation. Moreover, the conferees indicated that such a limitation on criminal prosecution should apply only if the person acted in good faith to report the audit results and to correct the deficiencies identified in the audit.[593] The Justice Department's July 3, 1991, guidance on environmental criminal prosecutions largely follows this approach.[594]

Penalties for knowing violations of the CAA requirements for stationary sources include a maximum jail sentence of five years.[595] Fines imposed under these felony criminal enforcement provisions are determined pursuant to Title 18, the general federal criminal code, which establishes a maximum per violation fine of $500,000 for organizations and $250,000 for individuals. Unlike Title 18 sentences, however, the penalties can be doubled for repeat offenders. For a knowing failure to pay fees owed to the government pursuant to Titles I,

---

[589] §113(h), 42 U.S.C. §7413(h).

[590] *Id.*

[591] See Chapter 15, Environmental Audits.

[592] H.R. CONF. REP. NO. 752, 101st Cong., 2d Sess. 347 (1990).

[593] *Id.*

[594] See Chapter 16.

[595] §113(c)(1), 42 U.S.C. §7413(c)(1).

III, IV, V, and VI, the maximum jail sentence is one year, which doubles for repeat offenders.[596] The penalty levels prescribed in the CAA also makes these offenses felonies. There are a variety of ways under Title 18 and the federal sentencing guidelines where these monetary penalty levels can be further increased, especially against organizations.

Many of the new CAA provisions depend on accurate and complete reporting in order to carry out the objectives of the statute. Consequently, any knowing actions to falsify reports, improperly maintain monitoring records, omit material data from reports, or tamper with monitoring equipment can be prosecuted, though the House-Senate Conferences on the 1990 Amendments make clear that "these provisions are not meant to penalize inadvertent errors."[597] Violations also include failure to install required monitoring equipment properly and failure to comply with notifications or reporting requirements.[598] The maximum prison sentence for these violations is two years, a sentence which doubles for repeat offenders.[599]

2. *Knowing Endangerment*

Similar to criminal provisions added to the CWA in 1987 and RCRA in 1984, the 1990 Amendments added the criminal offense of knowing endangerment. Under revised section 113, criminal liability can be imposed for knowingly releasing any section 112 HAP or any EPCRA section 302(a) EHS into the ambient air, if at the time of such release, the person knew that it placed another person in imminent danger of death or serious bodily injury.[600] Although the standard for *individuals* requires *actual* knowledge at the time of the offense, such knowledge can be inferred from circumstantial evidence which suggests that the individual took affirmative steps to be shielded from relevant information.[601] As with negligent endangerment, releases authorized under the terms of an operating permit are not considered criminal offenses.[602]

The maximum jail sentence for knowing endangerment is 15 years for individuals and fines of up to $1 million for corporations.[603] Potential penalties, including imprisonment, double for repeat offenders.

3. *Negligent Endangerment*

With the 1990 Amendments, Congress, for the first time, expressly imposed criminal liability for negligent acts under the CAA's stationary source provisions.[604] Negligent acts are defined narrowly as the negligent release of any section 112 HAPs or any EPCRA's section 302(a) EHSs into the ambient

---

[596] §113(c)(2), 42 U.S.C. §7413(c)(2).

[597] H.R. CONF. REP. NO. 952, 101st Cong., 2d Sess. 346 (1990). The conferees further noted that "for criminal sanctions to apply, a source owner or operator must be on notice of the record keeping, information or monitoring requirements in question." *Id.* at 346–47.

[598] §113(c)(2), 42 U.S.C. §7413(c)(2).

[599] §113(c)(2), 42 U.S.C. §7413(c)(2).

[600] §113(c)(5), 42 U.S.C. §7413(c)(5).

[601] §113(c)(5)(B), 42 U.S.C. §7413(c)(5)(B).

[602] §113(c)(5)(A), 42 U.S.C. §7413(c)(5)(A).

[603] *Id.*

[604] §113(c)(4), 42 U.S.C. §7413(c)(4). EPA published a proposed guidance on use of §112(r)(9) enforcement authority in May 1991. 56 Fed. Reg. 24,393 (1991).

air in a manner that places another person in imminent danger of death or serious bodily injury. The statute does not prohibit prosecutions for endangering employees who are injured by exposure to dangerous concentrations of air pollutants. The definition of "ambient air," however, ordinarily refers to outdoor air, leaving prosecutions for exposing employees to unsafe indoor concentrations to OSHA and state law.[605] Moreover, unless the defendant proves otherwise, it may be enough that employees or the surrounding community had to be evacuated following the release of specified HAPs to demonstrate negligent endangerment.

Like the knowing endangerment provisions, criminal liability for negligent endangerment may not attach if the HAP release was authorized pursuant to permit provisions. The maximum jail sentence is one year, but the sentence can double for repeat offenders.[606] A fine under the general federal criminal code, Title 18, also may be imposed.

4. *Contractor Listing*

Section 306 prohibits federal agencies from contracting with companies convicted of CAA violations for work to be performed at the facility where the violation occurred if the facility is owned, leased, or supervised by such company.[607] This facility-specific debarment from federal contracting continues until EPA certifies that problems arising from the violation have been remedied.[608] Federal contracts typically require contractors to certify that they have not been convicted of Clean Air as well as Clean Water Act violations. Furthermore, EPA is authorized under the 1990 Amendments to debar any other facility that the convicted party owns or operates from entering into contracts with the federal government. For any company seeking government contracts, this provision provides a powerful incentive to comply with CAA requirements.

B. Civil Enforcement Authority

Although the 1970 Amendments authorized the United States to obtain injunctive relief, Congress did not provide for civil penalties for CAA violations until the 1977 Amendments, when it added a provision allowing courts to assess civil penalties of up to $25,000 per day "for each violation."[609] The 1977 Amendments also added section 120, an elaborate provision that allows a court to impose a penalty intended to deprive a violator of the economic benefits of noncompliance. This economic benefit, under the statute, is intended to reflect the interest costs saved from delayed investment in necessary control equipment, the foregone operation and maintenance expenses, as well as any other savings.[610] Although EPA's implementing regulations were upheld by the court

[605] *See* United States v. Borowski, 977 F.2d 27 (1st Cir. 1992) (limiting prosecutions for knowing endangerment under the Clean Water Act to exposures suffered by people other than employees).

[606] §113(c)(4), 42 U.S.C. §7413(c)(4).

[607] 42 U.S.C. §7606(a).

[608] In addition to debarment from contracts, the EPA List of Violating Facilities bars the offending facility from access to federal grants or loans. 56 Fed. Reg. 64,786 (1991).

[609] §113(b), 42 U.S.C. §7413(b).

[610] §120(d)(2), 42 U.S.C. §7420(d)(2).

of appeals,[611] EPA has not used this authority much, in part because it is cumbersome, and in part because EPA ordinarily seeks to recover the economic benefit of noncompliance as part of penalties assessed under section 113(b). Moreover, the potential penalties, calculated at $25,000 per day for each violation, are ordinarily greater than the calculated economic benefit.[612]

The potential severity of civil penalties is increased by two statutory presumptions, one of which was added to section 113(e) by the 1990 Amendments. Under section 113(e)(2), when EPA or a state air pollution control agency makes a prima facie case that a violation continued after the Agency provided notice to the violator, there is a rebuttable presumption that the violation continued from day to day until there is a demonstration that it was remedied. The burden shifts to the violator to prove that the violation was not continuous by showing, for example, that operations ceased during a certain time period. If this demonstration is not made, each day of an ongoing violation constitutes a separate offense and penalties are assessed accordingly. EPA further assumes that multiple violations can take place on the same day, for exceedances of different pollutant limits.

When assessing penalties, EPA is directed to consider several factors including

- The size of the business,
- The economic consequences of the penalty on the business,
- The business's compliance history,[613]
- Good faith efforts of the violator to remedy violations promptly,
- The duration of the violation,
- Previous penalties assessed for similar violations,
- Economic benefits of noncompliance,
- The severity of the violation, and
- Other relevant factors.[614]

Pursuant to section 113(g), added in the 1990 Amendments, and the DOJ public participation policy, going back to the early 1970s, settlements reached between EPA and the violator are subject to public comment.[615]

In the Conference Report, the conferees made clear their view that EPA and DOJ have discretion *not* to bring civil or criminal enforcement action for technical or de minimis violations.[616] This comment is important because language in sections 113(a) and (b) suggests that enforcement action is mandatory in the case of violations by major stationary sources.

---

[611] Duquesne Light Co. v. EPA, 698 F.2d 456 (D.C. Cir. 1983) (upholding 40 C.F.R. pt. 66).

[612] *E.g.*, United States v. Chevron, 639 F. Supp. 770 (N.D. Tex. 1985) (the government recovered penalties of over $6 million for Prevention of Significant Deterioration (PSD) violations).

[613] EPA may take into consideration the violator's compliance with other environmental statutes as well as the CAA violation at issue under the Agency's new multimedia approach to enforcement.

[614] §113(e)(1), 42 U.S.C. §7413(e)(1). EPA integrated its civil penalty policy applicable to stationary sources that violate the CAA with civil penalty procedures for other environmental statutes in February 1992. 57 Fed. Reg. 4316 (1992).

[615] 42 U.S.C. §7413(g).

[616] H.R. CONF. REP. NO. 952, 101st Cong., 2d Sess. 347 (1990).

C. Administrative Enforcement

With the 1990 Amendments, EPA authority to issue administrative orders (AOs) was increased to address numerous categories of CAA violations. EPA's civil enforcement authority is applicable to: (1) SIPs and their permit programs, (2) states that fail to administer their programs, and (3) other federal violations specified in the CAA. Administrative penalties may be sought for virtually any stationary source violation. They are not applicable, however, to mobile source violations.[617] When EPA identifies SIP requirement violations, the Agency must issue a notice of violation to the affected source and the state where the source is located.[618] The state has 30 days to enforce its SIP provision. If the state fails to act, EPA is authorized to issue an AO that requires compliance or assesses a civil penalty. In addition, EPA is authorized to commence civil enforcement action.[619] At the same time, citizens are authorized to bring private suits to enforce compliance.[620]

Upon EPA's determination that a state has been unable or unwilling to administer and enforce SIP provisions and that there are widespread violations of the SIP, EPA may enforce the SIP directly.[621] This authority has rarely, if ever, been invoked. Furthermore, EPA may issue an AO banning construction of new sources or modifications of existing sources, if EPA determines that a state has failed to administer NSPSs requirements.[622]

Pursuant to section 113(d), EPA may impose civil penalties through administrative penalty orders and proceedings. Proceedings may be initiated for either current or past violations. There is a $200,000 upper limit on the penalties that may be imposed by EPA in such an administrative proceeding unless EPA and DOJ jointly agree that a larger penalty is appropriate. EPA must assert its administrative cause of action within a year of the violation.[623]

Those subject to penalty proceedings have an opportunity for a public hearing on the record before an administrative law judge (ALJ) in accordance with sections 554 and 556 of the federal Administrative Procedure Act (APA). Such proceedings must ensure due process protections such as a right to counsel, and the right to summon and cross-examine witnesses. Once the ALJ's decision is issued, parties have 30 days to challenge the ALJ's order in United States district court.[624] Consistent with the APA, rather than conduct an independent review, the district court only reviews the administrative proceedings to determine whether the record reflects substantial evidence to support the ALJ's order.[625]

---

[617] §113(d)(1)(B), 42 U.S.C. §7413(d)(1)(B).

[618] §113(d)(1)(A), 42 U.S.C. §7413(d)(1)(A).

[619] §113(a)(1), 42 U.S.C. §7413(a)(1).

[620] Unlike the Clean Water Act, citizens suits are not prohibited while administrative proceedings are pending. *See* CWA §309(g)(4) and (6).

[621] §113(a)(2), 42 U.S.C. §7413(a)(2).

[622] §113(a)(5), 42 U.S.C. §7413(a)(5).

[623] §113(d)(1), 42 U.S.C. §7413(d)(1). The limits are *not* the statute of limitations; the statute of limitations for federal civil penalty actions is five years from the date of violation. 28 U.S.C. §2462.

[624] §113(d)(4), 42 U.S.C. §7413(d)(4).

[625] *Id.*

Those subject to AOs must correct violations as quickly as possible within a year of the date that the AO is issued.[626] In addition, if the violator fails to pay AO penalties, the government may initiate collection proceedings in district court. For each quarter that a penalty remains unpaid, the district court can assess an additional 10 percent above the amount of the penalty as well as court costs, U.S. attorney's fees, and interest at the statutory rate.[627]

1. *Field Citations*

For minor violations detected by EPA field officers and other designated employees, EPA may assess maximum daily penalties of up to $5,000 for each day of a violation.[628] Even though a citation is paid by a violator, it may still face other enforcement action, such as citizen suits. Although section 113(d)(3) establishes an appeal procedure, the process is not subject to APA requirements.[629] EPA is still developing its field citation program and proposed rules are expected in early 1994.

2. *Emergency Powers*

The 1990 Amendments broadened EPA's authority to protect public health and the environment during emergency situations. EPA is authorized to issue an AO or file a civil action to immediately enjoin emissions from stationary or mobile sources that are causing or contributing to an emergency. EPA's section 303 emergency power extends to public welfare and environmental protection as well as public health concerns in emergency situations.[630]

Prior to the 1990 Amendments, EPA's emergency authority permitted emergency restraining orders for two day periods. EPA has rarely exercised its emergency powers largely because sources will usually voluntarily curtail operations to avoid imposition of a restraining order. EPA emergency restraining orders can now be issued for a maximum period of 60 days pursuant to section 303.[631] If EPA commences a civil suit for injunctive relief, EPA can extend an emergency restraining order another 14 days, and the courts are permitted to extend the order while litigation is pending.

3. *Information Gathering Authority*

In order to ensure compliance with CAA provisions, Congress has granted EPA extensive authority to compel the regulated community to create and maintain records, test air pollution emissions, and report data to EPA. Moreover, EPA inspectors are authorized to perform tests and observe operations at sources. EPA officials will be required to obtain search warrants in the event that an owner or operator of a source denies entry to Agency personnel.[632] EPA's subpoena power was also extended in the 1990 Amendments to cover

[626] §113(a)(4), 42 U.S.C. §7413(a)(4).

[627] §113(d)(5), 42 U.S.C. §7413(d)(5).

[628] Only EPA personnel have authority to issue field citations.

[629] 42 U.S.C. §7413(d)(3).

[630] 42 U.S.C. §7603.

[631] *Id.*

[632] *See* Marshall v. Barlow's, Inc., 436 U.S. 307 (1978) (requiring Department of Labor inspectors to obtain search warrants when they were denied entry at a facility).

any investigation, monitoring, or compliance inspection, or administrative enforcement proceeding.[633] Although the statute allows affected parties to challenge subpoena or certification demands,[634] those parties should object only to those demands for which they have a legal basis to do so, and comply with all other requests. Failure to comply with reasonable Agency demands could result in a penalty of $25,000 for each day of noncompliance with administrative actions and subpoenas.

Under the 1990 Amendments, EPA has broad authority to compel manufacturers of air pollution or process equipment to inform the Agency about the equipment's performance parameters. In addition, major stationary sources must submit compliance certifications and enhanced monitoring data. Other air pollution sources may be required to submit compliance certifications and enhanced monitoring data.[635] The certification must (1) specify requirements subject to certification, (2) identify the method used to determine compliance, (3) report on compliance status, (4) indicate whether compliance is continuous or intermittent, and (5) include any other information EPA specifies.

EPA was required to issue rules for enhanced monitoring and compliance certifications by November 1992. Pursuant to court order, EPA agreed to issue overdue regulations for states' enhanced monitoring of ozone, NO_2, and VOC by April 30, 1993. EPA did not propose regulations until October 22, 1993.[636]

Data collected pursuant to section 114 is available to the public, unless it contains trade secrets. Emissions data, however, cannot be classified as a trade secret because Congress intended such information to provide the basis for action under the citizen suit provisions.[637]

D. Citizen Suits

Congress included provisions in the 1970 CAA to encourage private citizens to act as watchdogs and force sources to comply with the Act as well as challenge EPA when it neglects to enforce the Act. Under section 304(a), citizens are authorized to take action against any person allegedly violating "emissions standards" or constructing or proposing to construct new sources in violation of PSD, nonattainment, or permit provisions.[638] Enforceable emission standards include those covered under most substantive parts of the CAA, including SIP and permit requirements.[639] Where EPA is required to exercise its nondiscretionary authority, citizens also may bring suit to compel the Agency to take action.[640] This authority has been extensively used by environmentalists to force court supervision of EPA implementation of the Act. For example, in 1972, the Sierra Club successfully used this authority in an action to invalidate

---

[633] §307(a), 42 U.S.C. §7607(a).

[634] If the violator has adequate reason to violate or refuse compliance with administrative subpoenas or actions, no penalties will be assessed. §113(e)(1), 42 U.S.C. §7413(e)(1).

[635] §114(a)(3), 42 U.S.C. §7414(a)(3).

[636] 58 Fed. Reg. 54,648 (1993).

[637] *See* NRDC v. EPA, 478 F.2d 875, 893 (1st Cir. 1973) (finding that information gathered pursuant to §114 must be disclosed to the public).

[638] 42 U.S.C. §7604(a).

[639] §304(f), 42 U.S.C. §7604(f).

[640] §304(a), 42 U.S.C. §7604(a).

all SIPs because EPA had not mandated inclusion of nondegradation provisions in them.[641] Citizens are also authorized, upon 180 days notice, to bring action against EPA when the Agency has unreasonably delayed promulgation of regulations in accordance with statutory deadlines.[642]

The 1990 Amendments created greater opportunity for effective use of the citizen suit provisions. Unlike its counterpart in section 505 of the Clean Water Act, section 304 has not often been applied in actions against violators as opposed to actions to force EPA to perform nondiscretionary duties. Without a comprehensive federal permit program in which stationary sources were required to conduct periodic monitoring and to comply with reporting requirements, citizens often lacked data to support their claims. The addition of the Title V permit program, stricter section 114 monitoring and compliance certification provisions, and section 110(a)(2)(f) periodic reporting requirements ensure that citizens will have access to data necessary for initiating a cause of action and that such data will be created in the first place.[643] Mobile source emissions data also must be made available to the public pursuant to section 208(c), which provides an additional basis for citizens suits.[644]

Prior to initiating a citizen suit, the claimant must provide written notice to EPA, to the state in which the violation is occurring, and to the alleged violator 60 days before commencing suit.[645] Claimants similarly must provide EPA with 60 days notice before bringing action to compel the Agency to undertake its nondiscretionary duties.[646] The 1990 Amendments further require citizens to serve the United States in any action, and authorize the United States to intervene in all section 304 cases.[647] The United States has 45 days to submit comments to the court on proposed settlements of section 304 cases.[648] Contrary to Clean Water Act provisions, there is no bar to citizens' suits if EPA has initiated an administrative penalty proceeding to remedy a CAA violation. Private citizens may not bring suit, however, if the state or federal authorities are taking action to enforce compliance, but citizens are entitled to intervene in the state or federal action.[649]

The 1990 Amendments clarified certain citizen suit penalty provisions. The new version of section 304 expressly authorizes recovery of civil penalties in citizen suit cases in addition to injunctive relief. Rather than limit recovery to ongoing violations, citizens are authorized to recover civil penalties for past violations upon a showing that the claimed violation had been repeated.[650] Civil penalties assessed under section 304 are paid to the Treasury and deposited into

---

[641] Sierra Club v. Ruckelshaus, 344 F. Supp. 253 (D.D.C. 1972), *aff'd without opinion by equally divided court sub nom.* Fri v. Sierra Club, 412 U.S. 541 (1973).

[642] §304(a), 42 U.S.C. §7604(a).

[643] 42 U.S.C. §§7414, 7410(a)(2)(f).

[644] 42 U.S.C. §7542(c).

[645] §304(b), 42 U.S.C. §7604(b).

[646] §304(b), 42 U.S.C. §7604(b).

[647] §304(c)(3), 42 U.S.C. §7604(c)(3).

[648] *Id.*

[649] §304(b), 42 U.S.C. §7604(b).

[650] In so doing, Congress implicitly repudiated the Supreme Court's decision in Chesapeake Bay Found. v. Gwaltney of Smithfield, Inc., 484 U.S. 49 (1987) (interpreting Clean Water Act's citizen suit provision to preclude such actions to recover civil penalties for wholly past violations).

a fund to finance future EPA enforcement activity.[651] A portion of civil penalties assessed—up to $100,000—may be used upon the court's order for beneficial mitigation projects to enhance public health or the environment.[652]

E. Judicial Review

Those affected by EPA regulations that implement the CAA have limited recourse to the courts. In an effort to expedite judicial review of EPA's regulations, Congress provided for direct review of all final nationally applicable regulations in the United States Court of Appeals for the District of Columbia Circuit.[653] Only regulations that apply to local or regional areas, such as EPA decisions on SIP provisions, may be challenged in the court of appeals for that circuit.[654] Challenges ordinarily must be brought within specific time limits, including decisions by EPA to defer a nondiscretionary action to a later time.

In most cases, petitioners must file for review within 60 days after EPA promulgates a rule.[655] If grounds for a challenge arise after the 60-day period has passed, the petitioner has 60 days from the date that the new basis for a challenge arose.[656] Courts have generally declined to review challenges filed outside the allotted time period on jurisdictional grounds.[657] Judicial review of regulatory actions during enforcement proceedings cannot be obtained if such review was available during the usual 60-day period.

EPA must observe specific requirements when promulgating rules. Each notice of a proposed rule EPA publishes in the *Federal Register* must include (1) factual data supporting the rule, including any material supplied by the Scientific Review Committee and the National Academy of Sciences; (2) methodology employed to obtain and evaluate data; (3) the rule's major policy considerations; and (4) a legal interpretation of the rule's provisions.[658] Any comments made by other agencies must be included in EPA's administrative record.[659] These detailed rulemaking requirements were largely added in the 1977 Amendments and are similar but somewhat more specific than those required under the APA. Interested parties may submit written comments and the Agency must address significant comments in the final rule.[660] The final rule may not consider data not included in the administrative record.[661]

---

[651] §304(g)(1), 42 U.S.C. §7604(g)(1).

[652] §304(g)(2), 42 U.S.C. §7604(g)(2). The Internal Revenue Code expressly prohibits tax deductions for penalties assessed, but it is less clear whether the Code would prohibit tax deductions for payments made towards beneficial mitigation projects. A party settling such a case may wish to seek tax counsel on such effects, including possibly obtaining a private letter ruling from the Internal Revenue Service.

[653] §307(b), 42 U.S.C. §7607(b).

[654] *Id.*

[655] *Id.*

[656] *Id.*

[657] City of Seabrook v. EPA, 659 F.2d 1349 (5th Cir. 1981). The Eighth Circuit has ruled that rejection of a petitioner's late challenge did not violate due process rights. Lloyd A. Fry Roofing Co. v. EPA, 554 F.2d 885 (8th Cir. 1977).

[658] §307(d)(3), 42 U.S.C. §7607(d)(3).

[659] §307(d)(4)(B)(i), 42 U.S.C. §7607(d)(4)(B)(i). Section 307(d) outlines record requirements for EPA rulemaking.

[660] §307(d)(6), 42 U.S.C. §7607(d)(6).

[661] §307(d)(6)(C), 42 U.S.C. §7607(d)(6)(C).

The courts of appeals largely review EPA rulemaking in accordance with APA standards for review of agency rulemaking. Under section 307(d)(9), courts may reverse an EPA action if the action is (1) arbitrary, capricious, an abuse of discretion, or otherwise unlawful; (2) inconsistent with constitutional right, power, privilege, or immunity; (3) beyond EPA's statutory jurisdiction, authority, or short of statutory right; and (4) without observance of procedure required by law, provided that such failure was arbitrary and capricious.[662]

Petitioners must overcome strict standards of judicial review to successfully challenge agency rules on substantive grounds. In *Chevron, U.S.A. v. NRDC,*[663] the Supreme Court stated that "considerable weight should be accorded to an executive department's construction of a statutory scheme it is entrusted to administer." Though courts generally are deferential in their review of EPA's actions, they have required EPA to provide a substantial explanation of legal and policy considerations underlying the Agency's decisions.[664]

If a challenge to a rule is made on procedural grounds, the petitioner must demonstrate that the procedural objection was raised with reasonable specificity during the rulemaking proceedings.[665] Moreover, the procedural error must be "so serious and related to matters of such central relevance to the rule that there is a substantial likelihood that the rule would have been significantly changed if the errors had not been made."[666] This standard is demanding and courts have rarely reversed EPA actions on procedural grounds.

[662] 42 U.S.C. §7607(d)(9).

[663] 467 U.S. 837, 844 (1984).

[664] Riverside Cement Co. v. Thomas, 843 F.2d 1246 (9th Cir. 1988); Sierra Club v. Costle, 657 F.2d 298 (D.C. Cir. 1981); Portland Cement Ass'n v. Ruckelshaus, 486 F.2d 375 (D.C. Cir. 1973).

[665] §307(d)(7)(B), 42 U.S.C. §7607(d)(7)(B).

[666] §307(d)(8), 42 U.S.C. §7607(d)(8).

Appendix A

Classified Ozone Nonattainment Areas

Nonattainment Areas	*Classification*
Albany-Schenectady-Troy, NY	Marginal
Allentown-Bethlehem-Easton, PA-NJ	Marginal
Altoona, PA	Marginal
Atlanta, GA	Serious
Atlantic City, NJ	Moderate
Baltimore, MD	Severe-15
Baton Rouge, LA	Serious
Beaumont-Port Arthur, TX	Serious
Birmingham, AL	Marginal
Boston-Warren-Worcester (E. MA), MA-NH	Serious
Buffalo-Niagara Falls, NY	Marginal
Canton, OH	Marginal
Charleston, WV	Moderate
Charlotte-Gastonia, NC	Moderate
Cherokee Co., SC	Marginal
Chicago-Gary-Lake Co., IL, IN	Severe-17
Cincinnati-Hamilton, OH-KY	Moderate
Cleveland-Akron-Lorain, OH	Moderate
Columbus, OH	Marginal
Dallas-Fort Worth, TX	Moderate
Dayton-Springfield, OH	Moderate
Detroit-Ann Arbor, MI	Moderate
Door Co., WI	Marginal
Edmonson Co., KY	Marginal
El Paso, TX	Serious
Erie, PA	Marginal
Essex Co. (Whiteface Mtn.), NY	Marginal
Evansville, IN	Marginal
Grand Rapids, MI	Moderate
Greater Connecticut	Serious
Greenbrier Co., WV	Marginal
Greensboro-Winston Salem-H. Point, NC	Moderate
Hancock & Waldo Cos., ME	Marginal
Harrisburg-Lebanon-Carlisle, PA	Marginal
Houston-Galveston-Brazoria, TX	Severe-17
Huntington-Ashland, WV-KY	Moderate
Indianapolis, IN	Marginal
Jefferson Co., NY	Marginal
Johnstown, PA	Marginal
Kansas City, MO-KS	Submarginal
Kent and Queen Anne's Cos., MD	Marginal
Kewaunee Co., WI	Moderate
Knox & Lincoln Cos., ME	Moderate
Knoxville, TN	Marginal
Lake Charles, LA	Marginal
Lancaster, PA	Marginal
Lewiston-Auburn, ME	Moderate
Lexington-Fayette, KY	Marginal
Los Angeles-South Coast Air Basin, CA	Extreme
Louisville, KY-IN	Moderate
Manchester, NH	Marginal
Manitowoc Co., WI	Moderate
Memphis, TN	Marginal
Miami-Ft. Lauder.-W. Palm Beach, FL	Moderate
Milwaukee-Racine, WI	Severe-17
Monterey Bay, CA	Moderate
Muskegon, MI	Serious
Nashville, TN	Moderate
New York-N, NJ-Long Is., NY-NJ-CT	Severe-17
Norfolk-Vir. Beach-Newport News, VA	Marginal
Owensboro, KY	Marginal

Classified Ozone Nonattainment Areas

Nonattainment Areas	*Classification*
Paducah, KY	Marginal
Parkersburg, WV	Moderate
Philadelphia-Wilm.-Trent., PA-NJ-DE-MD	Severe-15
Phoenix, AZ	Moderate
Pittsburgh-Beaver Valley, PA	Moderate
Portland, ME	Moderate
Portland-Vancouver AWMA, OR-WA	Marginal
Portsmouth-Dover-Rochester, NH	Serious
Poughkeepsie, NY	Marginal
Providence (All RI), RI	Serious
Raleigh-Durham, NC	Moderate
Reading, PA	Moderate
Reno, NV	Marginal
Richmond-Petersburg, VA	Moderate
Sacramento Metro, CA	Serious
Salt Lake City, UT	Moderate
San Diego, CA	Severe-15
San Francisco-Bay Area, CA	Moderate
San Joaquin Valley, CA	Serious
Santa Barbara-Santa Maria-Lompoc, CA	Moderate
Scranton-Wilkes-Barre, PA	Marginal
Seattle-Tacoma, WA	Marginal
Sheboygan, WI	Moderate
Smyth Co., VA (White Top Mtn.)	Marginal
South Bend-Elkhart, IN	Marginal
Southeast Desert Modified AQMA, CA	Severe-17
Springfield (W. MA), MA	Serious
St. Louis, MO-IL	Moderate
Sussex Co., DE	Marginal
Tampa-St. Petersburg-Clearwater, FL	Marginal
Toledo, OH	Moderate
Ventura Co., CA	Severe-15
Walworth Co., WI	Marginal
Washington, DC-MD-VA	Serious
York, PA	Marginal
Youngstown-Warren-Sharon, OH-PA	Marginal

Classified Carbon Monoxide Nonattainment Areas

Nonattainment Areas	*Classification*
Albuquerque, NM	Moderate <=12.7 ppm
Anchorage, AK	**Moderate >=12.7 ppm**
Baltimore, MD	Moderate <=12.7 ppm
Boston, MA	Moderate <=12.7 ppm
Chico, CA	Moderate <=12.7 ppm
Cleveland, OH	Moderate <=12.7 ppm
Colorado Springs, CO	Moderate <=12.7 ppm
Denver-Boulder, CO	**Moderate >=12.7 ppm**
Duluth, MN	Moderate <=12.7 ppm
El Paso, TX	Moderate <=12.7 ppm
Fairbanks, AK	Moderate <=12.7 ppm
Fort Collins, CO	Moderate <=12.7 ppm

Classified Carbon Monoxide Nonattainment Areas

Nonattainment Areas	*Classification*
Fresno, CA	**Moderate >=12.7 ppm**
Grants Pass, OR	Moderate <=12.7 ppm
Hartford-New Britain-Middletown, CT	Moderate <=12.7 ppm
Klamath Falls, OR	Moderate <=12.7 ppm
Lake Tahoe South Shore, CA	Moderate <=12.7 ppm
Las Vegas, NV	**Moderate >=12.7 ppm**
Longmont, CO	Moderate <=12.7 ppm
Los Angeles South Coast Air Basin, CA	**Serious**
Medford, OR	Moderate <=12.7 ppm
Memphis, TN	Moderate <=12.7 ppm
Minneapolis-St. Paul, MN	Moderate <=12.7 ppm
Missoula, MT	Moderate <=12.7 ppm
Modesto, CA	Moderate <=12.7 ppm
New York-N., NJ-Long Is., NY-NJ-CT	**Moderate >=12.7 ppm**
Ogden, UT	Moderate <=12.7 ppm

Classified Carbon Monoxide Nonattainment Areas

Nonattainment Areas	*Classification*
Philadelphia-Camden Co., PA-NJ	Moderate <=12.7 ppm
Phoenix, AZ	Moderate <=12.7 ppm
Portland-Vancouver, OR-WA	Moderate <=12.7 ppm
Provo, UT	**Moderate >=12.7 ppm**
Raleigh-Durham, NC	Moderate <=12.7 ppm
Reno, NV	Moderate <=12.7 ppm
Sacramento, CA	Moderate <=12.7 ppm
San Diego, CA	Moderate <=12.7 ppm
San Francisco-Oakland-San Jose, CA	Moderate <=12.7 ppm
Seattle-Tacoma, WA	**Moderate >=12.7 ppm**
Spokane, WA	**Moderate >=12.7 ppm**
Stockton, CA	Moderate <=12.7 ppm
Syracuse, NY	Moderate <=12.7 ppm
Washington, DC-MD-VA	Moderate <=12.7 ppm
Winston-Salem, NC	Moderate <=12.7 ppm

Bold type for emphasis only

PM-10 Nonattainment Areas

Region	*Nonattainment Area*
I	New Haven, CT
I	Presque Isle, ME
II	Guaynabo, PR
II	New York County, NY
III	Clairton, PA
III	Brooke County, WV
III	Follansbee, WV

PM-10 Nonattainment Areas

Region	*Nonattainment Area*
III	Hancock County, WV
V	Cuyahoga County, OH
V	Detroit, MI
V	Granite City, IL
V	Lake County, IN
V	Lyons Township, McCook, IL
V	Mingo Junction, OH

PM-10 Nonattainment Areas

Region	*Nonattainment Area*
V	Oglesby, IL
V	Rochester, MN
V	St. Paul, MN
V	Southeast Chicago, IL
V	Vermillion County, IN
VI	Anthony, NM
VI*	Bernalillo County, NM
VI	El Paso, TX
VIII	Aspen, CO
VIII	Butte, MT
VIII	Canon City, CO
VIII	Columbia Falls, MT
VIII	Denver Metro, CO
VIII	Kalispell, MT
VIII	Lamar, CO
VIII	Lame Deer, MT
VIII	Libby, MT
VIII	Missoula, MT
VIII	Pagosa Springs, CO
VIII	Polson, MT
VIII	Ronan, MT
VIII	Routt County, CO (part)
VIII	Salt Lake County, UT
VIII	Sanders County, MT (part)
VIII	Sheridan, WY
VIII	Tulluride, CO
VIII	Utah County, UT
IX	Ajo, AZ
IX	Coachella Valley, CA
IX	Douglas, AZ
IX	Gila County, AZ (part)
IX	Hayden/Miami, AZ
IX	Imperial Valley, CA
IX	Las Vegas, NV
IX	Mammoth Lake, CA
IX	Mohave County, AZ (part)
IX	Nogales, AZ
IX	Owens Valley, CA

PM-10 Nonattainment Areas

Region	*Nonattainment Area*
IX	Paul Spur, AZ
IX	Phoenix, AZ
IX	Reno, NV
IX	Rillito, AZ
IX	Sacramento County, CA
IX	San Bernardino County, CA (part)
IX	San Joaquin Valley, CA
IX	Searles Valley, CA
IX	South Coast Basin, CA
IX	Yuma, AZ
X*	Benton County, WA (part)
X	Boise, ID
X	Bonner County, ID
X	Eagle River, AK
X*	Frankling County, WA (part)
X	Grants Pass, OR
X	Juneau, AK
X	Kent, WA
X	Klamath Falls, OR
X*	Kootenai County, ID (part)
X	LaGrand, OR
X	Lane County, OR (part)
X	Medford, OR
X	Olympia/Tumwater/Lacey, WA
X	Pinehurst, ID
X	Pocatello, ID
X	Seattle, WA
X	Shoshone County, ID (part)
X	Spokane, WA
X	Springfield/Eugene, OR
X	Tacoma, WA
X*	Walla Walla County, WA (part)
X	Wallula, WA
X	Yakima, WA

*Indicates proposed PM-10 nonattainment areas 9/9/92.

Lead Nonattainment and Unclassifiable Areas

County	State	Whole/Part County	Designation
Listed by Area			
Bexar	TX	Part	Unclassifiable

Lead Nonattainment and Unclassifiable Areas

County	State	Whole/Part County	Designation
Collin	TX	Part	Nonattainment
Cuyahoga	OH	Part	Unclassifiable
Dakota	MN	Part	Nonattainment
Dent	MO	Whole	Unclassifiable
Douglas	NE	Part	Nonattainment
East Baton Rouge	LA	Whole	Unclassifiable
Fayette	TN	Part	Unclassifiable
Hillsborough	FL	Part	Unclassifiable
Holt	MO	Whole	Unclassifiable
Iron (2 areas)	MO	Part	Nonattainment
Jefferson	MO	Part	Nonattainment
Lewis & Clark	MT	Part	Nonattainment
Marion	IN	Part	Unclassifiable
Marion	IN	Part	Nonattainment
Muscogee	GA	Whole	Nonattainment
Onondaga	NY	Whole	Unclassifiable
Shelby	TN	Part	Nonattainment
Williamson	TN	Part	Nonattainment
Listed by State			
Jefferson	AL	Part	Nonattainment
Hillsborough	FL	Part	Unclassifiable
Muscogee	GA	Whole	Nonattainment
Marion	IN	Part	Nonattainment
Marion	IN	Part	Unclassifiable
East Baton Rouge	LA	Whole	Unclassifiable
Dakota	MN	Part	Nonattainment
Dent	MO	Whole	Unclassifiable
Holt	MO	Whole	Unclassifiable
Iron (2 areas)	MO	Part	Nonattainment
Jefferson	MO	Part	Nonattainment
Lewis & Clark	MT	Part	Nonattainment
Douglas	NE	Part	Nonattainment
Onondaga	NY	Whole	Unclassifiable
Cuyahoga	OH	Part	Unclassifiable
Fayette	TN	Part	Unclassifiable
Shelby	TN	Part	Nonattainment
Williamson	TN	Part	Nonattainment
Bexar	TX	Part	Unclassifiable
Collin	TX	Part	Nonattainment
Listed by Designation Then Area			
Collin	TX	Part	Nonattainment
Dakota	MN	Part	Nonattainment
Douglas	NE	Part	Nonattainment
Iron (2 areas)	MO	Part	Nonattainment
Jefferson	MO	Part	Nonattainment
Jefferson	AL	Part	Nonattainment
Lewis & Clark	MT	Part	Nonattainment

Lead Nonattainment and Unclassifiable Areas

County	State	Whole/Part County	Designation
Marion	IN	Part	Nonattainment
Muscogee	GA	Whole	Nonattainment
Shelby	TN	Part	Nonattainment
Williamson	TN	Part	Nonattainment
Bexar	TX	Part	Unclassifiable
Cuyahoga	OH	Part	Unclassifiable
Dent	MO	Whole	Unclassifiable
East Baton Rouge	LA	Whole	Unclassifiable
Fayette	TN	Part	Unclassifiable
Hillsborough	FL	Part	Unclassifiable
Holt	MO	Whole	Unclassifiable
Marion	IN	Part	Unclassifiable
Onondaga	NY	Whole	Unclassifiable

Sulfur Dioxide Existing Nonattainment Areas

Alabama
Colbert Co. [s]*
Lauderdale Co. [s]

Arizona
Cochise Co. (Douglas) [p]
Gila Co. (Miana/Globe) [p]
Greenlee Co. (Morenci) [p]
Pima Co. (Ajo) [p]
Pinal Co. (Hayden) [p]
Pinal Co. (San Manual) [p]

District of Columbia
**(Two areas) (part)

Illinois
**Madison County (part)
Peoria Co. (part) [ps]
**St. Clair County (part)
Tazwell Co. (part) [p]

Indiana
Lake Co. (part) [p]
Laporte Co. (part) [p]
Marion Co. (part) [p]
Vigo Co. [p]
Wayne Co. (part) [p]

Kentucky
Boyde Co. (part) [p]
Muhlenberg Co. [s]

Maine
AQCR 109 (Penobscot Co. (part) Millinocket) [p]

Minnesota
AQCR 131 (Minneapolis-St. Paul) [p]
Olmsted Co. (Rochester) [p]

Montana
Lewis and Clark Co. (East Helena) [ps]
Yellowston Co. (Laurel) [p]

Nevada
White Pine Co. (Central Steptoe Valley) [p]

New Jersey
Warren Co. (Upper Delaware Valley) [ps]

New Mexico
Grant Co. (part) [p]

Ohio
Coshocton Co. (Franklin Township) [p]
Cuyahoga Co. (part) [p]
Gallia Co. (Addison Township) [s]
Jefferson Co. (part) [p]
Lake Co. (part) [p]
Lorrain Co. (part) [p]
Lucas Co. (part) [p]
Morgan Co. (Center Township) [s]
Washington Co. [s]

Pennsylvania
Allegheny Co. [p]
Armstrong Co. [p]
Warren Co. [p]

Tennessee
Benton Co. (surrounding TVA Johnsonville) [ps]
Humphreys Co. (surrounding TVA Johnsonville) [ps]
Polk Co. [ps]

Utah
Salt Lake Co. [ps]
Tooele Co. (part) [ps]

West Virginia
Hancock Co. (part) [p]

Wisconsin
Brown Co. (Green Bay) [p]
Dane Co. (Madison) [p]
Marathon Co. (Rothschild) [ps]
Milwaukee Co. (Milwaukee) [p]
Oneida Co. (Rhinelander) [ps]

Guam
Piti-Cabras [p]
Tanquisson [p]

---

*''p'' means particulate; ''s'' means SO_2; ''ps'' means both.

**Indicates proposed SO_2 nonattainment areas 9/9/92.

Appendix B

Hazardous Air Pollutants

CAS Number	*Chemical Name*
75070	Acetaldehyde
60355	Acetamide
75058	Acetronitrile
98862	Acetophenone
53963	2-Acetylaminofluorene
107028	Acrolein
79061	Acrylamide
79107	Acrylic acid
107131	Acrylonitrile
107051	Allyl chloride
92671	4-Aminobiphenyl
62533	Aniline
90040	o-Anisidine
1332214	Asbestos
71432	Benzene (including benzene from gasoline)
92875	Benzidine
98077	Benzotrichloride
100447	Benzyl chloride
92524	Biphenyl
117817	Bis(2-ethylhexyl)phthalate (DEHP)
542881	Bis(chloromethyl)ether
75252	Bromoform
106990	1,3-Butadiene
156627	Calcium cyanamide
105602	Caprolactam
133062	Captan
63252	Carbaryl
75150	Carbon disulfide
56235	Carbon tetrachloride
463581	Carbonyl sulfide
120809	Catechol
133904	Chloramben
57749	Chlordane
7782505	Chlorine
79118	Chloroacetic acid
532274	2-Chloroacetophenone
108907	Chlorobenzene
510156	Chlorobenzilate
67663	Chloroform
107302	Chloromethyl methyl ether
126998	Chloroprene
1319773	Cresols/Cresylic acid (isomers and mixture)

Hazardous Air Pollutants

CAS Number	*Chemical Name*
95487	o-Cresol
108394	m-Cresol
106445	p-Cresol
98828	Cumene
94757	2,4-D, salts and esters
3547044	DDE
334883	Diazomethane
132649	Dibenzofurans
96128	1,2-Dibromo-3-chloropropane
84742	Dibutylphthalate
106467	1,4-Dichlorobenzene(p)
91941	3,3-Dichlorobenzidene
111444	Dichloroethyl ether (Bis(2-chloroethyl)ether)
542756	1,3-Dichloropropene
62737	Dichlorvos
111422	Diethanolamine
121697	N,N-Diethyl aniline (N,N-Dimethylaniline)
64675	Diethyl sulfate
119904	3,3-Dimethoxybenzidine
60117	Dimethyl aminoazobenzene
119937	3,3′-Dimethyl benzidine
79447	Dimethyl carbamoyl chloride
68122	Dimethyl formamide
57147	1,1-Dimethyl hydrazine
131113	Dimethyl phthalate
77781	Dimethyl sulfate
534521	4,6-Dinitro-o-cresol, and salts
51285	2,4-Dinitrophenol
121142	2,4-Dinitrotoluene
123911	1,4-Dioxane (1,4-Diethyleneoxide)
122667	1,2-Diphenylhydrazine
106898	Epichlorohydrin (1-Chloro-2,3-epoxypropane)
106887	1,2-Epoxybutane
140885	Ethyl acrylate
100414	Ethyl benzene
51796	Ethyl carbamate (Urethane)

Hazardous Air Pollutants

CAS Number	*Chemical Name*
75003	Ethyl chloride (Chloroethane)
106934	Ethylene dibromide (Dibromoethane)
107062	Ethylene dichloride (1,2-Dichloroethane)
107211	Ethylene glycol
151564	Ethylene imine (Aziridine)
75218	Ethylene oxide
96457	Ethylene thiourea
75343	Ethylidene dichloride (1,1-Dichloroethane)
50000	Formaldehyde
76448	Heptachlor
118741	Hexachlorobenzene
87683	Hexachlorobutadiene
77474	Hexachlorocyclopentadiene
67721	Hexachloroethane
822060	Hexamethylene-1,6-diisocyanate
680319	Hexamethylphosphoramide
110543	Hexane
302012	Hydrazine
7647010	Hydrochloric acid
7664393	Hydrogen fluoride (Hydrofluoric acid)
123319	Hydroquinone
78591	Isophorone
58899	Lindane (all isomers)
108316	Maleic anhydride
67561	Methanol
72435	Methoxychlor
74839	Methyl bromide (Bromomethane)
74873	Methyl chloride (Chloromethane)
71556	Methyl chloroform (1,1,1-Trichloroethane)
78933	Methyl ethyl ketone (2-Butanone)
60344	Methyl hydrazine
74884	Methyl iodide (Iodomethane)
108101	Methyl isobutyl ketone (Hexone)
624839	Methyl isocyanate
80626	Methyl methacrylate
1634044	Methyl tert butyl ether

Hazardous Air Pollutants

CAS Number	*Chemical Name*
101144	4,4-Methylene bis(2-chloroaniline)
75092	Methylene chloride (Dichloromethane)
101688	Methylene diphenyl diisocyanate (MDI)
101779	4,4′-Methylenedianiline
91203	Naphthalene
98953	Nitrobenzene
92933	4-Nitrobiphenyl
100027	4-Nitrophenol
79469	2-Nitropropane
684935	N-Nitroso-N-methylurea
62759	N-Nitrosodimethylamine
59892	N-Nitrosomorpholine
56382	Parathion
82688	Pentachloronitrobenzene (Quintobenzene)
87865	Pentachlorophenol
108952	Phenol
106503	p-Phenylenediamine
75445	Phosgene
7803512	Phosphine
7723140	Phosphorus
85449	Phthalic anhydride
1336363	Polychlorinated biphenyls (Aroclors)
1120714	1,3-Propane sultone
57578	beta-Propiolactone
123386	Propionaldehyde
114261	Propoxur (Baygon)
78875	Propylene dichloride (1,2-Dichloropropane)
75569	Propylene oxide
75558	1,2-Propylenimine (2-Methyl aziridine)
91225	Quinoline
106514	Quinone
100425	Styrene
96093	Styrene oxide
1746016	2,3,7,8-Tetrachlorodibenzo-p-dioxin
79345	1,1,2,2-Tetrachloroethane
127184	Tetrachloroethylene (Perchloroethylene)
7550450	Titanium tetrachloride
108883	Toluene

Hazardous Air Pollutants		*Hazardous Air Pollutants*	
CAS Number	*Chemical Name*	*CAS Number*	*Chemical Name*
95807	2,4-Toluene diamine	106423	p-Xylenes
584849	2,4-Toluene diisocyanate	0	Antimony Compounds
95534	o-Toluidine	0	Arsenic Compounds (inorganic including arsine)
8001352	Toxaphene (chlorinated camphene)		
120821	1,2,4-Trichlorobenzene	0	Beryllium Compounds
79005	1,1,2-Trichloroethane	0	Cadmium Compounds
79016	Trichloroethylene	0	Chromium Compounds
95954	2,4,5-Trichlorophenol	0	Cobalt Compounds
88062	2,4,6-Trichlorophenol	0	Coke Oven Emissions
121448	Triethylamine	0	Cyanide Compounds[1]
1582098	Trifluralin	0	Glycol ethers[2]
540841	2,2,4-Trimethylpentane	0	Lead Compounds
108054	Vinyl acetate	0	Manganese Compounds
593602	Vinyl bromide	0	Mercury Compounds
75014	Vinyl chloride	0	Fine mineral fibers[3]
75354	Vinylidene chloride (1,1-Dichloroethylene)	0	Nickel Compounds
		0	Polycylic Organic Matter[4]
1330207	Xylenes (isomers and mixture)	0	Radionuclides (including radon)[5]
95476	o-Xylenes	0	Selenium Compounds
108383	m-Xylenes		

NOTE: For all listings above that contain the word ''compounds'' and for glycol ethers, the following applies: Unless otherwise specified, these listings are defined as including any unique chemical substance that contains the named chemical (i.e., antimony, arsenic, etc.) as part of that chemical's infrastructure.

[1]X′ CN where X=H′ or any other group where a formal dissociation may occur. For example KCN or $Ca(CN)_2$.

[2]Includes mono- and di- ethers of ethylene glycol, diethylene glycol, and triethylene glycol $R—(OCH_2CH_2)_n—OR'$ where n = 1, 2, or 3; R = alkyl or aryl groups; R′ = R, H, or groups which, when removed, yield glycol ethers with the structure: $R—(OCH_2CH)_n—OH$. Polymers are excluded from the glycol category.

[3]Includes mineral fiber emissions from facilities manufacturing or processing glass, rock, or slag fibers (or other mineral derived fibers) of average diameter 1 micrometer or less.

[4]Includes organic compounds with more than one benzene ring, and which have a boiling point greater than or equal to 100°C.

[5]A type of atom which spontaneously undergoes radioactive decay.

4

Water Pollution

By Russell V. Randle
with Suzanne R. Schaeffer

I. Introduction

A. History and Background

Federal regulation of water pollution began with enactment of the Rivers and Harbors Appropriations Act of 1899, commonly known as the Refuse Act.[1] This early statute was designed and administered to protect navigation, but also contained a flat prohibition against discharges that is broad enough to cover pollution of surface waters. In 1948, the first precursor to the present federal water pollution control statute, the Clean Water Act,[2] was passed. This statute was based primarily on a water quality approach, stressing state enforcement with some federal involvement, including federal government assistance to state and local governments for construction and operation of waste treatment plants.

In the 1960s, as public awareness of water quality and pollution problems increased, federal water pollution control efforts became serious and more focused. In 1965, the Water Quality Act[3] was enacted by Congress. Under this statute, the states were to establish water quality standards for various bodies of water, including interstate waters. The federal government was authorized to act in case of state inaction. The standards were to be used to determine allowable limits for each individual discharger into the water body. Although this approach seemed theoretically sound, it worked poorly for several reasons. For one thing, state authorities had difficulty in accurately determining if a discharge exceeded the applicable standards. The states also failed to make the load allocations necessary to set enforceable discharge standards. In addition, the statute contained unwieldy enforcement mechanisms and required state consent before initiation of federal enforcement action.

Although the federal-state water quality approach did result in the gradual adoption of federally approved water quality standards by most states, it became evident after a few years that an effective nationwide pollution control program would have to include a permit program based on federal effluent criteria—i.e.,

[1] Act of March 3, 1899, ch. 425, §13, 30 Stat. 1151, 33 U.S.C. §407 (1988).
[2] Act of June 30, 1948, Pub. L. No. 80-845, ch. 750, 62 Stat. 1155.
[3] Water Quality Act of 1965, Pub. L. No. 89-234, 795 Stat. 903 (1965).

source-specific standards enforceable directly against the discharger. Congress revisited the Refuse Act and its broad prohibition against discharges without a permit in order to provide such an approach. In late 1970, President Nixon ordered implementation of the Refuse Act permit program, concurrent with rules published by the Corps of Engineers.[4]

Section 13 of the Refuse Act prohibits the majority of discharges into navigable waters, unless the discharger obtains a permit from the Corps of Engineers before initiating the discharge.[5] Although this section previously had not been given much attention, with the commencement of the permit program, the government began to actively use this authority to require that all industrial dischargers apply for and obtain permits. The permits were granted or denied on the basis of environmental factors. In addition, the Refuse Act provided a "bounty" to citizens who provided information to the government allowing it to bring criminal actions to enforce permit requirements. Violations of the Act were enjoinable and subject to criminal penalties.

The lack of civil enforcement authority, and other problems encountered in administering the permit program, arose because the Refuse Act was not written as a comprehensive water pollution control statute. Though the Act absolutely prohibited unpermitted discharges, it had no standards for the grant or denial of permits; nor were they provided in Corps rules. Moreover, as the result of a court decision, the government had to go through the burdensome preparation of environmental impact statements for every permit application;[6] which further burdened the limited staff allocated to the program. Finally, there was an inherent tension between the effluent discharge approach of the 1899 Refuse Act and the water quality approach of the 1965 Water Quality Act, and confusion about how these two programs related to each other and to other federal and state water pollution control cfforts.

The difficulties and shortcomings encountered under the Water Quality Act and the Refuse Act made it clear that some sort of comprehensive, coordinated legislative approach was necessary for effective nationwide water pollution control. In 1972, Congress responded by passing the Federal Water Pollution Control Act (FWPCA or the 1972 Act),[7] as well as the Marine Protection, Research and Sanctuaries Act (MPRSA),[8] to regulate ocean dumping.

The FWPCA focused on nationwide, uniform, technology-based effluent standards for each industry. It charged the Environmental Protection Agency (EPA) with the task of setting such standards. EPA was to consider the technological capability and cost of pollution control technology with respect to the regulated industry, on an industry-by-industry basis. EPA was required to follow a stringent timetable in setting these effluent standards. The FWPCA

---

[4] 33 U.S.C. §407 (1988); Exec. Order No. 11,574, 35 Fed. Reg. 19,627 (1970).

[5] The only exception recognized by the statute is for "refuse matter . . . flowing from streets and sewers and passing therefrom in a liquid state." Therefore, the Refuse Act does not apply to storm water discharges. Regulation of such discharges is addressed under the Clean Water Act, as discussed below in section VI.

[6] *See* Kalur v. Resor, 335 F. Supp. 1 (D.D.C. 1971). Environmental impact statements and other National Environmental Policy Act (NEPA) requirements are discussed in detail in Chapter 11, Protection of Natural Resources. The relationship between NEPA and the Clean Water Act is discussed more fully in section IV, below.

[7] 33 U.S.C. §§1251–1376 (1972).

[8] 33 U.S.C. §§1401–44 (1972).

also continued requirements for water quality standards, though these had practical effect only in areas where application of effluent standards alone would not achieve the desired water quality. The Act replaced the Refuse Act permit program with the National Pollutant Discharge Elimination System (NPDES) requiring every "point source" discharge of water pollutants to obtain a federal permit. Administration of the NPDES is to be taken over by the states and territories as their permit programs meet rigorous federal standards; so far 39 out of 54 states and territories have done so. In addition, the 1972 Act updated the 1970 Water Quality Improvement Act,[9] which established reporting obligations and a prohibition on the discharge of harmful quantities of oil. The 1972 Act also added restrictions on the discharge of hazardous substances. The political heart of the 1972 Act was the generous construction grant program for publicly owned treatment works (POTWs). These basic elements continue to provide the framework for federal water pollution regulation today.

In 1977, the Clean Water Act Amendments[10] significantly amended the FWPCA, and thereafter the Act became popularly known as the Clean Water Act (CWA).[11] The CWA focused primarily on rigorous control of toxic water pollutants using technology-based standards. The Amendments also addressed a number of definitional and policy issues raised by several court and EPA decisions in the 1970s.

In 1987, the Act was again extensively amended[12] to improve water quality in areas where compliance with the national minimum discharge standards had not resulted in attainment of the Act's water quality goals, to address largely unregulated discharges such as storm water, and to strengthen the enforcement provisions. These amendments thus returned to a focus on water quality similar to that contained in the early versions of the statute by requiring that discharge standards be tightened beyond technology-based minimums to assure that water quality standards for toxic pollutants would be met.

Finally, in 1990, Congress passed the Oil Pollution Act,[13] parts of which amended the CWA by strengthening the oil spill provisions to include more stringent reporting and cleanup requirements and more severe penalties for discharges.

Like the CWA, the MPRSA has also been amended several times, most recently in 1988. This has resulted in an effective prohibition against ocean dumping of all wastes other than dredge spoil; dredge spoil discharges are regulated rather than prohibited.[14]

---

[9] Water Quality Act of 1970, Pub. L. No. 91-224, titl. I, §§101–07, 109–12, 84 Stat. 91 (1970).

[10] Pub. L. No. 95-217, 91 Stat. 1567 (1977).

[11] 33 U.S.C. §1251 *et seq.* The statute was also amended in 1978 to more effectively handle spills of hazardous substances, Federal Water Pollution Control Act Amendments of 1978, Pub. L. No. 95-576, 92 Stat. 2467 (1978), and in 1981 primarily to revise the grant program for publicly owned treatment works. Municipal Wastewater Treatment Construction Grant Amendments of 1981, Pub. L. No. 97-117, 95 Stat. 1623 (1981).

[12] The Water Quality Act of 1987, Pub. L. No. 100-4, 101 Stat. 76 (1987).

[13] Oil Pollution Act of 1990, Pub. L. No. 101-380, 104 Stat. 484 (1990).

[14] The 1977 and 1980 Amendments prohibited almost all ocean dumping of industrial wastes and sewage sludge after 1981. MPRSA Amendments of 1977, Pub. L. No. 95-153, 91 Stat. 1255 (1977); MPRSA Amendments of 1980, Pub. L. No. 96-572, 94 Stat. 3344 (1980).

B. Basic Elements of the Clean Water Act Regulatory Program

Like most statutes, the CWA contains a declaration of goals and policy: a general statement of the broad objectives that the statute is intended to achieve. These objectives are set out in Title I, in addition to provisions for reseach and other study programs. The other five titles of the CWA contain provisions that set out the various regulatory mechanisms designed to achieve the statutory goals.

1. *Declaration of Goals and Policy*

Section 101(a) of the CWA states:

> The objective of this Act is to restore and maintain the chemical, physical, and biological integrity of the Nation's waters. . . .

In order to achieve this objective, statements of national goals and policies are set forth as follows: (1) eliminate the discharge of pollutants into the navigable waters by 1985; (2) achieve a level of water quality that "provides for the protection and propagation of fish, shellfish, and wildlife and provides for recreation in and on the water to be achieved by July 1, 1983"; (3) prohibit discharge of toxic pollutants in toxic amounts; (4) provide federal financial assistance to build publicly owned treatment works; (5) develop adequate waste treatment management planning to adequately control sources; (6) perform research to develop technology necessary to eliminate discharge of pollutants; and (7) develop and implement programs for controls of nonpoint sources such as storm water.

Although the "no discharge" goal contained in the statute has obviously not been achieved, nor is it likely to be achieved in the near future, its inclusion is significant both as a policy matter and as a practical matter, because it does influence the stringency of standards set under the Act.

2. *Primary Regulatory Components*

The substantive provisions of the Act substantially mirror the CWA's policy goals. These provisions are best understood as comprising seven components of a regulatory system designed to achieve the primary prohibition driving the CWA: to prevent unpermitted "discharges of pollutants" into "any waters of the United States" from any "point source."[15] The primary regulatory components of the CWA are as follows:

1. Technology-based effluent limitation standards establishing the minimum treatment required for direct industrial dischargers (existing and new sources) and for POTWs with complementary pretreatment standards for dischargers to POTWs (Title III).

[15] Although one of the national policies in §101 specifically addresses nonpoint sources, this was only added in 1987, and the primary focus of the Act for most of its history has been point sources. Pursuant to the 1987 Amendments, a comprehensive system for control of nonpoint sources is now being implemented under the statute, and will be discussed in section VI, below.

2. More stringent water quality-based effluent limitation standards, applicable to dischargers in areas where such standards are necessary to achieve water quality objectives (Title III).
3. A prohibition on discharges of harmful quantities of oil and hazardous substances, with complementary reporting and clean up obligations that became the model for the Comprehensive Environmental Response, Compensation and Liability Act (CERCLA section 311).
4. A permit program requiring dischargers to disclose the type and volume of discharges, providing EPA with authority to specify limitations imposed on discharges, requiring dischargers to monitor and report compliance with limitations, and authorizing enforcement by EPA or by citizen suits in the event of noncompliance. The NPDES permit program regulates industrial (direct and indirect) and POTW discharges and also storm water discharges; other specialized permit programs exist for ocean discharge, dredge and fill, and disposal or use of sewage sludge (Title IV).
5. EPA state and citizen enforcement of the statutory standards, permit limitations, and specific deadlines for compliance with such limitations, with stringent civil and criminal penalty provisions (section 309, general enforcement provisions; section 505, citizen suit provisions).
6. Funding programs to assist states and local governments with construction and operation of POTWs in order to achieve the applicable effluent standards (Title II and Title VI).
7. Various research and study provisions to support development of treatment technology and other means of controlling and/or eliminating discharges and preservation of the integrity of the country's waters (Title I).

The following sections will discuss the development of these various components, the impact of underlying definitional and policy decisions, the coordination of these components as part of a comprehensive water pollution regulatory system, and how the system applies to control various sources and discharges in particular situations.

II. Technology-Based Effluent Limitations and Pretreatment Standards

The CWA embodies a two-part approach to establishing effluent limitations for industrial discharges: (1) national minimum treatment levels for each particular industry, based on an assessment of what is technologically and economically achievable; and (2) more stringent treatment requirements for specific plants where necessary to achieve water quality objectives for the particular body of water into which the plant discharges. According to some commentators, Congress intended EPA to implement these standards in a matter that would force control technology innovation.[16] This section will focus on the

[16] *See, e.g.*, Chemical Mfrs. Ass'n v. NRDC, 470 U.S. 116, 134 (1985) (Marshall, J. dissenting) (and sources cited therein).

development and current status of the uniform, nationwide, technology-based effluent standards for direct industrial dischargers and POTWs and the complementary pretreatment effluent standards for industrial indirect dischargers.

A. Pollutants and Sources Regulated

EPA's initial implementation of the technology-based effluent standards required under the 1972 Act focused almost completely on high-volume "conventional" pollutants such as suspended solids (SS), oil and grease, acidity and alkalinity (pH), and biochemical oxygen demanding (BOD). The focus on conventional pollutants resulted largely because prior to 1977, the Act provided little guidance with respect to toxic pollutants, although defining the term "pollutant" very broadly.[17] Monitoring and modeling were also far more advanced for conventional pollutants than for toxics. While section 307(a) authorized EPA to identify and regulate toxics on a chemical-by-chemical, rather than on an industry basis, EPA had to prove that the substance would have toxic effects on identified organisms in affected waters before exercising this authority. Because of the stringent burden of proof, the extensive procedures required, and EPA's limited resources, only a small number of substances were identified as toxic under section 307(a), and there were long delays before effluent standards were adopted for them. As a result, EPA's pre-1977 promulgation of effluent limits and permit requirements overemphasized removal of solids and oxygen-demanding materials in conventional wastes,[18] while failing to adequately address the risks posed by low-volume, more toxic pollutants such as chlorinated organic compounds, heavy metals, pesticides, and other substances.

EPA's failure to develop adequate regulations to control toxic pollutants under the 1972 Act prompted the Natural Resources Defense Council (NRDC) to bring a lawsuit against EPA.[19] In the course of settlement of the litigation, EPA and NRDC developed a policy that concentrated the Act's regulatory mechanisms on the effective control of toxic or "priority" pollutant discharges. EPA and NRDC identified (1) the primary pollutants to be regulated, (2) the industries of principal concern in applying the regulations, and (3) the methods for regulating toxic discharges using the legal procedures available in the Act. The agreements reached in these negotiations were memorialized in a consent decree in 1976,[20] and were subsequently adopted by Congress as a blueprint for the toxics control strategy in the 1977 Amendments to the Act. As a consequence of this decree, for the next decade water pollution regulation under the CWA revolved around EPA's efforts to promulgate technology-based effluent

[17] Section 502(6) defines the term "pollutant" to mean "dredged spoil, solid waste, incinerator residue, sewage, garbage, sewage sludge, munitions, chemical wastes, biological materials, radioactive materials, heat, wrecked or discarded equipment, rock, sand, cellar dirt and industrial, municipal, and agricultural waste discharged into water." 33 U.S.C. §1362(6) (1972). The term excludes sewage from vessels under §312, and material used in oil and gas production injection wells, where approved by the state in which the well is located.

[18] It should be noted, however, that conventional treatment frequently removes substantial amounts of more toxic wastes.

[19] *See* NRDC v. Train, 8 ER Cases 2120 (D.D.C. 1976), *modified,* 12 ER Cases 1833 (D.C.C. 1979).

[20] *Id.*

limitations and pretreatment standards for the identified toxic pollutants and industries.

The NRDC consent decree directed that all regulatory tools available under the Act be used to control discharges of identified "priority pollutants." EPA was to develop a program to regulate 65 categories of "priority pollutants"[21] (these now include at least 126 specific substances) discharged by 34 industry categories[22] (now reduced to 26), which include more than 700 subcategories. Over 70 percent of the country's industries were affected by the decree.

The decree mandated adoption of "best available technology" (BAT) effluent limitations for each priority pollutant: the standard the 1972 Act required EPA to set and each industry category to meet by June 30, 1983. Under the decree the limitations were required to be applicable to at least 95 percent of the point sources in each industry category or subcategory, and similar technology-based limitations had to be promulgated for new sources and sources discharging into POTWs (indirect dischargers). The decree provided only a very limited basis for excluding a category of point sources from this regulatory system.

In addition to these industry-by-industry toxic effluent limits, the consent decree provided for full implementation of more stringent water-quality-based effluent standards, applicable on a waterway segment-by-segment basis. However, this aspect of the decree was largely ignored until 1987, as discussed below in section III.B.

The 1977 Amendments largely adopted the technology-based aspects of the decree and enacted them into law. The Amendments codified the consent decree list of priority pollutants, which were to be given primary attention in implementation of the CWA. The Amendments also continued to require adoption of effluent limits based on BAT for each listed pollutant and authorized EPA to add to or remove pollutants from the list of toxics. For substances subsequently added to the list of toxic pollutants, compliance with BAT effluent limitations was required within three years of their development. The Amendments also provided a new system for tightening and enforcing pretreatment regulations, based on effluent limitations on the discharge from POTWs as well as the intended use of the sludge from the facilities. Finally, EPA was authorized to adopt regulations establishing best management practices, to control toxic pollutant discharges occurring as runoff or other uncontrolled discharges from industrial plant sites, parking lots, and so forth.

Although the 1977 Amendments adopted many of the requirements of the NRDC consent decree, they did not fully replace the decree. In fact, the decree has served as the primary vehicle for modification and updating of the toxics control program. It was amended in 1979 to reflect the changes made by the 1977 Amendments and to respond to operational problems encountered by EPA in implementing the original decree.[23] Challenges to the decree have twice been rejected by the courts.[24]

---

[21] See Appendix A to this chapter.

[22] See Appendix B to this chapter.

[23] NRDC v. Train, 12 ER Cases 1833 (D.D.C. 1979).

[24] Environmental Defense Fund v. Costle, 636 F.2d 1229 (D.C. Cir. 1980); Citizens for a Better Environment v. Gorsuch, 718 F.2d 1117 (D.C. Cir. 1983), *cert. denied*, 467 U.S. 1219 (1984).

The modified consent decree also expanded the permissible bases for exclusion of substances and industry categories from regulation. Pursuant to the revised decree, EPA is authorized to exclude industry categories from regulation of certain substances where only "trace amounts" of the substances are found. Seven industry categories have been so excluded. EPA may also exclude pollutants from regulation under direct discharge effluent limitations if the amount and toxicity of such pollutants within an industry category or subcategory does not justify the development of nationally applicable regulations. EPA was given additional authority to exclude a pollutant from application of pretreatment standards, where it finds that the amount and toxicity of all incompatible pollutants discharged by a category or subcategory on a cumulative basis are so small that regulations of national applicability for pretreatment of those substances are not justified. Three pollutants of the originally listed 129 have been excluded on this basis.

The modified decree also extended the deadlines for promulgation of and compliance with effluent limitations. However, the revised decree had little effect with respect to water-quality-based effluent standards because of EPA delays in identifying wastes and developing a control program. This inaction was subsequently addressed in the 1987 Amendments, which imposed deadlines for implementing the water quality approach.

In sum, the consent decree, as modified by the court and confirmed by the 1977 and 1987 Amendments, has transformed the entire CWA program and focused EPA and industry attention on the most dangerous pollutants. The industry-by-industry technology-based effluent limitations have been transformed from limited requirements focused on three or four conventional pollutants to a very specific system of limitations potentially applicable to approximately 125 different pollutants for each industry category. To date, EPA has promulgated effluent limitations for all 34 industry categories. How this was accomplished is the focus of the following section.

B. Technology-Based Effluent Limitations

1. Standards for Direct Industrial Dischargers

There are three categories of effluent standards applicable to direct industrial discharges under the CWA. Their application depends on whether the discharge is of conventional, toxic, or nonconventional, nontoxic pollutants:

1. best practicable control technology (BPT)—initially used for all substances, but now primarily used as a benchmark for other standards;
2. best available control technology (BAT)—used primarily for priority or toxic pollutants, but also used for nonconventional, nontoxic pollutants; and
4. best conventional technology (BCT)—used for conventional pollutants.

The Act provides criteria for EPA to consider in developing these categories of effluent limitations.

The first two categories—BPT and BAT—were established by the 1972 Act. Section 301(b) contains the mandate to establish nationwide technology-based effluent limitations on an industry-by-industry basis, and provides that minimum effluent standards for existing sources of direct discharges in every significant industrial category be proposed in two phases: the first phase deadline of July 1, 1977, applied to attainment of the effluent limitations requiring application of the best practicable control technology currently available; the second phase deadline of July 1, 1983, applied to achievement of effluent limitations requiring application of the best available control technology economically achievable. As explained below, the deadlines were pushed back twice, ultimately to March 31, 1989.

a. Best Practicable Control Technology. Section 301 requires EPA to define BPT in conjunction with the criteria set out in section 304(b) of the statute. Section 304(b)(1)(B) requires that EPA consider several factors in its assessment of the BPT currently available, including the "total cost of application of technology in relation to the effluent reduction benefits to be achieved from such application." Thus, in construing the term "practicable" consistently with section 304(b)(1)(B), EPA had to justify effluent limitations in terms of total industrywide costs and total amount of reductions achieved. In essence, EPA was to perform a rough cost-benefit analysis.

Section 304(b)(1)(B) also requires EPA to consider specific engineering and process-related factors in developing BPT effluent limitations, including "the age of equipment and facilities involved, the process employed, the engineering aspects of the application of various types of control techniques, process changes, and non–water quality environmental impact (including energy requirements)." These criteria made it clear that EPA, while developing best "control" technology standards that stressed end-of-pipe treatment, also had to consider the alternatives of in-plant process changes, and other specific engineering factors, at least insofar as determining whether a proposed limitation would be "practicable."

EPA defined BPT pursuant to the 1972 Act as the "average of the best existing performance by well-operated plants within each industrial category or subcategory," and this definition and the relevant criteria were not substantially affected by the 1977 Amendments. Although promulgated in 1977, these standards continue to play an important role as baselines for setting other standards, such as the nonconventional, nontoxic pollutant standards discussed in subsection d., below.[25]

b. Best Available Technology. The second phase of the directive in section 301 of the 1972 Act required that by 1983, the best available technology economically achievable was to be achieved by existing industrial sources. EPA defines BAT as the "very best control and treatment measures that have been or are capable of being achieved." In setting BAT standards, EPA is to establish regulations pursuant to section 304(b)(2)(A), which directs EPA to identify "the degree of effluent reduction attainable through the application of the best

---

[25] EPA recently used the BPT provisions to set revised standards for the organic chemicals industry. *See* Chemical Mfrs. Ass'n v. EPA, 870 F.2d 177 (5th Cir. 1989).

control measures and practices achievable including treatment techniques, process and procedure innovations, operating methods, and other alternatives." Thus, EPA must consider process-related changes as available alternative controls, in addition to end-of-pipe controls, in establishing the BAT effluent limitations.

Section 304(b)(2)(B) requires that EPA consider "the cost of achieving such effluent reduction," or the affordability to industry of BAT limitations; however, there is no requirement for any cost-benefit balancing as in the case of the BPT criteria. Section 304(b)(2)(B) also specifies that the same engineering factors (age of equipment, for example) are to be considered in determining what is the best available technology economically achievable.

Although the BAT limitations were applicable to pollutants from all industrial sources (mainly conventional pollutants) under the 1972 Act, the 1977 and 1987 Amendments shifted the focus of the BAT standards to concentrate primarily on the priority or toxic pollutants listed in the NRDC consent decree or identified pursuant to section 307 of the Act. The 1977 and 1987 Amendments also amended section 301 to extend the date for attainment of BAT standards to March 1989. The BAT effluent limitations now have been promulgated for all industry categories, as noted above. Compliance with the limitation is required three years after promulgation, but in no event later than March 31, 1989.[26]

c. Best Conventional Technology. Another change made by the 1977 Amendments was to specifically exclude so-called conventional pollutants, the primary focus of EPA's pre-1977 BAT effluent limitations, from coverage under the BAT limits to be promulgated pursuant to the 1977 Amendments. The Amendments established BCT, an entirely new treatment standard for conventional pollutants. The BCT effluent limitations were, like the BPT and BAT limitations, to be adopted on an industry-by-industry basis, but were to apply with respect to each affected industry only to pollutants that were identified as "conventional." Section 304(a)(4) was amended in 1977 to specifically define "conventional pollutants" as "pollutants classified as biological oxygen demanding (BOD), suspended solids (SS), fecal coliform, and pH," and any additional pollutants designated as conventional by EPA. The Administrator designated oil and grease as additional conventional pollutants pursuant to this authority.[27] The definition also provides that "the thermal component of any discharge shall not be identified as a conventional pollutant," as there are specific provisions applicable to thermal discharges elsewhere in the Act.[28] A compliance deadline of July 1, 1984, was set for the BCT effluent limitations in section 301 of the 1977 Amendments, and this deadline was extended by the 1987 Amendments to three years after promulgation or March 31, 1989, whichever is sooner.

Section 304(b)(4) contains the criteria to be "taken into account in determining the best conventional pollutant control technology measures and practices," and requires that EPA consider "the reasonableness of the relationship between the costs of attaining a reduction in effluents and the effluent reduction

---

[26] CWA §301(b), 33 U.S.C. §1311 (1988).

[27] 40 C.F.R. §401.16.

[28] CWA §316, 33 U.S.C. §1326 (1988); see Section VII.B, below.

benefits derived.'' In examining reasonableness, EPA is to compare the cost and level of reduction of such pollutants from the discharge from POTWs to the cost and level of reduction of such pollutants from a class or category of industrial sources. Thus, the statute suggests that Congress expected the cost of providing treatment to comply with BCT limits would be generally comparable to the cost of achieving secondary treatment limitations for POTWs. Congress also expected that EPA, in developing the BCT limits, would review the old BAT limits for conventional pollutants and reduce their stringency to the extent indicated by the required consideration of reasonableness and comparison of costs of secondary treatment requirements. Section 304(b)(4)(b) additionally requires EPA to consider the same engineering factors considered in establishing BPT and BAT limits.

EPA's first attempt at promulgating BCT standards was reversed by the Court of Appeals for the Fourth Circuit because the agency failed to consider cost-effectiveness sufficiently in developing the regulations.[29] In response, EPA developed a new methodology and revised the BCT standards so that they were much less costly than the original limits. Thus, in most industry categories, BCT limitations are now no more stringent than those established under BPT, which also remain in force.

d. Standards for Nonconventional, Nontoxic Pollutants. The final category of effluent limits for existing industrial direct discharges, which was included in section 301(b)(2)(A) of the 1977 Amendments, is essentially a catch-all to cover those substances not covered by the other categories of effluent limits: the nonconventional, nontoxic pollutants. Section 301(b)(2) provides that BAT standards shall be promulgated for any such substances, and requires compliance with these standards by March 31, 1989, or within three years of establishment, whichever is sooner. EPA to date has regulated only about 10 substances under the standard, including ammonia, chlorine, color, iron, and total phenols. Section 301(g) provides that EPA, with the concurrence of the state, may modify the standards for nonconventional pollutants on a source-specific basis, so long as the modified standard complies with BPT requirements at a minimum and does not result in any additional requirements on other point sources or interfere with water quality standards. This provision has been of help primarily to the steel industry.

2. *Standards for New Sources of Direct Industrial Discharges*

Section 306 governs the promulgation of national standards of performance applicable to ''new sources'' of direct discharges. New sources are defined as any facility or major modification of an existing facility, ''the construction of which is commenced after the publication of proposed regulations prescribing a standard of performance under this section which will be applicable to such source.'' Section 306 contains the list of industry categories for which effluent guidelines are promulgated and provides that standards for new sources in those categories are to be established within a year of including the relevant source category on the list. The new source performance standards, while similar in

[29] American Paper Inst. v. EPA, 660 F.2d 954 (4th Cir. 1981) (holding that two-part cost-reasonableness test required under statute).

some respects to standards for existing sources, differ in several important ways, particularly with respect to the level of treatment required and the applicability of the standards. These differences are all the more significant because EPA has delayed in promulgating some BPT and BAT standards, and new source standards will be applicable to the addition or replacement of certain equipment at an existing discharger.[30]

Section 306(a)(1), in language parallel to that in the BAT standard, provides that a standard of performance for new sources shall be

> a standard for the control of discharge of pollutants which reflects the greatest degree of effluent reduction which the Administrator determines to be achievable through application of the best available demonstrated control technology, processes, operating methods, or other alternatives, including where practicable, a standard permitting no discharge of pollutants.

These criteria make it clear that EPA is to consider process-related alternatives to end-of-pipe controls in setting new source standards, similar to the requirements for establishing BAT standards, but that EPA is not required to perform any cost-benefit analysis or take account of specified engineering and technological factors. Although section 306 does provide that EPA shall consider "the cost of achieving the effluent reduction, and any non-water quality environmental impacts and energy requirements" in setting new source performance standards, there is no requirement that the performance standards be "economically achievable," as is the case with BAT limits. This allows EPA much more discretion in choosing appropriate standards, and means that more expensive alternatives may be used, if they significantly reduce the amount of potential discharges. This difference is based on the presumption that a new source not yet constructed will have more flexibility in altering production or other in-plant processes.

Another distinction between the new source performance standards and effluent standards for existing industry sources is that there is essentially no flexibility in application of the standards to a particular new or modified facility. No variances or other authority for modification are applicable to new sources under the Act, and strict and immediate compliance is required once applicable new source standards are promulgated.

Moreover, if EPA is the regulatory entity issuing a permit for a new source discharge (as opposed to the state), issuance of the permit is subject to review under the National Environmental Policy Act (NEPA).[31] Under NEPA, if issuance of the permit is a "major federal action" with a significant impact on the environment, an environmental impact statement must be prepared. Thus, there will be potentially lengthy delays in issuing the permit, and the permit may include requirements regarding environmental impacts not related to effluent or water quality considerations.[32] As might be expected, these potentially costly consequences resulting from application of new source performance standards have created a great deal of controversy over when a facility "commences construction," within the meaning of section 306. Although the issue has been

---

[30] 40 C.F.R. §122.29(b).

[31] CWA §511(c), 33 U.S.C. §1371 (1988); 40 C.F.R. pt. 6.

[32] There are serious questions concerning the propriety of including additional environmental requirements in an NPDES permit pursuant to NEPA. *See* NRDC v. EPA, 822 F.2d 104 (D.C. Cir. 1987).

addressed at length in the permit regulations, court decisions, and the opinions of EPA's general counsel disputes continue to arise because each case is fact-specific. For this reason, companies intending to build new facilities, or planning to add or change equipment at existing facilities, should become thoroughly familiar with the new source requirements before taking any action.

Section 306 does provide some relief to new and modified sources from its somewhat rigid and stringent requirements. It provides that any new facility constructed to meet all applicable new source performance standards in effect at the time of construction may not be required to comply with any more stringent standards for 10 years from the date construction is completed, or for the period of depreciation or amortization under the Internal Revenue Code, whichever is shorter. Under EPA's reading of the Act, however, this protection is not applicable where the stricter standards subsequently coming into effect are not technology-based, such as stricter water-quality-based effluent standards, permit conditions applicable to pollutants not controlled by the new source performance standards in effect at the time of the source's construction, or toxic pollutant prohibitions. In addition, at the expiration of the 10-year protection period, immediate compliance with the more stringent standards is required—no implementation period is allowed.

3. *Pretreatment Standards for Dischargers to POTWs*

Unlike direct dischargers, industrial facilities that discharge into POTWs[33] are regulated by a parallel set of effluent limits for indirect dischargers contained in section 307(b) of the Act. These pretreatment standards have two basic purposes. The first is to protect and prevent interference with the proper operation of the POTW. The second is to prevent the discharge of pollutants that pass through the POTW without receiving adequate treatment. As a result of these dual objectives, the pretreatment program is comprised of a two-part system of controls: (1) general pretreatment requirements applicable to all indirect dischargers,[34] and (2) requirements specific to particular industries, called categorical pretreatment standards, that are developed and promulgated with the other effluent guidelines for each industry category.

a. General Pretreatment Standards. The first part of the pretreatment program consists of general pretreatment standards. They are primarily directed at preventing the discharge of pollutants into POTWs that will interfere with the operation of the receiving treatment works. The regulations prohibit the introduction into any POTWs of the following:

1. Pollutants that create a fire or explosion hazard in the POTW, including but not limited to waste streams that meet the Resource Conservation and Recovery Act (RCRA) test for characteristic ignitable waste;
2. Discharges with a pH lower than 5.0 unless the POTW is specifically designed to accommodate such discharges;

[33] It should be noted that the Federal Facilities Compliance Act, (Pub. L. No. 102-386, 106 Stat. 1505 (1992) (to be codified at 42 U.S.C. §6961)) revised the definition of publicly owned treatment works to include federally owned treatment works.

[34] *See* 40 C.F.R. pt. 403.

3. Solid or viscous pollutants in amounts that obstruct the flow in a sewer system;
4. Discharges, including conventional pollutant discharges, of such volume and concentration that they upset the treatment process and cause a permit violation (such as very high concentrations of BOD pollutants);
5. Heat in amounts that will inhibit biological activity in the POTW resulting in interference, but in no case heat in such quantities that the temperature influent at the receiving POTW exceeds 40°C (104°F) unless the POTW is designed to accommodate such heat;
6. Petroleum oil, nonbiodegradable cutting oil, or products of mineral oil origin in amounts that will cause interference or pass through;
7. Pollutants that result in the presence of toxic gases, vapors, or fumes within the POTW in a quantity that may cause acute worker health and safety problems; and
8. Any trucked or hauled pollutants, except at discharge points designated by the POTW.

These general pretreatment regulations were revised and made more stringent in 1990, after review of the Pretreatment Implementation Review Task Force.[35] The revisions were designed to close the domestic sewage loophole in RCRA section 1004(27)[36] and impose a number of requirements on dischargers to POTWs, in addition to the discharge prohibitions listed above. The revised regulations require that industrial dischargers to POTWs must provide written notice to the appropriate authorities at EPA, the state, and the POTW "of any discharge which is otherwise disposed of, would be a hazardous waste under 40 C.F.R. part 261."[37] If the discharge is more than 100 kilograms a month of such RCRA waste, the industrial discharger must include information about the hazardous waste constituents, mass, and concentration, and estimate what these amounts will be for the next 12 months. The discharger must also certify in its discharge notice that it has a RCRA waste minimization program.

Pollutants that are addressed in existing discharge monitoring reports are exempt from the RCRA-related notification requirement. Thus, when RCRA waste notifications are filed, revisions to some pretreatment permits and enforcement actions for discharge of materials not addressed in the permits could result.

b. Categorical Pretreatment Standards. The second type of pretreatment requirements for indirect dischargers—categorical pretreatment standards—are intended to improve the effluent discharge and sludge quality of the POTW, by ensuring that no pollutants pass through without adequate treatment. These pretreatment standards, which are issued by industrial category, apply only to "incompatible" pollutants, or nonconventional pollutants that are not adequately treated by the POTW.[38] Thus, the categorical pretreatment standards

---

[35] 55 Fed. Reg. 30,082 (1990), amending 40 C.F.R. §403.5.

[36] *See also* 40 C.F.R. §261.4(a)(1).

[37] 40 C.F.R. §403.12(p)(i).

[38] "Compatible" pollutants to which categorical pretreatment standards are inapplicable are generally conventional pollutants such as BOD, SS, pH, and fecal coliform bacteria. Additional pollutants may be identified as compatible for a particular POTW if it is shown that the POTW adequately treats those pollutants.

focus on the 65 toxic (priority) pollutants and 34 industry categories addressed by the BAT effluent guidelines for direct dischargers. Section 307 requires that the categorical pretreatment standards achieve the same level of treatment for each discharger into the POTW as that required for direct dischargers. In other words, the indirect discharger must achieve a level of treatment equivalent to the BAT effluent guidelines (or new source performance standards) in meeting the applicable pretreatment standard. Compliance with pretreatment standards is required three years after promulgation.

The stringency of these categorical standards can potentially be reduced through application of removal credits, a mechanism provided by the statute to account for removals of a pollutant by the POTW.[39] These credits must be requested for each pollutant by the receiving POTW, to be applied against each applicable pretreatment standard. Removal credits are granted based on the POTW's demonstrated ability to consistently remove a particular pollutant in its treatment process. In order to be granted a revision, the POTW must provide consistent removal of each pollutant for which a discharge limit revision is sought, and its sludge use or disposal practices must be and remain in compliance with all applicable sludge use and disposal criteria.[40] This includes compliance with EPA's long-awaited final sewage sludge regulations, which were recently promulgated under CWA section 405, and authorize the granting of removal credits for certain pollutants.[41]

c. Enforcement. The pretreatment standards are currently enforceable by EPA and by states with NPDES permitting authority. The pretreatment regulations anticipate that responsibility for administration and enforcement of the program eventually will be taken over by the individual POTWs, with EPA and the state playing only a secondary role.

The regulations provide that any POTW or group of POTWs operated by the same authority with a total design flow greater than five million gallons per day, that receives incompatible waste, must have developed and implemented a pretreatment program by July 1, 1983. An approved pretreatment program is a prerequisite to the issuance of removal credits, although the POTW may be granted conditional removal credits while EPA is considering approval of its pretreatment program.

The regulations also require that pretreatment programs meet funding, personnel, legal, and procedural criteria sufficient to allow the POTW to meet its enforcement responsibilities. Once a POTW program has been approved, the POTW is responsible for enforcement of the applicable national pretreatment standards. POTWs have a number of means to exercise their enforcement authority, including contracts, joint powers agreements, and ordinances. The pretreatment regulations also establish extensive reporting requirements for both industrial dischargers and POTWs, as an aid in monitoring and demonstrating compliance with the standards.

---

[39] CWA §307(b)(1), 33 U.S.C. §1317(b)(1) (1988).

[40] EPA modified its removal credit criteria in an effort to take into account POTW process variations, *see* 49 Fed. Reg. 31,221 (1984), but was reversed by the U.S. Court of Appeals for the Third Circuit. NRDC v. EPA, 790 F.2d 289 (3d Cir. 1986), *cert. denied,* 479 U.S. 1084 (1987).

[41] 58 Fed. Reg. 9248 (1993) (to be codified at 40 C.F.R. pts. 257, 403, and 503). The removal credit provisions will be codified in 40 C.F.R. pt. 403. The standards for use and disposal of sewage sludge are addressed in detail in section IV.C, below.

4. *Updating Effluent Guidelines for Industry*

Section 304(b) requires EPA to periodically revise the effluent guidelines for industry categories, consistent with changes in technological and economic factors. Section 304(m) was added to the CWA by the 1987 Amendments and specifically requires EPA to establish and publish biennially a schedule for the annual review and revision of the promulgated effluent guidelines, in accordance with section 304(b).[42]

Section 304(m) also requires that EPA identify categories of sources discharging toxic or nonconventional, nontoxic pollutants for which effluent guidelines and new source performance standards have not previously been promulgated, and establish a schedule for promulgation of such guidelines.[43] The guidelines were to be promulgated no later than February 1991 for sources in the first published plan, and no later than three years after publication of subsequent plans for categories identified in those plans.[44]

EPA published its first two section 304(m) plans in 1988 and 1990. According to these plans, EPA was to issue new or revised guidelines for eight source categories and study 11 additional source categories for revision of existing limitation guidelines or promulgation of new guidelines.[45] The dates for these revisions and new standards under the plans were as late as 1995.

Because the dates for revision and promulgation of new standards in the 1988 published plan were several years behind the statutory deadline, and because there are additional source categories that EPA failed to include in the plan, NRDC brought suit in 1989 to force acceleration and expansion of EPA's schedule.[46] The settlement of this litigation resulted in a consent decree, which was entered by the court on January 31, 1992.[47] EPA subsequently published a new section 304(m) effluent guidelines plan in September 1992, in compliance with the terms of the decree.[48]

As reflected in EPA's 1992 plan, the decree commits EPA to schedules for proposing and taking final action on seven effluent guidelines already under development and four guidelines that have not yet been started.[49] In general,

---

[42] CWA §304(m)(1)(A), 33 U.S.C. §1314(m)(1)(A) (1988).

[43] CWA §304(m)(1)(B) and (C), 33 U.S.C. §1314(m)(1)(B) and (C) (1988).

[44] CWA §304(m)(1)(C), 33 U.S.C. §1314(m)(1)(C) (1988).

[45] *See* 53 Fed. Reg. 32,584 (1988); 55 Fed. Reg. 78 (1990).

[46] NRDC v. Reilly, No. 89-2980 (D.D.C. Oct. 30, 1989). NRDC filed an amended complaint additionally challenging EPA's 1990 plan on January 19, 1990.

[47] *See* 57 Fed. Reg. 19,750–55 (1992).

[48] 57 Fed. Reg. 41,000 (1992).

[49] The consent decree schedule for the seven guidelines currently under development is as follows:

Point Source Category	Proposal	Final Action
1. Pesticide Manufacturing	3/92	7/92
2. Pesticide Formulating & Packaging	1/94	8/95
3. Centralized Waste Treatment (Phase I)	4/94	1/96
4. Machinery Manufacturing & Rebuilding (Phase I)	11/94	5/96
5. Pharmaceutical Manufacturing	8/94	2/96
6. Organic Chemicals, Plastics & Synthetic Fibers*	12/91	5/93
7. Coastal Oil & Gas	1/95	7/96

---

*Remand issues in Chemical Mfrs. Ass'n v. EPA, 870 F.2d 177 (5th Cir. 1989).

The four identified new categories include waste treatment (Phase II), industrial laundries, transportation

EPA is required to start two guidelines per year throughout the 1990s, with deadlines for final action on each rule between four and five years after work has begun. EPA retains discretion to select guidelines for development based on Agency priorities.

EPA is also to conduct preliminary studies of 11 industries to determine whether effluent guidelines would be appropriate; eight of these industries are identified in the decree. Two such studies must be commenced per year in each of the years 1992 through 1995, with three studies to be commenced in 1996. The decree requires EPA to propose and take final action on at least 12 effluent guidelines, in addition to those currently under development, by December 31, 2003.

Pursuant to the consent decree, EPA proposed effluent guidelines, pretreatment standards, and new source performance standards in the pesticide chemicals manufacturing industry category in 1992.[50] The deadline for another set of effluent guidelines not addressed in the consent decree, but the subject of other litigation[51] —the pulp, paper, and paperboard source category—has been pushed back to October 1993 to allow EPA to attempt to develop an integrated rule combining effluent guidelines under the CWA and emissions control technology standards under the Clean Air Act (CAA).[52]

5. *Variances*

The statutory provisions that authorize variances from technology-based standards are very limited in their application. The most broadly applicable provision is section 301(n), which prescribes the requirements for granting a variance based on fundamentally different factors (FDF). There are also other provisions in section 301 that allow for variances to recognize use of innovative control technology and for variances from BAT limitations, in certain limited circumstances. No variances other than the FDF variance are allowed from toxic pollutant standards,[53] and no variances at all are allowed from discharge

---

equipment cleaning, and metal products and machinery (Phase II). EPA is also committed to propose and take action on eight effluent guidelines that are to identified at a later time. 57 Fed. Reg. at 41,000.

[50] *See* 57 Fed. Reg. 12,560 (1992). Since publishing its first two effluent guidelines plans, EPA has also promulgated final effluent limitations for the organic chemicals, plastics, and synthetic fibers category, 57 Fed. Reg. 41,836 (1992), and final effluent guidelines for the offshore oil and gas extraction category, 58 Fed. Reg. 12,454 (1993), pursuant to litigation in NRDC v. EPA, Civ. No. 79-3442 (D.D.C. 1979). *See, e.g.,* NRDC v. EPA, 781 F. Supp. 806, 34 ER Cases 1471 (D.D.C. 1992).

[51] Environmental Defense Fund v. Thomas, 657 F. Supp. 302, 25 ER Cases 1777 (D.D.C. 1987).

[52] EPA will also be faced with the task of rewriting some of its effluent guidelines, given the holding in Chemical Waste Mgmt., Inc. v. EPA, 976 F.2d 2 (D.C. Cir. 1992). In attempting to integrate its RCRA "third-third" land ban requirements with CWA requirements, EPA amended its regulation prohibiting dilution of wastes in lieu of treatment to allow aggregation of certain waste streams in instances where it was addressed by CWA requirements and EPA had not specified a particular treatment method. *See* 40 C.F.R. §268.3. The effect of the amended rule was to allow CWA treatment facilities to continue to use unlined surface impoundments, with treatment at point of discharge. The D.C. Circuit ruled that the amended dilution rule is valid only where the waste is "decharacterized" prior to placement in a surface impoundment and subsequently treated in accord with RCRA standards. 976 F.2d at 19. In other words, wastes must be treated to RCRA standards before placement in a lagoon or other impoundment in order to avoid the land ban prohibitions. This case illustrates potentially serious difficulties in attempting to mesh two regulatory regimes that address wastes quite differently—RCRA regulates waste-by-waste, and the CWA regulates industry-by-industry. See Chapter 6 for a discussion of RCRA land ban requirements.

[53] *See* CWA §301(1), 33 U.S.C. §1311(1) (1988).

limitations set to meet water quality standards or from new source performance standards.

The FDF variance evolved as a byproduct of the demands of the process used by EPA in setting effluent standards under the Act. Because it is impossible for EPA to fully consider every factor required under section 304 in revising or setting new effluent standards for each type of plant in every industry category in a timely manner, there had to be some way to weigh factors not properly considered in development of the effluent standards at the point where those standards were applied to a particular facility in an NPDES permit. Thus, the FDF variance evolved through EPA and court interpretation.

The FDF variance was initially applied to modify BPT effluent limitations by including a variance clause in each set of effluent limitation regulations. The clause provided that a discharger could obtain a variance from the applicable effluent limitations for its facility if it could demonstrate that there existed factors fundamentally different from those considered by EPA in developing the effluent limitations. The scope of this variance clause was expanded in 1976 in *Appalachian Power Co. v. Train,*[54] and the Supreme Court approved EPA's administrative recognition that some type of variance mechanism was necessary to take account of fundamentally different factors.[55]

An FDF variance may be obtained with respect to the categorical pretreatment regulations, the effluent standards for existing direct dischargers under the NPDES permit program and the effluent limitations for toxic pollutants.[56] An FDF variance is not available, however, from new source performance standards or from water-quality-based effluent standards. The FDF variance was codified in section 301(n) by the 1987 Amendments.

Section 301(n) tightens the FDF variance and requires that the discharger demonstrate to EPA's satisfaction that the facility is "fundamentally different with respect to the factors (other than cost) specified in sections 304(b) or 304(g) and considered by the Administrator" in setting the effluent limitation guidelines or categorical pretreatment standards.[57] Under the statute and applicable regulations,[58] factors to be considered in making a "fundamentally different" determination are (1) the nature and quality of pollutants contained in the waste load of the discharger's process water; (2) the volume of the discharger's process waste water and effluent discharge; (3) non-water quality environmental impacts of treatment and control of discharger's waste load (including energy requirements); and (4) age, size, land availability, and configuration as they relate to the discharger's facility and processes and other engineering aspects of control technology. If EPA finds that the discharger has established that its facility is fundamentally different, the facility may be eligible for alternative effluent limits. Based on the language of section 301(n), as amended in 1987, it appears that cost of compliance is specifically excluded from

---

[54] 545 F.2d 1351 (4th Cir. 1976).

[55] E.I. DuPont de Nemours & Co. v. Train, 430 U.S. 112 (1977). The Supreme Court subsequently again upheld EPA's FDF variance approach prior to its inclusion in the statute in Chemical Mfrs. Ass'n v. NRDC, 470 U.S. 116 (1985).

[56] *See* Chemical Mfrs. Ass'n v. NRDC, 470 U.S. 116 (1985).

[57] 33 U.S.C. §1311(n)(1)(A) (1988).

[58] 40 C.F.R. §125.31.

consideration as a factor warranting an FDF variance,[59] although one might argue that disproportionate cost is evidence that one of the other factors considered is fundamentally different.

In addition, the 1987 Amendments require that applicants for FDF variances must submit an application within six months of the effective date of the particular standard in question. For standards that had been established prior to the effective date of the Amendments, EPA allowed applicants six months from the date of promulgation of the implementing regulations, that is, until July 3, 1989. In addition, an appeal to the courts for improper application of factors considered during development of guidelines must be filed within 90 days of promulgation of final guidelines. Failure to comply with these procedural rules may result in waiver of the discharger's right to raise the FDF issue. Such rules make it imperative for affected industries to monitor and participate in the development and revision of applicable effluent standards lest this variance mechanism become unavailable.

Apart from the FDF variance provision, there are several additional variance provisions in section 301. Sections 301(c) and (g) provide for variances applicable to discharges of nonconventional, nontoxic pollutants. Section 301(c) grants EPA authority to modify the BAT requirements or the related pretreatment requirements affecting nonconventional, nontoxic pollutants if it can be shown that the economic capability of the discharger necessitates less stringent limitations. A further prerequisite to this modification is showing that it will result in further progress toward elimination of the discharge of pollutants. Although the basis for granting this variance is reasonably broad, the circumstances in which it can be granted are strictly limited: The section 301(c) variance does not apply to BCT effluent limitations, and section 301(l) of the Act precludes the modification of any effluent limitation regulating a toxic or priority pollutant by this mechanism.

Section 301(g) is the second variance mechanism applicable to BAT limitations for several nonconventional, nontoxic pollutants, including ammonia, chlorine, color, iron, and total phenols, but excluding heat. Modifications will be granted only if the discharger demonstrates that the modification (1) will at a minimum result in compliance with applicable BPT effluent or pretreatment standards or any applicable water-quality-based effluent standards, (2) will not result in any additional requirements on other sources, and (3) will not interfere with attaining or maintaining sufficiently protective water quality standards.

The final statutory basis for modification of BAT and BCT effluent limits and pretreatment standards is set forth in section 301(k). As amended in 1987, section 301(k) authorizes the appropriate permitting authority to issue a permit providing for a compliance date extension of two years if a source seeks to achieve the applicable limits through the use of innovative technology that has the potential for industrywide application and has a substantial likelihood of achieving greater effluent reduction than the effluent limitations or will result in

---

[59] Under case law interpreting the statute prior to 1987, an FDF variance was not available simply because cost of compliance would result in plant closure, EPA v. National Crushed Stone Ass'n, 449 U.S. 64 (1980). The costs of compliance with effluent limitations was relevant in determining whether fundamentally different factors existed at a plant and the cost effectiveness of alternative effluent limitations. Weyerhaeuser Co. v. Costle, 590 F.2d 1011 (D.C. Cir. 1978).

significantly lower costs. It is debatable, but possible, that this innovative technology variance may be granted for toxic pollutant limits, despite the prohibition against modification of toxic pollutant effluent limitations set forth in section 301(l).

III. Water-Quality-Based Effluent Limitations

The 1972 Act made technology-based effluent limitations the nationwide minimum level of treatment. The CWA provides several mechanisms by which these discharge limitations are to be tightened in order to protect or maintain adequate water quality in specific bodies of water. These water-quality-based effluent limits are developed by the state (or EPA) initially setting numerical limits for allowable pollutant concentrations for each specific body of water. The more stringent water-quality-based limitations are most often an issue along bodies of water where there is a heavy concentration of industrial discharges (such as the Houston Ship Channel), where receiving waters need to be maintained at a very high quality for recreational or other purposes (such as a trout stream), or where hydrologic modifications for navigation (such as lock and dam systems) have reduced the capacity of receiving waters to assimilate pollutants. After the water quality standards are developed, modeling is used to allocate allowable pollutant loads to each discharger to the body of water. The allowable pollutant loads translate into effluent discharge limits applicable to each discharger to a particular body of water.

Sections 301(b)(1)(C) and 302 of the CWA apply to all categories of pollutants and provide the basic mechanisms by which water quality standards are established and modified. Pursuant to the 1987 Amendments, section 304(l) has been the most important statutory mechanism for tightening discharge standards over the last five years. This provision requires tightening of priority and toxic pollutant discharge limitations to meet water quality standards. Other sections of the Act provide for periodic review of water quality by the states and reports to EPA, efforts to preserve lakes and estuaries, and efforts to develop controls on nonpoint sources of pollution affecting water quality.

A. General Water Quality Standards

Sections 301(b)(1)(C) and 302 are the most important of the general water quality provisions in the CWA and form the basis of the water quality approaches that have been part of the Act since 1972. Section 301(b)(1)(C) requires industrial dischargers and POTWs to achieve any effluent limitations more stringent than the minimum technology-based standards that are necessary to meet applicable federal or state water quality standards. Sources were to meet this requirement no later than July 1977, through incorporation of such water-quality-based standards in permits issued by EPA or through the state certification requirement under section 401 of the Act.[60]

[60] Section 401 requires that, prior to EPA issuing a federal permit, the state certify that the discharge will comply with all applicable state water quality standards, or other state-established treatment standards or compliance requirements. See Section IV.D., below.

Section 302 authorizes EPA to establish effluent criteria more stringent than the applicable BAT limits where necessary for the attainment or maintenance of water quality in a specific water body that

> shall assure protection of public health, public water supplies, agriculture and industrial uses, and the protection and propagation of a balanced population of shellfish, fish and wildlife, and allow recreational activities in and on the water. . . .[61]

Although this language has great potential impact, as it authorizes EPA to adopt its own effluent limitations for any body of water for which a state fails or refused to adopt water quality standards sufficient to maintain swimming, fishing, and other recreational uses, EPA has not made much use of it to date, interpreting its authority as providing only a selective tool to protect important water resources.

The water-quality-based effluent standards imposed by these two provisions can require levels of treatment considerably higher than those required by the technology-related effluent standards, particularly for water bodies with heavy concentrations of dischargers or exceptionally poor water quality, or water bodies with limited assimilative capacity resulting from hydrologic factors such as dams for navigation and water supply. (These hydrologic modifications are more likely to be a factor with respect to conventional pollutants such as BOD, which break down relatively fast, than with respect to more persistent toxic pollutants.) The potential stringency of these limitations is increased by the absence of any variance provisions applicable to section 301 water-quality-based effluent standards. Section 302 contains a limited variance mechanism for standards imposed under its mandate, including a potential five-year variance from certain toxic pollutant standards. Nevertheless, compliance with water-quality-based standards is essentially mandatory and relatively inflexible, increasing the importance of carefully following the development of such standards applicable to particular water bodies and dischargers to them.

Setting the water quality standards that are translated into effluent limitations for dischargers is a complicated undertaking, both procedurally and substantively. The pollutants required to be addressed by state water quality standards are primarily the priority pollutants specified in the NRDC consent decree, conventional pollutants, and listed nonconventional, nontoxic pollutants—over 140 substances in all. Pursuant to the procedures set out in 40 C.F.R. §131.20, states must hold public hearings every three years for the purpose of reviewing and revising state water quality standards. Although EPA issues guidance documents about the effects of various pollutants, it does not set specific minimums for state standards; instead the rules require that such standards specify and protect appropriate water uses (e.g., water supply, fish, wildlife),[62] and set specific numerical criteria where possible to attain these ends.[63] This is rarely an uncomplicated undertaking, given the limited understanding of pollutant transport processes, poorly quantified nonpoint sources, and weak hydrologic data that must often be employed in the process.

---

[61] 42 U.S.C. §1312 (1988).
[62] 40 C.F.R. §131.6, .10.
[63] 40 C.F.R. §131.11.

State water quality standards must attain the CWA's goal of fishable, swimmable waters wherever attainable, and must, at a minimum, maintain the uses designated in the standards and current uses,[64] unless the state can demonstrate that the designated use is unattainable or infeasible for any of several specified reasons, primarily concerning other physical or biological aspects of the water body.[65] In addition, no degradation of "outstanding national resource" waters, such as those in national and state parks, is permitted.[66]

Adoption of water quality criteria and standards for priority pollutants have no effect until these standards are translated into end-of-pipe effluent limitations that are imposed on dischargers. Section 303(d) of the Act requires states to identify all waters within their jurisdiction as to which BAT and other technology-based effluent limits are not stringent enough to promote and maintain compliance with water quality standards (water-quality-limited waters), to establish maximum loadings for water-quality-limited waters (called total maximum daily loads or TMDLs), and to provide a system for allocating those maximum loadings among all dischargers to the affected waters.

The permitting authority may not issue a permit for a discharge to a water-quality-limited body of water unless it finds that the discharge will not cause or contribute to the violation of water quality standards applicable to the water body into which the discharge is made. Section 305(b) requires biennial reviews of water quality by the states and reports to EPA. These biennial reviews are intended to be used as part of the periodic update of water quality standards by the states under section 303(d) and now 304(l), with resultant tightening of discharge standards where needed.

In implementing the general water quality approach under the CWA, EPA also borrowed the "bubble" concept from its Clean Air program. Under this approach, EPA permits facilities to cumulate the discharges from different sources within the plant and meet a single effluent limitation, rather than meet limitations for each source of discharge within the facility. This approach could result in cost savings, depending on whether it can be used in water-quality-limited areas and whether it applies to toxic pollutants. So far, it has been limited to steel plants.[67] Two subcategories in the steel industry—coke making and cold forming—were not permitted to use the bubble, in part because of toxic pollutant concerns.[68]

B. Water Quality Standards for Toxic and Priority Pollutants

The 1976 NRDC consent decree contained several provisions addressing water quality standards as they relate to priority pollutants. These provisions required EPA to issue water quality guidance for states to use in setting additional, more stringent discharge standards for toxic or priority pollutants. In addition, the decree required identification of so-called toxic "hot spots," where the application of technology-based standards would not achieve water

[64] 40 C.F.R. §131.10(h).
[65] 40 C.F.R. §131.10(g).
[66] 40 C.F.R. §131.12(a)(3).
[67] 40 C.F.R. §420.03.
[68] 47 Fed. Reg. 23,265, 23,266, 23,271–74 (1982); 40 C.F.R. §420.03(b)(3).

quality standards. For a variety of reasons, including EPA's slow pace in issuing the technology-based standards and the inherent scientific complexity of establishing water quality standards, these provisions of the consent decree had little effect on individual dischargers.

The 1987 Amendments added section 304(l), which is essentially a more tightly focused version of the general water-quality-based approach in section 303(d) discussed in section III.A., above. Section 304(l) also adopts the "hot spots" concept from the consent decree and places enforceable deadlines on implementation of water quality standards at the individual discharger level.

Section 304(l) requires that each state identify waters within the state where the application of technology-based effluent limitations is not expected to achieve or maintain water quality standards for toxic pollutants or attain the goals of the Act. EPA interpreted the Act to require that, where noncompliance results substantially from point source discharges of toxic pollutants, the state must determine which point sources are responsible and develop individual control strategies (ICSs) for each of these point sources to bring the body of water into compliance with water quality standards. By February 4, 1989, states were required to submit the list of identified water bodies, together with the affected point sources and the individual control strategies. EPA had 120 days, or until June 1989, to approve or disapprove. If EPA approved the strategy, then the affected dischargers had up to three years, or until June 1992, in which to comply. If EPA disapproved the control strategies, or if a state failed to submit them, EPA then had one year in which to promulgate substitute control strategies.[69] Sources affected by these changes then had three years, or until June 1993, to comply.

EPA issued lengthy guidance documents concerning implementation of section 304(l).[70] State assessments of impaired water bodies were made primarily on the basis of existing water quality data, as time did not permit substantial additional monitoring to be conducted to identify these water bodies. In addition, EPA's guidance indicated that ICSs should address *all* pollutant parameters creating water quality problems (e.g., ammonia, chlorine, and "whole effluent toxicity"), not simply the toxic pollutants identified in the NRDC consent decree.

EPA treated implementation of section 304(l) as a high priority, and as a result completed its review of state plans and individual control strategies on time in June 1989. Pursuant to this review, EPA listed 595 water bodies as substantially impaired as a result of toxic discharges from 879 point sources, including 240 POTWs. Individual control strategies, embodied in NPDES permit proposals, were established for all these point sources.[71] Many of the permits were challenged and are in various administrative appeal stages. Nevertheless, as a result of EPA's regulations, POTWs will require additional pre-

---

[69] Note that one appellate court has ruled that the decision of EPA approving an individual control strategy proposed by the state is not reviewable by either the district court or the court of appeals. Roll Coater, Inc. v. Reilly, 932 F.2d 668 (7th Cir. 1991).

[70] 54 Fed. Reg. 1300 (1989).

[71] The EPA regulations implementing section 304(l) were initially published at 54 Fed. Reg. 258 (1989), and 54 Fed. Reg. 23,868 (1989).

treatment by thousands of indirect industrial dischargers, and many other direct dischargers will have to comply with ICS requirements in NPDES permits.[72]

Some environmental groups filed suit to challenge EPA's regulations, contending that section 304(l) requires EPA to revise NPDES permits for *all* discharges of toxic pollutants to impaired waters, an interpretation that would significantly increase the number of NPDES permits that would have to be revised and tightened for toxic pollutants. The Court of Appeals for the Ninth Circuit agreed in part with this position, holding that section 304(l) requires the listing of many more bodies of water as impaired by toxic pollutants.[73] The court also found that, after listing additional impaired water bodies, EPA was to reconsider its decision not to impose individual control strategies on a number of sources.

In response to the court's decision, EPA revised its section 304(l) regulations to require that states identify *all* point sources discharging any toxic pollutant believed to be impairing or preventing the water quality of any water segment listed under section 304(l), not just those sources discharging into waters not achieving water quality standards due to point source discharges of priority pollutants.[74] EPA also proposed several options for dealing with the issue of whether ICSs would have to be developed for the additional sources designated under the revised rule: (1) no additional ICSs would be required, but permit updates will include more stringent requirements to address toxic pollutants identified under section 304(l); (2) additional ICSs would be required on a case-by-case basis; or (3) ICSs would have to be developed for all new sources listed pursuant to the revised regulations.[75] Regardless of which option is chosen, the upshot of EPA's revised regulations is that there are potentially a large number of additional sources subject to the section 304(l) program that will have to comply with either ICSs or tightened permit requirements.

Another important aspect of section 304(l) implementation is that the amended statute requires that states have standards in place for toxic pollutants. For such standards, states normally rely on EPA guidance that has been issued pursuant to section 304(a). EPA has issued guidance documents for most pollutants identified in the NRDC consent decree.

The 1987 Amendments also revised section 303(c)(2)(B) to require that states adopt numerical water quality standards for toxic pollutants where possible, with narrative standards to be retained as a back-up. EPA has announced that where states fail to adopt either numerical toxic water quality standards or mathematical methods to calculate toxic effluent limitations appropriate for water quality, EPA water quality guidelines will become the new state standard.[76] This policy effectively nationalizes water quality standards unless states act to recognize local variations. EPA recently promulgated final regulations implementing this policy, providing numeric criteria for all priority toxic

---

[72] Bleached kraft paper mills were the most commonly listed industrial source because of dioxin discharges; refineries and chemical plants were also listed often. The most frequently appearing toxic pollutants regulated under the individual control strategy program are metals, various hazardous organic substances, cyanide, and polychlorinated biphenyls (PCBs).

[73] NRDC v. EPA, 915 F.2d 1314 (9th Cir. 1990).

[74] 57 Fed. Reg. 33,040 (1992).

[75] 57 Fed. Reg. 33,051 (1992).

[76] 55 Fed. Reg. 14,350 (1990).

pollutants not adequately addressed in state water quality standards, thereby bringing the 14 states that had not adopted such standards into compliance with section 303(c)(2)(B).[77] These standards became effective on February 5, 1993.

Where numerical standards are impractical, the Act requires EPA to issue guidance on biological monitoring methods and for states to use such methods in setting standards and assessing compliance under the Act. EPA regulations promulgated in June 1989 authorize permitting authorities to set whole effluent toxicity limitations in specified circumstances,[78] and EPA is also requiring biomonitoring and whole effluent toxicity testing for POTWs discharging more than one million gallons per day and for smaller POTWs if major industrial dischargers are present.[79] EPA issued guidance in December 1989 on biomonitoring using five species, three for fresh water and two for salt water.[80] Some states, such as North Carolina, began implementing such requirements even before EPA's formal guidance was issued, and others have since followed suit.[81] This promises to be an area of regulatory growth and dispute in the coming years.

In summary, it seems clear that, both as to industrial direct discharge and pretreatment requirements, the water quality required under section 304(l) and EPA's revised implementing regulations can be expected, during the next 5 to 10 years, to increase the stringency of treatment requirements imposed on many industrial and other dischargers. The toxics orientation of the water quality standards, together with the policy changes and enforcement mechanisms discussed, merit careful consideration by potentially affected companies. Those companies would be well advised to participate actively in state proceedings related to the review and revision of existing water quality standards and the implementation of the planning process under sections 303 and 304(l).

IV. Permitting Under the Clean Water Act

The permit is the primary mechanism for imposing and enforcing limitations on pollutant discharges under the CWA. In particular, the permit program established under section 402, the national pollutant discharge elimination system (NPDES), provides the foundation for the entire regulatory system discussed previously. The scope, administration, and various terms of these permits are discussed in detail in the following sections. In addition, the Act contains provisions governing permits for ocean discharges in section 403, dredge and fill operations in section 404, and the disposal and use of sewage sludge in section 405. While these provisions are less central to the Act's system of water pollution control, they are important for controlling specific types of

---

[77] 57 Fed. Reg. 60,848 (1992). Forty-three states had already achieved compliance with §303(c)(2)(B), with approved state water quality standards in place, as of the date the final rule was signed.

[78] *See* 54 Fed. Reg. 23,868 (1989) (codified at 40 C.F.R. §122.44(d)(1)).

[79] The D.C. Circuit upheld EPA's whole effluent toxicity standards in a challenge brought by industry groups and sewage officials in American Paper Inst. v. United States, 966 F.2d 346 (D.C. Cir. 1993).

[80] 54 Fed. Reg. 50,216 (1989).

[81] *See, e.g.*, 56 Fed. Reg. 8973 (1991) (Colorado Aquatic Life Biomonitoring Regulation submitted to EPA for approval as revision to NPDES program).

discharges not easily addressed by generally applicable permit provisions and effluent limitations.

A. National Pollutant Discharge Elimination System

1. Definitions and Scope of NPDES Program

The primary prohibition of the CWA is against unpermitted "discharges of pollutants" into "any waters of the United States" from any "point source." Persons responsible for any such discharge must apply for and obtain an NPDES permit, or they may be subject to enforcement action or civil suit and potentially serious penalties under the Act. The terms of the prohibition against unpermitted discharges are defined in the statute and regulations and have been broadly construed in litigation interpreting their meaning and the scope of EPA's regulatory authority under the CWA.

The term "discharge of a pollutant" is defined in section 502(12) of the Act to include any addition of pollutants into navigable waters from any point source and any addition of pollutants to waters of the contiguous zone or the ocean from a point source other than a vessel or floating craft. Because a discharge must entail "addition of pollutants," in situations where the introduction of pollutants is solely the result of the presence of intake water drawn from the same body of water into which the discharge is made, regulation as a "discharge" may be avoided.[82] A "discharge" does not include discharges of water from dams, even if the dam discharge adversely affects the temperature or oxygen content of the receiving water.[83] As noted above, the term "pollutant" is also broadly defined in section 502(6) of the Act and includes substances one might not normally consider to be pollutants, such as sand, rock, munitions, colored water, chlorinated water, and even higher temperature water.[84]

The term "waters of the United States" is defined by EPA regulations as (1) navigable waters; (2) tributaries of navigable waters; (3) interstate waters; (4) intrastate lakes, rivers, and streams that are (a) used by interstate travelers for recreation and other purposes, or (b) a source of fish or shellfish sold in interstate commerce, or (c) utilized for industrial purposes by industries engaged in interstate commerce.[85] "Navigable waters" includes not only rivers and lakes, but also may be construed to include ditches that only contain storm runoff. The broad definition and the judicial construction of these terms ensures that almost all surface waters over which the federal government can constitutionally exercise jurisdiction are covered by the Act.

Finally, a "point source" is defined in section 502(14) as "any discernible, confined and discrete conveyance, including but not limited to any pipe,

---

[82] This distinction, which applies only if the pollutants present in the intake water are not removed by the discharger as part of its normal operations, forms the basis of EPA's net/gross rule, codified at 40 C.F.R. §122.45(g).

[83] *See* National Wildlife Fed'n v. Gorsuch, 693 F.2d 156 (D.C. Cir. 1982).

[84] See section II.A., above, citing definition of pollutant in §502(6), 33 U.S.C. §1362(6) (1988). *See, e.g.*, Weinberger v. Romero-Barcelo, 456 U.S. 305 (1982) (bombs dropped on naval target range held to be pollutants). Sewage from vessels, governed by §312 of the Act, and certain waste from oil and gas injection wells reinjected into wells and regulated under the Safe Drinking Water Act, are excluded from the definition.

[85] 40 C.F.R. §122.2.

ditch, channel, tunnel, conduit, well, discrete fissure, container, rolling stock, concentrated animal feeding operation, or vessel or other floating craft, from which pollutants are or may be discharged.''[86] This broad definition was specifically amended in 1977 and 1987 to exclude irrigation return flows and agricultural storm water discharges.[87] In addition, the discharge of sewage from vessels regulated under section 312 of the Act and certain discharges of dredge or fill material regulated under section 404 are exempted from the point source definition and regulation under the NPDES program.

Other discharges not subject to NPDES permit requirements are discharges to a POTW capable of meeting its effluent limits and discharges to privately owned treatment works. Discharges to separate storm sewers or sewage systems not connected to an operable treatment works must be permitted under the NPDES program. There are flexible permit requirements for discharges to privately owned treatment works that give EPA substantial discretion to consolidate or issue separate permits as needed to meet effluent standards. Also, discharges authorized by a governmental agency pursuant to CERCLA or CWA section 311 regulations do not require NPDES permits.[88]

In sum, despite several important exemptions, the scope of the NPDES permit program is exceedingly broad. The program essentially regulates all pollutants discharged from all facilities into virtually all surface waters in the United States.

2. *Permit Issuance and Administration*

Section 402 of the CWA provides that EPA is the issuing authority for all NPDES permits in a state until such time as the state elects to take over program administration and obtains EPA approval of its program. As of September 1992, 39 states and territories had approved NPDES programs and were functioning as the issuing authorities for permits in their jurisdictions.[89] The number of states administering their NPDES programs has not increased much over the last five years, despite the 1987 Amendments giving EPA authority to approve partial state permit programs as long as the program was complete within five years of submission.[90] Where the state is the issuing authority, procedures for judicial review of permit issuance are those provided under the state's administrative procedure act rather than those contained in the CWA and the federal Administrative Procedure Act (APC). State permit issuance is not a federal action subject to the requirements of the National Environmental Policy Act (NEPA).[91]

---

[86] 33 U.S.C. §1362(14).

[87] The 1977 Amendments excluded irrigation return flows, and agriculture storm water was excluded in the 1987 Amendments to §502(14).

[88] *See* 40 C.F.R. §122.3(d).

[89] States with NPDES authority as of September 1992 are Alabama, Arkansas, California, Colorado, Connecticut, Delaware, Georgia, Hawaii, Illinois, Indiana, Iowa, Kansas, Kentucky, Maryland, Michigan, Minnesota, Mississippi, Missouri, Montana, Nebraska, Nevada, New Jersey, New York, North Carolina, North Dakota, Ohio, Oregon, Pennsylvania, Rhode Island, South Carolina, Tennessee, Utah, Vermont, Virgin Islands, Virginia, Washington, West Virginia, Wisconsin, and Wyoming. 57 Fed. Reg. 43,733 (1992).

[90] *See* CWA §402(n), 33 U.S.C. §1342 (1988).

[91] *See* Chesapeake Bay Found. v. Virginia State Water Control Bd., 453 F. Supp. 122 (E.D. Va. 1978).

Permits issued by states are subject to review by EPA, and a state permit may not be issued if the EPA Administrator objects within 90 days after the state's proposed issuance. EPA must notify the state of the reasons for its objections and any revisions or modifications that are necessary to conform the permit to the Act's requirements. States are entitled to a public hearing regarding EPA's objections to the proposed permit. If the objections are not resolved at the hearing or otherwise, EPA may issue its own permit to the discharger.[92] EPA also has the authority to withdraw its approval of a state program and take over administration of the entire program if it finds that the state is not carrying out the program in accordance with the Act's requirements, after providing written public notification of the reasons, if the state fails to take corrective action within 90 days. This authority has not been exercised, although EPA periodically threatens it.

The general procedures for permit issuance begin with a discharger's submission of a completed permit application to the issuing authority (EPA or the state) at least 180 days in advance of the date on which the discharge is to commence or the discharger's current permit expires. EPA requires new dischargers to submit a new source questionnaire before the permit application is processed, so that EPA can determine whether the facility is a "new source." If the facility is determined to be a new source, the Act requires that the applicant prepare an environmental assessment for EPA's use in determining whether an environmental impact statement will be required under NEPA.[93]

After the application is filed, EPA, the Corps of Engineers's district engineer, and other federal agencies review the application to evaluate the impact of the permit issuance on areas within their respective jurisdictions. Where EPA is the issuing authority, the state where the discharge is to occur must be given an opportunity to review the application as well. Before EPA may issue such a permit, the state must certify under section 401 that the permitted discharge will comply with applicable water quality standards, treatment standards, and compliance deadlines provided by the Act and state law. If a state fails to certify or denies certification within a reasonable time (not to exceed one year) of receiving a permit application, the certification is deemed waived and EPA may issue the permit. Because the time period for waiver starts to run when the state receives the permit application, it is advisable for the applicant to send a copy of its application to the state for certification, rather than wait for EPA to do so.

Upon review of the application, the issuing authority will make tentative determinations regarding whether a permit should be issued, the required effluent limitations, compliance schedules, monitoring requirements, and so on, and will use these to develop a draft permit. The discharger and the public are

---

[92] CWA §402(c), 33 U.S.C. §1342 (1988). *See* Champion Int'l Corp. v. EPA, 850 F.2d 182, 28 ER Cases 1013 (4th Cir. 1988), which upheld EPA's veto of a North Carolina permit on the ground that it failed to assure compliance with water quality standards downstream in Tennessee. EPA then issued a more stringent permit.

[93] *See* CWA §511(c), 33 U.S.C. §1371 (1988). Section 511(c) makes NEPA review requirements applicable only to the issuance of permits to new sources. The issuance of permits to an existing source is not subject to NEPA.

given an opportunity to comment on this draft.[94] The discharger should carefully examine the terms of the draft permit to ensure that compliance at all times is possible, and if not, the discharger should negotiate different terms or request a variance or other relaxation of generally applicable effluent limits, monitoring and reporting requirements, or other terms.

The NPDES regulations require that a comment period of no less than 30 days be provided to allow the public to submit comments and request a hearing on a draft permit. The issuing authority must hold a public hearing if "significant" interest is shown in a proposed permit, and also must allow 30 days for preparation before the hearing. After the hearing or comment period, the issuing authority will issue a final determination on the permit issuance, taking into account the comments received on the draft. If the final determination substantially changes the tentative determinations and the draft permit, public notice is required. Any interested person has 30 days after notice of the final determination to request a reconsideration of the determination through an evidentiary hearing or legal review.

If reconsideration of the final determination is granted, the effective date of all contested provisions of the permit is stayed at that point.[95] The evidentiary hearing is an on-the-record adjudicatory proceeding presided over by an administrative law judge (ALJ). The ALJ's decision may be appealed to the EPA Administrator.[96] Where EPA is the issuing authority, the entire permit proceeding is subject to the requirements of the federal APA, and the review of the final determination takes place in the court of appeals, rather than district court. Under the APA's standard of review, the court of appeals is to uphold the ALJ's decision if it is supported by "substantial evidence in the record of the proceedings, taken as a whole." Where the state is the issuing authority, the permit proceedings will generally be governed by the state administrative procedure act. Upon completion of these review procedures, all contested provisions of the permit become effective and a final permit is issued.

In order to cover the costs associated with processing and administering NPDES permits, EPA has considered collecting fees from permittees, but no rule on this subject has yet been proposed.

3. Permit Terms

After the permit has been issued, the discharger's focus shifts from preparation for the application proceeding to ensuring compliance with permit terms and to keeping the permit up to date, in order to account for any modifications or changes in discharge that may occur. Permit terms not only establish specific limits and requirements for discharges based on the provisions of the Act, but also require that the permit holder report any failure to comply with those terms to the appropriate regulatory authority. Therefore, as noted in the preceding section, careful examination of permit terms at the draft stage,

[94] If the issuing authority determines that the permit should not be issued, it will issue a notice of intent to deny the permit.

[95] 40 C.F.R. §124.16(a).

[96] 40 C.F.R. §124.91.

where they are usually subject to negotiation and modification, is advisable. Some of the more important permit terms are discussed below.

a. Effluent Limitations and Variations. The NPDES regulations specify the manner in which effluent limitations are to be included in permits and imposed on permittees.[97] In general, effluent limits are imposed at the point of discharge. Where effluent limitations have not yet been promulgated for a particular pollutant or industry, the decision as to which effluent limits are to be included in a permit is based on "best engineering judgment," which is obviously more flexible than published rules. Once a permit has been issued on the basis of best engineering judgment, however, the Act's antibacksliding provision prohibits the relaxation of permit terms where the effluent limit subsequently promulgated proves to be less stringent, except for a few instances.[98]

Even after effluent limitations for a pollutant or industry have been published, there is considerable room for discussion regarding the limits actually set in the permit. Although EPA sets effluent limitations by industry category, whether a plant fits within a particular category is not always obvious, as EPA sets its effluent limitations based on the actual industrial processes not simply the end product manufactured. Thus, while a company's primary line of business may fall squarely within an industry category, there is no assurance that the particular processes at a plant do. The proper classification of a plant in an industry category is a matter that should be carefully checked, particularly because it is an area where regulators will defer more to an industrial discharger than is otherwise the case.

Even if the applicable industry category is clear, the applicant may seek to have certain limits modified, and the permitting authority often may seek to impose more stringent discharge limitations than those set by the effluent limitations guidelines where necessary to meet water quality standards, water quality related effluent guidelines, particular state requirements,[99] or other applicable standards. For this reason, careful engineering analysis of the proposed effluent limits is generally worthwhile.

For example, variations from the uniform effluent limitation guidelines may be allowed if a permittee can establish that its facility is eligible for an FDF variance, or one of the other modifications provided in section 301 discussed in section II.B.5., or can establish that it cannot comply with effluent limitations solely because of the presence of pollutants in its intake water, as discussed in section IV.A.1., above.

Permits also now specify a far greater number of pollutants subject to effluent limitations as a result of EPA's toxics strategy. The NPDES regulations require extensive waste stream analysis and extensive cataloging of virtually

[97] 40 C.F.R. §§122.44–.45.

[98] CWA §402(o), 33 U.S.C. §1342 (1988). Section 402(o)(2) permits backsliding only in six specified circumstances. Section 402 was added by the 1987 Amendments and codified to extend EPA's long-standing antibacksliding approach which was part of the NPDES regulations. EPA's program had a number of differences from §402(o). The regulatory program has now been amended to conform with the statute. *See* 40 C.F.R. §122.44(l).

[99] Under the Act, states are free to set more stringent effluent limits if they so choose. CWA §510, 33 U.S.C. §1370 (1988).

every chemical in the waste stream prior to filing permit applications and during the duration of the permit. Implementation of these requirements complicates the setting of limits and the permit process, and requires not only careful consideration at the application stage, but more extensive monitoring during the life of the permit.

With respect to the time allowed for compliance, while the Act establishes deadlines for achievement of the required levels of treatment, the permitting authority has considerable latitude to require compliance at an earlier date or interim steps toward early compliance. There are also a few provisions in the Act that may authorize the extension of deadlines, for example, where innovative technology is involved. Most of these provisions, however, have expired.

b. Monitoring and Reporting. The effectiveness of the permit program in assuring compliance with applicable effluent limitations, water quality standards, pretreatment standards, and other requirements depends primarily on the effectiveness of monitoring and data maintenance requirements included in permits. Section 308 of the Act reflects the central role of monitoring and reporting requirements and provides EPA with broad authority to require the owner or operator of any point source to (1) record and maintain records as prescribed; (2) make specified reports; (3) install, use, and maintain specified monitoring equipment or methods, including biological monitoring (biomonitoring); (4) sample effluents according to specified methods, locations, and intervals prescribed by EPA; and (5) provide other information that EPA may require in order to carry out the objectives of the Act. States may administer their own monitoring program, and once approval by EPA is received, the state becomes the monitoring authority for all point sources within its jurisdiction.

Section 308 also provides the monitoring/enforcement authority (for either EPA or the state) with the right to enter the premises of a discharger at any reasonable time to inspect the required records or the monitoring equipment or to take samples of effluent. All data obtained pursuant to section 308 must be available to the public, except where disclosure would divulge trade secrets or confidential business information. By statute, effluent data cannot be withheld as confidential business information.[100] The public disclosure requirement provides the foundation for citizen enforcement actions that may be brought against dischargers that are not in compliance with permit terms.

The NPDES regulations also contain monitoring requirements that are intended to ensure compliance with the effluent limits and other limitations included in the permit terms.[101] The regulations provide that monitoring is to take place at the point of discharge except in rare situations where this is infeasible. The permitting authority may require monitoring of internal waste streams where the final discharge point is inaccessible, where wastes at the point of discharge are so diluted as to make monitoring impracticable, or where interference among pollutants at the point of discharge would prevent detection or analysis. A permittee must monitor according to the permit terms to deter-

---

[100] CWA §308(b), 33 U.S.C. §1318 (1988).

[101] 40 C.F.R. pt. 22.

mine compliance with the limitations on amount, concentration, or other pollutant measures in the permit and to determine the total volume of effluent discharged and any other determination required by permit.[102]

Consistent with the requirements of section 308, the regulations provide that the permit must include requirements for installation and maintenance of equipment and testing and sampling methods. The regulations put the burden on the discharger to ensure that the monitoring requirements provided in the draft permit are adequate to provide accurate data; compliance with the limits in the permit will be assessed based on the methods contained in the permit. In enforcement proceedings, permittees are not allowed to attack the validity of monitoring techniques required in their permits. This further emphasizes the importance of careful evaluation of draft permit terms during the application phase.

Monitoring records must be retained for a minimum of three years, but that period may be extended by the monitoring authority at any time.[103] In addition, since the statute of limitations for permit violations is five years,[104] it would be prudent to retain the records for at least a five-year period.

Reporting requirements include periodic reporting to the permitting authority on forms provided by the authority. Reporting frequency is governed by the permit terms, but it must be at least annual. In addition, certain toxic discharges must be reported within 24 hours.[105] Under a currently proposed rule, discharges in violation of permit terms and in excess of reportable quantities under CWA section 311 or CERCLA would also have to be reported to the National Response Center.[106] Failure to properly monitor or report is a violation of the permit terms, and any person who makes a false statement in any monitoring record, or falsely represents that a facility is in compliance, may be subject to substantial fines and/or prison sentences under both the CWA and the federal criminal statute prohibiting false statements.[107]

The extensive and often complicated requirements for monitoring and reporting that are imposed by the Act and the NPDES regulations, as well as the potentially serious penalties for noncompliance, require that considerable time and money be devoted to compliance with these permit terms.

c. Duration and Revocation. Generally, permits are valid for a period of five years, although EPA may issue permits for shorter terms.[108] Permits also may be revoked, modified, or transferred on the basis of fairly insignificant changes in process or minor violations of permit terms. It is usually wise to have the possible bases for modification and revocation of the permit spelled out as specifically as possible in the permit terms. Although EPA recently proposed to

---

[102] 40 C.F.R. §122.44(i).

[103] 40 C.F.R. §122.41(j).

[104] The applicable statute of limitations is 28 U.S.C. §2462 (1988). *See, e.g.*, Atlantic States Legal Found. v. Al-Tech Specialty, 635 F. Supp. 284, 287 (N.D.N.Y. 1986); Chesapeake Bay Found. v. Bethlehem Steel Corp., 608 F. Supp. 440, 446–50 (D. Md. 1985).

[105] 40 C.F.R. §§122.41(k)(6), 122.42(a). These sections are part of the noncompliance reporting requirements, which are very specific and should be carefully reviewed by all permittees.

[106] *See* 53 Fed. Reg. 12,868 (1988).

[107] CWA §309, 33 U.S.C. §1319; 18 U.S.C. §1001 (1988).

[108] 40 C.F.R. §122.46(a).

revise its regulations to expand the types of minor modifications that would be allowed without public notice and issuance of a new permit, the rule was apparently withdrawn because of disagreement over what modifications should be allowable.

Once a permit expires, the permittee must have the permit reissued by demonstrating compliance with any more stringent requirements that became effective during the life of the permit. The permittee must file a completed application for reissuance at least 180 days before the current permit expires. If EPA fails to reissue a permit in a timely manner and the current permit expires prior to renewal, the current permit will continue in force until EPA renews the permit, even where the reissued permit will contain more stringent terms. It is good practice to file the completed renewal application well before the expiration date of the current operating permit, even earlier than the 180 required days. EPA's rules make clear that the application must be complete when submitted, including the burdensome data requirements.[109] Thus, ample time should be planned to prepare such applications.

d. Other Terms. Other terms that may be included in a permit depending on the nature of the discharger's operations are bypass and/or upset provisions, start-up exclusions, and the like. For example, EPA's bypass regulation provides a defense to noncompliance with permit terms, allowing intentional diversion of waste to prevent loss of life, personal injury, or severe property damage, where there is no feasible alternative.[110] The upset provision allows a permittee to defend a permit violation where an exceptional incident results in unintentional and temporary noncompliance with technology-based effluent limits, for reasons beyond the control of the permittee.[111] Where no bypass or upset provision is included in the permit, some courts have held those defenses to be unavailable to the permittee. The utility of such provisions in dealing with compliance problems that arise over the duration of the permit again counsel in favor of careful evaluation of permit terms and consideration of potential future problems at the outset of the permit process.

B. Ocean Discharge Provisions

Section 403(c) of the Act directed EPA to promulgate guidelines for determining the effects of pollution discharges on ocean water quality, aquatic life, and other aesthetic, recreational, and economic values of the oceans. No permit for a discharge into the "territorial sea, the waters of the contiguous zone, or the oceans" may be issued under section 402 unless the permit issuing authority determines that the discharge will not cause unreasonable degradation of the environment consistent with the guidelines, and permit conditions may be imposed to ensure that such degradation will not occur.[112] An ocean discharge permit applicant may be required to submit substantial information about receiving waters, in order to ensure that limitations are relaxed only in situations

[109] 40 C.F.R. §122.21.
[110] 40 C.F.R. §122.41(m).
[111] 40 C.F.R. §122.41(n)(1).
[112] 40 C.F.R. pt. 125, subpart M.

involving deep, fast-moving marine waters that result in the rapid mixing of quantities of water with the discharge of pollutants.

The 1981 Amendments extended the time for municipalities to apply for waivers of secondary treatment requirements for ocean discharges. The 1987 Amendments tightened the requirements in section 301 so that waivers are granted only in unusual circumstances. Section 301(h) now allows the granting of modifications only where the POTW applicant has demonstrated that its discharge, alone or in combination with other sources, will not interfere with the water quality of marine waters, that it has an adequate pretreatment program, that the receiving waters are sufficiently deep to mix rapidly with the volume of effluent discharge, and that it has a monitoring system and has taken adequate precautions against the entry of toxic pollutants from nonindustrial sources into the treatment works. Regulations governing such marine discharges are expected in the near future.

C. Provisions Governing Disposal or Use of Sewage Sludge

The 1987 Amendments revised section 405 of the Act, which prohibits disposal of sewage sludge from the operation of publicly owned or other treatment works where it would result in pollutants from the sludge entering the navigable waters, except in accord with an NPDES permit. Section 405 authorizes the Administrator to issue regulations governing permits for sewage sludge disposal and use, and states may administer their own sewage sludge permit programs where approved by EPA in accord with section 402. EPA promulgated regulations governing sewage sludge permits and state program requirements in 1989.[113]

In February 1993, EPA finally issued regulations providing guidelines for the disposal and use of sewage sludge, 15 years after they were due.[114] Pursuant to section 405, these regulations identify toxic pollutants that may be present in sludge and provide appropriate management standards, numeric criteria, and other standards necessary to protect public health and the environment.

EPA's final regulations establish requirements for the final use and disposal (but not processing) of sewage sludge: (1) where the sludge is applied to the land for a beneficial purpose (such as fertilizer), including products for use in home gardens; (2) where the sludge is disposed on the land by placing it in surface disposal sites (such as landfills);[115] and (3) where the sludge is incinerated. The standards apply to publicly and privately owned treatment works that generate or treat sewage sludge, as well as any person using or disposing of sludge, and are expected to cover nearly 35,000 entities.

The final standards include specific numerical limits for a total of 10 pollutants, which limits apply to some or all of the use or disposal methods specified, depending on the pollutant. A second round of rulemaking will address additional pollutants that EPA determines to be present in sewage

[113] These are codified in 40 C.F.R. pts. 122 and 501.

[114] 58 Fed. Reg. 9248 (1993) (to be codified at 40 C.F.R. pts. 257, 403, and 503).

[115] This does not include sewage sludge that is disposed with municipal solid waste in a municipal solid waste landfill, which is regulated under RCRA. The rule also does not apply to sewage sludge that is determined to be a hazardous waste under RCRA (40 C.F.R. pt. 261).

sludge and to be potentially harmful. Use or disposal must also be in accord with operational standards, which include requirements for control of pathogens in sludge (i.e., bacteria, viruses, protozoa, and helminth ova), as well as measures for reducing the attraction of carriers of disease such as birds, rats, and other animals (called vector attraction reduction). In the case of sewage sludge that is incinerated, an operational standard for total hydrocarbons is included in addition to the numerical limits. General requirements and management practices are specified for each end use and disposal practice, and the rule also includes monitoring, recordkeeping, and reporting requirements. Compliance with most provisions is required by February 19, 1994, or February 19, 1995, if new construction is required in order to comply with the new standards. Entities subject to the rule should be aware, however, that compliance with the monitoring, recordkeeping, and reporting requirements, other than for incinerator total hydrocarbons, is required by July 20, 1993.

These sludge use and disposal standards will in most cases be included in section 402 permits, but may also be implemented through permits issued under RCRA, the Safe Drinking Water Act, the MPRSA, or the CAA. If a treatment works is not subject to section 402 and none of the other programs are applicable, the Administrator is authorized to issue a permit solely to impose the sewage sludge use and disposal requirements.[116] The rule also provides for the granting of removal credits for certain pollutants[117] and revises the current regulations to provide a staggered schedule for permit applications, depending on the current permit status of the treatment works.

D. Section 404 Dredge and Fill Permits

Section 404 sets up a separate permit program for regulating the discharge of dredged or fill material and dredging activity, rather than regulating these activities under the general permit program in section 402. The Corps of Engineers is authorized to designate disposal areas and issue permits to discharge dredged or fill material at specified disposal sites. This section will only briefly describe a few general aspects of this regulatory program. Section 404 permitting and wetlands issues are discussed in detail in Chapter 11, Protection of Natural Resources.

The section 404 dredge and fill permit program has a broad reach, extending to all waters of the United States including wetlands, which are themselves broadly defined.[118] In addition, the Corps has interpreted its regulatory authority to extend beyond disposal to the use of dredge and fill material for development and construction. Although the Corps has authority to issue less burdensome "general" permits for certain types of activities, and other activities are exempted under section 404(f), a large number of projects are potentially subject to section 404 permitting requirements. Section 404 permits also are subject to

[116]CWA §405(f), 33 U.S.C. §1345(f) (1988).

[117]*See* section II.B.3.b., above.

[118]*See, e.g.,* United States v. Riverside Bayview Homes, Inc., 474 U.S. 121 (1985), upholding the Corps definition of wetlands under §404: "wetlands inundated or saturated by surface or groundwater at a frequency and duration sufficient to support, and that under normal circumstances do support, a prevalence of vegetation typically adapted for life in saturated soil conditions."

NEPA review and require preparation of an environmental assessment and possibly an environmental impact statement before issuance.[119]

There has been significant enforcement of the section 404 permit requirements, much of it directed toward wetlands destruction. The Corps, through the U.S. Attorney for the district in which the violation occurs, has the authority to bring enforcement actions with potential penalties of up to $25,000 per day of violation and to compel restoration of areas that have been dredged or filled without obtaining the necessary permit or in violation of permit conditions.[120] Pursuant to the 1987 Amendments, the Corps may also bring administrative penalty proceedings under CWA section 309(g).

As discussed in more detail in Chapter 11, wetlands definitional issues continue to create a great deal of controversy. In 1989, a wetlands delineation manual was issued by EPA and the Corps embracing what has been called the "no net-loss policy." Amendments were proposed to the manual in 1991 that would significantly restrict this policy, and over 80,000 comments were received in response. While EPA and the Corps continue to wrangle over the appropriate policy for determining what should be called a wetland, these issues will remain in the spotlight for the foreseeable future.

V. Pollution From Oil and Hazardous Substance Spills

A. The Oil Pollution Act of 1990

When Congress enacted the Oil Pollution Act of 1990 (OPA),[121] it replaced the prior haphazard system of overlapping federal statutes and inadequately funded response mechanisms for dealing with oil spills. Congress enacted this statute in response to the massive Exxon *Valdez* oil spill that occurred in Prince William Sound in 1989. That tragic incident, and the strong political consensus that it should never be allowed to recur, is reflected throughout the new statute in its stringent regulatory requirements, harsh liability scheme, and comprehensive approach to oil pollution problems.

Until the 101st Congress and the *Valdez* spill, Congress had attempted without success since 1975 to enact comprehensive oil spill liability legislation. These efforts often cleared committees and individual chambers, but differences over federal preemption of state regulations, the role of international conventions, and the stringency of regulation necessary to prevent oil spills precluded a reconciliation between House and Senate versions of the various bills. The *Valdez* incident sufficiently galvanized public opinion so that these differences were finally resolved after a lengthy and difficult conference. Because of this long genesis, courts will likely rely more heavily on the statutory text in interpreting the statute and view legislative history cautiously as an aid to interpretation.

---

[119] Section 511(c) excludes only permits issued by EPA from NEPA requirements, and therefore does not apply to §404 permits issued by the Corps.

[120] *See* United States v. Krilich, No. 92-C-5354 (N.D. Ill. Aug. 7, 1992) (consent decree imposing $185,000 civil penalty and ordering restoration of destroyed wetlands or creation of new wetlands, where developer acted without dredge and fill permit). Jail terms have been imposed in some instances.

[121] Pub. L. No. 101-380, 101 Stat. 484 (1990) (to be codified in scattered sections of 14, 16, 23, 26, 33, 43, 46 U.S.C.).

OPA mandates a comprehensive federal oil spill response system and establishes the Oil Spill Liability Trust Fund to provide much greater federal resources for oil spill response and cleanup and for prompt and adequate compensation for those harmed by oil spills. It also provides an effective and consistent system of assigning liability. OPA significantly strengthens requirements for the proper handling, storage, and transportation of oil and for a complete and prompt response in the event a discharge occurs. Many of these changes have potentially significant effects that reach far beyond the oil industry.

OPA is a lengthy statute that will be codified in scattered portions of the *United States Code.* Part of OPA is a free-standing statute, but many of its requirements will be found in amendments to section 311 of the CWA, in addition to a number of provisions in Title 46 (governing navigation safety), the Deepwater Ports Act, the Outer Continental Shelf Lands Act (OCSLA), and the Trans-Alaska Pipeline Authorization Act (TAPAA).[122] OPA's major provisions are as follows:

Title I is a free-standing statute, establishing the strict liability standards and the billion dollar Oil Spill Liability Trust Fund to pay for oil spill responses and to compensate for damages not recovered from responsible parties. The Fund is financed through a tax imposed under sections 4611 and 9509 of the Internal Revenue Code of 1986, as amended by Title IX of OPA. A tax of five cents per barrel is imposed on oil delivered at the refinery.

Title IV contains the regulatory standards. Subtitle A contains numerous amendments to the vessel manning, equipment, construction, and operating standards codified in Title 46 of the *United States Code.* These amendments provide for the phase-out of tankers without double hulls, the use of overfill protection and tank pressure monitors, and more stringent licensing of merchant marine officers and seamen, including reviews of criminal and driving records and drug and alcohol testing. The Coast Guard has promulgated rules implementing many of these requirements, including regulations governing the double hull standards and chemical drug testing programs.[123]

Subtitles B and C drastically amend section 311 of the CWA to improve federal responses to oil spills, to make spill prevention control and countermeasure (SPCC) plan requirements more stringent and coherent, and to impose severe penalties for violations including spills. These penalties are much higher than those provided under prior law.

Title III concerns international cooperation; however, it does not require the United States to adopt any international convention concerning oil spills. Moreover, as is made abundantly clear in the legislative history, OPA intentionally does not preempt state law. Thus, states are free to impose more stringent liability schemes and to set up their own response funds. At the time of enactment, 24 states had some form of oil spill statute, many with response funds of various kinds.

The other titles are generally of less immediate concern to the regulated community. Title II contains conforming amendments transferring money from

---

[122] Respectively, 33 U.S.C. §1501 *et seq.* (1988), 43 U.S.C. §1331 *et seq.* (1988), and 43 U.S.C. §1651 *et seq.* (1988).

[123] 56 Fed. Reg. 31,030 (1991) (drug testing); 57 Fed. Reg. 36,222 (1992) (double hulls).

funds under OCSLA, the Deepwater Port Act, and the CWA's oil spill funds to the new Oil Spill Liability Trust Fund. Title V concerns Prince William Sound; Title VI contains savings provisions and unrelated provisions concerning drilling offshore Louisiana and North Carolina; Title VII provides for a comprehensive federal research program; Title VIII amends TAPAA to make it consistent with OPA, but TAPAA continues to govern spills that occur in transporting oil to or through the Trans-Alaska Pipeline System. Spills suffered once oil is transferred to a tanker are governed by OPA.

1. Liability Under the Oil Pollution Act

Under section 311 of the CWA, the owners and operators of vessels and onshore and offshore facilities from which oil is discharged to navigable waters, shorelines, or into the exclusive economic zone are strictly liable for the cost of conducting the cleanup of that spill and for natural resource damages suffered as a result of it. Section 311 prohibits discharges of oil in harmful quantities, which are defined to mean those which caused a sheen on the water. This sheen test means that virtually no discharge of oil is permissible, and virtually every discharge is reportable. These rules have been the law since section 311 of the CWA was first enacted as part of the Water Quality Improvement Act of 1970.

OPA continues these rules, but eliminates some of the few defenses previously available under the CWA and increases liability limitations to levels that are so high that they are almost meaningless. OPA does not rewrite or amend the liability provisions of section 311 of the CWA; rather it establishes a separate liability scheme, explicitly modeled on section 311 and implicitly modeled on CERCLA section 107.

Section 1002(a) makes responsible parties—owners and operators, and in the event of vessels, charterers as well—liable for removal costs and damages. The same standard of strict liability applicable under CWA section 311 is applicable here.[124] This standard, the same as applied under CERCLA, is one of strict, joint and several liability, at least as the courts have interpreted it to date.

Unlike generator liability under CERCLA, however, the owners of the oil are not secondarily liable for cleanup costs and damages. The defeat of this provision in conference, which had been passed by the House, is important because its practical result would have been to eliminate almost completely the petroleum exclusion under CERCLA as far as generators were concerned. Instead, OPA as enacted contains a definition of petroleum modified to exclude fractions of petroleum specifically designated as hazardous substances under CERCLA.[125] The distinction is intended to prevent overlap between CERCLA and OPA and may become important because the cleanup and compensation mechanisms under the two statutes have some important differences.

Defenses to liability by responsible parties under OPA are limited to (1) an act of God; (2) an act of war; (3) an act or omission of a third party, other than an employee, agent, or party in a contractual relationship with the responsible party; or (4) some combination of these three. These are also defenses under section 311 of the CWA. Case law interpreting these defenses under section 311

[124] OPA §1001(17) (to be codified at 33 U.S.C. §2701(17)).
[125] OPA §1001(23) (to be codified at 33 U.S.C. §2701(23)).

and their counterparts under CERCLA suggests that these defenses are extremely limited. For example, predictable bad weather causing a release is not an act of God. Similarly, actions by vandals resulting in discharges is not an act of a third party amounting to a defense where security precautions were inadequate. One defense formerly available under section 311 that is not available under OPA is negligence on the part of the U.S. government.

OPA excludes from liability discharges permitted by a federal, state, or local permit. This "federally permitted release" concept, first developed in the 1978 Amendments to section 311 and continued in CERCLA section 101(10), is extremely important in the oil pollution area because oil and grease are such common pollutants. This language places a premium on compliance with effluent standards and pretreatment permit terms, and on assuring that adequate bypass and upset provisions are included in such permits. Otherwise, discharges in violation of a permit might be interpreted to give rise to liability under OPA.

Responsible parties under OPA are liable for removal costs and damages. Removal costs means the costs of removing, containing, and cleaning up an oil discharge, or of mitigating or preventing a discharge or substantial threat of discharge. These costs are recoverable by federal, state, and local governments, as well as by private parties that have to incur them.

Damages also are recoverable from responsible parties. These damages include natural resource damages, loss of tax and other revenue, and increased service costs. These categories are recoverable by governmental bodies, with natural resource damages recoverable by the properly designated governmental trustee. Private parties may recover damages to real and personal property (including loss of use), lost profits or earning capacity, and loss of subsistence use of resources.

OPA places limitations on liability, but these limits may be of little help to responsible parties because they are set at such high levels. In addition, the limitations can be overcome by a showing that a discharge resulted from a violation of a safety or operating standard and state law liability schemes may provide unlimited liability. The limits under section 1004 of OPA are as follows:

- $1,200 per gross ton for tank vessels or $10 million, whichever is higher, unless the vessel is less than 3,000 tons, in which case the limit is $2 million;
- $600 per gross ton for nontank vessels or $500,000, whichever is greater;
- $75 million plus all removal costs for offshore facilities, and no limit for Outer Continental Shelf facilities; and
- $350 million for onshore facilities and deepwater ports licensed under the Deepwater Port Act.

The limits for onshore facilities can be adjusted downward based on size, throughput, storage capacity, type of oil, discharge history, and other factors. The limit for onshore facilities may be lowered on these bases to $8 million. As is true under the CWA and CERCLA, these liability limits are not applicable if the discharge resulted from gross negligence, willful misconduct, or a violation of an applicable federal safety, construction, or operating regulation. The limited defenses discussed above—act of God, act of war, act of unrelated third party—are also lost in the event of such negligence, misconduct, or violation.

Claim procedures under OPA are different from those found in other environmental statutes. They emphasize that responsible parties are to be the primary sources of compensation, not the Oil Spill Liability Trust Fund. Under section 1014, the federal government is to designate the source or sources of an oil discharge (or threat of discharge) as soon as possible. The designation can be made because of the mandatory reporting requirements for oil discharges that remain in force under section 311 of the CWA.

A party designated as a source under section 1014 has only five days to deny such designation if it believes there is a basis for denial. If the designation is not denied, the responsible party is to begin advertising claim procedures within 15 days of receipt of the designation and continue advertising for at least 30 days. If no designation can be made, or the designation is denied, or if a public vessel has caused the discharge, then the federal government is to advertise claim procedures under the Oil Spill Liability Trust Fund.

As was true previously under section 311, vessels are required by section 1016 to establish and to maintain evidence of financial responsibility (e.g., an insurance policy and appropriate certificates) up to the maximum liability limitation. The sharp increase in these limits, however, makes it likely that vessels will pay far higher insurance premiums and may have difficulty finding adequate insurance.

Where a responsible party pays claims made against it under OPA, it is subrogated to all of the reimbursed party's rights against other responsible parties.[126] Section 1009 of the Act allows actions to be brought for contributions by responsible parties, and these actions may include all claims arising from the incident, including common law and admiralty claims, not just those arising under OPA. Such contribution claims must be initiated within three years of payment of a claim by the plaintiff.[127]

Where the Oil Spill Liability Trust Fund pays claims, it is subrogated to the claimants' rights and may bring actions against the responsible parties to recover these claims. Injured parties are to present claims to responsible parties first, before presenting them to the fund. If responsible parties do not act within 90 days, the claimants may then present them to the fund. Claimants have three years to file damage claims against the fund, and six years after the removal action is completed to file claims involving removal costs.

The fund also is to recover removal costs and natural resource damages from responsible parties. Removal and other costs must be determined to be consistent with the National Contingency Plan (NCP) in order to be compensable. Removal costs include the costs of "monitoring" private cleanup efforts,[128] making this the equivalent of "oversight costs" under CERCLA. Unlike CERCLA, however, the government's entitlement to "indirect costs," an often significant charge for government overhead in connection with cleanup and oversight, is highly debatable under OPA, in part because the statute

[126] OPA §1015 (to be codified at 33 U.S.C. §2715).

[127] OPA §1017(f)(3), (4) (to be codified at 33 U.S.C. §2717(f)(3), (4)).

[128] OPA §1012(a)(1) (to be codified at 33 U.S.C. §2712(a)(1)).

contains separate authorizations to pay such administrative costs out of the Oil Spill Liability Trust Fund.

Natural resource damages are broadly defined under section 1006(d). The legislative history makes clear that the broad definition is intentional and meant to follow the 1989 court of appeals decision in *Ohio v. Department of the Interior.*[129] The replacement cost of the resource is to be the primary basis for determining natural resource damages. Under section 1006(d), natural resource damages include the cost of assessment; the costs of restoring, replacing rehabilitating, or acquiring the equivalent of the damaged resources; and any diminution in value of those resources. Restoration is the preferred alternative and is to take place according to a restoration plan prepared and approved by the designated natural resource trustee. The plan is to be subject to public comment before approval and may function much like a record of decision or remedial investigation/feasibility study in a CERCLA cleanup.

2. *Oil Spill Removal Actions*

OPA rewrote CWA section 311(c) and (d), which govern federal action to assure oil spill removals. Under the revised provisions, the federal government is required to take action to ensure that proper removal is conducted, either by undertaking such action with federal resources, or by monitoring state, local, or private actions. These removals are to ensure the "effective and immediate removal of a discharge, and mitigation and prevention of a substantial threat of discharge."[130] Removals must be consistent with the NCP; contractors hired to conduct such removals have immunity from damages actions brought resulting from removal actions taken consistently with federal orders or the NCP. This immunity does not extend to responsible parties conducting such a removal action.

Section 311(b) is amended to give strong enforcement powers to the on-scene coordinator or other appropriate federal official. Any responsible party who, "without sufficient cause, fails to properly carry out removal of a discharge" under a federal order, is subject to a $25,000 per day fine, or treble damages based on the costs incurred by the Oil Spill Liability Trust Fund as a result of such a refusal. This language is based on similar CERCLA provisions.[131]

3. *Contingency Plan Requirements*

Congress was highly critical of the unrealistic and unworkable contingency plans in place for Prince William Sound when the *Valdez* spill occurred. The plans overlapped, they were uncoordinated, and they assumed far too small a spill and far too quick a response time. Many of these problems had been identified in drills but not corrected. As a result, the spill cleanup for the *Valdez* became a multiyear shore cleanup, at a cost of over $2 billion dollars.

Section 4202 of OPA rewrites requirements governing national, area, and facility contingency plans. The NCP was to be revised by August 1991 to reflect

---

[129] 880 F.2d 432 (D.C. Cir. 1989).

[130] CWA §311(c)(1), 33 U.S.C. §1321(c)(1) (1988).

[131] CERCLA §§106(b)(1), 107(c)(3), 42 U.S.C. §§9606(b)(1), 9607(c)(3).

the many changes in the statute; area contingency plans were to be prepared or revised by February 1992; individual facility SPCC plan requirements must be prepared and considerably updated. Revision of the NCP and publication of area plans, however, have not yet been completed.

Prior to OPA, CWA section 311(j) required facilities to prepare SPCC plans if they stored more than 1,320 gallons of oil aboveground or 42,000 gallons below ground.[132] Facilities subject to this requirement included those storing vegetable or mineral oils, not simply petroleum products. Thus, many food processing companies were subject to these rules.

Section 311(j)(5) now requires tank vessels and offshore and onshore facilities to prepare SPCC plans and specifies requirements for these plans. An onshore facility is required to prepare SPCC plans if it handles, transports, or stores oil, and if, "because of its location, [the facility] could reasonably be expected to cause substantial harm to the environment by discharging into or on the navigable waters, adjoining shorelines, or the exclusive economic zone."[133] Given the broad definition of navigable waters used under the CWA, a potential oil discharge to a storm sewer could be sufficient to require preparation of SPCC plans.

The SPCC plan must respond, to the maximum extent practicable, to a worst case discharge, and to a substantial threat of such discharge, of oil or hazardous substances.[134] The plan must

1. Be consistent with the NCP and area contingency plans;
2. Identify the person in charge of the facility, who must have authority to implement the plan;
3. Require immediate communication between the person in charge and appropriate federal officials and response action contractors;
4. Ensure by contract (or other means allowed under regulation) that adequate private personnel and equipment will be available to remove the worst case discharge to the maximum extent practicable;
5. Require training, periodic unannounced drills, and equipment testing necessary to ensure effective response actions;
6. Be updated periodically; and
7. Be resubmitted for approval with each significant change.[135]

The SPCC plans are to be submitted for federal approval. The language of the statute suggests that all such plans must be submitted and approved in order for facilities to continue operations. The legislative history suggests that only a fraction of these will have to be submitted and reviewed; otherwise the Coast Guard or EPA, as the case may be, would be overwhelmed with SPCC plans for small facilities.

The statute requires vessel and facility SPCC plans to be submitted for approval by February 1993, and the Coast Guard and EPA have promulgated rules governing the requirements for such plans.[136] Without the submission of

[132] 40 C.F.R. pt. 112.

[133] CWA §311(j)(5)(B)(iii), 33 U.S.C. §1321(j)(5)(B)(iii) (1988).

[134] CWA §311(j)(5)(A), 33 U.S.C. §1321(j)(5)(A) (1988).

[135] CWA §311(j)(5)(C), 33 U.S.C. §1321(j)(5)(C) (1988).

[136] *See* 58 Fed. Reg. 7330 (1993) (USCG rule); 58 Fed. Reg. 8824 (1993) (EPA proposed rule). The Coast Guard rule is an interim final rule, and subject to change. The EPA proposal will be used as guidance until the final rule, which may change, is finalized.

an SPCC plan, vessels and facilities are not permitted to continue to operate. Vessels and facilities submitting such plans may continue to operate for up to two years pending approval. If the statutory time period expires without action by the regulatory agency, or if approval is denied, the vessel or facility may not continue to store, transport, or handle oil.

These new requirements place a premium on the early preparation or update of SPCC plans, in part because these plans must ensure that a response action contractor is ready to bring adequate cleanup equipment in the event of a spill, and in part because the approval process may be slow. Although it seems unlikely that enforcement officials would in fact require facilities to shut down if regulatory delays slow plan approvals, the facility is in a better position to argue against such a shutdown if it has timely prepared and filed the needed plans and has a reputable cleanup contractor ready.

4. Spill Reporting and Enforcement

Since 1970, section 311(b)(5) has required that the person in charge of a facility or vessel must immediately report discharges of harmful quantities of oil to navigable waters to the appropriate federal agency. In practice this means that any discharge of oil to the waters must be reported to the National Response Center, which is operated by the Coast Guard. Such reports may not be used as the basis for any criminal prosecution against the person reporting, except for false statement or perjury. Failure to report is a criminal offense, punishable by up to five years in jail. OPA limited the immunity for reporting violations to "natural" persons, not corporations, so that immunity corresponded to the limits in the Fifth Amendment, which also does not protect corporations from self-incrimination. Additionally, evidence developed from such a report may be used against a natural person in a criminal case, even if the report itself cannot.[137]

OPA completely revised the penalties applicable to discharges of oil and violations of the SPCC plans and other regulations. A new provision, section 311(b)(6), was added, allowing the government to seek administrative penalties of up to $125,000 for violations of regulations or for discharges. This provision is similar to the administrative penalty provision in section 309(g) of the CWA and will probably be implemented using the same procedural rules.

Section 311(b)(7), as added by OPA, allows much larger civil penalties to be assessed in civil penalty actions brought in federal court. Any owner, operator, or person in charge may be fined up to $25,000 per day for a discharge, or $1,000 per barrel of oil discharged, or per unit of reportable quantity of a hazardous substance discharged, as discussed below. Although the daily penalty level is consistent with that provided for violations of other provisions of the CWA, the quantity-based penalty is new and may reach extremely high levels quickly in the event of a large spill. Civil penalties may be trebled where a discharge results from gross negligence or misconduct. The minimum penalty in such cases of gross negligence or misconduct regardless of quantity is $100,000.

New criminal penalties also are provided to punish dischargers. This change was accomplished simply by making the CWA's criminal penalty

---

[137] *See* OPA §4301(a)(3) (to be codified at 33 U.S.C. §1321).

provision applicable to discharges in violation of section 311(b)(3). Where such a discharge is negligent, the penalty could be a year in prison and a $25,000 fine; where the discharge was done "knowingly," the penalty could be three years in prison and a $50,000 fine; where the discharge resulted in placing others in imminent danger of serious bodily injury or death ("knowing endangerment"), the prison term is 15 years and the fine is $250,000 for an individual and $1 million for an organization. These criminal penalties may be difficult to obtain in practice from individuals, however, because of the mandatory self-reporting in section 311(b)(5), and the immunity from prosecution for compelled reports that is written into the statute and provided by the Fifth Amendment. As noted above, this immunity is limited to the reports themselves and not evidence developed from them.

B. Hazardous Substance Spills

Section 311 of the CWA also governs the discharge of hazardous substances. EPA was slow to implement the hazardous substances provision, and significant parts of its regulations were enjoined by a court shortly after the regulations became effective in March 1978. Congress reported by amending section 311[138] to simplify and clarify its provisions consistent with the compromise reached by EPA and the industry plaintiffs in the lawsuit.[139] The 1978 Amendments were directed toward the two most significant problems identified by the court: what factors should be used to establish what was a "harmful quantity," and the relationship of section 311 to the NPDES program.

Pursuant to these amendments, EPA promulgated regulations designating approximately 300 substances as hazardous and subject to the section 311 program.[140] In addition, the Agency has determined what quantities of these substances may be harmful (reportable quantities).[141] EPA places hazardous substances in one of five categories: X, A, B, C, or D. Reportable quantities are one pound of a category X substance, 10 pounds of a category A substance, 100 pounds of a category B substance, 1,000 pounds of a category C substance, and 5,000 pounds of a category D substance.[142]

The second significant aspect of EPA's hazardous substance regulations is that they exclude discharges made in compliance with an NPDES permit. A principal purpose of the 1978 Amendments was to limit section 311 to "classic" hazardous substance spills, and accordingly, EPA's regulations are not applicable to chronic discharges of designated substances, if the discharge complies with an NPDES permit.[143] Such discharges, of course, remain subject to regulation under the NPDES program.

If an NPDES facility has intermittent, anticipated spills of hazardous substances (i.e., into plant drainage ditches), it should evaluate whether these discharges should be regulated under the terms of its NPDES permit. The regulations give the facility the option of having such discharges regulated

[138] Pub. L. No. 95-576, 92 Stat. 2467 (1978).
[139] *See* Manufacturing Chemists Ass'n v. Costle, 451 F. Supp. 902 (W.D. La. 1978).
[140] 40 C.F.R. pt. 116.
[141] 40 C.F.R. pt. 117.
[142] 40 C.F.R. §117.3.
[143] 40 C.F.R. §117.12.

through the NPDES program or pursuant to section 311. In addition, a facility owner or operator that spills a harmful quantity of a hazardous substance must report the spill; failure to do so will subject the owner/operator to criminal penalties.

Discharges of hazardous substances may also reach navigable waters through municipal sewers and publicly owned treatment works. However, discharges from industrial facilities to a POTW are not covered by the regulations. The regulations do apply to all discharges of reportable quantities of hazardous substances to publicly owned treatment works by mobile sources such as trucks, unless the discharger has met certain requirements.[144]

OPA makes spills of hazardous substances to navigable waters, even if reported, subject to criminal prosecution. Section 309(c), the CWA's criminal penalty provision, was amended to include discharges in violation of section 311(b)(3), which forbids discharges of oil and harmful quantities of hazardous substances. In addition, SPCC plan requirements are applicable to facilities and vessels handling hazardous substances as well as oil.

New judicial civil penalties—based on the volume of the hazardous substances discharged—are now provided in section 311(b)(7). For every unit of reportable quantity of a hazardous substance discharged, a penalty of $1,000 may be assessed. Thus, for example, if the reportable quantity is 10 pounds and 1,000 pounds are discharged, the discharger could be subjected to a $100,000 civil penalty. Civil penalties triple if the discharge results from gross negligence or willful misconduct. Alternatively, EPA may seek the standard civil judicial penalty of $25,000 per day of violation or seek administrative civil penalties for discharges of hazardous substances.

Finally, it should be noted that the reporting requirements for spills of hazardous substances (as well as other defined wastes) have been substantially supplemented by CERCLA and by the Emergency Planning and Community Right-to-Know Act (EPCRA).[145] For a fuller description of these requirements, see Chapter 12 on reporting and monitoring requirements.

The nature of these regulations and the potential penalties that they provide place a premium on developing compliance procedures before a spill occurs. A facility should be evaluated to determine whether it may discharge a reportable quantity of any hazardous substance to the waters of the United States. If there is a risk of such an unpermitted release, it may be advisable to develop a pollution prevention program to prevent such discharges. Further, it is essential to implement a contingency plan capable of assuring a prompt and appropriate response in the event of a nonexempt reportable discharge of a hazardous substance.

VI. Nonpoint Source and Storm Water Pollution Control

It has been apparent since the early 1970s that discharges from nonpoint sources would likely prevent attainment of the water quality standards and the "fishable, swimmable" water goal provided in section 101(a)(2) of the

---

[144] *Id.*

[145] Also referred to as Title III of the Superfund Amendments and Reauthorization Act (SARA) of 1986, 42 U.S.C. §11001 *et seq.*

CWA.[146] Even where technology-based effluent limitations for point sources are met, and even after point source standards are tightened to protect water quality in particular water bodies, the volume of pollutants and the episodic nature of most nonpoint source discharges makes them a leading cause of water quality impairment.[147]

Nonetheless, regulation and control of nonpoint source discharges and storm water have proven difficult, in part because there are a huge number of such discharges. Economic and administrative burdens, as well as legal problems all complicated the development of a workable system for regulating these sources. In particular, EPA was faced with the dilemma of how to regulate all the storm water discharges from point sources: testing them in the same manner as process wastes from major industries would be incredibly burdensome and expensive for industry, local governments, and EPA; leaving them unregulated would result in serious adverse environmental effects. EPA's attempt in 1973 to resolve this dilemma by exempting certain discharges in its regulations started a long and heated regulatory battle.[148]

The regulatory controversy surrounding nonpoint, diffuse sources and storm water was not resolved in the statutory language until 1987, when Congress passed the Water Quality Amendments, adding section 402(p) to the Act.[149] The 1987 Amendments for the first time provided a coherent system of regulatory controls specifically applicable to nonpoint source discharges and storm water. That is not to say that all nonpoint source regulatory issues have been resolved—instead the controversy now is centered on EPA's attempts to implement the storm water provisions in section 402(p). Nevertheless, final rules for general storm water permits have now been promulgated, and EPA is investigating how to address additional sources of storm water discharge. The storm water rules and other aspects of the supplemental regulatory controls in place to address nonpoint source discharges are the subject of this section.

A. General Provisions

In the 1972 Act, Congress attempted to address nonpoint source discharges primarily through the areawide waste treatment planning and regulatory provisions under section 208. Although some effective plans grew out of this program, few actual controls on nonpoint sources were adopted. Indeed, Congress stopped funding the program in 1980.

The 1977 Amendments included section 304(e), which requires the use of best management practices (BMPs) for point sources handling hazardous sub-

---

[146] *See* National Commission on Water Quality, Staff Draft Report, at V-14 to V-16 (November 1975).

[147] A number of national assessments of water quality and other government-sponsored research has indicated that diffuse sources, including storm water point source discharges, such as urban runoff conveyances, construction sites, feedlots, resource extraction sites, and land disposal facilities, are a major source of water quality problems. *See* 56 Fed. Reg. 40,948 (1991); 57 Fed. Reg. 11,394 (1992) (discussing results of NOAA and state-sponsored studies and National Water Quality Inventories in 1988 and 1990).

[148] NRDC challenged EPA's 1973 storm water regulations in NRDC v. Train, 396 F. Supp. 1393 (D.D.C. 1975), *aff'd,* NRDC v. Costle, 568 F.2d 1369 (D.C. Cir. 1977). The court found that EPA could not create categorical exemptions from regulation for storm water discharges, although it had flexibility in shaping permits for such discharges. Following this litigation, EPA proposed regulations covering storm water discharges in 1979, 1980, and 1984. NRDC challenged these rules both administratively and in court.

[149] CWA §402(p), 33 U.S.C. §1342(p) (1988).

stances and toxic pollutants. The BMP requirements are intended "to control plant site runoff, spillage or leaks, sludge or waste disposal, and drainage from raw material storage which the Administrator determines are associated with or ancillary to" the industrial activities, and which "may contribute significant amounts of [toxic or hazardous] pollutants to navigable waters."[150] Thus, this provision requires regulation of incidental leaks, spills, and process losses, as well as plant runoff, and anticipates treatment and operating requirements as well as management practices.

EPA's regulations implementing the BMP provisions[151] are applicable to all dischargers who use, manufacture, store, handle, or discharge any pollutant that is listed as toxic under section 307 or as hazardous under section 311. The BMP regulations primarily stress procedural measures like preventive maintenance and housekeeping requirements.[152]

EPA also may include BMPs in effluent guidelines for particular industry categories. Section 304(e) provides that any BMP required as part of an effluent limitation under that section must be included in the discharger's NPDES permit. The regulations also require that a permittee develop a BMP program, which must be submitted as part of the permit application. All BMP programs must include toxic and hazardous substance control objectives with specific BMPs to meet those objectives. Programs must also include measures addressing inspections, preventive maintenance, housekeeping, materials inventory, employee training, and security measures. Many of these requirements will overlap with the provisions of other regulatory programs under the Occupational Safety and Health Act (OSH Act), RCRA, and EPCRA, as well as the provisions of the storm water regulations.

Although the BMP requirements are a useful means of controlling particular toxic and hazardous discharges from industrial facilities, they serve only a limited, supplemental role. Comprehensive regulations of nonpoint source discharges and storm water did not come about until after the 1987 Amendments were enacted. Indeed, Congress amended section 101 to include a new policy specifically addressing nonpoint sources, which stated that

> [i]t is the national policy that programs for the control of nonpoint sources of pollutants be developed and implemented in an expeditious manner so as to enable the goals of this Act to be met through the control of both point and nonpoint sources of pollution.[153]

In order to accomplish this new policy, the 1987 Amendments made three basic changes in the Act: (1) states were required to develop regulatory controls over nonpoint sources under a new section 319; (2) special planning mechanisms for estuaries emphasized nonpoint source controls for these areas under section 320; and (3) section 402(p) was added to bring poorly regulated discharges such as industrial and municipal storm water under effective control as point sources.

---

[150] CWA §304(e), 33 U.S.C. §1314(e) (1977).

[151] 40 C.F.R. pt. 125, subpart K.

[152] Although EPA intended to require additional BMPs in the future, RCRA and CERCLA requirements for handling hazardous wastes and releases of hazardous substances may in large part supplant any further BMPs under the CWA, and these programs have, in fact, helped to reduce nonpoint source loadings of toxic and hazardous pollutants.

[153] 33 U.S.C. §1251(a)(7) (1988).

Section 319 authorized $400 million to fund state efforts to plan control measures for nonpoint source controls. States are required to identify water bodies that fail to meet toxic pollutant standards as a result of nonpoint source discharges as part of their effort to identify bodies of water failing to meet water quality standards under sections 303 and 304(1).[154] Congress, however, appropriated only a fraction of this money.

Section 320 established the National Estuary Program, which requires states to plan and implement additional controls on both point and nonpoint sources of pollutants to those estuaries included in the program.[155] While the program is voluntary, states with ecologically important estuaries are taking its provisions seriously. Most important, Congress enacted section 402(p), which specifically addresses the requirements for storm water regulation.[156]

B. Storm Water Discharges

1. Statutory Provisions

Section 402(p) sets up a schedule of deadlines by which certain storm water dischargers must apply for permits, EPA or states must approve or disapprove permits, and compliance with permits must be achieved. ''Storm water'' means storm water runoff, snow melt runoff, and surface runoff and drainage.[157] This staggered regulatory schedule was intended to allow EPA to address sources of storm water discharge in order of relative importance. Basically, there are five categories of storm water discharges given regulatory primacy, for which an NPDES permit was supposed to be obtained before October 1, 1992:

1. A discharge with respect to which a permit has been issued under section 402(p) before February 4, 1987.
2. A discharge associated with industrial activity.
3. A discharge from a municipal separate storm sewer system serving a population of 250,000 or more.
4. A discharge from a municipal separate storm sewer system serving a population of 100,000 or more but less than 250,000.
5. A discharge for which the Administrator or the state determines that the storm water discharge contributes to a violation of a water quality standard or is a significant contributor of pollutants to the waters of the United States.[158]

Storm water discharges other than those listed above were subject to a statutory moratorium on regulation, which prohibited requiring permits for such sources before October 1, 1992. These provisions, when fully implemented may quadruple or quintuple the current number of NPDES permittees from the current number of about 60,000. This increase will probably choke the NPDES permit system for some years to come.

---

[154] CWA §319, 33 U.S.C. §1329 (1988).
[155] CWA §320, 33 U.S.C. §1330 (1988).
[156] CWA §402(p), 33 U.S.C. §1342(p) (1988).
[157] 40 C.F.R. §122.26(b)(13).
[158] CWA §402(p)(2), 33 U.S.C. §1342(p)(2) (1988).

For storm water discharges associated with industrial activity, NPDES permits must meet the applicable effluent limitations (BAT and BCT) imposed under section 301 of the Act. Those discharges from plant yards and other ancillary areas that are already regulated under an industrial discharger's NPDES permit continue to be regulated under that permit. For those industrial discharges not already regulated, the Act required EPA to promulgate regulations governing applications for permits by industrial dischargers by February 1989 (two years after enactment of the Amendments). Permit applications were to be filed no later than February 1990 (three years after enactment), permits were to be issued by February 1991, and compliance is required "as expeditiously as possible," but no later than February 1994 (had the permits been issued on schedule).[159]

The statute set the same schedule with respect to regulation of storm water discharges from large municipal storm sewer systems (serving a population of 250,000 or more). For medium municipal systems (serving between 100,000 and 250,000), EPA was to issue permit regulations by February 1991, with permit applications to be filed by February 1992, permits to be issued by February 1993, and compliance required by February 1996. For discharges from municipal storm sewers, the Act gives EPA flexibility to issue permits on either a system- or jurisdictionwide basis. The permit must also "include a requirement to effectively prohibit non-storm water discharges into storm sewers."[160] Substantive requirements also are imposed on the permitted discharges from municipal systems, and such permits

> shall require controls to the maximum extent practicable, including management practices, control techniques and systems, design and engineering methods, and such other provisions as the Administrator or the State determines appropriate for the control of such pollutants.[161]

2. *Regulatory Provisions*

EPA failed to comply with the statutory schedule in section 402(p), but managed to belatedly issue its final storm water permitting regulations on November 16, 1990, and amended rules on March 21, 1991, and April 2, 1992.[162] The regulations address permit application requirements for storm water discharges associated with industrial activity and for discharges from municipal separate storm sewer systems serving a population of 100,000 or more. The final rules require direct permit coverage for all storm water discharges associated with industrial activity, *including* those that discharge through municipal separate storm water sewers.[163]

---

[159] CWA §402(p)(4)(A), 33 U.S.C. §1342(p)(4)(A) (1988).

[160] CWA §402(p)(3)(B), 33 U.S.C. §1342(p)(3)(B) (1988).

[161] CWA §402(p)(3)(B)(iii), 33 U.S.C. §1342(p)(3)(B)(iii) (1988).

[162] 55 Fed. Reg. 47,990 (1990); 56 Fed. Reg. 12,098 (1991); 57 Fed. Reg. 11,394 (1992).

[163] 55 Fed. Reg. at 47,998. The final storm water rules were challenged successfully by NRDC on several grounds, including EPA's failure to include deadlines for permit approval and compliance, the exclusion of certain construction activities disturbing less than five acres from regulation, and the exclusion of many industrial facilities from regulation where "significant materials" were not exposed to precipitation. NRDC v. EPA, 966 F.2d 1292 (9th Cir. 1992). Those portions that remain intact and in force and those sections that have been invalidated are discussed in detail in this section. Pursuant to the *NRDC* opinion, EPA promulgated deadlines for permit approval and compliance that are noted below. *See* 57 Fed. Reg. 60,444 (1992) (to be codified at 40 C.F.R. pt. 122)

The rules are not applicable to all industrial discharges of storm water, only storm water discharges "associated with industrial activity" defined in the regulations to mean "the discharge from any conveyance which is used for collecting and conveying storm water and which is directly related to the manufacturing, processing or raw materials storage areas at an industrial plant."[164]

For a majority of the industry categories subject to regulation,[165] storm water discharges associated with industrial activity include, but are not limited to, storm water discharges from

1. Industrial plant yards;
2. Immediate access roads and rail lines used or traveled by carriers of raw materials, manufactured products, waste materials, or byproducts used or created by the facility;
3. Material handling sites;
4. Refuse sites;
5. Sites used for the application or disposal of process waste waters (as defined in 40 C.F.R. pt. 401);
6. Sites used for the storage and maintenance of material handling equipment;
7. Sites used for residual treatment, storage, or disposal;
8. Shipping and receiving areas;
9. Manufacturing buildings;
10. Storage areas (including tank farms) for raw materials, and intermediate and finished products; and
11. Areas where significant materials remain from past industrial activity.

Storm water discharges from these areas are subject to regulation regardless of whether materials or equipment are actually exposed to precipitation.[166]

For a larger number of "light industry" categories,[167] however, the regulations define "storm water discharges associated with industrial activity" to include storm water discharges from all the above-noted areas only "where material handling equipment or activities, raw materials, intermediate products, final products, waste materials, by-products, or industrial machinery are exposed to storm water." EPA justified the light industry distinction on the assumption that industrial activity in these industries would take place indoors.[168] The NRDC challenged this regulation in a lawsuit against EPA, and the Ninth Circuit found that there was no support in the record for EPA's assumption. Therefore, the "light industries" portion of the rule was remanded to the Agency as invalid.[169] EPA intends to reopen the rulemaking and use some

---

[164] 40 C.F.R. §122.26(b)(14).

[165] Identified at 40 C.F.R. §122.26(b)(14)(i) through (x).

[166] 40 C.F.R. §122.26(b)(14). Section 122.26(b)(14)(i)-(x) facility categories include specified industry segments within the lumber and wood industry, paper mills, chemical producers, petroleum and coal industry, leather tanning, stone, glass and clay products, metal smelters, refiners, and fabricators, ship and boat building, and construction activities.

[167] Identified at 40 C.F.R. §122.26(b)(14)(xi).

[168] Section 122.26(b)(14)(xi) facilities included food processors, cigarette manufacturers, clothing producers, printers, furniture makers, paint manufacturers, and pharmaceutical producers.

[169] NRDC v. EPA, 966 F.2d at 1305.

other means to exempt sources without significant materials exposed to precipitation.[170]

The NRDC also challenged EPA's exclusion of certain construction sites from the construction industry category for which storm water discharges are regulated. EPA defined the category as "construction activities (including clearing, grading, and excavation activities) that result in the disturbance of five or more acres of total land area, including areas that are part of a larger common development or sale."[171] Thus, the rule excludes construction sites of less than five acres from the definition of storm water discharges associated with industrial activity. The Ninth Circuit found the exclusion of smaller construction sites to be arbitrary and capricious and invalidated and remanded that portion of the rule to EPA.[172]

Notwithstanding the uncertainties created by the *NRDC* remand, any facility that discharges storm water associated with industrial activity must either (1) apply for an individual permit; (2) apply for a permit through a group application; or (3) seek coverage under a promulgated storm water general permit. Which of these permits is best for a source depends heavily on site-specific factors. The time to participate in group permit applications has now expired, leaving individual permits or in some cases general permits issued by EPA or the state, as the available choices for compliance.

a. Group Permits. Dischargers of storm water not eligible for coverage under a general permit are required to file either a group or individual permit application. Absent special circumstances, the time to participate in group permit applications has expired. Many facilities such as scrap yards and railroad facilities did participate in the group permit process, often through trade associations. A facility's ability to obtain a permit under the group application procedure depended on whether the facility was in the same effluent guideline subcategory or was sufficiently similar to other members of the group to be appropriate for group permit coverage. Generally, if the facilities involve similar types of operations, discharge the same types of wastes, have the same effluent limitations or similar monitoring requirements, the facilities may be appropriate for a group application.

A group application consists of two parts. Part 1 requires information concerning the participants in the application and their industrial activities and identification of the applicants who will provide data in Part 2. Based on the information contained in Part 1 about the representativeness of the group members chosen for monitoring and other factors, within 60 days of receipt EPA was to reject the group application as inappropriate or approve it for further processing. After EPA approval of Part 1 of a group application, the applicants must submit Part 2 data within no more than 12 months. Part 2 requires a percentage of the applicants (usually 10 percent, unless there are fewer than 20 group members) to provide the detailed quantitative data that all individual permit applicants must ordinarily provide.[173] If a group application is

[170] *See* 57 Fed. Reg. 60,444, 60,446 (1992).
[171] 40 C.F.R. §122.26(b)(14)(x).
[172] NRDC v. EPA, 966 F.2d at 1305–06.
[173] 40 C.F.R. §122.26(c)(2), as amended by 57 Fed. Reg. 11,394 (1992).

rejected, group members have 12 months from the date they are so notified to file individual permit applications.[174] Existing industrial facilities rejected from a group application had until October 1, 1992, to submit an individual application or avail themselves of a general permit, if one were available.[175]

Under the final rules, Part 1 of all group applications for industrial storm water discharges was to have been submitted to EPA by March 18, 1991, but this deadline was first extended to September 30, 1991, by EPA's amended rules.[176] Part 2 of the group application was to be submitted no later than 12 months after the date of approval of Part 1, and EPA issued a final rule extending the Part 2 group application deadline to October 1, 1992.[177] The Ninth Circuit found this extension to be illegal in the NRDC challenge to the storm water regulations, holding that the statute provided explicit and unambiguous deadlines for the submission of permit applications (February 1990) and for EPA approval of permits (February 1991) for industrial storm water discharges. The court ordered that these statutory deadlines be incorporated into the regulations.[178]

In response to this holding, EPA promulgated a final rule incorporating the statutory deadlines to the extent possible, given the already-existing extensions.[179] Thus, the regulations provide that EPA must issue permits for industrial dischargers who submitted group permit applications by October 1, 1993 (one year after the deadline). The statutory language regarding compliance (as expeditiously as possible, but no later than three years after issuance) is also incorporated into the regulations.[180]

As should be apparent from the above discussion, the requirements for EPA's two-part group permits were cumbersome. Moreover, states are not bound to accept the group permit option if they have approved NPDES programs, though most seem likely to do so.

b. Individual Permits. To obtain an individual permit, the applicant must provide detailed information about the facility, including a topographic map of the facility, estimates of impervious surfaces and total area drained by each outfall, and a narrative description of certain activities at the facility such as materials and waste management practices. Applicants must also certify that no process waste water will be mixed in with its storm water discharge, a requirement taken directly from the statute and also found in group and general storm water permit applications.[181] In addition, individual permit applicants

[174] 40 C.F.R. §122.26(e)(2).

[175] 57 Fed. Reg. 60,444, 60,447 (1992).

[176] 56 Fed. Reg. at 12,098.

[177] 57 Fed. Reg. 11,394 (1992).

[178] NRDC v. EPA, 966 F.2d 1292, 1298–1301 (9th Cir. 1992).

[179] 57 Fed. Reg. 60,444 (1992).

[180] 57 Fed. Reg. at 60,447. The rules also provide that for industrial activities owned or operated by a municipality of less than 250,000 people, Part 2 of the group application must be submitted by May 17, 1993, and permit issuance is required by May 17, 1994.

The rules also provide deadlines for discharges from municipal separate storm sewer systems. Large municipal systems (greater than 250,000 people) must have submitted Part 2 of their permit applications by November 16, 1992, and permit issuance is required by November 16, 1993. For medium municipal systems (between 100,000 and 250,000), Part 2 of the application must be submitted by May 17, 1993, and permit issuance must be completed by May 17, 1994.

[181] 40 C.F.R. §122.26(c)(i)(A)-(D).

must present quantitative data based on samples of storm water discharges collected during representative storm events from all outfalls containing a storm water discharge associated with industrial activity. The sampling must be performed in accordance with elaborate requirements in 40 C.F.R. §122.21(g)(3) and (7), and testing must be conducted for the parameters specified in 40 C.F.R. §122.26(c)(i)(E).[182]

The gathering of this information is very costly as well as time consuming for the individual permit applicant. EPA's regulations provide that individual permit applications were to be submitted to EPA or the permitting state by November 18, 1991, and the deadline was further extended to October 1, 1992.[183] This extension was accomplished during the Ninth Circuit's consideration of the *NRDC* case, which subsequently held that the earlier November 18, 1991, deadline was unlawful.[184] Nevertheless, the EPA regulations promulgated in response to the *NRDC* opinion include the October 1, 1992, deadline and require EPA to issue or deny applications for individual permits by October 1, 1993. For new facilities, permit applications must be submitted 180 days prior to commencement of industrial activity that may cause a storm water discharge, and EPA must issue or deny a permit within one year of receipt of the application.[185]

c. General Permits. It should be apparent from the above discussion of EPA's regulations for group and individual storm water permits that application, preparation, and administration of these permits is burdensome for EPA and industry alike. Therefore, EPA developed a baseline general permit scheme[186] and recently promulgated several general permits for storm water discharges associated with industrial activity and for storm water discharges associated with industrial activity from construction sites.[187] These permits formally apply only to the 15 states and territories where EPA is the permitting authority. It seems likely, however, that many states will also use them or impose similar requirements.

(1) Coverage. The general storm water permits for industrial activity and construction sites were issued for certain states and territories in Regions I, II, III, IV, VI, VIII, IX, and X, where the states or territories do not have approved

[182] For example, the regulations require a grab sample taken during the first 30 minutes (or as soon thereafter as practicable) of the storm water discharge. A flow-weighted composite must also be taken. 40 C.F.R. §122.21(g)(7).

[183] 56 Fed. Reg. 56,548 (1991).

[184] 966 F.2d at 1298–1301.

[185] 57 Fed. Reg. at 60,447.

[186] EPA began development of the general storm water permit program in 1991, as it was becoming apparent that the final storm water permit regulations would be administratively onerous. *See* 56 Fed. Reg. 40,950 (1991) (draft general permit for industrial discharges).

[187] 57 Fed. Reg. 41,176 (1992); 57 Fed. Reg. 44,438 (1992) (industrial activity); 57 Fed. Reg. 41,236 (1993); 57 Fed. Reg. 44,412 (1992) (construction sites). Although construction sites are an industry category under the regulatory definition of storm water discharges "associated with industrial activity," EPA chose to address storm water discharges associated with industrial activity from these sites in separate general permits. It should be noted that EPA retained its definition of construction sites excluding sites under five acres in the general permit, although this regulatory definition was remanded by the Ninth Circuit in the *NRDC* case. Thus, the general permits apply only to storm water discharges from construction sites greater than five acres.

NPDES programs.[188] The general permits establish requirements for notices of intent (NOIs) to be bound by the permit requirements, development of storm water pollution prevention plans, inspections, and certain other special requirements.[189]

Basically, any facility in a covered industry that seeks coverage under the general storm water permits must submit an NOI in order to receive authorization for its storm water discharges. An NOI for discharges associated with industrial activity must include information that identifies the location and activities at the facility, the operator of the facility, any existing NPDES permits, the receiving waters, any data on concentration of pollutants, whether the facility previously participated in the group application process, and, where the storm water discharge commenced after October 1, 1992, a certification that a pollution prevention plan has been prepared.[190] Similar information is required for storm water discharges from construction sites.[191] As discussed below, sources that already have an NPDES permit and sources that cannot certify that their storm water discharge is not mixed with process waste water may not use a general permit.

Once the NOI is submitted, a facility or construction site may discharge storm water under the terms and conditions of the general permit, although EPA may deny coverage based on the information contained in the NOI and require the facility to apply for an individual permit. Those industries covered by the general permits published by EPA on September 9 and September 25 must have submitted their NOIs by October 1, 1992, in order to be authorized to discharge under the general permits. Facilities may file later, but are subject to enforcement action for doing so. As a practical matter, however, EPA is more interested in encouraging facilities to file for coverage under this program, even if they do so late, than in bringing enforcement actions for late filings.

There are several types of discharges that are not authorized by the general storm water permits. With respect to storm water discharges associated with industrial activity, the general permits do not authorize the following:

1. Discharges of storm water mixed with process waste water, or other nonstorm water, unless the mixture is authorized by a separate NPDES permit or meets the general permit requirements for such mixtures;[192]
2. Discharges already subject to an existing effluent limitation guideline;[193]

[188] The general permits are for storm water discharges associated with industrial activity or construction sites in Alaska, Arizona, District of Columbia, Florida, Idaho, Louisiana, Maine, Massachusetts, New Hampshire, New Mexico, Oklahoma, South Dakota, Texas, and several of the territories including Guam and American Samoa. Authorized states must issue their own general permit regulations, but are likely to rely heavily on EPA's general permits for guidance.

[189] 57 Fed. Reg. at 41,236.

[190] 57 Fed. Reg. at 41,306.

[191] Construction sites must also provide estimates of project start and completion dates and the number of acres on which soil will be disturbed, and a certification that a storm water pollution prevention plan has been prepared that complies with approved state or local sediment and erosion plans or permits. Copies of the NOI must be sent to the state and local authorities responsible for such plans or permits. 57 Fed. Reg. at 41,218–19.

[192] The permissible mixture sources for storm water discharges associated with industrial activity are identified at 57 Fed. Reg. at 41,305–07. These same mixtures are allowed for storm water discharges associated with construction sites. 57 Fed. Reg. at 41,217–19.

[193] For purposes of the general permit, the following effluent limitation guidelines address storm water or a mixture containing storm water: cement manufacturing, feedlots, fertilizer manufacturing, petroleum refining, phosphate manufacturing, steam electric, coal mining, mineral mining and processing, ore mining and dressing, and asphalt emulsion. 57 Fed. Reg. at 41,305.

3. Discharges from facilities with existing NPDES permits for such discharges, until the permit expires;
4. Discharges from a construction site;[194]
5. Discharges associated with industrial activity that EPA has determined to be or may reasonably expect to be contributing to a violation of a water quality standard;
6. Discharges associated with industrial activity that may adversely affect a listed or proposed endangered or threatened species or its critical habitat; and
7. Discharges from inactive mining, landfills, or oil and gas operations occuring on federal lands where an operator cannot be identified.

The general permits for storm water discharges from construction sites similarly do not cover discharges of nonstorm water or unauthorized mixtures of storm water and nonstorm water, storm water discharges covered by an existing NPDES permit, discharges determined to be contributing to violation of a water quality standard, or discharges likely to adversely affect endangered or threatened species. In addition, storm water discharges that originate from the site after construction activities have been completed and the site has undergone final stabilization are not covered.[195]

(2) Pollution prevention plans. All industrial facilities and construction sites subject to EPA's general permits must prepare a storm water pollution prevention plan by April 1, 1993. Implementation is required by October 1, 1993, and the plan must be periodically revised so it is kept current. The regulations provide detailed requirements for such plans, which in general must (1) identify potential sources of storm water pollution and (2) describe and ensure implementation of practices that are to be used to minimize and control those pollutants.

The regulations for storm water discharges associated with industrial activities require that pollution prevention plans identify pollution prevention team personnel and their duties, and describe potential storm water pollution sources. This description must include maps indicating drainage patterns, water bodies, and existing structural measures to control pollutants; a narrative description of materials handling practices and locations; inventories of exposed materials; a list of significant spills of toxic or hazardous pollutants in the prior three years; and a certification that the discharge has been tested for the presence of non-storm water discharges. In addition, the plans must specify measures for good housekeeping, preventive maintenance, spill prevention and response, inspections, employee training, sediment and erosion control, and recordkeeping. The plan must also provide for comprehensive site inspections, to be performed annually in most cases. The plan provisions must be consistent with any section 311 SPCC plans, as well as the BMP rules.[196]

Pollution prevention plans for construction sites subject to the general permit must contain a detailed site description including the nature of the construction activity; the intended activities that disturb soils for major portions of the site; estimates of total area of disturbance; runoff coefficients; the name of

[194] These discharges are those covered separately in the general permits for construction activity.
[195] 57 Fed. Reg. at 41,218.
[196] 57 Fed. Reg. at 41,308–11.

receiving waters; and a site map indicating drainage patterns, location of impervious features, stabilization areas, water bodies, and soil piles. In addition, the plan must include a description of controls to reduce pollutants, including erosion and sediment controls, storm water management measures, controls to ensure no nonstorm water solid materials are discharged, and a certification that the plan reflects state and local sediment and erosion requirements. Maintenance and inspection provisions are also required.[197]

(3) Other requirements. An important condition of both the industrial activity and construction site general permits pertains to releases of reportable quantities of hazardous substances and oil. Where a permitted storm water discharge contains a hazardous substance or oil in an amount equal to or in excess of a reportable quantity established under 40 C.F.R. §§110, 117, or 302, the facility must take a number of actions specified in the rule, including notification of the National Response Center, revision of the pollution prevention plan to provide detailed information regarding the release and measures to prevent such releases, and submission of the release information to EPA.[198] If a discharge of hazardous substances or oil is the result of a spill or some other nonstorm water discharge, that discharge is not authorized by the permit and the discharger must report the discharge in accordance with 40 C.F.R. §§110, 117, or 302. Those sections of the CWA applicable to spills (sections 311, 301, and 402) also continue to apply.

A related provision in the general permits for discharges from industrial activities establishes special, additional requirements for certain permittees subject to reporting requirements under EPCRA section 313. In addition to meeting the baseline requirements, these facilities must provide appropriate containment, drainage control, and diversionary structure for areas where section 313 water priority chemicals are stored, processed, or otherwise handled.[199] Additional detailed requirements for containment, drainage, and recordkeeping are provided for areas considered "priority areas," which include liquid storage areas, other material storage areas, truck and rail car loading and unloading areas, and other transfer, process, or handling areas. These requirements are detailed and quite extensive.[200]

The general permits for industrial storm water discharges also include monitoring and reporting requirements for section 313 facilities and other facilities in specified industries. These requirements are only applicable to

---

[197] 57 Fed. Reg. at 41,220–22.

[198] 57 Fed. Reg. at 41,307.

[199] 57 Fed. Reg. at 41,310–11, 41,319. For purposes of the general permits, EPA identifies approximately 175 chemicals as "section 313 water priority chemicals" from those chemicals that are (1) listed in 40 C.F.R. §372.65; (2) manufactured, processed, or otherwise used at or above threshold levels at a facility subject to EPCRA §313 reporting requirements; and (3) meet at least one of the following criteria: (a) are listed in Appendix D of 40 C.F.R. pt. 122 in either Table II, III, or V, (b) are listed as a hazardous substance under CWA §311 at 40 C.F.R. §116.4, or (c) are pollutants for which EPA has published acute or chronic toxicity criteria. A list of these chemicals is provided at Addendum B, 57 Fed. Reg. at 41,331–35.

[200] Other, less burdensome special requirements in the general permits for storm water discharges associated with industrial activity include the following: (1) storage piles of salt for deicing or other purposes must be enclosed or covered to prevent exposure to precipitation; (2) permittees that discharge storm water through large or medium municipal systems are required to submit a signed copy of their NOI to the municipal system operator; and (3) permittees must comply with effluent limitations for coal pile runoff. 57 Fed. Reg. at 41,311–12, 41,315.

certain types of storm water discharges from these facilities. The rule specifies the parameters, as well as the required frequency of monitoring and reporting for each type of facility.[201]

C. Other Developments

Other sources of storm water discharges, such as municipal sewer systems serving less than 100,000 people (called Phase II sources), are now subject to regulation since the statutory moratorium on regulation of these sources expired October 1, 1992. Although EPA was to issue regulations applicable to additional sources of storm water discharges no later than October 1 under section 402(p)(6), former President Bush signed legislation before he left office extending the October 1, 1992, deadline and allowing EPA one additional year to develop its Phase II regulatory program.[202] EPA is currently in the process of developing control strategies for these other sources of storm water discharges.[203]

Apart from the storm water program and the other regulatory provisions discussed,[204] EPA has also been looking at economic-based approaches for controlling nonpoint source pollution. EPA Administrator Reilly had initiated an inquiry into a point and nonpoint source pollutant trading scheme, which would trade tightened controls on nonpoint sources for more relaxed controls on point sources.[205] According to some preliminary assessments, the program has the potential to save dischargers a good deal in terms of compliance costs. However, it is not known whether the new EPA Administrator will pursue this program.

Regardless of what approaches are adopted, it is likely that EPA will continue to focus on nonpoint source regulatory programs in the near future, and create additional controversy in the process. From a water quality perspective, the effort is well justified, though the timing and means of implementation is open to some question.

---

[201] The facilities for which additional monitoring and reporting are required include the following: EPCRA section 313 facilities, primary metal industries, land disposal units and incinerators, wood treatment facilities, industrial facilities with coal piles, battery reclaimers, airports (over 50,000 flights per year), coal-fired steam electric facilities, animal handling and meat packing facilities, chemical and allied product and rubber manufacturers, automobile junkyards, lime manufacturing facilities, oil-fired steam electric power generators, cement manufacturers and kilns, ready-mix concrete facilities, and ship building and repairing facilities. 57 Fed. Reg. at 41,312–15.

[202] The Water Resources Development Act of 1992, Pub. L. No. 102-580, 106 Stat. 4797 (Oct. 31, 1992) (to be codified in scattered sections of 10, 16, 26, 33, 42, and 43 U.S.C.).

[203] *See* 57 Fed. Reg. 41,344 (1992).

[204] With respect to other means of addressing nonpoint source pollution, EPA recently issued a guidance document addressing management of coastal nonpoint source pollution, which is largely regulated under the Coastal Zone Management Act, 16 U.S.C. §1451–64, 57 Fed. Reg. 26,845 (1992). EPA also recently published a draft general permit for discharges from animal feeding operations (feedlots), which is another example of a diffuse source of pollutants defined as a point source under the Act. The permit applies to all wastewaters from feedlot areas, including those generated by precipitation, placing feedlots in the same category of effluent guidelines as storm water. 57 Fed. Reg. 32,475 (1992).

[205] *See* 57 Fed. Reg. 21,244 (1992).

VII. Other Provisions

A. POTW Construction Grant/Loan Program

The 1972 Act established the POTW construction grant program in Title II to assist municipalities with construction necessary to comply with the stringent treatment requirements applicable to POTWs. This program was one of the largest public works programs ever funded by the federal government. The objective of the program was to fund the construction of plants that would most efficiently meet the applicable treatment requirements. Initially, the federal government covered 75 percent of the cost of approved treatment works, but decreased this amount to 55 percent in 1981. Apart from the reduction in federal aid, EPA's regulations implementing the grant program impose a number of requirements for sharing of costs by users and plant eligibility that may increase the cost of POTW treatment for industrial users.[206] These requirements are discussed below.

In 1987, the CWA Amendments converted the grant program, beginning in 1990, into a revolving loan program under which the federal grants are made to states. States disburse the federal funds for construction in the form of loans to municipalities or other POTW owners. The repayment of these loans in turn funds additional construction. Although this loan program was to replace the construction grant program, Congress has sometimes disregarded the loan program requirements in the appropriations process. The Clinton Administration has indicated a willingness to change this approach, at least in the short term, to provide some extra federal money in an effort to stimulate the economy. The POTW construction loan program requirements are discussed in the next section.

1. *The Revolving Loan Program*

The 1987 Amendments added Title VI of the CWA, which governs federal grants to states for sewage treatment plant construction. Section 601 provides that EPA is to make capitalization grants to the states to establish revolving loan programs for POTW construction. Funds may also be lent to help with nonpoint source controls and estuarine management plans under sections 319 and 320. The loan program is administered by the states pursuant to agreements with EPA, which require states to pay an additional 20 percent above the federal grant into the state fund.[207]

The designated state agency is to make loans for POTW construction through 1995 according to most of the same substantive criteria used previously to make grants under Title II, including requirements to minimize infiltration and inflow, to have sufficient reserve capacity, to minimize combined storm water and sanitary sewer overflows, to encourage use of innovative technology, and to achieve at least secondary treatment levels.[208] The state must also

---

[206] EPA's construction grant regulations are located at 40 C.F.R. §§35.900–.970. The construction loan regulations, promulgated in 1990, are at 40 C.F.R. §§35.3000–.3170.

[207] CWA §602(b)(2), 33 U.S.C. §1382(b)(2) (1988).

[208] CWA §602(b)(6), 33 U.S.C. §1382(b)(6) (1988).

establish requirements for the "expeditious and timely" obligation of loan moneys, which must be used first to assure progress toward compliance with enforceable deadlines, goals, and requirements of the Act.[209] Loans are made at or below market rates for a term not longer than 20 years, and repayment begins within one year of project completion. Loan recipients must establish a dedicated source of revenue to repay the loans.

States are required, after notice and opportunity for public comment, to prepare annual plans for the use of loan funds. States must also submit to EPA annual reports documenting how such funds were in fact used. EPA must also conduct or require the state to conduct regular auditing and accounting of state funds.[210] EPA can withhold future federal grant money and reallocate funds from any state found not to be administering its loan program in compliance with the Title VI requirements.[211]

EPA promulgated regulations implementing the Title VI loan program requirements in 1990.[212] The regulations require states to enter formal delegation agreements with EPA, which identify the state agency administering the loan program, the program costs, the personnel needed, and the accounting system to be used, among other things. These agreements have a five-year term. Under the regulations, states perform virtually all of the functions for loan review that EPA formerly performed for grants. The regulations also require that construction projects receiving grant assistance undergo state environmental review similar to NEPA scrutiny.[213] Recipients of loans have the right to dispute state decisions before the EPA Regional Administrator.

2. *Eligibility for State or Federal Funding*

An important consideration in any effort to minimize costs of industrial participation in a loan or grant-funded POTW program is whether all elements of the POTW are eligible for federal or state funding. Treatment costs that are not eligible must be funded by the grantee, without benefit of state loan programs. This will often result in higher municipal bond costs, of which industrial users generally will have to pay a proportionate share. Thus, where a portion of the treatment works is not eligible, industrial users will be assessed with their share of the bond interest at market rates on that facility, as well as the user charges for operation and maintenance discussed below. These costs may significantly increase the overall cost of discharging to a POTW.

Moreover, as both federal and state funding problems increase, EPA and state review of grant and loan applications will become more rigorous in an attempt to limit eligibility and reduce funding necessary under the program. For example, EPA regulations exclude from eligibility costs for lines constructed almost exclusively to serve industrial users and costs allocable to treatment of

---

[209] CWA §602(b)(4), (5), 33 U.S.C. §1382(b)(4), (5) (1988).

[210] CWA §606, 33 U.S.C. §1386 (1988).

[211] CWA §605, 33 U.S.C. §1385 (1988).

[212] 40 C.F.R. §§35.3000–.3170.

[213] 40 C.F.R. §35.3140. The regulatory provisions track many federal NEPA requirements including public participation, consideration of alternatives, and careful documentation of the decision process. Although nothing in the statute provides for state environmental review, EPA relied on §511(c), which sets forth EPA's NEPA obligations for POTW construction grants, as authority for this requirement.

pollutants in waste water that have been introduced by industrial users, unless the applicant already must remove such pollutants introduced by nonindustrial sources. EPA has the discretion to narrowly interpret provisions such as these so that industrial users will have to shoulder more of the costs of treatment.

3. User Charges

User charges may be a significant expense for industrial participants in federally or state-funded treatment works. Title II provides that industrial dischargers must repay the portion of the construction grant allocable to them and also pay their proportional share of operation and maintenance costs. These provisions were originally included to allay concerns that grant assistance to municipalities could function as an indirect subsidy to industrial users of POTWs, giving them an unfair advantage over direct industrial dischargers.

The so-called industrial cost recovery (ICR) requirement provides for repayment of capital costs by industrial POTW users. The provision was difficult to administer, however, and was repealed in 1980. Nevertheless, some local communities continue to assess ICR payments, despite the fact that they are not required by law and are often of questionable legality under state law.

The user charge provisions require industrial sharing of the annual operating and maintenance charges for a facility. Section 204 conditions approval of a construction grant on a finding that an applicant for federal funds has adopted or will adopt "a system of charges to assure that each recipient of waste treatment services . . . will pay its proportional share of the costs of operation and maintenance (including replacement) of any waste treatment services provided by the applicant."[214] EPA regulations provide:

> A grantee's user charge system based on actual use (or estimated use) of waste water treatment services may be approved if each user (or user class) pays its proportionate share of operation and maintenance (including replacement costs) of treatment works within the grantee's service area, based on the user's proportionate contribution to the total waste water loading from all users (or user classes). To insure proportional distribution of operation and maintenance costs to each user (or user class), the user's contribution shall be based on factors such as strength, volume, and delivery flow rate characteristics.[215]

Although volume is one of the factors for determining the allocation of user costs, EPA policy does not allow user charge systems to offer quantity discounts to large volume users. Nevertheless, this policy would not seem to preclude recognition of volume-related efficiencies such as flow equalization, which large volume users provide to the treatment facility to which they discharge. User charges also may only be based on a percentage of the charge for water usage where such charges are based on a constant cost per unit of consumption, so as to reasonably reflect the waste water discharge amount. In addition, an industrial user that discharges waste water containing toxic pollutants to a treatment works must pay for any increased costs of effluent or sludge management caused by that discharge.[216]

---

[214] CWA §204(a)(4), 33 U.S.C. §1284(a)(4) (1988).
[215] 40 C.F.R. §35.929-1.
[216] 40 C.F.R. §35.929-2(c).

EPA has detailed guidelines for user charge computations set out in the regulations. The guidelines are technical and complicated, and dischargers that are large contributors to a treatment works should pay close attention to the municipality's use of such guidelines in adoption of a user charge system. If the municipality or other treatment works operator improperly calculates proportionate share in its user charge system, it does not fulfill its obligation under section 204. An affected discharger could challenge EPA or state approval of any construction grant or loan application on this basis.

EPA has recently announced that it is considering making policy and regulatory changes to the POTW grant/loan program to encourage private investment in POTWs as a means of addressing the increasing concerns about POTW efficiency and funding.[217] EPA is soliciting public comment on this approach, and it remains to be seen whether partly or wholly privately owned POTWs will be feasible and efficient. In the meantime, it is apparent that POTW users are not insulated from the potentially significant costs of compliance with the CWA. In many circumstances, industrial users may want to examine other alternatives before relying on discharge to a POTW as a method of compliance.

B. Thermal Discharges

Heat is defined as a pollutant under the CWA and, as such, is subject to the effluent limitations provided in the statute. Thermal discharges are also addressed specifically by section 316, which provides that, after opportunity for public hearing, if a source demonstrates that the effluent limitations applicable to thermal discharges are more stringent than necessary to ensure "the protection and propagation of a balanced, indigenous population of shellfish, fish, and wildlife" in the body of water in which the discharge will occur, the Administrator or the state may impose less stringent standards that will ensure such protection and propagation.[218] These provisions are primarily of import to the electricity generating sector, because heat comprises such a major part of power plant discharges. EPA attempted to establish a no-discharge BAT level for heat, but was unsuccessful.[219] Nonetheless, some state permitting authorities may still initially propose no-discharge levels for heat in permits.

Proceedings under section 316 are complex and require submission of substantial scientific data. Obviously there are many difficult issues raised by the terms "balanced, indigenous population," and determining what is adequate "protection and propagation." Despite these problems, section 316 does provide thermal dischargers with an opportunity to avoid compliance with effluent standards that may be unnecessary to protect the environment and aquatic life.

---

[217] 57 Fed. Reg. 28,867 (1992).

[218] CWA §316, 33 U.S.C. §1326 (1988).

[219] Appalachian Power Co. v. Train, 545 F.2d 1351 (4th Cir. 1976).

C. Groundwater Pollution

Because of the large amount of potentially hazardous substances as well as nonhazardous solid waste generated and disposed by American industry, and despite various federal and state attempts to regulate treatment, storage, and disposal of waste, there has been increasing pressure to dispose of such waste on or below the land, with a concomitant increased threat to groundwater pollution. In response to this threat, EPA initially tried to regulate underground discharges pursuant to the CWA. The Act, however, does not clearly include aquifers in the definition of "waters of the United States," and the federal courts could not agree whether EPA had authority to regulate disposal into wells under the Act.[220]

EPA now relies on the authority of the Safe Drinking Water Act (SDWA)[221] and RCRA's land ban provisions to regulate such discharges through state hazardous waste and underground injection control programs. The state programs have broad application and are administered pursuant to Part C of the SDWA and RCRA.[222] Waste lagoons and ponds will continue to be regulated by EPA under RCRA and the states pursuant to hazardous waste programs. Therefore, many sources exempt from regulation under the CWA because they do not discharge to navigable waters are subject to waste water discharge requirements under RCRA or the SDWA.

D. Ocean Dumping

Pollution resulting from ocean dumping is almost entirely governed by the provisions of the Marine Protection, Research and Sanctuaries Act (MPRSA),[223] enacted in 1972. The MPRSA essentially applies to all dumping of materials (defined the same as CWA "pollutants") into the territorial sea or contiguous zone of the United States and all dumping by U.S. entities or vessels into the ocean.[224] The few exemptions from this coverage are oil spills, discharges from outfall structures, construction of a fixed structure for other than disposal purposes where otherwise regulated (i.e., oil exploration and drilling), fish wastes, deposits of oyster shells or other materials used to maintain fisheries if otherwise regulated, marine sanitation devices, and routine discharges from motor driven equipment or vessels.[225] Oil spills, outfalls, fish wastes, and marine sanitation devices are governed by the CWA.

As the result of amendments over time, the MPRSA now prohibits ocean dumping of practically all materials. This includes sewage sludge and industrial

[220] Section 402(b)(1)(D) does provide, however, that states must control the discharge of pollutants into wells.

[221] 42 U.S.C. §300 *et seq.* See Chapter 5, Safe Drinking Water Act, for a discussion of the SDWA provisions.

[222] The relevant SDWA regulations are found at 40 C.F.R. pt. 146, the RCRA regulations at 40 C.F.R. pts. 271, 272.

[223] 33 U.S.C. §§1401–44 (1988).

[224] MPRSA §101, 33 U.S.C. §1411 (1988). The territorial sea is a belt adjacent to the U.S. coast extending outward three miles, and the contiguous zone is an area extending 12 miles seaward from the territorial sea baseline.

[225] *See* MPRSA §3(f), 33 U.S.C. §1402(f) (1988).

wastes, except in exigent circumstances.[226] In addition, the dumping of radiological, chemical, and biological warfare agents and high level radioactive wastes is prohibited.[227] Amendments to the Act in 1982 also imposed restrictions on dumping of low-level radioactive wastes.

Basically, the only dumping activity of any consequence that is permitted by the amended MPRSA is the disposal of dredged spoil. The statute authorizes the Corps of Engineers to issue permits for ocean disposal of dredged materials.[228] The Corps must notify EPA prior to issuing a permit, so that EPA may approve or veto the decision, or waive application of its substantive review criteria.[229] EPA and the Corps developed a manual known as the "Green Book" in 1991, which specifies testing procedures for determining whether dredged material should be approved for ocean disposal.[230]

The statute also requires EPA to establish criteria for designation of sites where dumping of dredge material will be permitted and to designate sites where dumping will and will not be allowed, based on the factors specified in section 102 of the Act.[231] EPA promulgated regulations and initially designated marine dump sites that were already in use on an interim basis, pending completion of the required baseline or trend assessment surveys.[232] Environmental groups challenged this practice, and a consent decree was entered that imposed schedules for EPA to conduct the studies and decide whether to designate 22 interim dredge spoil sites.[233] EPA has now designated some 140 interim dredge material dump sites, and the designations have been sustained over the objections of environmental groups.[234]

EPA is also authorized to establish various categories of permits for ocean disposal of other than dredged material and has done so by regulation.[235] EPA has issued a number of general permits under these regulations for material having "minimal adverse environmental impact" that is disposed in small

---

[226] MPRSA §102a, 33 U.S.C. §1412a (1988, 1992 Supp.) Industrial waste means any solid, semisolid, or liquid waste generated by a manufacturing or processing plant the ocean dumping of which may unreasonably degrade or endanger human health, welfare, or amenities, or the marine environment, ecological systems, and economic potentialities. *Id.* The prohibition on dumping of sewage sludge became effective in 1991 and terminated an exemption for sewage sludge for New York City created by the decision in City of New York v. EPA, 543 F. Supp. 1084 (S.D.N.Y. 1981).

[227] MPRSA §102, 33 U.S.C. §1412 (1988).

[228] MPRSA §103, 33 U.S.C. §1413 (1988). The Corps has promulgated regulations applicable to dredge spoil disposal at 33 C.F.R. pt. 324.

[229] MPRSA §103(b)-(d), 33 U.S.C. §1413(b)-(d); 40 C.F.R. pt. 225.

[230] EPA's related efforts to address contaminated sediments in the ocean and other water bodies has caused some friction with the Corps. EPA recently developed nationally applicable interim sediment quality criteria, and hopes to publish final sediment criteria for certain pollutants in the near future. The Corps, however, believes EPA's "equilibrium partitioning" sediment criteria are overly stringent, and that the bioassays developed are too conservative and unrepresentative of any real risk. This controversy may cause problems not only with respect to EPA's sediment remediation efforts in conjunction with the Corps, but also in other regulatory programs where the Corps and EPA work together.

[231] MPRSA §102(a), (c), 33 U.S.C. §1412(a), (c) (1988).

[232] 40 C.F.R. §228.12.

[233] National Wildlife Fed'n v. Costle, Civ. No. 80-0405 (D.D.C. Oct. 1980).

[234] *See, e.g.,* National Wildlife Fed'n v. Costle, 629 F.2d 118 (D.C. Cir. 1980). EPA has further delayed the final designation process, however, by requiring NEPA environmental impact statements for all site designations. 39 Fed. Reg. 16,186 (1974); 39 Fed. Reg. 37,419 (1974); 40 C.F.R. §228.6(b).

[235] MPRSA §102(b), 33 U.S.C. §1412(b) (1988); 40 C.F.R. pt. 220. The EPA regulations provide for issuance of (1) general permits, (2) special permits, (3) emergency permits, (4) interim permits, and (5) research permits.

quantities at designated sites.[236] Special permits cover most other types of ocean dumping for materials meeting EPA's discharge criteria.[237] The other types of permits are used relatively infrequently.[238]

Enforcement provisions in the MPRSA generally parallel those in the CWA. Violations of any provision or permit term may result in civil penalties of up to $50,000 per day of violation, and/or revocation or suspension of the permit. The Attorney General may sue in court for injunctive relief, and any vessel used in a violation is subject to seizure. A knowing violation is a criminal offense, punishable by a fine of up to $50,000 or imprisonment of up to one year, or both. Citizens may also bring actions for injunctive relief and may be awarded attorney's fees.[239] The Coast Guard is responsible for detection of violations of the Act.[240]

VIII. Enforcement

The CWA provides a number of enforcement options to EPA and to states administering their own federal water pollution control programs and also bestows enforcement powers upon citizens with its citizen suit provision. Enforcement policy under the CWA and other environmental statutes is discussed generally in Chapter 18. This section will touch only on certain aspects of enforcement that are specific to the CWA. Because the potential exposure for companies and individuals under these enforcement provisions can be significant, even for infractions that cause little actual harm, it is important for all regulated entities to understand fully the criminal, civil, administrative penalty, and citizen suit provisions of the CWA.

A. Civil Enforcement of the Clean Water Act

The CWA provides EPA and the Justice Department with several avenues for civil enforcement against entities that violate either a provision of the Act, the implementing regulations, or the terms of NPDES and other permits. States generally have these same options, as provided in state procedural rules.

---

[236] 40 C.F.R. §220.3(a). The regulations generally authorize ocean dumping for the purposes of burial at sea, the sinking of Navy target vessels, and disposal of vessels (subject to specified limitations).

[237] 40 C.F.R. §220.3(b). These permits may be issued for three-year terms.

[238] Research permits may be issued for a term of 19 months where EPA determines that the scientific merit of the project outweighs the potential effects on the environment. 40 C.F.R. §220.3(e). These have been granted for ocean incineration (considered ocean dumping) in the past, but more recently have been denied pending EPA regulations addressing incineration.

Emergency and interim permits are not very clearly defined and are seldom used. Emergency permits may be approved, even if the material poses an unacceptable risk to human health, if there is no other feasible solution and the situation requires "urgency." 40 C.F.R. §220.3(c). Use of interim permits has essentially fallen by the wayside since their disapproval in the *City of New York* case noted above, and EPA has not redefined this type of permit.

[239] MPRSA §105, 33 U.S.C. §1415 (1988). The Supreme Court in Middlesex Sewage Auth. v. National Sea Clammers, 453 U.S. 1 (1981), held that the Act does not create a private right of action for damages for fishermen or others economically harmed by violations of the Act, although monetary damages presumably could be sought under common law and admiralty law theories.

[240] MPRSA §107, 33 U.S.C. §1417 (1988).

EPA may seek both injunctive relief and civil penalties in a civil enforcement action. Both section 504 and section 309(b) provide for injunctive relief, although EPA usually relies upon section 309(b). Section 309(b) authorizes the Administrator to have the court enter a temporary or permanent injunction to restrain and abate any violation of the statute, regulations, or permit terms, including state NPDES permits.[241] A party that violates an injunction issued by the court is subject not only to the criminal and civil penalty provisions of the CWA, but also the criminal and civil contempt powers of the court. Often, an injunction will be in the form of a consent decree that provides stipulated penalties for violation of the decree.

Section 504 gives EPA emergency powers to bring suit in district court to immediately restrain any person causing or contributing to pollution that presents an imminent and substantial endangerment to the health, welfare, or livelihood of persons.[242] A previous version of this provision was used to restrain the discharge of taconite tailings in the famous *Reserve Mining* case[243] in Minnesota, but the emergency powers provision generally receives little use.

Other options available to EPA include referral to the Department of Justice for civil enforcement action in district court under CWA section 309,[244] which provides for civil penalties of up to $25,000 per day of violation. A defendant in such an action has a constitutional right to a jury trial,[245] but the jury only decides liability. The district judge decides the amount of the penalty once a violation is found by the jury. In assessing the appropriate penalty, the court is to consider several factors including (1) the seriousness of the violation, (2) the economic benefit (if any) resulting from the violation, (3) any history of such violations, (4) any good faith efforts to comply with applicable requirements, (5) the economic impact of the penalty on the violator, and (6) such other factors as justice may require.

Section 309 also specifically addresses the issue of how process upsets should be treated for purposes of penalty assessment, where the upset causes a number of pollutant parameters listed in the permit to be simultaneously exceeded. The statute provides that a "single operational upset that leads to simultaneous violations of more than one pollutant parameter shall be treated as a single violation." Violations of multiple parameters that do not result from an identifiable operational upset will be treated as multiple violations.

Finally, dischargers should be aware that civil penalties assessed in CWA civil cases are often very large. There are several federal enforcement cases where the government has collected more than a million dollars. In fact, in one case involving several sewage treatment plants in Puerto Rico, the court assessed a penalty of more than $32 million.[246] In a recent settlement of a suit against a paper products company for discharges of carbon disulfide in violation

---

[241] CWA §309(b), 33 U.S.C. §1319(b) (1988).

[242] CWA §504, 33 U.S.C. §1364 (1988). Section 504 specifically refers to an inability to market shellfish as a factor constituting endangerment to livelihood warranting emergency action.

[243] Reserve Mining Co. v. EPA, 514 F.2d 492 (8th Cir. 1975). The court of appeals modified the district court's injunction to allow the discharger additional time to comply rather than to require immediate cessation of operations. *Id.* at 538.

[244] CWA §309(d), 33 U.S.C. §1319(d) (1988).

[245] United States v. Tull, 481 U.S. 412 (1987).

[246] United States v. Puerto Rico Aqueduct and Sewer Auth., 25 ER Cases 1921 (D.P.R. 1987).

of the CWA, the company agreed to pay $7.2 million in civil penalties, as well as $1.8 million in civil penalties under RCRA and $4 million in criminal penalties.[247] This case illustrates EPA's increasing emphasis on multimedia enforcement—in particular, combining CWA and RCRA enforcement actions. Civil and criminal penalties also are not deductible business expenses for federal income tax purposes, increasing their financial impact on companies. These trends illustrate EPA's continuing emphasis on stringent environmental enforcement, and it is likely that civil penalties assessed in these cases will continue to increase, as will the attention dischargers must pay to compliance.

B. Criminal Penalties

The increased enforcement emphasis under the CWA is even more apparent with respect to criminal penalties. Section 309(c), which provides for criminal penalties, was revised and made more stringent by the 1987 Amendments. Section 309(c) provides for several categories of violations:

- Negligent violations (§309(c)(1))—subject to criminal penalties of not less than $2,500 or more than $25,000 per day of violation, as well as up to one year imprisonment per day of violation. Penalties and length of imprisonment are doubled for a second offense.
- Knowing violations (§309(c)(2))—subject to fines of not less than $5,000 or more than $50,000 per day of violation and up to three years imprisonment per day of violation. As with negligent violations, penalty levels double for second offenses.
- Knowing endangerment (§309(c)(3))—where a person knowingly violates a permit or other requirement and "knows at that time that he thereby places another person in imminent danger of death or serious bodily injury," he or she is subject to fines of up to $250,000 and up to 15 years imprisonment, or for organizations, a fine of not more than $1 million. Fines and penalties are doubled for second offenses. Convicting an individual of knowing endangerment under the Act requires proof of "actual awareness or actual belief" that may be shown by "circumstantial evidence, including evidence that the defendant took affirmative steps to shield himself from relevant information."
- False reporting (§309(c)(4))—anyone who files false reports or who knowingly falsifies, tampers with, or renders inaccurate any monitoring device is subject to fines of up to $10,000 and imprisonment of up to two years; penalties double for a second offense.

Several aspects of these criminal provisions should be noted. First, the express wording of the statute makes negligent violations a potentially criminal offense. This broadens the scope of criminal violations under the CWA. Second, the degree of knowledge required to satisfy the requirement for "knowing" violations may include situations where a discharger is aware of a violation, for example, after being issued an administrative order, but continues to operate while attempting to abate the violation. Third, the "knowing endan-

[247] United States v. Dexter, No. H-89-39 (D. Conn. Sept. 3, 1992).

germent'' provision subjects a party to severe penalties, usually in cases where water supplies are contaminated, pretreatment requirements for toxics are deliberately violated, or hazardous substances are purposefully dumped in sewers or waterways.

In fact, knowing endangerment prosecutions have been initiated for violations of pretreatment requirements that allegedly endangered employees.[248] At least one such prosecution, in the *Borjohn* case, resulted in convictions of the company and its president, which were subsequently overturned on appeal.[249] The First Circuit held in vacating the convictions that the knowing endangerment provisions were not intended to punish knowing violations that resulted in imminent danger to employees, before the pollutant reached a publicly owned sewer, treatment works, or other downstream location. The court reasoned that the company's employees were endangered solely by virtue of handling the wastes at their place of employment, not by the illegal discharge, and that such endangerment was the province of the OSH Act, not the CWA. It remains to be seen whether other circuits will interpret this provision as narrowly.

Notwithstanding the *Borjohn* case, there is no dearth of successful criminal prosecutions against major industrial dischargers, including corporations and their officers, under the CWA. For example, Chevron was recently assessed $6.5 million in criminal penalties for a number of ''knowing'' violations of permit requirements and for bypassing the waste water treatment system,[250] and Bristol-Meyers pled guilty and paid a $3.5 million criminal fine for illegal discharges into POTWs in violation of the Act and state law.[251] Under the sentencing guidelines such convinctions ordinarily result in imprisonment. Imprisonment is a threat in particular for corporate officers, who may be convicted for knowing endangerment if the government proves that the officers deliberately shielded themselves from knowledge of violations.[252] States also provide criminal penalties for violations of their statutes implementing the CWA, and these may also include prison sentences.

C. Administrative Orders and Penalties

Another enforcement option under the CWA is for EPA to issue administrative compliance orders to dischargers for violation of permit terms or other CWA obligations, pursuant to section 309(a). Such orders may require compliance with an interim compliance schedule or an operation and maintenance requirement within 30 days. Permanent compliance is required within the time EPA determines to be reasonable under the circumstances. Receiving an EPA compliance order is a serious matter for a discharger, as failure to comply or at least to make good faith efforts to comply may be the basis for criminal prosecution or civil enforcement proceedings.

---

[248] *See, e.g.*, United States v. Borjohn Optical Technology, Inc., Cr No. 89-256 (D. Mass. Nov. 7, 1990).

[249] United States v. Borowski, 977 F.2d 27, 35 ER Cases 1729 (1st Cir. 1992) (vacating judgments of conviction in *Borjohn*).

[250] United States v. Chevron, U.S.A., No. CV-88-7836 (C.D. Cal. May 18, 1992). Chevron also had to pay $1.5 million in civil penalties.

[251] United States v. Bristol-Myers Squibb Co., No. 92-CR-123 (N.D.N.Y. Apr. 24, 1992).

[252] CWA §309(c)(3)(B), 33 U.S.C. §1319(c)(3)(B) (1988).

Section 309(g), added by the 1987 Amendments, also authorizes EPA to initiate administrative penalty proceedings against violators, and the Corps of Engineers to initiate such proceedings for violations of dredge and fill permits under section 404. The statute provides for Class I and Class II penalties. The upper limit on a Class I penalty is $25,000 total for the proceeding and $10,000 per violation, and the defendant has the right to an informal hearing. For Class II proceedings, the upper limit on penalties is $125,000, with a maximum of $10,000 per day of violation. The defendant also is entitled to a more elaborate hearing before an independent ALJ. The ALJ (or EPA in Class I proceedings), in determining the amount of penalties to be imposed, is to consider the same factors the district court is required to consider in assessing civil penalties under section 309(d).[253]

Section 309(g)(6) further provides that administrative penalty proceedings serve as a bar to section 505 citizen suits for the same violations if the administrative penalty proceeding is initiated prior to notice of filing of a citizen suit. Although this provision significantly limits citizen suits, citizens still may participate in the administrative proceeding.

Judicial review of EPA or Corps penalty decisions may be obtained in district court for Class I penalties and in the court of appeals for Class II penalties. In addition to the parties involved, any citizen who commented in the administrative proceeding may also seek judicial review. Although the statutory language is not clear, it appears that a court has the discretion to *increase* penalties where it finds that the penalty assessed by EPA or the Corps is too low.

In addition to the standard administrative penalty proceedings, EPA is currently considering developing a CWA "field citation" program under section 309(g), similar to that being developed under the 1990 Amendments to the CAA. A field citation would basically involve an inspector issuing a complaint and simultaneously offering a settlement to a facility, primarily for minor violations. No decisions have been made on the scope of violations that might be covered, the range of penalties, or the specific mechanisms to be used, but this type of program would certainly mean quicker enforcement action and potentially greater exposure to penalties.

D. Citizen Suits

The citizen suit provision in section 505 of the CWA has been used more than any other provision of its kind under the environmental laws. Citizen suits often involve national environmental groups such as the Sierra Club or NRDC, working through local grassroots organizations such as state public interest research groups (PIRGs). The numerous citizen suits brought under the CWA have been successful in bringing about increased enforcement action by EPA and have also resulted in the imposition of harsh penalties on dischargers found to be in violation of the Act's requirements. Thus, these suits should be considered an important enforcement tool under the CWA, in addition to EPA's enforcement powers.

---

[253] The Oil Pollution Act gives the Coast Guard similar administrative penalty authority under CWA §311 for discharges of oil or hazardous substances.

Section 505 provides that any person "having an interest which is or may be adversely affected" may bring a civil action against a discharger for violation of an effluent standard or order pertaining to such standard or against EPA for failure to perform its duties under the Act. In order to file a citizen's suit, a citizen must first give notice of the complaint to EPA and the Attorney General, the state, and the alleged violator (or only to the government, where the suit will be against EPA).[254] Generally evidence of violations is no obstacle, as discharge monitoring reports and other information required to be reported by the Act are a matter of public record.

Section 505 gives EPA a right to intervene in any citizen suit brought for violations of standards under the Act, and no consent decree may be entered in an action without EPA review and approval.[255] EPA has 45 days to object to a proposed decree.[256] Most consent decrees will include penalties (often severe) for the violations and schedules of compliance and will additionally provide for attorney's fees and costs to plaintiffs.

The courts have generally resolved procedural issues that could be obstacles to citizen suits in favor of the citizen-enforcers. One of the most important of these issues is standing. It is fairly well established that in most cases members of local environmental groups will have standing to bring citizen enforcement actions. Similarly, courts have found that citizen suits may be brought for injunctive relief, as well as civil penalties.

In fact, the primary restriction that courts have placed on citizen suits under the CWA is found in *Gwaltney of Smithfield, Ltd. v. Chesapeake Bay Foundation,* where the Supreme Court held that section 505 does not authorize suits for wholly past violations.[257] This ruling is not necessarily a significant impediment to citizen suits, given the Court's further ruling that allegations of ongoing or continuous violations need not be proven to give a court jurisdiction under section 505. Indeed, the district court on remand easily found sufficient evidence to infer a continuing likelihood of intermittent violations and reaffirmed the $1.3 million civil penalty.[258]

Large fines such as that imposed in *Gwaltney* are not uncommon in CWA citizen suits. For example, in a suit brought by NRDC, a fine of $1,680,000 was imposed against Texaco for violations of effluent limits and permit reporting requirements.[259] Another citizen suit brought for violations of an NPDES permit was settled for $1 million, in addition to another $300,000 in attorney fees.[260] These large fines serve to emphasize that citizen suits are a means of enforcement that should not be taken lightly.

---

[254] CWA §505(b), 33 U.S.C. §1365(b) (1988); 40 C.F.R. §135.4.

[255] CWA §505(c)(3), 33 U.S.C. §1365(c)(3) (1988); 40 C.F.R. §135.5.

[256] CWA §503(c)(3), 33 U.S.C. §1365(c)(3) (1988).

[257] 484 U.S. 49 (1987).

[258] Chesapeake Bay Found. v. Gwaltney of Smithfield, 688 F. Supp. 1078, 27 ER Cases 2230 (E.D. Va. 1988), *aff'd in part & rev'd in part,* 890 F.2d 690 (4th Cir. 1989).

[259] NRDC v. Texaco Refining and Mktg., Inc., 800 F. Supp. 1, 35 ER Cases 2095 (D. Del. 1992).

[260] Massachusetts PIRG v. ICI Americas, No. 89-1334-H (D. Mass. May 19, 1992).

IX. Conclusion

The CWA is probably the most mature and time-tested of our federal environmental regulatory programs. Most of the regulatory tools and mechanisms have been tested and have evolved to the point that they serve as models for many other environmental statutes. Nevertheless, there are continuing regulatory challenges such as control of nonpoint source pollution, pollution prevention, and the need for additional funding that necessitate new and different approaches and ensure that the Act will continue to be revised and expanded. In fact, Congress apparently intends to try to address these issues in legislation in 1994, though the legislative gauntlet may be hard to run with reauthorization of CERCLA occurring at about the same time.

In addition, ongoing disputes such as wetlands definitional issues and implementation of storm water controls illustrate that the Act is far from well settled with respect to many of its various components. Finally, the continuing presence of, and in many instances, the worsening of water pollution clearly demonstrates that the nation has far to go to fully achieve the Act's objective of restoring and maintaining the chemical, physical, and biological integrity of the nation's waters.

Appendix A

Section 307 Toxic Pollutants

Acenaphthene
Acrolein
Acrylonitrile
Aldrin/Dieldrin
Antimony and compounds*
Arsenic and compounds
Asbestos
Benzene
Benzidine
Beryllium and compounds
Cadmium and compounds
Carbon tetrachloride
Chlordane (technical mixture and metabolites)
Chlorinated benzenes (other than dichlorobenzenes)
Chlorinated ethanes (including 1,2-dichloreothane, 1,1,1-ethane and hexachloroethane)
Chlorinated naphthalene
Chlorinated phenols (other than those listed elsewhere; includes trichlorophenols and chlorinated cresols)
Chloroalkyl ethers (chloromethyl, chloroethyl, and mixed ethers)
Chloroform
2-chlorophenol
Chromium and compounds
Copper and compounds
Cyanides
DDT and metabolites
Dichlorobenzenes (1,2-, 1,3-, and 1,4-dichlorobenzenes)
Dichlorobenzinine
Dichloroethylenes (1,1- and 1,2-dichloroethylene)
2,4-dichlorophenol
Dichloropropane and dichloropropene
2,4-dimethylphenol
Dinitrotoluene
Diphenylhydrazine
Endosulfan and metabolites
Endrin and metabolites
Ethylbenzene
Fluoranthene
Haloethers (other than those listed elsewhere; includes chlorophenylphenyl ethers, bromophenylphenyl ether, bis-(dichloroisopropyl) ether, bis-(chloroethoxy) methane, and polychlorinated diphenyl ethers)
Halomethanes (other than those listed elsewhere; includes methylene chloride, methyl chloride, methyl bromide, bromoform, dichlorobromomethane, trichlorofluoromethane, dichlorodifluoromethane)
Heptachlor and metabolites
Hexachlorobutadiene

Hexachlorocyclohexane (all isomers)
Hexachlorocyclopentadiene
Isophorone
Lead and compounds
Mercury and compounds
Naphthalene
Nickel and compounds
Nitrobenzene
Nitrophenols (including 2,4-dinitrophenol, dinitrocresol)
Nitrosamines
Pentachlorophenol
Phenol
Phthalate esters
Polychlorinated biphenyls (PCBs)
Polynuclear aromatic hydrocarbons (including benzanthracenes, benzo-pyrenes, benzofluoranthene, chrysenes, dibenzanthracenes, and indenopyrenes)
Selenium and compounds
Silver and compounds
2,3,7,8-Tetrachlorodibenzo-p-dioxin (TCDD)
Tetrachloroethylene
Thallium and compounds
Toluene
Toxaphene
Trichloroethylene
Vinyl chloride
Zinc and compounds

---

*The term ''compound'' shall include organic and inorganic compounds.

Appendix B

Industry Categories

1. Adhesives and Sealants
2. Aluminum Forming
3. Asbestos Manufacturing
4. Auto and Other Laundries
5. Battery Manufacturing
6. Coal Mining
7. Coil Coating
8. Copper Forming
9. Electric and Electronic Components
10. Electroplating
11. Explosives Manufacturing
12. Ferroalloys
13. Foundries
14. Gum and Wood Chemicals
15. Inorganic Chemicals Manufacturing
16. Iron and Steel Manufacturing
17. Leather Tanning and Finishing
18. Mechanical Products Manufacturing
19. Nonferrous Metals Manufacturing
20. Ore Mining
21. Organic Chemicals Manufacturing
22. Pesticides
23. Petroleum Refining
24. Pharmaceutical Preparations
25. Photographic Equipment and Supplies
26. Plastic and Synthetic Materials Manufacturing
27. Plastic Processing
28. Porcelain Enamelling
29. Printing and Publishing
30. Pulp and Paperboard Mills
31. Soap and Detergent Manufacturing
32. Steam Electric Power Plants
33. Textile Mills
34. Timber Products Processing

5

Safe Drinking Water Act

By Russell V. Randle and Peter D. Robertson

I. Introduction

Like the Clean Air Act before it, the Safe Drinking Water Act (SDWA)[1] was enacted by an environmentally minded Congress of the 1970s. The 93rd Congress passed the Act in 1974, federalizing drinking water protection in a comprehensive manner for the first time. Prior to enactment of the SDWA, Congress regulated only drinking water used on interstate carriers, exercising its powers under the Commerce Clause of the Constitution, in order to prevent the spread of communicable diseases.

The 93rd Congress, responding to concerns that contaminants had fouled both surface sources and groundwater, determined to implement a more extensive drinking water protection regime. The reported pollution of major aquifers—most notably the Edwards aquifer in Texas—through surface pollution and underground injection of waste (which was prominent in, but not exclusive to, the oil and gas industry) further moved Congress to action. Finally, its concern that public water systems were a threat to public health and safety because they were old, improperly maintained, and inadequately funded also helped prompt congressional activity.

In the 1974 version of the Act, Congress required the Environmental Protection Agency (EPA) to establish national standards for acceptable levels of contaminants in drinking water delivered by public water systems. It also established programs for the regulation of underground injection wells and for the protection of sole source aquifers. As with portions of the Clean Air Act, however, EPA was slow to implement the requirements of the SDWA. Further, enforcement actions were infrequent because the Agency was hesitant to use its enforcement powers against units of local government—the most common drinking water providers.

Mimicking its action to strengthen other environmental statutes to force EPA's hand, Congress revised the SDWA extensively in 1986[2] with the objective of accelerating the pace of drinking water regulatory and enforcement activity. The Act, as amended in 1986, is structured as follows:

---

[1] 42 U.S.C. §300f *et seq.* (1991).

[2] Pub. L. No. 99-339, 100 Stat. 666.

- Part A sets forth the definitions used in the Act.
- Part B sets forth the program for regulating drinking water contaminants through national drinking water regulations applied to public water systems. It vests primary enforcement responsibility in the states. It also establishes procedures for variances and exemptions from those regulations under certain circumstances.
- Part C provides for the protection of underground sources of drinking water through state-administered programs to control underground injection wells. It also establishes a sole-source aquifer demonstration program and a wellhead area protection program.
- Part D sets forth certain emergency powers of EPA.
- Part E sets out general provisions of the Act that, *inter alia,* work to assure availability of supplies of chemicals necessary to treat water; provide for research, technical assistance, information, and personnel training; authorize appropriations for grants to states; provide for studies, demonstration projects, recordkeeping, a national drinking water advisory council, and for the regulation of federal agencies falling within the ambit of the Act; set forth requirements for judicial review and for citizens suits; and allow EPA to treat Indian tribes as states for purposes of the Act.
- Part F deals with lead in drinking water systems and coolers.

II. Regulation of Public Water Systems

The 1986 Amendments to the SDWA dramatically expanded the requirements on EPA to regulate the levels of contaminants in drinking water delivered by public water systems. The Amendments set out 83 individual substances for which EPA had to set both hortatory goals and enforceable limits.[3] Those substances are listed below in Table 1.

The statute also allowed EPA to substitute up to seven chemicals on the list with other compounds the regulation of which is more likely to be protective of public health than would the regulation of the originally listed contaminant.[4] EPA has made those substitutions as noted below in Table 2.[5]

A. Public Water Systems

The statutory scheme requires public water systems to meet specified objectives. The SDWA defines public water systems as a system delivering piped water to the public for human consumption that has at least 15 service connections or regularly serves at least 25 individuals.[6] The regulations further require that these systems serve their consumers at least 60 days per year.[7] The Act does not apply, however, to public water systems that (1) consist only of

[3] §1412(b)(1), 42 U.S.C. §300g-1(b)(1) (1991).
[4] §1412(b)(2), 42 U.S.C. §300g-1(b)(2) (1991).
[5] 53 Fed. Reg. 1892 (1988).
[6] §1401(4), 42 U.S.C. §300f(4) (1991).
[7] 40 C.F.R. §141.11(e).

Table 1.
EPA-Designated Substances Having Advisory and Enforceable Limits

Volatile Organic Chemicals	
Trichloroethylene	Benzene
Tetrachloroethylene	Chlorobenzene
Carbon tetrachloride	Dichlorobenzene
1,1,1-Trichloroethane	Trichlorobenzene
1,2-Dichloroethane	1,1-Dichloroethylene
Vinyl chloride	transl,2 Dichloroethylene
Methylene chloride	Cis-1,2-Dichloroethylene
Microbiology and Turbidity	
Total Coliforms	Viruses
Turbidity	Standard plate count
Giardia lamblia	Legionella
Inorganics	
Arsenic	Nitrate
Barium	Selenium
Cadmium	Silver
Chromium	Fluoride
Lead	Aluminum
Mercury	Antimony
Molybdenum	Nickel
Asbestos	Zinc
Sulfate	Thallium
Copper	Beryllium
Vanadium	Cyanide
Sodium	
Organics	
Endrin	1,1,2-Trichloroethane
Lindane	Vydate
Methoxychlor	Simazine
Toxaphene	PAHs
2,4-D	PCBs
2,4,5-TP	Atrazine
Aldicarb	Phthalates
Chlordane	Acrylamide
Dalapon	Dibromochloropropane
Diquat	1,2-Dichloropropane
Endothall	Pentachlorophenol
Glyphosate	Pichloram
Carbofuran	Dinoseb
Alachlor	Ethylene dibromide
Epichlorohydrin	Dibromomethane
Toluene	Xylene
Adipates	Hexachlorocyclopentadiene
2,3,7,8-TCDD (Dioxin)	
Radionuclides	
Radium 226 & 228	Uranium
Beta particle & photon radioactivity	Gross Alpha particle activity

Table 2.
Substitutions

Substitutions
Aldicarb Sulfone replaced Zinc
Aldicarb Sulfoxide replaced Silver
Ethylbenzene replaced Aluminum
Heptachlor replaced Sodium
Heptachlor Expoxide replaced Dibromomethane
Nitrite replaced Molybdenum
Styrene replaced Vanadium

distribution and storage facilities and that do not have any collection and treatment facilities; (2) obtain all of their water from regulated public water systems but are not owned or operated by those systems; (3) do not sell water to any person; or (4) are not interstate carriers of passengers.[8]

1. Statutory Requirements

For each contaminant identified by the statute, EPA must promulgate a maximum contaminant level goal and a national primary drinking water standard (which is usually a maximum contaminant level (MCL)).[9] The maximum contaminant level goal (MCLG) is not binding on public water systems, but is used to determine the enforceable maximum contaminant level. The MCLG is to be set at the level at which no known or anticipated adverse human health effects occur and must include an adequate margin of safety.[10]

The enforceable National Primary Drinking Water Standard (NPDWS) must specify a maximum contaminant level if EPA determines it is economically and technologically feasible to ascertain the level of the contaminant in drinking water.[11] Where EPA determines it is not technologically or economically feasible to do so, the Agency may instead specify each known treatment technique that would prevent to the extent feasible known or anticipated adverse human health effects.[12]

EPA normally finds that it is economically and technologically feasible to ascertain the level of contaminants in drinking water and thus promulgates an MCL as the national primary drinking water standard. Thus, it is common to use the abbreviation MCL when one is referring to the national primary drinking water standard, and we do so in this chapter.

In addition to the 83 contaminants identified by Congress for regulation, the Act also requires EPA to establish a drinking water priority list of contaminants that may have any adverse human health effects and that are known or anticipated to occur in public water systems.[13] The list must be revised at least every three years.

[8] §1411(1), (2), (3), and (4), 42 U.S.C. §300g(1), (2), (3), and (4) (1991).
[9] §1412(b)(3), 42 U.S.C. §300g-1(b)(3) (1991).
[10] §1412(b)(4), 42 U.S.C. §300g-1(b)(4) (1991).
[11] §1401(1)(C)(i), 42 U.S.C. §300f(1)(C)(i) (1991).
[12] §§1401(1)(C)(ii) and 1412(b)(7)(A), 42 U.S.C. §§300f(1)(C)(ii) and 300g-1(b)(7)(A) (1991).
[13] §1412(b)(3)(A), 42 U.S.C. §300g-1(b)(3)(A) (1991).

Two years after each revision of the list, the Agency must propose MCLGs and MCLs for at least 25 contaminants from the list.[14] A year after proposal EPA must promulgate final MCLGs and MCLs for those contaminants.[15] Thus, final standards are to be promulgated at the same time as the Agency revises the drinking water priority list.

EPA published its 1991 version of the list containing 77 substances or classes of substances. EPA included in the list the seven contaminants it had dropped from the original list of 83. This priority list is reproduced below at Table 3.

While EPA also published a 1988 version of the list, it has not yet acted to regulate any of the substances from that list and evidently will not do so. The Agency's semiannual regulatory agenda indicates that it plans to propose its first set of regulations for substances drawn from the priority list in June 1993 and to promulgate such regulations by June 1995.[16] These regulations will presumably draw on substances from the 1991 version of the priority list. This schedule was mandated to EPA as a result of litigation in the federal courts.[17]

B. Establishing MCLGs

As noted above, the SDWA requires EPA to set MCLGs at the level at which no known or anticipated adverse human health effects occur. EPA has adopted a system of categorizing substances and regulating them according to their categorization. A proper understanding of this categorization system requires a review of EPA's Guidelines for Carcinogen Risk Assessment.

1. Guidelines for Carcinogen Risk Assessment

In 1986 EPA adopted the *Guidelines for Carcinogen Risk Assessment*[18] (Guidelines) to assist it in hazard identification involving environmental pollutants. The Guidelines are intended to guide Agency evaluation of suspected carcinogens in line with the policies and procedures established in the statutes administered by EPA. The Guidelines are used for a variety of functions in the administration of a number of statutes, including the SDWA.

Table 3.
1991 Version of the Drinking Water Priority List

Inorganics	
Aluminum	Cyanogen chloride
Boron	Hypochlorite ion
Chloramines	Manganese
Chlorate	Molybdenum
Chlorine	Strontium
Chlorine dioxide	Vanadium
Chlorite	Zinc

[14] §1412(b)(3)(C), 42 U.S.C. §300g-1(b)(3)(C) (1991).
[15] §1412(b)(3)(D), 42 U.S.C. §300g-1(b)(3)(D) (1991).
[16] 57 Fed. Reg. 52,062–63 (1992).
[17] 58 Fed. Reg. 25,034 (1993).
[18] 51 Fed. Reg. 33,992 (1986).

Table 3.
1991 Version of the Drinking Water Priority List (cont'd)

Pesticides	
Asulam	Metalaxyl
Bentazon	Methomyl
Bromacil	Metolachlor
Cyanazine	Metribuzin
Cyromazine	Parathion degradation product (4-Nitrophenol)
DCPA (and its acid metabolites)	Prometon
Dicamba	2,4,5-T
Ethylenethiourea	Thiodicarb
Fomesafen	Trifluralin
Lactofen/Acifluorfen	
Synthetic Organic Chemicals	
Acrylonitrile	2,2-Dichloropropane
Bromobenzene	1,3-Dichloropropane
Bromochloroacetonitrile	1,1-Dichloropropene
Bromodichloromethane	1,3-Dichloropropene
Bromoform	2,4-Dinitrophenol
Bromomethane	2,4-Dinitrotoluene
Chlorination/Chloramination byproducts (misc.), e.g., Haloacetic acids, Haloketones, Chloral hydrate, Mx-2 [3-chloro-4-(dichloromethyl)-5-hydroxy-2 (5H)-furanone], N-Organochloramines	2,6-Dinitrotoluene
Chloroethane	1,2-Diphenylhydrazine
Chloroform	Fluorotrichloromethane
Chloromethane	Hexachlorobutadiene
Chloropicrin	Hexachloroethane
O-Chlorotoluene	Isophorone
P-Chlorotoluene	Methyl ethyl ketone
Dibromoacetonitrile	Methyl isobutyl ketone
Dibromochloromethane	Methyl-t-butyl ether
Dibromomethane	Naphthalene
Dichloroacetonitrile	Ozone byproducts, e.g., Aldehydes, Epoxides, Peroxides, Nitrosamines, Bromate, Iodate
1,3-Dichlorobenzene	1,1,1,2-Tetrachloroethane
Dichlorodifluoromethane	1,1,2,2-Tetrachloroethane
1,1-Dichloroethane	Tetrahydrofuran
	Trichloroacetonitrile
	1,2,3-Trichloropropane
Microorganisms	
Cryptosporidium	

The Guidelines currently divide chemicals into five main groups depending on the overall weight of scientific evidence of their carcinogenic risk: Group A (human carcinogens based on sufficient evidence from epidemiological studies); Group B (probable human carcinogens);[19] Group C (possible human

[19] Group B is subdivided into Group B1 and Group B2. Group B1 is reserved for substances for which there is limited evidence of carcinogenicity from epidemiologic studies. Group B2 is reserved for substances for which there is inadequate or no data from epidemiologic studies. 51 Fed. Reg. 33,400.

carcinogens based on limited evidence of carcinogenicity); Group D (not classifiable based on lack of data or inadequate evidence of carcinogenicity from animal data); and Group E (no evidence of carcinogenicity for humans [no evidence for carcinogenicity in at least two adequate animal tests in different species or in both epidemiological and animal studies]).[20]

EPA has begun a process to revise its cancer classification Guidelines. EPA's Science Advisory Board recommended that EPA undertake such a process, noting that the Guidelines were insufficient to characterize accurately the cancer risk posed by many substances.[21] The Agency has a draft paper on changing the Guidelines that discusses the possibility of providing narrative characterization discussions for each part of a risk assessment for a particular compound.[22] If such a change were adopted, it could cause major revisions in the way the Agency categorizes substances for purposes of the SDWA.

2. *SDWA Categorical Contaminant Ranking System*

EPA's process for regulating the permissible level of contaminants in drinking water relies, in part, on a categorical ranking of the contaminants' carcinogenic risks. This categorical ranking system in turn is based on EPA's Guidelines for Carcinogen Risk Assessment described above.

EPA fashioned and first applied the drinking water contaminant ranking system in a November 13, 1985, rule promulgating recommended maximum contaminant levels (RMCLs—the name was changed in the 1986 SDWA amendments to maximum contaminant level goals (MCLGs)) for a number of synthetic organic chemicals.[23] That same categorization system has been used by the Agency consistently since 1985 and is still in use today.

The November 1985 rule established three categories in which drinking water contaminants would be placed based on the weight of evidence of carcinogenicity via ingestion. Category I is today labeled "Strong evidence considering weight of evidence, pharmacokinetics and exposure" and is reserved for substances falling into Guidelines Group A and Group B. Category II is labeled "Limited evidence considering weight of evidence, pharmacokinetics and exposure." EPA places Group C substances into Category II. Category III—inadequate or no animal evidence—contains compounds found in Guidelines Groups D and E, which have limited or no evidence of carcinogenicity.

3. *The MCLGs for Carcinogens*

When contaminants are categorized according to this system, EPA can then assign an MCLG. For contaminants exhibiting strong evidence of carcinogenicity—SDWA Category I compounds—EPA assigns an MCLG of zero.

---

[20] *Id.* at 33,999–34,000.

[21] Science Advisory Board, Environmental Protection Agency, Health Effects Assessment of Perchloroethylene—Review of the Office of Research and Development's Draft Document: Response to Issues and Data Submissions on the Carcinogenicity of Perchloroethylene by the Environmental Health Committee, EPA-SAB-EHC-91-013, August 1991 at 8.

[22] Environmental Protection Agency, Working Paper for Considering Draft Revisions to the U.S. EPA Guidelines for Cancer Risk, EPA/600/AP-92/003, November 1992.

[23] 50 Fed. Reg. 46,880, 46,885–86 (1985). The SDWA categorical ranking system is based on a draft of the Guidelines published in 1984. 50 Fed. Reg. 46,884 (1985).

EPA believes the statutory mandate that MCLGs be set "at the level at which no known or anticipated adverse effects on the health of persons occur and which allows an adequate margin of safety"[24] can only be met if it assigns suspected carcinogens an MCLG of zero.[25] EPA has rejected a number of requests in rulemakings to abandon this conservative approach,[26] and its decisions to set zero MCLGs have been upheld in federal courts.[27]

4. *The MCLGs for Noncarcinogens*

For toxic substances not considered to have carcinogenic potential, the process of assigning an MCLG is far more complicated. The Agency reviews or undertakes toxicological analyses in order to establish a "no effect" level. The "no effect" level is based on chronic, lifetime periods of exposure and includes a margin of safety.

EPA refers to this exposure level as the reference dose (RfD). The RfD is considered to be the exposure level estimated to be without significant risk to humans when received daily over a lifetime.

The RfD is drawn from the highest no-observed-adverse-effect level (NOAEL) or lowest observed-adverse-effect level (LOAEL) identified in either epidemiological or animal studies. This level, measured in milligrams of the contaminant per kilogram of body weight per day, is based upon data from ingestion studies, when this information is available. When it is not, inhalation or other types of studies are used and conversion factors are applied to convert the exposure.

The RfD is calculated as follows:

$$\text{RfD} = \frac{(\text{NOAEL or LOAEL})}{(\text{Uncertainty factors})} = \_\_\_ \text{ mg/kg body weight/day.}$$

The uncertainty factor, which ranges from 100 to 1000, is used to accommodate, among other variables, (1) extrapolation of animal data to humans, (2) the existence of weak or insufficient data, (3) intraspecies variabilities, (4) the application of the RfD to a large and diverse population which includes sensitive subgroups, (5) the small numbers of test subjects compared to the exposed population, (6) the potentially synergistic action between the contaminant involved and other chemicals that could be ingested.

From the RfD, a drinking water equivalent level (DWEL) can be calculated. The DWEL is the medium-specific calculation for drinking water exposure to a contaminant. The DWEL can be expressed in a calculation as follows:

$$\text{DWEL} = \frac{(\text{RfD}) \times (\text{Body Weight in kg})}{(\text{Drinking Water Volume in 1 day})} = \_\_\_ \text{ mg/liter.}$$

DWELs are normally based upon a 70 kg adult body weight. For chemicals for which analyses have shown children to be a sensitive subgroup, the DWEL

---

[24] §1412(b)(4), 42 U.S.C. §300g-1(b)(4) (1991).

[25] *See, e.g.,* 54 Fed. Reg. 22,068 (1989), 50 Fed. Reg. 46,895–96 (1985); 49 Fed. Reg. 24,347–48 (1984).

[26] *See, e.g.,* 54 Fed. Reg. 22,068 (1989).

[27] International Fabricare Inst. v. EPA, 972 F.2d 384 (D.C. Cir. 1992); NRDC v. Thomas, 824 F.2d 1211 (D.C. Cir. 1987).

is instead based upon a 10 kg child. DWELs further assume a drinking water volume of two liters per day.

The DWEL assumes that 100 percent of a contaminant comes from drinking water exposure. Before calculating the MCLG, EPA determines the contribution of the contaminant from other sources, including air and food.

In instances where sufficient data are available on the relative contributions of other sources, EPA uses that data and factors those amounts out of the DWEL to arrive at an MCLG. The Food and Drug Administration (FDA) has studied many inorganic chemicals in its market basket surveys and other studies; therefore, adequate data on inorganic compounds are usually available.

For most organic chemicals, however, such data do not exist. In such instances EPA estimates that drinking water contributes 20 percent of total exposure. The DWEL is, therefore reduced by a factor of five in calculating the MCLG for such compounds. EPA considers this value protective and conservative and assumes it accounts for the range of unknown exposures from different sources.[28]

When data indicate that drinking water exposure is below 20 percent, the Agency has determined to keep a 20 percent estimate as a floor. A higher relative source contribution (from sources other than drinking water) would yield a lower MCLG, supposedly offering greater protection. EPA has determined, however, that in such instances the most appropriate course of action would involve efforts to reduce exposure from these other sources rather than forcing MCLGs lower in an attempt to control the small contribution from drinking water.

When data indicate that drinking water exposure is greater than 80 percent, EPA caps the drinking water source contribution at 80 percent. It believes that this 80 percent ceiling on the relative source contribution of drinking water will provide an additional uncertainty factor that will further protect sensitive populations, will accommodate future changes in the distribution of the contaminant in the environment, and will guard against potentially faulty data on exposure.[29]

Finally, in setting the MCLGs for Category II contaminants (limited evidence of carcinogenicity), the Agency uses one of two additional calculations: (1) applying an additional uncertainty factor of up to 10 to the RfD/DWEL derived number, or (2) setting the goal based upon a nominal lifetime cancer risk calculation between 10^{-5} and 10^{-6} (or between 1 in 10,000 and 1 in 1,000,000) using a conservative calculation model. The first approach is the one normally used. The second is used when valid noncarcinogenicity data are not available and data are available to quantify the cancer risk.

Category III contaminants (inadequate or no evidence of carcinogenicity via ingestion) are assigned an MCLG through the RfD approach described above, without the additional uncertainty factors applied to Category II compounds. Substances that are not classified under the Cancer Risk Assessment Guidelines, and which therefore have no automatic categorization under the SDWA, are assigned an MCLG through the RfD/DWEL process described above.

---

[28] 54 Fed. Reg. 22,069 (1989).

[29] 56 Fed. Reg. 3535 (1991); 54 Fed. Reg. 22,069 (1989).

While the Agency had faithfully followed the process described above for for developing MCLGs since 1985, it has recently shown a willingness to depart, at least slightly, from this process. In a final rule promulgated in January 1991,[30] the Agency noted for the first time that when there was additional information on cancer risks from drinking water ingestion separate from the evidence associated with the compound's classification under the Guidelines, it would conduct additional scrutiny. This scrutiny might place the contaminant into a different SDWA category than it would have under the usual categorization system.[31] Asbestos and cadmium received such scrutiny and were given different MCLGs than they would have received under the process EPA has followed since 1985.[32]

C. National Primary Drinking Water Standards

The Act requires promulgation of a national primary drinking water standard to accompany the MCLG for each regulated contaminant.[33] While the MCLGs are unenforceable goals, the NPDWSs are enforceable.

National primary drinking water standards are usually numerical maximum contaminant levels derived from the MCLG. The only guidance or requirement that the SDWA gives to EPA in setting the MCL is that it be as close to the MCLG as is "feasible."[34] The Act defines "feasible" as "feasible with the use of the best technology, treatment techniques and other means." The technology or treatment techniques must have been tested under field conditions and cost must be taken into consideration.[35]

If it is not economically or technologically feasible to ascertain the level of a contaminant in drinking water, EPA may identify as the NPDWS a specified treatment technique that can control the contaminant sufficiently to prevent known or anticipated adverse human health effects.[36] If the Agency decides to promulgate a treatment technique instead of an MCL, it must identify each treatment technique known to it that can meet the standard.[37]

When it promulgates MCLs EPA must also identify, but may not specify, the technology, treatment techniques, or other means that it finds feasible to meet the MCL.

In determining what represents best available technology or BAT (as the requirement for technology, treatment techniques, or other means is generally known), there is a requirement for field testing. EPA does not, however, require that a technology be field tested for each particular contaminant. It is sufficient

[30] 56 Fed. Reg. 3526 (1991).

[31] *Id.* at 3532.

[32] Ingested asbestos had a Guidelines ranking of Group C but was placed in SDWA Category I and given an MCLG of zero. Cadmium had a Guidelines ranking of Group B2, but was placed in Category III. 56 Fed. Reg. 3532, 3535–36.

[33] §1412(b)(1), 42 U.S.C. §300g-1(b)(1) (1991).

[34] §1412(b)(4), 42 U.S.C. §300g-1(b)(4) (1991).

[35] §1412(b)(5), 42 U.S.C. §300g-1(b)(5) (1991). Paragraph (5) goes on to note that granular activated carbon shall be considered "feasible" for control of synthetic organic chemicals. Thus, any other technology, treatment technique, or other means for the control of synthetic organic chemicals must be at least as effective as granular activated carbon.

[36] §§1401(1)(C)(ii) and 1412(b)(7)(A), 42 U.S.C. §§300f(1)(C)(ii) and 300g-1(b)(7)(A) (1991).

[37] §1412(b)(7)(A), 42 U.S.C. §300g-1(b)(7)(A) (1991).

that the technologies themselves have been field tested and that a laboratory demonstration or pilot program show that the technology will remove the individual contaminant at issue.[38]

In determining what constitutes BAT, EPA does not confine itself to technology that is in widespread use. The pre-1986 version of the SDWA required the use of the "best technologies generally available." Congress removed the modifier "generally" to assure that MCLs "reflect the full extent of current technology capability."[39] EPA has concluded that the 1986 version of the Act allows it to select a technology that is not necessarily in widespread use, as long as it has been tested beyond the laboratory.

EPA evaluates the availability, the removal capabilities, and the cost of the BAT candidates under consideration. The Agency's initial step is an engineering assessment of technologies capable of removing a contaminant. EPA seeks to determine which technologies have the highest removal efficiencies, are compatible with other water treatment processes, and are not limited to a particular geographic region.

Cost is an important consideration in determining MCLs. EPA analyzes whether the technology under consideration is reasonably affordable by large metropolitan and regional public water systems. EPA also calculates the total national compliance costs for each contaminant. These costs vary according to the number of systems that must install BAT in order to meet the MCL, which is in turn dependent upon the concentration level chosen for the MCL.

The feasibility of any MCL is also dependent on the ability to detect and measure the level of the contaminant. This factor is particularly important for compounds for which the MCLG is set at zero—a number which by definition cannot be measured. In these cases EPA must carefully balance the reduction capabilities of BAT and the ability to detect the contaminant to establish an appropriate MCL.

The levels chosen for MCLGs and MCLs have been and continue to be driven primarily by health risks. EPA reviews MCLs to ensure that they fall within a 10^{-4} to 10^{-6} range for excess individual lifetime cancer risk. This goal for the range of risk is consistent with other EPA regulatory programs.

D. Promulgation of Standards

While the 1986 Amendments have greatly accelerated the pace of regulation under the Act, EPA has not come close to meeting the timetables imposed by the statute for promulgating regulations. Section 1412(b)(1) required EPA to propose MCLGs and national primary drinking water standards for each of the 83 contaminants listed in the statute by June 1989. In addition, under section 1412(b)(3)(A), EPA was required to promulgate regulations covering 25 contaminants from the drinking water priority list by January 1991. EPA has failed to meet either of these goals. The 1986 Amendments have been the basis for successful suits seeking to impose judicial timetables on EPA's promulgation of

[38] *See, e.g.*, 56 Fed. Reg. 3547 (1991).

[39] S. Rep. No. 56, 99th Cong., 1st Sess. 6 (1985).

SDWA regulations.[40] The Agency is now under court order to promulgate the remaining standards[41] but has also missed some of the deadlines set by the court.[42]

EPA has promulgated standards for nearly 80 of the 83 contaminants named by the statute. In its semiannual regulatory agenda it announced plans to propose the first set of standards for 25 of the substances from the drinking water priority list by June 1993. In addition, as noted above in section II.A.1., EPA stated that it will revise the MCL for arsenic by November 1994 and propose a standard for sulfates by December 1993.[43]

The Act requires EPA to revise national primary drinking water standards whenever changes in BAT permit greater human health protection, and the regulations are to be reviewed at least once every three years. The EPA must analyze the changes in BAT over the prior three-year period, and if the Agency finds that such changes are not feasible, it must explain its findings in the *Federal Register.*[44]

E. Filtration and Disinfection

Section 1412(b)(7)(C) of the Act requires EPA to promulgate filtration requirements for public water systems supplied by surface water sources. These provisions further allow EPA to determine which systems will be required to filter drinking water. Section 1412(b)(8) requires similar action by EPA on disinfection as a treatment technique for all public water systems, and grants EPA authority to establish procedures for variances.[45] In June 1989, EPA promulgated disinfection and filtration requirements for public water systems supplied by surface water sources.[46]

These complex and controversial requirements direct systems relying on surface waters (or groundwater under the direct influence of surface waters) to use disinfection and filtration unless the water quality meets certain standards for microbiological contamination, turbidity, and protection of surface waters. Variances for filtration may be granted only if the source surface waters have low coliform counts and consistently low turbidity, and if the public water systems

- Disinfect and provide redundant disinfection capacity or automatic cut-off systems if residual disinfectant levels drop too low;
- Successfully control virtually all *Giardia lamblia* cysts and viruses;
- Institute an effective watershed control program to avoid contamination from *Giardia lamblia* cysts and viruses;
- Establish annual inspections to verify these requirements;
- Prevent outbreaks of waterborne disease; and

---

[40] *See, e.g.,* Miller v. Reilly, CA No. 89-6328-E (D. Or. June 25, 1990).

[41] *Id.*

[42] *See, e.g.,* 57 Fed. Reg. 52,063 (1992).

[43] 57 Fed. Reg. 52,062–63 (1992). See notes 16–17 and accompanying text, *supra.*

[44] §1412(b)(9), 42 U.S.C. §300g-1(b)(9) (1991).

[45] EPA has determined not to grant variances, however, from disinfection rules. 54 Fed. Reg. 27,513 (1989).

[46] 54 Fed. Reg. 27,486 (1989).

- Comply with total coliform and trihalomethane MCLs.

This costly rule ($3.1 billion by EPA's estimate with annual costs exceeding half a billion dollars) has its greatest impact in the northeast where many public water systems rely on surface sources for drinking water and had not previously instituted filtration.

EPA plans to propose disinfection requirements for public water systems using groundwater in August 1994, and to promulgate those rules in September 1996.[47] In addition, the Agency plans to adopt MCLGs and national primary drinking water standards for disinfection byproducts as part of its rulemaking on substances from the drinking water priority list. EPA planned to propose these rules in June 1993 but failed to meet that deadline.[48]

F. National Secondary Drinking Water Standards

The Act requires EPA to promulgate national secondary drinking water standards. Such standards are designed to protect public health by controlling contaminants that may adversely affect the odor or appearance of drinking water and thereby cause users of the public water system to seek other potentially less protected sources of water.[49]

These standards are advisory only, which may explain why EPA has set only 15 of them since 1986. The substances for which standards have been set are listed below in Table 4.

G. State Primary Enforcement Responsibility

The Act allows EPA to grant primary enforcement responsibility to a state if the state

1. Has adopted drinking water standards no less stringent than the federal standards;
2. Has adopted adequate enforcement procedures;
3. Will keep such records and make such reports as EPA may require;

Table 4.
Substances Chosen for National Secondary Drinking Water Standards

Aluminum	Manganese
Chloride	Odor
Color	pH
Copper	Silver
Corrosivity	Sulfate
Fluoride	Total Dissolved Solids
Foaming Agents	Zinc
Iron	

[47] 57 Fed. Reg. 52,062 (1992).

[48] *Id.* at 52,063.

[49] §§1401(2) and 1412(c), 42 U.S.C. §§300f(2) and 300g-1(c) (1991).

4. Has variance and exemption requirements, if at all, that are at least as stringent as those required by sections 1415 and 1416 of the Act; and
5. Has adopted and can implement a plan for provision of safe drinking water under emergency circumstances.[50]

As most states had preexisting drinking water enforcement programs in place, it was relatively easy for them to bring their regulations in line with federal standards and nearly all states have assumed responsibility for enforcement of the SDWA.

H. Variances and Exemptions

The Act allows EPA or a state that has assumed primary enforcement responsibility to grant variances[51] or exemptions[52] from national primary drinking water regulations (NPDWRs). States may grant variances from MCLs if the public water system cannot meet the MCL because of the characteristics of the raw water sources, but only after the application of BAT and only if the state determines that the variance will not result in an unreasonable risk to health.[53] When a state grants a variance, it must also prescribe a schedule for compliance with the regulations[54] and an implementation schedule for additional control measures designed to ensure such compliance.[55]

EPA may review a state's variance activities. If it finds that a state has abused its discretion in a number of instances in granting variances, or has failed to specify compliance and implementation schedules, it shall so notify the state.[56] After public hearings EPA may revoke particular variances or impose additional requirements on individual public water systems.[57] The state may take corrective action before EPA acts to revoke or modify a variance.[58]

Exemptions may be granted from NPDWRs[59] if EPA finds that the public water system cannot meet the requirements "due to compelling factors" (including economic considerations)[60] and the exemption will not result in unreasonable human health risk.[61] The exemption provisions contain compliance requirements similar to those for variances, but compliance must take place within three years of the issuance of the exemption.[62]

---

[50] §1413(a)(1)-(5), 42 U.S.C. §300g-2(a)(1)-(5) (1991).

[51] §1415, 42 U.S.C. §300g-4 (1991).

[52] §1416, 42 U.S.C. §300g-5 (1991).

[53] §1415(a)(1)(A), 42 U.S.C. §300g-4(a)(1)(A) (1991). If EPA adopts NPDWRs that specify treatment techniques rather than MCLs, states will be able to grant variances from such treatment techniques if the technique is not necessary to protect human health because of the nature of the raw water sources. §1415(a)(1)(B).

[54] §1415(a)(1)(A)(i), 42 U.S.C. §300g-4(a)(1)(A)(i) (1991). Compliance must be as expeditious as practicable. §1415(a)(1)(A). This statutory mandate has been rendered nugatory by EPA's regulations, which allow EPA to specify "an indefinite time period for compliance" while awaiting the development of new treatment technology. 40 C.F.R. §142.43(e).

[55] §1415(a)(1)(A)(ii), 42 U.S.C. §300g-4(a)(1)(A)(ii) (1991).

[56] §1415(a)(1)(G)(i), 42 U.S.C. §300g-4(a)(1)(G)(i) (1991).

[57] §1415(a)(1)(G)(ii), 42 U.S.C. §300g-4(a)(1)(G)(ii) (1991).

[58] §1415(a)(1)(G)(iii), 42 U.S.C. §300g-4(a)(1)(G)(iii) (1991).

[59] §1416(a), 42 U.S.C. §300g-5(a) (1991).

[60] §1416(a)(1), 42 U.S.C. §300g-5(a)(1) (1991).

[61] §1416(a)(2), 42 U.S.C. §300g-5(a)(2) (1991).

[62] §1416(b)(2)(B), 42 U.S.C. §300g-5(b)(2)(B) (1991).

Small systems[63] may receive one or more two-year extensions if the system must make capital improvements that cannot be finished in time[64] or the system needs financial assistance for the improvements and has entered into an agreement to obtain such assistance, and the system is taking all practicable steps to meet the compliance requirements.[65] The exemption provisions contain review authority for EPA identical to that in the variance provisions.[66]

I. Enforcement

Section 1414 of the SDWA sets forth the enforcement authorities available to the states and EPA. Both administrative orders[67] and civil enforcement actions[68] are available, and civil penalties may reach up to $25,000 per day of violation.[69] EPA may assess civil penalties up to $5,000 per day;[70] all others must be assessed by a United States district court in a civil action.[71] The court assessing such penalties must consider the seriousness of the violation, the population at risk, and other appropriate factors.[72]

An unusual feature of the SDWA's enforcement provisions is its requirement for public notification of violations.[73] The owner or operator of a public water system must give notice to the persons served by the system of any failure to comply with an MCL, treatment technique, testing procedure, required monitoring, or of the existence of a variance or exemption or the failure to comply with a variance or exemption.[74] Notice must take place in general circulation newspapers, and in press releases to electronic media and individual mailings (such as customer bills) where appropriate.[75]

Section 1414(c) distinguishes between the notice required for intermittent or infrequent violations and those that are frequent or continuous. Violations of MCLs or other violations posing a "serious potential adverse health effect" must be made within 14 days of the violation. Notice of a continuous violation of a regulation other than an MCL must be given at least every three months. Notice of "less serious" violations must be given at least annually.[76]

The notice must give a clear and readily understandable explanation of the violation, its potential health effects, corrective steps being taken, and the need to seek alternative sources of water. Violation of the notice requirements is subject to civil penalties up to $25,000.[77]

---

[63] Fewer than 500 service connections.
[64] §1416(b)(2)(C), 42 U.S.C. §300g-5(b)(2)(C) (1991).
[65] §1416(b)(2)(B), 42 U.S.C. §300g-5(b)(2)(B) (1991).
[66] §1416(d), 42 U.S.C. §300g-5(d) (1991).
[67] §1414(g), 42 U.S.C. §300g-3(g) (1991).
[68] §1414(b), 42 U.S.C. §300g-3(b) (1991).
[69] *Id.*
[70] §1414(g)(3)(B), 42 U.S.C. §300g-3(g)(3)(B) (1991). Such penalties may only be assessed after a hearing.
[71] §1414(g)(3)(C), 42 U.S.C. §300g-3(g)(3)(C) (1991).
[72] §1414(b), 42 U.S.C. §300g-3(b) (1991).
[73] §1414(c), 42 U.S.C. §300g-3(c) (1991).
[74] §1414(c)(1) and (2), 42 U.S.C. §300g-3(c)(1) and (2) (1991).
[75] §1414(c), 42 U.S.C. §300g-3(c).
[76] *Id.*
[77] *Id.*

Regulations implementing the notice requirement mandate that such notice be given through electronic media within 72 hours of an acute violation, notice in a general circulation newspaper within 14 days of the violation of an MCL or related requirements, and written notice to customers of those same violations within 45 days.[78] The regulations even dictate certain mandatory language on the health effects of some chemicals.[79]

J. Recent Consideration of Changes to the SDWA

Communities forced to comply with the Act have become increasingly critical of it over the past several years. They point to the SDWA as another burden forced on localities by the federal government without any federal funding to pay for the burdensome testing and treatment requirements. They criticize the Act as misdirected in part, pointing particularly to those provisions requiring the addition of 25 chemicals to the list of regulated substances every three years and the concomitant requirements for testing for those substances. State and local officials have complained that it makes little sense to spend money on unnecessary testing requirements for contaminants that do not exist in some systems. The disproportionate burden that the Act places on smaller communities has been particularly noted by many critics.[80]

Indeed, the burden is great enough that many states are considering abandoning primary enforcement responsibility under the Act and returning that responsibility to the federal government. California has announced it will do so, and other states could follow.

It has been these criticisms, and other similar complaints, that have informed congressional consideration of the SDWA of late. That these arguments are viewed seriously is clear in the battle over one amendment in the 102nd Congress.

Senator Pete Domenici (R.-N.M.) offered an amendment to the funding bill for EPA that would have placed a moratorium on the enforcement of many national primary drinking water standards. The amendment gained considerable support in the Senate and might well have passed had Senator John Chafee (R.-R.I.), the ranking Republican on the Senate Environmental and Public Works Committee, not offered a substitute amendment that gutted Senator Domenici's amendment and preserved the SDWA intact.

The Clinton administration viewed the criticisms seriously enough to propose the first federal financial assistance for communities to assist them in carrying out the requirements of the Act. When President Clinton proposed his economic stimulus plan in February 1993, he included a recommendation for a $600 million state revolving loan fund to be created in the fiscal year 1994 budget.

Not surprisingly, response from local officials has been supportive. But as many pointed out during hearings on the administration's proposal in early

---

[78] 40 C.F.R. §141.32(a).

[79] 40 C.F.R. §141.32(e).

[80] *See, e.g.,* Regional Administrator Wynne Focuses on Cleaning Up U.S. Mexico Border Area, Int'l Env't Daily (BNA), Aug. 17, 1992; Daily Rep. for Executives (BNA), Sept. 16, 1992, A-26.

1993, the financial needs of the communities related to SDWA implementation far exceed the funding contemplated in the Clinton plan.

Many note that they still believe substantial changes are needed in the Act in order to reduce the burdens on local governments. They intend to continue to press Congress to make such changes. As such pressure has been the prime moving force behind the first congressional steps to reauthorize and amend the SDWA, it is likely that pressure will continue to build in the 103rd Congress to revisit the Act.

III. Underground Sources

The regulation of public water systems primarily affects units of state and local governments. The Act's protection of underground sources of water, however, directly affects the waste disposal practices of industry. The Act strictly controls the underground injection of waste in order to protect usable aquifers from contamination. Underground injection is the subsurface emplacement of fluids through a bored, drilled, or driven well, or through a dug well where the depth is greater than the width or breadth.[81] Fluids are any materials that flow or move whether in a solid, liquid, or gaseous state.[82]

A. The Regulatory Scheme

The Act required EPA to list states in which underground injection control (UIC) may be necessary[83] in order to prevent underground water from violating a national primary drinking water regulation or otherwise adversely affecting human health[84] and to publish regulations governing the approval of state UIC programs.[85] The minimum requirements for approval are that the state program must

1. Prohibit any underground injection not authorized by permit or rule;
2. Require that permitted injections not endanger drinking water sources;
3. Include inspection, monitoring, recordkeeping, and reporting requirements; and
4. Apply to injections by federal agencies.[86]

Congress did place limits on EPA's regulatory authority, recognizing the burden such regulations would place on existing state UIC programs and particularly on the oil and gas industry. First, EPA's regulations may not entail requirements that interfere with the underground injection of brine and other fluids brought to the surface as a result of oil or gas production or natural gas storage, nor with underground injection for secondary or tertiary oil or gas recovery, unless such interference is essential for the protection of public

---

[81] §1421(d)(1), 42 U.S.C. §300h(d)(1) (1991), and 40 C.F.R. §144.3.

[82] 40 C.F.R. §144.3.

[83] §1422(a), 42 U.S.C. §300h-1(a) (1991). EPA listed all states as requiring UIC programs. 40 C.F.R. §144.1(e).

[84] §1421(d)(2), 42 U.S.C. §300h(d)(2) (1991).

[85] §1421, 42 U.S.C. §300h (1991).

[86] §1441(b)(1), 42 U.S.C. §300j(b)(1) (1991).

health.[87] Second, EPA's regulations are to take cognizance of varying state geological, hydrogeological, and historical conditions.[88] Finally, EPA's regulations may not disrupt state UIC programs in effect in a substantial number of states unless such disruption is necessary to protect underground sources of drinking water.[89]

EPA was authorized to allow states to issue temporary permits for underground injection if the state was unable to process all permit applications or if the technology for safe injections was not generally available and other available means of disposal were more harmful than injection. Such temporary permits expired, according to the statute, in June 1990.[90]

If a state program were disapproved by EPA, or if a state failed to develop a program, or if a state's program were or ever became inadequate, EPA would be required to prescribe a program for the state within 90 days.[91]

B. UIC Permits

Once the state or federal government has put a UIC permit program in place, no underground injection is permitted except by a valid permit or as generally allowed by rule promulgated pursuant to the UIC program.[92] EPA authorized by rule injections into wells existing when the regulations were adopted, but those authorizations expire (usually when the permit is granted or denied). Substantive requirements similar to those required when permits are issued must be followed by those covered by the grant of authority for existing injections.[93]

The permit application, issuance and appeal procedures, and permit conditions are similar to those of the National Pollutant Discharge Elimination System of the Clean Water Act. Permits may be issued for individual wells or may be issued for an entire area if the wells are identified, are within the same well field, and are operated by a single owner or operator. Area permits may not be used, however, to approve hazardous waste injections.[94]

Emergency temporary permits are allowed if an imminent and substantial endangerment to human health will result or if a substantial loss of or delay in production of oil or natural gas will occur unless the permit is granted. As with other exceptions, the injection cannot result in the contamination of underground sources of drinking water. These permits are for no longer than is necessary to avoid the human health hazard, or 90 days or less (in the case of permits to avoid an oil or gas loss), or until EPA acts to approve or disapprove a permit application (in the case of oil or gas production delays).[95]

EPA may exempt underground aquifers from the regulations if such aquifers do not currently serve as sources of drinking water and will not in the

[87] §1421(b)(2), 42 U.S.C. §300h(b)(2) (1991).
[88] §1421(b)(3)(A), 42 U.S.C. §300h(b)(3)(A) (1991).
[89] §1421(b)(3)(B), 42 U.S.C. §300h(b)(3)(B) (1991).
[90] §1421(c), 42 U.S.C. §300h(c) (1991).
[91] *Id.*
[92] 40 C.F.R. §144.11.
[93] 40 C.F.R. §144.21-.28.
[94] 40 C.F.R. §144.33.
[95] 40 C.F.R. §144.34.

future because (1) they are sources of commercially producible energy or minerals, (2) they are too deep to be commercially or technologically feasible as drinking water sources, (3) the water is contaminated, (4) they are over a mineral or energy well that could collapse, or (5) the total dissolved solids content is too high.[96] In certain circumstances, EPA may authorize a well with less stringent requirements than normally called for if such requirements will not result in an increased risk of contamination of the aquifer. Such relaxation of requirements is not allowed if the well injects into, through, or above an aquifer.[97]

C. Well Classification

The regulations separate wells into one of five classes, as detailed below. The primary objective of injection well regulations for all classes is to ensure the mechanical integrity of the injection apparatus and to ensure that injected wastes do not migrate into and contaminate underground drinking water sources.

Class I	Wells used for injection of hazardous and nonhazardous waste beneath all underground sources of drinking water within one quarter of a mile of the well bore.
Class II	Wells that inject fluids brought to the surface in oil or gas production or natural gas storage, or that inject fluids as part of the enhanced recovery process of oil or gas, or that inject fluids for storage of liquid hydrocarbons.[98]
Class III	Wells that inject for extraction of minerals.
Class IV	Wells that inject hazardous or radioactive wastes into or above formations that contain drinking water sources within one quarter of a mile of the well.
Class V	Wells not included in the above classes, including septic tanks and drainage wells.

EPA estimates that there are approximately 173,000 Class V shallow injection wells divided into more than 30 subcategories. EPA is planning a regulatory regime for Class V wells that "will protect against groundwater while recognizing the difficulties of this diverse well class."[99] EPA intends to focus on providing maximum flexibility to state and local governments to deal with these wells, and will characterize risks associated with various Class V wells because data are unavailable for risk assessments on individual subcategories of wells in this class.[100]

[96] 40 C.F.R. §§144.7 and 146.4.

[97] 40 C.F.R. §144.16.

[98] Fluids brought to the surface during oil or gas production may be mixed with waste waters from gas plants that are an integral part of production operations unless such waters are classified as a hazardous waste.

[99] 57 Fed. Reg. 52,064 (1992).

[100] *Id.*

D. Class I Wells

Class I wells are subdivided into hazardous and nonhazardous wells and, not surprisingly, EPA promulgated more stringent requirements for hazardous wells. The requirements for nonhazardous wells formerly applied to *all* Class I wells. EPA added requirements in 1988 for Class I hazardous wells to existing requirements for nonhazardous wells. Thus, the requirements described below for nonhazardous wells effectively continue to apply to all Class I wells.

1. Nonhazardous Class I Wells

The requirements for Class I nonhazardous wells are found at 40 C.F.R. pt. 146. Class I wells must be located such that they inject into a formation beneath all underground sources of drinking water within one quarter of a mile of the well bore. All Class I wells must be cased and cemented to ensure that wastes do not migrate, and must have a packer set or fluid seal on the tubing immediately above the injection zone. Logs must be kept and other tests must be conducted during the drilling and construction of Class I wells.[101]

EPA's minimum requirements specify a number of operating, monitoring, and reporting provisions. Wellhead pressure must be maintained so as to avoid fracturing the injection zone (except in cases where the fracturing is done intentionally in order to increase capacity) or the confining zone[102] above it. Injection is prohibited between the outermost casing protecting the aquifer and the well bore.[103]

There must be annular fluid between the injection tubings and the casings and it must be maintained and monitored to ensure it remains at an approved pressure. Continuous recording devices must be used to monitor injection pressure, flow rate, volume, and annular fluid pressure. Demonstrations of mechanical integrity must take place at least once every five years. Monitoring wells must be maintained in order to measure migration of wastes into, and pressure in, the underground sources of drinking water.[104]

Reporting requirements are to include quarterly reports on (1) the physical, chemical, and other characteristics of the injection fluids; (2) monthly average, maximum and minimum injection pressures, flow rates, volumes, and annular fluid pressure; and (3) the results of monitoring described above. In addition, reports must be made on the periodic tests of mechanical integrity, any other tests required of the permitee, and any well workover.[105]

Additional monitoring based on conditions at individual sites must be required, including annual tests of the pressure build-up in the injection zone. Additional requirements may include continuous monitoring for pressure changes in the first aquifer overlying the confining zone, the use of indirect geophysical techniques to determine the position of the waste front, periodic monitoring of the water quality in the first aquifer overlying the injection zone, periodic monitoring of the water quality in the lowermost underground source

[101] 40 C.F.R. §146.12.

[102] The confining zone is the zone above the injection zone.

[103] 40 C.F.R. §146.13(a).

[104] 40 C.F.R. §146.13(a) and (b).

[105] 40 C.F.R. §146.13(c).

of drinking water, or such other monitoring as is necessary to determine whether waste is moving into or between underground sources of drinking water.[106]

Class I wells must be plugged at the end of their useful lives. The regulations specify the methods to be used which are designed to prevent migration of wastes from the injection zone into underground sources of drinking water.[107] In addition, owners of Class I wells must establish sufficient financial ability to close the wells in accordance with the regulations.[108]

2. *Additional Requirements for Hazardous Class I Wells*

In 1988, EPA promulgated regulations implementing the Resource Conservation and Recovery Act (RCRA)[109] that impose additional requirements on the injection of RCRA hazardous wastes. The requirements distinguish between existing and new hazardous waste injection wells, with the more stringent requirements applied to new wells.

Class I wells into which RCRA hazardous wastes are injected are RCRA disposal facilities and therefore are subject to RCRA treatment, storage, and disposal permitting requirements. However, the RCRA program has deferred to the UIC program and UIC Class I permitted wells are therefore exempt from RCRA permitting and interim status regulations.[110] Related surface storage, treatment, or disposal facilities are not similarly exempt. Certain RCRA requirements, such as waste minimization, do apply to Class I well owners and operators.[111]

The more stringent requirements for Class I hazardous waste wells affect minimum siting criteria, the area of review, construction, logging and sampling, operations, and other matters. For example, all Class I hazardous waste wells must demonstrate that the area is geologically suitable for hazardous waste injection. This requirement for geological suitability contains detailed requirements for both the injection and confining zones.[112]

The area of review around Class I wells to be monitored for effects on underground sources of drinking water is much larger for hazardous waste wells than for nonhazardous waste wells. Previously the area was usually measured as a one quarter mile radius from the well bore. The rules for hazardous Class I wells increase this to a two mile radius.[113] If the zone of influence of the injection well is greater than than two miles, then the area of review is increased to reflect that greater distance.

Construction of new hazardous waste injection wells must be done with materials compatible with the injection wastes. In addition, the regulations establish elaborate logging requirements to assure that information presented in the permit application is correct.[114]

---

[106] 40 C.F.R. §146.13(d).

[107] 40 C.F.R. §146.10.

[108] 40 C.F.R. pt. 144, Subpart F.

[109] 42 U.S.C. §6901 *et seq.* See Chapter 6, for a discussion of hazardous and solid waste regulation under RCRA.

[110] 40 C.F.R. §§264.1(d), 265.1(c)(2), and 265.430.

[111] 40 C.F.R. §144.14.

[112] 40 C.F.R. §146.62(b) and (c).

[113] 40 C.F.R. §146.63.

[114] 40 C.F.R. §146.65-.66.

Additional operating requirements for hazardous waste Class I wells mandate automatic shut-offs and alarms to warn of lost pressure or the violation of other operating parameters. In the event that a shut-off occurs or an alarm sounds, the permittee must notify EPA or the state within 24 hours and injection operations at the well must cease until the problem is corrected. Contamination of an underground source of drinking water triggers a requirement to report the contamination in a local newspaper.[115]

The testing, monitoring, and reporting requirements for hazardous Class I wells are substantially similar to those for nonhazardous Class I wells.[116] As with nonhazardous wells, the operator of a hazardous well must have a post-closure plan and demonstrate financial capacity sufficient to fund the plan.[117]

E. Implementation of the RCRA Land Ban

The 1984 RCRA amendments contain provisions relevant to Class I hazardous injection wells. Under one of these provisions, EPA must review each RCRA-listed hazardous waste and determine whether injection or other disposal in land of these wastes may continue. Should EPA fail to make the decision by the schedule mandated in the statute, injection is automatically prohibited.[118]

EPA's regulations implementing these provisions are found at 40 C.F.R. pt. 148. Those regulations now ban injection of (1) wastes containing more than 1 percent of certain listed solvents, (2) wastes containing dioxins, (3) the so-called "California list wastes," (4) wastes containing more than 50 parts per million of PCBs, and (5) wastes containing more than 10,000 parts per million of halogenated organic compounds. The regulations also ban injections of the "first third," "second third," and "third third" RCRA wastes.[119] Exhaustive lists of the wastes contained in each of these umbrella groups are found in the regulations.[120]

Hazardous Class I well operators can petition to be exempted from these prohibitions, but exemptions rely on difficult demonstrations that there will be no migration of the injected wastes into underground sources of drinking water for as long as the wastes remain hazardous. This requires a showing that the wastes will not migrate for 10,000 years or that before the fluids migrate from the injection zone they will no longer be hazardous because of attenuation, transformation, or immobilization of the hazardous constituents in the waste stream due to hydrolosis, chemical interaction, or other means.[121] These petitions are expensive and time-consuming to prepare as the demonstration threshold is a high one.

EPA has approved a number of petitions for exemptions. In some cases EPA has granted extensions of the land-ban requirements where exemption

[115] 40 C.F.R. §146.67.
[116] 40 C.F.R. §146.68-.69.
[117] 40 C.F.R. §146.71-.73.
[118] RCRA §3004(f)-(g), 42 U.S.C. §6924(f)-(g) (1993).
[119] These terms are defined in Chapter 6, Section IX.
[120] 40 C.F.R. §148.10-.16.
[121] 40 C.F.R. §148.20(a)(1).

petitions were pending when the land-ban took effect. EPA has also rejected some exemption petitions on substantive grounds.

F. UIC Regulatory Enforcement

The 1986 Amendments provided vastly expanded enforcement authority to go with the expanded regulatory regime. While giving authority to the states to pursue enforcement actions, it did leave open a federal enforcement role. In those instances in which EPA becomes aware of a violation of the UIC program, it is required to so notify the state. If the state takes no enforcement action within 30 days, the statute gives EPA a nondiscretionary duty either to issue an administrative order requiring compliance with the UIC program or to undertake a civil enforcement action.[122]

EPA may issue administrative orders requiring compliance or assessing fines of up to $10,000 for each day of any past or current violation, up to a maximum of $125,000. When the requirements at issue deal with injection of fluids (1) brought to the surface during oil or gas production or (2) injected for secondary or tertiary recovery of oil or gas, the maximum daily penalty is halved to $5,000. The maximum total penalty, however, remains $125,000.[123] Administrative hearings are required when penalties are to be assessed, but need not afford the full process of the Administrative Procedure Act.[124]

Civil action fines can reach up to $25,000 per day of violation. If the violation was willful, criminal penalties could also apply.[125]

G. Protection of Sole Source Aquifers

Section 1424(e) of the Act allows EPA to determine, either on its own initiative or on petition, that an area has an aquifer that is its sole or principal source of drinking water. When such a designation has been made, the provision prohobits any federal financial assistance to a project that might contaminate the designated aquifer so as to create a significant hazard to public health.[126]

The 1986 Amendments added section 1427 which creates a sole source aquifer demonstration program. The program is designed to establish procedures for the development, implementation, and assessment of demonstration programs designed to protect such sole source aquifers—or ''critical aquifer protection areas'' as they are denominated in section 1427(b).[127] The demonstration program section was designed to provide federal grants to such areas for their demonstration programs, but Congress has not appropriated funds for this purpose.

The lack of funding has not rendered the provisions useless. The designation authority has been used by environmental groups, local governments, and citizens groups as they have sought to have aquifers designated as critical

[122] §1423(a), 42 U.S.C. §300h-2(a) (1991).
[123] §1423(c)(1) and (2), 42 U.S.C. §300h-2(c)(1) and (2) (1991).
[124] §1423(c)(3)(A), 42 U.S.C. §300h-2(c)(3)(A) (1991).
[125] §1423(b), 42 U.S.C. §300h-2(b) (1991).
[126] §1424(e), 42 U.S.C. §300h-3(e) (1991).
[127] 42 U.S.C. §300h-6(b) (1991).

aquifer protection areas to demonstrate the value of the aquifer. Such designations are used as ammunition in political struggles to block development projects deemed harmful by such groups.

The basis for designation as a critical aquifer protection area is EPA's finding that the aquifer supplies drinking water to 50 percent or more of an area's population and that, if contaminated, the aquifer would present a significant risk to the public health. EPA has designated more than 50 such areas, most after the 1986 Amendments. The timing suggests that these designations were sought primarily because of the potential for the demonstration grant funding authorized in section 1427. The large number of designations also reflects the fact that EPA delegated authority for the designations to Regional Administrators, cutting months, perhaps even years, off the time that it would otherwise take for such designations to be issued by the Agency.

In addition to the sole source aquifer protection program, states are required to adopt and submit to EPA a wellhead protection program.[128] The program must identify all "wellhead protection areas," which are the surface and subsurface areas surrounding wells or wellfields supplying a public water system through which contaminants are likely to migrate and therefore contaminate the well or wellfield.[129] The program must also identify technical assistance, financial assistance, implementation of control measures, education, training, and demonstration projects, as appropriate, to protect the waters within the protection area.

When a program is approved and implemented, EPA is authorized to make grants to states of between 50 percent and 90 percent of the cost of developing and implementing the protection program, but this has been another program that Congress has been hesitant to fund.

This regulation of groundwater protection, historically an area primarily of local concern, is an important federal step in this arena. The protection plans involve complicated issues of land use planning and other local matters. In addition, federal agencies will be required to bring any facilities within the wellhead protection area into compliance with the state plan, unless the President determines it is not in the "paramount" interest of the United States.[130]

IV. Emergency Powers

If EPA believes there exists an imminent and substantial endangerment to public health caused by a drinking water contaminant, Part D of the Act authorizes the Agency to take any actions deemed necessary. EPA is required to consult with state and local authorities to the extent practicable on the scope of the problem and their intended actions.[131]

EPA may issue administrative orders, which may include requirements for the provision of alternative water supplies by those who caused or contributed to the public health endangerment. Failure to comply with an administrative

[128] §1428(a), 42 U.S.C. §300h-7(a) (1991).
[129] §1428(e), 42 U.S.C. §300h-7(e) (1991).
[130] §1428(h), 42 U.S.C. §300h-7(h) (1991).
[131] §1431(a), 42 U.S.C. §300i(a) (1991).

order could subject the violator to fines up to $5,000 per day. The Agency may also ask the Justice Department to undertake civil enforcement actions.[132]

Part D also authorizes criminal[133] and civil[134] penalties for those who tamper with a public water system or attempt to tamper with such a system. Tampering is defined as introducing a contaminant or otherwise interfering with a public water system with the intention of harming persons.[135]

V. General Provisions

A. Judicial Review and Citizens Suits

Part E of the act places exclusive jurisdiction over all petitions for review of the establishment of national primary drinking water regulations in the U.S. Court of Appeals for the District of Columbia Circuit, and for review of any other action taken pursuant to the SDWA in the federal court of appeals in which the petitioner resides or transacts business.[136] District courts have jurisdiction over actions regarding variances and exemptions.[137]

Citizens suits are authorized against any person, including the United States, who is in violation of the SDWA.[138] Actions are also authorized specifically against EPA if the Agency has failed to take action required by the Act.[139] The plaintiff must give 60 days' notice of the suit to EPA, the alleged violator, and the state in which the violation occurs.[140] These citizens suits have been used effectively to force EPA to promulgate regulations under the Act where EPA had been slow to act, but, as noted above, the Agency has even missed court-ordered deadlines.

B. Other Provisions

Other general provisions establish a system to ensure that public water systems have sufficient chemicals to treat drinking water supplies. Public water systems may apply for a certification of need that, when granted, can require manufacturers, processors, and sellers to provide treatment chemicals to public water systems.[141]

Section 1442 authorizes EPA to conduct research, provide technical assistance to states, study and report to Congress on the costs of carrying out the Act, and collect information to support such activities. Section 1443 authorizes grants to states to carry out public water system supervision programs and section 1444 authorizes drinking water study and demonstration project grants.

---

[132] *Id.*
[133] Up to five years imprisonment.
[134] Up to $50,000 fines.
[135] §1432, 42 U.S.C. §300i-1 (1991).
[136] §1448(a), 42 U.S.C. §300j-7(a) (1991).
[137] §1448(b), 42 U.S.C. §300j-7(b) (1991).
[138] §1449(a)(1), 42 U.S.C. §300j-8(a)(1) (1991).
[139] §1449(a)(2), 42 U.S.C. §300j-8(a)(2) (1991).
[140] §1449(b), 42 U.S.C. §300j-8(b) (1991).
[141] §1441, 42 U.S.C. §300j (1991).

Section 1445 allows EPA to prescribe recordkeeping requirements for public water systems. It also authorizes EPA to inspect public water systems to ensure compliance with the Act.

Other sections establish a National Drinking Water Advisory Council,[142] make federal agencies subject to the Act,[143] and authorize EPA to treat Indian tribes as states under the SDWA.[144]

VI. Regulation of Lead in Drinking Water

Part F of the SDWA strictly limit the use of lead in drinking water systems and coolers.[145]

A. Public Water Systems

The Act requires the use of lead-free pipes, solder, or flux in the installation or repair of a public water system or plumbing systems connected to public water systems.[146] Lead-free solders and flux are those containing no more than 0.2 percent lead; lead-free pipes can contain no more than 8.0 percent lead.[147]

Public water systems have an affirmative obligation to identify and notify persons that may be affected by lead contamination because of the lead content of the materials used in the public water system or the corrosivity of the water supply being sufficient to cause the leaching of lead. This notice is required irrespective of any violation of the MCL for lead.[148] The notice must state:

- The potential source of the lead,
- The potential adverse health effect,
- Methods to mitigate the lead content,
- Mitigating steps being taken by the water system, and
- Any necessity for seeking alternative water supplies.[149]

In promulgating regulations to implement these lead requirements, EPA determined that it could not easily measure water quality parameters and correlate them with lead concentrations at the consumers' tap. The Agency's studies indicated that even with optimal treatment there is a high probability of leaching lead if there is any lead-containing material in the water system. Thus, EPA concluded that *all community water systems* should provide public notice of possible lead contamination unless they could affirmatively demonstrate to the state that there is no lead-containing material in the water system.

EPA included in its definition of water system the residential and nonresidential portions of the system. Thus, if residential systems already in place had been built with lead-containing material, EPA ruled that the public water system

[142] §1446, 42 U.S.C. §300j-5 (1991).
[143] §1447, 42 U.S.C. §300j-6 (1991).
[144] §1451, 42 U.S.C. §300j-11 (1991).
[145] §§1461–65 and 1417, 42 U.S.C. §§300j-21–300j-25 and 300g-6 (1991).
[146] §1417(a)(1), 42 U.S.C. §300g-6(a)(1) (1991).
[147] §1417(d), 42 U.S.C. §300g-6(d) (1991).
[148] §1417(a)(2)(A), 42 U.S.C. §300g-6(a)(2)(A) (1991).
[149] §1417(a)(2)(B)(i)-(v), 42 U.S.C. §300g-6(a)(2)(B)(i)-(v) (1991).

would have to provide the lead notice to all residential users, in spite of the fact that the water system may well have had no control over the materials used in the residential systems when they were installed. Local communities complained that they should only be responsible for the parts of the water system over which they could exercise direct control, but EPA required them to go further with the notice provisions.[150]

B. Drinking Water Coolers

EPA was required to publish a list of drinking coolers that were not lead-free (using the same definition of lead-free that applies to public water systems).[151] It did so on January 18, 1990.[152] Since then the sale or manufacture of water coolers that are not lead-free has been prohibited.[153] Criminal penalties are provided for knowing violations; civil penalties are available for all violations.[154] For coolers containing lead that were already in service, the SDWA required their recall by the Consumer Product Safety Commission.[155]

The Act provides special provisions governing lead contamination of drinking water in schools. EPA was required to publish a guidance document and a testing protocol to assist schools in determining the source and level of lead contamination.[156] States were then required to prepare a remedial action program to test for and remedy such contamination.[157]

VII. Conclusion

The SDWA has undoubtedly resulted in significant increases in the protection of public health. Some critics have complained that the health benefits have come, and continue to come, at costs too high for local governments to bear.

The "ripple effects" of the SDWA are felt far beyond the confines of drinking water regulation. The Superfund law has incorporated MCLGs as its cleanup standards in remedial actions.[158] Thus, Superfund cleanups could be required to reach levels of nondetectability for carcinogens.[159] The costs of the SDWA are therefore felt not only in that Act but in another wide-reaching environmental statute.

Thus, the SDWA is central to one of the growing controversies in environmental debate—"how clean is clean?" This question, and the growing financial burden engendered by the Act, will remain central topics as Congress turns to the reauthorization and possible amendment of the SDWA.

[150] 52 Fed. Reg. 41,544 (1987).
[151] §1463(a), 42 U.S.C. §300j-23(a) (1991).
[152] 55 Fed. Reg. 1,772 (1990).
[153] §1463(b), 42 U.S.C. §300j-23(b) (1991).
[154] §1463(c) and (d), 42 U.S.C. §300j-23(c) and (d) (1991).
[155] §1462, 42 U.S.C. §300j-22 (1991).
[156] §1464(b), 42 U.S.C. §300j-24(b) (1991).
[157] §1464(d), 42 U.S.C. §300j-24(d) (1991).
[158] Comprehensive Environmental Response, Compensation and Liability Act (CERCLA), §121(d)(2)(A), 42 U.S.C. §9621(d)(2)(A) (1993).
[159] In fact, where the Agency has established MCLGs of zero, it uses the MCL as the cleanup standard under Superfund.

6

Resource Conservation and Recovery Act

*By Duane A. Siler**

I. Introduction

The Resource Conservation and Recovery Act (RCRA),[1] originally enacted in 1976,[2] reflected Congress's concern about the growing problem of pollution of land by ordinary solid waste, i.e., garbage, as well as serious environmental damage resulting from unregulated hazardous commercial and industrial wastes. Congress had already addressed the problems of air and water pollution in, respectively, the Clean Air Act of 1970 and the Federal Water Pollution Control Act of 1972. In RCRA, Congress ''closed the loop,'' turning its attention to, among other things, hazardous residues resulting from modern air and water pollution control systems.

As originally enacted, RCRA comprised a broad array of provisions. Among the most important were a comprehensive regulatory framework for virtually all hazardous wastes (Subtitle C); an ambitious program to encourage states to adopt extensive plans for the management of nonhazardous solid waste and the elimination of ''open dumps'' (Subtitle D); mandates for the Secretary of Commerce to promote the consumption of recycled materials (Subtitle E); requirements for federal agencies to buy recycled products (Subtitle F); a program of federal projects and grants for research and demonstration of resource recovery systems (Subtitle H); and miscellaneous other provisions relating to enforcement, judicial review, and other procedures under the statute.

In the nearly 20 years since RCRA's enactment, some of these provisions have become extremely significant features of the environmental law landscape. For example, the Environmental Protection Agency (EPA) has used its authorities under Subtitle C to establish a complex cradle-to-grave system of controls over hazardous waste generation, transportation, treatment, storage, and dis-

*The author would like to thank Michael N. Romita for his assistance in the preparation of this chapter.

[1] 42 U.S.C. §6901 *et seq.* (1988).

[2] Pub. L. No. 94-580, 90 Stat. 2795 (1976). RCRA extensively amended and expanded the Solid Waste Disposal Act of 1965, Pub. L. No. 89-272, 79 Stat. 992 (1965), as amended by the Resource Recovery Act of 1970, Pub. L. No. 91-512, 84 Stat. 1227 (1970).

posal. Few U.S. businesses have not felt the impact of Subtitle C in their operations.

By contrast, EPA took no action directly to regulate solid waste under Subtitle D until the adoption of regulations governing municipal solid waste landfills in 1991. Management of nonhazardous industrial wastes remains largely unregulated by the federal government. Similarly, most observers would agree that federal efforts to promote the recycling of solid wastes and to develop markets for recycled materials have lagged far behind federal implementation of RCRA's strictly regulatory provisions, especially those relating to hazardous waste management.

Moreover, the focus of RCRA has changed and sharpened as a result of periodic amendments over the past 15 years. In particular, the Hazardous and Solid Waste Amendments of 1984[3] extensively amended and strengthened Subtitle C and mandated several new regulatory programs, including a program for the comprehensive regulation of underground storage tanks and new requirements for management of recycled used oil. Subsequent amendments, in 1988, added a demonstration program for the tracking of medical wastes.

There is no reason to believe that RCRA's evolution is complete. Congress has repeatedly amended and elaborated on the basic statute to meet emerging problems. Whenever Congress next undertakes a major reauthorization of RCRA—possibly in 1994 or 1995—new programs and priorities likely will occupy center stage. For example, the long neglected Subtitle D mandate for states to more effectively regulate and plan for solid waste management may be revived and strengthened in response to a perceived waste disposal capacity crisis. States may be given new power to prevent or limit the transportation of garbage across their borders. New controls may be placed on the use of toxic materials in manufacturing operations so as to reduce the amount of hazardous waste generated. What is certain is that for the foreseeable future, RCRA will remain among the most complex of the federal environmental laws and will require careful and continuing efforts on the part of businesses in order to ensure compliance.

Section II. of this chapter provides an overview of all of the subtitles of RCRA. Sections III. through XI. provide a detailed view of the most important part of RCRA, the standards for management of hazardous waste. Section XII. provides more detailed information about RCRA's standards for the management of nonhazardous solid waste, and Section XIII. offers some conclusions about RCRA's history and its future.

II. Overview of RCRA's Subtitles

A. Subtitle A

Subtitle A[4] includes general provisions and definitions. It recites Congress's concern about a growing solid waste problem due to "an evermounting

[3] Pub. L. No. 98-616, 98 Stat. 3221 (1984).
[4] 42 U.S.C. §§6901–07 (1988).

increase'' in discarded consumer products and ''a rising tide of scrap, discarded and waste materials.'' Congress found that inadequate control of hazardous waste had created ''substantial risks to human health and the environment'' and, if continued, would result in the need for ''expensive, complex and time consuming'' corrective action.[5] The basic objectives of RCRA, according to this subtitle, are ''to promote the protection of health and the environment and to conserve valuable material and energy resources'' by eliminating improper solid waste management (i.e., open dumps) and by requiring the minimization and proper management of hazardous waste.[6]

B. Subtitle B

Subtitle B[7] established within EPA a new Office of Solid Waste, headed by an Assistant Administrator reporting to the Agency's Administrator. In effect, Subtitle B elevated solid and hazardous waste programs to the same level within EPA as the clean air, clean water, and other programs headed by an Assistant Administrator.[8] This subtitle also requires that at least 30 percent of the funds appropriated by Congress to EPA to carry out RCRA be spent on Subtitle C hazardous waste programs.[9]

C. Subtitle C

Subtitle C[10] contains virtually all of the provisions (except definitions) relating to hazardous waste control. It directs EPA to adopt regulations for classifying solid waste as hazardous, including both criteria for identifying waste as hazardous and lists of known hazardous wastes, depending on factors such as toxicity, flammability, corrosiveness, or other hazardous characteristics. It requires EPA to establish standards for generators of hazardous waste identified or listed under section 3001 as may be ''necessary to protect human health and the environment,'' including requirements that generators use a manifest system to ensure that all hazardous waste is sent to an authorized facility. Subtitle C mandates standards for transporters of hazardous waste, including a prohibition on transportation of such wastes to any facility not designated by the generator.[11]

This subtitle requires EPA to adopt ''performance standards'' for all facilities for the treatment, storage, or disposal of hazardous wastes to protect human health and the environment, including standards for the location, design, and construction of such facilities and for operating methods, techniques, and practices. Under the 1984 Amendments, these standards prohibit the disposal of most hazardous wastes in landfills or other land-based facilities without prior treatment. Specific technical and design standards are prescribed for some types

---

[5] 42 U.S.C. §6901(a), (b) (1988).
[6] 42 U.S.C. §6902 (1988).
[7] 42 U.S.C. §§6911–17 (1988).
[8] 42 U.S.C. §6921 (1988).
[9] 42 U.S.C. §6916 (1988).
[10] 42 U.S.C. §§6921–39a (1988).
[11] 42 U.S.C. §§6921, 6922, 6923 (1988).

of disposal facilities, including landfills, and for groundwater monitoring and corrective action in response to contamination at virtually all hazardous waste facilities.[12]

Subtitle C also requires every hazardous waste treatment, storage, or disposal facility—whether new or existing—to obtain a permit from EPA or an authorized state in order to operate the facility. It also includes standards for existing hazardous waste facilities while they temporarily operate without a permit under "interim status." As amended in 1984, Subtitle C contains particularly detailed and stringent standards for existing hazardous waste surface impoundments.[13]

Subtitle C established a cooperative federal-state role in hazardous waste regulation, under which any state may be authorized to administer its own equally stringent hazardous waste program in lieu of the federal program and to issue permits for hazardous waste management facilities.[14]

Subtitle C contains its own enforcement provisions. EPA is authorized to inspect any place where hazardous wastes have been generated, stored, treated, disposed of, or transported from. EPA and authorized states are required to inspect all treatment, storage, and disposal facilities at least every two years. If EPA determines that a person has violated any Subtitle C requirement, the Agency can issue a compliance order and impose a daily civil penalty of up to $25,000. It is a crime knowingly to violate any RCRA requirement, punishable by fines and imprisonment. Violations of law that result in the knowing endangerment of another person are subject to even more severe criminal penalties.[15]

Other significant provisions of Subtitle C require persons who handle hazardous waste to notify EPA of their activities within 90 days of becoming subject to the Subtitle C regulations.[16] Another important provision, added in 1984, prohibits the export of hazardous wastes without the prior consent of the receiving country.[17] The 1984 Amendments also directed EPA to decide whether to classify used oil as a hazardous waste and to regulate used oil under a special set of standards that would protect public health and the environment without discouraging the recovery or recycling of used oil.[18]

D. Subtitle D

The objectives of Subtitle D,[19] set forth in section 4001, are to develop environmentally sound methods for the disposal of solid waste. These methods are supposed to maximize the utilization of valuable resources, including energy, which are recoverable from solid waste. This objective is to be achieved through "Federal technical and financial assistance to States . . . for comprehen-

---

[12] 42 U.S.C. §6924 (1988).
[13] 42 U.S.C. §6925 (1988).
[14] 42 U.S.C. §6926 (1988).
[15] 42 U.S.C. §§6927, 6928 (1988).
[16] 42 U.S.C. §6930 (1988).
[17] 42 U.S.C. §6938 (1988).
[18] 42 U.S.C. §6935 (1988).
[19] 42 U.S.C. §§6941–49a (1988).

sive planning pursuant to Federal guidelines.'' Section 4002 requires EPA to adopt guidelines for state solid waste plans. Section 4003 lists minimum requirements for EPA-approved state plans, the most important of which in practice is a requirement that all ''open dumps'' be upgraded to become ''sanitary landfills'' and that all new solid waste disposal facilities meet criteria for sanitary landfills under section 4004.

Other sections in Subtitle D mandate procedures for development of state solid waste plans and for EPA review and approval. As originally enacted, section 4008 authorized appropriations of up to $40 million for EPA grants to states to assist their planning process. However, this authorization expired at the end of fiscal year 1988.

Most of the requirements in Subtitle D pertain to states' adoption of solid waste management plans and, as such, do not impose direct requirements on private individuals or companies. Section 4005 is a notable exception. It prohibits any ''solid waste management practice or disposal of solid waste'' that constitutes ''open dumping'' under EPA's standards, and gives EPA the power to enforce the prohibition against any violator under section 7002 of RCRA.

E. Subtitle E

Subtitle E[20] directs the Secretary of Commerce to ''encourage greater commercialization of proven resource recovery technology'' by developing specifications for recovered materials and stimulating thc development of markets for such materials.[21] The Department has historically done little to implement this mandate. It has left the setting of specifications for regulated materials and products largely to EPA pursuant to Subtitle F of the Act. No federal agency has done much to stimulate private sector demand for such materials and products.

F. Subtitle F

Subtitle F[22] establishes the responsibilities of agencies of the federal government under RCRA. The first requirement is for every federal agency with jurisdiction over any facility that generates or manages any solid or hazardous waste to comply with all federal, state, and local requirements relating to the control of hazardous waste to the same extent and in the same manner as any other regulated person.[23]

A second requirement is for every federal agency to establish a program for the procurement of recovered or recycled materials, based upon EPA guidelines designating items that can be produced with recovered materials and recommended procurement procedures.[24] The 1984 Amendments specifically directed EPA to adopt guidelines for procurement of recycled paper by mid-

[20] 42 U.S.C. §§6951–56 (1988).
[21] 42 U.S.C. §6951 (1988).
[22] 42 U.S.C. §§6961–64 (1988).
[23] 42 U.S.C. §6961 (1988).
[24] 42 U.S.C. §6962 (1988).

1985 and for tires and two other product categories by October 1, 1985.[25] This section requires every federal agency, when procuring an item for which EPA has adopted a guideline (and whose value exceeds $10,000), to procure items that are composed of the "highest percentage of recovered materials practicable," consistent with maintaining a satisfactory level of competition. Every federal agency is required to develop an "affirmative procurement program," including a preference for purchases of recovered materials.

G. Subtitle G

Subtitle G[26] contains miscellaneous provisions, the most significant of which are enforcement provisions applicable to all enforceable requirements under RCRA. Under section 7002, any person may bring a "citizen suit" in the appropriate U.S. district court against anyone who allegedly is violating any permit, standard, regulation, prohibition, or order under any provision of RCRA, as well as against any person who, acting as a generator, transporter, or owner or operator of a hazardous waste management facility, has contributed or is contributing to any past or present handling of any hazardous waste that may present "an imminent and substantial endangerment to health or the environment."[27] In such an action the district court has jurisdiction to enjoin a violator from continuing such handling or to take other action as may be necessary to abate the hazard. No such lawsuit can be filed unless the plaintiff has given the alleged violator at least 60 days written notice.

In addition, under section 7003, EPA can sue any person whose current or past handling of hazardous waste may present an "imminent and substantial endangerment."[28] EPA also can issue orders as may be necessary to protect public health and the environment, and willful failure to comply carries a fine of up to $5,000 per day.

Subtitle G directs EPA to "encourage" the public to participate in the adoption of EPA regulations and programs under RCRA and makes this obligation applicable to any state program under RCRA. EPA is specifically required to give public notice in newspapers and on the radio of any proposal to issue a permit for a hazardous waste treatment, storage, or disposal facility and to hold a public hearing in the event of any opposition to the permit.[29]

H. Subtitle H

Subtitle H[30] established the framework for an ambitious program of federally assisted research and development on a wide array of waste manage-

---

[25] EPA has adopted guidelines for federal procurement of building insulation products containing recovered materials (40 C.F.R. pt. 248); cement and concrete containing fly ash (40 C.F.R. pt. 249); paper and paper products containing recovered materials (40 C.F.R. pt. 250); lubricating oils containing re-refined oil (40 C.F.R. pt. 252); and retread tires (40 C.F.R. pt. 253).

[26] 42 U.S.C. §§6971–79 (1988).

[27] 42 U.S.C. §6972 (1988).

[28] 42 U.S.C. §6973 (1988).

[29] 42 U.S.C. §6974 (1988).

[30] 42 U.S.C. §§6981–87 (1988).

ment and recycling issues.[31] It mandated a series of EPA studies relating to the feasibility of resource recovery from solid waste, including a study of the composition of the nation's solid waste stream. EPA was directed also to study the recovery of glass and plastic, the effects of source separation of municipal waste, the management and use of old tires, the economics of and impediments to resource recovery (waste-to-energy) facilities, the use of sewage sludge as fertilizer, and extending the life of municipal landfills. Subtitle H also mandated EPA studies of the adverse effects of a number of special, potentially hazardous wastes. These include wastes from petroleum exploration and drilling, ash and other residues from burning coal, cement kiln dust, and mining wastes. EPA has completed most of these studies.

This subtitle directed EPA to collect and disseminate extensive information, including information on methods for reducing and recycling solid waste, recovering energy from solid waste, financing of resource recovery facilities, and availability of markets for recovered materials.[32] It also authorized EPA to fund, through grants or contracts, facilities to demonstrate new solid waste technologies or processes; to conduct demonstration projects to test a range of methods and techniques for reducing wastes, including imposing charges on products to recover the full social costs associated with their disposal; and to give grants to state and local governments for up to 75 percent of the cost of new or improved solid waste facilities.[33] However, Congress has never authorized or appropriated funds for EPA specifically to carry out Subtitle H. Thus, like most of RCRA's solid waste programs, the ambitious research and demonstration program envisioned under this subtitle remains largely unrealized.

I. Subtitle I

Subtitle I[34] regulates underground tanks that store hazardous wastes, hazardous substances, or petroleum. These regulations are discussed in Chapter 13, Standards for Storage Tank Facilities.

J. Subtitle J

Subtitle J,[35] enacted in 1988[36] in the wake of widely publicized reports of medical wastes washing up on East Coast beaches, established a demonstration program for tracking such wastes. Congress limited the program to 24 months duration. Under EPA implementing regulations,[37] the program was in effect for two years in the states of New York, New Jersey, Connecticut, and Rhode Island, as well as Puerto Rico. It expired June 22, 1991.

The program included a list of regulated medical wastes, including laboratory wastes, pathological wastes, waste blood, sharp objects, and other wastes

[31] 42 U.S.C. §6982 (1988).
[32] 42 U.S.C. §6983 (1988).
[33] 42 U.S.C. §§6984, 6985, 6986 (1988).
[34] 42 U.S.C. §§6991–91i (1988).
[35] 42 U.S.C. §§6992–92k (1988).
[36] Pub. L. No. 100-582, 102 Stat. 2950 (1988).
[37] 40 C.F.R. pt. 259.

that had been in contact with infectious agents. EPA established a tracking system for such wastes from the point of generation to the point of disposal or destruction, using a standard form akin to a hazardous waste manifest. Neither EPA nor Congress has taken steps to reinstate such a tracking program since the demonstration program ended.

III. Identifying Hazardous Waste Under Subtitle C

Subtitle C of RCRA applies only to "hazardous wastes" and persons who manage it. This section outlines the methods and standards for determining whether a facility generates or handles "hazardous waste," as defined by the statute and EPA's regulations. As explained, the first step is to determine if a material is a "solid waste" under RCRA. If so, it must be determined whether the solid waste is further classified as "hazardous." If so, it must be determined whether the waste falls within one of a number of complete or partial exemptions from regulation.

A. Statutory Definitions

Section 1004 of RCRA defines "solid waste" very broadly as

> [a]ny garbage, refuse, sludge from a waste treatment plant, water supply treatment plant, or air pollution control facility and other discarded material, including solid, liquid, semisolid, or contained gaseous material resulting from industrial, commercial, mining, and agricultural operations, and from community activities. . . .[38]

This definition provides a number of significant exceptions from the definition of solid waste. These include

> solid or dissolved materials in domestic sewage, or solid or dissolved materials in irrigation return flows or industrial discharges which are point sources subject to permits under section 402 of the Federal Water Pollution Control Act, as amended (86 Stat. 880), or source, special nuclear, or by-product material as defined by the Atomic Energy Act.

Section 1004 then defines "hazardous waste" as

> [a] solid waste, or combination of solid wastes, which because of its quantity, concentration, or physical, chemical or infectious characteristics may—
>
> (A) cause, or significantly contribute to an increase in mortality, or an increase in serious irreversible, or incapacitating reversible, illness; or
>
> (B) pose a substantial present or potential hazard to human health or the environment when improperly treated, stored, transported, or disposed of, or otherwise managed.[39]

Thus, in principle a waste can be hazardous either because it has inherently dangerous qualities or because it is potentially capable of posing a threat if mismanaged.

---

[38] RCRA §1004(27), 42 U.S.C. §6903(27) (1988).

[39] RCRA §1004(5), 42 U.S.C. §6903(5) (1988).

Congress directed EPA to develop regulations establishing criteria for identifying the general characteristics of hazardous waste and for listing specific wastes the Agency considers hazardous.[40] EPA must consider a waste's toxicity, persistence, and degradability in nature, and the potential for its accumulation in tissue, as well as related factors such as flammability, corrosiveness, and other hazardous characteristics.[41] Thus, a waste may be defined as hazardous: (1) because it is expressly listed as a hazardous waste in EPA's regulations, or (2) because it exhibits any of the general characteristics of hazardous waste. Though the regulatory framework for "listed" and "characteristic" wastes is basically the same, there are some important differences in specific regulatory requirements, which are discussed below.

B. Regulatory Definition of Solid Waste

EPA's regulations implementing Subtitle C of RCRA are codified at 40 C.F.R. parts 260–80. While most other important Subtitle C terms are defined in part 260 of EPA's regulations, the definitions of "solid" and "hazardous waste" appear in part 261.[42] "Solid waste" includes "any discarded material" not covered by a regulatory exclusion or an EPA recycling variance. A "discarded material" is any material that is "abandoned," "recycled," or considered "inherently waste-like."[43] These latter terms are further defined in part 261.

Conceptually, the universe of solid waste under EPA's regulations can be split into two groups: materials that are recycled and those that are not. The definition of "abandoned" covers all nonrecycled materials. Thus, a nonrecycled material will be considered a "solid waste" if it is disposed of, burned or incinerated, or stored or treated before or in lieu of those activities.[44] For recycled materials, the determination is more complicated.

Recycled materials are classified in one of the following five categories:

1. Spent materials, defined as "any material that has been used and as a result of contamination can no longer serve the purpose for which it was produced without processing."
2. Sludges, that is, any wastewater treatment or air pollution control residue that is expressly listed as a hazardous waste in EPA's regulations.
3. Byproducts, defined as "a material that is not one of the primary products of a production process and is not solely or separately produced by the production process . . . i.e. slags or distillation column bottoms."

---

[40] RCRA §3001, 42 U.S.C. §6921 (1988).

[41] *Id.*

[42] 40 C.F.R. §261.2 (1991).

[43] 40 C.F.R. §261.2(a). Properly defining the relationship between regulations and solid waste has been an ongoing process for EPA. EPA's 1980 regulations defined all materials as solid waste if they were "sometimes disgarded" by any generator, regardless of the fact that some materials of that type were destined for recycling. EPA revised the solid waste definition significantly in 1985 in order to tailor it to specific types of material and methods of recycling. *See* 50 Fed. Reg. 664 (1985).

[44] 40 C.F.R. §261.2(b).

4. Discarded commercial chemical products expressly listed in EPA's regulations.
5. Scrap metal.[45]

Whether any particular type of material is a "solid waste" depends on how it is recycled. EPA's regulations recognize four different methods of recycling materials. The first is "use in a manner constituting disposal," that is, placing a material on land or using it to make a product placed on land. All five of the foregoing materials are considered solid waste if they are used in a manner constituting disposal. The second method of recycling a material is to burn it for energy recovery. Again, all of the foregoing materials are solid waste if burned for energy recovery.

The third method of recycling is holding material for an excessive length of time in anticipation of recycling. All of the foregoing materials except discarded commercial chemicals are considered solid waste if they are "accumulated speculatively," that is, if less than 75 percent of the material being accumulated at a facility is recycled in a calendar year.

The fourth—and most important—method of recycling is through reclamation, that is, processing a material to recover a usable product or regenerating the material. However, not all materials are considered solid waste if reclaimed. The definition captures spent materials, "listed" (but not characteristic) sludges, "listed" (but not characteristic) byproducts, and scrap metal.[46]

Notwithstanding this recycling-based classification scheme, EPA's regulations provide a blanket exemption for materials that are recycled by being used, reused, or returned to their original production process. This exemption does not apply, however, if the materials undergo reclamation or are used in a manner constituting disposal, burned for energy recovery, or accumulated speculatively. On the other hand, EPA has defined some materials as inherently waste-like. These materials are solid wastes no matter how they are recycled. Inherently waste-like materials include a small number of listed hazardous wastes.[47]

Certain waste streams are exempt from the definition of solid waste altogether, irrespective of whether they are recycled or disposed of.[48] If a material or process meets one of these exemptions it does not matter whether it might otherwise be categorized as a hazardous waste. From the standpoint of potentially regulated industries, the most important exemptions probably are: (1) domestic sewage, (2) regulated industrial point sources, and (3) closed-loop recycling.

The regulations define domestic sewage as untreated sanitary wastes that pass through a sewer system.[49] Under the domestic sewage exception, any industrial or commercial waste that passes through a sewer system in combination with, or where it will be mixed with, sanitary wastes is not subject to RCRA

[45] 40 C.F.R. §261.2(c).

[46] 40 C.F.R. §261.2(e), Table 1. Characteristically hazardous sludges and byproducts thus are exempt from regulation if they are or will be reclaimed to recover usable products. This is an important exemption for many industrial waste streams that would otherwise be subject to regulation.

[47] 40 C.F.R. §261.2(e).

[48] The exclusions are for domestic sewage, industrial wastewater regulated under the Clean Water Act, irrigation return flows, certain nuclear materials as defined by the Atomic Energy Act, in-situ mining wastes, reclaimed pulping liquors, spent sulfuric acid, closed-loop recycling materials, reclaimed wood preserving solutions, and recycled EPA listed hazardous waste K087. 40 C.F.R. §261.4(a).

[49] 40 C.F.R. §261.4(a)(1).

regulation, provided that the mixture is conveyed to a publicly owned treatment works (POTW).[50] EPA has long interpreted the domestic sewage exemption as covering all wastes that are discharged to a sanitary sewer system, even prior to the point at which they are mixed with sanitary wastes.[51] However, the precise "upstream" limit of the exemption has never been judicially interpreted, and one appeals court has held the exemption to apply only at the point in a sewer system where wastes first mix with sanitary waste from households, as distinct from sanitary wastes from an industrial facility.[52]

The industrial point source exemption likewise reflects congressional intent not to regulate a waste under two different regulatory schemes. Thus, solid or dissolved materials in industrial discharges that are point sources subject to permits under section 402 of the Clean Water Act are not solid wastes under RCRA. It should be emphasized that, unlike the domestic sewage exemption, the scope of which is subject to varying interpretations, the regulations clearly exempt industrial wastewaters only at the point of discharge. Industrial wastewaters upstream from the point of discharge (surface impoundments, tanks, lagoons, holding ponds, and other facilities used to treat or store wastewater) may be considered hazardous waste management facilities if the wastewater otherwise meets the definition of hazardous waste.[53]

The closed loop recycling exemption applies to any material that is returned to the original production process, but does not qualify for the exemption discussed above because it is reclaimed. Provided that the material is handled in an enclosed system of tanks and pipes, and is not burned or used to make fuel, it will not be considered solid waste.

C. Regulatory Definition of Hazardous Waste

Determining whether one handles solid waste is only the first step. If so, the next step is to determine whether the solid waste is categorized as hazardous waste as defined in 40 C.F.R. §261.3.[54] Solid waste that is not otherwise exempted (as discussed in Section D., below) is considered hazardous waste if it meets any of the following four criteria:

1. It is listed on EPA's hazardous waste list at 40 C.F.R. §261, Subpart D and has not been delisted.

[50] The restriction reflects the congressional intent embodied in the legislative history of the Solid Waste Disposal Act, which RCRA amended. Because sewage was already subject to treatment requirements under the Federal Water Pollution Control Act, under which states and municipalities were given federal funds to construct treatment works and study combined sewer systems, Congress decided that regulation of sewage under RCRA would be redundant. 45 Fed. Reg. at 33,098–99 (1980).

[51] 45 Fed. Reg. 33,097 (1980).

[52] Comite Pro Rescate De La Salud v. Puerto Rico Aqueduct and Sewer Auth., 888 F.2d 180, 30 ER Cases 1473 (1st Cir. 1989), *cert. denied,* 110 S. Ct. 1476, 30 ER Cases 2134 (1990).

[53] "The obvious purpose of the industrial point source discharge exclusion . . . was to avoid duplicative regulation of point source discharges under RCRA and the Clean Water Act. . . . These considerations do not apply to industrial wastewaters prior to discharge since most of the environmental hazards posed by wastewaters in treatment and holding facilities—primarily groundwater contamination—cannot be controlled under the Clean Water Act or other EPA statutes." 45 Fed. Reg. at 33,098 (1980).

[54] Under 40 C.F.R. §262.11, the generator itself is responsible for determining if it produces hazardous waste. The regulations do not impose any requirement for testing of waste, provided that the generator has sufficient knowledge of the waste's contents to be able reasonably to determine whether it is listed on a relevant list or has a hazardous waste characteristic.

2. It is a mixture of a solid waste and a Subpart D listed hazardous waste and it has not been delisted.
3. It is a mixture of a solid waste and hazardous waste that is listed in Subpart D solely because it exhibits a hazardous waste characteristic identified in Subpart C and the mixture exhibits a hazardous waste characteristic.
4. It exhibits a characteristic of hazardous waste as identified in Subpart C.[55]

If the material in question is not a solid waste, then it is not regulated at all under Subtitle C, regardless of its characteristics or properties.

1. "Listed" Hazardous Wastes

Section 3001(a) of RCRA directed EPA to promulgate criteria for listing hazardous wastes. Section 3001(b) required the Agency to then list particular hazardous wastes based on these criteria. Under section 3001(a), EPA established three criteria under which a solid waste may be listed as a hazardous waste:

1. It exhibits any of the characteristics identified as a hazardous waste characteristic in Subpart C of part 261 of the regulations (ignitability, corrosivity, reactivity, EP toxicity);
2. It has been found to be fatal to humans in low doses or, in the absence of human data, has been shown to be dangerous in animal studies; or
3. It contains any of the toxic constituents listed in appendix VIII of 40 C.F.R. part 261 and EPA has concluded, after consideration of certain other listed factors, that the waste is capable of presenting a substantial present or potential hazard to health or the environment when improperly managed.[56]

EPA has generated three separate lists of hazardous wastes. Section 261.31 of the regulations lists some 28 types of solid waste, e.g., spent halogenated solvents, which are considered hazardous, regardless of their source. Section 261.32 lists approximately 100 wastes from specific sources in specific industries, e.g., distillation bottoms from the production of acetaldehyde from ethylene. Section 261.33 lists several hundred "commercial chemicals" that, if discarded, are considered hazardous, regardless of their particular source. These listings cover the pure form of each listed chemical, as well as off-specification products (but not such products after they have been used or that were formulated to include other substances).[57]

Unless "delisted," a waste appearing on one of these lists is presumed to be a hazardous waste regardless of the particular composition or properties of the waste as generated at a particular facility. However, any person can petition

[55] 40 C.F.R. §261.3(a).

[56] 40 C.F.R. §261.11. The referenced app. VIII includes substances that have been shown in scientific studies to be toxic, carcinogenic, mutagenic, or teratogenic to humans or other species. In listing specific wastes, EPA may list classes of wastes that meet any of its criteria. 40 C.F.R. §261.11(b).

[57] This third list comprises two separate sublists, one for toxic chemicals ("U" wastes) and one for acutely hazardous wastes ("P" wastes). Acutely hazardous "P" wastes are subject to more stringent regulations.

EPA to exempt a listed waste from a particular facility.[58] Upon receiving a delisting petition, EPA must publish an initial determination in the *Federal Register* where it will be available for public comment. Following an evaluation of any such comments, EPA will publish its final decision in the *Federal Register* as a regulatory amendment or a denial of the petition.[59]

To succeed, a petitioner must first demonstrate that the waste does not meet any of the criteria under which the waste was listed. Second, EPA must be satisfied that the waste does not belong on the list due to factors other than the ones for which it was originally listed.[60] For example, for any "toxic" waste, the applicant must show that the waste does not contain any hazardous constituent.[61] If a waste has been listed because it exhibits a hazardous waste characteristic, e.g., corrosivity, then the petition must show that samples taken at the facility where the waste is to be delisted are not, in fact, corrosive using the same tests the EPA used to make the original determination. In addition, the petition must demonstrate that the samples are also not reactive, ignitable, or toxic using the appropriate EPA test for listing under those characteristics. As of early 1994, EPA had delisted wastes from about 100 facilities around the country, including multiple waste streams at many facilities.[62]

2. *"Characteristic" Hazardous Wastes*

A solid waste that is not listed is nevertheless a hazardous waste if it has one or more of the four hazardous characteristics identified in Subpart C of part 261 of the RCRA regulations. Pursuant to RCRA sections 3001(a) and (b), EPA adopted two criteria for identifying hazardous waste characteristics:

1. A solid waste that exhibits the characteristic may cause, or significantly contribute to, an increase in mortality or an increase in serious irreversible, or incapacitating reversible, illness; or may pose a substantial present or potential hazard to human health or the environment when it is improperly treated, stored, transported, disposed of or otherwise managed.[63]
2. The characteristic is one that can be measured by an available standardized test method available to generators of solid waste.[64]

---

[58] 40 C.F.R. §260.22.

[59] 40 C.F.R. §260.21(d)-(e). If granted, the exclusion will only apply to the specific facility to which the delisting petition pertained. The hazardous waste remains listed for all other facilities. In addition, a partial exclusion may be granted if EPA finds that the composition of the sampled waste may vary. 40 C.F.R. §260.22(k), (l).

[60] A successful petition does not automatically exclude a material from the definition of hazardous waste. If the waste still exhibits a hazardous waste characteristic, it remains subject to regulation. 40 C.F.R. §260.22(a).

[61] Such petitions must include information on the manufacturing process producing the waste, the average amount of waste produced, and lab sampling and testing techniques used. 40 C.F.R. §260.22(i). EPA will use this information to help evaluate whether the waste displays any other hazardous characteristics.

[62] 40 C.F.R. pt. 261, Tables 1 and 2.

[63] This is the statutory definition of the term hazardous waste provided in RCRA §1004(5), 42 U.S.C. §6903(5) (1988).

[64] 40 C.F.R. §261.10(a). RCRA §3001(b) requires EPA to identify additional wastes that may be carcinogenic, mutagenic, or teratogenic. This is because such testing cannot be readily performed by hazardous waste generators. 42 U.S.C. §6921(b) (1988).

Based on these criteria, EPA established four hazardous waste characteristics: ignitability, corrosivity, reactivity, and toxicity. In practice, the toxicity characteristic is by far the most significant in terms of causing solid wastes to be considered hazardous.

a. Ignitability. The ignitability characteristic regulates wastes that are capable of causing fires under normal working conditions. If any one of the following four requirements is met, the waste is hazardous: (1) it is a liquid other than an aqueous solution containing less than 24 percent alcohol by volume and has a flash point less than 60°C; (2) it is not a liquid and can cause fire through friction, absorption of moisture, or spontaneous chemical changes at standard temperature and pressure and it burns so vigorously and persistently when ignited that it creates a hazard; (3) it is an ignitable compressed gas; or (4) it is an oxidizer.[65]

b. Corrosivity. The corrosivity characteristic is designed to ensure regulation of wastes that could escape their own containment and eat through other containment devices, thereby releasing other chemicals with which they have been codisposed. A solid waste exhibits corrosivity if it either (1) is aqueous and has a pH less than or equal to 2 or greater than or equal to 12.5 or (2) is a liquid and corrodes steel at a rate greater than 6.35 millimeters per year at a temperature of 55°C.[66]

c. Reactivity. The characteristic of reactivity is designed to prevent unstable wastes from exploding during management. A solid waste will be deemed reactive if a sample of the waste has any one of eight listed properties. Among the eight are whether the material is capable of detonation or explosive decomposition and whether it is potentially explosive, or reacts violently or generates toxic gases when mixed with water.[67]

d. Toxicity. EPA's toxicity characteristic (TC) is designed to prevent the leaching of excessive amounts of specific toxic constituents into groundwater from a solid waste in the event that the waste is improperly managed. A solid waste is considered toxic if simulated leachate from the waste contains excessive amounts of any of 40 contaminants. The simulated leachate is produced by exposing a sample of the waste to a mildly acidic extraction fluid in accordance with a prescribed procedure, the Toxicity Characteristic Leaching Procedure (TCLP). The TCLP is intended to mimic the leaching process that occurs in a municipal landfill, thereby predicting what hazardous constituents might escape from a waste, and in what concentrations, if if were not classified as hazardous and were instead managed as ordinary solid waste. The limits for each toxic constituent, which are derived from the National Primary Drinking Water Standards under the Safe Drinking Water Act, range from 0.03 milligrams per liter to 400 milligrams per liter.[68]

---

[65] 40 C.F.R. §261.21(a).

[66] 40 C.F.R. §261.22.

[67] 40 C.F.R. §261.23.

[68] 40 C.F.R. §261.24(a). The TCLP test is set forth in detail in app. II of part 261.

The toxicity characteristic rule has undergone significant changes since it was first promulgated as part of EPA's 1980 RCRA regulations. RCRA §3001(g), part of the 1984 Amendments, directed EPA to examine the deficiencies of the preexisting procedure (known as the Extraction Procedure) and make appropriate

D. Exempt Hazardous Wastes

EPA's definition of hazardous waste provides for a number of exemptions, many of them reflecting exemptions created by Congress in section 3001 of RCRA.[69] These exemptions should not be confused with the exemptions from the definition of "solid waste," discussed earlier, although their net effect—an exemption from regulation—is the same. Perhaps the most significant exemption, at least in terms of the amount of waste excluded, is the exemption of all household waste. Primarily intended to exclude waste streams generated by consumers at the household level, this exemption also applies to waste streams generated at hotels, motels, and recreation areas. The exemption also covers materials derived from household solid waste, such as refuse-derived fuels. If, however, household wastes are mixed with other hazardous wastes, the entire waste stream is regulated as hazardous waste (unless the other waste is produced by small quantity generators as discussed below in Section J).[70]

Other significant exemptions cover residues generated from the burning of coal or other fossil fuels, including fly ash, bottom ash, slag, and flue gas emission control waste; wastes from petroleum drilling operations;[71] and wastes from the extraction, benefication, and processing of ores and minerals.[72]

E. Partially Exempt Hazardous Wastes

Certain hazardous wastes are exempted from some, but not all, RCRA regulations. These include hazardous wastes that are generated in a product or raw material storage tank, transport vehicle or vessel, pipeline, or manufacturing process unit.[73] Absent this exemption, many industrial tanks, pipelines, and process units would be considered hazardous waste management facilities

---

changes. In an attempt to refine and broaden the scope of the hazardous waste regulatory program, EPA made two basic changes. First, it replaced the Extraction Procedure (EP) leach test with the TCLP. Second, it added 25 organic chemicals to the list of contaminants tested for and established health-based regulatory levels for the new constituents. 55 Fed. Reg. 11,798 (1990). The overall effect of these changes was to capture many generators of hazardous waste (especially those dealing with organic compounds) under the RCRA regulatory scheme for the first time.

[69] Thus, under 40 C.F.R. §261.4(b) the following solid wastes are not "hazardous waste" and are not regulated by RCRA:

Household waste
Agricultural wastes returned to the ground as fertilizer
Mining overburden returned to the mine site
Fly ash and other wastes generated by coal combustion
Oil drilling wastes
Certain hexavalent chromium wastes
Mining and mineral processing wastes
Cement kiln dust wastes
Arsenical treated wood and wood products
Petroleum contaminated media and debris
Injected groundwater from oil refining equipment (until 1/25/93)
Reclaimed CFCs from heat transfer equipment
Drained oil filters

[70] This is important primarily for resource recovery facilities managing municipal solid wastes. If such facility manages only household wastes, it is not subject to RCRA, even if those household wastes have a hazardous characteristic. 40 C.F.R. §261.4(b)(1).

[71] 40 C.F.R. §261.4(b)(4) (fly ash, bottom ash, slag, flue gas emission control waste); 40 C.F.R. §261.4(b)(5) (petroleum drilling, operations waste).

[72] 40 C.F.R. §261.4(b)(7). EPA adopted the exemption for mineral processing wastes, which include a variety of specific wastes from specific types of mineral operations, pursuant to congressional mandate in RCRA §§3001(b)(3) and 8002(p), added to the original Act by the so-called Bevill Amendment. These Bevill wastes are exempted due to their large volume and inherently low hazard.

[73] 40 C.F.R. §261.4(c).

because of the presence of sediments or sludges with hazardous characteristics. Under the exemption, such material is not regulated unless it exits the tank, pipeline, or unit, at which point it becomes fully regulated, or unless the hazardous material remains in the tank, pipeline, or unit for over 90 days after the tank, pipeline, or unit is taken out of service.

A second exemption is for samples of solid waste that are tested to determine whether they are hazardous waste or for "treatability."[74] Such hazardous wastes are exempt from regulation during initial collection, shipment to a laboratory, testing, and return to the generator. They are not exempt once returned to the generator.

F. Mixtures of Hazardous and Nonhazardous Wastes

Much industrial and commercial solid waste consists of multiple waste streams that are generated together or become mixed during process operations. Where a hazardous waste becomes mixed with other wastes, the critical question is whether the resulting mixture is subject to regulation. To answer this question requires knowledge of EPA's "mixture" rule.[75]

For mixtures that do not include any listed hazardous waste, the criterion is relatively simple: Such a waste mixture is hazardous waste only if it exhibits a characteristic of hazardous waste. More complex issues arise, however, if such mixing is performed for the purpose of diluting or neutralizing a hazardous characteristic. In that case, the mixing may be considered "treatment" of a hazardous waste. If so, the facility at which the mixing occurs would be required to have a hazardous waste treatment facility permit. In general, to ensure that the treatment issue does not arise, it is advisable that there be some independent, process related reason for the mixing of such wastes.

The analysis is more complex for mixtures that contain a listed hazardous waste. As a general rule, any waste mixture that contains a listed hazardous waste is itself considered hazardous waste (unless it has been delisted). There are two exceptions to this rule. First, if the listed waste in the mixture is listed solely because it exhibits one of the four characteristics of hazardous waste identified in part 261, then the mixture is not hazardous if the mixture no longer exhibits any identified characteristic of hazardous waste. For example, section 261.32 lists a number of wastes from explosives manufacturing operations as hazardous because they are explosive. If a mixture of those wastes and other solid wastes is no longer explosive (and does not exhibit some other hazardous characteristic), then the mixture would not be considered hazardous.

The second exception is for certain mixtures of wastewater and very low concentrations of listed wastes. Provided that the wastewater discharge is "subject to regulation" under either section 402 or 307 of the Clean Water

---

[74] 40 C.F.R. §261.4(d), (e), (f).

[75] *See generally* 40 C.F.R. §261.3. The mixture rule, which appeared in the original 1980 RCRA regulations, was invalidated in 1991. Shell Oil Co. v. EPA, 950 F.2d 741, 34 ER Cases 1049 (D.C. Cir. 1991). EPA has repromulgated the rules as interim final rules, pending further review by the agency. 57 Fed. Reg. 7628 (1992); 57 Fed. Reg. 49,278 (1992). It is possible that EPA will substantially revise the rules, possibly to create specific standards for determining whether any particular mixture is hazardous.

Act,[76] such a mixture is not hazardous waste if it contains any of a number of specific hazardous wastes in specified concentrations.[77] The language of the regulations presents some significant ambiguities, including whether a discharge must actually be pretreated under section 307 of the Clean Water Act before it qualifies for the exception.

G. Wastes Derived From Hazardous Wastes

Any solid waste generated from the "treatment, storage or disposal" of hazardous waste is generally considered also to be hazardous waste.[78] As with the "mixture rule" described in Section F., above,[79] a waste that is derived from a characteristically hazardous waste is not hazardous if it does not itself exhibit the relevant characteristic. Similarly, if a waste is derived from a listed hazardous waste, it remains legally hazardous unless delisted.

It should be noted that the derived-from rule does not apply to materials that are reclaimed from hazardous waste and used beneficially, unless the reclaimed material is burned for energy recovery or is applied to the land. Thus, a reclaimed solvent, for example, that is returned to service would be considered a new product, not a waste. On the other hand, a material reclaimed from a listed waste and applied to land as a dust suppressant would be hazardous waste.

H. The PCB Exemption

Since their original promulgation in 1980, EPA's hazardous waste regulations have excluded polychlorinated biphenyl (PCB) wastes, the management and disposal of which are regulated under the Toxic Substances and Control Act (TSCA). EPA has recognized that some PCB-containing electrical equipment,

---

[76] Section 402 requires a National Pollutant Discharge Elimination System (NPDES) permit for all discharges directly to surface waters. Section 307 imposes general and categorical pretreatment requirements on discharges of wastewater to publicly owned sewer systems.

[77] These are:

> (1) the spent solvents carbon tetrachloride, tetrachlorethylene, and trichoroethylene where the maximum total weekly usage of these solvents divided by the average weekly flow of wastewater into the facility's treatment or pretreatment system is no greater than one part per million;
>
> (2) certain other spent solvents listed as a nonspecific source hazardous waste where the maximum total weekly usage of these solvents divided by the average weekly flow of wastewater into the facility's treatment or pretreatment system is no greater than 25 parts per million;
>
> (3) heat exchanger bundle cleaning sludge from the petroleum refining industry;
>
> (4) discarded commercial chemical products or chemical intermediates listed in 40 C.F.R. §261.33 arising from *de minimis* losses of these materials from manufacturing operations in which these materials are used as raw materials or are produced in the manufacturing process; or
>
> (5) wastewater resulting from laboratory operations containing toxic (T) wastes provided that;
>
> (a) the annualized average flow of the wastewater is not greater than one percent of total wastewater flow to the facility's treatment or pretreatment system, or
>
> (b) the combined annualized average concentration does not exceed one part per million in the headworks of the facility's treatment or pretreatment system.

40 C.F.R. §261.3(a)(iv).

[78] 40 C.F.R. §261.3(c)(2). Because "treatment" is defined broadly to include virtually all types of processing of hazardous waste to recover material resources (*see* 40 C.F.R. §260.10), this rule affects virtually all materials derived from hazardous waste. For this reason, it is known as the "derived-from rule."

[79] The "derived-from rule" was overturned in the same appellate decision that invalidated the mixture rule. EPA also reinstated the derived-from rule as an interim final rule pending further consideration.

e.g., transformers, may also contain organic constituents that would independently cause them to fail the TCLP. To avoid duplicative and perhaps inconsistent regulation, EPA excluded such units from regulation under RCRA, so long as they are separately regulated under EPA's TSCA regulations, 40 C.F.R. part 761.[80]

I. The Empty Container Rule

To protect against the unauthorized disposal of hazardous waste in containers while avoiding unnecessary regulation of containers that formerly held hazardous waste, EPA created an exemption for "empty" containers. Under this exemption, any hazardous waste residue remaining in either an "empty" container or an inner liner removed from an "empty" container is not subject to the RCRA program.[81]

The term "empty" has a technical, and variable, meaning, depending upon what hazardous waste the container previously held. As a general rule, a container holding a hazardous waste is "empty" when all wastes have been removed that can be removed using practices commonly employed to remove materials from such containers. In addition, no more than 2.5 centimeters of residue may remain on the bottom or, in the alternative, no more than 3 percent by weight of the container's full capacity of the hazardous substance (0.3 percent for a container over 110 gallons) remains. Special rules apply to containers holding hazardous waste as a compressed gas, which are considered empty when the pressure in the container approaches atmospheric. A container holding a listed acute hazardous waste is "empty" only when the container has been triple rinsed using the appropriate solvent, or by another method shown by scientific literature or tests to achieve equivalent removal, or the inner liner itself has been removed.

It must be emphasized that the empty container exemption covers hazardous wastes only while they are contained in such containers. Hazardous waste residues, once removed from a container, are subject to regulation. If, for example, an "empty" drum that contained a listed hazardous waste is then steam cleaned, the resulting residue would be considered a hazardous waste if it contained detectable amounts of the listed waste.

J. Conditionally Exempt Small Quantity Generators

EPA's original 1980 RCRA regulations exempted from substantially all regulatory requirements wastes that, although hazardous, were generated by generators who produce less than 1,000 kilograms per month of hazardous waste. This small quantity generator exemption was based on, *inter alia,* EPA's belief that only a relatively small amount of waste in total was attributable to such generators. The exemption also reflected the Agency's concern about excessive regulation of small businesses.

When Congress revisited RCRA in 1984, there was growing concern about the potential environmental impacts of the continued management of these

[80] 40 C.F.R. §261.8. *See* 55 Fed. Reg. at 11,805.
[81] 40 C.F.R. §261.7.

small quantity wastes as ordinary solid waste. Thus, the 1984 RCRA amendments created two classes of small quantity generators, dropping the threshold for exemption to 100 kilograms per month and mandating an intermediate regulatory scheme for wastes generated or accumulated in quantities greater than 100 but less than 1,000 kilograms per month.[82]

EPA regulations implemented this two-tier scheme by completely exempting generators of less than 100 kilograms per month of *nonacute* hazardous waste.[83] The exemption is conditioned upon the generator either treating or disposing of the waste on-site, or else sending it to an authorized municipal or industrial solid waste facility or to a facility that beneficially reuses or legitimately recycles the waste.[84] (The generator also is free to send its small quantity wastes to a fully approved RCRA hazardous waste treatment, storage, or disposal facility.) Such a conditionally exempt small quantity generator may also *accumulate* up to 1,000 kilograms of hazardous waste and remain exempt. If more than that amount is accumulated at any time, the entire amount is subject to the regulations applicable to generators of between 100 and 1,000 kilograms per month.[85]

For generators of *acutely* hazardous wastes, the threshold is lower. Such generators are conditionally exempt only if no more than one kilogram of acute hazardous waste is generated per month. A 100 kilogram threshold still applies to any residue or contaminated soil, waste, or other debris resulting from the cleanup of a spill of acute hazardous waste.[86]

Intermediate quantity generators, that is, of between 100 and 1,000 kilograms per month, are exempt from some, but not all, regulatory requirements. These exemptions, for example, from the requirement to use an EPA-prescribed manifest when shipping hazardous wastes to certain recyclers, are discussed below in connection with the requirements to which they pertain.

IV. Standards for Generators of Hazardous Wastes

The RCRA cradle-to-grave scheme separates waste handlers into three categories: generators, transporters, and owners or operators of hazardous waste treatment, storage, or disposal (TSD) facilities. Though the rules for each differ, they are linked in purpose. RCRA is designed to track hazardous waste from its origin, through all phases of transport, to its final destination at an approved facility for treatment or disposal.

A hazardous waste generator is the person at a specific facility whose act or conduct first brings hazardous waste under RCRA's regulatory scheme. The term "person" includes individuals, corporations, and governmental entities.[87] Identifying who is a generator of hazardous waste is usually a straightforward process. Typically, a generator is the person who controls the facility or process in which waste is generated. Most often, this is the individual or corporation that

[82] RCRA §3001(d), 42 U.S.C. §6921(d) (1988).
[83] 40 C.F.R. §261.5.
[84] 40 C.F.R. §§261.5(f), (g).
[85] 40 C.F.R. §261.5(g).
[86] 40 C.F.R. §261.5(e).
[87] 40 C.F.R. §260.10.

owns the facility. However, complex questions can arise where a single facility comprises separately owned operations, or where part or all of the facility is operated under a lease. Moreover, because the definition is site specific, one who owns or operates multiple facilities may be a generator at some but not all of them.[88]

A generator of waste is responsible for determining whether it is hazardous waste, what are the hazardous constituents of the waste, how the waste will be handled, and to whom it will be sent. A misapplication or misunderstanding of the regulations could result in improper or inadequate management of a hazardous waste after it leaves the generator's facility. At worst, a hazardous waste may be incorrectly defined as nonhazardous and escape regulation altogether.

RCRA section 3002 and part 262 of EPA's regulations apply to generators of hazardous waste. The statute required EPA to promulgate regulatory standards necessary to protect human health and the environment. Among the statutory requirements are recordkeeping that identifies the quantity, constituents, and disposition of generated hazardous wastes; labeling of containers; use of appropriate containers; gathering information and forwarding it to persons transporting, treating, storing, or disposing of such wastes; manifesting of the wastes; and biennial reports to the implementing federal or state agency.[89]

A. Waste Determination and Identification

A generator's initial responsibilities are to determine if the solid waste generated is hazardous waste and, if so, to obtain an EPA identification number. This number is used to track the waste from generation to treatment and disposal and to ensure that the waste is not improperly disposed of without knowledge of the Agency. The regulations prohibit a generator from offering hazardous waste to anyone for treatment, storage, disposal, or transport unless the generator has received an identification number.[90]

A generator must apply to EPA for a hazardous waste identification number by using a special form.[91] It is also possible to obtain an identification number by phoning the EPA regional office. This can be done only in emergencies, such as a spill, and EPA will require the generator to fill out the form at a later date.[92]

To make a hazardous waste determination, the generator is directed to check the hazardous waste lists in Subpart D of 40 C.F.R. part 261 and, if the waste is not listed, to determine whether it has a hazardous characteristic.[93] The generator may test the waste with the methods prescribed in the regulations. Alternatively, the generator may make a determination by applying knowledge of the hazardous characteristic of the waste in light of the materials or the processes involved in its use. The regulations do not provide a specific standard

---

[88] The term "generator" is not defined in the statute. The regulations define "generator" as "any person, by site, whose act or process produces hazardous waste identified or listed in part 261 of this chapter or whose act first causes a hazardous waste to become subject to regulation." 40 C.F.R. §260.10.

[89] The division of regulatory authority between EPA and the states is discussed below.

[90] 40 C.F.R. §262.12.

[91] EPA Form 8700-12. 40 C.F.R. §262.12.

[92] 45 Fed. Reg. 85,002 (1980).

[93] 40 C.F.R. §262.11.

that the generator must meet if it elects to forgo testing. If a generator erroneously determines that its waste is not hazardous but did not test the waste, EPA could take enforcement action if the determination was unreasonable.

B. Hazardous Waste Manifest Requirements

All generators that do not treat or dispose of their own hazardous waste on site must prepare a manifest. The manifest accompanies the waste at all times. It is a guide to where the waste is expected to travel and how it will get there, and lists all persons who will handle it. Improper use of the manifest (like other violations of Subtitle C) can result in civil and criminal liability.[94]

In 1980, EPA originally prescribed a manifest form for hazardous waste shipments. However, some states that operate their own hazardous waste plans (as authorized under RCRA section 3006 and 40 C.F.R. part 271) also adopted their own individual forms. Because no standard form existed, generators and transporters were often directed to fill out numerous forms and comply with various, differing requirements. In 1988, EPA and the Department of Transportation (DOT) published the Uniform Hazardous Waste Manifest form in order to end the confusion and duplication caused by the numerous state forms.[95] For each manifest, the generator must: (1) obtain the signature of the original transporter; (2) personally sign the manifest certification;[96] (3) retain one copy for his or her own records; and (4) give the initial transporter the remaining copies of the manifest.

Special procedures must be followed for generators shipping hazardous wastes by rail or water. For such shipments, the generator must send three copies of the signed and dated manifest to the designated TSD facility or the last water or rail transporter to handle the waste in the United States. Intermediate rail or water transporters do not have to be provided with copies as their signatures are unnecessary.[97]

Generators who dispose of their hazardous waste out-of-state should be alert to the fact that states may require additional information to be included on the Uniform Manifest. If the consignment state (the state to which the shipment is manifested) supplies the manifest and requires its use, then that manifest must be used. If not, and the generator's home state supplies the manifest and requires its use, then that manifest must be used. If neither state supplies a manifest, then the generator may use a manifest procured from any source.[98]

---

[94] RCRA §3008, 42 U.S.C. §6928 (1988).

[95] This form requires the generator to provide the following information: the generator's name, phone, and ID number; the manifest document number; the name and ID number of all transporters of the waste; the name, address, and ID number of the designated hazardous waste TSD facility; the DOT description of the waste; the number and type of containers used for each waste; the total quantity of each waste; and a certification that all applicable regulations have been followed. 40 C.F.R. §262, app. X.

[96] RCRA §3002(b), added by the 1984 Amendments, requires every manifest to contain a waste minimization certification to be signed by the generator. The certification reads: "I have a program in place to reduce the volume and toxicity of waste generated to the degree I have determined to be economically practicable and I have selected the method of treatment, storage, or disposal currently available to me which minimizes the present and future threat to human health and the environment." *See* EPA Form 8700-22 (Rev. 9-88).

[97] 40 C.F.R. §262.23(c)-(d).

[98] 40 C.F.R. §262.21.

The most important information to be included on the manifest is the names of the waste transporters and the designated TSD facility. The generator may also designate a backup TSD facility to handle the waste in an emergency. If, for some reason, the waste cannot be delivered to either of the designated facilities, the generator must either designate another facility or instruct the transporter to return the waste. The number of transporters and waste management facilities specified will dictate the number of copies of the manifest to be prepared. The generator, each transporter, and the designated facility must keep one copy, and an additional copy must be returned to the generator.[99]

Special manifesting regulations apply to persons who deal with international shipments of hazardous waste. Importers and exporters must substitute information about foreign generators, transporters, and TSD facilities and directions concerning proper handling that parallel the requirements of domestic transport and disposal. In addition, exporters must comply with special notification requirements. Primary exporters must provide EPA with specified information at least 60 days before the initial shipment of hazardous waste for each 12-month period.[100] EPA will forward this information to the receiving country for approval. If approved by the receiving country, EPA will provide an EPA Acknowledgment of Consent to the domestic exporter for attachment to the manifest before initial transport.[101]

C. Pretransport Requirements

It is the generator's responsibility to prepare hazardous waste properly for transportation. The waste must be packaged, labeled, and placarded in accordance with EPA standards. EPA has adopted by reference relevant DOT regulations on hazardous materials under 49 C.F.R. parts 172, 173, 178, and 179.[102] In addition to applicable DOT requirements, each container of 110 gallons or less used in transport must be marked with a special warning.[103]

D. On-site Accumulation of Hazardous Waste

EPA recognizes that generators cannot be expected to immediately move wastes off-site. The regulations therefore permit temporary on-site accumulation. If waste is stored in larger quantities or for longer periods of time than permitted under the rules for on-site accumulation, the generator will be subject to the much more stringent regulations applicable to hazardous waste storage

---

[99] 40 C.F.R. §262.22.

[100] In addition to information about the exporter itself, the following must be provided by consignee for each individual waste: (1) information on the hazardous waste; (2) the estimated rate and time period over which export will take place; (3) the estimated total quantity of waste to be exported; (4) all foreign points of entry and departure; (5) all means of transport; (6) all manners of treatment, storage, and disposal; (7) the name and location of all consignees; and (8) the name of all transit countries, the duration of stay, and the nature of handling of the waste while in each country. 40 C.F.R. §262.53.

[101] These procedures are streamlined under bilateral agreements with Canada and Mexico, such that shipment-specific prior approval by the receiving country is not required. *See* T.I.A.S. 11099 (Nov. 8, 1986) [U.S.-Canada]; T.I.A.S. 10827, Annex 3 (Jan. 29, 1987) [U.S.-Mexico].

[102] 49 C.F.R. §262.30-.32.

[103] The words, as specified in 40 C.F.R. §262.32 are: "HAZARDOUS WASTE—Federal Law Prohibits Improper Disposal. If found, contact the nearest police or public safety authority or the U.S. Environmental Protection Agency."

facilities.[104] The amount of waste and the time permitted for on-site accumulation depends upon whether the generator qualifies as a conditionally exempt small quantity generator or an intermediate quantity generator.

Normally, a generator may accumulate any amount of hazardous waste on-site for up to 90 days without a storage permit (or interim status as a storage facility) provided the generator complies with certain of the standards otherwise applicable to a storage facility.[105] The hazardous waste must be kept in containers or tanks or on drip pads that meet the technical requirements for these types of storage facilities in 40 C.F.R. part 265. The containers and tanks must be clearly marked or labeled with the words "Hazardous Waste." Each container must be clearly marked with the date upon which each period of accumulation began. In addition, during the period of accumulation, the generator must comply with the regulations at 40 C.F.R. part 265 Subparts C and D, which set forth generally applicable standards for "interim status" TSD facilities. These involve, among other controls, emergency procedures, contingency plans, employee training, and notice to local authorities.

Unless an extension has been granted by EPA, any longer period of storage will result in status as an operator of a storage facility. Such extensions are granted for unforeseen, temporary, or uncontrollable circumstances. Extensions of up to 30 days may be granted at the Regional Administrator's discretion on a case-by-case basis.[106]

A generator may collect and store lesser amounts of hazardous waste at satellite accumulation areas.[107] Typically, up to 55 gallons of hazardous waste or one quart of acutely hazardous waste may be so collected, provided it is stored in containers that are compatible with the waste, are in good condition, and are kept closed except when necessary to add or remove waste.[108] Additionally, the storage containers must be marked with the words "Hazardous Waste" or with other words that identify the contents of the containers. If more than 55 gallons of hazardous waste or one quart of acutely hazardous waste is accumulated, the generator has three days to move the excess waste to the primary collection area and mark the excess waste with the date the excess amount began accumulating. There the waste may be stored for 90 days from the date of accumulation under the normal 90-day storage regulations.

Generators of 100 to 1,000 kilograms of hazardous waste per month are subject to more relaxed accumulation rules. Such generators may store up to 6,000 kilograms of hazardous waste for up to 180 days without a permit or interim status.[109] If the waste must be transported more than 200 miles for off-site treatment, accumulation may take place for up to 270 days. All containers must meet the relevant technical requirements for containers and tanks.[110]

---

[104] EPA regulations define storage as any temporary holding of hazardous waste, no matter how brief. 40 C.F.R. §260.10.

[105] 40 C.F.R. §262.34.

[106] The regulations do not clearly indicate whether the Regional Administrator may renew such an extension or, if so, how many times.

[107] 40 C.F.R. §262.34(c).

[108] 40 C.F.R. §262.34(c)(1), which requires compliance with C.F.R. §§265.171, 265.172, and 265.173(a).

[109] 40 C.F.R. §262.32(d).

[110] 40 C.F.R. §265 Subpart I governs the use and management of containers. Small quantity generators accumulating hazardous wastes must comply with these regulations in full. 40 C.F.R. §265 Subpart J contains special rules on tank management for small quantity generators at §265.201. This is the only part of 40 C.F.R. §265 Subpart J that must be followed in this circumstance.

Although the regulations at 40 C.F.R. part 265 Subparts C and D are not applicable here, the intermediate quantity generator is also responsible for implementing less stringent, alternative controls on emergency response, employee training, and notification of the appropriate authorities.[111]

As with normal generators, the EPA may grant extensions to these intermediate quantity generators to permit a greater period of accumulation for unforeseen, temporary, and uncontrollable circumstances. An extension of up to 30 days may be granted at the discretion of the Regional Administrator on a case-by-case basis.[112]

E. Recordkeeping and Reporting Requirements

As a general rule, hazardous waste generators must keep all records generated for compliance with RCRA for a period of three years. If an enforcement action is taking place, the period is tolled until the action has been resolved. This requirement applies directly to: (1) all manifests; (2) all Biennial and Exception Reports; and (3) the results from all tests, analyses, and hazardous waste determinations performed in accordance with 40 C.F.R. §262.11.[113]

The Biennial Report is a statement of a generator's hazardous waste activities that must be submitted to the Regional Administrator by March 1 of each even numbered year. The report must be certified by an authorized representative and must include the following information: (1) the EPA ID number, name, and address of the generator; (2) the calendar years covered by the report; (3) the name, EPA ID number, and address of each TSD facility used by the generator; (4) the name and EPA ID number of each transporter used by the generator; (5) a description of each hazardous waste transported for treatment off-site; and (6) a description of efforts to reduce the volume and toxicity of waste generated and the changes actually achieved.[114] Small quantity generators are not required to submit Biennial Reports.[115]

If a generator does not receive a signed copy of the manifest from the designated TSD facility for the manifested waste within 35 days of the date the waste was accepted by the initial transporter, the generator must contact the transporter and the TSD facility to check on the status of the waste. If the generator cannot procure a signed copy of the manifest in an additional 10 days (a total of 45 days), the generator must file an Exception Report with the EPA Regional Office. Generators of 100 to 1,000 kilograms of hazardous waste per month who do not receive a completed manifest from a TSD facility are not required to contact the transporter or TSD facility but are required to notify EPA if no manifest is received for more than 60 days after the shipment occurs.[116]

---

[111] 40 C.F.R. §262.34(d).

[112] 40 C.F.R. §262.40(f).

[113] 40 C.F.R. §262.40. The EPA may require additional reports concerning the quantities and disposition of hazardous wastes as deemed necessary. 40 C.F.R. §262.43.

[114] 40 C.F.R. §262.41.

[115] 40 C.F.R. §262.44.

[116] 40 C.F.R. §262.42.

V. Standards for Transporters of Hazardous Waste

RCRA section 3003 governs transporters of hazardous waste. As with most other parts of Subtitle C, Congress spelled out general areas of control and left it to EPA to adopt implementing regulations.[117] The statute and implementing regulations do not place as many specific requirements on transporters of hazardous waste as on generators and TSD facilities. However, the regulation of hazardous waste transport remains crucial to the statute's regulatory framework. One of Subtitle C's primary aims was to eliminate improper disposal, or "midnight dumping." A transporter's failure to follow the regulations set forth at 40 C.F.R. part 263 can result in the transporter being classified as a hazardous waste generator or as an operator of a TSD facility. As with all requirements under EPA's hazardous waste regulations, failure to comply also can result in civil or criminal penalties.

A transporter, though not defined in the statute, is defined in the regulations as "a person engaged in the off-site transportation of hazardous waste."[118] The regulations specifically exclude those generators and TSD facilities that transport wastes on-site, for example, moving hazardous wastes from one portion of a plant site to another. Further, these regulations apply only to the transport of manifested hazardous waste. Therefore, if one transports waste only from conditionally exempt small quantity generators (less than 100 kilograms per month), these regulations do not apply, even if the waste would otherwise be considered hazardous.

In certain circumstances, transporters are required to comply with the regulations applicable to hazardous waste generators. This will occur if the transporter imports hazardous waste, mixes hazardous wastes of different DOT shipping descriptions, or allows wastes to accumulate and subsequently cleans out the transport vehicle.[119] A transporter who stores shipments of hazardous waste at a transfer facility for more than 10 days becomes subject to full-blown regulation as a hazardous waste treatment facility.[120]

A. Compliance With the Manifest System

Transporters have a duty to ensure that a proper manifest accompanies each waste shipment and that the party from whom the waste is received is provided with proof of delivery.[121] A transporter may only accept hazardous waste that is accompanied by a manifest signed by the generator.[122] The

[117] Section 3003 of RCRA requires EPA to promulgate regulations governing: (1) recordkeeping, (2) labeling, (3) manifesting, and (4) using only permitted TSD facilities. 42 U.S.C. §6923 (1988).

[118] 40 C.F.R. §260.10. The term "transportation" applies to "the movement of hazardous waste by air, rail, highway, or water." *Id.*

[119] 40 C.F.R. §263.10(c). In these circumstances the transporter is seen as injecting a new waste stream into the regulatory system, albeit through unconventional means. This is consistent with RCRA's policy of fully regulating all hazardous wastes regardless of how they are created.

[120] 40 C.F.R. §263.12.

[121] 40 C.F.R. §263.20, .21.

[122] For exports of hazardous waste, the transporter must also ensure that the shipment conforms to and is accompanied by the EPA Acknowledgment of Consent for that shipment. 40 C.F.R. §263.20. This form should be attached to the manifest at all times.

transporter must sign and date the manifest and return a copy to the generator before transport. If the waste is received from another transporter, all previous transporters must also have signed and dated the manifest. The receiving transporter must again sign and date the manifest to acknowledge receipt and leave a copy with the prior transporter.

When the waste is delivered to a designated TSD facility, the transporter must retain a copy of the manifest, signed by the owner or operator of the facility to acknowledge receipt. The facility will send an additional signed copy to the generator. This final copy will contain the signatures of the owner or operator of the TSD facility, the hazardous waste generator, and all transporters and the dates on which the shipment changed hands. It is a record of who had possession of the waste at all times. All signed copies must be maintained for three years from the date the hazardous waste was accepted by the initial transporter.[123]

For exports of hazardous waste, the last transporter within the United States is responsible for returning a signed copy of the manifest to the generator, reflecting delivery to an exporter. Such transporter must also indicate on the manifest the date the hazardous waste left the United States and provide a copy to the U.S. Customs official at the point of departure.[124]

Special provisions apply to transportation by water (bulk shipments) and rail.[125] Both types of shippers are permitted to use a ''shipping paper'' in lieu of a hazardous waste manifest, so long as the shipping paper contains all the information that is required in a hazardous waste manifest. After receiving and signing for waste from a nonrail transporter or generator, the initial rail transporter must forward at least three copies of the manifest to the next nonrail transporter or, if there will be no further nonrail transport, to the designated TSD facility. Upon delivery to a nonrail transporter or designated facility, the rail transporter must acquire a signed and dated copy of the manifest.

Transporters dealing with waste from intermediate quantity generators (100–1,000 kilograms per month) will be exempt from these requirements provided they have a reclamation agreement with the generator and maintain certain information on a log or shipping paper for at least three years after termination or expiration of the agreement.[126]

All hazardous waste accompanying the manifest must be delivered to the next transporter or to one of the designated facilities. If an emergency prevents delivery to the primary designated facility listed on the manifest, the transporter must make delivery to the alternate designated facility. If a problem arises with delivery to the alternate facility, the generator must be contacted and the manifest revised in accordance with the generator's instruction.

---

[123] 40 C.F.R. §263.22.

[124] 40 C.F.R. §263.20(g).

[125] 40 C.F.R. §263.20(e), (f).

[126] The following information must be maintained on the log or shipping paper and must be carried when transporting waste to the reclamation facility: the name, address, and EPA ID number of the generator; the quantity of waste accepted; all DOT-required shipping information; and the date the waste is accepted. 40 C.F.R. §263.20(h).

B. In-Transit Hazardous Waste Discharges

Transporters who discharge hazardous waste, accidentally or intentionally, are responsible for containing the discharge, notifying the authorities, and cleaning up.[127] The regulations specifically require the transporter to take "appropriate immediate action to protect human health and the environment."[128] This policy concern outweighs other requirements imposed elsewhere by the regulations. Thus, in emergency spill situations, a government official may authorize removal by transporters who do not have EPA identification numbers and without preparation of a manifest.

Regardless of government authorization, a transporter must follow certain DOT rules on reporting and notification incorporated by reference into the RCRA Subtitle C regulations.[129] These DOT regulations require notice to the National Response Center if as a direct result of hazardous materials one of the following occurs: (1) a person is killed, (2) a person receives injuries requiring hospitalization, (3) estimated damage to property exceeds $50,000, (4) radioactive materials are involved, (5) etiologic agents are involved, or (6) a continuing danger to life exists at the scene of the discharge.[130] A report must also be submitted to the DOT Office of Hazardous Materials Regulations, Materials Transportation Bureau, located in Washington, D.C., within 30 days of the release.[131]

VI. Standards for Hazardous Waste Treatment, Storage, and Disposal Facilities

Treatment, storage, and disposal facilities (TSDs) are regulated under section 3004.[132] As with generators and transporters of hazardous waste, Congress directed EPA to promulgate rules for TSDs "as may be necessary to protect human health and the environment." Specific standards under section 3004 include the following:

- Maintenance of records of all hazardous wastes handled by TSD facilities;

---

[127] 40 C.F.R. §263.30. Cleanup must be adequate to ensure that the hazardous waste discharge "no longer presents a hazard to human health or the environment." 40 C.F.R. §263.31.

[128] *Id.*

[129] 40 C.F.R. §263.30(c).

[130] 49 C.F.R. §171.15(a). The National Response Center can be reached at (800) 424-8802 or (202) 426-2765.

[131] 49 C.F.R. §171.16(a).

[132] "Treatment" is broadly defined in §1003 as "any method, technique, or process, including neutralization, designed to change the physical, chemical, or biological character or composition of any hazardous waste so as to neutralize such waste or so as to render such waste nonhazardous, safer for transport, amenable for recovery, amenable for storage, or designed to change the physical form or chemical composition of hazardous waste so as to render it nonhazardous." 42 U.S.C. §6903.

"Storage" is defined as "the containment of hazardous waste, either on a temporary basis or for a period of years, in such a manner as not to constitute disposal of such hazardous waste." *Id.*

"Disposal" is defined as "the discharge, deposit, injection, dumping, spilling, leaking, or placing of any solid waste or hazardous waste into or on any land or water so that such solid waste or hazardous waste or any constituent thereof may enter the environment or be emitted into the air or discharged into any waters, including ground waters." *Id.*

- Reporting, monitoring, inspection, and compliance with the manifest system;
- Operating methods, techniques, and practices for the treatment, storage, and disposal of hazardous waste;
- Location, design, and construction of TSD facilities;
- Contingency plans;
- Maintenance and operational qualifications and financial responsibility for TSD facilities; and
- Compliance with RCRA's TSD permit system.[133]

Section 3004 also includes restrictions on certain types of disposal in specific facilities and geologic formations and technical standards concerning land disposal of hazardous waste. These standards are discussed below.

EPA's TSD regulations, published at 40 C.F.R. part 264, apply to all TSD facilities with the following exceptions:

1. Persons who dispose of hazardous waste by means of ocean disposal subject to a permit issued under the Marine Protection, Research, and Sanctuaries Act;
2. Persons who dispose of hazardous waste by means of underground injection subject to a permit issued under the Safe Drinking Water Act's Underground Injection Control Program;
3. Owners or operators of POTWs;
4. Owners or operators of TSD facilities located in a state with its own RCRA hazardous waste program;[134]
5. Owners or operators of facilities permitted, licensed, or registered by a state to manage municipal or industrial solid waste, if the only hazardous waste handled by the facility is excluded from regulation elsewhere in the RCRA program;
6. Generators accumulating waste on-site who fulfill the requirements for exemption;
7. Farmers disposing of waste pesticides from their own use;
8. Owners and operators of totally enclosed treatment facilities as defined in the regulations;
9. Owners and operators of elementary neutralization units or wastewater treatment units as defined in the regulations;
10. Persons engaged in immediate response to a discharge or imminent and substantial threat of a discharge or hazardous waste;
11. Transporters storing manifested shipments of hazardous waste in proper containers at a transfer facility for 10 days or less; and
12. Persons who add absorbent material to waste in a proper container or who add waste to absorbent material, provided this mixing takes place when the waste is first placed in the container.[135]

---

[133] 42 U.S.C. §6924.

[134] In order to be approved by EPA, a state program must regulate TSDs at least as stringently as do EPA's regulations. Procedures and standards for approval of state programs are discussed elsewhere in this chapter.

[135] 40 C.F.R. §264.1.

The TSD standards are enforceable primarily through incorporation in the permits that EPA (or authorized states) issues to hazardous waste management facilities. The part 264 regulations do not apply to TSD facilities that qualify for "interim status" under RCRA section 3005(e).[136] Interim status covers certain facilities that were in operation before the initial RCRA regulations were promulgated in 1980 or before subsequently promulgated regulations subjected existing facilities to the RCRA management system. Interim status is temporary and all TSD facilities eventually become subject to full regulation. Pending issuance of a permit for such a facility (or its closure), the facility must comply with similar, but different, standards set out in part 265 of EPA's regulations. Those standards are described elsewhere in this chapter.

A. General Facility Standards

The regulations contain standards applicable to all facilities, as well as standards that apply to specific types of TSD facilities. The general standards include requirements for identification, notice, waste analysis, inspection, personnel training, special care for special wastes, and facility location.

All TSDs are required to apply for an EPA identification number, which can be used by generators to identify the destination of hazardous wastes on a manifest.[137] TSDs are also required to give various forms of notice to the Regional Administrator.[138] If hazardous waste is received from a foreign source, the facility must notify EPA in writing at least four weeks in advance of the date the initial shipment is expected to arrive. Notice of subsequent shipments from the same source is not required. If a facility receives hazardous waste from an off-site source, the generator must be informed in writing that the facility is properly permitted and will accept the waste. A third type of notice is required during the sale of a TSD facility. Before transferring ownership or operation of a facility, the new owner or operator must be informed, in writing, of the relevant RCRA regulations.

A general hazardous waste analysis must be conducted before a facility may manage a particular type of waste.[139] This analysis must be in accordance with a written plan, developed by the facility, and must be repeated as often as necessary to ensure that it is accurate and up to date. The regulations include minimum standards for both the development of the plan and the circumstances of its use. For off-site facilities, in addition to the standards applicable to on-site facilities, the waste analysis plan must specify procedures for inspecting and tracking the movement of hazardous waste at the facility.

In order to minimize the possibility of unauthorized entry of persons or livestock onto the active portion of a facility, certain security steps must be taken.[140] Facilities must be equipped with either a continuous surveillance system, monitoring and controlling entry to the active portion of the facility, or a barrier that completely surrounds the active portion of the facility and with

---

[136] 40 C.F.R. §264.3.
[137] 40 C.F.R. §264.11.
[138] 40 C.F.R. §264.12.
[139] 40 C.F.R. §264.13.
[140] *Id.*

which access can be controlled. Signs warning against trespass must be posted at and about all entrances to the facility's active portions. These security measures will not be required if the owner or operator can demonstrate to the Regional Administrator that physical contact with the waste will not be injurious and disturbance of the waste will not cause a violation of the regulations.

Owners or operators are required to inspect facilities regularly to prevent the release of hazardous waste and the threat to human health.[141] A written inspection schedule and inspection log must be developed and maintained for all types of equipment. If deterioration or malfunction is reflected by the schedule, steps must be taken to ensure against any environmental or human health hazard. Where a hazard is imminent or has already occurred, remedial action must be taken immediately.

To ensure compliance with the regulations, a program of on-the-job training of facility personnel must be conducted.[142] The program must be in accordance with a written training description for each employee who deals with hazardous waste and must be directed by a person trained in hazardous waste management procedures. At a minimum, the program must be designed to ensure that facility personnel are able to respond effectively to emergency situations.

Special precautions must be undertaken and documented to prevent accidents involving ignitable and reactive wastes.[143] Such wastes must be protected from sources of ignition and reaction. Some preventive measures, such as keeping the waste clear of flames and posting "No Smoking" signs, are obvious. Other measures, like avoiding spontaneous ignition from chemical reactions, must be carefully followed. Any management of ignitable or reactive waste and any mixing of incompatible waste must be undertaken in a manner that does not threaten human health or the environment. These threats include (1) the generation of extreme heat or pressure, fire or explosions, or violent reactions; (2) the production of uncontrolled toxic mists, fumes, dusts, or gases; (3) the production of uncontrolled flammable fumes or gases; and (4) damage to the structural integrity of the device or facility.[144]

The regulations include restrictions on where TSD facilities may be located.[145] Seismic considerations dictate that portions of *new* facilities where hazardous waste will be managed must not be located within 200 feet of a fault that has been displaced during the recent geologic past. To protect against the contamination of groundwater and surface water supplies, any facility located in a 100-year floodplain must be designed, constructed, operated, and maintained to prevent washout of any hazardous waste by a 100-year flood unless the Regional Administrator determines that (1) the waste can be safely removed before arrival of the flood waters or will not be vulnerable to the flood waters; or (2) for existing surface impoundments, waste piles, land treatment units, landfills, and miscellaneous units, no adverse effects on human health or the environment will result from washout. EPA's regulations also prohibit the

[141] 40 C.F.R. §264.15.
[142] 40 C.F.R. §264.16.
[143] 40 C.F.R. §264.17.
[144] 40 C.F.R. §264.17(b).
[145] 40 C.F.R. §264.18.

placement of any noncontainerized or bulk liquid hazardous waste in any salt dome formation, salt bed formation, underground mine, or cave.

B. Preparedness and Prevention Standards

EPA has promulgated preparedness and prevention standards, applicable to all TSDs, to minimize the possibility of a fire, explosion, or any unplanned release of hazardous waste capable of threatening human health or the environment.[146] These rules require the presence and maintenance of certain equipment and the preservation of numerous additional safeguards, such as unobstructed aisle space and immediate access to an emergency communication or alarm device. Unless the Regional Administrator determines otherwise, all facilities must be equipped with the following: (1) an internal communication or alarm system; (2) a communications device capable of summoning emergency assistance by a government agency; (3) fire, spill control, and decontamination equipment; and (4) adequate water or foam producing equipment.[147] All such equipment must be tested and maintained to ensure proper operation during an emergency.[148]

Facilities must attempt to make special arrangements with local authorities (police, fire, and emergency response teams) and local hospitals.[149] The specific type of arrangement will depend on the nature of the waste handled at each facility. Generally, all authorities should be provided with a layout of the facility, the properties of the hazardous waste handled, normal location of personnel, and facility access and exit routes. If the state or local authority refuses to make such plans, the facility must document the refusal in the operating record.

C. Contingency Planning and Emergency Procedures

Contingency plans designed to minimize hazards to human health or the environment must be implemented at all TSD facilities.[150] The plan will set forth the procedures to be followed in an emergency. It must describe any arrangements made with state and local authorities, information necessary to contact all persons qualified to act as emergency coordinators, a list of all emergency equipment (fire extinguishers, spill control equipment, and so forth), and an evacuation plan. Copies are to be kept at the facility and provided to state and local authorities. The rules require amendment as necessary whenever changes occur in the applicable regulations, the facility permit, the list of emergency equipment or coordinators, or the facility itself. Amendment is also necessary if the plan fails in an emergency.

---

[146] 40 C.F.R. §264.31.

[147] 40 C.F.R. §264.32.

[148] 40 C.F.R. §264.34.

[149] 40 C.F.R. §264.37.

[150] 40 C.F.R. §264.51. If the facility already has a Spill Prevention Control and Countermeasures (SPCC) plan in accordance with the Clean Water Act or some other emergency plan, that plan may be amended to incorporate hazardous waste management provisions in lieu of developing an entirely new plan. 40 C.F.R. §264.52(b).

Emergency coordinators, as specified in the contingency plan, are employees responsible for coordinating all emergency procedures.[151] Such coordinators must be familiar with plant operations and activities and the kinds of wastes managed and must be able to reach the facility in a short period of time. Importantly, the coordinator must have the authority to commit the resources needed to carry out the emergency plan. In the case of an imminent or actual emergency, the coordinator must see to it that all alarms are activated and all government authorities are properly informed. This includes immediate notification to the National Response Center, reachable at (800) 424-8802. A facility's emergency coordinator should be intimately familiar with these and all other emergency responsibilities under the regulations.[152]

D. Compliance With the Manifest System

Upon receipt of a manifested shipment of hazardous waste, the owner or operator of a TSD facility or its agent must sign and date each copy of the manifest and note any significant discrepancies in the shipment on the document.[153] One copy must be retained by the facility for at least three years, one copy must be given to the transporter, and one copy must be returned to the generator within 30 days of the delivery.

As with transporters, special rules apply to delivery by rail or water. Primarily, the regulations again allow the substitution of shipping papers for the manifest.

If there are any significant discrepancies[154] in the quantity or type of hazardous waste on the manifest and the actual shipment, the facility must attempt to reconcile the discrepancy with the generator or transporter. If this cannot be accomplished in 15 days, a letter must be submitted to the Regional Administrator describing the discrepancy and attempts to reconcile it. This notice must be accompanied by a copy of the manifest.

E. Recordkeeping Requirements

All facilities must keep a written operating record until closure (longer if an unresolved enforcement action regarding the facility is pending or if requested by EPA). The following information must be maintained in the record:

1. A description of the type and quantity of hazardous waste received and the date and method of the waste's treatment, storage, or disposal;
2. The location and quantity of all hazardous waste, cross-referenced to each waste's manifest;
3. Results of all waste analyses;
4. Incidents that require implementation of the facility's contingency plan;

[151] 40 C.F.R. §264.55.

[152] These responsibilities are found at 40 C.F.R. §264.56.

[153] 40 C.F.R. §264.71.

[154] A significant discrepancy involves one of the following: (1) for bulk waste, variations greater than 10% in weight; (2) for batch waste, any variation in piece count (such as a missing containment drum); or (3) obvious differences in waste type that can be discovered by inspection or waste analysis, such as the presence of unmanifested toxic constituents. 40 C.F.R. §264.72.

5. Results of self-inspections of the facility;
6. Monitoring, testing, or analytical data, and corrective action;
7. Notices to off-site generators that the facility is properly permitted and will accept the waste being sent and any further notice as required by the RCRA land disposal restrictions;
8. All closure and postclosure cost estimates;
9. Annual certifications that the facility has a program in place to reduce the volume and toxicity of hazardous wastes and has taken steps to minimize the present and future threat to human health and the environment; and
10. The specified use of land disposal units under an extension to the effective date of any land disposal restrictions.[155]

All records must be made available for inspection by EPA at all reasonable times.[156]

The regulations require the filing of a number of additional reports with the Regional Administrator. Notice of fires or other emergencies and facility closures are required as necessary.[157] As for generators, a Biennial Report must be submitted by March 1 of each even numbered year addressing facility activities during the previous calendar year.[158] In addition to the general information required of generators, the report must include (1) the most recent closure estimates for treatment or storage facilities and postclosure cost estimates for disposal facilities; and (2) the signed certification.

An unmanifested waste report is required for all waste received that is not properly manifested.[159] Such reports must be submitted to the Regional Administrator within 15 days following receipt of the waste.

F. Releases From Waste Management Units

When Congress enacted the 1984 Amendments, it mandated an extensive new program of corrective action at all TSD facilities.[160] EPA's implementing regulations, 40 C.F.R. part 264, Subpart F, require a monitoring and response program for every hazardous waste management facility. The requirements cover not only "regulated units," that is, hazardous waste treatment, storage, and disposal units, but also every "solid waste management unit" (SWMU) located at such, regardless of whether the unit manages hazardous or nonhazardous solid waste and regardless of when waste was placed in the SWMU. Pursuant to these rules, facilities with hazardous waste management units must conduct various monitoring and release response programs, as specified in the facility's RCRA permit.[161] Thus, EPA (or a state) will specify conditions in the facility permit designed to ensure that specified hazardous constituents from each of the facility's hazardous waste management units do

[155] 40 C.F.R. §264.74.

[156] *Id.*

[157] 40 C.F.R. §264.77.

[158] 40 C.F.R. §264.75.

[159] 40 C.F.R. §264.76.

[160] Section 3004(u), (v); 42 U.S.C. §6924(u), (v) (1988).

[161] A "solid waste management unit" is any surface impoundment, landfill, waste pile, or land treatment unit that receives solid waste. 47 Fed. Reg. 32,291 (1982).

not contaminate groundwater at levels in excess of specified concentration limits.[162] The facility owner/operator will be required under the facility permit to monitor, by means of a system of wells, groundwater quality at a specified "compliance point" (usually the limit of the facility's waste management area extending in the direction of groundwater flow).[163] EPA will generally specify concentration limits equivalent to any applicable drinking water quality limitation, although an alternate concentration limit can be established if EPA determines that a more lenient standard will not pose a threat to human health or the environment.[164]

EPA regulations require a three-stage groundwater protection program for all TSDs. First, every TSD must implement a "detection monitoring program," under which groundwater is sampled at intervals prescribed by the facility's permit to detect any statistically significant increase in the concentration of certain generic contaminants in the groundwater that might indicate a leaking unit. If such increases are detected, the facility must notify the Regional Administrator and implement a "compliance monitoring program," involving more specialized monitoring to confirm that hazardous constituents from the facility's units are contaminating the groundwater. If so, the facility must implement a corrective action program to find and correct the source of contamination so that groundwater at the compliance point will meet the applicable concentration limits.[165] The owner/operator of the TSD must perform corrective action beyond the facility boundary, that is, on other persons' property, if necessary to protect human health and the environment.[166] In addition to these programs with respect to a facility's hazardous waste units, the owner or operator has a blanket obligation to take corrective action for any SWMU at the facility "as necessary to protect human health and the environment."[167]

G. Closure and Postclosure Requirements

EPA regulations prescribe detailed standards for the deactivation or "closure" of a hazardous waste treatment, storage, or disposal facility and for its continued monitoring and maintenance subsequent to closure.[168] The regulations include a general "closure performance standard" under which a TSD must be closed in a manner that minimizes the need for further maintenance and prevents the escape of hazardous constituents that could present a hazard to human health or the environment. Every facility must, from its inception, have a closure plan describing how this standard will be met in the event of closure. The plan must accompany the facility's permit application and, upon approval by the Regional Administrator, becomes a condition of the permit.[169]

---

162 40 C.F.R. §264.93.
163 40 C.F.R. §264.95.
164 40 C.F.R. §264.94.
165 40 C.F.R. §264.91(a), .100.
166 40 C.F.R. §264.100.
167 40 C.F.R. §264.101.
168 40 C.F.R. §264.110.
169 40 C.F.R. §264.112.

Closure plans must include all steps necessary to close the facility at any time during its active life. The plan must include a description of the methods that will be used to remove hazardous wastes from the facility, steps to decontaminate the facility and its equipment, groundwater monitoring procedures, and a schedule for implementing the plan. The plan must be kept on file at the facility and can be changed only if approved by the Regional Administrator.[170]

The facility owner/operator must notify the Regional Administrator in writing at least 60 days before beginning closure of a TSD that includes a land disposal or storage unit (only 45-days notice is required for other facilities). Closure must begin not longer than 30 days after the known final receipt of hazardous wastes at the TSD, unless there is a reasonable expectation of further shipments. However, a facility must begin closure if no hazardous wastes have been received for at least one year after the most recent shipment (unless the Regional Administrator extends the deadline).[171]

EPA prescribes deadlines for completing intermediate steps towards closure. Thus, within 90 days of receiving the final volume of wastes (unless the Regional Administrator allows longer), a TSD facility must treat or remove all hazardous wastes at the facility or dispose of them on-site. Within 180 days, closure normally must be complete. Within 60 days of completion of closure, the owner or operator must submit to the Regional Administrator a certification, signed by an independent registered professional engineer, that the facility has been closed in accordance with the approved closure plan. In the case of a hazardous waste disposal facility, at the same time, the owner or operator must file with local zoning authorities a survey plat showing the location of hazardous waste disposal units and including a notation indicating that no subsequent owner will be permitted to disturb the closed unit.[172]

The owner or operator generally must provide postclosure care for a TSD facility for 30 years following closure.[173] This care must include continued groundwater monitoring and maintenance and monitoring of any waste containment systems, such as a cap. Again, postclosure care must be provided in accordance with an approved postclosure plan that is a part of the facility's RCRA permit. The plan must identify the maintenance and monitoring activities and identify who will be responsible for carrying out the postclosure activities. Within 60 days after completion of the postclosure period under the plan, the owner or operator must submit to EPA a certification by an independent registered professional engineer that the postclosure was performed in accordance with the EPA-approved plan.[174]

H. Financial Assurance

To ensure that facilities will have the resources necessary to complete proper closure and postclosure standards, EPA has promulgated extensive

[170] 40 C.F.R. §264.112(b).
[171] 40 C.F.R. §264.112(d).
[172] 40 C.F.R. §264.113–.116.
[173] 40 C.F.R. §264.117.
[174] 40 C.F.R. §264.118–.120.

financial requirements under the authority of RCRA section 3004(t).[175] The owner or operator of a TSD facility must prepare a detailed written estimate of the cost of closing the facility in accordance with the closure plan, as well as the cost of implementing any required postclosure care. The owner or operator must also establish "financial assurance" for the costs of closure or postclosure using one of several financial instruments prescribed by EPA's regulations.[176]

Closure cost estimates must equal the cost of final closure at the point in the facility's active life at which closure would be most expensive. The estimate must assume that the owner or operator will receive no allowances for the salvage value of wastes or waste equipment, and that third party contractors will perform the closure. Adjustments must take place annually for inflation and any time the facility closure plan is modified.

A facility may choose any of four financial instruments to assure accountability (or may, in some circumstances, use a combination of instruments): a closure trust fund, surety bond, letter of credit, or insurance policy. EPA has developed extremely detailed forms for each of these instruments. Alternatively, an owner or operator may, in effect, self-insure the closure by demonstrating to EPA that the company has a tangible net worth of at least $10 million and meets other criteria relating to net working capital, ratios of liabilities to assets, and total assets. Any person who is liable for financial assurance for closure or postclosure of a TSD facility should carefully review the relevant regulations, which are set forth at 40 C.F.R. §264.143–.147.

Similar requirements exist for liability coverage during the active life of a facility.[177] For all facilities, coverage must be maintained for bodily injury and property damage to third parties caused by sudden accidental occurrences arising from facility operations. The present minimum coverage is $1 million per occurrence with an annual aggregate of $2 million, exclusive of legal costs. Owners and operators of surface impoundments, landfills, land treatment facilities, or a miscellaneous disposal unit that is used to manage hazardous waste must also have coverage for damage to third parties caused by nonsudden accidental occurrences. The present minimum coverage for these facilities is $3 million per occurrence with an annual aggregate of $6 million. In both cases, the Regional Administrator may adjust coverage as necessary to protect human health and the environment. As with the authorized financial assurance instruments, EPA has prescribed a detailed form of Hazardous Waste Facility Liability Endorsement for such insurance.

I. Construction Quality Assurance

Every surface impoundment, waste pile, or landfill unit constructed after January 29, 1992, must have a construction quality assurance (CQA) program.[178] The CQA program must ensure that the new unit meets or exceeds all design criteria and specifications in the permit. The program must be developed

[175] 40 C.F.R. §264.140.
[176] 40 C.F.R. §264.142–.143.
[177] 40 C.F.R. §264.147.
[178] 40 C.F.R. §264.19.

and implemented by a registered professional engineer. A written CQA plan must be prepared, including schedules for observations, inspections, tests, and measurements, to ensure the proper construction and structural integrity of the new unit. The CQA officer must certify in writing to EPA that the unit meets all requirements before it commences operations.

J. Standards for Specific Types of TSD Facilities

In recognition of the varying circumstances under which hazardous waste is handled, EPA has provided additional regulations for numerous specific types of treatment, storage, and disposal facilities, including containers, tanks, surface impoundments, waste piles, land treatment facilities, landfills, incinerators, drip pads, and miscellaneous units, and for emissions of hazardous waste to the air from certain hazardous waste facilities. It is important to realize that one TSD site may include more than one type of management facility and be subject to multiple facility regulations. As with the general facility standards discussed above in Sections VI.A. through E., these standards are incorporated into permits for such facilities. As discussed in Section VIII, corresponding standards exist under EPA regulations governing interim status facilities pending issuance of permits to such facilities.

1. Containers

EPA standards for the use and management of containers[179] apply to every facility that stores hazardous waste in containers. A container is defined in the regulations as a "portable device in which a material is stored, transported, treated, disposed of, or otherwise handled." Containers must be made of a material that is compatible with the contents. Containers must always be closed, except when waste is added or removed. Containers must be inspected at least weekly. Areas where containers are stored must be sufficiently impervious to deter leaks of spilled material and must have secondary containment systems such that leaking wastes or precipitation run-on can be collected. All containers holding ignitable or reactive waste must be located at least 50 feet from the facility's property line. Incompatible wastes must be separately containerized and stored in separate areas. At closure, all hazardous waste and waste residues must be removed and the containers must be decontaminated or removed.

2. Tank Systems

When Congress amended RCRA in 1984, it required EPA to establish a new regulatory regime for tanks in which hazardous wastes are managed. Under EPA's implementing regulations, adopted July 14, 1986, every hazardous waste tank—whether above or underground—must meet specific standards for design, operation, inspection, and spill control.[180] For purposes of these standards, a tank is defined as a "stationary device, designed to contain an accumulation of

---

[179] 40 C.F.R. §264.170–.178.

[180] 40 C.F.R. §264.190–.199. Underground tanks that contain petroleum or nonhazardous waste chemicals are regulated under EPA's Underground Storage Tank (UST) regulations. 40 C.F.R. pt. 280. The UST regulations are discussed in Chapter 13, Standards for Storage Tank Facilities.

hazardous waste, which is constructed primarily of nonearthen materials (for example, wood, concrete, steel, plastic) which provide structural support." Partial exemptions apply to tank systems that are used to store or treat hazardous waste that contain no free liquids and are situated inside a building with an impermeable floor, as well as for tanks that are part of a secondary containment system.[181]

The regulations establish different requirements for new tanks and for existing tanks, that is, those in existence before EPA adopted the regulations on July 14, 1986. New tank systems must, of course, receive an EPA permit. As part of the permit application, the owner or operator must certify in writing that the new system has sufficient structural integrity and is otherwise acceptable for storing hazardous waste. Installation must accord with rules for materials, ancillary equipment, and corrosion protection and must be closely supervised by both the owner or operator and by a qualified installation inspector or professional engineer. The tank must be tested for tightness before being covered or placed in service. The owner or operator must maintain on file at the facility written statements from the professionals involved that the tank was properly designed and installed.[182]

New tank systems must have a secondary containment system designed and installed to prevent any migration of wastes from the system to the environment and capable of detecting and holding releases until they can be cleaned up.[183] Secondary containment systems must include a leak-detection system capable of detecting a leak soon enough to permit the cleanup of leaked wastes within 24 hours. Secondary containment structures must include an external liner, vault, double-walled tank, or equivalent device. The regulations specify design and performance standards for each of these types of containment.[184] Ancillary equipment, such as connecting pipes, also must be equipped with secondary containment systems.[185]

EPA regulations provide for a phased upgrading of existing hazardous waste tank systems to include secondary containment. Existing tanks storing certain specified wastes were required to have secondary containment systems by January 12, 1989. All existing tanks known to be more than seven years old must install secondary containment by January 12, 1989, or when the tank is 15 years old, whichever comes later. All other tanks must have secondary containment by January 12, 1995.[186]

In addition, any existing tank that does not have secondary containment was required to have on file by January 12, 1988, a written certification by an independent, qualified registered professional engineer that, based on a leak test or inspection, the tank is not leaking and is fit for use. This evaluation is also required for tanks holding newly designated hazardous wastes within 12 months of the hazardous waste designation. Pending the installation of secondary containment systems, every existing tank must be tested for leaks at least

---

[181] 40 C.F.R. §264.190(a), (b).
[182] 40 C.F.R. §264.192.
[183] 40 C.F.R. §264.193(b).
[184] 40 C.F.R. §264.193(c), (d).
[185] 40 C.F.R. §264.193(f).
[186] 40 C.F.R. §264.193(a).

annually or in accordance with a schedule developed by an independent engineer.

EPA regulations require the owner or operator of a tank system to operate the unit so as to prevent spills and overflows. Every aboveground tank and its containment system must be inspected for leaks daily. Inspections must be documented in the facility's operating record.

Any tank—new or existing—from which there has been a leak or spill must be removed from service immediately (unless the leak or spill is of less than one pound of hazardous waste and is cleaned up immediately). The owner or operator must stop the flow of waste into the tank and determine the cause of the release. The leak must be reported to EPA and leaked wastes cleaned up within 24 hours of detection. A more detailed follow-up report must be submitted to EPA within 30 days of the incident. Unless the tank system is repaired and provided with secondary containment for any underground portion of the system that leaked, the system must be closed.[187]

When a tank system is removed from service, closure requirements similar to those generally applicable to all TSDs apply. Significantly, if contaminated soils remain at the site after removal or decontamination of the system, the owner or operator must provide the same postclosure care that would be required for a closed hazardous waste landfill.[188]

3. *Surface Impoundments*

EPA regulations impose detailed design and operating requirements on the owners and operators of surface impoundments that are used to treat, store, or dispose of hazardous wastes.[189] For surface impoundments in existence prior to November 8, 1984, final permit standards do not require a liner for existing portions of such impoundments. However, every new surface impoundment, or new or replacement surface impoundment unit at an existing facility, must have a double liner system and a system to collect leachate between the liners. The upper liner must be designed and constructed to prevent the migration of any hazardous waste constituent through the liner, for example, a geomembrane. The lower liner must consist of at least two components, including an upper component through which hazardous constituents cannot penetrate, for example, a geomembrane, and a lower component designed and constructed of materials that will minimize further migration in the event of a breakthrough in the upper component. This lower component must be constructed of at least three feet of compacted soil with a permeability of no more than 1×10^{-7} centimeter per second.[190] The leachate collection system between the upper and lower liners must also be capable of detecting, collecting, and removing leaks of hazardous constituents from the upper liner. The regulations specify design and construction standards for such a system, including the drainage materials that should be placed between the liners and a pumping system to remove liquids from backing up into the drainage layer.[191]

---

[187] 40 C.F.R. §264.196.

[188] 40 C.F.R. §264.197.

[189] 40 C.F.R. §264.220–.231.

[190] 40 C.F.R. §264.221(c).

[191] 40 C.F.R. §264.221.

EPA's Regional Administrator may waive the double liner requirement for a surface impoundment if the owner or operator demonstrates that an alternative design, together with the location characteristics, will prevent the migration of any hazardous constituents into groundwater or surface water at least as effectively as would the double liner system.[192]

All surface impoundments must be constructed and operated to prevent overflows of wastes. All such facilities must have dikes sufficient to contain any such overflows, with an independent engineer's certification as to the dikes' structural integrity.[193] While a surface impoundment is in operation, it must be inspected weekly for evidence of deterioration of the impoundment or its dikes and for sudden drops in the level of the impoundment's contents.

The owner or operator of a new surface impoundment must record weekly the amounts of liquid removed from the leak detection system. All such new impoundments are subject to an "action leakage rate" to be set by the Regional Administrator.[194] The action leakage rate is the maximum flow of liquid that the leak detection system can effectively remove so as to prevent accumulation in the space above the bottom liner. If this rate is exceeded, the owner or operator must notify EPA and implement a response action plan to determine the source of the leak and, if necessary, repair it.

If a problem is detected, the impoundment must be removed from service and emergency procedures undertaken in accordance with the facility's contingency plan. If the impoundment is found to leak, it must be lined or closed. In any case, the impoundment cannot be returned to service without an independent engineer's certification of its integrity.[195]

At closure of an impoundment, whether scheduled or not, the owner or operator must remove or decontaminate all waste residues, equipment, liners, and underlying soils. If such "clean closure" is not feasible, the impoundment's remaining contents must be stabilized and the impoundment must be covered with a final cover that will minimize migration of liquids through the closed impoundment and is no more permeable than the underlying bottom liner or subsoil. If wastes remain in or under the impoundment after closure, the facility is subject to the standards for closure and postclosure care (including groundwater monitoring) as if it were a landfill.[196]

4. *Waste Piles*

Owners and operators of facilities that store or treat hazardous waste in piles must comply with standards for design, operation, monitoring, and inspection.[197] A pile is defined as "any non-containerized accumulation of solid,

---

[192] 40 C.F.R. §264.221(d). Under certain conditions, the Regional Administrator also may waive the double liner requirement for a surface impoundment that is a monofill containing only hazardous wastes from foundry furnace emission controls or metal casting molding sand that are hazardous only due to the toxicity characteristic. 40 C.F.R. §261.221(e).

[193] 40 C.F.R. §264.221(f), (g).

[194] 40 C.F.R. §264.222–.223.

[195] 40 C.F.R. §264.227. In addition to the requirements applicable to all hazardous waste impoundment, certain hazardous wastes cannot be managed in a surface impoundment without special approval of a management plan by the EPA Regional Administrator. *See* 40 C.F.R. §264.231.

[196] 40 C.F.R. §264.228.

[197] 40 C.F.R. §264.250–.259.

nonflowing hazardous waste that is used for treatment or storage." The regulations contemplate that hazardous waste will be held in piles temporarily for storage and/or treatment. If wastes are left in a pile permanently, the pile is subject to regulation as a hazardous waste landfill.[198] Waste piles that are located indoors or under roof are subject to reduced requirements.

Any permitted waste pile (except existing portions of a waste pile) must be placed on a lined surface that will prevent migration of hazardous constituents through the liner. The liner must be constructed of appropriate material, have adequate support, and cover all surrounding earth likely to be in contact with the waste or leachate. Waste piles must also have a leachate collection and removal system to protect against soil, groundwater, and surface water contamination. The leachate control system must be constructed so as not to be damaged by the weight of wastes or of operating equipment.

New waste piles or expansions of existing ones must have at least two liners and a leachate collection system. These liner and leachate collection/treatment standards are substantially identical to those applicable to surface impoundments, discussed above. As with new surface impoundments, every new waste pile is subject to an action leakage rate that will trigger a requirement for investigation and possible remedial action to repair a leak in the upper liner.

Waste piles also must have a system to control stormwater run-on and run-off and to treat collected precipitation.[199] If the pile contains particulate matter, it must be covered or other steps taken to prevent wind dispersal.[200] The Regional Administrator is authorized to specify any additional design or operating practices necessary to achieve the standards of the regulations applicable to piles.[201] Conversely, all of these controls can be waived if the facility demonstrates an equally effective alternative to the Regional Administrator.

Construction and installation of liners must be monitored for uniformity, damage, and imperfections. Inspection will continue during the life of the waste pile for evidence of deterioration or malfunctions in run-on/run-off and leachate collection systems.[202]

Ignitable or reactive wastes must be treated so that they no longer exhibit these characteristics or placed in a pile in such a way that the waste is not exposed to conditions that could trigger ignition or reaction.[203] Incompatible wastes may not be placed in the same pile without taking precautions against a reaction.[204] Some specific hazardous wastes may not be placed in piles that are not enclosed unless the owner or operator employs a special management plan approved by the Regional Administrator in addition to all other applicable requirements.[205]

Closure of a hazardous waste pile requires the removal or decontamination of all waste residues, contaminated containment system components, contaminated subsoils, and structures and equipment contaminated with waste and

---

[198] 40 C.F.R. §264.250(b).
[199] 40 C.F.R. §264.250(d), (e).
[200] 40 C.F.R. §264.250(f).
[201] 40 C.F.R. §264.251(k).
[202] 40 C.F.R. §264.254.
[203] 40 C.F.R. §264.256.
[204] 40 C.F.R. §264.257.
[205] Hazardous wastes F020, F021, F022, F023, F026, and F027. 40 C.F.R. §264.259.

leachate. These must be managed as hazardous waste. If decontamination of the subsoil is not practical, postclosure in accordance with the landfill regulations will be required.

5. *Land Treatment Facilities*

EPA's standards for land treatment reflect the fact that this is not a favored form of hazardous waste management.[206] A land treatment facility is defined in the regulations as "a facility or part of a facility at which hazardous waste is applied onto or incorporated into the soil surface; such facilities are disposal facilities if the waste will remain after closure."[207] In general, this management system contemplates a process—the placement of hazardous wastes directly into the environment—that EPA's regulations for other types of facilities seek to avoid.[208]

Any land treatment program must ensure that all hazardous constituents are degraded, transformed, or immobilized within the surface and subsurface treatment zone.[209] Such a program, which is included in the facility's permit, must include three components. First, the program must identify those wastes that the unit is capable of treating. The owner or operator must demonstrate that the hazardous constituents in each waste can be completely degraded, transformed, or immobilized in the treatment zone.[210] Second, the program must specify design measures and operating practices necessary to maximize the success of degradation, transformation, and immobilization processes. These measures include elements such as rate and method of waste application, measures to minimize leaching, and inspection procedures. As with waste piles, a run-on and run-off program must be established.[211] Third, a facility permit must include a program for monitoring the unsaturated zone to determine whether hazardous constituents will migrate from the treatment zone.[212] The monitoring program must include soil cores and soil-pore liquid monitoring devices (lysimeters) in the treatment zone. The details of the monitoring program, including the frequency of sampling, are determined by the Regional Administrator. If a statistically significant change over background levels of any relevant constituent is discovered that is attributable to the land treatment operation, the owner or operator must modify the facility's operating practices to improve the effectiveness of the degradation, transformation, or immobilization processes in the treatment zone.[213]

The Regional Administrator must specify in the facility permit the location and depth of the authorized zone of treatment. The zone may not be deeper than

---

[206] 40 C.F.R. §260.270–.283.

[207] 40 C.F.R. §260.10.

[208] For example, see the regulations applicable to tank systems and waste piles. 40 C.F.R. §264.190–.199, .250–.259.

[209] 40 C.F.R. §264.271.

[210] 40 C.F.R. §264.272. The "treatment zone" is the portion of the unsaturated zone below and including the land surface in which the owner or operator intends to maintain the conditions necessary to achieve the requirements of the regulations. The zone can be no greater than five feet underground and no less than three feet above the water table. 40 C.F.R. §264.271(c).

[211] 40 C.F.R. §264.273.

[212] 40 C.F.R. §264.278.

[213] 40 C.F.R. §264.278(a), (b), (c), (d), (g).

five feet below the surface and must be at least three feet above the seasonal high water table.[214]

The permit must forbid the farming of food-chain crops on the land treatment facility unless the owner or operator demonstrates that there is no substantial risk to human health caused by the growth of such crops.[215] It must be shown that the hazardous constituents in the waste will not be transferred to the crop by uptake and will not be ingested by grazing animals, or will not be transferred in concentrations greater than found in the same crop grown on untreated soils in the same region. In addition, EPA further limits strictly the application of cadmium-bearing wastes to crop lands on which animal feed is grown, including a maximum application rate of 0.5 kilograms per hectare.[216]

EPA regulations also restrict the application of ignitable, reactive, or incompatible hazardous wastes to the land treatment zone unless the waste is rendered nonhazardous or isolated from substances that may trigger a reaction.[217]

Closure of a land treatment unit consists largely of establishing a vegetative cover. Principal requirements during the postclosure period include maintenance of the facility's run-on/run-off systems and continued unsaturated zone monitoring.[218]

6. *Landfills*

EPA regulations impose detailed design and operating requirements on the owners and operators of hazardous waste landfills.[219] Most important, every new landfill, or new or replacement landfill unit at, or lateral expansion of, an existing facility, must have a double liner system and a system to collect leachate both above and between the liners. These liner and leachate collection/treatment standards are substantially identical to those applicable to surface impoundments and waste piles discussed above. As with those facilities, every new landfill is subject to an action leakage rate that will trigger a requirement for investigation and possible remedial action to repair a leak in the upper liner.

EPA's Regional Administrator may waive the double liner requirement for a landfill if the owner or operator demonstrates that an alternative design, together with the location characteristics, will prevent the migration of any hazardous constituents into groundwater or surface water at least as effectively as would the double liner system.[220]

Operational requirements for landfills include a system to prevent the run-on or run-off of stormwater from a 25-year peak storm.[221] The rules generally

---

[214] 40 C.F.R. §264.271(c).

[215] 40 C.F.R. §264.276.

[216] 40 C.F.R. §264.276.

[217] 40 C.F.R. §264.281.

[218] *See* 40 C.F.R. §264.280.

[219] 40 C.F.R. §264.300–.317.

[220] 40 C.F.R. §264.301(d). No waiver is permitted for any landfill located in Alabama. 40 C.F.R. §264.301(1). Under certain conditions, the Regional Administrator also may waive the double liner requirement for a landfill that is a monofill containing only hazardous wastes from foundry furnace emission controls or metal casting molding sand and which are hazardous only due to the toxicity characteristic. 40 C.F.R. §261.301(e).

[221] 40 C.F.R. §264.301(f).

forbid placement of ignitable or reactive wastes in landfills, although an exception is made for properly containerized ignitable wastes. Significantly, bulk or noncontainerized liquid waste or waste containing free liquid is prohibited. Containers holding free liquid can be landfilled only if the free liquids are first removed or mixed in the container with absorbent materials.[222]

In order to close a landfill (or cell within a landfill), the owner or operator must cover it with a final cover that will minimize over the long term the migration of liquids into the landfill and is no more permeable than the underlying bottom liner or subsoil. In addition to the generally applicable postclosure care required under 40 C.F.R. §264.117 for all TSD facilities, the owner or operator must continue to operate the leachate collection system, monitor the groundwater, and maintain the integrity and effectiveness of the final cover throughout the postclosure period.[223]

7. *Incinerators*

EPA's regulations for hazardous waste incinerators are the most complex of all of the TSD facility requirements.[224] For purposes of the regulations, an "incinerator" is defined as any "enclosed device that . . . [u]ses controlled flame combustion and neither meets the criteria for classification as a boiler, sludge dryer, or carbon regeneration, nor is listed as an industrial furnace."[225] First, every hazardous waste incinerator must meet a basic performance standard, viz., it must be designed, constructed, and maintained so that it achieves a destruction and removal efficiency (DRE) of 99.99 percent for each principal organic hazardous constituent (POHC) in the facility's waste feed, as specified in the facility's permit.[226] Second, incinerators that emit more than 1.8 kilograms per hour of hydrogen chloride (HCl) must either meet that limit or achieve a 99 percent reduction in HCl emissions through treatment of stack gas. Third, incinerators may not emit particulate matter in excess of 180 milligrams per dry standard cubic meter.

A hazardous waste incinerator may burn only wastes specified in its permit and only under operating conditions specified for those wastes. Development of permit terms and conditions is a two-step process. The first step is to conduct a trial burn. The owner or operator must apply for a trial burn permit by providing the EPA with a trial burn plan, containing information on the wastes to be burned, including hazardous organic constituents, and detailed information regarding waste feed rates and operating conditions.[227] The Regional Administrator must approve the trial burn plan if he or she finds that the trial burn is likely to demonstrate whether the incinerator can meet the required DRE for POHCs designated by the Regional Administrator, provided that the trial burn will not present an imminent hazard to human health or the environment.[228]

---

[222] 40 C.F.R. §264.312, .313, .314. For special provisions relating to disposal of small containers of hazardous waste in overpacked drums (lab packs), *see* 40 C.F.R. §301.316.

[223] 40 C.F.R. §264.310.

[224] 40 C.F.R. §264.340–.351.

[225] 40 C.F.R. §260.10. The definition also explicitly includes an infrared incinerator or plasma arc incinerator.

[226] 40 C.F.R. §264.343. An incinerator burning hazardous wastes FO20, FO21, F022, FO23, FO26, or FO27 must achieve a DRE of 99.9999% for each POHC.

[227] 40 C.F.R. §270.62.

[228] 40 C.F.R. §270.62(a)(5).

Based on the results, the second step is for the Regional Administrator to set operating requirements in the final permit. For each waste feed, the permit will specify operating limits including carbon monoxide level in the stack exhaust gas, waste feed rate, combustion temperature, combustion gas velocity, allowable variations in system design or operation, and such other operating requirements as are necessary to ensure that the performance standards are met.[229] When the facility is operating, the owner or operator must monitor combustion temperature, waste feed rate, combustion gas velocity, carbon monoxide, as well as visually inspect the incinerator and associated equipment daily and test the emergency waste feed cutoff system at least weekly.[230] Unless it is subsequently determined that the operating procedures specified in the permit are not achieving the performance standards applicable to the facility, compliance with the operating procedures is deemed to be compliance with these performance standards.[231]

As with all other types of TSD facilities, incinerators must comply with the generally applicable closure standards. In addition, the owner or operator must remove all hazardous waste and residues, such as ash, scrubber sludges, and scrubber waters, from the incinerator site.[232]

8. *Drip Pads*

EPA regulations include specific standards for drip pads that convey treated wood drippage, precipitation, or surface water run-on to an associated collection system, where such material is a hazardous waste.[233] The definition of "drip pad" elsewhere in the regulations limits the application of these standards to drip pads located at wood preserving plants.[234] Design and operational standards govern both previously existing and newly installed drip pads. For existing drip pads, the owner or operator must conduct an evaluation, reviewed and certified by an independent engineer to ensure compliance with the standards. All necessary upgrading, repairing, and modifying must be accomplished in accordance with a certified, written plan within the time specified by the regulations.

Closure and postclosure requirements are similar to the parallel rules for waste piles discussed above. All waste residues, contaminated containment system components, contaminated subsoils, and structures and equipment contaminated with waste and leakage must be removed or decontaminated and managed as hazardous waste. If total removal or decontamination of the subsoil cannot be practicably accomplished, closure in accordance with the landfill regulations will be required.

---

[229] 40 C.F.R. §264.345.

[230] 40 C.F.R. §264.347.

[231] 40 C.F.R. §264.343(d).

[232] 40 C.F.R. §264.351.

[233] 40 C.F.R. §224.570–.574.

[234] A "drip pad" is "an engineered structure consisting of a curbed, free-draining base, constructed of non-earthen materials and designed to convey preservative kick-back or drippage from treated wood, precipitation, and surface water run-on to an associated collection system at wood preserving plants. 40 C.F.R. §260.10.

9. Process Vents and Equipment Leaks

In 1990, EPA expanded its hazardous waste facility standards to regulate, for the first time, emissions of hazardous wastes to the air at certain facilities. EPA adopted air emission standards for process vents associated with distillation, fractionation, evaporation, solvent extraction, or air or steam stripping operations conducted at a permitted TSD facility or hazardous waste recycling facility that handles hazardous waste with an average total organic concentration of at least 10 parts per million.[235] Basically, the owner or operator of such a facility must either reduce total organic emissions from all process vents below specified limits (3.0 pounds per hour and 3.1 tons per year) or reduce, through emission controls, total organic emissions from such vents by 95 percent.[236]

Extensive recordkeeping is required to document compliance with the standard, including data identifying all affected process vents, throughput and operating hours for each unit, emissions rates and reductions achieved by add-on control devices based either on engineering calculations or tests, and a performance test plan for acquiring such test data.[237] Owners and operators must submit a semiannual report to EPA on the control device's performance, including dates when emissions exceeded allowable limits.

A companion standard, also applicable to permitted hazardous waste management facilities or hazardous waste recyclers, is intended to control air emissions from equipment leaks. The standard applies to specified equipment that contains or contacts hazardous wastes with organic concentrations of at least 10 percent by weight.[238] In general, the standard requires that every affected pump be visually inspected weekly and tested monthly for leaks. Compressors must be sealed and operated in a manner that will prevent emissions to the atmosphere and must be equipped with a leak sensor and alarm system. Leaks from pumps or compressors must be repaired within 15 days of detection.[239] Inspection, monitoring, and repair standards also are prescribed for pressure relief devices, sampling connections, and certain valves.

As in the case of process vents, the owner or operator of an affected facility containing such equipment must maintain a record of all such equipment in the facility and the materials to which the equipment is exposed, and a log of all inspections, monitoring, tests, and repairs.[240] A semiannual report must be submitted to EPA with information about any unrepaired valve, pump, or compressor.[241]

10. Miscellaneous Units

EPA has promulgated standards applicable to those types of TSD facilities not covered elsewhere by the regulations.[242] Because specific design and operational standards are not possible, these regulations focus on environmental

[235] 40 C.F.R. §264.1030–.1036.
[236] 40 C.F.R. §264.1032.
[237] 40 C.F.R. §264.1035(b)(2).
[238] 40 C.F.R. §264.1050–.1065.
[239] 40 C.F.R. §264.1051, .1053.
[240] 40 C.F.R. §264.1064.
[241] 40 C.F.R. §264.1065.
[242] 40 C.F.R. §264.600–.603.

performance standards that will ensure protection of human health and the environment. Permits for such facilities are required to contain such terms and provisions as are necessary to protect human health and the environment, including any of the standards applicable to other types of TSD facilities as may be appropriate. The performance standards are primarily designed to prevent the migration of hazardous waste into and through (1) the groundwater and subsurface environment, (2) the surface water or wetlands or surface soil, and (3) the air.

VII. RCRA Permit Process

RCRA sections 3005(a)–(d) provide for the permitting of TSD facilities. A nonpermitted facility may not operate unless it qualifies for interim status while awaiting final permit approval. (Requirements for interim status are discussed in Section VIII. below.)

EPA's regulations prescribe a two-part permit application process.[243] The owner or operator of a facility must submit a Part A application as soon as it falls under RCRA's waste management scheme.[244] For preexisting facilities, this submission is sufficient, if coupled with proper notification, for operation under interim status until the date set by the regulation for submission of the Part B application.[245] New facilities must simultaneously submit both the Part A and Part B applications at least 180 days before physical construction is expected to begin.[246]

A. The Part A Application

The Part A application is the less burdensome step in the application process. It provides EPA with basic notice and operational information and is intended as a precursor to the much more involved Part B application. Part A consists of Forms 1 and 3 of the EPA's Consolidated Permit Application Forms.[247] Form 3 must include the following information:

1. The activities conducted by the applicant that require it to obtain a permit under RCRA.
2. The name, address, and location of the facility.
3. The name, address, and telephone number of both the owner and the operator of the facility.
4. Whether the facility is new or existing. Existing facilities must also include photographs and drawings of the complex delineating all past, present, and future treatment, storage and disposal areas.
5. The types and quantities of hazardous wastes to be managed.

---

[243] 40 C.F.R. pt. 270.

[244] 40 C.F.R. §270.10.

[245] Under 40 C.F.R. §270.10, EPA may request the Part B application in advance of this deadline.

[246] 40 C.F.R. §270.1(b).

[247] 40 C.F.R. §270.1(b). Form 1 is a general information form filled out by applicants for permits under any one of a number of federal environmental statutes. These are RCRA, the Safe Drinking Water Act, the Clean Water Act, the Clean Air Act, and the Marine Protection, Research, and Sanctuaries Act.

6. A description of the processes to be used for managing the hazardous waste, and the design capacity of these items.
7. A topographic map (or other map if unavailable) of the facility and surrounding area.[248]

B. The Part B Application

New TSD facilities must submit a Part B application simultaneous with the Part A application and must receive a final RCRA permit before construction begins. Facilities operating under interim status must submit Part B of the permit application according to the statutory schedule for the various types of facilities or when requested to do so by EPA or the authorized state.[249] The regulations provide a list of the information necessary in the Part B application. All such information must be included unless the owner or operator can demonstrate that it cannot be provided to the extent required. A case-by-case determination of the information provided will be made in these circumstances. The following is a partial list of information to be included in a Part B application:

1. A description of the facility and surrounding area, including its location, topographic studies of the area, the geologic history of the area, aerial photographs of the area, and traffic patterns.
2. Emergency and safety information, including security and inspection procedures, the contingency plan, accident prevention and response procedures and equipment, and employee training programs.
3. Information about hazardous waste use and management at the facility, including chemical and physical analyses of the wastes handled, the waste analysis plan, the management and operation of each solid waste management unit, and the closure and postclosure plans.[250]

In addition to the above data, some of which must be provided by a registered professional engineer, specified data for each type of TSD facility must be provided.[251]

C. Procedure for Review

RCRA permits are issued in accordance with EPA's consolidated permit regulations at 40 C.F.R. part 124, Subpart A. However, before processing may begin, the applicant must fully comply with the requirements at 40 C.F.R. §§270.10 and 270.13.[252] Thus, a completed Part A application must be properly signed and filed with EPA. EPA has the authority to request any information necessary for completion.

For "major new facilities," EPA must prepare and mail to applicants a project decision schedule specifying key target dates. The schedule specifies

[248] 40 C.F.R. §270.13.
[249] 40 C.F.R. §270.10(f).
[250] 40 C.F.R. §270.14.
[251] 40 C.F.R. §270.15–.26.
[252] 40 C.F.R. §124.3.

target dates for the issuance of a draft permit, public notice, completion of the public comment period, and issuance of the final permit.[253]

EPA must then tentatively decide whether to issue a notice of intention to deny the permit or to issue a draft permit. If a draft permit is issued, it must include the following:

1. All conditions, compliance schedules, and monitoring requirements under the RCRA regulations at 40 C.F.R. §270.31–.33.[254]
2. Either a statement of basis or a fact sheet. A statement of basis is a short description of the derivation of the conditions of the draft permit or, in the casc of permit denial, an explanation of the reasons for denying the permit.[255] A fact sheet, required for all major facilities, is a more extensive explanation of the methodology used by EPA in reaching its tentative decision to accept or deny the application.[256]

Public notice and an opportunity for public comment will follow for tentative denials or grants of a draft permit.[257] Public notice and comment is unnecessary when a request for permit modification, revocation and reissuance, or termination is denied. RCRA permit decisions require a 45-day comment period. A public hearing may be held at EPA's discretion and must be conducted whenever EPA finds, on the basis of requests, a significant degree of public interest in a draft permit or whenever EPA receives written notice of opposition to a draft permit. Public notice must be given at least 30 days before any public hearing.[258]

Following the public comment period, EPA must issue a response to comments and a final permit decision.[259] Any interested person may petition EPA for review within 30 days of a final permit decision.[260] Any person may petition for review of those portions of the final permit decision that are different from the draft permit. However, only the applicant and persons who file comments or participate in the public hearing may petition for review of any other portion of the permit decision. Within a reasonable time thereafter, EPA may deny the petition for review (in which case the relevant conditions of the final permit decision become final agency action), grant the petition for review and remand the proceedings, or defer consideration until the completion of any simultaneous National Pollutant Discharge Elimination System (NPDES) permit proceedings. Persons dissatisfied with EPA's denial of a petition for review may ultimately seek judicial review of the final agency action.

---

[253] 40 C.F.R. §124.3(g). Whether a new TSD facility is a "major" facility is determined by EPA or the relevant state agency. 40 C.F.R. §124.2(a).

[254] *Id.*

[255] 40 C.F.R. §124.7.

[256] 40 C.F.R. §124.8.

[257] 40 C.F.R. §124.10.

[258] 40 C.F.R. §124.12.

[259] 40 C.F.R. §124.15, .17.

[260] 40 C.F.R. §124.19.

D. Permit Conditions

Subpart C of 40 C.F.R. part 270 prescribes conditions applicable to all RCRA permits. Every permit must require the permittee to

1. Properly operate and maintain all facilities and systems of treatment and control in accordance with the permit;
2. Provide relevant information to EPA upon request;
3. Allow access to and inspection of the facility and facility records upon reasonable request by EPA;
4. Monitor and keep records of all monitoring information, for the purposes of assuring permit compliance or as otherwise authorized by RCRA, of any substance or parameters at any location; and
5. Report any planned physical or operational changes at the facility.[261]

The express purpose of these conditions is to achieve compliance with the Act and the permit must include terms necessary to protect human health and the environment.[262] To achieve this goal, EPA or the authorized state agency may establish additional conditions on a case-by-case basis.[263] Compliance with these specified conditions need not always be immediate and may be in accordance with a written schedule of compliance, complete with interim compliance dates and reporting requirements.[264] Noncompliance, unless authorized in an emergency permit, is a violation of the Act and grounds for enforcement action, revocation, modification, or for denial of a permit renewal application.[265]

By contrast, compliance with a RCRA permit expressly constitutes compliance with RCRA Subtitle C for purposes of enforcement.[266] Such compliance does not, however, cover requirements not included in the permit that become effective by statute or concern placement of hazardous waste on the land under 40 C.F.R. part 268 or leak detection systems under part 264.

E. Permit Modification, Revocation, and Reissuance

EPA may unilaterally modify or revoke and reissue a RCRA TSD permit for cause or when EPA receives notice of a proposed transfer of the facility.[267] Causes for permit modification or revocation include prior permit noncompliance, misrepresentation or lack of full disclosure by the permittee, or a determination that the permitted activity endangers human health or the environment. If no cause exists, modification or revocation and reissuance may only take place at the request of the permittee when

1. There are material and substantial alterations or additions to the permitted facility or activity;

---

[261] 40 C.F.R. §270.30.
[262] 40 C.F.R. §270.32.
[263] *Id.*
[264] 40 C.F.R. §270.33.
[265] 40 C.F.R. §270.30(a).
[266] 40 C.F.R. §270.4.
[267] 40 C.F.R. §270.41(b).

2. Information received by EPA since issuance of the existing permit would have justified the application of different permit conditions;
3. New statutory requirements or regulations exist; or
4. EPA determines good cause exists for modification of a compliance schedule.[268]

If modified, only those conditions subject to modification are reopened. If revoked and reissued, the entire permit is reopened.

The regulations contemplate three different types of permit modification depending on the extent of the permitted changes. The simplest changes are categorized as Class 1 modifications. This covers circumstances such as administrative and information changes and other minor changes to conform with Agency guidance or regulations.[269] If EPA rejects a requested Class 1 modification, EPA must notify the permittee of such rejection. Generally, such changes are allowed without express EPA approval.

Class 2 modifications require agency approval following a formal submission by the permittee and a chance for public comment.[270] Such modifications may involve changes to emergency procedure and more significant Class 1 type changes. If EPA determines that the changes are important enough to warrant full-scale administrative procedure, the more extensive Class 3 procedure may be implemented.

Class 3 modifications are the major changes to the TSD facility or its operation. They require a formal submission by permittee and full notice and a 60-day comment period complete with public hearing.[271] At the conclusion of the comment period, EPA must grant or deny the modification request and respond to all significant public comments.

F. Expiration and Continuation of Permits

Unless otherwise specified by EPA for a shorter period, RCRA TSD permits are effective for 10 years from the date of issuance.[272] Land disposal facility permits must be reviewed and modified as necessary after five years. During review or following expiration, the conditions of the previously existing permit remain fully effective and enforceable.

G. Permits by Rule

Certain facilities are deemed to be permitted without formal application.[273] This system applies to ocean disposal barges or vessels that are permitted for ocean dumping under the Marine Protection, Research, and Sanctuaries Act, so long as such facilities are in compliance with the dumping permit and a small

---

[268] 40 C.F.R. §270.41(a).

[269] 40 C.F.R. §270.42(a). Changes are categorized by class in app. I to §270.42. If a change is not listed in the appendix, it will be categorized Class 3 unless EPA determines, based upon submissions by the permittee, otherwise. 40 C.F.R. §270.42(d).

[270] 40 C.F.R. §270.42(b).

[271] 40 C.F.R. §270.42(c).

[272] 40 C.F.R. §270.50.

[273] 40 C.F.R. §270.60.

number of minor RCRA requirements. Injection wells with underground injection control (UIC) permits under 40 C.F.R. part 144 or 145 are also permitted by rule. Lastly, a publicly owned sewage treatment works that accepts hazardous waste for treatment is deemed to have a permit if the POTW possesses and is in compliance with an NPDES permit under the Clean Water Act.

H. Special RCRA Permits

The regulations provide for a number of special permits to fit various circumstances. Among these are emergency permits, temporary operating permits for hazardous waste incinerators, permits for land treatment demonstrations, and research, development, and demonstration permits.[274] All special RCRA permits are likewise subject to immediate termination if necessary to protect human health and the environment.

An emergency permit may be issued by EPA to allow a nonpermitted facility to treat, store, or dispose of hazardous wastes in order to prevent an imminent and substantial endangerment to human health or the environment.[275] Such permits may be issued for up to 90 days and can be terminated by EPA at any time without notice or hearing when appropriate to protect human health and the environment.

Temporary hazardous waste incinerator permits may be issued to allow temporary operation of a new facility in order to determine operational readiness.[276] EPA may issue this permit for the minimum time required to bring the incinerator to a point of operational readiness to conduct a trial burn, not to exceed 720 hours operating time for the treatment of hazardous waste. When cause is shown, EPA may extend the permit once for up to an additional 720 hours.

Permits for land treatment demonstrations are issued by EPA to allow an owner or operator to meet the treatment demonstration requirements of 40 C.F.R. part 264, Subpart M.[277] As with incinerator permits, the conditions included will serve as the basis for the final facility permit.

Research and development permits may be issued to facilities that propose to use an innovative and experimental hazardous waste treatment technology.[278] Such permits may be issued for up to one year, renewable for three additional one-year periods.

VIII. Interim Status Facilities

Section 3005 of RCRA generally requires every TSD facility to obtain a permit. However, under section 3005(e), facilities that were in existence as of November 19, 1980 (or such later date upon which they first become subject to

---

[274] Also included are interim permits for UIC wells and temporary permits for boilers and industrial furnaces burning hazardous waste. *See* 40 C.F.R. §270.61–.66.

[275] 40 C.F.R. §270.61.

[276] 40 C.F.R. §270.62.

[277] 40 C.F.R. §270.63.

[278] 40 C.F.R. §270.65.

the permit requirement) may, under certain conditions, operate (or close) without a permit pending issuance of a final facility permit.[279] In order to obtain such "interim status," a preexisting TSD must also have notified EPA of its hazardous waste activities under section 3010 of RCRA and have made application for a permit to EPA or an authorized state.

The requirements for interim status TSD facilities, while similar to those for permitted facilities, are less stringent. The 1984 Amendments reflected congressional frustration with the delay involved in subjecting these interim facilities to full regulation. As amended, section 3005(e) required land disposal facilities that had interim status when the 1984 RCRA Amendments were adopted, within 12 months of enactment, to apply to EPA for a final determination of their permit status and certify their compliance with all groundwater monitoring and financial responsibility requirements. Section 3005(c) created a statutory timetable for permit issuance and, for the most part, such status was to be phased out by November 8, 1992.[280] However, interim status may still apply thereafter to existing facilities that become subject to RCRA because of a change in the statute or regulations after 1984.[281]

Interim status facilities may file Part A of RCRA's two part application process prior to Part B and must comply with the interim standards while awaiting Part B approval. All other facilities must submit Part A and Part B of the permit application simultaneously and must receive permit approval before operation commences.

Part 265 of the EPA's Subtitle C regulations provides the standards for owners and operators of TSD facilities operating under interim status.[282] Until interim status facilities receive permits, the part 265 standards are the only requirements applicable to them. Interim status requirements of general applicability to all types of TSD facilities, for example, general facility standards, preparedness and prevention, contingency planning, use of manifest system and recordkeeping, closure and postclosure care, and financial assurance are quite similar to the corresponding standards in part 264.[283] However, groundwater monitoring requirements for interim status facilities are substantially less stringent and do not include requirements for corrective action, nor apply to solid waste management units at the interim status site.[284]

Standards for particular types of interim status facilities also are similar to those for new facilities, although significantly less stringent in some respects. For example, groundwater monitoring requirements for surface impoundments, waste piles, and landfills are substantially less detailed and do not contain an explicit response action requirement in the event that leakage is detected from

---

[279] 42 U.S.C. §6925(e).

[280] RCRA §3005(c), 42 U.S.C. §6925(c), provides a timetable for permitting both interim status and new facilities. Permits for land disposal facilities with applications pending as of November 8, 1984, must be issued within four years after the enactment of the 1984 Amendments (November 8, 1988). Permits for incinerators must be issued within five years after the enactment of the 1984 Amendments (November 8, 1989). EPA or the authorized state agency was granted eight years after the enactment of the 1984 Amendments to issue permits for all other facilities for which applications were pending in 1984 (until November 8, 1992).

[281] RCRA §3005(e)(1)(A)(ii), 42 U.S.C. §6925(e)(1)(A)(ii) (1988).

[282] 40 C.F.R. §265.

[283] 40 C.F.R. pt. 265, Subparts A-E, G, H.

[284] 40 C.F.R. pt. 265, Subpart F.

the unit.[285] Requirements for interim status incinerators are also far less detailed.[286]

IX. Restrictions on Land Disposal of Hazardous Waste

In the 1984 Amendments to RCRA, Congress directed EPA to impose sweeping limitations on the disposal of untreated hazardous wastes in landfills or land treatment facilities. Under section 3004, as amended, EPA was required to review each listed hazardous waste under section 3001, and all wastes having a hazardous characteristic, and to prohibit all methods of land disposal of each such waste except those that would protect human health and the environment. EPA could approve continued land disposal only upon a demonstration that the disposal method would ensure that no hazardous constituents could escape from the disposal unit. Congress laid down a schedule for EPA action, based on review of all hazardous wastes, in three installments. If EPA failed to act in accordance with the schedule, the ''hammer'' provisions of section 3004 resulted in an automatic ban on all land disposal of the relevant wastes.[287]

Congress also directed EPA to adopt treatment standards for every type of hazardous waste while reviewing land disposal methods. Such treatment, whether expressed as a method of treatment or as a level of hazardous constituents in treated wastes, must substantially diminish the toxicity of the waste or substantially reduce the likelihood of migration of hazardous constituents from the waste. Only hazardous waste that is treated to the specified standard can be disposed of in a RCRA-permitted hazardous waste landfill or other land disposal facility.[288]

In a series of rulemakings between 1986 and 1990, EPA implemented these land disposal restrictions, also known as the ''land ban.''[289] For purposes of these regulations, EPA defines ''land disposal'' as ''placement [of hazardous wastes] in or on land.''[290] As an initial step, EPA banned, with limited exceptions, land disposal of a number of untreated spent solvent wastes;[291] land disposal of so-called ''California'' wastes, including highly corrosive liquids, PCB wastes, and liquid wastes containing between 0.1 percent and 1.0 percent halogenated organic compounds;[292] and land disposal of virtually all untreated wastes that contain dioxin.[293]

Subsequently, in proceedings known as the first-, second-, and third-third rulemakings, EPA reviewed the entire universe of hazardous wastes,

---

[285] 40 C.F.R. pt. 265, Subparts K, L, N.

[286] 40 C.F.R. pt. 265, Subpart O.

[287] *See generally* §3004(g), 42 U.S.C. §6924(g) (1988).

[288] *See generally* §3004(m), 42 U.S.C. §6924(m) (1988).

[289] *See generally* 40 C.F.R. pt. 268.

[290] 40 C.F.R. §268.2(c). The term includes placement in a landfill, surface impoundment, waste pile, injection well, land treatment facility, salt dome formation, salt bed formation, underground mine or cave, or concrete vault or bunker.

[291] 40 C.F.R. §268.30. This ban covers hazardous wastes F001, F002, F003, F004, and F005. It exempts solvent wastes generated by small quantity generators of 100–1,000 kg/mo of hazardous waste, as well as certain solvent-contaminated wastes generated from corrective action or cleanup.

[292] 40 C.F.R. §268.32.

[293] 40 C.F.R. §268.31.

adopted treatment standards for most such wastes, and banned land disposal of wastes not so treated. There are three types of treatment standards that can apply to a specific waste. The first is a limit on the concentration of particular hazardous constituents in the treated waste, i.e., absolute concentration.[294] The second is a limit on the concentration of particular hazardous constituents in an *extract* of the treated waste generated by a prescribed extraction procedure.[295] The third is a requirement for use of a specified treatment technology.[296]

Compliance with the land disposal restrictions is the responsibility, in the first instance, of the person who generates hazardous waste.[297] The regulations explicitly forbid dilution of a restricted waste as a substitute for treatment.[298] EPA can grant a variance from an applicable treatment standard if the generator demonstrates that its waste is physically or chemically different from the wastes that EPA considered in developing the treatment standard and therefore cannot be treated to the specified levels or by the specified methods.[299] Alternatively, a generator may obtain a site-specific waiver of a land disposal restriction by demonstrating to EPA, with a reasonable degree of certainty, that if the waste is disposed of in a particular land disposal unit, there will be no migration of hazardous constituents from the unit for as long as the waste remains hazardous. EPA has specified detailed requirements for waste analyses and monitoring data in support of such a no-migration petition.[300]

The status under EPA's land disposal program of contaminated materials resulting from response actions under the Comprehensive Environmental Response, Compensation, and Liability Act (CERCLA) and RCRA has undergone a complex evolution. Land disposal restrictions for soil and debris contaminated by solvent wastes, dioxin wastes, and California list wastes took effect in 1990. However, not until 1992 did EPA establish generally applicable land disposal restrictions for contaminated soils and other materials generated during hazardous waste spills or cleanups. Under the final restrictions, effective May 8, 1993, hazardous soils that the regulations would otherwise require to be treated by incineration, mercury restoring, or vitrification (as well as certain soils that are contaminated by mixed radioactive wastes) are prohibited from land disposal without treatment. Similarly, hazardous debris that is contaminated with any listed waste or exhibits a hazardous characteristic is banned from land disposal without treatment, effective May 8, 1994.[301]

EPA's standards for treatment of hazardous debris generally require deactivation of any hazardous waste characteristic, for example, ignitability, and

---

[294] *See* 40 C.F.R. §268.43.

[295] *See* 40 C.F.R. §268.41. For most wastes, the extract is obtained by use of TCLP in 40 C.F.R. pt. 261, app. II.

[296] *See* 40 C.F.R. §268.42.

[297] Hazardous wastes generated by a conditionally exempt small quantity generator, i.e., less than 100 kg/mo of hazardous wastes, are exempt from the land disposal requirements. 40 C.F.R. §268.1(e)(1). Indeed, such wastes can be disposed of in an authorized nonhazardous waste facility.

[298] 40 C.F.R. §268.3.

[299] 40 C.F.R. §268.44.

[300] 40 C.F.R. §268.6. The no-migration exemption is not available for any waste containing more than 500 parts per million of PCBs.

[301] 40 C.F.R. §268.35(e). "Debris" is defined as any natural geologic material or manufactured material that exceeds a 60 millimeter particle size and is intended for disposal. It includes stone, rock, brick, concrete, contaminated machinery or equipment, and similar materials from the demolition of buildings.

prescribe treatment for any other constituent for which the regulations establish a concentration-based limit in waste or extract.[302] Such treatment must be by a specified technology, e.g., abrasive blasting or solvent washing of contaminated surfaces, chemical destruction of surficial contamination, or encapsulation of the debris. If contaminated debris merely exhibits a hazardous characteristic, and if that characteristic is eliminated through a specified extraction or destruction method, the treated debris can be disposed of as ordinary solid waste. Similarly, treated debris from which contaminated surfaces have been removed generally can be managed as nonhazardous solid waste.

X. Special Requirements for Recycled Hazardous Wastes

Under EPA's regulations, hazardous wastes that are recycled generally are regulated in the same manner as are hazardous wastes that are treated or disposed of.[303] Thus, recyclable materials that would otherwise be hazardous waste are subject to all requirements for hazardous waste generators and transporters, and hazardous waste recyclers are subject to permitting and other requirements for hazardous waste storage facilities. However, EPA has created a large and complex body of exemptions from this general rule.

Some materials that would otherwise be classified as hazardous wastes are entirely exempt from regulation if recycled in certain ways because they are not considered solid waste.[304] Another set of hazardous recyclables is considered hazardous waste but is wholly or partly exempt from regulation. These include reclaimed industrial alcohol, used batteries returned to a battery manufacturer for regeneration, used oil recycled in some manner other than burning for energy recovery, scrap metal, and certain fuels recovered from petroleum refining wastes.[305] A third group of recyclable materials is regulated under specific requirements set forth in part 266 of the regulations. These include materials that are recycled by being applied to land (for example, fertilizers); hazardous wastes and used oil burned in boilers and industrial furnaces; recyclable materials from which precious metals are reclaimed; and spent lead-acid batteries that are reclaimed.[306] In all these cases, the actual recycling process is exempt from regulation, although recycling facilities will be regulated as hazardous waste storage facilities if they hold the recyclable materials prior to recycling.

A. Recycled Products Applied to Land

EPA's part 266 regulations apply to recyclable materials that are placed on the land with or without mixing with other materials.[307] Such materials are

[302] 40 C.F.R. §268.45.

[303] 40 C.F.R. §261.6.

[304] 40 C.F.R. §264.1(c). Materials that are not considered solid waste, and thus escape regulation entirely, include principally sludges or byproducts that exhibit a hazardous waste characteristic and are reclaimed.

[305] 40 C.F.R. §261.6(a)(3).

[306] 40 C.F.R. §261.6(a)(2).

[307] 40 C.F.R. §266.20–.23.

subject to all requirements for generators or transporters of hazardous waste, and the facilities at which such materials are placed on land are subject to all applicable standards for TSD facilities. However, to the extent that hazardous waste is used to produce a product for the general public's use, such as fertilizer, it is not subject to regulation if two conditions are met: first, that the waste has undergone a chemical reaction rendering the waste inseparable from that with which it is mixed; second, that the resulting product meets the applicable treatment standards for the constituent waste under EPA's part 268 land disposal regulations.

B. Hazardous Waste Burned in Boilers and Industrial Furnaces

Detailed and complex regulations govern the burning of hazardous waste in boilers and industrial furnaces (BIFs), including burning for energy or for recovery of materials or as an ingredient.[308] The regulations require all such facilities to apply and obtain a permit in the same manner as a hazardous waste incinerator, as discussed above in Section VII. Boilers and industrial furnaces must meet the same DRE standards as incinerators. Such facilities also are subject to most of the general facility standards applicable to all TSD facilities. The facility may burn only those hazardous wastes specified in its permit, in accordance with operating conditions specified in the permit on the basis of a trial burn.

BIFs must meet specific limits on emissions of hazardous constituents to the atmosphere. Such devices generally must achieve a DRE of 99.99 percent for all organic hazardous constituents in the waste feed, as demonstrated by a trial burn. Limits are also imposed on carbon monoxide and, in some circumstances, on dioxin and furan emissions.

Emissions of heavy metals are controlled by means of limits on the allowable amounts of heavy metals in waste feed material, which are in turn based on the height of the facility's stack and the local terrain and land use. The limits are expressed as maximum feed rates per hour of the relevant metals (Tier I and II feed rates). More stringent feed rates (Tier III) apply to facilities that have special features, such as short stacks, or are located in a narrow valley or near a large body of water. The regulations also impose corresponding Tier I, II, and III limits on the feeding of free chlorine and hydrogen chloride into the burner. Concentrations of particulate matter in the emissions from a BIF also are limited.

Generators and transporters of hazardous waste that is burned in a BIF are fully regulated under, respectively, parts 262 and 263 of EPA's regulations. All facilities that store hazardous waste that is to be burned, including intermediate processors or blenders, are subject to permitting and all other requirements applicable to a TSD facility.

Finally, the residues or products generated in a BIF are considered hazardous waste unless, in the case of a boiler, at least 50 percent of the heat input

---

[308] 40 C.F.R. §266.100–.112. These regulations, which were adopted February 21, 1991, replaced substantially less restrictive regulations applicable solely to the burning of hazardous wastes for energy recovery.

comes from coal and, in the case of a furnace or cement kiln, 50 percent of the raw material inputs are normal, nonhazardous raw materials. In addition, in order to escape continuing regulation as hazardous waste, the products of a BIF may not contain significantly higher concentrations of hazardous constituents than would be present in residues generated without burning hazardous waste.

C. Precious Metals Recovery

EPA has adopted minimal requirements for hazardous wastes from which precious metals are recovered.[309] Generators and transporters of such wastes must notify EPA under section 3010 of RCRA and use a standard hazard waste manifest for each shipment. The owner or operator of any facility where such wastes are stored prior to recycling must notify EPA under section 3010 and maintain records documenting that the materials are not being speculatively accumulated, i.e., not being held for more than a year before undergoing reclamation.

D. Spent Lead-Acid Batteries

EPA also regulates spent lead-acid batteries minimally prior to reclamation of lead values.[310] Persons who generate, transport, collect, or store such batteries without engaging in reclamation are entirely exempt from regulation. Facilities at which batteries are stored and reclaimed are subject to the notification requirement of section 3010 and to most of the general facility standards applicable to TSDs, as well as those relating to corrective action, closure and postclosure, financial assurance, containers, tanks, impoundments, and waste piles under part 264.

E. Management of Recycled Oil

In section 3014 of RCRA, added by the 1984 Amendments, Congress instructed EPA to address the difficult issue of how recycled oil should be regulated. EPA was directed to decide within two years whether or not to list used automobile and truck crankcase oil and other used oil as a hazardous waste. Congress further directed EPA to adopt such regulations as EPA deemed necessary to protect public health and the environment from hazards associated with used oil, while ensuring that such regulations do not discourage the recycling of used oil. Congress specifically mandated that such regulations exempt generators and transporters from manifesting and recordkeeping requirements if they send or transport used oil to a permitted recycling facility and that such recycling facilities be eligible for permits-by-rule.

Some eight years later, EPA adopted detailed final regulations on the management of used oil.[311] The regulations cover the recycling of used oil, defined as any petroleum or synthetic oil that has become contaminated by

---

[309] 40 C.F.R. §266.70.
[310] 40 C.F.R. §266.80.
[311] 40 C.F.R. pt. 279. 57 Fed. Reg. 41,611 (1992). The standards were effective March 3, 1993.

impurities through use. They are applicable to used oil generators, transporters, and "marketers," as well as to owners and operators of facilities that reprocess or re-refine used oil. Used oil that is burned for energy recovery also is regulated, but only if it exceeds EPA's "specification" for maximum permissible amounts of certain contaminants.[312] A generator, transporter, or burner may determine through analysis or other information that such used oil fuel meets EPA's specification. Such oil is not subject to further regulation if burned for energy recovery. Used oil that is not recycled by either processing/re-refining or burning for energy recovery must be managed as a hazardous waste.[313]

Generators of used oil that is destined for recycling are subject to minimal requirements. They must ensure that their used oil is transported only by a transporter who has an EPA identification number, although this requirement does not apply if the generator itself transports its own used oil, or used oil collected from household do-it-yourselfers, to an approved used oil collection center. No manifest is required for used oil shipments. (Generators may not, however, mix used oil with any hazardous waste.) If a generator also ships used oil to a burner, the generator must keep a record of each shipment, including shipments of both specification and off-specification oil.

Owners or operators of used oil collection centers are not subject to regulation, provided that they comply with the requirements applicable to a generator of used oil, do not accept used oil in greater than 55-gallon quantities, and are authorized by a state or local government.

Persons who transport more than 55 gallons of used oil must notify EPA under section 3010 of RCRA and secure an EPA identification number. The transporter may deliver used oil only to another transporter, to a used oil processing or re-refining facility, or to a used oil burner, provided that the person to whom the oil is delivered also has an EPA identification number. Used oil transporters must keep a record of each shipment, showing the name, address, and identification number of the generator and the person to whom the oil was delivered. Both the generator and the recipient must sign this record. If oil is discharged during transportation, the transporter must take immediate action to notify the National Response Center and other authorities and to contain and clean up the spill.

The regulations create a rebuttable presumption that, if used oil contains more than 1,000 parts-per-million of halogens, it has been mixed with hazardous wastes. It is the transporter's responsibility to determine whether used oil that it transports exceeds this limit. The transporter may make this determination either by testing the oil or by applying its knowledge of the halogen content of the used oil in light of the materials or processes used by the generator. The transporter must retain records of this determination for at least three years after the shipment to which the determination applies.

---

[312] The limits are: arsenic, 5 ppm; cadmium, 2 ppm; chromium, 10 ppm; lead, 100 ppm; total halogens, 4,000 ppm; flash point, 100 degrees F minimum.

[313] The regulations forbid the use of used oil as a dust suppressant, except in states that demonstrate to EPA that they have in place an adequate program to minimize the environmental impacts of such land application. Currently, EPA has not authorized the use of used oil as a dust suppressant in any state. 40 C.F.R. §279.82.

Transporters may temporarily store used oil in used oil transfer facilities, that is, transportation-related facilities such as loading docks, for up to 35 days without a TSD facility permit. The oil must be stored in tanks or containers that are properly labeled, in good condition, and equipped with a secondary containment system sufficient to prevent used oil from migrating to the environment.

Owners and operators of facilities that process used oil, including re-refining, must notify EPA and obtain an identification number. Each such facility must comply with general facility standards that closely parallel those for permitted TSD facilities, including requirements for contingency planning and emergency response. The facility must store used oil only in tanks or containers that meet the same requirements as are applicable to oil transfer facilities.

Used oil processors/re-refiners, like transporters, must determine whether the oil they handle has a halogen content greater than 1,000 parts-per-million, such that it is presumed to have been mixed with hazardous waste. Unlike a transporter, the facility must have a written analysis plan describing how this determination is made. The plan must specify whether sampling will be used and, if so, sampling and analytical methods. The records and results of all analyses must be maintained in a facility operating record.

Finally, owners and operators of processing or re-refining facilities must keep a record of the date and quantity of each used oil shipment received, including the name, address, and EPA identification number of the generator and transporter. Similar records must be maintained for each delivery of used oil shipped off-site from such a facility. (Re-refined lubricants, however, are no longer considered used oil.)

''Off-specification'' used oil generally may be burned as a fuel only in an industrial furnace or in an industrial or utility boiler. Such oil also may be burned in certain small space heaters that consume only oil generated on-site or from household do-it-yourself generators. Such oil also may be burned in a hazardous waste incinerator regulated as a TSD facility under part 264 of EPA's regulations.

Used oil burners are subject to substantially the same requirements as used oil processors. They must obtain an EPA identification number, store used oil only in tanks or containers with secondary containment, determine through analysis or by means of other information whether the oil they burn contains less than 1,000 parts-per-million of halogens, and maintain records identifying the source of each used oil shipment accepted for burning.

Any person who directs a shipment of off-specification used oil to a burner (or who claims that used oil that is to be burned meets the EPA specification) is subject to regulation as a ''used oil fuel marketer.'' A marketer that is not a generator or transporter must independently notify EPA.

XI. Role of State Hazardous Waste Programs Under RCRA

Under section 3006 of RCRA, any state may apply to EPA for authority to administer and enforce a hazardous waste program in lieu of the federal program, including issuing and enforcing permits for TSD facilities in that state.[314] EPA has adopted procedures and criteria for approving, revising and, if necessary, withdrawing approval of state programs.[315] A state program must cover all the hazardous wastes controlled by the federal program under part 261 and may delist wastes under procedures equivalent to EPA's.[316] A state program must cover all generators covered by federal regulations and require them to comply with requirements equivalent to those under part 262, including use of EPA's manifest form.[317] A state program must cover all transporters covered by EPA's regulations and require compliance with the federal manifest system and in-transit cleanup requirements, among other requirements under part 263.[318]

Authorized state programs may impose more stringent requirements or cover more wastes than the federal program. States may not, however, under cover of an approved federal program, unreasonably restrict, impede, or ban the free movement of hazardous waste into the state. Nor may a state adopt any requirement that has no basis in human health or environmental protection and that acts as a bar on treatment, storage, or disposal of hazardous waste in the state.[319]

With respect to regulation and permitting of TSD facilities, an authorized state program must have standards for such facilities that are equivalent to parts 264 and 265 of EPA's regulations. State law must require permits for all TSD facilities for which EPA requires a permit under part 270 and may authorize preexisting facilities to operate in interim status.[320]

Authorized programs must have minimum procedures for detecting and investigating noncompliance with regulations. This must include a program of periodic inspection of regulated facilities. The state also must encourage the public to submit information about suspected violations and investigate such reports.[321] The state program must be backed up with adequate enforcement authority, including the power to restrain violations by administrative order or legal action; to assess civil penalties of at least $10,000 per day of violation; and to obtain criminal penalties, including imprisonment, against a person who knowingly violates the state's hazardous waste laws.

States seeking authorization must apply to EPA under RCRA section 3006. Applications must include a detailed description of the state's program and an opinion from the state attorney general that the state has the required legal authorities needed to administer and enforce the program. The state also must submit a memorandum of agreement with EPA's Regional Administrator under which the state undertakes to submit required information and reports to EPA and coordinate its compliance monitoring activities with EPA's continuing inspections in the state. Prior to submitting its application to EPA, the state must afford the public an opportunity to comment on the proposed submission.

---

[314] A majority of states have received final EPA authorization for at least those federal requirements that were in effect prior to the 1984 Amendments to RCRA. 40 C.F.R. pt. 272.

[315] 40 C.F.R. pt. 271.

[316] 40 C.F.R. §271.9.

[317] 40 C.F.R. §271.10.

[318] 40 C.F.R. §271.11.

[319] 40 C.F.R. §271.1(i), §271.4.

[320] 40 C.F.R. §271.13.

[321] 40 C.F.R. §271.15.

EPA is required to approve a state program that conforms to the applicable requirements. Upon approval, EPA terminates its permit issuance activities in that state.[322] An approved state program must be revised if and when the federal program is changed. The state program must be revised by July 1 of each year to reflect changes in federal requirements during the 12 months preceding the previous July 1. All changes must be submitted to EPA for approval.[323]

EPA may withdraw approval of a state program if the state's legal authority no longer meets the requirements for approval, for example, because of a state court decision invalidating the state's authority, or because the state is not properly operating the program, for example, by issuing permits without required conditions.[324] To withdraw a state program, EPA initiates proceedings by issuing an order to the state. Following a hearing on the record before a presiding officer, the Administrator must list the deficiencies in the program and provide the state a reasonable period of no more than 90 days to correct them. Only if the state fails to correct the deficiencies can the Administrator revoke the state program approval, in which case the state may obtain judicial review of the withdrawal order.

XII. Solid Waste Regulation: Open Dumps and Municipal Landfills

Under Subtitle D of RCRA, EPA has adopted a program of partial regulation of the nation's nonhazardous solid waste. Pursuant to its authority under section 4005 to ban open dumping, EPA adopted criteria in 1979 for classifying solid waste disposal facilities as either sanitary landfills or open dumps.[325] In general, a facility will be considered an open dump if is situated in a floodplain and is subject to washout of solid waste; causes a discharge of pollution to surface waters without a permit; contaminates an underground drinking water source beyond the facility boundary; involves application of waste containing excessive amounts of cadmium to land that is used to grow food-chain crops; harbors excessive rodents, flies, or mosquitoes; engages in open burning of wastes; generates excessive amounts of explosive gases; is prone to fires; or presents a bird hazard to aircraft.

In 1991, pursuant to the statutory prohibition on open dumps, EPA adopted comprehensive regulations governing municipal solid waste landfills (MSWLF).[326] Failure to comply with these standards renders a municipal solid waste landfill an open dump, against which EPA can take enforcement action.

The MSWLF regulations impose more detailed location restrictions than EPA's older part 257 open dump standards, including severe restrictions on locating such facilities in wetlands, fault areas, seismic impact zones, or otherwise unstable areas. The newer regulations establish detailed operating criteria,

[322] 40 C.F.R. §271.1.

[323] 40 C.F.R. §270.21.

[324] 40 C.F.R. §271.22–.23. EPA regulations also include procedures whereby a state may, upon 180 days notice to the Administrator, voluntarily transfer its program responsibilities back to EPA.

[325] 40 C.F.R. pt. 257. All subsequent citations to RCRA's regulations are to the *Code of Federal Regulations* revised as of July 1, 1991.

[326] 40 C.F.R. pt. 258; 56 Fed. Reg. 51,016 (1991).

including requirements for excluding hazardous waste from MSWLFs, ensuring daily cover, monitoring methane generation, controlling precipitation run-on and run-off, limiting bulk liquid disposal, and keeping operating records.

MSWLF units must meet standards very similar to those for hazardous waste management facilities under EPA's Subtitle C regulations. New MSWLF landfills are required to have either a composite (flexible membrane plus compacted soil) liner and a leachate collection system or state-approved equivalent. Every MSWLF unit must monitor groundwater quality, unless the owner or operator can demonstrate that there is no potential for migration of hazardous constituents to groundwater. The regulations require more stringent monitoring if a statistically significant increase in contamination is detected and, if necessary, corrective action.

As with hazardous waste management facilities, MSWLFs must be properly closed, with a final cover system designed to minimize infiltration and erosion. Closure must be in accordance with a closure plan, and state authorities must be given at least 30 days notice of closure. Closure must be certified by an independent registered professional engineer, and a notation of the facility's status as a closed landfill must thereafter be included on the deed to the facility. The owner or operator must provide postclosure care and maintenance of the final cover for up to 30 years, as well as operating the leachate collection system. Financial assurance for proper closure and postclosure care, as well as for any necessary corrective action during the facility's active life, must be maintained through any of a number of prescribed financial instruments, including a trust fund, surety bond, letter of credit, insurance, or state government assumption of liability.

XIII. Conclusion

RCRA is without question one of the most important statutes in the federal system of environmental laws. Few commercial or industrial operations, no matter how small, do not generate at least some residuals that are considered hazardous waste. RCRA's requirements for management of these wastes probably affect more American businesses directly than either air or water pollution control laws, which are generally aimed at larger industrial operations.

Few observers would dispute that EPA has made a conscientious, even valiant, effort to implement Congress's comprehensive mandate under Subtitle C of RCRA. Unfortunately, this has resulted, perhaps inevitably, in regulations that are as complex and detailed as any in the entire *Code of Federal Regulations.* EPA has made commendable efforts since 1980 to assist the business community in understanding and complying with the RCRA regulations. However, the regulations are constantly evolving, both through subtle refinements and, sometimes, dramatic changes. Now and for the foreseeable future, every business, large and small, must plan to stay abreast of changing RCRA requirements. This will require expertise and, above all, vigilance.

7

Superfund

By John C. Martin and Timothy A. Vanderver, Jr.[*]

Well, here's another fine mess you've gotten me into.
—Oliver Hardy, *Sons of the Desert*

I. Introduction

In response to the national outcry over the environmental disasters at Love Canal and elsewhere, the 96th Congress enacted the Comprehensive Environmental Response, Compensation and Liability Act (CERCLA)[1] in the last days of the 1980 session. Congress intended to provide the government with broad powers to clean up abandoned hazardous waste sites, to address hazardous waste spills, and to force those who poison the land to pay for its remediation.

In order to further these goals, Congress drafted an act that was far broader in its scope than any previous federal environmental statute. Prior to the passage of CERCLA, federal environmental laws were media specific, in that they addressed pollution problems in only one of the environmental media—air, water, and so forth. In contrast, Congress intended CERCLA to encompass all media within its ambit. Thus, CERCLA becomes operative on the release of hazardous substances from a facility to the land, air, or water. Moreover, unlike prior environmental statutes, CERCLA was not limited to a specific industry or group of industries. Instead, Congress intended that CERCLA apply to any disposal activity involving hazardous substances.

In general, Congress attempted to address the problems of hazardous waste sites by proceeding on two tangents. First, Congress created a rolling fund, the "Superfund,"[2] to pay for the initial expense of response. Second, in recognition of the limits of the fund, Congress devised a liability scheme intended to visit the cost of the remediation on entities bearing some responsibility for these problems.[3]

---

[*] The authors would like to thank John A. Gillan for his assistance in the preparation of this chapter.

[1] 42 U.S.C. §9601 *et seq.*

[2] During 1980 the fund was composed of approximately $1.6 billion; in 1986, the fund was increased to about $8.5 billion.

[3] S. REP. NO. 848, 96th Cong., 2d Sess. 13 (1980), *reprinted in* [1980] U.S.C.C.A.N. 6119; General Elec.

Despite all the good intentions, the haste with which the final version of the bill was put together and the compromises that were necessary to ensure passage resulted in a statute that was vague and had an indefinite, if not contradictory, legislative history.[4] While the Superfund Amendments and Reauthorization Act of 1986 (SARA)[5] addressed some of the gaps in the statute, many issues remained unresolved. The numerous ambiguities and the statutory liability scheme have spawned a large volume of litigation but only a small number of site remediations.[6]

Moreover, both in 1980, and again in 1986, Congress did not truly appreciate the severity of the problem confronting the regulators who would implement CERCLA's broad mandate. Only after years of administering the program has the true magnitude of the task confronting Superfund come to be realized. Thus, currently some estimate that there are 450,000 sites that may be destined for Superfund cleanup.[7] Of these potential sites, approximately 1,207 are on the National Priorities List, signifying that EPA considers these sites' cleanup to be of the highest priority.[8] The average cost of cleaning up such sites has been estimated at well over $25 million, with the ultimate cost of the Superfund program currently estimated at more than $500 billion.[9]

The magnitude of the hazardous waste problem and the difficulties with the implementation of the statute have generated a steady stream of criticism for CERCLA and the EPA Superfund program from both environmentalists and industry. Criticism from these groups is likely to factor significantly in the Superfund reauthorization process scheduled to begin in the near future.

II. Classes of Liable Persons

Liability under CERCLA attaches to four classes of "persons" who, by statute, are responsible for a "release" of "hazardous substances" from a "facility."[10] The term "person" includes corporate and government entities along with individuals.[11] Section 107 specifically provides that present owners and operators, certain past owners and operators, transporters, and generators will be liable under the Act.

Co. v. Aamco Transmissions, Inc., 962 F.2d 281, 285 (2d Cir. 1985); Dedham Water Co. v. Cumberland Farms Dairy, Inc., 805 F.2d 1074, 1081 (1st Cir. 1986).

[4] *See* Exxon v. Hunt, 475 U.S. 355, 363 (1986); Hopkins v. Elano Corp., 30 ER Cases 1782, 1785 (S.D. Ohio 1989); United States v. Conservation Chem., 619 F. Supp. 162, 204 (W.D. Mo. 1985).

[5] Pub. L. No. 99-499, 100 Stat. 1760 (1986).

[6] A. Light, CERCLA Law and Procedure 282 (1990). In fact, by 1990 only 52 Superfund sites or 4% of the 1,000 plus sites then on the National Priorities List had been cleaned up. *Id.*

[7] Light, *supra* note 6, at 282 (citing letter from Sen. Sasser to William K. Reilly, EPA Administrator, Aug. 8, 1990).

[8] 57 Fed. Reg. 47,180 (1992).

[9] Light, *supra* note 6, at 232.

[10] The terms "release" and "hazardous substances" have been defined in the statute and by case law. They will be discussed in detail in Section III of this chapter.

[11] 42 U.S.C. §9601(21). Generally liability under the Act attaches to corporate entities. However, traditional rules governing corporate liability are not always applied under CERCLA. Thus there are instances where corporate structure does not preclude liability for individuals and related corporate entities.

A. General Parameters of Liability

1. Present Owners and Operators

a. Generally. Section 107(a)(1) provides that the "owner and operator of a . . . facility" will be liable for the consequences of a release or threatened release from its facility. Courts have interpreted this provision to impose liability on the owner or operator of the facility at the time contamination is discovered.[12] The statute does not qualify the term "owner" to limit liability to only "responsible" owners or "participatory" owners or "managing" owners. Courts have acknowledged the breadth of this term by decreeing that owners are liable under the statutory scheme regardless of their culpability for the contamination. Thus in a 1984 case, *United States v. Argent Corp.,*[13] a New Mexico district court held that a remote landlord was liable for the cleanup of a site even though the landlord had no direct responsibility for the site. Indeed, even a minimal ownership interest can yield Superfund liability. In *United States v. Allied Chemical Corp.,*[14] the District Court for the Northern District of California held that one who owns a right-of-way across property is liable as an owner under the statute. Other decisions coincide with these rulings.[15]

b. Lender Liability. Acquisition of an ownership interest through what had been a security interest has long been held to render the new owner liable. Thus, in *United States v. Maryland Bank & Trust Co.,*[16] the court ruled that when a bank took title to properly through a foreclosure sale, it became liable as an "owner" under CERCLA.

Despite CERCLA's secured creditor exemption,[17] lenders with interests in contaminated property short of actual ownership, may in certain instances have owner/operator liability. In *United States v. Fleet Factors Corp.,*[18] the court held that "a secured creditor will be liable if its involvement with the management of the facility is sufficiently broad that it could affect hazardous waste disposal decisions if it so chose."[19] This decision expanded liability beyond what until then had been the primary test—namely that liability would attach only if the lender had actually participated in the day-to-day management of the facility.[20]

---

[12] United States v. Monsanto, 858 F.2d 160, 168 (4th Cir. 1988), *cert. denied,* 109 S. Ct. 1356 (1989); Tanglewood East Homeowners v. Charles Thomas, Inc., 849 F.2d 1568 (5th Cir. 1988); United States v. Shaner, Civ. No. 85-1372 (E.D. Pa. June 25, 1985).

[13] 21 ER Cases 1356 (D.N.M. 1984).

[14] No. C-83-5898-FMS (N.D. Cal. June 27, 1990).

[15] United States v. Stringfellow, 661 F. Supp. 1052, 1063 (C.D. Cal. 1987); Monsanto, 858 F.2d at 168.

[16] 632 F. Supp. 573 (D. Md. 1986).

[17] CERCLA §101(20)(A), 42 U.S.C. §9601(20)(A) (owner and operator does not include any "person, who, without participating in the management of a . . . facility, holds indicia of ownership primarily to protect his security interest in the . . . facility").

[18] 901 F.2d 1550 (11th Cir. 1990), *cert. denied,* 111 S. Ct. 752 (1991).

[19] *Id.* at 1558.

[20] *See* United States v. Mirabile, 1985 WL 97 (E.D. Pa. 1985).

Fleet Factors and a subsequent decision by the Ninth Circuit, which applied the "actual participation" test,[21] caused an uproar in the lending community and, in reaction, EPA issued a rule in April 1992 clarifying the scope of the secured creditor exemption.[22] The rule provides that a lender may undertake activities to protect a security interest without incurring CERCLA liability: (1) actions taken prior to the inception of the loan or other transaction; (2) facility inspections; (3) policing the loan; and (4) loan workouts.[23]

These activities do not trigger liability only insofar as they fall short of participation in management of the debtor. The "participation" necessary for liability is either (1) exercising decision-making control over the borrower's environmental compliance, or (2) exercising control over operational functions at a level comparable to that of a manager.[24] Exercising financial or administrative functions (acting as credit manager, chief financial officer, or other similar role) as opposed to operational functions, will not constitute participation in management for the purposes of CERCLA liability.[25]

Upon forclosure, a lender may also retain the secured creditor exemption under the new rule. In order to remain exempt, the lender must attempt to dispose of the property quickly using reasonably available commercial means and must be able to demonstrate that the property is held to protect a security interest and not for investment purposes.[26] The lender can show it is motivated to protect its security interest by listing the property with a broker within 12 months of foreclosure.[27] The rule also requires that the lender accept, within 90 days, any bona fide offer of fair consideration received within six months of the foreclosure date.[28] The new rule was applied in *Ashland Oil Inc. v. Sonford Products Corp.*,[29] where its provisions were cited in denying liability against a foreclosing lender.

c. Innocent Purchaser. A number of early decisions found that liability as an owner does not require active participation in or management of hazardous waste activities.[30] While it retained this general rule, Congress created an exemption from liability for a small segment of owners classified as "innocent landowners" by the SARA provisions of 1986. In general, this defense requires that an otherwise liable owner demonstrate (1) that the owner acquired the property after the disposal occurred; (2) that it did not know or have reason to know of the presence of hazardous substances when it purchased the property;

---

[21] Bergsoe Metal Corp. v. East Asiatic Co., 910 F.2d 668 (9th Cir. 1990) (adopting the traditional common law rule that a corporate officer's participation in wrongful acts will render him liable for the consequences of those acts).

[22] 57 Fed. Reg. 18,344 (1992).

[23] 40 C.F.R. §300.1100(c)(2)(ii).

[24] 40 C.F.R. §300.1100(c)(1).

[25] 40 C.F.R. §300.1100(c)(1)(ii)(B).

[26] 40 C.F.R. §300.1100(d)(1).

[27] 40 C.F.R. §300.1100(d)(2)(i).

[28] 40 C.F.R. §300.1100(d)(2)(ii)(B).

[29] 810 F. Supp. 1057 (D. Minn. 1993).

[30] *E.g.*, United States v. Argent Corp., 21 ER Cases 1356 (D.N.M. 1984); United States v. Allied Chem. Corp., No. C-83-5898-FMS (N.D. Cal. June 27, 1990).

and (3) that the owner made appropriate inquiry into the past owner's use of the property.[31]

For a defendant to establish that it had no reason to know of the contamination at the time of purchase:

> [T]he defendant must have undertaken, at the time of acquisition, all appropriate inquiry into the previous ownership and uses of the property consistent with good commercial or customary practice in an effort to minimize liability. For the purposes of the preceding sentence the court shall take into account any specialized knowledge or experience on the part of the defendant, the relationship of the purchase price to the value of the property if uncontaminated, commonly known or reasonably ascertainable information about the property, the obviousness of the presence of or the likely presence of contamination at the property, and the ability to detect such contamination by appropriate inspection.[32]

Defendants that fit the narrow parameters of the innocent landowner classification are rare. However, in *United States v. Pacific Hide & Fur Depot, Inc.,*[33] the court found that shareholders who received stock in a closely held scrap metal business through a familial gift were innocent landowners. The court found that the releases at the property were caused solely by third parties, the shareholders had no reason to suspect that such releases had occurred, and that they had undertaken appropriate inquiry into the condition of the property under the circumstances.[34]

2. *Past Owners and Operators*

In addition to present owners and operators, CERCLA imposes liability on those who owned or operated the facility at the time of disposal.[35] As in the case of present owner/operators, no causal link between conduct of the past owner or operator and the contamination at issue is necessary. Instead the court need only determine that hazardous substances were "released" during the tenure of the past owner/operator.[36]

Whether some minimum period of past ownership is necessary to establish CERCLA liability remains unsettled. *In re Diamond Reo Trucks, Inc.*[37] found that a corporate entity that had owned the site for a single day during the disposal period was not liable under section 107(a)(2). In the court's view, holding the corporation (which was in essence a vehicle through which the property passed to four individuals) liable would extend the statutory language to an "absurd plateau" and subvert the intent of the drafters.[38] By contrast, the court in *Nurad Inc. v. William Hooper & Sons, Inc.,*[39] found that a short duration of ownership (four months) was sufficient for liability under section

---

[31] CERCLA §101(35)(A), 42 U.S.C. §9601(35)(A).

[32] CERCLA §101(35)(B), 42 U.S.C. §9601(35)(B).

[33] 716 F. Supp. 1341 (D. Idaho 1989).

[34] *Id.* at 1346–47.

[35] CERCLA §107(a)(2), 42 U.S.C. §9607(a)(2); Smith Land & Improvement Corp. v. Celotex Corp., 851 F.2d 86 (3d Cir. 1988), *cert. denied,* 488 U.S. 1029 (1989).

[36] Westwood Pharmaceuticals, Inc. v. National Fuel Gas Distrib. Corp., 737 F. Supp. 1272 (W.D.N.Y. 1990); United States v. Moore, 698 F. Supp. 622 (E.D. Va. 1988).

[37] 20 CWLR 660 (W.D. Mich. 1990).

[38] *Id.* at 667.

[39] 966 F.2d 837 (4th Cir. 1992).

107(a)(2) where the ownership coincided with disposal at the site. Although the court indicated that the relatively short period of ownership might be considered in the allocation of liability, there was nothing in the statutory definition of owner and operator to suggest that a minimum time limit is essential to finding past owner liability.[40]

The question of whether liability attaches to an owner whose ownership begins after the time that the hazardous substances were discarded on the property and before a response action is initiated is also unsettled. In *In re Diamond Reo Trucks,*[41] the court confronted the argument that leaking, which occurred during the time that the defendant owned the property, amounted to the "disposal" necessary to confer liability under the statute. The court rejected the argument, noting that to premise liability on the theory would extend liability to include all owners from the time the site became polluted. According to the court, this reading is beyond the intended scope of the statute.[42] However, in other cases courts have found that leakage or the migration of chemicals through the environment amounts to disposal under the statute.[43]

3. *Transporters*

Section 107(a)(4) of CERCLA imposes liability upon any person who accepts or accepted hazardous substances for transport to a facility, selected by such person, from which there has been a release. Prior to the enactment of SARA in 1986, there was some question about whether site selection by the transporter was required to establish liability in every instance.[44] However, the consensus now appears to be that site selection is a required element of transporter liability.[45] EPA's current enforcement policy reflects this consensus.[46] Although at least one court has concluded that transportation of hazardous waste within the same facility is sufficient to give rise to transporter liability,[47] there are conflicting decisions on this point.[48]

4. *Generator/Arranger Liability*

The final category of potentially liable parties under CERCLA are those persons who arranged for transportation, treatment, or disposal of hazardous substances which they owned or possessed.[49] While generally referred to as "generator" liability, in fact the liability might more properly be called "arranger" liability. Typically, arranger liability is visited upon a waste generator

---

[40] *Id.* at 844.

[41] 20 CWLR 660 (W.D. Mich. 1990).

[42] *See also* Ecodyne Corp. v. Shah, 718 F. Supp. 1454 (N.D. Cal. 1989); Cadillac/Fairview v. Dow Chem. Co., 21 ER Cases 1584 (C.D. Cal. 1984), *rev'd in part,* 840 F.2d 691 (9th Cir. 1988).

[43] Nurad, 966 F.2d at 845–46; New York v. Shore Realty Corp., 759 F.2d 1032, 1052 (2d Cir. 1985).

[44] LIGHT, *supra* note 6, at 121.

[45] United States v. Western Processing Co., 756 F. Supp. 1416 (W.D. Wash. 1991); United States v. Hardage, 750 F. Supp. 1460, 1473 (W.D. Okla. 1990).

[46] ENVIRONMENTAL PROTECTION AGENCY, POLICY FOR ENFORCEMENT ACTIONS AGAINST TRANSPORTERS UNDER CERCLA (Dec. 23, 1985).

[47] Kaiser Aluminum & Chem. Corp. v. Catellus Dev. Corp., 976 F.2d 1338, 1343 (9th Cir. 1992).

[48] Donahey v. Bogle, 23 CWLR 806 (E.D. Mich. 1991), *rev'd on other grounds,* 1993 WL 59296 (6th Cir. 1993).

[49] CERCLA §107(a)(3), 42 U.S.C. §9607(a)(3).

that arranged with a waste hauler for its own waste to be taken to a site for disposal or treatment. When the site becomes the subject of a Superfund response, the company is exposed to liability for having "arranged for" disposal or treatment of its waste.

Though liability is expansive within this category, the person in possession of the waste must take some affirmative step to arrange the disposal or treatment of the substance at issue and must have some duty or obligation with respect to the waste materials. Courts have not enunciated a clear demarcation of where arranging for liability ends.

In *AM International, Inc. v. International Forging Equipment Corp.,*[50] the Sixth Circuit made clear that "arranging for liability" demands some element of affirmative action. There, the court found that when a manufacturer abandoned hazardous electroplating baths in a property sale and the wastes were ultimately released into the environment, the manufacturer had not "arranged for" disposal. In that case, several years had passed and weather conditions over time caused the release of the hazardous materials into the environment.

The court rejected the contention that the manufacturer was liable under section 107(a)(3) noting

> Even if [the manufacturer] owned the chemicals at issue, it did not incur liability under section 107(a)(3), because it did not "arrange for their disposal." "Disposal" . . . is deemed to take place only at the point at which there is a threat that hazardous wastes will be emitted into the environment, air, soil, or groundwater. . . . The district court concluded that events at the facility after [the manufacturer] left it were entirely responsible for the "disposal" of the wastes.[51]

In *United States v. Aceto Agricultural & Chemical Co.,*[52] suppliers who sent chemicals to independent formulators and retained ownership of raw materials and final products were held liable for cleanup of the formulator's facility. The court found that despite the fact that the supplier had no knowledge of the formulator's disposal practices, its retention of ownership and the fact that the generation of waste was known to be inherent in the formulation process gave rise to liability. The court analogized the case to common law liability arising from an agency relationship for an ultrahazardous activity.[53]

---

[50] 982 F.2d 989 (6th Cir. 1993).

[51] *Id.* at 998. *See also* Amcast Indus. Corp. v. Detrex Corp., 2 F.2d 746, 1993 U.S. App. LEXIS 20634 (7th Cir. Aug. 12, 1993) (shipment of solvents that were occasionally spilled was not an arrangement for disposal); Jersey City Redevelopment Auth. v. PPG Indus., 655 F. Supp. 1257, 1261 (D.N.J. 1987) (sale of property that contained contaminated soils which were subsequently disposed of by the buyer did not constitute an arrangement for disposal of the soils by the original seller); Kelley v. Arco Indus. Corp., 739 F. Supp. 354, 360 (W.D. Mich. 1990) (rejecting argument that when supplier forwarded materials which supplier knew would be discharged at the end of the manufacturing process, supplier had arranged for disposal of discharged materials); Dayton Indep. School Dist. v. U.S. Mineral Prods. Co., 906 F.2d 1059 (5th Cir. 1990) (no arrangement for disposal of asbestos sold in transfer of building); Prudential Ins. Co. v. United States Gypsum Co., 711 F. Supp. 1244 (D.N.J. 1989) (same); Edward Hines Lumber Co. v. Vulcan Materials Co., 685 F. Supp. 651 (N.D. Ill. 1988), *aff'd,* 861 F.2d 155 (7th Cir. 1988) (finding no arrangement for disposal of hazardous materials in wood treatment chemicals); Florida Power & Light Co. v. Allis-Chalmers Corp., 893 F.2d 1313 (11th Cir. 1990) (no liability for PCBs in products supplied); C. Greene Equip. Co. v. Electron Corp., 697 F. Supp. 983, 987 (N.D. Ill. 1988) (same).

[52] 872 F.2d 1373 (8th Cir. 1989).

[53] *Id.* at 1379–82. *See also* United States v. Velsicol Chem. Corp., 16 CWLR 118, 121 (W.D. Tenn. 1988).

Merely characterizing the transaction as a sale will not insulate parties from liability.[54] Indeed, actual ownership or possession may not be required for a finding of liability.[55] The key to determining arranger liability in such instances appears to rest either in actual control of disposal or in a duty to exercise control over such disposal. Thus, in *General Electric v. Aamco Transmissions, Inc.,*[56] the court affirmed a lower court ruling that an oil company had not arranged for disposal of its tenant service stations' waste oil, where the oil company did not require tenants to do oil changes and did not assume responsibility for waste oil disposal. Sale of virgin oil products and leasing of tanks in which used oil was stored was not an arrangement for disposal. The court stated "it is the *obligation* to exercise control over hazardous waste disposal, and not the mere ability or opportunity to control the disposal of hazardous substances that makes an entity an arranger. . . ."[57]

B. Extended Liability

1. Personal Liability

Generally, "corporate individuals"[58] have been found liable if they fall within one of the four classes of responsible parties under section 107(a). While the breadth of liability under section 107 is not well-settled,[59] it is clear that corporate individuals may be individually liable for hazardous waste cleanup under CERCLA in certain circumstances.[60] However, "[n]ot all employees or managers of a close corporation will necessarily, absent special factors, be liable for a section 107 claim."[61] Instead, liability of a corporate individual for response costs under CERCLA generally will be determined by reference to the degree of authority and control over the activity that gave rise to the release of the hazardous substances involved.[62]

Some courts have phrased the inquiry into individual authority and control as whether the corporate individual could have prevented or significantly abated

---

[54] New York v. General Elec. Co., 592 F. Supp. 291, 297 (N.D.N.Y. 1984). *See also* United States v. Pesses, 1992 WL 111887 (D. Pa. 1992) (sale of scrap metals to reclaimer where evidence showed that reclaimers generally processed materials received by melting, shearing, and so on, was treatment, and seller was liable as arranger).

[55] United States v. Bliss, 667 F. Supp. 1298 (E.D. Mo. 1987) (defendant who acted as a broker between a chemical manufacturer and a disposal company had arranged for disposal; key fact was that the broker had a sufficient degree of control over the waste and the ultimate disposal thereof to meet the intent of the statute); CPC Int'l v. Aerojet Gen. Corp., 759 F. Supp. 1269, 22 CWLR 172, 179–80 (W.D. Mich. 1991) (finding that liability under CERCLA does not require ownership or possession of the hazardous substances and may extend to those who assumed responsibility for determining the fate of the hazardous substance).

[56] 962 F.2d 281, 285 (2d Cir. 1985).

[57] *Id.* at 286–87.

[58] Including directors, officers, trustees, employees, and stockholders.

[59] Conductron Corp. v. Williams, 785 F. Supp. 271, 274 (D.N.H. 1991).

[60] Kelly v. Thomas Solvent Co., 727 F. Supp. 1532, 1541–42 (W.D. Mich. 1989).

[61] *Id.* at 1543.

[62] *Id.;* Conductron Corp. v. Williams, 785 F. Supp. at 274; Quadion Corp. v. Mache, 1991 WL 111170, n.5 (N.D. Ill. 1991); Riverside Mkt. Dev. Corp. v. International Bldg. Prods., 1990 WL 72249, *3–4 (E.D. La. 1990); United States v. Carolina Transformer, 739 F. Supp. 1030, 106–38 (E.D.N.C. 1989), *aff'd,* 978 F.2d 832 (4th Cir. 1992); United States v. New Castle County, 727 F. Supp. 854, 869 (D. Del. 1989); United States v. Northeastern Pharmaceutical & Chem. Co., 810 F.2d 726, 745 (8th Cir. 1986), *cert. denied,* 484 U.S. 848 (1987); Shore Realty, 759 F.2d at 1052.

the hazardous substance discharge that forms the basis of the claim.[63] Other courts have asked whether the individual had direct responsibility for and control of the disposal practice at issue.[64] Regardless of the question's formulation, the inquiry is ultimately the same: did the individual have a sufficiently close nexus to the disposal activity giving rise to harm, either through actions or responsibilities, for a court to justify imposition of individual liability for acts carried out on behalf of the corporation?

In order to determine an individual's degree of involvement with and ability to control the disposal practices at issue, the courts have employed a balancing test composed of the following factors: sizable stock ownership in the corporation; active participation in the management of the corporation; whether the individual holds the position of officer or director, especially where there is a co-existing management position; presence at and supervision of the facility; distribution of power or ability to control waste disposal practices within the corporation; evidence of responsibility undertaken for waste disposal practices (including evidence of responsibility undertaken and neglected); power to negotiate regarding the disposal and handling of hazardous waste; and ability to prevent and abate the damage caused by the disposal of hazardous waste.[65] Courts have specifically held that an individual with responsibility for waste disposal cannot avoid liability by deliberately remaining ignorant of disposal practices.[66]

The case law, however, does not provide clear guidance on how these factors are to be weighted. Instead, this judgment is left to the courts on a case-by-case basis. Because of the subjective nature of the inquiry, exposure of corporate individuals cannot be assessed with great accuracy. In all of the cases addressing this issue, however, the courts were presented with for-profit, close corporations, or situations in which individuals were actively involved in the business at issue. Thus, although dicta from the test enunciated is certainly broad enough to encompass many situations, the law has not progressed to impose liability upon remote corporate individuals.

2. *Related Entity Liability*

Unlike assessments of individual liability, common law rules apply, for the most part, in assessing the environmental liability of corporate entities related to the principal "responsible party." This issue generally arises where the corporation directly involved at the site is either insolvent or defunct. In such situations, plaintiffs have attempted to establish that a corporate entity related to the defunct defendant may be held liable for the acts of that defunct corporation. This section will discuss the assessment of liability in the CERCLA context against (1) successor corporations and (2) parent and subsidiary corporations.

a. Liability of Successors. A successor corporation's liability for its predecessor's acts depends on the nature of the ownership transfer. In the event of a *de jure* merger or consolidation, the surviving corporation assumes the

[63] Thomas Solvent, 727 F. Supp. at 1541–42.

[64] Conductron, 785 F. Supp. at 274.

[65] *See* Thomas Solvent, 727 F. Supp. at 1543; Carolina Transformer, 739 F. Supp. at 1036–38.

[66] Quaidon, 1991 WL 111170, at n.5; Aceto, 872 F.2d at 1382.

debts and liabilities of the merged or consolidated corporation.[67] In contrast, a corporation acquiring the assets of a second corporation ordinarily does not assume the acquired corporation's debts and liabilities. The four exceptions to this general rule governing asset sales are

1. The express or implied assumption of the predecessor's liabilities by the acquiring corporation;
2. A *de facto* merger or consolidation in which the shareholders remain the same;
3. The mere continuation by the successor of the predecessor's business (same shareholders, directors, and officers); or
4. A fraudulent transaction designed to avoid the liabilities of the predecessor.[68]

With limited exceptions, the general rules of corporate successor liability have been applied in CERCLA contribution actions. In *Smith Land & Improvement Corp. v. Celotex Corp.,*[69] for example, the defendants were successor corporations to the company that originally had generated an asbestos pile on the plaintiff's land. In its discussion of whether the case against the successors to the original generators could proceed, the Third Circuit noted that the general common law principles governing the liability of a corporation for the torts of its predecessor are "equally applicable to the assessment of responsibility for clean-up costs under CERCLA." The court reasoned that the policies underlying CERCLA required courts to apply traditional common law rules in assessing the liability of successor corporations:

> Congressional intent supports the conclusion that, when choosing between taxpayers or a successor corporation, the successor should bear the cost. Benefits from use of the pollutant as well as savings resulting from the failure to use nonhazardous disposal methods inured to the original corporation, its successors, and their respective stockholders, and accrued only indirectly, if at all, to the general public. We believe it in line with the thrust of the legislation to permit—if not require—successor liability under traditional concepts.[70]

In applying the general rule of successor liability in asset sales, Superfund decisions have focused on two of the exemptions listed above. In *Michigan v.*

---

[67] Smith Land & Improvement Corp. v. Celotex Corp., 851 F.2d 86 (3d Cir. 1988), *cert. denied,* 488 U.S. 1029 (1989); New Jersey Transp. Dep't v. PSC Resources, 175 N.J. Super. 447, 419 A.2d 1151 (1980); 15 W. Fletcher, Cyclopedia of the Law of Private Corporations §7121, at 185 (rev. perm. ed. 1983).

[68] Philadelphia Elec. Co. v. Hercules, Inc., 762 F.2d 303, 310 (3d Cir.), *cert. denied,* 474 U.S. 980 (1985); Bud Antle, Inc. v. Eastern Foods, Inc., 758 F.2d 1451, 1457–58 (11th Cir. 1985); Leannis v. Cincinnati, Inc., 565 F.2d 437, 439 (7th Cir. 1977).

[69] 851 F.2d 86, 91 (3d Cir. 1988), *cert. denied,* 488 U.S. 1029 (1989).

[70] *Id.* at 92. The majority of courts addressing this issue have similarly held that traditional rules of corporate liability should apply in the Superfund context. *See* Louisiana-Pac. Corp. v. Asarco, 909 F.2d 1260 (9th Cir. 1990); GRM Indus., Inc. v. Wickes Mfg. Co., No. G89-30388 (W.D. Mich. Feb. 19, 1990); Michigan v. Thomas Solvent, 29 ER Cases 1119 (W.D. Mich. 1988); United States v. Crown Roll Leaf, Inc., 29 ER Cases 2018 (D.N.J. 1988). *But see* Anspec Co. v. Johnson Controls, Inc., 30 ER Cases 1672, 1674 (E.D. Mich. 1989) (court refused to expand CERCLA liability beyond the four categories of potentially responsible parties enumerated in CERCLA §107(a) in order to trace liability to the successors, this reasoning was expressly rejected in the *GRM Indus.* case).

Thomas Solvent Co.,[71] the District Court for the Western District of Michigan discussed the circumstances giving rise to a finding of successor corporate liability following an asset sale under the "mere continuation" theory. The case involved the "spinoff" of several corporations from the original Thomas Solvent Company following notice to Thomas Solvent of its potential CERCLA liability. In finding the spinoff corporations to be mere continuations of the original corporation, the court noted the presence of the following factors: a common identity of officers, directors, and stockholders between the purchasing and selling corporations, and a continuity of staff and operations.

The second exception to the asset sale rule that has been applied in the CERCLA context is the "continuing business enterprise." This theory is essentially an expansion of the "mere continuation" exemption. Rather than requiring some combination of identity between officers, directors, and stockholders, continuing business enterprise liability follows from the continuation by the successor corporation of the predecessor's business line. When applying this exemption, courts look to the following criteria: (1) continuity of employees, supervisory personnel, and physical location; (2) production of the same product; (3) retention of the same name; (4) continuity of general business operations; and (5) the purchaser's holding itself out as a continuation of the seller.[72]

Applying this exemption, the court in *United States v. Distler,*[73] found a successor corporation liable where the successor company retained the same employees and management, operated out of the same plant and produced the same product, and held itself out to the public as the same company. A similar result was affirmed by the Fourth Circuit in *United States v. Carolina Transformer Co.*[74]

While the continuing business enterprise liability theory has yet to become widely accepted in environmental litigation before federal courts, EPA has adopted the theory in an effort to broaden Superfund liability. In 1984, EPA issued a policy statement in which the agency announced that it would seek to hold a successor corporation liable for the environmental torts of its predecessor corporation if the successor acquires assets of the predecessor and continues substantially the same business operations as the predecessor.[75] In its June 1984 memorandum, EPA adopted the continuing business theory as its primary successor liability theory:

> In establishing successor liability under CERCLA, the Agency should initially utilize the "continuity of business operation" approach of federal law. However, to provide additional support or an alternative basis for successor liability, the

---

[71] 29 ER Cases 1119, 1129–30 (W.D. Mich. 1988). *See also* United States v. Vertac Chem. Corp., 671 F. Supp. 595 (E.D. Ark. 1987).

[72] Louisiana-Pac. Corp. v. Asarco, 909 F.2d 1260 (9th Cir. 1990) (refusing to apply the exception where corporate successor did not in fact continue predecessor's business); Mozingo v. Correct Mfg. Corp., 752 F.2d 168, 175 (5th Cir. 1985).

[73] 741 F. Supp. 637 (W.D. Ky. 1990).

[74] 739 F. Supp. 1030, 1036–38 (E.D.N.C. 1989), *aff'd,* 978 F.2d 832 (4th Cir. 1992).

[75] Courtney M. Price, EPA Memorandum, Liability of Corporate Shareholders and Successor Corporations for Abandoned Sites Under CERCLA 13–14 (June 13, 1984).

Agency should be prepared to apply the traditional exemptions to the general rule of nonliability in asset acquisitions.[76]

b. Liability of Parents and Subsidaries. As in the case of successor corporation liability, the liability of parent and subsidary corporations for the actions of related corporate entities under CERCLA will be decided by reference to common law concepts.[77] The test used by the courts in determining whether a parent will be held liable is whether the parent had pervasive control of the subsidary. Pervasive control is a function of nine factors: (1) whether the parent and the subsidiary have common stock ownership, directors or officers, common business departments, or consolidated financial statements and tax returns; (2) whether the parent finances the subsidiary; (3) whether the parent caused the incorporation of the subsidiary; (4) whether the subsidiary is undercapitalized; (5) whether the parent pays the salaries and expenses of the subsidiary; (6) whether the subsidiary receives business only from the parent; (7) whether the parent uses the subsidiary's property as its own; (8) whether the daily operations of the two corporations are kept separate; and (9) whether the subsidary observes basic formalities of the corporate form.[78]

Applying this test, the court in *United States v. Kayser-Roth Corp.*,[79] found that the parent corporation exercised pervasive control over its subsidiary. It based this finding on a number of conditions pointing to the parent's control over the subsidiary: (1) total monetary control; (2) restrictions on the subsidiary's financial budget; (3) a directive to the subsidiary that all contact with the government on environmental issues be funnelled through the parent; (4) the requirement that purchases, lease of or sales of real estate by the subsidiary be approved by the parent; (5) a policy that the parent approve all expenditures over $5,000; and (6) the placement of parent personnel in almost all director and officer positions.[80]

C. Governmental Liability

1. Federal Government

Like any other party, the federal government may be held liable under CERCLA if it falls under one of the four categories of responsible parties.[81] Generally, such liability will be visited on one of the agencies of the federal government through its ownership and operation of a federal facility.[82] Facilities operated by the Department of Defense or the Department of Energy are most often the prime targets for such liability.[83]

---

[76] *Id.* at 16.

[77] Joslyn Corp. v. T.L. James & Co., 696 F. Supp. 222, 224–25 (W.D. La. 1988), *aff'd,* 893 F.2d 80, 83 (5th Cir. 1990), *cert. denied,* 111 S. Ct. 1017 (1991).

[78] *Id.*

[79] 724 F. Supp. 15 (D.R.I. 1989), *aff'd,* 910 F.2d 24 (1st Cir. 1990).

[80] *See also* Idaho v. Bunker Hill Co., 634 F. Supp. 800 (D. Idaho 1986).

[81] *See, e.g.,* F.M.C. Corp. v. Department of Commerce, 786 F. Supp. 471 (E.D. Pa. 1992), *aff'd* 1993 WL 489133 (3d. Cir. Nov. 26, 1993).

[82] *Cf.* United States v. Monsanto, 858 F.2d 160, 164 n.2, 170–71 (4th Cir. 1988), *cert. denied,* 109 S. Ct. 1356 (1989).

[83] LIGHT, *supra* note 6, at 142–43.

One of the most significant debates in regard to federal governmental liability has been the extent to which governmental regulatory activity will give rise to owner or operator liability. Courts generally have been unwilling to impose owner or operator liability on the federal government solely on the basis of regulatory activities.[84] This is true even where EPA arguably has been negligent in performing a cleanup, and this has caused increased contamination at a site.[85] There is one exception to this general rule, however.

In *F.M.C. Corp. v. Department of Commerce,*[86] a Pennsylvania district court found that the government could be held liable as an owner or operator based on regulatory activities that amounted to control of the day-to-day operations of a facility. At issue in the case were the activities of the War Production Board (WPB) in regulating the rayon industry during the Second World War. The WPB controlled the day-to-day activities of the industry in general and the site's operator in particular. The court found that the WPB's activities went beyond mere regulation and conferred operator status on the government.

2. *State and Local Governments*

As with the federal government, state and local governments are liable under CERCLA.[87] The conditions meriting a finding of liability are similar: mere regulation often will not be enough to impose liability on a state,[88] but where there is clear evidence of control of day-to-day operations at a site, liability may attach. Thus in *United States v. Freeman,*[89] a state that took over daily operations of a facility for a period of two years was determined to have operator liability under CERCLA.[90]

Although clearly within that class of persons who may be considered an owner under the statute, a state or local government is exempt from liability if it obtained the property involuntarily through the exercise of its sovereign powers.[91] In such circumstances, the present owner and operator is not the governmental entity, but is "any person who owned, operated or otherwise controlled activities at such facility" immediately prior to a conveyance of the facility to a state or local government through bankruptcy, foreclosure, or other similar procedure.[92]

---

[84] *In re* Paoli Railyard PCB Litig., 790 F. Supp. 94, 95–97 (E.D. Pa. 1992); United States v. Skipper, 781 F. Supp. 1106 (E.D.N.C. 1991); United States v. Western Processing, 761 F. Supp. 725, 728–30 (W.D. Wash. 1991).

[85] United States v. Dart Indus., 847 F.2d 144, 146 (4th Cir. 1988); United States v. Azrael, 765 F. Supp. 1239 (D. Md. 1991); Paoli Railyard, 790 F. Supp. at 95–97.

[86] 786 F. Supp. 471 (E.D. Pa. 1992).

[87] B.F. Goodrich v. Murtha, 958 F.2d 1192, 1197–98 (2d Cir. 1992) (municipal arranger liability); Transportation Leasing Co. v. California, 23 Env't Rep. (BNA) 1151 (Aug. 8, 1992) (municipalities liable as arrangers); Pennsylvania v. Union Gas, 491 U.S. 1, 8–9 (1989) (state liable as owner/operator); United States v. Stringfellow, 19 CWLR 1034, 1040–41 (C.D. Cal. 1990) (state liable as owner/operator).

[88] United States v. New Castle County, 727 F. Supp. 854, 869 (D. Del. 1989); United States v. Carolawn, 698 F. Supp. 616, 621–22 (E.D.N.C. 1987); Dart Indus., 847 F.2d at 146; *cf.* United States v. Stringfellow, 19 CWLR 1034 (C.D. Cal. 1990).

[89] 680 F. Supp. 73, 79 (W.D.N.Y. 1988).

[90] *See also* CPC v. Aerojet Gen. Corp., 759 F. Supp. 1269, 22 CWLR 172, 179–80 (W.D. Mich. 1991).

[91] CERCLA §101(25)(D), 42 U.S.C. §9601(25)(D).

[92] CERCLA §101(20)(A), 42 U.S.C. §9601(20)(A).

Although a state or local government may escape liability when it comes into possession of property involuntarily, active responsibility for the disposal activity at a facility will void the exemption.[93] However, the exercise of regulatory power, by itself, will not give rise to governmental responsibility for a release.[94] Yet, the distinction between regulatory action and more active participation is not always apparent. In *United States v. New Castle County,*[95] the court denied plaintiff's motion for summary judgment for liability against the state which had been deeply involved in the planning and regulation of a model disposal site. The court found that the state's actions did not exceed its regulatory function and was not the hands-on participation in day-to-day management necessary for liability.[96]

Recently, local governments concerned about CERCLA liability, particularly arranger liability,[97] have contested their liability legislatively, as well as in the courts and before EPA. Local governments argue that they cannot afford to shoulder such liability, especially in those situations in which they only performed the governmental function of arranging for disposal of household and other municipal wastes at sites they neither owned nor operated.

A number of local governments first pressed EPA for a rulemaking which would limit their exposure at Superfund sites. When this effort failed in 1992, these governments turned to Congress. Senator Lautenberg (D-N.J.) and others sponsored several bills that would have limited the liability of local governments and precluded contribution actions against them. Lautenberg's bill passed the Senate but died in the House.

Municipal liability continues to be a controversial topic, with several bills currently under consideration in Congress. However, a number of approaches that differ from Senator Lautenberg's have developed, and it is difficult to predict whether consensus will emerge. In any event, this is likely to be one of the controversial topics in the upcoming Superfund reauthorization debate.

III. Liability-Triggering Events

A. Release or Threat of Release

As a predicate to a finding of liability, a CERCLA plaintiff must prove that there has been a "release" or "threat of release" of a hazardous substance.[98] The statute defines the term "release" very broadly to encompass any "spilling, leaking, pumping, pouring, emitting, emptying, discharging, injecting, escaping, leaching, dumping, or disposing into the environment."[99] Courts have concluded that a number of activities amount to "releases" within the meaning of the statute. Thus, for example, hazardous substances released in soil

---

[93] Stilloe v. Amery Bros., 759 F. Supp. 95 (N.D.N.Y. 1991).

[94] Dart Indus., 847 F.2d at 146; Carolawn Co., 698 F. Supp. at 621–22.

[95] 727 F. Supp. 854, 869 (D. Del. 1989).

[96] *Id.*

[97] Such concern arises out of the findings of liability in cases like B.F. Goodrich, 958 F.2d at 1197–98 and Transportation Leasing Co., 23 Env't Rep. at 1151.

[98] CERCLA §107(a), 42 U.S.C. §9607(a).

[99] CERCLA §101(22), 42 U.S.C. §9601(22).

or groundwater,[100] or leaking from drums,[101] amount to the requisite "releases" necessary to trigger liability. It is not necessary that the release occur offsite;[102] the release need only be to the "environment" which includes surface and groundwater, land surface or subsurface, or ambient air.[103]

Moreover, the Superfund plaintiff need only prove a "threat" of release to invoke CERCLA jurisdiction.[104] Thus, response actions can be initiated and cleanup undertaken even though no actual release of hazardous substances has occurred. Such a threat of release can be proven merely by a history of past releases.[105] Thus, as a general proposition, proof of release is not a difficult burden for the plaintiff.

B. Hazardous Substance

In addition to proving that there has been a "release" or "threat of release," the Superfund plaintiff must also establish that any substance which has been released or which poses a threat of release is a "hazardous substance." The phrase "hazardous substance" is one of the broadest terms employed in CERCLA, as it is defined by reference to a wide array of other environmental statutes. Thus, section 101(14) provides that "hazardous substance" includes materials designated under various provisions of the Clean Air Act (CAA), the Resource Conservation and Recovery Act (RCRA), the Toxic Substances Control Act (TSCA), and the Clean Water Act (CWA).[106] In addition to materials specified in these statutes, CERCLA permits EPA to designate other materials as hazardous substances if they "may" present a substantial danger to health and the environment.[107] Thus, the hazardous substances within CERCLA's ambit includes a wide universe of substances.[108]

---

[100] *E.g.,* United States v. Northernaire Plating Co., 670 F. Supp. 742, 746 (W.D. Mich. 1987), *aff'd sub nom.* United States v. R.W. Meyer, Inc., 889 F.2d 1497 (6th Cir. 1989), *cert. denied,* 110 S. Ct. 1527 (1990).

[101] Emhart Indus., Inc. v. Duracell Int'l, Inc., 665 F. Supp. 549, 574 (M.D. Tenn. 1987).

[102] *E.g.,* United States v. Mottolo, 695 F. Supp. 615 (D.N.H. 1988).

[103] CERCLA §101(8), 42 U.S.C. §9601(8).

[104] *E.g., In re* FCX, Inc., 96 B.R. 49, 51–52, 19 Envtl. L. Rep. (Envtl. L. Inst.) 20,849, 20,850 (Bankr. E.D.N.C.), *cert. denied,* 109 S. Ct. 1118 (1989).

[105] New York v. Shore Realty Corp., 759 F.2d 1032, 1045 (2d Cir. 1985).

[106] Hazardous substance is defined to mean:

> (A) any substance designated pursuant to section 1321(b)(2)(A) of Title 33, (B) any element, compound, mixture, solution, or substance designated pursuant to section 9602 of this title, (C) any hazardous waste having the characteristics identified under or listed pursuant to section 3001 of the [RCRA] (but not including any waste the regulation of which under the Solid Waste Disposal Act has been suspended by Act of Congress), (D) any toxic pollutant listed under section 307(a) of the Federal Water Pollution Control Act, (E) any hazardous air pollutant listed under section 112 of the Clean Air Act, and (F) any imminently hazardous chemical substance or mixture with respect to which the Administrator has taken action pursuant to section 7 of the Toxic Substances Control Act.

CERCLA §101(14), 42 U.S.C. §9601(14).

[107] CERCLA §102(a), 42 U.S.C. §9602(a).

[108] The statute also includes the term "pollutant or contaminant" that can be any other substance which is not a hazardous substance but which "will or may reasonably be anticipated to cause" various adverse effects on the environment. CERCLA §101(33), 42 U.S.C. §9601(33). The significance of the term is limited in that a pollutant or contaminant cleanup does not give rise to liability; liability only attaches for cleanup of hazardous substances. In addition, one does not have reporting obligations arising from releases of pollutants or contaminants.

The universe of "hazardous substances" under CERCLA is much larger than the universe of "hazardous wastes" under RCRA. While under RCRA a waste must be either listed as a hazardous waste or evidence a characteristic in order to be "hazardous," the same is not true for "hazardous substances" under CERCLA. Though the RCRA determination will require a certain concentration in many instances, EPA has taken the view that for CERCLA any concentration is sufficient to trigger liability. And, in fact, a number of courts have held that very small concentrations of listed substances within a solution constitute a "hazardous substance," notwithstanding the arguments that the materials were not RCRA "hazardous wastes" or environmentally harmful.[109]

Two exemptions from the broad definition of hazardous substances have generated great controversy. First, the "petroleum exclusion" exempts from the definition of hazardous substances

> petroleum, including crude oil or any fraction thereof which is not otherwise specifically listed or designated as a hazardous substance under subparagraphs (A) through (F) of this paragraph, and the term does not include natural gas, natural gas liquids, liquefied natural gas, or synthetic gas usable for fuel (or mixtures of natural gas and such synthetic gas).[110]

All petroleum naturally contains some constituents which would otherwise render the petroleum a hazardous substance (*i.e.,* benzene or toluene). Apparently recognizing that to designate petroleum as hazardous by virtue of the presence of these constituents would eviscerate the exclusion, EPA has taken the view that petroleum is not per se a hazardous substance. Instead, EPA and the courts have concluded that only if a petroleum solution includes materials that are not normally found in petroleum does it fall outside the exclusion from CERCLA liability. Thus, petroleum contaminated with other wastes has been held to be a "hazardous substance" the release of which can trigger CERCLA liability.[111]

Second, the "Bevill Amendment" exemption carved out in the parenthetical of section 101(14)(C) has proved troublesome. Within the list of materials covered by the term "hazardous substance," Congress included "any hazardous waste having the characteristics identified under or listed pursuant to section 3001 of [RCRA] *(but not including any waste the regulation of which under [RCRA] has been suspended by Act of Congress).*"[112] The parenthetical is a reference to a series of wastes the regulation of which was exempted from RCRA under an amendment to RCRA offered by Congressman Bevill in 1980.[113]

---

[109] *E.g.,* United States v. Alcan Aluminum Corp., 964 F.2d 252, 260–62 (3d Cir. 1992); Amoco Oil Co. v. Borden, Inc., 889 F.2d 664, 669 (5th Cir. 1989); City of New York v. Exxon Corp., 766 F. Supp. 177, 184–85 (S.D.N.Y. 1991); Arizona v. Motorola, Inc., 774 F. Supp. 566 (D. Ariz. 1991); United States v. Conservation Chem. Co., 619 F. Supp. 192, 238 (W.D. Mo. 1985); *but see* United States v. Ottati & Goss, Inc., 22 ER Cases 1736, 1739 (D.N.H. 1984) (granting motion to dismiss because defendant "did not cause or contribute to cause the disposal of any hazardous wastes . . . which exceeded the threshold established by the EPA for hazardous wastes"), *aff'd in relevant part,* 900 F.2d 429 (1st Cir. 1990).

[110] CERCLA §101(14), 42 U.S.C. §9601(14).

[111] *E.g.,* Alcan Aluminum, 964 F.2d at 266–67; Wilshire Westwood Assoc. v. Atlantic Richfield Corp., 881 F.2d 801, 803–05 (9th Cir. 1989); City of New York v. Exxon, 766 F. Supp. at 184–85.

[112] CERCLA §101(14), 42 U.S.C. §9601(14) (emphasis added).

[113] RCRA §3001(b)(2), 42 U.S.C. §6921(b)(2).

In the leading decision on the Bevill Amendment under CERCLA, *Eagle-Picher Industries v. EPA,*[114] the U.S. Court of Appeals for the District of Columbia Circuit addressed the exemption. The court ruled that if a substance is within the list of Bevill Amendment wastes, it is exempt from CERCLA coverage as a RCRA waste. However, if the substance is among those listed elsewhere in the provision, under another of the environmental statutes which form a part of the definition of hazardous substance, the material remains regulated under CERCLA.[115] While several other courts have adopted this analysis,[116] the District Court for the Eastern District of California reached a different conclusion in *United States v. Iron Mountain Mines, Inc.*[117] The court analyzed the legislative history of the CERCLA definition and concluded that its drafters intended that the special mining wastes that were included in the Bevill Amendment were not to have been considered hazardous substances under CERCLA. The court focused on language from the Senate Report where the exemption originated. There, the drafters noted that "any substance or material for which regulation is specifically suspended by Act of Congress under [RCRA] is excluded from designation as a hazardous substance for the purpose of S.1280, notwithstanding the presence in such substance of any hazardous or toxic chemical."[118] The CERCLA reauthorization process or additional litigation may well be necessary to settle the conflicting views.

IV. The National Contingency Plan

CERCLA liability extends to (1) any costs of response incurred by a government (federal, state, or Indian tribe) "not inconsistent with the national contingency plan"[119] and (2) "any other necessary costs of response incurred by any other person consistent with the national contingency plan."[120] Although the statute speaks in terms of the consistency of "costs" with the plan, in fact the inquiry is really whether the response actions giving rise to the claimed costs are consistent with the plan.

A. Background

The National Contingency Plan (NCP) establishes the standards that are to be used in responding to releases or threatened releases at a given site. The NCP does not set out detailed technical standards governing the type of cleanup methods to be used in particular situations. Instead, it governs the process

[114] 759 F.2d 905 (D.C. Cir. 1985); 822 F.2d 132 (D.C. Cir. 1987).

[115] Thus in *Eagle-Picher,* ore-mining waste, which is among the materials listed under the Bevill Amendment, was considered a CERCLA hazardous substance because components of mining waste are also regulated under the other provisions listed within the definition (*i.e.,* the Clean Water Act or TSCA).

[116] Idaho v. Hanna Mining Co., 699 F. Supp. 827, 833 (D. Idaho 1987); Bunker Hill Co., 634 F. Supp. at 673; United States v. Metate Asbestos, 584 F. Supp. 1143, 1147 (D. Ariz. 1984).

[117] 812 F. Supp. 1528 (E.D. Cal. 1992), *reaff'd,* reconsideration granted, summ. judgment denied, 1993 U.S. Dist. LEXIS 1665 (E.D. Cal. Jan. 22, 1993).

[118] *Id.* (citing S. Rep. No. 848, 96th Cong., 2d Sess. 28 (1980)).

[119] CERCLA §107(a)(4)(A), 42 U.S.C. §9607(a)(4)(A); 40 C.F.R. pt. 300.

[120] CERCLA §107(a)(4)(B), 42 U.S.C. §9607(a)(4)(B).

through which the ultimate technical approach to a particular site or problem is chosen.

Prior to the passage of CERCLA in 1980, the NCP (published first in 1968) dealt mainly with oil spills under the Clean Water Act.[121] The first post-CERCLA amendment of the NCP came in 1982 in response to the requirements of section 105 of the Act. Section 105 required that the NCP include

1. Methods to ascertain the locations of hazardous substance facilities;
2. Methods for evaluation and remediation of releases or threatened releases of hazardous substances that pose a substantial threat to public health or the environment, including analyses of costs;
3. Methods and criteria for determining the appropriate extent of removal or remedial actions authorized by the statute;
4. The appropriate roles of federal, state, and local governments and of interstate and nongovernmental bodies affecting the NCP;
5. Provisions for the identification, procurement, maintenance, and storage of response equipment and supplies;
6. A method for assigning reporting responsibility for "facilities" that may be located on federal property;
7. Means of assuring that remedial action measures are cost-effective throughout their active lives; and
8. Criteria for determining priorities among releases or threatened releases throughout the United States and evaluating potential urgency in order to take removal actions.

On November 20, 1985, EPA amended the NCP to require strict compliance in both private and governmental cleanups with the response requirements originally mandated by section 105.[122] Thus 40 C.F.R. §300.71(a)(2) provided that a private cleanup would be consistent and a governmental cleanup would not be inconsistent with the NCP if (1) in circumstances warranting a removal action, the removal was done in accordance with 40 C.F.R. §300.65, or (2) in circumstances warranting a remedial action, there was appropriate site investigation and analysis of remedial alternatives under 40 C.F.R. §300.68; compliance with subsections .68(e) through (i); selection of a cost-effective remedy; and opportunity for appropriate public comment under subsection .67(d) (unless applicable, relevant, and appropriate state or local requirements provided for a substantial equivalent). The regulations incorporated detailed response requirements that had to be followed.[123]

In addition, the 1985 NCP amendments added two other important requirements. First was the requirement that response actions comply, to the greatest extent possible, with all applicable or relevant and appropriate public health and environmental requirements. Second, the 1985 NCP added provisions that

[121] 42 U.S.C. §1251 *et seq.;* 40 C.F.R. pt. 300.

[122] County Line Inv. Co. v. Tinney, 933 F.2d 1508, 1513 (10th Cir. 1991). (The Tenth Circuit rejected the contention that the district court need only have "considered whether [the parties'] remedial action was cost efficient, environmentally sound, and appropriate under the circumstances[.]" Rather, the court chose to read the language of the 1985 NCP and EPA's interpretation of it to require strict compliance with the NCP's standards and procedures.) The amendment to the NCP was originally published at 30 Fed. Reg. 47951 (1985), and may now be found at 40 C.F.R. §300 *et seq.*

[123] *See* 40 C.F.R. §§300.65 (removals), 300.67 (community relations), and 300.68 (remedial actions).

required EPA preapproval before any response action could be paid by Superfund.[124]

The second post-CERCLA amendment occurred in 1990. Although much of the NCP's structure in regard to response actions was retained, EPA made a number of important revisions.[125] First, public comment requirements were amended such that a party could now hold either a public hearing or have a public comment period.[126] Second, and most significantly, the 1990 amendments dropped the strict compliance standard imposed in 1985. Thus, 40 C.F.R. §300.700 now requires "substantial compliance" with the NCP in order for parties to recover response costs. Moreover, the section notes that

> [A]ny response action carried out in compliance with the terms of an order issued by EPA pursuant to section 106 of CERCLA or a consent decree entered into pursuant to section 122 of CERCLA, will be considered consistent with the NCP.[127]

This new standard essentially inquires into whether the "cleanup has, when evaluated as a whole, achieved substantial compliance . . . and resulted in a CERCLA-quality cleanup."[128] EPA's change was a reaction to a concern that the strict compliance standard of the 1985 version of the NCP would discourage private party cleanups at the expense of the Superfund.[129] Revision of the strict compliance standard was intended to "remove unnecessary obstacles to [private parties'] ability to recover their cost from parties that are liable for the contamination."[130]

Courts have been inconsistent in their determinations of what will be considered substantial NCP compliance. In *General Electric v. Litton Business Systems, Inc.*,[131] the court essentially applied a substantial compliance standard even though it was dealing with the 1985 NCP. In so doing, the court found that the absence of public hearings as required by the 1985 NCP would not bar plaintiff's recovery of response costs.

In contrast, the court in *Channel Master Satellite v. JFD Electronics Corp.*[132] found that even under the substantial compliance standard, failure to hold public hearings or to provide public comment prevented recovery of response costs by the plaintiff. Moreover, the court rejected out of hand the contention that consultation with EPA on the cleanup satisfied the public hearing requirement.

Neither the 1985 nor the 1990 versions of the NCP defined the term "consistent"; however, the 1990 version sets forth nine criteria for evaluating consistency with the NCP. The regulations make clear that these factors are to be used as guidance only, and not followed slavishly in each instance.[133]

---

[124] These requirements were later upheld in Ohio v. EPA, 838 F.2d 1325 (D.C. Cir. 1988).

[125] 55 Fed. Reg. 8666 (1990).

[126] 40 C.F.R. §300.700(c)(6). Under the 1985 provisions a party was obligated to hold a public hearing.

[127] 40 C.F.R. §300.700.

[128] 55 Fed. Reg. at 8793.

[129] *See* 55 Fed. Reg. at 8666, 8792–93.

[130] 55 Fed. Reg. at 8792–93.

[131] 715 F. Supp. 949, 961 (W.D. Mo. 1989), *aff'd*, 920 F.2d 1415 (8th Cir. 1990).

[132] 748 F. Supp. 373, 389–90 (E.D.N.C. 1990).

[133] 55 Fed. Reg. at 8793. The NCP instructs a claimant to evaluate the following: (1) worker health and safety; (2) removal site evaluation; (3) remedial site evaluation; (4) documentation of costs; (5) determination

B. Distinction Between Private and Public Cleanups

When the government seeks to recover its costs of response it is entitled to all costs of response "not inconsistent with" the NCP.[134] In practice this means that the government's response costs are presumed to comply with the NCP and the burden shifts to the defendant to prove inconsistency.[135] This requires the challenging defendant to examine the detailed requirements of 40 C.F.R. part 300 to search out areas that the government might have ignored.

In contrast, as part of its prima facie case[136] the private plaintiff must prove that its costs are both (1) consistent with the NCP and (2) necessary.[137] Although the shift to the substantial compliance standard eases this burden, the private plaintiff must be prepared to demonstrate that it has, in fact, substantially complied with the requirements of the NCP. The presence of this requirement means that private claimants must consider carefully each cleanup step because the presumption of compliance afforded the government is not available to them. Moreover, as neither the NCP nor the case law has defined the term "necessary," private plaintiffs can expect further challenges to the necessity of various costs.

C. General Procedural Requirements

Consistent with the statute, the NCP divides response actions into two distinct types, removal actions and remedial actions. The procedural requirements differ for each category, with removal actions being subject to less stringent requirements.

1. Removal Actions

Removal actions are

> the cleanup or removal of released hazardous substances from the environment, [and] such actions as may be necessary to be taken in the event of the threat of release of hazardous substances into the environment, such actions as may be necessary to monitor, assess or evaluate the release or threat of release of hazardous substances, the disposal of removed material, or the taking of such actions as may be necessary to prevent, minimize or mitigate damage to the public health, welfare or to the environment, which may otherwise result from a release or threat of a release.[138]

These actions are not designed to implement permanent solutions but rather to alleviate imminent hazards.[139] Because of the potentially imminent nature of

---

of the need for fund-financed action and identification of Applicable Relevant and Appropriate Requirements (ARARs); (6) whether release reporting requirements have been met; (7) removal actions; (8) operation and maintenance; and (9) development of the Remedial Investigation/Feasibility Study (RI/FS) and selection of the remedy.

[134] CERCLA §107, 42 U.S.C. §9607; 40 C.F.R. §300.700.

[135] 55 Fed. Reg. 8794 (1990).

[136] County Line Inv., 933 F.2d at 1513–15; Ambrogi v. Gould, Inc., 750 F. Supp. 1233, 1253 (M.D. Pa. 1991); Amland Properties Corp. v. Aluminum Co. of Am., 711 F. Supp. 784, 794 (D.N.J. 1989).

[137] 55 Fed. Reg. 8794 (1990); CERCLA §107, 42 U.S.C. §9607.

[138] CERCLA §101(23), 42 U.S.C. §9601(23).

[139] Versatile Metals, Inc. v. Union Corp., 693 F. Supp. 1563, 1577 (E.D. Pa. 1988).

the threat and because the response is not designed to be permanent, the NCP does not require the plaintiff seeking recovery of removal costs to clear all of the hurdles set out for remedial actions. Instead the NCP employs a two-step process.

Prior to implementation of a removal, the NCP requires that a party undertake a Removal Site Evaluation, which is essentially an initial reconnaissance of the site. The Removal Site Evaluation is required in order to identify sources and potential migration and exposure pathways, and to evaluate the threat to determine if a removal action is necessary.[140]

In addition to this site evaluation, a party may also undertake a Removal Site Inspection.[141] The Removal Site Inspection, which is a more detailed inspection of the site, follows up and builds upon the Removal Site Evaluation. It has the same objectives as the Removal Site Evaluation and is required only where the inspecting party believes that the first evaluation has not provided sufficient information to evaluate the threat posed by the site.[142]

After completion of the preliminary inspection phase, the party is required to review the Removal Site Evaluation and Inspection (if necessary) to ascertain actual or potential harm to human health and the environment; potential for migration of hazardous substances; weather conditions that might increase the threat of release or migration; and the threat of fire or explosion. The evaluating party must determine whether the nature of the threat presented warrants immediate action.[143]

If after completion of the evaluation, the party determines that the magnitude of the threat requires removal, the NCP directs that the removal be carried out as quickly as possible.[144] If it will take six or more months after completion of the evaluation for work to begin, an Engineering Evaluation/Cost Analysis must be conducted and a sampling plan must be developed.[145] Neither of these steps is necessary where work begins prior to the six-month deadline.

Community involvement in the removal process is mandated by the NCP.[146] The degree of community involvement necessary is dependent upon the time it will take to begin work: the greater the lead time, the more community participation is required.[147] Community involvement requirements are first triggered in the removal process upon completion of the threat evaluation stage. A spokesperson whose job is to keep the community informed about the removal process should be designated at this juncture.

In cases where the removal begins in less than six months after completion of the removal site evaluation, the following community relations steps must be taken:

1. A notice of availability of the administrative record must be published in a major local paper of general circulation;

---

[140] 40 C.F.R. §300.410(b).
[141] 40 C.F.R. §300.410(d).
[142] *Id.*
[143] 40 C.F.R. §300.415(a)(1) and (b).
[144] 40 C.F.R. §300.415(b)(3).
[145] 40 C.F.R. §300.415(b)(4).
[146] 40 C.F.R. §300.415(m).
[147] *Id.*

2. Public comments must be accepted on the threat evaluation for 30 days after the publication of the notice of availability; and
3. A written response to significant comments must be prepared.[148]

For removal actions that are expected to last more than 120 days, the following additional community relations steps must be taken:

1. Interviews must be conducted with local officials and citizens to determine their concerns and information needs;
2. A formal community relations plan detailing all planned community relations activities must be prepared; and
3. An information repository where all documents of public record relating to the removal will be available for inspection must be established.[149]

Finally, where it is anticipated that the removal will not begin for at least six months, the party engaged in removal must

1. Carry out the requirements of the preceding two paragraphs;
2. Publish a notice of availability of the required Engineering Evaluation/Cost Analysis; and
3. Provide a public comment period of not less than 30 days.[150]

The community involvement provisions have consistently tripped up cost recovery plaintiffs under both the strict and substantial compliance standards.[151] Therefore, whether a party is undertaking a removal or defending a cost recovery action, intimate knowledge of and attention to these provisions is warranted.

2. *Remedial Actions*

Remedial actions are

> those actions consistent with permanent remedy taken instead of or in addition to removal actions in the event of a release or threatened release of a hazardous substance into the environment, to prevent or minimize the release of hazardous substances so that they do not migrate to cause substantial danger to the present or future public health, welfare or the environment.[152]

Because of their permanent nature, remedial actions have more regulatory requirements.

a. Remedial Preliminary Assessment and Inspection. Under section 101(24), the first steps in preparing for a remedial action are the Remedial Preliminary Assessment and the Remedial Preliminary Inspection. The Remedial Preliminary Assessment is an evaluation of the existing written information available regarding the site. It does not require an actual site visit or any other

---

[148] 40 C.F.R. §300.415(m)(2).

[149] 40 C.F.R. §300.415(m)(3).

[150] 40 C.F.R. §300.415(m)(4).

[151] Channel Master, 748 F. Supp. at 389–90; Amland Properties, 711 F. Supp. at 795. *But see* General Elec., 715 F. Supp. at 949.

[152] CERCLA §101(24), 42 U.S.C. §9601(24).

work at the site although both off- and on-site reconnaissance is authorized. Remedial Preliminary Assessments are only required for sites contained on the list of priority Superfund sites maintained by EPA.[153] However, a private party can petition EPA to have a Remedial Preliminary Assessment performed at any site.[154]

Upon completion of the Remedial Preliminary Assessment, the first actual site work begins with the Remedial Preliminary Inspection. Building upon the information already developed, the Remedial Preliminary Inspection requires the development and implementation of a sampling plan. It also requires a detailed report summarizing the findings of the Remedial Preliminary Assessment and Remedial Preliminary Inspection and recommendations as to whether and how to proceed.[155]

b. Remedial Investigation/Feasibility Study. The next step in the remedial process is the Remedial Investigation/Feasibility Study (RI/FS).[156] The overarching purpose of the RI/FS is to collect further site data that will enable the implementing party to select the most appropriate remedial action that fosters the goal of the remedy selection process, namely "to implement remedies that eliminate, reduce or control risks to human health and the environment."[157] The RI/FS is intended to present the decision maker with a reasonable set of cleanup alternatives based upon site conditions. Essentially, the RI is the process by which necessary data about the site is collected, and the FS used the data to develop alternatives, and set cleanup goals and standards derived from Applicable Relevant and Appropriate Requirements (ARARs), and Maximum Contaminant Levels (MCLs).[158]

Prior to initiating field work for the Remedial Investigation, the party engaged in the cleanup must conduct several community relations activities.[159] These include

1. Conducting interviews with local officials and citizens to solicit their concerns and information needs regarding the remedy;
2. Preparing a community relations plan in order to foster public involvement in the remedial process;
3. Establishing a local information repository; and
4. Informing the community of the availability of technical assistance grants.[160]

c. Remedy Selection/The Record of Decision. The next step in the remedial process is the actual selection of the remedial alternative to be implemented. At this juncture the decision maker must evaluate the alternatives presented in the RI/FS based upon five criteria:

---

[153] This list is known as the Comprehensive Environmental Response Compensation and Liability Information System or CERCLIS.

[154] 40 C.F.R. §300.420(b).

[155] 40 C.F.R. §300.420(c).

[156] 40 C.F.R. §300.430(a)(2).

[157] 40 C.F.R. §300.430(a)(1).

[158] 40 C.F.R. §300.430(d) and (e).

[159] 40 C.F.R. §300.430(c).

[160] *Id.*

1. Overall protectiveness of human health and the environment;
2. Balance of short- and long-term effectiveness;
3. Review of how each alternative will reduce toxicity at the site;
4. Implementability; and
5. Cost.[161]

The final step in remedy selection is identification of the preferred alternative and publication of the Record of Decision (ROD). After the preferred alternative remedy is selected, the party engaged in cleanup must publish a proposed plan for public comment. This plan must discuss the alternatives considered and the information relied upon to select the preferred remedy. The regulations set forth detailed public comment procedures for the proposed action.[162]

After close of the public comment period on the proposed plan, all comments must be reviewed to determine if the preferred alternative remains the most appropriate remedial action for the site.[163] Upon completion of this analysis, a final remedy is selected. This selection, along with responses to public comments, is documented in the ROD. This document sets forth the alternatives considered, the evaluation made of each, and the final decision on the remedy.[164] The ROD is to be made available for inspection and copying, and a notice of that availability should be published in a major local newspaper of general circulation.[165]

d. Implementation. The final phase in any remedial action is implementation of the remedy. The first step of this phase is designated the Remedial Design/Remedial Action (RD/RA).[166] This portion of the implementation phase includes the design and development of the treatment program, including both short-term "removal" type activities and longer term treatment. Once the design and development of the remedy is complete, the next step in the process is the actual implementation and construction of the remedy. The RD/RA is followed by the operation and maintenance period during which time the long-term treatment systems at the site (usually groundwater cleanup systems) are maintained, together with any physical improvements.

V. The National Priorities List

CERCLA section 105(a)(8)(B) requires that EPA develop criteria for and designate those sites that are of the highest priority for remediation in what is

[161] *Id.* States may substitute their own criteria if more stringent.

[162] Thus, the party engaged in cleanup is instructed to (1) publish a notice of availability and short summary of the proposed plan in a major local newspaper of general circulation; (2) place the proposed plan in the administrative record; (3) provide reasonable opportunity for public comment on both the proposed plan and the RI/FS; (4) provide an opportunity for a public meeting; (5) keep a transcript of the public meeting; and (6) prepare a written summary of the comments received. 40 C.F.R. §300.430(f)(ii)(E)(3).

[163] 40 C.F.R. §300.430(f)(ii).

[164] 40 C.F.R. §300.430(f)(ii)(E)(6).

[165] *Id.*

[166] 40 C.F.R. §300.435.

termed the National Priorities List (NPL). Under EPA's regulations, only sites on the list may be the subject of fund-financed remedial actions.[167]

After EPA performs a "site inspection" at a given facility, a site may become a candidate for a more thorough evaluation. Under its Hazardous Ranking System (HRS), EPA scores sites according to the perceived danger to the environment.[168] A set of criteria is examined to measure the risk associated with the migration of hazardous substances from the site via groundwater, surface water, or air. If the Hazard Ranking System score derived from examining these criteria is equal to or exceeds 28.5, the site is placed on the NPL.[169]

Periodically, EPA revises its list of sites on the NPL. Currently, there are approximately 1,208 sites on the list and approximately 28 sites proposed for inclusion on the list.[170] Once a site is proposed for listing, the public has a formal opportunity to comment on the listing.[171] Subsequently, a commenter may challenge EPA's listing of a site in an action brought in the U.S. Court of Appeals for the District of Columbia Circuit.[172]

In general, challenges to NPL listings have not fared well.[173] However, in two 1992 cases, *Kent County v. EPA*[174] and *Anne Arundel County v. EPA,*[175] the D.C. Circuit overturned EPA determinations that sites should be listed on the NPL. In both cases, the court noted that EPA's sampling methodology was contrary to EPA's stated policy on the subject and that there was no explanation in the administrative record for a departure from EPA methodology.[176] In addition, in *Anne Arundel,* EPA had used in its sampling calculations a private drinking well, the existence of which had not been disclosed to commenters. Accordingly, the D.C. Circuit remanded the listing determinations to EPA so that the sampling might be done properly and the newly discovered well could be considered in the comment period.[177]

VI. Standard of Liability Under CERCLA

During the legislative process prior to passage of CERCLA, a reference to "strict" liability was excised in favor of language which decrees that the liability is to be "construed to be the standard of liability which obtains under [section 311 of the Clean Water Act]."[178] Courts had already construed this

[167] 40 C.F.R. §300.425(b)(1).

[168] 40 C.F.R. §300.425(c)(1).

[169] *See* 40 C.F.R. pt. 300, App. A; *see also* Tex Tin Corp. v. EPA, 935 F.2d 1321, 1322–23 (D.C. Cir. 1991).

[170] 57 Fed. Reg. 47,180 (1992).

[171] CERCLA §113(a), 42 U.S.C. §9613(a).

[172] *Id.*

[173] *E.g.,* City of Stoughton v. EPA, 858 F.2d 747, 750 (D.C. Cir. 1988); Northside Sanitary Landfill, Inc. v. Thomas, 849 F.2d 1516, 1519 (D.C. Cir. 1988), *cert. denied,* 489 U.S. 1078 (1989); Eagle-Picher Indus. v. EPA, 759 F.2d 905 (D.C. Cir. 1985); 822 F.2d 132 (D.C. Cir. 1987).

[174] 963 F.2d 391 (D.C. Cir. 1992).

[175] 963 F.2d 412 (D.C. Cir. 1992).

[176] Kent, 963 F.2d at 395–99; Anne Arundel, 963 F.2d at 417–19.

[177] The court noted that if the well were closed for reasons other than as a response to the site at issue, the HRS score would have to be adjusted. Anne Arundel, 963 F.2d at 419.

[178] CERCLA §101(32), 42 U.S.C. §9601(32).

provision of the Clean Water Act to impart strict liability.[179] Not surprisingly, courts have ruled that CERCLA visits strict liability upon responsible parties.[180] Thus, responsible parties who meet the statutory criteria will be liable under CERCLA irrespective of fault or negligence.

Liability under CERCLA has also been found to be retroactive. Although the statute does not expressly speak to this issue, numerous courts have found that Congress clearly intended retroactive application.[181] The policy basis for this finding lies in the overwhelmingly remedial nature of a statute designed to, among other things, force the cleanup of abandoned hazardous waste sites.[182] Some decisions even indicate that recovery of response costs incurred prior to the enactment of CERCLA is authorized.[183]

Whether CERCLA liability is joint and several (i.e., each responsible party can be held liable for all costs of cleanup) has been among the most contentious issues in Superfund litigation. The controversy began in the legislative effort prior to passage of the statute. As a compromise, explicit references to joint and several liability were deleted from the bill. According to the most widely accepted legislative history, the deletion was intended to permit courts to decide the issue on a case-by-case basis. Senator Jennings Randolph (D-W.Va.) explained that joint and several liability was omitted so that

> issues of liability not resolved by this act, if any, shall be governed by traditional and evolving principles of common law. An example is joint and several liability. Any reference to these terms has been deleted, and the liability of joint tort feasors will be determined under common or previous statutory law.[184]

Thus, courts have followed the drafters' direction that joint and several liability should be determined based upon "traditional and evolving principles of common law."[185]

Perhaps the leading source for determining "traditional and evolving principles of common law," has been the *Restatement (Second) of Torts.*[186] Section 433A of the *Restatement* notes that:

> Damages for harm are to be apportioned among two or more causes where (a) there are distinct harms, or (b) there is a reasonable basis of determining the contribution of each cause to a single harm.[187]

---

[179] *E.g.,* Steuart Transport Co. v. Allied Towing Corp., 596 F.2d 609 (4th Cir. 1979).

[180] *E.g.,* United States v. Northeastern Pharmaceutical & Chem. Co., 810 F.2d 726, 732 (8th Cir. 1986), *cert. denied,* 484 U.S. 848 (1987); United States v. Monsanto, 858 F.2d 160, 167 n.11 (4th Cir. 1988), *cert. denied,* 109 S. Ct. 1356 (1989).

[181] Northeastern Pharmaceutical, 810 F.2d at 732–34; United States v. Conservation Chem. Co., 619 F. Supp. 162, 220 (W.D. Mo. 1985); United States v. Shell Oil Co., 605 F. Supp. 1064, 1069–73 (D. Colo. 1985).

[182] Northeastern Pharmaceutical, 810 F.2d at 732.

[183] Colorado v. Idarado Mining Co., 735 F. Supp. 368, 370–71 (D. Colo. 1990); United States v. Hooker Chems. & Plastics Corp., 680 F. Supp. 548, 557–58 (W.D.N.Y. 1988); Shell Oil, 605 F. Supp. at 1069–73.

[184] 126 CONG. REC. 30,932 (serial ed. 1980); *see also* 126 CONG. REC. 31,965 (serial ed. 1980) (statement of Rep. Florio).

[185] United States v. Chem-Dyne Corp., 572 F. Supp. 802, 808 (S.D. Ohio 1983); *see also* United States v. Alcan Aluminum Corp., 964 F.2d 252, 268 (3d Cir. 1992); O'Neil v. Picillo, 883 F.2d 176, 178 (1st Cir. 1989); Monsanto, 858 F.2d at 171 n.3.

[186] *See* Alcan Aluminum, 964 F.2d at 268–69; O'Neil, 883 F.2d at 179; Monsanto, 858 F.2d at 172; Chem-Dyne, 572 F. Supp. at 810.

[187] RESTATEMENT (SECOND) OF TORTS §433A (1965).

The *Restatement* also notes that:

> If two or more persons, acting independently, tortiously cause distinct harms or a single harm for which there is a reasonable basis for division according to the contribution of each, each is subject to liability only for the portion of the total harm that he has himself caused.[188]

In 1986, when Congress passed SARA, joint and several liability remained a critical issue. In response to criticism from many quarters, the legislation came to include three provisions intended to ameliorate the harsh effects of joint and several liability. First, Congress added section 113(f)[189] which specifically authorized a contribution action "during or after" a cost recovery action. Second, EPA was provided with authority to enter into de minimis settlements whereby the agency would be able to settle the liability of small contributors.[190] And third, SARA authorized EPA to provide a "nonbinding preliminary allocation of responsibility" under which the agency could allocate liability among responsible parties in order to expedite settlement.[191]

In addition, in testimony before Congress, the government acknowledged that if the harm at a site is divisible, joint and several liability should not attach.[192] More important, the government committed to exercise discretion in selecting defendants to a CERCLA enforcement action such that minor parties would not bear a disproportionate burden.[193] Thus, the compromise that permitted joint and several liability to be the subject of "traditional and evolving principles of common law" remained intact after enactment of SARA in 1986.

The government has generally taken the view that apportionment is a matter to be addressed in the contribution phase of the litigation. Hence, in the government's view, once it has demonstrated an indivisible harm, it is entitled to a joint and several liability judgment against the defendants. After the direct defendant's liability is resolved, it may bring an action in contribution against other responsible parties to recover that portion of the judgment attributable to the responsible parties who were not direct defendants.[194]

Despite the government's perspective, the prevailing view appears to be that once liability is proven in other respects, a defendant has the opportunity

[188] *Id.* at §881.

[189] 42 U.S.C. §9613(f).

[190] CERCLA §122(g), 42 U.S.C. §9622(g).

[191] CERCLA §122(e)(3), 42 U.S.C. §9622(e)(3).

[192] "If the harm at the site is divisible, joint and several liability would not apply. . . . The purpose behind joint and several liability is not to punish; it is not to be punitive. . . ." *S. Rep. No. 415, Hearings on S. 51 before the Senate Judiciary Comm.* (Serial J-99-30), 99th Cong., 1st Sess. 36–37 (1986) (testimony of F. Henry Habicht, Assistant Attorney General, Land and Natural Resources Div., Department of Justice).

[193] "We have not imposed and certainly don't intend to impose liability grossly out of proportion to someone's actual contribution . . . joint and several liability is not a rigid hard and fast rule. It is a rule based on equity, and parties will argue if they feel that liability is being imposed grossly out of proportion with the factual contribution." *S. Rep. No. 61, Hearings before the Senate Environment & Public Works Comm.*, 99th Cong., 1st Sess. 13–14 (1980) (testimony of F. Henry Habicht, Assistant Attorney General, Land and Natural Resources Div., Department of Justice). "[The possibility that] the Government could sue the generator of a single drum of waste found at a massive site for the entire cleanup of that site[,] in practice . . . does not happen." *Oversight Hearings Before the Subcomm. on Administrative Law and Governmental Relations (Serial No. 19) of the House Comm. on the Judiciary,* 99th Cong., 1st Sess. 13–14 (1986) (testimony of EPA Administrator Lee Thomas).

[194] Some courts have suggested adherence to the government view on the matter. *E.g.,* Monsanto, 858 F.2d at 171 n.22.

and burden to prove a reasonable basis for division of the harm. Using this approach, once the plaintiff demonstrates the defendant's liability as a responsible party for the release of a hazardous substance from a facility, courts will generally shift the burden to the defendant to establish that the harm is divisible or capable of apportionment.[195]

United States v. Alcan Aluminum Corp.[196] is the leading case on the subject of divisible harm. There, the court reviewed the prior precedent and legislative history, as well as the *Restatement of Torts,* and concluded that the defendant must be permitted the opportunity to demonstrate that the harm associated with the site is capable of reasonable allocation. The court reasoned that:

> [I]f the defendant can prove that the harm is divisible and that it only caused some portion of the injury, it should only be held liable for that amount. In our view, the logical consequence of delaying the apportionment determination may well be drastic, for it seems clear that a defendant could easily be strong-armed into settling where other defendants have settled in order to avoid being held liable for the remainder of the response costs.[197]

The nature of proof necessary for demonstrating divisibility has been difficult to discern. In *O'Neil v. Picillo,*[198] the First Circuit rejected a per se rule that if there is one environmental harm, it cannot be apportioned according to costs incurred. The *O'Neil* court ultimately ruled against the generator's divisibility argument and held the generator jointly and severally liable because it was unable to demonstrate that it had not generated some unidentified waste at the site.[199]

In re Bell Petroleum Services, Inc.,[200] the Fifth Circuit cast light on the nature of the proof necessary to demonstrate the requisite basis for apportionment. The court reasoned that

> [e]ssentially, the question whether there is a reasonable basis for apportionment depends on whether there is sufficient evidence from which the court can determine the amount of harm caused by each defendant. If the expert testimony and other evidence establishes a factual basis for making a reasonable estimate that will fairly apportion liability, joint and several liability should not be imposed in the absence of exceptional circumstances.[201]

Confronted with the apportionment of harm among successive owners of a facility emitting only one hazardous substance, the court opined that expert testimony on a volumetric approach to apportionment was sufficient to demonstrate the requisite "reasonable basis" for apportionment.[202]

---

[195] *E.g.,* O'Neil v. Picillo, 883 F.2d at 178–79; 858 F.2d at 172; United States v. Marisol, Inc., 725 F. Supp. 833, 842 (M.D. Pa. 1989).

[196] 964 F.2d 252, 260–62 (3d Cir. 1992).

[197] *Id.* at 270 n.29; *see also* In re Bell Petroleum Services, Inc., 3 F.3d at 901 (5th Cir. 1993) (early resolution of joint and several liability is preferable but should be left to trial court's discretion); *but see* United States v. Alcan Aluminum Corp., 990 F.2d 711, 723 (2d Cir. 1993) ("when to address divisibility and apportionment are questions best left to the sound discretion of the trial court in the handling of an individual case").

[198] 883 F.2d 176, 178 (1st Cir. 1989).

[199] *Id.* at 182–83.

[200] 3 F.3d 889 (5th Cir. 1993).

[201] *Id.* at 903.

[202] *Id.* at 904.

In some decisions there is an implication that once waste is "commingled," one cannot prove divisibility.[203] The government would argue that since each molecule of waste cannot be traced to its generator, there is no way to distinguish the harm caused by any particular generator's waste, and, hence, there is no basis to prove divisibility. The *Alcan* court rejected this view, noting that " 'commingled' waste is not synonymous with 'indivisible' harm."[204] Yet the court did not elucidate the nature of proof necessary for a divisibility determination once waste has been "commingled."[205]

Nor have cases delineated the nature of proof required to demonstrate divisibility in other contexts. In *United States v. Monsanto,*[206] perhaps because the toxicity of the waste at the site varied wildly, the court noted that evidence of volume would not, by itself, prove divisibility. Instead, a defendant would have to demonstrate that relative volumes at the site are "probative of contributory harm" and show the "relationship between waste volume, the release of hazardous substances, and the harm at the site." In another early case, a court suggested that the divisibility determination be decided based upon an analysis of "comparative causation."[207] Still others have suggested that it is a matter that must be proved at trial based upon a complex factual inquiry.[208]

While it is probable that the nature of the burden associated with proving divisibility will vary from case to case, courts are not likely to charge CERCLA defendants with proving an exact divisibility of harm or allocation. Certainly, there is nothing in "traditional and evolving principles of common law" which would suggest that the courts should demand exact precision before accepting a divisibility argument. In one comment in the *Restatement,* its drafters noted that

> [t]here may difficulty in the apportionment of some elements of damages, but this does not mean that one defendant must be liable for the distinct harm inflicted by the other. It is possible to make a rough estimate which will fairly apportion damages.[209]

In an example which seems applicable, the *Restatement* points out:

> [W]here two or more factories independently pollute a stream, the interference with the plaintiff's use of the water may be treated as divisible in terms of degree, and may be apportioned among the owners of the factories, on the basis of evidence of the respective quantities of pollution discharged into the stream.[210]

Accordingly, as in *Bell Petroleum Services,* there will be times when courts will reject joint and several liability based upon a volumetric analysis of the

---

[203] *E.g.,* Michigan v. Thomas Solvent Co., 29 ER Cases 1119 (N.D. Mich. 1988).

[204] 964 F.2d at 270 n.29.

[205] *Id.* at 270. The *Alcan* decision notes that if the generators were considered on a per capita basis, the defendant's share would have been disproportionate. In addition, the court noted that the liability was disproportionate to the defendant's volumetric contribution. *Id.* at 270 n.29.

[206] See *supra* note 180.

[207] United States v. Argent Co., 21 ER Cases 1356, 1357 (D.N.M. 1984).

[208] *E.g.,* Idaho v. Bunker Hill Co., 634 F. Supp. 800, 805 (D. Idaho 1986); United States v. Conservation Chem. Corp., 619 F. Supp. 162 (W.D. Mo. 1985).

[209] RESTATEMENT (SECOND) OF TORTS, *supra* note 187, §433A cmt. b. In *Bell Petroleum Services* the court compared the inquiry to an apportionment of fault under comparative negligence statutes noting that it "should not be difficult" for one accustomed to such decisions. 3 F.3d at 903, n. 16.

[210] *Id.* at cmt. d; *see also* RESTATEMENT §433 cmt. d, illus. 4 and 5; §881 cmt. d, illus. 1.

contributions of each of the parties.[211] Similarly, one would expect that the courts will adopt some reasonable methodology to divide liability among different classes of responsible parties (*i.e.*, owners versus generators). In other instances, courts will recognize that there is no reasonable basis for allocation of responsibility and, hence, joint and several liability will attach.

VII. Liability to the Government

CERCLA provides EPA with mechanisms to recover costs of cleanups or force cleanups. In general, the cost recovery provisions of the statute are employed to recover outstanding costs and obtain declaratory relief as to future costs.[212] The endangerment provisions of the statute permit the government access to an injunction or an administrative order.[213] In each instance, the four classes of responsible parties are liable in an action for costs or an injunction.[214]

A. Government Cost Recovery Authority

A company that falls within one of the four classes of responsible parties can be held liable to EPA, a state, or an Indian tribe for recovery of past and future response costs that are caused by the release or threat of release of hazardous substances. The statute confers liability for ''all costs of removal or remedial action . . . not inconsistent with the national contingency plan.''[215]

In general, the government has argued that it is entitled to all of its response costs—not simply those that are ''reasonable''—so long as the costs are not inconsistent with the NCP. Referring to the language of section 107(a)(4), some courts have adopted the government's position. In *United States v. Hardage,*[216] the Tenth Circuit considered costs incurred to further a remedy that the trial court ultimately rejected as inconsistent with the NCP. Because the subsequent rejection of the government remedy was not before the trial court at the summary judgment phase, and because affidavits submitted in response to the motion were conclusory, the Tenth Circuit declined to hold these costs to be inconsistent with the NCP.[217]

Hardage and other cases have held that the burden of demonstrating the inconsistency of government costs rests with the responsible party. The courts examined language contained in the government liability provision and compared it to the language governing private cost recovery. Since the government is entitled to recover costs ''not inconsistent with'' the Plan, and because other parties may recover costs ''consistent with'' the NCP, the court reasoned that Congress intended different burdens of proof. Accordingly, the party challeng-

---

[211] *See* Alcan Aluminum, 964 F.2d at 270 n.29.

[212] CERCLA §107(A)(1)-(4), 42 U.S.C. §9607(a)(1)-(4).

[213] CERCLA §106(a), 42 U.S.C. §9606(a).

[214] The four classes discussed in Section II, above, are present owners and operators, certain past owners and operators, generators, and transporters. See Section II.A.

[215] CERCLA §107(a)(4)(A), 42 U.S.C. §9607(a)(4)(A).

[216] 982 F.2d 1436, 1442 (10th Cir. 1992); United States v. R.W. Meyer, Inc., 889 F.2d 1497, 1500 (6th Cir. 1989), *cert. denied,* 110 S. Ct. 1527 (1990).

[217] Hardage, 982 F.2d at 1442–44.

ing governmental costs must bear the burden of demonstrating their inconsistency with the NCP.[218]

Courts have developed a very lenient standard for judging the government's adherence to the NCP. In *United States v. Northeastern Pharmaceutical & Chemical Co. (NEPACCO),*[219] the Eighth Circuit determined that the standard governing the evaluation of EPA's adherence to the NCP is the "arbitrary and capricious" standard applicable to governmental administrative actions. Other courts have also adopted this view.[220] Yet, at least one other court has inquired into the individual costs to determine whether they are reasonable and not inconsistent with the NCP.[221]

The issue of causation, however, has created some difficulty for cost recovery by the government. The language of section 107(a)(4) clearly implicates causation in some form. There, CERCLA specifies that liability attaches when a release or threat of release "causes" the incurrence of response costs.[222] The provision does not require that the government fingerprint particular chemicals that were sent to the site to demonstrate that they were the substances which were remediated at the site.[223] However, there certainly must be some form of causation; if nothing else, the government must demonstrate a causal nexus between the release and the incurrence of costs. For example, when a guard was hired on a site before the release was discovered, the court ruled that the release had not "caused" the incurrence of the response costs of hiring the guard.[224] Unless some element of causation is imposed as a prerequisite to liability, the word "causes" would be effectively read out of the statute.

B. Endangerment Injunctions

CERCLA authorizes the agency to file an action against responsible parties seeking an injunction where there is an "imminent and substantial endangerment."[225] While, over the past several years, EPA has been disinclined to file section 106 actions and, instead, has relied on its administrative order capacity, the provision remains among the government's enforcement tools.[226]

---

[218] Hardage, 982 F.2d at 1442. *See also* Northeastern Pharmaceutical, 810 F.2d at 747; Hopkins v. Elano Corp., 30 ER Cases 1782, 1785 (S.D. Ohio 1989); Cf. City of New York v. Exxon, 633 F. Supp. 609, 616 (S.D.N.Y. 1986) (court queried whether the two different formulations regarding consistency conveyed any real difference or were instead merely "the fruit of a semantic quibble").

[219] 810 F.2d 726, 747 (8th Cir. 1986).

[220] *E.g.,* Hardage, 982 F.2d at 1442; United States v. Bell Petroleum, 734 F. Supp. 771, 781 (W.D. Tex. 1990).

[221] *E.g.,* United States v. Ottati & Goss, 900 F.2d 429, 434–36 (1st. Cir. 1990).

[222] CERCLA §107(a)(4), 42 U.S.C. §9607(a)(4).

[223] *E.g.,* United States v. General Foods Corp., No. 1:90-CV-397, U.S. Dist. LEXIS 17,157 (W.D. Mich. 1990); United States v. Fairchild Indus. Inc., 766 F. Supp. 405 (D. Md. 1991).

[224] Amland Properties Co. v. Aluminum Corp. of Am., 711 F. Supp. 784, 795 (D.N.J. 1989).

[225] CERCLA §106(a)(1), 42 U.S.C. §9606(a)(1).

[226] The statute limits the capacity to bring a §106 endangerment action to the federal government. However, CERCLA §310(a)(2), 42 U.S.C. §9659(a)(2), permits a citizen suit that would, under limited circumstances, allow an action which seeks an injunction from the court for a "violation of any standard, regulation, condition, requirement, or order" under CERCLA. Courts have jurisdiction to order enforcement of such provisions and "to order such action as may be necessary to correct the violation." CERCLA §310(c), 42 U.S.C. §9659(c).

EPA has found it easy to demonstrate the endangerment necessary for an action under section 106(a). EPA may bring an action against responsible parties when it:

> [D]etermines that there *may* be an imminent and substantial *endangerment* to the public health or welfare or the environment because of an actual or *threatened* release of a hazardous substance from a facility.[227]

Given that this provision uses the term "may" and requires only an "endangerment" from a "threatened" release, courts have accepted EPA's determination that the requisite endangerment exists in circumstances where the threat to the environment is remote.[228]

Courts have been less inclined to defer to EPA's remedy selection in a section 106(a) court action than in other circumstances. In *United States v. Ottati & Goss, Inc.,*[229] the First Circuit noted that, by the wording of the statute, a court presiding over an action brought under section 106 has jurisdiction over the grant of relief. Thus, the First Circuit reasoned, a trial court is authorized to select the remedy using its discretionary legal power to consider the equities and the public interest. In turn, the court need not defer to EPA's remedy selection under the "arbitrary and capricious" standard employed when reviewing an administrative action.[230]

C. Administrative Orders

Section 106(a) also permits EPA to issue an administrative order where the requisite endangerment to the public health, welfare, or environment is present. EPA has used this administrative order authority extensively over the past several years. Indeed, it is common practice for EPA to issue an administrative order requiring potentially responsible parties to implement the remedy prescribed by the Agency's ROD. In addition, EPA often employs the administrative order to mandate performance of a removal action.[231]

The endangerment conditions necessary for issuance of an order are the same as those necessary for a section 106(a) judicial action: wherever EPA determines that there "may" be an imminent and substantial "endangerment" caused by a release or "threatened" release. Thus, courts will defer, in some substantial measure, to EPA's determination that the requisite endangerment conditions are present.

By the terms of section 106(a), EPA may issue "such orders as may be necessary to protect public health and welfare and the environment." Thus, an EPA-ordered response must be "necessary" in order to pass muster under the statute. If one compares the wording under section 106(a) with the wording under section 104(a) (which authorizes EPA to conduct response actions), there

---

[227] CERCLA §106(a), 42 U.S.C. §9601(a) (emphasis added).

[228] Conservation Chem., 619 F. Supp. at 192–95; *In re* FCX, Inc., 96 B.R. 49, 19 Envtl. L. Rep. (Envtl. L. Inst. 20), 849 (Bankr. E.D.N.C.), *cert. denied,* 109 S. Ct. 1118 (1989); B.F. Goodrich v. Murtha, 958 F.2d 1192, 1195–96 (2d Cir. 1992).

[229] 900 F.2d at 435.

[230] *Id; see also* United States v. A & F Materials, 578 F. Supp. 1249, 1257–59 (S.D. Ill. 1984).

[231] In some instances, EPA will negotiate an administrative order on consent with the potentially responsible parties. See Section X, below.

also appears to be a difference in the agency's authority. Under section 104(a), EPA may take whatever response the agency "deems necessary"[232] while section 106(a) demands that which is "necessary." One might well conclude that the section 106(a) standard applies an objective test as to what is "necessary" while section 104(a) permits EPA to determine the necessity of a response action.

This distinction would also conform to the different purposes reflected in the two provisions. If EPA issues an order under section 106(a) with the attendant penalties and bar on preenforcement review, sound congressional policy would hold the agency to a higher standard than that permitted for a government response under section 104(a). Conversely, when the Agency seeks to collect its costs following an EPA response conducted pursuant to section 104(a), the government is entitled to greater deference in selecting a remedy.[233]

There is a serious risk in declining to perform an administrative order. Generally, EPA may advance the threat that a company refusing the order will pay (1) a penalty of $25,000 per day of violation,[234] and (2) three times the cost of a response conducted by the government.[235] Indeed, courts have imposed penalties for failure to abide by the terms of an administrative order.[236]

A respondent to an administrative order may refuse to comply so long as it has "sufficient cause."[237] The nature of a sufficient cause defense was elucidated in the 1986 legislative history:

> We mean by "sufficient cause" an objectively reasonable and good faith belief either that the party is not liable under CERCLA or that the required response action is inconsistent with the National Contingency Plan. The court must base its strict scrutiny of the defendant's belief on objective evidence of the reasonableness and good faith of that belief.[238]

Based on this language, courts have ruled that the measure of whether a respondent has sufficient cause to decline performance of an administrative order is "the objective evidence of the reasonableness and good faith" of a belief that there is no liability.[239] Courts have ruled that inability to pay for the cleanup does not qualify for the "sufficient cause" defense to liability for penalties.[240] By contrast, an allegation that EPA had undertaken the response action and thereby preempted a respondent's performance was enough to

---

[232] CERCLA §104(a)(1), 42 U.S.C. §9604(a)(1). Other language in section 104(a) mandates that the response action be "consistent with the national contingency plan."

[233] Of course any response selected under the statute must be consistent with the NCP. See Section IV, above.

[234] CERCLA §106(b)(1), 42 U.S.C. §9606(b)(1).

[235] CERCLA §107(c)(3), 42 U.S.C. §9607(c)(3).

[236] Solid State Circuits, Inc. v. EPA, 812 F.2d 383, 391 n.11 (8th Cir. 1987); United States v. Lecarreaux, 1992 WL 108816, at *12–16 (D.N.J. 1992).

[237] A violation must also be "willful" in order to impose a $25,000 per day penalty. CERCLA §106(b)(1), 42 U.S.C. §9606(b)(1). *See* Wagner Seed Co. v. Daggett, 800 F.2d 310, 317 (2d Cir. 1985) (equating "willful" in the pre-SARA statute with bad faith).

[238] 132 Cong. Rec. H9624 (daily ed. Oct. 8, 1986).

[239] Solid State Circuits, 812 F.2d at 391 n.11; Lecarreaux, 1992 WL at 108816, *12–16.

[240] Lecarreaux, 1992 WL 108816, *12–16; United States v. Parsons, 723 F. Supp. 757, 763 (N.D. Ga. 1989), 738 F. Supp. 1436 (N.D. Ga. 1990), *rev'd on other grounds,* 936 F.2d 526 (11th Cir. 1991).

prevent the court from entering summary judgment as to the respondent's liability for penalties in *United States v. Parsons.*[241]

CERCLA permits a respondent who complies with the terms of an administrative order the option of petitioning EPA for reimbursement of response costs from the Superfund if it can demonstrate either that (1) it is not liable, or (2) EPA's selection of a particular response was arbitrary and capricious or otherwise unlawful.[242] The petitioner bears the burden of proof. Further review of EPA's decision in selecting the response action is confined to the administrative record. If EPA declines to grant the petition for reimbursement, the petitioner may file an action in federal court seeking reimbursement.[243]

Because the statute requires that the response action be completed prior to the petition for reimbursement, respondents are likely to be caught in the difficult position of waiting for completion of complex remedial actions before they are able to petition for reimbursement of costs incurred in responding to unfounded administrative orders. Thus, to date, the reimbursement provision has not been utilized to any great extent by parties responding to administrative orders that require long-term remedial actions.

D. The Bar to Preenforcement Review

The availability of preenforcement review of EPA action under CERCLA is governed by section 113(h).[244] Although EPA had always argued that its decisions regarding response actions are not subject to judicial review except in the context of either an action for injunction or for cost recovery initiated by EPA, judicial decisions on this issue were mixed prior to the enactment of the foregoing provision. Whereas some courts had fully embraced this position and rejected preenforcement review,[245] others held that they would assert jurisdiction over challenges to CERCLA's daily penalty and treble damage provisions even if they did not have preenforcement jurisdiction over the merits of EPA's administrative orders.[246]

---

[241] 723 F. Supp. 757, 763 (N.D. Ga. 1989), 738 F. Supp. 1436 (N.D. Ga. 1990), *rev'd on other grounds,* 936 F.2d 526 (11th Cir. 1991).

[242] CERCLA §106(b)(2), 42 U.S.C. §9606(b)(2).

[243] CERCLA §106(b)(2)(B)-(D), 42 U.S.C. §9606(b)(2)(B)-(D); *see also* EPA's OSWER DIRECTIVE NO. 9833.4, GUIDANCE ON PROCEDURES FOR SUBMITTING CERCLA SECTION 106(b) REIMBURSEMENT PETITIONS AND ON EPA REVIEW OF THESE PETITIONS (June 20, 1992).

[244] Section 113(h) of SARA bars judicial review except in the context of one of the following:

> "(1) An action under section 107 for damages or for contribution; (2) An action to enforce an order issued under section 106(a) or to recover a penalty for violation of such order; (3) An action for reimbursement under section 106(b)(2); (4) An action under section 310 [of SARA] (relating to citizens suits) alleging that the removal or remedial action taken under section 104 or secured under section 106 was in violation of any requirement of this chapter. Such an action may not be brought with regard to a removal where a remedial action is to be undertaken at the site; (5) An action under section 106 in which the United States has moved to compel a remedial action."

[245] Lone Pine Steering Comm. v. EPA, 777 F.2d 882 (3d Cir. 1985), *cert. denied,* 476 U.S. 1115 (1986) (upholding the lower court's across-the-board denial of jurisdiction for preenforcement review); Wagner Seed Co. v. Daggett, 800 F.2d at 315 ("to introduce the delay of court proceedings at the outset of a cleanup would conflict with the strong congressional policy that directs cleanups to occur prior to a final determination of the party's rights and liabilities under CERCLA"); Wheaton v. EPA, 781 F.2d 354, 356–57 (3d Cir. 1986) ("preenforcement review of EPA's remedial actions . . . [is] contrary to the policies underlying CERCLA); and J.V. Peters & Co. v. Administrator, EPA, 767 F.2d 263, 265–66, 22 ER Cases 2073 (6th Cir. 1985).

[246] Aminoil, Inc. v. EPA, 599 F. Supp. 69 (C.D. Cal. 1984); *see also* Aminoil II, 646 F. Supp. 294 (C.D. Cal. 1986); Wagner Elec. Corp. v. Thomas, 612 F. Supp. 736 (N.D. Ind. 1986); and SCA Servs. of Ind. v. Thomas, 634 F. Supp. 1355 (N.D. Ind. 1986).

Section 113(h) was enacted in an effort to resolve those inconsistencies and to "preclude piecemeal review and excessive delay of cleanup."[247] To achieve this end, Congress added broad language in section 113(h) which governs *all* claims against EPA CERCLA actions. "The timing of the review section is intended to be comprehensive. . . . [It] covers all issues that could be construed as a challenge to the response, and limits those challenges to the opportunities specifically set forth in the section."[248]

Since the passage of section 113(h), challenges to EPA filed prior to an enforcement action have met with little success.[249] Thus, although at least one court has suggested that challenges may be permitted when there is a risk of irreparable harm to human health or the environment,[250] the chances of obtaining preenforcement review are slim.

VIII. Liability to Private Parties and Nonfederal Governments

A private party (as opposed to the government) may recover CERCLA costs in several ways. Where the private party has already incurred response costs, it may bring a cost recovery action against the potentially responsible party (PRP). If the private plaintiff is a direct defendant, it may bring a contribution action against another PRP. Finally, a private party may institute a citizen suit under the statute's citizens suit provision.

A. Cost Recovery Actions

Section 107(a)(4)(B) provides that a PRP shall be liable for "any other necessary costs of response incurred by any other person consistent with the national contingency plan." As discussed in Section IV of this chapter, consistency with the NCP differs depending on the type of cleanup involved and the stage of the cleanup at issue. In a section 107 action, the burden of proving consistency with the NCP will initially be on the plaintiff.

B. Contribution Actions

When suit is brought against a private party under section 107, that party may in turn bring a contribution claim against one or more PRPs "during or following" the plaintiff's action against it.[251] Such actions are governed by section 113(f) which simply provides that "in resolving contribution claims, the court may allocate response costs among liable parties using such equitable

[247] Chemical Waste Mgmt., Inc. v. EPA, 673 F. Supp. 1043, 1055 (D. Kan. 1987).

[248] 132 CONG. REC. S14929 (daily ed. Oct. 3, 1986) (statement of Senator Thurmond), *quoted in* Cabot Corp. v. EPA, 677 F. Supp. 823, 827 (E.D. Pa. 1988).

[249] *E.g.*, Barmet Aluminum Corp. v. Reilly, 927 F.2d 289 (6th Cir. 1991); Cooper Indus. v. United States, 775 F. Supp. 1027 (W.D. Mich. 1991); Reynolds v. Lujan, 785 F. Supp. 152, 153–54 (D.N.M. 1992); Reardon v. EPA, 949 F.2d 1509, 1513 (1st Cir. 1991); Dickerson v. EPA, 660 F. Supp. 227, 231–33 (M.D. Ga. 1987), *aff'd*, 834 F.2d 974 (11th Cir. 1987).

[250] Cabot Corp., 677 F. Supp. at 828–29.

[251] CERCLA §113(f)(1), 42 U.S.C. §9613(f)(1).

factors as the court determines are appropriate.''[252] Unfortunately, since few CERCLA cases have actually gone to trial, interpretation of the equitable factors issue is limited.[253]

Although the legislative history makes clear that courts are free to consider any relevant criteria, the following factors may serve as a baseline: (1) the amount of hazardous substance involved; (2) the toxicity or hazard presented by the materials at issue; (3) the degree of involvement of the parties in the activities at issue; (4) the degree of care exercised by the parties; and (5) the degree of cooperation with the government.[254] These factors are to be used so that ''the relative culpability of each responsible party be considered in determining the proportionate share of costs each must bear.''[255]

Although PRPs are subject to a contribution claim under section 113, a settlement by the PRP with the state or federal government may end contribution liability. Sections 113(f)(2) and (f)(3)(B) provide that a PRP shall not be liable for claims for contribution if those claims have been settled with the government or a state. Such a provision is consistent with CERCLA's goal of promoting settlements, but this limitation on liability only goes to those items specifically covered in the settlement agreement with the government. Thus a PRP may find itself subject to contribution actions for noncovered items at a later date.

C. Citizen Suits

Under section 310 a private party may bring an action against ''any person . . . who is alleged to be in violation of any standard, regulation, condition, requirement, or order'' promulgated under CERCLA.[256] This section expressly sanctions citizen suits against both the government and private parties[257] seeking injunctive relief, penalties, and attorney's fees and costs.[258]

Prior to commencing any action, the plaintiff must provide 60-days notice to both the private party and the government. This notice must describe the claims, the facts underpinning those claims, and the name of the attorney representing the citizen.[259] If the government moves or has moved to undertake an enforcement action, the private party is then barred from suit.[260]

D. Liability to State and Local Governments

State and local governments may also maintain actions under CERCLA. The litigation authority of a state is broader than that of a local government.

[252] CERCLA §113(f)(1), 42 U.S.C. §9613(f)(1).

[253] LIGHT, *supra* note 6, at 145.

[254] H.R. REP. NO. 2817, 98th Cong., 2d Sess. §113(b) (1985); H.R. REP. NO. 253, 99th Cong., 1st Sess., pt. 3, at 19.

[255] United States v. Monsanto, 858 F.2d 160, 168 n.13, 178 n.29 (4th Cir. 1988), *cert. denied,* 109 S. Ct. 1356 (1989).

[256] CERCLA §310(a)(1), 42 U.S.C. §9659(a)(1).

[257] *Id.*

[258] CERCLA §310(c) and (f), 42 U.S.C. §9659(c) and (f).

[259] CERCLA §310(d)(1), 42 U.S.C. §9659(d)(1).

[260] CERCLA §310(d)(2), 42 U.S.C. §9659(d)(2).

States have authority akin to EPA in terms of the types of cost recovery actions they can bring and the burdens of proof imposed. Thus, in *Colorado v. Idarado Mining Co.,*[261] the court stated: "Like the U.S. and EPA, states can sue responsible parties to recover remedial and removal costs. To prevail, the state's response efforts must be 'not inconsistent with the NCP.' "[262]

In contrast to the state, municipal governments, may maintain cost recovery actions following the same procedures as a private party.[263] Thus, municipalities may have to prove that any response action that they take is consistent with the NCP, and, in some instances, they may be unable to bring a claim for natural resources damages.[264]

IX. Natural Resources Damages

In addition to the costs of response, the federal government, states, and Indian tribes may recover their "natural resource" damages in a CERCLA cost recovery action.[265] "Natural resources" is broadly defined to include "land, fish, wildlife, biota, air water, ground water, drinking water supplies, and other such resources."[266] The Act requires that the federal government and the states designate "trustees" to assess damages to natural resources. For the federal government, the trustees are normally the Department of the Interior and the Commerce Department acting through the National Oceanographic and Atmospheric Administration.[267] Whether a local government can qualify as a trustee for the purpose of recovering natural resource damages remains unsettled.[268]

Because there is a potential for very large awards and because the trustees' assessments of natural resource damages have the effect of a rebuttable presumption, the regulations governing the assessment of natural resource damages are critical.[269] Under the 1980 version of CERCLA, the Department of the Interior was to have promulgated regulations for assessment of natural resources damages by late 1982. In late 1983, several states and environmental groups sued the Department to force promulgation of the regulations necessary for assessments. Finally, in August 1986, the government published its final

[261] 735 F. Supp. 368 (D. Colo. 1990).

[262] *Id. See also* Vermont v. Staco, 684 F. Supp. 822, 831 (D. Vt. 1988), *revised,* 31 ER Cases 1814 (M.D. Pa. 1990).

[263] *See* City of Philadelphia v. Stepan Chem., 18 CWLR 667, pp. 1 & 2 (E.D. Pa. 1989); Town of Bedford v. Raytheon Co., 755 F. Supp. 469, 469–73 (D. Mass. 1991); Werlein v. United States, 746 F. Supp. 887, 908–10 (D. Minn. 1990).

[264] *Id. But see* City of New York v. Exxon Corp., 633 F. Supp. 609 (S.D.N.Y. 1986); Town of Boonton v. Drew Chem. Corp., 23 ER Cases 1859, 1862–63 (D.N.J. 1985).

[265] *See* CERCLA §107(a)(4)(C) and (f), 42 U.S.C. §9607(a)(4)(C) and (f). More specifically, the appropriate plaintiffs are able to recover "damages for injury to, destruction of, or loss of natural resources, including the reasonable costs of assessing such injury, destruction, or loss resulting from such a release." *Id.*

[266] CERCLA §101(16), 42 U.S.C. §9601(16). The statute proscribes "double recovery" for "natural resource damages, including the costs of damage assessment or restoration, rehabilitation, or acquisition for the same release and natural resource." CERCLA §107(f)(1), 42 U.S.C. §9607(f)(1).

[267] 40 C.F.R. §300.600(b).

[268] *See* City of New York v. Exxon Corp., 633 F. Supp. 609 (S.D.N.Y. 1986) (city may qualify as a trustee); Mayor & Bd. of Alderman v. Drew Chem. Corp., 621 F. Supp. 663 (D.N.J. 1985) (same); Raytheon Corp., 755 F. Supp. at 469–73 (city does not qualify as trustee); Artesian Water Co. v. New Castle County, 659 F. Supp. 1269, 1287–88 (D. Del. 1987) (same).

[269] CERCLA §107(f)(2)(C), 42 U.S.C. §9607(f)(2)(C).

natural resource damages rule[270] which quickly became the subject of a legal challenge culminating in the District of Columbia Circuit's remand to the Department in *Ohio v. Department of the Interior.*[271]

In general, assessment of natural resources is intended to address three subjects: (1) identification of the natural resources and the extent of their injury; (2) the damages owed to the trustee; and (3) identification of the method necessary for restoration, replacement, or other rehabilitation of the resources.

Actions taken in response to damages to natural resources have a different objective than the "response" actions taken under CERCLA. In general, response actions are intended to clean up a site in order to eliminate or mitigate the threat to the environment.[272] By contrast, restoration, rehabilitation, or replacement efforts are intended to return a natural resource to a state that approximates its condition prior to the release of hazardous substances.

In their original form, the 1986 natural resource damages regulations required a demonstration of a clear nexus between the release at issue and an injury to natural resources. In addition, the trustee was required to select the lesser of either (1) restoration, replacement, or rehabilitation, or (2) the damages occasioned by the "lost use" of the resource. The regulations used a market-based method to determine the damages resulting from lost use: plaintiffs were required to prove the replacement value of the resource.

The natural resource damages rule is composed of two general sets of directions: the "Type A" simplified rules applicable to minor releases; and the "Type B" rules for serious releases.[273] The *Ohio* decision remanded the original rules on the ground that they called for assessment based solely on loss of use without consideration of replacement or restoration costs.[274] For the more critical Type B regulations, the court rejected Interior's use of market values to assess lost use[275] and its measure of damages as the lesser of restoration or replacement expense, or loss of use.[276] In addition, the *Ohio* court rejected Interior's limitation of recovery for damages to publicly owned resources.

In 1991, Interior proposed amended natural resource damages rules in response to the *Ohio* decision.[277] The rules instruct trustees to balance a series of 10 factors in determining the restoration, rehabilitation, or replacement value of natural resources.[278] In addition, the trustee is to employ the "compensable value" concept in evaluating the loss of use. Compensable value means the quantum of money necessary to compensate the public for the loss in services from the injured resource from the time that the release occurred to the time that

---

[270] 51 Fed. Reg. 27,674 (1986).

[271] 880 F.2d 432 (D.C. Cir. 1989).

[272] *See* CERCLA §104(a), 42 U.S.C. §9604(a).

[273] 53 Fed. Reg. 5166 (1988) (Type A rules); 52 Fed. Reg. 9042 (1987) (Type B rules).

[274] Ohio, 800 F.2d at 490–91.

[275] *Id.* at 463–64.

[276] *Id.* at 432, 442.

[277] 56 Fed. Reg. 19,752 (1991).

[278] The factors include: (1) technical feasibility; (2) the relationship of the expected costs of the proposed actions to the expected benefits; (3) cost-effectiveness; (4) the results of any actual or planned response actions; (5) potential for additional injury resulting from the proposed actions; (6) natural recovery period; (7) ability of resource to recover without alternative actions; (8) acquisition of equivalent property where restoration is impossible; (9) potential effects of the action on human health and safety; and (10) consistency with federal and state laws and policies. *Id.*

the resource is restored to its prior condition. Compensable value includes loss of public use plus "lost nonuse values such as option, existence, and bequest values."[279]

The nonuse element of the proposed rule may create significant controversy both because of its subjectivity and the methodology for assessment. By way of illustration, "option value" is the value a natural resource has to one who does not use the resource but nonetheless sees value in retaining the option to use it. On an even higher level of abstraction, an "existence" value is one derived from the value a person places on a natural resource even though he or she never intends to use the resource. Finally, the "bequest" value of a resource is the value one ascribes to a natural resource because it may be used by future generations.[280] The proposed rule suggests that determination of these "nonuses" should be done through a contingent valuation technique of surveying a population to determine the dollar value placed upon the nonuses.[281]

The proposed rule does not resolve directly the public/private resources controversy. Acknowledging that there may be circumstances where a privately owned resource is used by the public, the proposed regulations leave it to the trustees to decide under what circumstances privately owned resources might give rise to natural resource damages. The trustees will be required to document a clear public interest in a resource that is not publicly owned before it is considered within the scope of the regulations.

Perhaps because the regulations have been in flux and because the statute does not permit recovery of damages that occurred wholly before its passage in 1980,[282] there have been relatively few cases decided on the subject.[283] However, because this element of damages has the potential to give rise to very large judgments, and because there are significant ambiguities in the proposed rule, natural resource damages are likely to remain a serious issue in litigation, regulatory efforts, and in the Superfund reauthorization legislative process.

X. Negotiations

CERCLA has spawned a great deal of litigation in recent years both among private parties and between private parties and the government. However, nearly everyone involved in the Superfund process has come to realize that the costs of Superfund litigation in terms of wasted resources and cleanup delays can outweigh the benefits of litigation. Thus, parties have negotiated settlements concerning hundreds of Superfund sites and billions of dollars in remediation expense. This section will examine the current climate for negotiations both with the government and among private parties, highlighting those stages in the CERCLA process where negotiations are critical.

---

[279] 56 Fed. Reg. 19,772, proposed §11.83(c)(1).

[280] 52 Fed. Reg. 9042 (1987).

[281] 56 Fed. Reg. 19,772, proposed §11.83(b)(2).

[282] *See* CERCLA §107(f)(1), 42 U.S.C. §9607(f)(1).

[283] United States v. Seattle, 33 ER Cases 1549 (W.D. Wash. 1991); Ohio, 800 F.2d 432 (D.C. Cir. 1989); Colorado v. Department of the Interior, 880 F.2d 481 (D.C. Cir. 1989).

A. Governmental Negotiations

In order for EPA to obtain response actions for the large number of Superfund sites across the country while meeting congressionally mandated deadlines,[284] the Agency must continue to encourage settlement with private parties. In recent years, however, the agency's position may have discouraged settlement. In late 1991, EPA began using "model" consent decrees and administrative orders on consent (AOCs) which, due to their onerous terms, have effectively derailed the settlement efforts of many parties otherwise predisposed toward settlement. Rather than accepting the one-sided terms of these documents, many PRPs have decided either to litigate or to accept a unilateral administrative order (UAO). Yet, while these form agreements will certainly continue to limit the number of disputes settled amicably, negotiation will probably remain the more common method of resolving CERCLA liability. While each site will have unique issues, the following presents some guidelines that may be of use in such negotiations.

1. Stages of Negotiation on Liability Issues

a. Before EPA Exercises CERCLA Jurisdiction. Among the most effective methods of avoiding significant CERCLA liability is to conduct a cleanup outside the EPA CERCLA process. Response actions outside of EPA's Superfund control may streamline and hasten the cleanup and thereby eliminate many costs.

The prospect that, at the end of the cleanup operation, EPA will find that the site is not sufficiently clean after remediation and require a second cleanup poses the most significant risk in this approach.[285] However, EPA appears disinclined to add a site to the National Priorities List if it is undergoing a cleanup and if the state does not advocate including it in the EPA CERCLA process. On balance, the transaction costs saved by avoiding the CERCLA process often outweigh the risks involved.

PRPs may legitimately argue to the state that a cleanup performed outside of the formal CERCLA process used for NPL sites will be completed significantly faster than an EPA-governed CERCLA cleanup. In addition, the PRPs may appeal to the state's desire to retain control over activities within its boundaries.

While the chances of prevailing are diminished, even after a site has been scored for the NPL, a PRP may negotiate with EPA and a state to avoid the CERCLA cleanup process.[286] If the PRP has a reasonable basis for challenging the scoring of the site or can demonstrate that the site should not be placed on the NPL, it may avoid a CERCLA response and the consequent costs. One may argue that the site would be better treated under a different statute, preferably one where the cleanup would be less costly.

---

[284] *See* CERCLA §116, 42 U.S.C. §9616.

[285] This can, of course, be avoided if the party doing the cleanup complies substantially with the NCP. See Section IV, above.

[286] *See* CERCLA §121(f)(1)(A), 42 U.S.C. §9621(f)(1)(A); 40 C.F.R. §300.66.

b. The Remedial Investigation/Feasibility Study. The next stage at which PRPs often negotiate with EPA is prior to the RI/FS. A PRP will usually learn of its potential liability through a section 104(e) information request issued prior to commencement of the RI/FS. EPA has authority to provide a 90-day moratorium on site action if it believes that such negotiation would facilitate an agreement and expedite cleanup.[287] If it chooses to invoke this provision, the Agency must provide the PRPs with information regarding other PRPs, waste volumes, and types of waste. PRPs will have 60 days from commencement of the moratorium to submit a proposal for conducting the RI/FS.[288] Even if EPA refused to invoke the moratorium, it will often entertain negotiations with the PRPs to conduct the RI/FS.

Traditionally, the advantage of a PRP-conducted RI/FS is that the PRPs will be able to exert more control over the RI/FS, both in terms of its costs and its outcome. Use of the model AOC may have done away with much of the incentive for PRPs to undertake the RI/FS. Under the model's terms, EPA retains the authority to change or modify any of the PRPs' decisions, and EPA is free to choose a remedy that is different from the preference expressed in the PRPs' Feasibility Study. Indeed, EPA has done so on more than one occasion.

c. Remedial Design/Remedial Action. After the RI/FS, the government proceeds through its decision-making process and issues the Record of Decision, which designates the selected remedy. At this point, EPA often entertains negotiations from PRPs concerning performance of the Remedial Design/ Remedial Action and may invoke a negotiation moratorium.[289] The moratorium can extend for 120 days, and PRPs are given 60 days from the notice date to submit a proposal to EPA concerning the RD/RA.[290] EPA is free, however, to proceed with the remedial design for the site during this period.[291]

As with the RI/FS, the principal benefit of the PRPs of performing the RD/RA is the potential cost savings in a private as opposed to a public cleanup. However, like the Administrative Order on Consent now mandated by EPA, the one-sided nature of the model consent decree argues against its acceptance. Thus, PRPs must consider other alternatives: (1) accepting a unilateral administrative order; (2) permitting EPA to conduct the remedy and defending a cost recovery action; and (3) defending against an endangerment action or enforcement of a unilateral administrative order.

The determination of whether to accept a unilateral administrative order or sign a consent decree is dependent upon the facts of each case. In the eyes of many CERCLA attorneys, however, the balance has shifted in recent years toward accepting the order and rejecting the model consent decree. First, unlike the model decree, the UAO does not set stipulated penalties. Thus, should a dispute arise, the PRP will not have agreed to a set penalty schedule and will be able to rely on the court's discretion in penalty assessment. Second, the order cannot require payment of past costs[292] and thus gives the PRP the option of

---

[287] CERCLA §122(e)(1) and (2), 42 U.S.C. §9622(e)(1) and (2).

[288] CERCLA §122(e)(2)(B), 42 U.S.C. §9622(e)(2)(B).

[289] *See* CERCLA §122(e)(1) and (2), 42 U.S.C. §9622(e)(1) and (2).

[290] CERCLA §122(e)(2)(B), 42 U.S.C. §9622(e)(2)(B).

[291] CERCLA §122(e)(2)(A), 42 U.S.C. §9622(e)(2)(B).

[292] In some instances, EPA has claimed authority to provide for recovery of past costs in a unilateral administrative order. However, there is no authority for the claim. *See* CERCLA §106(a), 42 U.S.C. §9606(a).

litigating cost recovery in a separate action. Third, positions taken in the model consent decree and EPA's unwillingness to negotiate on many of the provisions of the decree argue in favor of accepting the order. Finally, a PRP may also be able to recover its costs if, after completion of the remedy, it can demonstrate that it was not liable or the order was arbitrary and capricious.[293]

The Agency may also perform the remedy itself if the PRPs will not sign the model decree.[294] Depending on the facts of each case there may be some advantage to allowing EPA to perform the remedy and defending a subsequent cost recovery action. PRPs will avoid paying both for their own contractor and for EPA's oversight contractor. In addition, a PRP may believe it has a good defense to the Superfund action and may have enough potential liability that litigation will be a worthwhile risk.

In rare instances, the agency may seek an injunction for cleanup, claiming imminent and substantial endangerment at the site.[295] PRPs may well have an advantage in this setting since there is no presumption that EPA's proposed remedy is appropriate, and a court may impose a remedy based upon the exercise of its equitable discretion in fashioning an injunction.[296] In addition, PRPs do not risk imposition of penalties and fines unless they disobey any injunction that ultimately issues. Thus, if there are disputes as to the remedy selected by EPA, the PRPs may have more impetus to litigate in this context.

Finally, in unusual circumstances, a PRP may decline to negotiate a consent decree and decline performance of all or part of a unilateral administrative order. The strategy carries with it the risks of incurring $25,000 per day in penalties and, if EPA ultimately performs the remedy, a treble damage assessment. Thus, the approach will be used only in rare circumstances.

2. *Negotiation of Settlement Documents*

Once the PRPs have determined that they wish to settle liability, negotiations turn to the documents which will effectuate the settlement. With the use of the model consent decree and model AOC, many of the items that were formerly open to negotiation are either completely eliminated or require clearance from EPA headquarters before a change from the model can be made. Nevertheless, PRPs will pay particular attention to each term of the agreement, and even if the terms are nonnegotiable, the assessment of the settlement's terms will drive the determination as to whether settlement is really in the PRPs' best interest.

The factual predicate of the settlement document found in the statement of facts can be critical. Often the Agency's version of the factual background contains commentary on toxicity and pathways of contamination that is not essential to the agreement. Thus, EPA may have worded the predicate in such a way that it could be used against the PRPs in a separate toxic tort suit. Because many of these provisions are not essential to the settlement, EPA is often willing to edit the section to omit some of the offending language.

---

[293] CERCLA §106(b)(2), 42 U.S.C. §9606(b)(2).

[294] Whether EPA is able to perform the remedy itself is often a function of the state's willingness to pay its statutory share of the cost. *See* CERCLA §104(b)(3)(C), 42 U.S.C. §104(b)(3)(C).

[295] CERCLA §106(a), 42 U.S.C. §9606(a).

[296] United States v. Ottati & Goss, Inc., 900 F.2d 429, 436 (1st Cir. 1990).

Liability releases, though generally of limited utility, should also be reviewed carefully. Such covenants not to sue go only to matters covered by the agreement and thus the PRPs must be aware of exactly what protections the agreement as a whole provides. The more comprehensive the remedy, the stronger is the PRPs' argument for a more complete release.[297]

"Reopeners" are of great importance to the Agency. PRPs generally must accede to the presence of reopeners, but may negotiate on their terms and conditions. Once again, a more complete remedy provides the PRPs with more leverage for limiting reopeners.

Like the reopener provisions, most agreements will contain a narrow force majeure clause allowing PRPs to limit settlement obligations if an event beyond their control prevents compliance with the agreement. The Agency often insists on a clause which allows it to determine the "definition" of such an event and thus these clauses may have little utility. A similar result obtains in the dispute resolution provisions where the agency often seeks to have one of its own serve as the arbitrator of disputes. Appointment of a truly neutral party would be a more equitable mechanism for resolving such disputes.

The past costs recovery provision of a settlement agreement is usually the focus of hard negotiation. Settling parties often will argue that EPA should use its authority to force nonsettlers to pay a significant portion of past costs. Consequently, the settlers will argue that they should not pay all of the past costs. EPA has paid lip service to forcing nonsettlers to pay a portion of these costs, but it does not have a stellar record for implementing this policy. Settling PRPs will have better leverage on this issue if they convince EPA that the nonsettlers include at least one "deep pocket" with some genuine liability. Alternatively, settlers often argue for a reduction due to the infirmity of the government's case for recovery. More specifically, the settlers contend that the litigation risks attendant to the particular case justify cost concessions. In any event, the degree to which the Agency waives its past costs will often be a significant factor in determining the attractiveness of settlement agreement.

3. *De Minimis Settlements*

A de minimis settlement allows PRPs whose liability is seen as small due to low volume and to the relative toxicity of the waste they generated to buy out of liability. De minimis settlements are valuable to both the larger PRPs and the de minimis parties. Large PRPs benefit by avoiding the transaction costs associated with managing a large group and, more directly, through the premium paid by de minimis parties. For de minimis parties the advantages of avoiding the costs of the CERCLA process are obvious.

Generally, three central issues are the subject of negotiations: (1) the volumetric threshold by which de minimis status is determined; (2) the amount of any premium to be paid; and (3) the minimum buyout figure, if any. Each of the issues deserves the attention of both de minimis and larger PRPs.

---

[297] CERCLA provides that the agency is to be "guided by the principle that a more complete covenant not to sue shall be provided for a more complete remedy." CERCLA §122(c)(1), 42 U.S.C. §9622(c)(1).

Until recently, EPA had not acted with any great purpose on de minimis settlements. In recent years, the agency has begun to use its de minimis authority on a more routine basis.

B. Private Party Negotiations

In addition to negotiations with the government, PRPs in a multiparty site inevitably find that they must engage in negotiations among themselves. This process will consume at least as much time and resources as negotiations with the government and can be crucial to the viability of any overall settlement.

1. PRP Organization

The first critical stage of private party negotiation in the Superfund process is organization of a PRP group. If PRPs desire a settlement with the government, they usually must organize into a group in order to receive an ''audience'' from EPA.[298] As with governmental negotiations in general, early organization may benefit the PRPs collectively as it allows them more influence over Superfund decisions restricting the direction and setting the cost of cleanup.

Organization of a PRP group may not require a formal organizational agreement if the group is small. At larger sites with hundreds of PRPs, an agreement is essential. While there are model organizational agreements,[299] the terms of the agreement are always the subject of negotiation among the parties.

Of particular importance to potential signatories are the withdrawal provisions. Although these provisions usually allow a signatory to leave the group at any time, they often require the payment of outstanding assessments prior to withdrawal. The definition of the assessments that must be paid by a withdrawing PRP should be carefully scrutinized before signature.

Among the most critical provisions of any PRP agreement is the method by which voting power and structure is organized. These provisions often become a battleground between the de minimis PRPs and PRPs with larger volumes. The PRPs with the largest volumetric contribution to the site will generally argue for a proportional voting scheme, giving greater voting power to those parties with higher volume. In contrast, the de minimis parties will argue that voting power should be equally spread across the group. De minimis PRPs should recognize that if the proportional scheme is chosen, they will have to be concerned with dominance of the group by the large players. The large players will have similar concerns for any per capita voting authority. Often the issue is resolved on economic terms: voting power is allocated according to the percentages contributed in preliminary allocations. The voting power issue may also be defused by ensuring that both factions have adequate representation on the steering committee and its various subcommittees.

The role of the steering committee which acts on behalf of the group is central to any PRP organization. The committee's functions generally are (1) negotiating with EPA and other parties on all issues, including settlement; (2)

[298] EPA traditionally shuns individual settlers in favor of larger settling groups in order to save its resources and to assure that there will be enough resources to complete any cleanup.

[299] Information Network for Superfund Settlements, PRP ORGANIZATION HANDBOOK 4 (1989).

retaining and directing the activities of outside consultants and counsel; (3) appointing members of various subcommittees; (4) recommending a method of allocating costs, both procedural and substantive (i.e., how to pay for the cost of cleanup); (5) recommending a de minimis buyout proposal if appropriate; and (6) referring settlement matters to the group.[300] Adequate representation of all sides is crucial if the group is to operate smoothly.

Once the basic structure of the group is set and a decision is made to perform some part of the work, a second agreement implementing this decision is often drawn up. This document usually terminates the preexisting PRP group agreement and sets out the structure under which the group will carry out the work it agrees to perform for the government. Once again, a steering committee is formed which is delegated the day-to-day administrative tasks required to supervise the performance of the response action.

The settlement participation agreement[301] for conducting the remedy marks the point of no return for its signatories. Once PRPs sign, they are usually obligated to pay their allocated share of the costs involved in carrying out the work at the site. Because of the do or die nature of the agreement, PRPs are well advised to pay close attention to its terms. The same basic issues that arose in the PRP group agreement may surface here.

2. *Allocation*

Among the most important issues on which PRPs will negotiate is the method by which settlement costs are allocated. Allocation schemes generally are developed through the work of the steering committee or its allocation subcommittee. This group will devise a proposed scheme to present to the members of the group who will then comment on it and either ratify or reject it.

At this juncture, various coalitions of PRPs may form based on waste volume, toxicity characteristics, or some other consideration. The coalitions (and individual PRPs) will lobby the members of the allocation committee for a final scheme which they believe serves their interest.

There are a number of different ways to allocate liability. An element common to most allocations is a volumetric approach. Under a straight volumetric scheme, each PRP pays that portion of either cleanup or settlement costs based on the volume of waste it sent to the site. A permutation of this theme is a volumetric scheme with a multiplier based on the type of waste sent: the toxicity of the different waste streams is considered and a particular multiplier chosen for each. Such an approach seeks to assess the highest burden on those parties whose waste drives the cleanup—usually those with the highest toxicity.

Another approach to allocation is tiering. Under this scheme, PRPs are arrayed in tiers based upon volume or other characteristics and members of each tier either pay a sum certain or are assigned a percentage share on which their portion of ongoing cleanup costs will be calculated. Negotiation by individual parties is often critical to determine their places in the tiering structure.

---

[300] *Id.* at 8.

[301] In conjunction with the participation agreement there may also be a trust agreement that will enable the group to collect moneys in a trust account for payment of both administrative and work-related expenses.

A third allocation technique is known as the per capita approach. Under this approach, liability is assessed equally among all PRPs. Obviously, the approach is favored by high volume generators as it reduces an otherwise large proportional share of the liability. Pure per capita allocations are rare since, under ordinary circumstances, they are inequitable to lower volume participants. Where volume cannot be ascertained, however, there is often at least an element of per capita allocation.

There are as many allocation schemes as there are creative lawyers and environmental scientists. Regardless of the scheme chosen, negotiations are critical to obtaining an equitable division of the liability.

3. Alternative Dispute Resolution

Disputes will often arise which threaten to drive group members to litigate against one another. In order to prevent wasteful litigation, PRP agreements have made use of dispute resolution clauses with increasing frequency. Such clauses refer disputes to a neutral third party to render a decision or to engage in mediation. Usually, these alternatives are employed to resolve allocation disputes.

While the structure of alternative dispute resolution varies, often it will begin with an information gathering phase including distribution of an allocation questionnaire and marshalling of other information. The information is organized and parties are generally given the opportunity to argue their positions or, in some instances, to take testimony to resolve disputed facts. Again, there are as many dispute resolution schemes as there are lawyers and circumstances unique to particular sites. In designing a dispute resolution scheme, PRPs will balance the advantage of providing greater process and thereby permitting more thorough evaluation of issues against the cost of the process.

XI. Conclusion

The impact of CERCLA in the environmental arena has been dramatic. Industry has spent billions as a result of EPA's Superfund efforts, both in cleaning up problems and in transaction and litigation costs. As these costs have mounted, players on all sides have come to recognize that the statute has serious flaws.

Where this recognition will lead is uncertain. Although municipalities, lenders, and the insurance industry have been the most visible advocates of change in the liability scheme, other groups also oppose the existing system of liability and the levels of cleanup required. Yet at the same time, virtually all environmental groups oppose relaxation of liability and cleanup standards. The clash of these interests, the vast sums expended to meet arguably unrealistic cleanup levels, and the all-encompassing liability scheme guarantee a controversial and contentious Superfund reauthorization. Whatever the outcome of this debate, the statute will continue to have an impact wholly disproportionate to the problems it addresses.

8

Occupational Safety and Health Act

By Paul A. J. Wilson and J. Gordon Arbuckle
with V. Heather Sibbison

> He took me up a wet and rickety stair to a great light room, furnished with no visible thing but rude, manger-like receptacles running all round its sides: and up to these mangers, like so many mares haltered to the rack, stood rows of girls. Before each was vertically thrust up a long, glittering scythe, immovably fixed at bottom to the manger-edge. The curve of the scythe, and its having no snath to it, made it look exactly like a sword. To and fro, across the sharp edge, the girls forever dragged long strips of rags, washed white, picked from baskets at one side; thus ripping asunder every seam, and converting the tatters almost into lint. The air swam with the fine, poisonous particles, which from all sided darted, subtilely, as motes in sunbeams, into the lungs.
>
> "This is the rag-room," coughed the boy.
>
> "You find it rather stifling here," coughed I, in answer; "but the girls don't cough."
>
> "Oh, they are used to it."
>
> —H. Melville, *The Tartarus of Maids*

I. Introduction

The Occupational Safety and Health Act of 1970 (the OSH Act)[1] was enacted concurrently with the first of the modern federal environmental statutes. Particularly in the early years, the OSH Act's implementers emphasized the statute's safety, rather than the health, goals. As a consequence, one thinks of the OSH Act as a safety law, governing matters such as stair railings and machinery guards, rather than as a law profoundly affecting human health and the environment. Because worker safety was the concern, the OSH Act became the province of safety managers and labor lawyers rather than of those working in environmental fields. Thus, even though in recent years the Occupational Safety and Health Administration (OSHA) has radically increased its emphasis on worker health, and even though protection of worker health is inescapably intertwined with the workplace environment, many have been slow to recognize that in its health regulatory aspects, the OSH Act is an "environmental" statute. Indeed, the OSH Act is the only law that provides comprehensive protection for the workplace environment.

---

[1] 29 U.S.C. §651 *et seq.* (1988).

OSHA, which administers the OSH Act, has numerous environmental programs that are so inextricably interrelated to traditional environmental concerns, like toxic chemical control and inventory reporting, that it is essential to have a working knowledge of the health aspects of OSHA in order to effectively understand the other environmental programs.

This chapter discusses the OSHA programs most closely related to environmental concerns: training, hazard communication, process safety management, noise exposure, toxic and hazardous substance identification and control, carcinogen identification and control, and protection from exposure to bloodborne pathogens. Following the discussion on the substance of these major programs is some basic information on OSHA's establishment and enforcement of safety and health regulations.

II. Regulation of the Workplace Environment

OSHA regulates employee exposure to hazards in two ways. The first is through management standards that are generally applicable to all types of workplaces, such as employee training, hazard communication, and process safety management requirements. The second way that OSHA regulates employee exposure to hazards is through specialized regulations directed at specific environmental hazards. Examples of these specific regulations include worker exposures to noise, toxic and hazardous substances, carcinogens, and bloodborne pathogens. Both types of standards are discussed below.

A. General Management Standards

1. Training

Unlike other environmental laws, the OSH Act places a heavy emphasis on training to permit workers to recognize and avoid workplace hazards. Specific training requirements vary by industry and by the hazards to which employees may be exposed. There are, however, certain components that are common to all of OSHA's training standards. For example, employers are required to maintain records documenting that their employees received the training prescribed by the applicable regulations. Additionally, employers may be penalized for failing to give employees adequate training and for failing to maintain records documenting such training. Furthermore, an employer's failure to train an employee properly can be a factor in determining what penalty should be assessed against an employer should the employee be injured or killed.

2. Hazard Communication

The OSHA hazard communication (HazCom) standard is designed to reduce occupational exposure to harmful chemicals by training employees about the chemical hazards to which they may be exposed and how to implement measures to protect themselves from those hazards. The stated purpose of the HazCom regulations is "to ensure that the hazards of all chemicals produced or imported are evaluated, and that information concerning their hazards is transmitted to employers and employees.''[2] The HazCom standard applies to manufacturers, importers, and distributors of ''hazardous chemicals,'' and to all other employers whose workers are potentially exposed to such chemicals.[3]

A chemical will be deemed hazardous for purposes of the HazCom standard if it poses a ''*health*'' or ''*physical hazard.*''[4] A chemical poses a ''health hazard'' if ''there is statistically significant evidence based on at least one study conducted in accordance with established scientific principles that acute or chronic health effects may occur in exposed employees.''[5] A more comprehensive definition of health hazards can be found in Appendix A to the HazCom standard.[6]

A chemical is considered a ''physical hazard'' when ''there is scientifically valid evidence that it is a combustible liquid, a compressed gas, explosive, flammable, an organic peroxide, an oxidizer, pyrophoric, unstable (reactive) or water-reactive.''[7] These physical hazard terms are fully defined in section 1910.1200(c) of the HazCom regulation.[8]

The HazCom standard *does not* apply to any hazardous waste regulated by EPA; tobacco or tobacco products; wood or wood products; food, drugs, cosmetics, or alcohol for sale in a retail store or intended for personal consumption in the workplace; any consumer product or hazardous substance ''used in the workplace in the same manner as normal consumer use''; or any drug ''when sold in its final form for direct administration to the patient.''[9]

For additional help in determining whether a chemical is hazardous for purposes of the HazCom standard, an employer may refer to certain sources that list chemicals deemed by OSHA to be hazardous. Such sources include the 29 C.F.R. part 1910, subpart Z, listing of Toxic and Hazardous Substances; the American Conference of Government Industrial Hygienists' publication, *Threshold Limit Values for Chemical Substances and Physical Agents in the Work Environment;* the National Toxicology Program's *Annual Report on Carcinogens;* and the Monographs of the International Agency for Research on Cancer.[10]

The heart of the HazCom standard is its information generation and transmission system. First, chemical manufacturers, importers, and employers ''must evaluate chemicals produced in their workplaces or imported by them to determine if they are hazardous.''[11] The standard does not specify any particular procedure or method for evaluating hazards, but it does mandate that

[2] 29 C.F.R. §1910.1200(a) (1992). *See also* 48 Fed. Reg. 53,280 (1983) and 52 Fed. Reg. 31,877 (1987). For a description of the evolution of the HazCom standard, *see* Steelworkers v. Auchter, 763 F.2d 728, 731–32, 12 OSH Cases 1337 (3d Cir. 1985).

[3] 29 C.F.R. §1910.1200 (1992) and 52 Fed. Reg. 31,877 (1987). The HazCom standard defines ''chemical'' as ''any element, chemical compound or mixture of elements and/or compounds.'' 29 C.F.R. §1900.1200(c) (1992).

[4] 29 C.F.R. §1910.1200(b) (1992).

[5] *Id.* Health hazards include ''carcinogens, toxic or highly toxic agents, reproductive toxins, irritants, corrosives, sensitizers, hepatotoxins, nephrotoxins, neurotoxins, agents which act on the hematopoietic system, and agents which damage the lungs, skin, eyes, or mucous membranes.'' *Id.*

[6] *Id.* at app. A.

[7] *Id.*

[8] 29 C.F.R. §1910.1200(c) (1992).

[9] 29 C.F.R. §1910.1200(b)(6) (1992).

[10] 29 C.F.R. §1910.1200(d)(3)-(4) (1992).

[11] 29 C.F.R. §1910.1200(d) (1992).

manufacturers, importers, and employers "conduct a thorough evaluation, examining all relevant data and producing a scientifically defensible evaluation."[12] Criteria to be used to satisfy this requirement include carcinogenicity evidence, human data, animal data, the results of any scientifically valid studies, information available in company files, data obtained from a supplier, and relevant information from any other authoritative source.[13]

After an employer evaluates the hazard, it must then develop a written "hazard communication program" to inform employees and any downstream users of the risks associated with those chemicals deemed to be hazardous.[14] Each program must set forth criteria for (1) the labeling of containers; (2) the preparation and circulation of material safety data sheets (MSDSs); and (3) the training of employees.[15]

The labeling requirement mandates that employers affix labels or tags on containers indicating the identity of the chemical, a warning about its hazards, and the name and address of the manufacturer or importer of the chemical, or of some other responsible party.[16]

The MSDS requirement dictates that chemical manufacturers and importers develop a written or printed document containing information on hazardous chemicals, and that all employers maintain copies of MSDSs for each of the chemicals they use.[17] The MSDS for any given chemical must contain information detailing the identity, hazardous ingredients, physical and chemical characteristics, specific physical and health hazards, routes of entry to the body, permissible or recommended exposure limits, handling and use precautions, control measures, emergency and first aid procedures, the MSDS preparation date, and the name and address of the "chemical manufacturer, importer or other responsible party . . . who can provide additional information on the hazardous chemical and appropriate emergency procedures. . . ."[18]

OSHA's definition of hazardous chemicals is the most expansive of any such definition used by federal government agencies.[19] Employers should be aware that section 311 of the Emergency Planning and Community Right-to-Know Act (EPCRA)[20] requires that employers notify the local fire departments, the local emergency planning committee, and the state emergency response commission if they have on their premises more than 10,000 pounds of a hazardous chemical or more than 55 gallons or 500 pounds of an "extremely hazardous"[21] substance as defined by EPCRA.

[12] 29 C.F.R. §1910.1200 (1992), app. B.

[13] 29 C.F.R. §1910.1200 (1992), apps. B and C. To be considered scientifically valid, a study must be "designed and conducted according to established scientific principles." 29 C.F.R. §1910.1200 (1992), app. B.

[14] 29 C.F.R. §1910.1200(e) (1992). In multiple-employer workplaces (i.e., a construction site with a contractor and subcontractors), the principal employer must make sure that the written hazard communication program is available to the employees of every employer. *Id.* at §1910.1200(e)(2).

[15] 29 C.F.R. §1910.1200(e) (1992).

[16] 29 C.F.R. §1900.1200(f) (1992).

[17] 29 C.F.R. §1910.1200(g) (1992).

[18] *Id.*

[19] OSHA defines "hazardous chemical" in the context of its hazardous communication standard as "any chemical which is a physical hazard or a health hazard." 29 C.F.R. §1910.1200(c).

[20] 42 U.S.C. §§11,001, 11,011 (1988).

[21] *Id.*

Finally, the employee training requirement dictates that employees be provided with information identifying work areas where hazardous chemicals are present and describing labels, the MSDSs, chemical presence or release detection methods, potential health and physical hazards of work area chemicals, protective measures, and other relevant information on the hazardous chemicals to which the employee might be exposed in the normal course of his duties.[22] This employee training must be conducted in employees' "work area at the time of their initial assignment, and whenever a new hazard is introduced into their work area."[23]

In recognition of the importance of protecting the trade secrets of chemical manufacturers, OSHA has provided an exception to the ingredient disclosure requirements of the HazCom standard in situations in which a trade secret is involved.[24] A trade secret is defined as "any confidential formula, pattern, process, device, information or compilation of information that . . . gives the employer an opportunity to gain an advantage over competitors who do not know or use it."[25] This exception allows chemical manufacturers or importers to "withhold the specific chemical identity" from labels and MSDS, but the hazardous properties of the chemical and suggested precautions must still be disclosed.[26]

3. *Process Safety Management Standard*

The process safety management standard is OSHA's most recent general management regulation, having become effective in June 1992.[27] OSHA was in the process of developing this regulation when, in 1990, Congress provided OSHA with further instruction on what should be included in the process safety management standard. This instruction from Congress is of particular interest because it came in the form of a provision of the 1990 Clean Air Act Amendments,[28] rather than as an amendment to the Occupational Safety and Health Act. Inclusion of process safety management instructions in the Clean Air Act Amendments underscores the need to view the OSH Act as part of the interconnected web of environmental laws.

The process safety management standard is designed to protect employees from accidental releases of highly hazardous chemicals in the workplace that could occur due to failures in process, procedures, or equipment.[29] It represents an evolutionary step forward in OSHA regulatory practice, because prior OSHA

[22] 29 C.F.R. §1900.1200(h) (1992).

[23] *Id.*

[24] 29 C.F.R. §1910.1200(i) (1992).

[25] 29 C.F.R. §1910.1200(b) (1992). Any claim of a trade secret must be adequately verified for this exception to apply. 29 C.F.R. §1910.1200(i) (1992).

[26] 29 C.F.R. §1900.1200(i) (1992). This exception does not apply in situations involving a medical emergency. If an emergency exists, a chemical manufacturer may be required to confidentially disclose ingredients to a health professional. *Id.*

[27] Most of the process safety management standards became effective on June 1, 1992, but paragraphs (f), (h), (j), and (l) were stayed until August 26, 1992. The text of this regulation is now codified at 29 C.F.R. §1910.119 (1992). *See also* 57 Fed. Reg. 6356 (1991).

[28] *See* §304(a) of the Clean Air Act Amendments.

[29] 57 Fed. Reg. 6356 (1991). The term "catastrophic release" includes "a major uncontrolled emission, fire, or explosion, involving one or more highly hazardous chemicals, that presents serious danger to employees in the workplace." 29 C.F.R. §1910.119(b) (1992).

standards in the hazardous chemical area have focused on establishing technical requirements for dealing with "routine or daily exposures" of chemicals in the workplace.[30] The process safety management regulation breaks from this mold by not focusing on technical limits, but rather on the managerial and procedural "precautions necessary to prevent large accidental releases that could result in catastrophes."[31]

The process safety management regulation requires certain employers to implement management procedures to protect employees who work with or near any of over 130 "highly hazardous" chemicals. "Highly hazardous" chemicals include those substances "possessing toxic, reactive, flammable, or explosive properties" that present the potential for a catastrophic chemical accident in the workplace and consequent serious danger to employees.[32] The chemicals OSHA deems to be highly hazardous at or above certain threshold quantities are listed at Appendix A to the process safety management standard.[33]

Employers subject to the process safety management standard are those who use a manufacturing or other process involving either (1) the use of a prescribed amount of any of the listed highly hazardous chemicals; or (2) the on-site presence of 10,000 pounds or more of flammable liquids or gas stored in one location.[34] The regulations do not apply to "[h]ydrocarbon fuels used solely for workplace consumption," flammable liquids "kept below their normal boiling point without benefit of chilling or refrigeration," retail facilities, oil and gas well drilling/servicing operations, or "normally unoccupied remote facilities."[35]

By mandating management standards rather than technical standards, OSHA has attempted to give employers some flexibility to tailor safety measures to the realities of their operations. Nevertheless, all employers covered by the standard must satisfy certain basic requirements that OSHA deems essential to any safety system.[36] For example, employers must compile written process safety information "to enable the ... [persons] involved in operating the process to identify and understand the hazards posed by those processes involving highly hazardous chemicals."[37] This compilation must include information relating to the hazards, technology, and equipment used in the process.[38] In addition, employers are required to conduct a process hazard analysis to identify, evaluate, and control operations involving highly hazardous chemicals.[39] Such analyses are critical, in that they allow the employer to "determine where problems may occur, take corrective measures to improve . . . safety, and

---

[30] 57 Fed. Reg. 6356 (1991).
[31] *Id.*
[32] 29 C.F.R. §1910.119(b) (1992).
[33] 29 C.F.R. §1910.119(a) (1992), app. A.
[34] *Id.* Flammable liquid or gas is defined in 29 C.F.R. §1910.1200(c) (1992).
[35] 29 C.F.R. §1910.119(a) (1992).
[36] 29 C.F.R. §1910.119(e)-(o) (1992).
[37] 29 C.F.R. §1910.119(d) (1992). *See also* 57 Fed. Reg. 6356, 6374–75 (1991).
[38] 29 C.F.R. §1910.119(d) (1992).
[39] 29 C.F.R. §1910.119(e) (1992) and 57 Fed. Reg. 6356, 6375 (1991). The process safety evaluation must "be performed by a team with expertise in engineering and process operations[.]" 29 C.F.R. §1910.119(e) (1992).

preplan the actions that would be necessary if there were . . . [any] failures in the process.''[40]

Another key requirement of the standard is the training and education of employees.[41] Employers must provide initial and refresher training to employees who work with the chemicals covered by these regulations.[42] The training must emphasize ''specific safety and health hazards, emergency operations including shutdown, and safe work practices applicable to the employee's job tasks.''[43] Employers must prepare a written record to verify that employees have received and understood the proper training.[44]

Other mandatory components of the process safety management standard include the implementation of written operating procedures and practices, the establishment of maintenance systems for equipment, the development of a workplace emergency planning and response program, and the prompt investigation of every incident that caused or could have caused a release of highly hazardous chemicals in the workplace.[45]

B. Standards Regulating Workplace Exposure to Specific Environmental Hazards

1. Noise Exposure

The present occupational noise exposure standard was originally set forth in the Walsh-Healey Public Contracts Act[46] and applied to employees working on federal contracts.[47] The standard, which OSHA adopted under section 6(a) in 1971,[48] protects employees from the harmful effects of exposure to workplace noise exceeding the stated permissible levels described in Table G-16, published at 29 C.F.R. §1910.95.[49]

Any employer with employees subjected to sound levels in excess of the limits set forth in Table G-16, as analyzed over the course of an eight-hour workday, must take steps to reduce the noise to within the allowable limits by ''feasible administrative or engineering controls[.]''[50] Such controls include ''the installation of noise-damping materials[,] . . . the substitution of quieter machines, processes, or parts for noisy ones, and the rotation of workers to minimize their exposure to high sound intensities.''[51] An employer may substitute personal protective equipment such as earplugs or earmuffs to reduce noise

---

[40] 57 Fed. Reg. 6356, 6375 (1991).

[41] 29 C.F.R. §1910.119(g) (1992).

[42] *Id.*

[43] *Id.*

[44] *Id.*

[45] 29 C.F.R. §1910.119(f)-(o) (1992). *See also* 57 Fed. Reg. 6356 (1991).

[46] 41 U.S.C. §35 *et seq.* (1988).

[47] *See* Forging Indus. Ass'n v. Secretary of Labor, 773 F.2d 1436, 1440, 12 OSH Cases 1472 (4th Cir. 1985).

[48] 29 C.F.R. §1910.95 (1992) and 39 Fed. Reg. 23,502 (1974).

[49] Permissible noise limits for workers in the construction industry are found at 29 C.F.R. §1926.52 (1992).

[50] 29 C.F.R. §1910.95(b)(1) (1992). Administrative controls ''involve modification of work assignments to reduce employee exposure to noise'' and engineering controls ''involve modification of plant, equipment, processes, or materials to reduce noise. . . .'' *Forging Indus. Ass'n*, 773 F.2d at 1440 n.3.

[51] Marshall v. West Point Pepperell, Inc., 588 F.2d 979, 981, 7 OSH Cases 1035 (5th Cir. 1979).

exposure only if an employer can demonstrate that engineering controls fail to reduce sound exposure to within permissible levels.[52]

In addition to requiring engineering controls and personal protective equipment, the standard also requires employers to develop and implement "a continuing, effective hearing conservation program whenever employee noise exposures equal or exceed" allowable limits.[53] Every hearing conservation program must include strategies for monitoring noise levels, providing adequate employee notification, audiometric testing of employees to detect hearing loss, and recordkeeping of employee exposure measurements and audiometric tests.[54]

Whether an employer is subject to OSHA's noise mitigation requirements depends on whether its employees are exposed to sounds above specified decibel levels. OSHA's noise exposure limits are determined by calculating the decibel[55] levels in a workplace using a time-weighted average (TWA). The TWA essentially is a method of calculating worker exposure by "combin[ing] noise level and duration of exposure to measure the accumulation of noise levels experienced by an employee over a workshift."[56] OSHA's hearing conservation program requirement is triggered by an eight-hour TWA of 85 decibels, whereas the engineering controls requirements described in subsection 1910.95(b) are triggered at TWA levels of 90 decibels.

2. *Toxic and Hazardous Substances*

In individual rulemaking actions under section 6(b)(5), OSHA has promulgated over 30 standards to regulate employee exposure to toxic and hazardous substances.[57] OSHA's toxic and hazardous exposure standards[58] are becoming increasingly important in the modern workplace as the number of workers potentially exposed to such materials rises. Catastrophic accidents at Bhopal (1984), the Phillips 66 chemical plant (1989), the Arco Chemical facility (1990), and BASF (1990) have underscored the need for standards regulating toxic and hazardous substances.[59] Furthermore, exposure to these toxic and hazardous substances triggers a number of other federal regulations.

The goal of OSHA's regulatory program in this area is to establish routine or daily exposure limits for employees in the workplace. Such "permissible exposure limits" usually are expressed as TWAs, short term exposure limits

---

[52] 29 C.F.R. §1910.95(b)(1) (1992).

[53] 29 C.F.R. §1910.95(c) (1992).

[54] *Id.*

[55] Decibels "are a measure of sound loudness." *Forging Indus. Ass'n,* 773 F.2d at 1440 n.1. The full spectrum of audible sound loudness "can be compressed into a . . . scale of 0 to 140" decibels. *Id.*

[56] *Id.* at 1440 n.2.

[57] OSHA also attempted to promulgate more than 400 air contaminants standards in a single rulemaking which was vacated by the U.S. Court of Appeals for the Eleventh Circuit. AFL-CIO v. OSHA, 965 F.2d 962, 15 OSH Cases 1729 (11th Cir. 1992).

[58] 29 C.F.R. §§1910.1000–1919.1500 (1992). Substances covered include asbestos, coal tar pitch volatiles, 4-nitrobiphenyl, alpha-naphthylamine, methyl chloromethyl ether, 3,3'-dichlorobenzidine, bis-chloromethyl ether, beta-napthylamine, benzidine, 4-aminodiphenyl, ethyleneimine, beta-propiolactone, 2-acetylaminoflourene, 4-dimethylaminoazobenzene, n-nitrosodimethylamine, vinyl chloride, inorganic arsenic, lead, benzene, coke oven emissions, bloodborne pathogens, cotton dust, 1,2-dibromo-3-chloropropane, acrylonitrile, ethylene oxide, and formaldehyde. 29 C.F.R. §1910.

[59] In the Bhopal, India, accident there were more than 2,000 deaths; in Phillips 66 there were 24 deaths and 132 injuries; in Arco, 17 deaths; and in BASF 2 deaths and 41 injuries. 57 Fed. Reg. 6356 (1992).

(STEL), or "ceiling limits."[60] OSHA has defined TWA in the context of the toxic and hazardous substances rules as "the employee's average . . . exposure in any . . . work shift . . . which shall not be exceeded."[61] A STEL has been defined as "the employee's 15-minute time weighted average exposure which shall not be exceeded at any time during a work day. . . ."[62] Finally, OSHA has defined a "ceiling limit" as the employee's exposure limit "which shall not be exceeded during any part of the work day."[63]

If initial exposure monitoring of employees reveals that a permissible exposure limit for a regulated substance is being exceeded, an employer must institute control measures to reduce exposure to an acceptable level.[64] This requirement is consistent with OSHA's general hierarchy of controls policy, which specifies engineering and work practice controls as the preferred methods of reducing exposure.[65] OSHA favors these control options because both are designed to eliminate or minimize "the hazard at its source."[66] Engineering controls "encompass product substitution, process or equipment redesign . . . [and] enclosure, exhaust or dilution ventilation, and employee isolation."[67] Work practice controls alter "the manner in which a task is performed and often are necessary for the effective operation of engineering controls."[68]

If engineering or work practice controls are not feasible or successful, then an employer may provide employees with personal protective clothing and/or protective equipment (e.g., a respirator).[69] OSHA does not consider personal protective clothing or devices to be as desirable as engineering or work practice controls, because the effectiveness of the personal equipment is dictated by the employee's willingness and ability properly to fit, wear, and maintain the equipment, which is often uncomfortable and awkward.[70]

Other control methods recurring throughout OSHA's toxic and hazardous standards include continual monitoring of exposure levels; the use of warning labels on all entrances, work areas, and containers; employee information and training; improved hygiene and lunchroom facilities; and the implementation of a medical surveillance and examination program.[71]

Due in large part to the time-consuming procedural and substantive requirements of section 6(b)(5) and its limited resources, OSHA has promulgated individual standards for only "a small number of high priority substances and

---

[60] *See generally* 29 C.F.R. §1910.1000–.1048 (1992).

[61] 29 C.F.R. §1910.1000(a)(5) (1992).

[62] *Id.*

[63] *Id.*

[64] *See generally* 29 C.F.R. §1910.1000–.1048 (1992).

[65] *See* 29 C.F.R. §§1910.1001(f), 1910.1017(f), and 1910.1028(f) (1992). For a detailed discussion on OSHA's hierarchy of controls policy, *see* 51 Fed. Reg. 22,612, 22,692–93 (1986).

[66] 51 Fed. Reg. 22,612, 22,693 (1986).

[67] *Id.*

[68] *Id.* at 22,692.

[69] *See* 29 C.F.R. §§1910.1001(f), .1017(f), and .1028(f) (1992), and 51 Fed. Reg. 22,612, 22,693 (1986). A respirator is a personal protective device worn over an employee's face that filters harmful contaminants out of the air. 51 Fed. Reg. 22,612, 22,693 (1986). For an example of a typical respirator program, *see* 29 C.F.R. §1910.1001(g) (1992).

[70] 51 Fed. Reg. 22,612, 22,692–93 (1986).

[71] *See* 29 C.F.R. §1910.1001, .1017, and .1028 (1992) as examples of subpart Z standards requiring the implementation of these various control measures.

those with greatest public interest.''[72] For this reason, OSHA claims it neither has been able to address ''the many thousands of currently unregulated chemicals in the workplace nor to keep up with reviewing the several thousand new chemicals introduced since its creation.''[73] Therefore, in an effort to respond to this perceived backing of unregulated toxic and harmful substances, OSHA recently decided that, instead of approaching rulemaking on an individual substance-by-substance basis, it would begin promulgating regulations ''through the use of generic rulemaking, which would simultaneously cover many substances.''[74]

OSHA's initial effort at generic rulemaking was the so-called ''Air Contaminants'' proceeding in 1989 that attempted to set standards regulating 428 different materials.[75] This generic standard was challenged by various industry associations, a number of specific individual companies, and the AFL-CIO in *AFL-CIO v. OSHA.*[76] While the Eleventh Circuit held that ''nothing in the OSH Act would prevent OSHA from addressing multiple substances in a single rulemaking'' as long as the requirements of the OSH Act are not ignored,[77] it held that OSHA had indeed failed to meet the requirements of the OSH Act because it did not satisfy section 6(b)(5)'s substantive requirements:

> [W]e hold that OSHA has not sufficiently explained or supported its threshold determination that exposure to these substances at previous levels posed a significant risk of these material health impairments or that the new standard eliminates or reduces the risk to the extent feasible. OSHA's overall approach to this rulemaking is so flawed that we must vacate the whole . . . Air Contaminants Standard.[78]

OSHA decided not to petition the Supreme Court to review the Eleventh Circuit's decision on the air contaminants standard, although it is possible that legislation may be enacted to modify the OSH Act to authorize a more expedient method of standard-setting than currently allowed by section 6(b)(5).[79] In any event, the Eleventh Circuit's holding in *AFL-CIO v. OSHA* does not preclude the possibility of properly promulgated generic standards in the future.

3. *Carcinogens*

On January 22, 1980, OSHA promulgated rules to govern the procedures it must follow in regulating potential occupational carcinogens.[80] The rules, generally known as OSHA's Cancer Policy, are predicated on the recognition that ''responsible health regulatory policy requires that criteria should be specified for the identification of substances which should be regulated as posing poten-

---

[72] 53 Fed. Reg. 20,960, 20,963 (1988).
[73] *Id.*
[74] 54 Fed. Reg. 2332, 2333 (1989). *See also* 53 Fed. Reg. 20,960, 20,964–95 (1988).
[75] 54 Fed. Reg. 2332 (1989).
[76] 965 F.2d 962, 969, 15 OSH Cases 1729 (11th Cir. 1992).
[77] *Id.,* at 972.
[78] *Id.* at 986–87.
[79] *Id.* at 987.
[79] *Id.* at 987.
[80] 29 C.F.R. §1990.101–.152 (1992) and 45 Fed. Reg. 5001 (1980).

tial cancer risks to workers.''[81] The fact that OSHA terms its procedures for identifying and regulating potential occupational carcinogens a ''policy'' does not change the binding effect of these rules. The Cancer Policy has the force of law because, unlike other general statements of policy, it was the product of a full-fledged notice and comment rulemaking and is published in the *Code of Federal Regulations.*[82]

The first requirement for OSHA under the Cancer Policy is to identify and classify substances that pose potential carcinogenic risks to employees in the workplace. Potential occupational carcinogens include

> [A]ny substance, or combination or mixture of substances, which causes an increased incidence of benign and/or malignant neoplasms, or a substantial decrease in the latency period between exposure and onset of neoplasms in humans or in one or more mammalian species as the result of any oral, respiratory or dermal exposure, or any other exposure which results in the induction of tumors at a site other than the site of administration. . . . [Also included is] any substance which is metabolized into one or more potential occupational carcinogens by mammals.[83]

The scientific evidence whether a particular substance meets this definition may derive from human epidemiological studies and/or experimental studies in animal species.[84]

OSHA identifies several publications that it deems to be authoritative sources of evidence that the substances listed in them are carcinogens.[85] These include the 29 C.F.R. part 1910, subpart Z, list of Toxic and Hazardous Substances; the National Toxicology Program's *Annual Report on Carcinogens;* and the Monographs of the International Agency for Research on Cancer.[86]

When OSHA targets a substance as a potential occupational carcinogen for regulation, it must follow a three-step procedure: (1) publish an advance notice of proposed rulemaking (ANPR) indicating that OSHA is studying the feasibility of regulating the substance as a carcinogen;[87] (2) publish a notice of proposed rulemaking pursuant to section 6(b) of the OSH Act;[88] and (3) promulgate the final rule in accordance with established procedures and then publish it in the *Federal Register.*[89]

OSHA began reevaluating its Cancer Policy in 1982.[90] During the course of this reevaluation, OSHA stayed ''those provisions of the Policy requiring the establishment and publication of the Candidate List and Priority Lists (29 C.F.R. 1990.121, 1990.122, 1990.131 and 1990.133).''[91] The candidate list was

---

[81] 29 C.F.R. §1990.111(a) (1992).

[82] 29 C.F.R. §1990.101–.152 (1992) and 45 Fed. Reg. 5001 (1980).

[83] 29 C.F.R. §1990.103 (1992).

[84] 29 C.F.R. §1990.143 (1992).

[85] 29 C.F.R. §1200(d)(4) (1992).

[86] *Id.*

[87] 29 C.F.R. §1990.141(a) (1992). The purpose of the required ANPR is to solicit relevant information from interested parties about a substance's possible carcinogenicity, or lack thereof, at a very early stage in the agency's deliberations. *Id.* at §1990.141(a)(5) (1992).

[88] 29 C.F.R. §1990.142 (1992).

[89] 29 C.F.R. §1990.143–.147 (1992).

[90] 48 Fed. Reg. 241, 242 (1983).

[91] *Id.*

the first step in the priority-setting process and it targeted those substances that should "receive further study" for carcinogenicity.[92] The priority lists were the second step of the priority-setting process during which substances from the candidate list were further screened by using the priority factors specified in the Cancer Policy.[93]

OSHA takes the position that the remaining provisions have not been stayed and remain in effect.[94] It may be argued, however, that by staying the first two steps of the priority process, OSHA has effectively stayed the entire policy. This issue has yet to be resolved, and the enforceability of the Cancer Policy is still a question mark.

4. *Bloodborne Pathogens*

Responding to the growing concern over bloodborne diseases, OSHA recently promulgated a standard regulating occupational exposure to bloodborne pathogens.[95] This new standard recognizes the significant risk posed by these pathogens in the workplace, and it seeks to minimize or eliminate the risk by protecting employees from "exposure to blood and other potentially infectious materials. . . ."[96] This standard is especially relevant for employers in the health care and law enforcement professions.

Bloodborne pathogens are "pathogenic microorganisms that are present in human blood and can cause disease in humans."[97] Examples include hepatitis B virus (HBV) and human immunodeficiency virus (HIV). For purposes of this regulation, OSHA "assumes that all human blood and certain bodily fluids and tissues are potentially infectious . . . for bloodborne pathogens."[98]

The bloodborne pathogen standard applies to "each employer having an employee(s) with occupational exposure" to bloodborne pathogens or other potentially infectious materials.[99] Employees deemed to have "occupational exposure" are those who may reasonably be expected to have "skin, eye, mucous membrane, or parenteral contact with blood or other infectious materials that may result from the performance of an employee's duties."[100] Covered employees generally include those working in research laboratories, funeral homes, hospitals, prisons, and police and fire departments.[101]

---

[92] *Id.;* 29 C.F.R. §1990.121 (1992).

[93] 48 Fed. Reg. 242 (1978); 29 C.F.R. §1990.131 (1992).

[94] 48 Fed. Reg. 243 (1978).

[95] 29 C.F.R. §1910.1030 (1992). The bloodborne pathogens standard "represents OSHA's first regulation of occupational exposure to biological hazards." 54 Fed. Reg. 23,042 (1989).

[96] 29 C.F.R. §1910.1030 (1992).

[97] *Id.* Other bloodborne pathogens include syphilis, malaria, babesiosis, brucellosis, leptospirosis, arboviral infections, relapsing fever, Creutzfeldt-Jakob disease, human T-lymphotropic virus type 1, and viral hemorrhagic fever. 54 Fed. Reg. 23,042, 23,060–61 (1989).

[98] 54 Fed. Reg. 23,042, 23,081 (1989). The bodily fluids considered to be potentially infectious materials include "semen, vaginal secretions, cerebrospinal fluid, synovial fluid, pleural fluid, pericardial fluid, peritoneal fluid, amniotic fluid, saliva . . . , any body fluid that is visibly contaminated with blood, and all body fluids in situations where it is difficult or impossible to differentiate between body fluids." 29 C.F.R. §1910.1030 (1992).

[99] 29 C.F.R. §1910.1030(c) (1992).

[100] 29 C.F.R. §1910.1030(c). *See also* 56 Fed. Reg. 64,004, 64,101 (1991), in which OSHA notes that the regulation is not intended to cover "an employee . . . driving a bus down the highway or . . . processing insurance claims in an office setting."

[101] 54 Fed. Reg. 23,042, 23,081 (1989).

In each of these settings, employers must develop and implement an exposure control plan that "identifies . . . the tasks and work areas that are likely to present exposures to blood, or other potentially infectious products, . . . the employee positions that are involved, and . . . the controls that will be used to reduce the potential risk."[102] After identifying the hazards, the employer must take steps to minimize potential exposure. Exposure abatement methods available to employers include:

1. Engineering controls, such as sharps disposal containers and self-sheathing needles "that isolate or remove the bloodborne pathogens hazard from the workplace";
2. Work practice controls, such as handwashing, housekeeping and prohibitions against eating and drinking in work areas "that reduce the likelihood of exposure by altering the manner in which a task is performed";
3. Personal protective equipment, "such as . . . gloves, gowns, laboratory coats, face shields or masks and eye protection, and mouthpieces, resuscitation bags, pocket masks, and other ventilation devices";
4. Employee training on "the modes of transmission of bloodborne pathogens[,] . . . the use and limitations of methods that will prevent or reduce exposure" and other relevant information;
5. Hepatitis B vaccinations for employees; and
6. Prompt medical follow-up of exposure incidents.[103]

III. Employers and Employees Affected by OSHA Regulations

Almost all private employers, regardless of size, are subject to OSHA's safety and health regulations.[104] The only employers exempted are federal and state governments[105] and those private employers that are subject to another occupational safety and health law (e.g., the Mine Safety and Health Act).[106]

Employees also are encouraged to comply with applicable regulations[107] and to take an active role in making sure that their workplaces are safe. Accordingly, the OSH Act provides for the protection of "whistle-blower" employees who report, or provide testimony regarding, their employers' failure to comply with OSHA's safety and health standards. No such employees may be fired or otherwise discriminated against in retaliation for causing OSHA to inspect the premises of their employment, because they testify at hearings against their employers, or because they have chosen to exercise any right given them by the OSH Act.[108]

An employee who believes he or she has been subjected to retaliation by an employer may file a complaint with OSHA according to the procedures set forth

---

[102] *Id. See also* 29 C.F.R. §1910.1030 (1992).

[103] 29 C.F.R. §1910.1030 (1992).

[104] §5(a), 29 U.S.C. §654(a) (1988).

[105] However, the OSH Act specifically allows for the adoption of other federal or state legislation that would grant federal or state employees protections similar to those granted to private employees.

[106] Other examples include the Coal Mine Health and Safety Act, and the Atomic Energy Act of 1954.

[107] §5(b), 29 U.S.C. §654(b) (1988).

[108] §11(c), 29 U.S.C. §660(c) (1988).

in 29 C.F.R. §1977. An employee representative, such as a union, may file a complaint on an employee's behalf.[109] The employee's complaint may be in writing, or it may be made orally to the OSHA area director.[110]

A complaint must be filed within 30 days of the complained-of conduct, although this deadline may be relaxed if the employer has concealed the offending conduct or otherwise has misled the employee. The timing requirement also will be relaxed if the offending conduct is ongoing or continuous.[111] For example, in *Donovan v. Hahner, Foreman & Harness, Inc.,*[112] the court found the 30-day time limit not to be a jurisdictional prerequisite. Hence the court was free to extend the filing period, and chose to do so in that case because the offending employer had lied to the employee, telling him that he had been laid off rather than that he had been fired.[113]

After the complaint has been filed, OSHA will investigate the employee's charges, and if appropriate, bring suit against the offending employer in federal district court.[114] Indeed, even if the employee later chooses to remove himself from the suit, the government may continue to prosecute the action.[115]

Within 90 days of filing, the employee is entitled to a finding on the merits of his complaint.[116] If the court finds that the employee was the victim of prohibited retaliation the court may order his or her rehiring and the payment of back pay.[117] Conversely, however, OSHA generally will not seek to penalize an employee for failing to comply with OSHA's safety and health regulations. For a more detailed discussion on this subject, see *Atlantic & Gulf Stevedores v. OSHARC,*[118] in which the court found "with considerable misgivings . . . that the OSH Act's enforcement scheme is directed only against employers."

IV. Establishment of Safety and Health Regulations

Under the OSH Act, OSHA is authorized to develop and promulgate "mandatory occupational safety and health standards. . . ."[119] In establishing these standards OSHA has been granted considerable discretion. It may "determine whether or not there will be a standard; what the standard will be; . . . [and] the priorities between the various occupations that may require standards. . . ."[120] However, each of OSHA's standards must be "reasonably

---

[109] 29 C.F.R. §1977.15 (1992).

[110] *Id.*

[111] 29 C.F.R. §1977.16 (1992).

[112] 736 F.2d 1421, 11 OSH Cases 1081 (10th Cir. 1984).

[113] *See also* Donovan v. Diplomat Envelope Corp., 587 F. Supp. 1417, 11 OSH Cases 1956 (E.D.N.Y. 1984), *aff'd,* 760 F.2d 253 (2d Cir. 1985) (court refused to dismiss a complaint filed after 39 days because the employer had been late in raising the defense of untimely filing).

[114] §11(c), 29 U.S.C. §660(c) (1988). *See also* Marshall v. Whirlpool Corp., 593 F.2d 715, 7 OSH Cases 1075 (6th Cir. 1979), and the Supreme Court's consideration of that case, 445 U.S. 1, 8 OSH Cases 1001 (1980).

[115] 29 C.F.R. §1977.17 (1992).

[116] 29 C.F.R. §1977.16 (1992).

[117] 29 U.S.C. §660(c)(3) (1988).

[118] 534 F.2d 541, 553, 4 OSH Cases 1061 (3d Cir. 1976).

[119] §2(b)(3), 29 U.S.C. §651(b)(3) (1988). A comprehensive list of all standards that have been adopted since the enactment of the OSH Act can be found at 29 C.F.R. pt. 1910.1.

[120] National Cong. of Hispanic Am. Citizens v. Usery, 554 F.2d 1196, 1199, 5 OSH Cases 1255 (D.C. Cir. 1977).

necessary or appropriate to provide safe or healthful employment and places of employment.''[121] Once properly adopted, an occupational safety or health standard has the force of law. Each covered employer must comply or face possible civil and criminal penalties.[122]

A. OSHA's Authority to Promulgate Standards

Section 6 of the OSH Act[123] granted the Secretary of Labor[124] (and hence OSHA) the authority to promulgate three types of occupational safety and health regulations: (1) national consensus and established federal standards, (2) permanent standards, and (3) emergency temporary standards. Each of these has its own distinct procedural requirements.

1. Section 6(a) National Consensus and Established Federal Standards

Section 6(a) of the OSH Act granted OSHA powers of limited duration to ''promulgate as an occupational safety and health standard any national consensus standard, and any established Federal standard''[125] that was in effect on December 29, 1970.[126] These powers ''provided for an abbreviated procedure'' to allow OSHA to promulgate standards without the burden of complying with the notice and comment requirements of the Administrative Procedure Act.[127]

Congress authorized the section 6(a) procedure to ''establish as rapidly as possible national occupational safety and health standards ... [that] will be useful for immediately providing a nationwide minimum level of health and safety....''[128] The more formal notice and comment approach was bypassed because, in the view of Congress, consensus and federal standards ''have already been subjected to ... procedural scrutiny....''[129] OSHA was not required to adopt consensus or federal standards ''verbatim'' and had narrow ''promulgative leeway'' to make minor changes to those standards.[130]

OSHA was prohibited from using the abbreviated 6(a) rulemaking process to make any ''substantially meaningful modification'' to a national consensus or federal standard ''during its transformation into an OSHA requirement.''[131]

---

[121] §3(8), 29 U.S.C. §652(8) (1988). The interpretation of the ''reasonably necessary or appropriate'' clause has been the subject of much litigation. The main controversy centers on whether or not the clause imposes on OSHA an obligation to analyze each standard from a cost-benefit perspective. *See* American Textile Mfrs. Inst. v. Donovan, 452 U.S. 490, 512, 9 OSH Cases 1913 (1981) (clause does not require cost-benefit analysis for §655(b)(5) standard but ''might be construed to contemplate some balancing of costs and benefits'' for other standards); Industrial Union Dep't v. American Petroleum Inst., 448 U.S. 607, 667, 8 OSH Cases 1586 (1980) (plurality opinion) (Powell, J., concurring) (clause requires Secretary ''to determine that the economic effects of ... [a] standard bear a reasonable relationship to the expected benefits'').

[122] *See* Section V.D., below.

[123] 29 U.S.C. §655 (1988).

[124] This authority was delegated to OSHA in April 1971.

[125] 29 U.S.C. §655(a) (1988). This authority existed for only two years after the effective date of the OSH Act. *Id.*

[126] §3(10), 29 U.S.C. §652(10) (1988).

[127] *See, e.g.,* Deering Milliken v. OSHA, 630 F.2d 1094, 1096, 9 OSH Cases 1001 (5th Cir. 1980). (Administrative Procedure Act is found at 5 U.S.C. §551 *et seq.* (1988)).

[128] S. Rep. No. 1282, 91st Cong., 2d Sess. 6 (1970).

[129] *Id.*

[130] Deering Milliken, 630 F.2d at 1096.

[131] *Id.*

Such modifications could only be made according to the time-consuming notice and comment provisions of section 6(b).[132]

Although OSHA's 6(a) authority expired on April 28, 1973, most OSHA regulations in effect today were originally promulgated under section 6(a).

2. *Section 6(b) Permanent Standards*

Section 6(b) of the OSH Act authorizes OSHA, after public notice and comment, to "promulgate, modify, or revoke any occupational safety or health standard. . . ."[133] Since OSHA's rulemaking authority under section 6(a) expired in 1973, section 6(b) is now OSHA's only source of authority to set standards and regulations of a permanent nature.[134]

All standards promulgated, modified, or revoked under section 6(b) are subject to stringent procedural requirements. OSHA must "publish a proposed rule . . . in the Federal Register . . . and shall afford interested persons a period of thirty days after publication to submit written data or comments."[135] In addition, OSHA must hold a public hearing upon the request of any interested party filing written objections to the proposed rule.[136] Within 60 days after the period for filing comments or the completion of any hearing, OSHA may either "issue a rule promulgating, modifying, or revoking . . [a] standard or make a determination that a rule should not be issued."[137] Should OSHA decide to issue a rule, it must then publish a "statement of the reasons for such action" in the *Federal Register*.[138] Due in large part to section 6(b)'s burdensome and lengthy rulemaking process, OSHA has promulgated relatively few substance-specific and "generic" health standards.[139]

Section 6(b)(5) also requires OSHA to promulgate regulations governing safety in workplaces in which "toxic materials or harmful physical agents" are present.[140] In such circumstances, OSHA must issue a standard "which most adequately assures, to the extent feasible . . . that no employee will suffer material impairment of health or functional capacity even . . . [with] regular exposure to the hazard. . . ."[141]

The "material impairment" language in section 6(b)(5) imposes an important limitation on OSHA's authority to issue standards under that section. As the legislative history of the OSH Act indicates, an early version of subsection 6(b)(5) authorized the Secretary to adopt regulations to assure "that no employee will suffer any impairment of health or functional capacity."[142] Several senators, however, were "concerned that the phrase 'any impairment' would

---

[132] 29 U.S.C. §655(b) (1988). See Section IV.A.2., below.

[133] 29 U.S.C. §655(b) (1988).

[134] Section 6(b) standards are referred to as "permanent" so as to distinguish them from the emergency temporary standards provided for in §6(c), 29 U.S.C. §655(c) (1988). Section 6(c) emergency regulations may be effective for no longer than a six-month period. See Section IV.A.3., below.

[135] §6(b)(2), 29 U.S.C. §655(b)(2) (1988). OSHA's procedural requirements for standard setting are codified at 29 C.F.R. §1911 *et seq.* (1992).

[136] §6(b)(3), 29 U.S.C. §655(b)(3) (1988).

[137] §6(b)(4), 29 U.S.C. §655(b)(4) (1988).

[138] 29 U.S.C. §655(e) (1988).

[139] *See* discussion in AFL-CIO v. OSHA, 965 F.2d 962, 969, 15 OSH Cases 1729 (11th Cir. 1992).

[140] 29 U.S.C. §655(b)(5) (1988).

[141] *Id.*

[142] S. 2193, 91st Cong., 2d Sess. (1970). For a comprehensive analysis of §6(b)(5)'s legislative history, *see* American Textile Mfrs., 452 U.S. at 514–22.

require the Secretary to prevent insect bites''[143] and other ''frivolous harms that exist in every workplace.''[144] Thus, an amended version of section 6(b)(5) was adopted that modified ''impairment'' with ''material'' rather than ''any.''[145] This ''material impairment'' language was ''designed to prohibit the Secretary from regulating substances that create a trivial hazard to affected employees.'' An expanded discussion on this subject is found in *Industrial Union Department v. American Petroleum Institute.*[146]

The phrase ''to the extent feasible'' in section 6(b)(5) places yet another significant limitation on OSHA, and a considerable amount of litigation has arisen over the proper scope of this ''feasibility'' requirement. In *American Textile Manufacturers Institute v. Donovan,*[147] the Supreme Court provided some clarification of ''to the extent feasible'' language by holding that the phrase does not require a cost-benefit analysis for each prospective section 6(b)(5) standard:

> According to Webster's . . . Dictionary, ''feasible'' means ''capable of being done, executed, or effected.'' . . . Thus, §6(b)(5) directs the Secretary to issue the standard that ''most adequately assures . . . that no employee will suffer material impairment of health,'' limited only by the extent to which this is ''capable of being done.'' In effect then, . . . Congress itself defined the basic relationship between costs and benefits, by placing the ''benefit'' of worker health above all other considerations save those making attainment of this ''benefit'' unachievable. Any standard based on a balancing of costs and benefits by the Secretary that strikes a different balance than that struck by Congress would be inconsistent with the command set forth in §6(b)(5). Thus, cost-benefit analysis by OSHA is not required by the statute because feasibility analysis is.[148]

During the years since the Supreme Court's decision in *American Textile,* the lower federal courts have further refined the scope of the feasibility limitation. For example, in *Forging Industries Association v. Secretary of Labor,*[149] the U.S. Court of Appeals for the Fourth Circuit held that a feasibility analysis within the section 6(b)(5) context requires OSHA to show that a ''standard is both technologically and economically feasible.''[150]

Similarly, in a recent case, *AFL-CIO v. OSHA,*[151] the Eleventh Circuit explained that technological feasibility requires OSHA to ''demonstrate 'that modern technology has at least conceived some industrial strategies or devices

[143] Industrial Union Dep't. v. American Petroleum Inst., 448 U.S. at 720–21 n.34 (Marshall, J., dissenting).

[144] American Textile Mfrs. Inst. v. Donovan, 452 U.S. at 518. During a debate on the Senate floor, Senator Dominick argued that it is '' 'unrealistic to attempt . . . to establish a utopia free from any hazards. Absolute safety is an impossibility[.]' '' *Id.* at 517 (*quoting* 116 CONG. REC. 37614 (1970)).

[145] *Id.*

[146] 448 U.S. 607, 693, 8 OSH Cases 1586 (1980) (Marshall, J., dissenting).

[147] 452 U.S. 490 (1981).

[148] *Id.* at 508–09. The Supreme Court also pointed out that ''Congress uses specific language when intending that an agency engage in cost-benefit analysis'' and that no such language exists in §6(b)(5). *Id.* at 510–11.

[149] 773 F.2d 1436, 1452, 12 OSH Cases 1472 (4th Cir. 1985).

[150] *Id.* at 1452. *See also* National Cottonseed Prods. Ass'n v. Brock, 825 F.2d 482, 486, 13 OSH Cases 1353 (D.C. Cir. 1987), *cert. denied,* 485 U.S. 1020 (1988).

[151] 965 F.2d 962, 980, 15 OSH Cases 1729 (11th Cir. 1992), *quoting* Steelworkers v. Marshall, 647 F.2d 1189, 1266, 8 OSH Cases 1810 (D.C. Cir. 1981). *See also* Asarco v. OSHA, 746 F.2d 483, 11 OSH Cases 2217 (9th Cir. 1984); Boise Cascade Corp. v. Secretary of Labor, 694 F.2d 584, 11 OSH Cases 1010 (9th Cir. 1982).

which are likely to be capable of meeting the [standard] . . . and which the industries are generally capable of adopting.' " The *AFL-CIO* court defined economic feasibility as meaning that OSHA must establish a "reasonable likelihood" that the costs of a standard "will not threaten the existence or competitive structure of an industry, even if it does portend disaster for some marginal firms."[152]

An employer may apply to OSHA for an order granting a temporary or permanent variance from a section 6(b) standard.[153] OSHA will only grant a temporary variance if an employer demonstrates an inability to comply with the standard, takes all necessary measures to protect employees, and strives to develop an effective compliance program as soon as possible.[154] To receive a permanent variance, an employer must prove that its methods of operation "are as safe and healthful as those which would prevail if [it] complied with the standard."[155] Employers seeking either a temporary or permanent variance must also give affected employees notice and an opportunity for a hearing.[156]

3. *Section 6(c) Emergency Temporary Standards*

Section 6(c) authorizes the Secretary to adopt an emergency temporary standard if such a measure is necessary to protect employees from exposure to a "grave danger" from toxic or physically hazardous substances in the workplace.[157] Section 6(c) "does not require an absolute certainty as to the deleterious effect of a substance on man," and OSHA "need not wait until workers have actually been harmed to issue an emergency temporary standard."[158] The "mere speculative possibility" that a substance presents a danger, however, is not sufficient to call section 6(c) into effect.[159] An emergency regulation "must be supported by evidence" establishing a sufficient probability of harm to humans.[160] Such evidence may derive from "a body of reputable scientific thought,"[161] or it may be extrapolated from the results of animal experiments.[162]

If the conditions specified in section 6(c) are satisfied, an emergency standard may be issued without regard to the formal notice and comment provisions of the Administrative Procedure Act, and the standard will "take

---

[152] 965 F.2d at 982. *See also* Asarco v. OSHA, 746 F.2d 483, 11 OSH Cases 2217 (9th Cir. 1984); Steelworkers v. Marshall, 647 F.2d 1189, 8 OSH Cases 1810 (D.C. Cir. 1981).

[153] §6(b)(6) and (d), 29 U.S.C. §655(b)(6) and (d) (1988). *See also* 29 C.F.R. §1911 *et seq.* (1992).

[154] 29 U.S.C. §655(b)(6) and (d) (1988).

[155] §6(d), 29 U.S.C. §655(d) (1988).

[156] §6(b)(6) and (d), 29 U.S.C. §655(b)(6) and (d) (1988).

[157] 29 U.S.C. §655(c) (1988).

[158] Dry Color Mfrs. Ass'n v. Department of Labor, 486 F.2d 98, 104, 1 OSH Cases 1331 (3d Cir. 1973). *See also* Asbestos Info. Ass'n/N. Am. v. OSHA, 727 F.2d 415, 425, 11 OSH Cases 1817 (5th Cir. 1984) (OSHA "need not support its conclusion 'with anything approaching scientific certainty' ").

[159] Dry Color Mfrs., 486 F.2d at 104 n.9a.

[160] *Id.*

[161] *Asbestos Info. Ass'n*, 727 F.2d at 425, *quoting* Industrial Union Dep't v. American Petroleum Inst., 448 U.S. 607, 656, 8 OSH Cases 1586 (1980) (the Secretary " 'has the prerogative to choose between conflicting evidence of equivalent quality, and a court will consider a finding consistent with one authority or another to be supported by substantial evidence' ").

[162] *Dry Color Mfrs.*, 486 F.2d at 104. An extrapolation from animal experiments "will carry most weight in cases where it is the chemical substance itself that produces" the harmful effect and the animal being tested has a biological system that is "reasonably similar to that of man." *Id.* at 104 n.9.

immediate effect upon publication in the Federal Register. . . .''[163] OSHA must also publish in the *Federal Register* a ''statement of reasons'' for the emergency standard.[164] An emergency standard will lapse six months after publication if OSHA fails to convert it into a permanent rule by means of the section 6(b) procedure.[165] Furthermore, once an emergency regulation becomes effective, any employer may be granted a variance if that employer's operation methods ''are as safe and healthful as those which would prevail if he complied with the standard.''[166]

Because the purpose of section 6(c) is to give immediate protection to employees in an emergency situation, the exercise of Section 6(c) authority ''should be considered an unusual response to exceptional circumstances.''[167] As a result, OSHA's powers under 6(c) are restricted to rare situations in which a standard is necessary to avert grave danger.

When OSHA fails to establish satisfactorily that a grave danger exists, the courts have invalidated emergency standards to prevent section 6(c) from being misused ''as a technique for avoiding the procedural safeguards of public comment and hearings. . . .'' As the Third Circuit noted in *Dry Colors Manufacturers Association v. Department of Labor,*[168] ''the promulgation of standards under Subsection 6(b) is preferable since the procedure for permanent standards is specifically designed to bring out the relevant facts.''

In *Asbestos Information Association of North America v. OSHA,*[169] the Fifth Circuit struck down an emergency temporary standard relating to reduction of asbestos exposure levels because OSHA did not adequately demonstrate that the risk was ''grave,'' or even that the standard was ''necessary.'' Similarly, in *Florida Peach Growers Association v. United States Department of Labor,*[170] the Fifth Circuit invalidated an emergency pesticide residue standard because the Secretary failed to show ''by substantial evidence'' that exposure to the residue posed ''a grave danger . . . that must necessarily be protected by an emergency temporary standard.''

B. The National Institute for Occupational Safety and Health, and the Development and Drafting of OSHA Standards

Established by section 22 of the OSH Act,[171] the National Institute for Occupational Safety and Health (NIOSH) has been given the authority to ''develop and establish recommended occupational safety and health standards'' and to conduct research and experiments concerning occupational safety and health.[172] In exercising this authority, NIOSH may ''perform all functions

---

[163] *Id.* at 104 n.9.

[164] §6(e), 29 U.S.C. §655(e) (1988).

[165] *Dry Color Mfrs.*, 486 F.2d at 104.

[166] §6(d), 29 U.S.C. §655(d) (1988).

[167] *Dry Color Mfrs.*, 486 F.2d at 105 n.9a. *See also Asbestos Info. Ass'n*, 727 F.2d at 422 (section 6(c) emergency authority is only usable in ''limited situations'' and must be ''delicately exercised'').

[168] 486 F.2d 98, 105 n.9a, 1 OSH Cases 1331 (3d Cir. 1973).

[169] 727 F.2d 415, 427, 11 OSH Cases 1817 (5th Cir. 1984).

[170] 489 F.2d 120, 132, 1 OSH Cases 1472 (5th Cir. 1974).

[171] 29 U.S.C. §671 (1988).

[172] 29 U.S.C. §671(c) (1988).

of the Secretary of Health and Human Services'' relating to research, training, and employee education.[173]

The process by which NIOSH develops and establishes new standards for recommendation to OSHA is dictated by section 22(d) of the OSH Act.[174] The first step is for NIOSH to initiate and ''conduct such research and experimental programs as . . . are necessary for the development of criteria for new and improved occupational safety and health standards. . . .''[175] During this research phase, NIOSH may conduct inspections of workplaces, subpoena or question employers and employees, perform medical examinations and tests on employees, and require employers to measure, record, and report on employee exposure levels.[176]

After the results of these research and experimental programs are evaluated, NIOSH then has the authority to make recommendations to OSHA regarding the need for a ''new or improved'' OSHA standard.[177] NIOSH recommendations are ''immediately . . . forwarded'' to OSHA for consideration.[178] At that point, the fate of a proposed standard is left to the discretion of OSHA, which may follow, alter, or disregard NIOSH's advice.[179]

Although NIOSH is the main source of OSHA's standards development, section 6(b)(1) of the OSH Act allows new standards to be derived from ''information . . . submitted by an interested person, a representative of any organization of employers or employees, a nationally recognized standards-producing organization, the Secretary of Health and Human Services, . . . a State or political subdivision, or [from] . . . information developed by the Secretary. . . .''[180]

C. Preenforcement Judicial Review of OSHA Standards

Any person who believes himself to be adversely affected by a newly promulgated standard may challenge it in the federal courts of appeals under section 6(f) of the OSH Act.[181] An ''adversely affected person'' may either be an employee or an employer, although an employer may not obtain standing to contest a new regulation based on lost profits.[182]

---

[173] *Id.* The research functions of the Secretary of Health and Human Services, and of ultimately NIOSH, are specified in section 20 of the OSH Act, 29 U.S.C. §669. The training and employee education functions are contained in section 21 of the OSH Act, 29 U.S.C. §670.

[174] 29 U.S.C. §671(d) (1988).

[175] §22(d), 29 U.S.C. §671(d) (1988). The Director of NIOSH may initiate a research and experimental program ''upon his own initiative, or upon the request of the Secretary of Health and Human Services[.]'' *Id.*

[176] §20, 29 U.S.C. §669 (1988).

[177] §22(d), 29 U.S.C. §671(d) (1988).

[178] *Id.*

[179] §6, 29 U.S.C. §655 (1988). During the evaluation of a NIOSH recommendation or any other proposed standard, OSHA ''may request'' the assistance of an advisory committee. 29 U.S.C. §655(b) (1988).

[180] 29 U.S.C. §655(b)(1) (1988).

[181] 29 U.S.C. §655(f) (1988).

[182] *See* Fire Equipment Mfrs. Ass'n v. Marshall, 679 F.2d 679, 682, 10 OSH Cases 1649 (7th Cir. 1982), *cert. denied,* 459 U.S. 1105, 11 OSH Cases 1096 (1982). In some cases, trade associations have been held not to have standing to challenge OSHA regulations because ''[p]reserving the right of trade associations to promote their objectives is not an interest within the zone protected by the [OSH] Act.'' *Id.* In other cases, however, trade associations have been permitted to challenge standards. *See* AFL-CIO v. OSHA, 14 OSH Cases 1636 (D.C. Cir. 1990).

Such a preenforcement challenge may be brought by filing a petition for review in a United States court of appeals within 60 days of the date on which the standard was published in the *Federal Register.*[183] The Secretary of Labor is responsible for responding to the petition and for supporting the contested regulation. The filing of a petition does not relieve a person from complying with the challenged regulation. To obtain relief while contesting the validity of the regulation, the petitioner must also request, and have the court grant, injunctive relief.

A regulation may be upheld if it is "supported by substantial evidence in the record considered as a whole."[184] The "substantial evidence" test has been interpreted by the Supreme Court to require "such evidence as a reasonable mind might accept as adequate to support a conclusion."[185] This standard of review is much less deferential to OSHA than is the "arbitrary and capricious" standard of review prescribed in the Administrative Procedure Act.[186] As a result, the courts take a "harder look" at regulations promulgated by OSHA than they do at regulations adopted by most other agencies.[187]

D. The General Duty Clause: OSHA's Authority Over Activity Not Otherwise Specifically Regulated

Section 5(a)(1) of the OSH Act dictates that every employer

> shall furnish to each of his employees employment and a place of employment which are free from recognized hazards that are causing or are likely to cause death or serious physical harm to his employees.[188]

This so-called general duty clause was intended to ensure that OSHA would have the authority to protect those workers for whom no safety and health standards have been set.[189]

Under the general duty clause, an employer may be held accountable if OSHA can demonstrate that specific measures could have been taken to protect an injured employee from the hazardous condition that caused an injury, that such measures would in fact have provided protection, and that it would have

---

[183] *See* AFL-CIO v. OSHA, 14 OSH Cases 1636 (D.C. Cir. 1990), in which the court interpreted "within sixty days" as meaning that the petition must be filed by the 59th day after publication in the *Federal Register.*

[184] §6(f), 29 U.S.C. §655(f) (1988).

[185] American Textile Mfrs. Inst. v. Donovan, 452 U.S. 490, 522, 9 OSH Cases 1913 (1981), *quoting* Universal Camera Corp. v. NLRB, 340 U.S. 474, 477 (1951).

[186] AFL-CIO v. OSHA, 965 F.2d 962, 970, 15 OSH Cases 1729 (11th Cir. 1992); Steelworkers v. Marshall, 647 F.2d 1189, 1264, 8 OSH Cases 1810 (D.C. Cir. 1980), *cert. denied,* 453 U.S. 913, 11 OSH Cases 1264 (1981). *See also* Administrative Procedure Act, 5 U.S.C. §533 (1988).

[187] AFL-CIO v. OSHA, 965 F.2d at 970. *See also* National Grain & Feed Ass'n v. OSHA, 866 F.2d 717, 729, 13 OSH Cases 2007 (5th Cir. 1989); Asbestos Info. Ass'n, 727 F.2d at 421. An example of this less deferential standard of review is the Eleventh Circuit's recent decision invalidating OSHA's Air Contaminants Standard for 428 substances because OSHA failed to satisfy the "substantial evidence" test for each substance. AFL-CIO v. OSHA, 965 F.2d at 970.

[188] 29 U.S.C. §654(a)(1) (1988).

[189] *See* S. Rep. No. 1282, 91st Cong., 2d Sess., *reprinted in* 1970 U.S.C.C.A.N. 5177, 5185–87:

> The committee recognizes that precise standards to cover every conceivable situation will not always exist. This legislation would be seriously deficient if any employee were killed or seriously injured on the job simply because there was no specific standard applicable to a recognized hazard which could result in such a misfortune.

been "feasible" for the employer to implement those measures.[190] In determining whether or not safety measures are deemed "feasible," a court may look at what safety experts deem to be feasible from technology and cost-benefit perspectives.[191]

V. Enforcement

A. Monitoring Employer Compliance

1. Inspection

OSHA employs a large number of inspectors to determine whether employers are complying with applicable health and safety regulations.[192] There are two types of OSHA inspectors, safety officers, who normally inspect for physical safety hazards, and industrial hygienists, whose inspections are focused on compliance with occupational health standards. However, all OSHA inspectors are authorized to inspect workplaces for compliance with both safety and health standards, and occasionally there is some overlap. Both safety officers and industrial hygienists are generically known as compliance safety and health officers (CSHOs).[193] CSHOs work out of approximately 85 OSHA area offices located throughout the country. Each area office is run by a regional director.[194]

In addition to these federal inspection officers, the OSH Act provides for inspections by a large group of inspectors who are actually employed by those states to which OSHA has delegated primary responsibility for administering and enforcing the requirements of the OSH Act.[195] To obtain such authority, a state must develop a plan for implementing and enforcing the OSH Act, and it must obtain OSHA's approval of the plan.[196] At this writing, 21 states and two territories have been given the authority to administer their own safety and health programs.[197] Inspectors working for these states are also known as CSHOs.

Inspectors generally arrive for an inspection without a warrant. An employer may refuse to allow entry to the workplace if no warrant is produced, a right confirmed by the Supreme Court's decision in *Marshall v. Barlow's,*

---

[190] *See generally* National Realty and Constr. Co. v. OSHARC, 489 F.2d 1257, 1265–67, 1 OSH Cases 1422 (D.C. Cir. 1973).

[191] *Id.* at 1266 n.27.

[192] OSHA's emphasis on taking an active role in inspecting the premises of employers contrasts with the role usually taken by the Environmental Protection Agency, which more often concentrates its energies on passive regulation through permitting and reporting requirements and through educational initiatives.

[193] *See* 29 C.F.R. §1903.21(d) (1992).

[194] OSHA also has 10 regional offices, although inspections are not conducted from these offices. These offices are located in Atlanta, Boston, Chicago, Dallas, Denver, Kansas City, New York, Philadelphia, San Francisco, and Seattle.

[195] The federal government provides financial incentives to encourage states to take on the burden of OSH Act enforcement.

[196] *See* §18(c), 29 U.S.C. §667(c) (1988).

[197] These are: Alaska, Arizona, California, Hawaii, Indiana, Iowa, Kentucky, Maryland, Michigan, Minnesota, Nevada, New Mexico, North Carolina, Oregon, Puerto Rico, South Carolina, Tennessee, Utah, Vermont, Virgin Islands, Virginia, Washington, and Wyoming. *See* 29 C.F.R. pt. 1952 (1992).

Inc.[198] In that case, the Court found that the authority to inspect under section 8(c) to be unconstitutional under the Fourth Amendment "insofar as it purports to authorize inspections without a warrant or its equivalent." Of course, OSHA may obtain a warrant from a federal district court to compel the inspection.[199]

There generally are two types of inspections, those conducted randomly under authority of section 8(a)[200] and those conducted under authority of section 8(f)(1)[201] in response to a specific employee complaint. Under section 8(a), inspectors may "enter [any workplace] without delay and at reasonable times" to "inspect and investigate . . . all pertinent conditions, structures, machines, apparatus, devices, equipment, and materials therein, and to question privately any . . . owner, operator, agent or employee."[202]

Under section 8(f)(1), OSHA may respond directly to an employee complaint "that a violation of a safety or health standard exists that threatens physical harm, or that an imminent danger exists" by instituting an inspection.[203] These generally are referred to as special inspections, and they are limited to determining whether the conditions alleged in the employee's complaint in fact exist. Section 8(f)(1) inspections can be initiated only in response to an alleged failure to meet a specific standard; allegations of violating the general duty clause are not subject to special inspection.[204]

Section 8(e)[205] allows, but does not require, a representative of both the employer and the employees to accompany the CSHO on the inspection, although the OSH Act does not require that the employee representative be paid while accompanying the CSHO.[206]

2. *Recordkeeping Requirements*

Another way in which OSHA monitors the activities of employers (and helps employees to do the same) is through numerous rules requiring employers to maintain various types of records. The authority for implementing these recordkeeping requirements is found in sections 6(b)(7) and 8(c) of the OSH Act.[207]

Under section 6(b)(7), employers subject to OSHA's 6(b)(5) standards governing "toxic materials or harmful physical agents" are required to comply with regulations that "provide for monitoring or measuring employee exposure at such locations and intervals, and in such manner as may be necessary for the protection of employees."[208]

---

[198] 436 U.S. 307, 6 OSH Cases 1571 (1978).

[199] §8(b), 29 U.S.C. §657(b). *See also* Weyerhaeuser Co. v. Marshall, 592 F.2d 373, 376 n.2, 7 OSH Cases 1090 (7th Cir. 1979) ("[a] company has a right to conduct its business free of unreasonable administrative inspections").

[200] 29 U.S.C. §657(a) (1988).

[201] 29 U.S.C. §657(f)(1) (1988).

[202] 29 U.S.C. §657(a).

[203] 29 U.S.C. §657(f)(1).

[204] *See, e.g.,* Diamond Roofing Co. v. OSHARC, 528 F.2d 645, 648, 4 OSH Cases 1061 (5th Cir. 1976); Secretary of Labor v. Collier Keyworth Co., 13 OSH Cases 1209, 1214 (1987).

[205] 29 U.S.C. §657(e) (1988).

[206] *See, e.g.,* Chamber of Commerce v. OSHA, 636 F.2d 464, 8 OSH Cases 1648 (D.C. Cir. 1980).

[207] 29 U.S.C. §§655(b)(7) and 657(a) (1988).

[208] 29 U.S.C. §655(b)(7) (1988). See Section IV.A.2., above, for more information about §6(b)(5) standards.

The recordkeeping requirements promulgated under authority of section 8(c) are quite wide ranging. Of particular importance is the requirement that an employer maintain a log containing information about employees who are injured, killed, or have become ill from hazards associated with their jobs.[209] An injury or illness will be considered significant enough to warrant documentation if the affected employee is fatally injured, requires medical treatment, has suffered a loss of consciousness, has suffered an impairment in his or her ability to work or to move about, or if the employee's condition dictates that he or she be transferred to another job.[210] The employer must record this information within six days of receiving notice of the occurrence of such injury or illness.[211] Furthermore, the employer must compile and post for employees a summary of the injuries and illnesses that have occurred during each calendar year. These summaries must be posted from February 1 to March 1.[212]

Some employers are not subject to the injury/illness log requirement. These include employers with 10 or fewer employees, and most employers engaged in the retail trade, finance, insurance, and real estate industries.[213] More specifically, businesses classified in Standard Industrial Classiciation codes 55-69, 71-74, 77-78, and 81-89 are exempted.[214] Employers also may be

---

[209]*See* 29 C.F.R. pt. 1904 (1988). OSHA recommends the use of OSHA Form No. 200 for recordation of injuries and illnesses, although use of the form is not mandatory.

[210]29 C.F.R. §1904.12(c) (1992).

[211]29 C.F.R. §1904.2(b)(1) (1992).

[212]29 C.F.R. §1904.5 (1992).

[213]29 C.F.R. §1904.15(a) and .16 (1992).

[214]*See* 29 C.F.R. §1904.16 (1992). These Standard Industrial Classification (SIC) Codes represent the following industries:

SIC 55	Automotive dealers and gasoline service stations
SIC 56	Apparel and accessory stores
SIC 57	Home furniture, furnishings, and equipment stores
SIC 58	Eating and drinking places
SIC 59	Miscellaneous retail
SIC 60	Depository institutions
SIC 61	Nondepository credit institutions
SIC 62	Security and commodity brokers, dealers, exchanges, and services
SIC 63	Insurance carriers
SIC 64	Insurance agents, brokers, and service
SIC 65	Real estate
SIC 66	(reserved)
SIC 67	Holding and other investment offices
SIC 68	(reserved)
SIC 69	(reserved)
SIC 71	(reserved)
SIC 72	Personal services
SIC 73	Business services
SIC 74	(reserved)
SIC 77	(reserved)
SIC 78	Motion pictures
SIC 81	Legal services
SIC 82	Educational services
SIC 83	Social services
SIC 84	Museums, art galleries, and botanical and zoological gardens
SIC 85	(reserved)
SIC 86	Membership organizations
SIC 87	Engineering, accounting, research, management, and related services
SIC 88	Private households
SIC 89	Miscellaneous services

required to collect and maintain information to help OSHA study the causes and prevention of certain types of accidents or illnesses[215] or for specific enforcement purposes.[216]

Records maintained pursuant to the OSH Act may be reviewed by OSHA, NIOSH, or the Department of Health and Human Services.[217] There is precedent, however, suggesting that employers need not permit OSHA, NIOSH, or the Department of Health and Human Services to inspect records absent a subpoena.[218] OSHA, NIOSH, and the Department of Health and Human Services may also require employers to provide them with reports on the information found in the employers' records.[219]

B. Citations and Proposed Penalties

If OSHA believes an employer has failed to meet a safety or health standard, it may serve the employer with a citation that sets forth the violation(s) that OSHA alleges the employer has committed. Once the citation is received, the employer must place a copy of it at or near the location(s) of the alleged hazardous conditions.[220]

In situations in which OSHA believes employees are in "imminent danger" of injury or death, OSHA may petition a federal district court to order the employer immediately to abate the dangerous condition. If OSHA fails to bring such an action, any affected person may bring a mandamus action in federal district court to force OSHA to take action.[221]

Absent a finding of imminent danger, the citation will prescribe a time within which the employer must abate the alleged hazardous condition.[222] Both employers and employees may contest the reasonableness of the abatement period by filing a notice of contest within 15 business days of the date of the citation.[223] Within 10 days of receiving the notice of contest, OSHA must file a statement of reasons why the prescribed abatement period is reasonable.[224]

In almost all instances, the citation will be accompanied by a proposed penalty that OSHA thinks is an appropriate punishment for the alleged violation of the safety or health standard. As its name indicates, the proposed penalty is OSHA's initial assessment of what an appropriate penalty should be; it will, however, become an actual fine if an employer fails to contest it.[225] A cited employer has 15 working days from the date on which it receives the citation and proposed penalty to notify OSHA that it wishes to contest the citation

[215] §8(c)(1), 29 U.S.C. §657(c)(1) (1988); 29 C.F.R. pt. 1904.1 (1992).

[216] §8(c)(1), 29 U.S.C. §657(c)(1) (1988).

[217] *Id.*

[218] *See, e.g.,* Secretary v. Taft Broadcasting Co., 12 OSH Cases 1264 (1985), *affirmed sub nom.* McLaughlin v. Kings Island Div., Taft Broadcasting Co., 849 F.2d 990, 13 OSH Cases 1755 (6th Cir. 1988).

[219] §8(c), 29 U.S.C. §657(c) (1988). *See, e.g.,* G.M.C. v. Director, Nat'l Inst. Occupational Safety and Health, 636 F.2d 163, 9 OSH Cases 1139 (6th Cir. 1980).

[220] §9(b), 29 U.S.C. §658(b) (1988).

[221] *See* §13, 29 U.S.C. §662 (1988).

[222] §9(a), 29 U.S.C. §658(a) (1988).

[223] §10(c), 29 U.S.C. §659(c) (1988); 29 C.F.R. §1903.17(b) (1992).

[224] This and other procedural rules governing employee contests are governed by 29 C.F.R. §2200.38 (1992).

[225] 29 C.F.R. §1903.15(a) (1992).

and/or the proposed penalty.[226] Once the employer so notifies OSHA, its obligation to abate the alleged violative condition(s) is suspended until the question of whether there was an actual violation is resolved.[227] Employees may not contest the citation or an accompanying proposed penalty.[228]

C. The Occupational Safety and Health Review Commission

If an employer contests a citation or proposed penalty, it is entitled to present its case to the Occupational Safety and Health Review Commission (OSHARC). OSHARC is a federal judicial body that operates entirely independently of OSHA. OSHARC's sole purpose is to consider disputes between employers and OSHA regarding OSHA's citations and proposed penalties.[229]

OSHARC provides two levels of administrative review. At the lower level, an administrative law judge (ALJ) conducts hearings in which evidence is gathered. At these hearings, OSHA must prove the validity of its citations and proposed penalties. After considering the evidence and the arguments of both the employer and OSHA, the ALJ will render a decision sustaining, modifying, or overturning a citation. The ALJ will also decide whether a penalty proposed by OSHA is appropriate and may choose to modify it or reject it entirely. The ALJ may not order an employer to pay more than the penalty originally proposed by OSHA.

An employer who disagrees with an ALJ's decision may appeal all or part of that decision to OSHARC's second level of review, the three-member review commission. In turn, a final decision of the review commission may be appealed to the federal courts of appeals.[230]

D. Penalties

A proposed penalty will become final if the employer fails to contest the penalty or after there has been a final adjudication upholding OSHA's position. The amount of the penalty will reflect whether the violation has been deemed "nonserious," "serious," "willful," or "repeated." "Nonserious" and "serious" violations incur penalties of up to $7,000 per violation, while "willful" and "repeated" violations can incur penalties of up to $70,000 per violation.[231] "Serious" violations are the only ones specifically defined by the OSH Act, and are those that cause

> a substantial probability that death or serious physical harm could result from a condition which exists, or from one or more practices, means, methods, operations, or processes which have been adopted or are in use, in such place of employment unless the employer did not, and could not with the exercise of reasonable diligence, know of the presence of the violation.[232]

---

[226] 29 C.F.R. §1903.17 (1992).

[227] 29 C.F.R. §1903.18(a) (1992).

[228] *See* Secretary v. Boise Cascade Corp., 14 OSH Cases 1993 (1991); Secretary v. General Elec. Co., 14 OSH Cases 1763 (1990).

[229] *See* 29 U.S.C. §651(b)(3) (1988) and §12, 29 U.S.C. §661 (1988).

[230] §11(a), 29 U.S.C. §660(a) (1988).

[231] §17(a), (b), and (c), 29 U.S.C. §666(a), (b), and (c) (Supp. II 1990).

[232] §17(k), 29 U.S.C. §666(k) (1988).

An employer who fails to abate a violation within the allotted time period may be assessed fines of up to $7,000 per day for every day the violation has existed.[233] Employers may also incur penalties for failure to maintain proper records, for failure to post citations and other notices,[234] and for making false statements in official documents.

Furthermore, in situations in which an employee has been killed due to an employer's willful violation of the regulations, the employer may be prosecuted criminally and fined up to $10,000 or jailed for up to six months.[235] If that employer is found to be responsible for a second or subsequent employee death due to a willful violation, the employer will be subject to criminal penalties of up to $20,000 in fines or imprisonment for up to one year.[236] Similarly, local law enforcement officials may bring criminal charges of assault, battery, and even murder against an employer deemed responsible for the injury or death of an employee.[237]

VI. OSHA Standards and Private Litigation

A. Evidentiary Use of OSHA Violations

Congress did not intend that OSHA's regulations be used by employees as a means to bypass the exclusive remedies offered under state workers' compensation programs.[238] Section 4(b)(4) of the OSH Act precludes the use of OSHA regulations as an independent basis for a private cause of action against an employer:

> Nothing in this Act shall be construed to supersede or in any manner affect any workmen's compensation law or to enlarge or diminish or affect in any other manner the common law or statutory rights, duties, or liabilities of employers and employees under any law with respect to injuries, diseases, or death of employees arising out of, or in the course of, employment.[239]

Nevertheless, a number of federal and state courts have allowed plaintiffs to use OSHA's safety and health standards in negligence cases premised on common law or on other federal statutes. In such cases, the OSHA standard is used to establish the standard of care expected of employers in determining whether an employer has acted negligently. Under certain circumstances, moreover, some courts have viewed a violation of an OSHA standard as evidence of negligence per se. Examples of these cases, and of cases in which OSHA regulations have not been admitted as evidence of negligence, are discussed briefly below.

---

[233] §17(d), 29 U.S.C. §666(d) (Supp. II 1990).

[234] §17(g) and (i), 29 U.S.C. §666(g) and (i) (1988).

[235] §17(e), 29 U.S.C. §666(e) (1988).

[236] *Id.*

[237] *See, e.g.,* New York v. Pymm, 14 OSH Cases 1297 (1989).

[238] *See, e.g.,* Practico v. Portland Terminal Co., 783 F.2d 255, 265, 12 OSH Cases 1567 (1st Cir. 1985); Steelworkers v. Marshall, 647 F.2d 1189, 1235, 8 OSH Cases 1810 (D.C. Cir.), *cert. denied,* 453 U.S. 913, 11 OSH Cases 1264 (1981); Lowe v. General Metro Corp., 624 F.2d 1373, 1379 (5th Cir. 1980).

[239] 29 U.S.C. §653(b)(4) (1988).

1. OSHA Violations as Negligence Per Se

Well-established tort law principles support the notion that failure to comply with a statute designed to protect human safety and health constitutes negligence per se. *See,* e.g., the *Restatement (Second) of Torts:*

> The unexcused violation of a legislative enactment or an administrative regulation which is adopted by the court as defining the standard of conduct of a reasonable man, is negligence itself.[240]

In *Practico v. Portland Terminal Co.,*[241] the First Circuit found that a violation of an OSHA regulation may be deemed negligence per se when "an independent cause of action is established by either state or federal law which establishes"

1. The right of an employee to be free from negligence;
2. The duty of an employer to take reasonable precautions; and
3. The liability of the employer for injuries caused by the failure to take reasonable precautions.

All of these requirements were met by the plaintiff in *Practico,* who brought the action under the Federal Employee Liability Act (FELA). FELA makes a covered employer strictly liable for injuries caused as the result of the employer's failure to comply with safety standards. The court found that violation of an OSHA safety standard triggered FELA's strict liability provisions and accordingly reversed the lower court's decision that was based on a finding that the plaintiff had been contributorily negligent.

A similar test was used in *Walton v. Potlatch Corp.*[242] In that case the court found that a violation of an OSHA standard constitutes negligence per se if (1) the OSHA regulation clearly delineates the standard of conduct; (2) the OSHA regulation is intended to prevent the type of harm the defendant's act or omission caused; (3) the plaintiff is a member of the class protected by the OSHA regulation; and (4) the violation was the proximate cause of the plaintiff's injury.[243]

Another example of this type of analysis is found in *Teal v. E.I. DuPont de Nemours & Co.*[244] In that case, the court held that under Tennessee law, "a breach of a duty imposed by statute or regulation is negligence *per se* if the party impaired is a member of the class of persons the statute or regulation was intended to protect."[245]

---

[240] §288(B)(1) (1965).

[241] 783 F.2d 255, 265, 12 OSH Cases 1567 (1st Cir. 1985).

[242] 781 P.2d 229, 14 OSH Cases 1186 (Idaho 1989). *See also* Dixon v. International Harvester Co., 754 F.2d 573, 581 (5th Cir. 1985); Rabon v. Automatic Fasteners, Inc., 672 F.2d 1231, 1238 (5th Cir. 1982); Melerine v. Avondale Shipyards, Inc., 659 F.2d 706, 709, 10 OSH Cases 1075 (5th Cir. 1981).

[243] Walton v. Potlatch Corp., 781 P.2d 229, 14 OSH Cases 1186 (Idaho 1989); *see also* Rabon v. Automatic Fasteners, Inc., 672 F.2d 1231, 1238 n.13 (5th Cir. 1982), *quoting* Melerine v. Avondale Shipyards, Inc., 659 F.2d 706, 709–10, 10 OSH Cases 1075 (5th Cir. 1981) ("[t]o establish that the violation of a statute or regulation, including OSHA, is negligence *per se,* a plaintiff must prove 'th[e] violation of a statute which is intended to protect the class of persons to which the plaintiff belongs against the risk of the type of harm which has in fact occurred.' . . . If the plaintiff thus establishes negligence, he must then prove that the violation was the proximate cause of his injury. . . .")

[244] 728 F.2d 799, 10 OSH Cases 1857 (6th Cir. 1984).

[245] *Id.* at 805, *citing* Alex v. Armstrong, 215 Tenn. 276, 385 S.W.2d 110 (1964); Taylor v. Coburn, 597 S.W.2d 322 (Tenn. App. 1980); Berry v. Whitworth, 576 S.W.2d 351, 353 (Tenn. App. 1978).

2. *OSHA Violations as Evidence of Negligence*

In *Koll v. Mainatt's Transportation Co.,*[246] the Supreme Court of Iowa found that a violation of an OSHA standard constitutes negligence per se in cases where the injured plaintiff is an employee. The court further found, however, that if the plaintiff is not an employee of the defendant, such a violation "is evidence [only] of negligence. . . ."

In *Wendland v. Ridgefield Construction Services, Inc.,*[247] the Supreme Court of Connecticut found that a violation of an OSHA regulation may be used as evidence of negligence in a tort action. The *Wendland* court rejected decisions from other jurisdictions that a violation of an OSHA standard constitutes negligence per se on the grounds that the language of section 4(b)(4) of the OSH Act precludes such a result. *Rabon v. Automatic Fasteners*[248] allowed consideration of the safety standards set by OSHA regulations in a case involving a product liability action brought under Florida law and in *Johnson v. Niagara Machine & Tool Works,*[249] a case based on Minnesota state law, the court found that an OSHA standard was admissible and could be used to consider the comparative negligence of a nonparty employer.[250]

3. *OSHA Standards as Inadmissible Evidence*

The negligence cases in which OSHA standards have been deemed inadmissible as evidence generally involve plaintiffs who are not employees of the defendant, and hence are not deemed to be part of the class protected by the OSH Act.

For example, in *Cochran v. International Harvester Co.,*[251] the federal district court held that the OSH Act "does not enlarge the responsibility of owners of property to the employees of independent contractors." Hence, even though the defendant had violated some OSHA safety standards, the court entered summary judgment against the plaintiff, because he was an employee not of the defendant, but of the defendant's independent contractor. Similarly, there are cases that indicate that employees of subcontractors do not fall within the scope of protection.[252] The same reasoning also has been applied to invitees.[253]

---

[246] 253 N.W.2d 265, 270, 5 OSH Cases 1398 (Iowa 1977).

[247] 439 A.2d 954, 10 OSH Cases 1727 (Conn. 1981).

[248] 672 F.2d 1231, 1238 (5th Cir. 1982).

[249] 666 F.2d 1223 (8th Cir. 1981).

[250] *See also* Jupiter Inlet Corp. v. Brocard, 538 So.2d 857, 859, 13 OSH Cases 1896 (Fla. App. 1988).

[251] 408 F. Supp. 598, 602, 4 OSH Cases 1385, 1386 (W.D. Ky. 1975).

[252] In Horn v. C.L. Osborn Contr. Co., an employee of defendant's subcontractor was injured when the walls of a ditch in which he was working caved in. The employee brought a negligence action against the defendant claiming that the defendant had violated OSHA safety regulations. Reading the language of the OSH Act very strictly, the court found that an employer has a duty only to "his" employees, and concluded that the protections do "not extend to persons such as employees of subcontractors." Horn v. C.L. Osborn Constr. Co., 423 F. Supp. 801, 808, 5 OSH Cases 1045 (M.D. Ga. 1976).

[253] Trowell v. Brunswick Pulp & Paper Co., 522 F. Supp. 782, 10 OSH Cases 1028 (D.S.C. 1981); *see also* Sprankle v. Bower Ammonia & Chem. Co., 824 F.2d 409, 417, 13 OSH Cases 1382 (5th Cir. 1987).

B. Previous Citations as Evidence of Negligence

In at least one case a court has allowed evidence that an employer paid a fine for violating an OSHA standard to be entered as a declaration against interest in a tort action. In *Industrial Tile, Inc. v. Stewart,*[254] the Supreme Court of Alabama found that, "if the [OSHA] regulations are admissible as going to show a standard of care, then it seems only reasonable that the evidence of violation of the standards would also be admissible as evidence that the defendant failed to meet the standards that it should have followed."

VII. Conclusion

The number of recognized toxic materials in the present working environment will continue to increase with time, and OSHA can be expected to respond vigorously to these potential threats. Following its resounding defeat in *AFL-CIO v. OSHA,*[255] one can expect OSHA to redouble its efforts to reform the OSH Act to give the agency more flexibility than is currently provided under section 6(b).[256] These reforms should take cognizance of the scientific advances, such as physiologically based pharmacokinectic modeling, that have occurred in the field of risk assessment since the Act was initially passed. To the extent that OSHA takes full advantage of the latest and best scientific knowledge in evaluating the risks of the workplace environment, it should be able to assume that businesses' limited resources are spent in reducing real, not merely speculative risks to workers' health.

[254] 388 So.2d 171, 174 (Ala. 1980); *see also* Jupiter Inlet Corp. v. Brocard, 538 So.2d 857, 859 n.13, 13 OSH Cases 1896 (Fla. App. 1988); Dixon v. International Harvester Co., 754 F.2d 573, 581 n.5 (5th Cir. 1985).

[255] 965 F.2d 962 (11th Cir. 1992).

[256] One such piece of legislation has already been introduced. H.R. 1280 (S. 575) would, among other things, enact into law the 428 standards overturned by the Eleventh Circuit.

9

Toxic Substances Control Act

*By Marshall Lee Miller**

The Toxic Substances Control Act (TSCA) is potentially the most powerful and sweeping of all the environmental laws. When enacted in 1976, commentators claimed that if for some reason all the other environmental laws were repealed, the Environmental Protection Agency (EPA) could continue to regulate air, water, wastes, and the other media of pollution simply by using this one statute.

The reality has been more sobering: TSCA has erected a complex superstructure of regulations with, unfortunately, still scant environmental benefits to show for it. Moreover, some of the scientific assumptions about the pace of toxicological developments, on which the TSCA notification system was based, have proved over-optimistic. However, because EPA fines and penalties for even technical violations have soared so high, a thorough knowledge of TSCA's regulatory requirements is essential.

I. Background and Scope of the Act

A. Historical Reasons for the Legislation

National concern about the condition of the environment in the late 1960s led to the passage of a series of statutes. The Clean Water Act and the Clean Air Act gave federal and state authorities control over direct emissions into the environment, and the Federal Insecticide, Fungicide, and Rodenticide Act (FIFRA) regulated those chemicals, but there was no federal authority to require testing of most chemicals before they were manufactured and used. Tragic episodes in the early 1970s involving mercury, PCBs, kepone, asbestos, vinyl chloride, and a host of other substances led Congress in October 1976 to enact TSCA.[1]

Not all new chemical substances are subject to the Act. Some are excluded directly by the statute itself; others are exempted. There is a significant difference between the two categories.

---

*This chapter was prepared with the help of Pamela Hand of Baker & Hostetler.

[1] 15 U.S.C. §2601 *et seq.*

B. Statutory Exclusions

Excluded substances are those which are, by definition, kept outside the scope of the Act. This exclusion may be because they are regulated under other laws (such as pesticides under FIFRA) or by other agencies (such as the FDA). Other substances, such as tobacco and ammunition, are excluded for political reasons. Exclusions include the following:

- Any mixtures (though the component ingredients may be regulated);
- Pesticides regulated under FIFRA;
- Items regulated under the Food, Drug and Cosmetic Act (FDCA);
- Nuclear material regulated under the Atomic Energy Act;
- Tobacco and tobacco products;
- Certain obscurely identified items under the Internal Revenue Code.[2]

The exclusion of mixtures deserves special mention. The term "mixtures" is defined as any "combination of two or more chemical substances if the combination does not occur in nature and is not, in whole or in part the result of a chemical reaction. . . ."[3] The assumption underlying this exemption is that a mixture can be no more toxic than the sum of its component parts, but a chemical reaction creates a new substance which may have enhanced toxicity or adverse environmental effects. Be cautioned, however, that EPA sometimes considers a substance a "chemical substance" when common usage might be to regard it as a mixture.

C. Statutory Exemptions

Exempted substances are those that, by statute or regulation, are removed from coverage under all or part of the Act. The reason may be administrative convenience, a concession to business practicalities, or an exemption for substances that pose little environmental problem. The legal wording of the exemptions should be carefully noted, for they may apply to some portions of the Act but not to the others. For example, a category of chemicals might be exempted from section 5 but, if potentially harmful, might still be subject to sections 4 or 8, or other parts of the Act.

The most important exemptions occur under section 5, the Premanufacture Notification (PMN) provision of the Act. As described more fully below, these exemptions include chemicals in research and development. Most of the so-called exemptions, however, are really only partial exemptions. For example, substances manufactured for test marketing are supposedly exempt from the PMN requirements.[4] A test marketing exemption (TME), however, must be filed with EPA, which must review the TME within 45 days but has no time limit for a decision.

---

[2] TSCA §3(2) (definitions), 15 U.S.C. §2602(2).

[3] 40 C.F.R. §710.2(q).

[4] TSCA §5(h)(1), 15 U.S.C. §2604(h)(1).

D. Small Business

Under the Act, "small business" is treated in different ways in the various sections. In section 8(a), certain recordkeeping and reporting requirements, the level to qualify as a small business is $30 million; in section 8(b), inventory reporting requirements, the determinative amount is $5 million; and in section 5's provisions on supplementary reporting, the cutoff is a minuscule $1 million.

II. Premanufacture Notification Process

Although it is a widespread myth that TSCA only applies to new chemicals, the heart of the Act is indeed the notification program for new chemicals. The basic idea is to uncover and reject new chemicals that might pose a serious environmental risk. In the past, the danger of certain highly toxic chemicals was usually discovered only after workers and the public were exposed to the hazard for decades. TSCA's PMN goal was that there be "no more human guinea pigs."

A. Background

The manufacturers and developers of all new chemicals, that is, those chemicals not on the EPA Inventory (discussed below), unless otherwise exempted, must notify EPA at least 90 days prior to beginning production. In a separate category, notification may also be required for older chemicals, already on that list, if EPA determines that there is a significant new use that increases human or environmental exposure.[5]

The operative word in PMN is "notify." Following considerable debate, Congress in 1976 rejected the notion that each new chemical must be registered by EPA in a system akin to that for pesticides under FIFRA. The pesticide registration system requires detailed proof of both efficacy and environmental safety; the testing requirements can cost the manufacturers millions of dollars, and EPA's regulatory approval process can take years. Adopting this system to a full registration program for the thousands of new chemicals appearing annually would have snarled the American chemical industry beyond redemption.

Hence, the statute provides instead for providing information to EPA on the name and general nature of the new chemical. The sharp distinction between FIFRA's registration and TSCA's notification procedure is illustrated by the fact that EPA, when preparing the cost estimates to business for the TSCA premanufacture notification program, assessed the anticipated burden as zero. The Agency assumed that the data requirements for PMN would be minimal. This has not quite turned out to be the case.

[5]TSCA §5(a), 15 U.S.C. §2604(a). The criteria for a new use determination (Significant New Use Regulation (SNUR)) include the expected production volume, increased quantity or duration of human and environmental exposure, and hazards of manufacturing and distribution.

B. PMN Requirements

The essential PMN requirements are set forth in section 5(d) of the statute, which is cross-linked to section 8(a):

1. The common or trade name, the chemical identity, and molecular structure of the chemical or mixture;
2. The proposed categories of use;
3. The total amount of production and the estimated amount for each category of use;
4. A description of the byproducts from each process, use, or disposal;
5. The number of exposed individuals and the duration of exposure;
6. The manner or method of disposal;
7. Any test data in the possession of the notifier that bear on the environmental and health effects of the manufacture, distribution, use, or disposal of the chemical;
8. A description of any other health and environmental data known to the notifier.

There is no specific requirement that the applicant undertake scientific testing or generate environmental and health data. If the information already exists, it should be submitted. If the data appear in published scientific literature, a standard literature citation must be included with any information submitted in this form. But if data do not exist, section 5(d) does not require the notifier to create it. In theory, this is in marked contrast to FIFRA registration or drug approval by the Food and Drug Administration. In practice, EPA can use sections 5(e) and (f) to coerce a notifier into providing whatever additional information the Agency desires.

Accepted PMN substances are added to EPA's TSCA Inventory, discussed below, so that subsequent producers do not have to go through the process.

C. Importing and Manufacturing

A PMN is also required of any new chemical imported into the United States. Only manufacturers that are incorporated, licensed, or doing business in the United States may submit a notice.[6] This rule means that an importer, or broker, or even a company that replaces the middleman and begins purchasing directly from foreign suppliers is liable for PMN violations.

D. Methods of Extending the Review Process

A crucial way in which a notification differs from a registration is that the applicant does not have to await EPA approval. Instead, the applicant must merely wait for the elapse of the 90-day notification period and, if EPA has registered no objection, production may commence. In fact, EPA cannot wait

[6] 40 C.F.R. §720.22. On April 19, 1988, BASF Corp. agreed to pay a $1.28 million penalty for violating the import provisions of TSCA. Chem. Reg. Rep. (BNA) (Apr. 22, 1988).

until the 89th day to object. By regulation,[7] the applicant must be informed of EPA misgivings early in the process so the applicant can prepare its response and, in turn, EPA can prepare a rebuttal—all supposedly within the 90-day notification period.

The timetable of response and counter-response is specified in detail. EPA has to respond to the PMN within five days by publishing an acknowledgment of the notice in the *Federal Register.* This item must identify the chemical substance, listing its intended uses, and describe the toxicological tests required to demonstrate that there will be no "unreasonable risk of injury to health or the environment."[8] A decision to restrict any aspect of the chemical's production or distribution, described below, must be issued no later than 45 days before the expiration of the notification period, meaning that the Agency must respond very quickly. In turn, the manufacturer then has a month to offer its objections to the order.[9]

There are two ways that EPA can obtain more time for review. In special circumstances, the Agency is authorized by statute to take one additional 90-day review period. When TSCA was originally passed, there was concern that EPA would resort to the 180-day total review period as a matter of routine. That fortunately has not happened. Instead, EPA has used a second method, namely to declare the clock stopped when the quality or quantity of data in the notification is deemed inadequate.

E. Decision of PMN Insufficiency

Although TSCA may not specifically require the creation of any supporting scientific studies, the Agency has the authority to require them as a condition for the acceptance of a PMN.

Under section 5(e), EPA may determine that the information submitted is insufficient to make a "reasoned evaluation" of the environmental risks involved in a chemical.[10]

The manufacturer can prevent a proposed order of prohibition from taking effect merely by filing specific objections within 30 days. If EPA wishes to dispute these objections, the Agency must then seek an injunction from a federal district court, which will determine whether the data submitted were indeed insufficient.[11] If the manufacturer submits additional information which EPA continues to believe is inadequate, the Agency must take more drastic action under section 6(a) of TSCA (see below) or acquiesce in the district court's dissolution of the injunction.

F. Rejection of a PMN

Occasionally EPA may decide that the notified substance is so potentially hazardous that it should not be allowed on the market at all. Under sections

---

[7] 49 C.F.R. §720.25.

[8] 15 U.S.C. §2604.

[9] TSCA §5(e)(1), 15 U.S.C. §2604(e)(1). This description, although complex, is nevertheless an oversimplification.

[10] TSCA §5(f), 15 U.S.C. §2604(f).

[11] TSCA §5(e)(2)(A), 15 U.S.C. §2604(e)(C).

5(e) and (f) of the Act, if the Agency determines that manufacturing, processing, disposal, or other uses would "present an unreasonable risk of injury to health or the environment" and that the information provided is inadequate to make a "reasoned evaluation," it may prohibit chemical production.[12] If the Agency decides that there is an actual indication of hazard, rather than simply insufficient evidence to rebut, section 5(f) provides that it may prohibit, limit, or otherwise restrict production or use, as set forth in various portions of section 6.[13]

Initially, manufacturers' withdrawal of PMNs when challenged for more data was seen as a vindication of the program. However, for many chemical manufacturers, the costs of responding to anything more than a routine challenge to a PMN are not worthwhile. Thus, the number of withdrawn submissions may not be an indication of the value of the section 5 program.

The first section 5(e) notice, announced in April 1980, proposed delaying the manufacture of six new but questionable chemicals.[14] The firm dropped its manufacturing plans shortly thereafter. In September 1980, EPA issued another order to block production of a new chemical pending development of additional information on its human health rules.[15] That has been the pattern, and to date no manufacturer, either foreign[16] or domestic, has contested the EPA determinations as far as federal district court, as permitted in section 5(f)(3)(B).

As with an EPA determination of insufficient data, discussed above, the Agency may resort to a federal district court for an injunction that would prevent the manufacture or other utilization of the risky product.[17]

G. Notice of Commencement

EPA regulations require that a manufacturer must notify the agency twice, once for the PMN and the second time for the Notice of Commencement (NOC). The NOC announcing the beginning of actual production must be submitted within 30 days after commencement; it cannot be submitted even one day beforehand.[18]

The Agency's rationale for the NOC process is that it ensures that the TSCA Inventory will cover only substances that are, or recently have been, in active production. Actually, the entire NOC system is based on a misreading or a misunderstanding of the statute. Congress wanted to ensure that EPA added PMN substances to the Inventory list with minimal delay, so that other would-be producers would not needlessly submit PMNs for chemicals already listed. Instead, the Agency has converted this directive to it into a legal requirement imposed on manufacturers.

This NOC system is difficult to comprehend. No environmental hazard is created by a chemical that clears the PMN process but is never produced. Nevertheless, the substantial fines which EPA is currently imposing on compa-

---

[12] TSCA §5(e), 15 U.S.C. §2604(e).

[13] TSCA §5(f), especially (f)(2), referring to TSCA §6(a) and 6(a)(2)(B), 15 U.S.C. §2605(a) and (a)(B).

[14] 45 Fed. Reg. 27,817 (1980).

[15] *Id.*

[16] Chem. Reg. Rep. (BNA) 787 (Oct. 16, 1981).

[17] TSCA §5(f). See also Section VIII, TSCA Enforcement, below.

[18] 40 C.F.R. §720.102.

nies for violations, particularly for submitting a NOC prematurely, obliges manufacturers to follow the regulations closely.

H. Evaluation of the PMN Process

The whole PMN system presumes that EPA will be able to spot the most environmentally dangerous new chemical substances and prevent them from being produced. The dilemma is that many substances are toxic, and most chemicals are hazardous under some circumstances.

The framers of the Act had four chemical incidents in mind as examples of what they wished to prevent in the future; these were kepone, dioxin, asbestos, and polychlorinated biphenyls (PCBs). It is not clear, however, that the PMN process would have caught these villains. The first went through the more rigorous pesticide process; the second is a contaminant, not a commercial product; and the third is a natural rock material known for many centuries. Only the fourth would even have gone through the process.

The assumption underlying premanufacture notification was that scientific knowledge in the mid-1970s had made remarkable progress. Chemical specialists, it was thought, would soon be able to examine a chemical's structure and infer thereby its potential toxicological effects. Such optimism was unfortunately unfounded, or at least premature. More scientific studies might be required to support a PMN, and to a certain extent there has been such a trend. More important has been the growing EPA reliance on other portions of the Act, namely the reporting (section 8) and testing (section 4) provisions.

III. Exemptions and Special Rules in the PMN Process

A. PMN Exemption: Section 5(h)(4)

The statute provides that EPA can exempt a manufacturer or a new substance from all or part of the PMN process if it decides that the substance's production, distribution, use, and disposal "will not present an unreasonable risk of injury to health or the environment."[19]

In 1980, Polaroid petitioned EPA for a blanket exemption on minor changes made from time to time in the formulation of instant photographic film.[20] After similar requests from other companies, prolonged debate, and an initial rejection of the exemption by the Office of Management and Budget (OMB) as (ironically) too restrictive,[21] the agency finally approved the first section 5(h)(4) exemption in a rule published in June 1982.[22]

B. The Polymer "Exemption"

In July 1982, in response to industry petitions, EPA proposed other rules under section 5(h)(4) that would exempt about half of all new chemicals

[19] TSCA §5(h)(4), 15 U.S.C. §2604(f).

[20] *See* Chem. Reg. Rep. (BNA) 787 (Oct. 16, 1981).

[21] *Id.* at 803 (Oct. 23, 1981), and 819 (Oct. 30, 1981).

[22] 47 Fed. Reg. 24,308 (1982).

produced in the United States.[23] The rules would apply to the manufacture of certain polymers, chemicals used solely at the plant site, and low volume chemicals (defined generally by the companies as 25,000 pounds annually).[24] For chemicals produced in volumes under 1,000 kilograms a year, only a brief notice was to be submitted to EPA under the polymer exemption proposal: namely, manufacturer's name, location, chemical identity, and the polymer's molecular weight. Another category of polymers, those produced in quantities of between 1,000 and 10,000 kilograms annually, would have to be submitted with somewhat more information under an abbreviated 14-day PMN. Environmental groups, such as the Natural Resources Defense Council (NRDC), opposed the proposals.[25]

After an extended comment period and a review of approximately 1,000 polymer PMNs submitted by that date, EPA was reluctant to certify that no hazard at all existed, though none so far had been found. The agency therefore deferred a fuller exemption, pending longer experience, but did allow a shortened review period of 21 days for polymers. Under these circumstances, the careless use of the term "polymer exemption" has sometimes misled people into believing that a more comprehensive exclusion applies. So far, it does not.

C. Low Volume Chemicals

In April 1985, EPA published a rule expediting PMN review for low-volume chemicals (described as 1,000 kilograms or less a year).[26] A chemical eligible for this exemption undergoes a 21-day, rather than a 90-day, review and has fewer information requirements. Only the first manufacturer of a new chemical is eligible for the low-volume exemption (LVE). Subsequently, manufacturers must undergo the full PMN process.[27]

D. R & D Exemption

The manufacturer or importer of a chemical substance manufactured or imported only in small quantities[28] solely for research and development may be exempt from notification requirements if certain qualifications are met.[29] Among these qualifications are that the substance be used only under the supervision of a "technically qualified individual," and that all employees of the manufacturer or importer, or persons to whom it directly distributes the chemical substance who might come in contact with it, must be notified of any

---

[23] 47 Fed. Reg. 32,609 (1982).

[24] Section 26 provides that action taken for a single chemical may also be taken for a group. To grant a broad §5(h)(4) exemption, EPA must follow the rulemaking procedures of TSCA §6(c)(2) and (3). Within 5 days of receipt, EPA under §5(d)(2) must publish in the *Federal Register,* subject to §14 provisions on confidentiality, information on the new substance and its uses. Section 5(c) allows a 90-day extension period, if necessary, for good cause, subject to §5(e) and (f) regulatory triggers.

[25] Chem. Reg. Rep. (BNA) 555 (July 30, 1982).

[26] 50 Fed. Reg. 16,477 (1985).

[27] TSCA §5(h)(4), 15 U.S.C. §2604(h)(4).

[28] Small quantities means quantities of a chemical substance manufactured, imported, or processed or proposed to be manufactured, imported, or processed solely for research and development that are not greater than reasonably necessary for such purpose. A presumption for quantities under 1,000 pounds was in the original §5 proposed regulations but was dropped from the final version. This was retained for §8(b) inventory regulations, 43 Fed. Reg. 9254–55 (1978).

[29] 40 C.F.R. §720.36.

health risks that might be associated with the substance. Therefore, it would be necessary for the manufacturer or importer to have in its possession or control some information concerning the possible health and environmental effects of the chemical substance. No exemption is given for any substance distributed in commerce,[30] although the distinction may not be a clear one.

E. Test Marketing Exemption

Under TSCA section 5(h)(1), EPA may, at its discretion, grant approval of a test marketing exemption (TME), thereby granting the applicant an exemption from some of the PMN requirements if the Agency finds that the manufacture, processing, and distribution in commerce, and use and disposal of the substance for test marketing purposes "will not present any unreasonable risk of injury to health or the environment."[31] However, EPA may impose restrictions on testing marketing activities or may change the terms of or revoke an exemption if it receives new data that cast significant doubt on former findings.[32]

IV. Inventory of Existing Chemicals

A notification program for new chemicals must first answer the question: How do you know whether a chemical is a new chemical? The answer is that it cannot be found on EPA's Inventory of Existing Chemicals.

The basic concept is simple. For would-be producers, however, trying to determine whether a chemical is new and a PMN therefore necessary, the problem is becoming increasingly more difficult. The overwhelming majority of new chemicals placed on the Inventory have been put on a confidential list. Even for those items on the public list, the difficulties of terminology and concept mean that identical substances can be called different chemicals, while quite different substances can be termed the same chemical.

Determining whether complex chemicals are, or are not, on the Inventory can be a challenge. One reason is that the international terminology used by EPA and the private organization that characterizes chemicals may be logical but differs somewhat from that commonly used by many American companies. More important are the facts that there can often be quite different ways of identifying the more complicated substances, especially polymers, and that the rules are not always consistent.

A more serious problem is that EPA uses an "ingredients" approach, when in fact that might have little to do with the actual composition of the resulting chemical. Thus, EPA can characterize identical substances as different, and different substances as the same. The EPA Inventory needs drastic reevaluation. Although there are practical reasons for using the "ingredient" approach in characterizing chemical substances, EPA's policy lacks clarity of reason in classifying identical substances as different if they are made from slightly different intermediates. This might be tolerable simply as an Inventory

---

[30] 40 C.F.R. §720.36(d).
[31] 40 C.F.R. §720.38.
[32] TSCA §14(b)(1).

listing; the policy is difficult to understand when this unscientific peculiarity is used as the basis of significant EPA enforcement actions for violations of the PMN regulations.

A. Maintaining and Updating the Inventory

The Inventory is not an historical artifact, frozen in 1976. It is updated continuously, at least on computer, as new PMNs are received. The half-dozen volumes of the hardcopy version are revised every few years. In addition, substances may be altered or removed from the list if EPA or the manufacturer decides that the original submission is erroneous.[33] On rare occasions, a third party may supply the correction.

EPA has also removed a number of substances from the Inventory after determining that the original listing was fraudulent; usually this arises from the discovery that submitted chemicals were not actually in commercial production during the requisite period in the 1970s.

In 1986, EPA issued an Inventory Update Rule requiring manufacturers and importers to submit production volume and other information on certain chemicals. With a few exceptions, every four years this reporting must be provided anew to EPA. The exceptions include polymers, inorganics, microbes, and naturally occurring substances.[34]

B. Bona Fide Notice of Intent to Manufacture

There are three ways to determine whether a substance is already on the Inventory. The first, of course, is to check the published list, either by hardcopy or by computer. Since thousands of more recent substances are in the confidential listing, however, this search is not dispositive. The second way is to use a procedure known as "bona fide notice of intent to manufacture."[35]

In this approach, the manufacturer informs EPA in writing that it plans to produce a chemical and therefore has a valid need to know whether a substance requires a PMN or not. The problem is that, although in theory EPA must respond within 30 days,[36] there has been no effective time limit on EPA's response, and these notices have generally been accorded low priority. Many months can elapse before EPA answers.

For this reason, manufacturers suspecting that a substance is already on the confidential Inventory often prefer to submit a bare PMN. EPA responds almost immediately. The choice has become somewhat more difficult now that EPA requires a PMN fee of $2,500 (only $100 for small businesses) that might be forfeited if the manufacturer has guessed wrong and the submitted PMN is too meager to proceed further. Nevertheless, the time saved may be worth the risk. Ironically, this approach means that the best way to find out that a PMN is unnecessary is to file a PMN.

---

[33] *See, e.g.*, 53 Fed. Reg. 44,814 (1988) removing 45 substances.

[34] 40 C.F.R. §710.26 *et seq.* See Section IX, Reporting Requirements, below.

[35] 40 C.F.R. §720.25.

[36] 40 C.F.R. §720.25(b)(8).

V. Significant New Use Rules

Older chemicals may also be subject to section 5's PMN requirements. This can occur with existing chemicals that develop significant new uses or even an appreciable increase in their utilization for an existing purpose. The significant new use rules (SNURs) are discussed below.

A. Factors in Determining Applicability of SNUR

According to Section 5(a)(2), relevant factors include the following:

1. The projected volume of manufacturing and processing of a chemical substance;
2. The extent to which a use changes the type or form of exposure of human beings or the environment to a chemical substance;
3. The extent to which a use increases the magnitude and duration of exposure of human beings or the environment to a chemical substance; and
4. The reasonably anticipated manner and methods of manufacturing, processing, distribution in commerce, and disposal of a chemical substance.

B. SNUR in Practice

Determining when a use is a new one, especially for a chemical already having scores of applications, can be difficult. EPA found that drafting rules concerning a multitude of such situations was even harder than anticipated. After several unsuccessful attempts, the agency decided to issue SNURs on an ad hoc basis. Then, after a pattern perhaps developed, regulations could be prepared.

The first final SNUR, on two potassium phosphate chemicals, was issued only in September 1984.[37] Almost four years later, in July 1988, EPA decided it had sufficient experience to publish in the *Federal Register* amendments to the General Provisions of the SNUR.[38]

Once EPA determines the use of a chemical substance to be a ''significant new use,'' persons who intend to manufacture, import, or process the substance for that use must submit a proposed SNUR to EPA at least 90 days before beginning to manufacture, import, or process the substance for that use. Persons submitting a proposed SNUR must comply with the same regulations as those submitting a PMN for a new chemical.

A person may begin an activity that is designated as a significant new use in a proposed SNUR until such SNUR is promulgated and becomes effective, at which time the activity must stop, and the person must file a NOC, and then wait for EPA's review of the notice before resuming the activity.

---

[37] 49 Fed. Reg. 33,649 (1984).

[38] 53 Fed. Reg. 28,354 (1988).

Compliance with these new rules can be completed in advance if a company submits a proposed SNUR to EPA prior to the promulgation of the final SNUR. However, should EPA's 90-day review period of the SNUR extend beyond the final promulgation date of the SNUR, the person must still cease to manufacture, import, or process the chemical for the time remaining.

Provisions for an R&D exemption from the rule are identical to those for PMNs[39] as long as the manufacturer, importer, or processor notifies persons who will participate in the research and development of any and all possible health effects associated with the substance.

VI. Confidentiality

Although TSCA is designed mainly to collect information on chemical substances, there is grave concern over the issue of protecting secrets versus public disclosure.

Information regarding health and safety studies released to federal officials is subject to disclosure under TSCA.[40] Additionally, data that could protect "against an unreasonable risk of injury to health or the environment" may be divulged in a legal proceeding.[41]

However, information that is exempt from mandatory disclosure under the Freedom of Information Act (FOIA) may not be released by EPA.[42] And, despite the example of the kepone tragedy, EPA cannot release information to state health authorities unless they are defined as "contractors with the United States." Trade secrets and commercial or financial information obtained from a person is also confidential.[43] Although the Reagan Administration policy on section 5 supported industry's position that it could submit data labeled confidential without proving why,[44] EPA has consistently held that requests for confidentiality be coupled with an explanation, and Congress has threatened to pass legislation further regulating confidentiality if the business community abuses the privilege.[45]

EPA's September 1976 regulations for handling FOIA requests under various statutes, with the exception of FIFRA,[46] soundly favored disclosure,[47] but at that time EPA had few files with business secrets and few complaints from industry.

---

[39] 40 C.F.R. §720.36.

[40] TSCA §14(b)(1), 15 U.S.C. §2613.

[41] TSCA §14(b) and (a), 15 U.S.C. §2613(b) and (a). *See also* 40 C.F.R. §2.301(h), 43 Fed. Reg. 2637 (1978).

[42] TSCA §14(a), 15 U.S.C. §2613(a).

[43] Administrative Procedure Act §2(b)(4), 5 U.S.C. §552(b)(4).

[44] Chem. Reg. Rep. (BNA) 443 (Feb. 7, 1982).

[45] *See, e.g.,* Chem. Reg. Rep. (BNA) 483 (Aug. 3, 1984). The head of EPA's toxic office, John Moore, requested that companies claim less data as confidential to ease the evaluation by his staff. *Id.* at 3 (Apr. 6, 1984).

[46] Disclosure of certain information under the pesticide regulations has resulted in extensive litigation. *See* Mobay Chem. Corp. v. Costle, 447 F. Supp. 811, 12 ER Cases 1228 (W.D. Mo. 1978), *dismissed per curiam,* 439 U.S. 320, 12 ER Cases 1581 (1979).

[47] 41 Fed. Reg. 36,902 (1976).

Complaints that existing laws do not sufficiently protect confidential business information originated with the chemical industry. According to the Manufacturing Chemists Association (MCA), the trade secret exemption under FOIA does not assure the protection of privately developed information submitted to the government.[48]

In response to some of industry's concerns, EPA revised portions of the original inventory reporting proposal.[49] EPA established a task force to ensure computer security by protecting information on magnetic tape[50] and deleted the requirement that a toxicological bibliography be submitted.[51]

Polaroid Corporation was also concerned with the protection of chemical trade secrets and challenged EPA regulations.[52] In June 1978, a U.S. district court denied Polaroid an exemption from reporting the information in dispute, but also ordered EPA to restrict the information to within the Agency. That same year EPA amended its confidential business information regulations under TSCA to provide both substantial protection and notice to affected businesses before any confidential information is released outside the Agency.[53] Although Polaroid withdrew its suit and the court its order, confidentiality still remains a problem.

VII. Testing Requirements

A. In General

Testing of substances before they enter production was one goal of TSCA, as exemplified in the PMN process. But the Act also had the goal of mandating the testing of selected groups of existing chemical substances.[54] This development of health and environmental data is the primary purpose of TSCA section 4.

Under TSCA section 4(a)(1)(A), EPA may require testing of such a chemical (1) if the chemical is found to present unreasonable risk to human health or the environment,[55] (2) if there is insufficient data to reasonably predict the hazards of the chemical, and (3) if testing is the only avenue for pursuing this information. Additionally EPA may require testing if a chemical is produced in substantial amounts *and* substantial human and environmental exposure could result.[56]

When the testing of individual chemicals cannot predict the effects of a mixture in which they are contained, EPA may require the mixture as a whole to be tested as well.[57]

---

[48] Letter from former MCA President William J. Driver to Senator James Abourezk (D-SD), Jan. 18, 1978, *quoted in* Env't Rep. (BNA) 1468 (1978).

[49] 42 Fed. Reg. 13,130 (1977).

[50] *See, e.g.,* 42 Fed. Reg. 53,805 (1977), 43 Fed. Reg. 1836 (1978).

[51] 42 Fed. Reg. 39,182, 39,188 (1977), *reproposing* 40 C.F.R. §710.7(e).

[52] Polaroid Corp. v. Costle, No. 78-11335 (D. Mass. 1978).

[53] 40 C.F.R. pt. 2, 43 C.F.R. §3997.

[54] TSCA §2(b)(1), 15 U.S.C. §2601(b)(1).

[55] 15 U.S.C. §2603(a)(1)(A).

[56] TSCA §4(a)(1)(B), 15 U.S.C. §2603(a)(1)(B).

[57] TSCA §4(a)(2), 15 U.S.C. §2603(a)(2).

EPA must weigh the relative cost and availability of the testing protocol's parameters, and the period within which the test can reasonably be performed.[58] Each year EPA reviews all testing standards and makes any adjustments that may be necessary.[59] When a company plans to test a chemical for which EPA has no current standard, the company may formally request testing guidelines from EPA.[60] It is beneficial for a company to follow this procedure both to avoid possible additional charges because of testing inadequacies and non-compliance with EPA regulations and to assist a company in litigation with other parties, (i.e., OSHA), apart from the section 4(a) rule.

All tests requested by EPA must follow Good Laboratory Practice (GLP) standards. EPA's GLP requirements, issued in November 1983, provide that studies submitted to satisfy section 4 must explain whether they meet the standards, where they differ from GLP, or that the submitter did not conduct the tests and is not aware of the test conditions.[61] At a minimun, GLP requires very specific documentation of the personnel and organization conducting the tests, the equipment, the test protocol, including test and control procedures, and a description of every step in the testing process.[62] Failure to comply with GLP is itself a violation of the statute, namely TSCA section 15.[63]

EPA has published only a little more than 100 test rules over the past two decades. This slow pace led to a lawsuit filed by the NRDC in 1979 and a consent decree in 1986 that established informal procedures for issuing testing orders.[64]

B. Criteria for Testing Requirements

The obligation to test is based upon the showing of a need for testing that is determined from (1) the estimation of possible risk, (2) the inadequacy of existing scientific data to predict health and environmental effects, and (3) the need for testing to provide that data. The essential threshold is the first, namely, whether the chemical may present an unreasonable risk of injury to man and the environment.[65] This naturally raises the question of what level of risk is unreasonable.

Three federal appellate courts have considered this question and two have ruled on it. The U.S. Court of Appeals for the District of Columbia Circuit in *Chemical Manufacturers Ass'n. v. EPA*[66] held in 1988 that the risk had to be a "substantial probability," not merely a speculative or theoretical possibility;

---

[58] TSCA §4(b)(1), 15 U.S.C. §2603(b)(1).

[59] TSCA §4(b)(2), 15 U.S.C. §2603(b)(2). An earlier bill required EPA to propose test protocols within one year of enactment but this was not in the final version. *See* SENATE COMM. ON COMMERCE REPORT ON S. 426, TOXIC SUBSTANCE CONTROL ACT OF 1973, at. 7 (Comm. Print 1973).

[60] TSCA §4(g), 150 U.S.C. §2603(g). EPA has 60 days to grant or deny the petition. If granted, it has only 75 days to issue test standards; if denied, the agency must publish reasons for the denial in the *Federal Register.*

[61] 48 Fed. Reg. 53,992 (1983).

[62] 40 C.F.R. §792; 48 Fed. Reg. 53,992 (1983).

[63] Ironically, EPA's Office of Pesticides and Toxic Substances brought enforcement actions in the early 1990s against companies based on testing that failed to comply with GLP standards.

[64] NRDC v. Costle, 12 ER Cases 1833 (D.D.C. 1979).

[65] TSCA §4(a)(1)(A), 15 U.S.C. §2603(a)(1)(A).

[66] 859 F.2d 977 (D.C. Cir. 1988).

the toxicity at that level must be sufficiently high so that under those circumstances there would still be an unreasonable risk. In the same year, the Third Circuit in *Ausimont U.S.A. Inc. v. EPA*[67] held that the risk must be more than a "scientific curiosity."

Exposure is not an explicit factor in this risk determination, although the case law suggests that there has to be at least some possibility of exposure; otherwise, there would be no risk. Another type of EPA determination, however, relies much more on exposure or the production of the chemical substance in substantial quantities, even where there may be less evidence of toxicity. This is the difference between an estimation of possible risk type of determination under TSCA section 4(a)(1)(A), and an exposure or production determination under section 4(a)(1)(B). EPA has repeatedly declined to specify the meaning of the term "substantial quantities," preferring to make this decision on a case-by-case basis.[68]

C. Types and Procedures for Section 4 Studies

EPA has broad discretion to order testing for a variety of possible chemical effects. These range from acute, chronic, and subchronic toxicity to carcinogenicity, teratogenicity, mutagenicity, and neurotoxicity. Environmental effects also may be required, for which EPA has issued two dozen test guidelines, along with information on various mechanisms such as the transport process, biodegradation, chemical and physical properties, and chemical fate.[69]

When EPA issues a test rule, the affected parties must submit plans for the required studies within 45 days.[70] There are test standards for effects such as chemical fate, environmental effects, and health effects.[71] Only if and when they are incorporated into test rules for individual substances do they become mandatory.

D. Priority List for Chemical Testing

Because of the tens of thousands of potentially toxic substances that could be tested, Congress established in section 4(e) the Interagency Testing Committee (ITC) which recommends to EPA which chemicals should be tested.

ITC consists of eight members from different agencies within the federal government[72] and was given until 1977 to submit a list of chemicals for public comment and EPA approval. ITC gives priority consideration to chemicals that

---

[67] 838 F.2d 93 (3d Cir. 1988). The court did not rule on the threshold of risk but remanded the case to a lower court to review the actual exposure levels. *See also* Shell Chem. Co. v. EPA, 826 F.2d 295 (5th Cir. 1987).

[68] *See, e.g.,* 50 Fed. Reg. 20,664 (1985); 46 Fed. Reg. 30,300 (1981).

[69] TSCA §4(b)(2)(A), 15 U.S.C. §2603(b)(2)(A).

[70] 40 C.F.R. §790.

[71] 40 C.F.R. §§796, 797, and 798, respectively.

[72] These include EPA, OSHA, the Council on Environmental Quality, NIOSH, the National Institute of Environmental Health Science, the National Cancer Institute, the National Science Foundation, and the Department of Commerce. Several other agencies overlooked by the statute, such as FDA, have unofficially become a part of the committee. Others include the Consumer Product Safety Commission, and the Departments of Defense and the Interior. Members serve four years and may not have any financial interest or accept employment for one year from anyone subject to TSCA.

may cause cancer, gene mutations, or birth defects and also calculates the exposure and toxicity levels. EPA has 12 months to either initiate rulemaking under section 4(a) or publish reasons why not.

A priority list of chemicals that cannot contain more than 50 items at any time is then established.[73] The "list of 50" may name groups of chemicals in addition to individual substances. A chemical is listed until it is either designated for or found to be inappropriate for testing. To date, there have been several hundred substances on and off the list.

In order to develop the inventory priority list, an initial list of about 3,650 chemicals was compiled from 19 different sources. Those substances, which fell under the jurisdiction of other federal laws, were removed followed by other deletions. The list was narrowed down to a Master File of 1,700 and further scaled down through evaluating production volume and population exposure. A preliminary list of the remaining 330 chemicals was published in July 1977, and, in turn, reduced to a candidate list of 80.

In October 1978, a year after the publication of the initial priority list, EPA suffered harsh criticism by withdrawing the first group of 10 substances because it was not prepared to issue rules by the 12-month deadline, and by postponing the testing rulemaking until the appropriate standards were developed.[74] On May 8, 1979, the NRDC filed suit against EPA for not developing testing rules on the chemicals ITC initially recommended.[75]

In March 1982, the ITC chairman declared that the Committee would no longer review broad categories of chemicals although half of the first group listed were not individual substances but categories.[76]

E. Exemptions and Reimbursement

Manufacturers and others subject to a test rule may apply for an exemption within 30 days. One ground for exemption is that the tests for an "equivalent" substance would be a duplicate of those already done or those being performed by others.[77] Such an exemption, however, may obligate the manufacturer to reimburse the actual developer of the test data for being allowed to "piggy back."[78] An exemption is also available to manufacturers or processors who produce chemicals in small volumes, namely less than 500 kilograms.

This concept of test sharing was borrowed from FIFRA and helps relieve the burden of cost which companies may face.[79] The time allotment for reimbursement is generally five years after the date of submission but is subject to change at the EPA's discretion.[80]

---

[73] TSCA §4(e)(1)(A), 15 U.S.C. §2603(e)(1)(A).

[74] 43 Fed. Reg. 50,134 (1978).

[75] NRDC v. Costle, 14 ER Cases 1858 (S.D.N.Y. 1980); NRDC v. EPA, 595 F. Supp. 1255 (S.D.N.Y. 1984); 51 Fed. Reg. 23,713 (1986).

[76] Chem. Reg. Rep. (BNA) 1323 (Mar. 26, 1982).

[77] TSCA §4(c)(2), 15 U.S.C. §2603(c)(2); 40 C.F.R. §790.80.

[78] TSCA §4(c), 15 U.S.C. §2603(c); 40 C.F.R. §791.3(h). The reimbursement system for reliance on the data of others can be for TSCA, as with FIFRA, very complex.

[79] FIFRA §3(c)(1)(D), 7 U.S.C. §136a(C)(1)(D). This issue is discussed in Chapter 10, Pesticides.

[80] TSCA §4(c)(3)(B), 15 U.S.C. §2603(c)(3)(B).

EPA prefers that parties settle reimbursement disputes themselves, but is required to intervene, after consultation with the Attorney General and the Federal Trade Commission, if the disputes cannot be resolved.[81]

The reimbursement rule under TSCA section 4 dictates that the cost sharing amount is a direct proportion of each company's product volume. This section in FIFRA has generated more controversy, uncertainty, and administrative inconvenience than any other issue. It remains unclear yet whether the reimbursement scheme will be more successful under TSCA than FIFRA.

F. Determination of Significant Risk

The purpose of the testing is to determine whether a chemical might pose "a significant risk of serious or widespread harm to human beings." If the tests confirm that suspicion, EPA must then take appropriate regulatory action under one or more of TSCA sections 4 through 7 within 180 days, or the Agency must publish the reasons for not acting.[82]

The finding of significant risk is more severe than the standard for a TSCA section 6 action of "unreasonable risk"; it is similar to the finding of "imminent hazard" to man and the environment in section 7. Section 7 and section 4(f) resemble each other in another way: the agency seems reluctant to use either section in its regulatory program.

VIII. Enforcement

A. Civil Penalties

EPA determines the appropriate civil penalty for TSCA violations not to exceed $25,000 per violation per day.[83] "Nature, circumstances, extent, and gravity of the violation or violations and, with respect to the violator, ability to pay, effect on ability to continue to do business, any history or prior such violations, the degree of culpability, and such other matters as justice may require"[84] are all taken into account by EPA when making its decision. Before EPA issues the penalty, however, it is required to notify the violator and provide an opportunity for a hearing. The individual must respond within 15 days and may file a petition for judicial review within 30 days. Review is by the federal court of appeals for the circuit where the violator's business is located. If an individual does not file a petition or a final judgment has been entered and such person has not paid the specified penalties, the Attorney General can recover the amount plus interest in court.[85]

---

[81] TSCA §4(c), 15 U.S.C. §2603(c).
[82] TSCA §4(f), 15 U.S.C. §2603(f).
[83] TSCA §16(a)(1), 15 U.S.C. §2615(a)(1).
[84] TSCA §16(a)(2)(B), 15 U.S.C. §2615(a)(2)(B).
[85] TSCA §16(a)(4)(B), 15 U.S.C. §2615(a)(4)(B).

B. Criminal Penalties

Individuals convicted of violating TSCA provisions are not only subject to civil penalties but may in adaition to, or instead of, be subject to imprisonment for not more than one year.[86]

C. Private Right of Action

TSCA also provides an avenue for private citizens to file civil actions against anyone who is in violation of TSCA, or to sue EPA.[87] EPA must respond to either suit within 90 days. However, if the suit involves compelling the Agency to perform a nondiscretionary duty, EPA has the right to hold public hearings regarding the complaint and make a decision based on the findings within 60 days.[88]

In either circumstance, EPA must decide whether or not to grant the petition and then either begin the appropriate procedures or publish reasons for denial. If the result is the latter, the citizen may continue the suit at the federal district court level.[89] If the court so determines, a petitioner may be awarded compensation for legal fees accrued during litigation.[90] The award is not dependent on the success of a suit nor is it limited to public interest groups.

The Service Employees International Union (SEIU) successfully used section 20 to obtain asbestos standards for schools.[91] It was unsuccessful, however, in its opposition to the deletion of the inventory designation of inorganic glass as mixtures[92] and removal of PCB-contaminated soil in a mine shaft.[93] Very few private citizens have used this section.

IX. Reporting Requirements

Although the original rationale for TSCA had been that "human beings should no longer be guinea pigs," the implicit shortcomings of the PMN system have unfortunately meant that future toxic hazards will probably be detected the same way. As a former head of the EPA toxic program, Steve Jellinek, predicted almost two decades ago, the real environmental core of TSCA will shift from section 5 PMN to section 8 reporting.[94]

Recent EPA "reinterpretations" of sections 8(c) through (e) have dramatically changed the reporting requirements of TSCA.[95] After bitter complaints

---

[86] TSCA §16(b), 15 U.S.C. §2615(b).

[87] TSCA §21, 15 U.S.C. §2620. The citizen participation sections were missing in whole or in part from earlier versions of TSCA. For example, H.R. 5356 of 1973 had neither section, while the Senate bill (S. 426) had a citizens suit provision (§19) but only an oblique reference to citizen petitions (§24a). *See* H.R. REP. NO. 360, 93d Cong., 1st Sess. (1973) and S. REP. No. 254, 93d Cong., 1st Sess. (1973).

[88] TSCA §20, 15 U.S.C. §2619.

[89] TSCA §21, 15 U.S.C. §2620.

[90] TSCA §19(d), 15 U.S.C. §2618(d).

[91] EPA Office of Toxic Substances, *Bulletin*, Mar. 1984.

[92] *Id.* at May 1984.

[93] 49 Fed. Reg. 36,844 (1984).

[94] Personal conversation with author.

[95] EPA's new interpretation of merging sections 8(c), (d), and (e) is discussed in more detail in subsection E below.

from the chemical industry, EPA did declare an amnesty of sorts, but in practice the three subsections have been muddled into one.

A. Section 8(a): Inventory Update Rule

Chemicals that EPA has no immediate cause to regulate, but which harbor some concern over, are subject to data collection regarding production volume, use, and anything else affecting human exposure and the need for controls. Section 8 of TSCA specifies the chemicals on which the Agency can gather this information. Section 8(a) covers recordkeeping and reporting by manufacturers or processors of, or those proposing to manufacture or process, a listed chemical substance. The categories of manufacturers and processors encompass those who manufacture or process for "commercial purposes." Information on the chemical which EPA may require includes molecular structure, amounts produced, disposal methods, categories of use, description of byproducts, and all relevant data concerning health and environmental effects. Although section 8 usually exempts small manufacturers or processors from these provisions, there are some, such as those who manufacture or process mixtures in small quantities for research and development purposes, who are still covered.[96]

The first rules governing Section 8(a) were not proposed until February 1980,[97] three years after the time frame set in TSCA. Under the original proposal, chemical manufacturers, including mining companies, were required to report production and exposure-related data on chemicals with high risk toxicity and exposure levels. The information was to be used for risk assessment and for a chemical ranking of roughly 2,300 chemicals. The final section 8(a) regulation was issued in June 1982 and cut the original list of 2,300 to 245 chemicals.[98] EPA was to decide which chemicals needed to be further tested based on reports from manufacturers regarding production, release, and exposure data.[99]

The interpretation of Section 8(a) was broadened during the final reviewing process. EPA proposed a rule placing the responsibility of reporting data on chemicals on the processors instead of the manufacturers if the manufacturers' reports lacked accountability for the use of 80 percent of the chemicals. Through this expansion, 50 more chemicals were subsequently considered for the final reporting list.[100]

The final list of chemicals under section 8(a) to be reported by manufacturers and importers for information on current data on production volume, plant site, and site-limited status, was issued on June 12, 1986.[101] However, EPA did make provisions for some exceptions including polymers, microorganisms, and inorganic and naturally found substances. It also excepted companies that

---

[96] §8(a)(3)(A)(ii).

[97] 45 Fed. Reg. 13,646 (1980).

[98] 47 Fed. Reg. 26,992 (1982).

[99] *See, e.g.*, 50 Fed. Reg. 9944 (1985). The final list of chemicals appears at 51 Fed. Reg. 21,438 (1986).

[100] 47 Fed. Reg. 26,992 (1982); Chem. Reg. Rep. (BNA) 412, 413 (June 25, 1982); *Id.* at 3 (Apr. 2, 1982).

[101] 51 Fed. Reg. 21,438 (1986).

manufacture less than 10,000 pounds of the subject chemical. A report must be submitted every four years following the first.[102]

In October 1986, EPA proposed another rule pursuant to section 8(a), the comprehensive assessment information rule (CAIR). EPA would use CAIR to collect information regarding risk assessment and to generate regulatory strategies for 47 different substances.[103] EPA could also use CAIR to expedite the process of adding a chemical to the CAIR list and limit the collection of data to the Office of Toxic Substances.

B. Section 8(d): Reports of Health and Safety Studies

As a matter of course, companies test their chemical products to ensure safety and efficiency. Under section 8(d) any company manufacturing, processing, or distributing a chemical must furnish EPA with a copy of such studies. Additionally, if the company does not have copies of the studies but knows of them or can reasonably obtain copies of studies performed by another entity, the company must submit copies or lists of those reports as well. This subsection does provide for exceptions. If EPA decides that certain lists of studies are not required in carrying out the purposes of TSCA, then those limits are exempt from the rules governing section 8(d).[104]

In July 1978, EPA published the section 8(d) rules requiring commercial manufacturers, processors, and distributors of chemicals on the first Interagency Testing Committee priority list to submit lists and copies of health and safety studies to EPA.[105] In September, a petition was filed by the MCA soliciting EPA to amend or repeal the rule. With a few exceptions, EPA denied the petition.[106]

The Dow Chemical Company questioned EPA's right to collect studies on chemicals manufactured or processed for research and development and not for "commercial purposes." On September 15, 1978, Dow filed a petition for review with the Third Circuit, and on August 24, 1979, the court denied the petition.[107] Because of the issues raised regarding reasonable notice and comment, EPA revoked the rule.[108]

A revised rule of section 8(d) was proposed in December 1979 and made applicable to any records developed thereafter. Following a lengthy public comment period, the proposed reporting requirements were reduced, and a final rule was published in September 1982.[109]

A procedural definition indicating when an extensive search is necessary replaced the broad terminology "known to" and in the "possession of." The files that companies must search to find studies and records is now limited to those that usually contain such information, maintained by those responsible for

[102] 51 Fed. Reg. at 35,762.

[103] *Id.*

[104] TSCA §8(d)(1), 15 U.S.C. §2607(d)(1).

[105] 43 Fed. Reg. 30,984 (1978). Two minor corrections were made to the rule shortly thereafter (43 Fed. Reg. 36,249 (1978) and 43 Fed. Reg. 41,205 (1978)).

[106] 43 Fed. Reg. 56,724 (1978).

[107] Dow Chem. Co. v. EPA, 605 F.2d 673 (3d Cir. 1979).

[108] 44 Fed. Reg. 6099 (1979).

[109] 47 Fed. Reg. 38,780 (1982).

advising the company on the effects of the chemicals on health and the environment.

Under the final rule, even if a company is no longer manufacturing a chemical, if it did so within the past 10 years the company must submit copies of any relevant study to EPA. However, it is unnecessary for the company to submit lists of other known studies.[110]

The revised section 8(d) regulation exempts distributors from reporting because distributors do not usually conduct studies and because they were not required to report under section 8(d) in the past.

Seven types of studies, including studies of impurities, published studies, and studies previously submitted to a federal agency, are also exempt from reporting.[111] EPA found that these studies were not useful in assessing risk and were difficult to compile.

Additionally, companies must supply EPA with unpublished studies and other specific information on 40 chemicals and chemical categories.[112] Thirty-nine were recommended by ITC under section 4(e) and equal about 175 substances and the fortieth is asbestos which was added by EPA. EPA proposed an additional 65 chemicals which have since been recommended by ITC.[113]

Although EPA continues to argue that research and development studies are used for "commercial purposes" and not exempt, its final ruling argued that section 8(d) "is to give the agency access to information from which it can assess the nature and significance of chemical hazards and risks to health or the environment whether or not the chemicals are desired commercial products."[114]

After the *Dow* case in 1978, EPA faced another challenge to the validity of submitting studies conducted for research and development. The company argued that the language in section 8(d) means "manufacture or process for commercial purposes" excluding research and development and that the chemicals in question were produced in small quantities and not offered for sale.[115] The court of appeals, however, did not agree with the company's rationale and ruled in favor of EPA.[116]

Another issue involves the type of company governed by section 8(d). An independent testing laboratory supported by the industry held that it was not under any obligation to report to EPA, but eventually the Agency did obtain the information. With the court decisions supporting EPA's position, the controversy surrounding this subsection will not be easily resolved.

---

[110] EPA contends that past research uncovering potentially harmful chemicals may not have been disclosed to EPA at the time, and those chemicals may still be in use by other companies unaware of their hazardous effects.

[111] 40 C.F.R. §704.5.

[112] 47 Fed. Reg. 38,780 (1982).

[113] *Id.*

[114] *Id.* at 38,781.

[115] Dow Chem. Co. v. EPA, 605 F.2d 673 (3d Cir. 1979).

[116] 47 Fed. Reg. 38,780 (1982).

C. Section 8(e): Notification of Substantial Risk

There is an increasing realization that the expectation level for judging potential environmental hazards through section 5 PMN procedures was too high. Thus, hazard reporting requirements are becoming more important. This method of relying on section 8(e) permits the testing of the chemicals in question while allowing workers and the environment to be exposed, thus accomplishing the exact opposite of the basic premise of TSCA. TSCA is supposed to locate hazardous chemicals before their long-term exposure to the environment.

In 1987, EPA's Office of Toxic Substances changed its interpretation of the reporting law. After industry finally was becoming comfortable with the old reading of the law, EPA began enforcing the new one with severe penalties for noncompliance.

1. Notification

Because of the extensive notification requirements of TSCA, EPA is inundated with data it cannot process. Until comprehensive screening criteria are instituted, the information will remain on file while hazardous chemicals may continue to pollute and injure. Additionally, the authors of TSCA assumed that the field of chemical structure analogies would be a much better tool than it actually is. As a consequence, those who review the chemicals may not be able to distinguish the hazardous from the nonhazardous. Because of these problems, notification must be an integral part of the statute and may require more scientific sophistication.

Since EPA may not be able to predetermine health effects, it must rely on section 8(e) to learn of them as soon as possible. This section places the burden of reporting any indication of adverse effects on chemical manufacturers or individuals who acquire information to the effect that substantial risk of injury to health or the environment will result from a particular substance or mixture. If the individual knows that EPA already has this information, he or she need not resubmit it.[117]

2. Substantial Risk

The reporting requirement mirrors section 6 of FIFRA, but FIFRA uses the terminology "unreasonable, adverse effects on the environment,"[118] implying that the manufacturer will perform an adverse risk-benefit assessment and report it. TSCA mandates that all evidence pointing towards "substantial risk" must be reported. Noncompliance may be answered with civil penalties or criminal prosecution.[119]

Substantial risk does not take into account any social or economic benefits caused by using the chemical or any of the costs associated with restricting the

[117] TSCA §8(e), 15 U.S.C. §2607(e).

[118] FIFRA §6(a)(2), 7 U.S.C. §136d(a)(2), 15 U.S.C. §§2614(3), 2615, and 2616.

[119] TSCA §§15(3), 16, and 17. It is interesting to note that in the first major criminal case against a company for failure to disclose adverse data on the pesticides chlordane and heptachlor, the Justice Department chose to use the general federal criminal laws rather than FIFRA §6(a)(2). United States v. Velsicol Chem. Corp., 470 F. Supp. 1336 (N.D. IL. 1979).

use. Additionally, the extent of exposure is barely touched in assessing risks because "the mere fact the implicated chemical is in commerce constitutes sufficient evidence of exposure."[120]

Policies governing section 8(e) were issued in final form in March 1978 by EPA.[121] The responsibility for reporting adverse effects falls upon senior officers within a corporation.[122] However, the officials may not be responsible if the company establishes, internally promotes, and implements procedures through which an employee can submit and the company process any pertinent information in this regard.[123]

D. Section 8(c): Significant Adverse Reactions

Section 8(c), which is similar to section 8(e),[124] requires any manufacturer, processor, or distributor of any chemical to maintain records for 30 years of "significant adverse reactions" allegedly caused by the chemical. Comparatively, all other records need only be on file for five years. All of these records are subject to inspection and review by anyone that the manufacturer designates.

"Significant adverse reaction" was proposed by EPA in July 1980 to be defined as "reactions which may indicate a tendency of a chemical substance or mixture to cause long-lasting irreversible damage to health or the environment."[125] The rule required that both written and oral allegations be logged.

In September 1982, the final version was issued and supported the idea of less cumbersome regulations.[126] Moreover, the final version uses the section 8(e) concept of only recording previously unknown effects. Although this idea suits section 8(e), it does not complement 8(c) where the goal is to provide a record of health problems and complaints. Under the final ruling, oral allegations, the most popular form of complaints, no longer have to be recorded. In addition, the number of processors affected was reduced to those in Standard Industrial Classifications 28 and 2911,[127] and manufacturers of substances occurring naturally were completely exempt, reducing the number of those covered by more than 98 percent. Finally, there was no automatic reporting requirement to EPA.

---

[120] 43 Fed. Reg. 11,110 (1978). See discussion in Section II, above.

[121] Statement of Interpretation and Enforcement Policy; Notification of Substantial Risk. 43 Fed. Reg. 11,110 (1978).

[122] *See* United States v. Park, 421 U.S. 658 (1975).

[123] 43 Fed. Reg. 11,110 (1978).

[124] Section 8(e) requires "substantial risk of injury." Additionally, the evidence must be "information which reasonably supports the conclusion" and not simply alleged facts. And finally, the response for §8(e) is not to simply maintain records but to report to EPA immediately.

[125] 45 Fed. Reg. 47,008 (1980).

[126] 47 Fed. Reg. 38,780 (1982); "Significant adverse reaction" was defined in the final version to emphasize "significant" as follows: "reactions which may demonstrate the tendency of a chemical to be the cause of either irreversible or long-term harm to health or the environment." *See also* "EPA Concept Paper on Section 8(c)," released by EPA on July 8, 1982.

[127] Chemicals & Allied Products and Petroleum refining.

E. EPA Interpretation of Sections 8(c), 8(d), and 8(e)

In recent years, EPA has been following a stricter interpretation of section 8 reporting. Although companies continue to complain that EPA is ignoring the regulations, EPA has brought enforcement actions against many companies that violate the new interpretation of section 8(e). EPA's new approach combines all three subsections into one reporting requirement. This limits a company's ability to make health risk assessments and tends to classify cases as section 8(e) (substantial risk) even though these cases may have fallen under section 8(c) (worker and customer complaints) in the past. Through this mechanism, companies are now under the obligation to report to EPA and not simply keep records. Cases which would have previously fallen under (scientific studies) section 8(d) are also being categorized under section 8(e).

Although EPA's current interpretation may be changed, the safest course of action is to use section 8(e) and report any health and environmental suspicions to EPA even if they seem to be relatively minor.

X. Imports and Exports

Importers of chemical substances or mixtures are subject to the same regulations as manufacturers, and to TSCA section 13 as well. Exporters are subject to regulations dictated by section 12.

A. Section 13: Imports

EPA defines an importer as the individual responsible for paying duties on the imported goods or someone authorized to pay on his or her behalf.[128] When the imported goods reach the United States, the importer must file a form certifying that they are either subject to and complying with all rules and regulations under TSCA or are not subject to TSCA at all. The forms must be filled out using one of the sample statements provided. The certification may be included on the official entry form or commercial invoice, and the importer is required to keep all customs entry documentation, including the certificate, for five years.[129]

Under section 13, the Secretary of the Treasury must refuse the entry of a chemical import if any TSCA rules have not been complied with, or if the chemical is offered for entry in violation of a rule, order, or action under sections 5, 6, or 7. If any chemical import is refused entry into the United States, the Treasury Department must notify the responsible party and hold the merchandise for 90 days or until it is exported, whichever comes first.[130] The importer may submit a written explanation as to why the import should be allowed through customs. EPA must respond with a decision in 30 days. After the 90-day holding period, if the goods are not released, the Treasury Depart-

---

[128] 19 C.F.R. §101.1(1).
[129] 19 C.F.R. §162.1a(a)2, .1b, .1c.
[130] TSCA §13(a)(1)(B)(2), 15 U.S.C. §2612(a)(1)(B)(2).

ment will determine whether to dispose of or store the chemicals.[131] The importer must reimburse the United States for any charges incurred for storing, carting, or laboring on, and for disposing of the product. If the payments are delinquent a lien will be put on any future imports by that individual.[132] However, the Treasury Department may decide to release the merchandise to the importer "on execution of bond for the amount of the full invoice of such substance, mixture, or article (as such value set forth in the customs entry), together with the duty thereon,"[133] pending a review by EPA.

As with manufacturers, importers must judge if the import is on the TSCA Inventory. If it is unknown, the importer can file a bona fide intent request, and EPA will check the master inventory to determine if the chemical is on the list. If the chemical is not on the list or is a new chemical and its intended use is for "commercial purposes," section 5 PMN requirements must be complied with before the chemical is shipped to the United States. When a chemical is part of an article, it is exempt[134] if the chemical substance will not be removed from the article and will not be used for a separate "commercial purpose." Unsolicited free samples imported into the United States are also subject to TSCA provisions. Many companies, to avoid possible liabilities, return the samples to the shipper. Finally, imported hazardous and nonhazardous wastes must comply with TSCA because they are technically chemical substances. Thus, the importer is required to file a certification even if accompanied by a hazardous waste manifest as required by the Resource Conservation Recovery Act.[135]

When a chemical falls outside of TSCA jurisdiction, a negative certification must be filed or no certification at all.[136] The total exclusion from all certification requirements mandates that the chemical is imported solely for a non-TSCA purpose. Shipments containing chemicals being used for both TSCA and non-TSCA purposes must have the chemicals contained therein categorized specifically, according to use.[137] The importer must prove that the portion of the shipment under TSCA complies with section 13, and that the other part of the shipment is certified for an excluded purpose. If any import either totally or partially defined as excluded is used for a TSCA purpose, such an action could constitute a TSCA violation.[138]

B. Section 12: Exports

EPA defines an exporter as the individual who is responsible for determining and controlling shipment of a chemical out of the United States Customs territory.[139] The territory includes the 50 states, the District of Columbia, and Puerto Rico.

---

[131] TSCA §13, 15 U.S.C.A. §2612.
[132] *Id.*
[133] TSCA §13(a)(1)(B)(2), 15 U.S.C.A. §2612(6)(1)(B)(2).
[134] 40 C.F.R. §720.22(b)(1).
[135] 42 C.F.R. §6901–6992K.
[136] TSCA §13(B).
[137] TSCA §5(h).
[138] TSCA §15.
[139] 40 C.F.R. §707.65(a)(3).

Any chemical substance or mixture manufactured, processed, or distributed for the sole purpose of exportation is mostly exempt from TSCA regulations under section 12(a) and must bear a stamp or label indicating such.[140] The recordkeeping and reporting obligations under section 8 still apply to all exports. Regardless of the foreign purpose for the chemical (regulated under TSCA or not), exporters must notify EPA, in accordance with section 12(b), before exporting any chemicals if (1) test data are required under sections 4 or 5(b), (2) regulatory action has been proposed or followed under section 5 or 6, or (3) an action is pending or relief has been granted under section 5 or 7.

Under section 12(b), EPA must be notified of the first export to each country at the beginning of each year. The postmark on the notice must be the earlier of the exportation date or seven days from the forming of the "intent to export."[141] The basis for the "intent to export" a regulated chemical is either a contract or intra-organization agreement. After receiving the export notice, EPA has five days to submit to the importing country the following:

- what chemical is being exported;
- what regulatory action has been taken;
- the relevant *Federal Register* notice; and
- to whom in EPA the country should direct questions.[142]

New chemicals manufactured for the sole purpose of exportation as well as those in articles are exempt from notification requirements with a few exceptions. These exceptions include chemicals subject to the section 4 test rule; the section 5(b)(4) risk list; an order under section 5(e) or 5(f); a proposed final new order rule; or individual rules for specific articles. Finally, in order for an exporter to assert a confidentiality claim, it must be done when the notice is submitted and each page labeled as either "confidential business information," "proprietary," or "trade secret." Information labeled as such is treated respectively, but confidential information may be disclosed publicly through 40 C.F.R. §2 confidentiality claims procedures.[143]

---

[140] TSCA §12(a)(1)(B), 15 U.S.C. §2611(a)(1)(B).
[141] 40 C.F.R. §707.65(a)(1)-(3).
[142] 40 C.F.R. §707.60(a)(b).
[143] 40 C.F.R. §707.75(c). See Section VI, Confidentiality, above.

10

Pesticides

*By Paul A. J. Wilson**

> A little, wretched, despicable creature;
> a worm; a mere nothing, and less than
> nothing; a vile insect that has risen up in
> contempt against the majesty of Heaven and earth.
> —J. Edwards, *The Justice of God in the Damnation of Sinners*

I. Introduction

This chapter provides an outline of the federal regulation of pesticides, which is one of the most specialized areas of environmental law. Because of the complexity of the subject matter, this chapter is not intended to serve as a step-by-step guide to compliance with the registration and other programs administered by the Environmental Protection Agency's Office of Pesticide Programs. Rather, it provides an overview of the regulatory requirements that have been developed to implement the Federal Insecticide, Fungicide, and Rodenticide Act and will serve both as an introduction to the subject and as a general reference guide that the reader can use as a springboard for further research.

A. History of Pesticide Regulation

In the United States, pesticides were first subject to federal regulation under the Insecticide Act of 1910,[1] which set manufacturing and labeling standards for insecticides. The Act was designed chiefly to protect farmers from fraud rather than to protect public health. As a result, although products that were ineffective or mislabeled were subject to seizure, the Act neither set minimum safety standards nor required any type of pesticide registration.

Responding to the rapid increase in pesticide use that followed World War II, Congress passed the Federal Insecticide, Fungicide, and Rodenticide Act of 1947 (FIFRA).[2] Like the 1910 Insecticide Act, the 1947 Act required safety and

---

*The author would like to thank Molly E. Sullivan for her assistance in the preparation of this chapter.
[1] 36 Stat. 331 (1910).
[2] Pub. L. No. 80-104, ch. 125, 61 Stat. 163 (1947) (codified as amended at 7 U.S.C. §136 *et seq.*).

warning labels, but it also required, for the first time, federal registration of pesticides shipped in interstate commerce. Also like its predecessor, the 1947 Act had several shortcomings that made it largely ineffective. The first was its failure to permit the U.S. Department of Agriculture (USDA) to refuse to register a pesticide. The result was that every pesticide was registered regardless of its safety. The second was the statute's onerous burden of proof that effectively prevented USDA from bringing successful misbranding actions. Because of these inherent weaknesses, the Act did little to improve pesticide safety and ultimately led to the 1964 Amendments.

The 1964 FIFRA Amendments[3] permitted USDA to deny or cancel the registration of a pesticide if the pesticide or its label failed to comply with the statute and shifted the burden of proof in a misbranding action from the government to the registrant. Despite these improvements, though, little actually changed in practice. The USDA division in charge of registering pesticides rarely made use of the new tools provided by the amendments. USDA's regulatory inertia was due in large part to its conflicting roles: promotion of increased agricultural production through pesticide use on the one hand and protection of public health on the other. Consequently, by the late 1960s, frustrated by USDA inaction, numerous environmental groups sued the department for the cancellation or suspension of various pesticides in attempts to force USDA to act.[4]

The early 1970s also saw an increased awareness on the part of the American public of the many potential hazards to the environment, the regulation of which was scattered among various agencies. In response, President Nixon created the Environmental Protection Agency (EPA) in 1970 "to more effectively deal with problems in this area."[5] EPA thus became responsible for enforcement of FIFRA as well as those sections of the Federal Food, Drug, and Cosmetic Act[6] (FFDCA) that regulate pesticide residues in food.

Also reflective of the changing attitude toward the environment, Congress enacted the Federal Environmental Pesticide Control Act of 1972 (FEPCA)[7] to fill a number of the perceived shortcomings of FIFRA. That statute effectively rewrote FIFRA and serves as its framework today. Although requirements such as labeling and registration remained the heart of the statute, FEPCA reflected the growing congressional awareness of the potential threat to the environment and human health from pesticide use.[8] In fact, Congress's stated goal was to regulate "the use of pesticides to protect man and the environment. . . ."[9] This concern for human health and the environment is reflected most strongly in FEPCA's "unreasonable effects" standard under which a pesticide may be

[3] Pub. L. No. 88-305, 78 Stat. 190 (1964).

[4] *See, e.g.,* Environmental Defense Fund v. Ruckelshaus, 439 F.2d 584, 2 ER Cases 1114 (D.C. Cir. 1971); Environmental Defense Fund v. Hardin, 428 F.2d 1093, 1 ER Cases 1347 (D.C. Cir. 1970).

[5] S. Rep. No. 838, 92d Cong., 2d Sess., *reprinted in* 1972 U.S.C.C.A.N. 3993, 4001 (Reorganization Plan #3).

[6] 21 U.S.C. §§301–93 (1988).

[7] Pub. L. No. 92-516, 86 Stat. 973 (Oct. 1972).

[8] "Pesticides affect the food man eats, the water he drinks, the air he breathes and the flora and fauna that surround him. . . ." S. Rep. No. 838, 92d Cong., 2d Sess., *reprinted in* 1972 U.S.C.C.A.N. 3993, 3995.

[9] *Id.* at 3993.

registerd only if it does not cause "unreasonable adverse effects on the environment."[10]

FEPCA also required that pesticide registration applications be supported with safety and efficacy data, that manufacturers maintain detailed records of production and sales volume,[11] and that the use of a pesticide in a manner inconsistent with its labeling be prohibited.[12] Further, if EPA found pesticides sold in violation of the statute,[13] it was authorized to prohibit their sale or use and seek an order in federal district court for their seizure. Finally, the amendments also assigned EPA the task of reregistering all previously registered pesticides under new, more stringent registration standards in an effort to assure the safety of pesticides registered under older versions of the statute. Although FIFRA has subsequently been amended on a number of occasions, the changes instituted by FEPCA remain the core of the present system of pesticide regulations.[14]

B. Pesticide Regulation Today

Pesticides are currently subject to regulation under nearly a dozen diverse federal statutes,[15] the most important of which are FIFRA and FFDCA. Under those two laws, the regulation of pesticides can be divided into three broad areas: licensing (registration), provisions governing pesticide usage, and standards for pesticide residues in or on agricultural commodities, processed food, and animal feeds.

The heart of the regulatory scheme remains the registration program under which all new pesticides must be registered and all old pesticides reregistered with EPA. The registration program has several noteworthy aspects, including placement of the expense of generating data adequate to register a pesticide on the registrant rather than the government and the requirement that EPA employ a cost-benefit analysis in its registration decision. FIFRA also regulates pesticide usage through mechanisms such as use classifications and applicator certification that control access to certain more hazardous pesticides. The third mechanism by which pesticides are regulated is through the establishment of tolerances for pesticide residues on raw and processed agricultural commodities. To one degree or another, each of these three areas of regulation requires EPA to balance the costs and benefits derived from pesticide use. Under FIFRA

---

[10] *See, e.g.*, FIFRA §3(c)(5)(C) and (D), 7 U.S.C. §136a(c)(5)(C) and (D), Pub. L. No. 92-516, 86 Stat. 973 (Oct. 1972).

[11] S. Rep. No. 838, 92d Cong., 2d Sess., *reprinted in* 1972 U.S.C.C.A.N. 3993, 3994.

[12] *Id.* at 3993.

[13] A pesticide could violate the Act, for example, by being misbranded (bearing a false or misleading label), adulterated (strength or purity of pesticide is not in accordance with its label), or unregistered. Pub. L. No. 92-516, 76 Stat. 973 (Oct. 1972).

[14] Although FEPCA is actually the primary piece of pesticide legislation, the entire statute is still referred to as FIFRA.

[15] *E.g.*, Toxic Substances Control Act, 15 U.S.C. §§2601–29 (regulates pesticide ingredients); Occupational Safety and Health Act, 29 U.S.C. §§651–78 (regulates pesticides in the workplace); Hazardous Materials Transportation Act, 49 U.S.C. §§1801–12 (regulates transportation of pesticides); Federal Water Pollution Control Act, 33 U.S.C. §§1251–1387 (regulates pesticides in water); Poison Prevention Packaging Act, 15 U.S.C. §§1471–76 (regulates pesticide packaging).

today, it is intended that "any adverse effect ought not to be tolerated unless there are overriding benefits from the use of a pesticide."[16]

II. Registration

A. Data

Unless exempted, every pesticide sold or distributed in any state must be registered by EPA.[17] The term pesticide includes any substance that is used to destroy, repel, mitigate, or prevent any pest or a material used as a plant regulator, defoliant, or desiccant.[18] A pest is defined as "any insect, nematode, fungus, weed or any other form of terrestrial or aquatic plant and animal life or virus, bacteria, or other microorganism (except viruses, bacteria or other microorganisms on or in living men or other living animals) which the Administrator declares to be a pest."[19] The definition of pesticide does not include new animal drugs or animal feeds containing new animal drugs that serve pesticidal functions. Regulation of these substances is left to FDA under FFDCA.

Pesticides are defined by the Act so that a product's classification as a pesticide depends on its intended use, i.e., whether it has a pesticidal effect. EPA has established a three-part test to determine whether a product is a pesticide in which it considers both the seller's claims and the product's objective pesticidal properties.[20] EPA regulations also exclude from the definition of pesticides certain products with pesticide-like functions. These products include (1) those not used against pests, such as a product intended to control fungi, bacteria, or viruses in or on living humans or animals or products intended to control internal parasites in living humans or animals;[21] and (2) those products not used for a pesticidal effect, such as products that only present physical barriers against pest access and contain no toxicants.[22] Such products do not require registration.

EPA is not required to grant all applications for registration of a pesticide and may only register those that do not present an "unreasonable risk of adverse effects to the environment."[23] The burden and expense of generating information to meet this test is on the applicant, who must provide EPA with data on the pesticide's chemical and toxicological properties, residues remaining after application, performance, effect on the environment, and other information, including (1) the applicant's name and address; (2) the product name, complete chemical formula, and proposed label, including directions for use of the pesticide; (3) the proposed classification for general or restricted use; and (4) a

---

[16] S. Rep. No. 970, 92d Cong., 2d Sess., *reprinted in* 1972 U.S.C.C.A.N. 3993, 4095.

[17] FIFRA §3(a), 7 U.S.C. §136a(a). Prior to 1972, FIFRA only regulated pesticides placed in interstate commerce. However, in 1972 FIFRA was amended to "extend Federal pesticide regulation to actions entirely within a single state." S. Rep. No. 838, 92d Cong., 2d Sess., *reprinted in* 1972 U.S.C.C.A.N. at 3993.

[18] FIFRA §2(u), 7 U.S.C. §136u. *See also* 40 C.F.R. §152.15.

[19] FIFRA §2(t), 7 U.S.C. §136t. *See also* 40 C.F.R. §152.5.

[20] 40 C.F.R. §152.15.

[21] 40 C.F.R. §152.8.

[22] 40 C.F.R. §152.10.

[23] FIFRA §3(c)(5)(C), 7 U.S.C. §136a(c)(5)(C). *See also* 7 U.S.C. §136(bb).

full description of the tests performed with the pesticide and the results thereof or a reference to previously submitted data.[24]

An applicant either may submit data it has generated, or it may cite public data or data previously submitted to the EPA by another applicant for registration. Citation to data generated by others is commonly referred to as "me-too" registration. If an applicant cites data owned by another and previously submitted to EPA in support of an application, the citing registrant must offer to pay the data owner for such use.[25] EPA will not accept a reference to the data, i.e., will not consider it in support of the me-too application, unless the owner of the data has given permission to the subsequent applicant to use the data. If the parties are unable to agree on the amount of compensation required, the dispute is settled by binding arbitration.[26]

This portion of FIFRA is the result of a compromise between large manufacturers who wished to protect their often substantial investments and smaller ones who frequently lacked the funds necessary to generate the required data. It has also been the subject of litigation to determine the constitutionality and scope of the required compensation.[27] One particular sticking point was the retroactivity of the compensation provisions. When it was enacted in 1972, this provision was at odds with EPA's then-current practice of referring to data already in its files without compensating the data owner. The 1972 Amendments were unclear on such issues as whether data submitted prior to 1972 could be retroactively designated a trade secret, and whether a data owner was entitled to compensation if such previously submitted data were used by another in support of an application. In an effort to resolve these questions, Congress amended the provisions in 1975.[28] Yet uncertainty remained following the 1975 Amendments when, in *Mobay Chemical Corp. v. Costle,*[29] the Supreme Court found that Congress had neither endorsed nor denied EPA's uncompensated use of pre-1970 data. The Act was finally amended in 1978 to prohibit uncompensated use of data submitted after January 1, 1970, and to permit use of data submitted before that date without compensation.[30]

Persons who submit data in support of the registration of a pesticide that contains "new" active ingredients (ingredients first registered after September 30, 1978) are entitled to "exclusive use" of that data for 10 years.[31] Although an owner may choose to sell such data, during this period it may neither be forced to permit the data to be used by another nor to accept use compensation.

An applicant for registration may seek protection for data that it contends contains trade secrets or confidential commercial or financial information by

---

[24] FIFRA §3(c)(1), 7 U.S.C. §136a(c)(1). Note that this last requirement, submission of test result data, must be satisfied for each use for which the pesticide is to be registered. *See also* 40 C.F.R. pt. 158.

[25] FIFRA §3(c)(1)(D)(ii), 7 U.S.C. §136a(c)(1)(D)(ii).

[26] *Id.*

[27] *See* Thomas v. Union Carbide Agric. Prods. Co., 473 U.S. 568, 22 ER Cases 2033 (1985).

[28] Pub. L. No. 94-140, 89 Stat. 751.

[29] 447 F. Supp. 811, 12 ER Cases 1228 (W.D. Mo. 1978), *appeal dismissed per curiam,* 439 U.S. 320, 12 ER Cases 1581 (1979).

[30] *See* Chevron Chem. Co. v. Costle, 641 F.2d 104, 16 ER Cases 2004 (3d Cir. 1981), a case in which the court found that submitters of data have no property interest in the data submitted to a federal agency. *See also* Amchem Prods., Inc. v. GAF Corp., 594 F.2d 470 (5th Cir. 1979).

[31] FIFRA §3(c)(1)(D)(i), 7 U.S.C. §136a(c)(1)(D)(i).

clearly marking it or submitting it under separate cover.[32] EPA will not release that information unless disclosure is required to carry out the statute, in which case it may be released to a federal agency or at a public hearing. Before EPA can release such data, however, it must provide the applicant with 30-days notice. During that period, the applicant may seek a declaratory judgment in district court that the information may not be released.[33]

The types of data EPA considers "trade secrets" are few. Under the 1972 version of FIFRA, the task of defining what information could be claimed to be a trade secret was left to EPA. Although EPA's initial narrow definition of trade secrets was successfully challenged,[34] Congress amended the statute in 1978 to comport with EPA's definition. Consequently, the data considered to be trade secrets remain relatively narrow. For example, manufacturing and quality control processes, as well as detection methods for inert ingredients, may be subject to protection. Conversely, "all information concerning the objectives, methodology, results, or significance of any test or experiment performed on or with a registered or previously registered pesticide," its ingredients, and information regarding its effect on any organism may all be made available to the public.[35]

B. The Registration Decision

Pesticides may be exempt from registration under certain conditions. Pesticides that are (1) adequately regulated by another federal agency;[36] (2) of a character not requiring FIFRA regulation;[37] (3) merely transferred from one production location to another;[38] or (4) covered by an experimental use permit may not need to be registered.[39] Pesticides adequately registered by another federal agency include most biological control agents and certain human drugs, as described in 40 C.F.R. §152.20. Certain pesticides, such as treated articles or substances, pheromones and pheromone traps, preservatives for biological specimens, vitamin hormone products, and foods have been found to be of a character not requiring FIFRA regulation.[40]

If a potential registrant does not have adequate data to support its registration, it may obtain an experimental use permit (EUP) authorizing the temporary use of a pesticide in order to generate the data necessary to support its registration.[41] An EUP application requires information like that required for registration[42] plus additional information regarding the testing methods and procedures

---

[32] FIFRA §10, 7 U.S.C. §136h.

[33] FIFRA §10(c), 7 U.S.C. §136h(c).

[34] Mobay Chem. Corp. v. Costle, 447 F. Supp. 811, 12 ER Cases 1228 (W.D. Mo. 1978), *appeal dismissed per curiam,* 439 U.S. 320, 12 ER Cases 1581 (1979); Chevron Chem. Co. v. Costle, 443 F. Supp. 1024 (N.D. Cal. 1978); Dow Chem. Co. v. Costle, No. 76-10087 (E.D. Mich. Nov. 16, 1977).

[35] FIFRA §10(d), 7 U.S.C. §136h(d).

[36] FIFRA §25(b), 7 U.S.C. §136w(b).

[37] *Id.*

[38] FIFRA §3(b)(1), 7 U.S.C. §136a(b)(1).

[39] FIFRA §3(b)(2), 7 U.S.C. §136a(b)(2).

[40] 40 C.F.R. §152.25.

[41] FIFRA §5(a), 7 U.S.C. §136c(a).

[42] *See* 40 C.F.R. §172.4.

to be employed.[43] An EUP may be issued for up to three years. Small scale experiments not intended for actual pest control may not require an EUP. For example, if a land-use pesticide is tested on not more than 10 acres, and anything subsequently grown on the land is destroyed, no EUP is needed.[44]

EPA may register a pesticide if it determines that (1) the pesticide's composition warrants its proposed claims, (2) the proposed label and other submitted data comply with the statute, and (3) the pesticide presents no "unreasonable adverse effects" on the environment when used according to "widespread and commonly recognized" practice.[45] A registration will remain in effect for five years, at which time it will automatically expire unless the registrant seeks reregistration.

If EPA determines that the pesticide or its use does not meet any of these registration requirements, it must notify the applicant and state its reason for the proposed denial of registration. Unless the applicant corrects the defect(s) within 30 days and notifies the Agency, EPA may deny the application[46] and publish notice thereof in the *Federal Register*. The unsuccessful applicant or some other interested party having the permission of the applicant has 30 days in which to request an administrative hearing on the denial.[47]

A key aspect of EPA's decision to register a pesticide is the balancing of the risks and benefits presented by a particular substance. Although most pesticides are, after all, poisons and thus potentially dangerous, the benefits they provide may outweigh the dangers they present. As a result, EPA must determine that a pesticide does not cause "unreasonable adverse effects on the environment" prior to its registration.[48] Such effects are those that present an "unreasonable risk to man or the environment, taking into account the economic, social and environmental costs and benefits of the use of any pesticide."[49] EPA must, therefore, engage in a process of risk assessment, which involves a systematic effort to quantify the risks posed by such combined factors as a pesticide's toxicity and potential exposure, in its registration, cancellation, and suspension decisions. The Agency will also consider whether the risks posed by a pesticide can be mitigated, for example by restricting its use or by requiring warning statements in its labeling.

EPA's approach to risk assessment has been evolving, particularly with regard to carcinogens. Prior to 1972, FIFRA did not contain the "unreasonable adverse effects" standard. Consequently, when a pesticide such as DDT was found to be carcinogenic in animals and the available data could not disprove its possible human carcinogenic effect, its registration was cancelled without any assessment of risks and benefits.[50]

Over time EPA began to incorporate risk assessment procedures in its regulatory decision making. One example of this was EPA's ill-fated attempt to

---

[43] *Id.*

[44] 40 C.F.R. §172.3. For a discussion of EUPs, biotechnology, and proposed changes to 40 C.F.R. pt. 172 see Section V, below.

[45] FIFRA §3(c)(5), 7 U.S.C. §136a(c)(5).

[46] FIFRA §3(c)(6), 7 U.S.C. §136a(c)(6).

[47] *Id. See also* 40 C.F.R. pt. 164.

[48] FIFRA §3(c)(5)(C), 7 U.S.C. §136a(c)(5)(C).

[49] FIFRA §2(bb), 7 U.S.C. §136(bb).

[50] 37 Fed. Reg. 13,369 (1972).

mitigate the absolute language of the Delaney Clause—that section of the FFDCA that prohibits residues of any carcinogenic food additive.[51] The identification and elimination of any potential cancer hazard, as required by the plain language of the Delaney Clause, does not consider risk assessment or efforts to mitigate risks. Consequently, EPA developed a de minimis approach to the Delaney Clause, which allowed it to establish a tolerance for a carcinogenic pesticide where the "human dietary risk from residues of the pesticide is at most negligible."[52] An assessment of the carcinogenic risk of a pesticide is an inherent component of such standard. While its application in the Delaney Clause context has been rejected by the courts, this general approach to the regulation of carcinogens is an example of EPA's current policy on risk assessment. A similar transformation has occurred, for example, in determining the ecological risks of a pesticide.[53]

Registrants and applicants must provide EPA with information used to make risk-benefit calculations.[54] Thus, a registrant who obtains additional information regarding unreasonable adverse effects of a pesticide it has registered must then report the relevant information[55] to EPA within 15 working days[56] by certified mail.[57] EPA has promulgated detailed reporting rules that apply to information obtained from completed toxicological studies,[58] incomplete toxicological studies,[59] epidemiological studies,[60] and efficacy studies.[61] Failure to comply with these regulations may result in civil and/or criminal penalties.[62]

In some cases, even if there are inadequate data to allow it to make a final registration determination, EPA may grant conditional registration. The circumstances under which EPA may take this action are as follows: (1) the pesticide is identical or nearly identical to a currently registered pesticide and use; (2) the registration is sought for an additional use of a registered pesticide; or (3) the pesticide contains an active ingredient not contained in any currently registered pesticide and time is needed to generate the data necessary for registration.[63]

EPA recently adopted a more active role in encouraging the use of reduced-risk pesticides.[64] In the short term, EPA will attempt to reach this goal by permitting an applicant to request that its new product be considered a reduced-risk pesticide and provide information to support that claim in its

---

[51] 21 U.S.C. §348(c)(3).

[52] 53 Fed. Reg. 41,104 (1988). *See* Les v. Reilly, 968 F.2d 985 (9th Cir. 1992), *cert. denied sub nom.* National Agric. Chem. Ass'n. v. Les, 113 S. Ct. 1361 (1993), discussed in connection with the role of the Delaney Clause in setting residue tolerances at Section IV.B, below.

[53] *See* ENVIRONMENTAL PROTECTION AGENCY HAZARD EVALUATION DIVISION, STANDARD EVALUATION PROCEDURE, ECOLOGICAL RISK ASSESSMENT, EPA-540/9-85-0001 (June 1986); ENVIRONMENTAL PROTECTION AGENCY, SUMMARY REPORT ON ISSUES IN ECOLOGICAL RISK ASSESSMENT, EPA-625/3-91/018 (Feb. 1991).

[54] 7 U.S.C. §136d(a)(2). *See also* 40 C.F.R. pt. 153.

[55] 40 C.F.R. §153.66. Information is relevant if it would, by itself or in conjunction with other information, assist EPA in determining the pesticide's risks and benefits or the terms of its registration. *Id.*

[56] 40 C.F.R. §153.64.

[57] 40 C.F.R. §153.65.

[58] 40 C.F.R. §153.69.

[59] 40 C.F.R. §153.70.

[60] 40 C.F.R. §153.71.

[61] 40 C.F.R. §153.72.

[62] 40 C.F.R. §153.67.

[63] FIFRA §3(c)(7), 7 U.S.C. §136a(c)(7).

[64] 58 Fed. Reg. 5854 (1993).

registration materials. Reduced-risk pesticides will be entitled to special priority in the registration process. EPA's long-term approach to this goal includes the development of a more comprehensive reduced-risk policy. Elements of that policy will include determining the criteria that qualify pesticides as reduced-risk, streamlining registration for all pesticides, revising pesticide labeling to encourage the use of reduced-risk pesticides, and extending the exclusive use period for reduced-risk pesticides.[65]

C. State Regulation of Pesticides

States may also regulate the sale and use of pesticides, so long as state regulations do not permit the sale or use of any pesticide that is prohibited by FIFRA.[66] States may not impose labeling or packaging requirements that conflict with the federal statute, which prevents manufacturers from having to produce different labels for different states.[67] Finally, states may register a pesticide for additional uses beyond those for which it is federally registered in order to "meet special local needs," so long as that use has not been previously "denied, disapproved or cancelled by the Administrator" and, if needed, a tolerance has been established for that use under the FFDCA.[68]

The issue of federal preemption of state and local pesticide regulation has been one of the most litigated issues under FIFRA in recent years.[69] In *Wisconsin Public Intervenor v. Mortier,*[70] the Supreme Court determined that Congress did not intend FIFRA to preempt state and local regulation of pesticides. Instead, the Court found that "the more plausible reading of FIFRA's authorization to the States leaves the allocation of regulatory authority to the 'absolute discretion' of the States themselves, including the option of leaving local regulation of pesticides in the hands of local authorities."[71] The Court also found, based on the plain language of the statute, which mentions state regulation,[72] and the resulting regulatory framework, which leaves "ample room for States and localities to supplement federal efforts,"[73] that FIFRA did not sufficiently occupy the field so as to impliedly preempt state regulation. Therefore, currently, state and local regulation of pesticides is permissible so long as the regulations do not permit the sale or use of a pesticide prohibited under the federal law, or directly conflict with the federal law.

---

[65] *Id.* at 5854–55.

[66] FIFRA §24(a), 7 U.S.C. §136v(a).

[67] FIFRA §24(b), 7 U.S.C. §136v(b).

[68] FIFRA §24(c)(1), (3), 7 U.S.C. §136v(c)(1), (3).

[69] *See* Worm v. American Cyanamid Co., 970 F.2d 1301 (4th Cir. 1992); Hurt v. Dow Chem. Co., 963 F.2d 1142 (8th Cir. 1992); Chemical Specialties Mfrs. Ass'n v. Allenby, 958 F.2d 941, 34 ER Cases 2000 (9th Cir. 1992); Arkansas-Platte & Gulf Partnership v. Van Waters & Rogers, Inc., 959 F.2d 158, 34 ER Cases 1807 (10th Cir. 1992); Coparr, Ltd. v. City of Boulder, 942 F.2d 724, 33 ER Cases 1551 (10th Cir. 1992); Professional Lawn Care Ass'n v. Village of Milford, 909 F.2d 929, 31 ER Cases 1825 (6th Cir. 1990).

[70] 111 S. Ct. 2476, 33 ER Cases 1265 (1991).

[71] *Id.* at 2483.

[72] 7 U.S.C. §136v(b) states that "[s]uch [s]tates shall not impose or continue in effect any requirements for labeling and packaging in addition to or different from those required" by FIFRA.

[73] 111 S. Ct. at 2486.

D. Classification of Pesticides

When a pesticide is registered, it is classified for general use, restricted use, or in some cases, depending upon the specific use, for both. The applicant specifies which type of registration is sought in its application for registration, but EPA makes the final decision. Pesticides that do not cause unreasonable adverse effects on the environment when used according to practice and directions, including any warnings, may be classified for general use. These are commonly the "safer" products that are sold for general, common use. By contrast, a pesticide that, even when used in accordance with its directions, warnings, and cautions, may nonetheless present the potential for unreasonable harmful effects on human health or the environment, may be registered for restricted use only. The restricted use classification keeps the material out of the public's hands, imposes certain label and advertising restrictions, and requires that the pesticide be used by or under the direct supervision of a "certified applicator," a person having demonstrated some degree of specialized knowledge concerning pesticides.[74]

A pesticide's registration also may be changed from one classification to another. If EPA proposes to change the classification from general to restricted use, it must publish notice of its intent to do so and provide an opportunity for a hearing on the proposed change.[75] A registrant may ask EPA to change a pesticide's classification from restricted to general use by submitting a petition that states the basis for the change in classification. EPA must respond to such a petition within 60 days of its filing, either granting it or stating its grounds for denial. A denial is judicially reviewable.[76]

E. Reregistration

EPA is also charged with reregistering pesticides containing ingredients first registered before November 1, 1984.[77] Because many older pesticides were registered under the less demanding safety criteria of previous versions of FIFRA, this requirement is intended to ensure that all existing pesticides meet contemporary safety requirements. Although initial timetables proved unrealistic, reregistration is now on a rigorous schedule, taking place in five phases over a nine-year period.[78] Registrants are required to develop data to support reregistration comparable to that required if they were registering a new pesticide. Additionally, registrants now support the program through a one-time reregistration fee totalling $150,000, and annual maintenance fees.[79]

To secure reregistration, a registrant must show that "[t]he pesticide's data base is substantially complete . . . and . . . [t]he pesticide does not cause unreasonable adverse effects to people or the environment when it is used

[74] For a discussion of the regulation of certified applicators see Section III.A, below.

[75] FIFRA §§3(d)(2), 6(b), 7 U.S.C. §§135a(d)(2), 136d(b).

[76] FIFRA §3(d)(3), 7 U.S.C. §136a(d)(3).

[77] FIFRA §4(a), 7 U.S.C. §136a-1(a).

[78] New deadlines were imposed in the 1988 Amendments to FIFRA. *See* 7 U.S.C. §136a-1. *See* Environmental Protection Agency, Pesticide Reregistration, EPA-700-K92-004 (Pesticide Reregistration) (May 1992), for a description of the phases of reregistration.

[79] 7 U.S.C. §136a-1(i). *See also* Pesticide Registration, *supra* note 78, at 11.

according to the product label directions and restrictions.''[80] If a registration is found to have ''data gaps,'' i.e., to lack data considered essential by EPA, EPA may notify the registrant of its need for specific additional information. Upon such notification, the registrant is required to provide the missing data through independent studies or through the use of another's data, if they exist.

The large reregistration fees and potentially substantial data requirements pose a dilemma for registrants of minor-use pesticides, whose economic return often fails to cover reregistration costs. Consequently, minor usages are often dropped from labels, or registrants voluntarily cancel their entire registrations of minor-use products. To respond to this situation, there are several special programs designed to alleviate the burdens of minor-use registration, including data waivers, fee waivers or reductions, and third-party registrations.[81]

F. Fees

In 1988, FIFRA was amended to increase registration fees in order to fund the reregistration program.[82] The fees consist of an initial fee of $50,000,[83] a final fee of $100,000 to $150,000,[84] and annual maintenance fees of $425 per registration if a registrant has under 50 registrations.[85] For registrants with more than 50 registrations, the fee is $100 per registration for the next 150 registrations.[86] There is no additional fee if a registrant has over 200 registrations, and no annual fee is to exceed $20,000 per company.[87] Finally, EPA may waive or reduce the required fees for minor-use pesticides or fees imposed on small businesses.[88] During the reregistration period (October 25, 1988, to September 30, 1997) EPA ''may not levy any other fees for the registration of a pesticide under this subchapter. . . .''[89]

G. Cancellation and Suspension of Registration

EPA may terminate the registration of a pesticide through the mechanisms of cancellation or suspension. Despite the ordinary usage of these two words that suggests the converse, cancellation may be initiated on a lesser showing than suspension and does not prevent sale or use of a pesticide during the pendency of a cancellation proceeding. A suspension order, by contrast, is based on an EPA showing of ''imminent harm'' and imposes an immediate ban on the sale or use of the subject pesticide.

---

[80] PESTICIDE REREGISTRATION, *supra* note 78, at 6.
[81] *Id.* at 13.
[82] FIFRA §4(i), 7 U.S.C. §136a-1(i).
[83] FIFRA §4(i)(1), 7 U.S.C. §136a-1(i)(1).
[84] FIFRA §4(i)(2), 7 U.S.C. §136a-1(i)(2).
[85] FIFRA §4(i)(5)(A)(i), 7 U.S.C. §136a-1(i)(5)(A)(i).
[86] FIFRA §4(i)(5)(A)(ii), 7 U.S.C. §136a-1(i)(5)(A)(ii).
[87] FIFRA §4(i)(5)(C), 7 U.S.C. §136a-1(i)(5)(C).
[88] FIFRA §4(i)(4)(A)-(C), 7 U.S.C. §136a-1(i)(4)(A)-(C).
[89] FIFRA §4(i)(6), 7 U.S.C. §136a-1(i)(6).

1. Cancellation

EPA may cancel the registration of a pesticide should it fail to comply with the statute or cause unreasonable adverse effects on the environment.[90] As with other sections of FIFRA, the cancellation provisions require EPA to assess the risks and benefits of a pesticide before issuing a notice of intent to cancel it.[91] In deciding to initiate cancellation proceedings, EPA must consider the effect of cancellation on "production and prices of agricultural commodities, retail food prices, and otherwise on the agricultural economy"[92] and must consult with the Secretary of Agriculture. This balancing process is facilitated by the use of the "special review" process, which is an administrative mechanism for evaluating the pesticide's safety and fitness for continued registration.

"The purpose of the [s]pecial [r]eview process is to help the Agency determine whether to initiate procedures to cancel, deny, or reclassify registration of a pesticide product because uses of that product may cause unreasonable adverse effects on the environment. . . ."[93] The special review process may be initiated if EPA finds that a pesticide poses a risk of (1) serious acute injury to humans or domestic animals; (2) oncogenic, heritable genetic, teratogenic, fetotoxic, or reproductive effects of concern; (3) toxic residues in nontarget organisms; (4) a threat to the existence or habitat of an endangered species; or (5) a risk of sufficient magnitude to humans to offset any benefits gained by its continued use.[94] In determining whether to initiate special review, which EPA may do *sua sponte,* only risks, not benefits, are examined, and the burden of persuasion that a pesticide should continue to be registered is with the registrant.[95]

The special review proceedings are begun with private notification of the registrants, followed by public notice and request for comment.[96] Notice of special review proceedings alerts a registrant that EPA intends to initiate proceedings to cancel, suspend, or change the classification of a pesticide following the special review unless convinced otherwise.[97] The public comment period, which may include informal public hearings, is followed by notices of preliminary and final decisions that may initiate cancellation proceedings or impose a less drastic measure, such as different labeling requirements.

The special review process has been heavily criticized, in particular on account of its length, lack of openness, and alleged politicization.[98] In the early

---

[90] FIFRA §6(b), 7 U.S.C. §136d(b).

[91] One court has held that the standard under which registration may be denied (if a pesticide "generally" poses unreasonable adverse effects) requires a finding by EPA of considerable frequency of adverse effects. Ciba-Geigy Corp. v. EPA, 874 F.2d 277, 29 ER Cases 1721 (5th Cir. 1989).

[92] 7 U.S.C. §136d(b).

[93] 40 C.F.R. §154.1.

[94] 40 C.F.R. §154.7.

[95] 40 C.F.R. §154.5, .10.

[96] 40 C.F.R. pt. 154, subpart B.

[97] The issuance of this notice by EPA is not reviewable because it lacks finality. "[I]t merely sets in motion the administrative process that terminates in a reviewable final order." Environmental Defense Fund v. Ruckelshaus, 439 F.2d 584, 2 ER Cases 1114 (D.C. Cir. 1971). *See also* Dow Chem. Co. v. Ruckelshaus, 477 F.2d 1317, 5 ER Cases 1244 (8th Cir. 1973).

[98] *See* M. Lolley, *Carcinogen Roulette: The Game Played Under FIFRA,* 49 MD. L. REV. 975 (1990); J. Gasior, *Pesticide Safety Regulation under the Federal Insecticide, Fungicide and Rodenticide Act: Debacle at the EPA,* FORDHAM ENVTL. L. REP. 47 (1989).

1980s, special reviews often took the form of closed door meetings, but litigation challenging this practice[99] led to regulatory reforms to ensure more openness in the proceedings.[100]

Following special review, if EPA determines that cancellation is warranted, cancellation proceedings are initiated via notice of cancellation or intent to hold a hearing on the matter.[101] Within 30 days, those adversely affected may file a request for a hearing on the matter, which must include a party's objections to the proposed cancellation as well as the factual basis for those objections. Persons adversely affected may be user groups as well as registrants,[102] although users' rights may not be as extensive as those of registrants.[103]

EPA may deny a hearing request, a decision which is reviewable in federal court, although it is unclear whether original jurisdiction lies with the district or the appellate court.[104] If a hearing is granted, the case is heard before an EPA Administrative Law Judge (ALJ). Although EPA has the burden of going forward, the burden of persuasion ultimately rests with the registrants.[105]

Following briefing and argument, the ALJ renders a decision, which is included in the record from which the Administrator makes a final decision.[106] The Administrator's final decision is reviewable in a court of appeals if appealed within 60 days,[107] although history shows reversal is unlikely.[108]

2. *Suspension*

Suspension of registration is an immediate ban on the sale and use of a pesticide. EPA may initiate suspension of a pesticide at any time if it determines that the pesticide presents an "imminent hazard" to people or the environment.[109] Suspension may also be used if the risk underlying the imminent hazard decision may materialize during the pendency of cancellation proceedings. In this context, "imminent" is not equated with "immediate."[110] A harm is "imminent" if there is a "substantial likelihood that serious harm will be experienced during the year or two required in any realistic projection of the administrative process."[111] If EPA has not already initiated cancellation pro-

---

[99] NRDC v. EPA, No. 83-1509, *settlement approved* (D.D.C. Oct. 14, 1984).

[100] *See* 40 C.F.R. pt. 154.

[101] FIFRA §6(b), 7 U.S.C. §136d(b).

[102] *See* Environmental Defense Fund v. Costle, 631 F.2d 922, 15 ER Cases 1217 (D.C. Cir. 1980).

[103] *Id. See also* McGill v. EPA, 593 F.2d 631, 13 ER Cases 1156 (5th Cir. 1979).

[104] *Compare* Environmental Defense Fund v. Costle, 631 F.2d 922, 15 ER Cases 1217 (D.C. Cir. 1980) (original jurisdiction lies with appellate court) *and* Amvac Chem. Corp. v. EPA, 653 F.2d 1260, 15 ER Cases 1467 (9th Cir. 1980) (original jurisdiction lies with district court).

[105] Environmental Defense Fund, Inc. v. EPA, 548 F.2d 998, 9 ER Cases 1433 (D.C. Cir. 1976), *cert. denied,* 431 U.S. 925 (1977).

[106] *See* Environmental Defense Fund v. EPA, 489 F.2d 1247, 6 ER Cases 1112 (D.C. Cir. 1973).

[107] FIFRA §§6(h), 16, 7 U.S.C. §§136d(h), 136n.

[108] *See* Dow Chem. Co. v. Blum, 469 F. Supp. 892, 13 ER Cases 1129 (E.D. Mich. 1979).

[109] FIFRA §6(c)(1), 7 U.S.C. §136d(c)(1). *See* Environmental Defense Fund v. EPA, 548 F.2d 998, 9 ER Cases 1433 (D.C. Cir. 1976), *cert. denied,* 431 U.S. 925, 9 ER Cases 1575 (1977).

[110] *See* Environmental Defense Fund v. Ruckelshaus, 439 F.2d 584, 2 ER Cases 1114 (D.C. Cir. 1971) (court approved EPA findings that even a hazard whose effects might not be felt for years could be found to be "imminent").

[111] Environmental Defense Fund v. EPA, 465 F.2d 528, 540, 4 ER Cases 1523 (D.C. Cir. 1972).

ceedings for the pesticide at issue, it may do so simultaneously with the suspension proceedings.

There are two types of suspension, regular and emergency. The difference between the two lies largely in the notification requirements and hearing priority of each. A registrant is given advance notice of EPA's intent to begin regular suspension proceedings and has five days during which to request an expedited hearing.[112] If no hearing is requested during this time, EPA may issue an unreviewable suspension order.[113] If a hearing is requested, issuance of the suspension order is postponed during the pendency of the hearing, which is to be held within five days of the date of the request.

If EPA determines that an emergency exists, it may issue the suspension order before notifying the registrant.[114] In such a case, however, a hearing must be held within five days of issuance of the order if requested by the registrant. To date, however, this more drastic measure has only been used on three occasions, for the chemicals 2,4,5-T/Silvex, EDB, and dinoseb.[115] Dinoseb's registration was suspended after preliminary studies revealed possible serious health risks including birth defects and male sterility.[116] Similarly, 2,4,5-T and Silvex's registrations were suspended when studies showed fetotoxic and teratogenic effects from the pesticides as well as a correlation between exposure to the pesticides and spontaneous human abortions.[117]

3. *Indemnification of Registrants Upon Cancellation/Suspension*

In the event of a suspension or cancellation, registrants and end users who owned a quantity of the pesticide before the cancellation or suspension notice was issued, and who suffered losses as a result, may be entitled to reimbursement from EPA.[118] A 1988 amendment to FIFRA prohibits the making of indemnification payments without an advance line item appropriation for such payment.[119] This amendment was added after indemnification payments threatened to completely erode EPA's budget.[120] Further, EPA may exempt quantities of stocks in the user's possession on the date of the notice of cancellation or suspension from a suspension or cancellation order, and may provide a reasonable time for use or disposal of existing stocks of a pesticide in a final order of

[112] FIFRA §6(c)(1), (2), 7 U.S.C. §136d(c)(1), (2).

[113] *Id.*

[114] 7 U.S.C. §136d(c)(3). *See also* 40 C.F.R. pt. 164; Dow Chem. Co. v. Blum, 469 F. Supp. 892, 13 ER Cases 1129 (E.D. Mich. 1979).

[115] P. Finegan, FIFRA LITE: A REGULATORY SOLUTION OR PART OF THE PESTICIDE PROBLEM, 6 PACE ENVTL. L. REV. 615 (1989). One author has found EPA's infrequent invocation of suspension procedures to be the result of a FIFRA comprised of "overly broad and imprecise standards that can be manipulated by political ideologies and that shift with the tide of public sentiment. The result is inconsistent and inefficient pesticide regulation that leaves the public confused and uncertain about the health risks to which they may be exposed . . . and a suspicious regulatory system that sets no definite threshold on health risks imposed on the public." M. Lolley, *supra* note 98, at 990.

[116] Love v. Thomas, 858 F.2d 1347, 1350 (9th Cir. 1988).

[117] Dow Chem. Co. v. Blum, 469 F. Supp. 892, 13 ER Cases 1129 (E.D. Mich. 1979).

[118] FIFRA §15, 7 U.S.C. §136m.

[119] FIFRA §15(a)(4), 7 U.S.C. §136m(a)(4).

[120] Indemnification payments resulting from the cancellation of dinoseb, EDB, and 2,4,5-T/Silvex will cost the EPA over $100 million. H.R. REP. NO. 939, 100th Cong., 2d Sess., pt. 1, 78 (1988).

suspension. The value of the quantity used or disposed of during this time may be deducted from any subsequent indemnification.[121]

Dealers and distributors who, as a result of suspension or cancellation, cannot resell a pesticide, may seek reimbursement from the seller of the pesticide, unless at the time of sale the seller notified the purchaser that no reimbursement would be provided.[122]

H. Labeling and Packaging Requirements

As an essential element of FIFRA's risk management strategy,[123] all applications for registration must contain the proposed pesticide label, which must be approved as a condition of registration.[124] If the risk posed by a pesticide can be reduced by labeling containing explicit warnings and instructions, the labeling may make an otherwise unacceptable risk a reasonable one. The term "labeling" includes not only the label fastened to the container, but all accompanying written material.[125] EPA requires that labels include the name, brand, or trademark under which the product is sold, the name and address of the producer or registrant, the net contents, its EPA registration number, its producing establishment identification number, product ingredients, use classification warnings, precautions, including first aid treatment for exposure, and use directions.[126] Regulations require legibility and clarity and prescribe the smallest type face allowable for labels.[127]

Regulations proposed in 1984 but never promulgated would have extensively altered the current labeling requirements. The proposed changes included requiring use of a label with standardized placement of required label elements as well as changes to improve visibility and readability.[128]

As a corollary to the labeling requirements, to be eligible for registration pesticide containers and packages must generally meet the standards prescribed by the Poison Prevention Packaging Act[129] "in order to protect children and adults from serious injury or illness."[130] Child-resistant packaging is required when the product meets prescribed toxicity criteria and is recommended or permitted for residential use.[131] Packaging of products classified for restricted use or sold in large sizes and, therefore, unlikely to be accessible to children, need not be child-resistant.[132]

---

[121] FIFRA §15(c)(2), 7 U.S.C. §136m(c)(2).

[122] FIFRA §15(b)(2), 7 U.S.C. §136m(b)(2).

[123] For a discussion of risk management see Section II.B, above.

[124] FIFRA §3(c)(1)(C), 7 U.S.C. §136a(c)(1)(C).

[125] FIFRA §2(p), 7 U.S.C. §136(p).

[126] 40 C.F.R. §156.10.

[127] *Id.*

[128] 49 Fed. Reg. 37,960 (1984).

[129] 15 U.S.C. §1471 *et seq.*

[130] FIFRA §25(c)(3), 7 U.S.C. §136w(c)(3).

[131] 40 C.F.R. §157.22.

[132] 40 C.F.R. §157.24.

I. Regulation of Pest Control Devices and Inert Ingredients

Two peripheral areas of activity under the registration process are also worthy of brief comment—devices and inert ingredients. Although neither is required to be registered, FIFRA regulates both extensively. Pest control devices are devices designed to trap, destroy, repel, or mitigate any pest, not including equipment used to apply pesticides when sold separately from the pesticide.[133] EPA regulates pest control devices under a 1976 EPA policy statement.[134] Pesticide application devices that are sold with pesticides are regulated as pesticides.

Although pest control devices need not be registered, they are nonetheless regulated under FIFRA. They must be labeled[135] and may be found to be misbranded if they are not.[136] Further, EPA requires packaging for pest control devices to comply with the Poison Prevention Packaging Act.[137] Manufacturers and registrants are required to keep records regarding the production of devices,[138] and device manufacturing, sale, or distribution establishments are subject to EPA inspection.[139]

Inert ingredients, those materials found in pesticides that do not possess pesticidal qualities but are in the pesticide as fillers, solvents, carriers, and so forth are similar to pesticidal devices in that they need not be registered but are regulated under FIFRA and FFDCA. For example, tolerance levels must be established for inert as well as active ingredients found in pesticides if residues of those materials remain in or on raw agricultural commodities, processed foods, or animal feeds.[140]

Inert ingredients are an area of growing concern. "Inert" refers to an ingredient's lack of pesticidal qualities but does not indicate that it is harmless or nontoxic. In order to regulate inert ingredients, EPA has classified all inert ingredients found in pesticides into one of four categories based on its review of data concerning an ingredient's carcinogenicity and toxicity.[141] Those on List 1, the most toxic inert ingredients, are required to be labeled accordingly.[142] EPA has also strongly encouraged the substitution of nontoxic inert ingredients for inert ingredients found on List 1. List 2 consists of potentially toxic inert ingredients. EPA has made these items a high priority for testing and is collecting data. Once this data collection is complete, EPA will determine whether restrictions on their use should be imposed. List 3 contains inert ingredients of unknown toxicity—ingredients for which EPA lacks toxicity data, and for which no regulatory action has been taken. Those found on List 4

[133] FIFRA §2(h), 7 U.S.C. §136(h). *See also* 40 C.F.R. §153.240.

[134] 41 Fed. Reg. 51,065 (1976).

[135] FIFRA §2(p), 7 U.S.C. §136(p). This requirement is the same as that imposed on pesticides. Therefore, device labels must include the name, brand, or trademark, the name and address of the producer, its net contents, the producing establishment, warnings, and directions. 40 C.F.R. §156.10. *See also* 40 C.F.R. §153.240.

[136] FIFRA §2(q), 7 U.S.C. §136(q).

[137] 40 C.F.R. §157, subpart B. *See also* 7 U.S.C. §136w(c)(3).

[138] FIFRA §8(a), 7 U.S.C. §136f(a). *See also* 40 C.F.R. §169.2.

[139] FIFRA §9(a), 7 U.S.C. §136g(a).

[140] *See* 26 Fed. Reg. 10,640 (1961).

[141] 52 Fed. Reg. 13,305 (1987); 54 Fed. Reg. 48,314 (1989).

[142] *See* 54 Fed. Reg. 48,314 (1989) for a revised List 1.

are inerts of minimal concern, thought to be harmless and not subject to additional regulation.[143]

III. Pesticide Use and Enforcement

Although registration is the centerpiece of FIFRA, the statute also regulates virtually all aspects of pesticide usage.

A. Pesticide Applicator Certification

Pesticides that are classified for restricted use may be applied only by or under the "direct supervision" of a certified applicator.[144] EPA prescribes the requirements through which a person becomes a certified applicator, although a state may implement its own certification program if approved by EPA. Although a restricted use pesticide must be applied under the "direct supervision" of a certified applicator, that person need not be physically present when the pesticide is applied.[145]

Certification is granted to both the "private applicator," who applies pesticides on property the private applicator owns, rents, or which is rented or owned by his or her employer, and the "commercial applicator," who applies pesticides in situations not covered by the private applicator definition.[146] The competence of commercial applicators is determined on the basis of written examinations and performance testing,[147] including practical knowledge of the principles and practices of pest control, safety, environmental consequences of pesticide application, equipment, application techniques, applicable laws and regulations, and label comprehension.[148] Certification of private applicators may be based on either written or oral testing of the applicator's ability to recognize common pests, comprehend labels, apply pesticides correctly, recognize local environmental conditions of concern, and recognize symptoms of poisoning.[149]

B. Pesticide Storage, Transportation, and Disposal

The 1988 FIFRA Amendments required EPA to establish regulations concerning the storage, transportation, and disposal of pesticides and their containers. Prior rules in this area placed the burden of disposal on EPA and resulted in high costs to the Agency.[150] The 1988 Amendments changed a number of practices in order to shift this burden. As a result, EPA may now

---

[143] 54 Fed. Reg. 48,314 (1989).

[144] FIFRA §3(d)(1)(C), 7 U.S.C. §136a(d)(1)(C).

[145] FIFRA §2(e)(4), 7 U.S.C. §136(e)(4). The certified applicator must provide the applicator with detailed instructions for use and with information concerning where the certified applicator may be reached. 40 C.F.R. §171.6.

[146] FIFRA §2(e)(3), 7 U.S.C. §136(e)(3), 40 C.F.R. §171.2.

[147] 40 C.F.R. §171.4.

[148] *Id.*

[149] 40 C.F.R. §171.5.

[150] H.R. Rep. No. 939, 100th Cong., 2d Sess., *reprinted in* 1988 U.S.C.C.A.N. 3474, 3480–81.

require a registrant to provide data concerning safe storage and disposal prior to registration, require instructions concerning proper storage, transportation, and disposal to be included on the label, and, perhaps most important, require the registrant to have adequate finances to implement and complete a recall and disposal plan.[151] EPA is also authorized to require registrants to be responsible for the transportation, storage, and disposal of pesticides.[152] Implementing regulations for this provision have yet to be promulgated, but they are likely to contain cradle-to-grave pesticide management criteria. The regulations, once promulgated, will be found at 40 C.F.R. part 165.[153]

The 1988 Amendments also permit EPA to regulate pesticide container design to "promote the safe storage and disposal of pesticides."[154] These regulations, not yet promulgated, will be performance standards and will also be codified at 40 C.F.R. part 165.

C. Civil and Criminal Enforcement of FIFRA

FIFRA section 12 makes unlawful numerous acts, including the distribution or sale of an unregistered, cancelled, or suspended pesticide, label alteration, failure to keep and provide access to records, failure to advertise a restricted use pesticide as such, false guarantees, use of a pesticide in a manner inconsistent with its labeling, violation of a cancellation order, and falsification of registration documents or data.[155] Civil and criminal penalties for unlawful acts are described in section 14 of the Act and include fines and imprisonment.

States whose pesticide laws EPA has deemed adequate have primary responsibility for enforcing use violations, e.g., use of a pesticide not in accordance with its labeling.[156] Common EPA enforcement proceedings include actions for misbranding, failure to keep records, failure to obey cancellation orders, and use of unregistered pesticides. EPA has issued a number of interpretive rules regarding enforcement, particularly in the area of reporting requirements.[157]

An additional enforcement mechanism is the stop sale, use, or removal order. Such an order may be issued when EPA believes, on the basis of inspection or tests, that a pesticide or device intended for distribution or sale is in violation of the statute.[158] This enforcement mechanism is used frequently because it is comparatively quick and easy and may prevent human and environmental health hazards. EPA may also seize pesticides that are adulterated, misbranded, unregistered, mislabeled, improperly colored, misrepresented, or which will cause unreasonable adverse effects on the environment.[159]

---

[151] FIFRA §19(a)(1), 7 U.S.C. §136q(a)(1).

[152] FIFRA §19, 7 U.S.C. §136q.

[153] 54 Fed. Reg. 18,076, 18,084 (1989).

[154] FIFRA §19(e), 7 U.S.C. §136q(e).

[155] FIFRA §12, 7 U.S.C. §136j.

[156] FIFRA §26, 7 U.S.C. §136w-1. *See* United States v. Orkin Exterminating Co., 688 F. Supp. 223 (W.D. Va. 1988) (state's primary enforcement authority does not divest Attorney General of authority to bring criminal prosecution).

[157] *See* 50 Fed. Reg. 38,115 (1985), 44 Fed. Reg. 40,716 (1979), 43 Fed. Reg. 37,611 (1978).

[158] FIFRA §13(a), 7 U.S.C. §136k(a).

[159] FIFRA §13(b), 7 U.S.C. §136k(b).

Civil penalties of up to $5,000 per violation may be assessed at a hearing before an ALJ, who must consider the appropriateness of the fine based on the size of the business, the fine's effect on the business, the gravity of the violation, the defendant's exercise of due care, and the violation's effect on the environment.[160] EPA encourages voluntary disclosure of violations and may reduce penalties accordingly. A penalty may be reduced by up to 40 percent if disclosure is made prior to a discovery or announcement of inspection by EPA or appropriate state enforcement agency.[161] As an alternative to civil penalties, EPA may ask a court to issue warnings or enter settlement agreements, including settlements with conditions.

Criminal penalties may only be imposed by a U.S. district court following trial and conviction. Criminal penalties of up to $50,000 may be imposed for "knowing" violations of the Act.[162] Imprisonment of up to one year may also be imposed. Fines may be increased by invoking other federal statutes such as the Alternative Fines Act,[163] which allows the court to impose penalties of up to twice the amount gained by the defendant through the violation.

D. Regulation of Pesticide Exports and Imports

Pesticides and devices intended solely for export are largely exempt from FIFRA.[164] This policy has been criticized not only because of concern over the export of allegedly harmful products, but also based on concerns about international movement of pesticides through the atmosphere, water, and treated food products.[165] Nevetheless, U.S. manufacturers have been permitted to remain competitive overseas where they are required to do little more than meet the safety standards required by the countries to which they are exporting their products, which is all that is required of their foreign competitors.

EPA recently revised its pesticide export policy, in part in response to the above-noted criticisms.[166] Although several provisions remain unchanged, the policy imposes some new restrictions and makes other requirements more detailed. The policy still requires that pesticides intended for export must be labeled as such.[167] However, the new regulations require that labels must be multilingual, if applicable, rather than just bilingual as required under the old export regulations.[168] Other label information requirements include the product's manufacturer, use classification,[169] first aid treatment, and U.S. registra-

---

[160] FIFRA §14(a), 7 U.S.C. §136l(a).

[161] ENVIRONMENTAL PROTECTION AGENCY, FIFRA ENFORCEMENT POLICY 26 (July 2, 1990).

[162] FIFRA §14(b), 7 U.S.C. §136l(b). *See* United States v. Corbin Farm Serv., 444 F. Supp. 510, 12 ER Cases 1257 (E.D. Cal. 1978), *aff'd,* 578 F.2d 259, 12 ER Cases 1310 (1978) ("knowingly" required proof defendants knew they were dealing with a pesticide).

[163] 18 U.S.C. §3571 (1986).

[164] FIFRA §17, 7 U.S.C. §136o.

[165] *Federal Insecticide, Fungicide and Rodenticide Act: Hearing on S. 1516 Before the Senate Comm. on Agriculture, Nutrition, and Forestry,* 100th Cong., 1st Sess. 296 (1987) (testimony of Rick Hind, United States Public Interest Research Group).

[166] 58 Fed. Reg. 9062, 9063–65 (1993). The changes will be located at 40 C.F.R. pt. 168.

[167] 45 Fed. Reg. 50,274, 50,275 (1980).

[168] 58 Fed. Reg. 9062 (1993).

[169] The 1993 policy permits exporters to add explanatory language to use classification statements. 58 Fed. Reg. 9062 (1993).

tion status.[170] Further, exporters of pesticides not registered for use in the United States must obtain for each shipment a written acknowledgment from the export purchaser indicating its knowledge of the pesticide's lack of U.S. registration,[171] and that acknowledgment be submitted to EPA within seven days of receipt. Alternatively, an exporter may submit a purchaser acknowledgment to EPA at the beginning of each calendar year and an annual summary of exports to that purchaser.[172] EPA subsequently forwards that acknowledgment to the government of the country of import. EPA is also now required to provide the foreign government with notice of all regulatory actions taken with regard to a pesticide on the basis of health or environmental concerns and an annual summary of all pesticide regulatory actions.[173]

Pesticides imported into the United States must meet all testing and registration requirements imposed by FIFRA.[174] In addition, a pesticide importer must notify EPA of its intention to import pesticides or devices prior to their arrival in the United States via a notice-of-arrival form. EPA returns this form to the importer, who must present it to Customs upon arrival of the pesticides.[175] EPA may sample the imported pesticides and review their labels, circulars, and advertisements for compliance purposes.[176] If a pesticide is found not to comply with FIFRA, the importer will be notified and given up to 20 days to persuade EPA why the shipment should not be held and destroyed. Pesticides remaining in noncompliance are refused delivery and ultimately destroyed.[177]

IV. Standards for Pesticide Residues

The third area of EPA's regulatory authority over pesticide regulation is the establishment of standards for pesticide residues. Under the FFDCA,[178] EPA is charged with establishing "tolerances," the maximum pesticide residue allowable in or on raw and processed agricultural commodities as well as animal feed. If a pesticide remains in or on raw or processed commodities or

[170] 45 Fed. Reg. 50,274, 50,275 (1980). *See also* 58 Fed. Reg. 9062 (1993). If a pesticide is not registered for use in the United States the label must contain the statement "not registered for use in the United States of America." *Id.*

[171] FIFRA §17(a), 7 U.S.C. §136o(a).

[172] 58 Fed. Reg. 9062, 9074 (1993).

[173] 58 Fed. Reg. 9062 (1993).

[174] FIFRA §17(c), 7 U.S.C. §136o(c). *See also* 19 C.F.R. §12.110, .117.

[175] 19 C.F.R. §12.112, .114.

[176] 19 C.F.R. §12.116.

[177] 19 C.F.R. §12.117.

[178] FFDCA regulates numerous other aspects of pesticides besides residue tolerances. Although this regulatory regime is generally beyond the scope of this chapter, an example of other FFDCA pesticide regulation is illustrative of the statute's scope and the interagency coordination required. FFDCA regulates pesticides that are drugs. Absent agency coordination, pesticides that come within the statutory definition of "drug," "new drug," or "new animal drug" could be regulated by FDA under FFDCA as well as by EPA. FDA and EPA have, however, established procedures by which they coordinate their efforts to avoid wasteful duplication. In order to save time and resources, a registrant should determine whether one agency or both have jurisdiction over a pesticide before attempting to register.

The FDA-EPA procedures provide that pesticides that are new drugs intended only for human use are to be regulated only by FDA. 40 C.F.R. §152.20. Similarly, pesticides that are new animal drugs or feeds that contain new animal drugs are regulated solely by FDA and need not comply with FIFRA. 7 U.S.C. §136(u). Pesticides that are drugs but do not qualify as new drugs or new animal drugs are regulated by both FDA and EPA. Consequently, they must satisfy all applicable FIFRA requirements.

animal feed, unless a tolerance is established for that pesticide and the residue detected is within that tolerance level, a food is deemed adulterated and is, therefore, subject to seizure by FDA. Further, if data indicate residues will remain, EPA will not register a pesticide until either a tolerance is established for it or it is exempted from the tolerance requirement.[179] The goal of setting tolerances is to protect public health while allowing nonthreatening residues that result from the application of a pesticide according to its directions.

A. Raw Agricultural Commodity Tolerances

Section 408 of the FFDCA governs tolerance-setting for raw agricultural commodities, defined to be "any food in its raw or natural state, including all fruits that are washed, colored, or otherwise treated in their unpeeled, natural form prior to marketing."[180] EPA establishes a tolerance or grants an exemption for the pesticide on the basis of a petition filed by a registrant, registrant-applicant, or via rulemaking on its own initiative. This last option allows EPA to respond to a request for the establishment of a tolerance by an interested party. If EPA initiates rulemaking, the registrant or a registrant applicant may request that the proposal be referred to an advisory committee for review.

Regulations setting forth the required contents of a petition are set forth at 40 C.F.R. §180.7. The payment of fees to cover EPA expenses must accompany a petition.[181] Fees may be waived or refunded at EPA's discretion.

EPA makes very conservative assumptions when establishing a tolerance,[182] which include that (1) 100 percent of the crop for which a tolerance is sought is treated with the pesticide; (2) the residue level in the crop is at the maximum tolerance level; and (3) based on consumer consumption surveys, each consumer consumes the crop at the 90th percentile of consumption. With these assumptions in mind, EPA's goal is to set a limit such that if no commodity exceeds that limit, then no consumer will ever exceed the "reference dose," which is the daily safe consumption level for a 135 pound adult over the course of a lifetime.[183]

EPA sets a tolerance by determining the NOEL (No-Observable-Effect Level), the level of exposure at which no adverse effects occur, and dividing that level by a safety factor of 100. The resulting number is the reference dose. The reference dose is also subject to alteration by a safety factor as well. The reference dose is then multiplied by 60 kilograms, the assumed average weight of an adult. This number is compared to the TMRC (theoretical maximum residue contribution), the total theoretical amount of the pesticide's residue that might appear in one's daily diet. If the reference dose is higher than the TMRC, the tolerance is granted. If it is lower, further tests may be required.

---

[179] 40 C.F.R. §152.112.

[180] FFDCA §408, 21 U.S.C. §346a.

[181] FFDCA §408(o), 21 U.S.C. §346a(o). *See* 40 C.F.R. §180.33 for a complete fee schedule. Fees have been increased as of April 23, 1993. 58 Fed. Reg. 16,094 (1993). The fee for a petition for a new tolerance is now $56,175 plus $1,400 for each raw agricultural commodity over nine for which a tolerance is requested.

[182] Tolerance setting is pesticide specific. This methodology does not account for synergies that may occur from consumption of different foods which may be treated with different pesticides.

[183] While the 135 pound adult assumption may inadequately protect persons such as children or nursing mothers, the safety margins used in establishing a tolerance are designed to compensate for this.

EPA then publishes a proposed regulation establishing a tolerance, and anyone claiming to be adversely affected by the proposed tolerance may file written objections. If the objections are filed by someone other than the petitioner, the petitioner may respond and request a hearing, which will be held if questions of fact exist.[184] Following the hearing, EPA will issue a tolerance or an exemption by order, which is appealable at the appellate court level.[185]

Exemptions from the tolerance requirement are granted if the pesticide residue does not present a risk to public health.[186] An exemption may be obtained by submitting the same data that are required to establish a tolerance.

B. Food Additive Tolerances

Pesticides are also regulated as food additives under section 409 of the FFDCA when they appear in processed foods, including animal feeds, usually as a result of processing or packaging.[187] Processed foods that are derived from raw agricultural commodities containing pesticide residues below the tolerance set for the raw commodity need not have a tolerance established under section 409.

Many of the regulatory provisions under section 409 are similar to those found under section 408. Any person may petition for the establishment of a tolerance under section 409 or EPA may establish one on its own initiative. Any person adversely affected by an order that establishes a tolerance may file written objections, whereupon EPA must hold a public hearing. Following the hearing, EPA will issue an order, which is appealable at the appellate court level.

The Delaney Clause,[188] which prohibits residues of food additives that induce cancer in man or animals, plays a special role in the setting of tolerances for food additives. EPA attempted to ameliorate the strict prohibitions of the Delaney Clause, which the Agency considered unnecessarily restrictive, through several interpretive devices. The first of these was the de minimis exception, which EPA claimed permitted it to allow concentrations of cancer-causing pesticide residues greater than those tolerated for raw foods so long as the particular substances posed only a de minimis risk of actually causing cancer.[189] This interpretation was based on the notion that an administrative agency may avoid a literal application of a statute if the result of such literal application would be pointless.[190] This approach would allow EPA to apply the FFDCA flexibly when it came to pesticides that did not present a realistic safety concern. "The de minimis exception simply recognizes that the Delaney Clause should not be a bar to the use of a pesticide that satisfies the statutory standard of FIFRA for a carcinogenic pesticide which presents a trivial risk."[191]

---

[184] 40 C.F.R. §178.25. *See* 40 C.F.R. pt. 179 for detailed regulations governing public hearings.
[185] FFDCA §408, 21 U.S.C. §346a.
[186] 40 C.F.R. §180.1001.
[187] *See* 21 C.F.R. §170.19.
[188] FFDCA §409(c)(3), 21 U.S.C. §348(c)(3).
[189] 53 Fed. Reg. 41,104, 41,110 (1988).
[190] *Id.* at 41,107.
[191] 55 Fed. Reg. 17,560, 17,565–66 (1990).

The courts, however, have found that EPA's de minimis interpretation violates the FFDCA. In 1992, the Court of Appeals for the Ninth Circuit held that an EPA order permitting the use of four pesticides that posed a measurable yet de minimis risk of causing cancer violated the provisions of the Delaney Clause.[192] The court brushed aside EPA's argument that the interpretation is necessary for a more sensible approach to tolerance regulation and found the language of the Delaney Clause to be "clear and mandatory," and not subject to new interpretations or exercises of discretion. "[T]he Clause affords no flexibility once FDA scientists determine that these conditions are satisfied. A food additive that has been found in an appropriate test to induce cancer in laboratory animals may not be approved for use in food for any purpose, at any level, regardless of any 'benefits' that it might provide."[193] The Supreme Court recently upheld this decision when it refused to review the Ninth Circuit case.[194] Legislation that would, in effect, codify the de minimis exception has been proposed. The proposals would permit the Administrator to establish tolerances for carcinogens, including pesticide residues in processed foods, which pose a negligible cancer risk.[195]

Other approaches that EPA uses to circumvent the strictures of the Delaney Clause are the "constituents doctrine," which only requires the application of the Clause when a pesticide is carcinogenic as a whole, regardless of the carcinogenicity of the pesticide's individual ingredients, and the "sensitivity of method approach," under which EPA does not classify as a food additive any carcinogenic constituent that is undetectable by an approved method if the lifetime cancer risk of the constituent is below one in one million.[196] Although these approaches have not yet been challenged in court, given the holding in *Les,* it is questionable whether they would withstand judicial challenge.

FDA and USDA jointly monitor and enforce the tolerance levels established by EPA. Responsibility for poultry, meat, and egg products lies with USDA. FDA is responsible for other affected commodities. Monitoring and enforcement are carried out through regular sampling, testing, seizures, and injunctions.

V. Regulation of New Technologies

One expanding area of scientific development that is of significant and increasing public concern is the regulation of the products of biotechnology. EPA has regulatory authority over several of these, including microbial and

---

[192] Les v. Reilly, 968 F.2d 985 (9th Cir. 1992), *cert. denied sub nom.* National Agric. Chem. Ass'n v. Les, 113 S. Ct. 1361 (1993). *See also* Public Citizen v. Young, 831 F.2d 1108, 1112 (D.C. Cir. 1987) (court found EPA's de minimis interpretation to be contrary to law because the Delaney Clause prohibits the use of any carcinogenic food additive, regardless of the degree of risk).

[193] *Les,* 968 F.2d at 988 (quoting R. MERRILL AND P. HUTT, FOOD AND DRUG LAW 78 (1980)).

[194] 968 F.2d 985 (9th Cir. 1992), *cert. denied sub nom.* National Agric. Chem. Ass'n v. Les, 113 S. Ct. 1361 (1993). At the time of publication, EPA is in the process of complying with the zero-risk standard by identifying potentially affected carcinogenic chemicals. EPA is also seeking comments on a proposed policy that implements a zero-risk standard for carcinogenic pesticides used in foods. 58 Fed. Reg. 7470 (1993).

[195] H.R. RES. 872, 102d Cong., 1st Sess. (1993); S. RES. 331, 102d Cong., 1st Sess. (1993).

[196] 52 Fed. Reg. 49,752 (1987).

biochemical pesticides,[197] plants genetically engineered to possess pesticidal properties, and microorganisms that function as pesticides. Although data requirements for microbial and biochemical pesticides have been established,[198] EPA has not promulgated regulations covering all aspects of this new technology. As a result, many policies remain informal, and the Agency continues to operate under the federal Coordinated Framework for the Regulation of Biotechnology Products.[199]

The Framework requires companies to notify EPA prior to undertaking tests of genetically engineered pesticides and nonindigenous microorganisms. Under the Framework, products are classified either as high risk or low risk. Notification requirements depend on the classification assigned to the product. The notification procedure for tests with low risk microorganisms is relatively straightforward and much simpler than that required for high risk microorganisms.[200]

EPA is developing regulations to replace the 1986 Framework. An unpublished draft of the proposed amendments, circulated in 1988, proposed expanding the Framework's scope and excluding certain genetically modified organisms from notification requirements.[201] EPA recently proposed a rule that would implement this latter proposal.[202] The rule permits small-scale testing of certain microbial pesticides thought unlikely to pose unreasonable adverse effects in that setting without prior notification of EPA,[203] thereby actually reducing the scope of the 1986 Framework. However, the same rule would also require EPA notification of small-scale testing of certain genetically modified microbial pesticides.[204] Upon receipt of notification, which includes a data submission requirement, EPA would determine whether an EUP should be required. These regulations would amend 40 C.F.R. part 172.

EPA is also operating under the Report on National Biotechnology Policy of the President's Council on Competitiveness. The principles espoused in the Report include encouragement of review of biotechnology products based on their characteristics and risks rather than their origin, minimization of the regulatory burden on such products, accommodation of rapid advances in biotechnology, and regulation based on performance rather than design.

VI. Conclusion

As one of the oldest areas of environmental regulation in the United States, the history of FIFRA reflects the great expansion of scientific knowledge during this century. This is particularly evident in the evolving science of risk assess-

[197] Microbial pesticides include bacteria, fungi, viruses, and protozoans. Biochemical pesticides include semichemicals, hormones, plant and insect growth regulators, and enzymes. 40 C.F.R. §158.65.

[198] 40 C.F.R. §158.690, .740.

[199] 51 Fed. Reg. 23,302 (1986).

[200] *See* 51 Fed. Reg. 23,302, 23,321–22 (1986).

[201] Environmental Protection Agency, Unpublished Draft of Proposed Rule (November 1988). *See* 54 Fed. Reg. 7026 (1989).

[202] 58 Fed. Reg. 5878 (1993).

[203] *Id.* at 5881.

[204] Currently, there is a presumption that EUPs are not required for small-scale pesticide testing. 40 C.F.R. §172.3.

ment and its expanding role in the field of pesticide regulation as Congress and EPA attempt to strike a balance between the socially useful, yet potentially dangerous, use of pesticidal chemicals and the risk those materials present to public health and the environment. In this constantly changing legal regime, the greatest certainty is that the subject matter will not become less complicated with the passage of time. As in the past, advances in analytical technology will permit the reliable detection of increasingly small amounts of pesticide residues. This will pose increasing problems for regulators saddled with overbroad requirements such as the Delaney Clause that reflect the dark ages of risk assessment and analytical chemistry. The tension between the competing goals of FIFRA, however, is unlikely ever to be resolved, and its future, like its past, will reflect the dynamic balancing of maximizing production while minimizing environmental and public health risks.

11

Protection of Natural Resources

*By John C. Martin and Mary E. Bosco**
with Herbert W. Hecht and V. Heather Sibbison

I. Introduction

This chapter collects a variety of environmental laws designed to protect the nation's natural resources and the habitats vital to their survival. It begins with a discussion of wetlands protection, and then outlines the provisions of the National Environmental Policy Act, the Endangered Species Act, and other specific wildlife protection laws.

The laws discussed below are united by their breadth, the large number of federal agencies called upon to coordinate efforts to enforce their provisions, and their potential to affect a virtually limitless number of federal and private interests. Unlike other statutes discussed elsewhere in this book whose enforcement is focused on industry, the laws covered in this chapter have an impact on many of the federal government's building projects and other activities. As they also affect a substantial amount of private commercial activities, knowledge of their provisions and enforcement mechanisms is important in the planning phases of a wide variety of commercial projects.

II. Wetlands: A Regulatory Quagmire

Wetlands, once ignored and regarded as valueless, have in recent times become the subject of a major environmental and political battle. During the four years of the Bush Administration (1989–1993), few executive branch issues received as much attention and debate as the question of how to regulate the nation's millions of acres of wetlands.[1] The early months of the Clinton Administration reveal the same high level of interest in these national resources.

---

*The authors would like to thank Gregg A. Rothschild for his assistance in the compilation of this chapter.

[1] The Department of the Interior estimates that, as of the mid-1980s, approximately 104 million acres of wetlands existed in the conterminous United States. An additional estimated 170 million acres existed in Alaska alone. T.E. DAHL, U.S. DEP'T OF THE INTERIOR, FISH AND WILDLIFE SERV., WETLANDS LOSSES IN THE UNITED STATES 1970'S TO 1980'S, 9 (1990).

Although wetlands are primarily regulated on the federal level through section 404 of the Clean Water Act,[2] and through a variety of other statutory provisions,[3] states and localities often have a significant impact on the wetlands permit process. In addition, as the recent flood of wetlands-related litigation indicates, the courts are playing a central role in defining the regulatory parameters for activity on or about wetlands.[4]

Therefore, landowners, businesses, and others applying for dredge and fill permits, as well as those merely interested in the development potential of certain parcels of land, must look to numerous sources for regulatory guidance and compliance assurances.

This chapter does not attempt to discuss every issue or situation that applicants face during the permit process but instead highlights the major considerations that are likely to arise as a result of the structure and operation of the section 404 wetlands program.[5] By focusing on core practical concerns, such as procedural aspects of obtaining a permit, the definition of wetlands, mitigation requirements, appeal of permit denials, and judicial involvement in the wetlands process, this chapter tracks many of the central wetlands issues currently being debated on the national level and provides a picture of the potential regulatory and policy changes that may lie ahead.

A. Background

Scientific recognition of the functions and value of wetlands and the consequent emphasis on wetlands regulation are relatively recent occurrences.[6] The Rivers and Harbors Appropriations Act of 1899, among other things, prohibits dredging or filling of the navigable waters of the United States, including wetlands, without first obtaining a permit from the Army Corps of Engineers (Corps).[7] Although this statute later proved adaptable for wetlands

---

[2] 33 U.S.C. §1344 (Supp. II 1972). Section 404 of the Clean Water Act (CWA), 33 U.S.C. §1251 *et seq.*, establishes the statutory framework for the issuance of permits for discharges of dredged or fill material into the navigable waters of the United States. See Chapter 4 for a fuller discussion of the CWA.

[3] A great deal of federal legislation such as the National Environmental Policy Act of 1969 (NEPA), 42 U.S.C. §§4321–32, the Endangered Species Act of 1973 (ESA), 16 U.S.C. §1531 *et seq.*, and the Food Security Act of 1985, Pub. L. 99–198, 99 Stat. 1354 (1985), affects the various aspects of wetlands regulation. These and other wetlands-related statutes are discussed throughout this chapter.

[4] Lack of a formal wetlands administrative appeals process causes many permit applicants and other interested parties to turn to the courts for relief after the Corps of Engineers issues an unfavorable opinion. These legal challenges range from actions in which landowners assert takings claims to suits in which environmental groups challenge the federal government's application of wetlands protection laws. For a summary of the many recent private property takings cases, see the GAO's "Clean Water Act: Private Property Takings Claims as a Result of the Section 404 Program" (GAO/RCED-93-176FS).

[5] Brief reference is made herein to other types of wetlands permits, such as those issued by EPA pursuant to §402 of the CWA. This chapter primarily discusses the two most common forms of wetlands permits, general permits and §404 permits for activities involving the discharge of dredged or fill materials into the navigable waters of the United States. For a detailed survey of federal, state, and local wetlands issues, *see* W. Want, Law of Wetlands Regulation, Release #3, 5/92 (1989).

[6] Scientists from across the country discussed the functions and value of wetlands as part of a congressional hearing. *Science of Wetland Definition and Delineation, Hearings Before the Environment Subcomm. of the House Comm. on Science, Space, and Technology,* (November 12, 1991). Witnesses testified that wetlands provide buffer zones, flood-peak reduction, groundwater recharge, shoreline stabilization, food chain support, wildlife habitats, organic waste transformation, and toxic waste storage. *Hearings,* at 302. *See also* a detailed discussion of wetlands values by EPA in its 1990 Report to Congress on the National Water Quality Inventory 62–63 (April 1992) [hereinafter EPA 1990 Report to Congress].

[7] 33 U.S.C. §403 (1988).

protection purposes, it was long thought of as a law for protection of navigation only, and was never designed to provide a comprehensive wetlands regulatory framework.[8]

The statutory framework upon which the current wetlands permit system rests originated in 1972 as part of legislation amending the Federal Water Pollution Control Act (FWPCA).[9] The FWPCA, commonly referred to as the Clean Water Act (CWA), established a permit program for the discharge of dredged or fill material into the "navigable waters" of the United States (the section 404 program).[10] In addition, the Act created the EPA-supervised National Pollutant Discharge Elimination System (NPDES).[11] The section 404 program put in place a mechanism for addressing the majority of individual wetlands permit applications. Adoption of the NPDES, governing permits for the discharge of pollutants, the so-called EPA "veto" provision of section 404,[12] and the later-adopted section 404(b)(1) guidelines,[13] firmly established EPA's regulatory role for virtually all permit decisions.

Five years later, lawmakers made further important modifications to the federal wetlands program in the Clean Water Act Amendments of 1977.[14] Two of the changes with the greatest significance were the addition of the general permit program[15] and the carving out of statutory exemptions for several types of discharges including certain agriculture-related activities.[16]

---

[8] As the title of the Rivers and Harbors Act suggests, this provision was designed to cover a much broader area than just wetlands. Section 10 states in part that

> it shall not be lawful to excavate or fill, or in any manner to alter or modify the course, location, condition, or capacity of, any port, roadstead, haven, harbor, canal, lake, harbor of refuge, or inclosure within the limits of any breakwater, or of the channel of any navigable water of the United States, unless the work has been recommended by the Chief of Engineers and authorized by the Secretary of the Army prior to beginning the same.

33 U.S.C. §403 (1988).

[9] Pub. L. No. 92-500, 86 Stat. 816. The FWPCA, originally adopted in 1948, experienced a major rewrite as a result of the FWPCA Amendments of 1972. Congress again significantly amended the FWPCA in the Clean Water Act of 1977. These changes were signed into law on December 27, 1977. Pub. L. No. 95-217, 91 Stat. 1566.

[10] 33 U.S.C. §1344 (Supp. II 1972). As used in §404, "navigable waters" means waters of the United States. 33 U.S.C. §1362(7) (Supp. II 1972). EPA's §404(b)(1) guidelines include wetlands in the definition of "waters of the United States." 40 C.F.R. §230.3(s)(7) (1992).

[11] 33 U.S.C. §1342 (Supp. II 1972), CWA §402.

[12] 33 U.S.C. §1344(c) (Supp. IV 1974).

[13] CWA §404(b)(1) authorizes EPA to issue wetlands permit guidelines and, with regard to individual permit applications, to make comments to the Corps regarding its views on compliance with the §404(b)(1) guidelines. 33 U.S.C. §1344(b)(1) (Supp. II 1972). *See* Memorandum of Agreement between EPA and the Corps, August 11, 1992, at 2.

[14] Pub. L. No. 95-217, 91 Stat. 1566. In addition to the modifications discussed above, the 1977 Amendments established the Corps' lead role in the permitting process, §404(d), 33 U.S.C. §1344(d) (1982), and put in place certain notification procedures (i.e., public notices for permit applications are to be issued by the Corps not later than 15 days after receipt of a completed application), §404(a), 33 U.S.C. §1344(a) (1982). Furthermore, the 1977 Amendments added a provision requiring EPA, when denying permits, to issue a written objection containing limitations and conditions under which the permit would have been issued. §404(c), 33 U.S.C. §1344(c) (1982).

[15] CWA §404(e), 33 U.S.C. §1344(e) (1982); 33 C.F.R. §330.5 (1992).

[16] CWA §404(f), 33 U.S.C. §1344(f) (1982). Section 404 specifically excepts "normal farming, silviculture, and ranching activities such as plowing, seeding, cultivating, minor drainage, harvesting for production of food, fiber, and forest products, or upland soil and water conservation practices" from the general dredge and fill requirements. 33 U.S.C. §1344(f)(1)(A) (1982). *See also* 33 C.F.R. §323.4 (1992).

The Corps and EPA published a significant final rule on August 25, 1993, that, among other things, modified the definition of "discharge of dredged material." Commentors on the proposed rule had expressed concern that the new language might weaken the statutory exemptions provided for in 33 C.F.R. §323.4(a)(1)(b). The Corps and EPA responded to these comments by stating that the final "rule does not

In 1980, EPA finalized the section 404(b)(1) guidelines for the discharge of dredged or fill materials.[17] Although the early to mid-1980s were marked by significant court decisions involving topics such as the nationwide permit program and the definition of wetlands,[18] the present national attention on wetlands is largely derived from the high profile afforded wetlands and the environment during the 1988 presidential campaign. Then Vice-President Bush campaigned for a goal of "no net loss" of wetlands, a concept that energized both environmentalists and the regulated community.

Even before the Vice-President's "no net loss" statement, the Corps, EPA, the Soil Conservation Service (SCS), and the U.S. Fish and Wildlife Service (FWS) were nearing completion of a federal manual for the uniform identification of wetlands.

On January 10, 1989, these four agencies published the *Federal Manual for Identifying and Delineating Jurisdictional Wetlands* (the 1989 Manual).[19] The authors of the 1989 Manual had as their goal providing "a single, consistent approach for identifying and delineating wetlands from a multi-agency Federal perspective."[20] Reaction from the regulated community was immediate and severe.[21] Because of their lack of clarity and specificity, application of the manual's technical criteria for the three central wetlands characteristics—hydrology, hydrophytic vegetation, and hydric soils—was difficult and often inconsistent. In some regions application of the 1989 Manual resulted in a greatly expanded definition of wetlands.

The strong public reaction eventually led to the Administration's creation of extensive proposed revisions to the 1989 Manual.[22] These proposed revi-

change, in any way, the manner in which the Corps and EPA determine whether an activity is exempt under Section 404(f) of the CWA." 58 Fed. Reg. 45008, 45026–45027 (1993).

[17] 40 C.F.R. §230 (1992). Having operated under interim guidelines since 1975, EPA published final guidelines in the *Federal Register* on December 24, 1980. 45 Fed. Reg. 85,344 (1980).

[18] A settlement in National Wildlife Fed'n v. Marsh, 22 ER Cases 1417 (D.D.C. 1984), resulted in the determination that "isolated" wetlands of less than one acre qualify for nationwide permits and are not subject to the Corps' standard notification procedure. 49 Fed. Reg. 39,478–85 (1984) (to be codified at 33 C.F.R. pts. 320, 323, 325, and 330). In addition, the settlement agreement in *Marsh* led the Corps to revise its Nationwide Permit at §330.5(a)(26) to require notification before an applicant pursues activity in isolated wetlands areas of 1 to 10 acres, and to require individual permits for dredge and fill actions on isolated wetlands of over 10 acres. 49 Fed Reg. at 39,484.

The Supreme Court's ruling in United States v. Riverside Bayview Homes, Inc., 474 U.S. 121, 23 ER Cases 1561 (1985), greatly expanded traditional notions of jurisdictional wetlands. The Supreme Court held that the presence of groundwater alone could satisfy a wetlands determination. Prior to this decision, many in the regulated community had operated under the assumption that to be a wetlands, the land needed to be periodically covered by surface water.

[19] FEDERAL INTERAGENCY COMM. FOR WETLANDS DELINEATION, FEDERAL MANUAL FOR IDENTIFYING AND DELINEATING JURISDICTIONAL WETLANDS (USCOE, EPA, USFWS, and SCS (1989)). On March 20, 1989, the 1989 Manual was implemented.

[20] The 1989 Manual, Part I, Section 1.0, at 1.

[21] Landowners, developers, and representatives from local government petitioned the White House and Congress to withdraw the 1989 Manual. An interagency task force on wetlands headed by the White House Domestic Policy Council and composed of representatives from over a dozen executive branch agencies was formed and began to consider options to address the public outcry over the Manual. At the same time, the Administration faced extreme pressure from environmental groups and certain members of the scientific community to hold firm on the President's "no net loss wetlands" pledge. The Domestic Policy Council Wetlands Task Force received considerable public input as a result of extensive lobbying efforts and from public meetings conducted throughout the country. *See* 55 Fed. Reg. 30,279 (1990) and 56 Fed. Reg. 8560 (1991).

[22] The Administration partially blamed the 1989 Manual's failure on misconceptions about the manual's intent, misapplication, and "other factors." Proposed Revisions to the 1989 Federal Manual for Identifying and Delineating Jurisdictional Wetlands, 56 Fed. Reg. 40,446, 40,449 (1991).

sions, published in the *Federal Register* on August 14, 1991,[23] were referenced as part of a comprehensive wetlands plan announced by President Bush on August 9, 1991.[24] Not surprisingly, the 1991 revisions, like the 1989 Manual, evoked more criticism than compromise. An unprecedented number of public comments, both in support and opposition, caused the Corps, EPA, SCS, and FWS to extend the October 1991 comment period deadline to December 1991.[25] Then, in December, the four agencies once again extended the comment period on the 1991 revisions and released a proposed rule to incorporate some of these revisions into the 1989 Manual.[26] The comment period for the 1991 revisions and the December 19, 1991, proposed rule closed on January 21, 1992.[27] Political considerations and deep division over wetlands issues in his Administration ultimately forced President Bush to abandon efforts to formally implement the proposed revisions.[28]

Nevertheless, simultaneous with the formulation and release of the 1991 proposed revisions, Congress was pursuing alternate means of replacing the 1989 Manual. These efforts met with success when Senator Bennett Johnston (D-La.) championed passage of a provision in the 1992 Energy and Water Development Appropriations Act that prohibited the Corps from performing wetlands delineations using the highly controversial 1989 Manual.[29] The provision reads:

> [No Army Corps of Engineers funds] shall be used to identify or delineate any land as a "water of the United States" under the Federal Manual for Identifying and Delineating Jurisdictional Wetlands that was adopted in 1989 (1989 Manual) or any subsequent manual not adopted in accordance with the requirements for notice and public comment of the rule-making process of the Administrative Procedure Act.[30]

The practical effect of this language was to force federal regulators to officially readopt a wetlands manual published by the Corps in 1987 (the 1987 Manual).[31]

---

[23] 56 Fed. Reg. 40,446 (1991).

[24] White House Fact Sheet, Protecting America's Wetlands, August 9, 1991. The three-part plan was designed to "stop the net loss of wetlands" by strengthening wetlands acquisition programs, revising the 1989 Manual, and streamlining the regulatory system. Fact Sheet, at 1. One of the streamlining proposals involved refinement of the mitigation banking system, a topic of great significance for many permit applicants. *Id.* at 3–4. EPA and the Corps had previously signed a Memorandum of Agreement concerning mitigation guidelines under CWA §404(b)(1) (Feb. 6, 1990) (effective Feb. 7, 1990) (see mitigation discussion below at D.3.e.).

[25] Comments on the 1991 proposed revisions, and on a December 19, 1991, proposal to incorporate some of these revisions into the federal regulations, have exceeded 100,000 pages. 58 Fed. Reg. 4995 (1993). The notice extending the comment period from October to December 19, 1991, appeared in the *Federal Register* on October 16, 1991. 56 Fed. Reg. 61,868 (1991).

[26] 56 Fed. Reg. 65,964 (1991). The comment period on the proposed manual was extended to January 21, 1992. *Id.*

[27] *Id.*

[28] Unaltered, the 1991 proposed revisions would have greatly reduced the amount of land considered jurisdictionally "wet" by requiring independent evidence of all three technical criteria, by increasing the saturation period dramatically, and by changing the method for determining hydrophytic vegetation. Although it is unlikely that any of the 1991 proposed revisions will be adopted during the Clinton Administration, a January 1993 Corps/EPA notice in the *Federal Register* indicates that comments on the proposals are still being considered. *See* 58 Fed. Reg. 4995 (1993).

[29] Pub. L. No. 102-104, 105 Stat. 510 (1991).

[30] Pub. L. No. 102-104, 105 Stat. 510, 518 (1991).

[31] Environmental Laboratory, Dep't of the Army, Corps of Engineers Wetlands Delineation Manual (1987). Interestingly, the 1987 Manual also was not put through the public notice and comment procedure. *See* Royal C. Gardner, *Public Participation and Wetlands Regulation,* 10 UCLA J. Envtl. L. &

The Corps' adoption of the 1987 Manual took place immediately after President Bush signed the Energy and Water Development Appropriations Act of 1992 on August 17, 1991. Because this legislation provided only a partial and temporary solution, Senator Johnston inserted similar language in the Energy and Water Development Appropriations Act of 1993.[32] This language instructed the Corps to continue using the 1987 Manual until adoption of another wetlands delineation manual.

Despite the Corps' usage of the 1987 Manual, one troublesome question remained. Throughout 1991 and 1992 many in the regulated community were uncertain as to whether EPA was officially using the 1987 Manual or still applying the 1989 Manual standards. Apparently, EPA continued to use the 1989 Manual but "in judicial enforcement actions . . . confirm(ed) the jurisdictional status of a property under the 1987 Manual."[33]

Finally, in January of 1993, the Corps and EPA officially adopted the 1987 Manual through an amendment to the January 19, 1989 Memorandum of Agreement Concerning the Determination of the Geographic Jurisdiction of the Section 404 Program.[34]

The 1987 Manual has been largely successful in the regulated community but legislators on both sides of the wetlands question, many of whom are interested in non-Manual wetlands issues,[35] have vowed to continue seeking comprehensive changes to the federal policy.[36]

B. Wetlands Regulatory Structure

Although wetlands regulation, pursuant to section 404 of the CWA,[37] is largely carried out as a result of decisions made by the Corps in consultation with EPA, questions of policy and implementation extend across agencies and statutory sources.[38] In making sense of the wetlands permit process, an appli-

---

POL'Y, 1–39 (1991). Gardner points out that the 1992 Energy and Water Development Act does not technically prohibit the Corps from reissuing the 1989 Manual without public notice and comment because the 1989 Manual was adopted "in accordance with" the Administrative Procedure Act.

[32] Technically, the earlier wetlands provisions applied to funds appropriated for the Corps (and *not* EPA), and only for fiscal year 1992. The fiscal year 1993 language is contained in Pub. L. No. 102-377, 106 Stat. 1315 (1992).

[33] 58 Fed. Reg. 4995 (1993).

[34] *Id.*

[35] "Non-manual" wetlands initiatives being pursued administratively or through legislation include the revision of mitigation requirements, development of a compensation mechanism for wetlands-related takings (permit denials), streamlining the §404 permit process, and transfer of wetlands regulation from the federal government to state governments.

[36] Those in Congress who wish to reopen the question of the definition of wetlands are awaiting the release of a National Academy of Sciences (NAS) analysis of wetlands definition and of the existing wetlands delineation manuals. This study was approved as part of the fiscal year 1993 appropriation for EPA and is expected to be released in September of 1994.

[37] 33 U.S.C. §1344 (1988).

[38] In addition to the Clean Water Act, legislation having a significant impact on wetlands regulation includes the National Environmental Policy Act of 1969 (NEPA) §2, 42 U.S.C. §4321 (1988); "Swampbuster" (16 U.S.C. §3821 (1988)) and the Conservation Reserve Program, both enacted as part of the Food Security Act of 1985, Pub. L. No. 99-198, 99 Stat. 1354 (1985); the Coastal Barrier Resources Act, 16 U.S.C. §3501 (1988); the Water Bank Act, 16 U.S.C. §1301 (1988); the Migratory Bird Conservation Act, 16 U.S.C. §718(a) (1988); the Rivers and Harbors Appropriations Act of 1899, 33 U.S.C. §403 (1988); the Endangered Species Act of 1973 (ESA), 16 U.S.C. §1531 (1988); and other provisions. These wetlands provisions are generally discussed throughout this chapter.

cant should first become familiar with the basic wetlands regulatory structure. The following presents a brief overview of the relevant agencies, authorities, and guidelines used in the wetlands process. Special attention has been given to the issue of wetlands definition because of its crucial role in almost all wetlands permitting actions.

1. Principal Wetlands Regulators

In addition to the Corps and EPA, the Department of the Interior's FWS, the SCS and the Agricultural Stabilization and Conservation Service (ASCS) of the Department of Agriculture, the National Marine Fisheries Service (NMFS) of the Department of Commerce, and various state and local wetlands agencies are all heavily involved in the wetlands process.

a. The Army Corps of Engineers. As the federal agency responsible for the issuance of dredge and fill permits, the Corps is the most important contact for most wetlands permit applicants. The local Corps district office is available to offer assistance with general inquiries, help an applicant start the permit process, and advise of additional requirements that may involve other federal, state, or local authorities.[39]

If a general permit or permit exemption is not available,[40] a Corps' district engineer will coordinate the various elements of an individual permit application, including the consideration of other state and federal requirements. In so doing, the Corps uses a variety of methods to reduce duplication.[41] Beyond its general section 404 authority, the Corps' actions are dictated by a series of other laws, memoranda of agreement (MOA), and regulatory guidance letters (RGL).[42] Among the most important of the wetlands-related laws are the Endangered Species Act, the National Environmental Policy Act, the Coastal Zone Management Act, the Fish and Wildlife Coordination Act, the National Historic Preservation Act, and the Marine Protection, Research, and Sanctuaries Act of 1972.[43]

For instance, in considering a permit application, the Corps must be cognizant of section 7 of the Endangered Species Act that requires federal agencies to inform the Department of the Interior or the Department of Commerce if a proposed agency action would threaten an endangered species.[44]

Historically, the Corps has issued almost two-thirds of the wetlands permits which it has evaluated. A small percentage of permits are denied and the remainder are eventually withdrawn. An applicant should expect an application

[39] 33 C.F.R. §320 (1992). Although the Corps provides assistance during the permit process, the Corps officially is "neither a proponent or opponent of any permit proposal." 33 C.F.R. §320.1(a)(4) (1992).

[40] CWA §404(e), 33 U.S.C. §1344(e) (1988) addresses general permits and §404(f), 33 U.S.C. §1344(f) (1988) covers major nonprohibited discharges.

[41] 33 C.F.R. §320.1(a)(5) (1992).

[42] The Corps' general regulatory policy is found at 33 C.F.R. §320 (1992) *et seq.* Copies of MOA's or RGL's for specific wetlands issues may be obtained from the district engineer or, in most instances, from EPA.

[43] 33 C.F.R. §320.4(j)(4) (1992).

[44] 16 U.S.C. §1536 (1988).

review process of anywhere from several days to several months depending on the complexity of the case and the workload of the Corps district office.[45]

b. The Environmental Protection Agency. EPA performs a dual role in the administration of section 404 by developing the 404(b)(1) guidelines and by commenting on individual permit actions as part of the "public interest review."[46] EPA assists the Corps in determining the parameters of wetlands jurisdiction and in determining the structure of the section 404 exemptions. Most important from a major impact standpoint, EPA has "veto" authority pursuant to section 404(c).[47] This means that even if the Corps deems a permit application acceptable, EPA may independently deny its issuance. This extreme authority has only been exercised by EPA 11 times.

Other important wetlands tasks carried out by EPA include offering practicable measures to mitigate adverse impacts of certain permit activities, overseeing the state delegation program, and administering the NPDES permit program.[48]

c. The U.S. Fish and Wildlife Service. The FWS, pursuant to the Fish and Wildlife Coordination Act,[49] is afforded the opportunity to comment on section 404 permit applications. In addition, FWS is active in bringing new wetlands areas into the Coastal Barrier Resource System and in managing over 90 million acres of land in the National Wildlife Refuge System, of which a sizable percentage is wetlands.[50] Finally, FWS is responsible for creating national wetlands inventory maps, which although not definitive of wetlands jurisdiction, serve as a source for initially evaluating whether an area may be a wetland.

Because the FWS and several other branches of the Department of the Interior address wetlands issues, the Secretary of Interior has established an interdepartment task force on wetlands issues. Representatives from the Department of the Interior are equipped to offer advice and referrals to permit applicants on a wide range of wetlands subjects.

d. The Soil and Conservation Service and the Agricultural Stabilization and Conservation Service. At the Department of Agriculture both the SCS and the ASCS perform important wetlands-related functions. The SCS, among other responsibilities, identifies land that is covered by the Swampbuster provision of the Food Security Act and, where applicable, grants permit exemp-

---

[45] U.S. Army Corps of Engineers, Regulatory Program: Applicant Information, EP 1145-2-1 (May 1985), at 6, [hereinafter Corps Applicant Information]. The Corps Applicant Information pamphlet is currently being updated and is expected to be released during 1994.

[46] 33 C.F.R. §320.4(a), .4(b)(3) (1992).

[47] The veto provision, which allows EPA to deny a permit otherwise approved by the Corps, may only be invoked when EPA determines that the granting of a permit would result in certain "unacceptable adverse effect[s] on municipal water supplies, shellfish beds and fishery areas (including spawning and breeding areas), wildlife, or recreation areas." 33 U.S.C. §1344(c) (1988). On August 11, 1992, EPA and the Corps signed a Memorandum of Agreement addressing the minimization of duplication provision of §404(q), which among other topics, clarifies EPA's role under §404(c).

[48] *See* Memorandum of Agreement between EPA and the Corps, August 11, 1992, at 2, 40 C.F.R. §233 (1992), and 33 U.S.C. §1342 (1988).

[49] 16 U.S.C. §§661–66c (1988). *See also* 33 C.F.R. §320.3(e), .4(c) (1992).

[50] General Accounting Office, Wetlands Overview 34 (November 22, 1992) [hereinafter November 1991 GAO Report].

tions.[51] For permit denials, SCS has an extensive agency appeal mechanism.[52] Over the eight-year period since the Swampbuster provision was enacted, SCS has performed over two million wetlands delineations (involving nearly 15 million acres) requested by farmers.[53]

If a farmer illegally fills wetlands, or otherwise violates Swampbuster regulations, the ASCS is the agency responsible for enforcing this provision.[54] Additionally, the ASCS handles administrative appeals under Swampbuster.[55]

e. The National Marine Fisheries Service. The Fish and Wildlife Coordination Act authorizes the NMFS to comment on section 404 permits, especially with regard to coastal wetlands matters.[56]

f. State and Local Wetlands Involvement. In addition to the many federal entities involved in the wetlands process, state and local wetlands authorities often play an important role in permit evaluations. The CWA authorizes a state to assume the 404 program but, to date, only one state has chosen to do so.[57] Even if a state has not assumed the 404 program, the Corps will normally require a permit applicant to comply with the additional requirements imposed by the state in which the wetland is located.[58]

In some states, such as New Jersey, wetlands activity requires a state permit in addition to the federal section 404 permit.[59] Most of the state permit programs exist in coastal states and are designed to regulate loss of estuarine and marine wetlands.[60] More typical are states that only require water quality certifications or compliance with a coastal zone management plan.[61]

In some areas local governments become involved in thc permit process through local authorizations or certifications or as a result of zoning and land

---

[51] 16 U.S.C. §3821 (1988). Contained in the Food Security Act, the so-called "Swampbuster" provision denies various federal farm benefits to farmers who plant crops on wetlands that were converted after December 23, 1985. *Id.* A final rule issued by the Corps and EPA on August 25, 1993, clarified that "prior converted wetlands" (i.e., wetlands created before 12/23/85) are not waters of the United States for purposes of the Clean Water Act. 58 Fed. Reg. 45,008 (1993).

[52] November 1991 GAO Report, *supra* note 50, at 35.

[53] *Id.*

[54] *Id.*

[55] *Id.* The role of SCS in making wetlands determinations was discussed in an August 25, 1993, Corps/EPA final rule on the CWA Regulatory Programs. The final rule recognizes the need for farmers to be able "to rely on SCS wetlands determinations for purposes of complying with both the Swampbuster program and the section 404 program." 58 Fed. Reg. 45,032–33 (1993). In this regard, the Corps, EPA, SCS, and FWS are expected to issue a Memorandum of Agreement on one stop shopping for farmers seeking wetlands determinations, either late 1993 or early 1994.

[56] 16 U.S.C. §§661–66c (1988); *see also* 33 C.F.R. §320.4(b)(3), .4(c) (1992).

[57] CWA §404, 33 U.S.C. §1344 (1988), authorizes a state to carry out the regulations and procedures necessary to administer the wetlands permit program. Only the State of Michigan (Michigan Department of Natural Resources) has proposed a state program pursuant to the requirements of §404(g) and 40 C.F.R. §233, and has had its program approved by EPA pursuant to §404(h).

[58] 33 C.F.R. §320.4(j) (1992).

[59] New Jersey requires state permits for both coastal and freshwater wetlands. Coastal wetlands are regulated under the Wetlands Act of 1970, P.L. 1970, c. 272, N.J.S.A. 13:9A-1 *et seq.;* freshwater wetlands are governed by the Freshwater Wetlands Protection Act, P.L. 1987, c. 156, N.J.S.A. 13:9 B-1 *et seq.*

[60] As of 1990, 18 of 26 coastal states and territories had adopted permit programs for coastal wetlands. EPA 1990 Report to Congress, *supra* note 6, at 79.

[61] Section 305(b) of the CWA requires EPA to compile information on state wetlands programs. 33 U.S.C. §1315. In 1990, 42 states reported having programs in place to protect wetlands. EPA 1990 Report to Congress, *supra* note 6, at 78.

use decisions.[62] Corps regulations not only recognize this local interest but affirmatively state that local zoning and land use decisions will be accepted by the district engineer unless there are significant issues of overriding national importance.[63]

C. Definition of Wetlands

Both the Corps and EPA are quick to point out that they have been using the same general definition of wetlands since 1977.[64] EPA's guidelines for section 404 define wetlands as "areas inundated or saturated by surface or groundwater at a frequency and duration sufficient to support . . . a prevalence of vegetation typically adapted for life in saturated soil conditions."[65] Generally speaking, wetlands are "swamps, marshes, bogs, and similar areas."[66]

History is an excellent indicator of how confusing the science of identifying and delineating wetlands can be. Despite the existence of a "general" wetlands definition since 1977, prior to 1989 the various federal agencies participating in the process of delineating jurisdictional wetlands did so according to different methods and procedures. The Corps used the *Corps of Engineers Wetlands Delineation Manual* (the 1987 Manual),[67] EPA adopted the *Wetlands Identification and Delineation Manual,*[68] and the SCS derived its definition from the *Food Security Act Manual.*[69]

As a result of language placed in the 1992 and 1993 Energy and Water Development Appropriations Acts, section 404 wetlands delineations are now based on criteria contained in the 1987 Manual.[70] The wetlands definition contained in the 1987 Manual revolves around three principal characteristics: hydrology, hydric soils, and hydrophytic vegetation.[71]

Applicants that were denied permits as a result of delineations performed under the 1989 Manual may find different results under the current criteria

---

[62] 33 C.F.R. §320.4(j) (1992).

[63] 33 C.F.R. §320.4(j)(2) (1992). State law may also require such items as compliance with a coastal zone management plan or submission of a state water quality certification.

[64] ENVIRONMENTAL PROTECTION AGENCY, OFFICE OF WETLANDS, OCEANS AND WATERSHEDS, BACKGROUNDER ON THE PROPOSED REVISED FEDERAL MANUAL FOR WETLANDS DELINEATION, at 2 (August 14, 1991). *See also* 42 Fed. Reg. 37,122, 37,144 (1977).

[65] 40 C.F.R. §230.3(t) (1992). This definition also appears in the Corps' regulatory policies at 33 C.F.R. §328.3(b) (1992).

[66] 33 C.F.R. §328.3(b) (1992).

[67] ENVIRONMENTAL LABORATORY, DEP'T OF THE ARMY, CORPS OF ENGINEERS WETLANDS DELINEATION MANUAL (1987).

[68] WILLIAM S. SIPPLE, ENVIRONMENTAL PROTECTION AGENCY, WETLAND IDENTIFICATION AND DELINEATION MANUAL (1988).

[69] SCS uses a definition of wetlands taken from the Food Security Act of 1985. 16 U.S.C. §3801(a)(16). SCS performs wetlands delineations to determine whether certain acreage qualifies for agricultural subsidies. NOVEMBER 1991 GAO REPORT, *supra* note 50, at 35.

[70] The Corps began to use the 1987 Manual on August 17, 1991. Over the next six months, the Corps released three memoranda clarifying various issues relating to use of the 1987 Manual. These memoranda, dated October 7, 1991, February 20, 1992, and March 6, 1992, address issues such as wetlands technical criteria and wetlands indicators. The October 7, 1991, Memorandum states that EPA concurred in use of the 1987 Manual for "all actions." But, as discussed (in Section II.A.) above, until recently this was a point of some contention. October 7, 1991, Memorandum, at 3.

[71] The presence of water, measured by inundation or saturation to the surface for a specified number of days, indicates wetlands hydrology. Hydric soils, which are listed by the National Technical Committee for Hydric Soils, contain certain characteristics (such as organic or sulfidic material) found in wetlands. Plants that live in wet conditions are characterized by the term hydrophytic vegetation. 1987 Manual, at 16–17, 26, 30, 34.

because the the 1987 Manual differs from the 1989 Manual in several significant areas.[72] Most noteworthy, the 1987 Manual requires independent evidence of hydrology, hydric soils, and hydrophytic vegetation in order for an area to be classified a wetland.[73] The two manuals also differ in the way various types of vegetation are measured,[74] and as to the duration of inundation or saturation necessary to constitute wetlands hydrology.

To satisfy the hydric soil criteria under the 1987 Manual, an area usually requires inundation or saturation to the surface and a water table within 1.5 ft. from the surface for a significant part of the growing season (usually seven or more consecutive days).[75] Similarly, the hydrology criteria is satisfied only if soil is inundated or saturated to the surface for at least five percent of the growing season.[76] The criteria for hydrophytic vegetation requires that more than 50 percent of the dominant species must be obligate (always found in wetlands), facultative wetland (usually found in wetlands), or facultative (found equally in wetlands or non-wetlands).[77] Stated another way, hydrophytic vegetation is present "when the dominant species in a plant community are typically adapted for life in anaerobic (the absence of oxygen) soil conditions."[78]

Understanding the specifics of the technical criteria for wetlands is not necessary in order for an applicant successfully to apply for and receive a permit: whether or not wetlands indicators are present where the proposed activity is to occur is clearly beyond the control of the applicant. Nevertheless, general knowledge of the way in which the Corps and EPA technically define wetlands may help prepare an applicant for the sobering reality that jurisdictional wetlands are not always recognizably wet.

D. The Permit Process

1. General Information

An individual, business, or other party interested in obtaining a wetlands permit should become familiar with the Corps' general regulatory policies set forth in the Code of Federal Regulations (for "Navigation and Navigable

---

[72] Applicants receiving unsuccessful wetlands determinations under the 1989 Manual may petition the Corps for a new determination under the 1987 Manual.

[73] 1987 Manual, at 14. Because of confusing language in the 1989 Manual, some delineators took the position that a wetlands determination could be based solely on the existence of hydric soils (without even considering wetlands hydrology or hydrophytic vegetation). In these cases, delineators reasoned that the presence of hydric soils strongly suggested that an area contained wetlands hydrology and would support plant life normally found in wetlands conditions. The 1991 Revisions, 56 Fed. Reg. 40,446 (1991).

[74] The 1989 Manual includes facultative upland species (i.e., those plants that usually occur in non-wetlands but occasionally are found in wetlands) in the calculation of whether an area meets the hydrophytic vegetation criteria. The 1987 Manual includes only obligate wetland plants (almost always occur in wetlands), facultative wetland plants (usually occur in wetlands—more than a 67% probability), and facultative plants (occur equally in wetlands or non-wetlands) in the calculation of hydrophytic vegetation, and specifically excludes facultative upland plants. Army COE Memorandum, Implementation of the 1987 Corps Wetland Delineation Manual, at 4 (August 27, 1991). *See also* 1989 Manual, at 5, and 1987 Manual, at 16–26.

[75] 1987 Manual, at 26–32. A list of hydric soils, based on these criteria, has been established by the National Technical Committee for Hydric Soils. *Id.* at 32.

[76] *Id.* at 36–38, 50. Allowing for the nation's substantial regional differences, the Corps and EPA will require that some areas be inundated or saturated to the surface for 12.5% or more of the growing season in order to be called wetlands. *Id.* at 36.

[77] *Id.* at 17.

[78] *Id.*

Waters'')[79] and related federal and state wetlands materials. The Corps' regulatory policies generally discuss the rationale behind the permit program and the specific conditions that must be met before the Corps will issue an individual or general permit.[80]

Familiarity with wetlands regulations may be achieved in a variety of ways. As mentioned above, the many federal and state agencies responsible for wetlands issues serve as a wealth of information for the permit applicant. Personnel from these agencies are available for consultation and to provide applicants with guidelines for specific programs and requirements. Also, EPA has established a national toll-free hotline for general wetlands questions.[81]

For individuals and businesses with complex wetlands problems, environmental consulting services may prove useful in making initial wetlands assessments and in facilitating the application process.[82]

2. *Initial Evaluation and Considerations*

As the complex regulatory structure suggests, applying for and receiving a wetlands permit can be a time-consuming experience.[83] Advance planning and utilization of government-provided resources will greatly reduce the likelihood of costly permit delays. In certain situations, a preapplication consultation will determine that a wetlands permit is not necessary.

a. Preapplication Consultations. As a first step, a potential applicant for a section 404 permit should strongly consider participating in a preapplication meeting with a representative from the local Corps office. This prepermit consultation is encouraged by the Corps as a means to make the applicant aware of the permit process and to allow the Corps to involve, at the earliest possible date, other parties that may be affected by the proposed activity.[84] Other interested parties may include federal agencies, such as EPA and the FWS, state agencies, local agencies, and the public.

Corps personnel will routinely discuss potential alternatives to the proposed activity, outline the factors used in the permit decision-making process, and aid the applicant in complying with NEPA guidelines.[85]

The preapplication conference may also save an applicant time and money by establishing the existence of an applicable permit exemption or general permit, both of which alleviate the necessity for an individual permit.

---

[79] These General Regulatory Policies, found at 33 C.F.R. §320–30 (1992), include a description of the ''public interest review.'' The public interest review involves a balancing of the favorable and detrimental impacts of an action so as to achieve the protection and utilization of important resources. 33 C.F.R. §320.1(a), .4(a) (1992). The regulatory policies also outline the types of activities regulated (§320.1(b)), and give the general considerations for permit applications (§320.4).

[80] CORPS APPLICANT INFORMATION *supra* note 45, at 4.

[81] The national toll-free wetlands hotline number is 1-800-832-7828.

[82] This type of service varies widely in terms of price and experience of the delineators. The Corps district engineer may offer suggestions of reputable consultants upon request.

[83] ''Routine'' permit applications, involving public notice, normally take two to three months to be processed. CORPS APPLICANT INFORMATION *supra* note 45, at 4.

[84] 33 C.F.R. §325.1(b) (1992).

[85] *Id.* The application of NEPA to the permit process is referenced at 33 C.F.R. §320.3(d). *See also* 42 U.S.C. §§4321–47 (1988).

b. Permit Exemptions. Under the CWA, certain discharges of dredged or fill material are permissible.[86] Activity that does not require a permit includes discharges of dredged or fill material from normal farming, silviculture, and ranching, from dam and bridge maintenance, from farm pond and road construction and maintenance, and from forest road construction and maintenance.[87] These exemptions do not apply if the activity has as its purpose bringing an area of navigable waters into a use to which it was not previously subject, where the flow or circulation of these waters is reduced or impaired.[88] Additionally, these exemptions are limited by the Corps' extensive, narrowly drawn guidelines governing their use.[89]

c. General Permits. General permits, issued on a state, regional, or nationwide basis, form the other major category of exemption from the wetlands permit requirements.[90] The general permit program authorizes the Corps to issue activity-specific permits if the discharge is of such a type that it will result in only minimal adverse environmental effect.[91] Of these general permits, there are numerous nationwide permits (NWPs) covering a wide range of activity.[92] Although many of these permits do not require the applicant to notify the Corps before beginning the listed activity, notification is advisable and may save an applicant from later difficulties brought about from excessive or noncovered discharges.[93]

The Corps lists 13 general conditions, and nine specific conditions (applying only to section 404 activities), of which applicants for NWPs must be cognizant.[94] General conditions relate to navigation, proper maintenance of structure, erosion control, aquatic life movement, heavy equipment, regional conditions, wild and scenic rivers, tribal rights, water quality certification, coastal zone management, endangered species, historic properties, and notification.[95] Additional conditions imposed specifically on wetlands permit applicants include prohibitions on discharges near a public water supply, discharges in a concentrated shellfish area, discharges of unsuitable material, discharges in spawning areas, discharges obstructing high flows, discharges causing adverse impacts from impoundments, discharges into waterfowl breeding areas, dis-

---

[86] CWA §404(f), 33 U.S.C. §1344(f) (1988).

[87] CWA §404(f)(1), 33 U.S.C. §1344(f)(1) (1988). The CWA also exempts from permit requirements congressionally authorized federal construction projects that comply with NEPA (contain an environmental impact statement). 33 U.S.C. §1344(r) (1988).

[88] CWA §404(f)(2), 33 U.S.C. §1344(f)(2) (1988).

[89] 33 C.F.R. §323.4 (1992).

[90] CWA §404(e), 33 U.S.C. §1344(e) (1988).

[91] *Id.*

[92] 33 C.F.R. §330, App. A (1992). For a comprehensive discussion of general permits and the relationship between general permits and various environmental regulations, *see* W. WANT, THE LAW OF WETLANDS REGULATION, *supra* note 5. As part of the comprehensive wetlands plan announced by the Administration on August 24, 1993, the Clinton Administration is currently working on adding additional nationwide permits. See a discussion of the Clinton wetlands plan in Section II.G of this chapter.

[93] *See* 33 C.F.R. §330.6 (1992) for a general discussion of the Corps' authorization process for nationwide permits. Some NWPs, such as NWP 26, require an applicant to notify the district engineer and to include a wetlands delineation in the notification. 33 C.F.R. §330, App. A, (B)(26) (1992).

[94] 33 C.F.R. §330, App. A, (C) (1992).

[95] *Id.*

charges that are contrary to established mitigation procedures, and discharge activity that does not result in the removal of all temporary fills.[96]

d. Preliminary Assessment. Finally, a potential applicant should make certain that its seemingly "wet" proposed area of activity is actually a jurisdictional wetland. During the preapplication conference, a potential applicant will be notified that it must obtain a wetlands determination if a preliminary assessment has not already been performed. Although an applicant may request the Corps to perform this wetlands determination, using an outside consultant may save a considerable amount of time.[97]

3. *Obtaining an Individual Permit*

After receiving a wetlands determination, and eliminating the possibility of a permit exemption, an individual wishing to fill wetlands must seek an individual wetlands permit. The permit process generally involves submission of a permit application, followed by public notice, a comment period, a public hearing, a public interest review and section 404(b)(1) evaluation, and ultimate notification that the permit has been approved or denied.[98]

a. Permit Application Form. An applicant may obtain a permit application from the local Corps district office. The Corps uses a standard application form,[99] which requires a complete description of the activity proposed, including drawings, the location, purpose, and need for the proposed activity, the scheduling of the activity, the names and addresses of adjoining property owners, the location of adjacent structures, and a list of authorizations required by other federal, state, and local agencies for the work, including approvals received or denials already made.[100] Detailed engineering plans are not required but the drawings and application answers must be descriptive enough to allow the Corps to issue a public notice.[101] The district engineer may request additional information necessary to conduct the public interest determination and to determine compliance with the section 404(b)(1) guidelines.[102] A nominal fee, usually $10, is charged for permits but no fee will be charged if the application is withdrawn or denied.[103]

b. Public Notice. If the application is complete, the Corps will issue a public notice of the proposed activity. The Corps is required to issue this notice within 15 days of receiving a completed application,[104] but this schedule may be

---

[96] *Id.*

[97] District engineers are authorized to determine whether an area is jurisdictionally a wetland except in instances where EPA has made a §404 jurisdictional determination under its authority. 33 C.F.R. §325.9 (1992).

[98] 33 C.F.R. §325 (1992). Some permit applications do not necessitate each of these procedural steps, such as the public hearing.

[99] Some areas utilize local variations of the application form to facilitate coordination with federal, state, and local agencies. 33 C.F.R. §325.1(c) (1992).

[100] 33 C.F.R. §325.1(d)(1) (1992).

[101] 33 C.F.R. §325.1(d)(1), .1(d)(2) (1992).

[102] 33 C.F.R. §325.1(e) (1992).

[103] 33 C.F.R. §325.1(f) (1992). Additional fees may be required if the application is a joint federal/state submission.

[104] 33 C.F.R. §325.2(a)(2) (1992).

extended if the project is complex or for administrative purposes. The public notice is designed to put a variety of interested parties, including individuals, other federal agencies, local agencies, and state agencies on notice of the proposed activity and to solicit from those parties the comments necessary to evaluate the probable impact on the public interest.[105] The public notice will normally include the basic information contained in the permit application plus applicable statutory authorities, the Corps' contact employee, a list of other governmental authorizations sought and obtained, and information regarding NEPA, historic properties, endangered species, and/or coastal zone management plans.[106]

c. Comment Period. Following the Corps' issuance of a public notice, interested parties have an opportunity to provide comments on the permit application. This is the stage where an applicant is likely to find out if other federal or state requirements need to be satisfied. For instance, the state may require a water quality certification or may deem the proposed permit to be in violation of coastal zone management plans. On the federal side, the FWS may be concerned about a specific endangered or threatened species.

Interested parties having real or potential problems with the proposed permit will direct their comments to the Corps, and the Corps, in turn, will notify the applicant of these problems. At this point an applicant may wish to contact the concerned parties and try to resolve their differences in order to keep the permit application on track.

Normally, the comment period will last from 15 to 30 days depending on the nature of the activity, but this review period may be extended if information is missing or if a related law requires a longer time period.[107] If the problem requires additional compliance work, the permit process will be delayed. This underscores the need to explore the various federal and state areas of wetlands involvement during the preapplication meeting.

d. Public Interest Review and the 404(b)(1) Guidelines: Regulatory Approach and Criteria. Evaluation of the comments received from interested parties is an important part of what the Corps has termed the "public interest review." This review, which is a central element of the permit application evaluation, involves the consideration of the full public interest by balancing the favorable and detrimental impacts.[108] Specifically, the public interest review involves "an evaluation of the probable impact, including cumulative impact, of the proposed activity and its intended use on the public interest."[109] Specific factors considered include conservation, economics, aesthetics, general environmental concerns, wetlands, historic properties, fish and wildlife values, flood hazards, flood plain values, land use, navigation, shore erosion and accretion, recreation, water supply and conservation, water quality, energy needs, safety, food and fiber production, mineral needs, considerations of property ownership

---

[105] 33 C.F.R. §325.3(a) (1992).
[106] 33 C.F.R. §325.3 (1992).
[107] CORPS APPLICANT INFORMATION, *supra* note 45, at 7.
[108] 33 C.F.R. §320.1(a) (1992).
[109] 33 C.F.R. §320.4(a) (1992).

and, in general the needs and welfare of the people.[110] The activity must also comply with the EPA section 404(b)(1) guidelines.

The district engineer will be particularly concerned with the public and private need for the proposed work, the practicability of alternative locations and building methods, the extent and permanence of the beneficial and/or detrimental effects, the effect on wetlands in general, on fish and wildlife, on water quality, on historic cultural scenic and recreational values, on coastal waters, and on state and local requirements.[111]

e. Mitigation. During consideration of the permit application, the district engineer will discuss mitigation possibilities. Corps regulations direct the district engineer to discuss mitigation possibilities at the preapplication meeting and throughout the entire application process to minimize adverse project impact.[112] Mitigation is an important part of this process and may ultimately determine whether the application is approved or denied.

Mitigation can come in many forms and is only generally discussed in the Corps' regulatory policies.[113] The Corps' comments on mitigation complement the mitigation requirements that are required in connection with the Clean Water Act section 404(b)(1) guidelines. In this regard, the Corps and EPA signed a Memorandum of Agreement in February 1990 that was designed to clarify the mitigation requirements of section 404(b)(1). This memorandum sets forth a sequencing process that must be followed to determine the type and level of mitigation necessary to comply with section 404 of the CWA. In short, mitigation requires the avoidance of adverse impacts, minimization, or compensatory mitigation.[114]

f. EPA "Veto." The EPA permit veto, found in section 404(c) of the Clean Water Act, is an infrequently used, but extremely powerful authority. Pursuant to the section 404(b)(1) guidelines, EPA may initiate the veto process at any time during the Corps' consideration of a permit application.[115] Normally, EPA exercises the veto only after the Corps has decided to approve a permit application. EPA may only invoke this veto if the granting of a permit would result in certain "unacceptable adverse effect[s] on municipal water supplies, shellfish beds and fishery areas (including spawning and breeding areas), wildlife, or recreation areas."[116] The EPA veto is an important topic in the continuing political discussions over reform of the wetlands program.

g. Final Decision. Normally, district engineers will make a final decision on applications not later than 60 days after receipt of a completed application.[117] Exceptions to this 60-day rule are made when the comment period is extended, when submittal of information is not timely, when an application has been

---

[110] 33 C.F.R. §320.4(a)(1) (1992).

[111] 33 C.F.R. §320.4 (1992).

[112] 33 C.F.R. §320.4(r) (1992).

[113] *Id.*

[114] Memorandum of Agreement betweeen EPA and the Department of the Army concerning mitigation guidelines under CWA §404(b)(1) (February 6, 1990).

[115] 40 C.F.R. §231.1 (1992).

[116] CWA §404(c), 33 U.S.C. §1344(c) (1988). *See also supra* note 47.

[117] 33 C.F.R. §325.2 (1992).

suspended at the request of the applicant, or when information needed by the district engineer cannot be obtained within the 60-day period.[118]

E. Wetlands Appeals and Enforcement

1. Appealing a Corps Permit Denial

District engineers are specifically authorized to deny permits under section 404 of the Clean Water Act and under other Acts for which they have permit issuing authority.[119] A permit denial must contain the district engineer's name, detailed reasons for the permit denial, and a Statement of Findings that conclusively justifies the denial decision.[120] Furthermore, district engineers may deny permits without issuing a public notice or taking other procedural steps if other applicable permits have been denied or the proposed activity clearly interferes with navigation.[121]

A district engineer may also modify, suspend, or revoke an individual or regional permit if such action is necessary to protect the public interest.[122] If the district engineer suspends a permit, the applicant will be given 10 days to request a meeting with the district engineer and/or ask for a public hearing to challenge or comment on the suspension.[123] Following the meeting, hearing, or passage of a "reasonable period of time," the permit will be reinstated, modified, or revoked.[124]

Permit revocations and denials, with few exceptions, constitute final agency action.[125] Thus, an applicant wishing to appeal the Corps' decision, must do so in the appropriate district court. The district engineer's findings, pursuant to the public interest review and application of the section 404(b)(1) guidelines, will be taken as given by the court.

Recently, a large number of applicants denied wetlands permits have challenged the Corps' actions as unconstitutional takings in violation of the Fifth Amendment.[126] Takings challenges are predominantly made in the United States Court of Federal Claims.

---

[118] *Id.*

[119] 33 C.F.R. §325.8(a), .8(b) (1992). District engineers are also authorized to deny permits under §§9 and 10 of the Rivers and Harbors Appropriations Act of 1899, *supra* note 38, and §103 of the Marine Protection, Research and Sanctuaries Act of 1972, as amended, 33 U.S.C. §1401 *et seq. Id.*

[120] *Id.*

[121] *Id.*

[122] 33 C.F.R. §325.7 (1992).

[123] *Id.* at §325.7(b)-(d) (1992).

[124] 33 C.F.R. §325.7(c) (1992). Corps regulations do not specify the meaning of a "reasonable period of time."

[125] A district engineer's decision to deny a permit will be referred to the Corps' division engineer if a referral is required by written agreement, when the Governor from the state where the proposed activity is to occur has objected (in writing) to the denial, when substantial doubt exists as to the applicable authority, when requested by a higher authority, or when the district engineer is precluded by law from taking final action. 33 C.F.R. §325.8(b)(1-5) (1992).

[126] Lucas v. South Carolina Coastal Council, 112 S. Ct. 2886, 34 ER Cases 1897 (1992), one of the most important takings cases, does not involve a wetlands permit denial, but does contain circumstances generally applicable to wetlands and §404. *See* discussion below. Also, see GAO Report on takings cases, *supra* note 4.

2. *Appeal of a Section 404(c) Veto*

As mentioned above, EPA may under certain extraordinary circumstances veto the Corps' decision to issue a permit.[127] Before making a final determination to veto a project, EPA will meet with the Corps, the property owner, and the applicant to discuss EPA's recommendations and to give each of these parties an opportunity to correct any unacceptable adverse impacts. After a specified period of time, the EPA Administrator will make a final determination regarding the Regional Administrator's recommendations. A decision to exercise the veto authority constitutes final agency action and may only be appealed to the courts.[128]

3. *Wetlands Enforcement*

Somewhat distinct from but important to the permit process is the issue of wetlands enforcement. The Corps and EPA share the responsibility for enforcing the laws against unauthorized discharges of dredged and fill material and discharges that exceed the scope of an individual permit.[129] Corps and EPA enforcement authority derives primarily from the CWA and the Water Quality Act of 1987.[130]

Wetlands violations may be enforced through a variety of means including civil penalties, criminal penalties, and mandated restoration.[131] If the unlawful action is a knowing violation of the CWA, penalties may be severe. For instance, courts may assess fines of up to $50,000 per day of the violation, jail sentences of up to three years, or both.[132]

F. Significant Wetlands Litigation

Over the past several years the courts have been heavily involved in wetlands-related cases. These cases have addressed issues such as whether denial of a permit constitutes an unconstitutional taking, the range of EPA's jurisdiction, and the monetary value of wetlands on state and local tax rolls. Because of their importance to the overall permit process, several of these cases are briefly discussed below.

1. *The* Lucas *Case*

With the exception of wetlands definition, perhaps no wetlands-related issue has received more attention in recent months than the question of whether denial of a permit constitutes a compensable taking. Congress has debated and

---

[127] CWA §404(c), 33 U.S.C. §1344(c) (1988).

[128] 40 C.F.R. §231 (1992).

[129] CWA §309, 33 U.S.C. §1319 (1988). *See also* Memorandum of Agreement between the Department of the Army and EPA concerning federal enforcement for the CWA §404 program (Jan. 19, 1989) [hereinafter Wetlands Enforcement Memorandum].

[130] Pub. L. No. 100-4, 101 Stat. 7, 33 U.S.C. §1251 *et seq.*

[131] CWA §309, 33 U.S.C. §1319 (1988).

[132] CWA §309(c)(2), 33 U.S.C. §1319(c)(2) (1988). *See also* United States v. Ellen, 961 F.2d 462, 35 ER Cases 1165 (4th Cir. 1992), and Wetlands Enforcement Memorandum *supra* note 129.

continues actively to consider the question,[133] and the Clinton Administration inherited a Bush initiative that calls for incorporating a takings analysis into the federal wetlands program.

Although not specifically about wetlands, a takings case presenting virtually identical issues reached the U.S. Supreme Court in early 1992. In *Lucas v. South Carolina Coastal Council,*[134] the state court found that a South Carolina law that prohibited Lucas from building on two beachfront lots for which he had paid $975,000 acted as a "taking" and entitled Lucas to $1.2 million in compensation.[135] On appeal, the South Carolina Supreme Court reversed the decision, holding that beach areas are valuable public resources and that the state law in question was necessary to prohibit construction and prevent public harm.[136]

In June 1992, the U.S. Supreme Court ruled in favor of Lucas. The Court held that a property owner must be compensated when a law or regulation deprives that owner of all economically beneficial use of the property unless the use constitutes a nuisance or violates state common law property principles.[137]

The decision generated a wide range of comment from both environmental and development interests with both sides viewing the decision as a victory. Organizations and individuals with environmental advocacy groups have taken comfort in the fact that the decision requires a landowner to meet the very difficult burden of proving a *total* loss of economic value if he or she expects to be compensated for the inability to develop a regulated parcel of land. Past judicial decisions reveal few instances in which courts or administrative bodies have found that denial of a permit has resulted in the loss of all economic value of a piece of property.

On the other hand, private property rights advocates are encouraged by the Supreme Court's recognition that severe governmental actions designed to halt development clearly give rise to compensable takings. There is likely to be a flood of new litigation challenging government action and regulations that have the effect of denying property owners the use of their land without compensation. In addition, more and more states are likely to consider proposals that require a takings impact analysis to be done in instances where laws and regulations deny a property owner use of his or her land.

In late September 1992, the U.S. Supreme Court chose not to review a wetlands regulation case, *Tull v. Virginia,*[138] which involved the calculation of compensable takings in situations where wetlands regulations caused the loss of property values. Both the trial court and the Virginia Supreme Court determined that the denial of a permit in Accomack County, Virginia, did not constitute a compensable taking because the permit denial did not deprive the property owner of *all* economically feasible use of the property. The U.S. Supreme

[133] Senator Symms (R-Idaho) introduced S. 50 (The Private Property Rights Act of 1992) during the 102d Congress and nearly succeeded in gaining its passage. The measure was included in the Senate version of the 1992 Transportation Appropriations bill, but was ultimately removed during the conference on this legislation.

[134] 112 S. Ct. 2886, 34 ER Cases 1897 (1992).

[135] Lucas v. South Carolina Coastal Council, Order filed Aug. 14, 1989 (Court of Common Pleas).

[136] Lucas v. South Carolina Coastal Council, 404 S.E.2d 895 (S.C. 1991).

[137] 112 S. Ct. 2886, 34 ER Cases 1897 (1992).

[138] 113 S. Ct. 191, No. 92-112 (Oct. 5, 1992), *cert. denied.*

Court's decision not to review *Tull* may signal that the narrow view of *Lucas*—that only complete loss of value gives rise to a compensable taking—is the standard that courts will generally adopt for wetlands cases.

2. *EPA's Role in the Permit Process*

Another consistently litigated issue has been the nature and scope of EPA's involvement in the wetlands permit process. This type of suit usually arises because a permit applicant believes EPA has exceeded its statutory authority or because an interested third party[139] (or EPA itself) complains that EPA has been unlawfully restricted from becoming involved in an individual permit decision. The latter situation recently occurred in *Hoffman Homes v. EPA.*[140]

In this case, the Court of Appeals for the Seventh Circuit reversed a decision by EPA to impose an administrative penalty of $50,000 on a development company in Illinois that filled a 0.8 acre isolated wetland.[141] EPA had attempted to exercise jurisdiction over the land on the basis of the Commerce Clause, arguing that "migratory birds could, potentially, use the wetland as a place to feed, or nest or as a stopover on the way to the Gulf States for the winter months." The Seventh Circuit refused to give this broad a reading to the Clean Water Act. In early September 1992, the court vacated its decision, granted EPA a rehearing, and called for settlement negotiations.

3. *Other Wetlands-Specific Litigation*

Given the large number of permit applications and subsequent Corps' decisions, it is not surprising that many applicants have chosen to seek judicial relief as it often represents their only means of reversing an unfavorable decision. The sometimes unexpected and harsh practical effect of wetlands regulation has given rise to some unusual causes of action as well. One such example of a potential alternative means of relief is a petition by an unsuccessful applicant to have his or her jurisdictional "wetland" valued on the tax rolls to reflect the limited uses of the property. Throughout the country, tax assessors have been forced to reduce drastically the tax valuation of wetlands tracts.

Recently, a borough in New Jersey found itself litigating just such an issue. In *Bergen County Ass'n v. Borough of East Rutherford,*[142] the Tax Court of New Jersey reassessed local property taxes downward by more than $19 million for a 240-acre area of wetlands in northern New Jersey. The court found that severe restraints on development, imposed by EPA under the CWA, rendered the land far less valuable than its previous assessment.

4. *Litigation Considerations*

Reviewing some of these "tough to call" recent court decisions underscores the difficult challenges permit applicants often face when judicially attacking a permit denial. As a general rule, litigation should be a last resort for

[139] Often, environmental organizations such as the National Wildlife Federation or the Sierra Club, will bring suit to ensure that federal and state wetlands regulatory authority be given broad interpretation.

[140] 961 F.2d 1310, 34 ER Cases 1865 (7th Cir. 1992).

[141] *Id.*

[142] Docket No. 02-11-2122-90D (N.J. Tax Ct. Apr. 27, 1992).

In addition to the power to impose civil and criminal penalties, those government officials or agents charged with enforcement of the Act have at their disposal a number of other powers. For example, conviction of a crime under the Act empowers the government to modify, suspend, or revoke certain federal licenses or agreements previously held by the defendant. The types of permits or agreements subject to this power include those authorizing the person to participate in the import or export of fish, wildlife, or plants, those permitting the person to make certain uses of federal lands such as for grazing,[362] or those granting federal hunting or fishing permits.[363]

c. Inspection, Seizure, Forfeiture, and Injunctions. The Act also confers considerable powers to police the importation and exportation of protected species by authorizing the inspection and seizure of items upon importation and exportation.[364] The Act specifically provides that the enforcing officer shall have the right to make arrests and to conduct searches and seizures with or without a warrant, but only to the extent otherwise authorized by law. Fish, wildlife, plants, or other properties so seized shall be held pending disposition of any civil or criminal proceedings or pending an action *in rem* for forfeiture. In some cases, in lieu of seizure, the alleged violator may be able to post bond and retain the property in question.[365]

The Act also provides for forfeiture of any fish, wildlife, or plants once it is determined that they are or have been "taken, possessed, sold, purchased, offered for sale, transported, delivered, received, carried, shipped, exported, or imported" contrary to the provisions of the Act or its regulations.[366] In some cases, particularly for lesser violations and violations by unknowing tourists or others, the legislative history of the Act makes clear that forfeiture is considered the preferred and sometimes exclusive remedy.[367]

In the case of criminal violations, the forfeiture provisions can be severe. In the case of a criminal conviction, all equipment, vessels, and vehicles used to aid in the taking or transport resulting in the conviction are also subject to forfeiture.[368]

To the extent that they are not inconsistent with the explicit seizure and forfeiture provisions, the Act incorporates U.S. customs laws regarding seizure and forfeiture.[369] For example, the government must first establish probable cause for believing that grounds for seizure exist,[370] thus shifting the burden of

---

[362] ESA §11(b)(2), 16 U.S.C. §1540(b)(2) (1988).

[363] *Id.*

[364] ESA §11(e)(3), 16 U.S.C. §1540(e)(3) (1988).

[365] *Id.*

[366] ESA §11(c)(4)(A), 16 U.S.C. §1540(e)(4)(A) (1988).

[367] *See* H.R. CONF. REP. NO. 740, 93d Cong., 1st Sess. 28 (1973), *reprinted in* 1973 U.S.C.C.A.N. 2989, 3006; H.R. CONF. REP. NO. 1804, 95th Cong., 2nd Sess. 26 (1978), *reprinted in* 1978 U.S.C.C.A.N. 9453, 9493. However, in Carpenter v. Andrus, 485 F. Supp. 320, 14 ER Cases 1630 (D. Del. 1980), the court refused to enforce the forfeiture provisions against an owner who had no knowledge of the provisions against importation into the United States of a leopard legally shot by the owner in Kenya.

[368] ESA §11(e)(4)(B), 16 U.S.C. §1540(e)(4)(B) (1988).

[369] ESA §11(e)(5), 16 U.S.C. §1540(e)(5) (1988).

[370] "Probable cause is defined as a reasonable ground for belief of guilt supported by less than prima facie proof, but more than mere suspicion." United States v. One 1983 Homemade Vessel Named Barracuda, 625 F. Supp. 893, 898 (S.D. Fla. 1986).

proof to the defendant to establish a defense in order to retain his or her property.[371]

Finally, recognizing that violations of the Act often caused irreparable and irreversible harm to protected species, Congress added injunctive powers to the government's enforcement capabilities. In 1982, the Act was amended to provide the Attorney General the power to seek to enjoin any person alleged to be in violation of the Act or its regulations, because "[i]njunctions provide a greater opportunity to attempt resolution of conflicts before harm to a species occurs."[372]

2. *Citizens Suits*

In drafting the Act, Congress "encouraged citizens to 'bring civil suits . . . to force compliance with any provision of the Act.' "[373] The provisions governing "citizens suits" under the Act are codified at section 1540(g). The federal district courts have jurisdiction over these claims without regard to the amount in controversy or the citizenship of the parties.[374]

Most citizen suits under the Act seek to enjoin a person, including a government entity, from violating any provision or regulation of the Act. While private actions most often are maintained against the federal government, a private party may seek to enjoin a state government as well, "to the extent permitted by the 11th amendment to the Constitution."[375] In fact, such suits have in the past been successful. In *Palila v. Hawaii Department of Land and Natural Resources,*[376] a group of citizen and environmental groups concerned about the habitat of the endangered Hawaiian bird known as the Palila, successfully enjoined the state of Hawaii from maintaining feral goats in the endangered bird's habitat.[377]

Because of the congressional preference to use injunctive relief as a way of avoiding violations of the Act that may result in irreparable harm to species,[378] the test for granting injunctions under the Act is more permissive than the traditional balancing test used in other types of civil injunctive actions. Whereas a court typically will weigh factors such as the likelihood of irreparable injury absent an injunction, the competing harm that may be caused by the injunction, and the likelihood of the party seeking the injunction ultimately succeeding on the merits of his or her claim, in suits under the Act, Congress already has "decided that the balance of hardships and the public interest weigh heavily in

---

[371] *See* United States v. 2507 Live Canary Winged Parakeets, 689 F. Supp. 1106, 1113 (S.D. Fla. 1988). *See also* 19 U.S.C. §1594 *et seq.* (customs law provisions).

[372] S. REP. NO. 418, 97th Cong., 2d Sess. 24 (1982).

[373] Defenders of Wildlife v. Administrator, EPA, 882 F.2d 1294, 1300, 30 ER Cases 1460 (8th Cir. 1989), *quoting* Tennessee Valley Auth. v. Hill, 437 U.S. 153, 181, 11 ER Cases 1705 (1978).

[374] ESA §11(g)(1), 16 U.S.C. §1540(g)(1) (1988).

[375] ESA §11(g)(1)(A), 16 U.S.C. §1540(g)(1)(A) (1988). The 11th Amendment has been interpreted to prevent suits against states in federal court. The restriction may be circumvented, however, by naming a state officer as a defendant in seeking to enjoin him or her in the conduct of his or her official duties.

[376] 471 F. Supp. 985, 14 ER Cases 1204 (D. Haw. 1979), *aff'd,* 639 F.2d 495, 15 ER Cases 1741 (9th Cir. 1981).

[377] *See also* Fund for Animals, Inc. v. Florida Game & Fresh Water Fish Comm'n, 550 F. Supp. 1206 (D. Fla. 1982).

[378] S. REP. NO. 418, 97th Cong., 2d Sess. 24 (1982) ("[i]njunctions provide a greater opportunity to attempt resolutions of conflicts before harm to a species occurs").

favor of endangered species.''[379] Thus, in *Tennessee Valley Authority v. Hill,*[380] the Supreme Court rejected the usual balancing of equities in deciding whether or not to grant an injunction under the Act:

> We have no expert knowledge on the subject of endangered species, much less do we have a mandate from the people to strike a balance of equities on [one side or the other]. Congress has spoken in the plainest of words, making it abundantly clear that the balance has been struck in favor of affording endangered species the highest of priorities. . . .

Thus, Congress has eliminated the usual test of discretion that a court in equity would weigh in considering an injunction. Oncc a violation of the Act is found, ''the remedy must be an injunction.''[381]

The Act also specifically provides for a private action against the relevant agencies to compel them to enforce the Act.[382] First, the Act authorizes a private right of action to compel the Secretary to apply the Act's prohibitions against the taking, selling, importing, or exporting of endangered or threatened species on an emergency basis.[383]

Second, a private right of action may be maintained to compel the government to perform any nondiscretionary duties under section 4 of the Act.[384] These duties include making determinations regarding the threatened or endangered status of a species; subsequently monitoring the species; taking certain steps regarding proposed regulations; publishing a list of endangered and threatened species; conducting a review of that list; and developing and implementing ''recovery plans.''[385]

There are certain procedural requirements with which citizens bringing suit must comply. The Act requires in most cases that private enforcers provide 60 days' notice to the government and to relevant private parties prior to filing suit. The Act also prohibits the commencement of a private suit while the government is prosecuting an enforcement action over the same subject matter.[386]

Another requirement facing citizens seeking to bring suit under the Act is standing. Very often, the most difficult hurdle for plaintiffs to overcome in the Endangered Species Act context is demonstrating an ''injury in fact,'' particularly after the Supreme Court's decision in *Lujan v. Defenders of Wildlife.*[387] In *Defenders of Wildlife,* the Court stated that it was particularly difficult for a plaintiff to satisfy the injury in fact test when the plaintiff's asserted injury arises from the government's alleged failure adequately to regulate or constrain a third party. In that case, which is discussed in Section III.E., above, the

---

[379] Sierra Club v. Marsh, 816 F.2d 1376, 1383 (9th Cir. 1987), *citing* Tennessee Valley Auth. v. Hill, 437 U.S. 153, 174, 11 ER Cases 1705 (1978).

[380] 437 U.S. 153, 194, 11 ER Cases 1705 (1978).

[381] Thomas v. Peterson, 753 F.2d 754, 764, 22 ER Cases 1608 (9th Cir. 1985).

[382] ESA §11(g)(1)(B) and (C), 16 U.S.C. §1540(g)(1)(B) and (C) (1988).

[383] ESA §4(g)(1)(B), 16 U.S.C. §1533(g)(1)(B) (1988).

[384] 16 U.S.C. §1533 (1988)..

[385] *Id.*

[386] ESA §11(g)(1) and (2), 16 U.S.C. §1540(g)(1) and (2) (1988). The 60-day notice requirement does not apply to suits seeking review of decisions of the Endangered Species Committee. §7(m), 16 U.S.C. §1536(m) (1988).

[387] 112 S. Ct. 2130, 34 ER Cases 1785 (1992).

Secretaries of the Interior and Commerce repealed regulations that sought to extend the prohibitions of the Act to certain parties conducting activities overseas. The Court found that the plaintiff environmental organization lacked standing to complain because the affidavits presented by the plaintiff demonstrating the "intent" of its members to return to places abroad which might suffer due to the repeal of the regulations, were "simply not enough" to establish injury in fact.[388]

It remains to be seen how *Defenders of Wildlife* may ultimately constrict standing for environmental groups litigating under the Endangered Species Act. Courts have, in the past, held that an environmental group's member's aesthetic interests to enjoy natural areas are the type of interests "which have always enjoyed protection under standing analysis."[389] While Justice Scalia, in the *Defenders of Wildlife* opinion, did not clarify the continuing vitality of standing based on interests such as those that are "aesthetic," an analysis of that case certainly suggests that would-be litigants should emphasize and demonstrate "direct" or "imminent" injury with as much explicitness as possible.

Because the federal government is deemed to be the best suited protector of the public interest, and because the government is still meant to be the primary enforcer and steward of the Act,[390] the Act gives the Secretary, acting through the Attorney General, an absolute right to intervene in private lawsuits.[391]

Finally, Congress granted reviewing courts broad discretionary authority to reward costs and fees to "any party whenever the court determines such award is appropriate."[392] In the past, some courts have awarded fees even where the litigants in question lost on the merits.[393] The prevailing wisdom seems now to be that litigants must have some success on the merits of their ESA claim, and the litigants arguably must further the goals of the Act.[394]

H. Conclusion

The Act provides a unique scheme for multiple federal agencies and the states to work together to recover endangered and threatened species. Its potential to affect the outcome of many federal and private projects makes it an important statute to factor into project planning.

---

[388] *Id.* at 2138.

[389] Humane Soc'y of the U.S. v. Hodel, 840 F.2d 45, 52 (D.C. Cir. 1988). *See also* National Wildlife Fed'n v. Hodel, 839 F.2d 694, 27 ER Cases 1153 (D.C. Cir. 1988); Sierra Club v. Morton, 405 U.S. 727, 3 ER Cases 2039 (1972).

[390] *See generally* Hallstrom v. Tillamook County, 493 U.S. 20 (1989).

[391] ESA §11(g)(3)(B), 16 U.S.C. §1540(g)(3)(B) (1988). Private party intervention, however, is subject to the normal intervention tests under Fed. R. Civ. P. 24. Humane Soc'y of the U.S. v. Clark, 109 F.R.D. 518 (D.D.C. 1985).

[392] ESA §11(g)(4), 16 U.S.C. §1540(g)(4) (1988). In deciding whether or not to award attorney's fees under the Act, the court will consider the public benefit bestowed by the plaintiffs in advancing the policies of the Act in the "private Attorney General" capacity anticipated by §11(g), 16 U.S.C. §1540(g) (1988). *See* Carpenter v. Andrus, 499 F. Supp. 976, 15 ER Cases 1653 (D. Del. 1980).

[393] *See* Village of Kaktavik v. Watt, 689 F.2d 222 (D.C. Cir. 1982); North Slope Borough v. Andrus, 507 F. Supp. 106, 15 ER Cases 1793 (D.D.C. 1981).

[394] Carson-Truckee Water Conservancy Dist. v. Secretary of the Interior, 748 F.2d 523, 21 ER Cases 2115 (9th Cir. 1984), *cert. denied sub nom.* Pyramid Lake Paiute Tribe v. Carson-Truckee Water Conservancy Dist., 471 U.S. 1065 (1985).

V. Other Wildlife Conservation Statutes

A. Lacey Act

The Lacey Act[395] was enacted in 1900 and was originally intended "to outlaw interstate traffic in birds and other animals illegally killed in their State of origin."[396] Generally, the Lacey Act aids enforcement by federalizing most independent state, tribal, and foreign wildlife laws.

The Lacey Act outlaws trafficking in intrastate and interstate commerce if the "fish or wildlife or plant" was "taken, possessed, transported, or sold in violation of any law, treaty, or regulation of the United States or in violation of any Indian tribal law."[397] Notably, the Lacey Act alone does not prohibit unlawful takings. Rather, it prohibits the trafficking of wildlife that has *previously* been obtained in violation of another law.

The Lacey Act also outlaws trafficking in interstate commerce if the fish, wildlife, or plant was "taken, possessed, transported, or sold in violation of any law or regulation of any State."[398] In order to prosecute a case under this section, one must prove a violation of a valid state law. It is not necessary, however, that the person who violated the Lacey Act be the same person who violated the underlying state law. For example, in *U.S. Fish & Wildlife Service v. Picard*[399] a Connecticut fur dealer was prosecuted under the Lacey Act for transporting animal skins from Connecticut to New York, although he had purchased the skins from a hunter who had taken the animals illegally in Vermont.

The Lacey Act prohibits various related activities. For example, there are provisions that make it unlawful to attempt to commit a Lacey Act violation[400] or to traffic containers or packages containing fish or wildlife if they have not been plainly marked in compliance with Lacey Act regulations.[401]

The largest civil penalty for a Lacey Act violation is $10,000, although criminal penalties can be a $20,000 fine, five years imprisonment, or both. The Lacey Act is a general intent statute. It requires proof that the individual should have known, in the exercise of due care, that the specimen was taken, possessed, transported, or sold in violation of another law.[402] A violator may, however, be found to have committed a felony if he knowingly violates the Lacey Act.[403]

B. Marine Mammal Protection Act

Congress enacted the Marine Mammal Protection Act[404] (MMPA) in 1972 largely as a response to the realization that dolphins had been killed and

---

395 16 U.S.C. §§3371–78 (1988); 18 U.S.C. §42 (1988).
396 S. Rep. No. 123, 97th Cong., 1st Sess. 2 (1981).
397 16 U.S.C. §3372(a)(1) (1988).
398 16 U.S.C. §3372(a)(2) (1988).
399 DOI Dkt. No. Boston 79-4 (ALJ ID dated April 19, 1979).
400 16 U.S.C. §3372(a)(4) (1988).
401 16 U.S.C. §3372(b) (1988).
402 16 U.S.C. §3373(d)(2) (1988).
403 16 U.S.C. §3373(d)(1) (1988).
404 16 U.S.C. §§1361–1407 (Supp. II 1972 & 1988).

discarded by tuna fishermen. The MMPA coupled a management program with a moratorium in order to reduce the unnecessary killing of marine mammals.

The MMPA's stated "primary objective" for its management program is "to maintain the health and stability of the marine ecosystem."[405] Whenever consistent with that primary objective, the goal of the management program is to maintain marine mammals at their "optimum sustainable population,"[406] defined as "the number of animals which will result in the maximum productivity of the population or the species, keeping in mind the carrying capacity of the habitat and the health of the ecosystem of which they form a constituent element."[407]

The MMPA further states that: "[t]here shall be a moratorium on the taking and importation of marine mammals and marine mammal products." The moratorium is, however, subject to some exceptions.

The Secretary (of Commerce or the Interior) may waive the moratorium and allow both the taking and importation of marine mammals in certain cases.[408] The courts may invalidate the waivers if they fail to comply with statutory policies. For example, in *Kokechik Fisherman's Ass'n v. Secretary of Commerce,*[409] the court invalidated the Secretary's waiver because the government had no evidence that seals were at the "optimum sustainable population," and therefore could not make findings, which the court called an "absolute requirement," for the issuance of a waiver. Exemptions from the moratorium include, but are not limited to, an exemption for Alaskan natives,[410] for scientific research, public display, and enhancement of survival,[411] for the U.S. tunaboat industry,[412] and for other commercial fishermen.[413]

Any person who violates the Act, the regulations, or a permit is subject to a civil penalty of up to $10,000. Violators may also be subject to criminal penalties for knowing violations.[414] In addition, the government may seize the entire cargo of any U.S. vessel or other conveyance used in an unlawful taking.[415]

The MMPA has had a global impact because it directs the U.S. government to negotiate "to encourage the development of international arrangements for research on, and conservation of, all marine mammals."[416] Likewise, the U.S.

---

[405] 16 U.S.C. §1361(6) (1988).

[406] 16 U.S.C. §1361(2) (1988).

[407] 16 U.S.C. §1362(8) (1988).

[408] 16 U.S.C. §1371(a)(3)(A) (1988).

[409] 839 F.2d 795 (D.C. Cir. 1988), *cert. denied sub nom.* Verity v. Center for Envtl. Educ., 488 U.S. 820 (1988).

[410] 16 U.S.C. §1371(b) (1988). The exemption allows Alaskan natives to take marine mammals for subsistence purposes as well as for "purposes of creating and selling authentic native articles of handicrafts and clothing."

[411] 16 U.S.C. §1371(a)(1) (1988).

[412] 16 U.S.C. §1371(a)(2) (1988). Under this exemption, the Secretary may award permits for the incidental taking of marine mammals in the course of commercial fishing. *See also* Committee for Humane Legislation v. Richardson, 540 F.2d 1141 (D.C. Cir. 1976), *aff'd in part* 414 F. Supp. 297 (D.D.C.).

[413] 16 U.S.C. §137(a)(4) (1988). This exemption directs the Secretary to allow incidental takings if he finds that the takings would have a negligible impact on the mammal. It appears that Congress intended this exemption for U.S. fishermen whose takings are infrequent, unavoidable, or accidental. *See* H.R. REP. NO. 970, 100th Cong., 2d Sess. 14, 17 (1988), *reprinted in* 1988 U.S.C.C.A.N. 6154, 6158.

[414] 16 U.S.C. §1375(b) (1988).

[415] 16 U.S.C. §1376(a) (1988).

[416] 16 U.S.C. §1361(4) (1988).

government has and presently encourages foreign nations to prohibit fishing methods that result in large scale deaths of marine mammals. In response to U.S. pressure, South Korea and Japan agreed to ban drift-net fishing operations in 1991, and in 1992 Venezuela and Mexico agreed to ban purse-seine netting of dolphins by tuna fishermen.

C. Bald Eagle Protection Act

Congress enacted the Bald Eagle Protection Act[417] in 1940 to protect the species from extinction. The Act makes it unlawful to "take, possess, sell, purchase, barter, offer to sell, purchase or barter, transport, export or import, at any time or in any manner, any" protected birds, alive or dead.[418] The Act defines "take" as "pursue, shoot, shoot at, poison, wound, kill, capture, trap, collect, or molest or disturb."[419] The person must violate the Act "knowingly, or with wanton disregard for the consequences of his act."[420]

The exemptions to the Bald Eagle Protection Act include those for pre-Act products and for activities authorized by the Secretary of the Interior.[421] The agency may authorize the taking of bald and golden eagles for scientific research, for the protection of wildlife in a particular locale, or for religious purposes of Indian tribes.

Eagles are protected under several statutes. They are encompassed in the Migratory Bird Treaty Act, and bald eagles are protected under the Endangered Species Act. The government may elect to prosecute under any of the above statutes.[422]

D. Migratory Bird Treaty Act

In 1916, President Wilson signed a treaty with Great Britain (on behalf of Canada) for the protection of the "[m]any species of birds [that] in their annual migration traverse certain parts of the United States and . . . Canada."[423] Congress implemented the treaty with Great Britain in 1918 by enacting the Migratory Bird Treaty Act.[424] Later, by amendments, Congress incorporated the treaties of Mexico, Japan, and the USSR into the statute.[425]

Generally, the Migratory Bird Treaty Act and its corresponding legislation obligates the United States to preserve and protect migratory birds through the regulation of hunting, the establishment of refuges, and the protection of bird habitats. The Act forbids killing, possessing, or trading in migratory birds except in accordance with regulations prescribed by the Secretary of the

---

[417] 16 U.S.C. §668–68d (1988).

[418] 16 U.S.C. §668 (1988).

[419] 16 U.S.C. §668c (1988). *See also* 50 C.F.R. §22.3 (1990).

[420] 16 U.S.C. §668(a) (1988).

[421] 16 U.S.C. §668a (1988). The Secretary can issue permits only if the activity is compatible with the species' preservation, according to the regulations governing requests for permits.

[422] United States v. Mackie, 681 F.2d 1121, 1122–23, 19 ER Cases 1049 (9th Cir. 1982).

[423] Convention for the Protection of Migratory Birds, 1916, 39 Stat. 1702.

[424] 16 U.S.C. §§703–11 (1988).

[425] Ch. 634, §1, 49 Stat. 1555–56 (1936); Pub. L. No. 93-300, 88 Stat. 190 (1974); Pub. L. No. 101-233, §15, 103 Stat. 1968, 1977 (1989).

Interior. The Act protects species of migratory birds that are included within the terms of the treaties with Great Britain, Mexico, and Japan,[426] and the regulations contain a list of migratory birds protected by the Treaties and the Act.[427] Unlike most wildlife statutes, Migratory Bird Treaty Act violations are only punishable by criminal sanctions (and forfeiture).

The implementing[428] regulations forbid certain hunting methods such as traps, snares, nets, shotguns capable of holding more than three shells (unless the extra capacity is plugged), shooting birds from motorized vehicles or sailboats, or using live birds as decoys.[429] There are also various exemptions, including the sale of migratory birds which have been bred for the purpose of increasing food supply,[430] the acquisition of migratory birds by public parks, zoos, or scientific institutions,[431] and the killing of migratory birds by Native Americans whose tribes have treaty rights to hunt them.[432] Individuals may not, however, kill protected wildlife in defense of property. In *United States v. Darst,*[433] the Court rejected the defendant's assertion that he had a right to set traps to kill great horned owls in order to protect his chickens.

VI. Conclusion

The environmental laws grouped together in this chapter are diverse, involving a host of federal agencies and enforcement schemes. They are united, however, by their goal of protection of wildlife and other resources, and their consequent ability to have an impact on a virtually limitless number of federal and commercial projects and activities. Knowledge of these statutes' implementation, therefore, is critical in the planning stages of many construction and other projects.

[426] 16 U.S.C. §703 (1988).
[427] 50 C.F.R. §10.12 (1990).
[428] 16 U.S.C. §704 (1988).
[429] 50 C.F.R. §20.2 (1990).
[430] 16 U.S.C. §711 (1988).
[431] 50 C.F.R. §21.13–.14 (1990).
[432] *See* United States v. Bresette, 761 F. Supp. 658 (D. Minn. 1991).
[433] 726 F. Supp. 286 (D. Kan. 1989).

12

Reporting and Disclosure Requirements for Releases of Oil and Hazardous Substances

By Paul A. J. Wilson
with Parker E. Brugge

> The chapter of knowledge is a very short,
> but the chapter of accidents is a very long one.
> —Letter from P.D. Stanhope, Earl of Chesterfield, to Solomon Dayrolles (Feb. 16, 1753)

I. Introduction

This chapter is an effort to lengthen somewhat Lord Chesterfield's "chapter of knowledge" as it pertains to the "chapter of accidents" by providing a guide to two categories of reporting requirements related to the environmental release of hazardous materials. The first concerns the overlapping reporting requirements for unplanned or accidental releases of oil and hazardous substances under section 311 of the Clean Water Act (CWA),[1] section 103 of the Comprehensive Environmental Response, Compensation, and Liability Act (CERCLA),[2] section 304 of the Emergency Planning and Community Right-to-Know Act (EPCRA),[3] and section 112(r) of the Clean Air Act (CAA).[4] The second set of reporting requirements are those of sections 311, 312, and 313 of EPCRA which largely concern nonaccidental reporting related to emergency response planning and community awareness issues.

To describe the requirements of the first group, Section II of this chapter examines the reporting provisions of each statute through a common matrix. Under this approach, we compare the analogous individual components of each statute and present the various lists of reportable substances as well as a flow chart as a guide to assist in determining which reporting requirement(s) a

---

[1] 33 U.S.C. §1321.

[2] 42 U.S.C. §9601 *et seq.*

[3] 42 U.S.C. §11001 *et seq.* EPCRA was enacted as a free-standing statute within the Superfund Amendments and Reauthorization Act of 1986 (SARA). As a consequence, it is often referred to as "SARA Title III."

[4] 42 U.S.C. §7412(r).

release might trigger. As a result, the chapter can be used in two ways: it may simply be read as an introduction to the various statutory reporting requirements or it may be used as a reference tool to determine if reporting is required in response to a particular release by consulting the flow chart, lists of substances, and referenced regulatory materials.[5]

In general, each statute requires entities falling within its scope to notify federal, state, and/or local emergency planning and response authorities of environmental releases and discharges (planned or accidental) of hazardous substances covered by the statute. To assure compliance, each statute contains a variety of enforcement mechanisms, including civil penalties, authorizations for citizens' suits, and criminal sanctions.

Section II.A. of this chapter analyzes the general scope of reporting obligations under each statute, focusing on the question: what types of reporting requirements are triggered by the release of oil or chemical substances from facilities, vessels, and/or other sources? Section II.B. outlines the types of releases, spills, and discharges that are reportable under the various statutes. Section II.C. identifies the persons responsible for reporting, the entities to whom reports must be made, and the types of information that each statute requires to be reported. Section II.D. lists the various sanctions for nonreporters and briefly identifies penalties for unlawful releases or discharges.

Part III of this chapter describes in narrative form the material safety data reporting obligations under sections 311 and 312 of EPCRA and the annual Toxic Release Inventory reporting provisions of section 313 of that statute. Then, as in Part II, it briefly describes the enforcement mechanisms and penalties that are available to compel compliance with the various reporting requirements.[6]

II. Reporting Unplanned or Accidental Releases

A. Scope

The underlying approaches in CERCLA, EPCRA, the CWA, and the CAA to release reporting are more similar than they are different. All are defined by the chemical substance and facility or vessel from which the substance is released or discharged. Generally, section 311 of the CWA and section 103 of CERCLA cover releases and discharges from vessels (i.e., all types of watercraft) and offshore and onshore facilities. Section 304 of EPCRA and section 112(r) of the CAA cover releases from onshore facilities only.

With regard to reportable substances, CWA section 311 requires reporting of releases of "oil" and "hazardous substances." CERCLA excludes petroleum and applies only to "hazardous substances." The CERCLA definition of "hazardous substances," however, includes all CWA hazardous substances plus many more materials. The emergency release reporting provisions of

---

[5] These materials are not intended to be viewed as a comprehensive legal treatment of this subject and should not be used as a substitute for consultation with competent counsel.

[6] For a state-by-state guide to the reporting requirements covered in this chapter, *see* R. Abbott & J. Leeman, Spill Reporting Procedures Guide (J. Kimmel, ed. 1992).

EPCRA apply to "extremely hazardous substances" (EHSs), some of which are also CWA and/or CERCLA "hazardous substances." Moreover, EPA used the list of EPCRA EHSs as a guide to promulgate the list of CAA "regulated substances." Figure 1 illustrates the relationships of the materials governed by each statute.

EPA recently promulgated the list of substances reportable under section 112(r) of the CAA.[7] This list comprises 77 acutely toxic substances, 63 flammable gases and volatile flammable liquids, and certain explosives designated by the Department of Transportation.

Additionally, regulations to make reporting of releases of CERCLA hazardous substances and EPCRA EHSs co-extensive have yet to be promulgated.[8] Note also that under some circumstances releases of EHSs regulated under section 304 of EPCRA may also need to be reported as "toxic chemicals" on the annual Toxic Release Inventory (TRI) under EPCRA section 313.[9]

1. Substances and Facilities Under the CWA

Section 311 of the Clean Water Act (CWA) regulates discharges of oil and hazardous substances. For this purpose, "oil" means "oil of any kind or in any form, including, but not limited to, petroleum, fuel oil, sludge, oil refuse, and oil mixed with wastes other than dredged oil."[10] Reporting under the CWA, however, is not triggered simply by virtue of the release of any amount of oil. Instead, the statute provides that the discharge of oil, to be reportable, must (a) violate applicable water quality standards; (b) cause a film, sheen,[11] or discoloration of the water surface or adjoining shorelines; or (c) cause a sludge or emulsion to be deposited beneath the water surface or upon adjoining shorelines.[12]

Hazardous substances are defined as those substances, other than oil, designated by EPA that

> when discharged in any quantity into or upon the navigable waters of the United States or adjoining shorelines or the waters of the contiguous zone . . . or which may affect natural resources belonging to, appertaining to, or under the exclusive management authority of the United States . . . present an imminent and substantial danger to the public health or welfare, including, but not limited to, fish, shellfish, wildlife, shorelines, and beaches.[13]

EPA has designated as hazardous approximately 300 substances, thus rendering them subject to the section 311 reporting requirements.[14] EPA also has determined the quantity of each substance that may be harmful if discharged.[15] For this purpose, the quantity of a hazardous substance that will

---

[7] 59 Fed. Reg. 4478 (1994).

[8] The proposed regulation appears at 54 Fed. Reg. 3388 (1989).

[9] See discussion in Section III.C., below.

[10] 33 U.S.C. §1321(a)(1); 40 C.F.R. §110.1.

[11] The "sheen test" means that the presence of an oil sheen creates a rebuttable presumption that the oil spill is harmful, thereby creating an obligation to report. *See* United States v. Chevron Oil Co., 583 F.2d 1357, 1363–64, 12 ER Cases 1726 (5th Cir. 1978).

[12] 40 C.F.R. §110.3.

[13] CWA §311(b)(2)(A), 33 U.S.C. §1321(b)(2)(A).

[14] 40 C.F.R. §116.4.

[15] 40 C.F.R. §117.3.

FIGURE 1
RELATIONSHIPS OF MATERIALS
GOVERNED BY STATUTE

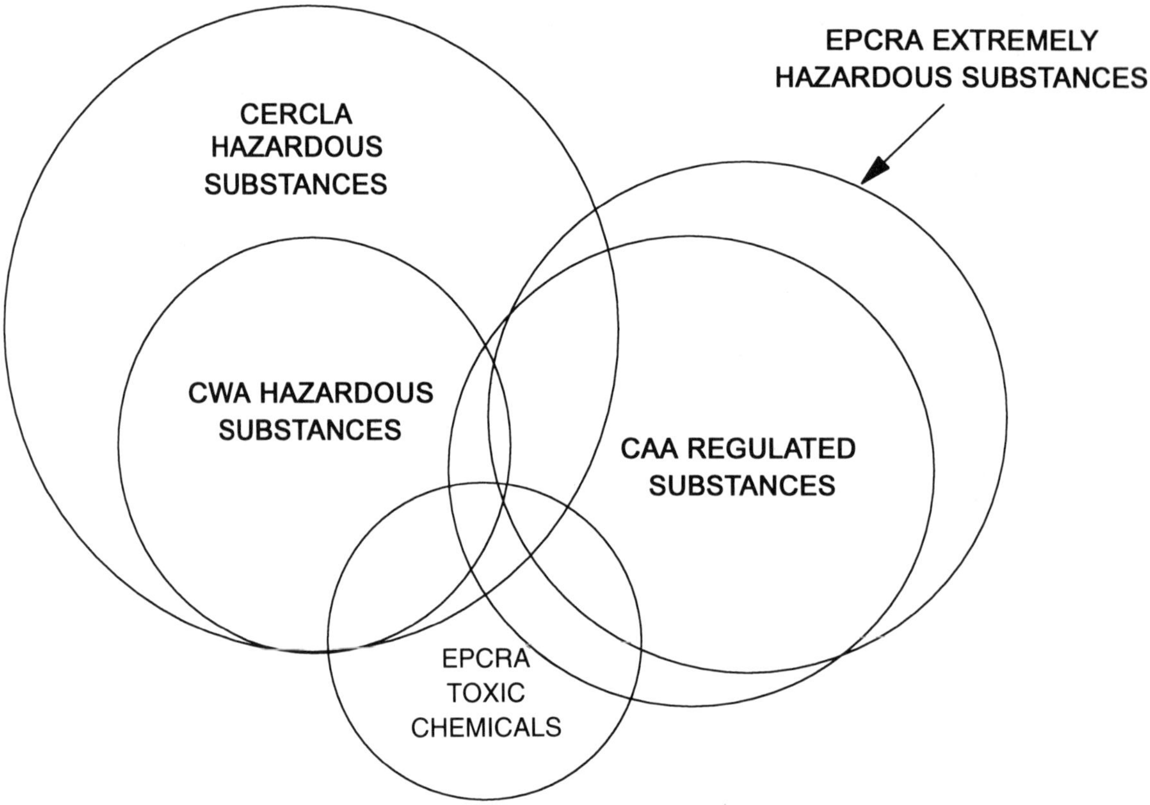

trigger reporting varies according to that substance's ranking on the following five-tier toxicity scale:

Category	*Harmful Quantities*[16]
X	1 pound
A	10 pounds
B	100 pounds
C	1,000 pounds
D	5,000 pounds

The person in charge of "a vessel or of an onshore facility or an offshore facility" must report discharges of harmful quantities of oil or hazardous substances to navigable waters to the appropriate federal agency.[17] The term

[16] *Id.*

[17] CWA §311(b)(5), 33 U.S.C. §1321(b)(5). For CWA purposes, these reports are to be made to the National Response Center of the United States Coast Guard. *See* Section II.C.1., below.

"vessel" includes "every description of watercraft or other artificial contrivance used, or capable of being used, as a means of transportation on water other than a public vessel."[18] The terms "onshore" and "offshore" facilities are defined so as to cover essentially all structures and vehicles on land or navigable waters.[19]

In terms of reporting obligations, there is no real distinction among these three classes of facilities. In some circumstances, however, onshore and offshore facilities must prepare a Spill Prevention Control and Countermeasure (SPCC) plan, which is a written plan for responding to a worst-case discharge or the substantial threat of such discharge of oil or hazardous substances.[20]

2. *Substances and Facilities Under CERCLA*

Under CERCLA,[21] the "hazardous substances" subject to reporting are any materials EPA has designated as hazardous pursuant to section 311 of the Clean Water Act;[22] any "toxic pollutant" listed under section 307(a) of the Clean Water Act;[23] any "imminently hazardous chemical substance or mixture" listed under section 17 of the Toxic Substances Control Act (TSCA);[24] any "hazardous air pollutant" listed under the section 112 of the Clean Air Act;[25] and any "hazardous waste" having the characteristics identified or listed under section 3001 of the Resource Conservation and Recovery Act (RCRA).[26] EPA is also obliged to designate additional substances as hazardous that, when released, "may present substantial danger to the public health or welfare or the environment."[27] The list of CERCLA "hazardous substances," along with their respective "reportable quantities,"[28] can be found at 40 C.F.R. §302.4.

By contrast to the CWA, however, CERCLA specifically excludes petroleum and natural gas from its reporting obligations.[29] EPA has limited this petroleum exclusion to petroleum that contains only those "hazardous sub-

---

[18] CWA §311(a)(3), 33 U.S.C. §1321(a)(3); 40 C.F.R. §110.1. A public vessel is defined as "a vessel owned or bareboat-chartered and operated by the United States, or by a State or political subdivision thereof, or by a foreign nation, except when such vessel is engaged in commerce." CWA §311(a)(4), 33 U.S.C. §1321(a)(4); 40 C.F.R. §110.1.

[19] "Onshore facility" means "any facility (including, but not limited to, motor vehicles and rolling stock) of any kind located in, on, or under, any land within the United States other than submerged land." CWA §311(a)(10), 33 U.S.C. §1321(a)(10); 40 C.F.R. §110.1.

"Offshore facility" means "any facility of any kind located in, on, or under, any of the navigable waters of the United States, and any facility of any kind which is subject to the jurisdiction of the United States and is located in, on, or under any other waters, other than a vessel or a public vessel." CWA §311(a)(11), 33 U.S.C. §1321(a)(11); 40 C.F.R. §110.1.

[20] For an analysis of SPCC plans, see Chapter 4, Clean Water Act, and Chapter 14, Risk Assessment.

[21] CERCLA §101(14), 42 U.S.C. §9601(14).

[22] 33 U.S.C. §1321(b)(2)(A).

[23] 33 U.S.C. §1317(a).

[24] 15 U.S.C. §2606.

[25] 42 U.S.C. §7412.

[26] 42 U.S.C. §6921.

[27] CERCLA §102(a), 42 U.S.C. §9602(a).

[28] "Reportable quantities" (RQs) under CERCLA are analogous to "harmful quantities" under the CWA. A report must be filed under CERCLA if an amount of a hazardous substance equal to or greater than its listed RQ is released into the environment within any 24-hour period. 40 C.F.R. §302.6.

[29] "The term [hazardous substance] does not include petroleum, including crude oil or any fraction thereof which is not otherwise specifically listed or designated as a hazardous substance under subparagraphs (A) through (F) of this paragraph, and the term does not include natural gas, natural gas liquids, liquefied natural gas, or synthetic gas usable for fuel (or mixtures of natural gas and such synthetic gas)." CERCLA §101(14), 42 U.S.C. §9601(14).

stances'' indigenous to petroleum (e.g., benzene, toluene, xylene).[30] As a result, the petroleum exclusion does not exclude from reporting any material that contains substances that are not normally found in refined petroleum fractions or that are present at levels higher than those normally found in such fractions. Courts have agreed with EPA's interpretation of the petroleum exclusion.[31]

The person in charge of ''a vessel or of an offshore or an onshore facility'' must report the release of a ''reportable quantity'' (RQ) of a hazardous substance as soon as that person has knowledge of such a release.[32] CERCLA defines the term ''facility'' broadly as

> (A) any building, structure, installation, equipment, pipe or pipeline (including any pipe into a sewer or publicly owned treatment works), well, pit, pond, lagoon, impoundment, ditch, landfill, storage container, motor vehicle, rolling stock, or aircraft, or (B) any site or area where a hazardous substance has been deposited, stored, disposed of, or placed, or otherwise come to be located; but does not include any consumer product in consumer use or any vessel.[33]

The definitions of ''offshore'' and ''onshore'' facility in CERCLA are identical to those in the CWA,[34] and courts have interpreted this definition with equal breadth to encompass virtually any area where hazardous substances are present.[35]

3. Substances and Facilities Under EPCRA

The ''extremely hazardous substances'' subject to reporting under section 304 of EPCRA are listed, along with their respective reportable quantities, at 40 C.F.R. part 355, Appendixes A and B. There are currently approximately 360 listed EHSs.[36] Unlike CERCLA, EPCRA does not contain a petroleum exclusion. Thus, a release of oil that contains one of the listed extremely hazardous substances in excess of its RQ would have to be reported pursuant to EPCRA requirements.

EPCRA imposes obligations for EHS release reporting on the owner or operator of a ''facility.''[37] The statute broadly defines the term ''facility'' as

> all buildings, equipment, structures, and other stationary items which are located on a single site or on contiguous or adjacent sites and which are owned or operated

---

[30] EPA Memorandum, Scope of the CERCLA Petroleum Exclusion Under Section 101(14) and 104(a)(2), from Francis S. Blake, General Counsel, July 31, 1987.

[31] *See, e.g.,* Wilshire Westwood Assoc. v. Atlantic Richfield Corp., 881 F.2d 801, 30 ER Cases 1065 (9th Cir. 1989); Mid Valley Bank v. North Valley Bank, 764 F. Supp. 1377 (E.D. Cal. 1991).

[32] CERCLA §103(a), 42 U.S.C. §9603(a).

[33] CERCLA §101(9), 42 U.S.C. §9601(9).

[34] CERCLA §101(17), 42 U.S.C. §9601(17) (''offshore facility''); CERCLA §101(18), 42 U.S.C. §9601(18) (''onshore facility''). Also, CERCLA defines the term ''vessel'' in the same manner as the CWA, i.e., ''every description of watercraft or other artificial contrivance used, or capable of being used, as a means of transportation on water.'' CERCLA §101(28), 42 U.S.C. §9601(28). However, while the CWA excludes from its definition ''public vessels,'' CERCLA does not. Thus, public vessels are subject to reporting under CERCLA, but not under the CWA.

[35] *See, e.g.,* United States v. Ward, 618 F. Supp. 884, 23 ER Cases 1391 (E.D.N.C. 1985) (CERCLA ''facility'' is broad enough to encompass roadside area where transporter spread PCB-contaminated transformer fluid); United States v. Hardage, 761 F. Supp. 1501, 32 ER Cases 1073 (W.D. Okla. 1990) (presence at site of hazardous substances renders site a ''facility'' for CERCLA purposes).

[36] Note, however, that regulations mandating EPCRA reports on releases of *all* CERCLA hazardous substances have been pending since January 23, 1989. 54 Fed. Reg. 3388 (1989).

[37] EPCRA §304, 42 U.S.C. §11004.

by the same person (or by any person which controls, is controlled by, or under common control with, such person).[38]

EPCRA section 304 is applicable to facilities "at which a *hazardous chemical* is produced, used, or stored. . . ."[39] The term "hazardous chemical" is defined by regulations promulgated by the Occupational Safety and Health Administration. EPCRA's extremely hazardous substances comprise a small subset of that universe of materials.[40]

4. *Substances and Facilities Under the CAA*

The Clean Air Act Amendments of 1990 completely revised section 112 of the Clean Air Act (CAA). In particular, the new section 112(r) now provides an elaborate program to prevent, reduce, and respond to accidental releases of toxic air pollutants and EPCRA extremely hazardous substances.

Section 112(r) creates general duties to prevent accidental releases of EPCRA EHSs and additional "regulated substances" to be listed pursuant to CAA section 112(r)(3), and to minimize the effects of such accidental releases. EPA has promulgated a list of "reportable substances" subject to reporting under section 112(r) of the CAA.[41] EPA also established "threshold quantities" for each of the reportable substances based on the following factors:

> [T]oxicity, reactivity, volatility, dispersibility, combustibility, or flammability of the substance and the amount of the substance which, as a result of an accidental release, is known to cause or may reasonably be anticipated to cause death, injury or serious adverse effects to human health.[42]

Owners and operators of "stationary sources" producing, processing, handling, or storing a threshold quantity of a regulated substance are required to minimize the damage caused by accidental releases by preparing and implementing "risk management plans."[43] The term "stationary source" includes the following:

> [A]ny buildings, structures, equipment, installations or substance emitting stationary activities (i) which belong to the same industrial group, (ii) which are located on one or more contiguous properties, (iii) which are under the control of the same

---

[38] EPCRA §329, 42 U.S.C. §11049(4). For this purpose, EPCRA's general exemption of motor vehicles, rolling stock, and aircraft from reporting, does not apply.

[39] 42 U.S.C. §11004 (emphasis added).

[40] The term "hazardous chemicals" refers to chemicals that meet the criteria for "health" or "physical" hazard under the worker hazard communication regulations promulgated by OSHA. 29 C.F.R. §1910.1200. See Chapter 8, Occupational Safety and Health Act; *see also* 42 U.S.C. §11049(5). All EHSs will meet OSHA's definition of hazardous chemical.

[41] 59 Fed. Reg. 4478 (1994) codified at 40 C.F.R. §68.130. The list includes 77 toxic substances, 63 flammable gases, volatile flammable liquids, and explosives. Explosives will be covered under CAA §112(r) if they are classified by the Department of Transportation in Division 1.1 (49 C.F.R. §172.101) (explosives that have a mass explosion hazard), and are present on-site in quantities greater than 5,000 pounds. The statute required the initial list to include at least 100 substances that posed the greatest risk of causing death, injury, or serious adverse effects to human health or the environment from accidental releases. The statute also expressly named the following 16 substances that must appear on the list: chlorine, anhydrous ammonia, methyl chloride, ethylene oxide, vinyl chloride, methyl isocyanate, hydrogen cyanide, ammonia, hydrogen sulfide, toluene di-isocyanate, phosgene, bromine, anhydrous hydrogen chloride, hydrogen fluoride, anhydrous sulfur dioxide, and sulfur trioxide. 42 U.S.C. §7412(r)(3).

[42] CAA §112(r)(5), 42 U.S.C. §7412(r)(5).

[43] CAA §112(r)(1), 42 U.S.C. §7412(r)(1). *See* 58 Fed. Reg. 54,190 (1993).

person (or persons under common control), and (iv) from which an accidental release may occur.[44]

B. Reportable Releases

1. CWA Reportable Discharges

Under section 311 of the CWA, a "discharge" of oil or hazardous substances into or upon the navigable waters of the United States,[45] the contiguous zone,[46] or adjoining shorelines[47] generally triggers CWA reporting obligations. The term "discharge" includes "any spilling, leaking, pumping, pouring, emitting, emptying, or dumping,"[48] but excludes certain authorized discharges, e.g., those subject to a National Pollutant Discharge Elimination System (NPDES) permit or in some manner related to permitted conditions of operations.[49]

A discharge complies with an NPDES permit if the permit contains an effluent limitation that either specifically applies to the substance discharged or applies to a different waste parameter identified in the permit and is intended to limit the discharge of that substance, *and* the discharge is in compliance with the effluent limitation.[50]

If a discharge does not comply with a permit limit (e.g., the amount of oil in wastewater exceeds that allowed under a facility's permit), it may still qualify for an exemption. In such a case, the permit application, the permit itself, or another portion of the public record must contain documents that specifically identify the discharged substance, the amount thereof, its origin and source, and the treatment to be provided to the discharge.[51] Alternatively, if a discharge of oil or hazardous substances exceeds the applicable effluent limits, it might not be deemed a reportable discharge if it originates from a point source that has a valid permit or a pending permit application and results from (i) contamination of noncontact cooling water or storm water (provided such contamination does not result from an on-site spill of a hazardous substance); (ii) a continuous or anticipated intermittent discharge of process waste water that originates within the manufacturing or treating systems; or (iii) an upset or failure of a treatment system or process that produces a continuous or intermittent discharge due to a number of causes, such as system failure or production schedule change, so long

---

[44] CAA §112(r)(2)(C), 42 U.S.C. §7412(r)(2)(C).

[45] The term "navigable waters" is defined at 40 C.F.R. §110.1. EPA has interpreted this term to cover *all* waters of the United States, whether navigable in fact or not. This has been upheld by the courts. *See, e.g.,* United States v. Ashland Oil & Transp. Co., 364 F. Supp. 349, 6 ER Cases 1991 (D. Ky. 1973), *aff'd,* 504 F.2d 1317, 7 ER Cases 1114 (6th Cir. 1974); *see also* United States v. Texas Pipe Line Co., 528 F. Supp. 728, 11 ER Cases 1465 (D. Okla. 1978) (the definition also covers a ditch leading to a river, regardless of whether there was a continuous flow of water in the ditch), *aff'd,* 611 F.2d 345, 13 ER Cases 1120 (10th Cir. 1979).

[46] The contiguous zone is "the entire zone established or to be established by the United States under article 24 of the Convention on the Territorial Sea and the Contiguous Zone." 33 U.S.C. §1321(9); 40 C.F.R. §110.1.

[47] 33 U.S.C. §1321(b)(3)(i).

[48] CWA §311(a)(2), 33 U.S.C. §1321(a)(2).

[49] *Id.;* 40 C.F.R. §110.1.

[50] 40 C.F.R. §117.12(b).

[51] 40 C.F.R. §117.12(c). Additionally, the permit must require that the wastewater containing the substance be treated as specified in the permit and that the treatment to be provided is in place. *Id.*

as the upset or failure is not caused by an on-site spill of a hazardous substance.[52] If any of these requirements is met, a discharge is not reportable under section 311.[53]

Even if none of the section 311(a)(2) exclusions applies, for a release to be reportable it also must be of sufficient magnitude that a "harmful quantity"[54] of the oil or hazardous substance is released. For oil, discharges meeting this criterion include: (a) discharges that violate applicable water quality standards; (b) discharges that cause a film, sheen, or discoloration of the water surface or adjoining shorelines;[55] or (c) that cause a sludge or emulsion to be deposited beneath the water surface or upon adjoining shorelines.[56]

For each hazardous substance, EPA has determined the RQ at which a release may be harmful.[57] A discharge within any 24-hour period of any listed substance equal to or in excess of its designated RQ *must* be reported *unless* the discharge

1. Complies with a permit issued under the Marine Protection, Research, and Sanctuaries Act of 1972 (33 U.S.C. §1401 *et seq.*);
2. Complies with approved water treatment plant operations as specified by local or state safe drinking water regulations;
3. Is made pursuant to label directions for application of a pesticide registered under section 3 or section 24 of the Federal Insecticide, Fungicide, and Rodenticide Act (FIFRA) (7 U.S.C. §136 *et seq.*), or pursuant to the terms of an experimental use permit issued under

---

[52] 40 C.F.R. §117.12(d).

[53] A discharge of oil or hazardous substances that is not in compliance with a facility's NPDES permit, but is exempt from reporting under subparagraph B or C of §311(a)(2), may still have to be reported under separate provisions of EPA's NPDES regulations. Those regulations, which are set forth at 40 C.F.R. pt. 122, make it a condition of every NPDES permit that "[t]he permittee shall report any non-compliance [with its permit] which may endanger health or the environment." 40 C.F.R. §122.41(l)(6). The information must be communicated to EPA orally within 24 hours after the permittee becomes aware of the circumstances, and must be followed up within five days by a written submission. 40 C.F.R. §122.41(l)(6)(i). The regulations require reporting within 24 hours for any "unauthorized bypass" or "upset" in the facility's operations that exceed the effluent limits in the facility permit, as well as for violation of the maximum daily discharge limitation set forth in the permit for any toxic pollutant or hazardous substance. 40 C.F.R. §122.41(l)(6)(ii). Instances of noncompliance with permit limits not covered by this 24-hour reporting requirement must be reported in the facility's regularly submitted discharge monitoring reports.

[54] "Harmful quantity" is defined as that "quantity of oil and any hazardous substances the discharge of which may be harmful to the public health or welfare of the United States." CWA §311(b)(4), 33 U.S.C. §1321(b)(4).

[55] The so-called sheen test, though prompting much litigation in the past, has now evolved into the proposition that the presence of a sheen creates a rebuttable presumption that the spill is harmful. *See* United States v. Chevron Oil Co., 583 F.2d 1357, 1363–64, 12 ER Cases 1726 (5th Cir. 1978).

[56] 40 C.F.R. §110.3. The same criteria apply to discharges of oil to the waters of the contiguous zone or to waters seaward of the contiguous zone in connection with activities under the Outer Continental Shelf Lands Act, 43 U.S.C. §§1331–51 (*e.g.*, oil and gas production beyond contiguous zone) or the Deepwater Port Act, 33 U.S.C. §1501 *et seq.*; 40 C.F.R. §110.4, .5. The general ban on the discharge of oil, however, does not apply to discharges permitted in the contiguous zone and seaward under the International Convention for the Prevention of Pollution from Ships, 1973, as modified by the Protocol of 1978 relating thereto (MARPOL) 73/78, Annex I, as provided in 33 C.F.R. §151.09. *See* 40 C.F.R. §110.6.

Some other discharges of oil are permitted for practical reasons. For example, while oil discharges from a ship's bilge are not exempt, discharges from a ship's properly functioning engine are permitted. 40 C.F.R. §110.7. Additionally, EPA may also permit the discharge of oil in connection with research or demonstration projects relating to the prevention, abatement, or control of oil pollution. 40 C.F.R. §110.9.

[57] 40 C.F.R. §117.3.

FIFRA section 5, or pursuant to an exemption granted under FIFRA section 18;

4. Complies with regulations issued under RCRA section 3004 or with permit conditions issued pursuant to RCRA section 3005;
5. Complies with instructions given by the On-Scene Coordinator pursuant to the National Oil and Hazardous Substances Pollution Plan or in accordance with applicable removal regulations as required by section 311 of the CWA;
6. Complies with a permit issued under section 165.7 of title 14 of the State of California Administrative Code;
7. Is from a properly functioning inert gas system when used to provide inert gas to a vessel's cargo tanks;
8. Is from a permitted source and is excluded by 40 C.F.R. §117.12;
9. Is to a publicly owned treatment works (POTW) and is specifically excluded or reserved in 40 C.F.R. §117.13; or
10. Complies with a permit issued under section 404(a) of the CWA or is exempt pursuant to section 404(f) or section 404(r) of the CWA.[58]

2. *CERCLA Reportable Releases*

Notification obligations under CERCLA arise when a person has knowledge of a reportable release,[59] which is defined as

> any spilling, leaking, pumping, pouring, emitting, emptying, discharging, injecting, escaping, leaching, dumping, or disposing into the environment (including the abandonment or discarding of barrels, containers, and other closed receptacles containing hazardous substance or pollutant or contaminant).[60]

For purposes of its definition of "release," CERCLA defines "environment" to include *all* environmental media.[61]

---

[58] 40 C.F.R. §117.11.

[59] CERCLA §103(a), 42 U.S.C. §9603(a).

[60] CERCLA §101(22), 42 U.S.C. §9601(22). The following releases are excluded from the reporting requirement:

> (A) any release which results in exposure to persons solely within a workplace, with respect to a claim which such persons may assert against the employer of such persons,
> (B) emissions from the engine exhaust of a motor vehicle, rolling stock, aircraft, vessel, or pipeline pumping station engine,
> (C) release of source, byproduct, or special nuclear material from a nuclear incident, as those terms are defined in the Atomic Energy Act of 1954, if such release is subject to requirements with respect to financial protection established by the Nuclear Regulatory Commission under section 170 of such Act, or, for the purposes of section 104 of this title or any other response action, any reprocessing site designated under section 102(a)(1) or 302(a) of the Uranium Mill Tailings Radiation Control Act of 1978, and
> (D) the normal application of fertilizer.

42 U.S.C. §9601(22).

[61] The term "environment" means

> (A) The navigable waters, the waters of the contiguous zone, and the ocean waters of which the natural resources are under the exclusive management authority of the United States under the Magnuson Fishery Conservation and Management Act [16 U.S.C. §1801 *et seq.*], and (B) any other surface water, ground water, drinking water supply, land surface or subsurface strata, or ambient air within the United States or under the jurisdiction of the United States.

42 U.S.C. §9601(8).

Like the CWA, a CERCLA release is reportable only if the amount of a hazardous substance emitted exceeds its designated RQ in a 24-hour period.[62] The list of hazardous substances, along with their respective RQs, are found at 40 C.F.R. §302.4.

3. EPCRA Reportable Releases

Under section 304 of EPCRA, owners or operators of facilities at which hazardous chemicals are produced, used, or stored must give immediate notice of the release of a reportable quantity of an identified EHS.[63] For this purpose, the term "release" is defined as

> any spilling, leaking, pumping, pouring, emitting, emptying, discharging, injecting, escaping, leaching, dumping, or disposing into the environment (including the abandonment or discarding of barrels, containers, and other closed receptacles) of any hazardous chemical, extremely hazardous substance, or toxic chemical.[64]

The statute provides that notice need *not* be given if the release results in exposure to persons solely within the facility boundary.[65] Further, the reporting requirement does not apply to "federally permitted" releases (as defined by CERCLA §101(10), 42 U.S.C. §9601(10)) or to "continuous" releases (as defined by CERCLA §101(22), 42 U.S.C. §9601(22)). EPA has proposed regulations defining federally permitted releases[66] that have yet to be finalized and has promulgated regulations defining continuous releases.[67] Similarly, reporting is not required for releases excluded from reporting by section 101(22) of CERCLA, 42 U.S.C. §9601(22). As with CERCLA, EPCRA requires notification of reportable releases to any environmental medium, including "water, air and land."[68]

4. CAA Reportable Releases

Under section 112(r) of the CAA, EPA is directed to promulgate reporting requirements to address the prevention and detection of accidental releases of "regulated substances."[69] The term "accidental release" is defined as "an unanticipated emission of a regulated substance or other extremely hazardous substance into the ambient air from a stationary source."[70] Section 112(r) also

---

[62] 40 C.F.R. §302.6.

[63] 42 U.S.C. §11004. Like CERCLA, the statute directs EPA to set RQs for extremely hazardous substances. The extremely hazardous substances and their RQs appear at C.F.R. pt. 355, Appendixes A and B.

[64] EPCRA §329(8), 42 U.S.C. §11049(8).

[65] EPCRA §304(a)(4), 42 U.S.C. §11004(a)(4). Note that it is arguable whether the RQ of an EHS must be released beyond a facility boundary, or whether it is enough that an RQ of a substance is released within the boundary and exposure to any amount of the substance occurs outside the facility. EPA takes the position that release of the RQ outside the facility boundary is not a prerequisite to liability.

[66] *See* 53 Fed. Reg. 27,268 (1988).

[67] *See* 40 C.F.R. §302.8 (continuous release is defined as "a release that occurs without interruption or abatement or that is routine, anticipated, and intermittent and incidental to normal operations or treatment processes").

[68] Environment is defined as "water, air, and land and the interrelationship which exists among and between water, air, and land and all living things." 40 C.F.R. §355.20.

[69] 42 U.S.C. §7412(r)(7)(A). Implementing regulations were proposed on October 20, 1993, 58 Fed. Reg. 54, 190.

[70] CAA §112(r)(2)(A), 42 U.S.C. §7412(r)(2)(A).

establishes a new entity, the Chemical Safety and Hazard Investigation Board, that is to investigate and report on such accidental releases. The Board is authorized to establish regulations binding on responsible persons for reporting accidental releases into the ambient air.[71]

Under EPA's proposed regulations (to be codified at 40 C.F.R. Part 68) stationary sources at which regulated substances are present in excess of the threshold quantities listed at 40 C.F.R. §130 must prepare risk management plans that will provide facilities "with an integrated approach to identifying and managing the hazards posed by these regulated substances."[72] These plans, which include "worst-case scenarios," are to be provided to EPA, to the Chemical Safety and Hazard Investigation Board, to state and local planning authorities, and to the general public.

C. Responsible Persons, Appropriate Agencies, and Required Information

1. *CWA Reporting*

a. Persons Responsible for Making and Receiving Reports. Section 311 of the CWA requires that "[a]ny *person in charge* of a vessel or of an onshore facility or an offshore facility immediately notify the *appropriate agency* of the United States Government" of any reportable discharge of oil or a hazardous substance as soon as that person has knowledge of such discharge.[73] The federal agency receiving such a report must then "immediately notify the appropriate State agency of any State which is, or may reasonably be expected to be, affected by the discharge of oil or a hazardous substance."[74]

Under the statute, the term "person" is construed broadly and may be an individual, firm, corporation, association, or partnership.[75] Courts have expanded this definition to include cities and municipalities[76] and have made it clear that a corporation owning or operating a vessel or facility may be a "person in charge."[77]

The "appropriate agency" to which a release must be reported is the National Response Center (NRC) of the U.S. Coast Guard.[78] The NRC must be notified as soon as the person in charge has knowledge of any reportable discharge of oil. If direct reporting to the NRC is not practicable, the predesignated EPA On-Scene Coordinator (OSC) for the geographic area in which the discharge occurs may be notified.[79] In such cases, reports must be promptly relayed to the NRC by the notified OSC. If it is impossible for the person in charge to give immediate notice to the NRC or the OSC, he or she may

---

[71] CAA §112(r)(6), 42 U.S.C. §7412(r)(6).

[72] 58 Fed. Reg. 54,190 (1993).

[73] 33 U.S.C. §1321(b)(5) (emphasis added).

[74] *Id.* This is a new requirement of the Oil Pollution Act of 1990, Pub. L. No. 101-380, 101 Stat. 484, amending the CWA.

[75] CWA §311(a)(7), 33 U.S.C. §1321(a)(7).

[76] *See, e.g.,* United States v. City of New York, 481 F. Supp. 4, 14 ER Cases 1410 (S.D.N.Y.), *aff'd,* 614 F.2d 1292, 14 ER Cases 1420 (2d Cir. 1979), *cert. denied,* 446 U.S. 936 (1980).

[77] *See, e.g.,* United States v. Mobil Oil Corp., 464 F.2d 1124, 4 ER Cases 1405 (5th Cir. 1972).

[78] 40 C.F.R. §110.10.

[79] 40 C.F.R. §110.10.

notify the nearest Coast Guard unit on the condition that the person in charge thereafter notifies the NRC as soon as possible.[80] With regard to reporting on discharges of hazardous substances, the person in charge must notify the NRC "as soon as he has knowledge of any discharge of a designated hazardous substance . . . in quantities equal to or exceeding in any 24-hour period the reportable quantity."[81]

Thus, the distinction between reporting on releases of oil as opposed to hazardous substances is one of timing. Oil releases require notice as soon as the person has knowledge of the discharge, whereas a hazardous substance must have been released equal to or exceeding the RQ within a 24-hour period to be reportable.

For reasons relating to potential liability, however, it is generally preferable to report both hazardous substance and oil releases as soon as possible; the penalties for failure to report are far too severe to delay reporting. To do otherwise would permit contamination to become more widespread, thus increasing potential environmental damage and associated cleanup costs.

b. Information Required. Although the implementing regulations under the CWA are silent on what information must be reported, generally, the operator at the NRC responding to the call will want answers to the following questions:

1. Who is the caller filing the report? Is the caller the responsible party or is he or she calling on behalf of the responsible party?
2. What substance or substances were released?
3. How much of the substance(s) was released?
4. What was the source and cause of the release?
5. When and where were the substance(s) released, including the name of the county involved?
6. Has the release affected any water or is it confined to soil?
7. What is the extent of damages? Has any evacuation occurred?
8. Have any other entities been notified of the release (e.g., responsible state and local authorities)?

Since passage of the Oil Pollution Act of 1990, owners or operators of all tank vessels, all offshore facilities, and certain onshore facilities have also been required to prepare SPCC plans.[82] These are plans "for responding, to the maximum extent practicable, to a worst case discharge, and to a substantial threat of such a discharge, of oil or a hazardous substance."[83]

---

[80] *Id.*

[81] 40 C.F.R. §117.21.

[82] CWA §311(j)(5), 33 U.S.C. §1321(j)(5). Prior to the Oil Pollution Act of 1990, vessels were not subject to this requirement. In response to the Exxon *Valdez* spill, however, Congress required tank vessels to prepare SPCC plans. The term "tank vessel" is defined as

> a vessel that is constructed or adapted to carry, or that carries, oil or hazardous material in bulk as cargo or cargo residue, and that—
> (A) is a vessel of the United States;
> (B) operates on the navigable waters of the United States; or
> (C) transfers oil or hazardous material in a port or place subject to the jurisdiction of the United States.

46 U.S.C. §2101(39). SPCC plans are described in more detail in Chapters 4 and 14.

[83] CWA §311(j)(5)(A), 33 U.S.C. §1321(j)(5)(A).

The statute required vessels and facilities to submit SPCC plans for approval by February 1993. Those that submitted plans will be allowed to continue their operation for up to two years pending approval.[84] Those that do not will be barred from handling, storing, or transporting oil.[85]

2. *CERCLA Reporting*

a. Persons Responsible for Making and Receiving Reports. CERCLA provides that "[a]ny *person in charge* of a vessel or an offshore or an onshore facility shall, as soon as he has knowledge of any [reportable] release (other than a federally permitted release) of a hazardous substance from such vessel or facility, . . . immediately notify the National Response Center . . . of such release."[86] As under the CWA, CERCLA reporting is triggered by the release of a hazardous substance in an amount equal to or exceeding the RQ in any 24-hour period.[87]

The NRC, in turn, has an obligation expeditiously to convey the notification of such a release to "all appropriate Government agencies, including the Governor of any affected State."[88]

b. Information Required. CERCLA, like the CWA, requires the person in charge to notify the NRC immediately of a reportable release. The NRC will request the same type of information for a CERCLA release report as listed above for a CWA release report.

3. *EPCRA Reporting*

a. Persons Responsible for Making and Receiving Reports. Under EPCRA, "*owners or operators*" of facilities at which hazardous substances (as identified by 29 C.F.R. §1910.1200) are produced, used, or stored, may be required to give two different notices of the release of an RQ of specific hazardous materials.[89] If either (1) a CERCLA hazardous substance or (2) an EPCRA extremely hazardous substance that is also listed as a CERCLA hazardous substance is released in excess of the RQ and results in exposure beyond the facility boundary, notice must be given immediately[90] to the Local Emergency Planning Committee (LEPC), the State Emergency Response Commission (SERC), and the NRC. If the material released is an EPCRA EHS, but is not a CERCLA hazardous substance, notice need only be given to the SERC and LEPC. It should be noted, however, that EPA has proposed a rule designat-

---

[84] CWA §311(j)(5)(F), 33 U.S.C. §1321(j)(5)(F). If approval of the plan is denied, or if the two-year period lapses, that vessel or facility may not continue to store, transport, or handle oil.

[85] CWA §311(j)(5)(E), 33 U.S.C. §1321(j)(5)(E).

[86] CERCLA §103(a), 42 U.S.C. §9603(a) (emphasis added). The U.S. Court of Appeals for the Second Circuit has interpreted the term "persons in charge" to include those, even of relatively low rank, who were in a position to detect, prevent, and abate the release of hazardous substances. United States v. Carr, 880 F.2d 1550, 30 ER Cases 1128 (2d Cir. 1989).

[87] 40 C.F.R. §302.6.

[88] CERCLA §103(a), 42 U.S.C. §9603(a).

[89] EPCRA §304, 42 U.S.C. §11004 (emphasis added); 40 C.F.R. §355.40.

[90] Neither EPCRA nor the implementing regulations defines the term "immediately." However, in its Final Penalty Policy for Section 304 (OSWER DIR. # 9841.2), EPA suggests that in some circumstances, notification within one hour after the release may be untimely.

ing all EHSs as CERCLA hazardous substances.[91] If and when this proposal becomes final, all EHS releases must be reported to the LEPC, SERC, and NRC. As a practical matter, however, it would be prudent to report all releases to all three authorities even before the final rule is promulgated.

b. Information Required. Depending upon what type of substance is released, EPCRA requires reporting to the NRC and/or to the LEPC and SERC. For reports filed with the NRC, the information required for an EPCRA release will be identical to that required for a CWA or CERCLA release. With respect to providing notice of a release to the LEPC and SERC, the owner or operator of the facility must provide the following information:[92]

1. The chemical name or identity of any substance involved in the release;
2. An indication of whether the substance is an extremely hazardous substance;
3. An estimated quantity of the substance that was released into the environment;
4. The time and duration of the release;
5. The environmental medium or media (e.g., air, water, soil) into which the release occurred;
6. Any known or anticipated acute or chronic health risks associated with the release and, where appropriate, advice regarding medical attention needed for exposed individuals;
7. Proper precautions to take as a result of the release, including evacuation (unless this information is contained in an emergency plan that is readily available);
8. The names and telephone numbers of the person or persons to be contacted for further information.[93]

In addition, "as soon as practicable"[94] following the release, the facility owner or operator must give the LEPC and SERC a written follow-up report confirming the information provided in the initial notice. This follow-up report must update earlier information concerning actions taken to respond to and contain the release, known or anticipated health risks from exposure to the released material, and advice regarding medical attention necessary for exposed individuals.[95]

4. CAA Reporting

a. Persons Responsible for Making and Receiving Reports. Section 112(r) of the CAA grants EPA broad authority to promulgate regulations relating to "release prevention, detection, and correction requirements which may include monitoring, recordkeeping, reporting, training, vapor recovery,

---

[91] 54 Fed. Reg. 3388 (1989).

[92] Notice must be given "immediately . . . by such means as telephone, radio, or in person." EPCRA §304(b)(1), 42 U.S.C. §11004(b)(1); 40 C.F.R. §355.40(b).

[93] EPCRA §304(b), 42 U.S.C. §11004(b); 40 C.F.R. §355.40(b).

[94] There is no formal definition of the meaning of the term "as soon as practicable." In its Final Penalty Policy (OSWER DIR. # 9841.2), however, EPA indicates that under certain circumstances, failure to file a written follow-up within a week of the release may be deemed a violation.

[95] EPCRA §304(c), 42 U.S.C. §11004(c); 40 C.F.R. §355.40(b)(3).

secondary containment, and other design, equipment, work practice, and operational requirements.''[96] EPA failed to meet its November 15, 1993, deadline for promulgating regulations that specify procedures for informing the public and local response agencies of accidental releases, for emergency health care, and for employee training measures to respond to such releases.[97] Once final, ''owners and operators'' of stationary sources then will have three years to come into compliance with those regulations.[98]

Moreover, the newly established Chemical Safety and Hazard Investigation Board will have authority to impose requirements on owners and operators for reporting accidental releases into the ambient air.[99] Those regulations will require the reporting of releases to the Board or to the NRC. The NRC, if notified, is required to report to the Board any release within the Board's jurisdiction.[100]

Owners and operators of stationary sources at which more than a ''threshold quantity'' of a regulated substance is present will also be required to prepare and implement a risk management plan designed to prevent or minimize, detect, and respond to accidental releases of such substances.[101] The statutory specifications for these plans are very detailed and are similar to the SPCC plan requirements imposed by section 311 of the CWA.[102]

b. Information Required. Based on the Notice for Proposed Rulemaking (NPRM), these plans are likely to include step-by-step process hazard analyses, written process safety information to permit the identification of hazards posed by processes involving regulated substances, development of standard operations procedures, employee training programs, maintenance programs, plans to prepare for the introduction of new regulated substances or process changes, safety audits, accident investigation, emergency response programs, a risk management plan, and new recordkeeping requirements.[103]

Within three years after implementing regulations are published by EPA, risk management plans must be submitted to the appropriate state and local agencies as well as to EPA and Chemical Safety and Hazard Investigation Board.[104]

[96] 42 U.S.C. §7412(r)(7)(A). Proposed rules were published in October 20, 1993, (58 Fed. Reg. 54,190) (1993).

[97] CAA §112(r)(7)(B)(ii)(III), 42 U.S.C. §7412(r)(7)(B)(ii)(III).

[98] CAA §112(r)(7)(B)(i), 42 U.S.C. §7412(r)(7)(B)(i). The statute defines ''owner or operator'' as any person who owns, leases, operates, controls, or supervises a stationary source. CAA §112(a)(9), 42 U.S.C. §7412(a)(9).

[99] CAA §112(r)(6)(C)(iii), 42 U.S.C. §7412(r)(6)(C)(iii). The Board will consist of five members appointed by the President, by and with the advice and consent of the Senate. The terms of office of the Board members is five years.

[100] *Id.*

[101] CAA §112(r)(7)(B)(ii), 42 U.S.C. §7412(r)(7)(B)(ii).

[102] For a more complete analysis of the CAA risk management plans, see Chapter 3, Clean Air Act.

[103] *See* 58 Fed. Reg. 54,190 (1993).

[104] *Id.*

D. Penalties

1. Penalties Under the CWA

a. Penalties for Discharges. Section 311 prohibits the discharge of harmful quantities of oil or hazardous substances into navigable waters.[105] With the passage of the Oil Pollution Act of 1990, both EPA and the Coast Guard have authority to impose administrative, civil, and/or criminal penalties for such discharges.

Administrative penalties may be assessed by EPA or the Coast Guard against the owner, operator, or person in charge of any vessel or facility from which oil or a hazardous substance is discharged.[106] EPA or the Coast Guard can seek up to $10,000 per violation (the total penalty cannot exceed $25,000) for class I penalties, via informal proceedings.[107] For class II penalties, the alleged violator has the right to a hearing before an administrative law judge, and the penalty cannot exceed $10,000 per day for each day during which the violation continues (the maximum amount of the penalty is not to exceed $125,000).[108] The public is allowed a reasonable opportunity to comment on any proposed penalty in a class II penalty proceeding.[109]

The owner, operator, or person in charge of a vessel or facility from which oil or hazardous substances are discharged in violation of section 311 also is subject to a civil penalty. The penalty for such a discharge is not to exceed (1) $25,000 for each day in which the discharge occurs; or (2) $1,000 per barrel of oil discharged; or (3) $1,000 per unit of reportable quantity of the hazardous substance discharged.[110] Thus, if 100 barrels of oil are discharged, the maximum civil penalty would be $100,000. Similarly, for a hazardous substance with an RQ of 10 pounds, a spill of 10,000 pounds would subject the responsible person to a civil penalty not to exceed $1 million.

In a case involving gross negligence or willful misconduct by the owner, operator, or person in charge, the civil penalties are more severe. The mandatory penalty in such a case is at least $100,000. The upper limit is unfixed and is based on the number of barrels of oil or reportable quantities of hazardous substances discharged times $3,000.[111]

Moreover, the Oil Pollution Act of 1990 provides for criminal penalties for violations of section 311 of CWA. For negligent violations, EPA is authorized to seek a fine up to $25,000 per day of violation and/or imprisonment of that person for up to one year.[112] For knowing violations, the responsible party can be fined up to $50,000 per day of violation and imprisoned for up three years.[113] For knowing violations that place another person in imminent danger of death

---

[105] 33 U.S.C. §1321(b)(3).

[106] CWA §311(b)(6)(A), 33 U.S.C. §1321(b)(6)(A).

[107] CWA §311(b)(6)(B)(i), 33 U.S.C. §1321(b)(6)(B)(i).

[108] CWA §311(b)(6)(B)(ii), 33 U.S.C. §1321(b)(6)(B)(ii).

[109] CWA §311(b)(6)(C)(i), 33 U.S.C. §1321(b)(6)(C)(i).

[110] CWA §311(b)(7)(A), 33 U.S.C. §1321(b)(7)(A).

[111] CWA §311(b)(7)(D), 33 U.S.C. §1321(b)(7)(D).

[112] 33 U.S.C. §1319(c)(1) (the minimum fine is $2,500 per day). Subsequent convictions warrant the imposition of a fine up to $50,000 per day and/or imprisonment up to two years.

[113] 33 U.S.C. §1319(c)(2) (the minimum fine is $5,000 per day). A repeat offender faces a fine of not more than $100,000 per day and/or imprisonment for up to six years.

or serious bodily injury ("knowing endangerment"), the fine can be as high as $250,000 for an individual, $1 million for an organization, and imprisonment could be for up to 15 years.[114]

b. Penalties for Failure to Report. Section 311 of the CWA provides civil and criminal penalties for failure to submit required notice to the appropriate authorities. A responsible person who has knowledge of the discharge of a reportable quantity of oil or a hazardous substance, but fails immediately to report the discharge to the NRC, is guilty of a criminal violation, punishable by a fine and/or imprisonment for up to five years.[115] The fine for an individual can be as much as $250,000, and for an organization, as much as $500,000.[116]

While reporting a discharge automatically subjects the responsible person to a civil penalty, the release notification given by such person may not be used against the person reporting the discharge, except in a prosecution for perjury or for giving a false statement.[117] The Oil Pollution Act of 1990 amended this provision to apply only to criminal cases against "natural persons," thus extending corporations no protection.

Finally, EPA has the authority to seek criminal penalties against any person who knowingly makes any false material statement or representation in any report. Such person may be punished by a fine not more than $10,000 and/or imprisonment for not more than two years.[118]

2. *Penalties Under CERCLA*

Although CERCLA does not authorize penalties for discharges of hazardous substances, it does penalize failure to report those discharges to the appropriate agencies.

Pursuant to section 103 of CERCLA, a person in charge of a vessel or facility from which a reportable release occurs who fails to "notify immediately the appropriate agency . . . as soon as he has knowledge of such release," may be fined and/or imprisoned for up to three years (five years for subsequent convictions).[119] As with the CWA penalties for failure to report, the maximum fine is $250,000 for an individual and $500,000 for an organization.[120]

---

[114] 33 U.S.C. §1319(c)(3) (for subsequent convictions, the maximum punishment is double with respect to both fine and imprisonment).

[115] 33 U.S.C. §1321(b)(5). Prior to passage of the Oil Pollution Act of 1990, the penalties consisted of a fine of up to $10,000 and imprisonment for not more than one year.

[116] 18 U.S.C. §3571. In lieu of these fines, EPA also has the option to fine the responsible party twice the amount of the greater of (1) any gain derived from the violation by that party, or (2) any resulting loss to others. 18 U.S.C. §3571(d).

[117] CWA §311(b)(5), 33 U.S.C. §1321(b)(5).

[118] 33 U.S.C. §1319(c)(4) (subsequent convictions subject person to fine not more than $20,000 and/or imprisonment up to four years).

[119] 42 U.S.C. §9603(b). *See also* 18 U.S.C. §1001.

[120] 18 U.S.C. §3571. Again, as under the CWA, EPA instead can fine the responsible party two times the greater of (1) any gain derived from the violator by that party, or (2) any resulting loss to others. 18 U.S.C. §3571(d).

3. *Penalties Under EPCRA*

Under EPCRA, as under CERCLA, it is not illegal for a person to discharge extremely hazardous substances. Failure to report the discharge, however, can lead to the imposition of severe penalties.

EPCRA authorizes EPA to assess a civil penalty of up to $25,000 per day for each violation of EPCRA's section 304 reporting requirements.[121] Subsequent violations may result in penalties not to exceed $75,000 per day for each such violation.[122]

Moreover, knowing and willful failure to provide required notices of releases under section 304 of EPCRA is punishable by criminal penalties, including fines of up to $25,000 and/or imprisonment for up to two years.[123] Subsequent convictions are punishable by fines of up to $50,000 and/or imprisonment for up to five years.[124]

4. *Penalties Under the CAA*

a. Penalties for Discharges. The CAA provides for severe criminal penalties to be imposed upon those persons who negligently or knowingly release regulated substances into the ambient air. Negligent releases of any section 112 hazardous air pollutant or any EPCRA extremely hazardous substance, which place another person in imminent danger of death or serious bodily injury, are punishable by a fine of up to $100,000 for an individual, $200,000 for an organization, and/or imprisonment for up to one year.[125]

In knowing releases into the ambient air of any section 112 hazardous air pollutant or any EPCRA extremely hazardous substance where others are placed in imminent danger of death or serious bodily injury, the responsible person faces fines of up to $250,000 for an individual, $1 million for an organization, and/or imprisonment of up to 15 years.[126]

b. Penalties for Failure to Report. Once the reporting requirements of section 112(r) are effective, it will be unlawful for any person to fail to report any release of any regulated substance to the NRC or to the Chemical Safety and Hazard Investigation Board.[127] Failure to report may result in civil penalties up to $25,000 per day for each violation.[128] In determining the appropriate penalty, EPA is to take into consideration the size of the business, the economic impact of the penalty on the business, the violator's past compliance history, the

---

[121] EPCRA §325(b)(1)(A), 42 U.S.C. §11045(b)(1)(A). In determining the amount of such penalty, EPA is to consider the nature and gravity of the violation, the ability of the violator to pay, the violator's past history of violations, and whether the violator gained any economic benefit from the violation. EPCRA §325(b)(1)(C), 42 U.S.C. §11045(b)(1)(C).

[122] EPCRA §325(b)(2), 42 U.S.C. §11045(b)(2).

[123] EPCRA §325(b)(4), 42 U.S.C. §11045(b)(4).

[124] *Id.*

[125] CAA §113(c)(4), 42 U.S.C. §7413(c)(4); 18 U.S.C. §3571. If the release results in the death of another person, however, the fine for an individual can be as high as $250,000, and $500,000 for an organization. Subsequent convictions subject that person to double the fine and double the incarceration.

[126] CAA §113(c)(5)(A), 42 U.S.C. §7413(c)(5)(A); 18 U.S.C. §3571. If the person is facing a subsequent conviction, the maximum fine and imprisonment are double.

[127] CAA §112(r)(6)(O), 42 U.S.C. §7412(r)(6)(O).

[128] CAA §113(b), 42 U.S.C. §7413(b).

duration of the violation, the economic benefit of noncompliance, and the gravity of the violation.[129]

Further, any person who "knowingly" violates a reporting requirement under section 112(r) may be fined and/or imprisoned up to five years.[130] The maximum fine is $250,000 for an individual and $500,000 for a corporation.[131] Subsequent convictions are punishable by fine ($500,000 for individual, $1 million for organization) and/or imprisonment up to 10 years.[132]

Moreover, severe criminal penalties may be imposed upon any person who knowingly makes any false material statement or representation in any notification. Such person faces a fine of up to $250,000 for an individual and up to $500,000 for an organization and/or imprisonment for not more than two years.[133]

E. Unplanned or Accidental Release Reporting Flow Charts

The following charts provide a graphic outline of the reporting provisions described above. Because EPA has not yet promulgated regulations defining the reporting requirements of section 112(r) of the CAA, no flow chart has been prepared for that statute.

III. Material Safety Data and Toxic Release Inventory Reporting

A. Scope

The Emergency Planning and Community Right-to-Know Act of 1986 was enacted as Title III the Superfund Amendments and Reauthorization Act of 1986, although it is not part of CERCLA.[134] The statute has two basic purposes: (1) to cause governmental entities to plan for unexpected releases of hazardous chemical substances into the environment; and (2) to require businesses using or storing such substances to notify emergency planning and response entities of the presence of those materials at their facilities and to report on the inventories and environmental releases (both planned and unplanned) of those substances. These reporting obligations are enforced by a variety of means, including citizens' suits and criminal sanctions.[135]

EPCRA's reporting provisions are contained in Subtitles A and B. Section II of this chapter described the release notification requirements of Subtitle A, which also required state and local governments to establish emergency planning and response authorities to deal with situations involving releases of so-called extremely hazardous substances.[136]

---

[129] CAA §113(e), 42 U.S.C. §7413(e).

[130] CAA §113(c), 42 U.S.C. §7413(c).

[131] 18 U.S.C. §3571. EPA, in its discretion, can choose to fine the responsible party twice the amount of any gain by that party or loss by other parties. 18 U.S.C. §3571(d).

[132] 42 U.S.C. §7413(c).

[133] 42 U.S.C. §7413(c)(2); 18 U.S.C. §3571. Subsequent convictions warrant imposition of double the maximum fine and double the maximum imprisonment. *Id.*

[134] Pub. L. No. 99-499, October 17, 1986 (Title III of the Superfund Amendments and Reauthorization Act of 1986). EPCRA is codified at 42 U.S.C. §11001 *et seq.*

[135] EPCRA §§325 and 326, 42 U.S.C. §§11045 and 11046.

[136] EPCRA §§301–05, 42 U.S.C. §§11001–05; 40 C.F.R. pt. 355.

FIGURE 2
REPORTING CWA OIL DISCHARGES

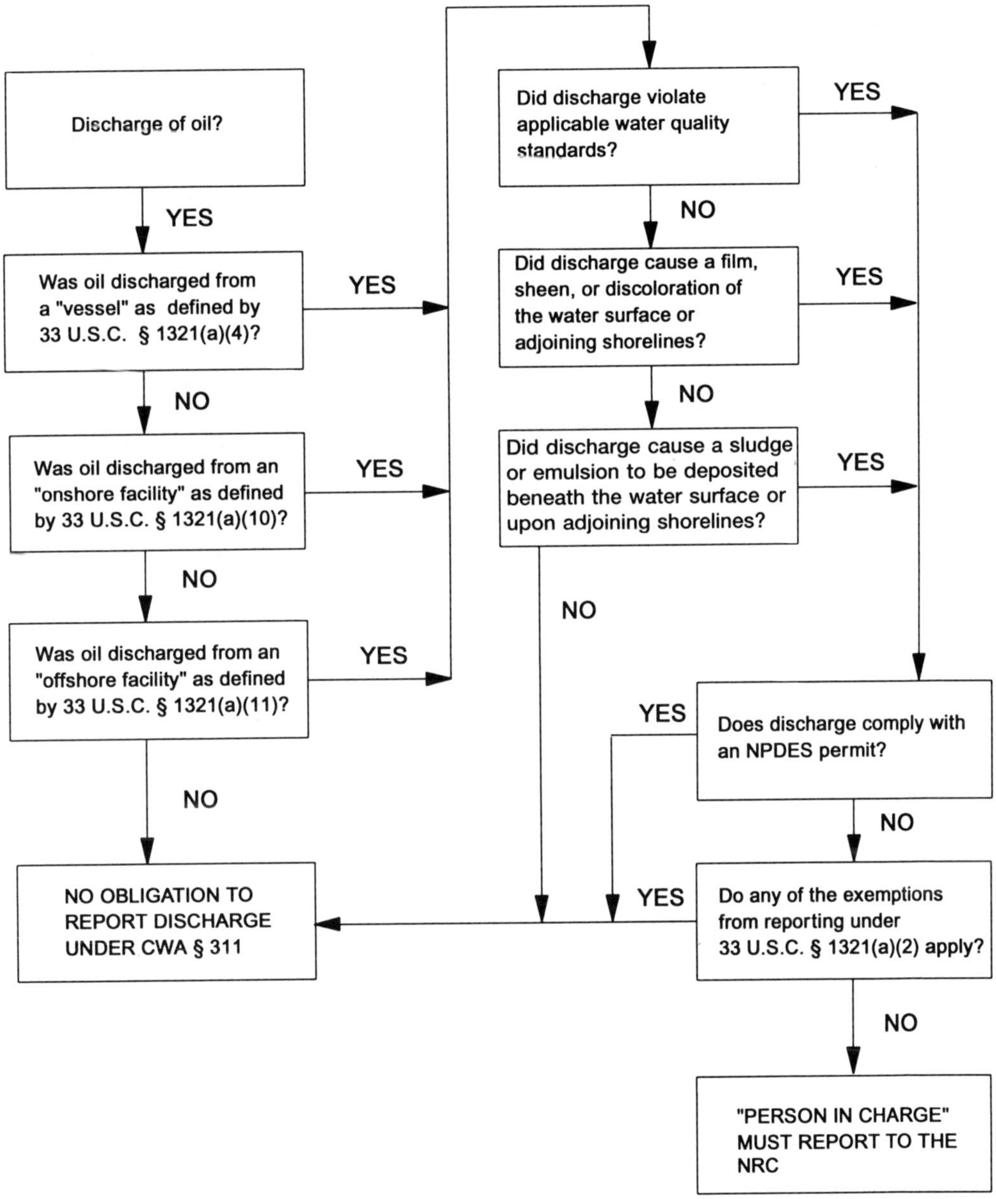

FIGURE 3
REPORTING FOR CWA
HAZARDOUS SUBSTANCE DISCHARGES

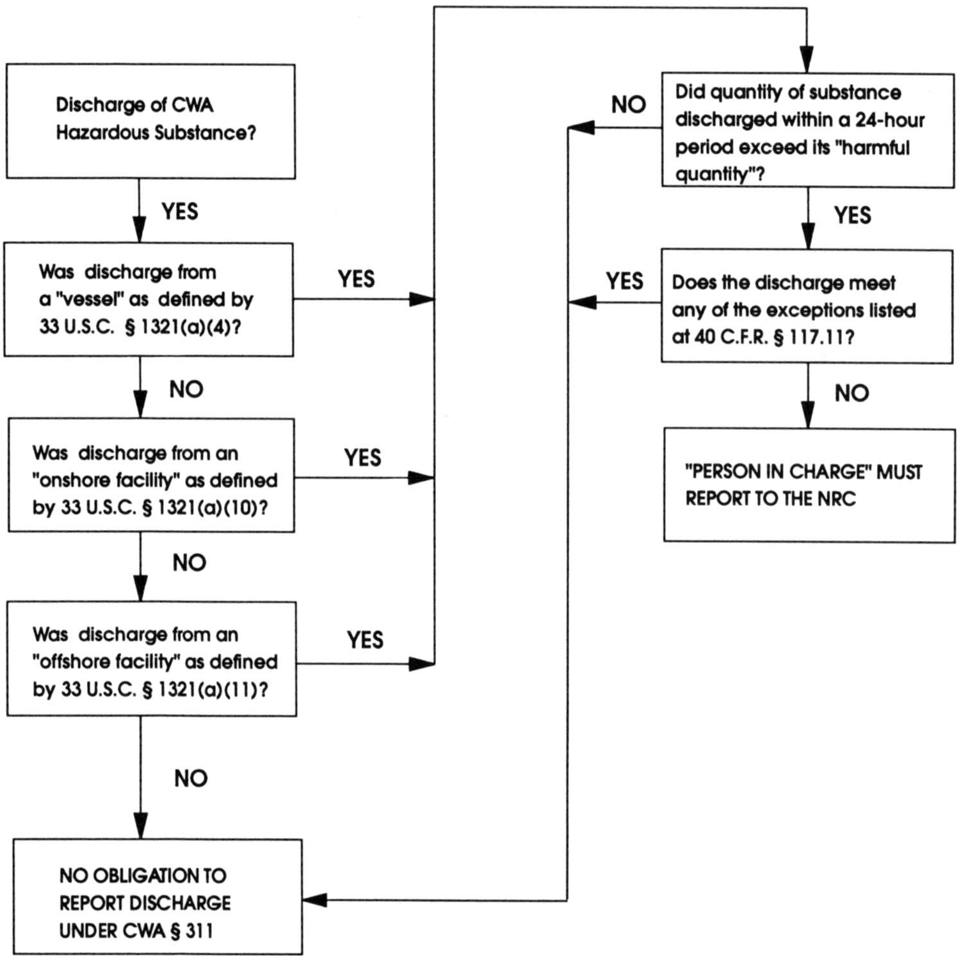

Under Subtitle B, three different sets of reports on two different groups of substances may be required.[137] Sections 311 and 312[138] require submission of information on inventories of "hazardous chemicals," i.e., those substances for which a Material Safety Data Sheet (MSDS) is required by the hazard communication regulations promulgated by the Occupational Safety and Health Administration (OSHA).[139] Section 313 requires persons who own or operate

[137] EPCRA §§311–13, 42 U.S.C. §§11021–23.
[138] 42 U.S.C. §§11021 and 11022; 40 C.F.R. pt. 370.
[139] 29 C.F.R. §1910.1200. See Chapter 8.

FIGURE 4
REPORTING FOR CERCLA HAZARDOUS SUBSTANCE DISCHARGES

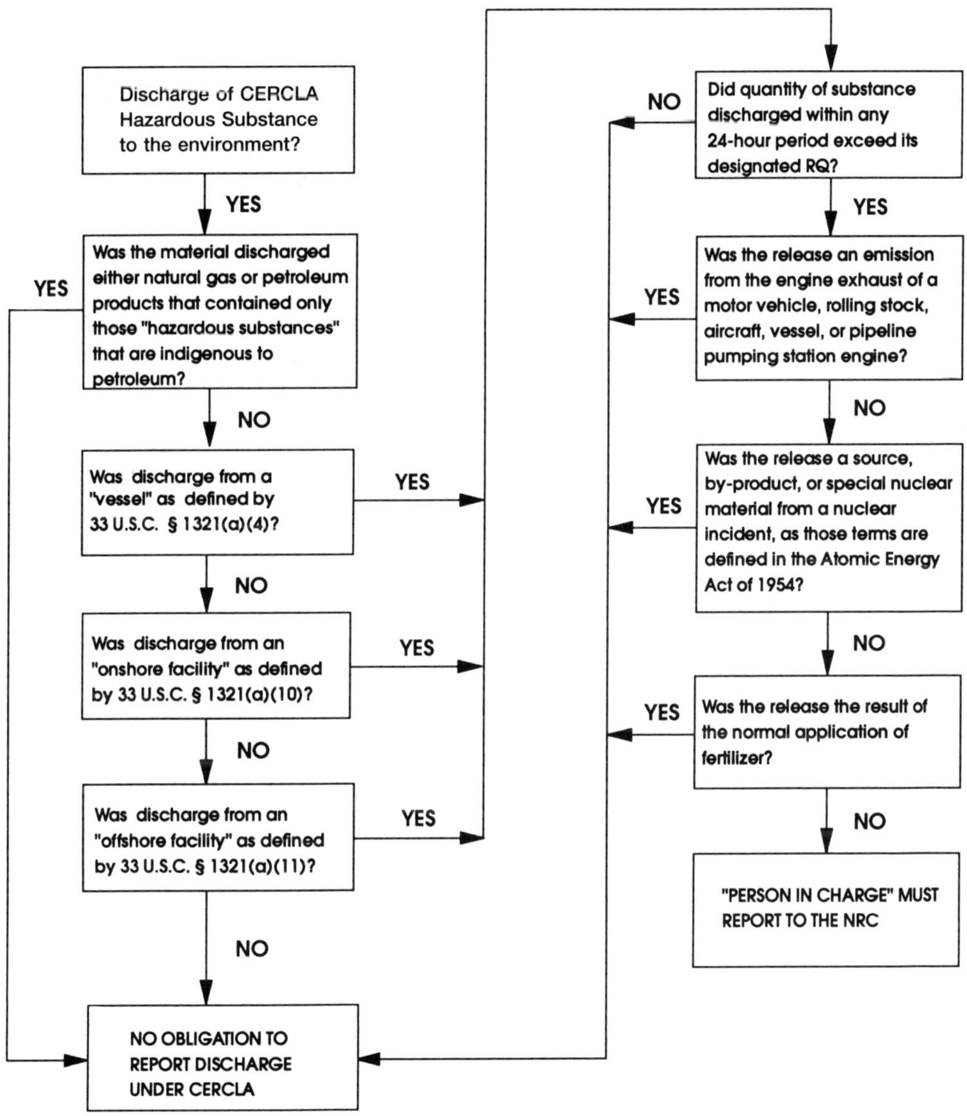

facilities within manufacturing sector Standard Industrial Classification (SIC) Codes 20 through 39 that manufacture, process, or otherwise use "toxic chemicals" in excess of specified quantities to file annual reports on the quantities of those substances at the facility, the manner in which they are

FIGURE 5
REPORTING FOR EPCRA EXTREMELY HAZARDOUS SUBSTANCE DISCHARGES

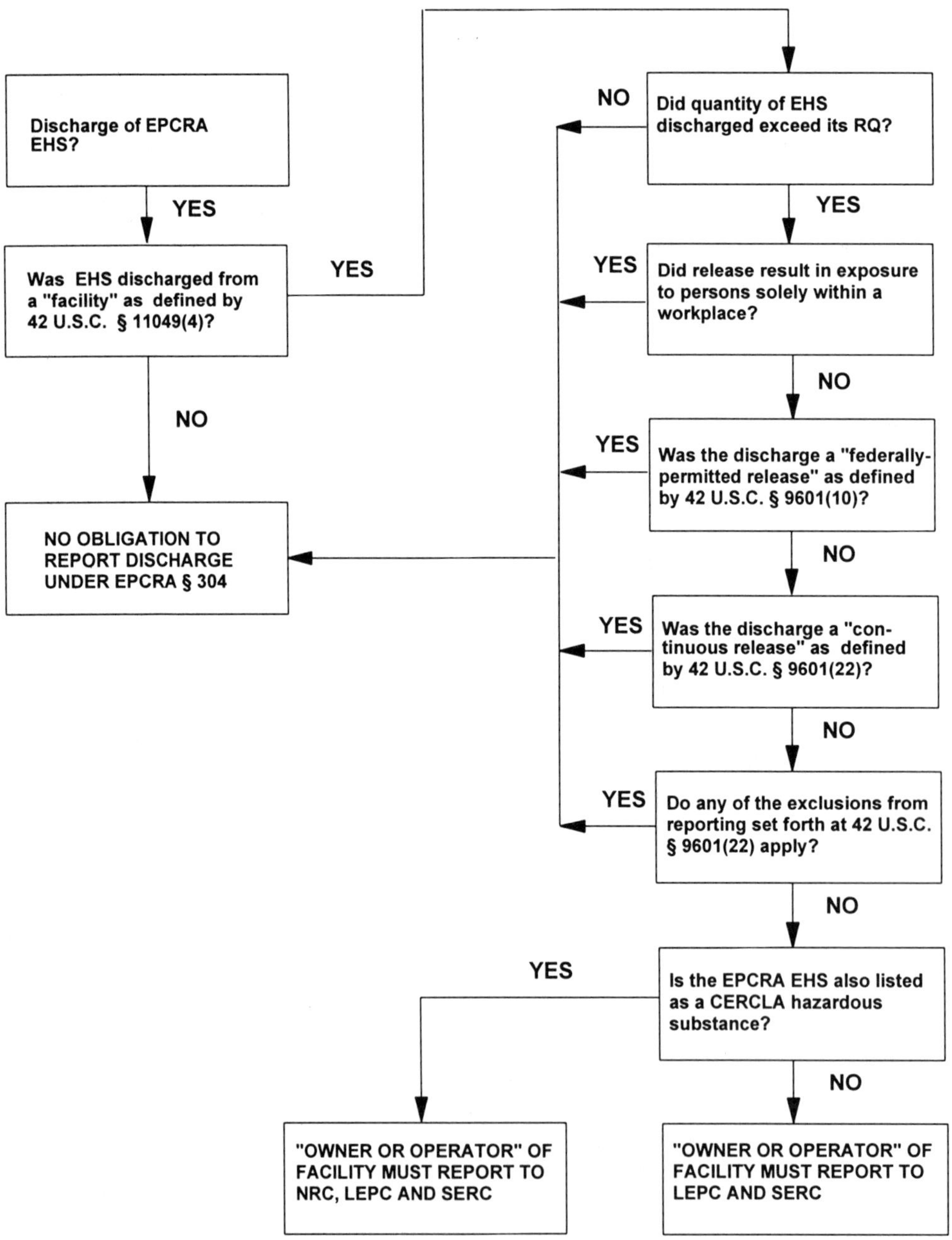

applicants and other interested parties involved in a dispute over wetlands matters. The Corps permit process, although cumbersome at times, affords applicants a variety of means to resolve conflicts and to pursue their proposed activity. Furthermore, the likelihood of success in wetlands-related actions is particularly difficult to predict in light of the complexity of the regulations and the tendency of different courts to emphasize different factors enumerated in the public interest review guidelines.

G. Conclusion

The White House and Congress continue to aggressively consider major revisions to the current federal wetlands program;[143] at the same time, the judiciary is faced with numerous cases involving interpretation of the myriad of wetlands regulations.

On August 24, 1993, President Clinton through his White House Office on Environmental Policy proposed "a comprehensive package of improvements to the Federal wetlands program that reflects a broad-based consensus among Federal agencies."[144] This 30-page report discusses many possible changes to wetlands policy and procedures such as streamlining the section 404 program, establishing a formal appeals mechanism for permit denials, increasing instances of states and localities assuming aspects of the federal permit program, establishing a uniform delineation methodology, refining the mitigation banking policy, and establishing regional criteria for the definition of wetlands.[145]

Some of the Administration and congressional wetlands initiatives will undoubtedly increase the amount of area considered jurisdictional wetlands, while others may reduce the remaining wetland acreage. Taken together, this ongoing policy and regulatory reexamination process will require parties planning wetlands permit applications to take into account constantly changing factors and considerations as they go through the permit process.

III. The National Environmental Policy Act

As the 1960s drew to a close, Congress became aware of the need for a strong national environmental policy.[146] The resulting legislation, the National

[143] In addition to its comprehensive wetlands package, the Administration is awaiting release in September 1994 of the NAS study on wetlands definition. *See* 58 Fed. Reg. 4995 (1993). A number of bills, such as the Clean Water Act reauthorization, have already been introduced in the 103d Congress that, if enacted, would significantly change the wetlands regulatory landscape.

[144] "Protecting America's Wetlands: A Fair, Flexible, and Effective Approach," White House Office of Environmental Policy, Aug. 24, 1993, at 2.

[145] *Id.* The Administration has already begun to act on a number of these wetlands initiatives. For instance, proposed regulations are currently being drafted that would expand the nationwide permits system, require the Corps to issue permit decisions in 90 days, establish a formal appeals process for Corps and EPA permit actions, and institute a wetlands certification training program for private delineators. In addition, the Corps and EPA published a final rule on August 25, 1993 that (1) modifies the definition of "discharge of dredged material," (2) clarifies when the placement of pilings constitutes a discharge of dredged material, and (3) codifies the current policies that prior converted wetlands are not waters of the United States. 58 Fed. Reg. 45,008 (1993).

[146] *See generally* 42 U.S.C. §4331(a) (Supp. V 1964).

Environmental Policy Act of 1969 (NEPA),[147] signified Congress' response to the environmental harm arising from decades of population growth, resource exploitation, and rapid industrial and technological expansion. The statute set forth a national policy that advocated environmental awareness and spoke of the responsibility of every generation to care for the environment so as to preserve it for succeeding generations to enjoy. On a more practical level, NEPA mandated that the federal government consider environmental concerns together with more traditional economic and social criteria in making major decisions such as where to build a highway or a hospital, whether to construct a power facility, or whether to lease a tract of park land for development.[148]

NEPA affords a statutory basis to force review of many federal decisions on environmental grounds. NEPA's impact has been particularly striking where the federal agency does not otherwise have distinct environmental responsibilities for which it can be held accountable. By injecting environmental concerns into federal decision making and permitting federal litigation challenging governmental actions, NEPA has not only elevated concern for environmental problems to a more prominent level in public discourse, but it has also generated a great deal of litigation.

Indeed, a large body of case law has developed as courts have struggled to clarify the statute's general provisions. As a result of NEPA decisions and regulations promulgated by the Council on Environmental Quality, many agencies have incorporated NEPA requirements into their routine procedures. The early flood of NEPA litigation testing the boundaries of the legislation has slowed to a steady stream of actions challenging agencies' decisions on the basis of whether or not they are in compliance with the statute's implementing regulations and those of the agency in question.

A. Overview of the Statute

NEPA is divided into two titles. Title I declares a national environmental policy, provides a method to attain the goals stated in the policy, and includes guidance on the fundamental question of how NEPA relates to other federal law. Title II creates the Council on Environmental Quality (CEQ). CEQ is charged with certain responsibilities by statute and, in addition, has promulgated the regulations which guide the NEPA process.[149] Its future appears uncertain, however, as President Clinton has proposed abolishing the CEQ and replacing it with the new White House Office of Environmental Policies.

1. Title I

The national environmental policy declared in Title I is the first ever legislated by Congress. Section 101(a) declares that "it is the continuing policy of the Federal Government . . . to use all practicable means . . . to create and

---

[147] Pub. L. No. 91-190, 42 U.S.C. §§4321–47 (1982), as amended by Pub. L. No. 95-52 (July 3, 1975) (appropriations) and Pub. L. No. 94-83 (August 9, 1975) (delegation to states to prepare environmental impact statements in certain limited cases).

[148] *See generally* NEPA §§101–02, 42 U.S.C. §§4331–32 (1988).

[149] *See generally* NEPA §204, 42 U.S.C. §4344 (1988), 40 C.F.R. §1500 *et seq.*

maintain conditions under which man and nature can exist in productive harmony . . . ."[150] Section 101(b) pronounces six related goals including assuring "all Americans safe, healthful, productive and esthetically and culturally pleasing surroundings."[151] Distilled to its essence, section 101 makes the federal government responsible for utilizing functional means to administer its programs in an environmentally sound fashion. Of course, such means must be consistent with other nationally defined objectives—NEPA does not elevate environmental concerns over other national goals.[152]

Section 102(1) furthers the purpose declared in section 101 by requiring that laws and policies be "interpreted and administered in accordance with the policies set forth in this chapter."[153] Prior to NEPA, an agency could contend that it lacked the statutory authority to consider environmental factors when making a decision. This section ensures that in most instances the agency has the authority, indeed the obligation, to weigh the environmental consequences of its actions.

Section 102(2), known as the "action forcing" section of NEPA, contains provisions designed to compel agencies to consider the environmental effects of their decisions. Subsections (A) and (B) direct federal agencies to integrate natural and social science and environmental design arts in planning and decision making and also to develop methods to ensure that environmental amenities are given appropriate attention alongside economic and technical considerations. If a proposal involves a conflict regarding alternative uses of available resources, subsection (E) directs the agency to develop and describe alternative courses of action. Subsection (F) mandates that agencies recognize the worldwide and long-range character of environmental problems, and directs them to furnish appropriate support to programs designed to foster international cooperation on environmental issues.[154]

The most significant provision in NEPA is section 102(2)(C), which forces agencies to account for environmental factors in a very concrete fashion when proposing a major federal action that may have significant environmental impact. The provision mandates that the agency prepare and distribute a detailed report explaining the environmental consequences of its proposed actions and of alternatives to those actions. The crucial language of the statute reads:

> The Congress authorizes and directs that, to the fullest extent possible: . . . (2) all agencies of the Federal Government shall—
> (C) Include in every recommendation or report on proposals for legislation and other major Federal actions significantly affecting the quality of the human environment, a detailed statement by the responsible official on—
> (i) The environmental impact of the proposed action,
> (ii) Any adverse environmental effects which cannot be avoided should the proposal be implemented,

[150] 42 U.S.C. §4331(a) (1988).

[151] 42 U.S.C. §§4331(b), 4331(b)(2) (1988).

[152] *E.g.*, Flint Ridge Dev. Co. v. Scenic Rivers Ass'n, 426 U.S. 776, 788, 8 ER Cases 2137 (1976) (stating that where NEPA is clearly in conflict with another statute, NEPA must yield).

[153] 42 U.S.C. §4332(1) (1988).

[154] *See generally* NEPA §102(2), 42 U.S.C. §4332(2) (1988).

(iii) Alternatives to the proposed action,
(iv) The relationship between local short-term uses of man's environment and the maintenance and enhancement of long-term productivity, and
(v) Any irreversible and irretrievable commitments of resources which would be involved in the proposed action should it be implemented.

Section 102(2) further requires the federal agency charged with preparing this environmental impact statement (EIS) to consult with other agencies which may have jurisdiction or special expertise in the matter and to make copies of the EIS available to the public.[155]

2. *Title II*

Title II of NEPA creates the Council on Environmental Quality (CEQ or Council).[156] This three-member body, housed in the Office of the President, is charged with monitoring progress toward achieving the national environmental goals proclaimed in section 101. Section 204 spells out the Council's specific statutory duties. First, CEQ is instructed to assist the President in the preparation of the Environmental Quality Report. Issues as broad as its title implies are addressed in this annual report, and an analysis of the need for additional environmental legislation is specifically required. The Council is also instructed to gather environmental information and to conduct studies on conditions and trends in environmental quality. CEQ is charged with developing and recommending to the President national policies to protect and improve the environment.[157] Finally, CEQ has the duty to provide guidance to other federal agencies on compliance with NEPA.[158] To this end, CEQ promulgated regulations in 1978 (amended in 1986) governing the NEPA process for all federal agencies.[159]

The Council has had a brief but turbulent history. Throughout the 1970s, CEQ played a prominent role in raising public awareness of such controversial issues as offshore drilling, toxic substances, and marine pollution. The Reagan Administration, as part of its effort to deregulate, cut the Council's budget to such a degree that it had few significant accomplishments other than issuance of amendments to its earlier regulations. CEQ became more active during the Bush Administration as its budget and staff were increased. During that period, efforts were made to consolidate the Council with EPA in a proposed cabinet level Department of the Environment.

The Clinton Administration has announced its intention to eliminate the CEQ and replace it with the White House Office of Environmental Policy.[160] In turn, the Council's responsibilities would most likely be transferred to EPA. However, because the CEQ was created by statute, arguably it cannot be dismantled unilaterally by a presidential order. The Clinton Administration's

---

[155] NEPA §102(2)(C), 42 U.S.C. §4332(2)(C) (1988).

[156] NEPA §202, 42 U.S.C. §4342 (1988).

[157] *See generally* NEPA §§201–04, 42 U.S.C. §§4341–44 (1988).

[158] Exec. Order No. 11,514, 35 Fed. Reg. 4247 (1970), *reprinted in* 42 U.S.C. §4321 app. (1988); Exec. Order No. 11,991, 42 Fed. Reg. 26,967 (1977), *reprinted in* 42 U.S.C. §4321 app. (1988).

[159] 40 C.F.R. §1500 *et seq.* (1992).

[160] Ann Devroy, *Clinton Announces Plan to Replace Environmental Council,* WASHINGTON POST, Feb. 9, 1993, at A6.

proposal must be approved by Congress before it can take effect. Legislation introduced in the Senate in 1993 also sought to eliminate CEQ, splitting its current responsibilities between EPA and the White House.

B. Regulations Under NEPA

Generally, Congress delegates the administration of a statute to one specific federal agency and that agency is authorized to promulgate regulations interpreting and implementing the statute. In contrast, NEPA places obligations and responsibilities on all federal agencies, but the statute does not delegate the power to adopt implementing regulations to any one agency. This omission was remedied in 1970 when President Nixon authorized the CEQ to issue informal guidelines to aid the agencies in the preparation of environmental impact statements.[161] The CEQ adopted guidelines in 1971 and 1973 but the guidance did not have the status of formal agency regulations.[162] In 1977, President Carter, by executive order, authorized the CEQ to adopt regulations rather than guidelines.[163] The Council adopted regulations implementing impact statement preparation the following year.[164] Those regulations have been amended once, in 1986, and govern the NEPA process today. In addition to those regulations, most federal agencies have adopted internal regulations covering their NEPA compliance.

Because NEPA is a very general statute, of necessity courts have considered its implementing regulations in order to infuse it with practical meaning. Lower federal courts held the initial CEQ guidelines to be purely advisory[165] but still accorded them considerable respect.[166] In its first NEPA decision after the adoption of the 1978 CEQ regulations, *Andrus v. Sierra Club,*[167] the Supreme Court cited the regulations 27 times and quoted extensively from them in footnotes.[168] Although the Court also relied on its own interpretation of NEPA and did not find the regulations to be controlling, the Court noted that "CEQ's interpretation of NEPA is entitled to substantial deference."[169] The *Andrus* ruling foreshadowed the deference given to the CEQ regulations in subsequent decisions. Since *Andrus,* lower courts have held that the CEQ regulations are controlling.[170]

---

[161] Exec. Order No. 11,514, 35 Fed. Reg. 4247 (1970), *reprinted in* 42 U.S.C. §4321 app. (1988).

[162] 36 Fed. Reg. 7724 (1971), 38 Fed. Reg. 20,550 (1973).

[163] Exec. Order No. 11,991, 42 Fed. Reg. 26,967 (1977), *reprinted in* 42 U.S.C. §4321 app. (1988).

[164] 43 Fed. Reg. 55,978 (to be codified at 40 C.F.R. §1500 *et seq.*).

[165] *See, e.g.,* Aertsen v. Landrieu, 637 F.2d 12, 15 ER Cases 2124 (1st Cir. 1980); Areene County Planning Bd. v. Federal Power Comm'n, 455 F.2d 412 (2d Cir. 1972), *cert. denied,* 409 U.S. 849 (1972).

[166] *See, e.g.,* Environmental Defense Fund, Inc. v. Hoffman, 566 F.2d 1060, 10 ER Cases 1987 (8th Cir. 1977); Silentman v. Federal Power Comm'n, 566 F.2d 237, 10 ER Cases 1796 (D.C. Cir. 1977).

[167] 442 U.S. 347, 13 ER Cases 1161 (1979).

[168] Note, *NEPA After* Andrus v. Sierra Club: *The Doctrine of Substantial Deference to the Regulations of the Council on Environmental Quality,* 66 VA. L. REV. 843 (1980).

[169] *Andrus,* 442 U.S. at 358.

[170] *See, e.g.,* Sierra Club v. Sigler, 695 F.2d 957 (5th Cir. 1983) (holding that CEQ regulations are binding on the courts and on federal agencies unless it can be shown that the regulations conflict with the language or legislative intent of NEPA or the teachings of the Supreme Court).

1. Categorical Determinations

The regulations promulgated by CEQ outline the procedures for implementing section 102(2)(C) of NEPA. First, the regulations permit federal agencies to prepare categorical guidance to determine whether or not a proposal is a major federal action that may have significant environmental impact. Based on the criteria set forth in these regulations, the agency determines that the proposal does or does not require an EIS, or that it falls neatly into neither category and, therefore, necessitates an environmental assessment.[171]

If based on the categorical exclusions within the regulations, the agency determines that its proposal will not require an EIS or an environmental assessment, then that action may proceed, in many instances, without the necessity of complying with further NEPA requirements. For many routine activities, such as personnel actions, agencies have specified that neither an EIS nor an environmental assessment is required.

2. Environmental Assessment

Many federal actions are neither categorically excluded nor included under the agencies' NEPA review regulations. In these instances, an environmental assessment is necessary.[172] An environmental assessment is a concise, public document that provides sufficient evidence and analysis to determine whether an agency proposal requires an EIS.[173] If the agency concludes, based on the environmental assessment, that the project does not significantly affect the environment, and, therefore, does not necessitate an EIS, then the agency must prepare a "finding of no significant impact" (FONSI) which briefly explains why an EIS is not necessary.[174] The FONSI must contain sufficient evidence to support the agency's finding of no significant impact. If it does not, courts can overturn it.[175]

3. Scoping and Drafting Processes

Once the determination is made that an EIS is necessary, the agency must publish a notice of intent in the *Federal Register* and begin to decide what will be included in the EIS. This so called "scoping" process is a preliminary step designed to foster participation and focus the EIS. The agency charged with preparing the EIS must invite other relevant agencies and the public to participate in the scoping process to determine what significant issues will be analyzed and how much depth to afford to each issue.[176] The regulations offer some guidance by specifying the types of actions, alternatives, and impacts that must be considered.[177] The scoping process provides an early opportunity for interes-

---

[171] 40 C.F.R. §1501.4(a), .4(b) (1992). Environmental assessments are discussed below.

[172] 40 C.F.R. §1501.4(b) (1992).

[173] 40 C.F.R. §1508.9 (1992).

[174] 40 C.F.R. §1501.4(e) (1992).

[175] *E.g.,* People *ex rel.* Van de Kamp v. Marsh, 687 F. Supp. 495 (N.D. Cal. 1988); State *ex rel.* Guste v. Lee, 635 F. Supp. 1107 (E.D. La. 1986).

[176] *See generally* 40 C.F.R. §1501.7 (1992).

[177] 40 C.F.R. §1508.25(a)-(c) (1992).

ted parties to influence the subject matter of the EIS and, thus, potentially affect its conclusions.

Once the scoping process is completed, the agency begins writing the EIS. Environmental impact statements are generally prepared in two stages—draft and final. The draft stage is designed to disclose all major points of view on the environmental impact of the proposal and the alternatives considered. The draft must "fulfill and satisfy to the fullest extent possible" the requirements of the final EIS.[178] The agency must then solicit comments from various governmental entities and affected parties.[179]

After completing the draft and examining its comments, the agency begins work on the final EIS. As mandated in section 102(2)(C) of NEPA, the final EIS must address the environmental impact of the proposed action, any unavoidable adverse environmental impacts of the proposed action, alternatives to the proposed action, the relationship between short-term uses of the environment and the maintenance of long-term productivity, and any irreversible and irretrievable commitments of resources involved in the proposed action. In doing so, the agency is obligated to respond to the comments on the draft EIS.[180]

4. *Delegation*

Section 102(2)(C) of NEPA implies, but does not specifically state, that the federal agency proposing the action in question is responsible for preparing the EIS. Agencies have consistently attempted to delegate that responsibility to state and local governments and, also, to private consultants. This issue has generated a great deal of litigation. In 1975, Congress amended NEPA to state that the responsibility of drafting the EIS could be delegated to state officials and agencies provided that the responsible federal official either participates in the preparation process or, at least, maintains some modicum of supervision over the final product.[181] The amended statute still holds the federal official ultimately responsible for the scope and contents of the document.

With a few exceptions, courts have permitted federal agencies to delegate the responsibility for preparing an EIS to private consultants so long as the agency maintained sufficient control or supervision over the process.[182] However, courts have not permitted an agency to delegate the responsibility to a private consultant who has an interest in seeing the project accepted or completed in a certain manner.[183]

5. *Lead Agency*

Many large federal actions involve the active participation of more than one agency. To streamline the EIS preparation process, the concept of the "lead agency" was developed so that there would be one federal actor with overall responsibility for the process. The CEQ regulations specify that, in situations

---

[178] 40 C.F.R. §1502.9(a) (1992).

[179] 40 C.F.R. §1503.1(a) (1992).

[180] *See generally* 40 C.F.R. §1502.9 (1992).

[181] 42 U.S.C. §4332(2)(D) (1982).

[182] *See, e.g.*, NRDC v. Callaway, 524 F.2d 79, 8 ER Cases 1273 (2d Cir. 1975).

[183] Greene County Planning Bd. v. Federal Power Comm'n, 455 F.2d 412, 3 ER Cases 1595 (2d Cir. 1972), *cert. denied*, 409 U.S. 849, 4 ER Cases 1752 (1973).

where more than one federal agency is involved in an action, the agencies must designate one to be the "lead agency." In making that determination, the most important factors to consider are the magnitude of each agency's involvement in the project, the authority each agency ultimately maintains over the decision to approve the project, and the expertise each agency holds regarding the project's environmental effects. CEQ maintains the authority to select the lead agency whenever those agencies involved cannot reach a consensus among themselves.[184]

6. *Contents of an EIS*

CEQ suggests a format for the EIS and provides guidance as to how it should read and look. More substantively, its regulations also dictate how certain topics, such as alternatives considered, the affected environment, and environmental consequences, must be addressed.[185]

The regulations characterize the alternatives section of the EIS as the "heart" of the document. They instruct the agency to present the environmental impacts of both the proposal and its alternatives in comparative form "sharply defining the issues and providing a clear basis for choice among options by the decision maker and the public."[186] The EIS must examine in detail, rigorously explore, and objectively evaluate the proposed action and all reasonable alternatives including the "no action" alternative. It must also identify the agency's preferred alternative, if one exists, and include appropriate mitigation measures which were not already included in the proposed action or the alternatives.[187]

The requirement to consider alternatives manifests the simple principle that a rational decision requires a knowledge of the available choices, including the choice of no action, and the consequences of each choice. A detailed discussion and consideration of alternatives that are remote or speculative is not required. However, an alternative may not be discounted merely because it is outside the jurisdiction of the agency or because it runs against an existing agency policy. Courts have held that the discussion of alternatives must be reasonable such that a reviewing court may conclude that a proposing agency has taken a "hard look" at the environmental consequences of its decision.[188]

Included in the EIS must also be a section that clearly and concisely describes the environment of all areas affected or created by either the agency's proposal or any of the alternatives being considered in the document.[189]

Finally, the EIS must include a section on environmental consequences. This section forms the scientific and analytic basis for comparing the alternatives to each other and to the proposed action. It should consolidate the discussions of those factors enumerated in NEPA section 102(2)(C) as they relate to the agency's proposal and to its alternatives.[190] It should include,

---

[184] 40 C.F.R. §1501.5(e), (f) (1992).

[185] 40 C.F.R. §1502.10–.18 (1992).

[186] 40 C.F.R. §1502.14 (1992).

[187] *See generally* 40 C.F.R. §1502.14 (1992).

[188] *See, e.g.*, Baltimore Gas & Elec. Corp. v. NRDC, 462 U.S. 87, 97 (1983); Vermont Yankee Nuclear Power Corp. v. NRDC, 435 U.S. 519, 11 ER Cases 1439 (1978).

[189] 40 C.F.R. §1502.15 (1992).

[190] 40 C.F.R. §1502.16 (1992).

among other topics, a discussion of the direct and indirect effects of the proposal and its alternatives, possible conflicts between the proposed action and other federal, regional, or state objectives, and any means to mitigate adverse environmental impacts.[191]

The problem of discerning which environmental effects the EIS must address reached the Supreme Court in *Metroplitan Edison v. People Against Nuclear Energy.*[192] The case was originally brought as a NEPA challenge to the proposed reopening of one of the reactors at Three Mile Island. The plaintiffs maintained that damage to psychological health and community well being were among the environmental effects which must be considered in an EIS. The Court, in rejecting this claim, held that NEPA was intended to address only effects on the "physical environment," and that while human health and welfare are goals of the statute, Congress intended to address them through protection of the physical environment.[193]

7. *Worst Case Analysis*

In 1986, CEQ amended the provision in the regulations governing instances when information on environmental consequences is lacking. Where there exists incomplete or unavailable information concerning reasonably foreseeable significant environmental effects of the proposal or an alternative, the agency must now disclose the lack of information. If the information is essential to a reasoned choice among alternatives and the overall cost of obtaining the information is not exorbitant, the agency must include the information in the EIS. If the costs of obtaining the information are, in fact, exorbitant, or the means to attain the information are unknown, the lack of information must be disclosed, and the agency must include in the EIS a description of the information, its relevance to evaluating significant environmental effects, and the agency's evaluation of such impacts based on generally accepted theoretical approaches to such determinations.[194]

Prior to the 1986 amendments, the CEQ regulations mandated that the agency include in its impact statement a "worst-case analysis" in such instances where essential information was lacking.[195] The new regulation[196] was interpreted by the Supreme Court in *Robertson v. Methow Valley Citizens Council*[197] where the Court upheld an agency determination not to provide a "worst-case analysis," stating that the amended regulation is entitled to substantial deference.

8. *Record of Decision*

Once the final EIS is completed, the agency is instructed to consider its conclusions when deciding what action to take on the proposal at issue. At the

---

[191] 40 C.F.R. §1502.16(a), (b), (c), (d), (h) (1992).

[192] 460 U.S. 766 (1983).

[193] *Id.* at 772.

[194] *See generally* 40 C.F.R. §1502.22 (1992).

[195] 40 C.F.R. §1502.22 (1992). *See also* Save Our Ecosystems v. Clark, 747 F.2d 1240, 20 ER Cases 1607 (9th Cir. 1984); Sierra Club v. Sigler, 695 F.2d 957, 972 (5th Cir. 1983).

[196] *See generally* 40 C.F.R. §1501.1 (1992).

[197] 490 U.S. 332, 354–56 (1989).

time of its decision, the agency must prepare a "record of decision" stating what the decision was and identifying all alternatives considered by the agency in reaching that decision.[198] The record of decision must also specify which alternatives were considered to be environmentally preferable, and state whether all means available to mitigate environmental harm have been adopted, and if not, why they were not. In most instances, the decision on the action may not be taken or recorded until the later of either 90 days after notice of the draft EIS is provided, or 30 days after notice of the final EIS is provided.[199]

C. Judicial Interpretation of NEPA

1. The Substantive Versus Procedural Debate

An important practical question about the policy and goals found in NEPA was whether they create any enforceable substantive rights. In other words, does NEPA require that a federal agency make a particular decision in certain circumstances, or does the statute only require that the agency consider certain specified environmental factors in its decision-making process. Although there was once disagreement among the various courts of appeals on this issue, the Supreme Court has since resolved the conflict.

In *Vermont Yankee Nuclear Power Corp. v. NRDC,*[200] the Court found that although "NEPA does set forth substantive goals for the nation, its mandate to the agencies is essentially procedural." Subsequently, in *Stryker's Bay Neighborhood Council v. Karlen,*[201] the Court reversed a decision which discerned in NEPA the substantive standards necessary to review the merits of agency decisions. In its holding, the Court ruled that once an agency has made a decision subject to NEPA's procedural requirements, the only role for a court is to ensure that the agency has considered the environmental consequences of its proposal. It would not be proper, the Court held, for a court to "interject itself within the area of discretion of the executive as to the choice of action to be taken."

Thus, in *Vermont Yankee* and *Stryker's Bay,* the Court clearly determined that NEPA does not create judicially enforceable substantive rights, but rather imposes a procedural duty on federal agencies to consider how their proposals would affect the environment. These holdings were extended in *Robertson v. Methow Valley Citizens Council.*[202] The *Robertson* court confronted a Ninth Circuit decision enjoining a National Forest Service decision which would have permitted construction to begin on a ski area in a national forest. The Ninth Circuit had ruled against the Forest Service because the mitigation measures relied on in the EIS were unenforceable and, thus, inadequate to satisfy NEPA's procedural requirements. The Supreme Court reversed, stating that courts are not to make substantive environmental decisions under NEPA regarding the

---

[198] 40 C.F.R. §1505.2(a), (b) (1992).
[199] 40 C.F.R. §1506.10(b), (c) (1992).
[200] 435 U.S. 519, 11 ER Cases 1439 (1978).
[201] 444 U.S. 223, 13 ER Cases 2157 (1980).
[202] 490 U.S. 332 (1989).

mitigation measures contained in the EIS. According to the Court, "NEPA merely prohibits uninformed—rather than unwise—agency action."[203]

In dicta, the *Robertson* court did note that although NEPA bestows only procedural requirements upon agency actions, that does not leave environmental plaintiffs without a judicial remedy. Rather, the remedy merely lies in other more substantive environmental statutes.[204]

2. *The Threshold Question: When Is an EIS Required?*

Section 102(2)(C) provides that an environmental impact statement must be prepared by federal agencies on "proposals for . . . major federal actions significantly affecting the quality of the human environment."[205] This relatively simple language has generated a very large volume of litigation.

The first word, "proposal," raises the issue of timing. A federal agency is not required to prepare an EIS until it has made a "proposal" for an action. The regulations state that a "proposal" exists at the stage when an agency "has a goal and is actively preparing to make a decision on one or more means of accomplishing that goal and the effects can be meaningfully evaluated."[206] The Supreme Court interpreted the term in *Kleppe v. Sierra Club.*[207] At issue in *Kleppe* were three studies, one of which was the Northern Great Plains resources program, a study undertaken by the Interior Department to assess the social, economic, and environmental impacts of resource development in five Great Plains states. The Department had already prepared an EIS for national coal development and had conceded that certain site-specific impact statements would be necessary on certain leases and activities in the Great Plains region. Plaintiffs argued that the Great Plains program and the two related studies constituted a regional program that required its own EIS discussing the program's impact on a regional level.

In rejecting plaintiff's contention, the Supreme Court held that a regional EIS was required only if there had been a recommendation on a proposal for a major federal action in the Great Plains region. The Court found that Interior's proposals were for actions either national or local in scope, and that there had been no proposal for any regional action. The Court, however, did not define the term "proposal" except to say that mere contemplation of an action or the study of a potential action is not enough.[208]

Another predicate for the EIS requirement is that the action at issue must be "federal." Federal action obviously includes what is undertaken directly by federal agencies including operation of programs, construction of facilities, and provision of funding to others. Federal action also includes a federal agency's decision granting permission for activities to others such as private businesses or state and local governments. The CEQ regulations describe a "major federal action" as one "with effects that may be major and which are potentially

---

[203] *Id.* at 351.
[204] *Id.*
[205] 42 U.S.C. §4332(2)(C) (1988).
[206] 40 C.F.R. §1508.23 (1992).
[207] 427 U.S. 390, 8 ER Cases 2169 (1976).
[208] *Id.* at 406.

subject to federal control and responsibility.''[209] This regulation includes within its definition ''circumstances where the responsible officials fail to act.''[210] It does not include general revenue sharing or judicial or administrative enforcement actions.[211] Such actions are not considered ''federal'' for NEPA purposes.

Once it is determined that an action qualifies as a ''proposal'' and that it is ''federal,'' the next step is to determine whether it ''significantly affects the quality of the human environment.'' This is an especially important threshold because demanding a high level of ''significance'' would allow many federal actions to escape NEPA's requirements altogether. Courts have taken a variety of approaches to this question. The Second Circuit, in *Hanly v. Kleindienst,*[212] adopted a two-part test to determine the significance of the impact. The *Hanly* test focused on the degree of change from current land use and the absolute quantity of the impact. The Fifth Circuit, in *Save Our Ten Acres v. Kreger,*[213] concluded that an agency action reaches the threshold whenever it ''may cause a significant degradation of some human environmental factor.''

The CEQ regulations provide a two-dimensional definition of ''significantly'' instructing the decision maker to consider the action's ''context'' and its ''intensity.'' When determining context, the regulations instruct the court or agency to analyze the action against several backgrounds such as society as a whole, the affected region, the affected interests, and the locality. The term ''intensity'' refers to the severity of the impact. In determining severity, the decision maker is to consider a number of factors, including any effects on public health and safety, the unique characteristics of the geographic area, and the cumulative effect of the proposed action in relation to other actions.[214]

3. *EIS Requirements for Special Types of Federal Actions*

Two types of agency actions deserve special attention in connection with the EIS requirement. They are proposals for legislation and ongoing agency programs.

In addition to requiring impact statements for proposals for agency action, section 102(2)(C) also requires an EIS to be prepared in connection with proposals for legislation.[215] Courts must determine whether an agency has sufficiently participated in the development of legislation so as to qualify the submission as a ''proposal for legislation'' under NEPA. The CEQ regulations seek to answer the question by defining legislation as any bill or legislative proposal, not including appropriation requests, ''developed by or with the significant cooperation and support of a federal agency.''[216]

---

[209] 40 C.F.R. §1508.18 (1992).

[210] *Id.*

[211] 40 C.F.R. §1508.18(a) (1992); *see also* Carolina Action v. Simon, 389 F. Supp. 1244, 7 ER Cases 1807 (M.D.N.C. 1975).

[212] 471 F.2d 823, 4 ER Cases 1785 (2d Cir. 1973), *cert. denied,* 412 U.S. 908, 5 ER Cases 1416 (1973).

[213] 472 F.2d 463, 4 ER Cases 1941 (5th Cir. 1972).

[214] *See generally* 40 C.F.R. §§1508.27(b)(2), (b)(3), and (b)(7) (1992).

[215] 42 U.S.C. §4332(2)(C) (1988).

[216] 40 C.F.R. §1508.17 (1992). Courts have interpreted this provision somewhat narrowly. In Environmental Defense Fund, Inc. v. Alexander, 501 F. Supp. 742 (N.D. Miss. 1980), the court held that an EIS was not required to accompany a feasibility report covering work on a waterway because the language of the report described future work and was of a preliminary nature. Similarly, in Citizens for Mgmt. of Alaska Lands v. Department of Agric., 447 F. Supp. 753, 11 ER Cases 2096 (D. Alaska 1978), the court held that Agriculture

A second type of agency action that merits special mention in connection with EIS requirements is an agency "program." Although NEPA does not specifically require the preparation of a "programmatic" EIS, the courts have required such an impact statement in certain instances where approval of the current proposal would foreclose decisions on whether to approve future projects that would in themselves require impact statements.

Scientists' Institute for Public Information v. Atomic Energy Commission[217] is a leading case dealing with EIS requirements for agency programs relating to future developments. In that case, the Commission had concluded that it did not need a programmatic EIS before proceeding with a breeder reactor demonstration program because the environmental impact of that program would be evaluated in individual EIS's on each demonstration plant. The District of Columbia Circuit, focusing on the potential future environmental effects of the decisions under review, held that a programmatic impact statement was required.

On a related subject, the applicability of the EIS to ongoing federal agency programs, the Eighth Circuit, in *Minnesota Public Interest Research Group v. Butz,*[218] held that Forest Service decisions, as part of an ongoing plan for the management of timber in a certain area, required an EIS to discuss the cumulative environmental impact of the decisions. The applicability of this EIS requirement appears to have significant potential for those who seek to change what they view as unacceptable, yet entrenched, agency policies and practices.

D. NEPA's Relationship With Other Federal Law

Because NEPA applies to all federal agencies, it is inevitable that conflict will occur between NEPA and other statutes that agencies are charged to enforce. When this happens, the Supreme Court has held that an agency's specific statutory obligations prevail over compliance with NEPA. The Court considered this issue in *Flint Ridge Development Co. v. Scenic Rivers Ass'n.*[219] There, the plaintiffs argued that an EIS was required for approval of a land development project on which an antifraud disclosure document had been filed with the Department of Housing and Urban Development pursuant to the Interstate Land Sales Full Disclosure Act. That Act provided that disclosure documents automatically become effective 30 days after filing (allowing sales to go forward in interstate commerce) unless suspended because of inadequate disclosure. The disclosure at issue was not found to be inadequate, nor was it in dispute that an EIS could not be prepared within 30 days. The Court held that the agency did not need to file an EIS, concluding that where NEPA and another

---

did not have to prepare an EIS to accompany its report on a congressional proposal to include certain lands in the national land system. In that case, the report was requested by the congressional committee, and not initiated by the agency. These cases suggest that an EIS will only be required if the agency itself initiates a formal legislative proposal.

[217] 481 F.2d 1079, 5 ER Cases 1418 (D.C. Cir. 1973).

[218] 498 F.2d 1314, 6 ER Cases 1694 (8th Cir. 1974), *rev'd,* 541 F.2d 1292, 9 ER Cases 1220 (8th Cir. 1976).

[219] 426 U.S. 776, 8 ER Cases 2137 (1976).

federal statute are in "clear and unavoidable conflict ... NEPA must give way."[220]

In NEPA actions where the challenged agency is EPA, courts have examined the environmental statute which EPA was acting under in order to determine whether EPA performed the functional equivalent of an EIS under the other statute. In performing this "functional equivalency" test, courts have concluded that most of EPA's regulatory activities under the Clean Air Act, the Federal Insecticide, Fungicide, and Rodenticide Act, the Ocean Dumping Act, and the Resource Conservation and Recovery Act, already require EPA to perform the functional equivalent of a NEPA review so that additional review under NEPA is unnecessary.[221]

E. Standing

The issue of standing, that is whether an individual or group bringing a NEPA action is properly before a federal court, has generated a great deal of litigation. Because environmental actions generally breed standing issues involving alleged injuries of a less tangible nature than standard commercial actions, federal courts have had to decide what types of indirect, noneconomic injuries are sufficient for a third party to bring an environmental action. Two Supreme Court decisions in the early 1970s left the courtroom door wide open for those representing environmental interests. By setting a low threshold for what constitutes judicially cognizable injury in environmental matters, these decisions afforded environmental groups the opportunity to challenge a wide array of government actions in the federal courts.

The earliest case, *Sierra Club v. Morton,*[222] involved a challenge to a National Forest Service decision approving construction of a $35 million resort in the Sequoia National Forest. The Sierra Club alleged that the proposal for development did not comply with federal laws governing the preservation of national parks and forests. Seeking to establish the principle that a membership organization with a "special interest" in the environment has standing to challenge actions that directly affect the environment, the Sierra Club did not claim to be directly injured by construction of the resort. Instead, the Sierra Club sought standing based on its status as a public interest group with a historic tradition of protecting and preserving the environment.

The Supreme Court rejected this theory of standing, holding that the mere allegation of a sincere and special interest in a problem is not sufficient to constitute the requisite injury and, therefore, to establish standing. However, the Court stated that such a showing of injury could be established merely by alleging that some of the Club's members used the area for recreational or aesthetic purposes.[223] The Court explained that the aesthetic injury suffered by members would be sufficient to confer standing not only upon those members individually but also upon the organization to which they belonged.[224]

---

[220] *Id.* at 788.
[221] *See* Alabamians for a Clean Env't v. EPA, 26 ER Cases 2116, 2121–22 (N.D. Ala. 1987).
[222] 405 U.S. 727, 3 ER Cases 2039 (1972).
[223] *Id.* at 734.
[224] *Id.* at 739.

Soon thereafter, in *United States v. Students Challenging Regulatory Agency Procedures (SCRAP I),*[225] the Court demonstrated how easily the standing requirements detailed in *Sierra Club v. Morton* could be satisfied. *SCRAP I,* among the most liberal standing cases, addressed a NEPA challenge against an Interstate Commerce Commission (ICC) action concerning railroads' collection of a surcharge on freight. The law students who filed the action claimed that their injury stemmed from the fact that the rate increase fell especially harshly on recycled goods. As a result, the price of such goods would increase, thereby causing people to consume fewer of them. In turn, plaintiffs argued, lower consumption of recycled goods would lead to increased mining and logging operations which would finally damage the aesthetic beauty of the land where the increased operations would occur. Despite this highly tenuous line of causation, the Court found that the students had standing to challenge the ICC's action in federal court. In rejecting the government's claim that the chain of causation was too attenuated, the Court stated that the allegation of a mere "trifle" of injury is sufficient to confer standing.[226]

Scrap I is often cited by environmental plaintiffs wishing to gain access to federal courts. Although that holding remains a leading precedent in the environmental area, subsequent cases have narrowed its application as the Supreme Court has begun to demand a more precise demonstration of actual injury before allowing NEPA actions to proceed. In *Lujan v. National Wildlife Federation*[227] and *Lujan v. Defenders of Wildlife,*[228] the Court reaffirmed the notion that recreational use and aesthetic enjoyment are sufficient noneconomic injuries to gain standing. However, in both instances, the Court denied plaintiffs standing, requiring in one instance that the plaintiffs demonstrate a much stronger nexus between the government action and the plaintiffs' injury, while holding in the second case that no sufficient injury had been alleged.

In *Lujan v. National Wildlife Federation,* the National Wildlife Federation brought action under two federal statutes, including NEPA, challenging the Interior Department's Land Withdrawal Review Program. The group alleged that the government's actions would lead to increased mining on public lands which would, in turn, damage the environment and result in diminished recreational opportunities and aesthetic enjoyment of federal lands in the vicinity of the areas to be mined. The Federation argued that these allegations were sufficient to receive standing under *SCRAP I.* The Court denied the Federation standing, holding that the facts did not demonstrate that its members were adversely affected by the government's actions. The flaw, according to Justice Scalia, was that the Federation's members averred only to have used federal lands in the vicinity of the lands which would be open to mining and not those lands themselves.

In *Lujan v. Defenders of Wildlife,* the Court found that the plaintiff lacked standing because it failed to state that its members were, in fact, injured by the government's actions. Defenders of Wildlife originally filed suit challenging a rule promulgated by the Secretary of the Interior interpreting a section of the

[225] 412 U.S. 669 (1973).
[226] *Id.* at 689 n.14.
[227] 497 U.S. 871 (1990).
[228] 112 S. Ct. 2130, 34 ER Cases 1785 (1992).

Endangered Species Act so as to narrow its application when applied abroad. Defenders of Wildlife alleged that promulgation of the rule would increase the rate of extinction of endangered and threatened species, therefore injuring its members who had traveled abroad to observe and study certain species and their habitats, and intended to do so again. The Court denied standing, holding that while the desire to observe and study a specific animal species is a cognizable interest for purposes of standing, such allegations, by themselves, were insufficient because they did not demonstrate that the Defenders of Wildlife's members were themselves among the injured.

In its connected discussion of standing generally, the Court plainly stated that it views standing in environmental cases as very difficult to establish, because the plaintiff is not the object of the government action that he or she is challenging.[229] In such an instance, where the government is regulating a third party, the Court appears to demand that the environmental plaintiff produce sufficient evidence of a judicially cognizable injury that is closely tied to the government action in question.

F. International Aspects of NEPA

Since its enactment, there has been considerable debate over whether NEPA's provisions apply to agency decisions concerning federal actions abroad.[230] In an attempt to end the confusion, President Carter signed Executive Order No. 12,114 requiring federal agencies to prepare environmental analyses for "major Federal actions significantly affecting the environment of the global commons outside the jurisdiction of any nation (e.g., the oceans or Antarctica)."[231] In essence, the compromise was designed to ensure that federal decision makers were informed of the environmental consequences of their actions which would have effects outside U.S. boundaries. In 1991, the Supreme Court reaffirmed what has become a general presumption against the extraterritorial application of congressional statutes.[232] The Court held that U.S. law generally should not be applied abroad so as to "protect against the unintended clashes between our laws and those of other nations which could result in international discord."[233]

However, in January 1993, the Court of Appeals for the District of Columbia Circuit narrowed this presumption against extraterritorial application, holding in *Environmental Defense Fund v. Massey* that instances do exist where NEPA must be applied to federal actions undertaken outside the United

---

[229] *Id.* at 2137.

[230] *See, e.g.,* Sierra Club v. Coleman, 405 F. Supp. 53, 8 ER Cases 1477 (D.D.C. 1975), *rev'd and remanded on other grounds sub nom.* Sierra Club v. Adams, 578 F.2d 389 (D.C. Cir. 1978) (holding that the Federal Highway Administration must prepare an EIS before commencing preliminary construction activities in connection with a road to be built through Panama and Colombia). *Cf.* Natural Resources Defense Council v. Nuclear Regulatory Comm'n, 647 F.2d 1345, 15 ER Cases 1857 (D.C. Cir. 1981) (holding that an EIS was not required to export a nuclear reactor to the Philippines because NEPA does not apply to actions where the impact is felt solely outside the United States).

[231] 44 Fed. Reg. 1957 (1979).

[232] EEOC v. Arabian Am. Oil Co., 111 S. Ct. 1227 (1991).

[233] *Id.* at 1230.

States.[234] At issue in *Massey* was a plan by the National Science Foundation to resume burning food waste in an open landfill in Antarctica after determining that the landfill contained asbestos. The Environmental Defense Fund argued that the planned incineration would produce highly toxic pollutants and that the Foundation had violated NEPA by failing to produce an EIS in order to evaluate fully the environmental consequences of its proposed actions.

In its decision, the court held that the presumption against the extraterritorial application of statutes does not apply in instances where the conduct to be regulated occurs within U.S. borders. In this case, even though the effect of the regulation would be felt outside the United States, the conduct to be regulated was the decision making process of a federal agency which, the court found, occurs primarily within the United States.[235] Therefore, the court reasoned, the federal agency must comply with NEPA. In support of its opinion, the court also recognized that the effects would be projected only onto Antarctica—an area which the court found to be without an individual sovereign.[236] The court stated that the rationale behind the presumption evaporated when applied to global commons because places like Antarctica, the oceans, or outer space were devoid of any laws with which U.S. law might clash.[237] For these two reasons, the court held that NEPA did apply to this agency action abroad.

Since NEPA is generally considered only to require research and consultation and not other substantive action, and since the court found that such conduct occurs primarily in the United States, this decision could bring within the purview of the statute many federal actions that are carried out abroad.

G. Conclusion

Although NEPA is a mature statute, recent decisions on standing and international impacts and the Clinton Administration proposal to abolish CEQ have raised significant questions about how the Act is to be implemented. Regardless of how these aspects of the statute are ultimately interpreted, NEPA is likely to continue to exert far-reaching impact upon governmental actions.

IV. The Endangered Species Act

The Endangered Species Act (ESA),[238] originally enacted in 1973, is intended to protect species whose survival is in jeopardy. The goal of the Act is to bring endangered and threatened species populations up to a level at which they may survive without the protections afforded by the Act. Over the years since enactment, the statute has been strengthened through various amendments providing for the designation and protection of critical habitat, the clarification of the definition of "species," and monitoring of candidate and recovered species.

[234] No. 91-5278, 1993 U.S. App. LEXIS 1380 (D.C. Cir. Jan. 29, 1993).
[235] *Id.*, 1993 U.S. App. LEXIS at *12.
[236] *Id.* at *3.
[237] *Id.* at *18–*20.
[238] 16 U.S.C. §1531 *et seq.*

What follows is a discussion concerning the process for protecting species under the Act, prohibited actions and penalties, exemptions, federal and state enforcement, and a brief discussion of other conservation laws.

A. Protected Species

1. Administration of the ESA

Protection under the Act requires the designation of a species as either "endangered" or "threatened." The Act entrusts implementation of this statutory scheme to the Secretary of Commerce and the Secretary of the Interior. The Secretary of Commerce, through the National Marine Fisheries Service, applies the dictates of the Act to most marine species.[239] The Secretary of the Interior, through the U.S. Fish and Wildlife Service, applies the Act to all other species. (In this section, the National Marine Fisheries Service and the U.S. Fish and Wildlife Service are collectively referred to as the Services.)

Almost any species of wildlife, fish, or plant may be protected under the Act if the species has been designated by one of the Services as "endangered" or "threatened." The Act defines an "endangered" species as one which "is in danger of extinction throughout all or a significant portion of its range."[240] A "threatened" species is defined as one which is "likely to become endangered within the foreseeable future[.]"[241] Under the Act, "species" may mean any species or subspecies of fish, wildlife, or plant, as well as any distinct "population segment of any species of vertebrate fish or wildlife which interbreeds when mature."[242] Species found only in other parts of the world are equally eligible for listing as U.S. species. (Indeed, as of January 1992, of the 1,204 species listed, 528 were foreign.[243]) The only creatures not eligible for listing as an endangered or threatened species are insects which have been determined to be pests "whose protection . . . would present an overwhelming and overriding risk to man."[244]

2. Listing of a Species as Endangered or Threatened

To benefit from the protections afforded by the Act, the species must have been placed on the list of endangered species or the list of threatened species by one of the Services.[245] The importance of listing cannot be overstated; the Act's prohibitions and penalties are applicable only to listed species (and in limited instances to species that have been proposed for listing).[246] Attempts to use the

---

[239] ESA §3(15), 16 U.S.C. §1532(15) (1988), indicates that the Secretary of Commerce shall have "program responsibilities" according to "Reorganization Plan No. 4 of 1970." Among other things, that Reorganization Plan vests in the Secretary of Commerce the authority and functions of the Secretary of the Interior as they relate to marine species. *See* Appendix to 5 U.S.C.A. Title 5 (1967 and Supp. 1992).

[240] ESA §3(6), 16 U.S.C. §1532(6) (1988). *See also* 50 C.F.R. §424.10(e).

[241] ESA §3(20), 16 U.S.C. §1532(20) (1988). *See also* 50 C.F.R. §424.10(m).

[242] ESA §3(16), 16 U.S.C. §1532(16) (1988).

[243] U.S. Fish and Wildlife Serv. Memorandum, Endangered Species: A Summary of the Act and Service Activities 6 (January 1992) [hereinafter U.S. Fish and Wildlife Serv. Memorandum].

[244] ESA §3(6), 16 U.S.C. §1532(6) (1988).

[245] Technically, the Act instructs the Secretary of Commerce to submit Commerce listings to the Secretary of the Interior, and directs the Secretary of the Interior to include the Secretary of Commerce's listings with those published by the Secretary of the Interior. ESA §4(a), 16 U.S.C. §1533(a) (1988).

[246] There are two provisions in the Act (both in §7, 16 U.S.C. §1536) which provide a small measure of protection for species that have been proposed for listing. (*See* Section C.2., below, for a further discussion).

Act to protect unlisted species have failed. For example, in *Wilson v. Block,*[247] plaintiffs sued under section 7 of the Act to enjoin development of a ski resort, arguing that the resort would threaten a particular plant known to grow only in that area. A federal appeals court rejected plaintiffs' claim because the plant had not been placed on either the endangered or threatened lists.[248]

When evaluating whether a species should be classified as endangered or threatened, the Act requires a consideration of whether the species suffers from

> (A) The present or threatened destruction, modification, or curtailment of [the species'] habitat or range;
> (B) The overutilization [of the species] for commercial, recreational, scientific, or educational purposes;
> (C) Disease or predation [affecting the overall survival of the species];
> (D) The inadequacy of existing regulatory mechanisms [to protect the species]; [and]
> (E) Other natural or manmade factors affecting [the species'] continued existence.[249]

The existence of any one of these factors may justify placing the affected species on either the endangered or threatened lists. The Act requires that the Services evaluate these factors "*solely* on the basis of the best scientific and commercial data available" (emphasis added).[250] The Act does *not* allow the Services to factor economic impact into their decisions on whether to list a species as endangered or threatened.[251] Indeed, Congress' clear intent that economic considerations not be a factor in the decision whether to list a species is evidenced by the legislative history:

> The Committee strongly believes that economic considerations have no relevance to determinations regarding the status of species and intends that the economic analysis requirements of Executive Order 12291, and such statutes as the Regulatory Flexibility Act and the Paperwork Reduction Act not apply.[252]

However, economic factors may be considered in other decisions affecting listed species, including the designation of critical habitat.[253]

The Act further dictates that the Services consider listing species that have been (1) "designated as requiring protection from unrestricted commerce by any foreign nation, or pursuant to any international agreement"; or (2) "identified as in danger of extinction, or likely to become so within the foreseeable future, by any State agency or by any agency of a foreign nation that is responsible for the conservation of fish or wildlife or plants."[254]

---

[247] 708 F.2d 735, 748–51, 19 ER Cases 1201 (D.C. Cir. 1983), *cert. denied,* 464 U.S. 956 (1983).

[248] *See also* Enos v. Marsh, 769 F.2d 1363, 1368, 23 ER Cases 1124 (9th Cir. 1985); Friends of Endangered Species, Inc. v. Jantzen II, 596 F. Supp. 518, 524, 20 ER Cases 1645 (N.D. Cal. 1984); Friends of Endangered Species, Inc. v. Jantzen I, 589 F. Supp. 113, 120 n.2, 20 ER Cases 1811 (N.D. Cal. 1984).

[249] ESA §4(a)(1), 16 U.S.C. §1533(a)(1) (1988). *See also* 50 C.F.R. §424.11(c)(1)-(5).

[250] ESA §4(b)(1)(A), 16 U.S.C. §1533(b)(1)(A) (1988). The legislative history of the Act makes clear that Congress used the term "commercial data" to "allow the use of trade data." It also makes clear that that term "is not intended, in any way, to authorize the use of economic considerations in [listing] the species." H.R. Rep. No. 5467, 97th Cong., 2d Sess. 19–20, *reprinted in* 1982 U.S.C.C.A.N. 2807, 2863.

[251] *See* H.R. Conf. Rep. No. 835, 97th Cong., 2d Sess. 19–21, *reprinted in* 1982 U.S.C.C.A.N. 2807, 2862–63.

[252] *Id.*

[253] *See* discussion in Section IV.A.3., below.

[254] ESA §4(b)(1)(B)(i) and (ii), 16 U.S.C. §§1533(b)(1)(B)(i) and (ii) (1988).

Finally, the Services may prescribe by regulation that a species be treated as endangered or threatened even though it is not listed as such, provided that (1) the species looks so much like a listed species that enforcement personnel have "substantial difficulty" distinguishing between the two species; (2) the "substantial difficulty" poses an additional threat to the listed species; and (3) such treatment of the nonlisted species will "substantially facilitate the enforcement and further the policy" of the Act.[255]

In practice, the listing process starts with a list of "candidate" species generated from formal petitions, informal letters from individuals and private groups, federal agency surveys, "and other substantiated reports on field studies."[256] From this list of candidate species (which in January 1992 numbered about 3,600 U.S. species),[257] the Services choose those for which they believe a listing is warranted, according to an established priority system.

The Fish and Wildlife Service's candidate species are categorized according to three classifications: "Category 1," which is the highest priority category, encompasses species for which there is sufficient scientific data to warrant designation as endangered or threatened; "Category 2," which encompasses species that appear to warrant listing but for which more supporting data are needed; and "Category 3" (or "inactive candidates"), which encompasses species that have recovered, are extinct, or have been found not to fit the Act's definition of "species."[258]

3. *Designation of Critical Habitat*

Congress has recognized that the greatest threat to the survival of endangered and threatened species comes from the diminution of the species' habitat. Accordingly, the Act requires the designation of a species' "critical habitat" concurrently with the listing of the species as endangered or threatened.[259] Once designated, a species' critical habitat may itself require special management considerations or protection in order to effect congressional intent that the Act "provide a means whereby the ecosystems upon which endangered species and threatened species depend may be conserved. . . ."[260]

"Critical habitat" is defined by the Act as meaning

> [T]he specific areas within the geographical area occupied by the species, at the time it is listed . . . on which are found those physical or biological features

---

[255] ESA §4(e), 16 U.S.C. §1533(e) (1988). *See also* 50 C.F.R. §17.50. Similarity of Appearance species are so noted in the endangered and threatened species list by an "(S/A)" following the name of the species on the list. 50 C.F.R. §17.11(b), .50(a).

[256] CONGRESSIONAL RESEARCH SERV., REPORT TO CONGRESS, ENDANGERED SPECIES ACT: THE LISTING AND EXEMPTION PROCESSES 4 (May 8, 1990). *See also* 50 C.F.R. §424.13.

[257] CONGRESSIONAL RESEARCH SERV., REPORT TO CONGRESS, *supra* note 256, at 4.

[258] U.S. FISH AND WILDLIFE SERV. MEMORANDUM, *supra* note 243, at 5.

> Species on these lists can move from one to another as more information becomes available. For example, species thought to be extinct . . . can, on occasion, be rediscovered after many decades and immediately move to the top . . . and *vice versa.* Typically, most species enter the list as [Category 2] and move either up or down as more information becomes available.

Id.

[259] ESA §4(a)(3), 16 U.S.C. §1533(a)(3) (1988); ESA §4(b)(6)(C), 16 U.S.C. §1533(b)(6)(C) (1988).

[260] ESA §2(b), 16 U.S.C. §1531(b) (1988).

> essential to the conservation of the species and . . . which may require special management considerations or protection.[261]

"Critical habitat" can also encompass "specific areas outside the geographical area occupied by the species at the time it is listed" if the Secretary determines that "such areas are essential for the conservation of the species."[262] Additionally, if the listed species is a *vertebrate* fish or wildlife, it may be designated as endangered or threatened only in certain geographical areas. Thus, it is possible for a species to be designated "endangered" in one area but only "threatened" in another. Critical habitat listings, and reference maps for fish and wildlife listed by the U.S. Fish and Wildlife Service, are published at 50 C.F.R. §17.95, and for plants at 50 C.F.R. §17.96. Critical habitat for species listed by the National Marine Fisheries Service are listed at 50 C.F.R. §226.

There are two situations in which the Act allows the Secretary to postpone designation of critical habitat until after a species has been listed. First, if the immediate listing of a species is deemed "essential to the conservation" of the listed species, then the Secretary may publish the decision to list a species immediately without the delay inherent in conducting the research necessary to designate the species' critical habitat.[263] In *City of Las Vegas v. Lujan,*[264] the reviewing court upheld the Secretary of the Interior's emergency listing of the Mohave Desert population of the desert tortoise as an endangered species, finding that such emergency regulations were subject to a less exacting scrutiny than if the Secretary had enacted the same regulation under nonemergency rulemaking procedures.

Second, the Secretary may postpone designation of a listed species' habitat if the critical habitat of the species is not "determinable" at the time of listing.[265] However, Congress intended this as a very narrow exception,[266] and the courts accordingly have frowned on the Services' attempts to use the "not determinable" provision of the Act as an excuse for failing to designate habitat. In *Northern Spotted Owl v. Lujan,*[267] a federal district court found that the Secretary of the Interior had an affirmative duty under the Act to seek out and identify the necessary biological and economic data for a critical habitat designation prior to publishing a final species listing decision. The court further found that the Secretary could not continue to avail himself of automatic extensions of time when he had made no effort to obtain the information necessary to designate the owl's critical habitat.[268]

However, the Services may decline to publish the actual location of a critical habitat if it is determined that disclosure of a species' critical habitat will

---

[261] ESA §3(5)(A)(i), 16 U.S.C. §1532(5)(A)(i) (1988).

[262] ESA §3(5)(A)(ii), 16 U.S.C. §1532(5)(A)(ii) (1988).

[263] ESA §4(b)(6)(C)(i), 16 U.S.C. §1533(b)(6)(C)(i) (1988). The emergency regulations expire, unless repromulgated, 240 days after publication. ESA §4(b)(7), 16 U.S.C. §1553(b)(7) (1988).

[264] 891 F.2d 927 (D.C. Cir. 1989).

[265] ESA §4(b)(6)(C)(ii), 16 U.S.C. §1533(b)(6)(C)(ii) (1988).

[266] H.R. Rep. No. 567, 97th Cong., 2d Sess. 19–20, *reprinted in* 1982 U.S.C.C.A.N. 2807, 2819–20.

[267] 758 F. Supp. 621, 33 ER Cases 1113 (W.D. Wash. 1991).

[268] *Cf.* Enos v. Marsh, 769 F.2d 1363, 23 ER Cases 1124 (9th Cir. 1985), in which the Ninth Circuit held that the Secretary of the Interior did not abuse his discretion for failure to designate the critical habitat of a plant species thought to be extinct where the species was discovered in a nonnative habitat. Therefore, the biological and physical features essential to its existence, which are required for a critical habitat designation, could not be determined at the time.

actually cause harm to the species (e.g., because it will disclose the location to poachers).[269]

Unlike the listing decision, the Services are allowed to consider economic factors when designating critical habitat. Indeed, the Services

> may exclude any area from critical habitat if he determines that the benefits of such exclusion outweigh the benefits of specifying such area as part of the critical habitat, *unless he determines,* based on the best scientific and commercial data available, *that the failure to designate such area as critical habitat will result in the extinction of the species concerned.*[270]

4. *Challenges to the Services' Listing and Critical Habitat Decisions*

Any person or organization may petition the relevant Service to add or remove a species from the endangered or threatened species lists, or to reclassify it from one list to the other.[271] Within 90 days of receiving such a petition, the involved Service must "make a finding as to whether the petition presents substantial scientific or commercial information indicating that the petitioned action may be warranted."[272]

The Service may then find that the petitioned action is unwarranted, in which case the petitioner may seek judicial review of the decision.[273] Alternatively, the Service may find that the petitioned action does appear to be warranted, in which case the Service "shall promptly commence a review of the status of the species concerned."[274]

This review must be completed and acted on within 12 months of the date on which the petition was filed.[275] Upon completion of this review, the affected Service has three options. First, it may find that the petitioned-for action is unwarranted. Second, it may find that the petitioned-for action is warranted and immediately (within 30 days) propose listing the species in the *Federal Register.* Finally, the Service may find that the petitioned-for action is "warranted but precluded," meaning that action on the petition must be delayed due to the processing of other, more pressing proposals to list. The Act requires that to reach a "warranted but precluded" finding, the Service must be making timely progress with the listing program in general. Further, the Service must reexamine the status of species designated as warranted but precluded each year on the anniversary of the initial finding until the species is either listed or rejected as unwarranted.[276]

Whichever of these three conclusions the Service reaches, it must give the public notice of its decision by publishing its determination in the *Federal Register.*[277] Furthermore, if it decides not to take the action requested, or if it decides that action is warranted but precluded, the petitioner may seek judicial

[269] 50 C.F.R. §424.12(a)(1) (1992).
[270] ESA §4(b)(2), 16 U.S.C. §1533(b)(2) (1988) (emphasis added).
[271] ESA §4(b)(3)(A), 16 U.S.C. §1533(b)(3)(A) (1988).
[272] *Id.*
[273] ESA §4(b)(3)(C)(ii), 16 U.S.C. §1533(b)(3)(C)(ii) (1988).
[274] ESA §4(b)(3)(A), 16 U.S.C. §1533(b)(3)(A) (1988).
[275] ESA §4(b)(3)(B), 16 U.S.C. §1533(b)(3)(B) (1988).
[276] *Id.*
[277] *Id.*

review.[278] For example, in *Northern Spotted Owl v. Hodel,*[279] plaintiffs sued on behalf of the northern spotted owl to force the Fish and Wildlife Service to list the owl as an endangered species. The federal district court found that the Service's decision not to list the northern spotted owl was arbitrary and capricious, as its conclusion that the owl had a viable population was contradicted by the agency's own scientific experts. On remand from the court, the Fish and Wildlife Service designated the owl as a threatened species.

An interested person may also petition the relevant Service to revise a critical habitat designation. Again, within 90 days the Service must determine "whether the petition presents substantial scientific information indicating that a revision may be warranted,"[280] and must publish that determination in the *Federal Register.*[281] Then, within 12 months of the date of the petition, it must determine "how [it] intends to proceed with the requested revision,"[282] and again, must publish that determination in the *Federal Register.*[283] Unlike petitions concerning the listing or delisting of species, the Act makes no provision for judicial review of decisions on petitions concerning critical habitat.

B. Protections Afforded by Section 9

1. Acts Prohibited in the United States

Section 9[284] of the Act sets forth in detail the protections afforded to endangered species. Almost all of these protections have also been extended by regulation to threatened species.[285]

Section 9 protects listed species of fish or wildlife by prohibiting any act which would further jeopardize the existence of the species. In particular, section 9 forbids the "taking" of any listed species in the United States, its territorial waters, or on the high seas.[286] To "take" a species is defined by the Act as "to harass, harm, pursue, hunt, shoot, wound, kill, trap, capture, or collect, or to attempt to engage in any such conduct."[287] The implementing regulations further define "harrass" and "harm" to encompass any activity that annoys the species or degrades its habitat to the extent that it disrupts behavioral patterns, including breeding, feeding, and sheltering.[288] Section 9

---

[278] ESA §4(b)(3)(C)(ii), 16 U.S.C. §1533(b)(3)(C)(ii) (1988).

[279] 716 F. Supp. 479 (W.D. Wash. 1988).

[280] ESA §4(b)(3)(D)(i), 16 U.S.C. §1533(b)(3)(D)(i) (1988).

[281] ESA §4(b)(3)(D)(ii), 16 U.S.C. §1533(b)(3)(D)(ii) (1988).

[282] *Id.*

[283] *Id.*

[284] 16 U.S.C. §1538 (1988).

[285] *See* ESA §4(d), 16 U.S.C. §1533(d) (1988):

> [W]henever any species is listed as a threatened species pursuant to subsection (c) of this section, the Secretary shall issue such regulations as he deems necessary and advisable to provide for the conservation of such species. The Secretary may by regulation prohibit with respect to any threatened species any act prohibited under section 1538(a)(1) of this title, in the case of fish or wildlife, or section 1538(a)(2) of this title, in the case of plants.

See also 50 C.F.R. §17.31(a) (fish and wildlife) and §17.71(a) (plants) (1992). Note, however, that regulations extending protections to threatened species may vary in states that have entered into cooperative agreements with the federal government. See Section IV.E., below.

[286] 16 U.S.C. §1538(a) (1988).

[287] ESA §3(19), 16 U.S.C. §1532(19) (1988).

[288] 50 C.F.R. §17.3 (1992).

also prohibits the possession, sale, transportation, importation, or exportation of members of an endangered species.[289] These prohibitions include "any part, product, egg or offspring" of endangered fish and wildlife, as well as "the dead body or plants thereof."[290] Plants listed as endangered are also protected under section 9 with prohibitions similar to those set forth for fish and wildlife.[291]

Violation of the taking provision is a general intent crime, meaning that it is not a prerequisite to liability that a violator know that the species taken by him or her was endangered or threatened. Hence in *United States v. Billie,*[292] a hunter was held liable under the Act for killing a panther even though he did not know the panther was endangered, because he had the requisite intent to kill the panther.

2. *Protection Abroad*

The Act does not prohibit the killing of endangered species outside of the United States. However, section 9 strictly prohibits the importation or exportation of fish and wildlife designated as endangered, or even a "part or product" of such animals.[293] The Services and the courts have adopted a very broad interpretation of the terms "import" and "export." In its regulations, the Fish and Wildlife Service directs that "*[a]ny* shipment in transit through the United States is an importation and an exportation, whether or not it has entered the country for customs purposes."[294] The courts have followed the Services' lead, finding in one case, for example, that crocodile hides aboard an airplane which was forced to make an unscheduled stop in the United States were properly seized by the government.[295]

As with the taking prohibitions, specific intent to violate the Act is not an element in the determination of whether the section 9 import/export ban has been violated. Tourists and hunters who unintentionally violate the ban because they were unaware that the species or species product they imported/exported was listed as endangered, nevertheless have been held liable under the Act.[296]

3. *Persons and Entities Subject to Section 9's Prohibition*

Section 9's prohibitions are applicable to "any person."[297] "Person" is defined by the statute as including

> an individual, corporation, partnership, trust, association, or any other private entity, or any officer, employee, agent, department, or instrumentality of the

---

[289] *See generally* 16 U.S.C. §1538(a) (1988).

[290] ESA §3(8), 16 U.S.C. §1532(8) (1988).

[291] *See generally* 16 U.S.C. §1538(a)(2) (1988).

[292] 667 F. Supp. 1485 (S.D. Fla. 1987).

[293] *See* the definition of "fish and wildlife" at ESA §3(8), 16 U.S.C. §1532(8) (1988), and the definition of "animal" at 50 C.F.R. §10.12 (1992).

[294] 50 C.F.R. §17.21(b) (emphasis added).

[295] United States v. 3,210 Crusted Sides of Caiman Crododilus Yacare, 636 F. Supp. 1281 (S.D. Fla. 1986).

[296] *See, e.g.,* United States v. Nguyen, 916 F.2d 1016 (5th Cir. 1990) (the defendant need not know that the sea turtle taken by him was a threatened species; he only had to know that he had possession of the turtle).

[297] 16 U.S.C. §1538 (1988).

> Federal Government, or any State or political subdivision thereof, or of any foreign government.[298]

Accordingly, federal agencies have often been the subject of a lawsuit under the Act.

For example, clear-cutting timber authorized by the Forest Service was halted by a federal court in *Sierra Club v. Lyng,*[299] because the court found that the clear-cutting was exacerbating the decline of an endangered woodpecker. The court deemed the Forest Service's actions to be a taking under the Act, and, accordingly, ordered the Forest Service to discontinue the clear-cutting.[300] In general, a factor in determining whether a governmental action will be deemed an unlawful taking under the Act appears to be whether the agency consulted with the Fish and Wildlife Service prior to commencing the action in question.[301]

Courts have also held the federal government accountable under section 9 of the Act for failure to take action that would prevent harm to a listed species. For example, in *Defenders of Wildlife v. Administrator, Environmental Protection Agency,*[302] plaintiffs used the Act to challenge EPA's continued registration of strychnine as an acceptable pesticide. Strychnine, which was used to control prairie dogs, was also killing black-footed ferrets and other endangered species. The court found that EPA's continued registration of strychnine constituted a taking under the Act.[303]

However, one federal appeals court has found that a municipality is not a "person" within the meaning given that term by the statute. In *United States v. City of Rancho Palos Verdes,*[304] the court interpreted the plain meaning of the language in the definition of "person" as reaching only to the officers, employees, agents, departments, and instrumentalities of political subdivisions of states—but not to the political subdivisions themselves. However, the court concluded that enforcement of the Act would not be jeopardized as applied to municipalities, "since any municipal corporation can only act through its officers, employees, agents, departments or instrumentalities, all of whom are clearly subject to prosecution under the [Act]."[305]

---

[298] ESA §3(13), 16 U.S.C. §1532(13) (1988).

[299] 694 F. Supp. 1260 (E.D. Tex. 1988), *aff'd in relevant part sub nom.* Sierra Club v. Yeutter, 926 F.2d 429 (5th Cir. 1991).

[300] For an example of a state being held liable for a taking under the Act, *see* Palila v. Hawaii Dep't of Land & Natural Resources, 852 F.2d 1106 (9th Cir. 1988) (state's program of maintaining sheep and goats in endangered species' habitat was destroying that habitat and constituted a taking under the Act).

[301] *See, e.g.,* Sierra Club v. Block, 614 F. Supp. 488 (D.D.C. 1985); Romero-Barcelo v. Brown, 643 F.2d 830, 835, 16 ER Cases 1593 (1st Cir. 1981), *rev'd on other grounds sub nom.* Weinburger v. Romero-Barcelo, 456 U.S. 305, 17 ER Cases 1217 (1982).

[302] 882 F.2d 1294, 30 ER Cases 1460 (8th Cir. 1989).

[303] *See also* National Wildlife Fed'n v. Hodel, 23 ER Cases 1089 (E.D. Cal. 1985) (the court found that the Fish and Wildlife Service's authorization of the use of lead shot ammunition resulted in the secondary poisoning of bald eagles; and that, accordingly, the Fish and Wildlife Service was guilty of a taking under the Act).

[304] 841 F.2d 329 (9th Cir. 1988).

[305] *Id.* at 331.

C. Responsibilities Imposed on Federal Agencies by Section 7

Section 7 of the Act dictates that federal agencies shall "utilize their authorities in furtherance of the purposes of [the Act] ... by carrying out programs for the conservation of endangered species and threatened species listed."[306]

1. Consultation on Listed Species

In particular, all federal agencies that plan actions that "may affect" listed species or critical habitat[307] must "consult" with the relevant Service to "insure that any action authorized, funded, or carried out by such agency . . . is not likely to jeopardize the continued existence of any endangered species or threatened species or result in the destruction [of designated critical habitat]."[308]

The consultation process starts with an inquiry from the agency to the Service regarding whether a listed species, proposed listed species, or candidate species may be present at the location of the agency's proposed action; if the Service indicates that no such species or critical habitat is present, the agency may move forward without completing a formal biological evaluation (see below).[309] However, if the Service indicates that such species or critical habitat is present at the site, then the agency must engage in consultation with the Service to ensure that the agency's action will not adversely affect the species' survival.

This process usually begins in a relatively informal manner with "early consultation." Early consultation generally involves meetings between the Service's representative and affected individuals and agencies regarding "whether any species which is listed or proposed to be listed may be present in the area of [the] proposed action."[310] Early consultation is "designed to reduce the likelihood of conflicts between listed species or critical habitat and proposed actions."[311] A preliminary biological opinion must be completed by the appropriate Service at this stage. As the result of this preliminary biological evaluation, the Service may determine that the federal agency's action "is not likely to adversely affect listed species or their critical habitat."[312]

2. Biological Assessment

If the Service determines that the agency's action may affect a listed species or a critical habitat, it triggers the second step in the process, and the agency will be required to conduct a formal "biological assessment"[313] to identify the impact the proposed agency action would have on any endangered

---

[306] 16 U.S.C. §1536(a) (1988).

[307] 50 C.F.R. §402.11(b).

[308] ESA §7(a)(2), 16 U.S.C. §1536(a)(2) (1988). *See also* U.S. FISH AND WILDLIFE SERV. MEMORANDUM, *supra* note 243, at 7.

[309] 50 C.F.R. §482(d).

[310] ESA §7(c)(1), 16 U.S.C. §1536(c)(1) (1988).

[311] 50 C.F.R. §402.11(a).

[312] U.S. FISH AND WILDLIFE SERV. MEMORANDUM, *supra* note 243, at 7.

[313] *See* ESA §7(c), 16 U.S.C. §1536(c) (1988), and 50 C.F.R. §402.12.

or threatened species, or species proposed for listing, likely to be affected by the agency's proposed action.

If from the biological assessment the Service determines that the proposed agency action is likely to adversely affect a listed endangered or threatened species, then a formal consultation process begins. The agency is forbidden from making any "irreversible or irretrievable commitment of resources" until the formal consultation has been completed. The formal consultation results in the Secretary's issuance of a formal "biological opinion." If in that opinion the Service concludes that the proposed agency action would jeopardize the survival of the listed species, then the agency may not take the proposed action unless the Service has been able to provide an acceptable alternative.

If from the biological assessment the Service determines that the proposed agency action is likely to adversely affect only species *proposed* for listing (or its critical habitat), section 7 requires the agency only to "confer" with the relevant Service before commencing with the proposed agency action.[314] The required "conference" is to identify problems early in an agency's decision-making process,[315] and may also encompass the biological assessment required under section 7(c).[316] Furthermore, the conference requirement is generally less formal than the "consultation" required after a species has been listed. Additionally, the regulations setting forth the "conference" requirement do not impose the same limitation on the "irreversible or irretrievable commitment of resources" as does the consultation requirement.

D. Recovery of Listed Species

All species that have been listed as endangered or threatened found in the United States are to benefit from a "recovery plan" to restore the species to the point where it is self-sustaining and can be removed from the protected lists. Such recovery plans are to incorporate research and management actions designed to reverse the species' decline and to ensure the species' long-term survival.[317] In descending order, the Services are to prioritize efforts in the plan as follows: (1) prevention of extinction, (2) avoidance of further decline, and (3) implementation of other activities necessary to effect recovery.[318] Hence, among other things, a recovery plan must identify the species population levels and/or habitat goals to be used to determine whether the species has recovered. If the recovery plan is successful, the Services may decide to remove the species from the endangered and/or threatened lists.

---

[314] 16 U.S.C. §1536(a)(4) (1988). *See also* Enos v. Marsh, 769 F.2d 1363, 23 ER Cases 1124 (9th Cir. 1985) for a detailed discussion of why proposed species are included in the biological assessment requirement.

[315] *See* implementing regulations published at 50 C.F.R. §402.10.

[316] 16 U.S.C. §1536(c) (1988).

[317] ESA §4(f), 16 U.S.C. §1533(f) (1988).

[318] U.S. FISH AND WILDLIFE SERV. MEMORANDUM *supra* note 243, at 9–10. *See also* Connor v. Andrus, 453 F. Supp. 1037 (W.D. Tex. 1978) (the Secretary of the Interior has an affirmative duty to bring endangered species to recovered status; he must promulgate regulations attacking the causes of the species decline); Defenders of Wildlife v. Andrus, 428 F. Supp. 167 (D.D.C. 1977); Carson-Truckee Water Conservancy Dist. v. Watt, 549 F. Supp. 704 (D. Nev. 1982), *aff'd,* 741 F.2d 257 (9th Cir. 1984); Sierra Club v. Clark, 577 F. Supp. 783 (D. Minn. 1983).

Generally the plan is drafted by "recognized experts under the direction of a Service employee" or is contracted out to an appropriate consultant on the species.[319] The draft plan must be approved by the relevant Service's Regional Office.[320] The Service will then publish a proposed recovery plan in the *Federal Register* for comment by the public, by experts, and by other interested federal and state agencies. Although the Act does not specify any particular time frame for developing a recovery plan, the Fish and Wildlife Service has indicated that it tries to publish draft plans within one year, and final plans within two-and-a-half years, of the date on which a species was listed.[321] In general, species recovery takes "several generations of successful reproduction" before a determination can be made that the species has become self-perpetuating.[322]

Periodically, the Services will review existing recovery plans and will revise the plans as needed. The status of any species delisted after implementation of a recovery plan must be monitored for at least five years.

Examples of successful recovery programs include those for the bald eagle, American and Arctic peregrine falcons, and eastern brown pelican. The decline of each of these species was reversed through aggressive habitat protection during mating season and through the banning of the pesticide DDT, which caused eggshell thinning and nest failures. The peregrine falcons also benefited from raising baby falcons in captivity and reintroducing them into the wild.[323] Other success stories include the American alligator and the red wolf.[324]

Conversely, the FWS has identified the northern spotted owl, among others, as a species whose recovery program development has been problematic. In particular, the FWS notes that "this species poses a large array of problems, many of which relate to the economic and social factors of the residents of the region."[325] Other problematic species include desert tortoise (Mojave Desert population), grizzly bear, gray wolf, California condor, black-footed ferret, and Florida panther.[326]

E. State Participation

In framing the Act, Congress recognized that it would be most effective if the states were included in the implementation of the Act. Indeed, before the Act's passage, most states were already regulating the taking of animals.[327]

The provision that primarily regulates cooperation between state and federal conservation personnel is section 6,[328] which dictates that the federal government "shall cooperate to the maximum extent practicable with the States

[319] U.S. FISH AND WILDLIFE SERV. MEMORANDUM, *supra* note 243, at 11.

[320] *Id.*

[321] GENERAL ACCOUNTING OFFICE REPORT TO CONGRESS, ENDANGERED SPECIES ACT: TYPES AND NUMBER OF IMPLEMENTING ACTIONS 17 (May 1992).

[322] U.S. FISH AND WILDLIFE SERV. MEMORANDUM, *supra* note 243, at 10.

[323] *Id.* at 12.

[324] *Id.*

[325] *Id.* at 13.

[326] *Id.* at 13–14.

[327] GENERAL ACCOUNTING OFFICE REPORT TO CONGRESS, WILDLIFE PROTECTION: ENFORCEMENT OF FEDERAL LAWS COULD BE STRENGTHENED 4 (GAO/RCED-9-44, 1991). Indeed, as of the date of the GAO report, state wildlife agents outnumbered federal agents 37 to 1.

[328] 16 U.S.C. §1535 (1988).

. . . for the purpose of conserving any endangered or threatened species.''[329] In order to effect that goal, the Act allows the federal government to enter into ''management agreements'' with the states governing ''the administration and management of any area established for the conservation of endangered species or threatened species.''[330]

Additionally, the federal government and states can enter into ''cooperative agreements'' under which states are authorized to administer the Act if the particular state ''establishes and maintains an adequate and active program for the conservation of endangered species and threatened species.''[331] States that have approved plans benefit from a significant amount of federal funding. Federal money is provided to cover up to 75 percent of a state's costs associated with implementing the Act, and up to 90 percent of the costs for conservation programs encompassing a joint effort among two or more states.[332]

States may continue to enforce their own wildlife conservation laws so long as those laws do not diminish the protections afforded by the Act.[333] In other words, the Act preempts state law only to the extent that the state law is less restrictive.[334] However, no state law may interfere with federal exceptions or permits specifically allowed under the Act.[335]

F. Exemptions

The Act does make provision for obtaining exemptions from its prohibitions and requirements.[336] The exemption provisions provide the principal opportunity for economic considerations to be involved in decision making under the Act.

1. The Endangered Species Committee

The primary exemption provision, section 7(g),[337] was added to the Act in response to the Supreme Court's decision in *Tennessee Valley Authority v. Hill.*[338] In that case, the Supreme Court affirmed a lower court's enjoining completion of the nearly finished Tellico Dam, where operation of the dam would have destroyed the critical habitat of an endangered species known as the snail darter. The Supreme Court read the plain language of the Act to preclude *any* economic considerations in the endangered species determination, even though the dam project was almost finished and there would be a ''sacrifice of the anticipated benefits of the project and of many millions of dollars in public

[329] ESA §6(a), 16 U.S.C. §1535(a) (1988).

[330] ESA §6(b), 16 U.S.C. §1535(b) (1988).

[331] ESA §6(c), 16 U.S.C. §1535(c) (1988).

[332] ESA §6(d), 16 U.S.C. §1535(d) (1988).

[333] ESA §6(f), 16 U.S.C. §1535(f) (1988).

[334] *See, e.g.,* State v. Billie, 497 So. 2d 889, 893–94 (Fla. App. 2 Dist. 1986), *review denied,* 506 So. 2d 1040 (1987); Cresenzi Bird Importers, Inc. v. New York, 658 F. Supp. 1441 (S.D.N.Y. 1987), *aff'd,* 831 F.2d 410 (1987).

[335] *See, e.g.,* Man Hing Ivory & Imports, Inc. v. Deukmejian, 702 F.2d 760, 20 ER Cases 1988 (9th Cir. 1983); H.J. Justin & Sons v. Deukmejian, 702 F.2d 758, 20 ER Cases 1993 (9th Cir. 1983); Fouke Co. v. Brown, 463 F. Supp. 1142 (E.D. Cal. 1979).

[336] ESA §7(i)-(p), 16 U.S.C. §1536(i)-(p) (1988).

[337] 16 U.S.C. §1536(g) (1982).

[338] 437 U.S. 153, 11 ER Cases 1705 (1978).

funds."[339] Congress responded to the *Tennessee Valley Authority* decision by amending the Act to include an exemption process which culminates in the review of exemption applications by the Endangered Species Committee (ESC)—commonly known as "the God Squad."[340]

Under this exemption, proponents of a project that is likely to jeopardize the continued existence of an endangered species or a threatened species, or destruction of a critical habitat, may apply to the Services for an exemption to the Act enabling the project to go forward. Parties that may apply for an exemption include any federal agency, the Governor of an affected state, or a "permit or license"[341] applicant. To be eligible to obtain an exemption, the applicant must be able to demonstrate that the consultations required under section 7 were made in good faith, that the applicant has made a reasonable effort to explore alternatives, that it has conducted any required biological assessments, and that it has refrained from making any irreversible or irretrievable commitment of resources.[342]

Within 20 days, the Service is to determine whether the applicant has met all of these criteria. If so, the Service must prepare a report and convene a formal hearing. Within 30 days of receiving the Report, the ESC is to grant or deny the exemption. That determination is to be based on whether "(i) there are no reasonable and prudent alternatives; (ii) the benefits . . . clearly outweigh the . . . alternatives; (iii) the action is of regional or national significance; and (iv) neither the agency nor the applicant [has] made any irreversible or irretrievable commitment of resources."[343]

2. *Incidental Take and Scientific Purposes Permits*

The Act allows for "Incidental Take Permits" which allow an individual, or an agency, to incidentally take listed species. The taking must be incidental to an otherwise lawful activity.[344] Applicants for this type of exemption must demonstrate that they have instituted adequate provisions in a "conservation plan" for maintaining, enhancing, and protecting the habitat affected by their actions. A draft conservation plan must be published in the *Federal Register* for public comment. The incidental take permit may be issued so long as doing so would not cause any appreciable reduction in the likelihood that the species will survive and recover.[345]

---

[339] *Id.* at 174.

[340] The ESC is composed of the Secretary of Agriculture, the Secretary of the Army, the Chairman of the Council of Economic Advisors, the Administrator of the Environmental Protection Agency, the Secretary of the Interior (who serves as chair of the ESC), the Administrator of the National Oceanic and Atmospheric Administration, and one person from each state affected by the proposed action. *See* ESA §7(e), 16 U.S.C. §1536(e) (1988), and 50 C.F.R. §453.05(d).

[341] The term "permit or license applicant" is defined in the Act as a person "whose application to such agency for a permit or license has been denied primarily because of the application of" the Act's taking prohibitions. ESA §3(12), 16 U.S.C. §1532(12) (1988); *see also* 50 C.F.R. §450.07.

[342] ESA §7(g), 16 U.S.C. §1536(g) (1988); 50 C.F.R. 450 *et seq.*

[343] ESA §7(h)(1)(A), 16 U.S.C. §1536(h)(1)(A) (1988).

[344] ESA §10(a)(1)(B), 16 U.S.C. §1539(a)(1)(B) (1988).

[345] GAO Report, Endangered Species Act, *supra* note 321, at 18.

Similarly, the Act authorizes special permits for otherwise prohibited actions taken for scientific purposes or to enhance a species' survival by, for example, the establishment or maintenance of experimental populations.[346]

3. Alaskan Natives

The Act allows Alaskan natives (and in some cases others) living in native villages to take endangered or threatened species for "subsistence" purposes so long as the taking is not done in a "wasteful manner."[347] Such Alaskan natives may also use the byproducts of such species to make "native articles of handicrafts and clothing."[348] However, the Act also allows the Services to promulgate regulations restraining natives from acts affecting a certain species if the Services believe such regulations are necessary to the survival of the species.[349] Finally, there is an "undue economic hardship" provision, which grants the Services discretion to allow the continued performance of a contract which would adversely affect an endangered species, where the contract was affective prior to publication in the *Federal Register* of the notice of consideration of an endangered species. To be eligible for this exemption, the proponent must be able to demonstrate that cancellation of the contract would cause it undue economic hardship.[350]

G. Enforcement Proceedings

1. Government Enforcement Proceedings

The Act is well armed with strong enforcement and penalty provisions. It may be enforced by the Secretary of the Interior, the Secretary of the Treasury, the Secretary of Transportation, or any federal or state agency or official to which authority is delegated for an enforcement function.[351]

The Act specifically provides that federal district courts shall have jurisdiction over "any actions arising under [the Act]."[352] The Act also includes a venue provision specifying that an enforcement action may be brought in any "district in which such person is found, resides, or transacts business."[353]

More typically, an enforcement proceeding will be in the form of an administrative action seeking civil penalties. The Act notes that "[n]o penalty may be assessed . . . unless such person [has been] given notice and opportunity for a hearing with respect to such violation."[354] These evidentiary hearings are handled by the Office of Hearings and Appeals within the Department of the Interior.

---

[346] ESA §10(a)(1)(A), 16 U.S.C. §1539(a)(1)(A) (1988).

[347] ESA §10(e), 16 U.S.C. §1539(e) (1988).

[348] *Id.*

[349] *Id. See also* Friends of Endangered Species, Inc. v. Jantzen II, 596 F. Supp. 518, 20 ER Cases 1645 (N.D. Cal. 1984).

[350] ESA §10(b), 16 U.S.C. §1539(b) (1988).

[351] ESA §11(e)(1), 16 U.S.C. §1540(e)(1) (1988).

[352] ESA §11(c), 16 U.S.C. §1540(c) (1988).

[353] ESA §11(a)(1), 16 U.S.C. §1540(a)(1) (1988).

[354] *Id.*

Once final within the agency, these decisions may be appealed to a federal district court.[355] Penalty assessments made during the hearing process are enforceable by the government in federal court.[356]

a. Civil Penalties. Although the dollar amounts have been amended over the life of the Act, there remains a basic three-tier structure to civil penalties that may be assessed in government enforcement actions. These tiers essentially break down according to (1) violations of the Act involving endangered species, (2) violations of the Act involving threatened species, and (3) inadvertent violations.[357]

The most severe level of penalties is reserved for violations of the Act affecting endangered species. The government may assess, after a hearing, penalties of up to $25,000 for "knowing" violations of the Act or its corresponding regulations protecting endangered (as opposed to threatened) species. This same penalty also may be assessed for knowing violations of any provision of a permit or certificate issued under the Act. Additionally, a person engaged in business as an importer or exporter of fish, wildlife, or plants may be subject to these more substantial penalties even for nonknowing violations of the Act, endangered species regulations, or a permit or certificate.[358]

The second tier of penalties comes into play for violations of the Act that do not involve endangered species. For any other regulations issued under the Act, the government may assess penalties up to $12,000 for knowing violations, or violations by a person engaged in the business of importing or exporting fish, wildlife, and plants.[359]

Finally, inadvertent violators of the Act may be assessed a civil penalty of no more than $500 for each violation.[360] This provision reaches noncommercial "inadvertent" importers or exporters, such as tourists importing a small item consisting of protected species parts.

b. Criminal Penalties. The Act also provides for criminal penalties. Upon conviction for crimes involving endangered species, a court may impose a fine of up to $50,000 and imprisonment for up to one year. For knowing violations of provisions other than those protecting endangered species, a defendant may be fined up to $25,000 and imprisoned for up to six months. As to defenses, in both civil and criminal cases, it is a complete defense for a person to have been acting in good faith to protect himself or someone else from bodily harm.[361]

---

[355] 43 C.F.R. §4.21 (1992).

[356] ESA §11(a)(1), 16 U.S.C. §1540(a)(1) (1988).

[357] *Id.*

[358] The 1978 amendments to the Act made commercial importers and exporters subject to civil penalties even if their violation was not "knowing." That amendment "subjects importers and exporters of fish and wildlife and plants to strict liability penalties" for noncriminal violations. H.R. Conf. Rep. No. 1804, 95th Cong., 2d Sess. 26 (1978), *reprinted in* 1978 U.S.C.C.A.N. 9453, 9493.

[359] ESA §11(a)(1), 16 U.S.C. §1540(a)(1) (1988).

[360] *Id.*

[361] ESA §11(b)(3), 16 U.S.C. §1540(b)(3) (1988). In Christy v. Hodel, 857 F.2d 1324 (9th Cir. 1988), *cert. denied sub. nom.* Christy v. Lujan, 490 U.S. 14 (1989), a defendant argued unsuccessfully that this defense should be expanded to the protection of personal property.

treated or disposed of, the quantities entering each environmental medium, and efforts made to reduce such releases.[140]

B. Material Safety Data Reporting

1. EPCRA Section 311—Material Safety Data Sheets

The owners or operators of facilities required by OSHA's hazard communication rules[141] to maintain MSDSs[142] for "hazardous chemicals" must give a copy of each MSDS, or a list of the chemicals for which an MSDS is maintained, to the LEPC, SERC, and the local fire department. "Hazardous chemical" has the same meaning given the term by the OSHA hazard communication regulations, with certain specified exeptions, i.e., "any chemical which is a physical hazard or health hazard."[143]

---

[140] 40 C.F.R. pt. 372. Subtitle C of the statute (42 U.S.C. §§11041–50) contains general provisions concerning such matters as penalties, enforcement, and trade secrets.

[141] *See* 29 C.F.R. pt. 1910.1200.

[142] EPCRA §329(6), 42 U.S.C. §11049(6) defines the term "material safety data sheet" as having the same definition as that promulgated by OSHA, i.e., "written or printed material concerning a hazardous chemical which is prepared in accordance with Paragraph (g) of this section." 29 C.F.R. §1910.1200(c).

[143] 29 C.F.R. §1910.1200(c). *See* EPCRA §329(5), 42 U.S.C. §11049(5). These terms are explained in the discussion of the hazard communication rules in Chapter 8. Many otherwise hazardous materials are excluded from this general definition by the OSHA regulations and EPCRA. For example, the OSHA definition excludes the following:

1. Any hazardous waste as that term is defined by the Solid Waste Disposal Act, as amended (42 U.S.C. §6801, *et seq.*), when subject to regulation under that act;
2. Tobacco or tobacco products;
3. Wood or wood products;
4. "Articles," defined as manufactured items that (a) are formed to a specific shape or design during manufacture; (b) have end use functions dependent in whole or in part upon their shape or design during end use; and (c) do not release or otherwise result in exposure to a hazardous chemical under normal conditions of use.
5. Food, drugs, cosmetics, or alcoholic beverages in a retail establishment that are packaged for sale to consumers;
6. Foods, drugs, or cosmetics intended for personal consumption by employees while in the workplace;
7. Any consumer product or hazardous substance, as those terms are defined in the Consumer Product Safety Act and the Federal Hazardous Substances Act, respectively, where the employer can demonstrate that such material is used in the workplace in the same manner as in normal consumer use and that such use results in an exposure which is not greater than that experienced by consumers in terms of duration and frequency; and
8. Any drug, as that term is defined in the Federal Food, Drug, and Cosmetic Act, when it is in its final form for direct administration to the patient. *See* 15 U.S.C. §2051 *et seq.;* 15 U.S.C. §1261 *et seq.;* 21 U.S.C. §301 *et seq.;* and 29 C.F.R. §1910.1200(b)(6).

EPCRA, in turn, excludes the following:

1. Any food, food additive, color additive, drug, or cosmetic regulated by the Food and Drug Administration;
2. Any substance present as a solid in any manufactured item to the extent exposure to the substance does not occur under normal conditions of use;
3. Any substance to the extent it is used for personal, family, or household purposes, or is present in the same form and concentration as a product packaged for distribution and use by the general public;
4. Any substance to the extent it is used in a research laboratory or a hospital or other medical facility under the direct supervision of a technically qualified individual; and
5. Any substance to the extent it is used in routine agricultural operations or as a fertilizer held for sale by a retailer to the ultimate customer. *See* 42 U.S.C. §11021(a)(1); 40 C.F.R. §370.21.

Section 311 reporting is required for hazardous chemicals present at the facility, as of the date the report is due, in quantities less than or equal to 10,000 pounds. Extremely hazardous substances have a reporting threshold of 500 pounds, 55 gallons, or the threshold planning quantity, whichever is less. These submissions must be made either within three months of the time a facility owner or operator is first required by OSHA's hazard communication regulations to have an MSDS for the substance or after the hazardous substance first becomes present in an amount exceeding the threshold quantity.[144]

The reporting party may either submit an MSDS or a list of hazardous chemicals for which MSDSs are maintained that are present in excess of the reporting threshold quantity to the LEPC, SERC, and the local fire department.[145] If a list is submitted in lieu of the MSDSs, it must provide the following three types of information:

1. The substances must be grouped into the five specified hazard categories.[146]
2. The chemical or common name must be listed for each hazardous chemical as provided on the MSDS.[147]
3. An identification must be made of any hazardous component of the substance as provided on the MSDS.[148]

If a person who has submitted an MSDS to satisfy the requirements of section 311 comes into possession of significant new information concerning that substance, he or she must provide a revised MSDS to the LEPC, the SERC, and the local fire department within three months of the discovery of such information.[149]

Two options have been provided for reporting on mixtures: an owner or operator may submit an MSDS or make a listing entry for the mixture itself[150] or an MSDS or listing entry may be submitted for each element or compound in the mixture that is itself a hazardous chemical.[151] If the first option is chosen, the total quantity of the mixture must be considered for determining the reporting threshold.[152] Under the second option, EPA has adopted a de minimis rule that provides for each component of a mixture that is a hazardous chemical present at more than 1 percent by weight (or 0.1 percent if the chemical is a carcinogen), that weight percentage is to be multiplied by the mass (in pounds) of the total mixture to determine the quantity of the hazardous chemical present in the mixture.[153]

---

[144] EPCRA §311(d)(1)(B), 42 U.S.C. §11021(d)(1)(B); 40 C.F.R. §370.21(c)(2).

[145] EPCRA §311(a)(2), 42 U.S.C. §11021(a)(2); 40 C.F.R. §370.21(b).

[146] These categories are (1) "Immediate (acute) health hazard"; (2) "Delayed (chronic) health hazard"; (3) "Fire hazard"; (4) "Sudden release of pressure"; and (5) "Reactive." 42 U.S.C. §11021(a)(2)(A)(i); 40 C.F.R. §370.21(b)(1); 40 C.F.R. §370.2.

[147] EPCRA §311(a)(2)(A)(ii), 42 U.S.C. §11021(a)(2)(A)(ii); 40 C.F.R. §370.21(b)(2).

[148] EPCRA §311(a)(2)(A)(iii), 42 U.S.C. §11021(a)(2)(A)(iii); 40 C.F.R. §370.21(b)(3).

[149] EPCRA §311(d)(2), 42 U.S.C. §11021(d)(2); 40 C.F.R. §370.21(c).

[150] EPCRA §311(a)(3)(B), 42 U.S.C. §11021(a)(3)(B); 40 C.F.R. §370.28(a)(2).

[151] EPCRA §311(a)(3)(A), 42 U.S.C. §11021(a)(3)(A); 40 C.F.R. §370.28(a)(1).

[152] 40 C.F.R. §370.28(b)(2).

[153] 40 C.F.R. §370.28(b). Note that these de minimis thresholds are analogous to those provided by the OSHA Hazard Communication rules. See Chapter 8.

2. *EPCRA Section 312—Emergency and Hazardous Chemical Inventory Form*

Section 312 complements the MSDS data called for by section 311 by providing emergency planning authorities with data on the quantities and locations of hazardous substances at the reporting facilities. All persons who make submissions under section 311 are required to submit inventory forms under section 312 to the LEPC, SERC, and local fire department.[154] Section 312 inventory reports must be filed annually by March 1. The same quantity-based reporting thresholds that apply to section 311 also apply to section 312 inventory reporting.[155]

Under section 312, "Tier I" information is to be submitted annually,[156] although "Tier II" information may be submitted instead.[157]

Tier I reports must contain the following three categories of information aggregated by health and physical hazard categories:[158]

1. An estimate, in ranges, of the maximum amount of hazardous chemicals in each of the five hazard categories present at the facility at any time during the preceding calendar year;
2. An estimate, in ranges, of the average daily amount of hazardous chemicals in each of the five hazard categories present at the facility during the preceding calendar year; and
3. The general location of hazardous chemicals in each of the five hazard categories at the facility.

Tier II reports require data on individual hazardous chemicals rather than on general categories.[159] EPCRA calls for the following information to be submitted in Tier II reports:

1. The chemical or common name of the hazardous chemical as given on the MSDS;
2. An estimate, in ranges, of the greatest amount of the substance present at the facility during the preceding calendar year;
3. An estimate, in ranges, of the average daily amount of the substance present at the facility during the preceding calendar year;
4. A brief description of the manner in which the substance is stored;
5. The location of the substance at the facility; and
6. Whether the owner or operator wishes to have the storage location of the substance withheld from public disclosure.[160]

---

[154] 42 U.S.C. §11022(a)(1)(A)-(C); 40 C.F.R. §370.25(a).

[155] 42 U.S.C. §11022(b); 40 C.F.R. §370.20(b)(2).

[156] 42 U.S.C. §11022(a)(2); 40 C.F.R. §370.25(8).

[157] 42 U.S.C. §11022(a)(2); 40 C.F.R. §370.25(b). Upon request of the LEPC, SERC, or fire department, an owner or operator who submitted a Tier I report must submit Tier II data within 30 days. 42 U.S.C. §11022(e), 40 C.F.R. §370.28(c).

[158] These are the same hazard categories established for Section 311, i.e., fire hazard, sudden release of pressure, reactivity, immediate (acute) health hazard, and delayed (chronic) health hazard. EPCRA §312(d)(1)(B), 42 U.S.C. §11022(d)(1)(B); 40 C.F.R. §370.40.

[159] EPCRA §312(d)(2), 42 U.S.C. §11022(d)(2).

[160] EPCRA §312(d)(2)(A)-(F), 42 U.S.C. §11022(d)(2)(A)-(F); 40 C.F.R. §370.41.

Just as the same reporting thresholds that apply under section 311 apply under section 312, the same provisions on mixture reporting apply under both sections.[161] To the extent practicable, the manner of reporting on mixtures under section 311 is to be followed by an owner or operator in section 312 reports.[162]

C. EPCRA Section 313—Toxic Chemical Release Reporting

The final reporting requirement of Subtitle B of EPCRA is the annual section 313 toxic chemical release report that is due every July 1.[163] Section 313 requires reporting on releases into each environmental medium of specified "toxic chemicals," i.e., those that can reasonably be anticipated to cause adverse human health effects or significant adverse effects on the environment.[164]

Reporting is only required if a facility meets a number of threshold criteria. The first of these is that the facility must have 10 or more full-time employees.[165] Second, the facility must be grouped in SIC codes 20-39.[166] Third, the facility must manufacture,[167] process,[168] or otherwise use[169] a toxic chemical in excess of the established reporting thresholds. EPA has elaborated on the statutory definition of the term "manufacture" ("produce, prepare, import, or compound a toxic chemical") to mean

> to produce, prepare, import, or compound a toxic chemical. Manufacture also applies to a toxic chemical that is produced coincidentally during the manufacture, processing, use or disposal of another chemical or mixture of chemicals, including a toxic chemical that is separated from that other chemical or mixture of chemicals as a byproduct, and a toxic chemical that remains in that other chemical or other mixture of chemicals as an impurity.

EPA expanded the definition to clarify its interpretation of the statutory definition to include coincidental production. In this context, however, EPA distinguishes toxic chemicals that remain as impurities in another chemical that

---

[161] EPCRA §312(a)(3), 42 U.S.C. §11022(a)(3); 40 C.F.R. §370.28.

[162] 40 C.F.R. §370.28(a)(2). *See also* H.R. Conf. Rep. No. 962, 99th Cong., 2d Sess. 289 (1986).

[163] 42 U.S.C. §11023(a); 40 C.F.R. §372.30.

[164] H.R. Conf. Rep. No. 962, *supra* note 162.

[165] EPCRA §313(b)(1)(A), 42 U.S.C. §11023(b)(1)(A); 40 C.F.R. §372.22(a). The term "full-time employee" means "2,000 hours per year of full time equivalent employment." 40 C.F.R. §372.3. To determine the number of full-time employees a facility has, the total number of hours worked by all employees, including contract employees, is totaled and that number is divided by 2,000. *Id.*

[166] EPCRA §313(b)(1)(A), 42 U.S.C. §11023(b)(1)(A); 40 C.F.R. §372.22(b). EPA interprets this requirement to relate to the primary SIC code of the facility. If the facility comprises more than one establishment, the applicability of §313 is based on a relative comparison of the value of products shipped and or produced at the establishments within Codes 20-39 as opposed to those grouped in other SIC codes. *Id.; see also* 53 Fed. Reg. 4500, 4501–04 (1988).

[167] EPCRA §313(b)(1)(C)(i), 42 U.S.C. §11023(b)(1)(C)(i); 40 C.F.R. §372.3.

[168] EPCRA §313(b)(1)(C)(ii), 42 U.S.C. §11023(b)(1)(C)(ii).

[169] EPCRA does not define the term "otherwise used." EPA, however, has defined the term to mean

> any use of a toxic chemical that is not covered by the terms "manufacture" or "process" and includes use of a toxic chemical contained in a mixture or tradename product. Relabeling or redistributing a container of a toxic chemical where no repackaging of the toxic chemical occurs does not constitute use or processing of the toxic chemical.

40 C.F.R. §372.3.

is processed, distributed, or used from those that are byproducts that are either disposed or processed, distributed, or used in their own right. If a toxic chemical is produced coincidentally as a byproduct in excess of the reporting threshold, reporting will be required. If, however, it is present as an impurity, EPA has applied a de minimis rule for determining threshold quantities. Thus, if a toxic chemical is present as an impurity in a concentration of 1 percent or less (or 0.1 percent if the toxic chemical is a carcinogen), the quantity of that chemical need not be considered for purposes of determining whether a reporting threshold has been met.[170]

EPCRA defines the term "process" as meaning

> the preparation of a toxic chemical after its manufacture for distribution in commerce—
> (I) in the same form or physical state as, or in a different form or physical state from, that in which it was received by the person so preparing such chemical, or
> (II) as part of an article containing the toxic chemical.

EPA includes in this definition "the processing of a toxic chemical contained in a mixture or tradename product."[171] The concept of processing means the preparation of a toxic chemical after its manufacture for distribution in commerce. This includes a number of different activities, such as blending, mixing, changing the physical state of the chemical, and incorporating the chemical into an article. A material is processed, if, after it has been manufactured, it is made part of another material or product. A toxic chemical can be processed if it is part of a mixture or tradename product, including such a chemical present as an impurity in a product. If a material containing an impurity is processed, the impurity is being processed, and if the impurity is a toxic chemical and the reporting threshold for that material is exceeded, it must be reported.[172]

A toxic chemical that is "otherwise used" is one that does not deliberately become a part of a final product, such as a catalyst, solvent, reaction terminator, lubricant, refrigerant, metal working fluid, cleaner, degreaser, or fuel.[173]

The statute specifies the following reporting thresholds:

1. 10,000 pounds for toxic chemicals *used* at the facility during the preceding calendar year; and
2. 25,000 pounds for toxic chemicals *manufactured* or *processed* at a facility during the preceeding calendar year.[174]

Subject to the 1 percent/0.1 percent de minimis concentration limits, release reports are also required for toxic chemicals that an owner or operator knows are components of tradename products that it imports, processes, or otherwise uses, if the quantity of such chemicals exceeds the applicable report-

[170] 40 C.F.R. §372.28.
[171] 40 C.F.R. §372.3.
[172] *Id.*
[173] *See* 53 Fed. Reg. 4505–06 (1988).
[174] EPCRA §313(f)(1), 42 U.S.C. §11023(f)(1); 40 C.F.R. §372.28. If more than one threshold applies, i.e., if a toxic chemical is both manufactured and otherwise used, reporting is required on all activities at the facility involving the chemical if any one of the reporting thresholds is exceeded. 40 C.F.R. §372.25(c). Also, if a facility reuses or recycles a toxic chemical on-site, the reporting threshold is determined by calculating how much of the chemical was added to the reuse/recycle system during the preceding year. 40 C.F.R. §372.25(e). *See also* 53 Fed. Reg. 4508 (1988).

ing threshold. The key to this requirement is the provision that release reports are required for substances exceeding the threshold reporting limits for "each listed toxic chemical known to be present at the facility."[175] An owner or operator has knowledge of the presence of a toxic chemical in a mixture or tradename product if it knows or has been told its identity or Chemical Abstracts Service (CAS) Registry Number, and that identity or CAS number corresponds to a toxic chemical listed in 40 C.F.R. §372.65. An owner or operator also has knowledge if it has been told by the supplier of the mixture or tradename product that the substance contains a toxic chemical subject to section 313 of EPCRA.[176]

1. *Reporting Alternatives*

There are a number of reporting alternatives based on the amount of information possessed by the owner or operator. For example, if the owner or operator knows both a toxic chemical's specific chemical identity and its specific concentration, the owner or operator is required to determine the weight of the chemical in the mixture or tradename product and to combine that with the weights of that chemical manufactured, processed, or otherwise used at the facility for purposes of determining the reporting threshold.[177]

If the owner or operator knows the specific chemical identity, does not know its exact concentration, but has been told the upper bound of its concentration, the owner or operator is required to assume that the substance is present in the mixture or tradename product at the upper bound concentration and to use that value for determining whether a threshold reporting quantity has been met.[178]

If the owner or operator knows the specific chemical identity and knows neither the specific concentration nor the upper bound concentration (and has not otherwise developed information on the composition of the chemical), it is not required to factor that chemical in the mixture or tradename product into its threshold reporting quantity calculations.[179]

If the owner or operator has been told that a mixture or tradename product contains a toxic chemical, does not know the specific chemical identity, and knows the specific concentration of the substance, it is required to determine the weight of the chemical as part of the mixture or tradename product. If a reporting threshold is met, the owner or operator is required to report using the generic chemical name of the toxic chemical or its tradename, if the generic name is not known.[180] If the owner or operator has been told that a mixture or tradename product contains a toxic chemical, does not know the specific chemical identity or the specific concentration, but has been told an upper bound concentration, it is required to assume that the toxic chemical is present at the upper bound concentration and, if the reporting threshold is crossed, to report using the generic name or tradename.[181]

---

[175] EPCRA §313(g)(1)(C), 42 U.S.C. §11023(g)(1)(C).

[176] 40 C.F.R. §372.30(a)(2). *See also* 53 Fed. Reg. 4508–11 (1988).

[177] 40 C.F.R. §372.30(b)(3)(i).

[178] 40 C.F.R. §372.30(b)(3)(ii).

[179] 40 C.F.R. §372.30(b)(3)(iii).

[180] 40 C.F.R. §372.30(b)(3)(iv).

[181] 40 C.F.R. §372.30(b)(3)(v).

If the owner or operator has been told that a mixture or tradename product contains a toxic chemical, does not know the specific chemical identity, does know specific concentration, and does not know the upper bound concentration, the owner or operator is not required to report on that chemical.[182]

2. Supplier Notification

To implement these obligations, EPA has established supplier notification requirements[183] that apply to facilities that manufacture or process products containing toxic chemicals sold or distributed in mixtures or tradename products to facilities that are also subject to reporting under section 313.[184] This notice, which is to be attached to an MSDS, if one is required, must contain the following elements of information:

1. A statement that the mixture or tradename product contains a toxic chemical subject to section 313 reporting;
2. The name and CAS number for each such toxic chemical; and
3. The percent, by weight, of each toxic chemical in the mixture or tradename product.[185]

Notification is not required if the concentration of such a toxic chemical does not exceed the applicable de minimis concentration, or if the commercial product is an article,[186] food, drug, cosmetic, alcoholic beverage, tobacco, or tobacco product packaged for distribution for the general public, or a consumer product as defined by the Consumer Product Safety Act.[187]

The contents of the required supplier notifications may also vary. If a supplier claims the specific identity of a toxic chemical in a mixture or tradename product to be a trade secret, the notice must contain a generic chemical name.[188] Similarly, if the supplier considers the specific percent-by-weight composition to be a trade secret, the notice must provide an upper bound concentration value.[189] These requirements do not apply to an owner or operator who does not know if its facility is selling or otherwise distributing a toxic chemical in a mixture or tradename product to another person.

3. Toxic Release Inventory Reports

Toxic release inventory reports are to be filed on EPA Form R, which calls for submission of the following types of information:

1. The facility's name, location, and principal business activities. This includes the facility's latitude and longitude, its Dunn & Bradstreet number, its parent's Dunn & Bradstreet number, technical and public

[182] 40 C.F.R. §372.30(b)(3)(vi).
[183] 40 C.F.R. §372.45.
[184] 40 C.F.R. §372.45(a).
[185] 40 C.F.R. §372.45(b).
[186] Article means a manufactured item (1) which is formed to a specific shape or design during manufacture; (2) which has end use functions dependent in whole or in part upon its shape or design during end use; and (3) which does not release a toxic chemical under normal conditions of processing or use of that item at the facility or establishments. 40 C.F.R. §372.3.
[187] 40 C.F.R. §372.45(d).
[188] 40 C.F.R. §372.45(e).
[189] 40 C.F.R. §372.45(f).

contacts, RCRA identification number, NPDES permit number, and underground injection well code. Streams or surface water bodies receiving toxic chemical discharges from the facility must be named, and off-site treatment, storage, or disposal facilities and POTWs to which wastes containing toxic chemicals from the facility were sent must be identified.

2. A "senior official with management responsibility for the person or persons completing the report," must certify the accuracy and completeness of the report.[190]
3. For each toxic chemical known to be present at the facility in excess of the applicable threshold, the report is to provide the chemical name and CAS number, and
   (a) A statement whether the toxic chemical is manufactured, processed, or otherwise used at the facility and the general category or categories of such use;
   (b) An estimate, in ranges, of the maximum amount of a toxic chemical present at the facility at any time during the preceding calendar year;
   (c) An estimate of the concentration of a toxic chemical in the influent to the waste treatment system, an identification of the waste treatment or disposal method used by the facility for each waste stream containing a toxic chemical, and "an estimate of the treatment efficiency typically achieved by such methods for that waste stream."[191] In this context, "treatment efficiency" means the mass percent by which a subject toxic chemical is removed from the waste stream rather than overall system efficiency; and
   (d) The quantity of every reportable toxic chemical released to each environmental medium. This requirement includes the off-site shipment of waste, including discharges to POTWs, on-site releases to land, and fugitive and point source air emissions. This requirement applies to both routine and accidental releases.[192]

Section 313 reports may be based on "reasonably available data," which include monitoring and emission measurements collected pursuant to other environmental statutes. If no such data exist, however, reasonable estimates rounded to no more than two significant digits may be used.[193]

---

[190] EPCRA §313(g)(1)(B), 42 U.S.C. §11023(g)(1)(B). Such an official is one with management responsibility for the person or persons completing a report, or the manager of environmental programs for the facility or establishments, or for the corporation owning or operating the facility or establishments responsible for certifying similar reports under other environmental regulatory requirements.

[191] EPCRA §313(g)(1)(C)(iii), 42 U.S.C. §11023(g)(1)(C)(iii).

[192] *See* 53 Fed. Reg. 4513 (1988).

[193] "[T]he owner or operator of a facility may use readily available data (including monitoring data) collected pursuant to other provisions of law, or, where such data are not readily available, reasonable estimates of the amounts involved. Nothing in this section requires the monitoring or measurement of the quantities, concentration, or frequency of any toxic chemical released into the environment beyond that monitoring and measurement required under other provisions of law or regulation." EPCRA §313(g)(2), 42 U.S.C. §11023(g)(2).

4. *Waste Minimization*

For a number of years EPA sought information relating to waste minimization. The Pollution Prevention Act of 1990 (PPA),[194] made pollutant source reduction and recycling reporting mandatory elements of the toxic release inventory report. As a consequence, facilities that must file TRI reports must now also provide information on the following:

1. The quantity of the toxic chemical (prior to recycling, treatment, or disposal) entering any waste stream or released to the environment;
2. Quantities of the chemical recycled at the facility and elsewhere;
3. Quantities of the chemical treated at the facility and elsewhere;
4. Information on source reduction activities and the method used to identify those activities;
5. Quantities of the toxic chemical released in a one-time event not associated with production processes;
6. Quantities of the chemical expected to enter any waste stream or be recycled in future years; and
7. Production ratio or activity index for the reported chemical.

5. *Exemptions*

Some uses of toxic chemicals are exempt from section 313 reporting. These include those used as structural components, products used for routine janitorial or facility maintenance, toxic chemicals in products used for personal purposes by employees or other persons at the facility as foods, drugs, cosmetics, or other personal items, products used for maintaining motor vehicles, and toxic chemicals contained in process water and noncontact cooling water or in air used as compressed air or as part of combustion.[195] Toxic chemicals that are manufactured, processed, or used in a laboratory under the supervision of a technically qualified individual need not be considered for reporting purposes, unless the activity involves specialty chemical production, pilot plant operations, or activities conducted outside the laboratory.

On its own initiative or upon petition by any person or state governor, EPA may start rulemaking to add or delete substances from the list of toxic chemicals.[196] The Agency may also modify by rule the reporting thresholds,[197] and it may alter reporting frequency, although it may not require that such reports be submitted more frequently than once per year.[198] The data collected pursuant to section 313 are kept in a computerized data base.[199] These data are accessible in the Toxic Release Inventory database through the National Library of Medicines's "TOXNET" database and through various other media.

---

[194] 42 U.S.C. §13101 *et seq.*, enacted as part of the Omnibus Budget Reconciliation Act of 1990, Pub. L. No. 101-508, 104 Stat. 1388.

[195] 40 C.F.R. §372.38(c)(1)-(5).

[196] EPCRA §313(d) and (e), 42 U.S.C. §11023(d) and (e).

[197] So long as the resulting reports cover a substantial majority of the aggregate releases of a chemical at a facility. EPCRA §313(f)(2), 42 U.S.C. §11023(f)(2).

[198] EPCRA §313(i)(1), 42 U.S.C. §11023(i)(1).

[199] 42 U.S.C. §11023(j).

D. Government Enforcement and Civil Actions

1. Governmental Enforcement

EPCRA section 325 arms EPA with a variety of sanctions it may employ against violators of the statute.[200] For example, any person other than a governmental entity who fails to satisfy any obligations under section 312 or section 313 is subject to a penalty of up to $25,000 per day of violation.[201] Persons who violate any provisions of section 311 are liable for a penalty of up to $10,000 per day for each day such violation continues.[202] EPA may assess these penalties administratively or through action in federal district court.[203]

A person against whom EPA has assessed an administrative penalty may file an appeal to federal district court within 30 days after the date of EPA's order.[204] If such person fails to pay the assessed penalty, EPA may ask the Department of Justice to bring suit to collect the penalty.[205] The Agency is given the power to issue subpoenas to compel testimony and document production. Failure to comply with such subpoenas is punishable as contempt by the federal district court for the district in which the person disobeying the subpoena resides, is found, or transacts business.[206]

2. Civil Actions

EPCRA also established a number of causes of action available to citizens and state and local governments.[207] A prevailing or substantially prevailing party may be awarded costs, including attorneys' fees.[208] A putative plaintiff must provide at least 60 days prior notice to an owner or operator, EPA, and the state in which the alleged violation occurred before filing suit.[209] Similarly, actions against EPA, a governor, or a SERC may not be filed without 60 days prior notice.[210] In any such action, the United States or a state may intervene as of right as may other persons if they have a direct interest that may be adversely affected by the action and that they may otherwise be unable adequately to protect.[211]

Actions against an owner or operator include suits for failure to submit an MSDS or list under section 311(a), failure to submit Tier I data on an inventory form under section 312(a), and failure to submit a toxic chemical release form under section 313(a).[212]

---

[200] Penalties for violation of EPCRA's emergency release reporting provisions were discussed in Section II.D. of this chapter.

[201] EPCRA §325(c)(1) and (3), 42 U.S.C. §11045(c)(1) and (3).

[202] EPCRA §325(c)(2) and (3), 42 U.S.C. §11045(c)(2) and (3).

[203] EPCRA §325(c)(4), 42 U.S.C. §11045(c)(4).

[204] EPCRA §325(f)(1), 42 U.S.C. §11045(f)(1).

[205] *Id.*

[206] EPCRA §325(f)(2), 42 U.S.C. §11045(f)(2).

[207] EPCRA §326, 42 U.S.C. §11046.

[208] EPCRA §326(f), 42 U.S.C. §11046(f).

[209] EPCRA §326(d)(1), 42 U.S.C. §11046(d)(1).

[210] EPCRA §326(d)(2), 42 U.S.C. §11046(d)(2).

[211] EPCRA §326(h)(1) and (2), 42 U.S.C. §11046(h)(1) and (2).

[212] EPCRA §326(a)(1)(A)(i)-(iv), 42 U.S.C. §11046(a)(1)(A)(i)-(iv).

The statute also provides that suit may be brought against EPA and local authorities for failure to meet statutory deadlines regarding response to petitions and information requests. However, an owner or operator may not be sued if EPA has brought an administrative or civil action to enforce the same requirement which the plaintiff would enforce.[213]

IV. Conclusion

> Accidents will occur in the best regulated families.
>
> —C. Dickens, *David Copperfield*

Hazardous materials are ubiquitous in our modern industrial society, and it is inevitable that at times, despite the best planning, they will be accidentially released. It was the object of this chapter to provide in summary form an overview of a number of federal statutes that deal with reporting and responding to such events.

Because accidents will occur, and given the significant potential liability that reporting errors can engender, it is advisable for businesses that handle materials subject to release reporting requirements to develop and adhere to a rigorous written compliance program. While such a program may not prevent all potential financial exposures, it will tend to mitigate them and, more important, will maximize the protection provided to human health and the environment.

---

[213] EPCRA §326(e), 42 U.S.C. §11046(e).

13

Standards for Storage Tank Facilities

By Mary Beth Bosco

I. Introduction

Disasters such as the Ashland Oil tank collapse and leaking underground tank farms throughout the country have focused the public's attention on the safety of the tank facilities used to store hazardous waste and petroleum.[1] The Environmental Protection Agency (EPA) estimates that there are somewhere near two million underground storage tanks nationwide—mostly constructed of unprotected steel and almost surely leaking.[2] Add to this figure the equally large number of above ground tanks and EPA is confronted with a daunting regulatory task. Development of comprehensive standards for the construction and operation of storage tanks is complicated further by the wide variety in the age and condition of these millions of existing tanks.

Not surprisingly, therefore, the legislative and regulatory response on the federal level has been to react to each specific situation, resulting in a maze of discrete and sometimes overlapping laws governing tanks and tank storage facilities and their management. Compounding the problem presented to tank owners and operators in managing their facilities in the face of these myriad regulations is the fact that many of these regulatory programs are still under development. This chapter therefore collects the various existing federal requirements relating to tanks and tank facility management. The first topic covered will be the design and operational standards imposed on both above ground and underground tanks. The second part of this chapter will discuss the facilities maintenance and management issues facing tank owners and operators (including the regulation of storm water runoff from industrial facilities). The chapter concludes with a discussion of special tank compliance and liability issues.

The various federal statutes and regulations governing storage tank operations and management most readily can be classified by the type of material being stored. There is a comprehensive set of regulations under the authority of

[1] *See* United States v. Ashland Oil, Inc., 705 F. Supp. 270, 29 ER Cases 1030 (N.D. Pa. 1989).

[2] Environmental Protection Agency, Publication No. 530, MUSTs for USTs 1 (July 1990). This figure does not include the millions of private heating oil tanks not subject to EPA's regulation.

Subtitle I of the Resource Conservation and Recovery Act (RCRA) for underground storage tanks (USTs) that store hazardous substances and petroleum.[3] This separate regulatory scheme covers all aspects of UST operation and management, providing technical performance standards, cleanup and closure requirements, financial responsibility criteria, and liability measures. While the federal UST regulations for the most part became final in 1988, the associated state enforcement programs are in varying stages of development.

There is no corresponding independent set of regulations for storage of all substances in above ground tanks (AGTs). Both AGTs and USTs used to store hazardous waste fall within the purview of RCRA Subtitle C's regulations. AGTs storing used oil fall under EPA's September 1992 used oil management regulations, while used oil USTs also are regulated under the RCRA Subtitle I UST regulations. Additionally, the Oil Pollution Act of 1990 (OPA)[4] contains certain provisions governing the management of onshore oil tank storage facilities. These provisions are summarized in this chapter.

This chapter will follow these general regulatory distinctions. Each section begins with the standards imposed on USTs, followed by any corresponding requirements for hazardous waste tanks or AGTs storing petroleum or used oil. The first regulatory area covered is tank design and construction standards.

II. Storage Tank Design and Construction Standards

RCRA Subtitle I required EPA to develop a comprehensive set of regulations for underground tank systems holding both petroleum and hazardous substances.[5] These regulations became final in 1988.[6] They contain technical standards governing tank design, installation and performance, closure and cleanup requirements, and financial responsibility obligations for UST owners and operators.

The operational standards imposed on AGTs are more diverse. Certain requirements for facilities using AGTs to store oil derive from the OPA. Hazardous waste storage in both above ground and underground tanks falls within Subtitle C of RCRA,[7] used oil AGTs are regulated under separate used oil management rules, while other above ground hazardous substance tank storage is not regulated separately on the federal level. The following sections focus on the technical standards for (1) tank installation, design, and performance, and (2) operational requirements for both USTs and AGTs.

---

[3] 42 U.S.C. §6901 *et seq.* Underground Storage Tanks that store hazardous wastes are regulated under RCRA Subtitle C.

[4] OPA §1001 *et seq.*, 33 U.S.C. §2701 *et seq.*

[5] RCRA §9001 *et seq.*, 42 U.S.C. §6991 *et seq.*

[6] 40 C.F.R. §270 *et seq.*

[7] RCRA §3001 *et seq.*, 42 U.S.C. §6921 *et seq.*

A. Technical Standards Governing the Design and Installation of Underground Tanks

1. Scope of UST Regulation

EPA's UST regulations under RCRA Subtitle I generally do not differentiate between the storage of hazardous substances and petroleum in underground tanks.[8] Rather, an underground tank is broadly defined as a tank or tank system the volume of which is 10 percent or more below ground and that contains either a CERCLA hazardous substance or oil.[9]

The breadth of this definition, however, is diminished somewhat by the number of USTs exempt from federal regulation. The following categories of underground tanks are not subject to EPA's UST regulations:

- Small (1,100 gallons or less) farm or residential tanks holding motor fuel for noncommercial uses;
- Heating oil tanks used only to heat the premises where stored;
- Septic tanks;
- Utility pipeline facilities regulated under other statutes;
- Surface impoundments, pits, ponds, or lagoons;
- Storm water or wastewater collection systems;
- Oil or gas gathering lines;
- Basement or other underground area tanks which rest on a floor;
- USTs storing hazardous wastes;
- Clean Water Act treatment tanks;
- Hydraulic lift tanks;
- Tanks with capacities of 110 gallons or less;
- Tanks holding a de minimis concentration of regulated substances; and
- Emergency spill and overfill containment systems.[10]

Any existing UST that does not fit within one of the listed exemptions must now be registered with the designated state or local agency.[11] Additionally, several states require the registration of home heating oil and farm fuel tanks and so go well beyond the federal requirements in this area. Underground tank owners also must notify the designated agency at least 30 days prior to bringing a new tank into use, and the notification must contain a certification that the tank installation meets EPA's standards.[12] Finally, there is a notification obligation imposed on tank sellers, who must advise their purchasers of the purchaser/

---

[8] The two areas in which EPA distinguishes between petroleum and hazardous substance USTs are release detection capability and owner/operator financial responsibility. See Sections III.A. and V.A., below.

[9] The Subtitle I UST regulations do not apply to tanks storing hazardous wastes. RCRA §9001(2), 42 U.S.C. §6991(2); 40 C.F.R. §280(10(b)(1).

[10] RCRA §9001(1)(A)-(I), 42 U.S.C. §6991(1)(A)-(I); 40 C.F.R. §280.10(b). EPA also has deferred regulation of five more tank types: wastewater treatment tanks not regulated under the Clean Water Act; systems containing radioactive material regulated under the Atomic Energy Act; power generation facilities regulated by the Nuclear Regulatory Commission; airport hydrant fuel distribution systems; and field-constructed tanks. 40 C.F.R. §280.10(c). However, these tanks are still subject to certain initial installation and cleanup standards. Accordingly, owners and operators of these tank types should be aware that leaks or suspected releases will trigger the full panoply of release reporting and cleanup obligations.

[11] 40 C.F.R. §280.22(a).

[12] 40 C.F.R. §280.22(f).

owner's obligation to register the tank with EPA. This requirement is one that often catches property owners unaware: if transferring land with USTs on it, the transferor must, as part of the transaction, advise the land purchaser that the purchaser is required to register the tanks with the state.[13]

2. *New and Existing UST Performance Standards*

EPA specifically has authorized installation of four general types of new underground tanks.[14] Because of the wide variations within each of these general categories, EPA determined to rely on existing industry performance codes to provide the standards for the design and installation of each of these four tank types, rather than develop a new set of installation requirements. Thus, if installing one of these four tank types, the owner generally need only follow established industry codes that are listed in the regulations in order to achieve compliance with EPA's standards as well.

The generally authorized tank types are (1) tanks constructed of fiberglass-reinforced plastic,[15] (2) tanks constructed of steel and cathodically protected,[16] (3) tanks constructed of steel-fiberglass-reinforced-plastic composite,[17] and (4) metal tanks without cathodic protection if installed at sites determined by a corrosion expert not to be corrosive enough to cause the tank to have a release due to corrosion during its operating life.[18] Any proposed alternate tank designs must receive agency approval, which is dependent on a finding that the alternate design, construction, and corrosion protection systems are not less protective of human health and the environment than the tank types expressly authorized by the regulations.[19] Piping associated with new tanks is subject to similar requirements.[20]

All new underground tanks must be equipped with spill and overfill prevention equipment, unless the UST system is filled by transfers of no more than 25 gallons at a time. The required spill prevention equipment must be designed to prevent product release to the environment when the hose is detached from the fill pipe. New overfill protection equipment must either shut

---

[13] 40 C.F.R. §280.22(g).

[14] 40 C.F.R. §280.20(a).

[15] The industry codes cited with approval in the regulations for fiberglass-reinforced plastic tanks are Underwriters Laboratories Standard 1316; Underwriters Laboratories of Canada CAN4-S615-M83; or American Society of Testing and Materials Standard D4021-86, *Standard Specification for Glass-Fiber-Reinforced Polyester Underground Petroleum Storage Tanks.* 40 C.F.R. §280.20(a)(1).

[16] The following standards and codes may be used to comply with this requirement: Steel Tank Institute, *Specification for STI-13 System of External Corrosion Protection for Underground Steel Storage Tanks;* Underwriters Laboratories of Canada Nos. CAN4-2603-M85, CAN4-G03.1-M85, CAN4-S631-M84; Underwriters Laboratories Standard 58; and National Association of Corrosion Engineers Standard RP-02-85. 40 C.F.R. §280.20(a)(2).

Approved cathodic protection measures are (i) coating the tank with a suitable dielectric material; (ii) field-installed cathodic protection systems designed by corrosion experts; (iii) impressed current systems that allow determination of current operating status; and (iv) other cathodic protection systems operated and maintained in accordance with the regulations. 40 C.F.R. §280.20(a)(2).

[17] The listed codes applicable to this requirement are the Underwriters Laboratories Standard 1746 and the Association for Composite Tanks ACT-100. 40 C.F.R. §280.20(a)(3).

[18] 40 C.F.R. §280.20(a)(1)-(4).

[19] 40 C.F.R. §280.20(a)(5). High-density polyethylene jackets regularly receive approval at the state level.

[20] 40 C.F.R. §280.20(b).

off the flow to the tank at 95 percent capacity or alert the operator through an alarm or flow shut-down when the tank reaches 90 percent capacity.[21]

In addition to new tank performance criteria, the Subtitle I UST regulations establish upgrade requirements for existing underground tanks. Within 10 years of the regulations' effective date (December 22, 1988) all existing systems must meet either the new tank performance standards or specific upgrade requirements, such as requirements for internal lining, or they must be closed down.[22] This upgrade requirement encompasses the above spill and overfill standards.[23]

Small businesses owning or operating USTs should pay particular attention to the pending 1998 upgrade requirement. Many state agencies expect an avalanche of tank closures in 1998 as many businesses opt to close existing tanks rather than assume the expense of upgrading. This strategy, however, may ultimately prove more expensive. As described in Section C below, tank closure requires a site assessment and cleanup of any contamination that such an assessment identifies, which may itself be a costly exercise. The expense of UST upgrade or closure therefore should be a contingency included in the tank facility manager's long-term budget planning strategy.

There is some cause for optimism, however, for UST facility managers facing the upgrade or closure decision. EPA currently is developing a rule that would clearly exempt lenders from liability for cleanup of leaking USTs. The purpose of this rule is to remove at least one of the hurdles facing UST owners in trying to obtain financing for tank upgrades.[24]

B. Technical Standards Governing the Design and Installation of Tanks Storing Hazardous Waste

1. *Scope of Regulation*

RCRA's Subtitle C regulates, among other matters, the storage of hazardous wastes in both above ground and underground tanks.[25] The general rule is that facilities that use tank systems to store or treat hazardous wastes must comply with the Subtitle C implementing regulations summarized below, with the exception of indoor AGTs situated on an impermeable floor that store hazardous wastes without any free liquid. Tanks used as secondary containment systems to collect releases need not comply with the requirements for release detection.[26]

2. *New and Existing AGT and UST Performance Standards*

All new hazardous waste tank systems are subject to two basic requirements: written certification of the tank's integrity and a secondary containment system. The written assessment must be submitted to the Regional Administra-

---

[21] 40 C.F.R. §280.20(c).

[22] 40 C.F.R. §280.21(a).

[23] 40 C.F.R. §280.21(d).

[24] EPA intends to issue a final rule on UST lender liability by July 1994. 58 Fed. Reg. 57,048 (1993).

[25] RCRA §3001 *et seq.*, 42 U.S.C. §6921 *et seq.;* See Chapter 6, Resource Conservation and Recovery Act, at Section VI.

[26] 40 C.F.R. §264.190.

tor and certified by an independent professional engineer.[27] The assessment generally must attest to the fact that the tank has sufficient structural integrity and is acceptable for the storing and treating of hazardous waste. More specifically, the certification is to include the following information:

- The applicable tank design and construction standards;
- The hazardous characteristics of the waste to be handled;
- A corrosion expert's report for steel tanks;
- A statement of design or operational safeguards against damage from any vehicular traffic for underground tanks; and
- A statement of design considerations to ensure the foundation integrity or stability if the tank is located in a saturated or seismic fault zone.[28]

In addition to this written certification as to the adequacy of the tank's design, the tank owner or operator must secure proof that the tank installation was conducted properly. This is to be accomplished by having an independent engineer inspect the tank system prior to its use and prepare a written report as to the components' integrity.[29] As the installation of new USTs storing petroleum and hazardous substances similarly must be certified, the safest practice now is to obtain an independent engineer's certification for any new tank installation. AGT systems must also be tested for tightness and a similar report prepared.[30] These reports must be kept on file at the facility.[31]

Unless a variance is obtained, all new tanks storing or treating hazardous waste must be equipped with a secondary containment system meeting certain requirements.[32] In addition to new tank systems, the secondary containment requirements apply to existing tanks according to the following schedule:

- January 1989—existing tanks used to store EPA Hazardous Waste Nos. F020, F021, F022, F023, F026, and F027;
- January 1989—existing tanks of known and documented age (or when the tank system is 15 years old, whichever is later);
- January 1995—existing tanks of uncertain age (unless the facility is older than seven years, in which case the operable date becomes the later of January 1989 or the facility's 15th anniversary);
- Within two years of a stored substance's first becoming hazardous.[33]

---

[27] 40 C.F.R. §264.192(a).

[28] *Id.*

[29] 40 C.F.R. §264.192(b).

[30] 40 C.F.R. §264.192(d). The regulations also contain requirements as to the type of backfill material permissible for use with underground tanks, as well as requirements for ancillary equipment. 40 C.F.R. §264.192(c) and (e).

[31] 40 C.F.R. §264.192(g).

[32] 40 C.F.R. §264.193. The variance must be approved by the Regional Administrator after a demonstration by the tank owner or operator that the proposed alternative design and operating practices either will prevent the migration of hazardous waste to the environment, or that in the event of a release, no substantial present or potential hazard will be posed to human health or the environment. 40 C.F.R. §264.193(g). Variances are not available for USTs storing hazardous wastes.

[33] 40 C.F.R. §264.193(a)(1)-(5). In lieu of a secondary containment system, the owner or operator of an existing tank may opt to obtain an independent written assessment of the tank's integrity. This assessment must include the following: (1) the tank's design specifications; (2) the hazardous characteristics of the stored wastes; (3) the existing corrosion protection measures; (4) either the documented or estimated age of the tank; and (5) the results of a tank leak or integrity test. 40 C.F.R. §264.191(b).

The general parameters governing the required secondary containment systems are that they be designed, installed, and operated so as to prevent any migration out of the system and that they be capable of detecting and collecting any releases.[34] More specifically, secondary containment systems for tanks storing hazardous wastes must contain at least one of the following devices:

- An external liner;
- A vault;
- A double-walled tank; or
- An equivalent device as approved by the Regional Administrator.

The regulations contain detailed operational parameters for each of these devices.[35]

C. AGTs Storing Used Oil

In September 1992, EPA published management standards for used oil generators, burners, and transporters.[36] These contain design requirements for tanks storing used oil.[37] Containers and tanks used to hold used oil generally must be maintained in good condition, without visible signs of corrosion, deterioration, or leakage and must have some type of secondary containment system.[38] At a minimum, the secondary containment system must consist of

- A dike, berm or retaining wall; and
- A floor covering the entire area within the dike, berm, or retaining wall, which all must be sufficiently impervious as to prevent any used oil released to the containment system from migrating to the environment.[39]

Additionally, the system, including fill pipes, must be clearly labeled as containing ''used oil.''

III. Operational Requirements for Storage Tanks

This section outlines the day-to-day operational requirements imposed on tank facilities. It discusses the inspection, maintenance, and repair requirements for both USTs and AGTs, along with release detection, closure, and cleanup regulations, including a discussion of the spill, prevention, and preparedness plan requirements applicable to certain tank storage facilities. It concludes with a discussion of the obligations placed on industrial tank storage facilities with respect to storm water runoff management.

Here, the requirements imposed on underground tanks storing petroleum and hazardous substances diverge somewhat from the requirements for above ground tanks storing hazardous wastes or petroleum in that the UST regulations

[34] 40 C.F.R. §264.193(b).

[35] 40 C.F.R. §264.193(d) and (e).

[36] 57 Fed. Reg. 41,566 (1992).

[37] USTs holding used oil are also subject to the general UST regulations discussed above. 57 Fed. Reg. at 41,624.

[38] 40 C.F.R. §279.64(b).

[39] 40 C.F.R. §279.64(c).

do not require a formal spill, prevention, and preparedness plan. However, it should be noted that, for facilities storing waste in both above ground and underground tanks, the requirements discussed below for hazardous waste storage tanks as a practical matter will generally extend to the facilities' underground hazardous substance tanks as well.

A. Operational and Maintenance Requirements for UST Systems

The day-to-day operational and maintenance requirements imposed on existing UST systems fall into four general categories: spill and overfill control, corrosion protection, tank repair, and release detection.

All owners and operators of existing USTs must guard against releases due to spills and overfills by ensuring prior to transfer that the available tank volume exceeds the volume of product to be transferred and by "constantly" monitoring the transfer operation.[40] Monitoring may be accomplished through electronic or mechanical means and does not require the physical presence of an attendant.

As to corrosion protection, such systems must be operated and maintained continuously[41] and must be tested by a qualified cathodic protection inspector within six months of installation and at least every three years thereafter.[42] UST systems with impressed current cathodic protection systems must also be inspected every 60 days to ensure proper operation of the equipment. Records of the inspections must be maintained.[43]

The third operational area of UST regulation is system repair of existing tanks. Generally, repairs to existing underground tanks must prevent releases due to structural failure or corrosion for the system's operating life and must be conducted in accordance with nationally recognized industry codes.[44] Specifically, repairs made to fiberglass-reinforced tanks must be made by a manufacturer's authorized representative.[45] Leaking pipes must be replaced if made of metal, but may be repaired if made of fiberglass.[46] Repaired tanks and piping must be tested or monitored within 30 days of completion of the repair. Again, records of the repair must be maintained for the life of the system.[47]

The UST regulations set forth general release detection standards, as well as specific requirements based on whether the system contains petroleum or hazardous substances. All new tanks must have release detection capability. Most existing tanks and piping were to be upgraded to have functioning leak detection systems by the end of 1992.[48] Current tank owners and operators should be aware that tanks that do not meet these release detection requirements must be closed down.

---

[40] 40 C.F.R. §280.30.

[41] 40 C.F.R. §280.31.

[42] 40 C.F.R. §280.31(b).

[43] 40 C.F.R. §280.31(c) and .31(d). The records must be maintained on site or at a readily available alternate location and are to be made available to EPA pursuant to RCRA §9005, 42 U.S.C. §6991d.

[44] 40 C.F.R. §280.33(a).

[45] 40 C.F.R. §280.33(b).

[46] *Id.*

[47] 40 C.F.R. §280.33(d) and .33(f).

[48] 40 C.F.R. §280.34(b) sets forth the phased-in schedule for release detection capability, which is based on the tank's age.

The general release detection requirements for all UST systems are that (1) the system must be able to detect a release from any portion of the tank and the connected underground piping; (2) the system must be installed, operated, and maintained in accordance with the manufacturer's instructions; and (3) the system must meet the performance requirements set forth in the regulations for petroleum-containing tanks and hazardous substance-containing tanks.[49]

As to the specific release detection system requirements for petroleum UST systems, tanks containing petroleum must be monitored at least every 30 days using one of the following methods:[50] (1) automatic tank gauging, (2) vapor monitoring, (3) groundwater monitoring, (4) interstitial monitoring, or (5) any other method that is capable of detecting a two-tenths of a gallon per hour leak rate or a release of 150 gallons within a month, with a probability of detection of 95 percent and a probability of false alarm of 5 percent or less.[51]

Piping associated with petroleum UST systems also must be equipped with release detection devices. Underground piping that conveys regulated substances under pressure must be equipped with an automatic line leak detector and have an annual line tightness test or monthly monitoring.[52] Suction piping must have either a line tightness test conducted at least every three years, or use a monthly monitoring method.[53]

All existing UST systems that contain hazardous substances must meet the requirements for petroleum UST systems set forth above. Additionally, by 10 years after the December 1988 effective date of the final regulations, all existing underground hazardous substance systems must meet specific requirements for secondary containment systems, double-walled tanks, and external liners.[54] Again, alternative release detection systems may be used for hazardous substance-storing tanks if approved by the implementing agency.

The UST regulations also set forth standards for the specific types of release detection methods chosen by the tank owner and operator to comply with the general outlines of the regulations. These release detection methods are inventory control, manual tank gauging, tank tightness testing, automatic tank gauging, groundwater monitoring, and interstitial monitoring. A summary of these technical requirements follows.

---

[49] 40 C.F.R. §280.40(a).

[50] When monthly testing is performed, a single release detection method may be used. When less frequent testing is performed, it must be backed up with monthly inventory control.

[51] 40 C.F.R. §280.41(a). There are three exceptions to these rules. First, petroleum underground tanks with capacities of 550 gallons or less may use weekly tank gauging. 40 C.F.R. §280.41(a)(3). Second, systems that now meet the new tank performance standards and use a monthly inventory control system or manual tank gauging may use tank tightness testing at least every 5 years for the 10-year upgrade period or 10 years after installation or upgrade, whichever is later. 40 C.F.R. §280.41(a)(1). Third, tank systems that do not meet the new tank performance standards may use a combination of monthly inventory controls and annual tank tightness testing for the upgrade period, at which time the tank must meet the new performance standards or be closed. 40 C.F.R. §280.41(a)(2).

[52] 40 C.F.R. §280.41(b)(1).

[53] 40 C.F.R. §280.41(b)(2). Suction piping, however, is exempt from release detection requirements if it is designed and constructed to meet the following standards: (1) the below-grade piping operates at less than atmospheric pressure; (2) the below-grade piping is sloped so that the contents of the pipe will drain back into the storage area if the suction is released; (3) only one check valve is included in each suction line; (4) the check valve is located directly below and as close as practical to the suction pump; and (5) a method is provided that allows compliance with these requirements to be readily determined.

[54] 40 C.F.R. §280.42(a).

Inventory control must be conducted on a monthly basis so as to be able to detect a release of at least 1 percent of the flow-through plus 130 gallons. The regulations require that an inventory control system must operate according to the following parameters: daily recording of inventory volume measurements for regulated substance inputs, withdrawals, and remaining volume; measuring equipment capable of measuring the level of product over the full range of the tank's height to the nearest one-eighth of an inch; reconciliation of substance inputs with delivery receipts before and after each delivery; deliveries through a drop tube that extends to within one foot of the tank bottom; metering and dispensing of product within the local standards for meter calibration or an accuracy of six cubic inches for every five gallons of product withdrawn; and measurement of any water level in the bottom of the tank to the nearest one-eighth of an inch at least once a month.[55]

Automatic tank gauging may be used in conjunction with inventory control if the automatic product level monitor test can detect a two-tenths of a gallon per hour leak rate from any portion of the tank that routinely contains product.

Manual tank gauging may only be used as the sole method of release detection for tanks holding 550 gallons of product or less.[56] It must be performed as follows: the tank liquid level measurements must be taken at the beginning and ending of a 36-hour static period; the tank liquid level measurement must be based on an average of two consecutive stick readings at both the beginning and ending of this period; the equipment used must be capable of measuring the level of product over the full range of the tank's height to the nearest one-eighth of an inch; and any variations between the beginning and ending measurements which exceed the regulatory standards must be treated as leaks.[57]

Tank tightness testing can be used only if capable of detection of a one-tenth of a gallon per hour leak rate from any portion of the tank that routinely contains product.[58]

Vapor monitoring release detection systems are subject to the following criteria: the materials used as backfill at the site must be sufficiently porous to allow diffusion of vapors from releases into the excavation area; the stored regulated substance must be volatile enough to result in a vapor level that is readily detectable by the monitoring device; the measurement of vapors by the monitoring device must be able to withstand moisture, such as groundwater, rainfall, or soil moisture; the background contamination level in the excavation area will not interfere with the release detection; the vapor monitors must be designed and operated to allow the threshold level to be preset specifically for the type of regulated substance stored in the tank system; a specific assessment must be made of the excavation area to ensure that the system can comply with the above five requirements; and the monitoring wells must be clearly marked and secured.[59]

---

[55] 40 C.F.R. §280.43(a).
[56] 40 C.F.R. §280.43(b)(5).
[57] 40 C.F.R. §280.43(b).
[58] 40 C.F.R. §280.43(c).
[59] 40 C.F.R. §280.43(e).

Groundwater monitoring release detection systems also must comply with the criteria set forth in the regulations. In order to meet these criteria, the tank owner/operator must first determine that the regulated substance stored in the tank is immiscible in water and has a specific gravity of less than one. Further, groundwater monitoring systems can only be used in accordance with the regulations in circumstances where the groundwater is 20 feet or less from the ground surface, and the hydraulic conductivity of the soils between the UST system and the monitoring well or device is .01 cm/sec or more. The monitoring well casing must ensure against migration of natural soils or filter pack into the well. The monitoring wells must be sealed from the ground surface to the top of the filter pack. The monitoring wells must intercept the excavation zone[60] or must be as close to it as is technically feasible. The continuous monitoring devices used must be able to detect the presence of at least one-eighth of an inch of free product on top of the groundwater in the monitoring wells. The site must be assessed to ensure compliance with these requirements and the monitoring wells must be clearly marked and secured.[61]

Interstitial monitoring systems must be capable of detecting a leak from any portion of the tank. For double-walled UST systems, the sampling or testing method must be able to detect a release through the inner wall and any portion of the tank that routinely contains product. For systems using a secondary barrier within the excavation zone, the sampling method must be able to detect a release between the system and the secondary barrier, and the barrier must be sufficiently thick and impermeable to direct a release to the monitoring point, yet installed so as not to interfere with proper operation of any cathodic protection systems.[62]

Finally, any other type of release detection method or combination of methods may be used so long as the implementing agency approves.[63]

The UST regulations also contain certain requirements for release detection for piping. Vapor monitoring, groundwater monitoring, or interstitial monitoring may be used for release detection from pipes only if they are used in accordance with the requirements for tank systems set forth above.[64] Automatic line leak detectors may be used only if they detect leaks of three gallons per hour at 10 pounds per square inch line pressure within one hour. Additionally, an annual test of the operation of the leak detector must be conducted.[65] A periodic line tightness testing of piping is acceptable only if it is capable of detecting a one-tenth of a gallon per hour leak rate at one and one-half times the operating pressure.[66]

---

[60] The UST regulations define the excavation zone for these purposes as "the volume containing the tank system and backfill material bounded by the ground surface, walls, and floor of the pit and trenches into which the UST system is placed at the time of installation." 40 C.F.R. §280.12.

[61] 40 C.F.R. §280.43(f).

[62] 40 C.F.R. §280.43(g).

[63] 40 C.F.R. §280.43(h). The standard for approval of such alternate methods is that the owner or operator must be able to demonstrate to the agency that the method is capable of detecting a release before it migrates beyond the excavation area and is as effective a method as any of the methods described above. In comparing methods, the agency is to consider the size of the release that the method can detect and the frequency and reliability with which it can be detected. *Id.*

[64] 40 C.F.R. §280.44(c).

[65] 40 C.F.R. §280.44(a).

[66] 40 C.F.R. §280.44(b).

Finally, system owners and operators must maintain records demonstrating compliance with the applicable release detection requirements. These records are to include written performance claims; the results of any sampling, testing, or monitoring; and written documentation of all calibration, maintenance, and repair of release detection equipment.[67] Again, the records must be maintained on site or be made readily available to the state implementing agency.

B. Operational and Maintenance Requirements for Hazardous Waste Systems

The RCRA Subtitle C operational regulations specifically applicable to AGTs and USTs storing hazardous waste are less detailed than their Subtitle I UST hazardous substance and petroleum counterparts and focus more on the waste being stored. The general rule for hazardous waste tanks is one of common sense: hazardous wastes or treatment reagents must not be placed in a tank system if they could cause the tank, its ancillary equipment, or the containment system to rupture, leak, corrode, or otherwise fail,[68] and incompatible wastes may not be stored together unless certain requirements are met.[69]

To ensure compliance with this general rule, prior to the storage, treatment, or disposal of hazardous waste in a tank, a detailed chemical analysis of the waste must be obtained.[70] The facility also must develop and maintain a written waste analysis plan designed to guarantee the currency and accuracy of the facility's sampling procedures.[71] At a minimum, this plan is to contain the following:

- A description of the test methods and parameters and a statement of the rationale for their selection;
- A description of the sampling method and statement explaining how it is designed to ensure a random sample;
- A statement of the sampling frequency and how it is designed to ensure currency;
- A description of any analyses to be performed of waste coming from off-site, if necessary;
- Any special waste analysis requirements; and
- Any surface impoundment procedures.[72]

In addition to analysis and documentation of the waste being stored at the facility, hazardous waste storage, treatment, and disposal facility owners and operators must comply with certain inspection obligations. First, the general physical security of the overall facility is subject to regulation, as a continuous

[67] 40 C.F.R. §280.45.

[68] 40 C.F.R. §264.194(a). Except for emergency conditions, ignitable or reactive wastes cannot be placed in a tank unless treated first or stored in such a way so as to preclude contact with any material that might cause an ignition or reaction. 40 C.F.R. §264.198(a). Facilities storing ignitable or reactive wastes also must comply with the National Fire Protection Association's *Flammable and Combustible Liquids Code,* Tables 2-1 and 2-6, as it pertains to protection of adjoining public or private areas.

[69] 40 C.F.R. §264.199. *See* 40 C.F.R. §264.17(b).

[70] 40 C.F.R. §264.13(a).

[71] 40 C.F.R. §264.13(b).

[72] 40 C.F.R. §264.13(a).

monitoring and security system with controlled entry is required, as are a facility fence or barrier and public warning signs.[73] Second, the storage tanks themselves must be regularly inspected according to a written schedule and plan.[74] These routine inspection results must be recorded in the facility operating log and maintained for at least three years.[75]

More specifically, the following must be inspected at least once each operating day:

- All areas subject to spill, such as loading areas;
- All above ground portions of tank systems;
- Data gathered from monitoring or release detection systems; and
- Construction materials or secondary containment systems surrounding the tank.[76]

Additionally, any cathodic protection devices must be inspected within six months of installation and annually thereafter, and all sources of impressed current are to be inspected or tested bimonthly.[77]

C. Release Detection, Cleanup, and Closure Requirements

The foregoing requirements are all aimed at monitoring for releases. The importance of recordkeeping at each stage of the process—installation of the release detection equipment, operation and testing, release confirmation, and repair—cannot be overemphasized. Tank facility managers therefore should ensure that the required records are maintained up-to-date and in an organized and accessible manner.

Oncc a ielease detection system is operational, there are very specific requirements as to the precise steps to be taken in the event a release from the system is detected. These are summarized below.

1. Release Detection and Reporting for UST Systems

The UST regulations under Subtitle I are quite specific as to the type of occurrence triggering the release reporting obligation. The following conditions must be reported to the implementing agency within 24 hours of their discovery:

- The discovery of released regulated substances at the site or in the surrounding area;
- Unusual operating conditions (such as sudden loss of product from the UST system, or an unexplained presence of water in the tank); and
- Monitoring results from a release detection method that indicate that a release may have occurred.[78]

---

[73] 40 C.F.R. §264.14(a). These requirements may be waived on demonstration to EPA's satisfaction that physical contact with the waste or equipment will not cause injury, or that disturbance of the waste by an unauthorized entrant to the facility will not cause an unknowing violation of the regulations.

[74] 40 C.F.R. §264.15.

[75] 40 C.F.R. §264.14(d) and .195(d).

[76] 40 C.F.R. §264.15(b)(4) and .195(b).

[77] 40 C.F.R. §264.195(c).

[78] 40 C.F.R. §280.50.

All suspected releases must be confirmed within a seven-day period.[79] This may entail a system tightness test to determine if a leak is occurring from the system. A confirmed release must be reported and contained within 24 hours of confirmation.

Specific procedures for reporting and cleaning up spills and overfills from USTs also exist. Spills and overfills must be reported to the implementing agency within 24 hours and immediate containment achieved.[80] The following spills and overfills are subject to these procedures:

- A spill or overfill of petroleum that results in a release exceeding 25 gallons or that causes a sheen on nearby surface water; and
- A spill or overfill of a hazardous substance that results in a release to the environment that equals or exceeds the reportable quantity for that substance under CERCLA.[81]

If the spill or overfill is less than these quantities, the owner and operator still must contain and immediately clean up the release. If cleanup cannot be accomplished within 24 hours, the owner or operator immediately must notify the implementing agency.

2. *UST System Cleanup and Closure*

Confirmation of a release by an UST owner or operator triggers certain immediate obligations for containment and identification and mitigation of any potential fire, explosion, or vapor hazards.[82] These immediate reactive measures are to be followed by abatement action, including emptying of the tank; performance of a visual inspection of any above-ground releases or exposed underground releases and prevention of further migration into surrounding soils and groundwater; monitoring of any safety hazards; remediation of any hazards posed by excavated contaminated soils; measuring for the presence of any further releases; and investigation to determine the possible presence of free product.[83] A report summarizing these initial abatement steps must be submitted to the implementing agency within 20 days after release confirmation.[84]

Additionally, where evidence exists that groundwater has been affected by the release, an investigation for soil and groundwater cleanup must be con-

---

[79] 40 C.F.R. §280.52.

[80] 40 C.F.R. §280.53(a).

[81] *See* 40 C.F.R. pt. 302. In addition to the UST reporting requirements, releases equaling or exceeding the CERCLA reportable quantity must be reported immediately to the National Response Center pursuant to §§102 and 103 of CERCLA, 42 U.S.C. §§9602 and 9603, and to the appropriate state and local authorities under Title III of the Superfund Amendments and Reauthorization Act of 1986, Pub. L. No. 99-499, 42 U.S.C. §9601 *et seq.*

[82] 40 C.F.R. §280.61. The requirements summarized above for release response actions for USTs also apply to *all* tanks storing used oil. 40 C.F.R. §279.64(g).

[83] 40 C.F.R. §280.62(a). Where free product is identified, it must be removed immediately, and a report submitted to the implementing agency within 45 days as to the type of free product recovery system utilized. 40 C.F.R. §280.64.

[84] 40 C.F.R. §280.62(b). Additionally, within 45 days of release confirmation, owners and operators must submit to the implementing agency all information assembled about the site and the nature of the release, including data on the nature and estimated quantity of release, data concerning possible receptors of the release, results of any site checks performed, and results of any free product investigations. 40 C.F.R. §280.63.

ducted and the results must be submitted to the agency as soon as practicable.[85] Finally, a corrective action plan may be required by the implementing agency. The regulations provide for public comment on the corrective action plan proposed by the site owner/operator.[86]

In order to close an underground tank following a release or otherwise, the tank must be emptied and cleaned by removing all liquids and accumulated sludges. The tank must be either removed from the ground or filled with an inert solid material. Additionally, the owner/operator must perform a site test and, if the results indicate contamination, initiate corrective action.[87] Notice must be given to the implementing agency at least 30 days prior to beginning the closure process.[88]

For a number of reasons, it is generally prudent to include to the greatest extent practical representatives of the state agency in the site check and cleanup process. In order to claim reimbursement from a state trust fund for cleanup or closure costs, the tank owner/operator must demonstrate compliance with all applicable regulatory requirements. This is discussed further in Section V.C.1., below. Involving the state in the process from the start obviously will aid in making such a demonstration. Even where a claim against the fund is not anticipated, however, early state involvement should minimize the need for repetitive testing or remediation measures.

3. Release Detection and Reporting for Hazardous Waste Systems

The RCRA Subtitle C release reporting requirements for tanks storing hazardous wastes are similar to those imposed on Subtitle I UST systems. Releases must be reported to the Regional Administrator within 24 hours of detection, unless the quantity is less than or equal to one pound, or it is immediately contained and cleaned up.[89]

In addition to the release reporting obligation, releases from hazardous waste tanks require immediate investigation and containment measures similar to those for USTs storing petroleum and hazardous substances. Any remaining product flow into the tank or secondary containment system must be closed, the tank removed from service, and the system inspected to determine the cause of the release.[90] Unless the owner/operator demonstrates to EPA's satisfaction that such is not practical, all remaining product must be removed from the tank or secondary containment system so that inspection and repair may proceed.[91] Next, a visual inspection must be conducted in order to prevent further migra-

---

[85] 40 C.F.R. §280.65.

[86] 40 C.F.R. §280.66 and .67.

[87] 40 C.F.R. §280.72. UST owners and operators facing closure and cleanup of a petroleum-containing UST should be aware that EPA has, at least temporarily, exempted from the hazardous waste Toxicity Characteristic rule petroleum-contaminated media and debris from USTs undergoing corrective action. 57 Fed. Reg. 36,866 (1992). This exemption greatly simplifies the procedures for disposal of contaminated soils from UST sites.

[88] 40 C.F.R. §280.71(b). Temporary closure also is regulated, as corrosion protection and release monitoring must continue during the temporary closure period. Absent an extension, temporary closure may not exceed 12 months. 40 C.F.R. §280.70.

[89] 40 C.F.R. §264.196(d). A report pursuant to CERCLA §§102 and 103 (42 U.S.C. §§9602 and 9603) under 40 C.F.R. §302 will satisfy this requirement.

[90] 40 C.F.R. §264.196(a).

[91] 40 C.F.R. §264.196(b).

tion of the released substance, and any visible, contaminated soil or surface water must be removed and disposed of properly.[92]

On a more long-term basis, the tank owner/operator has 30 days from detection of the release to submit a report to the agency, which is to include an analysis of the site characteristics and likely route of release migration, the results of any sampling or monitoring data, and a description of response actions taken or planned.[93]

4. Cleanup and Closure for Hazardous Waste

The release reporting and immediate containment measures must be followed by system repair or closure. The tank or secondary containment system from which a release has occurred *must* be closed *unless*

- The cause of the release was not one damaging the system's integrity;
- The cause of the release was from the primary tank system into the secondary containment system; or
- The cause of the release was from a portion of the system without secondary containment and secondary containment is then provided (unless the leak was from an above ground component susceptible of visual inspection).[94]

If the system is repaired in accordance with the above in lieu of closure, it may not be returned to service until an independent engineer certifies that the repaired system is capable of storing hazardous wastes without leakage for the intended life of the system.[95]

When a hazardous waste tank system is closed, the owner or operator is to remove or decontaminate all waste residues, contaminated containment system components or other equipment, and any contaminated soil, and manage them as hazardous waste.[96] A closure plan and cost estimate must be submitted to EPA. In the event that any contaminated soils cannot be removed or decontaminated as a practical matter, the postclosure requirements applicable to landfills will then attach to the tank site.[97]

IV. Tank Facilities Management

Hazardous waste storage tank facilities, as well as petroleum-containing tank facilities, are subject to certain requirements for emergency preparedness, prevention, and reaction. These include planning for responses to emergency spills and releases, employee training, and coordination with local emergency agencies.

These requirements, while usually consistent, vary somewhat depending on the substance stored in the tank. Accordingly, facilities using tanks to store a

[92] 40 C.F.R. §264.196(c).
[93] 40 C.F.R. §264.196(d).
[94] 40 C.F.R. §264.196(e).
[95] 40 C.F.R. §264.196(f).
[96] 40 C.F.R. §264.197(a).
[97] *See* 40 C.F.R. §264.310.

variety of regulated substances should undertake review and coordination of any applicable requirements both to ensure compliance and to avoid unnecessary duplication.

A. Hazardous Waste Storage Tank Facilities

Hazardous waste storage facilities

> must be designed, constructed, maintained, and operated to minimize the possibility of a fire, explosion, or any unplanned sudden or non-sudden release of hazardous waste or hazardous waste constituents to air, soil or surface water which could threaten human health or the environment.[98]

To this end, the federal regulations control personnel practices, equipment, and emergency preparedness plans for hazardous waste storage facilities.

All facility personnel are to be trained as to procedures in the event of an emergency. The facility must be equipped with an internal communications or alarm system capable of providing emergency instruction.[99] Employees also must have immediate access to a device capable of contacting emergency help (with advance arrangements with the local fire department and hospital already accomplished), as well as to portable fire control, spill control, decontamination equipment, and an adequate water supply. This equipment must be tested regularly.[100]

Most important, all hazardous waste tank storage facilities must prepare and maintain at the facility a Contingency and Emergency Preparedness Plan.[101] The Plan must be submitted to all local hospitals and police and fire departments that may be called on to provide emergency services.[102] It must contain

- A description of all actions to be taken in the event of an emergency;[103]
- Any necessary amendment to existing Spill Prevention, Control and Countermeasure (SPCC) Plans under section 311 of the Clean Water Act;
- A description of the advance arrangements with local emergency authorities;
- A listing of all personnel qualified to act as the facility's emergency coordinator;
- A listing of all emergency equipment; and
- A description of the facility's evacuation plan.[104]

---

[98] 40 C.F.R. §264.31.

[99] 40 C.F.R. §264.16 and .32.

[100] 40 C.F.R. §264.32.

[101] 40 C.F.R. §264.51 and .52.

[102] 40 C.F.R. §264.52.

[103] By regulation, these must include activation of the alarm or communication system, notification of the appropriate state and local authorities, identification of any released materials, assessment of any immediate hazards, proper notification if the release is outside the facility, containment and cleanup of the release, maintenance and reconstitution of any emergency or cleanup equipment used, and preparation of a report detailing the specifics of the release and response actions and submission to EPA within 15 days. 40 C.F.R. §264.56.

[104] 40 C.F.R. §264.52.

The provisions of the plan *must* be adhered to in the event of a fire, explosion, or release of hazardous waste that would threaten human health or the environment.

B. Oil Tank Storage Facilities

In reaction to the Exxon *Valdez* oil spill, Congress passed the OPA. Of note to tank facility managers is the OPA's requirement (as an amendment to section 311 of the Clean Water Act) for vessel and facility response plans. These new requirements, although not yet finalized, are expected to be significantly more elaborate than any preexisting SPCC plans for onshore oil transportation facilities. Facilities must prepare and submit plans if

- They handle, transport, or store oil or hazardous substances; and
- If the onshore facility, "because of its location, could reasonably be expected to cause substantial harm to the environment by discharging into or on the navigable waters, adjoining shoreline, or the exclusive economic zone."[105]

Under this definition, almost any onshore facility that could discharge oil to a storm drain or storm sewer may need to prepare a response plan.

The statute requires that the response plan

1. Be consistent with the National Contingency Plan and Area Contingency Plan;
2. Identify the individual at the facility with full authority to implement the plan and require immediate communication between that individual and appropriate federal and state officials and cleanup contractors;
3. Identify and ensure by contract (or other means acceptable under the regulation) the availability of private personnel and equipment necessary to remove the worst-case discharge, and to mitigate and prevent discharges (or substantial threats of discharge, including fires); and
4. Describe the training, equipment testing, periodic unannounced drills, and response actions to be carried out to prevent or mitigate discharges or substantial threats of discharge.[106]

Facilities must update these plans periodically to reflect changes in operations and lessons learned from drills and tests.

The response plan requirements overlap substantially with similar contingency plan and reporting requirements under the Emergency Planning and Community Right-to-Know Act (EPCRA or SARA Title III), RCRA, and CERCLA. The new contingency plan requirements do not supersede or supplant requirements under these other statutes, but are to be used in conjunction with and in supplementation of existing statutory requirements. This means that tank facility managers must coordinate the multiple planning requirements to ensure that all applicable obligations are met. This task is not an easy one,

[105] 33 U.S.C. §1321(j)(5)(B).
[106] 33 U.S.C. §1321(j).

particularly because the parameters of the Oil Pollution Act plans have not yet been finalized.

By August of 1992, the Coast Guard or EPA was to promulgate regulations governing tank vessel and facility response plans. The Coast Guard is responsible for the regulations governing response plans for worst case discharges of oil and hazardous substances from transportation-related onshore facilities, and EPA is responsible for preparing the necessary changes to the National Contingency Plan for nontransportation related facilities.[107] Neither agency met the deadline, although both have preliminary guidance in process.

On February 17, 1993, EPA published for comment a proposed regulation containing plan requirements for nontransportation related shore activities, such as oil wells, drilling, production equipment, and other fixed facilities that use and store oil.[108] The regulations propose to adopt a self-selection approach for determining what facilities "could reasonably be expected to cause substantial harm to the environment" and so are required to submit plans under the OPA. First, all facilities that store more than 42,000 gallons of oil and involve transfer over water or vessels must submit plans. Next, facilities that store less than one million gallons and involve no water transport would be exempted from the plan requirements under EPA's proposal. Finally, facilities that store over one million gallons and have no involvement with water transport would be required to respond to a series of questions in order to determine whether they must submit a plan. Facilities falling into this latter category would be subject to the plan requirements if one of the following is true:

1. The facility is located at a distance such that a discharge would shut down operations at a public water intake;
2. The facility is located at a distance such that a discharge would cause injury to an environmentally sensitive area;
3. The facility has insufficient secondary containment for above ground storage areas; or
4. The facility had a reportable spill of 10,000 gallons or more within the last five years.[109]

As an alternative to this somewhat experimental self-selection approach, EPA also proposed a second option for determining whether a facility would be required to submit a plan. Under this more conventional approach, all regulated facilities would be required to prepare plans, but smaller, low-risk facilities would be allowed to prepare abbreviated versions.[110]

On February 5, 1993, the Coast Guard published its interim final rule (effective as of that date) establishing the requirements for response plans for marine transportation-related facilities such as deepwater ports, certain Coast Guard–regulated onshore facilities, marinas, tank trucks, and railroad tank

[107] 57 Fed. Reg. 8708 (1992). Additionally, the Department of the Interior's Minerals Management Service is to prepare regulations governing response plans for nontransportation-related offshore facilities and transportation-related pipelines linking oil production platforms to onshore facilities.

[108] 58 Fed. Reg. 8824 (1993).

[109] 58 Fed. Reg. at 8826.

[110] 58 Fed. Reg. at 8829.

cars.[111] Unlike the approach taken by EPA, the Coast Guard regulations presume that both fixed and mobile marine transportation-related facilities that are used, or intended to be used, for transferring oil, in bulk, to or from a vessel with capacity of 250 barrels or more, reasonably could be expected to cause substantial harm to the environment and so are required to prepare and submit spill response plans. The rule does, however, contain a provision enabling facility owners or operators to apply for an exemption to the plan requirement.[112]

The dates for compliance established by the interim final rule are as follows:

- Facilities operating prior to February 18, 1993, must submit a response plan prior to that date and must be operating in compliance with the plan by August 18, 1993.
- Facilities beginning operation between February 18, 1993, and August 18, 1993, must submit a plan prior to handling, storing, or transporting oil, and must be operating in compliance with the plan by August 18, 1993.
- Facilities beginning operations after August 18, 1993, must submit their response plans not less than 60 days prior to handling, storing, or transporting oil at the facility.[113]

Finally, the Coast Guard regulations establish the general outlines for response plans, as well as requirements both for the designated individuals responsible for implementing the plan, and for ensuring that the appropriate equipment is available in the event of a worst-case spill or discharge.[114]

C. Storm Water Runoff Regulation

Industries storing hazardous materials on site now must also be concerned with the regulation of storm water runoff. The Water Quality Act of 1987 added section 402 to the Clean Water Act,[115] requiring that storm water discharges associated with industrial activity be permitted by October 1992.

On November 16, 1990, EPA published certain general National Pollutant Discharge Elimination System (NPDES) permit group and individual applications for industrial activity.[116] However, the regulatory burden of administering the program caused the Agency nearly a year later to issue a request for public comment seeking methods of implementing a more workable program.[117] The result was the establishment of baseline, general permits for storm water discharges from industrial sources.

---

[111] 58 Fed. Reg. 7330 (1993); to be codified at 33 C.F.R. §154.1015.

[112] 58 Fed. Reg. 7334 (1993); to be codified at 33 C.F.R. §154.1015.

[113] 58 Fed. Reg. 7337 (1993); to be codified at 33 C.F.R. §154.1025. The regulations also provide that a facility may operate for up to two years pending approval of a submitted plan so long as written certification is provided attesting that the facility has ensured the availability of equipment and personnel to respond to a worst case discharge.

[114] 58 Fed. Reg. 7338–39 (1993); to be codified at 33 C.F.R. §154.1026, .1027, and .1030.

[115] Pub. L. No. 100-4, 101 Stat. 65, 33 U.S.C. §1342 *et seq.*

[116] 55 Fed. Reg. 47,990 (1990).

[117] 56 Fed. Reg. 40,950 (1991).

As a result, on September 9, 1992, EPA Regions I, IV, V, VIII, IX, and X issued NPDES general permits establishing registration, storm water pollution prevention plan, and inspection requirements for facilities.[118] By October 1, 1992, covered industries within these regions[119] were to submit Notices of Intent (NOI) to be authorized to discharge under the general permit.[120]

1. Coverage of General Permits

Briefly, the NOI is to include the following: the address and identification of the facility, including a listing of SIC codes for the facility's principal products or activities; permit numbers for any existing NPDES permits or group application numbers; identification of the receiving water or storm sewer; identification of any existing data as to the concentration of pollutants in the storm water discharges; and, for any facility that begins to discharge storm water after October 1, 1992, a certification that a storm water pollution prevention plan has been prepared.

Unless notified by EPA to the contrary, facility owners or operators who submit such notification are authorized to discharge storm water associated with industrial activity under the terms and conditions of the general permit. If EPA denies coverage under the general permit on its review of the NOI, the facility must apply for an individual NPDES permit.

The following seven types of storm water discharges associated with industrial activity are not covered by the general permit:[121]

- Storm water discharges mixed with non-storm water, unless the mixture is authorized by a separate NPDES permit or meets the general permit's requirements for such mixtures;[122]
- Storm water discharges already subject to an existing industry effluent limitation;[123]
- Storm water discharges from facilities with existing NPDES permits for the storm water discharges until such time as the existing permit expires;
- Storm water discharges associated with industrial activities from a construction site;
- Storm water discharges determined by EPA to be contributing to a violation of a water quality standard;

---

[118] 57 Fed. Reg. 41,236 (1992).

[119] These regions include states that do not have approved state NPDES programs. Authorized states must issue their own regulations, which may be no less stringent than the federal regulations. 56 Fed. Reg. 40,950 (1991).

[120] Regardless of region, the NOIs are to be sent to: Storm Water Notices of Intent, P.O. Box 1215, Newington, Virginia 22122. A copy of the NOI form appears in the *Federal Register* at 57 Fed. Reg. 41,295 (1992).

[121] 57 Fed. Reg. 41,240 (1992). Dischargers that already had submitted an individual permit application or had participated in a group permit may also submit a NOI to obtain coverage under the general permit.

[122] The permissible mixture sources are discharges from fire fighting activities, fire hydrant flushings, potable water sources, irrigation drainage, lawn watering, routine detergentless building washdown, pavement washdowns (unless a spill of toxic or hazardous materials has occurred), air conditioning condensate, springs, uncontaminated ground water, and foundation drains. 57 Fed. Reg. 41,241.

[123] These are cement manufacturing, feedlots, fertilizer manufacturing, petroleum refining, phosphate manufacturing, steam electric, coal mining, mineral mining and processing, ore mining and dressing, and asphalt emulsion. 57 Fed. Reg. at 41,240.

- Storm water discharges that may adversely affect a listed or proposed to be listed endangered or threatened species or its critical habitat; and
- Storm water discharges from inactive mining, inactive landfills, or inactive oil and gas operations on federal land where an operator cannot be identified.[124]

2. *Pollution Prevention Plan Requirements*

All industrial facilities covered by the general permit for storm water discharges are required to prepare and implement a storm water pollution prevention plan. Generally, the planning requirement entails

- Formation of a team of qualified plant personnel responsible for plan preparation and implementation;
- Assessment of potential storm water pollution sources;
- Selection and implementation of appropriate management practices and controls; and
- Periodic plan evaluation.[125]

The measurement and controls section must contain descriptions of "good housekeeping" practices designed to keep contaminants out of separate storm sewers; a preventive maintenance and inspection program for all storm water management devices; spill prevention and response procedures;[126] a description of employee training programs; a description of documentation practices for plan status, implementation, and effectiveness; sediment and runoff containment measures; and an evaluation of the traditional storm water management practices.[127]

V. Financial Responsibility and Liability Issues

This chapter concludes with a discussion of liability, including special financial responsibility and cost issues. As with the preceding sections, the following discussion begins with the requirements for UST systems.

A. Financial Responsibility Requirements for Petroleum UST Systems

Petroleum system tank owners and operators (including municipalities) must demonstrate financial responsibility in the event of a release from the tank.[128] If the tank owner differs from the tank operator, only one need make the

---

[124] 57 Fed. Reg. at 41,240.

[125] 57 Fed. Reg. at 41,242. Facilities subject to §313 of the Emergency Planning and Community Right-to-Know Act (EPCRA), 42 U.S.C. §11001 *et seq.*, are subject to special requirements under the general permits for the areas where §313 water priority chemicals are stored, processed, or otherwise handled.

[126] In addition, where a permitted storm water discharge contains a hazardous substance or oil in excess of the CERCLA reportable quantity within a 24-hour period, it must be reported to the National Response Center and a report submitted to EPA within 14 days.

[127] 57 Fed. Reg. at 41,245.

[128] Excluded from these requirements, which are limited to petroleum-containing USTs, are the tanks not covered by EPA's technical tank performance regulations, or tanks removed from service prior to the financial responsibility compliance dates. 53 Fed. Reg. 43,327 (1988). EPA intends to issue a Notice of Proposed Rulemaking governing financial responsibility for hazardous substance tank owners and operators in the fall of 1994. 58 Fed. Reg. 57,049 (1993).

financial responsibility showing, although both would be liable for noncompliance.[129] In addition, a parent corporation may bear responsibility for a subsidiary's violation of these requirements.[130]

The timing and amount of a financial responsibility showing is dependent on the number of tanks owned. Petroleum tank owners and operators must demonstrate adequate financial responsibility both on a per-occurrence and annual aggregate basis. Owners and operators of USTs located at petroleum marketing facilities,[131] or that handle an average of more than 10,000 gallons of petroleum per month based on the average from the previous calendar year, must demonstrate financial responsibility for taking corrective action and for compensating third parties for bodily injury and property damage caused by accidental releases in the amount of $1 million per occurrence. All other UST owners and operators are subject to a $500,000 per occurrence amount.[132]

The annual aggregate amounts are based on the number of single containment units owned. Owners and operators of 1 to 100 petroleum USTs must demonstrate financial responsibility in the annual aggregate amount of $1 million. Owners and operators of 101 or more tanks are subject to a $2 million showing of financial responsibility.[133]

In recognition, however, of the difficulties faced by small businesses and other entities in obtaining adequate insurance at an affordable rate, EPA is proposing to extend the deadline for compliance with the financial responsibility regulations for certain tank owners and operators. These include small businesses, facilities that provide essential community services, facilities located in rural areas, local governments, and Indian tribes.[134]

The requisite level of financial responsibility may be shown by use of any one or a combination of the following mechanisms: a guarantee or surety bond (the form of which has been approved by the state attorney general's office), insurance or risk retention group coverage, a letter of credit, a trust fund, or a state-required mechanism that EPA has determined is at least equivalent to the preceding listed mechanisms.[135] Local governments have available to them special methods for demonstrating their financial responsibility. They are a bond rating test, a local government financial test, a governmental guarantee, and maintenance of a fund balance.[136] The regulations contain detailed standards and conditions for the use of all of these instruments. Additionally, owners or operators meeting stringent net worth and financial test requirements may act as self-insurers.[137]

Records evidencing compliance with the financial responsibility requirements must be maintained by the tank owner or operator.[138] An owner or

---

[129] 40 C.F.R. §280.90(e).

[130] 53 Fed. Reg. 43,326 (1988).

[131] A petroleum marketing firm is one that owns a petroleum marketing facility, which is a facility at which petroleum is produced or refined or from which petroleum is sold or transferred to other petroleum marketers or to the public. 40 C.F.R. §280.92(i) and (j).

[132] 40 C.F.R. §280.93(a).

[133] 40 C.F.R. §280.93(b).

[134] 58 Fed. Reg. 43,770 (1993).

[135] 40 C.F.R. §§280.94–103.

[136] 58 Fed. Reg. 9026 (1993).

[137] 40 C.F.R. §280.95.

[138] 40 C.F.R. §280.107.

operator may only be released from the financial responsibility requirements upon either proper closure of the tank or completion and approval of corrective action.[139]

B. Financial Responsibility for Hazardous Waste Systems

Hazardous waste tank owners and operators are subject not only to financial responsibility requirements in the event of releases or accidents, but also as to system closure. Owners or operators of all hazardous waste treatment, storage, or disposal facilities must demonstrate financial responsibility for injuries to third parties from an accidental occurrence in the amount of at least $1 million per occurrence and $2 million annually, exclusive of legal defense costs.[140] As with the UST regulations for petroleum tank owners and operators, hazardous waste system owners and operators may demonstrate their financial ability via a number of mechanisms: an insurance policy, self insurance, a letter of credit, a surety bond, a trust fund, or some combination of these means.[141] EPA must be notified of claims against these funds.

In addition, hazardous waste tank facilities must demonstrate adequate financial capability for tank closure. First, the facility must maintain a cost estimate for facility closure based on an operations level that would result in the most expensive closure and updated for inflation.[142] Next, the facility owner/operator must establish financial assurance for closure of the facility, based on one of the following means:

- A closure trust fund, submitted to EPA, into which periodic payments are made in specified amounts;[143]
- A surety bond guaranteeing payment into a standby closure trust find;
- A surety bond guaranteeing performance;
- An irrevocable letter of credit, issued for a period of at least one year, and backed up by a standby trust fund;
- A closure insurance policy issued for a face amount at least equal to the closure cost estimate;
- A self-financing test and corporate guarantee demonstrating compliance with certain capitalization requirements; or
- A combination of trust fund, surety bonds guaranteeing payment into a trust fund, letters of credit, and insurance.[144]

---

[139] 40 C.F.R. §280.109. Owners and operators filing as debtors under Chapter 11 of the Bankruptcy Code must notify the implementing agency by certified mail within 10 days after commencement of the proceeding. 40 C.F.R. §280.110.

[140] 40 C.F.R. §264.147(a).

[141] 40 C.F.R. §264.147(a)(1)-(6).

[142] 40 C.F.R. §264.142. The closure cost estimate also must be based on the assumption that a third party will perform the closure and may not adjust for proceeds from the sale of any equipment or product at closure.

[143] For example, for new facilities, the initial payment must equal the current closure cost estimate divided by the number of years in the pay-in period.

[144] 40 C.F.R. §264.143(a)-(g). It should be noted that, for tank facilities at which contaminated soil is left on site following closure, an additional showing of financial assurance for postclosure care must be made. 40 C.F.R. §264.145.

C. Financial and Liability Issues

1. Liability for UST Systems

EPA is authorized to clean up the release of petroleum into the environment from an underground storage tank if such action is necessary to protect human health and the environment.[145] In undertaking the cleanup action, EPA or states under cooperative agreements will use funds from the Leaking Underground Storage Tank Trust Fund, which is being financed by a tax on motor fuels.[146] The tank owner or operator, if he or she can be located, will be liable to EPA for reimbursement to the fund.

EPA may undertake such unilateral, emergency corrective action only if certain conditions are met. These are that (1) the owner or operator cannot be located within 90 days (or a shorter period if necessary to protect human health and the environment); (2) the situation is such that prompt action is required to protect human health and the environment; (3) the costs of the required corrective action exceed the amount of coverage called for by the financial responsibility regulations; or (4) the tank owner or operator has failed to comply with prior compliance orders.[147]

Section 9006 of RCRA also authorizes EPA to issue administrative orders to violators of Subtitle I or the UST regulations or to commence a civil action to force compliance.[148]

2. Liability for Hazardous Waste Systems

Section 3007 of RCRA[149] provides the mechanism for enforcement of the hazardous waste facility operations and management standards outlined above. It authorizes EPA or states with authorized hazardous waste programs to inspect the premises or records of hazardous waste facilities—even if the facility no longer handles hazardous waste. As with the underground tank program, violators are subject to several methods of enforcement under RCRA: administrative orders, injunctive relief, and civil and criminal penalties.[150]

3. Cost Recovery Issues

The news for UST owners and operators facing the upgrade or closure decision, however, is not all bleak. Nearly all of the states have authorized UST trust funds, funded by registration, permit, and compliance fees, to assist UST owners and operators in paying for tank closure or cleanup. The states have initiated these programs in recognition of the financial burden imposed on small businesses in particular by the UST release detection and upgrade requirements.

---

[145] RCRA §9003(h)(2), 42 U.S.C. §6991b(h)(2). The response program applies to releases which contain petroleum. Accordingly, petroleum-hazardous substance mixtures are subject to RCRA §9003(h) corrective action authority. *See* 53 Fed. Reg. 37,116 (1988).

[146] RCRA §9003(h)(1), 42 U.S.C. §6991b(h)(1).

[147] RCRA §9003(h)(2), 42 U.S.C. §6991b(h)(2).

[148] 42 U.S.C. §6991e(a). *See* Chapter 6, Resource Conservation and Recovery Act.

[149] 42 U.S.C. §6927.

[150] See Chapter 16 on Enforcement and Defense Strategies.

The procedures for which coverage is available, amounts, and eligibility requirements vary from state to state. However, state trust funds generally have one thing in common: in order to claim against the fund, the tank owner/operator must demonstrate compliance with all applicable regulations, including registration and the requirement for release detection systems. Thus, for businesses facing the upgrade or closure decision, a tank facility compliance review is an immediate necessity to any future claim for reimbursement of closure or cleanup costs.

VI. Conclusion

Tank storage facilities have been and will continue to be the subject of increasing regulation at the federal level. At a minimum, tank owners and operators must be aware of registration, installation, operation, closure, and financial responsibility requirements, all of which must be documented. Further complicating matters for the tank facility manager is the fact that these requirements are sometimes overlapping and continually evolving. The existence of this universe of regulations calls for periodic compliance reviews to ensure that all new regulatory requirements are met and that overlapping requirements are fulfilled as efficiently as possible.

14

Risk Assessment

By W. Caffey Norman III[*]

Quantitative risk assessment (QRA) is the name given to a quasi-scientific process used by regulatory agencies to predict the probability of developing a particular disease (most often cancer) as a result of exposure to a specific agent. QRA was used initially to evaluate carcinogenic risk in populations exposed to radiation.[1] With relatively little modification, the techniques and assumptions applied to radiation now form the basis for assessing carcinogenic risk from exposure to chemical substances. Such risk assessment, in turn, underpins regulatory standard-setting by federal and state regulatory agencies with responsibility for public health, the environment, the workplace, food and drugs, and consumer protection.[2]

This chapter describes the components of QRA. It then reviews some of the principal federal regulatory programs where QRA is applied in establishing regulatory standards.

I. Components of Carcinogenic Risk Assessment

A four-step process for carcinogenic risk assessment articulated by a National Academy of Sciences committee in 1983 is widely accepted throughout the federal government and by state regulatory agencies.[3] The first step, hazard identification, is intended to determine whether exposure to a given substance may increase a person's risk of developing cancer. The next step, dose-response evaluation, examines to what degree the likelihood of developing cancer changes as exposure increases. The third step, exposure assessment, attempts to quantify the amount of a carcinogen to which people may be exposed. The final step, risk characterization, combines these inputs to yield an

---

[*] The author would like to thank Gregg A. Rothschild for his assistance in the preparation of this chapter.

[1] *See* U.S. Nuclear Regulatory Comm'n, Reactor Safety Study: An Assessment of Accident Risks in the U.S. Commercial Nuclear Power Plants WASH-1400, NUREG-75/014 (1975) (also known as the Rasmussen Report).

[2] There are currently proposals before Congress that would tie the elevation of the Environmental Protection Agency (EPA) to the Cabinet to a mandate that EPA conduct risk assessment and cost-benefit analysis for all regulations.

[3] Committee on the Institutional Means for Assessment of Risks to Public Health, National Academy of Sciences, Risk Assessment in the Federal Government: Managing the Process (1983).

overall estimate of risk. This is typically expressed as a single numerical value representing the incremental lifetime risk of cancer from exposure to a particular substance at a specific level of exposure. Sometimes the risk characterization will be accompanied by a discussion detailing the assumptions and uncertainties underlying the risk estimate.

It is important to bear in mind that risk assessment involves statistical extrapolations of an unknown future rather than certain actuarial risks of a known phenomenon. Actuarial risks, such as the likelihood of dying in an automobile or airplane crash, can readily be computed from existing empirical data. This allows the prediction of future risks with a relatively high degree of certainty. Current QRA procedures, in contrast, employ highly conservative assumptions about an unknown future and then extrapolate probabilities based on those assumptions. Consequently, predictions derived from QRA should never be viewed as precise or accurate predictions of risk derived from empirical data.[4]

A. Hazard Identification

Hazard identification invariably relies on either epidemiology studies or long-term rodent bioassays. Epidemiology studies, which measure associations between exposure of defined human populations to an agent and the frequency of cancer in the study population, are by far the most reliable source of evidence.

Because risk managers wish to identify potential human carcinogens before human cancers have been caused, they often must resort to tests on animals. The most frequently used test, the long-term rodent bioassay, is conducted on the assumption that a substance that causes cancer in rodents will have the same effect on the human population. Since 1976, bioassays have been conducted by the National Cancer Institute (NCI) (subsequently this function was transferred to the National Toxicology Program (NTP) of the Department of Health and Human Services) under a standard protocol whereby 50 animals of two different species (usually mice and rats) are exposed to several dose levels of the suspected carcinogen for two years. The dose levels chosen are the maximum tolerated dose (MTD)—the highest dose that the species can tolerate—and fractions thereof (MTD/2, MTD/4).

Several hundred substances have been shown to be carcinogenic in mice or rats based on animal studies carried out by NCI, NTP, and elsewhere. Where a substance is shown to be carcinogenic in mice but not rats (or vice versa), the obvious question is which species is the better predictor of human effects. More fundamentally, if a bioassay in mice does not accurately predict the response in rats, rodents of similar size, diet, and lifespan, how can it be expected to predict the response in a much larger, longer-lived mammal with some very different biological parameters?

The relevance of animal bioassay results for humans depends on the accuracy of a great many assumptions, including some of questionable validity.

---

[4] Daniel Wartenberg & Caron Chess, *Risky Business: The Inexact Art of Hazard Assessment* 17, THE SCIENCES, March/April 1992.

A fundamental assumption underlying QRA is that a substance that induces an excess tumor at the MTD will also induce tumors at dose levels hundreds or thousands of times lower than the MTD, on the theory that cancer can be caused by a single molecule of a carcinogen interacting with deoxyribonucleic acid (DNA) in a single cell. Thus, regulatory agencies routinely extrapolate results of tests conducted at the MTD to the much lower levels of exposure that humans experience. There is considerable doubt within the scientific community that such extrapolation is accurate or appropriate,[5] and a growing feeling that the large sums of money spent conducting rodent bioassays could better be allocated to developing more sensitive, accurate, and cost-effective alternatives.[6]

Nevertheless, hazard identification based on animal bioassay results (and, occasionally, human evidence) continues to drive the regulatory process. Three of the more important listings of potential human carcinogens are briefly described below:

1. Annual Report on Carcinogens

In 1978, Congress amended the Public Health Service Act to direct the Secretary of Health and Human Services to publish an Annual Report on Carcinogens. This report, prepared by NTP on a somewhat less than annual basis, must contain a list of all substances that either are known to be carcinogens or that may reasonably be anticipated to be carcinogens.[7] In 1988, several associations brought an action challenging the methodology by which NTP lists substances in the report as reasonably anticipated to be carcinogens. Essentially, the associations alleged that NTP automatically listed any substance for which there was bioassay evidence of carcinogenicity in animals, without considering additional data that would indicate whether the bioassay results were relevant for humans. Such information might include evidence of a mechanism for the rodent tumors (e.g., a protein associated with kidney tumors in male rats that is not present in mice or humans) or of species differences in uptake, metabolism, and pharmacokinetics of a toxic substance.

In rejecting the associations' arguments, the court held that nothing in the 1978 amendments suggests that NTP must use such a "weight-of-the-evidence" approach in preparing the Annual Report.[8] The court held that "[p]harmacokinetics and mechanisms of action data are not relevant to determining the threshold question of whether a substance is a potential human carcinogen," thus blessing NTP's practice of mechanically listing any substance with positive results in a bioassay. The court recognized, however, that "[o]nce a substance has been determined to be a potential human carcinogen, pharmacokinetics and mechanisms of action data then become relevant to estimating the level or extent of the substance's cancer risk in humans for purposes of determining what regulation, if any, is appropriate."[9]

---

[5] Bryan E. Butterworth et al., *The Rodent Cancer Test: An Assay Under Siege* 1, Chem. Indus. Inst. of Toxicology, *Activities*, September 1991.

[6] Lester B. Lave et al., *Information Value of the Rodent Bioassay,* 336 NATURE 631, 633 (1988).

[7] 42 U.S.C. §241(b)(4) (1989).

[8] Synthetic Organic Chems. Mfrs. Ass'n v. Secretary, Department of Health & Human Servs., 720 F. Supp. 1244 (W.D. La. 1989).

[9] *Id.* at 1257.

2. IARC Monographs

In 1969, the International Agency for the Research of Cancer (IARC) initiated a program to evaluate the carcinogenic risk of certain substances to humans and to produce monographs on individual chemicals. The principal classifications used by IARC are as follows:

Group 1: Carcinogenic to humans
Group 2A: Probably carcinogenic to humans
Group 2B: Possibly carcinogenic to humans
Group 3: Not classifiable as to human carcinogenicity

Group 1 requires sufficient epidemiological evidence. Group 2 covers a broad range of agents, from those where the human evidence is almost sufficient to those with no human data at all but sufficient experimental evidence. Substances in Group 3 typically have only limited experimental evidence. The significance of the IARC listing for regulatory officials is the following statement:

> In the absence of adequate data on humans, it is biologically plausible and prudent to regard agents for which there is sufficient evidence of carcinogenicity in experimental animals as if they presented a carcinogenic risk to humans.[10]

Indeed, many state laws and the Hazard Communication Standard of the federal Occupational Safety and Health Administration tie labeling or regulation of substances as carcinogens to their classification by IARC or listing in the Annual Report on Carcinogens.[11]

3. EPA Guidelines

The Environmental Protection Agency (EPA) has adopted a somewhat less rigid approach in principle to the classification of substances with regard to potential human carcinogenicity.[12] The EPA guidelines require all data to be reviewed and the overall weight of the evidence to be evaluated. Both positive and negative evidence of carcinogenicity in humans and animals are to be considered. After all the evidence is weighed, a substance is assigned one of the following carcinogen classifications:

Group A: Known human carcinogen
Group B: Probable human carcinogen
Group C: Possible human carcinogen
Group D: Not classifiable as to human carcinogenicity
Group E: Evidence of noncarcinogenicity for humans.[13]

EPA's application of these guidelines in the past has tended to be fairly mechanical; substances with positive bioassay results have been classified in Group B, even where there is evidence of a mechanism or metabolic difference

[10] International Agency for Research on Cancer, IARC Monographs on the Evaluation of Carcinogenic Risks to Humans, Overall Evaluations of Carcinogenicity: An Updating of IARC Monographs Volumes 1 to 42, Supp. 7 at 30 (Lyon, France, 1987).
[11] *E.g.*, 29 C.F.R. §1910, 1200(d)(4).
[12] Guidelines for Carcinogenic Risk Assessment, 51 Fed. Reg. 33,992, 33,994 (1986).
[13] *Id.* at 33,996–34,000.

suggesting that effects in humans are unlikely. EPA is in the process of revising the guidelines with a view to improving its ability to take such data into account.[14] An EPA official recently indicated that revisions to the guidelines will not be made until EPA has an opportunity to review a congressionally mandated National Academy of Sciences report.[15]

B. Dose-Response Evaluation

Once it is determined that a substance poses a carcinogenic hazard, the next step in risk assessment is to determine the relationship between the dose to which a person may be exposed and the probability of inducing a response. In this step, the concept of a threshold—the dose of a substance below which no adverse effects will occur—is important. Dose-response relationships for a given substance are ordinarily determined by exposing rodents to a variety of doses of the substance and observing its adverse effects. The lowest dose producing such an effect on the animals is labeled the lowest-observable-adverse-effect level (LOAEL). The next dose tested below the LOAEL is labeled the no-observable-adverse-effect level (NOAEL). The threshold dose is assumed to lie somewhere in between these two dose levels. When regulatory agencies base standards on noncancer health effects, they routinely divide the NOAEL by a safety factor to account for potential differences in the human and rodent response levels and to protect more sensitive segments of the human population. The safety factor will generally be 100 or 1,000, resulting in a standard that is 1/100 or 1/1,000 the rodent NOAEL.

For carcinogens, the threshold model has generally been discarded by regulators because of the assumption that any dose of a carcinogen, no matter how small, can lead to cancer. Many scientists question the failure of the nonthreshhold approach to account for biological responses that would be expected to neutralize any toxic effect from low doses of relatively nontoxic substances, particularly where there is no effect on DNA.

The heart of the dose-response evaluation for carcinogens is the mathematical procedure used to extrapolate the effects seen at high doses. While several models are available, a linearized multistage (LMS) model is generally used by the regulatory agencies. While other models (e.g., Weibull, probit) sometimes provide a better fit to the data points, the LMS model is generally favored because it is a conservative method for developing unit risk estimates (or q_1*'s):

> Scientists derive the critical low-dose potency parameter, the so-called q_1*, by applying LMS to the tumor incidence data in rodents. The q_1* is the upper ninety-five percent confidence limit on the linear term of the dose-response function. This linear term is produced by the LMS model's linearization of the data: the model assumes that the dose-response relationship is linear at low doses, regardless of the shape of the dose-response curve within the range of tested doses. The q_1*, which is an estimate of the carcinogenic strength of a compound based on the LMS

[14] Office of Research and Development, Environmental Protection Agency, Working Paper for Considering Draft Revisions to the U.S. EPA Guidelines for Cancer Risk, November 1992.

[15] Pesticide & Toxic Chemical News, Sept. 29, 1993, at 5. See Section II.B. below.

model is an estimate of a substance's relative ability to cause tumors if it in fact is a carcinogenic agent.[16]

In addition to the 95 percent upper confidence limit, it is possible to use the LMS to derive so-called maximum likelihood estimates (MLEs). Use of the MLE results is a more realistic estimate of risk than the 95 percent upper bound.

C. Exposure Assessment

The next step, exposure assessment, is designed to determine the level of exposure of a given population to a substance. Exposure can take place through inhalation, ingestion of drinking water or food, or dermal absorption. Exposure assessment may be evaluated for two risk universes—population risk and maximum individual risk. Population risk represents the incidence of disease in the overall population related to a particular substance. The person at maximum individual risk is the person who suffers the largest incremental risk from a particular substance. This person, generally referred to as the Maximally Exposed Individual (MEI), is the person expected to receive the greatest lifetime exposure from a particular source (i.e., a person living on the fenceline of a chemical production facility). A risk assessment using the MEI will typically incorporate assumptions that the MEI is exposed outdoors to the source 24 hours a day, 7 days a week, 52 weeks a year for 70 years. Obviously, such a scenario never exists.

As a way to reduce the uncertainty inherent in this part of the assessment process, some have advocated using a Maximally Exposed Actual Person (MEAP) model rather than the traditional MEI approach. While the MEI is designed to estimate worst-case exposure, the MEAP allows for a more realistic estimate of exposure by focusing on the most exposed person while producing a central estimate of MEAP exposure as well as a distribution of possible MEAP exposures. Following the MEAP model, central estimates of exposure were found to be 1/30 to 1/300 of the predicted worst-case MEI exposures.[17] Most regulatory agencies have continued to use the MEI approach, however.

D. Risk Characterization

A numerical risk estimate is the product of the q_1* and the measured or predicted exposure. The calculation provides an estimate of the increased incidence of cancer (typically over a lifetime) from the particular level of exposure.

Because there is so much conservatism built into each risk estimate, EPA has stated that it should be viewed only as the upper bound of likely risk. The actual risk, according to EPA, is somewhere between the upper-bound estimate

[16] Alon Rosenthal et al., *Legislating Acceptable Cancer Risk from Exposure to Toxic Chemicals,* 19 Ecology L.Q. 269, 288 (1992).

[17] Neil C. Hawkins, *Conservatism in Maximally Exposed Individual (MEI) Predictive Exposure Assessments: A First-Cut Analysis,* 14 Regulatory Toxicology and Pharmacology 107–117 (1991).

and zero.[18] EPA also cautions that the full range of uncertainties must be provided along with a numerical estimate because of the imprecision inherent in the risk assessment process. Unfortunately, this rarely happens in practice. EPA typically develops risk estimates for substances in Group C under its guidelines, even though it may not regulate such substances as carcinogens. This naturally causes confusion for the public, which assumes that if a cancer risk can be computed, the substance must pose a significant public health risk.

II. Carcinogenic Risk Assessment Under Federal Statutes

Congress has been unwilling to provide specific guidance regarding the level of protection the regulatory agencies must provide against carcinogenic risk. Indeed, Congress has been so vague in this area that Justice Rehnquist, in a notable concurrence in *Industrial Union Department v. American Petroleum Institute*,[19] would have held parts of section 6(b)(5) of the Occupational Safety and Health Act to be void as unconstitutional under the nondelegation doctrine. This refusal to provide meaningful guidance has allowed Congress to avoid responsibility for difficult decisions on politically sensitive environmental questions while retaining the ability to criticize regulatory officials.

Aside from the zero-risk Delaney Clause described below, Congress has typically chosen to take one of two approaches: (i) technology-based standards, requiring equipment or practices that will limit, for example, emissions to a level of technological achievability; or (ii) health-based standards that require levels of a pollutant to remain below the concentration deemed to pose a risk to health or the environment. Some statutes blend the two approaches. Each has obvious flaws. A polluter may meet applicable technology-based standards using state-of-the-art equipment and still cause exposure to hazardous substances at unsafe levels. On the other hand, achieving a health-based standard may cost many billions of dollars to avoid a single theoretical cancer incidence. Indeed, it may be impossible to achieve a completely safe level for a ubiquitous contaminant at any price. The conservatism inherent in risk assessment adds to the difficulty faced by regulatory agencies that must adopt health-based standards.

One result of the diverse mandates driving regulation by different regulatory agencies is the adoption of divergent acceptable levels of risk by different agencies and even by the same agency in different statutory contexts. For example, at EPA, there appears to be a tendency to regulate substances in order to reduce lifetime cancer risk below the broad range of 10^{-4} to 10^{-6}. In other words, individual risks greater than 10^{-4} are highly likely to be regulated while risks less than 10^{-6} are rarely regulated. The Occupational Safety and Health Administration (OSHA), on the other hand, does not tend to regulate risk lower than 10^{-3} where there are feasibility constraints.[20]

---

[18] Guidelines for Carcinogen Risk Assessment, 51 Fed. Reg. 33,992, 33,997–98 (1986).

[19] 448 U.S. 607 (1980) (Rehnquist, J., concurring). The Supreme Court has not used this doctrine to invalidate a congressional enactment since the *Schecter Poultry* decision in 1935 (295 U.S. 495).

[20] Rosenthal, *supra* note 16, at 321.

A comparison of the way QRA has been used to implement a wide variety of statutes follows.

A. Occupational Safety and Health Act

In 1970, Congress enacted the Occupational Safety and Health Act.[21] Under this Act, OSHA is responsible for adopting and enforcing standards that limit workplace exposure to air contaminants that pose material health risks. Section 3(8) of the Act defines an "occupational safety and health standard" as a standard that is "reasonably necessary or appropriate to provide safe or healthful employment."[22]

The Act provides essentially three statutory mechanisms for establishing standards for protection from hazardous substances. Section 6(a) authorized OSHA to adopt standards already in existence as national consensus standards as "startup standards" to be effective during the first two years that the Act was in effect.[23] Section 6(b) authorizes OSHA to issue new permanent exposure standards in rulemaking proceedings.[24] And section 6(c) authorizes OSHA to issue emergency temporary standards that require immediate action to reduce a workplace hazard when employees are exposed to a "grave danger."[25] Standards issued under section 6(c) must be followed by the establishment of permanent standards under 6(b).[26]

Where toxic materials or harmful physical agents are concerned, section 6(b)(5) requires that OSHA set a standard "which most adequately assures, to the extent feasible, on the basis of the best available evidence, that no employee will suffer material impairment of health or functional capacity."[27] In the most important judicial decision concerning QRA, the Supreme Court held that OSHA had to demonstrate that exposure at the current permissible exposure limit presented a "significant risk" to workers before a lower limit could be adopted.[28] Because it had been established that benzene was a human carcinogen, OSHA had taken the position that no safe exposure level could be determined and therefore that section 6(b)(5) mandated the agency to set the exposure limit at the lowest feasible level as long as it would not impair the viability of the industries regulated. OSHA had set an exposure limit of 1 ppm (the consensus standard had been 10 ppm), maintaining that there can be no safe level for a carcinogen.

Rejecting the standard, the Supreme Court found that "the language and structure of the Act, as well as its legislative history, indicated that it never

[21] 29 U.S.C. §651 *et seq.* (1989).

[22] 29 U.S.C. §652(8) (1989).

[23] 29 U.S.C. §655(a) (1989); *See also* §3(9), 29 U.S.C. §652(9) defining the term "national consensus standard."

[24] 29 U.S.C. §655(b) (1989). From 1972 to 1988, OSHA adopted 24 standards under this authority. A recent effort by OSHA to follow short-cut procedures to update the limits for 428 workplace contaminants was overturned by the Eleventh Circuit, which held that the procedures resulted in inadequate findings for judicial review. AFL-CIO v. OSHA, 965 F.2d 962 (11th Cir. 1992).

[25] 29 U.S.C. §655(c) (1989).

[26] 29 U.S.C. §655(c)(3) (1989).

[27] 29 U.S.C. §655(b)(5) (1989).

[28] Industrial Union Dep't v. American Petroleum Inst., 448 U.S. 607 (1980) (*Benzene*).

intended to require the elimination, as far as feasible, of insignificant risks of harm.''[29] The Court held that, before promulgating a workplace standard under section 6(b)(5), the Secretary must make a threshold finding that the workplace in question is unsafe in the sense that significant risks are present and can be eliminated or lessened by a change in practices.[30] The Court noted that under OSHA's policy of regulating simply on the basis of carcinogenicity, evidence that a substance is a carcinogen at some level would justify the conclusion that the agent poses some risk of harm ''no matter how minute the exposure'' and ''no matter how many experts testified that they regarded the risks as insignificant.''[31] The Court then concluded that such an approach constituted an abdication of OSHA's ''threshold responsibility'' of demonstrating the necessity for more stringent standards.[32]

Under current practice, OSHA considers a number of factors when determining whether a substance poses a significant risk to workers. These factors include the type of risk presented, the quality of the underlying data, the reasonableness of the risk assessment, the statistical significance of the findings, and the significance of risk. OSHA also weighs whether the regulatory provisions being considered will substantially reduce the identified risks, and whether the provisions are cost-effective and technologically and economically feasible.[33] Once OSHA determines that such a significant risk does exist in a particular workplace, and that the risk can be reduced by regulatory action, it must then promulgate regulations which comply with section 6(b)(5). In *American Textile Manufacturers Institute v. Donovan,*[34] the Supreme Court interpreted this statutory responsibility as requiring OSHA to submit the most protective standard possible to eliminate a significant risk of material health impairment, subject to technological and economic feasibility.

B. Clean Air Act

The Clean Air Act (CAA),[35] when originally enacted in 1970, required EPA to set emission standards for carcinogens and other air pollutants listed as hazardous air pollutants under section 112. The emission standards were to be set at a level that would ''protect the public health'' with an ''ample margin of safety.''[36] EPA made extensive use of risk assessment analysis in its attempts to determine the extent of potential cancer risk attributable to various industrial sources of air toxics.

At the outset EPA had a great deal of difficulty implementing the ''ample margin of safety'' standard. This caused rulemaking under the CAA to proceed very slowly. If interpreted literally, the ''ample margin of safety'' standard could be construed to require zero emissions for carcinogens, at enormous

[29] *Id.* at 641.
[30] *Id.* at 642.
[31] *Id.* at 645.
[32] *Id.* at 659.
[33] Proposed Workplace Standard for Methylene Chloride, 56 Fed. Reg. 57,036, 57,100 (1991).
[34] 452 U.S. 490 (1981).
[35] 42 U.S.C. §7401 *et seq.* (1989 & Supp. III 1991).
[36] CAA §112(b)(1)(B), 42 U.S.C. §7412(b)(1)(B) (1989).

societal cost. Even if the language did not mandate a zero risk standard, many at EPA felt that the national emission standards for hazardous air pollutants (NESHAPs) were an inefficient use of resources given the enormous cost of reductions in relatively small potential risks.

The delay in rulemaking resulted in substantial litigation. In the most important of these decisions, *Natural Resources Defense Council v. Environmental Protection Agency* (*Vinyl Chloride*),[37] the U.S. Court of Appeals for the District of Columbia Circuit ordered EPA to adopt rules to set safe levels of carcinogenic emissions without regard to cost or technological feasibility. The court also expressed a view as to how EPA should determine what constitutes an "acceptable risk." The court endorsed risk assessment as long as it is "based on realistic assumptions and utilizes the best available scientific information" and noted that the use of QRA "will always be marked by scientific uncertainty."[38] The court also recognized that the evaluation of risk must be adjusted to reflect the inherent uncertainties in the process, especially when a straight-line extrapolation is used, because "there is no particular reason to think that the actual line of the incidence of harm is represented by a straight line."[39]

In response to *Vinyl Chloride,* EPA adopted a new approach for setting NESHAPs. The Air Office would regulate as carcinogens only those compounds classified in Category A or B under the guidelines for carcinogenic risk assessment. Risk assessments for stationary sources would be calculated using the theoretical MEI approach. When calculating risk for mobile sources, however, EPA chose to use a population risk approach rather than the individual risk approach. EPA chose the population risk approach in order to prevent a source from subjecting a large population to small individual risks, which would produce a high estimated population incidence of cancer while not greatly increasing individual risk. Under EPA's new policy, risk to the MEI could not exceed 10^{-4}, and as many people as possible would be protected from 10^{-6} risks.[40]

While EPA's policy was quite reasonable in light of the statutory language and *Vinyl Chloride,* Congress understood that a health-based approach to standard-setting under section 112 would continue to result in long delays in regulating sources of hazardous air pollutants. Therefore, in 1990, Congress amended the Clean Air Act to adopt a technology-based approach, requiring EPA to adopt a rigorous schedule of standards for various sources. The standards would, in turn, generally require such sources to attain the emission levels reached by the best-controlled sources in their sector using maximum achievable control technology (MACT).

Congress was concerned that even after application of a technology-based standard, emissions of air toxics might still pose a danger to public health. It therefore included a requirement for an additional round of standards to deal with this so-called residual risk. By November 1996, EPA must report to Congress on any remaining risks to public health or the environment after the

[37] 824 F.2d 1146 (D.C. Cir. 1987), *rev'g* 804 F.2d 710 (D.C. Cir. 1986).

[38] *Id.* at 1165.

[39] *Id.*

[40] Proposed NESHAP for Benzene, 54 Fed. Reg. 38,083, 38,089–91 (1989).

adoption of the technology-based standards.[41] If Congress fails to enact legislation based on the EPA report, EPA must promulgate standards dealing with residual risk if such standards are necessary to provide an ample margin of safety to protect public health or to prevent an adverse environmental effect (taking into account cost, safety, energy, and other relevant factors).[42]

To facilitate EPA's use of better science, Congress called for a review by the National Academy of Sciences (NAS) of risk assessment methodology used by EPA in determining carcinogenic and other risks associated with exposure to hazardous air pollutants.[43] The results of this review were to be reported to EPA and the Congress by May 15, 1993.[44] The NAS review was delayed, however, and the published report is expected in May 1994. A pre-publication version was released by NAS on January 19, 1994.[45] The report specifies a number of improvements the EPA should incorporate into its risk assessment process.

C. Safe Drinking Water Act

The Safe Drinking Water Act (SDWA)[46] requires EPA to establish drinking water standards. Standards generally consist of maximum contaminant levels (MCLs) for specified contaminants, although in some cases treatment technology is specified in lieu of MCLs. Before setting a MCL for a contaminant, EPA must establish a nonenforceable maximum contaminant level goal (MCLG). The MCLG must be set at the level where no adverse effects on the health of a person are believed to occur and which allows ''an adequate margin of safety.'' The MCL must then be established at a level as near the MCLG as is ''feasible with the use of the best technology, treatment techniques, and other means which the EPA finds after examination for efficacy under field conditions . . . are available (taking costs into consideration).''[47] As under the current Clean Air Act, Congress recognized that only by taking technological and economic feasibility into account could EPA develop a workable program of drinking water standards.

The Office of Drinking Water (ODW) has set MCLGs for substances that are known or probable human carcinogens (Groups A and B) at zero while it sets MCLGs for agents classified as possible human carcinogens (Group C) at a level above zero on the basis of a noncarcinogenic endpoint with additional safety factors.[48] In one of the few instances where EPA has taken into account mechanism of action data in standard-setting, EPA placed para-dichlorobenzene in Group C under its guidelines and assigned it a nonzero MCLG based on evidence that the mechanism by which it caused kidney tumors in rats was of limited relevance to humans.[49]

---

[41] CAA §112(f)(1), 42 U.S.C. §7412(f)(1) (Supp. III 1991).
[42] CAA §112(f)(2)(A), 42 U.S.C. §7412(f)(2)(A) (Supp. III 1991).
[43] CAA §112(f)(1)(A), 42 U.S.C. §7412(f)(1)(A) (Supp. III 1991).
[44] CAA §112(o)(4), 42 U.S.C. §7412(o)(4) (Supp. III 1991).
[45] NAS Press Release, Jan. 18, 1994.
[46] 42 U.S.C. §300f *et seq.* (1989).
[47] 42 U.S.C. §300g-l(b)(4), (b)(5) (1989).
[48] *See* 40 C.F.R. §141.50–.52 (1992).
[49] National Primary Drinking Water Regulations, 52 Fed. Reg. 25,690, 25,696 (1987).

More recently, EPA adopted a zero MCLG for perchloroethylene even though it had been unable because of resistance from its Science Advisory Board to classify perchloroethylene in Group B.[50] EPA had based its proposed zero MCLG for perchloroethylene on its expected classification in Group B.[51] The Agency took the position in the final rule that its decision as to potential carcinogenicity under the SDWA was separate from its classification of perchloroethylene under its guidelines for carcinogenic risk assessment. The U.S. Court of Appeals for the District of Columbia Circuit upheld this approach.[52]

D. Clean Water Act

The Clean Water Act (CWA)[53] requires EPA to publish a list of toxic pollutants and then adopt a set of technology-based limits for these pollutants.[54] Each toxic pollutant listed under the CWA must be subject to effluent limitations resulting from the application of the best available technology economically achievable.[55] Releases of toxic pollutants are regulated by industry-specific effluent guidelines and pretreatment standards that are developed within the limitations of the available control technologies.[56] Additionally, all publicly owned treatment works, as well as many generators of industrial wastewater, must obtain a national pollutant discharge elimination system (NPDES) permit that implements the effluent limits and may further limit releases of toxics in effluents beyond federal limits.[57]

In addition to technology-based regulations, the CWA also provides for water quality standards. Although primary responsibility for setting ambient water quality standards is placed on the states, the standards must be approved by EPA's regional offices.[58] To assist the states, EPA's Office of Water has set additional guidelines, called Ambient Water Quality Criteria, that recommend acceptable concentrations of toxics in waters that may support aquatic life for potential human consumption or may be used as a potable water source.[59] EPA relies on QRA in developing the water quality criteria.[60] Criteria for carcinogens are based on an acceptable level of individual risk of 10^{-6}.

E. Federal Insecticide, Fungicide, and Rodenticide Act; Federal Food, Drug, and Cosmetic Act—The Delaney Clause

Two statutes govern the use of pesticides in the United States. The Federal Food, Drug, and Cosmetic Act (FFDCA)[61] authorizes EPA to regulate the use

---

[50] National Primary Drinking Water Regulations, 56 Fed. Reg. 3526, 3541 (1991).
[51] 54 Fed. Reg. 22,068 (1989).
[52] International Fabricare Inst. v. EPA, 972 F.2d 384 (D.C. Cir. 1992).
[53] 33 U.S.C. §1251 *et seq.* (1989 & Supp. III 1991).
[54] 33 U.S.C. §1317(a)(2) (1989).
[55] *Id.*
[56] 40 C.F.R. §§401, 403 (1992).
[57] 40 C.F.R. §122 (1992).
[58] CWA §303(a), 33 U.S.C. §1313(a) (1989); 40 C.F.R. §131.5 (1992).
[59] CWA §304(a)(1), 33 U.S.C. §1314(a)(1), (3) (1989).
[60] See generally 33 U.S.C. §1314 (1989).
[61] 21 U.S.C. §301 *et seq.* (1989 & Supp. III 1991).

of pesticides deemed likely to appear on human foods. The Federal Insecticide, Fungicide, and Rodenticide Act (FIFRA)[62] requires EPA to decide what pesticide uses will be registered.

The Delaney Clause of the FFDCA establishes a clear and unambiguous standard. It prohibits any pesticide residue "if it is found . . . to induce cancer when ingested by man or animal, or if it is found, after tests which are appropriate for the evaluation of the safety of food additives, to induce cancer in man or animal."[63] On its face, therefore, the Delaney Clause forbids the use of any carcinogenic pesticide without regard to whether, by use of QRA or otherwise, a regulatory agency has judged that it is unlikely to pose a threat to human health.

Nevertheless, EPA has attempted to use QRA in regulating pesticides.[64] Because a finding of cancer risk would mean complete prohibition under the clause, EPA was especially concerned that a strict interpretation of the Delaney Clause as applied to new pesticides would damage industry and would serve to prevent the replacement of older pesticides with safer new ones. EPA began to divide pesticides into two categories—those that pose only a negligible risk and those that pose a greater risk and are worthy of greater scrutiny.[65] EPA came to rely on risk assessment in implementing this negligible risk policy, especially in the area of hazard identification. The EPA Office of Pesticide Programs (OPP) applied the Delaney Clause to Group C carcinogens only if the estimated risk would be greater than negligible.[66]

In 1992, however, the Ninth Circuit held that EPA's so-called negligible risk policy violated the clear and unambiguous language of the Delaney Clause and struck down EPA's interpretation of the Act.[67] In its ruling the court held that once EPA determines that a pesticide induces cancer in humans or animals, then the Agency loses all discretion and must prohibit its use as a food additive. In response to this decision, the Administration has proposed amendments to the FFDCA that would replace the Delaney Clause with health-based standards for pesticide residues.[68]

FIFRA provides EPA with the statutory mandate to regulate the use of all new pesticides in the United States,[69] and to suspend the use of pesticides already on the market. The statute directs EPA to withdraw permission to use a pesticide if there are "unreasonable adverse effects on the environment" which the statute defines as "any unreasonable risk to man or the environment, taking into account the economic, social and environmental costs and benefits of the use of any pesticide."[70] In 1971, the D.C. Circuit added teeth to this language by holding that the statute "places a heavy burden on any administrative officer

[62] 7 U.S.C. §136 *et seq.* (1989 & Supp. III 1991).

[63] 21 U.S.C. §348(c)(3)(A) (1989).

[64] Regulation of Pesticides in Food: Addressing the Delaney Paradox, Policy Statement, 53 Fed. Reg. 41,104 (1988).

[65] *Id.* at 41,112.

[66] *Id.*

[67] Les v. Reilly, 968 F.2d 985 (9th Cir. 1992), *cert. denied,* 113 S. Ct. 1361 (1993).

[68] Inside EPA, Sept. 24, 1993, at 5.

[69] FIFRA §2(a), 7 U.S.C. §136a(a), 136a(a) (1989).

[70] FIFRA §2(bb), 7 U.S.C. §136(bb) (1989).

to explain the basis for his decision to permit the continued use of a chemical known to produce cancer in experimental animals.''[71]

EPA has used risk assessment analysis to implement this broad regulatory authorization. The OPP closely examines all pesticides categorized as Group A or Group B while considering those in Group C on a case-by-case basis. When assessing exposure, OPP does not use the MEI approach, but instead uses a very conservative population-based approach. This approach makes assumptions about crop applications that are so high that they could never actually occur.[72]

F. Toxic Substances Control Act

The Toxic Substances Control Act (TSCA)[73] contains a narrative standard that is similar to the one contained in FIFRA. For example, TSCA's definition of substances considered ''hazardous,'' those which carry ''unreasonable risk of injury to health or the environment,'' is derived from FIFRA's definition of ''imminent hazard.''[74] EPA's Office of Toxic Substances (OTS) maintains responsibility for implementing TSCA. In so doing, OTS has made extensive use of QRA.

Instead of using the maximally exposed person approach described above, OTS considers a reasonable worst-case scenario in its assessment of potential cancer risk for new chemicals or new uses of existing chemicals. This approach is based on the potential risk a substance poses to a worker in an occupational setting or that of a consumer using a product. For example, in assessing potential cancer risk from chemicals used in paints, a reasonable worst-case scenario might be that of a professional painter who paints six or seven hours a day in a poorly ventilated room over a 35-year period. While risk assessments of new chemicals are based primarily on scenarios of individual risk, without regard to the potential size of the exposed population, OTS assessments of existing chemicals typically estimate both individual and population risks.

Although OTS has not yet formalized its risk management criteria, it has operated under certain general guidelines. OTS has interpreted TSCA to exclude situations in which lifetime individual risk is less than 10^{-6}.[75] And OTS considers both individual risk and population risk when deciding whether a substance requires regulation. For instance, in deciding to phase out the use of asbestos in almost all products over a seven-year period, OTS concluded that the rule would prevent 200 cases of cancer and would also relieve certain highly exposed individuals of a 10^{-3} lifetime excess cancer risk. OTS cited both of these factors when justifying the costs caused by suspending the use of asbestos.[76]

---

[71] Environmental Defense Fund v. Ruckelshaus, 439 F.2d 584, 596 n.41 (D.C. Cir. 1971).

[72] Rosenthal, *supra* note 16, at 305–06.

[73] 15 U.S.C. §2601 *et seq.* (1989 & Supp. III 1991).

[74] TSCA §6(a), 15 U.S.C. §2605(a) (1989), FIFRA §2(l), 7 U.S.C. §136(l) (1989).

[75] Rosenthal, *supra* note 16, at 308–09.

[76] *See* Asbestos: Proposed Mining and Import Restrictions and Proposed Manufacturing, Importation, and Processing Prohibitions, 51 Fed. Reg. 3738 (1986).

III. Conclusion

Agencies maintain considerable latitude in translating narrative legislative directives into specific risk assessment and risk management decisions. This discretion has spawned differences among and within agencies over what exposure levels of a substance constitute a human health risk.

In regulating human exposure to a variety of toxic substances, federal agencies rely heavily on a risk assessment process that is quite conservative in its assumptions. Whether data from high-dose animal experiments can be accurately extrapolated to human beings is a subject of continuing debate. Because of the conservative nature of the assumptions made in using these data in models upon which projections of human risk can be based, the risk estimate often far exceeds the actual level of risk. Agency officials responsible for risk management should bear in mind that the output of current risk assessment methodology generally represents the upper-bound level of risk. The actual risk lies somewhere between the risk estimate and zero.

15

Environmental Auditing

By Timothy A. Vanderver, Jr. and J. Gordon Arbuckle
with David J. Farber

I. Introduction

Preceding chapters have emphasized the increasing scope and complexity of environmental law. Concomitant with this development is the continuing rise in the intensity of government and private enforcement efforts. Companies of all sizes face increasing potential and actual criminal and civil liability. As a result, industry increasingly needs orderly processes for reliably answering a broad range of environmental questions. These include: "Is this facility in compliance?" "Does this facility have the management systems in place to achieve and maintain compliance?" "Does this facility or company we are about to acquire or this product we are about to sell bring with it environmental risks and attendant liabilities?"

To meet these needs, environmental assessments and audits have already been incorporated by much of American industry as an integral part of many business operations or transactions. These assessments and audits serve to inform management of the environmental strengths and weaknesses of current or future operations, and aid management in evaluating the viability of product lines or facilities. Environmental assessments are also routinely conducted as part of any property or business acquisition.[1]

Before discussing the practical aspects of auditing, it is important to distinguish how an audit differs both from operational activities and from environmental assessments. Unlike day-to-day environmental programs for a particular facility or company, which typically assign line managers the responsibility for obtaining permits and complying with governing environmental regulations, an environmental assessment is an organized manner of looking at a particular subject to determine whether or not the subject meets a certain

[1] Preliminary assessments, sometimes referred to as "Phase I" assessments, are often required by banks or other financial institutions as a prerequisite to an acquisition. While the focus of this chapter is on operational auditing as opposed to transactional auditing, many of the same principles apply. For more information about transactional audits, *see* EPA Lender Liability Rule, 40 C.F.R. pt. 300, Subpart L, 57 Fed. Reg. 18,343 (1992); EPA Guidance on Landowner Liability under Section 107(a)(1) and De Minimis Settlements under Section 122(g)(1)(B) of CERCLA and Settlements with Prospective Purchasers of Contaminated Property, June 6, 1989, supplemented May 1991.

compliance objective. An audit is a particular form of assessment intended to verify the existence (or nonexistence) of certain conditions.

Ironically, for all the attention given to environmental audits, the auditing process remains largely undefined. There is no industry consensus of what an audit must accomplish, how broad an audit's scope ought be, or even how an audit should be conducted. Rather, the audit has always been and remains an open-ended process with no set limits or guidelines. While EPA's auditing policy has defined an audit as "a systematic, documented, periodic and objective review by regulated entities of facility operations and practices related to meeting environmental requirements,"[2] neither its policy statement nor any statute or regulation sets out in detail any standardized audit requirements. Nor have such requirements been specified by any trade association or standards-setting organization.

Several general observations can be made. Typically, the audit is conducted by a third party professional for the purpose of validating or verifying circumstances at a particular point in time. An independent team usually performs a systematic review, based upon a methodology appropriate to the particular goals set by management and to the particular facility or group of facilities under review. Thus, audits are often designed to "verify compliance with environmental requirements; evaluate the effectiveness of environmental management systems already in place; or assess risks from regulated and unregulated materials and practices."[3] The ultimate objective is to advise management with respect to environmental compliance or liability exposure.

It must be emphasized that an audit cannot substitute for a comprehensive environmental compliance program. The audit is simply one of several tools in a compliance program, a tool which can be used by management to verify whether the compliance program is effective and meets management's needs. This purpose—informing management and identifying potential or current flaws in a compliance program—is relatively limited. Thus, this chapter assumes that a compliance program that manages day-to-day environmental issues is already in place.

This chapter is an introduction to environmental auditing. After reviewing in Section II why a company may implement an auditing program, Section III considers how to appropriately tailor the audit's scope. Section IV considers how to design an audit, including a discussion of relevant confidentiality issues, and Section V describes the audit team. Section VI outlines how an audit might be conducted, and Section VII describes the necessity for an audit report and its preparation.

II. The Purposes of Auditing

As noted above, management may decide to undertake an audit for a variety of reasons. Perhaps the foremost reason is to enable management to develop an understanding of the impact of environmental issues on business. While most audits only provide a "snapshot" review of current operating

[2] EPA Environmental Auditing Policy Statement (EPA Policy or EPA Auditing Policy), 51 Fed. Reg. 25,004, 25,006 (July 9, 1986).

[3] *Id.*

conditions (as opposed to reviewing historical practices or projecting future operations), they can provide management with a current perspective of the company's operations and levels of current compliance. Audits can also be performed to assess the viability of future investments, either with respect to upgrading current facilities, expanding operations, or acquiring new facilities or product lines.

A second reason for auditing is to evaluate the company's potential environmental liabilities. Federal enforcement powers under statutes such as the Resource Conservation and Recovery Act (RCRA),[4] the Safe Drinking Water Act (SDWA),[5] the Clean Air Act (CAA),[6] the Comprehensive Environmental Response, Compensation and Liability Act (CERCLA),[7] and the Toxic Substances Control Act (TSCA)[8] pose significant risks to any industrial operation. In addition to civil fines potentially reaching into the hundreds of thousands of dollars (whether for intentional conduct or not), many of these statutes also include criminal penalties that can be enforced against either the company or management. For example, under the Clean Air Act, any person who "knowingly" violates applicable environmental regulations may be fined up to $25,000 per day of violation and imprisoned for up to five years.[9] Under the SDWA, a "willful" violation of applicable law may be punished by comparable sanctions.[10]

In addition to governmental liabilities, management may want to evaluate the company's exposure to private parties. Potential third party liabilities may exist under the "citizen suit" provisions incorporated into such environmental statutes as CERCLA, RCRA, and the SDWA,[11] and under traditional common law theories of trespass, nuisance, strict liability, and possibly even ultrahazardous activity.

A third reason to conduct audits is to satisfy the current regulatory emphasis on self-audits and prevention. A company's demonstration of "environmental good faith" may limit or mitigate possible criminal or civil penalties the government may seek for a violation. EPA's auditing policy makes clear that

> [i]n fashioning enforcement responses to violations, EPA policy is to take into account, on a case-by-case basis, the honest and genuine efforts of regulated entities to avoid and promptly correct violations and underlying environmental problems. When regulated entities take reasonable precautions to avoid non-

[4] 42 U.S.C. §6901 (1988) *et seq.* RCRA §3008, 42 U.S.C. §6928, provides for civil penalties up to $25,000 per day for permit violations, and criminal penalties of $50,000 per day or two years in jail for "knowing" violations, and double such fines for repeat violations. An intentional imminent endangerment of others can trigger $250,000 per person and $1,000,000 per company of fines and up to 15 years in prison.

[5] 42 U.S.C. §300-f *et seq.* (1988). SDWA §1423(b), 42 U.S.C. §300-h(2)(b), provides for civil penalties of $25,000 per day or up to three years in prison for "willful" violations.

[6] 42 U.S.C. §7401 *et seq.* (1988 & Supp. II 1990). CAA §113, 42 U.S.C. §7413, provides for civil penalties of up to $25,000 per day, and criminal penalties of up to five years in prison for "knowing" violations.

[7] 42 U.S.C. §9601 *et seq.* (1988). CERCLA §103(c), 42 U.S.C. §9603(c), provides for penalties of up to $10,000 per day for each day of noncompliance with reporting and other requirements or a criminal penalty of up to three years imprisonment.

[8] 15 U.S.C. §2601 *et seq.* (1988). TSCA §16(b), 15 U.S.C. §2615(b), provides for up to $25,000 or one year in prison for violations of the Act.

[9] *See supra* note 6.

[10] *See supra* note 5.

[11] *See* CERCLA §310, 42 U.S.C. §9659; RCRA §7002, 42 U.S.C. §6972; SDWA §1449, 42 U.S.C. §300j-8.

> compliance, expeditiously correct underlying environmental problems discovered through audits or other means, and implement measures to prevent their recurrence, EPA may exercise its discretion to consider such actions as honest and genuine efforts to assure compliance.[12]

Similarly, the U.S. Department of Justice has indicated that it will take into account voluntary auditing and disclosure efforts in its criminal prosecutions of environmental crimes.

> It is the policy of the Department of Justice to encourage self-auditing, self-policing and voluntary disclosure of environmental violations by the regulated community by indicating that these activities are viewed as mitigating factors in the Department's exercise of criminal environmental enforcement discretion.[13]

Congress has also articulated its preference for self-auditing and voluntary disclosure. The Conference Report to the Clean Air Act Amendments of 1990[14] implicitly acknowledges the beneficial purpose of an audit, noting that "knowledge gained by an individual solely in conducting an audit or while attempting to correct any deficiencies identified in the audit or the audit report itself should not ordinarily form the basis of the intent which results in criminal penalties."[15] Congressional and administrative pronouncements provide industry with little assurance that instituting a rigorous auditing program may have any real mitigating effect on subsequent enforcement actions, and the potential risks inherent in voluntary disclosure are not clearly compensated by these open-ended statements of potential mitigation. Even so, management should recognize that undertaking an auditing program may assist in any later enforcement action.[16]

A fourth reason to conduct an audit is to identify and prevent future problems. As EPA has noted, "[a]lthough environmental laws do not require a regulated facility to have an auditing program, ultimate responsibility for the environmental performance of the facility lies with top management, which therefore has a strong incentive to use reasonable means, such as environmental auditing, to secure reliable information of facility compliance status."[17] By undertaking a methodical review of operations and their potential impact upon the environment, management may prevent future noncompliance and possible attendant enforcement efforts.[18]

Finally, an audit may be required to fulfill certain legal requirements. In the past few years, EPA has required the implementation of an auditing program as

---

[12] EPA Policy, *supra* note 2, 51 Fed. Reg. at 25,007.

[13] U.S. Dep't of Justice, Factors in Decisions on Criminal Prosecution for Environmental Violations in the Context of Significant Voluntary Compliance or Disclosure Efforts by the Violator 1, 4 (July 1, 1991) (unpublished memo) [hereinafter Justice Policy]. See the discussion of this memorandum in Chapter 16, Enforcement and Defense Strategies.

[14] Section 113(c) of the 1990 Clean Air Act Amendments added certain criminal and civil penalties for both knowing and negligent violations of the Act's requirements. 42 U.S.C. §7413.

[15] H.R. Conf. Rep. No. 952, Conference Report to Accompany S. 1630 (Clean Air Act Amendments of 1990), 101st Cong., 2d Sess. 348 (1990).

[16] The existence of a regularized auditing procedure may also be used as evidence of due care in defense of any private party negligence claims.

[17] EPA Policy, 51 Fed. Reg. at 25,006–07.

[18] Both EPA and the Justice Department highlight this function of the audit as serving to evidence good faith. *See* Justice Policy, *supra* note 13, at 4 (prosecuting attorney should inquire whether "safeguards beyond those required by law [have] been developed and implemented to prevent noncompliance from occurring"); EPA Policy, 51 Fed. Reg. at 25,007 (same).

a condition of settlement agreements and consent orders reached with companies subject to both civil and criminal enforcement. EPA's Audit Policy makes clear that the Agency "may propose environmental auditing provisions in consent decrees and in other settlement negotiations where auditing could provide a remedy for identified problems and reduce the likelihood of similar problems recurring in the future."[19] In recent years, numerous companies, including several Fortune 500 companies, have entered into agreements containing auditing requirements.[20] Similarly, other companies have voluntarily agreed to conduct audits in an effort to avoid both governmental and private litigation.[21]

As with environmental enforcement in general, audits will increasingly make their way into settlement agreements and consent orders in the coming years. Although the federal government already has authority under Chapter 8 of the U.S. Sentencing Commission's Guidelines Manual to order a program to detect and prevent violations,[22] legislation has recently been introduced to expand that authority, and to explicitly give the courts the authority to require an environmental audit as part of any proposed criminal violation of numerous environmental statutes.[23]

The securities laws' disclosure obligations may also require undertaking an audit to ensure that the company has not inadvertently failed to disclose certain environmental liabilities.[24] Thus, by conducting an audit, the company

---

[19] EPA Policy, 51 Fed. Reg. at 25,007 (footnote omitted).

[20] *See, e.g.,* United States v. Browning-Ferris Indus. Chem. Servs., 704 F. Supp. 1355, 1360 (M.D. La. 1988) (including environmental audit as part of consent decree); United States v. Unichem Int'l, Inc., 1990 WL 264544 (D. Wyo. Nov. 5, 1990) (requiring audit as part of criminal settlement). The *Browning-Ferris* consent decree contains considerable detail addressing the scope of the audit, the selection of the audit firm, the preparation of an audit plan, audit report, compliance plan, and corporate management systems report, and finally outlines the uses of the audit by the regulatory agency. 704 F. Supp. at 1374–79. Other companies that have agreed to auditing provisions include Union Carbide, Eagle Picher Industries, E.I. DuPont de Nemours & Co., Menominee Paper Co., and Rhone-Poulenc. *See* Letter from Acting Assistant Attorney General Barry M. Hartman to Congressman Charles Schumer, February 7, 1992, *cited in* 7 Tox. L. Rep. (BNA) at 557 (Sept. 30, 1992).

[21] At least one company anticipating a major expansion of its facility has preempted the litigation process and negotiated an agreement with a local environmental group to conduct an independent audit. *See* 7 Tox. L. Rep. (BNA) at 413 (Sept. 2, 1992).

[22] *See* United States Sentencing Commission, *Federal Sentencing Guidelines Manual* §8D1.4(c) (1992); *see also Statement of Acting Assistant Attorney General for Department of Justice's Environment and Natural Resource Div. before House Subcomm. on Crime and Criminal Justice* at 17 (June 11, 1992).

[23] *See* Environmental Crimes Act of 1992, H.R. 5305, 102d Cong., 2d Sess. (1992); *see also* Omnibus Crime Control Act of 1991, S. 1605, 102d Cong., 1st Sess. (1991). Although the Environmental Crimes Act has been opposed by both the Justice Department and EPA on the grounds that there may be constitutional problems with having the courts administer environmental audits, these legislative efforts are a harbinger of increased statutory attention to environmental auditing.

[24] In SEC v. United States Steel Corp., [1979–80 Transfer Binder] Fed. Sec. L. Rep. (CCH) ¶82,319 (Oct. 18, 1979), the SEC, relying on Securities Act Release No. 5170 (July 19, 1971), Securities Act Release No. 5386 (Apr. 20, 1973), and Securities Act Release No. 5704 (May 6, 1976), found that U.S. Steel failed to comply with applicable disclosure statutes in filing its Form 10K and Form S-7 by not disclosing material environmental liabilities or potential outlays necessary to comply with environmental statutes. In approving U.S. Steel's settlement offer, the Commission required it to conduct a comprehensive environmental audit which would identify its environmental problems and recommend solutions to be reviewed and enacted by the company's audit committee. *See also* SEC v. Occidental Petroleum Corp., [1980 Transfer Binder] Fed. Sec. L. Rep. (CCH) ¶82,622 (July 16, 1980); Regulation S-K, Item 101(c)(1)(xii), 17 C.F.R. 229.101(c)(1)(xii) (requiring disclosure of environmental conditions).

For a discussion of how the disclosure of environmental liabilities can be used in the tender offer and proxy fight context, *see* Koppers Co. v. American Express Co., 689 F. Supp. 1371, 1406–07 (W.D. Pa. 1988); Paperworkers v. International Paper Co., 1992 WL 198430 (S.D.N.Y. Aug. 17, 1992).

can readily have the knowledge necessary to include in its 10K or other Securities and Exchange Commission (SEC) filings, and may save time and expense of dealing with the SEC in the context of an enforcement action related to nondisclosure of material facts.

III. Scope of the Audit

The above discussion makes clear that there are a variety of reasons a company may decide to undertake an audit. Obviously, management's objectives in seeking an audit will dictate, in large measure, the scope and type of work to be performed. Even within the parameters set by management, however, the audit can be conducted in a variety of ways. This section outlines several different ways of defining the scope of an audit.

No two audits will be alike. Some audits may review operations at an entire subsidiary or division, while others may focus solely on a single plant or facility. Others may be broadened to include the entire company, while yet others may be narrowed to a particular function or operation.[25]

Even if an audit only examines a particular function or operation, its scope can vary. Thus, an audit could focus on (1) whether the company has an effective compliance assessment and validation program in effect, (2) whether systems are in place to manage environmental issues and crises, (3) an assessment of the environmental liabilities associated with a particular product line, (4) potential liability as a transporter/disposer of hazardous materials, (5) the health and safety implications of operations, (6) the company's waste minimization efforts, or (7) how the company optimizes material uses. For example, if the company was a generator of a significant waste stream that has given rise to CERCLA liabilities, it may be interested in auditing its past and present waste streams and disposal practices to evaluate and project future liabilities. Similarly, if a particular operation involves the handling of volatile chemicals, an evaluation of the operation from a health and safety perspective, as well as from a liability assessment perspective, may be appropriate.

Because the audit only provides a "snapshot" of operations, its value may be limited even if appropriately tailored in scope. To compensate for this, management should consider broadening the applicability of the audit beyond the particular operation or facility at issue and using the audit to identify ongoing (or generic) compliance problems. By conducting a historical review and making recommendations that apply to the entire company, rather than just addressing a particular facility or specific operation or division, the value of the audit can be greatly enhanced. Thus, if the audit addresses such issues as whether (1) monitoring is being done in compliance with applicable requirements, (2) proper agency notification procedures are in place, (3) all necessary environmental controls are in effect, and (4) appropriate and effective corporate

---

[25] EPA's definition of the audit as a review of "facility operations and practices related to meeting environmental requirements," EPA Policy, *supra* note 2, 51 Fed. Reg. at 25,008, gives little, if any, guidance on what the Agency views the proper scope of an audit to be and implicitly recognizes the elusive nature of standardizing audits.

policies exist and are being implemented, the company will be able to maximize the return on its investment in the auditing process.[26]

Particularly if a company is interested in evaluating its potential legal exposures, reviewing past operations is critical to any audit. This is particularly true since environmental liabilities under CERCLA can be retroactive, and yesterday's acceptable practices can be the subject of today's enforcement activity.[27]

As broad as the audit process is, it cannot replace an ongoing environmental compliance program. In the environmental field, where continuous and daily compliance should be the rule, using the audit as a sporadic "find it and fix it approach" will fall dramatically short of the requirements imposed by law and regulation. Although audits may be effective in pointing management in the right direction, even the broadest audit cannot fulfill the functions of an effective continuing compliance program.

IV. Designing the Audit

A. Methodology

Once the company has decided upon the goals and scope of the audit, the audit team (discussed below) can begin to design the audit. The team must choose a methodology to be applied to the range of facilities or operations under consideration. There are at least five principal methodologies that can be used: (1) the substance-by-substance approach, (2) the unit process approach, (3) the disposal method approach, (4) the legal requirements analysis, and (5) the management systems approach. Although there is some overlap between these methods, each yields a different focus of evaluation, and the use of these overlapping methodologies assures far greater effectiveness in identifying problems or "soft spots"—areas where risk is high and improvement is needed.

1. Substance-by-Substance Approach

The substance-by-substance approach focuses on the uses of a particular substance or group of substances, and considers the implications of their use. This approach is particularly effective in evaluating potential liability under CERCLA, RCRA, EPCRA (the Emergency Planning and Community Right-to-Know Act), and TSCA, which regulate "lists" of substances and waste streams.

The first step in a substance-by-substance evaluation is to identify the relevant substances. CERCLA, RCRA, and numerous other environmental

---

[26] The Justice Department's prosecution policy specifically addresses the "questions [that] should be asked [by] any program: Was there a strong institutional policy to comply with all environmental requirements? Had safeguards beyond those required by existing law been developed and implemented to prevent noncompliance from occurring? Were there regular procedures, including internal or external compliance and management audits, to evaluate, detect, prevent and remedy circumstances like those that led to the noncompliance? Were there procedures and safeguards to ensure the integrity of any audit conducted? Did the audit evaluate all sources of pollution (i.e., all media), including the possibility of cross-media transfers of pollutants?" Justice Policy, *supra* note 13, at 4–5.

[27] *See* CERCLA §107, 42 U.S.C. §9607.

statutes regulate substances either as toxins, carcinogens, or hazardous substances, and these lists should be reviewed prior to beginning any audit design.[28] In addition, because CERCLA regulates certain waste streams as hazardous,[29] attention must also be given to potential waste streams. Once the "listed" substances have been identified, a review of the facility's operations can be conducted to "inventory" which substances the audit should address.

The inventory of substances should be as broad as possible, and consider the use of substances on the facility's production lines, in its laboratories, and as raw material. There also may be numerous nonproduction related uses in which the listed substances may be found. For example, PCBs may be found in electrical equipment unrelated to the operations or production lines at the facility. Similarly, garages or truck bays, which are only peripherally related to manufacturing operations, may also contain oils, waste oils, or solvents.

If the audit is being conducted to identify potential liabilities arising out of past disposal practices, a review of the substances and waste streams involved in the facility's past operations will also be needed. This review should focus on substances previously used in either discontinued or modified operations. Particularly given the retroactivity of CERCLA and some other environmental statutes, this historical review is essential if a proper evaluation of potential liability is needed. Finally, a review of past, current, and anticipated future disposal practices should be conducted to identify all waste streams and substances that are disposed from the facility, either during an intermediate step in the production process or at the end of the process.

Once the substance inventory is complete, the audit should undertake a comprehensive review of how each substance arrives, is used, and is disposed of. Particular attention should be focused on when the substance is introduced to the facility (i.e., how it arrives and where it is stored), when it is introduced into the manufacturing process, and how it is used. As noted above, any changes in the substance during the manufacturing process or any intermediate losses should be noted, so that the audit can properly account for potential liabilities or management processes relevant to these steps. The audit should identify how each substance is ultimately disposed of to ensure that the audit encompasses a "cradle-to-grave" analysis of the substance's use.

Lastly, the audit designer should keep in mind the legal ramifications of the substance's use at each point on the process line.[30] For example, because air emissions may implicate permit requirements under the Clean Air Act, storage of intermediate and final wastes may implicate the status of the facility as a

[28] *See, e.g.*, CERCLA List of Hazardous Substances and Reportable Quantities, 40 C.F.R. §302.4, Table 302.4 (1992); Conventional Water Pollutant List, 40 C.F.R. §401.16 (1992); National Primary and Secondary Ambient Air Quality Standards, 40 C.F.R. §50 (1992); Initial List of Hazardous Air Pollutants set by 1990 Clean Air Act Amendments, Title III of 1990 Clean Air Act Amendments §112, 42 U.S.C. §7412; Maximum Concentration of Contaminants for the Toxicity Characteristic, 40 C.F.R. §261.24, Table 1 (1992); Clean Water Act List of 126 Priority Pollutants, 40 C.F.R. §423, App. A (1992); RCRA Groundwater Monitoring List, 40 C.F.R. §264, App. IX (1992); RCRA List of Hazardous Wastes, 40 C.F.R. §261.33 (1992); National Primary Drinking Water Standards, Maximum Contaminant Levels and Maximum Contaminant Level Goals, 40 C.F.R. §141.11–.16, 141.50–.52 (1992); and National Secondary Drinking Water Regulations, Secondary Maximum Contaminant Levels, 40 C.F.R. §143.3 (1992).

[29] *See, e.g.*, CERCLA List of Hazardous Substances and Reportable Quantities, 40 C.F.R. §302.4, Table 302.4.

[30] The necessity of incorporating some of the legal requirements analysis is a good example of how the methodologies overlap.

treatment, storage, or disposal (TSD) facility under RCRA, use of the substance may trigger EPCRA notification requirements, and ultimate disposal may implicate CERCLA, the auditor must evaluate the substance under each of these statutory regimes.

2. *Unit Process Approach*

In contrast to the substance approach, the unit process approach addresses a particular product line or process within a facility. The focus of the audit is to understand the environmental risks associated with a particular phase or aspect of the manufacturing process.[31] Each aspect of the process under consideration should be examined to determine whether it is a closed system (i.e., whether there are no actual or potential releases from the system into the environment) or an open system (i.e., releases can or do occur). If the system is open, the audit must consider each point within the system that does or could cause a release.

The audit should account for each manufacturing, maintenance, disposal, mechanical, storage, raw material, and transportation element involved in the process. In this review, the design should identify and account for all interim and final discharge points, as well as all spill and other environmental controls that exist. Once identified, these unit components should be compared with the legal requirements for environmental hazards posed by the system.

For example, if a manufacturing operation was being analyzed, the audit should account for all on-site storage of materials (whether or not used in a particular process), the on-site energy generation equipment attendant to the unit, and all on-site laboratories involved in the manufacturing process. Even such "nonprocess" areas as the surrounding grounds, the parking areas, and administrative offices should be included in any unit process audit.

3. *Disposal Method Approach*

The disposal method approach reviews all interim and final disposal points, with little attention to the processes that generate the wastes or the inputs (such as raw materials and risks inherent in their storage and usage). Instead, the purpose of this type of audit is to identify the actual and potential waste streams from a particular facility.[32]

The audit should identify all air emissions, water discharges, and land discharges from the facility in an effort to characterize the release, the volume of the materials released, and the emission control devices in place to manage such releases. The audit should also compare the releases with applicable legal requirements, and assess exposures and current compliance status.

For water discharges, the audit should consider how much waste is being released into water sources, the waste's toxicity, whether the release is to a publicly owned treatment works (POTW) or to an on-site treatment system, the frequency of the discharge, the concentrations of the discharge, and any predis-

---

[31] The scope of the audit will define what "units" are to be analyzed. For example, if the scope of the audit is facilitywide, the unit analysis could be applied on a component-by-component basis. Alternately, if the focus of the audit is on a particular production line, the "unit" may be defined as that line.

[32] *See* Justice Policy, *supra* note 13, at 4 (noting that Department will consider whether the "audit evaluate[d] all sources of pollution (i.e., all media), including the possibility of cross-media transfers of pollutants").

charge treatments. The audit should also evaluate whether the releases comply with applicable national pollutant discharge elimination system (NPDES) permit limitations. If the water discharges are to a POTW, the audit should identify the POTW and address pretreatment of the waste, as well as any characteristics of the waste (either as a function of volume, concentration, or toxicity) that may affect the POTW's operations.

If air emissions are implicated, the audit should examine the quantity and quality of the emissions, and evaluate whether they are in compliance with limits imposed by state implementation plans (SIPs), federal prevention of significant deterioration (PSD) or nonattainment area permit requirements, or any new source performance standards (NSPS) that may apply. The air emissions should also be reviewed to identify the characteristics of emissions from each source and the controls in place to regulate these emissions.

For "solid waste" or land disposal subject to RCRA and CERCLA, the audit should ascertain whether each waste is a "hazardous waste." If so, the audit should assess compliance with the RCRA hazardous waste management regulations. Similarly, the audit should determine whether the facility qualifies as a "small quantity" or "reuse/recycle" generator, which may exempt it from certain RCRA requirements. The audit should also verify that each facility at which waste is being stored, treated, and disposed of has appropriate RCRA permits and meets all other applicable requirements. Finally, if the facility is transporting its own waste off-site, the audit should identify how such transportation is being carried out, and whether Department of Transportation and EPA authorizations have been obtained.

4. *Legal Requirement Analyses*

A fourth method is the legal requirements analysis. As its name suggests, this approach involves a review of all applicable federal, state, and local laws and regulations,[33] followed by a determination of which are applicable to the facilities under consideration.

EPA's 1986 Auditing Policy specifies the following statutes as applicable: the Clean Air Act, RCRA, Clean Water Act, the Hazardous Materials Transportation Act, TSCA, CERCLA, SDWA, FIFRA, the Marine Protection, Research, and Sanctuaries Act, and the Uranium Mill Tailings Radiation Control Act.[34] In addition, EPCRA should be an integral part of any legal requirements analysis, as well as all applicable state and local regulations, including those that have been delegated from EPA to the states.

Once a comprehensive review of potentially applicable laws is completed, the audit should determine which apply and whether these legal requirements are being met. The audit should also consider the facility's past legal problems, including any enforcement actions that may have been brought, in an effort to ascertain compliance history. The audit should also consider the facility's past operations in light of such retroactive statutes as CERCLA.

[33] Although this review is inherent in the three other methods listed above, this approach places far greater emphasis on the regulatory requirements, and only then compares those that are potentially applicable to facility operations.

[34] EPA Policy, *supra* note 2, 51 Fed. Reg. at 25,009 n.1.

Finally, the audit should account for statutory obligations requiring a facility to anticipate future problems. For example, the Clean Water Act requires a facility to prepare a Spill Prevention Control and Countermeasure (SPCC) Plan, which must include a series of contingency plans for potential spills. Thus, it is not enough for the audit to consider the facility's current or past operations. It must also consider future risks and analyze whether statutory obligations regarding these risks are being met.

5. Management Systems Approach

This evaluation approach is often most productive in terms of long-term contribution to an organization's ability to come into and stay in compliance. It does not substitute the auditors' judgment for that of management in determining how the organization should be structured. Instead, it simply asks whether the company has in place some assignment of responsibility and an orderly way of approaching the basic issues of environmental compliance such as the following:

- How do we determine what the laws and regulations require of us, make that information understandable to the employees who need to know, and communicate it to them effectively?
- What chemicals come into our plants and where do they go?
- What records do we keep and which do we destroy?
- How do we budget for environmental compliance and how are priorities determined?
- Who notifies when we have a release, who do they call, and what do they say?[35]

These questions are often both painful to ask and difficult to answer. However, from the perspective of long-term contribution to the organization's compliance status, they are often the most important part of the audit.

B. Organizational and Policy Issues

Once the audit's scope and methodology have been fixed, organizational and policy issues must be addressed. First, management must clearly communicate to the entire company its full support for the audit. All participants in the audit, including lower level managers and employees, must understand the serious nature of the audit and management's commitment to follow through on the audit's recommendations. As noted in the EPA Policy statement:

> Management support may be demonstrated by a written policy articulating upper management support for the auditing program, and for compliance with all pertinent requirements, including corporate policies and permit requirements as well as federal, state, and local statutes and regulations.
>
> Management support for the auditing program also should be demonstrated by an explicit written commitment to follow-up on audit findings to correct identified problems and prevent their recurrence.[36]

---

[35] These questions are illustrative. For other factors to be considered in the management systems approach, see Chapter 17, Compliance Management and Strategies, at Section II.E.

[36] EPA Policy, *supra* note 2, 51 Fed. Reg. at 25,009.

Second, the audit must determine what corporate policies addressing environmental issues already are in place. Such an inquiry should include investigating current procedures, written and oral policies, and historical corporate practices. If the audit finds such policies lacking, the audit team should consider proposing appropriate policies in the audit report. The audit should also determine what corporate lines of organization exist, and ensure that a chain of command is in place to effectuate the company's environmental policies.

The audit may also address implementation of corporate policies regarding (1) apparent or actual legal violations discovered by employees, (2) employee concealment of environmental information, (3) the filing of false reports and inaccurate compliance information, and (4) how and when the company will defend an employee accused of environmental crimes.[37] The EPA Audit Policy suggests several policies that should be developed, including, among others, organizational environmental policies to "implement regulatory requirements" and policies to "provide management guidance for environmental hazards not specifically addressed in regulations."[38]

C. Confidentiality

One critical issue that must be addressed prior to the initiation of the audit is confidentiality. The auditing process can often provide a company's adversaries with a road map to its environmental problems, and there is the potential for the audit's disclosure in an enforcement action or in litigation which can have significant adverse consequences. Accordingly, it is important to determine early in the auditing process whether the audit will need to be kept confidential and, if so, to take the necessary steps to ensure confidentiality.

EPA has recognized that in certain circumstances audits should be entitled to some degree of confidentiality: "EPA acknowledges regulated entities' need to self-evaluate environmental performance with some measure of privacy and encourages such activity."[39] Even so, no matter how confidential the audit is, it may uncover information that the company is statutorily obligated to disclose to EPA or others.[40] Further, a court may order disclosure of the audit in litigation, which might provide evidence of the company's noncompliance with environmental regulations. These adversary proceedings can include both private party

[37] The Department of Justice often reviews such policies in the enforcement context:

> Effective internal disciplinary action is crucial to any compliance program. The attorney for the Department should consider whether there was an effective system of discipline for employees who violated company environmental compliance policies. Did the disciplinary system establish an awareness in other employees that unlawful conduct would not be condoned?

Justice Policy, *supra* note 13, at 5.

[38] EPA Policy, *supra* note 2, 51 Fed. Reg. at 25,009 n.2.

[39] *Id.* at 25,007.

[40] EPA's policy states:

> [A]udit reports may not shield monitoring, compliance, or other information that would otherwise be reportable and/or accessible to EPA, even if there is no explicit "requirement" to generate the data.

EPA Policy, *supra* note 2, 51 Fed. Reg. at 25,007. Both state and federal environmental statutes often require a company to report to the regulating agency any known releases of hazardous wastes or other environmental problems. *See, e.g.,* CERCLA §103(a), 42 U.S.C. §9603(a).

actions based on documented noncompliance as well as administrative penalties for prior violations.[41]

There is at least one good reason not to preserve an audit's confidentiality and that is if the company intends to voluntarily disclose the audit report to EPA. Both EPA and the Department of Justice encourage the voluntary disclosure of the audit even where there is no statutory obligation to do so.

> It is the policy of the Department of Justice to encourage self-auditing, self-policing and voluntary disclosure of environmental violations by the regulated community by indicating that these activities are viewed as mitigating factors in the Department's exercise of criminal enforcement discretion.[42]

The discretionary nature of the government's reponse to voluntary disclosure will probably leave most companies feeling uncomfortable. To minimize this feeling, if disclosure is contemplated, a company may consider staging the audit by undertaking an initial informal assessment. Should significant problems be uncovered by this informal assessment, the problems could be corrected before the formal auditing and report stage. Admittedly, this is not the optimal way of using auditing to promote environmental compliance. However, given the government's attempt to require confession as a threshold requirement for the possibility of avoiding criminal prosecution, it may be the only approach available.

Alternatively, the company could take all necessary steps to ensure the confidentiality of the audit, and at the end of the process evaluate whether disclosure is warranted. Of course, this will ensure that the government is shown only audits of those facilities without significant problems, which could heighten the government's perception of the seriousness of problems at other facilities.

There are three privileges under which an audit's confidentiality might be preserved: (1) the attorney-client privilege, (2) the work-product privilege, or (3) the self-regulation privilege. As will be described below, taking the necessary steps under any of the theories does not by any means guarantee that the audit's confidentiality will be preserved. However, close attention to the elements of privilege will maximize the possibility of not being required to disclose. Consultation with counsel is recommended on whether to attempt to protect the report and, if so, how to maximize the likelihood of being able to maintain confidentiality.

1. Attorney-Client Privilege

The attorney-client privilege protects communications between a client and its attorney. The Supreme Court in *Upjohn Co. v. United States,*[43] noted that the privilege exists to allow a client to "giv[e] information to the lawyer to

---

[41] In its policy statement, EPA has specifically reserved the right to request auditing documents in litigation. EPA Policy, *supra* note 2, 51 Fed. Reg. at 25,007 ("EPA's authority to request an audit report, or relevant portions thereof, will be exercised on a case-by-case basis. . . . EPA expects such requests to be limited, most likely focused on particular information needs rather than the entire report").

[42] Justice Policy, *supra* note 13, at 1; *see also* EPA Policy, *supra* note 2, 51 Fed. Reg. at 25,007 ("EPA encourages regulated entities to notify appropriate State or Federal officials of findings which suggest significant environmental or public health risks, even when not specifically required to do so").

[43] 449 U.S. 383, 389 (1981).

enable him to give sound and informed advice,'' as well as to encourage clients to seek early advice.[44] The four elements of the privilege can be summarized as (1) use of an attorney to provide legal and not business advice, (2) communication between the attorney and client or prospective client,[45] (3) confidentiality of the communication, and (4) no waiver of the privilege by disclosure or otherwise.[46]

Although many companies have in-house counsel serve on the audit team to avail themselves of the privilege, it is by no means a guarantee that the privilege will stand if tested. In *United States v. Chevron,*[47] a Clean Air Act case, the court rejected Chevron's privilege claim in its attempt to avoid disclosure of an environmental audit on the grounds that the audit was not prepared by Chevron's attorney in his capacity as an attorney. Although Chevron's in-house counsel was one of the three audit team members, the court rejected Chevron's arguments and ordered disclosure of the audit on the grounds that ''[t]he communication must be between the client and attorney in his or her capacity as an attorney rather than as, for example, a business advisor. Additionally, the communication's primary purpose must be to gain or provide legal assistance.''[48] Although the use of outside counsel lends a heightened sense of confidentiality to the audit process, arguably the *Chevron* reasoning might also be applied to outside counsel.

Even if the audit satisfies the privilege's strictures, a company must carefully monitor participation in and distribution of the audit. All documents related to the audit, including the audit report, should reflect both their privileged nature and the fact that they were created to provide legal advice. Similarly, circulation beyond a limited group of senior corporate personnel could waive any privilege that might otherwise attach. Thus, any communications regarding the audit, as well as the audit report, should be circulated on a need-to-know basis. Again, a company should consult with counsel to create a distribution list of audit-related documents that will minimize the possibility of waiver of the privilege.

2. *Work-Product Privilege*

Similar to the attorney-client privilege, the work-product privilege may also provide a basis for keeping the audit confidential. The work-product privilege protects documents generated by an attorney ''in anticipation of

---

[44] *Id.* at 390.

[45] Communications between the attorney's agent, i.e., any consultants or engineers retained by the attorney, and the attorney are also privileged. *See, e.g.,* United States v. Cote, 456 F.2d 142 (8th Cir. 1972). Note that not every corporate employee may be considered the ''client'' for purposes of the privilege. *See Upjohn,* 449 U.S. at 383, 389. Other considerations, such as whether the privilege protects notes taken at a meeting with counsel or correspondence with counsel circulated within a company are not discussed here, but should be considered in designing the audit.

[46] *See, e.g.,* Admiral Ins. Co. v. United States Dist. Court for the Dist. of Ariz., 881 F.2d 1486, 1492 (9th Cir. 1989).

[47] 1989 WL 121616 (E.D. Pa. Oct. 16, 1989).

[48] *Id.* at *6; *see also* 5 Tox. L. Rep. (BNA), at 1200 (Feb. 27, 1991), *citing* Aerojet-General Corp. v. Argonaut Ins. Co., No. 262425 (Calif. Super. Ct., San Mateo County, Jan. 3, 1991) (ordering disclosure to insurers of environmental audit conducted by engineers on behalf of attorneys on grounds that audits were not prepared for remediation and not for litigation).

litigation.''[49] The leading case of *Hickman v. Taylor,*[50] noted: ''it is essential that a lawyer work with a certain degree of privacy,'' on the grounds that if the protection was not afforded, ''much of what is now put down in writing would remain unwritten.''[51]

Because the work-product document extends only to documents prepared in anticipation of litigation, documents prepared in the normal course of business will not be protected.[52] Thus, in *Diversified Industries, Inc. v. Meredith,*[53] the court found that a law firm's investigative report, which ''could have been performed just as readily by non-lawyers aided to the extent necessary by a firm of public accountants'' did not constitute legal advice. Documents prepared in reasonable anticipation of litigation, however, may be protected by the privilege.[54]

Audits, however, are typically not prepared in anticipation of litigation, or even with the expectation that litigation may ensue. Thus, it is likely that the work-product privilege will not protect an audit.[55] Another limitation of the work-product protection is that it applies only to an attorney's impressions and notes, and it does not apply to underlying facts. For example, if environmental testing is done during the audit, the test results would not benefit from the protection, even if an attorney's analysis of the test results might.

3. *Self-Evaluation Privilege*

In addition to the attorney-client and work-product privileges, a judicially created ''self-evaluation'' privilege may, in certain circumstances, protect an audit from disclosure. The privilege, first articulated in *Bredice v. Doctors Hospitals, Inc.,*[56] was created to permit entities to critically review their internal procedures without risking the possibility that their efforts would create future liabilities.

For example, in *Granger v. National Railroad Passenger Corp.,*[57] the court permitted disclosure of that part of an Amtrak Investigation Committee Report addressing the underlying accident that triggered the report's preparation while preventing disclosure of those sections of the report that contained recommendations designed ''for the purpose of protecting the public by instituting practices assuring safer operations.''[58] Like the report in *Granger,* it could be argued that since the purpose of an environmental audit is to protect the

---

[49] Fed. R. Civ. P. 26(b).

[50] 329 U.S. 495 (1947).

[51] *Id.* at 510–11.

[52] *See, e.g.,* Fed. R. Civ. P. 26(b)(3) Advisory Committee Notes; Simon v. G.D. Searle & Co., 816 F.2d 397, 401 (8th Cir.), *cert. denied,* 484 U.S. 917 (1987); 8 C. Wright & A. Miller, Federal Practice and Procedure §2024, at 198–99 (1970).

[53] 572 F.2d 596, 603 (8th Cir. 1977).

[54] *See* Fed. R. Civ. P. 26(b)(3); *Simon,* 816 F.2d at 397, 401.

[55] *See, e.g.,* 5 Tox. L. Rep. (BNA) at 1200 (Feb. 27, 1991), *citing* Aerojet-General Corp. v. Argonaut Ins. Co., No. 262425 (Calif. Super. Ct., San Mateo County, Jan. 3, 1991) (ordering disclosure of audit because it was not prepared for litigation).

[56] 50 F.R.D. 249 (D.D.C. 1970), *aff'd,* 479 F.2d 920 (D.C. Cir. 1973).

[57] 116 F.R.D. 507 (E.D. Pa. 1987).

[58] *Id.* at 510; *see also* Emerson Elec. Co. v. Schlesinger, 609 F.2d 898, 907 (8th Cir. 1979), which rejected the self-evaluation privilege because the documents sought were not prepared for internal use.

public by "instituting practices assuring safer operations," it too should be protected.

No court has yet ruled on the self-evaluation privilege in the environmental audit context.[59] Companies should, however, consider the possibility of invoking the privilege and correspondingly ensure that the audit includes a statement of the company's interest in the public's safety. To achieve this, the audit should also include a self-critical analysis divorced from any regulatory and litigation proceedings that may be pending. Finally, the factual and analytical aspects of the report should be separated to the extent possible.

V. The Audit Team

An integral part of any auditing process is the audit team. This team will determine which audit methodology should be employed, as well as address the other organizational and policy issues that must be resolved before the audit is undertaken.

The team should consist of a number of independent legal and technical personnel, each of whom brings a particular specialty to the audit process. The EPA Policy notes:

> The status or organizational locus of environmental auditors should be sufficient to ensure objective and unobstructed inquiry, observation and testing. Auditor objectivity should not be impaired by personal relationships, financial or other conflicts of interest, interference with free inquiry or judgment or fear of potential retribution.[60]

As noted above, counsel should be part of the audit team if confidentiality is a concern. Whether outside or in-house counsel is used, the attorney should have authority to specify who the audit team members may communicate with, how the audit should be conducted to preserve confidentiality, and who will receive copies of the audit report or parts thereof.

The audit team may also include either in-house or outside technical staff or consultants. Although using outside consultants and counsel may increase audit cost, outsiders will ensure the independence of the audit team and permit it to operate free of internal bureaucratic pressures that employees might otherwise be subject to. To control costs, one or more in-house counsel might be assigned to the team in order to ensure that the audit remains within budget.

It is essential for lines of communication to be kept clear both between management and personnel, as well as within the audit team itself. An "audit coordinator" should be appointed to create the bridge between the team and the facility or operation being audited. The coordinator should maintain regular communications with shop foremen and other line management to ensure that the audit team is engaged in an open, frank, and honest dialogue with the facility's employees.

A "team leader" should also be appointed to set goals and timetables for the audit team. It is important for the team leader to clearly articulate these goals

[59] There has been some debate between industry and government attorneys regarding the creation of a special self-evaluation privilege for environmental audits. *See* 7 Tox. L. Rep. (BNA) at 398 (Aug. 26, 1992). Presumably, this privilege would be proposed through legislation, which has yet to be introduced.

[60] EPA Policy, *supra* note 2, 51 Fed. Reg. at 25,009.

and timetables so that the audit team members have a realistic expectation and understanding of what is expected of them. Similarly, the team leader, in conjunction with the audit coordinator, should structure the involvement of facility personnel.

Each member of the audit team must develop sensitivities to issues of particular concern to the unit being audited. The audit team should be careful not to conduct an ''inquisition'' of facility staff, nor should the audit leave line employees with the impression that their jobs are at risk because of the audit's potential findings. Similarly, if the facility has recently experienced a significant release or other environmental accident, care should be taken not to place collective blame on the facility for the conduct of a few employees. Only by being sensitive to the particular needs of the facility at issue can the audit team ensure that the information collected will not be sanitized by employees for the perceived purpose of saving their jobs.

VI. Conducting the Audit

Once the audit team is in place, the audit can be designed and carried out. After determining the scope of the audit, designating who will participate in each phase, and choosing a methodology, the audit team can begin the actual audit. Before collecting data, the team should conduct a preliminary site inspection, which reviews the particular facility or unit to be audited from a physical and geographic viewpoint. The audit coordinator should also conduct preliminary interviews with facility management to obtain a sense of what information the employees will be able to provide, their level of sophistication, and any special concerns that will need to be addressed.

Once the preliminary interviews and site inspection are completed, detailed employee questionnaires should be drafted. The questionnaires should address such areas as the facility's layout, the processes used, any written and unwritten company policies in effect, the chain of command at the facility, the individuals responsible for environmental and related issues, a list of all environmental emergency procedures and contingency plans, all environmental training that occurs both on-site and off-site, and any other corporate policies that may affect the subject of the audit. Obviously, the form and scope of the questionnaires will depend upon the audit methodology chosen.

After the questionnaires have been completed and collected, the verification stage can begin. The initial compilation of the data should be completed, and the audit team should familiarize itself with the questionnaire responses. Once this information has been assimilated, a site visit should be conducted. During this visit, the audit team should inspect and review the physical layout of the facility and its operations. The plant manager, several supervisors (including environmental safety supervisors, if any) and selected employees should be interviewed, and their responses compared with the information collected in the questionnaires.[61] These interviews will also serve as a useful way to clarify

[61] Because the questionnaire is often a more effective way of gathering audit information, the site visit is of less importance. Thus, if budget constraints require limiting the scope of the audit process, site visits can be reduced, or, if necessary, even eliminated. Other quality assurance procedures should be in place, however, to ensure the accuracy of the information collected.

ambiguities or inconsistencies in questionnaire responses. The interviews should be coordinated with site visits, and the team members should ensure that they are not confrontational or accusatory in nature.

Further quality assurance might be appropriate even after the site visit and employee interviews. "Quality assurance may be accomplished through supervision, independent internal reviews, external reviews, or a combination of these approaches."[62] Care should be taken even during this stage to guard against the improper disclosure of conclusions that may be confidential, and counsel should be involved in any quality assurance check.

VII. The Audit Report

The final step in completing the environmental audit is preparing the audit report. EPA has defined the audit report as "a written report which candidly and thoroughly presents findings from a review . . . of facility environmental performance and practices."[63] The report should contain a summary stating the audit's goals, conclusions, and recommendations. It should also include photographs and diagrams where appropriate, as well as a section devoted to recommendations. The report should also include an appendix of relevant statutes and regulations, as well as copies of the questionnaire used and all interview notes taken.[64]

If confidentiality is desired, a limited number of copies should be made, and they should be distributed only to a select group of upper management. Plant managers and other facility employees should not receive copies of the report. Rather, extracts of information or recommendations contained in the report can be created for distribution to lower level employees. It may be appropriate to have the report compiled and issued by outside or in-house counsel to preserve any privilege that may attach.

VIII. Conclusion

Although confidentiality is not guaranteed, in today's world of increased legal enforcement, any company with significant environmental risks would be prudent to use the auditing process. While a significant tool in understanding and minimizing environmental risks, the environmental audit is only a small part of a comprehensive environmental compliance program. The auditing

---

[62] EPA Policy, *supra* note 2, 51 Fed. Reg. at 25,009.

[63] *Id.* at 25,007. The Policy also notes that an "audit report is not a substitute for compliance monitoring reports or other reports or records which may be required by EPA or other regulatory agencies." *Id.*

[64] The audit team may also consider creating an "audit manual" memorializing how the audit was conducted, who participated in the audit, and where problems were encountered. An audit manual is particularly useful to companies that have or intend to institute a regular audit program. EPA's ENVIRONMENTAL AUDIT PROGRAM DESIGN GUIDELINES FOR FEDERAL AGENCIES, EPA/130/4-89/001 (August 1989), and GENERIC PROTOCOL FOR ENVIRONMENTAL AUDITS AT FEDERAL FACILITIES, EPA/130/4-89/002 (August 1989), provide good models for such manuals, as well as indicate what EPA considers to be good auditing practices.

process, however, is one of the few steps a company can take to aid in defending itself against enforcement activities.

If the audit receives strong support from management and is executed in a careful and creative manner, it can also prove to be invaluable in educating management as to the risks inherent in an existing operation, as well as inform management's business judgment about the future. Finally, the audit can uncover flaws in current operations, and enhance safety as well as the environment.

16

Enforcement and Defense Strategies

*By Elliott P. Laws and Russell V. Randle**

I. Introduction

The tools Congress has given the enforcers of federal environmental statutes are quite impressive. The federal government has granted itself the authority to discover the most secret details of the operations and processes of an industry. It can force a business to submit to elaborate inspections. It can require, on pain of severe penalties, that expensive corrective measures be implemented. Almost no information is sacred, and with this knowledge the government can act with the aid of the courts. It can impose severe financial penalties and close businesses. It can, after a criminal trial, take away a person's freedom.

When these authorities are focused on a company, an individual, or both, they can be devastating. How can regulated entities respond to an environmental enforcement action? What is the enforcing entity seeking to accomplish? What is the strategy to be implemented? How is success defined?

One phrase aptly states what should be the goal of federal environmental enforcement authorities as well as the targeted company or individual: "To win without fighting is best."[1] There are few regulatory enforcement schemes more weighted in the government's favor and where the regulated entity is left feeling more helpless than under the federal environmental regime. Traditional defenses work badly in this area, and those who rely on them often make the situation worse rather than better for their clients. On the other hand, some of the most successful defenses to federal environmental enforcement actions have been those where no real or traditional "defense" was ever offered. The "triple A" approach of "admitting," "accepting," and "acting" has often left regulated entities in far better condition than those that fought regulators at every turn. As such, a vigorous and contentious defense to enforcement actions may poorly serve the targeted entity's long- (or short-) term best interest.

The federal government has tremendous statutory and regulatory authority to enforce compliance with environmental laws. Coupled with the authority Congress has provided the federal courts, a truly impressive arsenal is in place

---

*The authors would like to thank Anne B. Walton and Parker E. Brugge for their assistance in the preparation of this chapter.

[1] SUN TZU, THE ART OF WAR (SUN-TZU PING FA) (Thomas Cleary, trans., 1988).

to severely punish violations of these statutes and implementing rules, and increasingly to require remedial work to address the consequences of violations. Over the past decade, these powers have been exercised with greatly increased frequency, sophistication, and severity. These trends are demonstrated by the enforcement accomplishments at all three levels of enforcement described below: criminal, civil, and administrative. Moreover, the Environmental Protection Agency's (EPA's) role in enforcement has grown significantly as the Agency has dedicated more resources and developed better strategies for more effective enforcement.[2]

In addition to federal enforcement authorities, many state and local government agencies implement strict enforcement programs. In some instances, state public health and safety legislation covering civil and criminal penalties for environmental offenses is even broader in scope or more stringent than federal provisions. For example, California recently passed a law that would subject corporations and their managers to criminal prosecution for failure to detect and disclose serious concealed dangers, such as environmental or workplace hazards.[3] States such as New Jersey have developed rigorous cleanup requirements to address potential hazardous waste sites.[4] EPA has reported a significant number of state administrative actions and judicial referrals demonstrating many states' commitment to vigorous enforcement policies. For example, in fiscal year (FY) 1989, there were 12,126 administrative actions and 714 civil judicial referrals. The numbers decreased somewhat in FY 1991 with 9,607 administrative actions and 544 civil judicial referrals.[5]

This chapter will examine the following aspects of the federal environmental enforcement system:

- The authorities and policies that underlie general environmental enforcement strategies on the federal level;

---

[2] EPA has implemented a cross-program/multimedia approach to utilize its resources for enforcement more effectively. EPA's investigative strategy includes working closely with other federal agencies. For example, EPA has signed a memorandum of understanding with the Federal Bureau of Investigation that outlines plans for shared training, technical, legal, and investigative support. Similarly, EPA anticipates working with the Occupational Safety and Health Administration (OSHA) to inspect the petrochemical industry, lead smelters, polychlorinated biphenols (PCBs), and asbestos hazards; the U.S. Customs Service to investigate the international shipment of hazardous waste; and the Securities and Exchange Commission and Internal Revenue Service to gather background information on companies' ability to pay fines and whether companies are seeking to deduct fines as business expenses in violation of Internal Revenue Code §167.

In addition, EPA has developed the integrated data enforcement analysis (IDEA), a computer data base and software program that provides companies' compliance history under the air, water, the Resource Conservation and Recovery Act (RCRA), and the Toxic Substances Control Act (TSCA) programs. The program combines and collates information from several enforcement data bases that include geographic information, toxic release inventories under §313 of the Emergency Planning and Community Right-to-Know Act (EPCRA), Dun & Bradstreet, and other sources to detect patterns of pollution and waste emissions.

[3] CAL. PENAL CODE §387 (West 1993). Proof of actual knowledge by a manager or corporation only requires a demonstration that one has information that a "reasonable person in the circumstances in which the manager is situated [would know] that the serious concealed danger exists." *Id.* §387(b)(1)(B)(3). Violations of §387 are punishable by imprisonment for one to three years, fines up to $25,000, or both. A fine as high as $1 million can be assessed against a corporate offender.

[4] Environmental Cleanup Responsibility Act, N.J. STAT. ANN., TIT. 13, CH. IK (1988). Under the New Jersey statute a company targeted by enforcement authorities could be forced to close or change ownership.

[5] Only matters involving the Clean Water Act (CWA), Clean Air Act (CAA), and RCRA (or their state counterpart) are reflected in the number of judicial referrals. The number of administrative actions reflects actions under the Federal Insecticide, Fungicide, and Rodenticide Act (FIFRA) as well as the water, air, and RCRA statutes.

- The laws and court decisions that frame the liabilities that attach to every company and many individuals;
- The rationales that often lead companies and their counsel to depart from the traditional battle cry of "the best defense is a good offense."

In short, this chapter will take a close look at how the various enforcement agencies are likely to respond in a particular situation, and perhaps more important, why.

II. Criminal Enforcement

Clearly the centerpiece of the environmental enforcement regime is the use of the various criminal enforcement authorities. The increasing use of this power by the federal government has brought an added element to the manner in which corporate America conducts its business. Compliance with environmental provisions was initially a "bottom line" or "dollar" concern. Not any longer. With the real prospect of staggering criminal penalties and incarceration, business is being forced to constantly monitor the ever-changing environmental landscape and ensure that it is positioned to protect itself and its employees from violating criminal provisions.

A. Criminal Enforcement Trends and Records

The record of the Environmental Crimes Section[6] of the Department of Justice's Environment and Natural Resources Division reflects the federal government's increasing commitment to vigorous enforcement of environmental laws. Total criminal penalties assessed since the Environmental Crimes Section was created in 1982 through the time of this writing include more than $237 million in fines and imposition of more than 404 years of imprisonment.[7] The number of EPA referrals of criminal cases to the Department of Justice increased from 20 in FY 1982 to an all time high of 81 in FY 1991.[8] These criminal referrals ordinarily involved both individuals and corporations in the same case. The Department of Justice reports an increase from 40 indictments in

[6] Originally established as the Environmental Crimes Unit of the Environmental Enforcement Section, this office coordinates and monitors criminal referrals and their progress throughout the country.

[7] In 1992, the federal government obtained more than $163 million in criminal fines and penalties that included $125 million from a $250 million dollar criminal assessment against Exxon Corp. and Exxon Shipping Co. for the *Valdez* oil spill into the Prince William Sound. Half of that criminal sentence was forgiven in exchange for Exxon's pledges to other environmental safety projects, including its contribution to a response fund for oil spills and commitment of 25% of its total research budget to environmental safety.

[8] EPA implemented a new "bean-counting" method in 1991 that adds actions under cross-program/multimedia efforts separately resulting in a higher total number of referrals to the Department of Justice.

Prior to EPA's referral, a team of Agency personnel headed by a special agent-in-charge at one of the 10 regional offices investigates allegations of criminal wrongdoing. Once the regional attorney develops the case, the file is reviewed by the national enforcement office. If the evidence is sufficient, the case is referred to the Department of Justice. The Department of Justice then presents the matter to a grand jury for investigation and issuance of indictments.

Under a recent agreement proposed between U.S. Attorneys and the Department of Justice, regional attorneys may be permitted to prosecute certain routine environmental violations without first referring the case to the Department of Justice for its approval.

FY 1983 to 125 in FY 1991. During the first 10 months of 1992, the Department of Justice reported a record 191 indictments. Thus far, these figures include the criminal indictments of 1,019 corporations and individuals along with 716 guilty pleas and convictions.[9]

Those subject to environmental laws and regulations can expect the federal enforcement programs to become even more formidable. Since 1988, EPA's enforcement budget has increased over 70 percent. Under current plans, by 1995, EPA will have approximately 200 investigators compared to the 35 to 50 employed in 1990, largely as a result of the requirements of the Oil Pollution Act of 1990.[10] An ambitious environmental enforcement program is politically popular, especially when federal funds for environmental public works programs are stable or shrinking. The government will be devoting more resources to finding polluters, while encouraging public involvement in their efforts through rewards for informers and encouragement of citizen suits.

B. Criminal Enforcement Policy and Objectives

The imposition of severe fines, expensive remedial measures, and, more important, imprisonment for high ranking corporate and government officials are forceful deterrents to environmental crimes. Prosecutors target corporate officers and employees, as well as federal employees, in order to ensure personal accountability for serious environmental crimes. This approach recognizes that criminal convictions punish individuals much more severely than corporations. When threatened with jail, corporate and government officers and employees not only have a powerful incentive to comply personally, but also to prevent others under their supervision from engaging in activities that could result in liability being imputed to them or to their corporation.

For government regulators and prosecutors, the only way to "lose" in this context is to do nothing or to appear as if one is "soft" on environmental violators. It is popular socially and politically to prosecute the environmental polluter.

Few recall former Administrator William Ruckelshaus' comment that the question about enforcement action is not whether it is tough or weak, but whether it is wise or foolish. For instance, a single EPA enforcement action that targets a specific industrial practice for the first time could have a greater deterrent effect than bringing a large number of actions which are similar to cases the Agency has been prosecuting for many years. The fact that the Agency is now prosecuting a violation for the first time will likely cause many companies to conduct a very detailed evaluation of their practices in that area.

By the same token, for the corporate or individual defendant faced with an environmental charge, the severity of the charge is somewhat beside the point. It

---

[9] Corporations account for 315 of the 1,019 indictments, while individuals account for the remaining 704 indictments. These figures do not include another powerful enforcement mechanism—civil injunctive relief—which is especially costly to some environmental offenders. For example, through a settlement agreement, USX, a steel manufacturer with operations in Gary, Indiana, was required to perform corrective and preventative measures that will cost the company over $32 million. *See* United States v. USX Corp., No. H88-558 (N.D. Ind. Oct. 22, 1991).

[10] Pub. L. No. 101-380, 101 Stat. 484 (1990).

is, to some extent, an exercise in minimizing losses. There is virtually no public support or sympathy for the environmental defendant. There is a widely held perception that the offense committed, while perhaps not directed against an identifiable individual, is a violent crime that causes significant harm and is callously aimed at the public in general. In the court of public opinion, a defendant often loses as soon as such charges are brought. EPA and the Department of Justice consciously use public opinion in an effort to assist the effectiveness of the enforcement program.

In addition to the loss of prestige and good will in the community, corporations can and do suffer severe and tangible consequences if convicted. Along with the obvious impact of fines imposed, consider also a company's potential exposure to derivative shareholder suits when it fails to disclose environmental liability. Corporations convicted under the criminal provisions of the Clean Air and Clean Water Acts may not enter into any contract with the federal government for the procurement of goods, merchandise, or services if the contract is to be performed at a facility that committed the violations or is supervised by a person so convicted.[11] The debarment continues until EPA certifies that the conditions leading up to the conviction have been corrected.[12] Additionally, felony convictions of any kind *may* lead to contractual debarment, and other criminal environmental violations, such as under RCRA, have led to such punishment.[13] Moreover, under ordinary government contracting procedures, an indictment can be cause for suspension from government contracting or subcontracting until the indictment is resolved.

The Department of Justice has established guidelines for prosecution of environmental violations.[14] The policy is designed to encourage self-policing, self-auditing, and voluntary disclosure. These actions are mitigating factors for prosecutors to consider in deciding whether to seek indictments, and if so, for what kind of violations. Under the guidelines, the Department of Justice evaluates six primary factors in determining whether to prosecute violators, including

1. Whether the violating entity made a voluntary disclosure of the matter under investigation;
2. The extent and timeliness of the violating entity's cooperation;
3. Preventive measures and compliance programs instituted by the violating entity;
4. The violating entity's compliance record;

[11] CAA §306(a), 42 U.S.C. §7606(a) (Supp. III 1991); CWA §508(a), 33 U.S.C. §1368(a) (1988). The Clean Air Act also allows EPA to extend the ban to other facilities owned or operated by the convicted person.

[12] *Id.*

[13] CAA §306, 42 U.S.C. §7606 (Supp. III 1991); CWA §508, 33 U.S.C. §1368 (1988); Federal Facilities Compliance Act, Pub. L. No. 102-386, 106 Stat. 1505 (1992) (to be codified at 42 U.S.C. §6961). If a contractor is convicted under one of those sections, the facility owned, operated, or managed by the convicted contractor is placed on the EPA List of Violating Facilities that bars the facility from any contracts, grants, or loans. The facility is only removed after the condition giving rise to the conviction is corrected. *See* 56 Fed. Reg. 64,786 (1991). The amended Clean Air Act allows debarment of the entire company and not just the offending facility.

[14] U.S. Dep't of Justice, Factors in Decisions on Criminal Prosecutions for Environmental Violations in the Context of Significant Voluntary Compliance or Disclosure Efforts by the Violator (July 1, 1991) (unpublished memo).

5. The existence of an internal system within the violating entity for disciplining employees who commit violations and the effectiveness of that system; and
6. The violating entity's efforts to correct ongoing compliance problems.

All of these factors are evaluated on a continuum. In theory, this approach is intended to provide greater leniency to companies that satisfy more of the criteria, while making prosecution more likely for companies that satisfy fewer criteria. Prosecutors are to consider gradations within each of these factors with the result of the greater a regulated entity's good faith cooperation, the more leniency it should expect.[15] In practice, however, these considerations are anything but mechanical. The Department of Justice guidelines are just that, guides to Justice Department attorneys. Deviations are allowed and often occur. The federal government cannot be forced to adhere strictly to them, so caution should rule in basing action solely on an interpretation of the guidelines.

Nonetheless, through these guidelines the Department of Justice has attempted to promote uniformity in enforcement. At the same time, Congress has attempted to standardize statutory penalty provisions, and has done so at very high levels—felonies—for most violations.

C. Criminal Enforcement Authority

Congress has included criminal liability provisions in most statutes that address environmental, natural resource, and conservation concerns.[16] Moreover, prosecutors are armed with additional criminal authorities under the general federal criminal code—Title 18—that enhance their environmental enforcement power. One effective tool with severe penalties available to prosecutors is the false statement statute.[17] Because the success of environmental regulation largely relies on self-reporting, the Department of Justice and EPA take an extremely serious view of false or misleading statements and failures to

---

[15] The Department of Justice guidelines parallel the sentencing guidelines for corporate criminal sentencing to a large degree. The policy is intended to reduce concern among regulated entities that perform voluntary and mandatory audits that reveal environmental violations. It is doubtful that the policy has achieved that goal. Many companies fear that full disclosure will provide factual support for prosecutors seeking evidence of intent to commit or knowledge of violations. The Department of Justice policy does not guarantee that an audit will remain privileged. Furthermore, the attorney-client and work product privileges usually apply only to legal counsel and not to the underlying facts in an audit. The audit is only covered by the work product doctrine if it is prepared in anticipation of litigation. See Chapter 15, Environmental Auditing.

[16] CAA, 42 U.S.C. §7413(c) (Supp. III 1991); CWA, 33 U.S.C. §§1319(c) and 1321(b)(5) (1988); Comprehensive Environmental Response, Compensation, and Liability Act (CERCLA), 42 U.S.C. §9603(b) and (c) (1988); Deepwater Port Act, 33 U.S.C. §§1514 and 1517(b) (1988); EPCRA, 42 U.S.C. §11045(b) and (d) (1988); Endangered Species Act (ESA), 16 U.S.C. §1540(b) (1988); FIFRA, 7 U.S.C. §1361(b) (1988); Magnuson Fishery Conservation and Management Act, 16 U.S.C. §1859 (1988); Marine Protection, Research, and Sanctuaries Act, 33 U.S.C. §1415(b) (1988); Migratory Bird Treaty, 16 U.S.C. §707(b) (1988); Noise Pollution Control Act, 42 U.S.C. §4910(A) (1988); Ports and Waterways Safety Act, 33 U.S.C. §1232(b) (1988); RCRA, 42 U.S.C. §6928(d) (1988); Rivers and Harbors Appropriations Act, 33 U.S.C. §§406 and 411; Safe Drinking Water Act (SDWA), 42 U.S.C. §§300h-2(b) and 300i (1988); Surface Mining Control and Reclamation Act, 30 U.S.C. §1294(e)-(g); and TSCA, 15 U.S.C. §2615(b) (1988).

[17] 18 U.S.C. §1001 provides: "Whoever, in any matter within the jurisdiction of any department or agency of the United States knowingly and willfully falsifies, conceals or covers up by any trick, silence or device a material fact, or makes or uses any false writing or document knowing the same to contain any false, fictitious or fraudulent statement or entry, shall be fined not more than $10,000 or imprisoned not more than five years, or both."

report in response to statutory requirements.[18] Likewise tampering with monitors and test results are viewed as a grave matter. Other important federal laws that the government can use to prosecute environmental crimes include conspiracy,[19] mail and wire fraud,[20] aiding and abetting statutes,[21] obstruction of justice[22] and obstruction of administrative proceedings.[23] This enforcement authority combined with criminal provisions in the substantive statutes and the new federal sentencing guidelines discussed below make stiff penalties for convicted individuals and corporations very likely.[24]

D. Criminal Penalties

Fines for individuals and corporations under the defining statutes are severe. They range from maximum penalties of $10,000 for false reporting under the Comprehensive Environmental Response, Compensation, and Liability Act (CERCLA) and the Clean Water Act to $1 million for corporate knowing endangerment under the Resource Conservation and Recovery Act (RCRA) and the Clean Water Act.[25] With most environmental statutes, each day of a violation can be counted as a separate offense. Under the Clean Air and Clean Water Acts, and the Emergency Planning and Community Right-to-Know Act (EPCRA), criminal fines and sentences double for subsequent convictions. Moreover, in order to impose a greater financial burden on companies, criminal and court fines are not considered deductible business expenses under section 167 of the Internal Revenue Code.

1. Alternative Criminal Fines

Amendments to the federal criminal code in 1987 allow courts to impose fines that exceed those authorized under the defining environmental statutes. Under the Criminal Fine Improvements Act,[26] individuals and corporations are subject to an alternative fine structure that is based on the amount specified for the offense under the substantive statute, specific fines derived from different

---

[18] *See, e.g.,* United States v. Brittain, 931 F.2d 1413, 32 ER Cases 2084 (10th Cir. 1991) (upholding a conviction under 18 U.S.C. §1001 for false reporting of material facts to EPA where statements regarding wastewater treatment plant's pollution discharge monitoring reports were capable of influencing Agency enforcement action); United States v. International Paper Co., No. 9100051-B (D. Me. July 31, 1991) (company fined $2.2 million for two counts of making false statements to the government and three counts of storing and treating hazardous waste without a permit in violation of 18 U.S.C. §1001); United States v. Gold, 8 ER Cases 1239 (N.D. Ill. 1977).

[19] 18 U.S.C. §371. *See* United States v. Weitzenfoff & Mariani, CR 90-1568 (D. Haw. Oct. 2, 1991) (conviction for conspiracy and five counts of knowingly discharging pollutants and sewage sludge).

[20] 18 U.S.C. §1341.

[21] 18 U.S.C. §2.

[22] 18 U.S.C. §1501.

[23] 18 U.S.C. §1505.

[24] The guidelines for business entities currently do not apply to environmental crimes. *See* 56 Fed. Reg. 22,762, 27,786–94 (1991). The Sentencing Commission is in the process of revising guidelines that are applicable to environmental offenses. Revised guidelines are not expected to change the sentencing of individuals but could significantly impact corporate or other organizational defendants. The Sentencing Commission was scheduled to issue proposed amendments to the sentencing guidelines in early 1993. The commission, however, has only circulated a draft of the environmental guidelines, and missed its May 1 deadline to issue the guidelines in 1993. When the amendments are formally released, they will automatically take effect in 180 days unless Congress enacts legislation specifically rejecting the revisions.

[25] *See* 42 U.S.C. §9603 (1988); 33 U.S.C. §1321(b)(5) (1988); 42 U.S.C. §6928(e) (1988); 33 U.S.C. §1319(c)(3) (1988).

[26] Pub. L. No. 100-185, 101 Stat. 1279 (1987) (codified throughout Title 18 of the United States Code).

offense categories, or an amount determined by a new gain/loss formula set forth in the Act.[27] The Clean Air Act Amendments of 1990 specifically subject violators to Title 18 penalty provisions.[28] Several corporate defendants in violation of environmental statutes have been sentenced under the Act. For example, in *United States v. Orkin Exterminating Co.,*[29] the company was convicted of misdemeanor violations of the Federal Insecticide, Fungicide, and Rodenticide Act (FIFRA) for misuse of pesticides that resulted in two deaths. Orkin was fined $500,000, which far exceeded the maximum penalty specified under the statute.[30] The anticipated sentencing guidelines for corporate environmental offenses will almost certainly make higher fines the norm.

2. *Sentencing Commission Guidelines*

As with other federal crimes, for environmental, conservation, and wildlife offenses that occur after November 1987, the courts may sentence individuals in accordance with U.S. Sentencing Commission Guidelines.[31] The guidelines increase the length of incarceration, eliminate parole and suspended sentences, and restrict probationary sentences.[32] The courts have relied on the sentencing guidelines to impose actual jail time on defendants convicted of environmental crimes. For example, the Sixth Circuit required a federal district court to resentence an individual who pleaded guilty to numerous Clean Water Act violations, finding that the district court improperly considered the defendant's ownership of a business when it declined to impose a jail sentence. In *United States v. Rutana,*[33] the court stated that the federal sentencing guidelines do not allow the court to consider the effect of incarceration of an individual on the continuing operations of the individual's business.

---

[27] 18 U.S.C. §3571 (Supp. 1992). Maximum fines are derived from a grade assigned to the type of offense or the maximum prison term that the defining statute authorizes. The Act doubles the amount of fines that corporations pay as compared to individuals. The gain/loss formula calculates fines on the basis of the economic benefit obtained compared to the loss suffered as a result of the offense. This formula was used to calculate the penalties assessed in United States v. Ashland Oil, Inc., 705 F. Supp. 270, 29 ER Cases 1030 (W.D. Pa. 1989) (fining Ashland Oil $2,250,000 for the release of 500,000 gallons of oil when its poorly constructed storage tank collapsed). Ashland faced a potential fine of twice the clean-up cost—$15 million—but the court recognized Ashland's cooperation.

[28] *See* 42 U.S.C. §7613(c) (1990).

[29] 688 F. Supp. 223 (W.D. Va. 1988).

[30] *See* FIFRA, 7 U.S.C. §1361(b)(1)(A)(B) (1988). The maximum penalty is $25,000 for knowing violations by a commercial applicator of a registered pesticide and $50,000 for a registrant or producer.

[31] *See* 52 Fed. Reg. 18,046–99 (1987). The guidelines divide environment and natural resource crimes into four categories:

1. Knowing endangerment;
2. Hazardous or toxic substance violations;
3. Other pollutant violations; and
4. Conservation and wildlife violations.

There is a minimum penalty assigned to categories 3 and 4 that is increased if the offense is an ongoing violation.

[32] *See* 54 Fed. Reg. 47,063 (1989). In addition, multiple count violations are standardized under the sentencing guidelines because all violations that continue over a period of days are considered ongoing violations and receive the same increased penalty.

[33] 932 F.2d 1155, 1158–59, 33 ER Cases 1233 (6th Cir.), *cert. denied,* 112 S. Ct. 300, 33 ER Cases 1800 (1991). The Sixth Circuit noted that the district court failed to articulate other factors that would support a reduced sentence. Moreover, the court of appeals required the district court to reconsider the fine imposed on the defendant. The Sixth Circuit indicated that the district court mistakenly assessed the minimum fine of $5,000 for the Clean Water Act violation when it was authorized to fine the defendant $5,000 for *each* of the 18 violations to which he pleaded guilty. *Id.* at 1160.

In one recent case, the court upheld application of the guidelines to a first-time offender. In *United States v. Ellen,*[34] the United States Court of Appeals for the Fourth Circuit affirmed the conviction of a development project manager who violated the Clean Water Act by filling wetlands without a permit on the Eastern Shore of Maryland. Ellen argued that the guidelines that authorize upward adjustment of penalties for continuous releases of pollutants to the environment and discharges without a permit should apply only to violent or serious offenses and that alternative sentencing is more appropriate for first-time offenders. The Fourth Circuit rejected appellant's argument and noted "[t]hat Ellen believes . . . an offense of this magnitude is trivial or unimportant ironically exemplifies the need not to foreclose punishment by imprisonment in enforcing laws aimed at environmental protection."[35] The Fourth Circuit decision underscores the courts' ever-increasing willingness to adhere strictly to penalty provisions that will further congressional intent in public welfare statutes.[36]

E. Legal Standards for Criminal Prosecution

The legal standards for "knowing" violations of environmental statutes have been the subject of much litigation in the federal courts. The degree of intent and knowledge required to convict a defendant for an environmental offense often differs from what is required under other criminal statutes. For many crimes, the government must prove that the defendant had specific intent to act contrary to the law or violate a known legal duty. In environmental cases, however, courts have considered whether defendants acted knowingly and voluntarily,[37] and not whether the defendants acted with specific intent or actual knowledge that a statute had been violated by them. In addition, the self-reporting requirements of most environmental statutes often present prosecutors with an easier task in terms of establishing elements of the criminal offense.

1. Responsible Corporate Officer Doctrine

The responsible corporate officer doctrine demonstrates the government's policy of prosecuting the highest ranking company official against whom a case can be made. The doctrine originated from cases brought under the Food, Drug, and Cosmetic Act (FDCA).[38] In *United States v. Dotterweich,*[39] the Supreme Court found that those who ship adulterated foods are " 'punished by the statute

---

[34] 961 F.2d 462, 35 ER Cases 1165 (4th Cir. 1992). *See also* United States v. Irby, 949 F.2d 759 (4th Cir. 1991) (upholding application of sentencing guidelines that increased defendant's offense by six levels based on ongoing or repetitive releases of pollutants to the environment in violation of the Clean Water Act).

[35] 961 F.2d at 468.

[36] In response to some courts' application of the sentencing guidelines, the Sentencing Commission has proposed amendments that would eliminate double-counting factors used to increase penalties for certain environmental violations. *See* 57 Fed. Reg. 90 (1992).

[37] For example, RCRA imposes penalties on one who "*knowingly* transports or causes to be transported any hazardous waste . . . to a facility which does not have a permit . . . *knowingly* treats, stores or disposes of any hazardous waste . . . without a permit . . . in *knowing* violation of any material condition or requirement of such permit or in knowing violation of any material condition or requirement of any applicable interim status regulations or standards." 42 U.S.C. §6928(d) (1988 & Supp. 1992) (emphasis added).

[38] *See* 21 U.S.C. §1319(c)(6) (1988); Lisa Ann Harig, *Ignorance Is Not Bliss: Responsible Corporate Officers Convicted of Environmental Crimes and the Federal Sentencing Guidelines,* 42 DUKE L.J. 145 (1992).

[39] 320 U.S. 277 (1943).

if the article is misbranded [or adulterated], and ... the article may be misbranded [or adulterated] without any conscious fraud at all.' "[40] The Court found that any person, including a corporate officer or employee "standing in a responsible relation" to a violation, could be prosecuted.[41] No mental element or act in furtherance of a violation is necessary to sustain a conviction. It is only necessary that the officer had the power to prevent the violation from occurring.

The Supreme Court established the standard to be applied to responsible corporate officers in the landmark FDCA case of *United States v. Park.*[42] The *Park* case made it clear that a corporate officer can be held criminally liable if the officer had "by reason of his position in the corporation, responsibility and authority either to prevent in the first instance, or promptly to correct, the violation complained of, and that he failed to do so."[43] The responsible corporate officer doctrine is designed to prevent high level employees from escaping liability when they choose to ignore violations. The Justice Department can prove through circumstantial evidence that officers had knowledge of regulations, knowledge that violations occurred, and that they failed to take action to prevent those violations. Even before the *Park* case was brought, Congress had made responsible corporate officers subject to prosecution under the Clean Water Act. As if to remove any question of where Congress believed criminal corporate responsibility should lie after *Park,* the two most recently amended environmental statutes, the Clean Water Act and the Clean Air Act, both specifically identify responsible corporate officers as "persons who may be held criminally liable for violations."[44]

2. *Scienter Requirement*

Courts have considered violations of environmental statutes that involve toxic chemicals and hazardous waste serious and, in general, have presumed that these highly regulated industries and their officers and employees have knowledge of the regulatory requirements.[45] The Third Circuit outlined the government's burden of proof to establish criminal liability under RCRA in *United States v. Johnson & Towers.*[46] The company and two mid-level managers were convicted for disposing hazardous waste into the Delaware River

[40] 320 U.S. at 281 (citations omitted).

[41] *Id.*

[42] 421 U.S. 658 (1975). In *Park,* the president of a retail food chain was convicted of food adulteration under the FDCA. Park had been notified that food stored in the warehouse prior to its distribution had been contaminated by rats. Park was convicted even though he had delegated the responsibility for compliance with the applicable rules to other officials in the company. *Id.* at 673–74.

[43] 421 U.S. at 673–74.

[44] 33 U.S.C. §1319(c)(6) (1988); 42 U.S.C. §7413(c)(6) (Supp. III 1991).

[45] Appeals courts that have interpreted public welfare statutes generally agree that it is not necessary to prove the violator's actual knowledge of the statute's existence. United States v. International Minerals & Chems. Corp., 402 U.S. 558 (1971); United States v. Dee, 912 F.2d 741, 745, 31 ER Cases 1953 (4th Cir. 1990), *cert. denied,* 111 S. Ct. 1307, 32 ER Cases 2038 (1991); United States v. Hayes Int'l Corp., 786 F.2d 1499, 1503, 24 ER Cases 1282 (11th Cir. 1986); United States v. Johnson & Towers, 741 F.2d 662, 669, 21 ER Cases 1433 (3d Cir. 1984).

With respect to intent under RCRA, the courts of appeals have split on the issue of whether the prosecution must prove that a defendant who disposes of hazardous waste had actual knowledge of the receiving facility's permit status. *See* United States v. Hayes Int'l Corp., 786 F.2d 1499, 1504 (11th Cir. 1986) (not required); *but see* United States v. MacDonald & Watson Waste Oil Co., 933 F.2d 35, 55 (1st Cir. 1991); United States v. Speach, 968 F.2d 795, 35 ER Cases 1325 (9th Cir. 1992) (required).

[46] 741 F.2d 662, 21 ER Cases 1433 (3d Cir. 1984), *cert. denied sub nom.* Angel v. United States, 469 U.S. 1208 (1985).

without a permit. The court stated that the government must prove that each defendant had knowledge that the company did not possess a permit and that it was required to obtain one.[47] The court found, however, that "such knowledge, including that of the permit requirement, may be inferred by the jury as to those individuals who hold the requisite responsible positions with the corporate defendant."[48] The Third Circuit did not indicate, however, what other knowledge the jury could infer based on corporate position alone. When coupled with the *Park* analysis for responsible corporate officers, the *Johnson & Towers* decision should stimulate serious concern about regulatory requirements and compliance within management.

Several other appeals courts have liberally interpreted the criminal provisions that require knowing conduct so that criminal prosecution for knowing violations has become much easier. For example, in *United States v. Hayes International Corp.*,[49] the Eleventh Circuit addressed the degree of knowledge required to obtain a conviction under RCRA. Hayes International, through an employee, arranged to dispose of wastes generated at its aircraft refurbishing facility by contracting with a hauling company that did not have a permit to handle the material.

In the *Hayes* decision, the court considered several defenses to the RCRA charges. The Eleventh Circuit rejected arguments that the defendant was unaware of the hazardous nature of the waste generated by the facility and was unaware that a permit was necessary for its handling.[50] The court reasoned that those who operate in heavily regulated areas are presumed to have knowledge of the applicable regulations.[51] The court also addressed the government's burden of proof and found that the prosecution is not required to establish defendants' actual knowledge about the receiving facility's compliance with permitting requirements. It held that a conviction can be supported by circumstantial evidence that the defendant "willfully failed to determine the permit status of the facility."[52] Finally, the court suggested that a possible defense is defendants' erroneous good faith belief in a material fact that resulted in an environmental offense.[53]

---

[47] 741 F.2d at 670.

[48] *Id.*

[49] 786 F.2d 1499, 24 ER Cases 1282 (11th Cir. 1986).

[50] 786 F.2d at 1503.

[51] The Eleventh Circuit noted that "it is completely fair and reasonable to charge those who choose to operate in such areas with knowledge of the regulatory provisions." *Id. See also* United States v. Goldsmith, No. 92-8030 (11th Cir. Nov. 30, 1992) (government need not prove defendant had knowledge that drums transported contained hazardous substances where government proved defendant had knowledge of general hazardous character of chemicals); United States v. Dean, 969 F.2d 187, 35 ER Cases 1255 (6th Cir. 1992) (knowledge of permit requirement is not a prerequisite for a RCRA conviction); United States v. Baytank, Inc., 934 F.2d 599, 33 ER Cases 1825 (5th Cir. 1991) (allowing the presumption that a chemical storage company is knowledgeable about applicable regulations); United States v. Hoflin, 880 F.2d 1033, 30 ER Cases 1419 (9th Cir. 1989) (knowledge of permit requirement is not necessary for a conviction).

[52] 786 F.2d at 1504. For example, the Eleventh Circuit noted that "[i]f someone is willing to take away wastes at an unusual price or under unusual circumstances, then a juror can infer that the transporter knows the wastes are not being taken to a permit facility." *Id. But see* United States v. Speach, 968 F.2d 795, 35 ER Cases 1325 (9th Cir. 1992) (finding that knowledge of the receiving facility's permit status is a prerequisite to a RCRA conviction for unlawful transportation of hazardous waste).

[53] *See, e.g.*, United States v. International Mineral & Chems., 402 U.S. 558 (1971) (involving transportation of dangerous materials in violation of regulations under 49 C.F.R. §173.427 issued pursuant to 18 U.S.C. §834(a)); *compare* United States v. Buckley, No. 90-3615, 32 ER Cases 2081 (6th Cir. Apr. 30, 1991) (finding

In *United States v. Greer,*[54] the Eleventh Circuit expanded *Hayes* and *Johnson & Towers* in a decision that allowed the government to prove that the defendant knowingly disposed of or caused others to dispose of hazardous waste even when the government offered no direct evidence that the defendant arranged for the disposal. The court allowed the jury to infer from testimony that Greer had approved of dumping "as a way to meet storage squeezes" in the past and had done so in this instance as well.[55] Thus, a past pattern of conduct by responsible corporate officials can suffice to prove a violation when no direct evidence is offered.

Although the courts generally have permitted the government to prove defendants' knowledge of violations through circumstantial evidence, there is a split in the circuits on whether the government must prove defendants' actual knowledge of a receiving facility's permit status to obtain a RCRA conviction. In *United States v. MacDonald & Watson Waste Oil Co.*[56] the First Circuit reversed the conviction of an owner and president of a company that transported hazardous waste to a facility that had a permit to accept waste, but not the type of waste delivered. The First Circuit rejected instructions that allowed the jury to infer defendant's knowledge of the offense by virtue of his position in the company.[57] The government demonstrated that the defendant was involved in day-to-day management of a small company that previously had been warned about accepting this type of waste. In contrast to the Eleventh Circuit decision in *Greer,* which allowed the jury to infer knowledge based on evidence of the defendant's past misconduct, the First Circuit refused to affirm the conviction without direct evidence of the defendant's present misconduct.[58] Although the First Circuit stated that the government must prove a defendant's actual knowledge, those subject to regulations should be aware that most courts interpreting the knowledge requirement have imposed a less stringent burden of proof on the government.

The most serious criminal offense under environmental statutes involves knowing endangerment.[59] It applies to defendants who violate environmental

of good faith is immaterial when defendant caused asbestos to be emitted in violation of the Clean Air Act and failed to report the release in violation of CERCLA, because dealing with hazardous wastes gives individuals "constitutionally adequate notice that they may incur criminal liability for emissions-related actions").

[54] 850 F.2d 1447, 1452, 28 ER Cases 1254 (11th Cir. 1988).

[55] 850 F.2d at 1451–52.

[56] 933 F.2d 35, 55 (1st Cir. 1991). *See also* United States v. Speach, 968 F.2d 795, 35 ER Cases 1325 (9th Cir. 1992).

[57] The First Circuit stated that the district court's instructions allowed the prosecution to establish defendant's knowledge based on his "(1) status as an officer of the corporation; (2) direct responsibility for the activities that are alleged to be illegal; and (3) knowledge or belief that the illegal activity of the type alleged occurred." *Id.* at 55 n.20.

[58] "In a crime having knowledge as an express element, a mere showing of official responsibility under *Dotterweich* and *Park* is not an adequate substitute for direct or circumstantial proof of knowledge." *Id.* at 55. In part, the court was concerned that the *MacDonald* case was a felony matter, involving more severe consequences than *Dotterweich* and *Park,* which were misdemeanors. At the same time, the First Circuit upheld the conviction of other MacDonald & Watson employees who had signed documents that revealed the nature of the waste at issue. The court noted that this type of circumstantial evidence is sufficient for the jury to infer that the defendants, regardless of their position in the company, reviewed and understood the documents. *Id.* at 41.

[59] In knowing endangerment cases against individuals prosecuted under the CWA, RCRA, and the CAA, the government is required to demonstrate the defendant's "knowledge" of the wrongdoing. *See* 33 U.S.C. §1319(c)(3) (1988); 42 U.S.C. §6928(e) (1988); 42 U.S.C. §7413(c)(5) (Supp. III 1991). (In 1991, Congress

statutes with knowledge that the offense places others in danger of death or serious bodily injury. In these cases, for corporations but *not* individuals, "knowledge" can be proved by circumstantial evidence that the defendants willfully shielded themselves from evidence of wrongdoing.[60] So far, only one appeals court has upheld a knowing endangerment conviction.[61]

In *United States v. Protex Industries,*[62] the Tenth Circuit considered knowing endangerment under RCRA in which a hazardous waste handling company was charged with knowingly exposing its workers to solvents that caused intoxication and psycho-organic injury. The Tenth Circuit found that "[t]he gist of the 'knowing endangerment' provision of RCRA is that a party will be criminally liable if, in violating other provisions of the RCRA, it places others in danger of great harm and it has knowledge of that danger."[63]

The First Circuit recently overturned a conviction for knowing endangerment to employees under the Clean Water Act, but left open the possibility of applying RCRA knowing endangerment provisions to the violations. In *United States v. Borowski,*[64] the court found that a metal finishing company and its president could not be held criminally liable because the government failed to allege that individuals other than company employees were endangered by the illegal discharges. The court reasoned that, although the acts were egregious, the Clean Water Act protects U.S. waters from contamination, and not corporate employees from endangerment. The court determined that while the handling of pollutants is not the purpose of the Clean Water Act provision, criminal provisions under RCRA address the general handling, treatment, and storage of hazardous substances and these offenses were not charged.[65] Under the govern-

---

held hearings on a proposed environmental crimes bill that would have extended knowing endangerment provisions to CERCLA, FIFRA, TSCA, EPCRA, the SDWA, and the Ocean Dumping Act. While this legislation did not pass, it is safe to assume that the issue has not died and will be revisited in this or a subsequent Congress.)

[60] *See, e.g.,* RCRA §3008(f)(2), 42 U.S.C. §6928(f)(2) (1988) that provides:

> In determining whether a defendant who is a natural person knew that his conduct placed another person in imminent danger of death or serious bodily injury—
>
> (A) the person is responsible only for actual awareness or actual belief that he possessed; and
>
> (B) knowledge possessed by a person other than the defendant but not by the defendant himself may not be attributed to the defendant;
>
> *Provided,* that in proving the defendant's possession of actual knowledge, circumstantial evidence may be used, including evidence that the defendant took affirmative steps to shield himself from relevant information.

The Clean Air and Clean Water Acts have similar provisions. It should be expected that the fact that Congress specifically states that implied knowledge cannot be used as the basis for a knowing endangerment conviction for an individual will be used to counter the position adopted by the First Circuit in the context of less serious knowing violations. *See supra* note 58.

[61] The government recently appealed the dismissal of knowing endangerment charges against a company that released hepatitis tainted blood vials into the Hudson River in violation of the Clean Water Act. *See* United States v. Geronimo Villegas, 784 F. Supp. 6 (E.D.N.Y. 1991). The owner of the lab has appealed his conviction for two counts of knowing violations of the Clean Water Act that were not dismissed by the court.

[62] 874 F.2d 740, 29 ER Cases 1593 (10th Cir. 1989). The court firmly rejected the defendants' argument that psycho-organic injury did not constitute "serious bodily injury" within the meaning of the statute, noting that "[a]ppellants position demonstrates callousness toward the severe physical effect the prolonged exposure to toxic chemicals may cause or has caused to the three former employees." *Id.* 874 F.2d at 743.

[63] 874 F.2d at 744.

[64] 977 F.2d 27 (1st Cir. 1992).

[65] 977 F.2d at 31. The court noted that criminal sanctions apply to those who put another person in imminent danger of death or serious injury by knowingly violating pretreatment standards for pollutants entering publicly owned treatment works.

ment's multimedia enforcement approach, criminal charges under both RCRA and the Clean Air Act for such misconduct are now much more likely.

3. *Individual Culpability*

The courts have not limited the classes of individuals who will be criminally liable for environmental offenses. In *Johnson & Towers,*[66] the Third Circuit determined that knowing treatment, storage, or disposal of hazardous waste without a permit under RCRA applies broadly to employees as well as owners and operators. The appeals court reversed the district court's finding that only owners and operators could obtain permits and, therefore, only they could be prosecuted for disposing waste without a permit.[67] The court noted that the statute's definition of ''person'' includes individuals as well as other entities.[68] The court reasoned that had Congress intended a different result it could have specified otherwise in the law.[69]

Recent cases and legislation confirm that federal employees and federal government contractors are not immune from prosecution.[70] For example, in *United States v. Dee,*[71] the Fourth Circuit affirmed the conviction of two high level civilian employees of the Department of the Army who held supervisory positions at the Aberdeen Proving Grounds in Maryland. The Fourth Circuit rejected defendants' claim of immunity finding that they were ''individuals'' without RCRA's definition of ''person'' and noted that ''[t]he defendants . . . were . . . convicted as individuals, not as agents of the government. Suffice it to say that sovereign immunity does not attach to individual government employees so as to immunize them from prosecution for their criminal acts.''[72]

4. *Negligence Standard*

Criminal liability provisions for negligent acts or omissions are included in both the Clean Water and Clean Air Acts and may be added to other environmental statutes as they are amended.[73] Several criminal negligence cases have been brought for Clean Water Act violations. In *United States v. Frezzo Bros., Inc.,*[74] the Third Circuit considered the negligence standard. In *Frezzo,* two

---

[66] 741 F.2d at 664. Two employees of the defendant, Angel and Hopkins, who held mid-level managerial positions within the company, improperly discharged hazardous waste and directed others to do the same.

[67] The court stated that ''it would undercut the purpose of the legislation to limit the class of potential defendants to owners and operators when others also bear responsibility for handling regulated materials.'' *Id.* at 667.

[68] 741 F.2d at 666–67.

[69] *Id.*

[70] *See, e.g.,* Clean Water Act, 33 U.S.C. §1323 (1988); the Federal Facility Compliance Act, Pub. L. No. 102-386, 106 Stat. 1505 (1992) (to be codified at 42 U.S.C. §6961), specifically allows federal employees and agents to be held liable for their criminal activities under RCRA.

[71] 912 F.2d 741, 31 ER Cases 1953 (4th Cir. 1990), *cert. denied,* 111 S. Ct. 1307, 32 ER Cases 2038 (1991).

[72] *Id.* 912 F.2d at 744. In United States v. Carr, 880 F.2d 1550, 30 ER Cases 1128 (2d Cir. 1989), the Second Circuit upheld the convictions of a federal employee for failure to report a release of hazardous substances from the burial of paint cans. The court rejected defendant's argument that he, a mid-level federal employee, in charge of a rifle range at an Army base, could not be the ''person in charge'' of a ''facility,'' which is the operative requirement in the statute.

[73] *See, e.g.,* Clean Air Act, 42 U.S.C. §7413(c) (Supp. III 1991) and the Oil Pollution Act amendments to the Clean Water Act, 33 U.S.C. §1321(B)(5) (Supp. 1992).

[74] 461 F. Supp. 266, 12 ER Cases 1481 (E.D. Pa. 1978), *aff'd,* 602 F.2d 1123, 13 ER Cases 1403 (3d Cir. 1979), *cert. denied,* 444 U.S. 1074, 14 ER Cases 1033 (1980). The district court denied defendants' petitions for postconviction relief. 546 F. Supp. 713 (E.D. Pa. 1982).

officers in a small mushroom growing company were convicted for negligently discharging pollutants into a stream when the company's compost holding tank overflowed during a heavy rainfall. The court indicated that evidence demonstrating that the releases could have been prevented with adequate precautions was sufficient to satisfy the negligence standard.[75] This standard imposes stringent requirements on individuals and business entities to remedy existing problems and to discover and eliminate potential risks.

The amended Clean Air Act includes criminal provisions for negligent as well as knowing endangerment. Under that Act, an individual who negligently releases any of 189 "hazardous air pollutants" under the Clean Air Act or any of 366 "extremely hazardous substances" under EPCRA, into the ambient air that places another person in imminent danger of death or serious bodily injury is punishable by a fine under Title 18, imprisonment for up to one year, or both.[76]

Fines for negligent violations can be severe. For example, in *United States v. Pennwalt,*[77] the collapse of a 75,000 gallon storage tank led to the indictment and conviction of the company on a theory of negligent discharge of chemicals in violation of the Clean Water Act. Pennwalt was fined $1.1 million for its negligent maintenance of the tank and failure to report the spill correctly in violation of CERCLA.[78] The penalty was even more severe for Exxon Corporation when it plead guilty to a misdemeanor charge of negligently discharging oil into the Arthur Kill in New York harbor without a permit in violation of the Clean Water Act. Exxon agreed to pay a criminal fine of $5 million in addition to a civil penalty of $10 million.[79]

The legal standards applied to criminal prosecution of environmental offenses along with the trend towards increased enforcement should send strong warnings to the regulated community. If individuals engage in operations and hold managerial positions in fields subject to environmental, health, and safety regulations, they can be deemed to have knowledge of and consequently liability for violations.[80] In addition, knowing endangerment does not require much more evidence to convict a corporation than what is required for knowing violations. For example, under RCRA, a supervisor who directs illegal activity can be criminally charged with both a knowing violation and the more serious offense of knowing endangerment, if those who carry out the directive are personally placed at risk by the activity. Moreover, the negligence standard requires those in responsible positions to prevent accidental violations of environmental regulations. These standards are demanding and have severe consequences when they are not met. They reflect, however, the public's heightened

[75] 602 F.2d at 1129. The district court in *Frezzo Bros.* had stated that the government need only prove the essential elements of the crime: (1) the defendant discharged a pollutant, (2) negligently or willfully, (3) without a permit. 461 F. Supp. at 272 n.6.

[76] 42 U.S.C. §7413(c)(4) (Supp. III 1991).

[77] No. CR88-55T (W.D. Wash. May 2, 1989).

[78] *See also* United States v. Ashland Oil, 705 F. Supp. 270, 29 ER Cases 1030 (W.D. Pa. 1989) (imposing a fine of $2.25 million for negligent violations under the Clean Water Act).

[79] *See* United States v. Exxon Corp., No. 91-131 (D.N.J. Mar. 20, 1991); United States v. Exxon Corp., No. 91-1003 (E.D.N.Y. Mar. 20, 1991).

[80] *See* United States v. Brittain, 931 F.2d 1413, 1420 (10th Cir. 1991) (finding that willfulness or negligence of a subordinate actor can be imputed to the supervisor by virtue of his position and responsibility to act under the circumstances).

concern for health, safety, and the environment and the government's response to that interest.

III. Civil Enforcement

Even with the increased emphasis in criminal enforcement, most EPA enforcement resources remain targeted in the civil arena. EPA has over 20 years experience in running the various components of its civil enforcement program and has developed a relatively smoothly run operation. EPA's civil enforcement policy is designed primarily to remedy environmental problems and to deter violations of the law.[81] EPA also recognizes that for the policy to be successful in avoiding high litigation costs on both the Agency and the regulated community, it must be applied consistently to all parties.[82] Thus, the policy consists of rigid principles that are to be applied objectively with little room for discretion on the part of EPA—at least in theory.

A. Civil Enforcement Policies and Objectives

In the past, EPA's civil enforcement programs have been designed to address media-specific statutory compliance on primarily a region-specific approach. For example, Region II may not be aware that company X (alleged to be violating the Clean Water Act in upstate New York) has a history of committing similar violations in Region VI. If it did, Region II would likely impose a larger penalty based on the company's history of noncompliance. To deal with this problem, the programs have evolved into two conceptual approaches whereby EPA targets environmental programs based on geography and compliance.

Under a geographic-based approach, EPA can identify all polluters in a specific sensitive geographic area of concern, such as the Chesapeake Bay and the Great Lakes. Through this approach, the programs target noncomplying facilities contributing to pollution of that specific geographic area and take necessary enforcement actions in the form of orders and penalties to achieve compliance.

Under a compliance-based approach, EPA will be able to identify particular companies that have a pattern of noncompliance within or across media, including those companies that have facilities in several states or EPA regions. Through this approach, EPA may target those companies with a poor compliance record and take enforcement action accordingly. Nevertheless, whether EPA chooses to shift to these conceptual approaches, the underlying civil penalty policies will remain the same.

Basically, the civil penalty policies developed by EPA under the different environmental statutes attempt to assess appropriate penalties based on several factors, perhaps the most important being (1) the economic benefit that a

---

[81] EPA General Enforcement Policy #GM-21, Policy on Civil Penalties 1 (Feb. 16, 1984).
[82] *Id.*

noncomplying facility has realized and (2) the gravity of the violation.[83] The economic benefit component is designed to prohibit the violator from realizing an economic gain by not complying with a particular environmental statute. Thus, it attempts to place the violator in the same financial position as it would have been had it achieved compliance in a timely and lawful manner. The gravity component is included as a deterrence mechanism to ensure that the violator is monetarily worse off than it would have been if it had properly complied.

EPA has established a number of media-specific penalty policies under the various environmental statutes.[84] These policies provide guidance to EPA enforcers in calculating civil penalties under the various environmental statutes for certain types of violations. Generally, the penalty amounts arrived at under the policies for the calculated economic benefit of the alleged violation are the minimum settlement amounts that the Agency will accept in civil cases brought against the violators.

The monetary value of the gravity component for a particular violation is derived from a series of tables within these penalty policies according to the specific type of violation. As a general rule, this value will be adjusted (by not more than 10 percent) from the value listed in the table *only* if the violator shows good faith and makes efforts to quickly reach compliance.[85]

According to its civil penalty policies, EPA considers several objective factors in calculating the monetary value of the gravity component of the penalty. First, EPA will make a determination as to the actual or potential harm caused by the violation. For example, in a situation where the violation consisted of the illegal emission of a pollutant, the Agency may look at (1) the amount of pollutant emitted, (2) the sensitivity of the environment to which the pollutant was emitted, (3) the toxicity of the pollutant, and (4) the period of time over which the violation occurred. Second, the extent of deviation from a statutory or regulatory requirement will be examined, as well as the overall importance of the violation to the regulatory scheme. Finally, the Agency will look at the size of the corporate violator, and increase this component in proportion to the size of the violator's business or resources.

For the economic benefit component, EPA has developed the BEN computer model[86] to calculate the economic benefit accruing to a violator through avoided or delayed costs of complying with applicable environmental requirements. Examples of violations that may result in savings from *avoided* costs are the following: (1) failure to properly operate and maintain certain pollution control equipment, (2) failure to use registered waste transporters, and (3) failure to employ a sufficient number of adequately trained staff.

---

[83] *See, e.g.*, EPA, CLEAN AIR ACT STATIONARY SOURCE CIVIL PENALTY POLICY 1 (Oct. 25, 1991).

[84] *See, e.g.*, EPA, CLEAN WATER ACT PENALTY POLICY FOR CIVIL SETTLEMENT NEGOTIATIONS (Feb. 11, 1986); EPA, CLEAN AIR ACT STATIONARY SOURCE CIVIL PENALTY POLICY (Oct. 25, 1991); EPA RCRA CIVIL PENALTY POLICY, (Oct. 1990).

[85] *See, e.g.*, EPA, CLEAN AIR ACT STATIONARY SOURCE CIVIL PENALTY POLICY, *supra* note 84, at 1.

[86] BEN is the EPA computer software used to calculate the monetary value of the economic benefit component. The BEN model has been severely criticized for overstating the "actual" economic benefit of violations. Nonetheless, it remains an important aspect of EPA's enforcement program as EPA will not, barring extraordinary circumstances, settle for less than the economic benefit calculated using the BEN model.

Among the types of violations that may result in savings from *delayed* costs are the following: (1) failure to install equipment needed to monitor groundwater or to meet emission control standards, (2) failure to timely submit a permit application, (3) failure to perform a test where the regulation still requires the test, and (4) failure to timely develop and submit a spill prevention plan.

To calculate economic benefit of noncompliance using the BEN model, the following inputs are required: the initial capital investment and the annual operating and maintenance expense of any required equipment, the first month of noncompliance, the date of actual or assumed compliance, and the date of penalty payment.[87]

For avoided costs, the BEN model is designed to calculate the cost of compliance and then make adjustments to reflect anticipated rate of return and income tax effects on the violator. For delayed costs, since the violator eventually will have to spend money to achieve compliance, the model is programmed to calculate the amount of interest on the unspent money that reasonably could have been earned by the violator during noncompliance.[88]

EPA also may consider whether an adjustment in the civil penalty amount is justified on the basis of extreme financial hardship to the violator.[89] Upon a claim of such hardship, EPA may request from the violator tax returns and other financial information. This information then will be entered into a second computer program—named ABEL—that will project the probable availability of future internally generated cash flows to evaluate a violator's options for paying the penalty. If the ABEL analysis indicates that the violator indeed will suffer extreme financial hardship, EPA may in its discretion reduce the penalty amount accordingly.

B. Civil Enforcement Trends and Records

As EPA's statistics demonstrate, civil rather than criminal enforcement continues to be the most often used weapon in EPA's arsenal. In FY 1982, EPA referred 110 civil cases to the Department of Justice, compared to just 20 criminal referrals in that same year. By FY 1991, the number of civil referrals soared to 393,[90] compared to 81 criminal referrals. Moreover, in recent years, EPA has significantly stepped up its civil enforcement efforts. Since FY 1989, EPA has referred 1,132 civil cases to the Department of Justice; this amounts to nearly 30 percent of *all* civil referrals in the 20-year history of the Agency. By and large, EPA prefers civil enforcement actions over criminal, in part because

---

[87] EPA, Guidance for Calculating the Economic Benefit of Noncompliance for a Civil Penalty Assessment 3 (Nov. 5, 1984).

[88] While the resulting calculations of the BEN model are used extensively in settlements and litigations, some economists still believe that further refining of the model is necessary. *See, e.g.*, Fuhrman, *Getting It Right: EPA's "BEN" Model Still Needs Work*, 23 Env't Rep. 3100 (Apr. 2, 1993).

[89] EPA, Guidance on Determining a Violator's Ability to Pay a Civil Penalty (Dec. 16, 1986).

[90] While the 393 case figure is the highest total number ever referred to the Department of Justice in one year, EPA did not claim a record year. EPA implemented a new counting method in FY 1991 that adds actions under cross-program/multimedia efforts separately, which resulted in a higher total number of referrals to the Department of Justice. Under the old counting method, EPA would have had 366 referrals, slightly below the previous referral record of 375 cases in FY 1990, calculated under the old "bean-counting" method.

the burden of proof is lower, the cases are more likely to settle rather than go to trial, and other procedural requirements are much more relaxed.

As the number of civil referrals by EPA has increased, the overall amount of penalties assessed in terms of dollars has grown substantially. This is in large part due to an increase in the statutory civil penalty limits in the various environmental statutes that have been reauthorized over the past 10 years and an increased awareness on the part of the public as to the seriousness of environmental violations. However, this increase in penalty amounts also is due to an improvement in the quality of the cases being brought by the Agency. According to EPA personnel, this has resulted in the assessment of larger penalty amounts and EPA taking a tougher stance in settlement negotiations. Congress has also made a conscious effort to standardize penalty amounts so that violations of similar provisions of different laws will result in similar penalties. Still, increased efforts on the part of EPA cannot be discounted as a cause of this upswing in civil enforcement.

In FY 1991, EPA assessed a record of $41.2 million in civil judicial penalties. This represents a 21 percent increase over the previous year, and it also represents 23 percent of *all* civil penalties assessed in EPA's history. In the past three years, EPA has assessed 53 percent of all civil penalties ever assessed by the Agency.

In FY 1991, penalties for violations of the Clean Water Act dominated the civil penalties assessed by EPA with 36 percent of the total. Following the Clean Water Act, penalties under RCRA amounted to 24 percent and penalties under the Toxic Substances Control Act (TSCA) amounted to 15 percent.

In FY 1991, EPA obtained the largest civil penalty ever for a Clean Water Act violation.[91] In that case, a steel company agreed to pay nearly $6.2 million in civil penalties for committing thousands of violations of applicable Clean Water Act permit requirements, including repeated illegal discharges of wastewater containing various metals, cyanide, and oil and grease to the Ohio River. EPA in FY 1991 also assessed civil penalties for violations of the Clean Air Act, RCRA, the Safe Drinking Water Act, FIFRA, EPCRA, and CERCLA.

C. Civil Enforcement Authority

EPA has in place enforcement programs under each of the various environmental statutes that are briefly discussed in Chapters 3 through 10. Each statute has its own enforcement provisions that are used to assess civil and criminal penalties, as well as provide injunctive relief. Congress has, over the years, made a sustained effort to standardize the penalty provisions of the various environmental statutes. As such, most statutes have similar or identical civil penalty levels as well as standards for determining violations.[92]

[91] United States v. Wheeling-Pittsburgh Steel Corp., No. C2 88-598 (S.D. Ohio July 16, 1991) (the fine, the largest Clean Water Act penalty ever, was assessed as part of a settlement between the federal government and Wheeling-Pittsburgh).

[92] *See, e.g.*, CAA, 42 U.S.C. §7413(b) (Supp. III 1991); CWA, 33 U.S.C. §1319(d) (1988); CERCLA, 42 U.S.C. §9609 (1988); RCRA, 42 U.S.C. §6928(g) (1988); TSCA, 15 U.S.C. §2615(a) (1988); and SDWA, 42 U.S.C. §300g-3(b) (1988) (public water systems) and 42 U.S.C. §300h-2(b) (1988) (underground sources of drinking water).

Under most statutes, the maximum civil penalty for each violation is $25,000. Further, each day of violation constitutes a separate offense. Thus, significant penalties can accrue within a short period of time for companies that fail to quickly achieve and maintain compliance.

As with criminal enforcement, there are also other, more general civil authorities that are available to the government as it enforces environmental statutes. For instance, under the Federal Debt Collection Procedures Act (FDCPA),[93] the federal government has the right to obtain a prejudgment remedy where there is reason to believe that the party against whom the United States has asserted a claim will leave the jurisdiction, attempt to conceal or dispose of assets, or has avoided service of process.[94] The FDCPA also provides that a judgment in a civil action creates a lien in favor of the federal government on all real property of the debtor.[95] As such, the United States may force the sale of real property in order to satisfy a debt under a civil judgment.[96] Lastly, the FDCPA allows the federal government to void prior transfers of a debtor's property that were fraudulently made.[97]

In a recent decision under this provision, the court voided certain real estate transfers made by the defendant to his wife, even though they occurred prior to the enactment of the FDCPA.[98] The United States had filed a CERCLA cost recovery action against the defendant and sought to ensure that sufficient funds were available to satisfy the claim, even though the defendant disputed the claim and it had yet to be resolved by a court.[99] By this action, the federal government was able to ensure that the defendant had assets that could be used to satisfy the United States' claim when and if it prevailed in the CERCLA action.

1. Administrative Actions

As well as having authority to seek civil penalties through the judicial system, EPA has the option of bringing administrative actions to assess civil penalties. In assessing penalties pursuant to administrative mechanisms, EPA is not bound by all of the rules attendant to a court action. EPA must, however, provide certain procedural safeguards, the foremost being the opportunity for a hearing before an Agency administrative judge.[100] However, the administrative process, which may result in penalties as high as $25,000 per day of violation, is much less burdensome for EPA and provides less procedural protections to alleged violators than judicial proceedings. Some of the administrative provi-

---

[93] 28 U.S.C. §3001 *et seq.* (Supp. III 1991).

[94] 28 U.S.C. §3101(b) (Supp. III 1991).

[95] 28 U.S.C. §3201(a) (Supp. III 1991).

[96] 28 U.S.C. §3203 (Supp. III 1991).

[97] 28 U.S.C. §3304 (Supp. III 1991). Such a transfer is "fraudulent" if it was made without receiving a "reasonably equivalent value in exchange for the transfer," and the debtor is at the time or becomes insolvent because of the transfer; or the transfer is to an insider who had reasonable cause to believe the debtor to be insolvent. 28 U.S.C. §3304(a) (Supp. III 1991).

[98] United States v. Dickerson, 790 F. Supp. 1583 (M.D. Ga. 1992). 28 U.S.C. §3631 provides for the retroactive applicability of the FDCPA.

[99] 790 F. Supp. at 1584–85.

[100] *See, e.g.*, CWA §309(g)(2)(A) and (B), 33 U.S.C. §1319(g)(2)(A) and (B) (1988).

sions do place caps on the total amount of penalties that can be recovered by EPA, but others do not.[101]

As shown by recent activity, EPA strongly favors administrative over judicial actions in penalizing violators of most environmental statutes.[102] From FY 1982 to FY 1991, the annual number of administrative actions brought by EPA increased from 1,000 to nearly 4,000. Most of these actions were brought under the authority of the Clean Water and Safe Drinking Water Acts.[103] With the addition of administrative penalty authority under the 1990 Clean Air Act, this figure has continued to grow. In FY 1991, EPA assessed nearly $32 million in administrative penalties.[104] In FY 1991, EPA assessed an administrative penalty of $3,375,000 under RCRA and another of $2,220,000 under TSCA.[105]

The Agency's statutory administrative penalty authorities vary to some extent, mainly in terms of the specific violations to which the different penalty amounts apply. For instance, the Clean Water Act provides for Class I and Class II administrative penalties.[106] The main differences between the two classes of penalties are (1) the monetary limits on the penalties EPA or the Corps of Engineers can assess, and (2) the procedures EPA or the Corps must follow in order to impose the penalties.[107] The Safe Drinking Water Act provides for administrative penalty assessments under its programs regulating public drinking water systems as well as underground sources of drinking water.[108] However, under the public drinking water provisions the Agency's administrative assessment authority is limited to $5,000.[109] A $125,000 cap is in place for the underground drinking water program.[110]

For Class I Clean Water Act penalties, the upper limit on the penalty is $10,000 per violation, and $25,000 total for the proceeding. The alleged violator only has the right to an informal hearing. The upper limit on penalties in Class II Clean Water Act proceedings also is $10,000 per violation, but the maximum amount for the proceeding can be as high as $125,000. In a Class II proceeding, the alleged violator is entitled to a formal hearing before an administrative law judge (ALJ) in accordance with procedures set forth in the Administrative Procedure Act. In determining an appropriate penalty in either a Class I or Class

[101] Both the Clean Water Act and the Safe Drinking Water Act have administrative penalty caps of $125,000, while the Clean Air Act sets a cap of $200,000. *See* CWA §309(g)(2)(B), 33 U.S.C. §1319(g)(2)(B) (1988); SDWA §1423(c)(2), 42 U.S.C. §300h-2(c)(2) (1988); and CAA §205(c)(1), 42 U.S.C. §7524(c)(1) (Supp. III 1991). *But see* RCRA §3008(a)(3), 42 U.S.C. §6928(a)(3) (1988) (no limit on administrative penalty assessments).

[102] Out of all of the civil cases in FY 1991 under which EPA either assessed or won a penalty, 89% were from administrative enforcement actions. EPA, NATIONAL PENALTY REPORT 18 (Mar. 1992).

[103] *See* CWA §309(g), 33 U.S.C. §1319(g) (1988); SDWA §1414(g), 42 U.S.C. §300g (1988).

[104] NATIONAL PENALTY REPORT, *supra*, note 102, at 7. This total includes administrative penalties under the water, air (mobile sources), drinking water, and marine protection acts, along with RCRA, EPCRA, CERCLA, TSCA, and FIFRA. *Id.*

[105] *Id.* at 18.

[106] 33 U.S.C. §1319(g)(2) (1988).

[107] The Clean Water Act administrative penalty authorities also extend to the U.S. Army Corps of Engineers that administers the dredge and fill (wetlands protection) program under §404 of the Act.

[108] SDWA §1414(g), 42 U.S.C. §300g-3(g) (1988) (public water systems); SDWA §1423(c), 42 U.S.C. §300h-2(c) (1988) (underground sources of drinking water).

[109] SDWA §1414(g)(3)(A), 42 U.S.C. §300g-3(g)(3)(A) (1988).

[110] SDWA §1423(c)(2), 42 U.S.C. §300h-2(c)(2) (1988).

II proceeding, the ALJ or EPA is to consider the same types of factors that are considered by courts in assessing civil penalties.

Once these administrative penalty proceedings are initiated by EPA or the Corps of Engineers, they operate to bar citizen suits under the Clean Water Act for the same violations.[111] The proceedings, however, must have been initiated prior to EPA receiving notice that a citizen suit will be filed. Although the administrative penalty provision limits citizen suits significantly, citizens may nonetheless participate in the administrative proceeding.

Thus, while civil and criminal judicial actions are crucial to EPA's overall success in combatting violations of environmental statutes, administrative actions continue to be EPA's most widely used tool in enforcing compliance. These authorities are likely to continue to be used quite frequently, in part because of the control over the action exercised by EPA,[112] but also because of the fact that the average time to resolution is six months, rather than three or four years as in the case of civil actions. Administrative penalties have proved to be a valuable enforcement tool in effectively deterring companies from committing violations.

2. *Citizen Suits*

In addition to federal enforcement actions initiated by EPA, most environmental statutes provide private individuals and organizations the authority to participate in enforcement through citizen suits.[113] Although the scope of each statute's provisions vary, they generally authorize any person to bring a civil action against any alleged violator, or against EPA for a failure to perform a nondiscretionary duty.[114]

When suing the federal government, citizen suits normally proceed under two broad theories. The first theory is where the government, usually in the person of the EPA Administrator, has failed to perform a duty that is mandated by law. A typical example of this is where a statute directs EPA to promulgate a regulation implementing a statutory provision within a specific time frame, and the Agency fails to do so. Called a "deadline suit," this litigation usually results in EPA being placed on an enforceable schedule to promulgate the required regulations.

The second theory is where the federal government itself is alleged to be in violation of the statute. This type of action can arise in numerous circumstances but the most common is where a federal agency is in violation of a permit or

[111] CWA §309(g)(6)(B), 33 U.S.C. §1319(g)(6)(B) (1988). This provision was, in part, a response to court decisions stating that the Agency's pursuit of an administrative penalty proceeding was not an "action in court" sufficient to bar a citizen suit action. *See, e.g.,* Proffitt v. Commissioners, Bristol Tp., 754 F.2d 504, 22 ER Cases 1333 (3d Cir. 1985).

[112] Unlike civil and criminal actions that EPA must coordinate with the Department of Justice, administrative penalty assessments are handled solely by EPA.

[113] *See, e.g.,* CAA §304, 42 U.S.C. §7604 (Supp. III 1991); CWA §505, 33 U.S.C. §1365 (1988); CERCLA §310, 42 U.S.C. §9659 (1988); EPCRA §326, 42 U.S.C. §11046 (1988); RCRA §7002, 42 U.S.C. §6972 (1988); SDWA §1449, 42 U.S.C. §300j-8 (1988); and TSCA §20, 15 U.S.C. §2619 (1988).

[114] Citizen suit provisions have been incorporated into environmental statutes for more than 20 years and never have been declared unconstitutional. *See, e.g.,* Delaware Valley Toxics Coalition v. Kurz-Hastings, Inc., No. 92-5961 (E.D. Pa. Feb. 17, 1993) (in upholding the constitutionality of EPCRA's citizen suit provision, the court noted, "I will not be the first court to hold these provisions unconstitutional").

some other statutory requirement. Usually the remedy sought is injunctive relief to order the affected agency to comply with its permit requirements, or to otherwise comply with the law, and penalties.[115]

As a prerequisite to any citizen suit, the statutes normally require the private party to provide 60-days' notice to the federal government (both EPA and the Department of Justice), the state where the alleged violation took place, and the alleged violator prior to actually commencing the lawsuit.[116] The purpose of the notice requirement is to give the primary enforcement authorities the opportunity to initiate an action on their own and to avoid litigation by allowing the alleged violator to correct any infraction and to negotiate with the citizen any resolution of the threatened action.

As a second prerequisite, under some statutes, a citizen suit can only be initiated against an entity alleged to be in current violation of the particular statute. In other words, citizens may not maintain an action where they allege that violations of the law occurred wholly in the past.[117] The Supreme Court in *Gwaltney of Smithfield v. Chesapeake Bay Foundation*[118] held that federal court jurisdiction over citizen suits arises only where the citizens "make a good faith allegation of continuous or intermittent violation." That pleading requirement is usually easily met unless the alleged violating facility has closed. Interestingly, the 1990 Clean Air Act expressly allows citizen suits for wholly past violations.

Finally, as a third prerequisite, any person or organization bringing a citizen suit must establish proper standing by alleging an injury in fact. In *Lujan v. Defenders of Wildlife,*[119] the Supreme Court construed the citizen suit provision of the National Environmental Policy Act to require the following:

> [T]he "injury in fact" test requires more than an injury to a hypothetical interest. It requires that the party seeking review be himself among the injured.[120]

The *Defenders of Wildlife* case seems to have tightened the test for standing to bring a citizen suit. In the past, courts have held that an environmental organization's aesthetic interests to enjoy natural areas are the type of interests "which have always enjoyed protection under standing analysis."[121] Nevertheless, while the *Defenders of Wildlife* case did not clarify the continuing vitality of standing based on interests such as those that are "aesthetic," an analysis of that case certainly suggests that would-be litigants must be able to emphasize

---

[115] The Federal Facility Compliance Act, Pub. L. No. 102-386, 106 Stat. 1505 (1992) (to be codified at 42 U.S.C. §6961) specifically waives sovereign immunity under RCRA and also exempts federal employees and their agents from personal liability for civil penalties, which most environmental statutes already provided.

[116] *See, e.g.,* Hallstrom v. Tillamook County, 493 U.S. 20 (1989) (ruling that, under the citizen suit provision of RCRA, failure of plaintiff to give required 60-day notice required dismissal of the case).

[117] *See, e.g.,* Gwaltney of Smithfield, Ltd. v. Chesapeake Bay Found., Inc., 484 U.S. 49 (1987) (Clean Water Act §505(a) does not permit citizen suits for *wholly* past violations).

[118] 484 U.S. at 64. *See also* Comite Pro Rescate De La Salud v. PRASA, 693 F. Supp. 1324, 1334, 28 ER Cases 1769 (D.P.R. 1988) (in a Clean Air Act §304 citizen suit, allegations that show "continuing intermittent violations of the [Clean Air Act] in the past and a continuation of the conditions that led to those violations . . . satisfy the good-faith standard of *Gwaltney* and are sufficient to establish jurisdiction").

[119] 60 U.S.L.W. 4495 (1992).

[120] 60 U.S.L.W. at 4497 (quoting Sierra Club v. Morton, 405 U.S. 727, 734–35, 3 ER Cases 2039 (1972)). See Chapter 12, Reporting and Disclosure Requirements.

[121] Humane Soc'y of the U.S. v. Hodel, 840 F.2d 45, 52 (D.C. Cir. 1988). *See also* National Wildlife Fed'n v. Hodel, 839 F.2d 694 (D.C. Cir. 1988).

and demonstrate "direct" or "imminent" injury with as much specificity as possible.

Citizen suits normally may not be initiated if EPA or a state has commenced and is diligently prosecuting a civil action to require compliance with the law.[122] The statutes also make it clear, however, that any person may intervene as a matter of right in such an enforcement action brought by EPA or the state.[123] Likewise, EPA may intervene as a matter of right at any time in an action brought by a private citizen.[124]

Once all of the prerequisite procedural hurdles have been overcome, a private citizen is authorized to seek civil penalties. Most cases have held that penalties awarded by virtue of a citizen suit must be paid to the federal government and not to the citizens bringing the action. Generally, citizen suit provisions require that any such penalties recovered from a violator must be deposited in a special fund in the U.S. Treasury.[125] Alternatively, this money may sometimes be designated for use by EPA for an environmentally beneficial mitigation project. The Clean Air Act allows the court, in certain instances, to designate up to $100,000 of a citizen suit civil penalty for such projects that benefit public health or the environment.[126] The citizens can recover their attorney fees and costs of the litigation from the violating entity, including the federal government.

IV. Defense Strategies

As the previous sections of this chapter illustrate, federal, state, local, and citizen enforcers have an impressive array of weapons available to train on alleged violators of environmental laws. Not only are there a range of administrative, civil, and criminal authorities available, but with the various self-reporting requirements in the statutes and the deference afforded to EPA by the courts, the burden is more realistically on the accused to establish its compliance or innocence rather than on the government to prove violations.

As Chapter 17 explains in greater detail, the best defense for a company facing an environmental enforcement action is to be able to establish that a corporate policy existed that clearly established a commitment to comply with environmental laws and to ensure that its employees do the same. A company that treats environmental requirements as an unwelcome burden or an afterthought will, in addition to increasing the likelihood of violating the law, be unable to argue that any violation was an aberration from standard practices that is unlikely to recur. Thus, there is no reason for a company to wait until it receives a notice of violation or summons from EPA to prepare its defense to an environmental action. The basis for such a defense can and should be in place,

---

[122] *See, e.g.*, CAA §304(b)(1)(B), 42 U.S.C. §7604(b)(1)(B) (Supp. III 1991). Both the Clean Water Act and RCRA bar the continuation of a citizen suit if either a civil or criminal action has been commenced. *See* CWA §505(b)(1)(B), 33 U.S.C. §1365(b)(1)(B) (1988); RCRA §7002(b)(1)(B), 42 U.S.C. §6972(b)(1)(B) (1988).

[123] CAA §304(b)(1)(B), 42 U.S.C. §7604(b)(1)(B) (Supp. III 1991).

[124] *See, e.g.*, CAA §304(c)(2), 42 U.S.C. §7604(c)(2) (Supp. III 1991).

[125] *See, e.g.*, CAA §304(g), 42 U.S.C. §7604(g) (Supp. III 1991).

[126] CAA §304(g)(2), 42 U.S.C. §7604(g)(2) (Supp. III 1991).

in the form of a corporate philosophy that makes compliance with environmental laws, standards, and regulations an integral part of the standard operating procedures of the company.

Still, even the most conscientious of companies or individuals can find themselves in the crosshairs of an environmental enforcement action. There are many factors that will determine the type of action to be pursued by federal, state, and local enforcers. Usually, however, there will not be as many factors that will determine the response that the company or individual should make. While responses range from total capitulation to Agency demands to total defiance and forcing the enforcement action to its ultimate conclusion (usually a trial), the preferred response will fall somewhere between these two extremes in the vast majority of cases.

In the past, many traditional litigation tactics have had an exaggerated impact in the environmental arena. Many believed that environmental enforcers were tremendously overworked. Consequently, "bury them in paper" was often a defendant's response to a civil suit brought by the Department of Justice on behalf of EPA. Frequent motion practice and heavy discovery demands would be imposed on a Department of Justice or EPA attorney supposedly ill-equipped to respond. With the prospect of a trial looming in the background, and the knowledge that a caseload of 20 to 40 similar cases was waiting, the objective of this strategy was to wear down the government opposition and win a settlement more favorable to the defendant. Today, it is rare for this strategy to improve defendants' settlement prospects or chances at trial. This strategy could, however, prove more successful for an action brought by a citizen's group. Although, even with that class of case, national environmental advocacy groups are usually organized and sophisticated enough to survive such tactics.

To better understand what the proper defense to a civil enforcement action or criminal indictment should be, it is useful to review the enforcers' goals. There are certain common goals whether it is a federal, state, local, or citizen enforcement action, or a criminal indictment. Among these are prompt remediation of environmental violations, commitments to avoid such violations in the future, restitution, and some degree of punishment for violations. Clearly, the easiest way to accomplish these goals is to have a quick resolution of the allegations so that the primary goal, remediation of environmental harms, can be implemented. To that end, on the civil side it has long been the policy of the United States in general and EPA in particular to "[p]rovide incentives to settle and institute prompt remedial action."[127] Similarly, EPA is prepared to "[p]rovide disincentives to delaying compliance."[128] The primary "incentive" available to EPA in the civil or administrative context is the amount of money it seeks for a violation. Civil and administrative penalties range as high as $25,000 per day, with continuing violations resulting in very significant monetary exposure. While there are maximums for administrative penalties under some statutes, there are no such corresponding limitations on civil penalties imposed

[127] EPA General Enforcement Policy #GM-21, Policy on Civil Penalties, at 6, Feb. 16, 1984. In 1991, President Bush issued Executive Order No. 12,778 in response to the "tremendous growth" in civil litigation. Oct. 23, 1991, Civil Justice Reform. 56 Fed. Reg. 55,195 (1991). That Order directed that both before filing a civil action and during the pendency of such action attorneys for the United States shall make "reasonable efforts" to settle the matter. E.O. No. 12,778, §1(a) and (b).

[128] Policy on Civil Penalties, at 6.

in judicial actions. The Agency's clear message, therefore, is that it will seek higher or lower penalties based on the willingness of an entity to cooperate.

On the criminal side, corporate fines can range as high as $1 million per offense, while individuals face the highest "fine" possible, loss of liberty. But, as noted previously, one of the elements in the Department of Justice's guidelines for determining whether or not to prosecute violators is "the extent and timeliness of the violating entity's cooperation."[129]

EPA has developed a general civil enforcement policy as well as several media-specific policies.[130] Included in the various policies are guidances to Agency enforcers on the types of cases to be brought in different circumstances, along with a formula to calculate civil penalties that is intended to provide an objective basis for such penalties. It must be noted, however, that these policies are informal guidance to EPA employees and may not be relied upon to ensure a specific result.[131] It has also been held that the policy is inapplicable to lawsuits not prosecuted by the federal government.[132] Understanding what EPA is seeking to accomplish provides the best basis for deciding what defense to use in an enforcement action.

In defending a civil or criminal enforcement action, the choices are relatively simple: settle or fight. On the civil side, the Agency will normally notify a party of the pendency of an action and offer to settle either prior to or at the time of filing the complaint. EPA's settlement offer will be based on a number of factors enunciated in the appropriate penalty policy. Generally, they are "degree of willfulness and/or negligence"; degree of cooperation/noncooperation"; "history of noncompliance"; and "other unique factors specific to the violator or the case."[133]

On the criminal side, there may or may not be an indication that a company or individual is the target of a criminal investigation prior to the government's initiation of grand jury proceedings. However, under the Justice Department's guidelines it is likely that at least in the corporate context evidence of the existence of a criminal investigation will be readily apparent. In this situation, the government's "hand" arguably increases as the investigation progresses. Similarly, the chances of a resolution more favorable to the defendant usually decreases as the case makes its way through the system. As the Justice

---

[129] U.S. Dep't of Justice, Factors in Decisions on Criminal Prosecutors for Environmental Violations, *supra* note 14.

[130] *See supra* note 84.

[131] "The policies and procedures set out in this document and in the *Framework for Statute-Specific Approach to Penalty Assessment* are intended solely for the guidance of government personnel. They are not intended and cannot be relied upon to create any rights, substantive or procedural, enforceable by any party in litigation with the United States. The Agency reserves the right to act at variance with these policies and procedures and to change them at any time without public notice. . . ." POLICY ON CIVIL PENALTIES, *supra* note 81, at 7.

With such significant discretion in its implementation of the penalty policy, it has also been long suspected that the formula can be manipulated to justify virtually any penalty amount that EPA desires to reach.

[132] Sierra Club v. Electronic Controls Design, 909 F.2d 1350, 1354–55 n.6 (9th Cir. 1990). "The U.S. makes much of the fact that the proposed payments are also inconsistent with the Environmental Protection Agency's (EPA) settlement policy. That policy is irrelevant to this appeal. Because the policy also states that it is intended only to guide the EPA in cases *prosecuted by the government,* we need not decide whether the payments required under the proposed consent decree in a citizens' suit are within the four corners of the EPA's policy." *Id.* (emphasis in original).

[133] POLICY ON CIVIL PENALTIES, *supra* note 81, at 5.

Department's policy notes, "mitigating" factors will be reviewed "[w]here the law and evidence would otherwise be sufficient for prosecution."[134] Further, "mitigating efforts made by the regulated community will be recognized and evaluated. The greater the showing of good faith, the more likely it will be met with leniency. Conversely, the less good faith shown, the less likely that prosecutorial direction will tend toward leniency."[135]

Since it is the rare case where a total defense to an environmental action is present, the goal of whatever strategy employed should be to reduce the amount of the fine or prison sentence and/or limit the amount of remedial or corrective activity required. Arguments such as reasons for the violations, past history of compliance and cooperation with regulatory officials, voluntary corrective measures, prompt notification of violations, and a willingness to go beyond the minimum required by law or regulation must be prepared and presented to prosecuting officials. Depending on the responses from EPA and the Department of Justice, both formal and informal, a decision must be made whether the government or a court will be more receptive to such arguments. Unfortunately, there is no infallible formula to aid in that decision, and there are intangible human factors that will often be the deciding factor.

Many questions should be answered before an informed decision can be made regarding defense strategy. However, the primary defense should almost always be an attempt to reach some settlement with the government. Otherwise, the company or individual must determine if a court is willing to immerse itself in the technical morass that accompanies environmental matters. Does the judge's individual judicial record and reputation reflect a tendency to support the positions of administrative agencies? Would acceptance of the arguably technically or legally correct defense nonetheless require "sanctioning" an environmentally unpopular action on the part of the defendant? Does EPA have an enforcement policy goal that may go beyond the facts of the particular case? Is there some doubt that the company is actually guilty of the alleged violations? Do these violations merely represent the tip of the iceberg? Has the company corrected the violations as well as implemented measures to prevent their recurrence?

Added to the answers of these questions are certain other intangibles: which EPA regional office is prosecuting the action; which judge is likely to handle the trial; are there any district court decisions by that judge (or appellate decisions that the judge must follow) that give some indication of how the judge views cases of this type or how much deference a judge is to accord to EPA, particularly as to penalties and remedial requirements or in handling white collar criminal cases. After evaluating all of these issues, the defendant must make a decision by balancing the answers to the questions with the facts of the particular case.

Clearly, a decision to settle with the government amounts to an acknowledgment of culpability and that a better or cheaper deal probably could be obtained from the government rather than a judge, at least when litigation risks

[134] U.S. Dep't of Justice, Factors in Decisions on Criminal Prosecutors for Prosecutions for Environmental Violations, *supra* note 14, at 3.

[135] *Id.* at 14.

and costs are considered. It may also be a capitulation to the Agency's discretion in setting penalty levels and corrective requirements, or the Department of Justice's prosecutorial discretion in deciding what, if any, charges to bring. As such, this course should be well thought out before being pursued as a strategy. While there is clear deference to EPA and other agencies charged with administering technical statutes,[136] that deference is less pronounced when judges evaluate Agency penalty calculations. As judges assess penalties, fix damage amounts, and impose criminal sentences on a daily basis, they seldom think Agency personnel are better at calculating appropriate penalties than they are. "Assessment of the amount of a civil penalty is committed to the informed discretion of the Court."[137] As such, the court is free to accept, reject, or modify an EPA penalty calculation.

One of the major criticisms of the federal sentencing guidelines is that they take away or limit much of the discretion traditionally exercised by judges. As a result of these guidelines, however, it may actually be easier for a criminal defendant to predict what the outside risks of incarceration and fine are.[138] Knowing the maximum fines and periods of incarceration and determining whether the various enhancement or reduction adjustments apply can give a defendant a good idea of the best and worst case scenarios. Also of major concern is the fact that the defendant's level of cooperation with governmental authorities can raise or lower the sentencing range, or influence whether a prosecution is even brought. Thus, the clear possibility exists that a vigorous corporate or criminal defense strategy could result in a sentencing recommendation that includes an enhancement for lack of cooperation.[139] When, however, the defendant is cooperative, a relatively favorable sentence with innovative components can result.[140]

---

[136] *See* Chevron, USA, Inc. v. Natural Resources Defense Council, 467 U.S. 837, 21 ER Cases 1049 (1984).

[137] United States v. Environmental Waste Control, Inc., 710 F. Supp. 1172, 1242, 29 ER Cases 1757 (N.D. Ind. 1989), *citing* United States v. ITT Continental Baking Co., 420 U.S. 223, 230 n.6 (1975). "In exercising this discretion, the Court should give effect to the major purpose of a civil penalty: deterrence. . . . RCRA requires the Administrator to take into account the seriousness of the violation and any good faith efforts to comply with applicable requirements. In the absence of other statutory guidance, the Court may give consideration to these same factors in determining an appropriate penalty." United States v. Environmental Waste Control, Inc., 710 F. Supp. at 1242, *citing* United States v. T&S Brass & Bronze Works, Inc., 681 F. Supp. 314, 322, 27 ER Cases 1220 (D.S.C. 1988).

[138] *See supra* notes 28 and 32.

[139] In a recent, nonenvironmental case, a federal district court judge actually *added* six months to a defendant's criminal sentence for going to trial rather than pleading guilty. United States v. Jones, Criminal No. 90-00240-01 (D.D.C. 1993). Perhaps even more surprising, a divided Court of Appeals for the District of Columbia Circuit upheld the additional time, although an en banc review of that decision is now pending. United States v. Jones, 973 F.2d 928 (D.C. Cir.), *vacated in part,* 980 F.2d 747 (D.C. Cir. 1992).

[140] United States v. Environmental Indus. Research Assoc., Inc., CR-91-255-01-D (M.D.N.C. Apr. 6, 1993) (laboratory pleaded guilty to defrauding EPA and was fined $174,000 out of maximum $500,000; all of the fine was suspended based on company's cooperation during the investigation and its planned community service program).

EPA has also decided that in civil settlements, the acceptance of "environmentally beneficial projects" is useful to the furtherance of the Agency's enforcement goals. "In certain instances, additional relief in the form of projects remediating the adverse public health or environmental consequences of the violations at issue may be included in the settlement to offset the effects of the particular violation which prompted the suit." EPA, POLICY ON THE USE OF SUPPLEMENTAL ENVIRONMENTAL PROJECTS IN ENFORCEMENT SETTLEMENTS 1 (Feb. 12, 1991). Generally the acceptable types of projects are pollution prevention, pollution reduction, adverse public health/environmental consequences remediation projects, environmental auditing projects, and enforcement-related environmental public awareness projects. *Id.* at 2–5.

There is seldom a down side to attempting to negotiate an acceptable settlement with EPA. Even if negotiations fail, the court will almost always inquire about previous settlement efforts. If the defendant has refused to negotiate with the Agency or has been unwilling to show reasonable flexibility in such negotiations, it will be harder to obtain a favorable result from the court. Judges frequently pressure parties to settle, and parties who have refused or been reluctant to show movement ordinarily receive the most pressure.

For a defense litigation strategy to succeed, the defendant must ordinarily be postured as always willing to negotiate, always ready to respond to an EPA proposal with a counterproposal of its own, and be in possession of arguments and verifiable facts to support its theory of penalty level and corrective measures. Included in these facts should be examples of similar cases in which EPA has accepted desired settlement conditions.

In *United States v. Environmental Waste Control, Inc.*,[141] EPA argued that the court should "presume" that it must assess the maximum penalty of $25,000 per day for the company's RCRA violations and reduce that amount only upon a showing of "mitigating considerations."[142] The court rejected this argument, acknowledging that while EPA has the right to adopt regulations for its own administrative assessment of civil penalties, that right may not "impinge on the discretion Congress has afforded the courts."[143] The court then determined that the Agency was actually seeking a total of $60,350,000 in penalties.[144] Finding that EPA's penalty request "would be wholly punitive and would far exceed the scope of any proper deterrent purpose," the court ultimately imposed a penalty of $2.778 million.[145] Thus, the principle that the courts are not bound by EPA penalty calculations was upheld.

It sometimes makes sense to force EPA to prove its case in court because there are numerous instances where trials or court hearings resulted in the imposition of smaller fines than proposed by the Agency or in a handful of cases, vindication for the company.[146] Those cases are, however, infrequent.

Prior to and during negotiations with EPA, the best approach is to objectively evaluate and, if necessary, acknowledge the weaknesses of a defendant's case. That is, *admit* for settlement purposes to the violations if they in fact

---

[141] 710 F. Supp. 1172, 1242, 29 ER Cases 1757 (N.D. Ind. 1989).

[142] 710 F. Supp. at 1242.

[143] *Id.*

[144] *Id.* at 1244. The court also ruled that the actual number of days that the company was in violation of the statute was less than EPA had alleged. *Id.*

[145] *Id.* at 1245.

[146] United States v. Coastal Ref. & Mktg., Inc., 911 F.2d 1036, 32 ER Cases 1088 (5th Cir. 1990) (dismissing suit of the United States on appeal after trial court had initially found violation of Clean Air Act regulations); Katzson Bros., Inc. v. EPA, 839 F.2d 1396, 27 ER Cases 1425 (10th Cir. 1988) (remanding EPA penalty calculation under FIFRA, in part due to the "severity of the penalty" considering the violator's "spotless prior compliance record and the lack of harm caused to the environment by the violator"); Yaffe Iron & Metal Co. v. EPA, 774 F.2d 1008 (10th Cir. 1985) (upheld finding of violations but vacated and remanded to the Agency civil penalty imposed by EPA since it improperly considered certain evidence); United States v. Walsh, 783 F. Supp. 546, 34 ER Cases 1974 (W.D. Wash. 1991) (government sought over $825,000 from virtually indigent defendant, but court set penalty of $3,500); United States v. Louisiana-Pac. Corp., 682 F. Supp. 1141, 27 ER Cases 1621 (D. Colo. 1988) (rejecting as "arbitrary and simplistic" EPA's proposed methodology to calculate penalty and setting a $65,000 penalty for Clean Air Act violations); United States v. SCM Corp., 667 F. Supp. 1110, 26 ER Cases 1586 (D. Md. 1987) (rejecting Agency claims as to both number and duration of Clean Air Act violations and imposing penalty of less than Agency request for statutory maximum).

occurred. At the same time, however, there will likely be holes or shortcomings in the government's case. Often, actions taken by a company were informally discussed or even approved by Agency personnel. While these actions will likely be insufficient to legally bind the EPA, they certainly may serve to mitigate the severity of the company's actions. Emphasize those weaknesses as support for the position that the amount of penalties or scope of remediation sought by the government is excessive.

On the criminal side, realize that arguments that the defendant was not the perpetrator, that the crime did not occur, or that there was no criminal intent will likely have little impact in a criminal environmental prosecution. In the context of a corporate prosecution there will be few circumstances where the argument can be made that the wrong company was indicted. On the individual side, the concept embodied in the responsible corporate official doctrine virtually eliminates the chances of foisting responsibility off onto another employee of the corporation.[147] Still, weaknesses common to civil cases can and do exist on the criminal side as well. Levels of involvement, good faith, and advice received from government agencies are all examples of factors that, while not sufficient to cause dismissal, can be used to mitigate the severity of the sentence.

The company must also try to convince the Agency that the commitment and resources to ensure that these types of violations will not recur are present. *Accepting* that responsibility either by identifying changes in the corporate management structure or employee training procedure are ways to present evidence of that acknowledgment by the company to EPA. Instituting a voluntary environmental audit program is also an excellent method of ensuring confidence that violations will not recur. It is also consistent with policies promoted by both EPA and the Department of Justice. Obviously the costs of restitution or changes offered as evidence of a changed corporate attitude should not outweigh the severity of the accused violations, although a dollar for dollar trade-off is not always possible.

The company must also establish that any changes in corporate structure and philosophy are real. It should *act* quickly to implement them. It is not necessary to wait until a settlement or plea agreement is reached with the government to begin implementing necessary changes. Part of the aim of remediating problems is to accomplish changes quickly. As such, once a change in procedure or structure or the acquisition of new equipment is decided upon, the company should proceed whether or not an agreement has been reached with EPA. "Credit" for the changes can be obtained if it is made clear that they were done in response to the problems or violations identified by the enforcement action. Again, the company must be firm in its dealings with the Agency, since EPA will attempt to require additional measures beyond those implemented by the company. Even during negotiations, it will be wise to consult with EPA technical personnel regarding the scope of changes instituted. It will be more difficult for EPA to argue that not enough was done if it was consulted

[147] Of course, no avenue should be ignored in examining possible defense strategies. For example, an indicted employee of a corporation should investigate the possibility that the responsible corporate official doctrine places responsibility for the offense with some other corporate officer. Even if this approach is successful it is unlikely to result in exoneration of the employee but may add the corporate officer to the action. Additionally, it may result in making the employee appear to be less culpable at the time of sentencing.

every step of the way. "Admitting," "accepting," and "acting," if done with the proper safeguards will likely lead to a successful negotiation with the Agency.

Finally, there are other steps that a company can take even before a violation occurs that will leave it better situated to respond to an investigation, especially in the criminal context. Defense and indemnification policies should be in place to reassure employees that the corporation will stand behind them. Similarly, joint defense strategies should be considered where both the company and its employees are targets of an investigation or are indicted.

A company should make the corporate decision that it will assist its officers and employees if those people find themselves under criminal or civil investigation because of their activities in carrying out corporate environmental responsibilities. Responsible corporate officials, as well as line employees, need to know when, under what circumstances, and to what extent, the company will defend them if they are charged with a criminal offense or threatened with individual fines. Employees acting clearly outside the scope of their employment may be treated differently from employees facing sanctions for following corporate policies. Corporations should consider indemnifying employees for the costs of their defense counsel and providing insurance or the possibility of reimbursement for fines, if permitted by law. Payment of counsel costs cannot, however, be tied to cooperation by the employee or limitations on the type of testimony provided by the employee. These policies should be set out in advance by the corporations, both for the well being and comfort of the employees but also to avoid the possibility of tampering charges.

Joint defense strategies should also be considered if both the corporation and individuals are targeted. It is sometimes a prosecutorial tactic to pit the interests of the individual against those of the corporation. That is, either offer a better deal for the individual in exchange for his or her cooperation in the government's case against the corporation or entice the corporation to make more concessions in exchange for leniency against the individual. There is nothing wrong with this practice, and it should be considered as part of a potential joint defense strategy. At some point, however, corporate and individual interests can and do diverge. It should be acknowledged by both the corporation and the individual that at some point a joint defense strategy may not be proper—especially should the case go to trial. For example, at trial, the parties must be diligent that evidence properly introduced against only one defendant is so limited by the court. This will insure that inferences against any other defendant cannot be drawn by the jury. Corporate policy cannot, therefore, be devised so as to provide unlimited benefits and protections to employees.

V. Conclusion

The easiest way to avoid civil and criminal liability is to know what the law is and to comply with it. Also make sure that everyone in the company is aware of the legal requirements applicable to their work responsibilities. Even with the best of intentions, however, violations of the law can occur. Those entities and individuals that have operated in accordance with a process and structure that demonstrates knowledge, diligence, attention, and care will be in a far better position to survive. When faced with a criminal or civil prosecution, perform a worst and best case scenario and make defense strategy decisions accordingly.

This is an extremely serious area of the law. Companies can fail, careers can be ended, and the course of lives altered beyond recognition. The environment and the laws designed to protect it are intended to and should be taken quite seriously. There is not likely to be any relaxation of the government's efforts to make compliance in this area uniform. As the new EPA Administrator stated, ''[w]e must restore voluntary compliance with the nation's environmental laws by making them fair and efficient, *by forcefully executing them,* and by increasing public disclosure of environmental practices.''[148]

---

[148] *Opening Statement of Administrator Designate of the Environmental Protection Agency, Carol M. Browner, Before the Senate Comm. on Environment and Public Works,* Jan. 11, 1993, at 3 (emphasis added).

17

Compliance Management and Strategies

*By J. Gordon Arbuckle and Timothy A. Vanderver, Jr.**

I. Introduction

How well a company complies with laws and regulations designed to protect the environment is becoming more and more important as requirements become more pervasive and the consequences of noncompliance escalate. Effective environmental management has become a critical factor for organizations and the individuals working in them.

This need for effective management systems to assure compliance with environmental obligations has been reinforced, in the early 1990s, by continued escalation in the aggressiveness of governmental and private efforts to enforce environmental duties and to punish failure to perform them. It is further emphasized by the policies of the Department of Justice (DOJ), the Environmental Protection Agency (EPA), and new Federal Sentencing Guidelines, which give great weight to the existence or nonexistence of environmental management systems in deciding how strict enforcement will be. In addition, environmental statutes and regulations are becoming increasingly more stringent and detailed, requiring additional monitoring and reporting, more extensive prevention and response measures, and authorizing severe civil and criminal penalties for violation of statutory and regulatory requirements.

As a consequence, compliance management in the 1990s requires much greater day-to-day attention to compliance issues, a detailed knowledge of how a company and its pollution control equipment and policies are working, a full understanding of the results of monitoring and auditing, and the devotion of adequate resources to a comprehensive management system. Failure to take such steps can result in consequences that are wildly disproportionate to the time, money, and effort saved by stinting on the environmental program. Environmental compliance management is a crucial part of corporate management and merits the same priority attention as economic aspects of corporate performance.

*The authors would like to thank Suzanne R. Schaeffer for her assistance in the preparation of this chapter.

This chapter identifies areas of concern for compliance managers and suggests compliance concepts for consideration in developing an appropriate and effective environmental compliance strategy. This guidance is of necessity quite general in nature, and cannot serve as a substitute for the development of individualized, comprehensive compliance strategies tailored to the individual company. Nonetheless, it can be used as a starting point for the development of such specific strategies.

II. Areas of Concern

A. Criminalization of Environmental Violations

Criminalizing conduct in the environmental arena has been a major trend of the last decade. Criminal prosecution focuses on the individuals who cause or are responsible for corporate actions, and subjects these individuals to punishment for illegal corporate actions. Thus, the rationale behind this trend is that the threat of prosecution is far more effective in motivating individuals to comply with environmental standards than almost anything else. A maxim among criminal lawyers is that nothing focuses a person's attention as effectively or opens one's wallet as quickly as the possibility of losing one's personal liberty.

A related aspect of the movement toward criminalizing environmental violations is the political advantage that is perceived to be gained by supporting environmental crimes legislation. Many lawmakers apparently believe that supporting such legislation establishes their environmental credentials, and it is also difficult to oppose such legislation since this may be regarded as favoring pollution and polluters. These political pressures often lead to broad criminal provisions and stringent penalties.

Emphasis on environmental enforcement through the criminal process has also been generated by the Environmental Crimes Section of DOJ's Division of Environment and Natural Resources. Since the unit's inception in 1982, its size and the scope of its efforts have increased significantly. This is evidenced by the steadily growing number of criminal indictments each year, as well as the millions of dollars in fines and hundreds of years of jail time imposed on corporations and individuals who have been convicted of or entered guilty pleas to environmental violations.

The threat of prosecution, conviction, and increased sentences for individual employees and officers under environmental statutes is serious. While companies cannot be sent to jail and are not directly affected by the sentencing guidelines for environmental crimes, they are nevertheless liable for their employees' conduct, since a corporation can only act through its agents and employees. Thus, companies may be subjected to large fines and other serious penalties for criminal violations of environmental statutes,[1] and must be vigilant

[1] For example, a company may be fined up to $1 million for knowing endangerment under the Resource Conservation and Recovery Act and the Clean Water Act. *See* 42 U.S.C. §6928(e) (1988); 33 U.S.C. §1319(c)(3) (1988). For a detailed discussion of criminal penalties for environmental, see Chapter 16, Enforcement and Defense Strategies.

to assure that they have minimized the risk of criminal liability arising from employee conduct. A Department of Justice memorandum detailing the factors to be considered in prosecuting environmental violations looks to preventive measures and compliance programs as indicia that a company is trying to comply with the law.[2] It also notes that the pervasiveness of noncompliance, internal disciplinary actions, and subsequent compliance efforts are additional relevant factors that will be considered. A company's careful attention to these same factors is critical to effective compliance management.

The foregoing and the more detailed discussion of liability and enforcement in Chapter 16 established that a critical element of any compliance strategy must be an effort to minimize the risk of criminal prosecution for a company and its officers and employees. The potentially wide-ranging and serious consequences of a criminal proceeding justify giving considerable attention to this issue.

B. Escalation of Civil Fines

A second major trend in compliance enforcement is the recent escalation in the size of civil fines for environmental violations. The dollar amount of such penalties has increased to the point where the traditional wisdom that civil fines cannot be sufficiently large to get the attention of major corporations no longer bears much relation to reality. With each day of violation and each limit exceeded being considered a separate offense at $25,000 to $50,000 per offense, fines of several hundred thousand dollars have become common, actual penalties in the $10 to $20 million range are no longer exceptional, and there is the potential for fines in the $100 million range. For example, in a recent enforcement action for violations of the Clean Water Act (CWA) and the Resource Conservation and Recovery Act (RCRA), a company was required to pay $9 million in civil penalties as part of a settlement agreement.[3] Thus, even when prosecution is civil instead of criminal, fines can be of sufficient magnitude to threaten the very existence of a company. Compliance programs that at least avoid long-term or repetitive violations are therefore essential to preserve the viability of companies.

C. Monitoring and Reporting Requirements

A third major trend affecting compliance is the effective use of monitoring and reporting requirements under most federal environmental statutes. This puts the burden on the company to monitor its compliance and report its noncompliance. Like the Internal Revenue Code, environmental laws are largely self-policing, so that it is not necessary to wait for the enforcer's visit to start the violation clock running. For example, in 1990, the Clean Air Act Amendments included provisions that impose greatly expanded monitoring and reporting

[2] U.S. Dep't of Justice, Factors in Decisions on Criminal Prosecutions for Environmental Violations in the Context of Significant Voluntary Compliance or Disclosure Efforts by the Violator (July 1, 1991) (unpublished memo).

[3] *See* United States v. Dexter, No. H-89-39 (D. Conn. Sept. 3, 1992). The company also agreed to pay $4 million in criminal penalties.

requirements for sources as part of a new permit program. Previously there was no permitting of air pollution sources and only minimal monitoring and sampling requirements. Under the 1990 Amendments, sources must report monitoring results to the permitting authority at least every six months. EPA is to specify the monitoring procedures and methods to be used, and although continuous monitoring is preferred, it is not required if sufficiently reliable alternatives are available.[4] Continuous monitoring will be required, however, for sources subject to the Amendments' new acid rain provisions, and states may also choose to include continuous monitoring requirements for other sources in their permit programs, as long as EPA approves these as "additional permitting requirements not inconsistent with [the] Act."[5]

Additional reporting requirements for spills of hazardous substances, oil, wastes, and other potentially harmful materials are found in the Comprehensive Environmental Response, Compensation, and Liability Act (CERCLA), the Emergency Planning and Community Right-to-Know Act (EPCRA), and the Clean Water Act as amended by the Oil Pollution Act, each of which imposes fairly extensive reporting requirements on companies, facilities, or vessels handling such materials.[6] Moreover, reporting of information that toxic and other substances may present a "substantial" risk of injury or may have "unreasonable" adverse effects on the environment is required under the Toxic Substances Control Act (TSCA) and the Federal Insecticide, Fungicide, and Rodenticide Act (FIFRA).[7]

Because of the importance of these monitoring and self-reporting provisions, careful attention must be paid to the performance limitations of monitoring technology in the real world, in contrast with such technology's theoretical capability. Facilities frequently accept monitoring requirements without knowing whether the technology to meet those requirements is available. If monitoring equipment, for example, has an error factor of plus or minus 10 percent, that factor should be built into the permit. Otherwise, the facility will be liable for the 10 percent error factor. This emphasizes not only the importance of technological considerations, but also the need for diligence in the permit application process in an attempt to work some flexibility into permit requirements.

Other concerns related to monitoring and reporting involve accuracy. The accuracy and reliability of sampling and laboratory analysis may be suspect, which could result in either reporting a violation where none exists or failing to report a violation that does. A submission to the reporting authority that inaccurately shows compliance is likely to be considered a false statement, and, as discussed previously, can lead to criminal prosecution. On the other hand, incorrectly reporting noncompliance needlessly subjects a source to enforcement and penalties. Unfortunately, such incorrect reporting, as well as incorrect and perhaps unintentional false reporting of compliance, happens with surpris-

---

[4]CAA §504, 42 U.S.C. §7661c (Supp. II 1990); *see also* 57 Fed. Reg. 32,250 (1992) (final permit regulations to be codified at 40 C.F.R. pt. 70).

[5]CAA §§404, 412, 506, 42 U.S.C. §§7651c, 7651k, 7661c (Supp. II 1990).

[6]*See* CERCLA §103, 42 U.S.C. §9603 (1988); EPCRA §§311–13, 42 U.S.C. §§11021–23 (1988); CWA §311, 33 U.S.C. §1321 (Supp. II 1990).

[7]TSCA §8(c)-(e), 15 U.S.C. §2606 (1988); FIFRA §6(a)(2), 7 U.S.C. §136d (1988).

ing frequency. Many of these cases do not involve intentional conduct but are simply the result of carelessness, inattention, or lack of understanding.

Monitoring and reporting requirements in environmental statutes and the penalties for their violation, as well as the negative consequences of inaccurate reporting, underscore the importance of paying adequate attention to reporting requirements, the monitoring and reporting process, available technology, and monitoring results in establishing an effective compliance program.

D. Citizen Suits

The monitoring and reporting requirements in environmental statutes, and the availability to the public of reported information, have greatly assisted individuals or groups who want to bring "citizen" suits and to government enforcers as well. Citizen suits have been a major enforcement tool under the Clean Water Act in recent years, and the citizen suit provisions contained in CERCLA and RCRA are also being used with greater frequency. It is likely that such suits will similarly be used for enforcement of the Clean Air Act in the near future.[8]

Citizen suit provisions generally enable a citizen—typically an environmental group—to sue a company or facility for violating its permit, statutory requirements, or regulatory limits. In addition, citizens are usually authorized to sue EPA for failure to adequately enforce the provisions of the statute.[9] In view of the self-reporting requirements under most statutes, proof is often no obstacle in such suits. For example, under the Clean Water Act, the mandatory quarterly monitoring reports filed by permittees are a matter of public record and are often used as the evidentiary basis of liability in citizen suits. A monitoring report that shows discharges of pollutants in excess of allowable regulatory levels, as reported by the discharger, is not only easily accessible but is fairly conclusive evidence of violation. Likewise, the spill reporting requirements under CERCLA and EPCRA provide readily available proof of violations to the citizen seeking to initiate enforcement action against a company.

The increasing amount of fines awarded in citizen suits, some for millions of dollars, and the recovery of attorneys' fees and costs by the prevailing party through enforcement efforts that use publicly available reported compliance information have become major concerns for the regulated community. This development also emphasizes the necessity for an effective compliance plan to avoid such enforcement.

E. Environmental Auditing and Assessment

During the early 1990s, environmental auditing and its variants, which generally involve reviewing the compliance posture of a given facility or company with the object of bringing that facility or company into full compliance, received a great deal of attention. Not surprisingly, environmental

---

[8] *See* CAA §304, 42 U.S.C. §7604 (1988 and Supp. II 1990).

[9] *See, e.g.*, CWA §505, 33 U.S.C. §1365 (1988); RCRA §7002, 42 U.S.C. §6972 (1988); CERCLA §310, 42 U.S.C. §9659 (1988).

auditing has not met all expectations, but it has generally proved to be a useful compliance tool.

The advantages of auditing are clear: it identifies any shortcomings, and the shortcomings can then be promptly corrected. The drawbacks are equally clear and fall into two categories. First, where serious deficiencies are identified by the audit, the audit report can be a road map for the prosecution, unless it can be protected from disclosure. Second, and perhaps more serious, is the situation where deficiencies are identified and not remedied. Conducting business with notice of compliance shortcomings will likely stimulate extremely vigorous enforcement action and eliminate any prosecutorial problems with "knowledge," an issue discussed in Chapter 16, Enforcement and Defense Strategies.

The tension between discovery and the disclosure of what has been discovered has been a constant concern for companies and enforcement entities dealing with the issue of environmental auditing. It has also been considered in depth by EPA and DOJ over the past few years. These agencies want to encourage auditing as a means of promoting compliance, but they are not able, as a consequence of bureaucratic and political imperatives, to provide any sort of meaningful incentive for companies that identify compliance shortcomings and correct them. Instead, EPA and DOJ have adopted the posture that noncompliance should be disclosed, and the company that so discloses must rely on prosecutorial discretion to avoid being penalized for that noncompliance.[10]

While most companies probably feel uncomfortable with this approach, it is the official position of DOJ. It must be taken into account when considering whether to use auditing as part of a compliance strategy.

F. Relationship Among Environmental Laws

Not surprisingly, most companies are subject to a number of overlapping, statutorily mandated environmental programs. A fair-sized manufacturing facility using one or two common industrial solvents may be affected by a variety of federal statutes, including the Clean Water Act, the Clean Air Act, EPCRA, CERCLA, RCRA, TSCA, and the Occupational Safety and Health Act (OSH Act), among others. As discussed in Section II.C., above, more than one statute is likely to be involved with respect to reporting requirements alone. This pervasiveness of federal environmental regulation makes it apparent that a comprehensive, well-coordinated compliance program is necessary. The point is further reinforced by the fact that there are also state environmental programs that may complement or conflict with federal environmental statutes, as well as local enforcement programs that may affect the environmental requirements imposed on a facility or company.

The overlap among various federal and state environmental laws makes a strong case for integrating a facility's or company's overall compliance efforts. If a company approaches each type of requirement separately, it is likely that some will be missed and others may be satisfied only at the expense of not satisfying others. Thus, unless a comprehensive compliance management pro-

---

[10]This and other issues related to environmental auditing are discussed in detail in Chapter 15, Environmental Auditing.

gram is undertaken, compliance efforts are likely to result in overlooking some regulatory requirements and seriously increasing the risk of enforcement action by federal, state, and local authorities.

G. Economic Pressures

A final trend that should be mentioned is the use of environmental issues by competitors, consumers, investors, and even foreign governments as a reason for purchasing, investing, imposing import controls, or making other economic decisions. These approaches, arguably intended to use economic pressures and market consequences as ways of encouraging environmentally and socially responsible behavior by corporations, have in some instances been more successful in getting top management attention than even the threat of criminal prosecution.

The reason for this is that such approaches, as they become more widely used, have the potential to create serious adverse economic consequences. The process for evaluating the environmental "acceptability" or "responsibility" of a product or company is largely uncontrolled, so that organizational bias, misinformation, and poorly performed scientific testing may influence the outcome and result in misinformed or inaccurate evaluations. As more individuals and organizations consider such environmental evaluations in making economic decisions concerning a product or company, the effect of an adverse evaluation by a rating group, whether deserved or not, may have significant financial repercussions for the product or company involved. In addition, companies making environmental claims are likely to be more closely scrutinized than they have been in the past, and will need to carefully substantiate and review any such claims. This underscores the growing importance of demonstrating effective environmental compliance efforts, credible scientific support for environmental policies and practices, and "due concern" for the environment.

III. General Compliance Concepts

A. Integration of Compliance Efforts

There are numerous stories of facilities that have eliminated one environmental problem only to find that they have created other far greater problems. A classic example concerns the refinery that solved an air emissions problem by bubbling the contaminated air through its cooling water. Unfortunately, the cooling water then flowed, in an open trough, through the plant area before being discharged to a nearby stream. In effect, the refinery replaced a fairly minor air quality problem with more significant Clean Water Act and OSH Act violations. Stories such as this one are a better indicator of the need for an integrated compliance strategy than any series of unending lectures could possibly be. An integrated strategy becomes even more important as environmental requirements become more numerous, more stringent, and focus on in-plant processes.

The need for a comprehensive, integrated compliance approach is further reinforced by EPA's recent move to multimedia enforcement.[11] In this new strategy, the Agency is attempting to assess compliance and punish noncompliance under the Clean Water Act, the Clean Air Act, RCRA, and various other statutes in one fell swoop.

All of this argues for developing a coherent strategy for complying with all environmental laws. It also probably makes sense to factor in compliance with major OSH Act standards at the same time. Such an overall effort can avoid transferring violations from one environmental medium to another. Even more significantly, it can provide an overall view of a facility's or company's compliance situation and the need for improvements on an across-the-board basis.

B. Considering State and Local Governments in Developing Compliance Strategy

State and local governments have always been the front line with respect to assuring compliance with environmental requirements. As federal environmental regulation has grown, Congress has tended to impose increasing burdens on state and local governments for implementing and enforcing federal programs. For example, states are integrally involved in administering the federal RCRA program, the Clean Air Act, and the Clean Water Act, as well as the reporting requirements under EPCRA and CERCLA. Local governments are also involved in differing degrees, depending on the statute and the state, in enforcing federal statutory programs. An example is the increased enforcement responsibility for local governments under the 1990 Amendments to the Clean Air Act.[12]

In addition, most states have their own environmental programs that state and local governments have responsibility for administering and enforcing. These responsibilities create substantial funding needs for both state and local governments. Since these levels of government are perennially short of funds, this could prove significant. Both federal and state governments have attempted to address this resource problem by using new sources of funding, such as assessing fees from regulated entities under various compliance programs.[13] While such fees have been characterized by some as pollution taxes, they should improve the ability of state and local governments to administer the requirements of statutory programs.

Another aspect of these taxes is their impact on regulated entities, particularly those that are small businesses or marginal operations, since taxation at these levels may prove to be a significant burden. One aspect of a compliance strategy may be a focus on attempting to ameliorate the impact of such taxes.

---

[11] *See, e.g., Illegal Waste Importers, Exporters Targeted in EPA, DOJ "Cluster" Filing,* 22 Env't Rep. (BNA) No. 23, at 1404 (Oct. 4, 1991).

[12] CAA §110(a)(2)(E), 42 U.S.C. §7410(a)(2)(E) (Supp. II 1990).

[13] For example, under §112(l) of the Clean Air Act, states that develop hazardous air pollutant programs that meet certain requirements may qualify for federal grants. 42 U.S.C. §7412(l) (Supp. II 1990). An example of fee assessment is the permit fee provision in the new air permit program. CAA §502(b)(3), 42 U.S.C. §7661a(b)(3) (Supp. II 1990).

However the funding concerns for additional state and local government responsibilities are resolved, the basic compliance approach with respect to these entities will not change. When possible, a facility should maintain a close and continuing relationship with local and state agencies. These agencies are far more likely to be cooperative and sympathetic than EPA. Even if they are not overly sympathetic, they will still be the primary contact on many environmental compliance issues. Thus, a close relationship is essential, and a good relationship can never hurt with respect to any compliance management program.

C. Developing a Commitment to Compliance

Compliance involves a number of functional aspects: (1) assessing compliance (determining whether there are or might be problems and what level of effort may be needed to fix them); (2) achieving compliance (installing human and mechanical systems to comply with legal requirements and manage risks); (3) maintaining compliance (keeping the system operating); (4) assuring compliance (operating internal checks to confirm compliance, risk management, and proper system operation); and (5) validation of compliance (external checks and procedures to assure others that compliance is being achieved). The only way to assure that all of these compliance functions are being satisfied is to ensure that adequate personnel and institutional resources are dedicated to satisfying them every day on-site.

An important part of this effort is the development of an appropriate compliance culture that is based on an expressed commitment to developing appropriate programs for the achievement of suitable environmental compliance objectives. No matter how elaborate a compliance plan, unless it is formally adopted by the company and committed to by management as an essential corporate practice, it will not be successful. Nor will it be successful if management only pays lip service to the idea without allocating sufficient resources to developing and implementing compliance measures. A compliance management plan that is adequately supported and actually observed and implemented as a part of the day-to-day operations of the organization is well on its way to success.

D. Environmental Education

Perhaps the most vital aspect of ensuring that the various compliance functions are satisfied is the education of all relevant employees as to the compliance requirements: What are the notification requirements? What levels must be met to assure compliance? and What procedures are required for compliance? If a company does not ensure that employees, from managers to loading dock personnel, know and understand the requirements, there is little chance that compliance will be achieved, regardless of how well-developed the strategies are or how strong the commitment to compliance is.

Two steps are necessary to educate employees involved in or responsible for environmental compliance. The first is learning what is required and keeping current with respect to one's knowledge of such requirements. This can be accomplished through use of environmental handbooks, statutes, regulations, environmental seminars, trade publications, and so forth. Trade associations, local chambers of commerce, and even environmental agency programs can also be useful for this purpose.

The second and more difficult task, however, is to effectively communicate the requisite knowledge to those who need to know it. It is imperative that a company develop a mechanism to assure that those having responsibility for environmental compliance, including supervisors and senior personnel, have adequate, up-to-date knowledge for their jobs and for overseeing others. There is no magic formula for assuring effective communication to those who need to know. However, each company, division, or facility must be aware of this need to communicate and must develop effective methods for ensuring that it happens. Some suggestions for doing so will be discussed in Section V., below.

E. Demonstrating and Documenting Diligence

As the substantive and monitoring requirements in environmental statutes become more stringent, violations and their detection become far more likely. Demonstrating diligence becomes an important mechanism for minimizing or avoiding penalties and similar unpleasantness. Equally important is documentation of these demonstrations of diligence, so that there will be a means of convincing enforcement agencies, citizens' groups, and courts of a company's or facility's good-faith efforts to comply with the law.

This is complicated by the fact that the practice of demonstrating and documenting diligence is in its infancy. Few know how to approach this problem, which tends to be very company- or facility-specific in the absence of the overall development of the subject. As a result, each company or facility is largely on its own in this area. Because demonstrating and documenting diligence can be an important mechanism for minimizing the impact of occasional noncompliance, however, it should be pursued despite the absence of guidance on the subject.

Companies should keep in mind that regardless of the particular system employed, in order to be credible, demonstrations of diligence must involve responsible corporate officers and employees involved directly in compliance management, and documentation must be consistent and regularly performed. For more complex operations, computerized management information systems may be the only way to document diligence demonstrations. While this is a more difficult and potentially costly undertaking, it may have advantages pertaining to community right-to-know reporting and other aspects of environmental law. Thus, such computerized information systems could assist not only in diligence documentation but also in integrating an overall compliance strategy.

IV. General Suggestions

Over the last 20 years or so, the following concepts concerning environmental compliance have proved to be a useful general guide.

- *Devote as much time and effort to compliance as is necessary.* Compliance cannot be regularly scheduled for a one hour time block on alternate Wednesdays. Instead, a company must commit the time and effort (as well as other resources) that prove necessary, no matter how much or when it is required. The amount of time and effort required will depend on the complexity of the facility or company and its operations, and the significance of the compliance problems it faces.
- *Aggressive compliance is the best answer to aggressive enforcement and the best way to minimize environmental risks and their consequences.* Compliance efforts must be vigorous, and the importance of compliance must be forcefully communicated to all employees. Unless the organization is committed to compliance, even moderately aggressive enforcement will result in significant penalties.
- *Everyone is responsible for environmental compliance and the need to demonstrate due diligence and due concern in order to avoid and protect against potential consequences.* Individual employees represent either an organization's most valuable resource or its greatest vulnerability in its effort to fulfill environmental obligations and avoid liability. All employees, officers, and other management personnel must be aware of compliance requirements and efforts and take all steps to ensure and demonstrate that they are met.
- *You can never destroy all copies of a document.* There are a number of corollaries to this principle. First, if only one copy remains, it will most likely be in the hands of a whistleblower. Second, that one copy will have the marginal and unfortunate comments of the company's Chief Executive Officer. The suggested solutions are (1) not to create documents that you would not like to see in an enforcement agency's hands and (2) not to rely on secrecy and document retention as a way of limiting liability, but instead make aggressive compliance efforts and document those efforts.
- *Consultants can help but cannot do the job for you.* Most executives would die before letting a consultant run their business. The same should be true for environmental compliance. While consultants and lawyers can be extremely helpful in assisting a company with developing its compliance strategy and with coming into compliance under environmental statutes, the consultant alone cannot do this. The company's employees, and especially its management, must be deeply involved.

These guidelines are of use, in conjunction with the general concepts above, in establishing a solid foundation upon which to construct a successful compliance program. This foundation is crucial, as companies face a number of uncertainties and other difficulties created by the increasing volume of environmental statutes, regulations, and regulatory authorities with which a company must contend in compliance programs.

V. Specific Compliance Guidelines

While no number of guidelines can anticipate or remedy every compliance issue or serve as a substitute for an individualized compliance management program, the specific institutional guidelines set out below should provide a useful framework for the design, development, and evaluation of appropriate compliance program features, building on the more general principles discussed in Sections III. and IV., above.

- *A Policy Statement.* There must be a clear statement of policy on safety, health, and environmental compliance. It should be written, comprehensive, realistic, honest, well-communicated, and sufficient to achieve compliance in the face of critical scrutiny and hindsight. It must be committed to by top management and that commitment must be credibly conveyed to all responsible employees.
- *A Workable Management Structure.* The responsibility and authority for carrying out the compliance policy should be assigned to personnel with clear access to the highest levels of the organization who themselves have sufficient and clearly defined authority to ensure compliance. Persons responsible for compliance should be clearly designated as such, so that they and others are aware of their responsibilities and where the ultimate responsibility for compliance lies.
- *A Process for Knowing Specifically What Is Required.* This builds on the environmental education concept discussed in Section III.D., above, which suggests that management must have a workable system for keeping those responsible for compliance aware of the specific things they and the company must do or must not do to comply with the policy and the law. Suggestions for establishing and implementing a system include (1) continuing, internal, process-oriented compliance assurance programs; (2) participation from all responsible levels of the organization; (3) documentation of the process and identification of who has responsibility for knowing and implementing specific functions or requirements; and (4) external compliance assessments as a supplement to the internal process. It should be remembered, however, that excessive reliance on outside assistance, unless integrated properly into the organization's compliance program, can be expensive, inadequate, and dangerous.
- *A Communications Program to Make Sure Employees Know What to Do.* It is necessary to develop a manual of procedures, or comparable written materials to outline specific steps that each employee or unit of the company is expected to take in carrying out processes, procedures, and activities that affect compliance. The materials should be comprehensive and continuously updated, yet brief and expressed sufficiently clearly so that those who need to understand them can. The information must be communicated to all appropriate employees, with records kept to show this communication. Training should also be provided that emphasizes the seriousness of the program and of the failure to observe the procedures, with records kept of all training provided.
- *A System for Identifying and Locating Chemicals.* The increasing emphasis on the notification requirements of EPCRA, CERCLA, TSCA, and the CWA makes it essential for a company to know what potentially harmful chemicals are coming into the plant, where they are stored, what their use is, and what risks to human health and the environment are

presented. The system must meet EPCRA requirements and must demonstrate proper control and disposal in accord with statutory requirements. Communication of health risks to employees is required under OSHA and TSCA.

- *A Defined Procedure for Complying With Notification Requirements and Responding to Releases.* As discussed previously, EPCRA, OSHA, CERCLA, TSCA, and the CWA all impose incident, discovery, periodic, or noncompliance notification requirements that are enforceable by strict civil and criminal penalties. This makes it vital to have a written, conspicuously posted notification that (1) specifies notification and response requirements under all applicable statutes, regulations, and permits; (2) assigns responsibility for notification and response in compliance with applicable requirements; (3) lists phone numbers or addresses for making notifications and outlines when to call or write and what to say; and (4) provides a workable notification-response process that meets regulatory requirements. This process should concentrate on notification and response requirements and should ensure the availability of persons with a legal duty to report, or assurance that reporting will be done immediately.
- *A Clear Policy on Generation and Maintenance of Records.* A document retention policy needs to be formulated and implemented with the following considerations: (1) environmental statutes impose specific constraints on document retention programs; (2) it is not certain that any document can be kept confidential, or that all copies will be destroyed; and (3) improper document destruction is a common basis for criminal prosecution.
- *A Policy and Program for Communicating With Regulators and the Public.* In light of greater public awareness of environmental issues, it is important that companies develop effective ways to communicate to both the public and regulators their commitment to the protection of human health and the environment. This is especially true since both have increased access to information regarding companies' operations and compliance, thus creating the potential for misunderstandings and for increased enforcement. Persons with the most knowledge of compliance must be involved in communication with regulators and the public. These persons should try to maintain an atmosphere of openness, trust, and understanding, and try to foster an attitude that the company is working with authorities to solve any problems.
- *A Policy on the Right to Defense and to Continued Employment.* Responsible officers and employees need to know when and to what extent the company will defend them if they are charged with a criminal offense or threatened with individual liability or fines. Setting out the policy in advance will benefit both employees and the company. The company needs to determine the relevant legal and practical constraints on the scope of the policy and set out the policy either in the company's bylaws, employee contracts, or operations manuals.
- *A Waste Minimization Program.* For most companies, waste minimization programs are no longer a frill, especially if their operations involve

hazardous waste. Any such program should be in writing, consistent with EPA guidance on the subject, and effectively communicated and implemented.

- *A Process for Evaluating Environmental Effects of Products and Activities.* Detailed evaluation of the long-term, cradle to grave impact of new products or initiatives from an environmental as well as a liability or risk management perspective is becoming an increasingly common element of environmental management programs and is probably a major protection against severe unanticipated consequences.

VI. Conclusion

Like almost everything related to environmental regulation, compliance has become complex and significant. This chapter can generally help a company or facility in its efforts to comply with its obligations under the various environmental statutes that may affect it. However, this assistance is of necessity limited; it can only provide a few strategies and some ideas, and point out a number of pitfalls that can be avoided.

Successful environmental compliance management requires dedication to preventing and correcting violations. It also imposes a number of other requirements, such as maintaining good relationships with regulators and keeping them aware of potential problems. The significant potential penalties imposed by the environmental statutes, the stepped-up enforcement efforts and increased convictions for criminal violations, and the general negative consequences of violations make such diligence worthwhile.

List of Statutes

Administrative Procedure Act, 5 U.S.C. §501 *et seq.*

Clean Air Act (CAA), 42 U.S.C. §7401 *et seq.*

Clean Water Act (CWA), 33 U.S.C. §1251 *et seq.*

Coastal Zone Management Act of 1972 (CZMA), 16 U.S.C. §1451 *et seq.*

Comprehensive Environmental Response, Compensation, and Liability Act (CERCLA), 42 U.S.C. §9601 *et seq.*

Deepwater Port Act of 1974, 33 U.S.C. §1501 *et seq.*

Emergency Planning and Community Right-to-Know Act (EPCRA), 42 U.S.C. §11001 *et seq.*

Endangered Species Act of 1973 (ESA), 16 U.S.C. §1531 *et seq.*

Federal Environmental Pesticide Control Act of 1972 (FEPCA), Pub. L. No. 92-516, 86 Stat. 973 (1972)

Federal Facilities Compliance Act, Pub. L. No. 102-386, 106 Stat. 1505 (1992) (to be codified at 42 U.S.C. §6961)

Federal Food, Drug, and Cosmetic Act (FFDCA), 21 U.S.C. §301 *et seq.*

Federal Insecticide, Fungicide, and Rodenticide Act (FIFRA), 7 U.S.C. §136 *et seq.*

Federal Water Pollution Control Act (FWPCA), 33 U.S.C. §§1251-1387

Food Security Act of 1985, Pub. L. No. 99-198, 99 Stat. 1354 (1985)

Hazardous Materials Transportation Act (HMTA), 49 U.S.C. §1801 *et seq.*

Hazardous and Solid Waste Amendments of 1984 (HSWA), 42 U.S.C. §6901 *et seq.*

Marine Mammal Protection Act, 16 U.S.C. §§1361-1407

Marine Protection, Research, and Sanctuaries Act of 1972 (MPRSA), 33 U.S.C. §1401 *et seq.*

Migratory Bird Treaty Act, 16 U.S.C. §§703-11

National Environmental Policy Act of 1969 (NEPA), 42 U.S.C. §4321 *et seq.*

Occupational Safety and Health Act (OSH Act), 29 U.S.C. §651 *et seq.*

Oil Pollution Act of 1990 (OPA), Pub. L. No. 101-380, 101 Stat. 484 (1990)

Outer Continental Shelf Lands Act (OCSLA), 43 U.S.C. §1331 *et seq.*

Poison Prevention Packaging Act, 15 U.S.C. §1471 *et seq.*

Pollution Prevention Act of 1990 (PPA), 42 U.S.C.A. §§11071-78

Resource Conservation and Recovery Act (RCRA), 42 U.S.C. §6901 *et seq.*

Rivers and Harbors Appropriations Act of 1899 (Refuse Act), 33 U.S.C. §§403, 407, 411

Safe Drinking Water Act (SDWA), 42 U.S.C. §300f *et seq.*

Superfund Amendments and Reauthorization Act of 1986 (SARA), 26 U.S.C. §4611 *et seq.;* 42 U.S.C. §§6911, 9601 *et seq.*

Toxic Substances Control Act (TSCA), 15 U.S.C. §2601 *et seq.*

Trans-Alaska Pipeline Authorization Act (TAPAA), 43 U.S.C. §1651 *et seq.*

Glossary of Acronyms

AGT: above ground tank

ANPR: advanced notice of proposed rulemaking

AOC: administrative orders on consent

AQCRs: air quality control regions

ARAR: applicable or relevant and appropriate requirement

ATSDR: Agency for Toxic Substances and Disease Registry

BACM: best available control measures

BACT: best available control technology

BART: best available retrofit technology

BAT: best available technology economically achievable

BCT: best conventional pollutant control technology

BDAT: best demonstrated available technology

BIFs: boilers and industrial furnaces

BMP: best management practices

BOD: biochemical oxygen-demanding

BPT: best practicable control technology

CAIR: comprehensive assessment information rule

CAS: Chemical Abstract Service

CEMS: continuous emissions monitoring system

CER: continuous emissions reduction

CERCLIS: Comprehensive Environmental Response Compensation and Liability Information System

CFCs: chlorofluorocarbons

CMSA: consolidated metropolitan statistical area

CO: carbon monoxide

CQA: construction quality assurance

CSHIB: Chemical Safety and Hazard Investigation Board

CSHO: compliance safety and health officer

CTGs: control technology guidelines

DRE: destruction and removal efficiency

DWEL: drinking water equivalent level

EHS: extremely hazardous substance

EIS: environmental impact statement

EUP: experimental use permit

FDF: fundamentally different factors

FIP: federal implementation plan

FONSI: finding of no significant impact

GACT: generally available control technology

GLP: good laboratory practice

GVWR: gross vehicle weight rating

HAPs: hazardous air pollutants

HazCom: hazard communication standard

HC: hydrocarbon

HCFC: hydrochlorofluorocarbon

HCl: hydrogen chloride

HDV: heavy duty vehicle

HON: hazardous organic NESHAP rule

HRS: hazardous ranking system

ICR: industrial cost recovery

ICS: individual control strategies

IDEA: integrated data enforcement analysis

LAER: lowest available emission rate

LDV: light duty vehicle

LEPC: local emergency planning committee

LMS: linearized multistage (model)

LOAEL: lowest-observable-adverse-effect level

MACT: maximum achievable control technology

MCL: maximum contaminant level

MCLG: maximum contaminant level goal

MEAP: maximally exposed actual person

MEI: maximally exposed individual

MLE: maximum likelihood estimate

MOA: memoranda of agreement

MSDS: material safety data sheet

MSW: municipal solid waste

MSWLF: municipal solid waste landfill

MTD: maximum tolerated dose

NAAQs: national ambient air quality standards

NATIC: National Air Toxics Information Clearinghouse

NCP: national contingency plan

NESHAPs: national emission standards for hazardous air pollutants

NMOG: nonmethane organic gas

NO_2: nitrogen dioxide

NOAEL: no-observable-adverse-effect level

NOC: notice of commencement

NOEL: no-observable-effect level

NOI: notice of intent

NOx: nitrogen oxide

NPDES: national pollutant discharge elimination system

NPDWRs: national primary drinking water regulations

NPDWS: national primary drinking water standard

NPL: national priorities list

NPRM: notice for proposed rulemaking

NRC: National Response Center

NSPS: new source performance standards

NWP: nationwide permit

O_3: ozone

OBD: on-board diagnostics

ODS: ozone depleting substance

OSC: On-Scene Coordinator

Pb: lead

PCB: polychlorinated biphenyl

PIRGs: public interest research groups

PM: particulate matter

PMN: premanufacture notification

POHC: principal organic hazardous constituent

POMs: polycyclic organic matter

POTWs: publicly owned treatment works

PRP: potentially responsible party

PSD: prevention of significant deterioration

QRA: quantitative risk assessment

RACM: reasonably available control measures

RACT: reasonably available control technology

RD/RA: remedial design/remedial action

RfD: reference dose

RGL: regulatory guidance letter

RI/FS: remedial investigation/feasibility study

RMP: risk management plan

ROD: record of decision

RQ: reportable quantity

RVP: Reid vapor pressure

SERC: state emergency response committee

SIC: standard industrial classification

SIP: state implementation plan

SMSA: standard metropolitan statistical area

SNUR: significant new use rule

SO_2: sulfur dioxide

SPCC: spill prevention control and countermeasure

SS: suspended solids

STEL: short term exposure limit

SWMU: solid waste management unit

TC: toxicity characteristic

TCLP: toxicity characteristic leaching procedure

TMDL: total maximum daily load

TME: test marketing exemption

TMRC: theoretical maximum residue contribution

TRI: toxic release inventory

TSD: treatment, storage, or disposal facility

TSP: total suspended particulates

TWA: time-weighted average

UAO: unilateral administrative order

UIC: underground injection control

UST: underground storage tank

VMT: vehicle miles traveled

VOC: volatile organic compound

Table of Cases

References are to chapter and footnote number. Alphabetization is letter-by-letter.

B

D

E

H

I

J

K

L

Q

R

S

T

U

V

W

Y

Index

I

J

K

L

S

T